JOURNEY OF THE MIND

The National Library of Poetry

Cynthia A. Stevens, Editor
Nicole Walstrum, Associate Editor

Journey of the Mind

Library of Congress
Cataloging in Publication Data

ISBN 1-56167-263-7

Manufactured in The United States of America by
Watermark Press
11419 Cronridge Dr., Suite 10
Owings Mills, MD 21117

Editor's Note

As editor of Journey of the Mind, I truly enjoyed reviewing and interpreting the many artistic submissions accepted for this anthology. The variety of topics and styles is wonderfully overwhelming. Each poem within this anthology is an admirable contribution. However, there are some outstanding verses I wish to honor with special recognition.

Winning the Grand Prize with its weight alone is "A Storm at Dusk," by M. C. Guimond. With a brewing storm as the backdrop of the piece, Guimond presents a young girl awakening to the startling reality of death while killing insects for her collection. An outstanding array of unique descriptions is displayed in this masterpiece of poetic language, "as the red wind of dusk ruffled the mottled,/ mad, Van Goghish, sunflower swirls of her dress." And, as if mother nature herself were watching, "...tree shadows slowed to an earthworm's crawl/ while ants, crickets and beetles were bottled." Each line touches your senses. Guimond's words enable you to feel, see, hear and breathe the final realization, *death is serious*. "A Storm at Dusk," merits your attention.

"Romance," by Nyx, takes an in-depth look at the emotions evolving from the experience of love. The poet presents the aftershock of a broken relationship by using many abstract images, such as: "hoops dangle from shark-tooth ears/ like broken wrists in your handcuffs..."; and alluding to the blurry vision found in most romances, "Candlewax cataracts crust milky eyes...." The poem's overall question, *is romance nothing but a whimsical untruth?*

Another poem full of imagistic detail is "depression," by Laura M. King, which ponders upon the wish that *if only* one could go back and have prevented the awful tragedy of another's deep depression. King employs bold descriptive scenes like, "as it was you spent years in that sea/ cold rotting and shrinking from the salt/ drowned by the glass of water which was not half full but shattered." This poem is one of sincere remorse.

A few other outstanding poems touching upon the loss of loved ones are, "In Memory," by Marilyn Campbell Scala; "One Precious Jewel Was Loaned To Me," by Pauline H. Kammet; and Sheryl Singleton Lynch's "Alberta."

E. T. L. Evans presents us with "The Child Asleep," which is both beautifully rhythmic and picturesque. Evans portrays a parental view of a young child sleeping as the parent tiptoes into the child's room "to steal a kiss from petal-soft cheek." Also about a loving parent and child relationship is, "Sarah," by Maria Norris. While utilizing a great metaphor of a daughter as a butterfly Norris presents us with the heartbreaking acceptance all parents must go through - *letting their child fly free.*

Several more prominent poems you won't want to miss are: "Slow Dance," by Suzanne Czehut; "I Always Felt Cold," by Juan Jose Pena; and Theresa Wilhoit's "Shiloh, April 7, 1862."

Although I do not have the time or space to individually critique every eminent poem appearing within Journey of the Mind, you will notice that each piece of artistry is constructed with grave originality and design. May all of the artists within this anthology be renowned for their talents and efforts in creative writing.

I sincerely hope that you enjoy reading Journey of the Mind.

Cynthia A. Stevens, Senior Editor

Acknowledgments

The publication Journey of the Mind is a culmination of the efforts of many individuals. Judges, editors, assistant editors, graphic artists, layout artists and office administrators have all brought their respective talents to bear on this project. The editors are grateful for the contribution of these fine people:

Sheree Bernstein, Jeffrey Bryan, Chris Bussey, Keith Crummedy, Amy Dezseran, Chrystal Eldridge, Joy Esterby, Aundrea Felder, Ardie L. Freeman, Hope Freeman, Bob Graziul, Paula Jones, Steve Miksek, Diane Mills, Eric Mueck, Tanya Rayton, Lamont Robinson, Jacqueline Spiwak, Caroline Sullivan, Nicole Walstrum, Ira Westreich, and Diana Zeiger.

Howard Ely, Managing Editor

Winners of the 1994 North American Open Poetry Contest

(Held in connection with the anthology, Journey of the Mind.)

Grand Prize

M.C. Guimond / Clinton Township, MI

Second Prize

Suzanne Czehut / Hamilton Square, NY
E.T.L. Evans / New York, NY
Pauline H. Kammet / Las Vegas, NV
Laura M. King / Carlisle, PA
Sheryl Singleton Lynch / Hollis, NY
Maria G. Norris / Woodbury, NJ
Nyx / Louisville, KY
Juan Jose Pena / Albuquerque, NM
Marilyn Campbell Scala / Port Washington, NY
Theresa Wilhoit / Phoenix, AZ

Third Prize

Anne Armstrong / Atkins, IA
Anna Banaszak / New York, NY
Trisha Barry / New York, NY
Stephen A. Beck / Hazel Park, MI
Barbara Bloom / Owings Mills, MD
Barrington H. Bowser, Jr. / Richmond, VA
Kent Braithwaite / Palm Desert, CA
Kristina Breeding / Rolla, KS
Thomas Bruce / Webster, NY
Michael P. Byron / Irvine, CA
Jason Caldwell / Drayton, SC
Vincent Cardinale / Belmont, MA
Mark Chadwick / Parma, OH
Samantha-Lee Chaifetz / New City, NY
Laurie Christenson / Port Orchard, WA
Will Cline / Kalamzoo, MI
Bernard Criscuolo / Margate, FL
Pamella A. Cunningham / Brookfield, OH
Ellen M. Curtin-Contabile / Bedford, TX
Mort W. F. Cooper Elkind, Chestnut Ridge, NY
Pat Fischer / Fenton, MI
William John Giacofci / Easton, MD
Paul Granick / Keansburg, NJ
Steve Harper / San Francisco, CA
Richard T. Hartshorn / Iowa City, IA
Melisa Hayes / Littleton, CO
Jo Heinze / Chicago Heights, IL
Susan J. Johnson / Washington, DC
Daniel Kaufman / La Jolla, CA
W. E. Kendra / Ford City, PA
Anna Maria Kline / Jackson, NJ
Laura Laurent / Brampton, Ont. Canada
Dorothy Manley / Forest Grove, OR
Sandra Lee Messer / San Francisco, CA
Dorothy E. McClinton / Riverdale, GA
Joette McDonald / Vermilion, OH
Nick Menkee / Alturas, CA
Hanne E. Moon / Meridian, MS
John L. Mullins / Springfield, MD
Jesse Murphree / Brandon, MS
Helen Neely / Ellington, MO
Bill Olesky / Port Saint Lucie, FL
Colleen Phillips / Colma City, CA
David J. Ridley / Terrace Bay, Ont. Canada
Karen Lee Risley / Pensacola, FL
Xavier Alexander Robertson / Utica, MI
Lisle G. Russell / Staunton, VA
Nicola M. Shugars / Ellicottville, NY
Barbara Simpson-Lara / Riverside, CA
Mark Storer / Thousand Oaks, CA
Patricia C. Sturm / West Lafayette, IN
Jennifer Sullivan / Brecksville, OH
Linda Ross Swanson / Portland, OR
J. Symlar / Upper Marlboro, MD
Robert I. Thiel / Annapolis, MD
Sacha Wamsteker / West Hollywood, CA
Betty James Sexton Williams / Fresno, CA
Lyle K. Williams / Fort Worth, TX
Shoshanna Zuker / Bronx, NY

Congratulations also to all semi-finalists.

Grand Prize Winner

A Storm at Dusk

My niece examined her insect menagerie
as the red wind of dusk ruffled the mottled,
mad, Van Goghish, sunflower swirls of her dress.

Birds softly twittered in September fields,
tree shadows slowed to an earthworm's crawl
while ants, crickets and beetles were bottled.

Dark dialogues of thunder woke the nest,
crooked fingers of lightning clawed the west,
the horizons closed in, masked in rainy mist.

But she ignored the grumbling storm, gazing
in studious worship at her lifeless darlings,
counting, qualifying like a seasoned scientist.

My wrinkled arm wrapped around her thin waist.
Our faces engaged: blue ice filled her eyes.
"You seem so serious today, my dear,"

I said, as the sky groaned in grey sunset
and summer drew a sickly shallow breath.
She sighed and said, "As serious as death."

—M. C. Guimond

Hate The Wrong Reason

Eyes are of every shape and
color no one will hate you
because of your eyes.
Bodies are also every shape
and color, so why do
they hate you for your
difference in body and
not your eyes
Your eyes are a door to your soul and speak
your soul and speak
the truth
Your body says nothing
Listen to the truth and facts
and don't hate a person
for the difference in body.

Clariluz Perez

The Seed

We smash through the dark when we start our plight
colors, galor blinded by sight
The angels laugh with utmost delight
and reward us grandly when we do right
Shining us on into the night.

We'll never be angels try as we might
they are only guides upon our flight
We never make it far before the fires ignite
There's angels no more we have learned to fight

Langsam tod
There's no turning back the path we choose
with straight minds laced with booze
or what ever means you use
we come as ones and leave as two's.

With the angels gone the demons have bite
as they do best to fight Satan laughs
out of spite cause nothing you do is right
Then the moment arrives at last your future
joins the past leaving your soul in a cast

No time to fix it life went by too fast.

Jeff Walters

Our Garden's Woes

Rain, rain, please go away,
Come again some other day.
All this moisture, we don't need,
We can't get out to pull the weeds.

Now we need the sun to shine,
The tomatoes are rotting on the vine.
The ground is muddy as we pass,
And, the rain drops twinkle in the grass.

Chase the dark clouds, God, as you can do,
The sun will rise in the sky so blue.
And as the sun sends out it's rays,
We then will have much dryer days.

The rain did stop, as we all knew,
The sun did shine, and our garden grew.
We love gardening, as you can see,
And, we enjoy the beans and the peas.

Erma McVicker

They Come to Buy Death

Their death comes in needles. Their death comes in vials.
Come and take me. Come and take me.

Young rich suburbanites and poor young children of the night.
Being devoured by the power of the ever so greeting death.
Come and take me. Come and take me.
Absorb me, I am your life.

They come to buy death, but it's not alright.
The smile that's the vial...Oh so enchanting.
Calling. You're falling deeply into the infinite trance.
You won't be back.
Come and take me. Come and take me.

Calls the endless sleep, in a solacing voice inviting you to join.
No pain nor suffering, this method so buffering .
Just one try if you'd like to die.
You fall so fast and so deep into this zombie like sleep.
Awaken!, but you won't.
Come and take me, come and take me, come and take us.

Hear the posthumous cry of the fallen. Feel the pain we're all in.
We can't stop this!
Thanatopsies, a meditation of Death, a crack Hitler.

James Shones

Hurricane Dan

Through the violent rain,
Comes an unexpected, uninvited Hurricane.
Through the towns and villages it looks for more victims to claim.
And it leaves the same.
As if it's some sort of game.
But on again, it came and came.
Will this be a Hurricane you can tame?
As it leaves more towns burst into Flames.
But on day there came a man.
A hundred times strong as any man can.
He told the people, his name was Dan.
And he heard of the Hurricane from a far away land.
And the Hurricane heard of Dan.
And for a victim, it came to claim Dan.
And for a fight for victory, Dan defeated the Hurricane
with an ordinary frying pan.
The Hurricane explained, it didn't mean to hurt
anybody, it just wanted a name.
So the villages called him: Hurricane Dan.

Amanda Shreve

Quintessence

Some soft, bittersweet sort of Silence
Compels us, calls—and crying, we come.
Its assurance, endurance, unnerving, —but
Stark, gripping it is—and strong.

So here, this ancient Woodland,
Stoic, sympathetic with the Sun,
The wildly gentle, the patient Forest
Turns its back, and the sun goes down.

And Darkness hushes these wilds each evening.
In the twilight, they are still—
—standing humbly, unmoved,
As the sun lends its rest to the Silence—
The sober silence of the big earth's love.

Chris Vogel Haley

Turkey Tradition

Succulent turkey and sweet potato pie
cornbread dressing and calories that are high.

Thanksgiving day is a day to eat
take a little nap and then repeat.

It certainly seems strange.. because eating is such a pleasure,
that the very next day, you have this need to measure.

A pound of fat here, a pound of fat there,
before you know it.... Thanksgiving fat is everywhere.

It shows up on your arms and you wear it on your thighs,
it pooches out your belly and puffs out your eyes.

So beware on this day, when you are filling your plate,
after you stuff it in your mouth, it is then too late.

That's why stuffing the turkey is a holiday tradition,
the name sure fits as the mirror reflects your condition.

So Hurry... you have only four weeks to lose that Thanksgiving bulge
before you feast at Christmas time and again you overindulge.

Becky Benbrook

The Bird

Dark arabesque, hanging low in mist —
Crumpled kerchief, black and shaken-out
With tiny sketch of Oriental orange —
What do you think?
Does your heart beat high as you flash through
those tunnelling air ways?
Does your stomach flip with ecstasy?
Do your eyeballs and tongue go dry?
Must you blink and beak against the wind
As your feathers shuffle, freeing nits?
Does your bird flesh tingle with some pulse of fear?
Do you ever think of falling, down through the wild air?
Does your heart rattle in your breast
at the thought?
I wonder, as I watch you here...
And — I wonder — to you
Am I nothing here —
Or do you see me, seeing you?
And do I, unknowing, urge you on —
To flaunt that freedom so outrageously?

Elisabeth T. Hitchcock

Late Hours of the Night

Here in the late hours of the night I find myself in the darkness of my room. Where eyes stare beyond darkness trying to find peace and joy. In this frustrating world around me. This world full of pain and anger. Here in the late hours of the night I find my troubled mind once again. When will I rest, I ask? When will I have the peace of mind? Here in the late hours of the night in this four walls that surround me. When once they would let me see through them and me travel beyond distanced worlds. Once when I felt happiness around me. Wanting to yell for help but too weak to do it. Wanting out but too weak to try. Here in the late hours of the night. I feel a cold shiver surround me and my heart beat grows weak my eyes closed slowly. I finally put my mind to rest in a deep sleep to never awake.

Blanca M. Vallejo

A Tragedy

The Angel of Death swept o'er one day,
And as He passed my Father's way,
His left wing dipped, Dad's shoulder brushed,
And in an instant, A life was crushed.

Glenda Alger

Taproot

There is a root, fine and fleshy, begun in long ago
darkness when the drum sang alto and the moon
awakened over the lake of dreams.

Thin, straight at first, weaving root, pushed through
and married deep within the pure centers of the trees,
especially the shivered birches, down

into the earthy corporal, made sacred by her sharing;
a holy tap root, spread surging into star-strewn winter
nights. Curving root, arched along the spines

of mountain ridges; fringed and fearless sentries of stone,
cracked open, bloody tendril tumbling down and wild
along the way of ancient footfall. Surging root

of grandmothers, breaking through blue ice to feed
the young and turn its passion toward the soul of winter's
silence; tender shoot trembling beneath clear moonlight.

Frosted vine spirals in silver confusion, waiting for daylight
to burst forth its perfect coiled profusion, tap root leading
up beyond the eagle's flight into the sun's own artery.

Carol W. Bachofner

Thirty Two

Nothing up his sleeves.
David Copperfield? Who's he?
Elephants disappearing? Statue of Liberty gone?
Big Deal! Child's play!
Kid's stuff!

You ever have Stockton guarding you?
You ever have Jordan in your face?
Where's the ball?
Now you see it, now you don't.
He flashes that grin and shows you empty hands.
And Worthy dunks for two.

You want to see a REAL Magician at work?
Watch:
"You ain't got a chance to hang with me,
Five championship rings on my hand, you see.
Three times MVP, what have you done?
Before you know it, you'll be washed up, my son.

Presto! Chango! Abracadabra!
Without Magic around,
Showtime's left town!"

Jeff Daniels

Fifty Years and Holding

Kiss my lips before we settle down to rest.
Dawn will come but sleep could be eternal.
Your silver head will lie here close to mine.
Then darkness once again will turn to light.

Hold me just a moment longer my sweet love.
Let me hear you say once more you love me.
In this moment everything seems right.
Still I'm not ready yet to say "goodnight".

Carol Berry O'Shea

Among Others

Have you ever wondered what's among people?
Ask yourself.
People are people you can't tell what's among them.
You, yourself, can tell what's among you.
Have no fear to ask,
Someday you, yourself, will find what is among others.

Andy Garza

Daydreams

The modern sages tell you
Daydreams you should pursue,
That in the stress filled lives you lead
This is the thing to do
The dreams you dream at night are alright
But the daydream tried and true from the blue,
Gives a needful lift when you are all uptight,
In a daydream you can be
Anywhere you want to be,
Fortune smiles on every venture you may try.
You're the Captain of the Crew
All the orders given by you
Are obeyed within the twinkling of an eye.
Though your castles are of air
With a sunbeam for a stair
They'll endure the little while you would be king,
For you've other lands to see
Doctor, lawyer, merchant be,
And a daydream will grant you everything.

Gladys Loveland

Oh! This House

Oh! This house is lonely, love is absent;
Death is present.
But then, there was a noise which
bounced from the roof!
What is there, who is there?

Is it death, that has come to
capture me, or life fighting for me?
I don't want to go; I don't want to go.
Who calls for me;
Is there someone there?

I made it through the night once again;
Oh! this house is lonely, love is absent;
The night has come again, the noise is
present; who is there; who is there?

An answer bounced from the roof;
Love is here, love is here.
Oh! This house is lonely;
No more, life captured me.

Joyce B. Simelton

"Journey to Survival"

Looking out my window, I could see past the dawn...
Deep in my heart, I knew something was wrong.

My thoughts caught on tree limbs, like a kite on a windy day...
Tangled in knots, trying to get away.

They found a lump in my Breast, it would have to be removed...
Oh! The thought of it being cancer, how could life be so crude!

When they said that "it was," the tears welled in my eyes...
Oh couldn't it be mistake? Please tell me its a lie!!

The clouds hovered over, there was a storm coming in...
With lightning and thunder, the most violent of wind!

When the journey was over, and the roads were all dry...
The clouds had all passed, I was going to SURVIVE!!

Joanne Clurman

Emotions

An empty place in my heart is what I've found,
But then the music fills it with its sweet, sweet sound.
Instead of sorrow and depression, that is what I now lack,
I have a new frame of mind that I plan to keep intact.
Happiness is what it's called, and no one has it, anywhere,
So what's going to happen? Doesn't anybody care?

Carmen Fon

True Love

There is such a thing as love
Even though some people can't find it
People that can find it are very privileged
Because they have someone to love them back
Some people think they have found love but,
It just messes up their lives
So if you think you've found love
I just hope it's TRUE

Amy Jones

Obsidian Eyes

Your black curls muddle my thoughts, abysmal giant eyes
Denuded cosmic heart, livid captious gaze
Intransigent, sempiternal obstinate

Who would think that behind those innocent eyelashes
You encarcel a storm of passion

Tumult of sensuality that upon a touch of my skin on your skin,
Outbursts devouring fire, ravaging, asphyxiating

Multiple orgy of orgasms
Faces of a thousand colors surge suddenly from your essence in flames
Faces of terror, expressions of despair, Revolt of anxiety

A simple graze of my lips on your intoxicating flesh
Unleashes an ocean of tameless love, savage worship
While continuous eruptions prolong your celestial agony

Lips of immense tenderness, kisses of an insatiable desire
You are the most sublime, you are an explosion of eternal love
Repressed for millennia

My perdition you live
My salvation you are

Jorge Aragon

Winter

Winter, a blanket of white lay across the bare
deserted ground.
Streets sleep silently.
Cold air roams; winds whistle a low short tune.
Cold air guards keep people imprisoned in their homes.
Snowmen rest waiting for children to come out and play.
Smoke swirls and whirls out of chimneys like
ballerinas in motion.
Lakes keep to themselves as if they had no friends.
Winter, a blanket of white!

Jessica Polly

Estranged Other

Her leprosy pleads a cure.
Deterioration knots
A headache in her voice.
Her pointed gate.

She jailed, and thunder between her eyes-
Estranged other, face of two
Motherly cherry tree
Plumped in alcohol jars.

One child's avant-garde.
Sugar spun and spider kissed
Sticky limbs that beam glassy white
Are one in jilted trust.

Around the corner, and in swinging arms,
Dressed with smiles, the moments glory.
Shielded memory-cause in memory lapse

Forgive
A friendly pearl
Cast to form; while shelled.

Carrie McKenna

A Letter From God

Dear friend; I was watching you when you got up this morning and you did not even say good morning Lord. I was very disappointed because I didn't hear from you. I even brought the sunshine in and made the birds sing a song of joy to you. And even then you still didn't acknowledge my presence. Are you ashamed of me I sent the sunshine in, to show you that I am still the Creator of this world. And I am trying to show you that my love is real, I did not change, I am still the same God as I was yesterday, today and tomorrow. You're the one that has changed and I hope it is for the love of Jesus Christ and not for yourself. I don't want to hurt anybody's feelings in writing this letter, all I want to do is to tell you that I love you and I will take care of your needs if only you will ask. And try to acknowledge my presence and the beauty around you everyday if it is possible I am writing this letter from the bottom of my heart and if this letter does not touch your heart and moves you closer to God then I don't know what will happen. But I do hope that you will acknowledge one thing and that is, that I love you my friend.
From Jesus Christ, your loving Father.

Andy Martin

Did You Know You Were Always There

Did you know you were always there - somewhere near to me
Did you know our paths would cross and we were meant to be

For years and years you've walked before me
In the same paths that I have come
Was it that path you left for me that brought me to your arms
But, why couldn't my eyes see you?

Did you know that I was always there
Did you feel my presence
Do you believe our paths compared is equal to one in essence
And yet, you never saw me

Till on the day that we should meet - in the oddest sort of way
Just like in a fairy tale, my love
You stood that special day

One touch and I was doomed, my sweet
One touch and you were too
Paralyzed in each other's arms - I paralyzed to you
What is this feeling of overwhelmingness
What is it we're to do

How powerful this spell on us - how intoxicatingly wonderful this dream
What is this thing inside our hearts that begs our souls to scream.

Geraldine E. Morris

Man-Kind

We have climbed the highest mountains and reached deep into the dirt brought forth the precious mineral for use upon this earth.

We have spanned the mighty oceans and laid the railroad tracks and reaped the mighty harvest God's gift to man is right.

We have trapped our mighty rivers and seem to slow their flow but then the power is needed to make this country go.

We have laid a long, long cable across the ocean floor to talk and share with others and make our deeds worth more.

We have a wonderful vessel she sails the seven seas bringing hope and health to others our servicer to all Man-kind.

We have made another first we have taken another step for all the world to see. We placed a foot upon the moon and it was shown and seen by all Man-kind.

This is truly a great great country and it makes me feel so proud when I hear the Star Spangled Banner and see Old Glory waving in the breeze. Just to see a little boy scout bending on his knees - to raise to face the flag then be allowed to feel at ease. May it never change.

James A. Stephens

"Have You Opened the Door?"

Jesus knocked on the door of your heart today
Did you open and let him come in?
Did you listen to what he had to say?
Or did you shut the door on him?

Patiently he will stand and wait
To be invited into your heart
If you hurry, you'll find it's not too late
To accept him and make a new start.

The shadows of fear then will all fly away
Your life will begin a new
With him you are able to meet each day
And face life's challenges, too.

So ask Jesus now to enter your life
Hold out your hand to him.
It will mean the end of all sorrow and strife
Open and let him come in.

Jean C. Paul

How Much Will It Take

Didn't take much to get me.
Didn't take much to please me.
Took three words to make me melt,
Couldn't help the way I felt.
Took one minute, my dreams came true.
Took one moment, then I knew.
You don't love me anymore
My dreams, shattered. My heart, it tore.
I can't help thinking of the feelings you gave,
No matter what happens, my heart will save,
The good times we had as one.
The worst is over with; it's done.
It only took one tear to cry,
It only took one word—good-bye.

Jennifer Kerschner

Tabula Rasa

A child's observations, keen and right,
Dispel grimness, gloom, and blight
Of an old man's soul who's forgotten how
To love and to cherish life.

The three-year old sees a picture of a compeer
Dressed in cap and coat
Sitting nearby a grazing goat.
He says, "A car is not coming!"

Oh! What sense of goodness and protective
Preservation of life!

"Lest we become as little children...".
Heed the advice!
Surround yourself with the laughter,
The truth, and yes, with the innocent and
Pure Logic of the Tabula Rasa.

Christiane Gebauer Monroe

Eulogy

The Old Weaver that weaves life's ways
Determines the length of all our days;
Some are short and some are long,
Some have woes, others a song;
But when our life is through at last
A gold thread is woven through our past.

Elizabeth Stewart

Wings

With upward sighs, I cast my soul,
Dispensed with wings, which seldom grow.
Far from sight, they flew on tears,
Choked with emotion, knowing fate was near.

With Godspeed intended, I watched their flight,
These sentient beings, lost in the night.
Hopeful yet muddled, they approached their end,
I stood amazed, and without much chagrin.

Then they stopped, their path fell short,
As we witnessed, a truly celestial report.
An aurora borealis, spectacularly displayed,
Talked of passion and Love, from colors every shade.

"Assuage yourselves," the oracle decreed,
"Of the blind hate and lust, and sex with greed.
"I will not preach, just tell what I know,
"That Love cleanses all fears, and then we grow."

With soul renewed, I began to cry,
But listened intently, to one final reply,
"Spread your wings, fly back to earth,
"Remember this night, your eve of rebirth."

Deron Dahlke

Oh, Lord

Love, sincerity, and compassion are clear,
divine and dear.
For only you, Oh, Lord,
know life's cumbersome sword.
You lead and guide us in the right way,
tell us what to do and say.
The bond of love shows through,
both the old and new.
You forgive us of each and every mistake,
and guide us in the path to take.
To take the road less travelled,
or the one paved and graveled.
To find the better choice to make,
and not leave out hearts at stake.
Help us, Oh, Lord to see,
So we don't run into that dreaded tree,
of hate, jealousy, and sin,
To fight, over come, and win,
Thank you so very much, Oh Lord,
For helping me hold that sword.

Dustin Manshack

Untitled

Perhaps we grow old because we are sad and empty
Do wrinkles represent the pain in our hearts and the
tears in our souls
Does everything sag because we are almost ready to give up
our dreams
Knowing time is slipping away
Is it because we have forgotten how to hope
Does our vision weaken because there is not a future to plan
Do we shrink to hide our loneliness
Perhaps we finally give up when our spirit is broken
And we realize our secret longings - however simple -
never will be
We need to be surrounded with love
To be cherished and important to someone
Then our wrinkles become laugh lines
And we still think of life with joy and hope
Our vision will be of heaven and life ever after
And our memories will carry us gently into eternity.

Elaine Adams-Nichols

Now That You're In Heaven

Now that you're in heaven do you remember me
do you miss care or understand me

Do you hear what I'm saying
when I talk to you in my prayers.
Now that your in heaven do you still care

It's so confusing to think about because
I know I must still exist to you
but if so wouldn't you fell the way I do.....

Wouldn't you feel unhappy or sad but
in heaven your not suppose to fell bad.

Now that your in heaven do you hear this poem I wright
Do you feel the sadness in my words

Now that your in heaven do you know
what I am thinking every time of everyday or
Do you not know me at all in any way
I know I love you that's all I do know

Now that your in heaven everything
is so.....different
Nothing is the same

Now that your in heaven I fell so much pain

April Florey

A Good Man Died!

What happens when a good man dies.
Does an angel take his place?
Why are we left with less than goodness?
Upon a world that is going to waste.
We need the good men to help the bad,
Not the other way around.
If we continue to loose the good ones,
What will become of this town?
What happens here on earth when a good
man's put to rest.
I guess what they have always said is true,
God takes only the very best.

Anne Gleason

The Meaning of My Life

In a world so full of life, am I here?
Does anybody know life is? I do not.
Homeless people beg for food and money on the streets
yet none care. Why? Are no people caring enough?
Do people set by and watch people suffer? Is
the world a cruel joke? Somebody please tell me.
As I set and watch the world go by, I wonder
is this all that we are to people. Nameless faces.
Why doesn't someone help these less fortunate?
I would if I could. Am I the only who cares?

When will people realize the world isn't
going to get better unless we do something?
Never I suppose. I will probably never know
the meaning of life. I don't pretend to know.
Are we here by some divine power, or some
cruel joke? Does anyone have sympathy for
anyone else? Will the world get any better?
Will someone please tell me the meaning of life?
I just want to know why. Oh please someone
tell me. The meaning of life.

Adam Bonds

Is There Need?

The blood that flows from wounds of war
Does not differ from man to man.
Nor bones, dug up from graves of those
Who killed, were killed, are similar.
The suffering that rakes the heart
Has depth as deep in all of us,
No matter what our color, creed.

So why these lines, so sharply drawn
By bigot, hater and soured minds,
When sun and moon shine on us all,
For all, there is our birth, slow death.
Is there need for rape of lives?
Is there need for more scrambled brains?

Florence K. Wiener

The Weeping Rose

The yellow rose which represents our love
Does not stand so proud and tall anymore
But only weeps with great sorrow
We are all weeping with great sorrow
The once yellow petals have all turned to brown
The stem once strong is now bent over
As if crying
We all are crying like the rose
The petals now fall like tears
We all weep like the rose...

Elizabeth Elaine Allen

'Perfect Love'

Perfect love reaches out to those who
  don't need it.
It reaches out to those who don't want it.
Perfect love reaches out to those who
  can't handle it.
And perfect love reaches out to those who
  take advantage of it.
Perfect love never reaches out to those
  who are willing to commit to it.
It never reaches out to those who can
  express it.
Perfect love never reaches out to those
  who can feel it.
And perfect love never reaches out to
  those who would die for it.
Perfect love turns its back on those
  who are in need of it.
But always seems to reach out to those
  who try to destroy it.
Perfect love reaches out when it shouldn't.

Dawn Donaldson

Opaque Seas

The warmth of a summer breeze
Drifted across the opaque seas
The confounded clouds finally broke free
A few stray rays of sun were seen

A treasure that was held so tight
The sun did shine both day and night
Fields of green till the end of sight
The jewel withheld its natural light

The leaves fell and withered on the ground
No sign of life could be found
No birds or bees made a sound
The opaque seas rose as I slowly drowned

Garrett M. Moser

A Broken Dream

"Wait!," I said," Don't leave me alone,
Don't take my dreams, don't leave me cold;
I've tried my best, give me a chance,
To prove myself, to make you proud."

"You've had your chance, it's time to quit,
The waste of time, the days I spent;
Get out of here, do not come close,
Unless you crave, to lose some more."

It has been years, since I left Jack,
My manager, who wished me luck;
It was more than my life he took,
My heart, my soul, my eyes to look.

The dreams I had, to be famous,
A movie star a millionaire;
To have a place in society,
Seem to vanish — I was twenty.

There was passion, he failed to see,
That made others to search for me,
Here I am now, in my limousine,
Laughing at him, the man with Gin.

Bemnet Yohannes

Be Proud

Be proud of who you are
Don't waste time being jealous or rude.
Be kind when you speak of others
You'll get no where with a bad attitude.

Be proud of what you can do
Don't forfeit your chances to excel.
Take pride in the things around you
Be confident and you will do well.

Be proud of your family roots
It's the one thing you can not change.
You can choose your friends but not your family
Be respectful and proud to carry the name.

Be proud of your accomplishments
No matter how small the praise.
Do the best you can with what you have
You'll be rewarded in so many ways.

Evelyn S. Wallace

Poet's Dream

  Swiftly gliding in the air
  Down from tree to tree
  I sing a sweet melody,
  How lovely is the feeling
  but it is only a dream.

No sooner to be awaken with such thought
We can still be happy even if it's only in a dream.
If to hold to a dream is for a dreamer,
With this fondness a dreamy poet shares.
Taking not a thing for granted:

  He loves to seek beauty, secrets, and meanings;
  To his simple soul every answer he finds
  Sweetly he meets the greater soul.

For him there's music in the rustling waters,
He listens as leaves whisper or as winds whistle;
If he sees love in the winking of your eyes,
And if he feels pain when a child whimpers
Or feels the rage of an angry storm;
In his silent soul he dreams to reach the heart
  of every dreamless man.

Fatima Bantegui

Catching the Turtle

Two boys and their aunt went fishing one day.
Down the bottom, not far away.
One boy was deaf, could not hear,
But he loved to fish in the pond here.
The aunt baited their hook and line.
Five inch fish was all they caught every time.
The boys were about eight or nine.
Enjoying themselves and doing fine.
A turtle, one boy pulled in,
On his face came a great big grin.
The deaf boy wanted to take a look,
At the turtle on the other boys hook.
He ran to the turtle as quick as a tack.
While his aunt yelled, "Get back! Get back!"
He did not hear his aunt's call.
So, he didn't get back at all.
The turtle bit him on the shoe,
Now, what is the aunt going to do?
The turtle bite didn't break the skin,
But he never got that close to a turtle again.

Brenda Elaine Martin

Crayons Can Sing Too!

You, my baby girl,
Draw me a river.
Watch yourself.
Don't let the color stain the paper.
Instead, allow them to drip off the corners,
Onto the counter-top.
Let them splash in the pools of their own blood
and gather together bleeding
Into an endless sea.

Carlina Dawn Kohutek

Haunting Reservations

This harsh reservation is a magnet to me
Drawn to these people of history

Who once were free to roam this land
And now are boxed in, and I can't understand

Why this race of people, with such honor and power
Should be crushed underfoot like a delicate flower

The one time masters of forest and field
Forced now to harvest an earth that won't yield

The brave young warriors, unlike legacy
Must now fight with alcohol and poverty

The dark eyed children, so forlorn, it seems
As I walk by, and my conscience screams

For it's truly a prison where we've forced them to live
And I think to myself, "How can they ever forgive?"

Oppressed and forgotten, no one to care
But deep in their souls, the Spirit's still there

My head hung in shame, I turn to depart
And the tear on my cheek is like a knife in my heart

Donna M. Jones

To My Elusive One

I touch you in passing like the touch of a child's
I read you in rhymes that deafen the world
I see you in shadows of lingering smoke
I read you in stories left out in the rain
I walk with you into R. E. M. and through your transparency, I die
Ever so slowly, I whisper your rhyme

Erin E. Woodruff

Dream Land

Walking barefoot upon the sand,
Dreaming of some far off land.
A land without hunger, a land without pain,
A land filled with sunshine and no acid rain.
A land with no arguing, fighting or fear.
A land where the water always is clear.
A land full of happiness and nobody cries,
Where everyone lives and nobody dies.
A land where your neighbors are always your friends,
A land where there's laughter and love never ends.
A land full of harmony, peace and no strife,
Oh wouldn't that be a wonderful life?

Judy Glass

"Alone"

Here I lay all alone, silent and still like a stone.
Dreaming of you who I wish to hold,
When days get short and nights turn cold,
I dislike the thought of being away,
And very much dislike this place where I have to stay,
I want to come home more and more,
To have you meet me at the door,
When my workday's is over and all is done,
I want to come home to only you,
To all your hugs and all your kisses,
And so you can fulfill all my wishes.
My wishes that you could hold me tight,
When the day is over and turns to night.

Gary L. Anderson, Jr.

Memories

Memories of you and me keep running through my mind,
  driving me crazy with the loneliness I find.
Memories captured are put into my heart,
  looking through them, gives me hope to a new start.
Reviving the feelings of love stuck down deep inside,
  helps my insanity when remembering the times I desperately cried,
Memories of crying out because we were slowly drifting apart,
  and memories of special moments; quickly broke my heart.
Tear drops fell like rain that night, rolling with loneliness;
  draining all of my might.
Memories of our friendship seemed to good to end,
  hanging on with the hope of our hearts
  willing to mend,
Memories of your love being stronger
  than I have ever felt,
Along with your tender touch; has made
  me passionately melt.
Being in your loving arms would fulfill my needs again,
It is what I need, it is in my dreams,
  and it is in my prayers, Amen.

Joleen Manuel-Donley

Einsiedlen

Faces of God
colors of dimension,
dogs of fur and faith.
Lightening tickles
vision.

The stained-glass ceiling is not too low,
It's just that I'm too short
to dance
with the heavens.

And the fizz of life bubbles on.

Gretchen Glick

Untitled

An empty well on a hot summer day
dry and dusty full of hard clay
deep and unforgiving
never a hope to see the living
waiting only for the coolness of the clouds
with rain drops fillings it is allowed
to feel worth existing
water to turn and begin twisting

An empty well on a hot summer day
someone has made you feel this way
intoxication to evaporation
as you harden towards the separation
never let it drain you dry
within is the one you can always rely

Cheryl Dorstad

Blade of Grass

A blade of grass, it grows so low,
Dwarfed by all the neighboring sights,
Is not as impressive as a tree in a row
That towers toward the evening lights;
Nor like a mountain maintaining respect
For standing defiant, bold, and strong.
Even the sea is known as she effect
The melodious chant of a seaside song.
But a blade of grass so humble it be,
Eaten, ravaged, and trod under foot,
Was adorned with more than the eye can see
The miracle of life by which it took
It's uniqueness, like man, in full delight
Though only a blade there are no two alike.

Helmer Tietjen

What Is Fellowship To Me?

F - is for our fellow man to whom we should share the word
E - is for everyday in which God we should serve
L - is for being like-minded having the same love as Jesus
L - is for leading unbelievers to Christ because they really need us
O - is for the obligation we have to Testify
W - is for the willingness we should have on each other to rely
S - is for the sacrifices we sometimes must give
H - is for the honor we owe because Jesus still lives
I - is for the picture we should illustrate to sinners who are unaware (mostly)
P - is for a Christian's sincere prayer

Fellowship involves all these traits in which we should display,
so don't just fellowship once a week-fellowship everyday!
For if we fellowship with the Father, the Son, the Holy Ghost, and as well as with other believers, God will be pleased in watching this and forever He will keep us!

Erica M. Hubbard

Painting Lesson

Every spring Ma and I painted six kitchen chairs,
Each having 110 spokes with ridges,
Two high chairs and the table....white.
"Something so clean about white," Ma would say
Wrinkling her nose at the grease-spotted
Green and yellow gas stove with black burners,
Walls and curtains shaded gray by a coal furnace
That belched its dust through the registers.
On Saturday mornings forever I scrubbed the kitchen,
Scraped mud, mashed potatoes, gravy and peanut butter
Off those chairs and that table without complaint.
There was something so clean about white.

Jane Farrell

My Ocean

Alone I sit and wonder WHY,
Each hello ends in GOOD-BYE.

Does nothing last? Must it all FADE;
Like passing winds in waters WADE.

So often treasures are too soon GONE;
Like that moment of silver on oceans of DAWN.

Love and friendship come and GO,
When winds pick up and start to BLOW.

And those castles built up high of SAND,
Are destroyed in collisions of water and LAND.

What seems to be? Still hard to TELL...
Once complete... a shattered SHELL?

Sometimes the sun can steal our SIGHT.
And we become ships that pass in the NIGHT.
Then the heart hanging on is forced to let GO,
'Cause it's too hard to fight the strong UNDER-TOW.

So confusion sets in, and again I'm ALONE,
Dancing with tides in a sea of my OWN.

Jill Darby

Growing Things

From out of my windows I see growing things.
Each new pungent blossom, I note, with it brings
A fragrance so heady - my fair heart sings.
An' my spirits stretch wide, like the eagle's wings.

Choruses of star jasmine, a flutter on vines,
Whispering their bouquets, like rare, old fine wines -
This aroma, so enticing, on which spirit dines.
Jade-leafed, snowy blossoms, murmuring sweetly on vines.

Fruits will come later, with a sensual beauty -
Profusion of blossoms have promised with surety.
They grow - how they grow - with such elegancy!
I'm dumb-struck at such unparalleled beauty.

Tangelos, deepest orange, and shaped like a pear,
Weighing down branches, too heavy to bear.
They need watchful eyes, tender loving care.
Else - tumbling to the ground - they're the worse for wear.

Grapefruit, so plentiful - huge and so round.
Peaches - like fireballs - in clusters abound.
Oranges - sun-drenched - in mass, to be found.
My eyes drink in growing things - everywhere - all around.

Esther Utman

Out My Window

Out my window, I see the roof,
Each shingle no bigger than a horse's hoof.
Down some more I see a pipe,
And under it a fruit so ripe.
That means a tree,
So far that I can see.
Some bushes so green,
That is what I have seen.
Someone resting in a little cot,
And next to it, wildflowers in a pot.
The grass, so pretty, and freshly cut,
Everything is colorful like a rainbow, but —
One color is missing, it's in my room,
A colorful bottle of pink perfume.

Cristy Trancucci

Ice Around Her Heart

She shuffles through the snow,
each step a fight against weight.
The weight of time, the weight of cold,
heavy burden, like the weight of her heart.
She reaches the house, steps inside to warmth.
But the weight of cold remains in her heart,
frozen solid, to bear sown on her soul.
She's old, has fought many battles,
has the scars to prove her losses
and her victories.
But there can only be loss
with this war that rages inside her.
She stretches gnarled fingers to searing
heat of the bright flames of fire.
The ice around her heart crackles and groans
but remains cold. So very cold.
The ghost of her husband, so recently
taken from her, hovers, beckoning.
The ice thaw, ever so slightly.
The weight begins to lift away from her heart.

Helen Thomas

Untitled

Aliens from Mars have landed on Venus
Elvis clones are waiting to clean us
My dog is growing buy eyed tentacles
The computer's seeping through its ventricles

Pat's on the computer having fun;
Microchips are the only ones
Mutating hair is invading our planet
A large jar of hairspray would quickly can it

Oprah's thin, Joan Rivers is bald
Geraldo Rivera's just been mauled

Hey, watch out! What was that!
A naked guy wearing a hat
There are old folks with funny voices
And bums sleeping in Roll Royces.
Ross Perot is all ears
What has happened over the years

The world's a strange and funny place
A perfect dwelling for our human race

Catherine Mary Mackinnon

The Quiet Rose

The rain was slowly trickling down upon the stilled earth. The trees lacked wind, there was silence throughout.

The stone, out of cement and the letters engraved with patience. Tears from the Lord ran down the face of the stone and soaked within the freshly laid dirt. In mourn, I squeezed the rose with my ever trembling hand. My flesh was sliced and torn, blood escaped through my fingers. My hand was in pain, but also was my heart.

Looking down at one's earthly bedding of mud and raised dirt, remembering the one I once loved. Dropping the rose onto the soaked dirt, refraining from any tears. "Goodbye," I whispered in only a gentle voice. All I could do was walk away, so I did.

Ann Sable

Untitled

The sky rages with flashes of light
emerging from the clouds above.
Peace is in the air. The night
is still and filled with beauty so rare and deep.
The gentle soft breeze rustles through the trees.
And yet in the serenity of it all, there is someone,
Somewhere who was no peace, who is dying from hunger,
and homelessness.
Someone who can't understand the beauty of the night,
Because they find no comfort in it.
That one person who roams the paths of others,
In hope, that they might find some comfort,
Some peace on their way; where ever they may go.
They continue searching, but find nothing,
In the still of the night.

Carmen Valdes

Mama

You've seen my family in the Chevy,
Eight kids, little ones in the back.
Julio is on the radio
Singing to mama about love.
I see it in her eyes at night, tucking us in:
Miguel, Luis, Carlos,
Martin, Eddie, Ana,
Little Oscar,
And me.
I see it in her eyes
When she has to explain why
The moon is white,
The sun is yellow,
Thunder clouds are black,
And why dirt is brown.
"Because," she says,
"It's where life grows and is loved,"
Kissing our brown foreheads
With her brown lips.

Jamie Kmiec

What Is Black?

Black is an unlit room.
Empty space,
Shadows under the moon.
Everlasting darkness.
So thick no one can see.
Demons of greed
Creep through the night.
Silently we see shadows.
Moving in the dark, dark night.
Death. An unawakened sleep.
Cold.
Confused.
Frustrated.
Black tastes like nothing ever tasted before.
It feels like a gentle mountain breeze
Flowing through cold December air.
Black sounds like an owl hooting on a cold, dreary night.
And smells of the burning embers of an old fire.
If there were no black, it would always be white.

Cathy Cirrito

Gestalt

I am but a part of "ME"
Encompassed in the was and what is to be.
To dream of times that future holds,
couched in memories as life unfolds.
But to know this moment... NOW,
Is really all I have somehow.

As shadows from the yesterdays,
create their own though dubious ways
of thoughts that hold me to the past,
paths once traveled though did not last.
With experiences to teach me how,
to shape my life sprung from the ... NOW!

Today's thoughts create tomorrow,
filled with joys or abject sorrow.
For I alone can choose my life,
to learn that growing comes from strife.
And as struggle unlocks the creative me,
to be as much as I can be.

And fulfill within my soul
joining the pieces that makes me whole.

Doris F. Peach

Rebirth

If there is life after death, then I have been reborn into eternal life. For it was in my life before, that I became lifeless, and in becoming lifeless I became dead. My physical self, beaten, worn, and only able to function under a deep spell. The spell of Alcohol.

Not a man or woman on earth could pass this spell. Only through what I choose to call Hell could I see the light. Only through a life of utter confusion, and hopelessness could literally be reborn from utter death, to the incredible hope that my higher power helps me to see just for today. No spell hanging over my head, like a tight noose waiting for my neck. It is not like that any more.

GOD thank you for keeping me sober today. You have lifted the spell which haunted me, and I am not alone. Never forgetting that I am an alcoholic.

James E. Walker

Dedication

Each morning I arise with tears in my eyes from the night before.
Even now I cry a little more.
Sunshine hits my face with care, just as it had when you were there.
Living without you is one constant battle and I am only one.
Yet you give me the strength to fight and surrender to none.
Therefore I keep marching on, oblivious of the world around me I gaze
at the morning sun, just as you had done.
Whispering those words you lived to hear.
As the words flowed I felt you so very near.
Again I said them and in the distance I heard your reply.
Tears of joy began to trickle down from each eye.
Throughout the day, my thoughts are of you.
Thinking of all the good times we've been through.
My yearn for you grows move each day, as night falls I kneel and pray.
Dear God, take care of my mother dear,
Kiss her for me and hold her near.
She taught me how to find goodness in all.
From your arms she shall never fall.
But I long to feel the warmth of her hand against my skin when
she'd hug me goodnight and tuck me in.

Athena Towns

"Trust and Betrayal"

All the ones we love,
Even that special bird called a dove.
When sending my friendship, love, and trust,
Out to each and everyone,
It seems betrayal is all I have won.
Everyone and everybody out for themselves,
Hurting another person,
They just don't care.
There's not enough trust in my heart to even spare,
Only our good memories are packed onto our shelves.
Getting even is all you can hope for,
The hurting and aching they all gave to me.
Whenever I turn my head I always seem to get more,
Hoping soon someday we'll see
The trust that someone can put back in me.
So on flies that special dove over a path in the sky,
He has no more trust,
Now just like I.

Heather M. Neal

"A Daddy's Prayer"

Dear God,
Even though I may be far or near
Guide, bless and protect my precious children from fear,

For that time I am away may seem lonely and long
The love in my heart for them will always stay strong,

As time goes by my children will grow
There will be times they will miss me and their hearts will be low,

Give them courage and strength and leave them never
For I will always be their daddy forever,
Amen.

Clifford William Phillips, Jr.

"Now"

Truth, - is the best policy -
Even though, many look the other way
Honesty, is the answer,
If we plan to keep greed away.
Consistency, is the hammer -
Which we must use, even it's refused.
With Faith, as the fire -
We burn away the crude;
Making facts stand, clean and renewed!

We must do, what we must do.
"And God help us", every woman and man.
Make America, proud of me and you,
No forked tongued senators, no under the table plan.
"Knock" - those private pork barrels -
It's time, that we got tough!
Stop beating around the bush -
Both parties have argued enough!
Then, - we can -
"God Bless America!"

Carla Wahe

Paths Of Desire

Minds touched by the tentacles of desire-
Each word caressed -
gently pulled -
by a seemingly lunar presence
into the minds eye -
opening up visions of a more Earthly coupling
rejoicing in the unity of both body and spirit -
leaving a heavenly glow in its wake.

Arthur Feinberg

Mom

Though the traditional mother's day only comes once a year,
Every day belongs to mother dear.

The trials and tribulations that she must bear,
I'm sure to her, at times seem unfair.

Mom will worry as her children mature,
But enjoy immensely this blessed grandeur.

Were it not for Moms and their undying devotion,
Children would grow with little emotion.

The hearts of gold and smiling faces,
Go within their offspring to all places.

If tears ever come to Mom's beautiful eyes,
Its only evidence of joy and happiness from her face,
Which portray a ray of sunshine every place.

Children will learn as they grow old,
That the words Mom speak, turn to gold.

The wisdom she has and advice she gives, are all a glory,
And become a treasure in a lifelong story.

Bobby J. Bean

Lover's Lament

Every morning at sunrise, I feel so blue.
Every evening 'bout midnight, my dreams turn to you.
I see your smiling face, feel your warm embrace,
Whatever I do.
Wherever I go, you're there.

Every morning at sunrise, I wake to find
That you're not near me, but you're in my mind.
So, darling, please be true wherever you may be.
And when you dream dear, please dream of me.

Harvey J. Nozick

The Lost of a Love One

I had a dad who I loved very much, then one day he was turned to dust.
Everyone said it will get better! If that is so why am I so bitter
There isn't a day that I don't think of him.
But Lord why did you take him?
My kids have no Grandpa and I have no dad! the drunk driver
that killed him well he is mad! now he gets 10 years and I get life.
Thank God for my husband who helps me be a good wife
My kids they do wonder why papa isn't here, but I tell them he's all
right he's in heaven with God up above, looking down on us
Giving all his love!

Angie Gaston

Mystic World

Sunbeams shine through separated clouds above.
Everything bursting into color, as that of a new born dove.

As the day would pass on, everything grew.
Cool sprays sent from above like that of morning grass dew.

Night grows over the day, as of a black sheet.
In the darkness, a breeze would sweep fields of wheat.

Like a dream, how beautiful the moon would glow.
Mystic world as it will always remain, for all the world know.

Barbie S. Taylor

Freedom And War

Death be not proud,
Except to die in the name.
A death of honor,
And not one of shame.

I fight to be live,
And live to be free.
I give my life,
In service of thee.

I pledge allegiance
To the flag.
In hopes that I might obtain
The Freedom and Liberty in which it stands.

One nation under God,
There does Justice abound,
Where all men are crated equal,
That is the place where true Freedom is found!

Catra Lynette Smith

Grandma and Me

Hand to hand
Eyes the color of the sand,
Caring and loving above the sea,
There in a rocker sits grandma and me.

Grandma played games with me when I was bored,
She also brought me many things.
Grandma makes such good cookies,
And tells me things that happened long ago.

Grandma's been my friend for a long, long while.
As a baby she often changed my tears to a smile.
She has a way of making me feel good,
And doing the things that I should.

Julie Mueller

Shadows of Evening

Yearly, like a tide swelling into an ocean inlet
Fall colors wash spectacularly across the land
And seen through windows facing autumn's twilight
Is the death ritual of the leaves on every hand.

Now patient, leafless trees wait in quiet dignity
Weaving a tapestry of immutable and dominated dark
Like skeletons against the early winter's snow
Where once the flaming maple glorified the park.

Then noiselessly snowflakes mantle the landscape
Like whipped cream topping on bush and garden post
Transfiguring the orchard filled with peach trees
Into hooded sentinels gleaming dimly like a ghost.

As they keep their cold and lonely winter vigil
They rest and steel themselves to wind and snow
They're learned the blessings of winter solitude
Knowing with spring the breath of life will flow.

So let's accept the shadows of long evening hours
Let joy, love and faith upon our souls descend
And let us find solace in the assurance O Lord
That thou art counselor, hope of peace and friend.

Dorothy Manley

Forget

Why do you sit atop the tor,
And weep for what is no more?
Smile and face the new days sun,
And forget what will remain undone.

Gisela A. Telis

The Generation Chain

My memories automatically rewind
Far into the yesteryears.
My visions dance fast forward
Into the future years.
My grandchildren forever link me
With unknown tomorrows I will never see.
My memories connect them with past history.
Through our overlapping destiny
We will weave renewal and immortality.
Alike, but different,
Separate, but together,
Hand in hand
Through the generation span,
We will grow to know
More about life,
More about love,
More about God's plan.

Betty Fobair McDermott

Adopted

She laid in her room on the floor
feeling a bomb cram against her chest
she tasted the salt
that flooded her face
she felt the knot growing inside her throat
she shivered when she thought
about what could have been
to never know her mother
to never know her father
to never have had a chance
to take the breath of life
to never have had a chance
to have someone to love
what would she have done
if her mom had not chosen life?

Jessica Stalley

"Joys of Life"

Embracing life with loving care
feeling a gentle breeze tossing your hair-
Relishing the beauty of birds in a tree,
savoring the taste of the salty sea-
Delight in twinkling stars in the sky,
letting your hopes and dreams soar high-
Basking in the warmth of the sun by day,
and strolling in the moonlight along the way-
Enjoying the years as they come and go,
cherishing family and friends, and letting them know-
Running through the meadows picking flowers you love so,
wading in the pond - frolicking in the snow-
These are but a few joys of life you will know,
and love will surround you wherever you go.

Donna Mackey Perse

Untitled

Crazy and wild are my dreams
Filled with rage and many screams
I'm caught between a world beyond
A life of which I am so fond
Passion and fire, love and lust
A faraway desert amongst all of us
Nowhere to run, and no place to hide
A mystical journey into the sky
Do not turn around or you'll feel regret
It's too late now, you can never go back
Welcome to the land of the rising sun
You're already dead, though you thought you're won.

Heather M. Fish

Fiction

Fiction is what we call untrue
Fiction is not real, it is a fantasy.
It thrives on emotion and feeling and
without it fiction will end as carelessly
as it began.

If fiction should end,
then what would be true?
Nothing or everything?

Fiction is what brings life a
little twist, an exciting moment in
an eternity of moments.

What is real?
Only what we think matters.
Is fiction real?
Only in our dreams.

Jennifer Pesonen

The Return to Innocence

As I look around this cluttered room,
Filled with memories of years gone by,
I see the life of the child inside me
That I've somehow let silently die.

I've let the promises of the future entice me
And the hope of things that will last,
While forgetting the simple joys in life,
And the ones I've loved in the past.

I've forgotten the morals of my character,
While searching for satisfaction in vain.
And it's not whether you win or lose,
But how you play the game.

So now I think I'll go back in time
To the place that I know best,
Where innocence is still a virtue
Because this child needs a rest.

Angela G. Evans

Once As A Friend But Now As A Lover

Over the past few weeks, my feelings have grown stronger
flaming with desire, my heart denies you no longer.

When we face each other eye to eye, I can't escape the feelings
that I have deep inside.

Love is a passion that dwells from within, in the future as
a lover but now as a friend.

Taking a chance and reaching for my heart, we over came the fear
that was felt from the start.

After talking and listening we understand, love can always grow
stronger between a woman and a man.

If we loved in a life before this we live now, our
hearts have remembered and true love has been found.

So often our minds wonder and forget the past, but our love
is growing stronger and built to last.

A lover or friend which ever it maybe, our hearts will share
a feeling that will never be felt again.
The day a lover was made out of a friend...

Beth Foster

Untitled

'Tis like a vision of a silvery moon
floating high in the heavens over a blue lagoon.
The marsh hens are chirping, the gulls soar on high,
as the sun goes down and the darkness draws nigh.
The whippoorwill calls to his mate from afar,
while the sea turtle crawls out on the sand bar.
The tarpon are striking, the trout are grand,
what place in this world is like this land?
Although we never did like to boast,
there is no place like the Mississippi Gulf Coast.

Claude Howard Stone Sr.

The Passing

My Grandmother's body laid
for a long, long time in the
same room where I was baptized.
Her body was wrapped in white satin,
just as mine was.
But now offertory candles replace those of baptism —
their light fell on her face to
hide her years from prying eyes.
So when the Great Aunts gather,
none will know of her suffering.
No one else will see that her
coffin is the same color
as the nutritional drip
which force fed her through a tube in her side
Her only strength now was in her hands
bound together with her rosary,
the crucifix fell to her side
poised like a key
set to open the door.

Barbara Simpson-Lara

"My Friend, My Spirit"

I am no longer a member of your tribal entities.
For I co-exist with whom has made me free,
My soul.
It can take me far, it can take me beyond.
Along with my body, entwined, I walked the earth.
On two feet which loosened the dirt, I went on
Until my dark hour bestowed upon me.
Let the light shine, may darkness fall away.
Maybe as heavy as stone you say?
Immortal am I, or at least it seems that way.
Don't you think so?
Soul of mine, don't leave me in oblivion,
for darkness has so many corners which I'll never find.
And the light is open to roam freely without fear.
You and I can conquer together.
You and I shall always remain together.

Javier Espinoza

Don't Wait Till It's Too Late

Don't wait till it's too late to tell your loved ones you care
For in the next instance a heart beat they can no longer be there

For all of the feelings you hold close to your heart
Are nothing but a thought if not shared from the start.

Don't wait till they're sick or moving away, to say
I love you, I'll miss you, I wish you could stay.

In the world in which we live love is all so rare
So open up your heart and share tell your loved
ones you care.

For in the next instance a heart beat, they can no longer
be there.

E. Thomas

Angel

I know what it is like to feel the pain -
For I gave up a beautiful baby girl.
Sometimes I feel as though I'm going insane.
I lie in this room each day,
Crying many painful tears -
Remembering the angel I gave away.
Karen and Dave that angel is yours now forever,
She was mine for only one brief moment.
All I ask is you let her know I'll always love her.
That angel I named Sadie Lyn,
But that name she'll never know -
For you, her dear loving parent's, named her Alyson.
Yes, sometimes I feel as though I'm going insane -
Yet I know you'll love your angel dearly,
And someday a dim light will appear through all my pain -
For I know now Alyson was a gift from above!
Though unplanned as she was,
That angel I'll always love.

Chanda Staley

Riding On The Joy Of God

I walked in sin no joy within
For I was hooked on Satan's bag
My spirit lagged then I just dragged
Until the truth of Christ I grabbed.

Addicted now to Christ each day
He pointed out the upward way
He turned my night right into day
Then made my work just more like play.

My heart has wings I like to sing
For I have met the King of Kings
He took me from a world of sin
And put His love and truth within!

He rolled those dark clouds all away
Left only sunshine there to stay
My heart's now turned to praise my King
That's why I almost shout and sing

I sing because he gave me hope, my soul feels now like it can float
My joy just rides up in the sky my heart has wing's I'm flying high.

I'm flying high, up in the sky, I'm riding now on the joy of God.
My heart has wings, I like to sing I'm riding now on the joy of God!

Dorothy Wildt

The Streets Of My City

The streets of my city are a sad, holy place,
For it is there that the innocent die.
The streets of my city are like Christ crucified.
For it is there that mothers cry.

Victim meets Victim at the doorway of death
While the killers pursue the false gods of life.
And the Kings of the Streets and the Lords of the Night
Spread poison, and evil, and terror, and strife.

As the blameless look on in fear of it all,
The addicts, the whores, and the pushers of dope
Are used as the peons by the powers that be
To suppress and benumb and deny us all hope.

We must work as one in the streets of my city.
We must free our children from the power of dope.
We must stand firm against evil with the power of Faith.
And through Charity we shall find the promise of Hope.

If we have hope for our city we have found the way
To bring peace to my streets and friendship for all.
And the killings and strife and errors of today
Will be but a memory too sad to recall.

Allen F. Lyons

You

Grow and become the YOU you were meant to be,
For it's the only person you are, you see.

As you learn, as you grow, please remember for me
To become that person you were meant to be.

Be true to yourself, then you will truly be
God's spirit on earth; you will always be free!

Be proud of yourself, you are God's own creation.
God doesn't care for what reason, from what nation

You were born; but that you grow in steps, at each station,
For wisdom is better than wealth, education,

Is much more important for the world, for each nation.
When you're truly yourself you're a perfect creation.

Happiness and contentment is so simple and lasting;
It is sharing and giving, it is your's for the asking.

God wants you to find this, and His love everlasting.
Forgiving, not judging, is all God is asking.

Love life, people, flowers; love sunshine...just basking;
Use your talents, your time wisely; pray often, but not asking

For riches, for wealth can be lost, while God's love is YOU...
Everlasting.

Joyce Melaragno

Rainbow of Love

The rainbow of love show's God's meaning of racial harmony
For mankind.
The colors of the rainbow of love so brilliant, and bright
Showing God's assurance, and the promise of his love.
The colors of the rainbow of love are these: White, Red,
Orange, Yellow, Green and Blue, and Purple too.
White Oh! White, the color of the cloud from where the
Rainbow flows bringing joy, and love to mankind below.
Red Oh! Red, fiery red to show destruction, and the blood he shed.
Orange Oh! Orange, so radiant, and warm the rays flowing
Through a golden sun.
Yellow Oh! Yellow, so sunny, and bright the color of the
Golden sunlight.
Green Oh! Green, so cool, and serene the color of the trees,
And the grass in spring.
Blue Oh! Blue, majestic blue the color of the heavenly hue
So calm, and peaceful too.
Purple Oh! Purple, so regal, and royal denotes the birth
Of the heavenly child.
The colors of the rainbow of love.

Alice M. Teague

Mind's Peace

Life displays our struggle in many ways,
for the most part, we all settle on the search
for mind's peace.

Emotions run wild trying to find a gentle
harbor within which peace of mind can be
found.

I find my search, kind of jagged, so to
speak, a rugged trail out of reach by life's
highway, okay, I'm a path walker.

Somewhere, out in the vast wilderness
of the universe, contained in Eternity.
Mind's Peace for this one, is most likely
in the forth corner, under a chair, in a box,
wrapped in a gray cloth, tied with a yellow
ribbon.

Donna Rose Baldwin

Metamorphosis

Two caterpillars—alike, yet different.
For no two caterpillars are alike. Or are they?
Each ask for little: merely a chance: a chance to become a beautiful
butterfly. Then their chance arises.
Each begins its plight. The plight of the cocoon.
Its shell that will hide—hide now but soon display its beauty.
Or will it? One butterfly, beautiful,
cracks its shell and emerges to fly away—FREE.
But the other butterfly, equally beautiful, cracks its shell and
attempts to emerge—TRAPPED. Hindered it struggles—struggles
to escape the bonds, the bonds that hold fast. A voice in the distance,
"Don't give up little butterfly, this is the land of equals."
Equals, yes. But why the bonds? The trapped butterfly continues
its struggle—but time is running out. Soon the chance will be gone.
And so will the butterfly. Wasted. Beauty wasted. Why? Bonds.
Difference. Who is responsible? We are. America. The world.
Everyday we lose butterflies because our bonds grow stronger.
No. The wasting can be stopped. We must stop it. Or...
The world is a caterpillar, asking for a mere chance
A chance to become Free... Trapped-It is up to us to
free the butterflies.

Christina Smith

Pray

Would God be happy with the world if he came back today?
For some time to change things we better start to pray.
Christians always fighting like we're serving different Gods.
Praying for each other would increase our odds.
Finding out God's plan for us and filling our own shoes,
Forget about the don'ts and concentrate on the do's.
Be quick to listen and slow to speak,
And help your brother when he is weak.
None are perfect, always keep that in mind.
We are all a little different, but all the same kind.
I pray that though we have different lives,
And through troubles we have trod.
That when we finish our work here,
We will end up at home with God.

Darren Stockett

Adventure Seekers

A boy's will is the wind's will,
for they share a need to be free,
to scamper over the hilltops,
to sigh from the top of a tree.
No time for sleep for there's much to see,
and too many games to play,
and if in the end an outhouse falls,
well, that's just a perfect day.
They sneak around buildings, peer in at cracks
and whistle an eerie tune.
They know that capers succeed best at night,
and better yet when there's no moon.
A curious boy, a capricious wind,
O, what a whimsical pair.
If I was given just half a chance,
I'd follow them anywhere.

Jean Calkins

Love Again

I hear your heartbeat next to mine,
I try to tell you things won't be fine,
You love me so, you love me true,
Why, oh why, can't I love you?
You say you'll love me 'till the world's end,
Why can't you learn to love again?

Elizabeth Barry

With Love, From Sydney Carton

My soul it calls indulgence,
For this twisted burning lust,
This heart, only lives, for the girl whom I can trust.
She's a vision of beauty, catches the eyes of wonder,
As nightfall brakes, I dream to be you,
in the daylight of autumns slumber.
Sinking in agony, aching with passion,
'Til someday between whirlwinds will awaken my satisfaction.
Release this torture, answer my call.
As I look into those deep eyes of blue,
I risen into the fall.
Seep into my mind, control my every move,
For my love that I may prove.
When earth turns to dust, and we all are but the past,
This feeling which lifts me from bondage,
My love forever to last.

Ali Morris

"A Man Ain't S'posed To Cry"

There is much in life a man can't know,
For time just races by.
His deepest feelings never show.
Cause a man ain't s'posed to cry.

He must be strong and always grim
To hide the tears inside
His heart may break, but his face must grin.
Cause a man ain't s'posed to cry...

Oh what poor fool has made this rule.
That a mask must always show.
To hide his warmth and tenderness
So the world would never know...

Well, I guess that maybe I'm weak, it's true
That others are strong,... not I.
But to lose a love so great as you,
then a man can't help but cry.....

Jack Dailey

Uncontrolled Misery

I wish there was a pill that could take away my pain.
For when I lost my mother, life has never been the same.
Even though it's been four years, I still expect to see her.
My heart cannot accept the fact that I'm no longer near her.
Sometimes I scream, "Oh God why me, you know she's all I got!"
But there's this need inside of me, no one can fill her spot.
I thought by now the pain would ease, or maybe go away.
But the darkest day of my life, seems like only yesterday.
I've lost that smile, my easy style, that I once possessed.
Without my Mother's loving ways, there's such a loneliness.
I'd give a million yesterdays, to say those things I should have said.
But now they're only quiet thoughts, stored deeply in my head.
So for those who read what I just wrote.
Being without her is no joke.
You should feel lucky when you hear me say.
"If your Mom is alive everyday's a good day."

Brenda J. Thomas

For Wilkie

The day is ending -
  give me your hand in friendship.
    Forget the dissonances in life's music.
      Don't go.

Cold night comes swiftly -
  I need your warmth, forgiveness.
    Be more than husband on our common journey.
      Be friend.

Christina Courter

Festival

Spring has tatted it's tender lace of leaves.
Fresh new dogwood petticoats peep coyly
from under winter's long-leaf dress.
Hillsides display their panorama of delicate greens.
Azaleas open hungrily
as forsythias leave sleepily;
tulips frolic at the feet of tired jonquils—
each part expectant, patient, forbearing,
making way for the next.

Beth Cartwright

"Crystal Ritual"

His presence a vivid picture in my mind.
For when I retire my heart aches a lonely beat.
Raging emptiness sheds the crystal drops, tear after tear,
each screaming of loneliness, love, and fear.
Each yearning for his gentle.
embrace and sweet kisses.
Evening after evening the same.
Crystal ritual.
For I know soon he will
embrace me, and collect his
loneliness, love, and fear.

Adonia Yarbrough

Incomplete

In mourning for you I found happiness
For while engulfed in sorrow I searched my soul
In my soul I found an empty cage
The cage of obsession from which you escaped
Now I realize it was not you I loved
It was the image of love
The picture of my life is an incomplete collage
Missing from view is that which makes a man whole
Love is what makes a man complete
I need love
But I do not want you
To you I gave all I had
In return you forced rejection upon me
Now I am left empty
But through your mirage I have travelled
And I see with you I could have never been fulfilled
For you know not of the need for love
And your soul will forever be wandering
Through darkness
Desolate and alone

Joseph Greenwood

Life's Circle

The flowers in my garden most are gone
For winter days have come, and they are spent.
They will not bloom again for me to see;
They will live only in the seed they bear
Seeds which will bring new flowers in the spring.
One flower alone endures the winter's cold.
It blooms so bravely in the grasses tall
And dares to face whatever Winter brings.

The winter of my life has come, and I
Must take hope from that single flower that blooms.
I, too, must brave the winter's days ahead,
And, like the flower, I shall face each day
Knowing the seed that I will leave behind
Will flower in the years that are to come.

Bessie Richards Chapin

For Me In Heaven

In sweet at brightest
Forest on world,
Or Green at highest
Stepped on world...
My sight is clearest there, my look is fairest there,
I'm healthiest and energized,
But not happiest there.
A place for me beyond the mountain loom, outside of nature's room;
A higher place where Green can't get,
so stepped in thought my eyes forget
Where the song of flora is always near,
but quiet enough for me to hear.
Yes, in Sweet at brightest,
But place ever made,
And high on stepped
Where Green's not made
I do not have a look there, my eyes are sightless there
I'm lightest and brightest
And happiest there.

Cara Monica Blades

The Mask

My heart thumps in fury to be free
Free from my past and free from the present
So I could finally just be me
Without hiding behind this mask of lint

I'm forced to wear this putrid mask
By society and its stupid rules
It is the absolute worst task
To be working for these insolent fools

The mask is simply a smile or a kind word
To be expressed no matter what I think or how I feel
I must keep smiling and always walk forward
Or be trampled by others who have been dealt the same deal.

Celesta Flanigan

The Love of Books

It was through the love of books I found a
friend - it was through the love of books
I reached to heights I only dare to dream.

It was through the love of books I climbed
to heights above my peers and threw off the
scales of darkness, and shackles of poverty
that just seek to keep me bound in weights
of ignorance.

I see a new day dawn as the night vanishes
as it sees the light. So did my mind see
clarity as the shadows melt away. It was
through the love of books I finally found
my way.

Elizabeth Clarke

Today

We wake up each day
Not knowing whether it's our last.
For during the day the unknown could happen.
Live free for today we are alive
Today the sun will rise, the sun will fall,
but today could be our last for there may
be no tomorrow.

Jennifer Lucio

You and Me

Friendships mean more than fun and games;
Friendships mean more than tears and pain;

Friendships are strong they grow like a vine;
That's why our Friendship is one of a kind;

We came together, two lost souls;
and created a bonding friendship
like none other told;

We share our deepest secrets and dreams;
We share our intimate moments and schemes;

We make each other smile and glow;
We help each other in times of woe;

And even though we may disagree;
Just remember I have you and you have me;

Together we will travel down life's longest paths;
Through marriage and children our friendship will last;

And in the end when all is said and done;
Our friendship will carry on with the decades to come;

Christina A. Gingerelli

Frog

Small, green, lovable, stuffed
frog
Smaller, deadlier, rainbow, poisonous
frog
Killer of flies and death to man
frog
Slayer of all
frog
Disease, damnation, hail, and pestilence
frog
Ruler of the world
frog
Master of all reality
frog
Small, green
frog

Glenn Peeler

To Fly Away

I could turn away
From all this misery.
Endless abyss of burning sky
Devouring my pain.
Let this world drag me closer to the edge,
Until I awake to freedom...
Until I fly away.

I can love, but I can't feel
What's been left behind.
Down, down, pulling me into its wed,
Hate binds my hands
Before they turn to wings
And save me.
Still, I lack the courage
To simply fly away.

To die, leave it all behind -
Watch blue tears melt upon a cloud,
Kiss the moon, touch a star,
To hurt no more...
To fly away.

Christy Kidder

Christmas At My Grandma's House

After the two hour journey
From San Diego to LA.,
We unpack so much luggage
It seems like we came to stay.

After greeting our many relatives
And peeking under the tree.
the sights and smells of the holidays
Overcome us immediately.

Sweet potato pie, peach cobbler, and cupcakes,
My mom and her sisters stop their diets
until after Christmas break.
My cousins and I — we talk on the phone
While our mothers are in the kitchen—all day—
slaving over the stove.

Until the wee morning hours
My oldest cousin and I wrap gifts,
While my aunts sit around telling old stories and myths.

Once every other Christmas Eve,
My cousin and I sneak a peek at the presents we received;
then we hide them behind the tree and go back to sleep.

Arika Suber

I Love New York

The big apple seed has all of your needs
From the Jets to the Mets from Mazart to Getz
From Tahoe to Soho from plain to plain
It's the greatest of magnums of tasty champagne
So come taste the apple and let's pop the cork,
And join in the chorus of I love New York.

Evelyn Failla

My Ancestors

In the 1700's the story is told of those who were brave and oh so bold
From "The Polatinate Section of Germany", conditions,
however were just as bad returned home so very sad.
New york state was not that great.
Some stayed here sending word not to come
because conditions were very poor and sad.

In 1727, the refugees came again.
This time landing at the Port of Philadelphia.
On English ship's that had embarked from "The Port of
Rotterdam",
settlement was made in a roughly defined as
South Central and Eastern Pennsylvania.

There are twelve variations in spelling
the name Heistand five in pronouncing it.
Six were military men, four were Mennonite Ministers,
one became a Bishop in his church one a physician,
one had a lumber and coal business, one was a dentist,
one was an attorney, one was President
of the Exchange Bank of Marietta, the rest were farmers.
Some combined their farming with their profession.

Again strength and courage, knowing they succeeded at all costs.

Barbara E. Cook

A Night on the Town

Walking these lonely streets full of people
Searching for an answer to life's underlying question;
Loneliness is fulfilled through one's own decision
To ignore the most basic human feeling of love.

Dina M. Sinsay

Isolated

Isolated, my breath feeds
From the slope of his neck
To the base of his chin
Entangling its sacrifice
In the silent whisper of departing fear.
My lips speak throughout him
Submitting to the rhythm of this deafening heartbeat
Demanding nature echoes of my own.
Covering me slowly
His arms, legs, tongue melt throughout me.
Dripping down
Onto the palest reaches of naked skin.
Torrential stream unleashing its flood
As raging drops collect aimlessly
On flushed fingertips.
A tangling of hands, hair on my cheek
Planting its scent within my pores, my mouth, myself
Now will I know, now will I see, now... feel
Feel his smell, his sweat — I can feel everything
I am complete.

Alison Dickey

Emphasis

We'll all relax now, and get away
from the universe. The noises of the
airplanes will stop as the dust spreads
through the sky. We'll all multiply
and listen to the rules of space, leave
nothing behind but wasted ambitions
hopeless dreams that have left us in
distaste.
  Let the tidal wave ride over you, it's
  Sweet and swelling. While the mounds
  of waves are cold and jelling.
You wanted something new, you wanted
something bright, you wanted something
sweet, so leave your inhibitions home
tonight.
  Rinse away the bitterness of another
  fading day, and lighten up your darkest
  fears with sunlight that never
  goes away.

Josina Williams

Wayward Love

Are you found oh capricious beauty
Garrulously trooping the suitory
Benefourously from Tom to Dick to Harry
Does Christ effect whom you will marry

Ere my heart 'tis ere my booty
For Christ's repose rejoice in duty
Bound hearts adhesion regales of faith
As life without is travestied grace

Twang is loosed the arrow twain
Fraught dark not mischievous brain
As bite lack one is to be smitten
For garrulous is only the meow of a kitten

A seal secured not easily broken
Threw it's return a heart is shaken
Speaks volume though now unopen
The seal of love not likely a token

Through flaxen air skies be blue
Little doubt thought you he knew
Spirit's knowledge flow visions of fair
Oh rejection bits the maul of bear.

Joe C. Johnson

Roses and Pearls

Velvet petals, soft and warm,
gently curved in a circle of love
each holding the other in perfect form
Graciously sharing a fragrance
found in no other flower
the petals slowly uncurl
until the blossom
opens wide and full.
A Rose:
The loving, tender, giving heart of woman.

Iridescent, shimmering, lustrous,
patience begun as a tiny grain of sand
Irritations and adversities only serve
to lend growth and strength
until a lovely, perfect sphere
glows with inner serenity.
Exquisite to look at, it becomes even
more beautiful in service.
A Pearl:
The gentle, pure, serene soul of woman.

Frances Hatch Pershing

Water Words

Laugh little brook as you splash along
Giggling and gurgling your mirthful song
As you tumble and mumble across pristine pebbles
Sounding your high notes, minors and trebles
Sliding and gliding across slipp'ry stones
Rhythmic'ly humming your soothing tones

The sight of your pathways is a treasure to see
The sounds of your journeys captivate me
In memories of when I sat on your banks
Watching in wonder and giving my thanks

For the eloquent simplicity of your
Song of Freedom and Joy

For the ascending aspiration of your
Song of Hope and Faith

For the continual crescendoing of your
Song of God's Love

Jean C. Morrissey

Summons To A Poet's Heart

Activity: speak clearly, from the heart.
Give your friends your self and accept the beauty of the moment;
a touch of bright, and building bridges.
Walk, side by side, in equal places.
Run straight to the grounding you share in strengths and spirit.

Quiet: warm; listen to your soul and center your being within
the moment.
Offer all you are; share everything, but take away nothing.
Hold my spirit close to receive eternity translated in heartbeat,
rhythms of breathing and enjoined with all nature.

Pray: together; step into me and accept my blessing
of companionship.

Live: in touch; nurturing the excitement into ecstasy.

Love: each other.

David L. Standley-Farris

"Joy-Filled Living"

Fulfilling the purpose of our birth
Glorifying God, Creator of earth.
Revering the life to us He has given
Rejoicing in our daily living.

Seeing the good more than the bad
Praising others will make us glad.
Encouraging friends along the way
Sharing our burdens will brighten the day.

Remembering the joy instead of the pain
Discovering the rainbow after the rain.
Allowing our hearts to be more forgiving
These are the "secrets" of joy-filled living!

Glenda Cook Pickens

God Is A Peacemaker

God is a peacemaker, God is of love.
God is in heaven, God is above.

God watches us all through the day.
And he guides us every step of the way.

I'm glad you're always there for me.
You lift me up and set me free.

God you gave me more than I need.
Thank you god for loving me.

You brought me a family that I love with my heart.
You gave me friends from the start.

I hope you listen to all my prayers.
Thank you god for being there.

Charlene Byrne

"God Made"

"God made" the oceans
"God made" the seas
"God made" the birds
"God made" the trees
He spoke and said, let there be light
The sun for day, the moon for night
In heaven let stars come forth to shine
Upon this great big world of mine
When this was done he still wasn't through
There was one thing more
That he had to do
In his mind he had a plan
So from the dust "God made" man
He breathed into Adam's nostril's
The breath of life
Then took his rib and make his wife
He put them in
The garden of Eden to live
But they had to leave
All because "God made" Eve

Donnie A. Frederick

The Wrong Colors

Dancing green robins float through the air.
Maroon-gray blowfish walk with grace.
Blue crocodiles slither under the neon pink ground.
Greenish-yellow angels silently hang on violet trees.
Reddish-orange olives hover in the silky white sky.
The Netherworld is not so perfect to the human eye.

Davina F. Becker

God Means to Me

God means to me; the vibrant colors of the sea.
God means to me; the warmth a fire on a stormy night.
God means to me; the light in the eyes of my Sami.
God gave me Sami to love and adore and to teach of him evermore.
For when I'm with Sami, I'm filled with glee.
The feeling I feel with God in my heart, by the sea.
Sami's God child so all things to her are free.
There's no light like the light in a child's eyes.
The light of innocence that God has given children's eyes.
So you see God has given all a child, a Sami to teach of him evermore.
Teach of his love and how to be free and filled with the Glee,
like I retrieve from my Sami.
Like the colors of the beautiful sea.

Darlene Garceau

"Reality Check"

Last night a prayer for you came to mind, asking God to always keep you in my thoughts, and to forever be kind.

It wasn't a prayer to be touched by an angel's kiss, for that prayer has already been said. Instead it was a prayer for you to stay forever in my midst, and keep my heart exceedingly glad.

It was a prayer asking God for help for I can't love you by myself, for I need His Divine Spirit to guide me and to teach me to cherish your love, and to put my ego on the shelf.

If it wasn't for him answering my prayer your love would not have come to be, but instead my soul has been touched by a love only God and His Angel could possess and allow me to make each prayer that I pray a reality.

Darryl L. Williams

A Widow's Prayer

Time has gone by, on the wings of a dove;
Gone are the days shared, with the one that I love.

Remembered are good times, of things that occurred;
But somehow those memories are shattered and blurred.

Gone is the laughter, that so often was heard;
All I have left now are friends, with a comforting word.

Maybe some day, my heart I can mend;
Until that day comes, all I can do is pretend.

Time heals - or so they say; I guess I will just
have to wait for that day.
Some say it will come - but I don't know when;
I'll take it one day at a time, from now until then.

Jacqueline R. Corum

Graduation

I see the day when I will be gone,
Gone from all the troubles I now face.
I see the day when I will encounter a new life,
That will bring a fresh light to my day.
My own special day to be honored,
For all my hard work and good will.
I will then face my inner fear,
Living in my own desperation.
How do I resolve this fear of mine,
With no one around me to confide.
For now I will live in this world,
Scared and excited for my big day.

Jennifer Pope

Farewell

Time has come to say good-bye,
Good-bye to you dear old Dunbar High,
We've walked your halls with joy and pride,
Now by your standards, we'll abide.

Good-bye dear teachers loving kind,
No better ones we'll ever find,
You've helped to stir our inner drives,
And taught us how to live our lives.

No longer will the school bells ring,
Our Alma-Mater sing,
But we shall never you forget,
Nor joyous school days we have spent.

Farewell, Farewell to the, dear old Dunbar High.

Dorothy Drinkard-Hawkshawe

So Long

So long, I bid farewell to you
Good times gone by of my prime time life
Minus the days of work and strife
On to the golden years with no trace of tears
Upward and onward to the sunset years
Where I'll look forward to each sunrise in sight
I will look to the doves in flight
Against the rainbows in store
Waiting at my front door
To all of you, enjoy your life whatever it brings
Keep a song in your heart ready to sing.

Johnnie M. Rice

"The Beast"

There was fire on the mountain, "The Beast" was loose again.
Grab your saws and shovels all you women and men.
From everywhere they came, from every state and town,
They came to fight "The Beast" on his own ground.
One foot in the green, one foot in the black,
They have to stop "The Beast" or they won't come back.
Inch by inch, and foot by foot,
They fought "The Beast" in the smoke and soot.
There was borate bombers and choppers in the air.
You could tell it was a war going on out there,
Brave men and women, one and all
They fought "The Beast" and watched him fall.
He may be gone, but he's not dead,
On another hot day he'll raise his head.
Again, they'll come to knock him down,
And fight on land with no flat ground.
But in July of "94,"
These brave young folks have won once more.
So say a prayer for one and all,
Who will fight "The Beast" until it rains next fall.

Earl A. Selby

Eternity

So many nights we walked the beach
Hand in hand, side by side, a pair of one
All we wanted, needed, was in reach
Evening came, soon day would be done

We sat on the breakwall to watch the sunset
There were breezes, rolling waves, a quiet hush
The sun sank into the lake, I can't forget
We could stay here forever, your hand in mine

Time has gone on and you've gone ahead
You are loved and missed in every way
I can only follow now where you have led
Surely I'll find you and we'll meet again some day

Harold Reider

"My Dad"

The decisions that he makes are always his alone - some are grandiose, others are not obviously known.

He pays a heavy price for the mistakes that he makes along the way - but shows no one this accounting upon his face, for that would show all, and soon betray.
"My Dad"

But alas, the decisions he has made, and the fire breathing dragons he has slain, are the trials and conquest of no ordinary man.
"My Dad"

How can a man so broad, and proud, and true, love me as deeply as he does, yet hold it in so well, because,
He Is "My Dad"

How does this man bring out in me such fiery wrath, then break my heart the very next moment, and bring tears to my eyes because of my desperate need to be held by him,
He does, because He is "My Dad"

I love him, and admire him more than any other man on this earth, so please be careful dad, stay well, go with god, and I'll embrace you once again at another birth,
Because You Are "My Only Dad"...

Cary W. Hartmann

Truth

What is truth? Is it something that really
happens or is it just a word, can we as people
really comply with the meaning of the word truth,
can we live up to the standards that are bestowed
upon us with this meaning? Truth is far from being
a virtue which is used with a passion, or even a
glimpse of once in awhile, so I declare a solution
to the word truth, to change its meaning.
TRUTH - A virtue which is hard to comprehend and
impossible to live up to.

Carlos Vargas

Brotherly Inspiration

In just a few months away I will see you walk away, with all your hard determination of four long years. I know the tears will be swelling up in my eyes of courage and love. Then I will hear them call out your name ..., Then it will suddenly come over me.

As I look back on all the good times we've spent together, it's hard to think it won't be as easy to do things now. Whenever I look at you, you seem so intelligent in your ways, and so strong. But you often tell me your terrified to go out in that big world. I never see you getting down on yourself, and I know college must have been hard for you but you took it all with ease and determination.

You always told me, don't let anyone get you down, just look away and keep your head up. And whenever I was in trouble you always were willing to lend me your hand. You always had a love for your music and wanted to get me involved as much as you were.

I know we won't be calling each other as often and exchanging little jokes that only you and I understand!

Sometimes I sit and look at you ... and all your success and think to myself I would like to be in your place. But I strive to be the best I can do, just like you always do.

Bernadette Warner

Hate

Hate is like a storm, thundering through the sky.
Hate is like a vulture, getting ready to fly.
Looking across the vast sky for it's cowering prey.
Sneaking up on the animals that work and play.
Hate is an epidemic, spreading throughout the world.
Hovering over human hearts, it's power coming unfurled.
Hate is like a scorpion, with it's poisonous tail.
Striking innocent victims, even the young and frail.
Hate is like the Devil, for it is his pride and joy.
He plays and tricks the minds and hearts of every girl and boy.
Hate is like a viper, full of deadly venom.
Striking every second, every possible victim...

Jessica L. Wells

The Birth of War

A disagreement, turning to a conflict.
Hatred is born. Blood is shed.
The simple solution is buried.
The people live for war.
It becomes their entire lives.
They eat, drink, sleep the hatred.
Emotions become too powerful.
Innocents are killed.
The children lose their hopes and dreams.
They follow the warpath blindly.
Families are turned against themselves.
Parents kill their children, children kill their parents.
Once-friendly neighbors lust for each other's blood.
And the leaders do not stop it.
War is obsolete.
And so are the people.

Donna Jackson

Displaying Patience

The desirable discretion of the unknown dreams to come
Have created a sense of confusion in my uncontained mind
I have yet to comprehend the distant emotions I hold
I will soon display the content within my inner most self
The distant signs that only an immense power can feel
Will become clear in an honorable dimension of each it's own
A definite force shall push the other in a direction of peace
The persuasion put upon will devour for an everlasting time
I can't quite compete with the indifferences between
But I will forever hold stability in a deep desire of one's consent

Jamie Billich

Life

Pens and pencils with their ink and their lead
Have destroyed some books, have even saved books

Love trapped inside a wishful, hoping heart
Has destroyed some souls, has even saved souls

Guns thunderous blows that everyone knows
Have destroyed some lives, have even saved lives

Anything you find, even in your mind
Can destroy this world, can save this world

Britta M. Anderson

This Wonder

The iridescent color's are dancing in the sun,
The hue's are astonishing a painting to be done,
The movements a kaleidoscope to the eyes delight,
In awe of this wonder-a Hummingbird in flight.

John Glynn

God Steps In

What has happened to the world today?
Have love and compassion all flown away?
Did we need a hurricane, tornadoes, earthquakes, and such
To cause our return to values with which we were out of touch?

As the Lord looked down on us from above
Did He become disgusted with our lack of love?
Why should we worry if a neighbor has nothing to eat?
Our pantries are full and our lives are complete.

Serbs and Bosnians daily kill one another.
Not stopping to think "He is really my brother".
In African, people die of starvation, many thousands a day!
Don't think about them ... they're so far away!

Morals are gone! It seems everything goes.
Uncensored filth on T.V. and radios
Religion, to some, means church and praying on Sunday,
Then preying and preying on neighbors on Monday.

All over the world God's gotten our attention.
People came together as if to a convention.
The shaking, rumbling, and torrents from above
Have brought all kinds together under God's gracious love.

Claire B. Garrison

Untitled

Butterflies with gossamer wings
  Have to be the prettiest things,
And every here and there I see
  A flower where a busy bee
Is carrying off, with happy drone,
  The nectar to his honey comb.
A soft brown doe nudges her newborn fawn
  To exercise and build his brawn,
While high up in a lofty pine
  New hatchlings say it's dinner time.
All these and more make Spring abound
  In brand - new sights and brand-new sounds;
Tiny creatures, freshly born,
  In unison greet each coming morn
In their own feeble, little ways
  To welcome the dawning of each new day.

Jeaniece Taylor

Friends

Some friends are very near, and some are far away.
Have you done your part in making a brand new one today?

Just look, there is the telephone as it hangs upon the wall.
Did you use it, even once, today to make a friendly call?

We know it's there for business, but friends are business, too.
Did some one hear, "How are you? I hope you're fine," from you.

Did you walk across the street today to show someone your care?
Take a minute from your busy day another load to share?

Friends are jewels more precious, than either silver or gold,
We need as many as we can get, both the new ones and the old.

So help me, Lord this day to use, remembering a friend to be.
For having friends and being one is strictly up to me.

Elsie Mae Prettyman

Sacred Blood

Proposal of the heart can not bleed for if they do it stains the brain in uncommon vain. It sinks to the depths of our soul and exposes the sensitivity of our being. Like a child we are forced to sit and wait for the overwhelming sense of vulnerability to deliver its punishment. Vulnerability comes in the hands of its master and the bestower of pain, LOVE.

Joseph Thomas

A Plea To My Black Brothers

Oh Black Brothers
Have you gone completely mad?
You're killing more of your own
Than the white man ever has!

You're doing to yourselves
What the Ku Klux Klan couldn't do.
You're killing off your mothers and your fathers,
And your sisters and brothers too.

Somehow we've lost our God
Along the way,
And the whole Black race
Is having to pay.

Are you going to let dope
Accomplish what no man could do?
Turn your backs on a God
Who's been good to you.

So, are you gonna ask God
To come back into your lives,
Or go right on serving Satan
With your guns and your knives?

Eustatia Young

Blue Box

He runs his fingers along the side to the latches.
He begins to open one, then the other.
He pauses.
I say nothing; I mean nothing.
He eases the cover open and a musty scent fills the room.
I light a match and watch the flame.
He lifts one leg over the edge of the box, wavering slightly.
My finger burns and I reach for another match.
He brings his other leg into the box.
I strike the match against the book side.
He looks at me and grins.

At first I make no move to follow.
The match burns out and I pocket the rest.
Only then do I move to get off the bed and step into the box.

No one will look for us here, I say as I shut the door behind us.
He has already gone away.

I take the matches from my pocket.

Bethany Marchand

God Has His Reasons

God took our son on a cold winter morning.
He gave us no clue, He gave us no warning.
He took him so fast, in the blink of an eye.
Our son was gone we know not why.

God has His reasons for calling him home.
To be with Him in His heavenly dome.
To share His life with my little boy.
Brings me both, sadness and joy.

God has His reasons for everything.
I'm sure He had His Angels sing,
When our little Dennis joined Him there;
Without a worry, without a care.

God has His reasons for the things that He does.
He had His reason, whatever it was.
We don't know why and won't understand.
'Til we join Him in the Promise Land.

God has His reasons for what He does.
He's here in the lives of all of us.
He'll take care of us in His own way.
All He asks is that we pray.

Janet D. Bedel

The Awakening

The old man lay in darkness, alone upon his bed
he knew the end was nearing, and his heart was filled with dread
No one there to soothe him, to calm his mounting fears
He raised a trembling, feeble arm, and wiped away his tears
His wife and child, whom he adored, had perished long before
Now he lay dying in this room,, alone,.. unloved..ignored
He felt a sudden rush of air, and then a wondrous sound
A feeling he was falling, lights and colors all around
He saw that he was standing on a strange and misty shore
Was it something he imagined... or had he been there before?
Soon his eyes became accustomed to the blinding, brilliant light
There were figures coming toward him and his heart filled with delight
Arms outstretched, and faces shining, healthy, happy, full of life
Stood his darling little daughter, and his ever-loving wife
Is this death...This sweet reunion?
Oh! How far, this, from the tomb
Soon his woes were all forgotten
For at last he had come home!

Dorothy Drew

My Grandpa's Life

A young man worked hard all his life
He met a woman, she became his wife
Six children they did raise
Each one gives them all their praise.

As time went on
Eight grandchildren came along
He helped to teach them right from wrong.

Now 44 years later, his working days are done
No longer slaving in the hot summer sun
Repairing trains are in his past
It's time to have some fun at last.

So, written is just this thought
To show you all the love you've brought.

Cindy Evans

She Still Has Her Pride

He's the one she had always looked up to,
He was never there, though, to help her as she grew.
But he had been a hero in her eyes,
She had always been proud of her long distance family ties.
Until that day came and she never wanted to look at him anymore,
She ran into her room and closed the door.
Soon she left, not daring to look back,
For fear he'd see that her life full of colors had just turned black,
Memories haunted her from that day on,
Things that she hadn't remembered came to her in her dreams
from night until dawn.
Things of her childhood that she knew not,
She had been hurt, badly, she knew that much.
So what is she to do now?
He had broke her heart, but to break her spirit, she would not allow.
When that hand goes up in a rampage she will try to hide,
But, she'll live, because her spirit is unbroken,
and she still has her pride.

Deanna Ford

The Devil's Dinner

The devil runs wild inside our minds,
He feeds at your cells and lavishly he dines,
You let him inside and serve a plate,
For he has chosen you for his life long soul mate,
Each chance you give him he'll snatch it up
For the devil is here and he's here to sup!
So chose you guests wisely or you will soon suffer,
The wrath of the one you've invited for supper!

Beckie Marquez

Raindrops

Raindrops play music on the window pane
The drops run down the glass
Howling wind is knocking at my door
I can hear the thunder's roar
The room is quiet but is listening to the storm

Brianne Chandler

Deadly Secret

Long, flowing, pale
Head to toe bony
flesh transparent
inside and outside interchangeable
scared, trapped and panicked
Taking small amounts (the smaller the better)
excusing herself she leaves
Door locked
takes a deep breathe
Eyes closed
fingers down throat
pushing all the enemy out
Water running to hide the terror-
no one can know her deadly secret
On a daily basis
she struggles to keep it
People suspect
but there is nothing to do
She is living her death
from not having enough food.

Donna Marie Bucko

Daddy

There sits a 5 year old girl waiting to
hear her father's voice, but hearing the
words your "father's gone,"

Sitting in a chair waiting to
Say good-bye and lay her tear stained
Rose on his grave while listening
to the words people have to say!

With people watching her walk-up
slowly, with tears running down her cheeks.
She says a short whisper:

"I Love You, Daddy"

Amanda Pratt

Have You Ever...

Have you ever arose to see the sun glow
hear the cow moo or hear the rooster crow
or see the horses run in the pasture below.

Have you ever heard a hen clucking to baby chicks
or listen to the red bird sing, as you walk
and watch the graceful soaring of a hawk.

Have you ever had a taste of water from a well
or smell the honeysuckle at the front door
heard the ring in the distance of the school bell.

Have you ever watched ducks swimming in the pond
or want and hold a fluffy, cuddly sweet kitten
or a puppy dog as she chews upon your mitten.

Have you ever rolled on the cool green grass
watch downy white puffy clouds up above
count snow geese in formation as they pass.

Have you ever thought to take time to pray
for all things on earth God give us today
and guide us safely on our merry way.

Geneva Broddle

"My Letter to You"

Every moment you are beside me, my
heart flutters in breathless recourse, and
I am left with a loss for words ... So
I become inspired to write.
In Italy, they may define this as CAESURA;
The slight pause in reading beautiful poetry
aloud so one might catch a hesitant breath
before continuing. I would have to agree
With your lips close to mine I feel I could
paint the face of God and describe my sight
unto some grand libretto, to where even
the sourest of men would weep.
You are my reason to create, and for this I
shall always love you.

Joseph David Howell

In the Eyes of a Child

A little girl sits on a swing waiting...waiting.
Her blue eyes scan over the horizon,
as wind blows her curly hair into a frenzy.
The sky bright with the heavens
colors reflect the child's thoughts,
bright and vivid, her imagination
running wild and free as though it were the wind.
Then, as though the child's heart had stopped beating,
her imagination had died,
leaving only room for the pain of truth.
Her heart sank as she knew that her waiting had ended.
The little girl stood in a place of death and darkness,
holding a single red rose to her cheek,
as if the rose was her life support.
What happens when the rose wilts and dies?

A little girl sits on a swing looking empty,
her blue eyes tell the story of her pain.
Always remember in the eyes of a child,
for our pain lies within our souls.

Jamie Lee Bozyk

To Allison

In her soft eyes I drown with sweet resolve
Her features so arrayed as to enthrall
Impassioned by her beauty I evolve
Enamored with her charms I helpless fall
Like the wind I run through her dark tresses
Delight with each long sojourn on her lips
Visit I her cheek with soft caresses
The splendor of all things does she eclipse
The east beholds less radiance in the sun
My love's depth wakes the sea with jealous tide
With nothing twixt our hearts they are but one
A world in which unfettered loves reside
These words of love are rendered for her sake
Upon the breath that she does from me take

Bryan T. Graff

No Worries, No Cares....

The cinnamon colored tumble weeds go rolling off in the distance. Lime green cactus's sprinkle the plains. Grey clouds cover the once blue sky. Greenish, brown, musty colored lizards dot the desert. The sun hits the earth with great humidity. The animals hide under the once cool rocks trying to escape the sun's vicious rays. The buzz of the bees is carried across the cracked, parched earth as an occasional breeze blows across the plateau.
There are No Worries, No Cares, for even what you may think, it is peaceful here.

Jennifer Adamson

Old Memories

Brown wrinkled paper, wilted rose pedals,
her memories of yesteryear.
She remembers when she was young,
and before his hair turned silver.
Now she is left alone with faded memories
in a small book that has folded pages.

She turns the pages one by one,
reviewing the days that have been spent.
The time is gone,
but it feels like it was only yesterday.

She settles back in her easy chair
and slowly glances around the room
In her mind she turns the room back fifty years
to the sights and sounds that existed then.

Candida L. Cameron

A Special Farewell

How can I say goodbye to a mother?
Her place can never be filled by another.
God gives only one, to have and to hold,
It's painful at times to watch her grow old.
Then comes the day God says "Let go."
"I need her in heaven body and soul."
"She's so happy now, I wish you could see.
You loved her so much, now trust her to Me."
She told Me to tell you,
"Please don't you cry."
"We're having a wonderful time, your father and I."
Her memory will always live in my heart,
So you see, I'm not sad.
We're not really apart.

Dorothy J. Kumhall

Consuming Fire

Under a pale moon,
Her warmth and love comforting me,
A spark ignited into a roaring blaze.
Hungry it crackled,
Starving it spewed sparks.
Carefully I fed it,
One by one
Letters filled of lies.
It's appetite never satisfied,
It hungered for desert.
A picture of a beloved no more
Was gently laid to rest.
As yellow flames began to lick at his face,
My eyes met his for a final farewell,
Before the fire engulfed him,
And he was gone.
Tears flowed freely, splashing down,
Putting out the fire between us
Forever.

Carin Hershey

Casey

Bright blue eyes and golden hair
Her smile an artist's dream come true.
Though little time has touched her here
Because of her, old things seem new.

Age is taking another victim
The conflict fierce and battle lines hazy,
But tiny hands heal old war wounds.
Thank you God for our little Casey.

Elaine Moss

Mother

I have watched the years my mother take,
her withered hands makes my heart break.

Her cloudy blue eyes so tired and sad,
remembering the years both good and bad.

She sits alone as many hours,
her memories pop up like beds of flowers.

Her hands so worn, wrinkled and rough,
but gentle with love in her tender touch.

She's made her mark on the minds of all,
and will, until the Lord makes his call.

I write these words with all my love,
and love her I will until she is called above.

So bless her lord for the years she gave,
her solid old heart, please do save.

Take her in your arms with your merciful touch
for she's my mother and I love her so much.

Dorothy J. Edmunds

Sorrow, Tomorrow

Names and dates carved in ancient stone
hidden by tangled dry weeds and worried grass

Brown wilted flowers mingle with dandelions
dusty shattered vases left from centuries past

Short rusty iron fence frames a precious grave
marking the untimely passing of an infant born

Wind streaked clouds cold swirls threatening
the moonlight reflecting off warm desert sand

Life like a mirage shimmering forever just beyond
yesterday's sorrow and the promise of tomorrow

Annie J. Heart

Blue Moon

The cover of the moon so big and bright
hides the sadness of the night.
The tears will fall but no one will see
the sadness in our eyes you and me.
I remember a time when you said you
loved me underneath that big blue moon,
But now even as I speak you are saying
good-bye and leaving me weak.
I turned to the moon to ask what to
do as if I expected an answer from you.
The only response I got from the moon
was a sparkle of light on some dew.
I took a look closer at that piece of dew;
It was settled on a white rose,
but not any white rose,
It was planted in the middle of a bush of red roses.
As I walked away I thought about that single white rose
and how it compares to my life.
May be I was put in this world to be alone,
Just me, underneath my big blue moon.

Brandy Mathews

True Love!

I sit here thinking of Lee
Remembering the words he said to me
Were they true
'Cause it's got me blue
Crying, trying to get him out of my heart,
but I know that feeling won't depart

Brandy Wiley

The Master Leads

The master loves to lead
His children by the hand
O'er mountain top or valley low in any land
But sometimes we won't be led
By his goodness and his love
And sometimes the master tries another plan
He takes a lash and whippeth us to him
Like a loving father whips his child
When we doubt or when we stray
When we fail to watch and pray
He takes a lash and whippeth us to him
Sometimes his lash is sickness
Sometimes some other things
Sometimes a financial need
Disaster often brings many ways we can be whipped
To show us that we erred
To show us what not to do
But that his will to be preferred
So by this staff or by his rod
Either way is up to God

Flossie Hall

A Shore Pleasure

Together we walked on the wet sands, faded by the tides
His face glistened by the inflamed sun
A cool mist breezed our faces with refreshment
The gentle touch of his lips sliding down my neck, sparked jitters up my spine
His warm hands caressed my tanned flesh and his kisses sweet and passionate
It was paradise without a doubt
Nothing could part our romantic mood but a mere separation
With memorable moments to cherish, it was sad to say good-bye.

Ann Marie L. Betlow

Dancer

I can see his muscular build through his black and white coat.
His green eyes express the words he cannot speak.
What is he thinking when he looks into my eyes?

Tender is the touch he places upon me.
I look down upon him, smiling as I watch him sleep.
When he awakes, he gazes at me lazily.
Do you want breakfast? I ask. Meow! is his reply.

Donna L. Diaz

"Thinking of You"

Here is a rose that comes from my heart
Hoping that last for you a long, long time.

Within this time, I'll be thinking only of you
And I hope to be in your mind,
Because darling I love you.

Now that I pinned it on you
It is hard to tell you apart.
It looks so beautiful on you
Right beside your heart.

If I miss seeing you one day,
My heart will cry for you.
I just like to tell you if I may
If you ever go away,
My soul will be lost for you.

And within this time, I'll be thinking only of you.

And I hope to be in your mind, because darling I love you.

Jesse Govea

Grandpa

I watch you slowly drift away,
hoping you will be better one day.

You lie there silently sleeping,
last breaths of air you are seeking.

You then begin to forget my name,
and I know things will never be the same.

I listen to my Father say,
that you have already passed away.

I know and regret what I did not say,
that I loved you each and every day.

Amy Tschumperlin

The Flower

How beautiful
How beautiful is my green existence
To the heavens, I open my flawless wings.
The sun, its rays of life dance upon my glorious wings
The breeze, sweet as an angel's breath
One day it will gather beneath my flawless wings
and carry me from my nest to the profound, radiant sun.

How long
How long I have reached
To the heavens I have stretched until my spine has lost its
strength and the sun's scorching flames sear my now bent back
Bonded by the shackles of my existence, I feel the tide of
piercing wind continually wear at the shores of my sanity.

How weary
How weary I have become
A raindrop rolls from my face to chase my battered wings as
they fall to the ground.
As my shadow grows more powerful than the path before me,
I take a last look at the distant fading sun and imagine what
would have been if I could have broken my bonds and flown.

Eric Hall

Spring

Where does the stream flow when it flows?
How does the wind blow when it blows?
How does the tree grow when it grows?
What does your mind do when it knows?

Where does a bee go when it flies?
Where does a sob go when a baby cries?
Where does the look go out of your eyes?
Where is a lovers soul when he sighs?

What do the bells say when they ring?
Whom is the song for when you sing?
How does your heart beat in the spring?
This little poem, does it mean a thing?

Francis T. Bleidorn

The Man

The man standing on a corner
Huddled in the pouring rain.
I go to him as he looks lonely.
He against the world, the world him.
Within the clouded confines of his mind,
He harbors fond memories.
With rain drizzling down his face he looks at me.
No glimpse of recognition.

Bedelia Lind Lam

Untitled

In the forest among the weeds,
there stand beautiful trees.
Trees that will be sure to flourish
Trees that we should truly cherish.

Cherylanne Piegaro

The Mystery Behind the Pen

It's one of the mysteries the unfeeling don't know,
How the story of life is like a mystery show.

What thoughts lurk down deep, inside a man's mind?
What feelings are hidden; or deadened by time?

Are they real? Are they true? Are the questions you ask.
Who's to care, who's to know, so long as they last.

A man cannot say all the things that are there,
When the feelings are hot and there's no one to share.

It's easier to write with a mysterious pen,
Those fantasies and thoughts that are held deep within.

A shadow of life is on the delicate lines,
First a thought, then a tingle. It's often sublime.

Read with deep feeling, they're a lover's delight.
Read only words and they're cold, stark and trite.

To think these are wrongful is quite a mistake.
But to speak them in public is a risk we won't take.

To put words on paper is not such a deal.
And to hide them in darkness is to deny they are real.

Thus, the mysterious pen is no mystery at all.
It's my fountain of feelings, expressed with a scrawl.

Albert M. McCaig Jr.

Puppets of the Mind

I cannot yet begin to understand
How you and I fell into this vortex
Of love and adulation, but it's grand
To contemplate, that when we meet the nex'
We will have time to fondle and to kiss,
For me to run my fingers through your hair
And touch the hidden areas of your bliss.
It's great indeed to think, that like the air
We breathe, we will be free, to love and drink
Through the same straw at the same time, the wine
Reserved for the Deity, and think
Each other deified and just divine.
For in each other's presence we will find
That bodies are mere puppets of the mind.

John Gerson Davies

Caught Between Black and White

In this time of trouble unknown,
I absolutely refuse to become withdrawn,
I need to be with people and talk,
In time past I would take a walk,
Hours and days by myself I would spend,
waiting for the dark times to end,
I use to refuse help in times past,
but this mood I hope will not last.
Of dark times, places and faces I would think,
into the dark valley I would sink,
but with time and help I will rise above,
because I don't want to hurt those I love,
with Gods helping hand I will stand,
above all the dark spots in a distant land.

Everette D. Mullins

Broken Heart

When I looked into your eyes
I admit it took me by surprise
To see a face this sad
Wondering could it be that bad?
Could it be this one who hurt you so
That didn't stop or search your soul
It's time to rest these endless tears
For, I promise there's nothing to fear
Those who hurt you were not smart
Cause now they've broken your precious heart

Ashley D. Cummings

I Am

One as truth of reality, reality of truth as one
I am as one rewards for repentance
Repentance for rewards one as am I

I am as one not condemning;
Condemning not one as am I
I am as one fast redeeming
Redeeming fast one as am I

I am as one being balanced with power
Power with balanced being one as am I

Power that's healing and restoring
As I am. Am I as restoring and
healing that's power?!

Power that's healing and restoring
one as am I, I am as one
restoring and healing that's power.

Power that's purifying one am I... giving
strength to restore and increase the
healing for one... I am one for
healing; the increase, and restore to
strength giving, I am one, purifying that's power.

Gregory La Mont Baraat Mursalat

"The Sea Gull Odyssey"

The sea gull mimics in loud terrain
I am brotherhood to this kin
tranquility sets on shoulders of the ocean,
You trek the pattern-knitted ski-seven.

hypnotized where there is no pride
in the waves above and tide
behind the eyes of eden
and a soul unbeaten

A youth desire is ever seized here
the travel is the repetitive mirror
Ballads will play strongly wild
see the mountains we climbed child

singing
breathing
witnessing
with crossed arms

had this dream before
that the sea gull was my core
in the eve of Sunday
with the eve of the distant bay

John Boe

His Voice

I am not dead,
I am just further ahead.

I am not still,
For I am having a thrill.

Yes I have departed,
But really life has just started.

For you see,
I am with the Lord God Almighty.

So all of you who were close to me,
Do not weep.

But instead let this be a testimony:
To follow in order to seek and keep
the will of the Lord God Almighty.

And thus you will see,
By following the will of the Lord God Almighty,

That when you depart,
You will then share this thrill with me.

Gentry C. Sullivan

The Visitor

I asked Him if He'd come and sit beside me on the bed.
I asked Him if He'd hold my hand and gently stroke my head.
When I arose I shared with Him the bread He blessed and broke.
I filled my soul by listening to the heartfelt words He spoke.
We talked until He made my many troubles melt like snow,
And when He left, I cried because I found I loved Him so.
I could not say who'd been here for they'd laugh and think me odd;
But I'd spent my entire day just visiting with God.

Evelyn L. Wallace

Life On The Farm

I moved out of town and looked around
I bought a farm which could do me no harm
I greeted a bee and it stung me
I greeted a dog and he danced with a frog
I greeted a flea and it bit me
I greeted a mouse and it tore up the house
I greeted a hog and it barked like a dog
i greeted a pig and it chewed up my wig
I saluted the sky and a hawk flew by
I greeted a hen and she flew in the wind
Then a crow flew by and polluted the sky
I sat on a stump and out ran a skunk
A squirrel in a tree tried to out talk me
I put on my hat and out flew a bat
The man in the moon stepped out of the sky
He asked me my name and I started to cry
I walked down the road and was jumped by a toad
I Went back to town where I belonged
I Started to sing and the farm came along
We greeted each other happily and live together as one family.

Ida B. Seaborn

Fair

When the fair comes to town
I can let my hair down and
have a ball, when the fair comes to
town I can act like a clown
cause when I go to the fair
there I can be me, when the fair
comes to town I can play around, for when
the fair comes around everyone can
act like a clown!!!

Angie Jankovic

If As A Christian I Pray,—-

If, as a christian, I pray constantly
I can avail a whole lot in the world
So I must pray consistently
And spread God's word to all the world

If, as a christian, I pray constantly
This world will be a peaceful place to live in
So I will pray consistently
For all the powers that be
Especially in my own country

If, as a christian, I pray constantly
Temptations may come, but, certainly-
Not one of them could hold me captive still
Because, I, back to praying will flee

My walk with God and my life in this world
Will only succeed if I pray and not faint
So I will pray consistently
Until I reach eternity!!!!!!!

Claire Aboko-Cole

"Great To Look Back"

When I was little and growing up.
I can remember things like a little pup.
Among those wonderful; "sing-song", things
carefree moments and playing on swings.
Hide and seek and bike riding flings.
Grandma's sugar cookies that after school brings.
Memories well up and my heart fairly sings.
Those times with family and friends take wings.
One thing sort a funny and I can't say why?
My Mother had a LETTER on her sweater.
I never ask; or said why?
'Cuz I'm sure it was a High School thing;
Not sure how she got it; but the school
colors were there. From Dad or a boyfriend
or maybe she won it, herself from any number of things.
It was worn and She did not put it on a shelf.
I reflect on that "LETTER" on MOM's sweater in spite of myself.
'Cuz its just stamped on my mind and well's up Happy Thoughts of
how Great: "MY MOM".

Inghram Miller

Grandma

Little Old Woman... What do you see?
I caught you, glancing at me.

We are so alike in many ways
But do you have the strength to count the days?

I have the strength, but only in youth,
You have the wisdom which tells the truth.

I know, one day, that you will be gone,
But I will still be here to sing your song.

I will never forget who gave to me a life so pleasant,
As the one that you made for me.

I will hold you in my arms forevermore.
Until life closes it's golden door.

So, smile, Old Woman,
And I will tell you what I see...

When I glance at you,
I see me.

Denise Hauser Nave

"My Choice"

When I was just a young girl I lived my life my way
I did what I wanted to I went from day to day
But now I am a woman in the middle of my life
I look down at my children and wonder if I might
Have made a different choice back then
And chose a different life
But as they smile back at me I know my choice was right
I could have changed it long ago I could have been alone
I could have gone a different route but then I'd never known
The joy they bring into my life the love I've learned to show
My children are a part of me I see me as they grow
One day they'll look back at their past
And memories will live
They'll remember their own lives as I once did
And the love they learned throughout their lives
Will grow within their young
And as I see them growing now they'll see it in their own
My children are a part of me I see them as they grow
I thank the Lord above for these miracles I've known.

Cindy Issitt

I Do Remember

I do remember how it started, I do remember when,
I do remember why it happened,
and I remember what you said.

I do remember that first day,
I do remember the last, I do remember the memories,
that you have hidden in the past.

I do remember your words,
in that night of ecstasy,
I do remember wondering,
"Does he really love me?"

I do remember when, things started to go wrong,
I thought you said you wanted,
our relationship to be long.

I do remember that things change,
but I don't remember why,
I do know that it's over, between you and I.

I guess I'll always remember,
what we did, said, and went through.
But now the hardest part of all, is getting over you.

Janice Tucciarone

Windsong

Whispering winds won't you sing me a song
I don't care about this life, is that so wrong?

Please sing me a song, we're both lonely tonight
Don't keep the trees company, they have the next days sunlight
To shine upon them and life seem right
I have nothing but silence to keep me a flight

Whispering winds please share in my sorrow
It won't be to long before there is no tomorrow

When I am gone, do not fear
There will always be a soul who longs to hear
That silent song that brings the sky to tears

Whispering winds won't you please dry your eyes
It wasn't your song that made me realize

That where ever I go, I'll always whistle your tune
Whispering winds I am lonely too

So let us meet later in a world far away
Where dreams are remembered and reality is astray
So won't you sing me to sleep, my only friend
I promise I'll never ask you again

Julie McManus

Untitled

I went to sleep the other night and woke with a terrible fright
I dreamed I had lost control of the dearest treasure that I own

I saw my girls walking away
From the love and the dreams I had hoped for them someday
From caring and sharing with me and each other
I heard them say "they didn't have a Mother"

I sat and I trembled and sobbed for awhile
But then something touched me and I felt myself smile
If I continue to love them anyway, the day will come
That even though I am a mother, they'll see I'm not so dumb

I held them when they were little and they skinned their knee and as they grew older and away from me I reached out to guide them along life's way but somehow they didn't want that at least for today

With death, war and taxes it was such a relief I was to become a parent; no worry, no grief now I look at my children, they're still my greatest treasure and this love that I have no one will ever measure

The new year is here and all I ask for is hope and the blessing of God to help me COPE.

Judith E. Randlett

"Glitter"

Glitter, glitter, sparkle, shine, where did it all go!
I dreamed of diamonds, gold and jewels, I was a
fairy-tale queen.

I awoke, where did it all go!
I looked and I sought to no avail!
Then I slept and dreamed again, I was in my fairy-tale land again.
All sparkly jewels, gold and diamonds.
I also danced the night away with a handsome fairy-tale king.

Aren't dreams fun.

Gail Tamara Taylor

I Envy

I didn't know the meaning of envy until I met you
I envy the woman that lays by your side every night.
she has the kisses that I long for,
the nights that I desire,
the children that I'll never have, and
the man that I love.
She has everything, everything that I wish I could have.

Dalila Alcantara

Visions of You

Can you feel my body quiver, your arms around me holding tight
I feel a glow and start to shiver, being with you I know it's right

And tonight I'll lie beside you a rush of warmth runs through my soul,
No one else could make me feel the way I do,
making love that makes us whole

I'm filled with uncertainty now, feeling tormented and desolate
You cared for me and I for you, but we both knew our fate

An everlasting love affair, that it would never be
My only desire was to love you, your dream is of being carefree

I see your face in everything I do, I feel your arms around me tight
The way it started out to be, remembering your eyes in candlelight

The times we shared for they were few
Meant the world to me, rather than never having loved you

I've kissed your lips so many times, longing to touch you
And all I ever wanted was for you to love me the way I loved you.

Diane J. Shaw-Jones

My Feelings

I feel pain.
I feel sorrow.
I feel loneliness in my heart.
Though I never feels this when we are together
but when we are apart.
Yet two days have pasted and still you are not here.
My soul has only begun to hold you ever so near.
Tell me that you love me.
Tell me that you'll stay.
Tell me that you'll always be here
Until your dying day.
I think of tomorrow and what is yet to be.
But I know that in my heart someday
you'll see.
The hurt
The sadness
And the agony
That I have felt knowing you have
left and will never be with me.

Hollie Wilson

The Winds

The winds of change are upon me,
I feel the blessed Lord has renown me.
Strange the winds of change how they surround me.
Cool and comfortable flowing through my hair
Without a moment of despair
Things I'd put on a shelf I now find within myself
Look at the things the winds unite, when once
They may not have taken flight.
Strange how the winds change speed in desperate times of need.
Sometimes strong and full of rain just like our inner pain
Sometimes weak trying to get in the door,
Just like the times we had before.
Strange the winds of change.

Josefina Vargas

I Always Felt Cold

In my first awareness as a child
I felt the cold of a Winter's night
before the multicolored soda refrigerator
in my great uncle's corner store
watching the naked branches and shadows.

My first room upstairs was chilling
without a heater to warm the night
during the deep snows and freezing cold
of the long and frigid winters of Las Vegas
through whose snowy roads I often drove.

I felt the cold even in the Jungles of Vietnam
where we froze that night by edge of the river
as we waited in an ambush we set for the Vietcong;
I felt it again as I held the pale, lifeless cold body
of Larry Comis from Minnesota who had been my best friend.

And I felt the chill on that cold and rainy morning
when I stood watching as my son left my side
to go with his mother who started the divorce,
and I was left with the lonely emptiness of my soul
as the absence of my family left only the cold.

Juan Jose Pena

The Way It Was

On the twenty ninth of september in seventeen
I first made my appearance on the scene
'Twas one thirty by the clock one saturday morn
When doc came to the house and there I was born.
By the time I was seven five times we did move
We seemed to be in a moving groove
At fifteen a month for eighteen long years
We scraped and we saved and shed a few tears
What a relief for now we could breath with a sigh
As the folks got around and finally did buy.
Then one day just out of the blue
It really did sound to good to be true
As I then done something that did change my life
That's when I got married to my wonderful wife
Forty-nine years later and still on the go
As we very seldom would say no
Now I will tell you all at last
This has been a brief history of my past.

Gilbert Hedges

Eternal Landscapes

As I stand on the cliff of my mind
I gaze across the plains of my memories.
The slow wind caressing the hills of loss,
carried to the shore where I shed my tears.
I stand I watch my years go by,
Like the sudden bolt of a deer
running from the fear of a gun.
As the sun beats on my face
I feel the warmth of friendships come and gone
and smell the breeze of a new beginning.
As I take a step I can feel the cool grass
sooth all of my longing heartache
and I am swept away across the field of dreams
and run toward the sunrise of my future.
I am not scared,
for my mind is a beautiful place.

Jennifer Ally Hugg

"When the Twilight Fades"

When the twilight fades my shadow from blue to black,
I get that feeling deep inside the hollow of my fears.
The thoughts of what could be gained by innocent patience,
sometimes, the quiet revels in the comfort of troubled worries.
Refreshing concrete iron flash endures the earth light.
Then I saw your eyes sparkle crystalline reflections,
I so often look to acquire with longing strength.

I can't keep the kindred flame from involving you,
Unknown to what is instantly so precious to higher spirits.
The boring romantic rages inside
his thirst of crimson, circling around
My impacted enticements of moreover
Celestial quantities answering nothing unto everything.
Then the shimmering blonde flow of silk spun hair,
calms me to a delicate plane of color and delights.

Alan Rodriguez

Loneliness

There are times in each of our lives
Those times when nothing seems to go right
And we wish someone was there to care.

We feel the need to share our thoughts
But when we turn around and look
There are times when no one else is there...

James E. Bishop

The Last Word—An Epicurean Delight

When chicken like this is served, the wise man
never lingers; he puts away his knife and fork
and eats it with his fingers.

Dud Hopkins

Hour Glass

My mind is an hour glass, my memories take place of the sand.
I grab to hold them, but I watch them slowly slip through my hands.
Tears can fill an ocean, one to quietly drown yourself in.
Watch closely, the storm's about to begin.
The wind blows so hard, your mind begins to whirl. You thought you were a woman, but you stand there a frightened little girl.
Thoughts of yesterday still linger so close behind.
Happiness is not something we have, but something we try to find.
We think that if we can get back whatever it is we have lost,
then life would be better, no time to worry about the cost.
We hold on to ideas about what yesterday meant. We think about that certain one, we swear they were heaven sent.
But still the mind remains an hour glass that the sand slips so easily through. And the time for letting go of yesterday is now well over due.

Becky Kirby

Waiting for the One

I always wondered who it would be,
I guess I have to wait and see.
Whenever I think that I have found
the right one,
That relationship is gone and done.
I want to find the right kind of guy,
And let all the wrong ones pass on by.
I need to find someone who will treat me right,
Someone who won't just stay one night,
I can't believe their lies anymore,
Because it's my heart that needs to restore.
I guess I deserved what I got
But things they said meant a lot.
On the outside I cried,
On the inside I died.
So, as I wait for "Mr Right" to arrive,
I am the one who is deprived,
I always wondered who it would be,
I guess I have to wait and see.

Heather Ziolkowski

Because You Never Came

I waited months that turned into years
I had a place for you in my heart, my life, my home
But you never came.

It wasn't long before I realized that
There would be no packages wrapped in pink or blue
No first word, first step, or hear "mom."
Because you never came.

There would be no first day at school, prom or graduation
Nor would I ever see you dressed in white or handsome in your tuxedo
No grandchildren will I have to spoil and love
Because you never came.

Now as the years have gone by and I am growing old and gray
No one will be there when I'm ill
Or say "mom" come stay a spell.
No memories have I, only a void never filled and a love never given.
All this, because you never came.

Alfrida Vella-Turner

Untitled

I am a human
I have a human's heart and soul
But beyond others I ponder life
I nestle down a deeper hole.

I see the extinction of the beasts
I watch the acid rains
I have known poverty, hunger, and disease
I sorrow, filled with shame.

How could this insolent race of mine
Turn on those forbearing?
I sense the inner presence of hate
Am I the only one caring?

Those powerful tigers, skinned of hide
Coats dull, which once had glistened
Where are our morals, I ask again
But no one wants to listen.

Yet still there is a hope in me
That it is not too late
But first we must learn to love again
And turn away from hate.

Jessica Evans

Mother's Mission

A babble and coo replace my alarm clock.
I have a new boss now.
The pay is not money.
The hours are long.
ABC's and 123's are the most popular songs.
Magazines have been replaced by children's books.
Diapers and burp rags fill each nook and crook.
Take a good look at my new job description,
LOVE, PATIENCE, and KINDNESS are the prescription.
I am a nurse to fix all bruises and bumps.
I'm a chief whose cuisine is bananas without lumps.
I am a financial counselor clipping coupons to save a buck.
A swim instructor whose best friend is a rubber duck.
I am a teacher teaching basic life.
A loving mother with hugs to help strife.
My bank account is far from full,
but my heart is overflowing.
This has to be the best job I have ever had,
I am never bored, and the payoffs keep growing.

Brenda Lee Sasa

A Leaf

Here am I, look at the size of me,
I have grown as big as I could be.

I am a leaf, a leaf am I,
I use to live a way up high.

I lived up high, where the breezes blow,
they loosen me gently, and I fell below.

My color of green has faded past,
only one season, did it last.

Tossed here and there and everywhere,
my season has gone, the tree is bare.

Now I am still, I will forever rest.
Time will blend me, into earths crest.

Joann Crump

The Autumn Winds

I have seen the autumn winds.
I have seen from my door the first autumn winds.
And time is changing our love.
Our love that is passing with the time.
I feel like flying and going to where the autumn winds go.
Far, far to where someone is waiting, and feels the time passing by
September is our day to remember,
And now my love has passed me and left me.
Our love, that was so true, has now been untrue.
Now I am blue and my soul is going to where the autumn winds blow.
For I have seen the first autumn winds.

Irene A. Martinez

"One Man"

I have seen the sins that people do;
I have traveled across this land too.
I have seen kids who go unfed;
I have seen people who have no bed.
I have seen the unborn die in vain;
I have felt the anger and the pain.
I have seen the sick with little hope;
I have seen their families try to cope.
I have seen injustice everywhere;
I have seen people who really don't care.
I have seen the tragedy of mortal life;
I have felt the anger and the strife.
I have seen the plight of our youth;
I have seen them struggle in finding truth.
I have seen the evils of drug abuse;
I have seen vicious crime on the loose.
I have felt the need for a higher power;
I have seen the need for family hour.
I have tried to reason as best I can;
I have pondered long, but I'm just one man.

Dave Craddock

I Am

I wonder what life will be like in the future.
I hear my parents arguing and screeching at each other.
I see boxes full of belongings and bare walls.
I want to add my feelings to what they say.
I am a caring girl in pain.

I pretend no harsh words are being said to or around me, being thrown
like daggers at a minute's notice.
I feel helpless and at fault.
I touch my teddy bear in despair and she talks with words of
comfort.
I worry about all of the divorces in the world.
I cry not knowing if my parents will become one of every two
marriages that fail.
I am a caring girl in pain.

I understand that they are doing what they feel is right.
I say to myself that things will work out.
I dream of a world full of peace, love, and unity.
I try not to cry when I talk about my innermost feelings.
I hope I live life to its fullest and greatest, accomplishing many
goals.
I am a caring girl in pain.

Bretton Butilier

Singin' In The Gutter

Hurry in
I hear them say
Smokin' dew
Takes the blahs away
Then I find that speeding's great
But the world gets slow and I can't wait

Friends won't help
By giving me more
Got no cash
I rip off a store
Just one time more's all I crave
Maybe this gutter's a good final grave

Now I'm
Singin' in the gutter
  staring at the moon
Don't worry 'bout me
  I'll make it out soon
Yea,
Singin' in the gutter
  But Lord there ain't no tune

Don Bova

Sweet Love

In the depth of my soul
I hear Thy call
Oh Divine Friend
My heart trembles at Thy approach
Many lives I've waited for Thee
years of sweet longing
Tears of divine sorrow melted in Thy love.
At last You come to touch my lonely heart
Leave me no more
You are my all
Sweet Love, Sweet Love, You are my all.

Jorge Paulovich

Sand Hills of Flat Rock

While standing in the doorway of an old log cabin,
I heard footsteps of an old lady, hair white as snow
Jogging along a river road, smelling honeysuckles in the rain
While lilacs are waving plumes of fragrant, as the wind blow

Just beyond a covered bridge makes any man dream,
watching the tumbling waters along a winding stream,
In search of the hidden channel cats, and bluegill,
and even look for morel mushrooms growing on a hill.

Whisperin' wind blowing thru the willows sweep the sand,
Across the farmland that ripple and drift so grand.
From dawn to dusk the farmer harvest the corn to yield,
while a red-bird sitting on a rusty corn planter in a field.

I recall tailgate picnics and hayrides when I was a lad,
I watched a dipping bobber in the flat-rock stream.
That's as close to heaven as I'll ever get with Dad,
Cause Daddy worked long hours to give us all a dream.

The children is all sick and my wife's down with the flu,
And the mortgage on the old cabin is nearly due.
But we are still living in an old log cabin
In the rolling sand hills of flat rock.

Carroll Sears

A Walk with the Good Shepherd

Don't cry for me Mother, just look up.
I just took a walk with the Good Shepherd.
I know you'll live many days without me
And there will be days of sorrow, but
Mother I'll see you in the heavenly tomorrow.

I saw you at my grave weeping
And praying today, mother I had
My arm around you and stood with you all the way.

God has never left you he just took me home
To walk with the Good Shepherd.

Heaven is so beautiful, even more than we talk of.
Yes mother I did say, "I wish mother could see this."

And the Good Shepherd reply, "yes my son she will,
And you and her will stroll the street of heaven together."

So mother hold close to your faith for one day
You will walk with the Good Shepherd.
Until then I love you

Cindy Rogers

The Shiny Brass Ring

As a young child on the merry go-round
I kept trying to grab the brass ring from the crown
As I grew older, throughout my life, always reaching
For that brass ring, not in sight
Joys sorrows, trials and tears. Reaching for that
Brass ring, to grasp so clear
What I thought it would bring to me? I do not know
It was just like waiting for that slow boat to show
Then one time when I was so low. Down as far as I could go
I found myself praying, holding my arms way up high
Trying to grab strength from the sky
The more I did this the stronger I got
Of course this made me to never stop
Then one time to my surprise. I realized I had grabbed
That brass ring from the sky
I now know where it is all at. The shiny brass ring is
There for all to get. If you do it in the right way
Our Lord will lead you through each day
With your prayers and psalms you sing
You too can have the shiny brass ring

Jeanette E. Wiig

You

When I saw you standing there,
I knew that you were the one.
The one that I would give my heart to
But not expect yours in return.

I long to look into your dark eyes
And to feel your warm touch,
But this remains a dream
Because you won't give me a chance.

I would give up everything
for one touch of your fingertips.
I could never feel this way about anyone else
because you hold in your hands,
My heart and the golden key.

Elizabeth Woodrow

"In Love!"

Sherry is her name words. .
I know her differently!
Abstract thrill or tender thought
Is her for me to see.

A word in thoughts where thinking needs to language
Stands apart like a lighted sphere;
Be it the word for her, however,
Then all the light does disappear.

For who can see the light when blinded
By a globe whose instantaneous flash continues
And is always in the eye?

I can but see a bluish dot. .
Abstract, again, but clear.
It rides and bobs before me
Ere I look there. . or just right here.

Alan D. Johns

A Child's Nightmare

I hear the tune of a lost child's song
I know the nightmare he lives because of a system gone wrong
I know his worries and I see his fears
I feel his heartache and I cry his tears
why won't the courts try to understand
the suffering he endures at his mother's hand
a child so frightened, so scared, so alone
all he wants is to be with his father, at home

Bridget I. Carter

My Mother, My Friend

A mother's love is unconditional;
I know this because of my mother.
She is more to me than just a parental figure;
She is someone I look up to.
I admire her endurance and courage;
Her faith inspires me.
I respect her comments and criticisms;
She is a wise counselor, always offering prudent advice.
She is someone I can constantly depend upon;
whether it be a shoulder to cry on, or a listening ear;
She is continually extending he support.
She is an unique individual;
never a harsh judgment, never a cruel statement.
If hearts were made of gold,
my mother would have such a heart.
She is a precious gift from God,
And I am abundantly blessed to have this special person in my life.
My Mother, My Friend.

Johanna Faith Lapi

Untitled

As I walked through the white wintery snow,
I listened to the wind steadily blow.
Listening to my crunching shoes,
Hearing it as if it were a steadfast soldier leaving his post.
Watching the sunset fall,
As it painted many rich colors across the sky,
like a splashed picture.
The trees had winter green leaves,
Coated with a thin layer of white, like a snowy roof on a house.
Birds flying onward toward the south, to migrate and nest.
I knew it was time for me to rest,
I knew it was time for me to go into an everlasting rest.

Elizabeth M. Burger

The Game Of Life

The Winds of Change blew in today.
I listened to what they had to say.
"You're old," they said, "Too old to play.
You'll lose the game, you're in the way."
But I said, "No, I want to play.
I may be slow and cause delay."
To my surprise, they let me stay
And I knelt down and I did pray.
"Please Lord, help me, don't make them pay
Because I think that I can play.
Give me a chance before you say
'You're old, my dear, too old to play.'"
Well, I did win, I'm here to say.
"Thank You Lord, for seeing my way.
And thanks again for letting me play."
The Winds of Change blew out today.

Donna Jean Zeabart

In Good Time

Oh, to dream of a time with no sorrow,
I long for that to be tomorrow.
Why, oh why must the cruelties of life,
Be dealt out like the stab of a knife?
Rarely is it that I have seen,
Explanations that are not few and far between.
Speak to me! Speak to me! Is my cry,
But oh, how it seems they long for me to die.
Death though is not part of my dream,
I want to dwindle on like a stream.
To travel and visit through out the world,
While my mind and thoughts I unfurl.
Not 'til then will I pass from here,
And get the rest I hold dear.
Upon this I will take my last breath,
And until then, only then, will be my timely death.

Ben Walton

"The Life Inside"

I see the sad lonely faces with tombstone eyes,
I look in their hearts and hear their cries.
Some faces are hard yet still I see through,
Their crying inside like me and like you.
The harder the face the harder the cries,
Deeply hidden in the face of lies,
Everyone here must hold the crying frown,
Or everybody here would surely break down.
I've seen some people who made it home,
Their faces have changed, their minds seem to roam.
What has happened to these men so unique?
Their faces now soft their eyes so weak!
Will we all be the same when it's our time to go?
The fear burns inside of a change I will know.
But till then I must live, and live day by day,
Because when you live in prison, there is no other way.

George F. Boody

The Culprits

White flashes in the western sky,
Then rain
Telling its tinkling story on the pane;
Drops gathering in puddles in the street
To plan their next adventure, when to meet;
Then slowly disappearing as the sun
Comes out to see what mischief has been done
While he was gone.

Albert H. Martin

Carry On Gentle Shepherd

As I think back and reflect on the years,
I look up and smile, then I feel the tears.
... My heart is filled with fears ...
... I listen with heart and ears ...

I ask God, "Why now? Why does he have to go?"
He answers in silence ... it's not for me to know.
... With winter comes the snow ...
... In spring the waters flow ...

He has other lives that need preparing.
He has other ties for him to be wearing.
... They'll surely be staring ...
... He'll still be caring ...

Journey on Man of God wherever He leads.
Continue to sow and water your seeds.
... There are so many needs ...
... Keep up with the weeds ...

When we arrive at the condo in the sky,
no more questions; we won't be wondering why
... we had to say goodbye ...
... Now I think I'll cry ...

Jane Skipper-Martin

To My Son

While sitting on my porch daydreaming of yesterday,
I looked out across the yard
And could still see my children at play.
A little boy in shorts with cowboy boots
Striking just below his knee,
Was playing with his dog
Beneath the old apple tree.

It seems only a short time,
That I held you in my arms
And I can still hear your famous saying,
"Please scratch my back Mom."

My eyes have filled with laughter
And sometimes filled with tears,
As I have watched you accomplish
Many things with the passing of the years.

I thank God, as I look at the
Handsome man you became.
But, down deep within my heart,
You will always remain...
My Little Boy

Iris LeVault

My Life Was Like A Rollercoaster

Things Given And Taken Away

I loved my mother than I lost her..,
I loved my grandparents then I lost them...
to a very crucial disease

I finally met my father and
we got really close, oh my God!
Mr. Heart attack came along,
he left me without a note

God gave me a child that I love very much
then I found out again what joy can really be.

Now I know that life can't be but so bad,
because, it turned around for me....

Bernetta Melvin

I Cry

Missing someone is the worst feeling I've ever had
I miss you
I miss you all the time
But now it's too late to tell you I love you
It's too late to tell you how much I cared then
And how much more I care now
And there's nothing I can do
I can try
try to remember
try to believe
but never forget
never forget the way you were
never forget the way I felt when I was around you
And now that you're gone
and I'm only left with memories
I can't feel the happiness any longer
and not knowing what to do.
I CRY

Andrea Kenney

In Search Out of a Friend

It was a day just like this one but somehow different
I needed a friend but not just anyone
I search through the faded pages of my telephone book
And even through the dark corners of my once sharp memory
Alas, I found no one
I did find many names and I smiled as I remembered
The laughters we shared and the hands out that were made
Suddenly my heart grew sad and ache as I realized that
I could not confide, depend or trust any one of them
How could it be? I thought, could I be so wrong
Troubled and stupefied, I decided to search again
Hoping that in my haste I might of overlook a name or two
As my search ended in vain, I laid quietly alone
Suddenly I felt at peace for in the stillness of the hour
I confided to the only true friend I knew.

Jacques R. St. Juste

"The Wind"

Ire winds blow - long thru the night
I often long to see by sight
The wind, the breeze, that seems so light.

But no, I do not get to see
This thing that blows its breathe at me;
I long to hold it, feel outright, this thing I know to be.

It rustles briskly thru the leaves,
Sometimes I wonder if they're grieved
When to the ground they're heaved.

You hear it whistle, oh! So bold
I wonder of the tales it's told;
It knows no fright, it knows its way, because it is so old.

Sometimes it's strong and tricky, destruction is its name;
Taking all that's in its path the good and bad the same,
It takes all, none are exempt, it's just the wind's bad game.

You travel far, care not for miles;
You travel swiftly in streamline style
You twist, you bend, and seem to smile.

Thou unseen thing I know thou art, I know you're with us not to part;
You're here, you're there, you're everywhere, without a start.

Geneva Maxine White Cox

One Little Ring

With this little ring I do thee wed,
I pledge all my love until I am dead.
If you walk with you feet or ride in a chair,
Makes no difference to me, I'll always be there.
As I write down this poem with tear filled eyes,
Our hope is not lost, it's as high as the skies.
Life's not so nice, we know this is true,
I sure hope it helps when I say I love you.
When our life is over, all our dreams will come true,
Because the prayers that I said were especially for you.
With each new life comes the promise of death,
So we live to the fullest, until our last breath.
When life is unkind, like it has been to you,
don't you ever forget this guy loves you!

Greg Meier

In Remembrance of You

I said a prayer for you today,
I prayed "Why did you leave this way?"
You left us all without a clue,
and now we'll never know what was true.

It took us all by a wounding blow,
why did it happen, no one will know.
For you it was just another day,
the day you chose, to pass away.

You were a strong and talented man,
who lost all promise in the palm of your hand.
We would of helped in your time of despair,
But deep in your heart, you felt we didn't care.

Now time has passed and we must move on,
and say to ourselves, "He is really gone."
Help us to understand why it happened this way,
And strengthen our hearts from day to day.

So, please say a prayer for us today,
for we are uncertain why you past this way.
And strengthen our souls with your heavenly smile,
while journeying us down that untimely road, mile after mile.

Beth Clark

Duet in Harmony

As time flows by and life plays on
I realize that our existence is too short
for us not to stop and think.....
how melodious our lives have been
and all the wonderful days yet to come
for you and I are a never ending source
of beautiful songs that play
like a symphony on the strings of my heart
and our love is a timeless dance
to which we shall always waltz.

Evelyn Lewis-Isaak

"Spring"

Today I woke up with a start,
I felt strange stirrings in my heart.
I heard a soft breeze say to me.
Come on, come on, come on out and see -
Out I rushed to see the secret of the breeze.
  And there beneath the crust of melted snow.
Was a green carpet, new grass so green.
A crocus lifted face, kissed by the sun's first embrace.
The buds on limbs long dead,
  Had awakened and burst forth from sleeping buds.
Even the birds had a new song to sing.
And then I knew -
It's "Spring" "Spring" "Spring"

Juanita Knoll

Floating Down from Independence

Late last night and the night before
I realized
I have reached the end of all I know-
and still you're there, wanting to go!
You are my anchor!
Because I'm afraid I don't know who I am...
Don't get me wrong, I'm not hiding
behind formalities or other such doors.
To you, Silverfish, I have promises to keep...
And miles to go before I sleep.
So, before we exile into the night, pass
me the bottle,
and we'll be on our way-
Journeying through life our own way.

And you send be spinning -into thought - that is:
I guess I'm just addicted to the pain of delight.

Dianna L. Starkweather

Is This Love?

Is this love? I ask of you from above. How do I know if it's true?
I really don't know what to do. I am too confused with all these
feelings, I really need a lot of healing. I need to just wait it out,
I don't think I can, is my main doubt. Someday I hope I can figure out
what it is, so I can give him what all is his. I have so much pain
inside, that I just can't decide. I really need some help from
someone, but how can they help what is already done? Sometimes I
think
of just ending it all, but the wall is just too tall. So I still ask
of you from above, Is This Love?

Cynthia Darnell

Remember

I remember the time; I remember the place:
I remember the smile that was on your face;
I remember your lips as moist as dew. And
I wonder, do you remember me too!

I remember the time that seems so close;
I remember the guy I loved the most;
I remember the feelings I had
  when you were near;
Oh how I wish you were here!

I wrote this poem so you could see
  that you still mean so much to me.
I wonder, do you remember me?

Anita Kay Van Nordstrand

"A Father's Plea"

As I held that fragile hand, a tiny little pearl
I said O Lord don't take her now,
She's just a little girl
Her night-black eyes, her loving smile,
With life that's just begun,
If you must take another soul
Then let me be the one
If I should lose this precious gift,
The pain I could not bear
The damage to my broken heart
Would be beyond repair
Just once more before I go
I hope that you shall see
You mustn't take this little child
Away from her and me
But if it's so that you see best
To give her Heaven's care,
At least I'll have some peace of mind
Knowing that she's there.

Candice M. Anderson

Untitled

I saw a flower on my bed
I said that is just what I dread
It was a poisonous one
It was as dangerous as a gun
I was scared to death
And I was out of breath.
I screamed as loud as I could
But it was like I was talking to a wall of wood.
Finally someone said
There is nothing to dread about that flower on my bed.

Jill Feinman

Wind Sprints

Tortured by visions I could not ignore
I saw what I shouldn't and then I saw more
I stumbled and ran, tripping I screamed
I would die to end these terrible dreams.

Awakened to see that all was not gone
The horror would never end with the dawn
Out of my threshold with incredible speed
The rumble behind of the nightmare stampede.

Chased down and flogged, but seldom beaten
Can't stand and fight I'm always retreating
With an occasional hand I'm pulled to my feet
But I'm too fast from running for us to meet.

It's not my fault that my feet are so light
Don't think our friendship is not worth the fight
My neck strains to see you running behind.
My legs still sprinting does not mean I'm blind.

It's just that I'm scared to even slow down
And face the whirlwind of pain that is abound
There's reason to doubt, but know that it's true
When in my choked gasping breath I say I love you.

John Gordon

Her

When I am feeling confused, I look into the mirror to see who I am.
I see a young girl with grown up thoughts,
Who wishes that her number matched her mind.
I see a beautiful face longing for love,
And a wonderful sweet prince as handsome as a dream.
This girl believes in others, yet rarely herself.
She is radiant when others are around,
But when by herself her glow dims into nothing.
Many see her as a rose that is always in bloom,
But really she is wilting slowly as time goes on.
By day she is alive and by night she is dead,
As her thoughts keeps her awake even when asleep.
Her emotions are numb from the memories that she keeps.
I begin to realize that I am this girl.
I long for love and for a sweet prince.
I believe in others and not myself.
I am beaming with joy in front of others and dull when alone
I am the wilting rose that needs love and nurturing.
I am awake at night wondering who I am.
I am no longer confused for I am my own person.

Jamie Quint

"Walk With Me"

When you are feeling blue, and the weight is too great.
Walk with me in the glow of the moonlight.
If you feel troubled in life, and confusion is your guide.
Walk with me in comfort, that I'll try to ease your mind.
Then hopefully with tenderness, and love given only for you.
You will feel that you can walk with me your whole life through.

Cynthia J. Wilkinson

"A Road"

As my road in life comes to an end
I see heavens pearly gates in the distance.

And as I begin to remember my life and the things
I've accomplished, how I've walked through Hell,
Met the devil and called him a friend.
How I found Christ, or was it Christ found me?

When the darkness was a friend and the light an enemy,
When I was alone in the darkness, and when
I found happiness in the light.

True, I never was an angel, but I had faith.
And when they ask, "How did you know?"
I'll say:
"I always believed in you."

Clayton Dye

Golden Color

I see golden color.

As I close my eyes tonight -
I see the golden color of the leaves,
reflected by the sun.

I see golden color

Wrapped up in autumn's blanket;
cozy and heart-warming.
The glorious colors of Vermont's changing leaves.

I see golden color.

Tho, it's nearly October -
yet, the day is so alive with these colors,
that I'm basked in the warmth as of a summer's day.

I see golden color.

Cindy L. Palmer

SVN's blinding

I look at myself through the eyes of an hourglass
I see the meadows of all years past
finding moments which will last and last
The days of life will fly right by
blurs of heaven fill my mind
Your beauty filled me from left to right
a world without you never crossed my mind
Once you left me
I became blind.

Aaron DeVere Lau

Life

I see the darkness, I see the way.
I see the passage to another day.
A sign of hope, a word of praise.
A glow of happiness to fill my days.
A silent moon, a glowing flower.
A bird that sings on every hour.

I've seen the winter, I've seen the light
I've seen the brightness of the night.
Something lovely, something sure.
Something made from something pure.
Memories that dance, memories that shine.
Memories of life that will always be mine.

A breathless moment, a whispered name.
A person you know will remain the same.
A chocolate kiss, a golden flower.
A spoken word that gives you power.
Words that have sung, words that have flown.
Words that will always be your...own.

Alison Heldman

To Grandpa Mac with Love

Here you lay sound asleep, dreaming of the people you will soon meet. I see you playing and holding us kids, but most of all, helping us all. The Lord is are friend, in many way's he watches over us night and day. When he thinks, we have done are work, he calls us back to him. We try to pray, but its not easy. But little do we know, everything we say and do is a pray in every way. So here you lay for awhile and here you sleep in peace, You have nothing to do but sleep, and go and visited our Lord. You are in no pain and you are in no hurry, so just lay where you are and remain happy, and sleep in peace, and think of Our Lord, you will soon meet. The Lord will be with you for ever and a day. He is taking you with him for a nice long rest. we love and miss you, and you will always remain in our hearts.

Alice Sheppard

Under the Poet's Tree

When the work is done and there's time for me,
I steal away to the poet's tree.
A tranquil spot where the mind runs free.
Where thoughts have life and dreams can be.

Where merriment abounds and the senses believe
All manner of things that cannot be
Illusions unfettered by magical decree
Where reality is limited only by me.

Come dream with me if you can and leave behind all care
There's magic in my special place and thoughts that we can share.
Let your imagination flow and your soul float free
And meet me beneath the poet's tree.

Diana Taylor

The Echo of a Smile

In the quiet of the day, my mind wonders to past mistakes.
I sense the need to call them back as links in a chain.

Each one created a feeling or made me question an inner value.
Each one made a change to the person I am now.
Each one brings back a memory of events that I was unable to change.
Each one sets a course of action that led me to this day.

Looking down at the person I see, I smile at myself with kindness.
If I could change the past, would I? The answer
The answer is in the smile.

Diane Patterson

My Cries

As the rain falls from the clouds above,
I sit alone, hoping to find love.
It seems my life has been a mere dream
Alone and sad, like a lonely stream...
It runs silently into the night
And tries desperately to keep out of sight.
I'm tired of always being alone,
I sit by myself like a cold little stone.
Why is there a hole in my life?
I feel as though I always have to strife!
I wish there were something to be done...
So I will no longer have to shun.
Now slowly stops the silent rain
Which means to me it's time again...
Time to put this mask where it should be
To make my frown austere to see.
But if you look, deep within my eyes...
You'll almost swear, that you hear my cries.

Amanda Leming

The Picture

Wondering if you loved me
I sit here and stare.

Wondering why this wall is bare.

Where your picture used to hang.
All that left is a single stain.

From the nail that held your face.
So secure in that place.

But now your gone; never to return
And in my heart, your love will always burn.

Elly Maxwell

The Cane

Oftentimes while walking down the empty hall
I stop and listen for the slightest sound
But there is none.
I slowly open the door of his room;
To find it empty,
But for the cane lying there
Against the corner.
Memories flash before my eyes
As tears begin to form.
It's just a worn, wooden cane,
But it was his.
In my mind I can hear the steady clop
As he walked, across the wood floor,
In his old boots.
But there is no sound.
The cane is silenced now,
But in my mind he will never be.

Charity A. Bliss

Goodbye

When I think about you leaving,
I think about all the good times I'm gonna miss.
The time has come for me to learn,
That there will be many more as time goes on.
I don't know what I'll do,
When there is no one left for me to talk to.
All the times I've lied in bed,
And thought about how much I'd rather be dead,
was just an escape from the pain.
I suddenly realize,
The only way to leave this is to talk and cry.
The pain won't just go away,
Thinking about how hard it is to go on everyday.
Feel good about yourself,
It makes the pain heal much faster.

Allison Pastore

Never

I have never been here before.
I see your reflection in my mind,
your touch is so gentle,
your words are so kind.
As I sit here with nothing to
do except write this poem and think of you.
Your smile brings sunshine to me,
like petals of a rose, a beauty to see.
If only for a moment our lips could meet,
so soft and delicate, warm and sweet.
I love you more than you will ever know,
more than I could ever show.
Never before have I felt this way
never before until today.

Daina Christian

Garden Minstrel

Music floats beyond the confines of the screen
Upward melody joins (angelic) choirs strong;
Carefully selecting pearly keys
Praise and adoration crescendo.
Flowers nod in majestic appreciation
As I play in a gazebo for Him alone.

Cristy Copeland Nagle

My Man

Every morning I wake up with you on my mind,
I think how lucky I am to have a man so wonderful and kind.
Everything about you is just right,
You're on my mind from the beginning of the morning to the end of each night.
Every night in my dreams I see your face,
it takes me away to a warm special place.
You bring sunshine to my cloudy days,
you make me laugh with your funny little ways.
When I'm around you I can't help but smile,
even though I've been with you a short while.
I don't think anyone loves me as much you do,
and God only knows how much I love you.
you give my life all its meaning,
sometimes I have to pinch myself to make sure I'm not dreaming.
I'm going to love you and take care of you as best I can,
because I know out of all the guys I want you as my man.

Chrissy Yacoub

Untitled

I always wondered what life had to offer somebody like me,
I thought I was a loser definitely,
But when I got here I was told otherwise
They said their was hope and I saw it in their eyes,
To be cured of this fate, of dying in a bottle,
Were there was no hope only sorrow
And I slowly got better much to my surprise
But I thought I was cured, I thought I was wise
Well one day it happened alone and afraid,
I didn't reach out I tried to be brave,
Alone and unsure I set out to find
What I thought I was missing and putting aside,
So I picked up the bottle I thought I was cool,
And then I saw how I acted a fool,
So I walked through the doors alone and afraid,
And their were my friends still sitting the same,
I always wondered what life had to offer somebody like me,
But when I got here I was told otherwise
They said their was hope, but now I felt it inside.

Anna Maria Sardina

Present And Past

For it's been just yesterday, that
I thought we'd last, oh how time has past
For the present thoughts of today
Still brings about the past
Although the thoughts of you, still
brings out the Present and the past
it's hard to forget the things I
went thru, only to lose you
to start a new was hard to do
yet the thoughts of the past only
makes me wonder more of what
the present will be,
boy, it's hard to forget, but it's
now the present and it's not the past.

Angel Eyo

Little Marie

A little child came tugging at my arm
I turned around and looked with great alarm
"Read a story," she whispered softly to me
Of course I will, little Marie
A little child whose life had just begun
Was soon never to see the glorious sun
Why was I filled with so much self-pity
When my legs would soon heal and I'd walk again - all over the city
This little angel went to heaven the next day
I could not cry, for I knew that all her pain had been taken away!

Ann Marie Torielli

No One More Beautiful Than You

I've never known anyone more beautiful than you.
I walk behind you watching your every move in front of me.
Watching that still grace of hand and thigh.
Watching your face change with words that you do not say,
Watching your solemn eyes as they turn to me,
or turn away full of knowledge,
slow or fast, watching your lips part and smile,
or turn to a frown.
Watching your masculine waist, your proud hands in their grace,
your an animal, my animal to love for all eternity.
Never to be rejected, but abandoned as I am to you
Over hearing your perfect speech of motion, security,
or the love you are giving me.
You talk to and help everyone when they need it,
That is why I've never know anyone more beautiful than you.

Hilary Stanley

Lonely Cries

Sounds of a lonely bird's cry ring in my head,
brings back memories of times when I was alone.

The lonely cries increased as the memories
of a loved one now only a distant memory,
but only their spirit remains unknown,
unsure of where it has gone,
but sure of its happiness.

The memory still lingers in his heart.
Weeping bird cry no more for the loved one is
still alive in your heart.

Amardeep Sangram

"Because I Love You"

I'm writing this poem, because I love you.
I always wanted to be with you,
For the rest of my life.
I don't want to see tears' coming down your face,
Because I want to see a smile on your face,
Also I just wanted to say, I love you.
I know it's late now,
But tonight I just wanted to write this poem for you;
Because I never want to loose you.
I'll always be by your side, I'll always be in your heart,
Also; I'll always be there for you always,
Because I love you.
I'm writing this poem, to say I'll always be there
For you; no matter what; I'll always be there for you.
I love you so much, I don't know what or how too
Say this, but you're a part of my dream
This is what I dreamed of is having you with me,
For the rest of my life.
So I'll always be there,
Whenever you need me the most; because I love you.

Andy Lee James

The Dead End!

So you think you cool,
Just who you trying to fool?
Everyday you going and getting high,
What you thinking? you ain't never gonna fly!
Someday you'll join a gang,
You'll know it's over when you hear the bang!
You were a great guy,
Until the day you started getting high.
Now that your dead,
Who's gonna sleep in your bed?
Your family is really hurt,
They never thought they would see their
son be buried in the dirt!
Well everyone is missing you
But we did all we could do!
You wouldn't listen to what we said,
Now we lay here crying in our beds!
Just one last word before I say good-bye and start to cry.
Remember the day I told you Drugs End All
Dreams, will I guess you found it out!

Jennifer Karr

Aphrodite

The soft sea mist whispers to the breeze,
She is coming.
The birds' constant cheep chip ceases in the air,
She is coming.
Slowly the curtain of mist parts,
She is coming.
For a moment the world is silent,
She is coming.

Up, on a cushion of foam,
She is here.
Beautiful, golden-haired,
She is real.
Silently the breeze carries her to Cythera, her isle,
She is true.
There a chariot drawn by doves awaits her,
She is love.

Now on Mount Olympus, high,
She is peace.
Taken in by Zeus, her idol,
She is home,
The goddess of love.

Helen Griese

Reality

On a rainy street, the magician reached out to me
Igniting a mystical flame - a private show performed publicly

Everything we had ever been, or will ever know
Rushed between in an eternal flow

Mere mortals might not conceive of merging body and soul
Heart's beating as one while chests rise and fall

We touch without flesh meeting - he absorbs my every thought
And gives them back uncensored, agreed with or not

I search for earthly expressions of how it feels to stroll on a cloud
Love seems so insignificant to even say aloud

Magic without illusion, a time etched in my memory
Intimacy undefined ... our reality.

Gail Church

Earthly Illusions

If you stereotype me ... I feel saddened
For I am not your vision of me

If you judge my physical body ... I feel confused
For I am not the outer shell you perceive

If you label me ... or if I agree with your evaluation
We both lose for I may not be displaying
My full expression of God's spirit today

So don't be fooled or blinded by our misunderstandings
Ask me how I am and I'll tell you my truth
At this moment to the best of my ability

Let's celebrate the uniqueness of you being you
And me being me
Together ... yet separate

(A pegGwen original.)

Gwendolyn Eddy

Hills Beach

Greeted with a smile as I come through the door,
I run through the little house on the shore.
As I run to the beach, I throw off my shoes,
and see the beauty of so many different hues.
I am amazed every time I'm here
By the beauty that seems to be everywhere.
I see the island so far away,
The little children so hard at play.
The best times here are early in the night.
The beach is deserted, the sea gulls take flight.
I see the reflections of the setting sun,
Heaven and earth become one.

Heather Carrier

Death

A precious one from us is gone,
A voice we loved is stilled.
A place is vacant in our home that never can be filled.

Darcy Jean Lee

A Child's Eye

A child's eyes so big and bright
A Mother's cries as she leaves never to return.
One by one in a line they have come
to say Goodbye to a dear friend
Tear after tear they will cry for a friend
they once held near.

A sister's cries, a lover's dream all to
soon to be heard or seen a friend's fate, a lover's
cries many to say a sad embrace for a warm face.

A Father's goodbye, a lover's cry many say a
sad embrace a cold stare, sad eyes, hurting
hearts, a slow walk to a song
memories return of times
they where one. Dream's of times that
they were one how it plays back in her
mind a slow embrace, for a wonderful face
as she begin's to read a poem he once wrote!

Jennifer S. Combs

Moving Grandma

He was there when I drove up the old lane of the farm today,
Even though there were no cows to milk, or kittens that love to play.
There was no corn in the river bottom, or eggs that could be bought,
I crossed the Shoal Creek bridge, and thought of the first fish
that I had caught.

He was there when I drove up the old lane of the farm today,
I could feel him as we loaded the furniture and prepared to drive away.
Grandma's teary eyes told a story that needed no words,
And to think this place could return to it's glory days,
was a thought that was simply absurd.

He was there when I drove up the old lane of the farm today,
I was determined to be strong, and not let my emotions get in the way.
I kept thinking he would come up beside me with a story he needed to tell,
Like the time he killed that twelve-foot rattler, or the one about
the old "Milk Cow from Hell."

He was there when I drove up the old lane of the farm today,
His body was gone, but his spirit was here to stay.
None of us seemed to be able to think of something, anything to say,
When we loaded up Grandma, for the last time, and prepared to drive
away.

Chris Parris

Ode to the Professional Informant

Scorned by most of his fellow man,
A Lawman perhaps his only fan,
He stalks his target night and day,
In turnabout becomes their prey.

Take heed, the tightrope you walk wears thin,
Some criminal looks to do you in,
Flee from this unsavory field,
To ventures with more productive yield.

Some dangerous task for you is fine,
Your eyes blinded by the dollar sign,
Your purpose be the law to serve,
Our wish, more people had your nerve.

Hark Judas, Hey Fink, Oh Stool Pigeon,
Have heart for the transgressor a smidgen,
Think of all the cases that you made,
Because of you, John Law made his grade.

And when in the end your tasks are done,
What matter that the fight not be won,
What matter that the odds were great,
Some law breaker has met his fate.

Harold Wenig

An Optimist's Creed

For every hill there's a valley, for every up there's a down,
For each moment of joy there's a heartache, for every smile, a frown,
Just when the goin' gets easy, and you start to relax and kick back,
Fate steps in with the unexpected, and you find yourself flat on your back.
It's been so since the world began spinning, so it shouldn't surprise you, my friend.
If your heart is set upon winning, be prepared for a fight to the end.
For it's sorrow and tears, you'll discover, that comprise a great part of your life.
I learned this the day that my lover became another mans wife.
She had promised to love me forever, but "forever" came fleetingly soon,
And my world which had once been so happy, reverted to sadness and gloom.
Still I mustn't forget in the darkness there's surely a light up ahead.
And remember, you've only two choices: 'tis a better world living than dead,
So rise up, my friend, like the Phoenix, and brush off the ashes of fate.
If your goal in life is to find peace and love, then go for it - it's never too late!

John Charles Preston

I Thought Her So

It saddened me when I thought her so,
A lonely woman and her empty bed.
But perhaps there were unknown moments,
Moments which lived on in her head

Beyond her dark bare strife,
A memory to save her from her mundane life,
A hope kept hidden, a dream kept locked
In a most secure pocket within her heart.

It saddened me when I thought her so,
A broken woman, whose dreams had passed.
But perhaps there were unknown wishes,
Little wishes which her very soul cast;

Reaching farther than her solitary room,
Living beyond the pain and ordinary gloom.
Little wishes kept under strict lock and key,
Little wishes she'd always kept from me.

Amy Loren Maddrey

The Ball

High frequency. Resonance tinkles, bumbles
Glass ball. Circular cone rotates, vibrates
A red skirt on the prairie, a gold bracelet was found in a sewer
Five hundreds arhats, ants creep onto their naked chests

Sine curves, diagonal lines parallel to vertical rhombus
In a cardboard box, a ball of wire is crooking, embracing
Transparent flesh and virginal base. To smear with a scraper,
It turns the assorted pigment into fashioned color purple in the air

The vase has a soul, sunlight under the dense forest
The vase has an emotion, electrocardiogram ripple motion
The vase has an ideal, pragmatism plus dream
The vase has a life, the vase is living

When an octopus stretches countless feelers, wriggling in craziness
Those lubricant legs with a cocky tail, slip into the hell
A middle aged tulip in a mirror, she is looking for her error
Freud's admirers, with a pious pray, boisterously, each has a role to play

Frogs jump into a dark well with a dive, swans fly into the blue sky
It's lust luster, still, and an owl underneath the white firmament as well
Finally, there is only a loneness left, melting with a clock twisted
The porcelain vase in drawing room, it now weighs 0.04 ton

David C.

"Open The Door"

Open the door and you will see
A space in my heart which holds the key
Take that key and treat that it with care
With you I would go anywhere;

Open the door and you will see
A space in my heart which holds the key
Take that key and adore it for a while
And when you think of me, always smile;

Open the door and you will see
A space in my heart which holds the key
Take that key and hold it tight
Let me into your dreams every night;

Open the door and you will see
A space in my heart which holds the key
Take that key and hold it close
Of anyone I've loved - I love you the most;

Allison Patrice Johnson

You Touch My Life

You touch my life with sweetness that filled my heart inside,
your lovely smile that open my eye's to see such beauty so precious and divine, a beauty that will always remain on my mind.

You touch my life by your presence
with love I feel inside, my heart
yearns for your return this truth I
can't deny, I never in my life felt
like this before, to find someone so
special, someone I adore.

You touch my life with your eye's
that shine bright as the day, how
much I love to gaze into them,
how long, I dare not say. Oh a
nice warm summers day cannot compare
to the beauty in you I see, just the
very thought of you makes my whole world
complete. This my be strong but I know
it's not wrong the love I feel inside,
I know it's real this thing I feel
'Yes' for you I'll surely DIE!

Jose A. Fernandez

Fourth of July

A mass of land floating in an ocean
A baby reaching for the sky
Crime and anger twisted and tangled
When gun shots and ambulances chime
And even when you come down to it all
The rich the poor, enemies and friends, victims and criminals,
The weak and the strong, black or white, Muslim or Christian,
Spanish or Japanese.
There is one night when all people come together
And drive miles to look up in the sky to see a little spark of light
But as I look around above the Ooo's and the Ahh's
I don't see adults, I see children with big goofy grins
And even though it only lasts a few minutes
It's like a second in the sun, a moment of fame
When the last spark fizzles out and everyone gets up and leaves
When the children become adults again and the grins melt away
And even though everyone leaves empty handed and there was
no prize or money for coming such a long way
The satisfaction written on everyone's face and the reflection
of freedom in everyone's face is more than enough

Judith LePera

Daguerreotype

The old woman I saw, the one in long baggy gingham,
a bag of flowers on her arm - on a levy, somewhere,
near a boat: 150 years ago (or thereabouts),
two children by her side: Kinky-haired and smiling,
beautifully: en route to her promised land?
They did not know from what bond they sprang, or age,
they held to her arm.
Nor she - they loved and trusted.
But she - fearful in determination, hopeful in her fear -
longed to ride the lone tram away:
to unknown regions, northwards?
But the shadowed presence across the quay waited and waited:
He bought a white ticket for Himself:
Here, His chattel, would go along, duty paid, southward.
He trusted her (Long-time member of the family,
like U-No, the bird dog),
She hoped and dreamed: He knew.
Or was I dreaming looking at my Mother's mother's
faded picture?

Francis Browne

Untitled

I was riding on empty, an emotional low,
A barren desert my spirit's home.
The music along with the words had all disappeared.

You came along like a verdant oasis.
Your spirit captured mine in a loving embrace.
Your presence filled my cup.

I now leave refreshed in mind and body.
No longer afraid to face the hungry world once more.

Diane K. Corsaw

DuVona

As the winds carry a mist of enchantment on their endless flight
A beautiful creature named DuVona appears in the dark of the night
The sea lashes out its beckoned call to the fair young child
She turns and smiles then comes to the ground... her hair bathed in moonlight mild
She is Nocturnal's only daughter... his blessing and his curse
But she is wailing because of one great thirst
She is trapped in a doorway... forbidden to ever see sunlight
The beams of the day banished to her and she lives only in the night
She is frail and pale and so fragile to the touch
But she would brave a thousand battles just to have what she longs for so much
But it is never hers nor ever will it be
For she is damned to darkness throughout eternity
So if on some ebony night up in the sky there is a mist
It is the weary DuVona whom sunlight has never kissed...

Angela Bozorth

A Garden of Memories

In the park there are gardens of flowers.
A beautiful sight to see
where I'd go and set for hours.
On a bench neath the old elm tree.
Where the squirrels would chatter like magpies.
When the sun in the sky grew hot.
And the children played round my bench in the shade
and all of my cares were forgot.
It was just a garden of flowers.
A beautiful sight to behold.
There were poppies-petunia and
pansies chrysanthemums and marigolds.
Where the bees buzzed from blossom
to blossom and the birds chirped
a sweet melody.
A garden of eden all by itself
with beautiful memories.

Elizabeth Titus

Teddy Bear

A teddy bear's a simple thing-
A bit of fuzz, A bit of string.
But behind that bit of string
There's a lot of love in that simple thing.

A rose is like the teddy bear
that is in need of gentle care,
Yet day by day a rose will die
And a teddy bear might lose an eye.
But You'll always's remember the teddy bear
That is in need of gentle loving care,
So don't forget that bit of string
That makes up that simple thing.

Frankie Tallarida

To Papa:

A minister for the church is to bring peace.
A church is God's garden and the minister is just the gardener.
This does not be-little the man or the church,
but like all gardens they grow old and beautiful!
In that process the garden will find a new gardener,
He may be young or old, He could have lots of wisdom or only
experience, either way, he is there to tend the garden,
It will only grow if the garden tells the gardener what it needs
to live and the gardener tells the garden what he needs to
help it.
Some of the garden may be lost in the changing of hands but
the plants will always be in God's hands.
They only need to remember this and tell the gardener what
he needs to do and all will be well in our own Eden.
We only have to trust the Father and His new gardener.
Let the young farmer sow his field said the man, for he shall
reap the harvest himself. If he loves the land and his
Lord then the land will love him.

Love, Heath.

Heath McCaskill

Free Diamonds

Everyone needs a diamond.
A diamond as big as the mind can see.
A diamond, as big as the one,
in your own fantasy.

And then!!
A million diamonds, I did see,
sparkling out across the sea.
The evening sun was slipping low,
as I looked across, this wonder I behold.

If you have never owned a diamond,
this one is free to everyone.
All you need, is the evening sun,
shining down, upon the ocean so warm.

Some people say, what did God do for me.
Well, for one thing,
I was born, in the land of the free.

A place where I can take the time to behold,
these wonderful miracles, that unfold.
Miracles taken for granted, day by day,
and I pray that God never, TAKES THESE DIAMONDS AWAY.

Cathy Reeves "Misty"

The World As We Know It

The world as we know it is
A disgrace to God our creator.
The world as we know it is a world of hate,
Caused by ignorance and fear.
The world as we know it is a world of pollution;
Caused by the greediness of people and powerful companies.
The world as we know it is a world of destruction,
Destruction of the Earth, destruction of mankind.
The world as we know it is a nonlivable place.
The world as we envision it is a world of peace and harmony.
The world as we envision it is a world of beautiful nature.
The world as we envision it is a world of creation.
But all these things I've spoken of are unthinkable dreams,
And dreams are made to be broken.

Greta Olson

Soulfire

A torch, a light, a passion burning.
A drive that moves us down the path and a match that lights
the flame of love.
Running water, that brings a spiritual awakening from a dormant
thud to a glorified burst of pure light.
Heat, flame and love powered, it gives us wisdom to peer through
the clouds, see the sky and find peace in our hearts.

Soulfire ... the key to the door, a connection to all that's past
and future.
Soulfire ... an insight that grows love from a concept to a
fulfillment of all needs.
Soulfire ... the meaning of life, the strength to trust, the
the gravity that pulls us back to God.

Jeffrey R. Brock

To Heather - My Fourth Grandchild

"Your Mother's Child"
A duplicate copy, a little clone.
One yet so small, the other full grown.

You are your mother's image,
You are your mother's child.

The way you walk, the way you talk,
The sweet innocent look in your eyes.

As you get older, your own personality you'll gain,
But parts of your mother, will always remain.

Generation after generation, child after child,
many, many reproductions of your mother's child.

Bonnie Hoover

A Biological Father's Love

Pressed between the pages of an old and tattered book,
a few surviving photographs upon which we can look,
to recall the angelic face of a baby as she smiled,
in a long ago, distant time, when she was her father's child.

Nursery rhymes she must have song, when she was at play,
bedtime prayers she might have sang, once in a long ago day,
rhymes and prayers we never heard, at least not with our own ears,
but they echoed in our minds, as we drifted through the years.

Like shadows cast, from the east, by the morning sun at dawn,
as surely as the night's tears dry, when the morning dew is gone,
one's childhood is so fleeting, just a fraction of our time,
and so quickly her's was gone, we missed her uphill climb.

And as the days turn into weeks, and the weeks turn into months,
after all those years he proudly recalls, he was her daddy once,
and though her name is different, their blood and cells are one,
and there will remain through time and change, a bond that won't
be undone.

Dixie Harden

The Bridge Tender

In the light of a cafe candle
a pen scrawls blindly in the hand's shadow
as a lost sketch of random lines connected by random music,
a violin without strings.
These are broken measures that sing.
Candlelight that does not beam on you,
but through you.
Past you.
Leaving eyes rolling
on the waves of the Bay.
Enter the City but remember your name,
so as not to be lost in the breeze
generated by the blinking wings
of a sunset gull.

Austin Lin

Embers

At night when I am sleeping you visit in my dreams.
A glance, a touch, a passing trace a sense of peace upon your face.

What is it that death holds, that makes you sleep so deep?
Can it be so sweet and peaceful, that it keeps you away from me?

What makes you lie there so placid and so cold?
For this I need and answer.
Please tell me what death holds!

Never to touch you or feel your love's embrace
Just shadows in the nighttime to take your sacred place.

There is a dying fire in me now this pain my heart has never had.
I just lost my best friend I also called him Dad.

So, at night when I am sleeping I see him in my dreams.
Once again we'll be together, a child again I'll be.

April Johnson

Musing On The Ruins Of An Egyptian Shrine

Reduced to ashes, these columns of a one-time land
A land that lived in flashes of color
Now buried beneath the sand
The priestly paintings, once glow
Are dusty as faded youth
In these ancient fragments
Can we ever know
Their wisdom
Their morals
Their truth

Florence Pearson

A Bird in Flight

Soaring in the open skies,
A little black speck catches my eye.

The mechanics of its flight,

Is the most beautiful sight.

gliding on the wind,

It drops down then up again.
"He must see me" to myself I say,

As he turns, spins, and flies so gay.

Like a little kid with a new toy, he shows me,

How majestic he can be.

And as he flies away towards the setting sun,

I yell "show me your splendor again sometime beautiful one.

And I realize that this was a bird in flight.

Eric S. Ivasiecko

The Sunset

In the evening I go out to see,
A masterpiece of God's laying before my eyes.
Brushes of gold He dips gently into
Paints that are finer than the finest riches on earth.
With careful strokes He paints on His canvas sky.
The colors He chooses are more spectacular
Than the song of a thousand angles.
He paints with the experience of a thousand years,
And yet, everyday's sunset is different
From the one before it.
Oh how lucky are we to have a God
Able to paint such wonders for all the land to see.

Jill L. Wallace

The Lowly Criminal

On a misty morn in the middle of September,
A long time criminal was tarred and feathered.

His screams rose over the city,
But no soul ever took pity.

As he looked to the heavens and offered his prayers.
A low gold light rose up from his hair.

Everyone was frozen in their place,
A look of surprise on everyone's face.

Down came the hand of God,
And scattered the frightened mob.

His hand took the criminal to the sky,
And from now on he could fly.

For he was criminal no more,
But an Archangel evermore.

Chris Schmidt

My Mother's Day Prayer

In this old cruel world - it's so hard to find,
A mother like yours or a Mother - like mine.
Someone who's faithful and kind - honest and true
Someone who says I love you and Jesus does too!
Someone who gave everything and took nothing in return.
Someone whose greatest joy - was to see you learn.
Someone who went to work - when she really wasn't able.
To put clothes on our backs and food - on the table.
This is my prayer
My Mother's Day Prayer
Mother - may God bless you
Because you've always cared
  About my ups
  About my downs
  About my smiles
  About my frowns
I pray for you Joy
I pray for you Peace
I pray for you Love
From God up above.

Benford Hunter Jr.

"My World Is Your World, Too!"

Take a good look at the world around us!
A multitude of cultures and languages remind us,
Of how rich and vast is thin bounty we call life!
Red, yellow, black, and white, side by side,
These colors look quite nice!

Even though oceans may keep us apart,
We come into this world,
With an innocence of heart!
By looking beyond the color of our skin,
We can liberate our eyes,
And see the beauty that's within!

The message that I hope to relate,
Is to live and help live,
Start now, right this minute,
You know...
It's never too late!

Barbara Fadul-Cheon

Riddle

Rough, beautiful, soft:
a part of life enclosed in a bed of rocks.

As it falls, you can feel its energy;
you can see its form cascading freely.
It surrenders to the pull of the earth and sunders joyfully
just before it glides to the motionless glass below.

It is elegant, captivating, even breathtaking as it descends.
Once enclosed within the glass it is simply there.
It rests within the rocks as the rest of its
soft white body plunges with a roar of mist and foam.

It is enclosed by matter that can't feel its presence;
it is seen by golden eyes that also fall
and die on top of its darkened rocks.
Its is a journey through the world
to a place of silence among the leaves.

Elvira Ceja Oseguera

That Special Someone

A special person only comes once in a lifetime
A person you love
A person you need
A person you want
A person to share your dreams
A person who makes you angry, makes you cry, and makes you
Confused all at the same time
A person who laughs with you not at you, someone who will
Dry your tears, hold you tight, make everything alright,
Say sweet things in the night
This is my lifetime and I want to spend it with someone like you
No one can make me feel like you do
No one touches my heart like you do
No one will ever take the place of you
You are my special person, I love you
In my lifetime I always will

Carolann Melanson

The Senior Prom

One small drink led to the next,
a pile of roses lies on my chest.
It was prom night, the night to act wild.
Mamma was right, I'm just a child.
I thought I was old enough to choose,
but I was wrong, cause I chose the booze.
I thought that I was really cool.
Never again will I see my school.
My life was taken like the switch of a light.
So if you must choose make the choice which is right,
or your senior prom may be your last night.

Crystal Thompson

To Have A Heart

To have a heart I have found to be,
A private hell deep inside of me
The terrible games that people play on each other
Shows me that we no longer really love one another.
The Bible said We should turn the other cheek
But when we do people think that we are weak
I pray each day that people will turn around
Because when they do they will be heaven bound.
The terrible abuse I have had to endure
It's not Gods way of this I am sure.
If I knew how I would make people see
That Gods way is the only way to be. AMEN

Heather Collins

Autumn

The misty dawn,
A quiet morn.
A mother deer and her fawn
  tread lightly through leaves of gold.
Soon a warm sun would unfold.
Squirrels gathering nuts
  and scampering away,
And birds flying South for the winter to stay.

John Harrison Pollard

"God's Bouquet"

God searched here on earth to see if he could find,
A rose to put in his bouquet, It must be a special kind.
And then he saw it, a perfect one a blowing in the breeze.
It was bright and in full bloom
and beautiful to see,
It sparkled like a diamond and was fresh as the morning dew
and it bent ever so gently as the soft wind blew.
And he looked for imperfections
and there were none that he could see.
and without a moments hesitation.
he said dear come with me
now the moral of this story is right in plain view,
because don't you see my dearest mother the rose was you.

Betty June Norton Nicholl

Religion

A message of darkness, a vision of pain
a searing drop of tainted rain.

Confusion, delusion, a growing boys dream
a crack in the spotlight that can never be seen.

Those empty souls with their minds in the sky
Created a God that was created through lie.

But through the shroud of darkness
and the light of day,
some people ran while the rest of them prayed.

A single flower, a child in pain
a shocking answer to a mindless thing

Sudden reality exposed by doubt
hidden meaning in a tortured shout

Forty days and forty nights was
the time required to see the light.

But as the mind grows full
and patience runs out
A man of God becomes a man of doubt.

Chris D. Wheeler

Deflections

Tattered ribbons hug worn ballet slippers, reclining on
a shelf, very dusty.
A once vibrant voice incapable of thrilling anyone; especially
herself, so rusty.
Albums of pictures, posters pans and revues, yellowed and
dried; impressive.
Encore! Encore! Amid the applause, sustenance, waned and died,
depressive.
She traveled alone in her quest for adoration, fortune and fame,
too bad.
Denied herself pleasure, temptation and pursuit of loves' flame.
  That's sad.

Gerree Leslie

The Thought of You...

A stab to my feelings.
A shot to my soul.
I gave you my innocence my innocence you stole.

You squeeze my mind causing me
to think of things untrue. Falling into
yet one more thought of you.

Thinking I want you knowing that I
don't. Nothing left to say or do but
leave this loving note.

The pressure and strain you put
into me, making me feel unworthy
of love even from me.

Your content was hollow but you
were so deep. Your endless stare driving
me to a tormented sleep.

You swallow me into your hole
tragedy burnt throughout my soul

The lies you told me were somehow
true. How will I ever escape this thought of you.

Jessie Krill

A Tribute To Parents

You gave me a home, brought me in from the cold;
A shoulder to lean on, someone to hold.
You sheltered me when weather started getting too rough;
Counseled and advised me when life got too tough.
My attitude given from you was "be free";
In order to be happy, I've got to be me.
The manner you taught me are all very well;
It's evidenced by how all of your friends, they can tell.
They say "he a nice man" and make you feel good;
You've done a superb job and rightly should.
My parents give me so much, but ask for much less;
To them I attribute my life and success.
You're more than my Parents, you're also my friends;
I now have a love that never ends.

George J. Miller

The Forgotten Child

The forgotten child lives inside the woman,
A silent woman driven by perfection.
She cooks bacon, does dishes, and drinks cold coffee.

She stares out the kitchen window,
Her eyes are fearfully empty, the wind dances,
Her hands move automatically, the dishes are dried.

The bacon is consumed, the coffee reheated.
The child is locked away, a prisoner within.
She struggles with her pain, longs to laugh.

The forgotten child lays curled in a corner,
No longer willing to be quiet, to be ignored,
The child raises her angry fist, shakes it!

The forgotten child wants the woman
To listen,
To hear!
She just wants to be seen,
To dance with the wind!

Ana Swanson

Thoughts

Warm, humid, sultry nights and a gentle summer breeze.
A silver moon shines from the heights softly shining through the trees.

And from this place so far away my thoughts start to wonder
Across time and distance to another day, that I recall so much fonder.

In my mind, I see you so clear. A vision of beauty you are.
The power of your essence seems so near.
Shimmering constant and bright like the North Star.

I see your face high in the night sky.
Your voice is the breeze singing gently in the trees,
And makes my weary soul soar as if I could fly,
But leaves my body, weak, and trembling on bent knees.

I raise my hands to touch your shining face,
So wondrous, so glorious and so fair.
But suddenly away this vision seems to race
And here I must stay drowning in workday cares.

But my spirits are brighter,
And my steps so much lighter.
My smile so strong and true,
All because of this one little thought of you.

David P. Gaines

"The Plot"

I've always thought a privy thought, deserved a privy space;
A solitary, hidden spot where no one saw my face...
To look out on the hills of green and see the clouds and sky;
But, yet myself, be never seen - no matter who went by!

I searched the world for such a place, where I could lie and ponder
And feel the sun upon my face or watch the moon up yonder...
It wasn't easy, time went by; and though I searched the plain
And climbed the mountain to the sky, my hunt seemed all in vain

But then, I found a wooded nook, beside a quiet stream
I lay me down, along with book, to rest and sleep and dream
"Move on, you knave - you're on my Grave"!

Alice C. Hart

Untitled

If you listen to the wind you'll hear a song—
A song of love calling to be found.
A voice lost in the breeze, untouched by life.
Clutching at your heart
Tearing at your soul
Crying out in the darkness,
Screaming in pain.
Lonely, desperate
Seeking a place amongst the trees
For love
And understanding.
Who will be the comforter?
Will someone rise to take her hand,
Or will she rest among the trees for eternity?

Cynthia Dale

Our Tree House

Our tree house recalls days of youthful play
Adventures high above ground shared with someone for a day
A first house to own with no mortgage - no deed to record
Laughter - stories - and secrets too behind the boards.

Now in golden years our adventurous spirits still abound
But we keep our tree house safely on the ground,
You see - our wild stories and guffawing
Are replaced with peace - serenity - and a little snoring.

Chirpful sounds - woodpecker's rap - catbird calls - Zzzzzzzz.

Donald E. Gillis

Heritage: Memories of a Father

A gruff voice explodes from the midst of a white beard
A sparkle glitters in deep-set, dark eyes
Weathered lines cover an aging face
Rough hands and muscular arms reveal the man's livelihood

A baseball is slowly passed in front of a child
Laughter and excitement fill the air as the pair board the motorcycle
Later, their shadows, large and small, dance across the porch as
they swing
Strong arms carry a sleeping form to be laid gently to bed

The crinkling of parchment pages breaks the morning silence
Child's and adult's voices join in singing their favorite hymn
The child's steps become silent as the kneeling shadow becomes clear
The gruff voice now sounds hushed as the man talks with his God

A solitary figure steps between the sun and the grave marker
Tears stir the dust over the sleeping man's bed
The figure kneels and a strangled voice cries out
Questions without answer reverberate through this resting place

The sun sets, the mud dries, the figure rises
The face displays the memories of the lost companion and mentor
Deep-set, dark eyes focus on the freshly turned ground
Farewell, beloved father, until we meet again

Debbie A. Zenoby

Untitled

There is a lady I know who is friendly and nice,
A thoughtful and kind person,
Someone who you wouldn't have to ask twice for help.

A radiant, outgoing person who gives of herself for others,
An angel sent to earth to bring a little light to whomever she comes
in contact,
A soul free as the wind and as beautiful as the sunrise of each
morning.

This is my lady, my love, the woman of my dreams,
heart of my heart, soul of my soul,
My reason for going on day to day.

For it is her that has brought me life, vigor and a reason to love.
Ever since I've known her, all I could do is dream of her,
wanting to possess her, have her as my wife.

For this is my lady Deborah, my friend and my love.

Bill Hintz

"Recreation? Procreation?"

A word, a kiss,
A touch, then this!
Gasping! Reeling!
Consumed with feeling!
Bodies trapped in spastic motion!
Overwhelmed, within an ocean
Of wildly, incandescent passion!
Felt everywhere, in every fashion!
Crazy urges and mindless drives,
Unrelentingly, grip your lives!
And then, the end! A climactic daze!
Senses numbed and in haze!
The ultimate measure of physical pleasure,
Has loosed a horde of tiny invaders!
(Someone left off his latex waders!)
And now, they have a new place to dwell,
Hot on the trail and swimming like hell,
In a desperate race to one single cell!
Oh well. Time will tell.

Howard M. Pierce

What Is A Rose?

Picture a rose without the flower...what would you have?
A useless plant with very little natural beauty of its' own.
A plant that is susceptible to bugs and disease,
with no practical use or purpose.
A plant that every time you touched it, or even got too close to it,
you'd most likely get stuck by a thorn!

Now, if you can, picture just the flower...the flower, all by itself,
is a thing of great beauty and is worth having...but the flower finds
it very hard to survive for very long without the plant under it for
support and protection. The plant holds the flower up where it's
safe and where all can enjoy it's great beauty.

Separate, they are only two parts; but together, they are one,
and are complete as God intended them to be!

Honey, this is how I view our relationship. I am the plant and you
are the flower. Separate, we can function, but together our lives
will become a beautiful rose!

I love you very much!!

Bradley J. Matkins

You I Am Thinking Of

When our hearts first met I felt this warmth inside me
A warmth so concentrated that my soul felt so free

As I glazed into your eyes, I saw an ocean so blue
The moon, the stars could not symbolize the selectiveness
I saw in you

You were like that of a man Godsend from the clouds so far up above
My heart was palpitating simultaneously displaying signs of
nocturnal love

How I never wished to depart that evening as I was so burned
with fire inside
I needed an outburst immediately, Oh, How it was intensified

Next evening, yes the next evening, was like a fairy tale
Your touch, your smile, your gorgeous structure was like a
ship without a sail

I crept deep into the recesses of your imagination like a fire
is to a flame
Please understand this heated feeling of passion as I lose
myself in your frame

As the evening turned to a close tears of joy poured down my face
As I reminisced the previous evenings savoring every taste

Evonne Moye'

"Later Than Before"

He sat and thought,
about all of their good times.
And a tear touched his eye,
as he remembered his crime.
She had loved him so much from the start,
from the first touch,
with all of her heart.
Now he stands looking down upon her,
with the blood on his hands.
Why he did this, he does not know,
But through life without her he cannot go.
He walks to the bedroom,
Where they had slept.
He thinks of the blankets,
How warm they had kept.
He turns on the light,
Leans against the shelf,
Looks at her picture,
And turns the gun on himself.

Destiny Justice

My Dad

You know he taught me so many things
About the birds and bees and butterfly wings
Screwdriver's, hammer's and that kind of stuff
Boy! Some of those things were really tough
I remember the woods and hunting for deer
When things were slow, he would bend my ear
I'll never forget the good times we had
And now that he's gone, I'm really sad
I loved my dad, with all my heart
And it tears me up' that we're now apart
Go with God, My Father, My Dad
In his hands, I know you'll be glad
I'll miss you forever
My Father, My father, My Dad, My Dad

Ernest P. Schiffer

Untitled

I wish that I knew How to write
About the lovely earth I see,
Around me, stretching far and wide,
The blue of sky, the green of tree.

Here man diminishes from sight
With all his weaknesses and sin
When I behold by God's sunlight
All things created He, for man.

These are the things that cannot know
How to impart a blow or curse,
For they fulfill the need for which
God placed them here upon the earth.

Oh that men like trees could be,
To bring forth flower and fruit, and then
Give out to all who hungry be
Of loves pure fruit,
Man's love for man.

Grace W. Price

"Suffering Man"

Profoundly do I feel for you my fellow man!
Affliction and trial seem to be your fortune here
Relentless are the pains that court thee to the death
Pitiless that disease which cripples once strong limbs
Even from the start, life strikes her treacherous blow,
Intimate with hunger, as you take life's first breath.
Unstrained the sorrow, from loss of one you love
Depression lowers thee to Satan's dark abode
Profusely flows your blood on the field of battle
Loneliness caresses with none to ease your days,
And who shall guide your shaking hand when you are old?
Or kiss thy wrinkled face when you have reached the day?
And who will think thee fair, when beauty goes to rest?
Flirtatious is death, 'till she draws you close to her
Suffering is your spouse, but not a loving one
A world of tears have flooded man's heart through the years
A sky-full of dreams, suffocated to their grave!
Man's murdered hopes make an ocean of deep, red blood!
A mountain of tentacles feeling grief and woe!
Yet helpless do I stand, to aid thee wretched man!

Evelyn Olson

The Little Rain Drop

Down from the bottom, up from
the top I just seen a little rain
drop, it flew past me, and there it goes
a little rain drop with a little tiny nose.

April Renee Freeman

Untitled

Shuttered in the black hole of age she sits
staring, wizened and still
ever littling, ever less
as function fades
and life is left
unhinged

Betsy N. Rhodes

Rainbows And Sunshine

There are rainbows and sunshine
after the showers, there is God we
can lean upon during our darkest hours.
There are sunsets and the silvery
moon at night, there is a God
who will lead us by his eternal light.

There are lilies of the valley and
rose of sharon blooming everywhere,
there is a God who loves us and he
will always care.

Betty J. Furgison

Two Good Friends

Who is this guy named Al?
Al - don't you know? Al is my pal
Al is the one who knocks on my door and shouts,
"Hey, Sal, this's Al, your ol' pal -
Come on, come out, let's play for awhile."
"Okay," I say with a smile -
Just let me get dressed, ol' pal, ol' Al."

So, out comes Sal -
all dressed up to play with Al -
takes a deep breath, peers up in the air
and gloomily grunts "Oh my, oh my,
look at that sky, it's grey, I say -
What a perfectly dreary day."

"But hey," shouts Al, so happy and gay, -
"you know what we'll do, dear Sal?
The day is just perfect for fishing, my pal."

So, - off they run, the tomboys two -
Sally O'Grady and Alison Pooh. And now you know
that the two little pals, called Al and Sal
they were not at all boys but two little gals!

Edly Bussolotta

Three Strikes

There's a place in this great land, where men
all come to yell... Passing judgement on one
another, sending them straight to jail... They
play the game of politics, toying with-in our
live's... Changing laws daily, to hear us weep or cry..
Yet the biggest game, that they now play, is
simply one, two, three... one strike, two strike,
three your out, out of society... It may sound
funny, a great big joke, yet it's true, reality... When
they all pass judgement, what will the sentence
be... Twenty-five years to life, that's just what
three strikes face... Taken away from family,
over a piece of coffee cake... A candy bar, apple
stix, or whatever it may be... The third strike can
be anything, then they throw away the key...
Simply one, two, three, a change of laws we need...

Donald Hargrett

"Infinite Marble"

Numbers line the halls,
all empty before the first ring.
They wait for the sentences and notes they will hold,
both of study and of love.
But in these storage spaces of life,
some hold the key to death.
Different calibers and different shells combine to produce
a sentence of death for the souls they meet.
It was thought in times past,
they were a status symbol or a way of life;
But now they are there not to take away life - but to protect it.
The tool was made to destroy, not to help protect a creation.
What has happened is a generation of fear,
fear to live a life.
If we don't create a world where life is right and death is wrong,
our world will become a city, a metropolis,
of Tombstones.

Harden Barker

My Flying Lessons

I studied the book and I studied the sky
All I wanted to do, was learn to fly
I went out in the AM's and PM's for a lesson
As that was the best time for a session

To learn the ups and downs of flying
The take offs were easier planning
The landing were sometimes very rough
However those planes were made of pretty good stuff

The way they bounced around was no joke
I'm really surprised nothing ever broke
At times the wind was very brisk
When you hit air Pockets you take a risk

I often came in on a wing and a prayer
Knowing full well, I'd land some where
airport ahead, with wind sock blowing
Signals to me the way I should be going

The trial flight was very rewarding
Excusing mistakes, corrections and regarding
quick out of the plane to get my log book signed
Thinking and dreaming of the next flight sublime.

Irene G. Smith

Time

To every thing there is a Season,
All nature heeds the time and reason.
The hour of time passes bye,
Flowers nod and butterflies, fly.
The red cardinal bids us a last goodby,
A splash of color way up high.
Silent and quite as the dark of night,
Busy Bees sleep and turn out their light.
Brightly glows the Harvest Moon,
Its reign in heaven to end to soon.
Daylight grows shorter, the nights grow colder,
Winters ice and snow comes closer and bolder.
'Tis nature's way to span the year,
As she hurries along both far and near.
Man, also, lives one day at a time,
As he settles down for the long winters rhyme.
And now the sands of time are running out,
Time to stop all waiting, no doubt.
So another year, another season,
'Tis nature's plan, for time, the reason.

Edna Leonard

A Glimpse of God

At dawn, light from the radiant sun displays
all the exquisite delights of the earth.
I see the gentle gliding movements of the wings
of a golden eagle in flight;
A field of wild flowers with their brilliant colors
and I am filled with delight.
Hovering above a crimson flower, a tiny bumble bee
pollen ladened, darts from flower to flower.
With nuts in its cheeks, a tiny grey squirrel scampers
up an evergreen tree narrowly missing the gentle shower.
A mother holds her baby tenderly and he touches her hair
with his chubby fingers and smiles.
A field with corn tall and ripe is stretched out
before me for miles and miles.
Walking beside a pure flowing river, I see the water sparkle
in the sunlight like a carpet of diamonds
and I reach out and touch.
On a morning like today, I am filled with immense pease
because my soul God has touched.

Joanne Marie Lake

Blind

I drink my sorrows span
Alone my echo's fear
My heart bleeds with pain
And soul speaks in vain
How come however, it seems over
But all is not, I go on through
My horror diminished truth
To dream pleasure
Do not consist with realities desert space
The fire sparks
Whispers to die
All ends, for this time
Tears a woes waste
The tongue I once sought
Full moon, beautiful, deadly
Though the moon will not
Rise another day
To blind and deceased eyes
Blind in a way

Chace Guernsey

Untitled

I can still see that star
Alone, shinning brightly, in the dark sky
Hearing the gentle music that bounced
Softly into my soul
Moving along at just the right pace
Looking above the mountainous trees
Where anyone can be free
There were no thoughts of what had been
Or of what was to be
I was free
With that star
Alone in the dark sky, shinning
As bright as it could
Knowing it wasn't going anywhere
Or be anything
But what it already was.

Julie Heinzler

Two souls

Two separate entities
Alone they travel along different paths but how could they
Know
How could they sense the invisible force that would
Eventually connect the two paths like the last piece of a
Puzzle which creates a picture out of what was once just a
Couple hundred scattered pieces of cardboard

Two separate entities become one soul
One mind
Making whole that which used to be two halves of the same

Two lives destined to become one
One life of eternal bliss
The nirvana everyone dreams of but can never experience in reality

Distance cannot make one forget the unforgettable and though
We may be miles apart we will always share the same heart

Chelsie Dwello

Inner Peace

Where does the strength come from when you walk
Alone, where's the encouragement when there's no
Shoulder to cry on. No hand to brush away that
Tear.

My light shines from within me, my strength is of
God. I am not alone, but filled with inner peace.
My heart is filled with joy. My life is one of
Happiness, my fulfillment is in christ. For he is
Love and I am blessed.

These things I give unto you, are not of the world.
Only a blessed few shall receive my call. These are
The words I hear him say. For I know Jesus is the
Only way.

Gwenda Dexter

"A Friend Is Love"

The dear lady that I love
also is my dear friend my love
a friend who means so much to me
My lady love my friend is she
My lady, my friend is more than just a friend
My lady my companion until the end
All the things we do together
Because we care we love each other
My love for her is deep and wide
My lady my friend I want by my side
To ride the long, long trail
Together our love will prevail
To have my lady for my friend
That's what love is with my friend
Day by day our love we share
My friend my love is there
Two friends that share our love
Knowing love, love is a friend
We will share our love until the end
That's what a friend is. It's love

Eugene C. Sweet

Who Knows

Have you ever wondered how the world turns endlessly,
We should stop and think how precious life can be.
  Just think,
All of our childhood and teenage treasures,
Might be read in the future for someone's pleasures.

Genetta Marie Wynn

Always Remember

What can you do when nothing is going right?
Always remember, that when you are down,
  The only way to go is up.

When you get lost in the labyrinth of life,
Always remember, that there is someone who cares,
  Out there looking for you.

What's left when you feel you've reached the end of your road?
Always remember, that there is a paradise outside,
  Just waiting to be discovered.

When you feel like everyday is a rainy day,
Always remember, that without the rain,
  There would be no rainbow.

What can you do when a dream has shattered?
Always remember, that they are not all meant to be,
  But the most important ones are.

So, when you feel like you could just die,
Always remember, that no matter what,
  I'm here, and I'll always love you.

Denise Henckel

Handle With Care

Always wanted to know me?
Always thought you knew me?
You don't know shit about me...
Till you reach my heart

It's hard to find
but easy to see
just look deep inside my eyes - or my tears
if you ever see them fall

I have a lot of love
just not right away
I'm hard outside
yet soft inside

If I came with an instruction manual
it would say
rough at times
but don't let the outside fool you
or will make a fool of you!
Handle with care

Danielle Peters

"America" a Progressive Country

Of all the country in this world,
America is the richest of them all;
For rich is natural resources and gold,
Most pioneers and frontier men immigrate here all.

Over the snow-capped mountain,
People build a good life for their shelter,
A vast area of flat land in the center
Are riches farm in the region producers.

The most picturesque rural village,
Is New England located in the Northern corner;
The busiest harbor is in New York
Considered the largest city of the country in this world.

The fifty States of the Union,
Has different climatic condition;
Others experience warm, summer and cold,
With an average annual temperature.

God bless America, the land that we loved,
Stand beside here and guide us to be strong, happy and useful,
V - as Victory, a free new world;
God bless America, our home sweet home.

Carmen Lara Gonzales

All I Wish

All I've ever wished for
is to write just one poem
to match the beauty in your eyes
to match the softness of your touch
to match the warmth you give to me

Edmond Mullen

The Old Barn

The old barn stands untended now.
Among its relics a rusted plow.

The harness old Dick wore,
As through the earth the plow tore.

A storage place for the family trunk,
An iron bedstead, and bits of junk.

A pine tree grows through the roof
While to the side, the pecan stands aloof.

Who will clean and throw,
Pick and choose, and stow?

Or will it just remain
A picturesque memory of an old refrain?

Dorothy Melanson

Untitled

Day in and day out,
Among the blind madness of sameness I walk,
wondering when will things change.

Looking into eyes of lost desperation and futile hope,
crying for salvation.

Torn from dreams by harsh destitution,
and pushed into the darkness of loneliness.

From one door to the next hopeful entry, mocked for feelings,
or just pushed outside, away from warmth and love.

So I turn inward, away from all the madness, all the pain.

I cry in pitiful silence,
As the world roars on in its uncaring cruel madness called society,
and policies, and all the other false hopes and beliefs.

I wish in my lonesome desperation for relief,
For a hope brighter than the dull medley of life,
hoping for caring, warm escape from this madness.

Where shall I turn?
What world would take such a hopeless wonderer, as I?

So I walk on with eyes of lost desperation and futile hope,
Among the blind madness of sameness, alone, and hoping.

David Andrew Peterson Jr.

Our Swing Set

Our swing set was a doorway,
An access to the distant corners of imagination,
A highway to dimensions beyond grown-up comprehension
A toll booth in which we deposited time and creativity and
Ended up in a mystical kingdom.

Our swing set took us to far away lands,
Protected us from destructible forces,
Traveled at speeds dangerous to the weak,
Defended our sacred worlds.

Our swing set was a doorway,
An entry to worlds of mystery which we conquered,
An entrance to the deepest reaches of childhood fantasy,
A door now sealed because we grew up.

Carrie Wozny

Ode To Jackie Kennedy Onassis

Before his death, life was a dream come true
An image of what we had missed
You stand so strong, all night long
Blood stained clothes, meant a door would close
As we all stood in awe, of your strength at the core
You took up the pen, to write us all
For the support, and encouraged us to move forth
Your finesse would even the score
Your eyes had seen much more
Now that your gone we have to live with this void

Cathy Ann Dee Woolley

Partner for Life

It did appear when first we met,
an unforgettable time to say,
this is it, and now we're set,
to get life going again on its way.
I was sad and she was lonely,
the time was difficult to say the least,
but as I thought she was the one and only,
I felt she thought I was the best.
We took out thoughts and decided to marry,
The rings we found at our first stop,
Some would say we seemed in a hurry,
But we knew this could not be topped.
In just a flash we were as one,
It seemed nothing in the world could be that quick,
Now that the important part was done,
It now was time to celebrate our pick.
So let me relate this essential clue,
if you, sir, are seeking a wife,
wait for that special one for you,
and she will be your PARTNER FOR LIFE!

Daniel Verdino

There Is A Time for:

There is a time for crying,
and a time for laughing;
There is a time for sadness,
and a time for happiness;
There is a time loving, and a time for hating.
There is a time for sharing,
and a time for selfishness;
There is a time for marriage
and a time for divorce.
There is a time for war, and a time for peace.
There is a time for Jesus, and a time for sharing our sins.
There is a time for family, and a time for friends;
There is a time for working, and a time for resting.
There is a time for jealousy
and a time for making up.
There is a time for everything, but
there is only one thing that only
happens once in life. And that is the time of life.

Andrea Joy Clark

Passionate Innocence

I see into the glow of his eyes
and feel my soul being released into the air.
Soaring, we leave our bodies behind.
Our souls intertwine, music is composed in our passion.
Caressing in the blinding darkness, kissing in the empty contentment.
As the night ends and darkness dims, we fly.
Our souls part and fly to our bodies.
With a long dark day ahead,
to wait for night where we can be free once again.

Emily Coppess

Henry Adolph Kuhlman

When I was a wee tot, my father would set me on his knee,
and after church he would read the Sunday comics to me.

Sunday, it seems, was the only day he sometimes rested.
Farming for his family, was where his time was vested.

He slopped hogs, milked cows, and picked corn by hand.
With horses, then tractors, he dutifully tilled his land.

From his brow, much laborious sweat has tirelessly flowed.
From his heart, much love unselfishly has been bestowed.

Kindness and compassion blossom along my father's path.
Dad is contagiously congenial and rarely shows his wrath.

'Hello Hank.' 'Hi Henry.', he is greeted with affection.
Honesty and integrity have always been his direction.

I am very proud of my father and love him very much.
He EARNED my respect with his special caring touch.

Unequivocally, I can honestly say I have the best father in the world.
'Dad, you're the greatest', my banner would say as it is unfurled.

On occasion I am told, 'You are just like your dad.'
The highest compliment, I think, and I really feel glad.

So, happy birthday Dad, on this your 90th year.
Just know, I love you and hold you so very dear.

Brian Kuhlman

O Moon, O Moon

For when night hath come
And all is Dark
The feeling again arises inside my soul
As I stand alone in the quiet, empty space
My body is enveloped in a cold, quivering fear

Every sound intensified in my mind
The mere rustling of leaves like a plane overhead
Of my own shadow I am afraid
My heart racing, my mind playing tricks
All around me the terrifying scream of silence

O Moon, O Moon, O dastardly Moon
Why have you forsaken me?
Where have you gone? I cannot find You I am frightened and alone
Please, O Moon, come out and spread Your pale rays upon
this stricken land

Now night hath come
And all is Dark
Inside my soul the feeling burns
The fear, the cold, the silence, the Dark
And You, O Moon, my final hope, You have abandoned me too.

Brenda R. Lutovsky

Olympic Dream

Had I the gift of purebred athlete's gait,
And, free of ills and aches of old,
Could race the gay gazelle across the plain,
And summon strength to fast subdue the streaking train,
I then would not resign myself to wait,

To pine, imprisoned, caught in dumbstruck awe
By glee of graceful limb and soul.
Oh, if this one could only sprightly leap
The farmfield fence, and leave him there, a hulking heap,
That other struggling self whom last I saw

Bent plucking roses from a private plot,
And dreaming books were cakes of gold.
They say such possibilities exist.
If I could forego wisdom and succumb to this,
Then someday I could be what I am not.

Harold Reames

The Circus People

The crowd has gathered
and all settled in their seats,
Everyone eager and so happy,
Drum rolls increase with every beat.

Suddenly there's silence and the clowns begin their acts,
People get ready for action with those beautiful giant cats.

There is so much going on, plenty for all to see,
Acrobats swinging back and forth like monkeys in a tree.

With all that's happening on stage, color and excitement, too.
Peanut vendors manage to do their act, too.

Music in the background, creating a happy theme,
The air is filled with joy, in general a very happy scene.
The circus people make it happen,
entertainment for everyone,
Children of all ages,
that includes everyone!

Julia Lombardo

The Wind

I saw you toss the kites up high,
And blow the birds through the sky.
And all around I heard you pass,
Like pieces of paper blowing on the grass.

You blow all day for so long,
The wind that sings so loud a song.

I saw the different things you did,
But always yourself you hid.
I felt you push, I heard you call,
I couldn't see yourself at all!

You are strong and so very cold,
You are both young and old.
You first sing soft, then sing loud,
Like swirling circles all around.

You blow all day, for so long,
The wind that sings so loud a song.

Ashley Cohen

Autumn's Child

Autumn's wind is crisp and cool
And clears a path as we walk to school
Leaves spin and whirl around
Forming ghostly shapes floating across the old playground

Autumn leaves were never so much fun
As wrapped in a child's hair in the morning sun
Schoolyard trees are ablaze with a golden hue
Everything smells fresh bathed in the morning dew

The bell summons all that are still at play
In Autumn's morning light at the break of day
The room is warm, the smell inviting
As the teacher prepares for reading and writing

Autumn will pass with the blink of an eye
So short, so quiet, shall she die
Taking with her the leaves and wind
When winter shall come and autumn shall end

The school house windows frame the time
Of a season beckoning children with her rhyme
To come outside and continue to play
Before Autumn's Child has gone away

Jesse Murphree

No Revenge

Daily I deal with memories of pain,
And daily the blame goes straight down to hell.
Mirrors still haunt me like something insane.
I loathe you and curse the place where you dwell.

The bruises of fights and memories of tears
reoccur like night mares and twist my soul.
Your scorn has scarred my future years.
You took what you wanted while taking your toll.

I cried when I learned you had taken your life,
Not in mourning but because you were gone,
And revenge wasn't mine, just lonely strife.
A dead bastard can't pay for what he has done.

My heart doesn't know real love all the same,
but loathes a bastard in hell with no name.

April Kabler

Abuser

When frustration and anger turns into abuse
and danger, it raises the brows of relatives
and stranger. When a simple little fight
could trigger ones mind, nothing else matters
at that particular time. When the abuse
continues again and again, the day seem
longer and the nights pass on, you start
to realize that the violent acts are wrong.
Now you're afraid, your self-esteem is low,
your mind snaps and you have now taken
the final blow. Questions are being asked.
Answers are very little. How could you
possibly feel fit as a fiddle. Your body
has shut down, your heart has been ripped
apart and your love has been tested. Now
you must face being arrested. The only
thing that matters now, is that, you are free.
Free from your abuser. Now whose the loser?

Brenda White

Childhood Days

When the bird was in the nest,
And dusk was drawing near.
When my love ones laid down to rest,
Every sound in the night I could hear.

The soft breeze whispered in the trees.
The water rippled in the stream.
I could hear the rustle of the leaves.
It was like a midsummer dream.

The old wise owl would hoot away.
The sound of crickets chirping every were.
The rabbits that would hide by day,
Would come out to play with out a care.

When the moon would beam,
And the deep blue sky was clear.
I would wish for my dream,
When a shooting star would appear.

When I was young and every thing was new,
When I had not a worry or a care.
With much delight, I would embrace the night,
Till day light would appear.

Barbara Zanchelli

To Flossy

When I was just a little girl
And fairy tales came true
I dreamed a lovely dream so real
About a child I knew
This child was beautiful and bright and gay
With golden hair and eyes of grey.
She made the world a brighter place
For all who saw her precious face.

I longed to touch this child of dream,
This magic child I knew.
I wanted so to hold her close
To have her love me too.
And then one day when I grew up.
I felt afraid and sad.
I feared I'd lost this wondrous dream.
The best I'd ever had.
I prayed to God to make her real,
This child of dream I'd loved.
He let her come to life for me.
"I thank you, God above!

Hester Eddins

Gods Ministering Angels

As I awoke this morning
And glanced at the fleecy blue sky,
I wondered what God had for me, today, -
Then I saw two cloud-angels float by.

Their wings were open and powerful,
But so gentle and light, yet strong,
It gave me a measure of comfort
Just to glimpse them floating along.

I wanted to call to them: "Come now,
Tell me your mission, this time,"
But they floated on softly before me,
Their form so vibrant, sublime.

As I watched them, I thought how true
Was the saying "Angels among us,"
For earth has its human angels
To guide, comfort and bless.

It appeals especially to us oldsters
Whose time is slipping away,
To know God's ministering earth-angels
Walk with us, protecting, each day.

Dorothy Horton

A Touch

He felt so alone as he traveled that day
And he cries out, "Unclean," to those passing his way.
He longed for a touch from even one friend
Who would share in his pain and his loneliness end.

When Jesus came down from the mountain that day,
The man who had leprosy began to pray,
"Lord, if you're willing, you can make me clean."
The crowd was amazed by what was to be seen.

"Yes, I am willing," the Master replied,
And he reaches out and touched the man kneeling nearby.
Jesus did more than just make the man whole.
He lovingly touched him in body and soul.

So many in our world their own loneliness face.
They, too, need a touch or a gentle embrace
From a friend who will reach out, and so understand
That God's love may be felt through the touch of a hand.

Cheryl Davis

A Tear

A tear glistened in her eye;
  And her heart took and undying pace.
She looked into the darkened sky;
  As the tear descended down her face.

She rested her head into her hands;
  The minutes seemed like years.
Like an hourglass counting the sands;
  She had shed another tear.

Her heart ached with an increasing pain;
  She had cried so many nights.
Where was the love she wished to gain;
  Or was it to be an endless fight?

She sought to end this once and for all;
  The pain and sorrow to be no more.
She was tired of waiting for love to call;
  It felt like an unhealing sore.

She opened her eyes to revel one last tear;
  Her heart ending its pace
The end of this torture became more near;
For it was a tear of red rolling down her face.

Janet Lynn Young

Special Love

He's nice and warm
And he's kind and sweet.
He's the kind of guy
Any girl would love to meet
A couple of times, I gave him a call,
I did everything to get his attention.
I feel so stupid and sometimes mad.
But how could I lose something I never had.
He's tall and cute and there's no doubt.
He's got a smile that will knock you out.
But what am I doing all this for.
He never liked me, never will
And yet I am sitting here
Thinking about him still.

Al Gahagan

Dreams of You

Each night I dream sweet dreams of you
And hope some day those dreams will come true;
But when I near you my knees go weak,
Then you smile and I cannot speak;
For if one small smile is all it takes
To brighten any dreary day,
Then if on your lips it does rest
All my days will be the best;
I lose myself within your eyes,
My mind goes numb, my courage dies;
I smile in return and walk on past
And yearn for the day when at last-
  I can tell you of my dreams of you.

Daniel W. Patrick

Baby Jeffry

I was thinking of scripture
And I looked at your picture
And I saw the Lord in your face
That look in your eyes unknowing of lies
It reminded me of a place
A place we will be together all thee
Loved ones and people of kindness
And that's why I think
The Lord sent us you
A sweet way to subtlely remind us.

Bruce Usher

My Lonely Heart

My lonely heart is aching for you
And I find myself, feeling extremely blue.
I wish you were here holding me tight
For I could not bear being alone again
Tonight.

My lonely heart will be empty inside
Until I feel your touch and you are
By my side. I need to hear your
Tender voice and to kiss your lips
ever so moist.

Make a promise to me that you will be true
For I could not bear the thought of losing
You. When I see you again I hope you
Will say that you missed me and will
Want me to stay.

I will hold back my feelings as best as I can till I
Know that you want me in your life again.
For I have never felt this way but
With you and I hope throughout life
We will stay ever so true.

Janet Krasky

My Ex

Well, that was the third time that we have gone out
And I have to admit that I did have some doubt
To tell you the truth, it was hard to trust you
And it all began when I heard what you do
They said you were going out with someone besides me
But I loved you so much that I wouldn't see
The more attached that I became
The more I kept giving in to your game
You cheated on me and then you lied
But I thought it would get better the more I tried
I really believed that we could work it all through
But finally I realized, there was nothing I could do
And even if you had tried to let me
It wouldn't have worked, because we had drifted apart
Even after all we went through
I know that I will always love you

Amanda Hale

Kaleidoscope

Someone turned the knob
  and I moved.
Trapped in a vacuum,
  we move around
    forming different patterns,
      patterns of peace, war,
        love, hate, confusion, pain, joy,
And when one pattern is formed,
someone turns the knob
  at the bottom of the world
and we form another.
Like a kaleidoscope,
  the green envious lover,
  the red angry murderer,
  the black funeral marcher,
  the blue suicidal man,
  the white virgin bride,
We move together,
  a collage of color,
in tune with the knob of Fate.

Deborah Sherr

Designated Fool

I look at your face on the wall,
and I often wonder where you are now
that your life took the fall.
You lived your life, and now you
are gone. Why did everything have to
go so wrong?
"Life is precious," most people say,
so why did your's get taken away?
What happened to you was so unfair,
but I guess some people just don't care.
This world is selfish, this world is cruel,
and there is always a Designated Fool.
Why did you have to be the fool?
The one that fell into the trap?
I only wish that you could see how bad this
world is getting to be.
And there's always someone breaking a rule,
just to find a Designated Fool!

Andie Masciulli

"I Still Believe"

I still believe in America and the "good old-fashion way."
And I still believe in God above and our American right to pray.
I still believe in the Holy Bible; the "Good Book" from up above.
I still believe in law and order and God's eternal love.
I still believe in courage and serving our country during war;
It's our patriotic duty and our freedom is worth fighting for.
I still believe in marriage and I believe in family ties.
I believe in teaching children to refrain from telling lies.
I still believe in manners, whatever one's age may be;
And having respect for our elders and praying on bended knees.
I still believe in miracles for my own life is one, indeed;
And I believe in life itself and helping people who are in need.
I still believe in old-fashion love and being faithful to your spouse.
I believe that fathers should rule their family but God should rule
their house.
I believe in chasing rainbows and "hitching your wagon to a star."
I believe in setting goals in life and just being who you are.
For life is too short and too precious to waste it all away.
I believe life is worth living and I'll know on "Judgement Day."

Deborah L. Young

Always In My Heart

Every day I waited to watch you pass,
And I waited to hear you say hi.
I waited to see your irresistible face,
and now it seems that we'll be saying good-bye.

What will I do without hearing your voice,
what will it be like without having you here?
My heart will be filled with sorrow,
and my life will be empty without you near.

I'll never forget the love you gave,
or the times we shared together.
I'll always remember your smiles and laughter,
and you'll stay in my heart forever.

Dawn Champagne

Unicorns

Unicorns are such lustrous creatures, their values are no less. They gallop through the forest like the whisper of a song. Their long silky hair is like silver upon a needle. They drink from a stream with a breathless slurp. For they are like magical stars in a heavenly breeze.

Jennifer McDonough

Never a Goodbye

We have had many years to spend time together
And I will treasure those years forever
We have gone many places
Seen some sights and lots of new faces
Through the years so much has been shared
We have understood each other and always cared
I want you to know that I love you with all my heart
And understand I'm just growing up, but we will never grow apart
Sometimes there are things that I would like to do
However, please know that I will always have time for you
"It's hard to watch as your life is changing," I heard you say
But I can't stop that; just know that I'm ready for anything
that will come my way
There will be times when I am not here
But look towards the horizon and my vision will be clear
Don't think this is goodbye because together we'll always be
For in my heart I will see you, and in your heart you will see me

Julie Diane Conaway

A Teenager's Prayer

Oh Lord, oh Lord I'm just fifteen
And killing and violence is all I've seen
My sister's and brother's, they will not talk
And I'm afraid Lord to even walk.

I go to school so I can learn
And education I desire to earn,
We walk the halls in so much fear
Our mother's praying, their eyes full of tears

Tell me Lord, what's going on today
Why can't we all gather, hold hands and pray.

Our lives are so short; the children so few
What's going on Lord, don't they believe in you
Help us Lord, stop the killing
Because very soon I'll lose all my feelings

The blood is shed, the tears are flowing
Soon my Lord we all are going
I want them to stop, and come together
And end this war and blood shed forever
I pray to you Lord; my teenage prayer
It seems to me that no one else cares.

Annette M. Eccles

Freedom

Sometimes I just want to leave you
and lay in the warm sand
and have the cool wave wash over me
I want to fly with the bluebirds
and swim with the dolphins
I want to laugh with the crickets
and dance with the caterpillars
I want to laugh with the hyenas
and crawl with the snakes
but then I want to stay here with you
and hold you in my arms
whispering lullabies in your ear until you fall
into a soft, silent sleep
I want to hear your breath
and feel your warmth
I want to touch your eyes
and know your smile
and then I'll join you in your soft, silent sleep
and we'll stay that way forever

Gretchen Hill

My Childhood in the Park

As birds fly throughout the sky,
And little children are on the swings;
I look around the park and sigh.
I remember all the little things.

When I was just a little kid,
I'd get dizzy on the merry-go-round.
I would finish the slide with a skid
And get dirty on the sandy ground.

In the summer, I'd pick berries
After I climbed up into the trees.
Then in fall, when there were no berries,
I would stomp through the colorful leaves.

Even though my childhood has gone away,
Memories of it are here to stay.

Jennifer Griner

Us

A friend is wind that blows on a scorching summer day
and rain that quenches desert thirst.

Friends are shells that lie side by side on a sandy
beach and waves that bounce across seas together.

We are the river that has rushed with rain and trickled
in drought, always flowing on.

You, my friend, are the sky that's always there, and
the earth on which I stand.

Bradley J. Hamilton

"The One That Got Away!"

We took a picnic basket on a sunny August Day,
And sat within the meadow where our son could run and play.
But didn't realize until, beside the babbling brook,
Our little boy revealed a broken branch, and fishing hook!

"I want to be a fisherman, when I grow up, someday!"
"Okay, my son, but you can't cry each time one gets away!
As years went by we watched our little boy become a man,
Returning to this famous fishing hole, now and again.

We watched him make decisions, but the wisest of them all,
Was the day he chose to answer God, and His almighty call.
Often from the pulpit we can hear our son still say,
"God, please supply the proper bait, so none will get away!"

Cynthia J. Ruff

"Path Of A Man"

I look down at my hands
And see the wrath of the desert.
I feel the pain of the sands,
The stinging cuts and the pulsating hurt.

I can't relate to the life these people walk,
The path they choose everyday.
I don't understand the language that they talk
And the odd sounding words they say.

I ask myself how they can be.
How they can live beneath the scorching sun?
I wonder about the sights they will never see
And the experiences of life that they blindly shun.

Darin C. Ruhl

All Was Black

I stood alone in complete darkness
and silence

Surrounded by visions of horror

I tried to hide,but none of the
sweet dream clouds would
let me ride away with them

All was black, not a sliver of light
from the moon shone its
way through the dark clouds
of the wicked night

I felt myself fading to the heavens, but then I
heard his voice calling my name

He came to me ....

... I then awoke realizing, it was all a bad nightmare

Heather Dobson

Give Us a Chance

Love is the same for both young and old
and so the pain that love can hold.
So many people, mostly parents,
do not think that to the kids, it is apparent.
The teens of this world are smart
but some need a little push start.
We all know that everyone can love
So why hold back instead of shove?
Us teens need to learn on our own
The truth that has been grown.
No one gives us a chance to make the slightest glance
into the past and to help the future.
We all have it in us to get through the torture.
Because we are not weak and frail,
We can see a change is needed for us to sail.
Give us the chance to make a difference
and we will show you we have perseverance.
Just let us be, Don't try to make us see.
We know what has to be done,
But please for now just let us have our fun.

Barb Hughes

Rain

I hear the rain slowly,
and softly beat against my window.
Somehow it can sense and feel my pain.
And I want to run,
run far away.
Where no one can hurt or betray me again.
Calm and beguiling...it continues.
For a while I lay in the darkness...listening.
The rain reflects my emotions, and fears.
It provides security, and comfort...that I need badly.
And all the pain,
and suffering that I have inside,
just washes away...when it rains.

Corrina Huang

Goodbye Grandma

God looked down at my grandmother,
and saw a suffering sight.
He told her that he loved her
he said "Come Home Tonight."
"Oh how I hate to see my children suffer,"
he said to her that night.
The last six words were spoken,
"Nellie, please walk towards the light"

Angela M. Goderich, age 16

The Amber Curtain

The amber curtain slowly coming down,
and spreading out o'er all the ground.

Soon all the trees will be bare,
to find a leaf will be very rare.

When the last little leaf is hard to find,
winter and cold aren't far behind.

When all the trees dress up in their coats of white,
it won't be long till that late December night.

That last little leaf that once so fair,
can still be seen clinging there.

All through the sleet, the snow, and rain
I guess it was its fate that it remain.

Think what fall would be like,
without any trees,
and to see the beauty of, the silent, falling leaves...

Eugene H. McCollum

Untitled

It is upon the sand the water washes away
And takes back out to sea
The foot prints of laughter and castles of gold
To remain but memories

So we walk hand in hand upon the sand
The water washes to sea
In hopes that someday our footprints remain
More than just memories

Together we will build a castle of gold
To withstand the water and sea
Here our lives will begin to live out our dreams
And keep the memories

As we grow in strength and hold in our hearts
The precious memories
The water and sand will stay at our side
And our friend will become the sea

Joanne McDonough

Somewhere Special

When the cool air tickles
And the birds fly high
There is a place
For you and I.

In the forest
Beyond the trees
Past the butterflies
And the bees.

Where no one comes, where no one knows
About somewhere special where we always go.

Where we have a picnic
With bread and pie,
And talk and talk
As the day goes by.

Where we can share our secrets
Beneath our souls.

For no one hears and no one knows
About somewhere special where we always go.

Chandler E. Hinkson

The Last Dream

With death hovering near, just beyond my grasp,
And the calendar flips backward into my past.
I'm reminded of a story - my mother told me...
While patiently sitting, on her knee...

Of the grasshopper, who wiled his life away,
And, the ant that stored some food, each day.
As the grasshopper played...summer turned to fall,
Winter arrived - and he had nothing, at all...

Well, I was that grasshopper, who wasted his life,
I never saw the future, with its pain and strife
Now I must close any eyes, and sadly return,
To all those mistakes, too late to learn...

Each last day I only wish and dream,
About returning to yesterday, in a time machine.
To change "Just one thing", each day of my past,
This is my greatest wish - and it will be my last...

Daryl Gaertner

I Had A Dream

I had a dream
And the dream came true
I then awoke
And the dream was Life

I've closed my eyes inward into a memory
And watched the tears of the past flood a conscious soul
I've heard the wispy clouds of a thought disappear
Into a shadow of what would have been

I've built a castle of smiles visible to a wishful audience
While a pained mime shed a moat of tears
I've gauged my deeds by the clock of time
And found I'd finished nothing

I glimpsed the future in a dream
And reflected on this nightmare
I had a dream
And the dream was true
When I awoke
The dream was Life

Edwina Boykin

Just When I Think

Just when I think we have nothing more to show
And the feelings which we've shared have nowhere else to go
Just when I think I must be out of my mind
To believe after all we've been through love is what we'd find
Just when I think this is how it ends
In the great scheme of things we're nothing more than friends
Then a light glimmers in your eyes in that mischievous way
To say that what I've wanted for so long may not be far away
Then you lay your head against me and close your eyes so fine
That's just when I think you're mine!

Just when I think there must be someone else for you
A man who'll make you happier in a world that's bright and new
Just when I think the chance for us is past
And even if we took it things just wouldn't last
Just when I think we should just say goodbye
To the dreams I saw so often twinkling in your eye
Then that smile comes over your face which you only have for me
And feelings locked inside ourselves through love are finally free
As you become that special part of me I'll cherish through all time
That's just when I think you're mine!

David Allan Mitchell

God's Creation

As a bald eagle swoops through the Rocky Mountains
And the raging water gush in the Snake River
A green sea of trees by the millions
Almost hover over thousands of miles of the range

The deep and wide canyons, carved by the water
The glaciers fall and chip off the boulders
It reminds me that Lord, your work stops never
And this piece of art is of your splendor

As a huge black bear stands on it's hind legs
And makes it's "no trespassing" signs on the trees
And the beavers eat down the trees like pegs
And the prairies are open to a non-stop breeze

As a family of raccoons shelter in a hollow tree
And a mother grizzly bear protects her young
Lord, in you I have a shelter in thee
And for your glory praises are sung

For you, Lord are more mighty than the highest mountain
You are more gentle than a small, colorful butterfly
Though your wrath is hotter than the freshest lava
Like old faithful you I can rely

Jim Wilburn

Elusive Seasons

As the morning sun begins to warm
And the swallows sing and swoop
The young child begins his day
And Mom's start theirs...

The seasons are sure to change
With spring comes all that's new
And summer with it's sky so blue
Fall and winter offer color
and the sparkle of new snows.

The child knows of change
His toys become more alone
Moms peer out the windows
As their children join new friends...

As the sapling becomes a tree
And a caterpillar becomes a beautiful butterfly
The son is now a dad,
The daughter seeks her own being...

And as with the setting sun
The evening lily becomes magnificent
Now the grandchildren
Extend their hearts with love...

Dorothy Campbell

"Memories" Treasure Chest

My mother's trunk sat upstairs
and to her it was so dear ——

A treasure chest kept thru the years.

I opened it and as my eyes filled with tears,
I looked back at the memories that
happened down thru the years——-

Sadness and joy filled my heart
as I saw my mother and father's
dear smiling faces———

They were so young—where did the years go?

How fast they went——-
but they're together with God now,
with years well spent.

Eugene Thompson

Boundaries

Life ain't fair if you have to share
And there are boundaries that have fenced you.
But in the end the rules will bend
And the odds won't be against you.

Without a friend or without an end
Of a story in a book,
Life will pass by, in the blink of an eye
Without taking a second look.

Although it may seem that we live in a dream
What we have is all too real.
There is love, there's hate, there's destiny and fate
In between is the emotions we feel.

It's hard to explain the long road of pain
That through my life I have paved.
All I can say is that I've paid my way
And now I'm taking back what I gave.

Like I said in the end the rules will bend
And the odds won't be against you.
So hold on one more day, and you'll soon break away
Those boundaries that have fenced you.

Jenna Hood

In a Field of Weeds

In a field of weeds a flower grows,
and there, she stands alone.
Her roots grow twisted in the earth,
a soil of crumbled stone.
Her head held high in prejudice,
she knows what all eyes see.
Empty passion, yields this frustration.
Deserving of the weeds.

As seasons pass her colors wilt,
and turn a dulling grey.
With the snowdrifts on the winter's sky,
her beauty fades away.
The roots that struggle to survive,
twisted in the stone.
In a field of weeds a flower dies and there she dies
alone.

Jason Caldwell

A Vacation

I'd like to go on vacation
And walk in the woods once again
And listen to Catbirds and Blue Jays
And look for the little brown wren.

I know Foxy Fox in there hiding
As well as the deer and the hare
And blackberries grow in huge clusters
With plenty, and then some to spare.

I'd fill my pails quickly with berries,
Then turn and trudge onward toward home,
And I wouldn't ever be lonely
Or sad, or even alone.

The pies and the jams and the jellies
In winter will taste best I know
Because of the memories that linger
Of vacation days long ago.

Gyneth Griffin

A Tawny Port Autumn Afternoon

A lovely elfin girl wakes up
and walks barefoot
on a new silver carpet
She laughs silently
when her father turns
A disturbance in the force!
Someone new in his afternoon nap
Has turned the purring golf announcers silent
She lightly hops about the room
Mama cooks tomatoes and brown sugar and peppers
A wispy smell in a quiet kitchen tickles father's nose
He stretches in his racing t-shirt
and walks sock footed to the door
A bright red door opens to a tawny port afternoon
Our house is small surrounded by a giant oaks breathing
Taking in strength from the autumn afternoon
May this dusky afternoon be with us thru the winter

Gail Elaine Rose Rector

Untitled

What is this that takes the tender heart
And weaves around it a hard cocoon?
To protect it from the barbs of life
That might forever leave a bitter wound.

That thus entombs within this shell-like case
The spark that through strife stays true,
For the day when circumstance might change
And the spark spring to life anew.

Cliff Barnes

Life Goes On

The train is running over the track
And we're so far now
That I can't look back
I've left my old world behind
And a new world I'm left to find.
A world of laughter and of cheers
A world where I will have no fears
I thought I had once found that world
But that was when I was a very little girl
Now I've grown and things have changed
Every so often I feel a pain
To go back to the way things were
And be a little girl
With great big curls
And I guess I have to realize now
That once you've moved on down that track
There's really no use trying to turn back.

Cheryl Patchcoski

"Hands On"

If ever you're feeling downhearted
And you seem to be all alone
Take a minute, come by and see us,
Be a visitor in our nursing home

Take a hand from a wheelchair in your hand
Hold it gently as you would the wind
And before you realize what's happening
A small miracle will begin

You'll see a smile as wide as a river
A returning touch to your hand
And a wealth of love outpouring
As only the elderly can

If you ask how this miracle happened
How their love is much more than you see
Ask me and I'll tell you
This miracle happened to me

Josie H. Dykes

Just A Look

There's no need for talking, just look
and you will see.

All the emotions and feelings inside
of me.

Just a look that's all you'll receive, and you'll
feel the hurts that makes me grieve

You might not understand how the feelings
got there, without a word or sound disturbing
the air,

Look at my mouth, my nose and my eyes, you
will notice that there's no surprise.

A look that's all you'll see.

A look with all the feelings inside of me.

Jaime Buchanan

Untitled

When the tides of life are raging,
And your life seems torn into,
It's then the time to ask yourself
What would the Savior do.
Remember, He held His head up high,
Up there on Calvary,
Even though they hurt and scorned Him,
His tears were for you and me.
He cried "Oh Father, forgive them,
For they know not what they do,"
And as He breathed His last sigh of life,
He prayed for me and you.
His body was torn and bleeding,
As they dragged Him from the cross,
The world was sad and lonely,
For it knew a bitter loss.
The loss of one so holy,
Who for us had died upon the cross.

Jeannette M. Gutwein

Broken Tranquilities

Purple waves of sorrow
Anger like pearls of ice slip into my broken mind
Lost in nightmares of tomorrow
True peace my spirit shall never find
A river of nothingness flows deep in my heart
Disappearing sense lost in my days
Adversity rips my soul apart
My thoughts in a ghostly haze
Dark cries go unheard
From apathy this world does not wake
Drowning in every hate filled word
No love left to take
My real thoughts never to be free
Promises shattered in yesterday's light
Leaving self-told lies to be
Emotions trapped in each midnight
Falling to our tragic last breath
Like flowers resting in shame
Hysterical souls taunted before death
Tears frozen with no hope, like an ocean with no name

Crystal Lee Caswell

The Life of an Adopted Child

The girls went with our Mom; The boys went with our Dad.
Another family has split apart; Divorce is so sad.

Don't be angry with our Mom for giving me away.
She did her best for me-in her own way.
To me-she gave her most precious gift-the gift of life,
Even though she could no longer be our Dad's wife.
I know that she must have loved me with all of her heart.
She found me the perfect home so that I could have a new start.

My "new" Dad loved me dearly and thought I could do not wrong.
Friends called me his "little shadow" as we walked along.
Very deep within my heart, this nice man I came to adore.
Though he has passed on, he'll be my Dad forevermore.

My "new" Mom always gave me her tender, loving care.
Her arms gave me comfort when I had a nightmare.
She was the example of a perfect mother and wife.
From this wonderful woman, I learned the rights and wrongs in life.

Needless to say, I've had the best of both worlds, as you can see.
No little girl could have grown up better than me.

Your concern for me makes me love you so much.
Finding my "big brother" has enriched my life with that special touch!

Anne T. Fisher

Untitled

When an unborn child floats on the Godly liquid, destiny appears as an undecided genetic particle. Can the unborn tell 'essence' from 'substance,' does its pulse tick on an earthy zone or a divine one? Ancient memories pave their way to the womb where they can shelter and secure the message of God. And toe-to-toe with destiny, nature and man unfold the simplicity behind the routine of life. The freedom that God gave us haunts him. The choice that God gave us manipulates all aspects of life. It seems like whole generations pass by me and the youth of my children soothes my fear. The light of my forefathers that knocks on the door of my memory, shapes the character of my grand-children. I was waiting at the corner of life and without touching it, I have experienced the wait for death. The knight that fought for his loved one also experienced the wait for death when full of passion, he stood and waited at the corner of life. Once, a memory from another life awakened a memory of a familiar death inside me. The sword of the knight is not in use anymore. The Godly liquid becomes a firm substance in the gravity of life.

Haim Mizrahi

The Endless Sea

The ocean - the sea
Are drawing me.
Tall dry grasses swaying in the wind.
The blazing sun reflected in the surf
As it laps against the sandy shore.
The blue sky - the quietness
Behind the secluded dune.
All bring memories of the one I love
And shall see no more.

The sea beckons me
As I think of days gone by
And I yearn for the peace I find
In the sea of my memory.
Sometimes the surf is wild and rough.
Sometimes quiet as it laps against my toes.
Always it stretches endlessly to the sky
Where blue meets blue and we glimpse eternity.

Betty Hunt

If I Can't Sing Alleluias

When answers to my earnest prayers
Are not what I expected
May your grace so fill this heart of mine
That your higher ways may be accepted

In the loneliness of pain filled hours
That none but you can share
Lord help me know I'm not alone
For you are present there

If weakness ebbs away the strength
My grateful praises to impart,
If I can't sing Alleluias Lord
Then hear them from my heart

Intensify the fellowship
We share in grace divine
Until your thoughts become my own
Your higher ways be mine!

Carol Bousema

The Old Man and the Shoe

The old man bid me come near and asked why
are you not of good cheer a beautiful
woman of course said I has left a pain
like a poke in the eye she's gone and left
me high and dry and feeling like I could
just die well what did you expect asked he
a love to last for all eternity yes I said
is that too much to ask for a woman that's
no easy task said the old one who probably
knew he sat on a rock and took off a shoe
and pulled out a picture once new a
beautiful woman with a crooked smile from
that photograph did beguile from ages ago
to now its the same we struggle for
fortune and fame to please a face and a
form and wind up as food for the worms you
see where I carry that picture said he
it helps make up for her walking all over
me so if you're feeling abused and blue
put a picture of her in your shoe

Dennis A. Benson

"Techno-Misery"

What has this world come to today?
Artificial means rule our way.
When we're trapped they throw away the key.
Let's start a breed against technology.

I can't do that, and I can't do this.
Techno-misery gets us all pissed.

Machines are all of our bosses now.
You'll get fired if they see you scowl.
The president talks all contradictions.
Our lives are being replaced by science fiction.

Go to a warehouse and you here "beep beep."
This is what they call techno-misery.

Used to have a job that was O.K.
Replaced by something better is what they say.
Found out I was replaced by something steel.
Now they all want us not to make a big deal?

Techno-misery means we can't feed our folks.
Our jobs replaced by nuts and bolts.

Bradley W. Varner

Drinking and Driving

Close by the door he paused to stand,
as he slipped his class ring off her hand.
All who watched did not care to speak,
as a single tear ran down his cheek.
All through his mind memories ran,
of all the times they once had had.
He held his class ring and started to cry,
he kissed her cheek and wanted to die.
As the wind began to blow,
they lowered her casket down below.
This is what happens to many alive,
when friends let friends drink and drive.

Deanna Herald

Untitled

Close by the door he paused to stand,
as he took his class ring off her hand.
as a silent tear rolled down his cheek.
And through his mind the memories ran,
of the moments they laughed and walked in the sand.
But now his eyes were so terribly cold,
he never again would have her to hold.
And just as the wind began to blow,
they lowered her casket into the snow.
This is what happened to many alive,
when friends let friends drink and drive.

Clover Johnson

The Swing

I feel her delight from the little red swing,
As her giggles float by on the breeze,
And I faintly recall a similar laugh
As it beckons to me like a tease.

It's been years - I resist, I'm no longer a child,
to feel myself soar through the air,
A tree-ripened parent who's neglected her youth
And suppressed a cavalier flair.

But I climb on that swing - right up behind her.
Her expression takes on a new shine,
And we sail off together, and the giggles begin,
But this time they're both hers and mine.

Brenda Goins

I feel the wind lovingly caress my face, like a hug.

It twirls around my arms and legs with a little push and a little tug.
As I close my eyes and feel the wind gently weave through my hair,
I am filled with appreciation, for moments like these are rare.

I hear the waves ripple up against the side of the ship.
They crash against the boat, then do a backwards flip.
As I hear the waves ripple, prodding me to keep going,
I am filled with encouragement from the seed of support they are sowing

I see the sun color the tips of the waves gold.
It shines upon my cheeks and saves me from the cold.
As I see the sun shining, smiling down from the cloudless sky,
I am filled with a great love for its guiding and protecting eye.

And as I am feeling, hearing, and seeing,
I forget all about my strife,
For I am filled with a wonderful feeling,
as I realize I am full of life.

Danielle Krochak

Swoosh

"Look out below!"
As I fly through the snow.
"Get out of my way,"
I hear a voice say.

With a lightning-bolts speed,
this sport it does feed,
the souls who do dare
try to fly through the air.

The ones who aren't scared of braking their necks.
The ones who aren't worried of spills or wrecks.
And what single sport offers all this and more
skiing that is the one where you sore!!!

Eddie Hazelwood

The Most Passionate Love

As I stare out the window I see your face.
As I stare at the pale moon, you're what is on my mind.
I can't help but to love you, I can't help but to stare,
I can't help but to see your face everywhere.
The most precious sight I've ever seen,
It seems to be the most beautiful thing.
Your eyes like the sky, your smile like the wind.
For when we kiss I feel the chills rush in.
I've never had an experience quite like this,
I've never had so much passion in just one kiss.
Your love is something I won't forget,
For your love was the best of it.

Dawn Houck

December Reflections

The December morning was crisp and cold
As I walked through my old hometown,
While my thoughts went back to an eight-year old
And the hills that I sledded down.

Yet, as I looked at familiar things
Through the eyes of a returning friend
I realized that 'time on wings'
Is a fact that has no end.

Because as a child the small seemed big
Like the buildings, the streets, and the people,
But later in life a ' twig is twig'
And only a church has a steeple.

Those years of hometown may be gone now,
But the memories linger forever
Of Christmas, December, and snow,
Annually revived by the weather .

The seasons return in their order
While flowers come only in spring,
But Christmas, December, and Winter
All of these memories bring.

George Sendon

Hell-Binding Myopia

To ye who fail to see the world
apart from your own selves,
and ye whose lives are not unfurled
apart from where you dwell,
I say you live in hell.

No state of life can I conceive
as worse or less than that,
and those who in such straits must breathe
yet still do not combat,
from life no joy extract.

David Rudel

"The Greatest Gift"

The years have flown
As if not two minutes have passed
Since I held this wonderful creation in my arms.
As if it were only yesterday
That I held her hand
While she took those first trembling steps.
Now, Today, she holds my hand as I take my last steps.

Through it all I have tried to teach her the values of life
Never dreaming that she was teaching me something as well.
To try to think now how my life might have been
Without this rare and unique individual
Whom is neither my child nor my daughter
But someone whom I proudly call a friend.

My days on this earth are almost gone.
I approach the end of this chapter
Not with sadness or dismay
But with an all encompassing joy
For sitting at my side, holding my hand
Is my greatest gift from Heaven.

Janet Walker

Winter on the Soos Creek Trail

What signs of nature will I see on the trail today,
As I'm walking along on this brisk, cool December day?
A battered salmon slowly moving up the stream;
How he made it up this far, I could only dream.

The Great Blue Heron is quietly standing in the pond,
Looking for something good to eat that might come along.
The friendly Mallard Ducks don't really seem to mind,
Sharing their winter home with birds of another kind.

The Black-capped Chickadees in the bare willow tree,
Hopping around the branches, eating insects that they see.
Up ahead a pretty bird of blue and black flies away,
Making noisy screams and calls, the sounds of the Steller's Jay.

The Red-tailed Hawk up in the sky above the trees,
Soaring freely, this big bird, I wonder what he sees.
The densely growing spirea has all turned brown;
The lady ferns and horsetails have all died down.

The wetland marshes with the cattails standing tall,
Are waiting patiently for spring to come and warm them all.
This is what I saw as I was walking along the way;
The signs of winter nature on the Soos Creek Trail today.

Bonny Antonelli

The Candle

In a poetic way, the candle, it burns
As it flickers and flits, so too, my heart yearns
To hope it would shine, as a love, ever on
Yet to know all too soon that the flame will be gone

Maybe the image will be burned in my mind
Then again, maybe nothing will be left behind
Of a love, like the candle, that once burned so bright
But now, in abandon, can give me no light

It's a sad thing to watch, to see it all melt
The light reveals to me feelings I thought I'd never have felt
Wax runs down the candle as though it were my tears
Time subtracts from the candle as it adds to my years

There are times when I wonder that in time will I cope
I see the wick glowing - the glow gives me hope
But the candle burns down, silent, cold as a stone
As I stand here without, feeling old and alone

Now the fire has been snuffed and I see the smoke rise
Like my love, shadow love, as it fades out and dies
I'm bereft in my sorrow and the weight of my doubts
And I'm left like the candle, alone and put out

Jeffrey F. LeGore

"A Forever Gift"

The best things in life are free,
As my parents always explained to me
And apparent it came to be, as
I saw the waves rushing in to me.
With an eye on the sky,
And as I looked around, no lovelier
place could be found.
Forever more, I'll remember
the peace and tranquility, I found looking
at the sea.

Dava Anne Copenhaver Moyer

The Real Me

The real me does not show.
As not so many people know.
I get into mischief with honey bees,
While stealing apples from grandma's trees.

The real me does not care,
how many times I'm told to share.
Snatch it away, it's mine, it's mine,
I've done this ever since age nine.

The real me will not stop.
I run wild hip, hip, hop.
Without a scratch, without a scrape,
I fly around without a cape.

The real me has a secret side.
I can not tell you it will run and hide.
Shy and uncertain is its part.
This part of me is hidden deep inside my heart.

Brandy Hauptmann

The Old Plow, The Horse, The Man

He was tired, near exhaustion
As sweat beaded on his brow
and his aching hands were blistered
From the handles on the plow.

And his big old horse would give a snort
And shake his head around
As the plowshare made it's furrow
Through uncultivated ground.

And as they trudged across the land
The tracers you could hear
As they slapped against the breaching rings
And jerked the plowing gear

And the bumping sound of the singletree
As it bobbed across the land,
Set off a rhythm steady and soft
That eased both horse and man.

And the old plow, the horse the man
Worked that wondrous land all day
and tomorrow will be planting time
for a new harvest is under way.

Harold Brinig

All Is Well

I watch as the birds fly swiftly by.
As trees wave briskly; salute the sky.
As squirrels climb up and scathe the fence,
Not to see would be too dense.

I watch the wind blow every leaf.
A sprinkle here, a raindrop brief.
The silence breaks just me to tell
The silence breaks just me to tell
That life knows peace; and all is well.

Frankie Jackson

The Sea

It looks so clear and as if without a blemish lit,
As the moonlight throws its shining armor upon it,
And yet as the swirling rings unfold,
A story of depth is solemnly told.
It has lived its life often in glory,
And through the storms, it has a sad story;
The many fish that have lived and died,
In its waves of own self pride;
The ships which sailed and often sunk,
Its island holding trees with a crooked trunk,
Sailors and boatmen, divers and swimmers,
And astutely surrounded by the tall green timbers,
Its story is told as it slowly unravels,
And it will forever live to tell of its travels.

Frances Smith

The Bandit

Anticipation of the hunt through the body sent a fever and chills,
As the quite of darkness moves swiftly over the swamp and hills.

While frost laid heavy on the fields,
and sparkled like diamonds to the sight
A winter moon shown softly through the woods that night.

Then soft words are spoken, collars untied gone like a Spirit
the pursuit undenied.
With an eagerness to run or fight,
straining and pulling forward running with all their might.

The bandit moves quickly in hopes not to be found.
A nose strikes the scent, the air fills with sound.

The noise of the chase sounds miles away.
Then barks and a loud howl, the quarry is at bay.

What thrills of a hunt under the chill of a winters moon.
The sounds of hounds treeing that willey old coon.

While dozing in my rocker in my declining years.
Thrills of the hunt and sounds still ring in my ears.

Carl R. Higgins

Nature and God

Yes, I've heard the laughing trees
As their leaves are tickled by a passing breeze;
A branch supporting a trilling bird...
All this beauty I have heard!

The falling drops of rain in chorus
As they sing with joy of their heavenly source;
The waves of the ocean humming their song
As they caress the beaches all day long.

I've heard the love of a doe for her fawn
As they drink the dew of a brand new dawn;
The purring of a little contented kitten
As it licks the fur of its soft, white mitten.

I'm awakened each morn by a rooster's crow
To welcome the day as it starts to grow;
The beckoning fingers of outer space,
A wish to mingle with an alien race!

All mixed together in the blender of love
By our Heavenly Father Who reigns above!

Carol R. Mills

City

Constantly walking .. walking
as they walk murderously
  through dark unpaved streets
  marching to a beat, beat
(drums march on between intervals)
the machine city swallows
eat my factories!
  it dares!
It dares the outside world, forces
it kills slaughters and destroys
with mutilated ecstasy burned into the soil
  the city laughs
as the machine city weeps
  (into the dawn)
with an endless pulse
the machines beat on.

Daniel Frank

And On Mother's Day

And on Mother's day feelings ride on a joyful high
As thoughts of days of old go floating by.

And this day is special to us all
As we think of Mother's we treasure like a china doll.

And we think of how wonderful they are to behold
That we love them with a love that can't grow old.

And here I am with a special prayer of thanks to bestow
For my Mother who, by God's grace, was given to me not so long ago.

And I know that because of your love
Which fills me like the beauty of a dove,

That many agonies I am spared.
To the world I have declared,

That God has to me given
The greatest Mother that has even liven.

Douglas Landon Potts

Undying

One solitary tear rolls down my face
As we go our separate ways, I reminisce
I remember all the things we shared
All of our dreams, hopes, and aspirations
They start to fade
Getting more faint and distant with each step we take
The romance, the passion, the lust
It's drifting
Drifting away. Becoming distant and remote
It is gone
I no longer feel your touch or benign kiss
Everything has ceased
Vanished without a trace
Everything except for my love
It shall reach you from far and near
It is undying.

Jennifer Daniels

To Sascha

A long life
Well-lived in peace and beauty.
Love and loyalty
Given and received without end.
Leap in joy
Amid the tall grass and wildflowers,
Sweet dog,
Forever.

Jean M. Johnston

The Little Turtle

We watched it from the window
As we were 'dining in'
It came across the driveway-
"Come on, little turtle, you can win"

It hurried on along its way
To the house where there was shade
We knew that somewhere in its heart
The little turtle's plan were made

So on it went, and out of sight
Just where it went we cannot tell
But God in all his wisdom knows
That with the little turtle "all is well"

Jean Collins

Uncle

You left us in a world of anger and unforbidden pain
As you fought each moment like a world without fear
You cried and talked of reasons for holding on
Although you knew that death would soon be near
At your bedside I would always be
But trying to hide the pain and bitterness within me
Your wife and son mourned for you
As well as your family and the daughter you never knew
Death was by your side, but you could not see it
And afterwards, took possession of you
Now the memories of you will live forevermore
But an uncle like you, I will never again bore

Fernanda F. Pereira

No time for Mom

Mother is your greatest gift, she gave you life
At least until you took a wife, then time for
Mom you have no more.
No time to stop knock on her door, say hello, see her smile and
Stay a while. I don't have time,
I'll see you soon some afternoon, when I have time.
I got a call to day, mom had passed away, I
Had no time to see her alive, but you can
Bet I'll find time to see her dead.
The time was always there, but I wasn't
Oh to have a second chance, I'd knock on her
Door, see her smile and stay a long long while
But instead I'll see her dead.
Regrets, regrets, oh do I regret.
Go see mom before it's too late, see her
Smile and stay a long long while

Edward De Sabato

Night

As I lay there in my bed,
Basking in the darkness of my room,
feeling myself be swaddled in a blanket of inner peace,
I lay there listening to the sounds,
the cars driving by,
the occasional deep breath coming from elsewhere in the house.
Normal night noises of a city that never slumbers.
All those noises being interweaved into a great cloth.
A cloth woven from everything that had happened today or ever,
All of which were justified in my dreams.
As if someone had solved all my problems for me as I lay there.
As I slipped into a state of half consciousness,
I thought of how perfect today was and my pillow was like a cloud,
A cloud of angel's feathers.
Peace, quiet, contentment, tranquility, sleep.

Claire Kendrick

Menehunes?

Have you ever heard of a MENEHUNE? True!
At one time the Hawaiian Islands had quite a few.
It's fascinating to know what they really do,
Since they're always hiding from me and you.

They are Males, short and very small, like elves.
Having round fat bellies that seem to swell.
Round smiling faces of mischief which they won't tell.
Running barefoot very fast is what they do so well.
Their unkempt hair is so long—for on this they didn't dwell.

They were never seen.
Coming out only at night and being so keen,
Being very useful as we slept and dreamed.

Busy repairing stone walls,
Standing in lines, passing stones to one and all.
Completing fish ponds without a stall,
So much was accomplished by not being tall.

There was so much magic in whatever they did,
But their tiny footprints couldn't be hid.

It brought laughter and GOOD LUCK to all of us
Being sprinkled with the MENEHUNE'S magical dust.

Joann Knapp

My heart, heavy with caution and desire,
awaiting the contact of known strangers, met my guardian angel.
My mind, light from the emergence of old
friends, expanding, grasping, doubting the floor, met my
guardian angel.
My beliefs, reaching for dry land, seized
in uncertainty, met my guardian angel.
My soul, screaming for a drop of water,
all I receive are disease filled droplets of the devil's sweat.
My fingers, desiring a feel of solitude,
grope, and are satisfied by the splendor of roses.
My past is an exhausting travel, being retired
by the judge's gavel. My sentence is eternity.

Drew Lankford

Good-Bye

When you leave, please take care of you.
Be careful, for your life's not through.
While I'm in here and you're out there.
Don't forget that I still care.
Don't forget to smile, for you'll never be alone.
Even though you're out there, finally on your own.
I'm glad that I decided to let you in my heart,
Because now you'll still be with me, even though we're
Apart.
So now it's time to say good-bye
I will think of you as I cry.
So now you're gone and now you're free,
All I ask is that you please remember me...

Charlotte Valore

Starlight, Starbright

First star I see tonight
But what I see is not a star
Your lighted window leading me to
the sanctuary I find in your eyes.
You lie sick in your bed.
As I climb to my perch and gaze upon you.
Your body paled by your sickness your eyes closed
Fleeing in sadness I sit in the wet
Grass and stare at my first star
In your window

Ben McClain

Breakdown

My nerves are frayed;
All shattered, all tattered.
As we end another discussion,
Loud percussion.

Carol Ann Coughlin Candela

The Forgotten

Feelings blown away with old photographs, images soon to be forgotten.
"Sorry" is not accountable for anything. "Neither am I" you used to say.
My past fades away along with feelings I used to have.
I am again forgotten now.
I am only a face with pieces left to fit in the puzzle of my life.
I am one of the forgotten, I have no love left to give.
Along with faded photographs and memories blow away, a part of each one of us dies, the hurt will always stay.
I am one of the forgotten.

Bethany Zetterlund

It's Easier To Have A Crush Than To Be In Love

It's easier to have a crush than to
be in love.

My parents are in love. They worry
about money and the kids.
Billy and Christy didn't make it.
Di's and Charley's royal marriage
didn't last.
But I get to have the perfect
relationship...
In my head, I can imagine -
Chris O'Donnell, Lyle Lovett,
the boy in math class!
No arguments, no worries
the couple of the century.

It's easier to have a crush than
to be in love.

Judith Andiman

Dreams of a Child

Oh little heart hold on to your dreams,
be not afraid to ride on moon beams.
Youth is the time for your thoughts to fly free,
to climb a mountain or walk by the sea.

Your world can be a wonderful place,
just wear a smile of love upon your face.
For it will be a reflection of your soul,
a gift to carry through life more precious than gold.

For there's not a dream on earth which won't come true,
if you but have faith in the things you do.
Elves and fairies are as real as can be,
to the heart that can believe, to the heart that is free.

Nothing in this life can stand in your way,
unless you listen to the negative words people say.
They may run you down and tear your ideas apart,
but listen not, sticking to your dreams and following your heart.

Life is yours now to seek,
stand up strong and be not weak.
Time will tell that you were right,
if this life you tackle with all your might.

Donald T. Thorne

Vision Scape

Maybe 'tis the sun when the lively amber honey
beams below on your sweet face,
or 'tis the silk worms welcome with the touch
of my fingers within your hair's grace.

Asleep, your perfect curve of long lashes; like a
heaving tidal wave I ponder down in clashes,
or the spiritual joy like that of the meadowing grass,
flying high over knees, the horizon a thick rolling sash.

The innocent dew that dwells among the soft young rose,
is seen in your eyes might the sweet petals close?

For the dreaming is gone while my petals awake,
and the rhyme which I dwell is mine and to take,

To the abyss of my dreams, my heartened soul gets taken away,
Later!
Fair love!
In mine dreams once more another day.

Irene Vasquez

Yellow

Like the golden rays of the sun
beating down upon this vast green earth.

The third color of the rainbow as it appears
while the sun shines during the rain.

The color of mustard that is spread
upon a hot dog or hamburger.

It could be a tomato or someone's favorite color.
It could be as bright as the sun or as dull as a gloomy day.
It can be seen on some vehicles, bright as can be.

The color of yellow is everywhere if we take the
time to find it.

Amber Burton

"Memories"

As I sit here reminiscing over the many
beautiful memories you've given me,
I feel sad. A weird kind of sadness; one that
I'm sure I've never felt before.

It feels as if something has been taken
from me without my permission;
Like my insides have been ripped out.

It almost seems as if a beautiful part of
me has died. The part that loved you.
Even now, although it's been quite
sometime, my heart feels so heavy at the
mere thought of you.

Is it all possible to still love you?
And if that is at all possible, have you
already moved on?

Answers unknown, are always those
that hurt the most.

Erika T. Clench

A Rainbow of People

A rainbow of people, glistening,
Across the hemisphere,
The darkness strikes suddenly,
A sharp blackness appears,
Washing the vast colors away.

Constance L. Moy

Your Absence

When summer passes and autumn draws near, I reminisce about you because I've deeply missed you my dear. As tears well in my eyes it is no surprise that I won't see you as another year go by because I don't know when I'll see your smile again my dear special friend.

As sometimes when I think of you, you're my morning and evening flower because I always wonder what you're doing each and every hour, as seconds turns into minutes, minutes into hours, hours into days and days into weeks. I get so weak cause I've not seen your effervescent beauty for some time that's why I dedicate to you this rhyme.

But if you ever come back I surely won't say I haven't been missin' you at all cause I have and wouldn't tell you no lie. Cause while writing about you..... I cried.

Cleveland Adams

Athena During Wartime

Her statue, in the museum
beckoned across marble floors
with a hand as still and white
as the hand of a corpse.

Her gown, it was faded gray,
a smoking whisper
a shroud.

I could not meet her eyes:
two steely shields
edged with the fatigue of bitter campaigns.
My gaze rested, instead
on her soft, fettered breasts.

"Goddess,"
I breathed,
seeing him leagues
away
in the mud and clutching a gun.

my own dear Ares
and only eighteen.

Aleyna K. Pleva

Conscience

Inner voice is prodding pleading
Beckoning my brain be heeding
What imagination's breeding
Could be useful or misleading

Why this struggle is proceeding
When I'm rest so sorely needing
Must my spite be ever feeding
On a steady fare of reading

Meaning into all receding
Actions and forever weeding
Truth from false, good from bad? Creeding
The Almighty's interceding.

Edward J. Wild Jr.

My Life

My life is unhappy
Because of abuse
Abuse of no friends
Abuse of feeling trapped
Abuse of being so shy
My shyness has left me without any friends
I hate my shyness
I wish it would go away
But the more I wish the stronger it gets

Christy Rand

Eventide

There is a lull in the evening
Before the sun goes down.
When the air cools off
And the world slows down.

The breeze soft as a Kitten's breath
And the scent of flowers seem heaven sent.
The songs of the birds sweetly diminish
To the call of the nightingales beautiful finish.

Calm is the air in the evening hush
Before darkness comes in a final rush.
And the stars begin their nightly ride
After the quiet interlude called "Eventide".

Carl T. Roberts

Together

The star filled sky, the lonesome night.
Being with you can't feel more right.
The look in your eyes, the sparkle, the shine.
The fire burning, I'm so glad that you mine
To be with you, to have you close.
To kiss your sweet lips, is what I love most.
The touch of your hands, how it makes me feel.
The sweet sound of your voice
Makes all my pain heal.
Running my fingers through you hair,
In your beautiful brown eyes I stare.
Holding you close all through the night.
Saying I love you, while you hold me tight.
The moon, the stars,
The stormy weather.
We then close our eyes
And we dream together.

Jennifer Schrantz

Oblivia

The sky is weeping; I do see the tears.
Belief comes creeping; sentence, I do fear.
I have known the moors, and no more I need.
When the fog there lures my wounds shall not bleed.

There are the rumbles; then the sky does growl
For good reason. Again the clouds do howl
And loath what's beneath them. That is their woe.
They are above all humans. Such sorrow.

I look upward and see eyes of lightning.
And all is electrical, now striking
The west of my wasted mind, left little
That's mine but tearing tears, torn and trifled.

Ashton John Fischer Jr.

The Message Is Crystal Clear

I'm a young man, who made a mistake.
But God really gave me plenty of breaks.
I knew, I would pay, for my memory won't leave.
It's here everyday.
I saw the judge in his eyes.
And I promise Lord, I did not lie.
Though when the time came, I'd remember to cry.
This has a sad ending, that's easy to see.
But, I pray that you'll listen and open your mind.
For the message, I send is easy to find.

Fernando Olivas

Best Friend

My best friend let me now and I fell down
Best friend fell in love with some else and left me alone now
Well I cry again today because I lost my
best friend and only friend to someone else
Hope my best friend is happy
I my sad and down because I lost my
best friend to some other woman
But all my best friend thing's away he gave me but for went I burn
Well take time together over losing my best friend
As I start over and make a new and better
life for myself with out my best friend
Going to have to learn to do without my
best friend in my life

Dianna Dill

Respite

(For Darcy Sullivan)

once again I am torn
between love and logic and how things seem
between the blinding sensation of being reborn
bursting forth in joy and pain and light
and knowing it is short-lived like wisps of mist
in the first rays of the morn
twirling wheel of twilight fills my mind
distance and dependency struggle
lessened I have become—emptiness outlined
in frustration and the glimmer of tears
when you look back
to gaze upon what is left behind
shivering from the absence—I crawl into you
blazing eyes remove the glazing of ice
that smothers my body of deprived blue
"how like a winter my absence has been from thee"
this line of languish I hold inside as
the times of comfort scattered in my life are too few
so glows the truth in my eyes
despite my fleeting respite—I will feel so cold

Joshua McNeese

A Sister's Prayer

Dear God,
Bless my sister
For her loving kindness
She is not capable of saying no.
Bless her for the joy she brings me and others.
Bless her for the patience
She has in abundance.
Bless her for her humor
Which is delightful, never spiteful.
Bless her ears, you know how much I bend them.
She is always sure to listen
Without prejudice.
Bless her for always knowing
When to give advice and when to listen.
Thank you
For giving me a sister such as her.
And please,
Help me to be a good sister
To one so deserving.

Heather P. Gill

Street Symphony

Shots ring out in the night.
Blood fills the streets.
Women wail, sirens scream
To the background of a loud rap beat.

Bullets bounce off grafettied walls.
Gangs stand face to face.
Skidding cars add a cymbal crash.
The beat keeps on at a steady pace.

Painted lady hustle a trick.
Well dressed man hands her a five.
Pimp scowls and demands a twenty.
Bullets and knives to the sound of jive.

The body, cold, dead, young.
Ignored by the addict on his way to score
Met by the pusher at the corner bar.
Louder music from the crack house next door.

More sirens. More bullets. More blood.
The symphony ends. Total silence
Until the beat begins anew.
Wilder. Louder. More intense.

Jean L. Mowry-Everett

A Season In Hell

... so the flower in the desert lives;
blooming bloodied thorns upon its crown
the sun in its wrath, to each unknown
death stalks, can pain no more the heartless soul
leaves lament broken spirits it's tortured by time
life - blood flows through murderous veins, to reach the opened mind
fortitude no longer the root of saviors, dying for the sake of the living
seductive petals tainted with evil, choke the breath of life
slain dew drops chance nothing in death silence
tranquil absence quivers through its heart
the final edifice to senseless, sadistic death
live only to remember, forget, to die
in the winter, an ultimate sacrifice unto evil for love;
death becomes the flower in the desert....

Helen Chang

O' Wind

O' wind, O' wind,
Blowing and whispering
A sweet melody in my ear.

O' wind, O' wind,
How you blow the leaves across the bright blue horizon.

O' wind, O'wind,
It is time to say goodbye!
You have now calmed down and dropped the leaves,
And no longer sing your sweet melody.
Goodbye, goodbye, O' wind! O' wind!

Justin Frisque

Whispers of Death

Whispers of what used to be.
Black in the night, but still, white.
Two slivers of light dance around
Whispering to me.
The warmth of the breath, moistness of the nose.
Sounds in my ear that rumbled.
"What?" I used to say.
Whispers answered back
Always
They were mine, all mine until they went away
If only the whispers would come back
I'm drowning in grief without you.

Alison Undertheun

Of Florida and Fire Ants

Calamondin oranges cover bonsai size evergreen trees.
Blue heather trembles by the wall, astir in the Florida breeze.
Hibiscus faces redden next to the mulched over winding walk;
Brown stripe lizards blink in the sunshine waiting for a lunch to stalk.
Red eye periwinkles snuggle below purple crepe myrtle plants.
All would be perfectly lovely here, were it not for the fire ants.
In and among the calm flowers, swarming wild on top the dirt
Are the sizzle mouthed southern no-see-ems, whose bites guarantee hurt.
I'm sorry to have to tell you all this rumor for what it's worth:
The colonies don't just bite Floridians. These ants are heading north!

Charlotte Fahey

Shana (Girl of Dreams:)

Where the sky lies down a shade of
blue, where the sun shines up a day
of new, where only a few will go to cry,
Shana - it's you, in their eyes.
Shana is one who dream's alone,
She hears their cries for life;
She has wing's and can fly, an angel of the night sky.
She feels the love for the homeless,
the care for the hart,
the flower of forgiveness,
She would never depart;
She always here within our mind's
to share all our dream's all of the time.

Cindy Schlegel

Destiny

Born long ago, when the world was still new,
Born, but nobody wanted you.
Punished each day for being alive,
It's amazing at all that you even survived.

You were only a baby, what did you do wrong?
Even though you're older, these questions stay strong.
"Why didn't they love me? I tried to be good."
They'd stop you from crying; or feeling if they could.

The bruises and cuts have faded away.
The hurt and heartache still haunt you today.
"Why?" is the question. Why are you here?
To teach some lessons? To listen and hear?

Somewhere, some way, they'd been hurt too
But the cycle of pain has ended with you.
You're all grown up and you've learned how to live,
It took years of trying to finally forgive.

Connie Forte

"All the Silly Things"

All the silly things we do
Brings out my love for you
Life holds many things- some hard, some dear
But nothing else matters when you are near.

Playing with blocks, crawling on the floor
Or even holding your baby, it opens up the door.
A door that leads us down the road
To life's uncertain ways
And to watch you grow is such a pleasure
Every single day.

So later on in life
I hope you'll know it's true
That all the silly things we used to do
Opened up my heart to you.

Frank Cmara

The Goddesses Who Rule Me

Twins in the sense of their birth and existence
Both entities bear extreme attractiveness in their nature
Each can be deadly while in their clutch

One desires all which may make her happy
When she approaches I can feel her power and her evil
The ordeal is priceless for she tells me she loves me
I wish she would stay but she never does
Mania will return with her love for me

The other views all as bleak and morose
When I feel her near I try to overlook her presence...but I can not
She is very powerful in her methods
What commonly results is a test of whether I leave with Blue or wait
Wait for Mania and her cycle of love
By far it is more irresistible to leave with blue

While I do not know their purpose I know their affect
Both beautiful when alone though deadly if found in one consciousness
As both have their times with me I know I will have to leave with one

When that decision comes it will not be made in my mind but in my hands
Whichever one I choose the end will be the same

Hans-Juergen M. Harle

Moma's Love Light

May the memories of you, moma
bring a smile to my face,
through quivering lips, I know the
emptiness cannot be replace;
For moma, so dear and a love in
its purest form,
Gave me all you could. Since the
day I were born;
Hope time will help me get through each day,
Memories of your heart of Gold will
always be with me to stay:
Moma I miss you and your spirit lives on in me,
As you promised that's the way it
would always be;
You said to let your love light shine on
thru me to others,
So it could be passed down to
our young future mothers.

Ethel Brooks Marshall

Untitled

My first walk in the hospital
Brought me a visual gift
And an emotional gift.

Looking out the window at the end of my corridor,
My breath stops momentarily.
A smile floods my face.
I squeeze Peter's hand.

On a wire-enclosed roof top,
A group is gathered,
All dressed in the street clothes, except one.
Blue robe, blue pajamas, white socks, black shoes with a small heel, making her awkward.
She is the center of this picture.

The beautiful orange ball is tossed from one to the other.
The patients miss many times—-
But laugh and run about joyfully.
Childlike, she raises her head, throws it back and drinks in the fresh air and the sight of the sky so close.

She appears, even if momentarily, Happy.

Joan Redmond Imperiale

Center Stage and Beyond

The ground floor as patchwork set with pieces of
brown, there a pattern of red and more, some green some gold.
The sky dramatic with streaking paynes gray
hues and wandering clouds.
Colors of brilliant gold, orange, and crimson array the canopy.
Trees perform, their balleting limbs all
darkened in dampness and swayed against the azure sky.
Dervishing leaves struggle with life, birds
mime, squirrels at task, and evergreens
stand sentinel in quiet watchful waiting.
Crescendant time blends into life clothed in
ermined majesty, adorned in brilliance
of diamond and glitter as crystallite palaces.
At rest, the end? But no! Comes
peace, fulfillment, and the anticipated
reward of a job well done.
Soon will begin once again a new performance.

Jo Heinze

Inner I

Who is this person looking in
Burning to get out
Eternally fired by emotions
Wrought from sight, smells and sound
What is this conscience
That will never agree
Searching for empathetic hearts and souls
For lost goal
Healing sympathy
Are there words of reason
A therapeutic drug
Or spiritual enlightenment
For this strong need of lack love
Shared desires of the heart
Conflict in the mind
More than this is my wound
Impatiently passing time.

Bryan Shepherd

Flame

Out of the flames and into the fire,
Burns this deep candle lit desire.
No water so cool can quench this heat,
That burns in my heart.
Do I feel defeat?

All no my love it was meant to be,
These never ending feelings between you and me.
Hold dear my love this fever is rare.
Are we but a doomed lovers pair?

To feel the Ice, the snow, the rain,
Always in love but always in pain.
No it shall not be these never ending feelings
Between you and me.

My love is bold and brazen its true,
But will I always care for you.
This is a riddle of the mind?

Star crossed lovers, traveling through
Space and time always in love but always behind.

The flames still burn slowly and true
Desire and love I will always feel for you.

Jennifer L. Scarry

Monsters

"There's no such thing as monsters," the mother told her child.
"But come and climb upon my knee
and we'll rock a little while."

"The scary things you think you see, aren't really there at all.
It's just your imagination
dancing on the wall."

"But mom, he had an ugly face and fangs so big and sharp.
I'm really glad I have you here
to hold me in the dark."

"There's nothing in the darkness, son, that you should ever fear.
Just remember that I love you
and mommy's always here."

He closed his tired and heavy eyes, and drifted off to sleep.
"There's no such thing as monsters"
his mommy did repeat.

"There's no such thing as monsters, your mommy tells you true.
There's no such thing as monsters here
just mom and dad and you."

Elizabeth S. Campbell

Ol' Glory

Gallantly flying, it is you we often neglect,
but hats removed and covered hearts
still show our undying respect,
as you cover the caskets on horse-drawn carts.

Lazily waving o'er head each day,
seasoned by the test of time
you always volunteer to lead the way
day or night, you are sublime.

Only for the love of their country
which they have been taught,
do men and women battle and die for thee
without a moment's thought.

Red, white and blue contrast gray skies
with vibrant stripes and stars,
displaying the freedom you symbolize
which we claim as ours.

Yes, I salute you for what you stand
like patriots, minutemen and those who serve,
you are the one who is true and grand
always receiving the honor you deserve.

Jon Patrick Newell

A Love So True

There's so much a m an can do.
But he can do much more with a wife like you.
A good wife can make a man that is true.
But it's still left up to you.
You make choices everyday
Bad or good it's not going away
You always face troubles head to head
And pray to see daylight before you're dead
When we marry, we pray she's the best
We as Christians give God the rest.
There's no guarantees in this world
But God blessed us with two beautiful girls
Both had long beautiful curls
We pray for the best
But prepare for the worst
We never take nothing less
Trying very hard not to express
Our girls are married now and gone
Both have two kids of their very own
And we'd love having all of them home.

Jim Irick

I'm Going Home

Jesus is sharp like a two-edged sword
But He is my savior and He is my Lord
When I have this earth I won't be alone
Praise the Lord I'm going home.

Jesus is there and He is the light
So we'll always have day and we'll never have night.
There'll be no street or alleys to roam
Praise the Lord I'm going home.

When Jesus died He saved me from hell
So I won't have to go to it's cell
Cause he died on the cross to bear every sin
That I have without or I have within.

There is times that I'm going to stray
But He'll never let me get far away
Cause He is the shepherd that never does sleep
Praise the Lord I'm on of his sheep.

Joe Dunkin

D.W.I.

If I had the time I'd help, you're so low!!!
But I don't have the time, for self degrading fools like you!!!
Down, Down, you put yourself down...why?
It's sickening how you kill yourself, before it's time!!!
You've thought about it haven't you?
You're not worth it,
My time that is, everyone needs time, to realize.
Work it, don't kill yourself, kill the pain!!!!
That pain that burns in you
The hate, that you're not as good.
Sympathy,?! Ha, no time.
See the mirror!?
That's it...deal with it.
Then I'll have some...time.

Chad Christensen

The One Inside

I can not see you,
But I feel and know you are there.
I am not sure how you are or what you are doing.
It seems to me you are having fun.
Do you even know who I am?
The one inside.
So gentle, loving and kind,
Not a worry in the world.
A tear for not shedding
A feeling I will never forget
For I am your mother
and you are the one inside.

Cindy Tackett Gibson

Someday

She fills her heart with joy;
But it usually comes down as a toy.
Day by day she feels the pain inside;
Why, can't it just unwind.
People can tease her and pick on her in such a way;
That she sits back and thinks about her dreaded day.
As she thinks about the world going round and round;
She knows something has got to be abound.
Life will be better just give it time;
She thinks as she tosses a dime.
I will wait, listen, and learn;
Someday life will give me my turn.

Jamie Gladhill

Watch Our Children

It's a hurried world we live in, people rushing to and fro
But it's time to face the facts, about something we all know
It's time to watch our children, let's watch our children grow
Take the time to stop and listen, teach them things they need to know
Yes, you have to make the dollar there is food to buy and bills to pay
But a childhood passes quickly, take the time to stop and play
We can feed their little bodies, even buy them fancy clothes
But if they have no loving family life, will they be happy as they grow?
It's a challenge we all face, one to be treasured, not one to forget.
Make the time to help a child, let's all be sure their needs are met.
Children are such precious gifts, each one is heaven sent
The time you share with any child, is time wisely spent
So with faith in God and love for man let's do the best that we can do
If it's your child or someone's you don't know
Be there for them when they need you.............

Bonnie J. Anderson

Freedom

Life is a wonderful flower in the morning sun shine,
But life without freedom is like a bird in its cage.
A place where the sun comes and goes unexpectedly,
where the wind blows against your wish,
where a dream defers as you watch it.
Please nature! Let the cage be destroyed,
Let the bird fly again,
The sun will be bright,
The breeze will be gentle,
And life will be crystal clear like a chandelier
that shines brightly in the dark.

Joe Nguyen

Reflections

Once there was a garden,
but now it grows weeds.
Once there was an ocean,
once blue, now green.
Once there were trees,
as far as the eye could see,
but now there are buildings,
big tall, and lean.
Once there was love,
and now there is hate.
Once there was life,
now death is our fate.
Once you could dream,
and they would sometimes come true,
Once the world was exactly brand new.

Edward A. Padgett Jr.

Friends 'Til the End

Dedicated to Chrissy Toney)

You were once here,
But now you are gone.
I thought we'd always be together,
But I guess I was wrong.
I'm filled with sadness and no more pride.
I wish I could set those feelings aside.
You left without letting us say good-bye.
Now all I can do is cry.
It was so long ago we drifted apart,
But the memory of you will remain in my heart.
The ties that hold us together will never break or bend,
Because we'll be always friends 'til the end.

Hilaree Hawkins

The Search for a Rhyme for Orange Ends on a Sour Note

O, the juice that is an orange's!
(And other of its ilk)
Tastes so sweet, never tinges

Except after milk.

Dave Schmidt

Everyone Thinks

Everyone thinks that life is so bad
But people have more now than they've ever had
Everyone thinks that there is too much killing
Yes, it needs to stop, but how many on the streets are willing
Everyone thinks our children have gone astray
Well maybe parents, and not children, should lead the way
Everyone thinks our nation is so troubled
Stop blaming someone else and let your efforts be doubled
Everyone thinks the answer is someone else's job
While people continue to lie, steal, kill, and rob
Everyone thinks the solution lies with someone else
First the solution needs to start with yourself
Everyone thinks the other race is at fault
Why don't we live and love as Jesus taught
Because what everyone thinks doesn't matter you see
The true healing will come, when we all finally learn
If you give your thumb a backward turn
True healing will come with a nation of "Me"

Gladys R. Reynolds

"After the Storm"

Evening precedes the darkness of night, and dawn the light of day.
But sometimes there are storm clouds, to hide the sun away.
But no storm lasts forever, yes that is surely true.
And when the storm is over, the sun comes shining through.
But no storm is without its effect, on land, sea, or sky.
And our peace is often disquieted, while the storm is passing by.
But when the storm is over, with all its great to-do.
There is that golden sunlight, that comes shining through.
No storm is without purpose, that God allows to come our way.
For in the dark and stormy night, we learn the value of the day.
God our heavenly father wants to teach us, that He is the one, who,
Regardless be it rain or shine, will always see us through.

H. Fitzgerald Durbin

"The Eyes of Morning"

Not sons of my body
but sons of my soul, of my spirit joined
Sons of my choice
The children of promise
Rather than of fate, blind...
like eyes without morning

All that is eternal all that endures
Is that which I have to give
Not that of stone, of leaf or sky
But not without measure
But shaken, and pressed down

There is a window and all that look upon it
Face the illusion of life
Some see fear, some see hate
Some see injustice
Some see only themselves
Others all they long to be

We shall see more and we shall open each one together
Like young eyes in the morning

Jeffrey Burnett

Broken Heart

It can be weird sometimes, and sometimes confusing
but the one we fall in love with has nothing to
do with choosing
It's funny how things change when you have
a broken heart
Hoping people just leave you to die not push
you to start
Falling out of love is not easy to do
but falling right back in again is something that
makes you blue
tears fall
at his last call
he said his time had come
To move on the better things which made your heart feel numb
When he said he'd love you forever, you knew it wasn't a lie
But when you found out the truth, you started to cry
Broken promises, broken dreams, your heart will never be the same,
But I guess that's a lesson we all have
to learn, when we play this game

Andrea Syvertsen

The Prestigious Santa

I heard somebody say, Mom should be Santa Claus,
But the person that said it is just trying to start a war.

We take nothing from Mom, she is the first Santa on this earth,
Because she is the only one that can give a precious birth.

But little children and grown ups alike would think it's very weird.
To see a big fat woman hollering Ho! Ho! Ho! With no moustach
or beard.

For all you Moms who want to join this plan no matter how far or nea
Let man still be Santa Claus, he only get the prestige once a year.
Ho! Ho! Ho!

Charles McDuffie

My Dreamland

There is a land not far away, I cannot call its name;
But this place is very special, I go here every day.

When things go wrong and problems arrive;
When my heart is sore and red are my eyes.

I travel there so soothe my soul, I travel there for me;
There is never pain or sadness nothing horrible have I seen.

I am never scared or afraid for angels watch over me;
When I am in my special place made especially for me.

So many wonderful things I see that I cannot name them all;
But I have a name for my special place, my dreamland.

Summer, winter, spring, and fall.

Coryell LaRue

When the Lord is There

When times in your life are hard and depressing.
Call on the Lord and he'll come caressing.
When the walls seem to close and you feel your in a bubble.
Lean toward the Lord to carry your trouble.
When the fights, never ending and last for forever.
Come to me said the Lord, with your worst endeavors.
When ears are closed and you're begging to be heard.
The Lord listen's to all no matter how disturbed
When your laughter is tears, and tears are laughter.
Follow the Lord and pick the problems up after.
But the after is over when you return from his trip.
Because he'll refresh you with strength like a hot summers dip.

Derese Blanchard-Watkins

The Unheard Cry

Crucify him! The people cried. Crucify him!
But this time the mother did not stand by
silently weeping.
This time she joined in with the
screaming crowd.
A life was taken that day.
Not in the way in which we know it.
But in the blink of an eye
and the prick of a pin,
the life force that flowed in and
around him was drained.
All in the same amount of time it took
to create this life, so it was
to destroy it.
As the body was banished
and they took to disposing of it,
the people were seen leaving
the place of execution with smiles
of satisfaction disfiguring their
normally placid faces.

Dana Knorr

Friends

Tomorrow is another day,
but, today has just begun,
and we would like to spend it,
with the comfort of a friend.

For friends can be cheerful and sometimes even sad,
but for today, the friend I will spend it with,
will only make me glad.

For life is just too short to worry about the past,
we all should take our lives, just a little at a time.
For what we have today, tomorrow may be gone.

So take your life wisely, take it one day at a time,
be sure you know who your friends are,
the people you can count on.

So when you lie down in bed tonight,
you will have no worries or doubts.

Hang on to your heart, and be sure to keep your smile,
so the friends you have today,
will be your friends tomorrow.

Carol Coffee

Calories...

There are so many of them,
but where do they come from?
What is the real meaning of them?

They haunt me in the morning,
they haunt me during the day,
they tell me what to eat
it seems they even haunt me in my sleep.

They have a certain way of expanding my wardrobe.
They have taken control of my life.
They have taken over my mind.

You have to fight them,
you can't let them win.
Fore if you do they will attack.

They are evil, they never surrender,
you must be strong
or they'll take what they want, your body.....

Some people are lucky they don't see many
or have to count many in their lives.
But others like me,
will soon become prisoners of their world.....

Gwendolyn M. Bultron

Not Much Time

Today there are so many diseases
But who do you think it pleases.
Doctor's are always looking for a cure
But no one's ever really sure.
A little girl's dream of being a dancer
Will sadly be destroyed because of cancer.
A little boys hopes of making good grades
Will not come true because of AIDS.
Yes it's sad, but it's true
These children don't know what to do.
I think it's a rotten crime
Because they don't have much time.

Christal Cotton

Remembrance of a Tragedy

they went to bed happy cold night
but would be awakened by gunfire with fright
taken away in orderly fashion by death trains
but death and destruction was all that remained
jews were sentenced to die by the master race
so concentration camps is what they now faced
some would suffer and starve to death
others faced the gas chamber as it claimed their last breath
they would prey from their beds at night
that someone would stop the nazi third reich
the war is over and we remember what it has cost
that all of the loved ones that family's have lost
over six million Jews died and will be missed
but some have survived by being on Schindler's list

Carmen Kelly Jones

Before the Roses Die

I stopped and bought you some roses today.
But you aren't here and it's getting late.
The card attached says, "I Love You"
You're there with her and I'm getting the clue.
You won't say it out loud, so I won't get hurt.
Just a memory is all we are.
I know about the both of you.
Does she know about us?
Does she cry, or scream, or make a fuss?
I'm sorry to have let you down in the past.
I thought our love was meant to last.
Here I go again, I'm about to cry.
I just wish you'd come home
Before the roses die.

Carrie Thirsk

"Call Me"

If you ever need to talk,
call me - I'll answer.

If you ever need someone to lean on,
call me - I'll be the shoulder.

If you ever need a friend,
call me - I'll be your best friend.

If you ever need to cry,
call me - I'll bring the tissue.

If you ever need a hug,
call me - I'll give you a thousand.

If you ever need anything,
call me - I'll give you anything I can!

Cassandra E. Stinson

Ode to a Humming Bird — 'Tis Just a Small Miracle

'Tis just a small miracle of God that I see.
Buzzing and humming so merrily.

The nectar of the bloom it does crave.
Working and storing for a rainy day.

If I were to learn from this small creature divine.
It would be to sing in rain as well as shine.

Life isn't always happiness and joy.
Yet with a merry song the small bird does employ.

It is a song of praise, to the Lord on high.
For giving it patience and helping it fly.

It sings and flutters from one bloom to the other.
Taking time to smell the flowers as it hovers.

They come in a variety of colors, as does man.
Yet peaceful these small birds are, as is God's plan.

Not one is greater than the other.
Sharing and working with no bother.

Is it possible that we could from this small bird learn?
To treat each other with a kind deed turned?

Beverly Matthews

The Ten Commandments

Out of the night and out of the hills
Came a strange light of terror and thrills
Out of the mist and out of the clouds
Came a strange list that frightened the crowds

Out of the thorns and out of the fire
Melting the horns of the animal liar
Came the ten lines that altered the world
Mysterious signs of God's wrath unfurled

Out of the stone and into their hearts
Into their bones and all of their parts
seared on their minds and into their blood
the tie that binds above the dark mud

Alvin Miller

A Mother's Memory, A Father's Pride

"Mommy, I fell down and hurt my knee. Make it better?"
"Can I keep him, Mom? He won't eat much.
An' I promise I'll take care of him?"
"Mom, I'd like you to meet Susan."
"Don't worry, Mom, I'll be back before you know it."

"Watch me, Daddy, see?"
"Trainin' wheels are for sissies."
"Play catch with me, Dad?"
"It's a great car, Dad, thanks."
"Dad, this is Susan."
"Don't worry, Dad, I'll do us proud."

"Missing. . . Mekong Delta . . . presumed . . ."
"On behalf of the President and a grateful nation . . ."
Twenty-one reverberating explosions.
A soft, blue triangle with large white stars.
"For actions above and beyond . . ."
"Without regard for his own . . ."
A pale blue ribbon with small white stars.
A golden disk,
"Valor."

Dan Decker

"Hurt"

What do you do when the hurt stays?
Can you do anything, or does it always remain?
Its so hard to handle, so hard to bear,
Nothing to do, it's just always there.
How can you change it? I don't know.
I know if you leave it, the hurt will just grow.
Grow and grow until it can't grow anymore
and when it's done growing, your heart's still sore.
You can't change the pain, you can't change the hurt
your heart slowly crumbles into a form like dirt.
You can't stand the pain, can't last much longer,
but you must understand, hurt makes you stronger.
So don't give up, don't give up the fight
because at the end of your dark tunnel, there's a
ray of light.
So learn to deal with the hurt and the pain
and always remember, whenever you lose,
somehow you gain.

Doni Lynn Zolman

3-D

I can't see, can't you understand?
Can you feel it when you hold my hand?
I can't feel because of who I am
tell me what you see as you walk this land.
I don't know what to do
except to live my life through you
even though it seems fake
it makes up for your mistakes
All that surrounds me is faded light
no more colors just black and white
my pain needs a bath to wash the gray away
then maybe I'll see again someday
my love is my weakness, my world is now regret
guide dogs are no comfort, it's too hard to forget
I can't hear you from where I stand
Can you taste the freedom that I wish I had?
Cement feelings don't bother me
What burns behind my back, I can't see
My friends hate me and I'm not offended
The music inside my head has ended.

Jill Estronick

Memory Gone

Can you hear me,
Can you see me,
I am old, with faded memories.
My wife is gone, my children grown.
They had to put me in a home.
I can't remember anymore.
I forget who they are, before they go out the door.
Alzheimers, is what they call it.
A terrible disease that robs the mind.
A burglar inside your head.
Robbing you until your dead.
My pace is slow, my eyes are empty.
The words do not come out of my mouth.
There is no cure, just a lot for the family to endure.
I said goodbye, began to cry.
I love you Dad.

Charmaine Burton

Untitled

After all words have been exhausted
your love continues to
strum a variety of cords
on the strings of my heart.

Deborah Saunders

This Old House

Haven't time to fix the shingles
Can't keep the rain from coming in.
This old house aren't like it use to be,
As you will soon see!
The walls are getting black
To wash it off it all comes back
If we could have gotten us a heater
Our time here would have been much sweeter
Under the bed it is so damp,
Its a wonder while asleep we don't get a cramp
We're to open the windows and turn on the oven for more heat
That makes the house sweat and that isn't good or sweet
To wash clothes on a cold and foggy day.
Have to hang them close to the ceiling oh! what a way
The spiders and bees just love this old house
To top it off even a mouse
Wages good, but its almost around the clock,
Its from the house to the barn and back again, to some that's a shock
This old house will be ready soon
For someone else probably about noon.

Esther Carlos

"Teen Life"

It's sometimes not easy being a teen;
Can't really understand what people mean.

In a world of confusion with so many questions;
Who has all the answers, where do I go,
Sometimes I'll just never know.

Help is what you need in order to succeed,
Friends, family, boyfriends, you know what you need.

Talk, talk, talk, to learn the values of life;
You're now aware of those certain things that
Once gave you strife.

Now you can understand and feel a sense of growth;
Remember you never said I can't or I won't.

Just be bold and be daring;
Because this is one teen that calls for a cheering!

Carol Marie Pedroso

The Foundry

Hard by an open panel in the glass
Carboned o'er with smoke and sooty grime
A schoolboy stops short from his hurrying past
And presses closely for a fitting time
To watch the foundry-men working there
In the industrial interior.
He sees the "hot stuff" molten, fierce and bright
Which gingerly athletic they will pour
From long handled ladles to the bight
Of the sand's skillful shapen bore.
As cobbler shapes the leather to the last,-
In a doctrine's upright sandy bore
Lo! the molten soul of childhood's cast!
The molten stuff of laughter and of tears
Hardened in the foundry of the years,
Witnessed through a broken window pane.
By a schoolboy coming down the lane.

David D. Thomas

Born a Son

Wish I'd been born a son
If I had I might be closer to you
Maybe you'd look at me
I shouldn't stand out in crowds
I should of made my mother proud

Ann Peck

The Rosebud

(In loving dedication to my Grandmother, Martha Wallo)

The precious rosebud
Carefully dusted with tears
Lies upon the grave
Knowing it will never bloom
Yet understands the sorrow

Words never spoken
Carefully carved in his heart
Feelings never felt
Denials of emotion
Killed all but the strongest love

A silent knowledge
He knows, yet frustration builds
Realization
The key to all happiness
He knows all but the answer

Moist tears of sorrow
Furrowing down the petals
From the sweet rosebud
On his grave of emotions
Never to bloom in his heart

Angela M. Olsen

Memories

As each day journeys on,
Carrying me with the passing of life,
I call to mind the memories of childhood.
My friends.
My family.
And my loved ones, I'll someday see again.
I can recollect the smiles and the laughter,
As well as the heartache and the tears.
I remember the moments that shouldn't exist,
And those I'll cherish forever.
Even though I can't see tomorrow
And I can't see what my life has in store for me.
The days will journey on.
And there will come a time in my life,
When I look back one last time.
For that reason,
I pray to God,
Let my memories last forever.

David Michael Le Clear

Communism

Ten years pass the dead man's wrath,
Carving an almost ominous path.
Evolving with it a new world order,
Causing the destruction of several borders.
A fearsome world has engulfed them all,
Bringing to them feelings of gall.
Has hatred passed through all the commonalty,
And will death strive and cause more casualty?
As of now destruction is young,
And by the neck, humanity is strung.
The fate of tranquility lies amongst the youthful,
For their wisdom shall make the world more mirthful.

Anand Gupta

Cats

Cats are playful, cats are nice.
Cats are the sweetest thing I ever seen.

I had cats before, they were so pretty and nice,
But we got rid of them because everybody got sick.

I miss them, I really miss them. I cry day and night,
Wishing they would come back for another pretty sight.

I love them, they love me.
I want them to come back to me.

My cat was "bart", my cat was "studley"
And they love me.

"Studley" was black, "bart" was gray,
I'm in pain because they went away.

I think of them day and night
Hoping they will think of me on the same night.

They were good, never bad.
I've been good to them, I always have.

This love will never fade away,
Just because they went away.

I miss my cats, I really do,
And I'll miss them all the way through, because it's all true...
I love you two!

Courtney Munn

A Simple Promise

Have you ever been in love
Cause someone swept you off your feet
Have you ever made a promise
That you tried but just couldn't keep
I'd give anything just to be with you
Just to show you my heart is true
Are you scared to open up your heart again
Do you want me to be just another friend
I don't know why I said what I did
Was it in my heart or all in my head
What do you think about when we're together
Do you wonder why she didn't stay forever
She's gone can't you see
What's left is me
One thing I can promise
Even if we are apart
I can make this promise to you
I'll try not to break your heart

Amy Thomas

Drinking and Driving

Drinking and driving doesn't get you any where,
'cause when you drink and drive you don't care,
When the kids had a wreck,
One had hurt his neck.

As the days went by,
We tried not to cry,
We did the best we could,
Not much we could do.

One day we got the news he had died,
We all were upset and everyone cried,
We all did like we should,
But we all did the best we could.

The funeral was on a snowy day,
We were by the family all the way,
He would have graduated last year,
But he didn't just because of beer.

Carrie Anthony

The Magic In The Lighted Sky

I don't wanna go to sleep tonight
cause tomorrow it's all over
The sooner I would see the morning's light
when all of life is over

I heard a report on the radio
The newsman sounded sad
He said there'd be no place to go
And we would all be dead

The magic in the lighted sky
Will put us all to sleep
Little children asking why
While their mothers weep

I didn't think it would end this fast
But I guess He has his way
When something starts it cannot last
No nothing ever stays

I refuse to go to sleep tonight
I'll be awake when it's done
And it makes no sense to put up a fight
'Cause by losing life we've won.

Dennis Strimple

I Remember You

Life seemed so down to you
cause you never knew what to do,
I remember when you were cheerful and bright,
but now you're never happy and there is no light.
But there you lie,
and a tear begins to fall from my eye.
I want to scream,
hoping it was all a bad dream.
I can't find the courage to go to bed,
I just see my best friend lying on the floor dead.
Now things seem so black cause I know you won't be back

Erika Lathrop

New Beginnings

Memories fading away
Changes occurring every day
Many emotions encompass your life,
Saying good-bye to loved ones cuts like a knife,
And still we must go on.
Searching for the peace of mind we desperately rely on,
It seems impossible but it will not last.
Soon we'll stop living in the past
And look to the future.
Life is a roller coaster of ups and downs, twisting curves,
and uncertainty,
With opportunities and challenges waiting to be unlocked
by that one unique key
Special to each person.
Releasing anxiety is a necessity to ensure a happy ending,
Because every waking moment is a new beginning.

Carol M. Secrist

Untitled

Hold fast to life -
Then let it be -
For we are one step from eternity -
The very day we are born -

Beatrice S. Trupin

Letters To A Friend

Everyday I press my face against the window, squinting through the chips of black paint.
If there is light, come back in an hour.

If darkness prevails, then there is hope...
For I can pull happiness out of the dark.

Although many may be able to say the same,
I realize how fooled they are by the shallowness of it all.

And I savor how special I feel, while others are satisfied with the obligatory line...every now and then.
Across the miles only so many manifestations of friendship present themselves...I realize it's merely a symbol.

For the derived meaning is not confined to the ink from a pen.
Feelings elude description, so this is surely a poor attempt.

Synonyms are simply that, but "thank you" doesn't suffice.
In its lowest denominator it is part of a person's life.

So don't tell me "thank you" will do.
Only for those that smirk when I say she's my friend will such a remark be adequate.

Yet even I offer it so often I hazard the label of a flatterer, but I could not be more sincere;
I say it for the first time every time.

Friendship is not fleeting, and for me I know this one to be true.

Chad Green

Aurora Celebrates Christmas Eve

In a time, long before a million yesterdays, and the day before Christmas. Aurora strolled out onto the dance floor of the universe. The shimmering gown she wore twinkled with a billion rainbow-colored sparkles. She turned slowly, and winked at a star over her bare shoulder. A soft serenade was chiming across the wide heavens,...for her ears only. Slowly, she began to dance.

Lifting her soul to the heights of the universe, so all the world could see her beauty and hear her soft hum. Way up there, she danced for all to see. Higher and higher and higher, then down some, and up again....Oh! the pleasant performance so moves this weary ol' me.

Down in the middle of this snow-covered meadow I stand. It's cold out here, but my soul feels warmth from within.

Upon her rainbow-colored breast lies the soft aura of a bright Christmas dancing in the skies, warming our hearts, bringing good cheer and sweet joy to all mankind.

Our applause for Aurora's Christmas song is, to lend a helping hand, smile with the children, love our grandparents, and always giving thanks. Merry Christmas Alaska!

Eileen M. Stickman

"An Ode to Country Ham Days"

Come and listen to my story, I have a tale to tell;
About a county named Marion, whose festival I love so well!
The festival's known as Country Ham Days, a catchy sort of name;
With its devotion to great country ham, it has received statewide fame!
Country Ham Days is a two day event, held the last weekend in September;
One visit by anyone from far or near, makes it an event they will always remember!
From flea markets, crafts, and the PIGasus Parade, to lots of
country foods and the Pokey Pig Run,
No matter what you've come for, you're guaranteed to have fun!
Country Ham Days has been celebrated, 25 years to this day;
And through these years it has really grown, bigger and better in every way!
So with my heart full of great Kentucky pride, I must bring my special story to an end;
And wish a Happy Silver Hammyversary, to Country Ham Days, my friend!

Danielle Ford

The Pelican

Love guardian of the bay,
unblinking on timeless perch.
Before the pier,
Before the piling,
Where was thy watch?

Helen M. Henderson

Fast Moving Trains

Fast moving trains - sounds
click in my memory -
New York escapades, escapes
to Broadway.

The blue frocked conductor punches
my pass to heaven to
man of La Mancha madness.
In joy, I weep.

Click clicking the door opens -
air rushes - sounds charge hard
fast and real while I
breathe deeply the smells of trains.

Nothing compares as the wild, crazy
winds of time pass by outside
I sit in my soft couch-like chair
and drink scotch - straight and hard.

Christine Colaiacovo

Homelessness

Seeing people on the streets in old clothes tattered and torn, cold and helpless without a home to even keep them warm, Sick, tired, and hungry though no one knows their name, when you see people like this do you feel any shame? Some people beg but get no where in life, Upper classmen think their drunks but really they are full of strife, no one really cares if they live or die, when you see people like this does it make you want to cry? Children without parents to teach them right from wrong, children who are forced to keep themselves standing nice and strong, when you see a child like this look into his eyes, can you tell as you look within his helpless little heart cries? Next time you see these people remember this little part, Give To The Poor Listen To Your Heart.

Amanda Utley

I Love You When...

I love you in the morning,
I love you in the night,
I love you in the evening,
when all the stars gleam bright.

I love you in the summer,
I love you in the spring,
I love you in the fall with
All the fading leaves.

I love you when its April,
I love you when its May,
I love you when its June,
and every other day!

Jamie Meadows

A Dirge for the "Gay"

If I were a man or a woman gay, I'd write a poem and say
I don't know why I am this way, but some say a little gene went astray

To them I'm a freak, a fag, a queer, acceptable only when I'm not near
But I've got two legs, two arms, a mind, and I look a lot like all mankind

Do you suppose I can ever so bold as to claim God gave me a Soul?
You say all creatures God did make, do you suppose His hand did shake?

I'm one of ten in all the permanent, to nine of ten a "different"
With a man's body and a woman's mind, is it possible peace and joy to find?

Here am I you say, living in sin, but you divorce and marry again
You hate the man with color black and make him live in a rundown shack

If Jesus can your sins forgive, will he not accept my way to live?
If I don't drink and tell no lies, if I'm honest and pay my tithes

Why can't I sit in a pew, just like the rest of you?
How I wish you could see, half man half women, I just want to be me

Some of you are big, some are small, some are short, some are tall
and here am I not man, not woman, lucky you fully man and fully woman

Really it doesn't seem quite fair, your beautiful world I cannot share
When the reason I'm this way is a little gene that went astray.

Everett L. Williams

Dear God

You are always there to listen to me, I know you are always there,
Although you are not someone I can visually see.
Every time I kneel down to pray you have always heard everything that
I have to say.
You are the light of my life and the one who helps me make it through
every single day.
Sometimes it is hard for me to see,
but I am truly thankful for all you have given to me.
Please forgive me for all of the sadness and bitterness within my
heart, I know if I keep praying it will one day part.
I can not help wonder how long it is going to be,
but I guess that is just your way of strengthening me.
You are the only one who knows how I truly feel.
No one understands why it is taking my heart so long to heal.
You have been there with me every step of the way, you watched me fall
in love and you watched him walk away.

Angelica Aranda

Country Church Of My Childhood

(Dedicated to Newville Baptist Church, Waverly, Virginia.)

There's a little white church in the country, where I used to kneel and pray.
I'd give all I own to go back home, for one of those childhood days.
The little white church I remember, surrounded by bushes and trees.
Nothing fancy about it, no carpet for bended knees.

An old fashioned stove in the center, most of the church felt cold,
But, the friendly folks assembled there had hearts more precious than gold.
We met there every Sunday and everyone shook hands.
We learned the Ten Commandments, how God lived in foreign lands.

We learned of the birth of our Saviour, of a cross where he suffered and died.
We learned of the tomb where they lay him; how on Easter he rose to the skies.
We learned about God's species, two of each kind and kin.
About the Ark of Noah, that God had put them in.

I remember the wee, small grave yard close beside our little church
Where I would wander aimlessly some Sundays after church.
I could not understand it then or know the reason why,
That people died and left behind their loved one there to cry.

I wonder if our little church is standing just as tall
And are the people serving God, just like when I was small?
I hope they are, Would cause me pain to go back once again
And find and little church not used, where I received my name.

Emma Noon Reed

When Mommy Comes To Heaven

When mommy comes to heaven
I know she'll be surprised
When she sees, my angel wings
And my cute blue eyes.

She might not recognize me
With this halo around my head
When she had me aborted
I was tiny and so red.

I would have been her first born
But she aborted me
I would have been much in her way
And she wanted to be free.

I hope she's been forgiven
I've missed her oh so much
I long to be beside her
And feel her loving touch.

When mommy comes to heaven
I'll show her that I care
What, Lord? I didn't understand.
Lord don't let her go there.

John Wright

"Myself"

Each time I look into a mirror,
I like to see the face,
that is looking back,
or when I take a walk,
I like the friend,
that is following me.

Sometimes I do things,
and I feel like I can,
never face myself again,
or I get angry,
and I want to run,
from the world,
but I always stop myself and realize,
if I can't work this out with myself,
and have myself for a friend,
I realize I have no friends.

Myself, is the best friend I have,
and if I can't get along with myself,
I don't need any friends.

Tracy Sadler

Loving You

I love the way you look
I love the way you smile
I love the way you'd do anything
even go an extra mile
I love the way you hold me
I love the way you walk
I love the way you listen
when we sit and have a talk.
I love the way you stare at me
I love the way you sing
I love the way you said "I do"
when you handed me the ring.
But most of all, I love your touch
It brings me happy tears
To know I'll have only you to love
for the rest of our living years.
I love you.

Wendy Worrell

The Farm Home Windows Glow

The sun went down and the moon came up,
But there was no smiling moon-beam like a buttercup.
Shadows of the evening silhouetted the trees upon the ground,
The brisk hustling of heavily laden tree leaves made the only sound.
The farm home kitchen window dimly lit by a kerosene lamp,
Which was carried from room-to-room and users avoided getting it damp
Lest the hot glass chimney would break and the wick would make it smoke,
This is known to cause people to cough or possibly choke.
Stumbling around in the dark when getting up at night,
Falling into a door, a black eye, what a sight.
Trip over a chair hurrying to the telephone that would ring,
Catch or stub a toe how that would sting.
Then one bright day along came Nellie Benson (Gray),
A lovely farm neighbor lady serving on the board of directors of the Rea.
A "special night" was set, the time and place was now,
Electricity was turned on in all the farm homes, everyone went Wow!
One could see all over, every room in the house was lit,
Nellie Benson (Gray) and the board of directors really did their bit.
Pleased - Nellie parked her car on the table-land and looked down on
the valley below,
Praising the Lord, lights in all the farm home windows how they did glow.

Dorothea Ruth Lux

Creekwood

Tucked away deep into the foothills of the Smokes is a hiding place
apart from all the rest. Old, rustic and filled with eclectic
memories and charm is Creekwood.
We were welcomed by shouts from a gurgling creek not 10 feet from our doorstep.
It laughed and babbled and splashed along its way as if rushing to a
secret place, begging us to follow.
An old, hard door led us through the living room and a maze of
scents; old ashes in the fireplace, dried apples, bayberry, wood.
It was cool and damp. We struggled with windows that didn't want to
open; carefully stuffing holes in the screens with plastic.
The view from every window was life...woods, dozens of ferns growing
along the stone wall of the creek, flowers, water.
Once the sun found its way through the morning mist, suddenly
brilliant greens burst in the sunlight and glistening stones looked
up between branches to find light.
Nighttime always brought a final peace. Giant branches of pines
blanketed this little cottage, but the creek never slept. All night
long it laughed and babbled, almost assuring us we were not alone in the dark.
Memories of Creekwood...and of our days in May will long live in my
soul and ever remind me of a place apart from all the rest.

Donna M. Wakeman

Gwendolyn

I saw her today and it was the same. Out of a crowd of distraction she came, and there was a tingle of delightful surprise. A vision of beauty arresting my eyes. That childish grin appeared on my face. She sauntered and gestured with rhythm and grace. The butterflies were the same. Since the first time that I saw her this feeling remained. It was Gwendolyn, beautiful, blessed, pure and fair. She has imprisoned my heart, I know not where. He smiled at me once and my world was gone. Mysteriously cloaked in a mist or a fog, stopping my thoughts in mid-sentence. Like the clouded existence in a dream where nothing was real but her presence. And gone from the world was the evil and vile, blocked from my sight by a sea of white, and I was engulfed, blinded by her smile. She spoke to me once and it moved me. The sound overwhelmed me completely. Her voice was a musical instrument of pleasure. The tones could reach octaves that my ears could not measure. Like hearing my favorite song for the first time, I listened, trying to absorb every line. Trying to savor every note of every word, trying to remember each sound that I heard. But she spoke it too fast and I yearned for more of this melody. If I could reproduce such harmony, such sound, with a device, I would play it again and again. And I would call my new instrument, a Gwendolyn.

Gregory Perrin

A New Tomorrow

Each Day I Wake
I face a New Tomorrow
One that's Filled with Joy
To Bypass all my Sorrow

Step by Step
Like a New Born Child
I Break Free of your old Bonds
No longer Meek and Mild

No Longer do I Cry for You
Into my Pillow at Night
I learn to Trust and Hope Again
And not to run with Fright

Brick by Brick
The Wall comes Crashing Down
And Now a Smile lights my Face
Where you had left a Frown

Karen B. White

"Friends Again"

Since I started talking to God again,
I have discovered a long lost friend.
As silent as he may be,
There is always a sign to see.
I had to wipe my eyes of the devil,
And take myself back to God's level.
Now I try to talk to him everyday,
Looking for the signs of this way.
Even if life begins to look him,
I must remember to keep faith in him.

Norma Jean Avery

My Love

My love
I have loved you
and I will always love you
Although we can not be together
I will never forget the love
I felt for you

Until I met you I had never
felt real love,
And I will never feel this
love again

We must go our separate way
but there will always be
Something special between us
The love we felt for one another

You will always be my love
We shared a lot together,
happy times, sad times, and
most of all we shared love
Good bye for now
My love

Stacey Standridge

Untitled

I see a rainbow shine through
the light.
Tears come to my eyes,
For the sight I see,
The most beautiful thing that
can be.

Holly Jackson

Why Should I Live

Why should I live,
I have no more to give,
My life is a mess.
I no longer deserve the best.
My head is gone,
I've lost my pride,
I loved him so,
But then he died,
I hear no death,
I feel no pain,
Yet in this life I still remain,
I can't stand it anymore.
then,
Boom!
I hit the floor,
as blood flows from my head,
my agony's released,
and now I'm dead.

Margie Bentley

Mother

I am mother,
I have no name.
There is no other,
Who's quite the same.

Some say I am firm,
But not really strong.
The young ones must learn,
Between right and wrong.

I am like a bear,
Watching her cubs.
There's no need to share,
The warmth of hugs.

I love the smell of rain,
On a summers day.
I hate the smell of fear,
That let's the pain play.

My favorite time is night,
When I can forget.
The problems out of sight,
No cheeks are wet.

Laura Root

Brett

The first time that I saw you,
I knew we'd fall in love.
That special smile you gave me,
was like a message from above.

God was always telling me
those feelings for you were right,
But, I must admit, I had my doubts
until that warm spring night.

You became someone to talk with,
or just lovingly tease.
Your touch made me feel special,
and instantly at ease.

You knew just how to make my life
a natural and wonderful blend,
of the perfect love and romance
with the very best kind of friend.

So, on this day, one year ago,
I married you, my friend.
Our lives became inseparable,
one love; until the end.

Raelynne M. Dunn

Outside My Window

Outside my window,
I listen to the rain.
Hitting against the house,
And the window pane.

Outside my window,
I wish there, I could be.
Running and jumping in puddles.
Or sailing the open sea.

Outside my window,
Anything can happen.
Going from Mars to Pluto,
Or anywhere else I've been.

Sometimes I wish,
That I am up high,
In a spaceship,
Beyond the sky.

Outside my window,
Or sailing the open sea.
Anywhere but here,
I wish I could be.

Mendy K. Clouse

That Special Someone

That special someone
I long to find him
That special someone
Who I have lost

That special someone
His kiss so sweet
That special someone
Again, our lips will never meet

That special someone
I have found him
That special someone
Who is no longer lost

That special someone
Our kiss so long
That special someone
Who's love is strong

Rachel Faulk

"The Game Called Life"

I entered a contest.
I lost.
My sister cries.
"Why?", she asks.
The vase broke.
They are left to pick up the
pieces.
I entered a contest.
I lost.

Tara Das

Writer's Block!

Alas, alas, O, woe is me!
I meant to write a poem, you see.
So here am I, with pen in hand,
But with no words at my command.

Just thinking of the task to be,
Does some awful things to me.
My mind goes blank, I'm in shock,
I think they call it, "Writer's Block"!

Lovey S. Baldwin

For You, Mom And Dad

As time passes, Mom and Dad,
I realize how much you've done
for me over the years—
the patience
and understanding I could count on,
your wise and practical advice—
the effort you always made
to help me be a better person.

As time passes,
I'm more grateful than ever
for the gift you've given so often—
the gift of your own time,
your own life—
the great and generous gift of you.
But the greatest gift of all
is the gift that you both have given me
and that gift is of
your spiritual guidance and love.
But, the thing that I am most grateful for
is for having such caring, loving, and
understanding parents like you.

Theresa Le

"Fetal Murmurings"

I'm just a little baby
I really have no say;
But I'm to be aborted
And thrown away today!

I can't speak out for myself;
My "right to life's" a fight.
"Mama" has been brainwashed,
Into thinking "it's alright."

Because I'm still a fetus,
They think I'm not worthwhile;
Not enough to rearrange
Or change their own lifestyle.

Don't they know when I grow up,
A great help to man they'd see;
Perhaps, one day, cure cancer,
Or a great leader be?

Because they think I'm worthless,
They'll never know the joy,
One has when they are holding,
Their precious girl or boy!

Norma Jean Sauers

Who

Who walks this path with me.
I really need to know.
The one who shares my hopes and fears,
walks with me to and fro.

Who dreams this dream with me,
and shares my inner thoughts.
The one who sees my silent tears,
and battles that I've fought.

Who runs this mile with me.
Supports me like no other.
I should have known, you keep
me strong, its always you dear mother.

Janice Y. Akintewe

Without You

When I think about you and me
I remember how happy I can be
I still feel your touch,
I miss you so much
tell me these feelings,
are you feeling them, too
no one else compares
don't you see
My life without you is empty
My heart is torn, the tears still fall
I lay awake looking at the dark
life is over, empty, meaningless
no one else can save me
I'm slowly fading, dying.

Tracy A. Bogert

Because

Because of your authority
I respect you
Because of your accomplishments
I honour you
Because of your power
I serve you
Because of your might
I fear you
Because of your person
I love you
Because of your drinking
I miss you!

Tanya Ricci

Such Drama

Such drama with my body parts.
I scold my liver
I scold my spleen
I scold everything in between.
I praise my limbs
and hail my cells.
I praise my brain
for giving me such spells.
And, all, I praise
my loving soul within
keeping me pure and away from sin.

Martin Kornberg

My Child

When I look down at you,
I see life and love.
Your the gift I received,
from God above.

I know by your first years,
your future will be bright.
Your eyes lit up,
as you take in all the sights.

As you grow up,
and questions come from your mind,
The knowledge you seek,
is not always easy to find.

No matter what road,
you may take.
Your life is the best,
you can make.

The words, "I Love You,"
comes from my heart.
There is nothing and nobody,
that can ever tear us apart.

Linda S. Mallet

She Set The World Aflame

In a haunting dream at night,
I see my world aflame.
My little child cries in fright
she'll never be the same.
My hopes for her have toppled down.
I made my child cry,
and to my lips it brings a frown,
a dark tear to my eye.
And as my girl looks up at me
I'll never be the same
because this little girl I see
has set my world aflame.

Mike Benigni

Eddie

From the corner of my eye
I see your shadow.
Relentless intruder.
Forever encroaching
onto my thoughts.
In the stillness of the wee hours
I recall your smile.
Your green eyes
invade my reflection-
demanding recognition.
The years have not diminished
my memories of you.
My life is haunted
by your absence.

Margaret Polaczyk Bologna

The Tale

As you sit spinning this twisted tale.
I slip slowly into the darkness.
You take me down where many have
walked through the deep dark trail.
Your words are slipping through my mind.
I know there is no sympathy to be found
among those who do not love.
The story is taking its toll.
I cannot find my soul.
It is not there it has never been
there and now I am empty.
So I sit and listen.
I wait for the end.
Do you feel it?
The end is near.

Rachael Gibson

Untitled

You are my dream maker
I spent so many days with you
How could you not
  be in my dreams?
Did you hear me speak to you
  the other morning?
I promised you I would
  if I could
One never knows
So, for now
  you'll be in my dreams
Forever.

Joyce C. Burris

Endless Waters

Gazing out upon the endless sea,
I stand alone on an empty shore.
I watch the waters move in beauty,
A salty spray and a gentle roar.

The waters roll in, break and fall
Leaving whirlpools in the sand.
Walking alone, my prints soon gone,
Fresh and free, but I hold no hand,

These endless waters became a friend.
I sit for hours gazing with love,
But love is painful like never before.
My thoughts are deep and far beyond.

The glowing sun now at the horizon
Slowly slipping down from sight,
But still I watch the half lit sky
To hold its beauty for dreaming at night.

Kay A. Foster

The Pits

I've found myself at the bottom...
I think I was pushed in.
The towering walls are slick and black...
Each time I look up, I see toeholds
But they are constantly changing.
Each time I reach a ledge,
It gives way.

Sometimes I slip only a short way.
Yet other times I find myself
Once again at the bottom.
I look up and, at times, there is light,
I think I've even seen a helping hand,
But the arm is never long enough.

Once there was a ladder,
But it was set with dry rot.
Once there was a doorway,
But it was merely a broom closet.
And once there was hope,
But now only frustration
Festers in my soul.

Sunita Shinde

Sunset

I like to watch the sunset.
I think it's beautiful-
To see that golden glow
Or reflections on the snow.
As the sun goes slowly down,
I suddenly show a frown.
That glorious flame
has shown me no blame.
For that orangey-red,
is never the same.
It goes from orange to light blue.
As for the stars, there are only a few.
As the sky turns to black,
I turn to look back,
at our precious memories.
I know you can't take these.
There is many an instant,
When I think for just one moment,
We could be what we were before.

Tiffany Genovay

Untitled

When I lie in bed I think of you
I think of all the things
Me and you have been through.

When you held me in your arms
The first night we meet
It is something I'll never forget.

The first night was perfect
Everything right, you held me so tight.

I know we will grow stronger
In a matter of time
There no question in my mind.

When I think about what we shared
It brings a smile to my face
It makes me want to show you
How much I care.

I would do anything for you
I wish you knew
How much, I care about you!

Karen Feind

Cholesterol Fol De Rol

"Get thee to a cloister,"
I told the sexy oyster,
"Manhattan clam chowder
and New England, take a powder."
I broke into a gallop
To avoid the blue-eyed scallop.
Like every diet-conscious wimp
I confined myself to shrimp -
no mussels, seafood platter,
lobster maybe, but no matter!
Eating shellfish is no longer sin!
Nutritionally, it's in!
Early experiments were fishy,
so have bouillabaisse with your Vichy!
This news is just terrific
because it's scientific!

Marguerite Glotzer

I Was Afraid

When I wanted to hug you
I was afraid too
When I wanted to hold your hand
I was afraid too
When I wanted to kiss you
I was afraid too
When I wanted to hold you
I was afraid too

But now that I'd got you
I am afraid to lose you

Shawna Rowland

Alone

Alone in a world of pain,
I wonder without any clues.
Searching for that special girl
I pray that it is you.
Your hair, your eyes,
Shine so very bright,
Every time I see you,
You let out a special glow.
A glow so bright,
That shines my darken world.

Rafael Rodriguez Jr.

"Leaving"

As life goes on
I will leave
When you're yelling
I get scared
I think....
Maybe I should leave
But I don't want to leave
My friends I leave behind
I will never forget
I'll miss them dearly
But I must start over new
I'll miss my friends
And they'll miss me
But I must move on
I don't want to leave.

Tiffany Krueger

A Winter Dilemma

It's a blizzard, in full sway.
I won't get out, to work or play.
The electric's off, I'm all alone.
Can't even use the telephone.

The water tank is on the blink.
A pile of dishes, in the sink.
Impossible, to do any chores.
Drifts of snow, block the doors.

Winter's fury, is on display.
Its been a very hectic day.
One thing I'm thankful about.
Being snowed in, and not out.

Lucille Stromp

My Love

If you were a flower
I would be your soil

If you were a bird
I would be your nest

If you longed for a drink
I would be your water

If you longed for hunger
I would be your nourishment

If you become sad
I will make you smile

If you become angry
I will calm the fires

If you become weak
I will be your strength

If you lose your serenity
I will become the clouds

If I lose you
Then death will have my dominion.

Lacinda Riley

Even Though

Even though for a short while,
I'd come just to see your smile
Even though the days were few,
I'd come just to see the view.
Even though you aren't mine,
I have these feelings deep inside.
and even though you've gone away,
you're in my heart everyday.

Tanya Kay Walsh

Winter

Winter -
Icy cardboard scene -
Bleak landscape
Where spidery tree limbs
Hold hands,
An army of fence posts
Tied together
March in even strides
Across a snow-swept field...
Wind breaks the silence
As it hounds the edges
Of a mass of fleeting clouds,
Grinding their edges
Into softly falling powder;
And now silence again -
Storm ended
The sky clears
And the moon and stars appear.
Ice on velvet -
Winter...

William Maloney

If

If down you were
I'd raise you up
If on your face tears
I'd wipe them dry
If unhappy your mood
I'd make you laugh
If one were to strike you
I'd bear the blow
If your heart were diseased
I'd give you mine
If you lost all hope
I'd travel to find it
If pain was upon you
I'd take it away
If you found goodness
I'd share your smile
If ecstasy shook you
I'd tremble along
If you were mine
I'd finally find joy.

Troy E. Bentley

Being Different

Think how boring the world would be
if everyone was like you and me.
Same name, same face
even the same race.
Same math, same clothes
Same religions, same nose.
No matter if you pray at a
Church or steeple, we all
have one thing in common-
We all are people.

Lynanne Gelinas

In The Heart Of Silence

When I think I may die,
I give a lonely sigh,
To smell my lover in the air,
I stare and no ones there.

I cry in despair,
For no one is there,
Desperately I cry...
Then I said, "Good-bye."

Abigail Young

The Flight

Oh my look how high,
If I took a step to fly.

Would I hit the ground and die?
Or would I take the chance to soar.

Fly across the mountains to the shore,
Of the oceans to heaven's door.

I might float down to pay my toll,
For these few moments that I stole.

The price is simple.
It's my soul.

Wesley Cloud

I'm Always Wondering

I'm always wondering —
If I'm going out to play today,
If I'm playing goalie,
If I'm going to become a priest,
How old I'll be in the year 2,000,
When Father will die,
When I will die,
If I will become a saint,
What I'll get for my birthday,
What HEAVEN is like,
When this poem will end.
I don't know why I wonder that.
How will I know?
I'm always wondering —

Tully MacLiam O'Clisham

Love Poem that Rhymes

Oh to be in love.
If only one forever.
One night maybe,
Maybe one night never.

On all be the sun.
But as lovers know,
it is only love
for which the moon will glow.

If I find the one
that my heart she'll keep,
with night in love I'll live
with my love in day I'll sleep.

Timothy William Oates

Lethargic Bunnies

Trust is easy
if there's never been abuse
Finding the answers
I just can't refuse
Taking the long way home
Somehow losing your way
Slowly but surely
you find a brighter day
Forgiveness is forgotten
when it's taken for granted
It's always hard to read between
when the lines are somehow slanted
Knowing someday you'll find your way
to the place you'd like to call home
Hoping to God for the best
and not to be alone
Understand what you can
always live what you believe
Because someday you'll find it
and never want to leave.

Kristine Smailes

What Is Love?

What is love I do not know,
I think I'll just go with the flow
I hope I'll find my love soon.
For how about this afternoon.

Alicia Jones

Stones

Mostly they rest.
If they are large enough they loom.
To amuse themselves,
the flat ones skip over ponds.

Some have the knack
of growing green hair
or lie on lake bottoms
soothing to fish bellies.

Look at the possibilities
they give to mountains,
seashores, small birds touching.

Many are painfully shy,
sink from sight
in abandoned fields.

It is that particular moment
when the earth's heart beats
toward them some unseen love.

Boulder, mountain, planet, dust:
What fills the stone, fills us.

Orrin Bowers

My Shiny Old Dime

Since I have time,
I'll go for a stroll.
If I should fall
Right in to a hole,
I'll take my old dime
A shiny old dime it is.
And on my way home,
I'll buy me a drink.
But not with my dime,
If that's what you think.
Rum it will be,
With a tangy old twist
Of lemon and lime.
Then I'll walk home,
Along with my dime.
My shiny old dime.

Louis Colabella

Tears

You let go of my hand
  I'm crying can't you tell
Or don't you understand,
  You didn't treat me well
The pain I feel inside
  Is more than I can bear
There are rules to follow
  But you don't seem to care
You hurt me through and through
  You left me all alone
Right now I am so blue
  For me your love has never shone
  Have you ever felt a tear?
Have you ever felt the pain?
  You can't leave me standing
  All alone out in the rain

Stephany Garcia

The Stage

On the stage I feel at home.
I'm happier than I've ever known.
But why?
Is it because I cry?
I'm a different person up there.
Someone without a care.
Where I can have different eyes,
and lead other lives.

But I'm happy as me.
and my life is full of glee.

Yet, on the stage,
I can show rage.
I can have fears,
but shed no tears.

It's clear to me,
the stage is where I want to be.

Susan Werkheiser

No Time

No time to pray Dear Lord,
  I'm in a rush.
My hair's a mess and
  my teeth aren't brushed.
I don't want my friends
  to see me this way.
I'll say an extra long prayer
  later today.
I know you'll understand
  and forgive me.
And, so I'm off
  in a frenzied rush
But in my rush I hear,
  a voice speaking
  directly to me...
My dear child, where
  would you be.
If on the cross, I had
  no time for thee?

Sandra Whiteman Vernooy

"Phobia"

I'm not afraid of anger
  I'm not afraid of fear
I'm not afraid of unpleasantries
  Whispered in my ear
I'm not afraid of darkness
  I'm not afraid of death
I'm not afraid of the poison
  Which takes away my breath
I'm not afraid of the ocean
  I'm not afraid to jump in
I'm not afraid of drowning
  In a puddle of my own sins
I'm not afraid of danger
  I'm not afraid of being alone
I'm not afraid of the monsters
  Eating my flesh to the bone
I'm not afraid to know the answer
  I'm not afraid to cry
I'm not afraid of the day
  When God tells me it's time to die.

Wesson

Destiny

My journey must begin now,
  I'm told without a choice.
No map that leads to safety,
  my guide; my inner voice.
The road may lead to danger,
  that much I do not know.
Dreams will pass by quickly,
  Hopes will fade so slow.
When inspiration's lacking,
  I wish the end is near.
But what will happen after,
  that still is not so clear.
And if the finish proves,
  to be a whole new start.
I'll then know all the answers,
  kept within my heart.
So, let the future mold itself,
  and you may help it too.
But don't forget that stars won't shine,
  when the sky is blue.

Marisa Casey

Forget-me-nots
    in
daring   disarray
  grow
by the rickety bridge
that crosses the stream.
Stone
  steps
    head
a crazy pathway
cobbling
    down
to the weathered barn
that holds the secrets
of my greening years.
The orchard
flowers and fruits
nostalgia's twinge
I crunch its apple
    Remembering.

T. Stephanie Gottlieb

Requiem For Summer

Tarnished marigolds bravely standing
In a crystal field.
A robin in the snow,
Watching,
As summer's grass slowly dies.
Open milkweed pods,
Tattered Queen Ann's Lace
Betrayed by happy Japanese Lanterns.
Trees bare their limbs in sorrow,
Bending in the moaning wind,
As it sprinkles deadly snow
Over the garden and the field,
Covering up the corpses
Of summer and spring.
Breathless,
We await the resurrection.

Michelline I. Guimond

Goosedown Express

V-shaped formations
flap into a wet cornfield.
It's Goosedown Airlines!

Dee Whitmore Schick

A Hindrance Of Civilization

This continuance of FREEDOM
in a deficiency at forward motion
leads one to believe hindrance

The progress of mankind
is often stayed by circumstance
and inanimates this progress
When civilization is hindered
and said progress is inanimated
no proficiency is observed

Since no proficiency is observed
civilization is halted
progress is contemplated

A motion instituted
hindrance in civilization.

Michael Cook

Love Memories

When I'm sitting all alone
In a lonely little place
The shadows start to fall
My heart begins to ache

As the memories of my past
Come crowding round my heart
It's then I wish again
I could live the happy part

I use to think love just a game
And in it I took part
Never thinking of the end
Each time I gave my heart

Always taking never giving
Until I met you so divine
Now I've changed my way of living
Because you say your mine

But if you think love just a game
But are willing to play it fair
Let's you and I play the same
And fine happiness there

Pat Patterson

Life

It is like a white rose
in a patch of thorns
  It is as clear and fragile
  as a piece of glass.
It can be as cold as
a mountain stream.
  Or as warm as a fire
  in January.
It can leave as soon
as it pleases. Or stay as long as it
  wants.
It is mine and yours
if we choose to keep it.
  It is always next to
  its enemy. Death
It is all. It is life.

Monica Danielle Jones

Dank

Once upon a time, long, long ago,
In a place where the gods go,
On a hidden river bank,
Dreamed a child whose name is Dank.

While the dancing muses drank,
They played an innocent prank,
Blessing him gently on the flank,
As a dancer of great rank!

Then, in time, as the boy grew,
More and more his feet flew.
The winged feet, so jubilant,
Made his dance exuberant,
Dancing always with such might,
That his fame soared to great height!

All the muses far below,
Their sweet blessings still bestow,
To the star,
Shining brightly! High! Afar!

Raymond Sutherland

Nature's Chorus

The crickets join together
In chorus,
The birds sing in
Harmony.
The trees are black
In the moonlit night.
There's nothing but
Darkness, nature, and me.
Night time is peaceful,
But it won't last for long,
At dawn's early light,
All the music is gone.
For now all the creatures.
Are singing to thee,
There's nothing but
Darkness, nature, and me.

Tausha Feger

A Madman's Point of Insanity

To see a sight of sightly proportion,
In excess towards the distortion.
Sights unlimited and nowhere to be seen,
Your eyes seem to have a blind screen.
Come inside so you can see,
A madman's point of insanity.
Found out is a siege of wonder,
Look out, you might slip and blunder.
Are you lost inside this boxed maze,
Or just wandering around in a daze?
Come in friend so you can see,
This madman's point of insanity.
Are you happy that the tour is done,
Oops, now it's time to begin the fun.
Do you like the bars in the window sill,
Is the door behind you open still?
Walked into a trap is what you've done,
Don't take away a madman's sun.
Come inside so you can see,
Your brand new point of insanity.

Robin M. Virant

Pearl

The moon is like a pearl
In heaven's dusky dress.
A splendor of iridescence...
It glows with mellowness.

The stars are meshed in dewdrops,
They shed a silvery light
Upon a sleeping universe...
The hush of velvet night.

A spray of golden moonbeams,
Clings in soft caress.
The moon is like a pearl,
In heaven's dusky dress.

Virginia M. Heprian

First Love

How soon we lose the passion
in life's midstream
remembering our first love
at thirteen.
"But, Oh Mom, I love him!"
she says with such feeling
Pulling me against her
breast she sighs,
"Oh darling, I remember."

Janice Rayburn

"Season of Love"

Autumn is here dressed
In many colors,
and you are near
Dressed in love.
Rich and golden is my love
While the leaves are falling
My heart falls for you.

Autumn is an open door
Through it we all must go
But do not shatter
As we will not scatter;
For Indian Summer
Shall guide us.

Memories soon may fade,
But you are dear
When Autumn is near
Because your touch is real
And love sustains forever.

Marion F. Coleman

Comfort In Your Arms

There was a time
in my life when
I was into pretty pink bows.
But that was years ago,
and times have changed.
Now the thing,
that I want to be into is
you...and only you.
I want you to love me
as much or even more than,
I love you.
I want you to hold me like
you've never held anyone before.
I want to feel your,
strong yet comforting,
arms around me,
and when we dance,
I want to feel comfort in
you arms!!

Yvonne Hupe

Reflections

I see your reflection
in my mind as a
tear roles down my
cheek how can I tell you
I love you how can you know,
how can you see that I love you,
how can I show,
how deep my feelings are for you

Mandy Lords

The Universe Is Round

The farther we go
in our opposite directions.

I towards Science
You towards Religion.

I towards Enlightenment,
You towards True Faith.

I towards a non-violent society,
You towards making all actions Love.

I towards the Service of Humanity
You towards the Service of God.

The farther we go
In our opposite directions

The closer we come.

Matthew S. Vittucci

Would-Be Fiddler

The soul of you —
in sweet, frenetic strains —
sears the air with passion
beyond mere human words.
Something truly holy
went into your making —
as pure as an angel's voice;
soft and deeply sensuous.
I am but a mortal,
trying to do you justice.
You tolerate my clumsiness —
my laughable attempts
at bringing out my spirit through
the song in both of us.
Maplewood and ebony,
rosin-coated energy ...
Blessed, my experience —
unfold and blossom forth.

Jan Renfrow

Our Star

The light I see
in that great night sky
is always turning, yearning
up so high
So beautiful, peaceful, bright and new
green, yellow, red and blue
Often like the wind
it's always there
even when the clouds
are desolate and bare
I know that star
of yours and mine
will be like our love
and always shine

Jeffrey Gass

"The Chase"

Flying high
in the bright blue sky
there flew a feathered soul.

Down below
in the sifting snow
tip-toed a four-pawed foe.

The feathered soul
saw the four-pawed foe
and squawked in mere fright.

"Oh me, oh my,"
meowed the four-pawed foe,
"I just spotted quite the sight."

"Get back, get back,"
squawked the feathered soul,
"I will not play this game."

"As you wish,"
then he slyly hissed,
"I'll chase you just the same."

Shannon Darnell

Memory

I see the reflection of my heart
in the cracked mirror,
I see the flooded stream and remember
all the tears I have shed,
I hear the robins song and recall
the dances we shared
I sniff of a flower and smell
the fragrance of your cologne instead,
I awake, then to realize, that you
are nothing more than a sweet
memory in a bitter world.

Stephanie Kelly

"The Game"

I fail to see the logic,
in the games that women play
For the answers...
they never say

In the mind of one,
a sign of weakness
In the mind of another,
the show of strength

Privy to the damned
Denied to the fortunate
Are all the heartaches,
in the name and game of the chase

And for the Raven,
he has fallen from heaven
And without grace,
he has withdrawn from the Race

Joshua Eklund

Portrait of a Lost Love

Rushing Waters
Stormy Seas
Abandoned Oceans
Rescue Me
Forever Drowning
Loosing Breath
Constantly Fighting
Inevitable Death

Danielle Arellano

The Call of the Loon

An eerie, haunting sound
In the ghost-gray dawn
On a North Country lake
Taking one back
To a time primeval
To a time of birch-bark canoes
With campfires aglow
A time of fish-hooks made of bone
Arrows of feather, wood, and stone
To the time of the Chippewa
When the wilds were really wild
The call of the loon
An eerie, haunting sound
That takes one back
To a time of long ago

Talbott B. Hagood Jr.

Night's Bout

Night is the day's adversary
In the ring of the universe.
Day is garbed in sky-blue,
Night in midnight black.
When the bell of twilight sounds,
The opponents rise slowly,
And their daily encounter begins.
The cacophony of the day's weary world
Falls to the soothing strains
Of night's melodic intervention.
The encounter becomes softer
As its airs encircle all who exist
Beyond time and space...
Where slumber is smooth.
And gentle dreams, are...
This is your bounty
When night has vanquished day.

Sondra Weiss

Blind

I walk barefoot
In the tall grass
The trees moving
As the wind runs fast

All my life running
As my fear burns within me

Looking... Looking...
Someone please
Hold me close

Teach me to love
And protect me
Protect me from
The hate that surrounds me

Teach me to love others
Let me be blind to color
But let me see inside

Let me be blind...

Michele Goldstein

I Saw a Dog

I saw a dog sitting at the
dinner table eating his food and
tapping his tail that was as long
as a big snail but all you can
see he is not as pretty as me!

Carolyn Greiner

Always Remember

Children have a place
in this universe
whether it be
heaven or earth

Your child is
amongst us
in our hearts
and
in our minds
and
with the will of God
heaven will be
his place of birth.

Theresa Zarcone

Untitled

So many people
in this world full of fears
never show true feelings,
afraid of acid tears.

But they don't have much time
and when that time is gone
they sit and suffer in their pride
and wonder what went wrong.

When one day I lost a friend
I cried a thousand tears.
Each drop was for another time
when I should have held him dear.

I see the falling leaves outside
so beautiful and free.
Why can't our tears fall from our eyes
like leaves from a tree?

Valerie Furcha

The Garden House

The other day I met alone with death
  inside the old garden house
the sweet and innocent smell
  of blooming pansies
created the illusion of an ordinary
  lunch date

We spoke of righteous matters
and those that had plagued me
all of my years
  and finally, when all was said
all questions solemnly answered,

he slowly took my old and withered
hand in his
  and we left the little garden house
together.

Samantha-Lee Chaifetz

Untitled

Look deep
into my eyes
can you see the tears
cause by your lies
all that you wanted
was a second chance
all that I needed
was a little romance
why keep dreaming
why keep taking
you had my heart
and my soul you were taking

Jessica Cahill

"Cycle"

As the petals of youth drift
  into the roses of adulthood
The gap between being a child
  and being an adult is bridged
Forever.
Those petals herald our acceptance
  of our passions as a child
And our memories as we grow
Older and
Wiser.
We have become roses but
soon
new petals will look to us for
Guidance and
Nurturing.
And then it will begin
The cycle again.

Michelle W. Hummer

Friendship

I lurk in the shadows,
Invisible to some;
Only you can see me,
You're the only one.

I know who you are,
I even know your name.
I thought you were my friend,
But now it's not the same.

You changed through the minutes,
Seconds, hours and days.
I only asked for friendship,
And friendship never pays.

Victoria Hope East

The Contest

The only way to win this prize,
is apple pie and mother.
Or constant waving of the flag,
from one side to the other.

A poet almost has to be,
a patriotic bloke.
Or his dream of security,
goes like a puff of smoke.

So I sing a song on Mother's Day.
The apple pie I'll eat.
And constant waving of the flag,
To me is very neat.

I need the fame and fortune too,
of winning in this race,
A little recognition too,
would not seem out of place.

Run up the flag Hip-Hip-Hooray.
Break out the apple pie.
If I don't win a booby prize,
I'll sit right down and cry.

James W. Shaffer

Untitled

Devoid of a path
Knowing no lines
My live is a journey
Which one may define,
But where I rule
And the choice is mine.

Dagfinn Senturia

Gone Where

The cry for blood is deafening.
Is it the color red that enrages?
Gone where is the compassion
For all creeds, colors and ages.

The born, the unborn scream
For lives they were promised.
Gone where is the human love
The bygone times cherished.

Brains perish on so called highs
Of joy assaulting the masses.
Gone where is the want of a remedy
To ease the pain, ills that lashes.

Conscience is a thing passe.
Replaced by the great miasms.
Gone where is the beam's ray
To light the way to life's dignity.

Can it all be brought back?
In time to save creation's magic
Or has it all gone so far aslack
Its lost in yon fields of infinity.

Nell Taylor Bush

The call of the Crow
is letting us know
of springtime's final return
for wisdom is found
far below ground
the same rules the depth
of our soul

Tamah Frances Scoville

With You In My Life

With you in my life there
is sunshine and music.
There is wild storms and soft
summer breezes.
There is blue skies above
and star filled nights made for love.
There is quiet, fun filled days
Spent playing, talking, or just
enjoying the silence.
There is sunrises, sunsets,
and so much beauty to be found
with you in my life.

With you in my life there
is laughter an tears to chase
away all my fears.
There is honestly and trust.
There is hope, faith, and so
much understanding to be
found with you in my life.

Patricia Hanshaw

Silence Under A Crescent Moon

The ghostly glow is all I see,
Is there someone looking back at me?
Changing shapes without a care,
With hidden parts I know you're there.
Looking down on a place so small,
The view you have beats none at all.
Silently darkening the colors to blue,
The mystery at night is caused by you.
All is quiet under a crescent moon.

Ron J. Schmidt

Untitled

The line of love,
is only special
When it has been slightly erased...
...and redrawn.

Carrie Brummer

Him

Describing him -
is to tell of my feelings
to fling them starkly on the page
for all the world to see - I am naked.

Needing him -
what worse mistake can a woman make?
Letting down her guard,
revealing her true self.

Loving him -
yes, even when it isn't reciprocated,
we allow ourselves to fall - deeply -
body and soul.

Leaving him -
can someone please show me the way?
I'm wandering dazed and lost
in the maze that is my heart.

Korrel Crawford

Eyes That See

Eyes that see
is what I need
Eyes I have, but they can't see
They lust and wonder
they flirt and ponder
but I want eyes that can see
My eyes cry of jealousy
My eyes scream to criticize
My eyes love to deny
but I want eyes that can see
My eyes frown and blink
My eyes hurt with a wink
but I want eyes that can see
Eyes that can see
the hurt in someone else
not just in me

Marilyn Gipson Smith

Second Choice

Second choice,
Is what I'll be
Forever and a day.

Second choice,
For him to love.

Second choice,
For time with thee.

Second choice,
Is what I'll be
Forever and a day.

Second choice
For him to hug.

Second choice,
In making love.

Second choice,
Is what I'll be
Forever and a day.

Kristy Lee Keithly

When the Leaves Turn Green

When the leaves turn green
is when summer appears.

The bright sun shines on a
fawn and mother deer.

When tulips and roses
begin to bloom,

The snow will melt and meet
its doom.

When the lake melts down
from ice and cold,

The quilts and heavy blankets
we then shall fold.

Megan Lengerman

To My Mother

Love came softly from her arms.
It blanketed my life.
It exalted her charms
It brightened my day.

If ever a storm threatened my world,
If ever a dark cloud passed my way,
I knew where to run
I knew where to stay.

Protected by a love that was so great
Nothing could bring me harm.
My fears went quickly away, for
Love came softly from her arms.

W. James Dyber

Behind Closed Doors

I see the look about you,
It brings me to tears,
If only I knew your secrets
That you manage to hide from
The world.
If only you knew how much
I care for you, you'd know
It really isn't worth the
Time you spend in your room
Trying to make everyone happy.
I'll still love you, for always
It will be worth your while
To stay with me forever
'Til the end of the world.

Susan Davids

"Black"

It is the color - the color of death
it covers - so no one can see
it protects - us
from the good and - bad
of the world.

It is a blanket - of peace
so quiet and - soft
no love - no hate
can touch it.
This blanket - it's for me.

It stops us - from hearing
the anger, - the sadness,
the injustices, - the despair.
This blanket - it's for me...

Lorie Deamer

Suicide of the Year

When his music spoke
it fell heavy on my chest and
I opened my mouth to breath

He told me his hurts and
his failures and
I ran out and I bought them
via cash-money

Because his music is poetry
written by a man who was full of
teenage angst - growing old -
he couldn't fill the void

And the day I heard
He plugged it with a bullet...

My chest feels heavy
I open my mouth to breath
and everyone stands around with their
mouths open...

And he bleeds
and I breath.

Summer Johnson

Untitled

(Dedicated to Gerard Landry)

I had seen you once again,
it had been over a year.
I didn't even get upset,
didn't even shed a tear.
I didn't even think about,
all the times we've shared.
I don't love you anymore,
but I will always care.
There will always be a small place,
somewhere in the back of my heart.
That belongs to only you,
it was yours right from the start.
No matter what might happen,
I will always care for you.
But my love for you has died and gone,
and I know yours for me has too.
We have both went our separate ways,
and moved on with our lives.
We may not feel the same for one another,
but our memories will never die.

Shawn Stutes

Life

Life is coming.
It hits you like a tornado.
You better be ready.
It can be a breeze.
It can be a storm.
Life can dry you up
like a desert,
or you can be
as full as the ocean.
Who knows.
Watch out for the stone walls.
They may be hard to climb.
Just remember life is coming.

Kara Sauble

Caring

What is caring???
It is a way of life!
It is sharing.
It is relieving strife.

Why should we care???
To save our own souls!
To have less fear.
To reach eternal goals.

What do we do???
We love each other!
We make errors but few.
We help our brother.

When do we stop???
When we can no longer go!
When we have dirt on top.
When we make the flowers grow.

Joyce Rothlisberger

A Whisper

The black moon above
It lingers so low
Why is it black
No one would know.

Some say it's evil
Some say it's pride
I say it's magic
Lurking inside.

Then by surprise
One windy night
It descended from the heavens
And sent me on flight.

It spoke in a whisper
And called out my name
I stopped and turned
And to me it came.

Its voice was gentle
It held a soft glow
It asked me to follow
For no one would know.

Jacqueline Rose Sovde

Fall Leaves

My favorite season is fall
It makes me feel so merry,
With colors painted all around
Like lemon, lime, and cherry
The leaves are falling everywhere
And hurry on their way
To making piles in people's yards
As big as mountains of hay.
My father likes to rake them up
Until there's left not one
I'd rather jump into the leaves
To me that's much more fun!

Joy Wennerberg

Untitled

About the wreck of the hesperus,
And tied to them mast as it was;
Puking it out.
He said with a shout,
"I'm glad that it wasn't asparagus,"

Jay A. Johnson

Love

Love has its ups and downs.
It may bring happiness, it may
Bring frowns;
It may bring tears of sadness or
tears of a broken heart.
But always remember if it is a
love meant to be you shall never
part, and always remember also
love does not come from the outside,
but from inside; the heart.

Mandy Rogers

I Love You

It may not have been love at first sight
It may not have started out right,
But look how far it's gone;
It seems to be right now.
Problems come, Problems go
Still my love for you has only grown.
I want you to know that in the end
whatever makes you happy, can only
make me happy, too. No matter how
sad it really is.
Don't ever forget these simple yet so
powerful and meaningful words,
I Love You!
These are the most complicated words
I've ever known,
But the feelings they give me for you
makes them the most wonderful
and beautiful words I've ever known

Susan Keddie

Grandma

Have a happy birthday
It only comes once a year
Hope you have a great party
With lots of fun and cheer
I haven't seen you in a while
I hope you're coming down
Or maybe I could come up
And visit your ole town
I hope you like the poem
I wrote it from my heart
It may not be too long
But this is how you start
I love you with my heart
And really miss you too
I do hope to see you
Before the summer's end
I also wrote this card
To tell you you're my friend
Love,

Stephanie J. Olivieri

Blind

Love is a complicated subject
It's not taught in any schools
Maybe it's a skilled trade
And I have yet to find the tools

They say there's love at first sight
This type I have yet to find
Maybe it's really out there
And I am just blind

Rodney Dugan

The Sunken Ship of Hidden Treasure

Down under the silky blue.
It shines like golden sun.
The people there know very well
The bright and wealthy one.
It inhabits half the population there
From big as a shark to small as a seed.
It has supplies for everyone
And meets simple and complex needs.

It's hidden well beneath the seas
Not to be grasped by the eyes of man.
Hidden from the hurting above
From the endangered and polluted land.
Known about by only fish
It houses rarities none can measure.
Untouched by destroying man,
The sunken ship of hidden treasure.

Lauren Hovey

To Love

When we first met
it was most profound,
I knew at last
that I had found,
A person with whom,
I could share and trust,
To dream with, and live for,
and die, if I must

We've been married now
for a number of years,
We've had lots of laughter,
we've also had tears,
You've been the major
part of my life,
I feel very proud,
when I say I'm your wife

Life is beautiful,
when love is the core,
Especially when you're married
to the one you adore.

Katie Carlaftes

The Mystery of Love

Rose petals on pillows
It wasn't meant to be
Alluring sunsets
Holding Hands
An admiring smile
It wasn't meant to be
The pedal point of a tide
Simplicity
Small gestures
A gentle touch on the cheek
It wasn't meant to be
Snowflakes
Champagne
A dance by candle light
Making love in the rain
It wasn't meant to be
Unless you solve it for yourself.

Kristine M. Eisenbraun

My Special Place

There's a special place I go
It's an easy path to find,
I simply shut the world out
And dwell inside my mind

I gather all my memories when
life was so much fun
Spread them all before me
and count them one by one

I pick up all the happy ones
and with my arms embrace
Then stack the ones that sadden me
And meet them face to face
I linger there still clinging on
for I know that this must end
I step outside with a loving thought
that I'll visit there again.

Vera R. Seitz

You Haunt Me

You know,
It's been more than
Five years now.
I should have gotten used to
The lack of your laughter,
And the silence of your
Empty bedroom.
I shouldn't expect
To hear the arrival of your car
In the driveway
As you stop in to say hello.
And then
There's that brief instant
When I hear footsteps behind me
And I turn around
To ask you where you've been
To try to bring you home.
But all I've accomplished
Is scaring another
Pedestrian.

Shauna Wreschner

"The Years Are Gone"

The time has come,
It's finally here,
To end and complete,
Your high school years.

You're moving on,
To your college days,
You've grown and matured,
In countless ways.

I hope that in time,
We don't lose touch,
Our friendship, to me,
Means too much.

I'm proud of you,
For you have accomplished this.
A lifetime of love,
To you I wish.

Valerie Sanchez

Summer Rain

I see his reflection in the rain,
its mirror pouring silk before me,
the touch of his warm sleeve
upon me
pressed against the rose of night.

I taste the silver wine, the rain
laced upon my lips, its breezes
caressing ivory mist, his lips
drinking the quiet, flaming
like diamond stars, within.

It is the night, the washing rain
I breathe in rhythmed shadows
white against the ribboned sand
he echoes in its silence,
the flower

He embraces
in my hand.

Paula Davis

"Lucidity"

Life seems like a dream
It's over so fast
We walk around in a daze
Trying to make it last
It is really real
Everything we see
Everything we feel

Everyone we hate
Everyone we love
What's to be our fate
Take the time to look at the sky
Such a beautiful sight
But, do it quick, before you die

John Lake

Could It Be

Could it be,
I've finally found her;
The one I've dreamed of,
The one I prayed for.
Could it be,
Too good to be true;
No. If its true
It couldn't be better.
How did I ever get so lucky?
Or does luck have
Nothing to do with it?
Whatever or however it happened,
I don't want it to end.
Is it love?
Yes.... it is.

Jason P. Normandin

Current Thoughts

Ideas
like silvered fish
Dart to the surface
of imagination,
Snatch at a morsel,
Dive deep,
Lurk in silent dark spaces,
Leave only ripples
to mark their places
in time's murky stream.

Rebecca S. Mushko

Midnight Bridge

I cover the overpass and
I've got the world on a string -
many strings. It's a nice
night, but tonight who cares about
the weather - great music,
the hum of traffic - I like
sometimes not to think about tomorrow.
Above, distant suns and winking stars
but no meteors - a gentle night.
Is there a beautiful woman
on a parallel bridge?
No answer.
Only a sly white disc advertising
reflected light from the sun,
only the bridge rocking
imperceptively endless.
My mind, like the wind
swings on steel -
suspension bridges, saxophones,
six string guitars, whatever.

Shawn Moon

War Children — S. Wales, Nov. '43

Not far past the theater
Just before the Red Cross building
Was a cozy little tea room, she said,
Where they served sweet rolls.
If he could manage shore leave
That night she would meet him there.
He knew the Port by day,
The wreckage by the docks,
And the ruins along St. Helen's Road
So that even in the blackout
He would easily find his way.
Yet what later came to mind
More than any other aspect of the Port
And long after his ship put out to sea
Were the sounds of children playing
(When ordinarily children are abed)
Coming from the darkness and the ruins
Along St. Helen's Road instead.

Vincent Cardinale

'Pebbles'

Pebbles, that's what we are,
just blowing all around,
like shifting sand beneath us,
we have no solid ground.

We're always told, to hold on tight,
and never to let go, what, is it,
that we're holding to,
if we never know.

Could it be a dream we have,
or just a plain old rope.
Is this a question we must ask,
dear God, please give me hope.

He'll give us rest upon a rock,
we'll be adrift no more,
if we'll just take it to our Lord,
that lives on heavenly shore.

Mozelle Osborne

Untitled

Man with Two eyes
often sees double
Man with one eye
sees half as much
Man with no eyes
sees with heart

David R. Anderson

Delicate

Delicate is our relationship,
just like life, and flowers.
So I think of you,
only of the future.
Together I know we'll be together,
for a lifetime, and plus more.
We are slowly becoming one,
part of me is in you,
and so the other way.
Right now I couldn't imagine
life without you,
Delicate we both are,
as flowers, we could so
easily die, or be crushed.
For me, you are my food,
my survival to live,
Your all I need.

Sharon Gogolek

To Yourself and to Others

May your thoughts be good
Just like some heavenly food.
Set goals of ambition -
Let that be your inspiration.

Speak words that are uplifting,
Through the day be they fitting
As swords let your words be -
They are free and at no fee.

Do a good deed every day;
You'll be happy all the way.
Let "Prepared" be your guide -
Good deeds will always abide.

May your omissions be few;
They will keep you true.
Don't let things be omitted -
By them you'll be benefited.

Thaddeus Capek

The Cries

I'm lying awake at night,
just listening to the sounds,
and sometimes I hear the cries.
They come from far off in the
distance but close, nearby and
I don't know who it is that does cry.
I hear the crying from within
and I hear it without. I can hear
it like the piercing sound of a bright
light; The bright light that shines
into my tired eyes.
Although I am tired and want to
sleep I lay awake and listen to the
cries. The cries of the children, my
cries, your cries. Well all can hear
them if we listen.

Meghan Eve Graves

Daydreamer's Song

In a daze;
Just passing time;
I stare at nothing.
My eyes are too busy
Staring into my imagination
To focus on reality.
Like a child playing house,
I can see what tomorrow may bring.
Through my mind's eye,
I can forever envision
The future that may lie
Over the horizon of this moment.
And if, when I reach the future,
My eyes see skies
Darker than those I have envisioned,
I'll just stare at nothing,
And dream of the next horizon.

Rennetta Jenco

My Pain

I love you, girls,
Just the same
Even with all the pain.
I'll always remember.
When into this world, you came.
Know my love, is strong
Like chain,
Even when I feel the pain.
Will your love
Remain the same?
Two little girls
Who bear my name.
Our lives will never
Be the same
As I watch it rain
I ask.
Will it wash away
my pain.

Russell Charles Peake

Life

Sometimes I sit alone,
just thinking of how
life is. Wondering if
I'll make my life
what it's supposed
to be. Just thinking
about how I'm living
it now is right or
wrong. Someday I
want to be someone,
but not so sure how
I'll make it. Sometimes
I just sit alone
thinking of how life is.

Miranda Walker

Love Of Beauty

Beauty is sweet,
Like a blooming rose,
Death is sorrow,
To one that loved,
But age is death to beauty.

Amanda K. Perez

Together

Sometime together,
Just we two.

It takes two to be one.
(Not one, not three.)
Two.

A beach white.
A sun warm.
Beneath an umbrella,
Two books.

We'll read together.
In sun white, beach warmth
We'll read together.
read together.
together.

Robert L. McLaughlin

Prayer And Meditation

From dawn until sunset
Laboring through the day,
When the load gets heavy
Stop for a moment to pray.

Some say prayer is useless—
A waste of time,
They must learn prayer
Comes from the heart,
Not the mind.

A moment of meditation
Strengthens a weary soul,
When the heart is open
God's miracles unfold.

The journey is happier
When praying through the day,
Loads become lighter;
Clouds fade away.

C. J. Moore

Moonset

Daughter of the night
Laughed, skipped,
Tripped from the dying sun
Kissed the stars
Waltzed into
Chocolate dreams
Tossed her hair of moonlight
Scattered the diamond dew of dusk
Whispered cool breath
Into the listening breeze
Then fell
Silent
To meet the
Blushing
Breathless
Damask Dawn.

Lara Narcisi

Walking Home

Walking through a fall - plowed field
Looking
I assumed that if I broke enough
Clouds of powder - earth in my fist
Eventually destiny would find in
My hand an
Arrow - head

Michael B. Tripp

Death

Peacefully asleep
Lie, never to awaken
Drifting away to
An unknown mystical world
And rising to a new life.

As the sky brightens
Raindrops roll off the tree's leaves
While light peeks through
The dark clouds which are passing
To leave a rainbow behind.

God has created
More than just a human race
For there is nature
Which beautifies the whole world
And masks it of its sorrows.

Yvonne Lombardo Brown

One Hundred Stories

The field of dreams
lies deep beneath my wings,
for when we're young
with no worries, growing up
is like climbing one hundred
stories high above the clouds.

The blades of grass are so green,
sometimes the sky looks so mean.
But we must always remember that
life can be so short if we're not
on the same team.

For when we reach the goal
we've worked for just as we are,
all of our dreams will be there
forevermore.

So if you have a dream,
it's only an arms length away.
A dream is invisible until
you make it be seen.

Monte L. Kindell

Life

What is the meaning of life?
Life comes as fast as it goes
It dies as fast as it lives
It brings happiness and sadness
Love and hatred
Some say it's simple
Other say it's complicated
Life is a very meaningful thing
Some search high and low
To find the purpose,
And fulfill their mission
So what's the meaning, of this life?
Love is the answer to this question
It nourishes and feeds the soul

Meghan Parikh

Dreams

Reality suffocating;
Life overtaking.
Dying...Slowly...
Beside the happiness
Packed away in memory...
Buried beneath the others;
Forever.

Vincent C. Gilbert

"Thoughts of Seduction"

(Dedicated to "U the Man")

I would like to dim the
lights, throw on the jazz
and let my tongue dance
around your body like a
ballerina, not missing an inch
of your flesh!
While caressing you, in places
you weren't even aware of,
not stopping unless you gave
me the word, and leaving you
in complete satisfaction.
"I would turn the quiet storm
into an uncontrollable hurricane!"

Lisa Marino

"Essence"

An exquisite cluster of color
Lights upon a blossom fair
Reaching
For the essence of life.

She gathers seeds
Of love, into herself.
Spring holds promise
As she takes flight.

From flower to flower
She fulfills His plan,
The annual renewal
of creation.

Mary F. Forrester

Social Remorse

Suffocated dead flies in a jar
Like a collection of dead people
and reasons to come
An accelerated thought
turned into overdrive
A psychoanalysis of things to come
Of things to be
Of my life
Of my suicidal thoughts
Of my suicidal feelings
My life revolves around death
Around dying
Around being alone
My lonely life will change soon
I know it will
And I'm not sad

Ra King

You Go Together

You go together,
Like birds of a feather,
You've been through calm,
And stormy weather.

You stayed together,
For sixteen years,
Through the happiness,
And the tears.

With two children,
You became parents,
Every now and then,
You wonder,
Could we do it all over
again?

Nikki Morgan

"Who Is He?"

His face lights up
like the sun up above,
with a heart that is filled
with eternal and everlasting love.

His mind, oh how it knows
many different kinds of words,
and ears that can hear
things we haven't heard.

His world he wanted
So peaceful and clean.
Now look at it,
it's all dirty and mean.

But, he will fix it,
for I can feel it in my heart.
And, I know that this man
is very brilliant and smart.

Yes, he is a man.
And, you ask, "Who is He?"
He is the Lord Jesus Christ,
the creator of you and me.

Nicole A. House

This Place Called Home

Inside our hearts
Lives a plan
A special place
For you and me

Safe cozy and warm
A haven of love
Where anger doesn't last
And laughter rings clear

Tick-tock - moving hands
Music to my ears
A favorite chair
A beckoning novel

This place I know
Familiar faces on the wall
Collectibles on the shelves
Coffee mugs, spoons, or a Rembrandt

Chill winds may blow
Here you can rest
An eternal flame glows
In, "This Place Called Home!"

Lauren L. Young

Mother

Such noble and beautiful
living beings;
They live to tell
a thousand words
Preach and teach
the good and bad
Raise and praise
when happy or sad

Their hearts - glow
and show;
How much they care -
Passing love and hugs
in the air;

Yes, this special
being gave
BIRTH TO ME

Thomas R. Mason

Beyond the French Doors

Sitting at this table
looking straight at love
While I sip my java
with the full moon above
I stare beyond the French doors
I seem to look at you more
With a smile like pearls
and a face so fair
My love feels warm, but very bare
The honeymoon glows
The summer breeze flows
You're not but a step away
I feel as if . . .
but I will stay away
My last sip for tonight
My last glance for the evening
at your face so fair
but why should you care?

Lynne Baron

A Prayer for Granddaughter

For a little girl, tonight I pray
Lord, keep her safe upon her way

Through life's high and twisting path
Guide her hand upon the staff

Warm her face with summer's sun
This bright and shining little one

Pain, nor sadness weigh her heart
Faith and strength to her impart

Into your tender care endure
My precious precious granddaughter

Timothy A. Disbennett

Despair

Alone
Lost in a forest of
Fears
Too bewildered to
See a tiny
Leaf bud
Burst with
Hope.

Willa Crawford

Poem

Alex you are my
Love and my
Everything you bring me
Joy with
All that you do and also by just
being yourself and
Not someone you are not that is
why I love you
Dearly also for being caring, loving
understanding and
Respectful I would like you to know
that you will always be my
One and only true love.

Marjorie Martinez

The Other Day

Just the other day I met you.
You were laughing and smiling
I couldn't help but want to sit
closer to you.
Just the other day you asked me out.
I couldn't help but say yes and smile.
Just the other day we were married.
I couldn't help but smile a little brighter
and laugh a little more.
Just the other day our anniversary rolled around.
I couldn't help but love
you a little more then I did before.
Just the other day you passed away.
I couldn't help but cry and smile
because I had to thank you for all the other days.

Michelle Breault

God

A baby sleeps so soft and sweet,
Lying in lacy, white sheets.
It sleeps without a move,
For it is so tiny.

A mother watches in amazement
From a rocking chair.
Her young child is so wonderful,
That the mother cries a soft tear,

For God made a sweet,
Young,
Person,
Who will keep the circle of life
Going.

Misty Lee Barker

Envy

Two
Majestic in their frailty
paused before the window
of men's fine shoes.
"They're you," she said.

And my year's savings
of tears
fell on Newbury St.
blew around and down Clarendon
to boil the Charles.

Comfortable compliments
between winter branches
about fine men's shoes are
only for others.

M. Nakache

"Relax"

Let your Home be your
Sanctuary.
Where your mind finds
Peace
A place with Contentment
at Home
This special place....

Buddy Lee Olds

Good-Bye

The softness of your touch,
Makes me love you so much,
The sparkle in your eye -
Oh, it's hard to say good-bye,
I love the way you look at me,
I hope you know, boy
Can't you see.

Being with you makes me happy,
You've made me cry,
But then you held me tight,
You wiped the tear from my eye,
And then you kissed me and
said good-bye.

Melissa Garcia

The Allure Of Shapes

AN abstract design
Makes some excited.
THE same makes others
Feel unrequited.
IS it in the eyes,
Or is it in the wise.
Comprehending plans
The small and grand,
MADE by the Higher,
Synchronized by hand.
Fulfilling needs not
Only in our heart,
BUT in the maker
At history's start.

Marinna Mahon

The Love of My Life

Many have said they have loved me.
Many have said they have cared.
But you oh God have shown me.
what is meant by true love.
The death of your life on the cross
is much more than a man can ask for.
And this I awesomely declare!
Many have proclaimed their loyalty but
can turn around and be so cruel.
Many have claimed their faithfulness
but oh how they can stab you in the
back. But you oh Lord have shown me
that by your death for me you have
shown me the greatest love of all.
And by your loving grace for me you
have given me the greatest gift of all.
Thanks be to God who has given me
the free gift of eternal life. Amen!

Troy Nakamura

Nada

In the beginning there was Nada,
Nada was everywhere.
Nada was old and very wise,
Nada was deciding,
Nada was very brave,
Nada was doing her job,
Nada was aborting.
In time, Nada became reckless.
Nada was home,
Nada was a cockroach.

Timothy David Rice

Till We Find Love

May our lives improve with time.
May I hold your hand in mine.
May we help each other smile,
If only for a little while.

May we enjoy both sun and rain.
May we never love in vain.
Sharing lessons from our past,
May we find a love that last.

Together or apart may we,

Find a place where we can be,
Living happy ever after
Filled with smiles, joy and laughter.
Wherever our life's path may lead,
May we find the love we need.

Kathy Lusk

"When No One Cared"

As time goes by, I often cry, of
memories in my mind
and no matter how hard I try
to forget, it comes back time after
time.
I can forgive, but I cannot
forget the pain and hurt that
I feel.
It doesn't matter who believes
me or not, because I know
that the abuse was real.

Jennifer Myers

Ice Queen

Emptiness;
Memories stolen from my mind,
Feelings ripped from my heart.
Unable to feel
Trudging through life;
Searching for some sort of meaning,
A reason for being.
Feeling far away,being so close
Not able to reach out or speak
"I love you" echoes through my head.
Frozen in time, soundlessly deafening.
I want to run to you,
The walls around me are too high.
I call out your name,
You do not hear;
I am trapped inside myself
Cold and alone, waiting to thaw.

Kim Woessner

Poetic Phallacy

I am but
midwife of a poem
that grows
in mental womb,
Conceived by intercourse
of life and language.

Fear of misconception
or abortion,
Like local anesthetic,
Dulls the brain,
As fetal phrases
struggle to survive
and every cryptic clause
seeks to outrun
mental menopause.

Sandy Clarke

Midnight Stallion

Each night before I go to bed,
a horse jumps through my head.
Like a bolt of lightning in a
storm and disappears into the
light of the morn.

Ashley Hill

Don't Stop

We have everything for a
Moment - but not to keep
Inside our hearts and souls
This horror makes us weep
Growing together then
Drifting apart
Always an ending
Always a new start
Faces of old, faces of new
Can ignite forgotten pleasures
Love, be it one or the other
Is one of life's genuine treasures
In time, we all change
But the images of these
Special moments will keep the
Breath of life upon our hearts
Forever

Mark T. Hildenbrand

Soliloquy

Sunlight creates a blanket of leaves,
Moonlight creates a blanket of stars.
They are a part of my life,
Neither being more or less important.
I could not say,
"I love moonlight more."
Or, "Sunlight best."
Would life exist without the other?

But my love in you,
I find the answer.
Comparing your smile to moonlight
And your eyes to sunlight,
I know the reply.
Life would adjourn,
If either moonlight,
Or sunlight ceased to be.

Lee Ann McCann

"At Sunset"

We sat by the sea at sunset,
My dear sweetheart and I
We watched the wonderful beauties
Aglow in the far western sky

The sun was a great ball of fire
But clouds partly hid it from view.
They made the sunset more glorious
With color of every hue.

Years later we sat at the Sunset
of a long and beautiful life
and watched the glow of the evening
I and my sweetheart - my wife

And we knew as we saw the sun setting
and beheld its last golden ray
'Twas the clouds we had shared together
That made glorious the end of the day.

Ramona Broadie

Missing You

How I do still miss you
My dearest best friend,
Since God called you to heaven
And your life on earth did end.

So now you have peaceful rest,
Rather than more pain down here.
How I do still miss you,
Though tomorrow will be one year.

But I'll always remember our fun
As best friends we did play,
Until I can join you above
On that glad and happy day.

Because it isn't good-bye forever,
Only so long for a little while.
Yes, one day Jesus will greet me too
With open arms and a loving smile.

Mary Ann Riggleman

It's Here!!

Christmas, Christmas,
my favorite time of year,
Looking forward with anticipation
to fellowship and good cheer.

How good to see the tinsel,
to smell the scent of pine,
And, there's an open invitation
for visits and sips of wine.

The traditional tree is decorated,
and cookies baked in number,
Just waiting for the little ones
to awaken from their slumber.

The midnight star,
soft snow that's a caress,
Hush now, listen, it finally
arrived, it's ... Merry Christmas!

Sandra M. Novak Gecsi

Me

When I was a little girl
My hair had no curl.
At that it was better than Betsy,
A plastic mold for Wetsey.

To school I walked the lane.
Oh, how the boys were a pain.
Kicking rocks all the way,
Do it again at the end of the day.

School's out I became a wife.
Husband, home, a wonderful life,
Mom and Dad left behind,
To live this life of mine.

Along the way a mother,
Two children like no other,
A grandmother at forty —
not old fashion or corny.

A senior curly is my hair.
I didn't do it, I wouldn't dare.
years have brought modern things.
Perms and curling irons with a fling.

Lucille Sallee

Untitled

Slaughtered like cattle
politics ideology
perverted excuse

Art Lohman

You are...

You are the light
My life shines through.
My life could never be as great
As it is with you.
You are the sun
When my days are filled with rain.
Without you, my life
Wouldn't be the same.
You are the gold
In my blue-skied day.
All the things you've done
I could never repay.
You are the rainbow
After a storm of great night.
You brighten my day
And light up my night.
You are the light, the sun,
The gold, the rainbow.
Nothing could better explain
Why I love you so.

Jennifer Leiby

Parfait Amour

Oh, my darling, don't you know
My love for you forever will grow
Here on earth or above the blue
Eternally, I want to be with you
Just supposing someday soon
When men have landed on the moon
Or sailed away above the blue
And returned to tell us what they knew
That there is love and loveliness
and people live in happiness
Each is crowned with Heaven's Bliss
and greets his neighbor with a kiss
There is peace beyond compare
and each race is welcome there
No more worries, strife, or war
For it is love and loved you are
Oh, my darling, don't you know
My love for you forever will grow
Here on earth or above the blue
Eternally, I want to be with you

James P. Mareno Jr.

Facing The End Of Times

Bless me father for I have sinned
my sins are many
redemptions, few
and yet
I ask for mercy
I ask for pity
of your compassion, a grain.
of my repentance, a mount.
I see the end - I am frightened
I wait for God.
I see the Angels coming forth.
Blue eyes Angels with trumpets, horns,
the monks are chanting,
the heavens open
I wait for God.

Luis Garcia-Fino, Jr.

Identity

Perceptions fall to the ground,
Naked are the thoughts I have found.
Questions arise from within,
Allowing doubts to begin.
Confusion reigns in my head;
The truth has yet to be said.

Strange new sounds caress my ear,
And somehow seem to draw me near.
I fight the calling that prevails,
Yet I know that I will fail.
In my thoughts I have been trapped,
All my strength has been tapped.
Gently, I vanquish the fear.

Lisa Caraisco

"Watersedge"

Dozen days dry boned,
Nearer now,
Watersedge
Stand stone still,
Look, listen,
Watersedge
Friendless fogbank forbids,
Best bethink,
Watersedge
Deadmarch drowning driftwood,
Watch, wait,
Watersedge
Catlike cunning carefully,
Soundless sip,
Watersedge
Timeless tasty treat,
slowly savor
Watersedge

G. B. Adams

Being Italian

Being Italian to me it seems
Never reaching any of my dreams
Staying home and cooking too
Is what Italians want me to do
Leaving the house to play outside
Italians saying stay inside
Children playing all day through
Italians saying not you too
Friends come over to say hi
Italians come they say good-bye
All the boys are having fun
Italians saying get this done
It gets dark and this is true
Italians don't let you be you

Maria Favuzza

Promise Me Tomorrow

Promise me a sunrise,
Promise me a sunset,
Promise me a winter,
Summer, spring and fall
Promise me starry nights
And bright lights.
Promise me a rainbow
Promise me tomorrow.

Millie Katshulas

The Departure

I planned to leave without a thought,
No farewell or explanation;
My nature had as yet not taught
Me to cope with complication.

As I turned to go, however,
My troubled eyes could not contain
The fear that I might see you never;
So fast the sun consumes the rain.

But still I left, without a thought,
Or perhaps, without obvious qualm.
Yet inside I had never fought
So severely to keep calm.

My coat around my shoulder,
And my glove upon my hand,
I left one thing at your doorstep;
My heart you did demand.

Tylie N. Stricker

Only Us

No criticism.
No jealousy.
No pettiness.
No disagreements.
One conscience.
One mind.
Only tranquillity.
Only us.
Yeah, just the three of us:
Me, myself, and I.

Sydney Bantom

A Mother's Love

A mother's love is like no other.
No matter what you do, your
mother loves you.

She nurtures you through the
toddler years; and helps you
with teenage fears.

When your mother must go away,
I know it's kind of sad to say;
but you must go your own way.

You will always think of the old days.
You must accept the fact that she
is gone; and live your life happy and long.

But remember this on your way —
A Mother's Love is like no other
no matter what, you're with
each other.

Renay McCarthy

Street Resider

I'm always alone,
No need to be surrounded,
Don't throw me your bone,
Put it back where you found it.

I need not your sympathy,
I'll make do as I please,
A beggar...does not describe me,
I would never resort to my knees.

No...I have no residence,
But yes...I am free,
Fear not my presence,
For I am only me.

Miranda E. Merica

Revelation

On top of a mountain
No one but me
I asked my God to rescue me
There He stood just out of reach
Then a river of lava
Appeared at my feet
How can you do this God don't you care
He asked me softly
Why did you put that there?
Just relax He said what I say is true
You are welcome here
It's all up to you
The answer was simple
It was easy to see
My distance from God
Was put their by me

William Bunce

Sheltered Soul

I have a little secret.
No one can know the worth.
About my tiny child,
I lost before giving birth.

The doctors said "I'm sorry,
There's nothing we can do.
Your baby just didn't make it.
Our main concern is you."

I told them not to worry,
Even though I sat and cried.
Its little soul stayed with me,
Even though my child died.

This soul has been my comfort,
When I'm upset and when I'm down,
It even keeps me company
When no one is around.

And someday when I'm in heaven,
Little fingers and toes I'll see,
Of my tiny little child
Who's soul I've held in me.

Kelly Sue Moss

Time Tells

Judge not others
no opinion return.
Who knows the heart
or of its concern?

Deeds we judge
so easy to see.
Only a facade
shallow it be.

No vision have we
the heart within.
Know not its reason
or of its intent.

Stephen K. Hanson

Untitled

Your touch,
Plays a song on my heartstrings,
A melodious tune,
Refreshing soft and sublime,
Like warm, gentle rain
Falling,
On a dry and thirsty vine.

Norma L. Visage

You Gave Me

You gave me your heart
No questions asked
I received it gratefully
All pieces intact

You gave me your soul
So freely I accept
To keep it next to me
Is all for the best

You gave me your love
To handle with care
For there's no other
Than your life I want to share.

Tracy M. Marr

Remember

When you look into the sunset,
note the beauty of the sky.

When you look upon the ocean,
do you need to question why.

When you look at all the mountains,
do you see the wonder there.

When you look into the heavens,
know I'm watching you with care.

For you see, I'm always with you,
we will never be apart.

For no one can take the memories
that we cherish in our heart.

Melissa M. Garrett

Help

Sitting all alone
Nothing to do
No where to go
What's going to happen to me?
I'm scared
No where to run
No where to hide.

My parents are scaring me
They fight all the time
They yell all the time
What's going to happen to them?

Sitting all alone
Nothing to do
No where to go
What's going to happen to me?
I'm scared
No where to run
No where to hide.

Mandy Lynn Simmons

God Connection

Lovers gaze in state of grace
oceans caress the shore..
all species enjoying equal space
language needs no word for war...
Compassion received in a glance
feelings of joy point the way..
commune with genius
sharing love of perfection
acceptance of predator and prey..
Tho' reverence for life the game
All acclaimed -
is truly the God Connection.

Veronica Theuma

One Moment To Go

One moment to go,
  One more hour shall pass,
One more minute shall come,
  And we shall meet death
Face to face at last.

Candice Williams

The Indian's Anguish

Where once the earth was free, he stands
(Now reservation-bound),
His ancient face as weather-worn
And furrowed as the ground.

And in his eyes the past returns
And phantom warriors drift.
The ghostly horsemen gallop by
On silent steeds and swift,

The shadow shapes of stately souls,
That pass and slowly fade,
And on the baked and barren plain
He stands alone, afraid.

For will his children's children know
The past with love and trust?
And stopping down, he breathes his name
And writes it in the dust.

Sally Yocom

Untitled

Uncle Kevin
Now that you're in Heaven
What do you do?
Are you with God?
if not, with who?
Are you happy? Are you sad
Are you mad? Or are you glad?
So much to ask you
So little to know
Oh Uncle Kevin
Why'd you have to go?
I know now you don't suffer
But it's just so much tougher
Believing you're gone
Or do you live on...
I love you Uncle Kevin

Jessica Hale

The Door

As I lay upon my bed I hear the ocean roar,
As I fade into my dreams I see the mystical door,
As I open up the door and walk into the dark,
Inside my heart I feel a strange memory spark,
A memory of love not a memory of war,
But now i know it's just a dream and I'll have to close the door,
As I see it close behind me the pain starts to begin,
That the memory of love shall never be opened again.

Jessica Phillips

Enslaved

Encased in the skulls and souls
of all beings
is one passion
Some lie to camouflage failure
Some learn
Some never learn - or even care
Some - just escape
living lives for them
Detached and damned
They dictate
Comply without question
Selfless, not selfish
Even in love - what a farce
Why succeed
Why love
Why bother
Does it matter
And to who - and why
Does it really matter
Don't lie to the one you detest most.

Steven Lee Smock

"This Gift of Life"

This day is the beginning,
Of all I seek to find,
My hope will have no ending,
I've put all doubt behind...

This gift of life has reason,
in all thing I believe,
there is not one impossible,
If I choose to achieve...

So from this day forward,
I will live my dreams,
because I know just how much,
this gift of life really means.

Diamon

Tilcara

Wonderful memories
of by gone days,
recall it to me.

Tilcara,
a town with an accent
that is what you are.

A spot in the mountains,
a stain of different greens,
with high winds and breezes,
old an unchanged.

A town that is little
as strange is her name;
a name with an accent
of indian background.

My childhood, my youth,
my laughs and my sorrows.

I know that whenever,
wherever I'll go,
still I will hear
your whispering tones.

Nelida S. de Bregola

The Tree Of Creativity

As I sat underneath the tree
Of creativity,
I let my thoughts as leaves
Drift in the breeze of memory.
I rake the memories into a pile,
Inside my head,
Where these thoughts
May never be dead.
Memories of the past,
Thoughts of the future,
All alike.
And I think to myself,
"Just let it flow,
Let the breeze take you
Where you want to go."

Jeremy Lange

Loss

Absorbing the emptiness
of living in darkness
Without you here
there is an empty place
Inside of me
Being endlessly filled
with hate and sorrow
Pulling a black cover
over tomorrow
Feeling the desolation
of your nonexistence
Feeling no jubilation
over being free
Without you beside me

James Martin, Sr.

My Child

You are the poem I dreamed
  of writing,
The masterpiece, I longed
  to paint.
You are the shining star I
  reached for,
In my ever-hopeful quest
  for life fulfilled.
You are my child -
Now with all things
I Am Blessed.

Kim Guilfoyle

Dreaming

Dreaming, dreaming all the time
Oh how I wish you were mine.
To hold, to love, to live for
My heart and soul I'd give for
You, my darling, so it seems
But my wish is only dreams!

Dreaming, dreaming all the hours
Oh why can't true love be ours?
To have, to keep, to will for
To always, always thrill for
You, my love, it's plainly seen
I'll need to stay with my dream.

Dreaming, dreaming all the days
Let me count the many ways.
To love, to lust, to cope for
And I will always hope for
You, my sweetheart, and that means
I must keep on with my dreams.

Shyrlee Rueter Cole

Untitled

In my heart are
Secret places -
Shadowed chambers,
Misty faces -
Is it tomorrow
Waiting there,
Or only yesterday
Dark and bare?

Val Bishop

The Key

Your heart is like a lock
On a treasure chest, that's
Been swallowed by the sea.
Harden with corrosion, frozen
Solid by the death's of no boundaries.

Like the currents of the
Underwaters, that crushes anything that
Dares threaten to come near.

The beauty inside the chest will
Never be seen, because of the fear
To find the key.

But to all the heart's that's been
Broken and locked, the keys
Thrown away. Shall one day
Be open and the treasures, shall
Be reclaimed.

Louis S. Jackson

Legend Of Castle Manderley

Ere mornin's sea mist roll
On Manderley's essence atoll
Molten cloud forms gleaming air
Elegant endless floral care
Whispers sought her face
Elusive presence fluid grace
Clandestine wonder gossips told
Manderley's moments unfold
Love's Lady soul declare
Sir Manderley future heir
Ethereal essence at the gate
Shrouded shadows casting fate
Passion weapons wounded heart
Hidden anguish token part
Hushed memoirs revealing slate
True love's celestial mate
Love's last pleading call
A slip a push a fall
Grasping seconds ere so late
Elusive essence Manderley Gate

Mavis D. Wallace

Ribbon

You know I can still smell you
On that ribbon from your hair
I keep it in my wallet
To remember you so fair
You dropped it on the floor one day
And left it as you drove
A car that took you straight to God
And left me all alone
I come to see you all the time
As you sleep beneath a stone
The tombs do a mosaic make
Above a bed that's now your home.

Paul Loh

Widow's Mite

Penney, penney,
on the ground,
This poor ole widow
will bend down
to pick you up!
For God's Blessing
and a little luck!
Let this grow from
a penney to a buck!

Penney, penney,
That I found
If I should loose you,
let it roll around
too another ole widow,
to put in her shoe,
to bring her luck,
and many a buck too!

Mary Jo Carder Tolan

10:15

10:15 he comes home
plays with fire on my bosom
enters me with a knife
cutting my soul, taking my life
10:15 he's here again
makes me dance in the rain
forces me to drink his milk
wrapping me with a dirty silk
10:15 he lies on the bed
raises his hands, shakes my head
touches my face with his fist
agonizing body, he claims it's his
10:15 he kisses the floor
swims through his piss towards the door
closes his bewildered eyes
looking at me, I say goodbye

Ruperto V. Calon Jr.

The Gift

For a moment, you stood
on the threshold of our spirit;
awakening freedoms and passions
as yet unknown
in our limited focus.

At the inception of awareness,
you led us in our search
for vitality and being;
introducing experience and aspiration
where empty space had been.

And for a time, you made memories;
giving the essence of yourself
to be shared and treasured,
and entrusting your dreams
in the care of our souls.

Within your courage is our ambition
to achieve and defend excellence,
to be keepers of a priceless bestowal;
heirs to a gift
dedicated to the soul of life.

Sherry Eleanor Haynes

Gray

Who would have guessed?
Not I, not in a thousand years,
That something as small,
As the absence of your phone call,
Could reduce me to tears.

Chris Tice

Your Love

Thoughts of you drift to me
On those long, lonely nights,
Of how much I care for you
And long to hold you tight.

I wish that I could tell you
The things I'd like to say.
Like how much I need you,
And want you every day.

A woman like you doesn't come along
But once in a while.
That can take a heart of stone,
And melt it with a smile.

Richard C. Scott

Untitled

I feel a presence touch me
One I do not know
It covers me completely
And enters in my soul
The darkness comes to ease my pain
And take me to my home
For me this is the only gain
Of love that I have known
It takes away my self illusions
And fill the empty void
All that's left is pure confusion
And a picture of Sigmund Freud

Oxford S. Wiltshire III

The One I Love

My heart has reasons for loving you
one reason is 'cuz you love me, too.
I don't know what else I'm left to do
But I am sure that this one is true.

Is it the fate that keeps our heart beat
or is it the love that is so deep?
There's not much of a choice to keep
I just hope we both need not to weep.

I can not live through life without you
'cuz that will make me totally blue.
Everything I do, it's all for you
I love you, will always do, that's true.

Quennie R. Lanada

Untitled

As I look onto the memories I try to keep,
Only as I climb the mountain so steep.
The mountain of life I've tried to climb,
Only as I look onto the memories I find.
I look at the river flowing down,
And as I swim through, will I drown?
And of the river of life that flows away,
Will I look around and say?
As I climb the mountain so steep,
Will I find the memories I try to keep?

Susan Brincken

Untitled

I sometimes remember happiness
or sleeping by your side.

I sometimes remember how it was
with you all the time.

I sometimes remember your gentle face
with those clear blue eyes.

I sometimes remember sharing dreams
and making ours the future.

I sometimes remember your promises
of how you'd always love me.

But I always stop there, because,
you have forgotten.

Stephanie A. Weddell

What Is Life?

Life is it the sun that rises
or the sun that sets?
Is it the places we've went
or the people we've met?

Is it the things we accomplish or
the goals we make?
Is it what we give
or what we take?

Is it the wind that blows
or the rain that falls?
Is it the clouds that form
or the birds that call?

For all of these things
maybe so true,
But the real answer lies between
me and you.

Stacey Pardee

Adult Films

Some find them stimulating
others see them as titillating.
I think they're far from fascinating.
Indeed, I find adult films nauseating!

There's nothing romantic
about their spectacular antics.
Sex so raw, rough and profound
which knows no bounds
just drives me frantic.

We have freedom to express
and I don't mind undress
but so much distortion of sex
causes me distress.

Synoman Danish

Julian

A special baby, a
person I see.
Someone in Life that
means so much to me.
Someone I Love and care
for dearly.
This little guy is some
what a part of me, it's my
sister's baby and quite clear to
see why her son means so much
to me.
That Little Love is the
baby I call my Nephew "Julian."

Jennifer Branham

Memories

Thoughts of tender love,
Pain of what could of been,
Memories;
Yesterday, today, tomorrow
always a soft sorrow,
But memories still, memories
Today a cloud for my high
Tomorrow a life passing by
always a gentle sigh, memories;
Love now never let go;
the old ones know.
Passing will always show,
Memories.
Yesterday here, tomorrow gone
forgetting all pain
Remembering all love
Returning, Memories

Judy Brown

Cruelness

People are mean
People are cruel
They judge you before they know you
Just because you are different

Being different is good
What would this world be like
if everyone was the same
Boring, I tell you

So here's a caution
Don't judge a book by its cover
The person inside could be another

Morgan Sears

"Jealousy And Greed"

What happens to
people that are nice to you?

Suddenly it seems
stranger, they get sorta
funny as if it you.

You begin to feel
as if it a disease, you
know you don't! Oh
well! So! So!

Then you begin to
feel the big push, the
Mack truck. You say
to yourself, what's it all about.

By then it dawn's
on you self serving
attitude in your
life. Not brought on by you.

As it progresses
it begins to stink.
You think!! al-las-kapute.

Roland Ely

The Soul

The soul is like water
It cannot be seen
but can be touched
and can be felt
and it can be tasted

John Orlich

Sunshower (West Hill Pond)

Clear droplets
pitter patter
light green
neon ferns
twigs snap
pebbles scatter
raindrops pelt
sun fuses
iridescent rainbows
drops subside
green leaves gilded
luminous fallow saffron
resplendent radiance
amber daystar
afterglow

Ray Tedeschi

The Seasons

Tipsy gaited sea gull,
Playground gourmet,
Summer is coming.

A gathering of tall grasses
Stand rippled by
An early summer's wind.

Early morning composer,
Picasso of song,
White-tipped winged mimic!

Two swans parading
Through shallow moving streets
Of subtle stirred water,

A distant willow tree
Weepingly silhouetted
In sunset's moment.

Hillside resident
Outward branches diminishing
Roots growing strong.

Azure-tinted snow capped mountain
Sitting, waiting.

Norma Jean Manning

With America's Permission

Sweet little tender girl
Playing down by the tracks
Listening to the man, whose voice cracks
He gives her an innocent twirl

Gently, he pats her on the head
Asks her to ride in the car
He promises not to take her far
Oh! So soon she'll be dead

We let him go free
He's so, so, sublime
Knows he's not going to do time
For reasons, I just can't see

Already plotting his next mission
Mom and Dad experience the fears
Both will cry a thousand tears
And this is with America's permission

A. Page Melson

Dear God

Dear God,
Please forgive me for all my
wrongs, yet I know there are a lot,
but that's why I had to write this poem,
to wash away the sins
that I've sought. I don't know
how to redeem or exactly where
to begin, each one of my hours
has at least one sin. I try
to connect with you in every
way, crying and begging as
I pray, in my heart is
were I want you to stay.

Sherri Ross

The Wishing Well

Oh wishing well, wishing well
Please grant a wish for me
I've come to make a special wish
It's for my friend, you see

For he has known much sadness
Much sadness, for awhile
And I'd gladly give you all I have
Just to see him smile

So I offer you this golden coin
To make his wish come true
This is the only wish I have
And all I ask from you

Oh wishing well, wishing well
You truly must believe
This comes from deep within my heart
Please, grant this wish for me

Pamela S. Tucker

Mystical Prayer

Oh great creator of the world
Please grant us one more day
to perform our art;
Let the days turn into a bright
Sight in which children will use
your mystical soul coming from
the deepest clouds in the sky;
Let freedom and peace be a
part of our lives, and let us
expand our minds as we read your
book of wisdom words;
Let mystical Angels lead our
Children, and so they will not get
lost in the joy of darkness
and eve of destruction.
The Kingdom is ours.

Marco Antonio Zuniga

Press Time

Lives built on hype
Revolving around ink and paper
Skipping over truth and fact
Exploiting lies and hear say
Why?
Looking for the green
Buying the bigger wallet
Never letting real proof show
Always ready to label guilty first
Forgetting honestly
Letting dirt run a much
Where is the freedom?

Ray Dandurand

Just For The Taking

You cannot catch a moonbeam,
Pour it in a jar,
But glory is enchantment
Each moment where you are.

The fragrance of a rosebud
Bursting into bloom
Cannot be truly captured
In a vial of perfume.

The thrill when a toddler
First ventures it alone,
Never quite remembered
When that child is fully grown.

The heart was made for loving,
The senses to behold
The beauty that surrounds us
Just waiting to unfold.

Louise Carmack

My Mother

Pray for me
Pray for my mother.
If not for my mother.
I would not be here.

God made it so
That we have mothers
No other way
Life could ever be.

As life goes on
For me and all other
Praying for our mothers
Is a right thing to do.

God gave us mothers
So there would be other
To pray for our mothers
The right thing to do.

So pray for me
Pray for my mother
If not for my mother
I would not be here.

Opal J. Douglas

Cactus Flower

The juice from this succulent plant
produced an exquisite and fragile
blossom
It blooms once in its lifetime
with an affinity for love
It is becoming extinct
because that love has faded
The cactus life is consumed
as each day passes by
but this plant will stand humble
in the forsaken desert
its arms extending toward the sky
waiting for embraces
that will never come

This once enchanting blossom
will never bloom
again.

Van T. Bourgois

"Memories"

Yesterday rides a memory train
pulling into my today;
urging thoughts to track back
to old ghost towns
I left along life's way.

Yesterday belongs to someone
who doesn't live here anymore,
The past lies in old ghost towns
and time has boarded up the door.

Tho I've traveled back
down that track to visit
certainly is true!
It's here in today that
I wish to stay
Making memories totally new.

Lorraine Hiester-Smart

Candlelight Vigil

Here again
quiet in the shadows
one candle fighting
so tired
I am only one person
who will fight
when I am gone?

The lies continue
mother to daughter
it's ok
he means well
too subtle at times
more obvious later
whole lifetimes later

Gather to me, little ones
learn the strength
quiet the night
hear the silence
become the candle
light the match

Kimberly Wood Lianos

The Three Sisters

The three sisters
Quietly whispers
"Go back to the place
Where you left a trace,
of your, soul.
Now Go"
Marbles bound,
Where you found
Yourself,
By yourself
or with friends
She seems to send
comfort and peace,
Thru you, for at least,
A while
So smile!
In just a year
You'll see your dear
Mountains, again

Marguerite Smith

Rain

Whenever I smell
  rain,
It is early spring in Nebraska,
  and I am
  on the porch,
  smelling the dust

  and sticking out my tongue to catch
  a few rain drops.

But that is not my story.
My story is my Grandma,
  who can smell the sweet rain
  but would rather see
  the sun, because of
  old bones.

Melissa R. Sand

Captive Heart

Captive heart behind the walls
Raised by grief and lonely falls
One way out and no way in
Wondering how to begin

Wounded by the flagrant blasts
Of living with the fear that lasts
She holds the only key and asks
How to let them in

Stumbling 'round within her cell
Her daily living loveless hell
Ascending from the deepest well
Takes the spirit from within

Reminded that she's not alone
His quiet whisper, gentle tone
You cannot do it on your own
My power in your weakness wins

Paul D. Akers

Remember God

When many doubts and fears assail,
Remember, God will never fail.

When life's trials and troubles abound,
Remember, God is still around.

When in yourself no hope you see,
Remember, God brings victory.

And when you feel you must give in,
Remember, God is there to help you win.

Paul B. Candler

Memory Lane

I stroll down memory lane
Remembering only one name
I stroll down memory lane
Remembering one boys name
I think I loved him
But how shall I ever know
I know I miss him
But how shall I ever tell him
Now I hear a voice
It says it's time to go
I know it's time
Time to leave memory lane
Good-bye memory lane
Good-bye one boys name

Meranda Ward

Keeping In Touch

Just as the famed Toledo blade
  Required the hone for rustful wear,
So, too, the finest friendship made
  Needs patient periodic care.

Now ether sings with silent things,
  Faster than falcons words are flown;
Sound then the beat a greeting brings
  That joy you meet may be your own.

Matricaria

Mirrored Sunglasses

Mirrored sunglasses
resting upon your face.
Used to block out sunlight
and UV radiation.
(Need to protect those eyes)

Mirrored sunglasses
are a stylish thing.
People wear them to look
"cool," or make them look like
the man who began the trend.

Mirrored sunglasses
reflecting the wearer's
world back from where it came.
Preventing the world from
knowing what lies behind.

Mirrored sunglasses
are a good tool to use.
They stop the would be stones
from causing ripples in
your artificial lake.

Rick Gerry

Innocence Lost

A parade of young decomposing soldiers
return from their battle of death.
Millions were injured,
dying in overflowing rivers
of blood or feverish infections
Women crying
hysterically when letters arrive in
mail boxes declaring
how bravely a husband,
brother, son
fought and how hard
the doctors worked to
save them.
Folded up flags
given to wives
commemorate
men lost to senseless
killing.

Vanessa Agha

Abagail

Casually elegant
she rises
from her sunny sill
and laves each shining hair
patiently into proper place;
then turning olive eyes
upon me, thoughtfully,
allows one silken stroke
from nape to tail
before she leaves the room.

Patricia K. Menees

Rites of the Flower

Budding;
Rise into the light,
Grasp the sun.

Growth;
Bathe in the falling droplets,
Caress the loving earth.

Blossom;
Give forth the inner beauty,
Present the future bloom.

Withering;
Return to the birthplace,
Rejoice in the memory.

Wayne Chang

Storm

Frozen, fearless drops of rain
rolled suddenly from the sky
like bowling balls suspended,
then released to strike the pins
of trees and grain, of grass and
panes of glass enclosed in frames.

As each one smashed upon the next,
the THUD was heard across the land.
Hearts cried out with aching loss
of fruitful expectations and tears
fell flat upon the ground torn
into bits by one such stubborn storm.

Mary E. Fischer

Joy's Minstrel

Down from the hills he came,
Roving along.
Singing a glad little
Mad little song.

A lass at her window
Heard him ride by.
The grace of his rondel
Caused her to cry.

"Poet!" She called to him.
"Coulds't thou love me?"
Fair maid", he carolled back,
"Loves I have three!"

"Each of them beautiful,
Each of them kind.
These are their names, sweet miss:
God, Spirit, Mind."

Thus spoke joy's minstrel, then
Tugged at the reins,
And left the young damsel
Weeping again.

Theodore K. Lilley Sr.

Lonesome Moon

Don't the moon look lonesome,
  shining through the trees?
Don't the wind sound frightening,
  blowing with such ease?
Don't the shadows look haunting,
  like the evening's breeze?
Don't the air just freeze you,
  like the winter morning's kiss?
Don't the moon look lonesome,
  shining through the trees?

Laura Shankles

Untitled

"If only I could be
A dreaming personality
Who lives and behaves like me
In a poet's rhyme and rhapsody."

Harry E. Rothman

Leap

I have been running,
Running so long and far,
He keeps following,
I can't lose him,

Soon, I come to a creek,
He's still following, so I run through,
It's too deep, and I almost drown,
To my surprise, he saves me,

At the other side, I escape,
I'm very tired,
He's right at my heels,
Then, we come to a cliff,

I'm forced to choose,
Capture or death, so, I jump,
He cries "No", but it's too late,

I'm falling,
As I fall, I see him jump after me
I'm shocked, then my body hits the jagged rocks,
"Life after death, many colors, but he's chasing me!"

Stephanie Deitz

"Tiny Tack"

Tiny tack
rusted and overlooked
object

So alone
shoved deep into
the spacious wall

Diligent and strong
holding up
art

Never letting go
never masking beauty

Michelle Lynn Mitchell

The Beetle

It crawled under leaves,
sad, old.
Poked into flowers,
the ground.

Tired once, it
went to its young
Fat, sleepy, they
ignored.

Tired again, it
went to its mate
Restless, irritable,
she ignored.

Tired once more, it
went to bed.
Lying there, its
sleep eternal.

Shahana Mushtaq

Me And Am!

No other me and am can feel
the feelings I've within;
No other me and am can fit
precisely in my skin.

Bobby Roberts

Untitled

Everything
Said and done
In the
Wink
Of an eye
Touch and
Kiss me
And
Do it all
Again
Going over
All my days
I love
My love
I Love You
Throughout
These my thin
And whispering
Ebony Lines more.
and over

M. J. Kissel

Eyes In The Sand

When I look at the
sand after the hide
goes back out

Leaving the sand nice,
wet, and brown

Looking so smooth
and enticing

That it reminds me
of your beautiful
brown eyes

It also makes me
want to walk in it
and scrunch my
toes in the sand

Kathy Jones

Of Tassels in the Wind

The shimmering
Sea of grass with
Tassels held high
Are bending and bowing
Frolicking in the wind
What fun it must be
To be coaxed and tossed
To be swung and swayed
And twist and turn
And bend and bow
How I wish someday, somehow
I too, can join their play
Of tassels in the wind.

Yoshiyuki Otoshi

Clowns

Watch the clowns
laugh - fumble - cry
like pictures in a mirror
they reflect ourselves

Ernest J. Clarke

Edges

Dark edges of night
searing through the slats.
Delicately, silhouettes appear
and fade in the darkness of
sorrow.

Bright edge of day
slicing through the slats.
Starry shadows grace the walls
and fade in the light of
joy.

Glistening edge of twilight
falling crisply through the slats.
Fogging images light the canvas
and fade in the dusk of
repose.

Dewy edge of dawn
seeping through the slats.
Excitingly charming currents of light
fade in the new life of
day.

Linda A. Konitsney

Life Cycle

Time goes by,
Seasons change.
Some things die.
Others remain.
Clouds pass by with rushing wind.
Rain comes falling down again.
Sun comes out.
Life in bloom.
Will be over just as soon.
Old man dies, tattered, worn.
Just as quick baby is born.
Cycle of life continues on.
New beginnings with every dawn.

Laura Legg

Fear

I'm afraid of never
seeing the sun again
Having to play video play games,
by myself
Being the last to be chosen
on a sport team
I have fear
Fear is when you speak
as though you are paralyzed
as if you were afraid to look at anyone
you feel like being
left in an empty box
with no one or nothing
but yourself.
That is FEAR.

Noelle Navas

Mothers

Mothers:
Sees you through loving eyes
comes running when she hears your cries
loves you just the same
no matter what the blame
loves you from the day of birth
treats you like the best on earth
does the best for you
help when you're feeling blue
teaches you right from wrong
no matter how long.
She needs no introduction
just a lot of loving
let the bottom line be
a Mother's love is free

Theresa Ann Reay

Windows of Heaven

Beautiful music is your being
Sensual surreal breathtaking
and healing
Nothing is too much
Look up beyond this starry night
Somewhere so far out there
Pull the shade higher
Drawn towards the sky I stare
Past the sea
Pass tender melodies
Headlining the sun
Listen in perfect sigh
Heavens celebrate
Their solatium giving soulmate
Trapped in the crevice of time

Marie Roberts

Untitled

Lord let me be an eagle, who
shares the skies above — with
the wind the rain, the clouds,
the sparrow and the dove.

Or let me be a turtle who
calls the lakes and rivers
home — let me be a buffalo,
with no fences, free to roam.

Lord let me be a rabbit who
knows not hatred, war or greed
— let me be the bear who only
takes upon his need.

Or let me be the monkey who
swings carelessly among the
trees - BUT PLEASE don't make
me be a man who has forgotten
all of these.

Steven Castecka

Two Little Girls

With one pair of skates.
Should one have fun
while the other just waits?
That's no good! Here's what to do.
Give each girl one skate
and one tennis shoe!

Rolling down the sidewalk
laughing in the sun,
two having fun
instead of just one.

Lee Marlowe

Sophistocat

I like to watch Sophistocat
She always knows just where she's at
She never smiles or looks my way
But that is how she likes to play.

She sits upon the window sill,
With arching back and curving tail,
She preens her thick and shiny mane,
Then gazes thru the window pane.

She's so aloof; she's so stuck-up.
She's better far than Silly Pup;
He pants and jumps and licks my face.
To her he's just a cheap disgrace.

The only time she bothers me
Is for a choice "delicacy";
And then, she brushes round my leg,
the closest she will ever beg.

Oh! just one time I'd like to crack
My "queenly-type" Sophistocat;
But she knows I'm content to stay
Her humble servant every day.

Marian Whitehouse

Her Box

She sits alone in the box
She is told to call
Home
She tells them again
And again
That it was not her
But the box still remains her
Home
Weeks, months, years,
Time goes by
As she sits, waiting, in the
Box
Then one day her time comes
To pass on to the other side
To a better place
And that is when they find the
Maniac
Who did it.

Rena Schulman

Untitled

Don't mess with the kid ...
she knows what she is doing.
She might be young, and she
might look innocent, but you
need not do more than remind
her ... she knows ... right from wrong.

Don't mess with the kid ...
it's all a game to her.
She is just looking for the
line, where is that switch
that will set you off ...
So she'll know ... exactly
where to step.

Don't mess with the kid ...
She thrives on your direct correction.
Lead her by example, empower
her with knowledge of how
to properly use her skills ...
not to manipulate ...... but
to appreciate.

Philip Kiersten Sapienza

Why

Why is why?
Is why starry eyed
I don't know why?
Goodbye!

Darwin A. Minnis

Untitled

She sat ...
She saw ...
She heard ...
She had been here
or had she?
Maybe in dreams
Maybe in truth
But here

She walked ...
She ran ...
She embraced ...
This was real
as was before
Fore this was love
And it was hers
Now and always

Vicki L. Dennis

The Sea

Shells of brown
Shells of white
The land is so thin
Beneath the light.

I wonder what that noise is
Wush Wush

Why it's the sea coming a shore
The wind is blowing, blowing
The palm trees
The sun is shining, shining
Over all the land.

Rachel Hewson

The Love Of A Child

His eyes, the light it
shines within
His smile just looking
makes me grin.
The light caresses of
his touch;
no wonder I love my
son so much.
The joy I felt when he was born;
and also pain, my body worn.
His little giggles, when
his bottoms bare,
and all the private
moments that we share.
I'm sure my friends that
you're all aware;
THAT THIS IS THE
LOVE OF A CHILD.

Talaya Jenkins

First Snow

In your bed at night
breathing your breath
I learn to miss you

Anna Banaszak

Lost Creature

There's a creature lost in time
shrouded in legends now left behind
a harmonious blend of grace and
strength.
With a flowing mane of silky length
a symbol of legends now grown old
infused with purity and courage
bold.

Wild he ran free to roam
until a presence like a beacon shone
to tug his heart and spirit along
as she sang an innocent song.

In a sunlight glade she calmly sat
while he approached unaware the
trap.

That men of cunning secretly laid
to capture the magic that he made
this is why though you may seek
only a few know of what I speak...

Sandra Bjornn

Relate

Silent him,
Silent she.
Piercing silence,
more to be.

Move twice forward.
Move twice back.
Gaining nothing,
for what you lack.

A doctor heals.
A patient dies.
To heal a patient,
so no one cries.

Tomorrow comes.
Yesterday falls.
The now is lost,
and time just crawls.

Things you need.
Things you miss.
You know its gone,
relate to this.

Robert Derek Ashton

Lovepath

The world is such a hated place,
Since I let you walk away,
I thought you would come home again,
But time has got in our way.

Now many years of later gone by,
I think back and wonder why,
Why we had to leave it so bad,
When it started off so fine.

From the days of us arguing so loud,
To the tenderness of night,
Never seeming to amaze,
We couldn't go on without a fight.

Roaring thunder, crashing rain,
Nothing can get in my way,
For its your love that I want,
Not sorrow and pain,

Please don't let your feelings go
I will be back for you some day.

Sean J. Varner

Rose of Sharon

Rose of Sharon, a babe born of a virgin, wrapped in swaddling clothes
and lying in a manger.

Jesus, you were God's rosebud, perfect in beauty, crimson in color and
ravishing in fragrance.

You grew and the petals unfolded revealing yet a rarer beauty.
A beauty the world had never seen. Yet the fate of a wicked
and dying world awaited you. In their hands the rose was soon to be
bruised and crushed bringing forth the crimson flow, causing yet a
sweeter fragrance.

Destined for the cross the careless hands of cruel men beat the rose
until it lie in ruins to wither and die.

But oh! It didn't end there. Jesus you rose to bloom forever more.
You rose to ascend back to the throne where yet a sweeter fragrance
fills the air.

Oh! to behold the rose in this land until I can share the rarer
fragrance in Immanuel's land.

Anita Rutt

Love Has A Thousand Faces

Love has a thousand faces, you've heard it said before.
But which one is that special key that will open the heart's door.
Is it the worried frown on a mother's face in the wee hours of the morn.
As she lovingly wipes the tiny brow of the precious child she has born.

Or the sparkle of childish pride in the eyes of a strong, young lad.
When he announces to one and all, "Hey guys, come meet my Dad."
Maybe it's the calloused, caring hands of a farmer late at night.
That gently pulls a helpless calf by a lanterns's flickering light.

Is it the loyalty in an old dog's breast as he waits by an empty shack.
He knows nothing of death and such, but he's sure that they'll back.
Or can it be the love for a beautiful girl that makes a young man sure.
That a love as special as they have, could never have been known before.

But let's not forget the love of many years, shared by a man with his wife.
He sits by her bed with tear filled eyes, knowing that God has taken her life.
Is it the love in a soldier's heart that makes him go off to war.
And give his life for his country on some lonely, far off shore.

Or a simple trust between old friends, each knowing the other as true.
They've always been there for each other, down the years in the things they do.
It's all of these we meet in life as we travel here below.
For love does have a thousand faces that God has given us to know.

Telva Bolkcom

Forbidden Love

In her dreams she can feel his soft gentle touch, the tender way his
hands search for so much.
In his eyes a mysterious glimmer, comparable to moonlit shimmer.
Dreams of him behind closed eyes, cold and dark after love dies.
Love can't die when you feel so intense, when the memories remain ever immense.
Love so many different ways, which one serves ours in this paraphrase?
In her thoughts he's always there, her skin awaits his soft caress;
her hearts begins to race, a warmth covers her like his tender embrace.
A love that unites two into one, is rare in times for yet undone.
Their love must always be, wrapped inside only a memory.
As blowing breezes she'll always know, that in your heart you won't let her go.
Eternally the stars will shine, your love she'll have in her heart or mine.
As days go by and years entwine; their love remains an unforgivable
sign; a test of faith, a chance to grow, all of the principles we yearn to know.
Forbidden it shall always stay, alive in our hearts 'til judgment day,
when truth shall reign above all, the source of their love — it to will fall.
Until such a time; dreams keep them near, and in his eyes forever dear,
forbidden love will always appear.

Kim Learn

Flowers

Flowers bloom in the spring and wither in the fall
But in the summer they will bloom,
and bloom, and bloom until they're tall
In the spring they turn different colors
From shades of red, to shades of yellow
and even to shades of blue
But the most special flower of all
the flowers in the world
At least that's what I think
Is the rose that turns from shades
Of white, to shades of red, and
even to shades of pink
A rose can represent anything from
love or just being nice
Or it could mean "Let's have dinner
at my place, at 6:00, with
champagne on ice."

Tiffany Kimyetta Williams

"A Secret"

I want to write a novel
But it involves my family much
If I write or tell about it
People's heart it will surely touch

The aches and pains lingering in my heart
Seems like the arteries and veins are torn apart

You see, it's nothing that made me thrilled
But my mouth must remain sealed

I can't describe the feelings
It brought directly to me
But I do know
It's not the way it's supposed to be.

Valarie Roby

One Road

There is one road to be traveled,
But it must be traveled alone.
It is only traveled at one point in time,
And the time remains unknown.

There is no preparation,
you can not plan ahead.
All you can hope for at best,
Is to be later in life instead.

People teach you all of your life
About twists and turns you will take.
They tell you how to cope,
Or deal with every day.

So who is there for us in the end?
To travel now...To say goodbye.
For we know how to live our lives,
But no one can teach us how to die...

Karin Lee Risley

A Tree Of Deceit

Lies...spoken to comfort
Cause pain, mistrust and abandonment
One lie planted like the seed of a tree
Quickly blossoms into a forest
The life's light blocked by the forest branches
does not enter
And death is slow and painful.

Kathleen Flannery

Untitled

Here we sit in our picture perfect world
But look a little closer as reality's unfurled
From pot to acid the whole druggie bit
Everybody's doing it
There are people dying left and right
Who don't think life is worth the fight
As they pull the trigger of the gun at their head
Their last thoughts of how much better to be dead
The world around me continues to fall
and here I am in the midst of it all
Watch as Satan takes his bow
Should I shoot up or shoot myself now

Rae Schreib

To My Dear Wife

There may be times when tongues are sharp,
But loves great passion like a harp,
Persists and plays its melody,
And all harsh tones cease to be.
The love and devotion that we share,
Keeps all in tune when life seems bare.
And though the toil, hardships, and tears,
We strive to overcome our fears.
And share we will until the end,
A love that's strong and yet does bend.
A love fulfilled in every way,
To bring us through, day by day.

Nelson E. Cook

Alone Again

So they say that life goes on
but not for me now that you are gone.
I'd think about how you used to care
but now as you can see I have no one there
When I first saw you, I knew at a glance
that I shall get you while I still had the chance.

They all had tried to take you away
but you wouldn't listen to whatever they'd say.
You stayed with me as long as you could
and then you left me like I thought you would
But now I'm all alone again
I've lost my one and closest best friend.

Lisa Gouveia

Jerome

He was here.
But now he's gone and thought
the time his memory lives on.
Day after night, night
after day his love will
never fade away.
And he'll always hold a
special place in my
heart even though we are apart.
And if we shall ever meet again
our love will be special as it was back then

Peggy Wireman

Unanswered Prayers

There's a time when you're so scared
And you want to have faith.
But you can't, you just can't.
All you can do is pray
And just hope that it isn't
One of God's unanswered prayers.

Kelly Hubbard

The Black Roses

The roses were seal
But now they're black
once a sign of love
now loves what they lack

I gave you a rose when I thought you cared
it was our love
the love that we shared
love has it thrones, that it tries to hide
as did the rose that withered and died
a cut from a rose will always leave a scar
roses weren't meant to be picked
just viewed from afar.

A sign of beauty a sign of despair
roses should be hurled with special care
for ever though roses being out feelings inside
the thrones are still painful that can't be denied
Roses are seal, my tear's are blue
a throne struck my heart my roses died for you!

Karen Hall

A Search For Perfection

I thought I could find perfection in a rainbow.
But rainbows almost never complete in arc,
And when they do they never have consistency of intensity.
And they exasperate when they fade in and out.
And sometimes they double themselves, troublesomely.
And they claim a pot of gold is at their feet. But there isn't.

Hummingbirds became the subject of my next search,
But the little devils seldom are still enough to see. Clearly.
And they are elusive, sometimes they are here or there,
And sometimes they are nowhere at all.
Their colors are exquisite, but they are quarrelsome.
How lovely if they flew in a flock. But they don't.

Little children are so lovely and small and cuddlesome.
But you can't cuddle them unless they say so. They squirm.
And they spill things. Sometimes on themselves, or on the floor.
Then I thought about butterflies. But they flit about, purposely.
Kittens should be a candidate, but they have crying spells,
And they have to be taught not to bite or scratch.

As for perfection? I didn't find it.
But maybe I found something better.

Louis A. Presley

Sweet Revenge

A lot of time has passed away
but still I can't forget your face
Forget the girl I used to be
or all those careless, hopeful dreams

My heart's my biggest enemy
It harbors all those memories
It hones a knife that bears your name
and stabs me with remembered pain

And then...

I'm haunted by the happy times
and ache to love you one more time
At last you have your sweet revenge
you haunt me with what might have been

Kathryn B. Coonts

Homeowner's Blues

When we bought this house, we thought it would be fun,
But the extra bills...there must be a ton!!!
Water bill, trash bill, property and school taxes, too!
This is the "American Dream" we thought to pursue?

Cleaned out the septic tank which was disgusting!
Gas bill was high because the gas line was leaking.
Need to replace half of the roof by summer.
Gosh, all of these problems are such a bummer.

But there isn't a landlord to call anymore,
So we'll fix it ourselves and try not to get sore,
and while we try to find the money somewhere
we'll focus instead on the good things that are here.

Mary A. Rager

"Don't Ever Give Up Your Dreams"

I know sometimes life gets confusing,
but the way to go is to keep walking
with what our dreams are,
Life requires learning and going
Through head times,
but we must keep walking,
The road we see in front of us.

"Don't Ever Give Up Your Dreams"
We all see our dream in the sky
As we keep walking and dreaming
This is where we start to meet our dream,
I know there will be times of confusion,
but we must keep walking and shut
Those times out the door,
Into a peaceful passage of music and
The sound of wind caressing your face.

Stephanie M. Winger

A Little Red Wagon

I guess I've seen a lot from my childhood to a man,
but there's one thing I remember that I can't quite understand.
It was an Autumn day as the sun hid behind the clouds,
the wind blew a message, yet the leaves made not as sound.
I was standing on a hillside where in peace did people lay,
when I saw a Little Red Wagon that was rusted and decayed.
As I looked upon the tombstone, the boy had died at 5,
and a Little Red Wagon was laid gently by his side.
You know sometimes it takes a lot to make a grown man cry,
but as I knelt down on my knees, tears were in my eyes.
I don't know why I came here, for the past can cause much pain.
For you see the Little Red Wagon I gave him last Spring.
Push open life's door with a meaning if it's only for just
one day, and rest upon it's door step and God will lead the way.
I cry sometimes with heartache, but God always understands,
he tells me not to worry, that my son is in his hands.

Ronald R. Presser

In Their Shoes

If you think it's easy, walk a while in their shoes.
Because a child is different.
They have feelings too.
Walk a while in their shoes.
They have hopes and dreams just like you.
They may not speak or walk as you do, walk a while in their shoes.
Show the care and love of God.
Most of all walk a while in their shoes.

Jeanette Hacker

Reflections Of Love

I Love You,
But to just speak these words cannot possibly bring across my deepest and most inner feelings. The most motivations of my love for you are not just the utterance of words from my lips, but rather a feeling that swells deep from inside and brings forth a radiance of love, understanding and all that life has to offer you.

There are no problems, regardless of how deeply rooted they may seem, that enough love cannot overcome. I am at your side not only when I wish to be but, when you need me the most.

When you have tears, I'll be there to kiss them from your face. When your body aches, I'll be there to sooth you. When you become chilled from the cold, I'll be there to give you warmth. When you require my love through the satisfactions of your needs, I'll be there to give you fulfillment.

My love is not a gift randomly given to just anyone in passing. I seek a love to much my own - a mutual love of understanding one another. I love you, not fear you. I trust you, not question you. When we are silent who in this universe can count the words that pass between us.

Robert L. Thames Jr.

Little Brother

When we were small, we'd yell and we'd fight
but we'd forget why, so it was all right

If I needed a playmate, he'd always be there
we'd definitely fight, but we would also share

If someone else would pick on him
I'd be the one to stick up for him

If I needed a friend, I'd just go up stairs
he may not say it, but I know how he cares

When he was hurt, I felt so bad
and when he was happy, I was also glad

We've caused each other a lot of tears
but we'd also sooth each others fears

There will never be another,
than a big sisters love for her little brother

Rachel Breon

"Distance"

I see you there
but where?
You're talking,
but I'm not hearing.
You're crying? But why?
for I am dying.
Every thing goes black.
I wonder when I'll go back.
I see a light, but it I cannot fight.
The light is warm, but sounds like a storm
I am in your heart which
will never part.

Shauna Luke

Yellow Rose

Yellow rose are the symbol of our love to me.
Because you see,
like our love, they are rare.
You can not find them everywhere.
Like our love, most people think,
that others are better (like red or pink).
Like our love, they are alive and sunny,
and they pull us together, like bees to honey.

Jami Kiser

Untitled

High in the sky, so far to fall,
But you can see forever no cares at all.
Holding my head high, I see above the rain,
If you can't look to the future, there'll always be pain.
I reach out to feel the clouds, they just slip away,
You can't hold what's not there, dreams are what fills today.
Soaring, soaring, soaring, forever free,
Never touching the ground, everything to see.
So I open my eyes and experience it all,
Because you never know when you may fall.
No need to worry you're high in the sky,
Tomorrow is a new day, a new day to fly.

Karen Pelkey

On Eagles Wings

Her entire being consumed
by the thunderous lightening
she would search the sky
for the rainbows
breaking through the storms.

Her eyes drifting upward
drawn by the gentle whir of a plane's engine
she would dream of flying like the wind
and soaring with the eagles.
Oh, the freedom it would bring!

Her peace unearthed in His majestic creations
from a small child's laughter
to the warmth of a loving friend's embrace
to the calmest waters and the highest mountains.

Discovering her own rainbows
amidst the storms of life
uncovering the freedom
of her own eagle's wings
she becomes the majestic creation
Yahweh intended her to be.

Marykathleen O'Haver

Flow Lonely River

Glide peacefully oh lonely river
By the willows gentle hand
I had parted and will never
See again that lonesome strand.

Parted from the lisping river
And my dreams of long ago
Where the sunny waves do quiver
And the rainbows come and go.

Low the lonely night is falling
Soon the world will be asleep
With the songs of night birds calling
I will see you and will treasure mem'ries I will love to keep.

Marvin Gullett

Untitled

My life is dead, people and their children
come to near.
Greed my lead them on instead.
Our life is copulated with our fear.

How often have I heard, too many times to show,
You simply have no feeling, I think I need to know.

Why are you a big fat terd?

Katherine Plaisted

The Weeping Willow Tree

I am a willow tree bent with age
By the wind's cold blasts and the storm's cruel rage,
Many a year I've seen go by,
But for some strange reason, I just don't die.

A babbling brook by my feet does roll,
Its rippling laughter stirs the soul,
Of the weary traveller who stops on his way,
To rest his bones on a hot summer day.

The violets nestle around my feet,
Now one of my arms is a lover's seat,
The birdlings have their nests up there,
Hidden by my long green hair.

I hope that God will let me stay,
Just the way I am today,
Bending my head in service to,
The one who made both me and you.

Roberta Treiber

Untitled

Laura Ann Nickle, July 21st was your birthday, always celebrated in bygone years, with presents, song, a cake and hugs, for one we loved so dear. Today there's no celebration, a day that's devoid of mirth, you are with us only in spirit, your body has lift this earth. No presents can I give you, see you accept with anticipation, A smile on your precious face. I can't give a hug or sing you a song, as I always did on that day. There's no song in my heart, just sadness since you went away. I will go to visit a small grassy mound, place flowers at your feet, only god can understand such unrelenting grief. Your birthday was one of joy, best wishes for your dreams to come true, A profound emptiness prevails, no hope or joy, memories are all we have left of you. I am grateful for the short time, we were allowed to share, you led by example, you taught us how to love and care. I will forever be appreciative of things you would say and do, without you on this birthday, God knows how your family misses you. The years we had you with us, literally seemed to fly, helplessly, hopelessly, there's nothing left, but to cry,cry and cry.

Mildred R. Hipkins

"On To Chicago" 1968

Eating air with electronic vibrations,
cameras transform the event into a
tiresome chore. Through grainy color pixels
on CBS, Walter Cronkite greets America at 7 p.m. EST.
A slow motion rain of gauzy movement filters
behind the screen. Over-miked, badly amplified,
the candidate grins, his teeth slipping over
his slight bottom lip. A sharp shot from a
busboy assassin an inch behind his ear tries to
end the scene with a flash of black. The hum of
film and tape grows. My mother watched the funeral
train, annoyed. "We knew what happened, we didn't
have to see it all damn day."

Stephanie K. Moran

Graveyard Reflections

There stood... President Bill Clinton
Among the grave markers of our heroes...

Reflecting on the sacrifices
Our heroes had made...

Hoping that with the power he possessed,
He might prevent future sacrifices...

Or, at least, reduce the sacrifices
Believed necessary for our survival...

Russell Stevens

Mothers And Fathers

Oh father, oh father where is my dear mother?
Can mother be hiding, Can mother be climbing?
Oh dear father where is my mother? Oh mother,
Oh mother where are you? Oh father, oh father
where are you? Oh father, oh father I lost you.
I walk into a sunny, bright room. Where I find
my beautiful and tired mother and my excited and
handsome father. What is that? Could it be a dog
wrapped in colorful blankets? Could it be a doll?
Oh I don't know. How would I know.

Oh I know, I know it is a baby. Oh no, Oh no
I don't want a baby, because I'm the beautiful
baby. At least until "it" was born. Oh no, Oh no
I don't like it. All it does is eat, sleep, and
cry all night. I always hear that awful "thing"
crying or nagging. I am so tired of hearing "it".
Mother and Father get very tired of taking care of "it".
I don't understand why they had to have "it". "It"
is so tiring, but cute in some ways. Oh no, oh no,
Oh brother, it is a brother to me.

Tiffany Ohannesian

Can You Hear The Angels Crying?

Can you hear the angels crying?
Can you feel their awful pain?
Can you see their teardrops falling,
That it seems they shed in vain?
Can you smell the fear within them?
Can you touch upon their hurt?
They are bruised, and they are battered,
They are treated just like the dirt.

Take the time and try and listen,
don't tell me you can't hear,
a scream out in the darkness,
filled with pain and filled with fear.
Just another angel crying,
he could be one or ten,
and come tomorrow's dawning,
he'll be crying once again.

Another angel murdered
he's heading for the ground,
perhaps he'll find in heaven,
what on earth could not be found.

Mary Sanchez

My Soul Speaks

Can you hear me crying in the night?
Can you hear my laughter during the day?
Laughter, tears, conversations, and stories are all shared.
  I could have been a part of that.
My grandparents are spoiling my brothers and sisters.
Look at that woman- petite and so pretty.
Beside her- the tall, dark, striking man.
I could have been a combination of
  both mother and father.
Each holiday passes by- Christmas, Easter, Birthdays.
Do you remember mine?
To be a part of everyday life-
School, work, vacations, and quality time.
I will never know what it is like or to belong.
I felt life for a month - all warm and cozy in my quiet little world.
Why did you hurt me?
Why couldn't I be a part of your life?
Do you think about me everyday? I think about you.
I think about what my life could have been - would have been.
Why wasn't I given that chance?

Tracy Intondi

Sweet

Lying, lying in my bed,
Can't get to sleep memories flood my head.
Some are sad - some are good.
Some things I've never told anyone, but I think I should.
I think of how my life's turned out,
Not that bad I really don't think.
I'm only 14 but, the times gone by as fast as one blink.
When I'm overwhelmed by sad memories, tears start
rolling down my cheeks, splash! they hit the floor.
Then I think to the future and what's in store for me
A smile suddenly lifts up my cheeks,
I go on with my life week after week.
But sometimes all you have are those sweet memories,
You know the ones that keep moving you on through life's many
streets,
When you feel can't move on,
Just remember this,
Life is so precious so very, very, (sweet.)

Patrick Chipley

He Sent Rainbows

He sent rainbows, not one but two
Caressing the sky to bring to me
A message of love and caring
To show the path he longed to take.
Broken dreams and bitter tears
Forgotten.
The tortured body he never wanted
Reaching out for love not knowing why
He must endure this role in life
Not of his doing nor fault
Knowing the end was soon to come
The legacy of the rainbow, not one but two
Would tell of his love, joy yet to be
Purple, and red, yellow and green
More lovely than any they had ever seen
A message of peace so lovingly sent
The lifetime of sorrow, forgotten.
He left the rainbows, not one but two
Filling the earth for us to see
All the love and joy yet to be.

Rita Louise Monaco

Euphoric Melancholy

A tear trickles down from your silky skin
Cast from a saddened eye
The seasons are changing and rearranging
And it makes you ponder, why?

The summer ends... The Fall begins
And memories leave their mark
Leaves tumble off their parental stems
To be orphans in the dark

Each Summer casts reflections which
Gain strength throughout your dreams
The soothing warmth of sun filled days
And nights - sensual and serene

The bonding of two lovers souls
A treasure beneath the stars
The Summer has a mind of its own
And leaves its subtle scars

These tears of memory, that now, you cry
For soon will come to an end
The seasons will change and so will you
Though the melancholy lives on within.

Richard Meyer

Whisper

Strong scent
  caught in the breeze.
Firm features,
  tough yet strong.
Standing tall
  facing the Alaskan winds.
Reach out to me
  with your open arms.
Caress my face
  with your roughened fingertips.
Whisper your thoughts,
  let them soar with the eagles and the raven.
Spruce tree,
  you have captured me
  yet set me free.

Lara Hensley

God's Eye

He lifts an eyelid upon the world
  Cautiously, carefully......

He awakens and looks on
  To the earth held in His hands

He looks for the good and watches the bad
  Some making mistakes, some mending mistakes

By noon He is directly overhead
  Glowing with such love and warmth
   His children can not bear to look

When evening comes He still watches
  Watches the violence - the justice,
   The pollution - the cleansing, the frowns and the smiles

When night finally sets in, He closes His great eye
  Casting a flood of color over His world
   Of righteousness and sins

The lower His eyelid drops
  The more sins are forgiven

Then He is swallowed in sleep and leaves
  His millions of glowing angels to guard His
   Wonderful creation

LuCinda Hohmann

A Day Away

Sitting on the beach watching the waves roll in.
Children are dancing and prancing as if time will never end.
Birds and butterflies fill the air.

There's a sense of peace here without any cares.
The air so fresh on the crystal blue sea, oh how I wish
it were a part of me.

The water is filled with sailboats of every color,
oh what a beautiful sight, out on the water.

Not a cloud in the sky, just a big bright yellow light
way up in the sky.

Oh how I wish I could stay, forever under the sun.
But this is just a day away.

Lorelei O'Neal

A Winter Evening

White flakes falling from a powder blue sky.
Children throwing snowballs, with their eyes all a wide.
Hands cold and shivery with a lifeless touch of fear.
Knowing that summer will soon be near.
Making snowmen and angels in the freshly falling snow.
Running to the icy lands to and fro.
Holding hands, their mittens rub, as they end
Their day with a little hug.
Swinging hands and frolicking on as they sing a merry song —
'Good-bye good-bye' they shout with glee.
Sorry, but their day must end until winter comes again.

Yolanda Elizabeth King

Circles

There was a sunny day, once, when we all joined hands in ONE giant
circle.
Laughing
Dancing
Singing
Then a storm came, our hands let go,
and we all ran home.
Then when the rain had stopped,
we all returned and joined hands again.
Except, not in one giant circle.
As a look around,
I see that many circles were formed.
Why do I stand alone?

Shelley Polinsky

A Father's Lament

Fog, like vaporized milk drifting over cracker houses, dampened the city, not deterred by nighttime's ghostly veil, young teenage toughs raced past in cars along beer can-littered trails.
Their screeching tires, laughing girls, and hard-rock music blaring awakened me and took me back to a time without self-doubt or caring.
I recalled a youth of selfish pleasure — a birthright that would last forever, of adolescent toys and after-school joys and thinking I was so very clever.

But now former teenage thrills are chilled by a father's occasional waking fear, As my daughter grows older every year and pressures Dad for time to spend away from home with friends again.
From the other side of twenty-odd years I couldn't have anticipated the concern and fright of a parent waiting anxiously in the night, For hands to unlock the door and turn out the porch light's beacon bright. It is only now that I feel the loss of the laughter and the sharing, As my daughter finds other men more youthful and more daring.
But no matter how sophisticated she becomes; how sure of life's promises unfolding, A father will never lose the love, that tender sense of caring, and the early years of holding fast to someone soft and endearing.

Richard H. Peterson

Untitled

If it's an eagle, soaring thru the heavens,
come
fly with me for a moment;
If it's a cheetah, agile and lean,
come
run with me for an instant;
If it's a lion, steadfast and graceful,
come
stand by my side for a time;
If it's Marci,
come
lay beside me forever.

Lawrence Coggan

Death Creeps By Heaven's Door

Oh death!
Clad in your black woolen robe.
Why, my heart do you probe?

You ask me for answers, to questions
I have not known.
You beckon my heart with the sweetest croon.

Oh! My perturbed heart prays to you,
Day and night, hour by hour,
your sweetness grows sour.

You pick me up! Oh! Pale rider.
You take me to the Brimstone fire.
Then you pull me out and we ride higher.

You take me to a place so bright and warm.
Bright, so bright as the crystal light.

And oh, so slowly, death creeps by heaven's door.
A beautiful mansion,
and standing outside is the cheap whore.

Matt Crowe

"First Love"

Beauty unbridled sears the soul;
Clamoring conscience relinquished role.
Fear and fascination, increased intensity,
Amorous anticipation, release reality.

Free falling, distinction dimmed,
Ineffable insanity, serendipity skimmed.
Discovery dawns, embers endure;
Dangerously denied, tantalizing torture.

Fanned fire, unretractibly remain,
Past due payment, delivered domain.
Sizzling senses, soaring sensation,
Crashing crest, eternal elation.

Tender touch, lingering lips,
Soft sigh, burgeoning bliss.
Sated slumber, comforting closeness
Halves are whole, alleviate aloneness.

Kristin Johnson

Unwanted Dreams

I can never interpret dreams,
Cloudiness is all it seems,
Never do they go away.
Maybe skip a day,
Here or there,
Dreams are everywhere.
Unconsciously, you follow their advice,
Sometimes bad, sometimes nice,
Maybe a hysterical laugh to you,
But special ones they are few.
I always say follow your dreams
They may be the supporting beams,
Of your life ahead,
On to what you might be led,
Always follow your unconscious thoughts,
Even if there's rough spots,
Stay yourself, always be true,
To the one you knew,
Always do that and you will be strong,
Your dreams will always help you along.

Staci Flowers

Sunshine

A bright light peeks from the clouds.
And then, without a warning,
a spark and then a flash.
A golden ray of sunshine has been born.

Rob Capriccioso

"Nature"

Trees, flowers, bluebirds, and flies
Clouds and stars up in the skies.
These are the things of nature.

Pine trees, sitka, hemlocks, and fir
Listen to some of the sounds to be heard.

Bluebirds, sparrows, dragonflies, bees
Taste the pollen in the warm summer breeze.
These are the things of nature.

Samantha Langley

"Mother's in Tears"

They hardly open their eyes to the knowledge, dreaming, being in college to receive a diploma, for their graduation and be ready for communication. Hey wait a minute, why are my brothers looking sad with their head down, is it because I have become a very bad boy, or perhaps, an ignorant clown. Who are accusing me of doing a lot of crime saying, I never care a dime. Let me go, I want to be with my boys they promised me fun and lots of joys. Yo, I am young, I want to get married, have three kids and a beautiful wife. What are you saying to me, impossible because some one has ended my life? You mean, I am dead, that's why my mother, brothers and family are crying. That's why you said, nobody would like to rewind the bloody and ugly tape. Oh, sweet Jesus dozens of little girls have been abused, murdered and raped. Not always we have been kind, that sometimes, "We are very hard to find." We have to learn how communicate with our kids and "fulfill their needs." God, he only turned fifteen, didn't have a chance to learn what life means, but God, he don't know much about this life and already has lived in hell. Full of anguish, ignorance, violence, and never will hear the wedding bell. I refused this reality, I want him on my lap and his picture in the frame. Let me go back to the past, where he was learning how to smile and crawl. And with his tiny hand reaching my face, laughing at the sound of my call. I want my dream, please my friend. Let it end!! Let it end!! Let it end!!

Melvin Rojas

"Feelings"

You're like the morning sun,
coming across the hill,
Always shining bright, sharing
your rays of good will.

When all others fail me and there's
nothing left for me to do.
I know you'll be there Mom,
Have I told you lately, how much I love you?

Of all the many things in life that
I have lived to see,
You Mom, have shown me how special
Love can be.

You loved my hurts away,
Always told me there'd be a brighter day.
You gave all of yourself unselfishly to me
and one day I became a Mother just like you
trying to live and Love as you do.
But never can I fill your shoes,
Because Mom, No one can love like you!

Peggy Elaine Fonner

Marriage and the Fountain of Youth

Like a concrete slab it has two main ingredients
concrete and steel reinforcement.
With out the steel reinforcement
the concrete slab will soon start to crack, break, then fall apart,
crumble and finally turn back into dust which it originated.
But, with the steel reinforcement
even under extreme pressure and heavy load, it can withstand the all.
Even though it might crack it will never break or fall apart.
So are you my reinforcement.
Marriage to me is like the fountain of youth.
Like the concrete slab it will eventually get old on the outside.
But on the inside it's just as new as the day it was bound together.
So are you as new and alive as the day we were married.
Though, in many years to come I may grow old.
I will always be young at heart till death do us part.

Margarito D. Verver

Love

What is the meaning of Love?
Confusion?
Compromise?
Giving?
Taking?
It is a word thrown around freely
It is a feeling unexplainable, intangible
Is it sharing everything or is it sharing nothing?
Will you know when you fall in Love?
Or will you just fall flat on your face?
Will the feeling be erased?
Or will you be fooled by his warm embrace?

You feel on top of the world, but enjoy it while it lasts
Because when another comes along, that feeling fades fast
With just a blink of the eye
He's gone without even a goodbye
Into another girls arms he makes his rounds
While you're still searching for that steady ground
And that question remains to linger in the air
Was it a dream or did he care?

Jennifer Hogan

Over Again: Another 4th of July

Making love in the night's
cool wet air
By the side of the lake, that rippled across its lay,
new dry tears
Surrendering to panting passions that intoxicated dreams, that we
will always share
Gently still allowing the slow visions to pass, never forgetting how
much I cared
Remembering the fireworks, and how they reflected in your eyes, as we
sat on the rocks and stared
And even though the slippery slipping of time has slipped by so
quickly, it seems as if we were just there
Talking about Andy Griffith and feeding the ducks, enjoying
just having each other near
Sometimes secretly wishing for another 4th of July, and always
thankful for the one that we have shared
Because it's over again as I shake off the past, but at least in
my mind it remains alive and clear
As I quietly awake again remembering, that you're
no longer here

Thomas Bruce

Life's Balance

Can light be known, if dark has ne'er been seen?
Could love be felt, if hate had never been?
Who knows true peace, except it follow war?
Where is happiness, but grief has gone before?
The day that dawns with most welcome light,
Seems brightest after the darkest night.

Pity him who walks on level ground,
And never knows the joy of up and down.
Pity him who into wealth was born,
Who's never needed praise nor heeded scorn.
Life's pendulum must scribe a constant arc
Swinging freely from its center mark;
Life grows, for all, on both extreme,
But equally in a balanced scheme.
We learn the sound of Heaven, taste of Hell;
But we must know both to know either well.

Richard L. Carlton

Goodbye For Now

I called you, but you did not answer. I reached for you, yet I could not feel your touch. I searched for you, but only your footprints remained. I talked to you out loud, but you did not acknowledge that you heard me.

How am I supposed to deal with your absence? How do I say goodbye
to a unique masterpiece? Do I put you in a closet or hide in my deepest thoughts? Or will my memory of you just go away?

You allowed me to fall when necessary, yet you always picked me up. With your feet you led the way and with an eagle's eye you watched over me. You always listened when I felt I had something important to say, and your tongue was always swift to provoke me to action. With your heart you sought to make life better for those around you, and with your soul you devoured all of my pain.

I have to say goodbye now to the physical strength that you have shed. The bad times have disappeared for you have given me hope. Your hands have molded every part of my being. I say goodbye to you with a new understanding that you will always remain with me in my heart.

Tamika Zenice McIntosh

A Prayer "Old Chassis" "Beat-Up Chevy" and Cottonwood Tree

"Old chassis" sitting on your wheels
Could you kindly tell me how it feels
To sit here so proudly in this clean air
And not have a worry, a fret or a care
But instead give everything to Him in prayer?

"Beat-up Chevy," paint-a-peeling,
Tell me kind sir what you are a-feeling
Do you feel old, but still able and strong
Do you worry any longer about what is right or wrong
But instead, give everything to Him in song?

Oh Iris and Rose, magnificent Oak and Cottonwood tree
Your wondrous beauty touches a deep place in me
Give me the courage, wisdom and strength to see
What I long for to set me free
Tell me, is the key
To give everything to Him in prayer?

Madelaine Taffi

Grandma's Touch

As a tiny baby I was caressed by your loving hands and
cradled in your comforting arms.
As a little girl I was nurtured by your generosity and
unselfish ways.
As a young lady I was comforted from tragedies by your
understanding wisdom and never ending ability to listen.
You were always there...
As a grown woman I realize how much I was guided by your
fortitude, your strengths and constant praise.
You have touched my life in such a way no word could ever express.
Now it is for you that I must summon all those precious things
which you graciously bestowed upon me with your
"Grandmas Touch."
As I touch you now I can only pray that you are receiving some
of those precious things which I am trying to return to you
so that you might be comforted now
and find strength for what lies ahead.

Theresa L. Clements

Light Dreams

Peeling paint on weathered boards,
cross my windows, keeping out the light.
Hugging my knees, holding myself in.
Rotting plaster wall,
screaming out at me with words,
Of hate, anger, confusion.
Raising stick arms towards a
remembered sky - I see:
Small wounds, like tiny mouths. Mocking me.
Just another number, part of a statistic.
A shadow generation, wandering.
Bound by the weights of hopelessness and despair.
Movement from a swollen belly.
will you ever know love? My child.
Will anyone hold you and need you?
Will you live in the sunshine and have dreams of light?
I had a dream. Once
Time for me to work. Time for painted smiles;
Concrete and sweating palms.
Failing light and crystalline dreams.

Sarah J. Peterston

Untitled

I see pain in my mother's eyes, a distant worry, a lonely
cry, a dying dream to see her children strong, the worry that
she raised me wrong.
When she sees me make a mistake, its as if I'm drowning in a lake.
She tried to raise me to be wise, but all she got were looks
of despise.
When I'm angry I let her know, I try to make her let me go.
I'm thankless when she tries to help, then I run to her when
it doesn't work out.
She's always there thru thick and thin, to give me hope that
I can win.
Sometimes she can't help but get upset, but that doesn't mean
she loves me less.
I depend on her because you see, she means the world and all to me.
I couldn't have a better friend, on who I know I can depend.
I love my mother more than you'll ever know, and I never
want to let her go.

Kathy Gragg

Untitled

I am listening for sounds of life that do not
cry out in anger.
I am listening for the laughter of children
instead of the clashing of their
competition.
I am listening for adults to yell in excitement
and not in rage.
I am listening for a change.
I am listening for nature's seasonal messages.
I am listening for any message.
I am listening for God to break from the
heavens.
I am listening to a friend.
I am listening for a voice to tell me what to
do.
I am listening to myself.
I am listening for a sound in the night.
I am listening to the fear in human hearts.
I am listening for a way to calm them.
I am listening...

Leslie R. Sease

"Mama's Pearl"

I once had a vision sent from heaven, a beautiful gift to behold.

This vision came real, it was nothing to conceal, a beautiful
daughter all my own.

God gave forth to her the breath of life; just as he gave to me too.

How can we doubt our Messiah's love; his son gave sacrifice
for both me and you.

He gave us the sky, the mountains, the ocean, the earth, he bestow
his beauty for all to see.

So that none would ever doubt that he does exist; so we
may follow him and have life eternally.

Everywhere we look is God's fine art; written all over the world.

How can I doubt he made me this and much more, he gave
me a beautiful baby girl.

He gave her golden hair, big blue eyes, and a smile that
could light up the world.

He's given me a lifetime full of happiness through this little girl.

He's give me a precious pearl; yes "Mama's Pearl."

Terry L Provost

Lonely Heart

Night after night, I've cried for our love...
Day after day, I wonder what happen to us...
So hurt and alone I've been...
Going through mixed emotions, feeling no one loving me...
Alone, I said, "I would make it"...
Pretending and Denying, I didn't need you...
Fooling my heart, saying, "I didn't love you...
Wanting so much to be with you...
Even the hurt, you put me through...
Can't erase, what I really feel for you...
All the times we shared together...
Now, far apart from one another...
Tears that fall, with no meaning...
Dreams and wishes with no hope...
Shattered hearts, and broken promises...
All we are left with, are memories,
of the way we were...
That leave us with, a "Lonely Heart"

Olga A. Yanez

The Little Prince

My darling
Day by day you alternate between
Feisty adult
and crotchety old man
You're dying
and nothing in my power will alter your destiny
Soon, I will no longer hold you
feel your soft fur
your paws on my shoulder while we move
As one
through the changes and chances of this life
My darling
in our 18 years together you have become
Far more than my pet
You have become
My son
Do you know how much
Your mother
already misses you

Michelle L. Hufford

The Rose

I am the Rose just a small seed at that, I bloomed the
day I was put in with the dozen,
I was taken out of that dozen and left all alone...

I am a Rose fading away, slowly a departure coming someday
I was once the reddest of red and brightest of all,
but now I'm the Rose that has taken the fall.
I am a Rose that was supposed to live forever and
never to die the Rose that doesn't need water and yet is never dry

I am a Rose all solemn and standing alone,
That one Rose you threw away You did not know that
was the one with love, that was the one who cared, that was
the one single Rose that will always be.

That Rose was me...

Sheryl Marie Damron

How Do I Feel About You

How do I feel about you?
Day in and day out
I sit here and wonder
What is this
A chance at love or what!
I sit here and wonder
Am I good enough for you
Maybe you deserve someone better
and older too.
To me age is nothing but a number
Love is not based on age, color, or presents.
It is all based on feelings
I know my feelings are strong for you
but I don't deserve someone as good as you.
I'm also scared to grow to annoy you
Then I'll be scared to lose you.
Then I ask myself
what should I do
Back to the first question that came from you.
How do I feel about you?

Silvana Buono

Chainless Minds

Eternal spirits of the chainless minds.
Direct me thru these golden times
Throw at my feet endless joy of peace and love.
Show me the bitter sweetness of life,
So I may too give life.

Wanda Horner

Rescued

Confusion. Darkness. Despair. Anxiety. Loneliness. Gloom.
Days and nights filled with nothingness; meaninglessness.

Endless hours of waiting. Hoping. Wishing. Praying.
Then giving up; surrendering. Defeated. Dejected. Depressed.

I'd look outside to empty streets and inside to an empty house.
Wondering. Pondering. Questioning. And again and again no answer.

It had to be over. Done. Finished. Ended.
Leave it alone to wither and die.

Then from out of the night came a calling.
Loud. Intimidating. Strange. I was drawn to it.

A small light in my world of darkness.
In time the light grew. Glowing. Appealing. Exciting.

Soon, I was filled with warmth and passion;
joy and rapture! A love I've never known.

My darkness was filled with sunshine. Hope. Meaning.
Life and love. Thank you for giving me you!

Yvonne Belden

Friday Night In Fallon...

Friday night.

The old folks, and farmers know.
days-end finds them sleeping -
one with the sun seared and weary earth.

in town,
the girls don their follow-me-home-and-feel-me-up duds.
the cowboys cash their checks -
count their condoms -

in anticipation of the long Nevada night.

this,
the dance of the desert.

search for sensation -
for solace.

A last grab at life before the dusty dark descends and devours its own
- smothering the scorched, empty stretches of snake trailed sand.
a full moon hangs silent.
stones speak
timepassing...

Judith Carlisle

The Acts Of The Mind During The Holocaust

Sorrow. As I walk in line there are tears in my eyes I see
death and sorrow, fired and ashes, and a body on
the side. As I'm walking on I cry and cry praying to
God to let the nightmare go by.

Dazed. I am confused and dazed about the things that are happening
today. Will this night ever end or will it continue on again?

Fear. As I look around I see fear in everyone's eyes I look
up into the sky it is so bright red and hot
All I can hear are screams and guns going off.
Has the nightmare ended? No it has only begun.

Outrage. As the nightmare continues I feel something
inside is it sadness, no but is anger to those
who have done this to me all because I was
a Jew but some how I feel that this nightmare will be over soon.

Pity. Well The night is over and I have survived
but as I am walking the street I must cry.
I see piles of body's ready to be burned
and stains of blood on the earth. The nightmare
has ended and I pray that is will never happen again.

Mercedes Garza

Untitled

As I drown myself and my sorrows
Deep into the song playing on the radio
I feel the cold wet tears drip down my pale face.
What has happened to me?
I was broken by someone I loved.
Through all my sorrow though, I heard a voice
Calling through the mist of my tears
But the happy voice I heard simply faded away

My heart is getting weak from all this sorrow
All this sorrow inflicts deep wounds in my heart
I won't let his this happen again

I've been in a state of depression for much too long
So long I forgot what happiness is.
I have to get out before I sink
Below the earth
Deep deep below the ground I once ventured
A place I searched and searched for a mender
A mender to mend my heart of all its wounds
I did not succeed though
I will try again.

Serena Agnellini

Reflections of a Jet

They think I'm a wild girl
Denim and leather and flipped up collar
Tough street fight kid; Ghetto material...West Side Story material.

You think I'm Outrageous
Shining starlight, flickering firelight: Fire and ice
Racing to moonlit fantasies
Crazed into overdrive by overactive senses.

I think I'm Ordinary
Mediocrity at its most middle
Not wild or wonderful
Not silver studs or silk shirts
Mirroring myself
Checking pose, checking stance, checking my hair.

I sometimes wonder how anyone could find ME unusual.
I wear boots because they're comfortable (and make me a little taller than life).
Silk shirts are soft against my skin (and glisten in starlight).
The leather jacket is warm (and discourages prospective opponents).
And if I race to moonlit fantasies
It's only to see you.

Robin J. Melton

Men

Men why do you walk around in
Despair not knowing who you are
In Jesus's eyes you are a star
He created you to be strong in the power of his might
Realize that life is a spiritual fight
He has given you Dominion over the land
To fulfill his purpose and to carry out his plan
Drugs and violence is not the key
Come to Jesus he will set you free
His love is, unconditional he don't
See you as you are but as you can be
We need you all across the nation
To be leaders and positive role models
For the future generations.
Men in him you will find all you need
To help you to live and succeed

Sonja Grayson

Untitled

Marriage is a unique challenge, given to those individuals who are determined to complete a long journey through life together.
At times, the trip can be unsteady... but the commitment pulls them through, and brings many smooth and straightways to travel.
There are even times when the pathway splits...
Never for very long, for the two long to be together again walking side by side in love...
And each reminds the other to stop every so often along the way to reaffirm the love they share and regain the strength that is sometimes lost, but can always be found again on this wonderful journey called Marriage.

L. Darimont

Ruth

She had nine children to raise without riches
Did it with a prayer, scrap cloth and stitches
When she knew things were bad
Wouldn't shed a tear or let us see her sad

Everyday she wore the same old dress
but on Sunday she looked her very best

She gave us strength in her own caring way
to carry us through each and every day
In the memories I saw where I cried
I saw her faith carry her 'til she died.

Sue Campbell Fowler

Untitled

Did you want to be the first
Did you pray to be the last
Was the pain too much to bear
When you couldn't hold on to the past
Did you see the light in front of you
Did you feel the love we shared
We couldn't say it but we all knew
No longer could your precious life be spared
And so you left us on that cold day
To stand over you, staring at your shell
It was so hard to see you go that way
As your spirit was lifted, ours fell
You didn't want to leave without us
Yet you knew it was one or the other
Please remember we love you so
You're still our father and brother
And every day I look to the sky
I can see your smile in the sun's rays
I never really got to say goodbye
But I've done it in so many other ways.

Jennifer A. Bernstein

He Does Exist

There was a young man, who once among mortals
Died on the cross to open the portals.

Who upon his head, was cast a glowing beam
From his heavenly Father who reigns supreme.

He healed the sick, and in every way
Taught that love and truth should guide man each day.

Not all did he reach, but those by His side
Were promised by the Father an eternal place to abide.

So we must choose, which path to take
With the gift of free will, this decision we make.

Mary Della Lana

The One Who Waits

It is completely foreign,
different and alarming -
No conception of the emotions inspired;
Yet, I expect you to react.
There is the awareness of you -
and I will know you entirely,
then there can be no question.
Having the desire also for you to know me -
not only that person visible,
but the one within,
so full of fear that precious feelings
cannot be spoken;
the one inside, the one who waits.

Mechell Arant

My Room

At times it is a place of Exile to where I am banished by the
  Disgruntled Monarchy.
Indefinite periods of punishment, acquittal achieved
  only when contrition is affected and noble favor is regained.
Or perhaps my sequestration is self-imposed,
  an escape from the wrath of the angry Rulers,
  a time to shed the tears pride scoffs at.
It is then a lonely, painful Dungeon.

Often it is a Place of Labor, of work of an ever changing shift,
  where I must toil after mid-day and maybe into the evening.
My Supervisors are unmerciful, the duties unvarying, satisfaction low.
Rewards come but twice a year, cold comments on paper
  accompanied by number ratings.
Still I continue, for it is all I know, and the Alternatives
  unworthy of consideration.
It is then a dull, tiresome Office.

But it is always a Place of Sanctuary,
  a calm locale to relax, to forget the harshness of the Outsiders.
I am invulnerable here; in solitude I am safe.
It is a warm, peaceful Paradise.

Sheela Kamath

Brendan's Backyard

The lights glowed a lanternesque glow
distanced from the outstretched yard.
The house was bordered by a short
wooden fence.
The trees stretched beyond eye's sight,
stretching up into a sky open to its leaved arms.
Remnants of children's play lingered
in the makeshift wall of stones which lay half
scattered and tumbled in a kicked down style.
The huge, lofty houses hide a child's past,
A past only a story can reveal,
for the huge dwellings now reside where a child's
playground once thrived.
But to grow up is to let a smile of remembrance glimpse
upon your lips as you tell others of your past fun.
Your memory reveals in your mind's eye the life you ran
through as a child.

Michele Nosal

"The People We Love Hurt Us The Most"

I never knew you until that faithful
day you took me for all I had:
Then spent the rest of your days
With me showing me how little
you cared: or were you teaching me
A lesson for something I had done?

Maxine Humble

The Destiny of Friendship

So many friendships taken for granted;
Diversity and opinions so often slanted,
That when someone comes into your life,
And increases your joy, lessens your strife,
You realize this gift, the greatest ever,
And you feel you've known this soul forever.
Floating through all of space and time,
To hear your friendship in rhythm and rhyme,
And knowing two paths could be, as both your dreams may soar,
Realizing this friendship comes along once, then no more,
You grasp onto the bond of love and memory,
And carry it with you, so you can always see,
The colors of friendship, so vivid and bright,
That give you the wings for life's destined flight.

Theresa Starkey

Heavens Above

Look behind that cloud with the light illuminating...
Do you suppose that's heaven's door?
What might it behold?
Look at the sun shine it's so bright!
Could that be out heavenly Father's light?
Just a fraction of how warm His love is!
It might!! I might!!

Over there I see a rainbow...
Just reflections from angels teeth
the light of the Father bouncing off their smiles!
And now comes some rain...
tears from all who live in heaven
their crying for those of us who have fallen,
Get up! Get up! Look over there...
Do your see a cloud, do you see the sun!
Is that a rainbow you see?
Or is it perhaps the heavens above?

Jennifer M. Burns

City of Darkness

Does anyone out there care?
Does anyone care to lend an ear?
I guess not, but do not worry I am used to
it by now where I live in my own private city of darkness.
Where no one listens
and no one cares.
To caught up in their fancy new age world,
to caught up to care about me.
Me who is nothing more to them
than a speck of dirt on the feet on a homeless wanderer.

Maybe it would be easier to end it all.
What do I have to live for?
Everything I have ever loved has left or been taken away.

I guess I should go now.
Maybe to the next world, maybe even the future
to find my soul mate,
or maybe just to discover my true self.

Nikki Dudley

Dance Of Love

Reaching out to touch her hand
feeling so proud as we start to dance

Smelling her perfume on the breeze,
Sets the mood and puts me at ease,

Spinning around and holding her tight
the grip of love has found me tonight

And when the dance is finely through
I'll take her hand and say I do.

James E. Green

The Rock

Why so important the rock
does it stand the test of time
an object to become the envy of man
man who can only hope his dust can
gather the mass to become a small
part of the hardened rock

Is man so insignificant that the solid rock laughs
as his various forms attempt to shape it

As the various forms of man come and go
left behind is the reshaped rock
marking the time when touched by man

Rodger D. Murphey

Untitled

Once I was a little girl
Dolls and dreams and ribbons and bows
Living my time in castles with trolls
Gazing at the wonder of it all
Knowing my way would make it better

As time rolls on...

Once I had a little girl
Gone were the dolls and dreams and castles
Looking ahead in fear and silence
Wondering about my way...as she goes hers
And I look to see the future
I remember the past...

I see my mommy's face, I feel her touch
It all doesn't seem to hurt so much
And I can see again, the dreams

Once she has had a little girl
Perhaps she will remember me
And know that no one loves her like her mommy...

Valerie Wilhelm

Just Because

Don't be rude to me, just because I'm a child.
Don't abuse me, just because I'm a child.
Don't talk down to me, talk with me, because I'm just a child.
Don't expect to much from me, because yes I'm just a child.
I need extra love, and no not because I'm just a child.
Listen to me, I really do make sense.
Help me when I need it, and don't be so tense.
Correct me when I'm wrong, so I can learn from my mistakes.
Let us count on you, no matter what it takes.
It's a really tough world out there, so please prepare us.
We are all individual, so don't compare us.
Love us and cuddle us and protect us when were scared.
We are the future, we need to be nurtured. -

Olive Misceo

Misunderstood

I hate to be misunderstood.
Confusion sets in.
I should said this when I meant that.
I should have listened first and acted last
Other people kept changing what I said.
Other people kept changing what I meant.
I meant to tell you the truth.
I meant to be honest.
I meant to be definite on my goals.
I meant to speak to you face to face.
I do not need an interpreter.
Now hear me clearly.
Now I stand tall and speak out for myself.

Melody J. Thomas

The War of Loved Hate!

Many years have went by, and they say marines
don't cry. Well I am her to tell there's tears
in my eyes & you ask why.
Every time I think of my brothers and sisters
left behind from Vietnam. Tears fill my eyes
it is not hate or anger, it's sadness for those
and there families Vietnam should have never been
although it did end. Over 58 thousand did and over
2,000 left behind or missing, did we win so
did we lose (yes) we lost over 60,000 men
women and their families, it is, such a shame and
there gov't and ours to blame, the 60's and 70's was a
Time for peace and love how come the gov't never
caught the bug, what was the reason for
American Treason, did they trade lives for rice
money or drugs maybe that was the 60's and 70's
bug. There will never be another Nam but
There will be more and more, Sophisticated bombs
mankind will always fight even if it's not right.

Mike Teeling

"Missing You"

If all the stars should fall from the sky,
Don't ever worry, don't ever cry.
I'll be there to give a shoulder
to lean on,
Until the day you realize I'm gone.
I'll be sad on the day I go,
And no one will be able to stop the
tears that endlessly flow.
So until the day we meet again, I'll
miss you with all my heart,
From the day when we first part.

Lisa Fahlsing

True Freedom

When the veil of death, upon me rests
Don't shed your tears for me.
Just know one thing, within your heart
I am at last set free.

Free from my troubles and my woes.
Free from my pain and fears.
For now I am completely free,
Of what has plagued me, all my years.

The pain my body has endured.
The times my spirits broken.
The lonely days that I've lived through.
The sounds of harsh words spoken.

My eyes will never see again.
My body breathes no more.
For I am not here on Earth, you see,
But with the angels I do soar.

Linda Davis

"Your Journey"

Rejection lays like a dark and ominous
cloud over the lives of those you left behind
Guilt takes root in the doubts and unanswered questions.
Was it something we did, or something we didn't do?
Could we have helped you to chart a different course?
Why didn't we see the fork in the road,
or the danger signs along the way?
And where will you have traveled before we meet again?
Anxiously we await your return.
For the answers to all our questions
rest in you telling of the journey that took you away.

Shirley Gross

"Two True Hearts"

Two true hearts joined as one.
Can't you see true loves begun?
I looked around and saw your face,
It took me to a whole new place.
To think of something that I knew;
But whenever a thought came to mind,
It was that I loved you.

Josie Church

Where Was God?

Nights lingered on and the violence never ceased
dreadful screams yet still no peace.
The dreams and the nightmares of children young and old
the innocent minds being rotted into mold-
the ugly memories the terrifying thoughts
the brutality and anger the Jews suffering brought.
Every minute, every second waiting, waiting...
waiting for your life, for someone to live or die
the sun and the moon and the stars could be seen
but where was the God in the sky?
Everything's dead everything's gone
no reason to live for no one is strong
God is dead there is no hope
and the world is not round
for I know up on the rope
lies the terror of men
the sweetness of children...
is this all true will anyone heal
if it is I know,
that God is not real!

Kate Johnston

Trials

Oh my poor soul!
Dreary is the path I've strode,
Not of choice, but by God's design,
Lest I journey or fall behind.
Overwhelmed by grief and despair,
I keep my stride with only a prayer!
"Lift up thyself! An inner voice do say,
Life isn't sure, so waste away not the day,
Rip and run ye need not do,
But take the time to see things through.
Plan not so far ahead, and sleep not too long upon thy bed.
Life under the sun isn't always fun,
So be content with an effort well-done.
O'er death, and O'er pain,
But the joy you mete shall return again."

Lee Thornton

Fragile Flower

Fragile flower blowing gently in the soft breeze
drinking in the sunshine of life;
such a short time ago, you were a tiny seed
placed in the earth by loving hands.

From a sprout, you had become a thing of beauty
touching our lives with your being.
Too soon, the lovely petals fell upon the ground,
wrenched from our grasp by wayward winds.

We have searched to find a trace, but you must return
to the garden of memory.
In the mind we carry a shadowy image,
a kaleidoscope of color

Of a delicate blossom that faded too soon,
leaving all a hunger for spring.
To sustain you, our tears will become as the dew
that will greet each fresh new morning.

Ruth Warner

Alcohol

Daytime lows make nighttime highs.
Drown your sorrows in a flask of lies.

Drowning your pain and yourself.
Living for the drink,
The past is just goodbye.

A bottomless pit swallows you whole.
You smile blankly, your eyes like raindrops,
splashing and breaking; tiny droplets scattering to and fro.

Oblivious to the world you're all alone.

God bless you when you take a drink.
That much deeper in the bottle you'll sink.

Lisa M. Shaver

Don't Cry For Me

Don't cry for me, Mom, because it seems that I am gone;
Dry those tears from your eyes.

I will be with you when the sun is setting
and the moon begins to rise.

When you hear the birds singing,
It's a song from me to you.

And when you see the flowers blooming,
Yes, I'll see them too.

And when the leaves are changing colors,
And summer turns to fall;

Don't let your heart break anymore,
Because I too am watching it all.

Please don't let my absence tear your world apart;
I'm not really far away, I'm right here in your heart.

All the years you loved me, they were not in vain;
Because you see, Mom, it has helped to ease my pain.

Take care of my daddy and Jessie too;
And remember I'm in heaven and I'm waiting for you.

Linda Barker

Jobe

Jobe had many trials that he went through
During the most, his faith remained true
Jobe's trials at times were much for him
And at times things did seem dim
God knew that Jobe's faith was very strong
So it wasn't as bad when things went wrong
Some said the suffering was all from his sin
But Jobe knew the faith he had within
There was a time he thought that they were right
But he didn't let Satan win the fight
Deep down he knew God was there
And that He really did care
Through it all Jobe had lost everything
But he knew God would have blessings to bring
The Lord reminds Jobe of His wisdom
So he'd be ready when his time would come
Job defends the Lord from each ones accusations
He did this without any hesitation
For his love for the Lord was as strong as ever
He knew there would be a time they'd be together.

Margaret B. Belcher

Rose for a Would Be Queen

When I was young, I used to dream
Each day I would have one rose as a Queen.
I was that Queen who sat on my throne
Waiting patiently each day for a Rose fresh Grown.
Years past while waiting-then I soon understood
I could not be the Queen - that I thought I could.
But then I remembered as I slide into age -
One needn't be a Queen - to enjoy such praise.
For now late in life-A real dream come true.
My love grows me Roses - So - I need not feel blue
For a Rose a day - graces my vase on the table
Love is so beautiful - I'm the Queen of my fable!

Norma Dotson Payne

Our Love

Our love is like a tree of leaves —
Each gentle leaf is another way of growing —
Together in love, happiness, and harmony.

The roots are our hearts
because this is where love starts —
Deep down in our hearts.
The trunk is our respect for one another
For out of it sprouts the branches,
the little things we do and say,
the way we look at one another.

The leaves are what we reveal to the world
about ourselves —
To love, cherish, and respect one another —
As we are —
The colors in the leaves are the voices within us —
Our many different ways to show the happiness we've come to share together.

But most of all the tree as a whole
symbolizes a perfect love, a perfect way of life and total Happiness.

Linda M. Royall

Jersey Shore

Joys are the days of summer that last forever
Early morning breeze, that blow so soft
Rich are the days of sun, skies so blue
Sunsets on the coast, colors against the sky
Eternity of peace, troubles are so far away
Young are the hearts of all who come to see
Seas begin to rock and the wind begins to blow
Heavy are the clouds with rain, dark are the skies

Out of a clap of thunder, the rains begin
Rains seem to rage on and never end
Evening comes and a sense of serenity returns

Rose Marie Leach

Silent Voices

Silent voices crying to be heard, echo through the night,
Endless thoughts of broken dreams lie buried in the ground.
The nights accustomed to what it sees and never tells a lie,
For what we hide lies no deeper than the shadows the lurk throughout the night.
As far as what we foretell is only seen by those with perfect site,
And like a tree we stand and watch throughout the passing of time,
The erosion of the simple things we seem to leave behind.
And in the silence of the night we cry a thousand tears,
Silently the river flows that hides our deepest fears.
As you sit and listen to the voices throughout the night,
Ask yourself, "Is it I, who is truly blind of site?"

Olivia Kalcum

To My Wonderful Mother...

It all began when I was born;
Early on a sunny morn.
You gave me life, and so much more;
Of which I am ever grateful for.
In your arms, you held me near;
And shooed away my every fear.
Your gentle hands would lift me high
Whenever I would get hurt and cry.
With a magic touch, you could kiss away
the "boo-boos" found from day to day.
Though tired and weary you sometimes might be;
There was always time to spend with me.
As I became older, your love held strong;
Throughout my days of doing wrong.
I tried your patience and your will;
Disappointed and sad, you loved me still.
Soon enough, into an adult I grew;
Your support was there, and your friendship too.
I have always been thankful for the things you do;
And no one is prouder to have a mother like you.

Kimberly L. Frantz

Constancy

The endless vista swells with the light of the sun as it rises in the east, time infinitum represented here, in this wilderness of chaos, controlled only by the constant of presence; (is it absent when you are also?) Light represented by the colors it gives in its narrow bands as they bounce and touch, absorbed only by the welcoming hospitality of being, dark and light patches on a landscape black as midnight without them; Seas that ebb and flow constantly throughout their existence, tiny circles always, storms that add to their bountiful ecology, as if time could continue forever, unchanging in the course that they take, unknowing what is to come; Omnipresence of peace, constantly compromised, stable only in the minds of the ignorant, or the lucky, or the luckless, peace cannot be achieved even in seeming perfection, because only perfection is free; Everything follows a cycle, completing and beginning the constant struggle, the lovely phase of nature, where perfect is unneeded and is never missed because no one remembers if it ever was; (linear time sees perfection as folly) For now, the sun will rise over the hills in the east and approach the cliffs in the west in the chaotic order that is seen every day and has been seen since man was alive to witness it and will be seen to come. (Time will never cease until it ends.)

Rachel Graham

Untitled

Why bother with the trivial things, why dwell on the past,
enjoy each moment on this earth, for it may just be your last,
if you know what the truth is, hold it inside your heart,
you are the master of your fate, you have been from the start,
you chart out your map, looking for that personal treasure,
the trip will be lifelong journey, filled with pain and pleasure,
signs along your path, will guide you on your way,
twists and turns will teach you, just what you need to say,
to see what is approaching, there are obstacles you must face
dissolve your fear and anger, and put action in its place,
the straight and narrow path, is sometimes hard to find
you get misguided and sometimes lost, with delusions in your mind,
to discover your destination, you must simplify what you demand,
a steady course with gentle weather, and someone to hold your hand,
your map is filled with people and places, interacting and interwoven,
I hope that you are happy, with the path that you have chosen.

Melanie L. Smith

She Swoons To Nature's Violence

Lightning throws its metallic net across the sky.
Ensnaring the truthful eye.
Thunderous crack of the whip,
Talons flagellate perfumed flesh.
Thor steals a melodious sigh.
Rain a cathartic balm, cleanses sin
From the restless soul.
The winds haughty violence, wanes
Melancholy, softening the mortal blow.
Swirling mist blinds the naked light.
Clutching her veil immodestly,
She swoons with singular delight.
The serpentine beast lays translucent
pearls at her feet.
The siren seductively calls nature to abate.
Joyously, she has sipped from the glass vessel
with euphoric lips.

R. W. Anthony

Love Is Blue

How can you say to me our love's not eternity?
How is it that says you, and to say that love is blue.
As I walk the night, as I know that you weren't right.
I hope in morning dew that you find that love's not blue.
"Love is blue," that's what you said.
You were not sure that there was any cure.
I hope someday you see that our love be eternity.
I hope in morning dew that you find that love's not blue.
"Love is blue," that's what you said.
You were not sure that there was any cure.
How can you say to me our love's not eternity?
How is it that says you, and to say that love is blue.

Piper L. Gardner

Ugly

Embarrassed to be a part of your life
even if I did belong in there somewhere.
Too full of the feeling that you see
right through me, that you see me as ugly.
In front of you I cannot accept that
I don't always say the right thing
so I'll admit that I don't talk much.
I want you to know me on the inside ugly.
Through all of my actions - Jesus,
It's all for you and I don't mean
it to be. You're turning me around
and you're making me, you're making me ugly.

Jennafer L. Black

Shades Of Me

Sometimes I am springtime green -
energized and alive,
fully living each minute per day.
But other times I'm a distant grey -
silent and low-key,
keeping quiet and to myself, letting each minute slip away.
My colors change from day to day,
Sometimes green and others grey.

Lisa Spencer

"Little One"

Little one we love you so.
Even though you know not this.
Inside my womb you grow and grow.
You'll love us too, this is our wish.

Little one we love you so.
Little lad or little miss
Maybe twins we do not know.
Only God knows of this.

Little one we love you so.
Dear God we pray, please grant our wish.
Locks of brown and eyes of a doe
In time we know your lips we'll kiss.

Phyllis Doty

Heaven's Doorstep

I see heaven's doorstep every night
Ever beckoning for me to bare the light.
My soul sorrows when it is lost to sight
- Yet I see Heaven's doorstep every night.

Greater than the stars does it shine
For all destinies in its brilliance are combined.
Somehow I know it shall never be mine
- Yet greater than the stars does it shine.

It is the end of all bitterness and pain.
Often the quest of it is questioned by the sane.
Away it washes tears like the coming rain.
- Yet it is the end of all bitterness and pain.

At its threshold the purity of truth is told.
Those that cross are the spirits grown old.
Younger they grow as such joy they behold.
- Yet at its threshold the purity of truth is told.

Like the great wheel of the night sky
Promising the paradise that could never turn to lie,
Waiting for the day fate chooses for us to die
- Yet ever like the great wheel of the night sky.

Kara Sutton-Jones

I Find Truth...

I find truth... when I see a family
Ever simulating normalcy
Always being
The epitome of dysfunction

I find truth... when I peer into dead eyes
That once shone with life
Now are blank
From senility and apathy

I find truth... when I experience a world
Dying from neglect and corruption
Knowing it is our lot
The good and the bad

I find truth... when I stare into a mirror
At a face once familiar
Now scarcely known
Scarred from feast and famine

I find truth...
In unexpected places

Wednesday A. Scott

Shameless Eyes

I see I'm not the same
Every time I see or hear your name
And inside, I want you... satisfaction's guaranteed
Your shameless eyes, is all I'll ever need

Each time it's never the same, thus naked
truth and darkened eyes, I know your name
All along it's made me blush, and I can see
with you, I can finally love and be free

You know, you've touched me
and it made me feel like fire
It's something that just happens
the pounding of a long awaited desire

So when you're ready, and sooner or later
I think it's already cast to be
To look into your shameless eyes
that will love only me.

Tommy Lee Stine

Crossroads

Sometimes you need a hand to hold and you don't know where to turn;
Every time you make a move it leads to another burn.
Nobody tells you just what seems to be going on;
They are trying to protect you, but that's the last thing that you want!
They are trying not to hurt you, but it's just a bit too late;
'Cause they don't seem to realize that they are holding on to your fate.
Your standing at the crossroads and don't know which path to choose;
It's a really simple choice one is win and one is lose.
No matter how hard you try you just can't understand;
that not every one has the answers, you just salvage what you can

Mandy E. Cekine

The Greatest Gift

It is the time of year again.
Every year it is the same.
We go shopping long before December, day
after day,
So we have gifts for our loved ones on Christmas day.
The children say "Mom, Dad, for Christmas
I want this, and I want that."
What is Christmas all about? Did we forget?
Jesus our savior was born.
What would we be without him?
Nothing... we would forlorn.
Look around you.
Open your heart, open your eyes.
The world is so beautiful, like paradise.
The ugliness that we see,
We did it, you and me.
We need no money, gold or fame.
With our Father we are all the same.
The greatest gift we have is free.
God gave His son for you and me.

Margaretha Murphy

A Lonely Rose

A single, pink rose on a grassy hill,
Droplets of dew on the petals,
It sat just beyond the painted'ol mill,
About 35 feet from stinging neddle,
A thorny, green stem stuck into the ground,
Where tiny, black insects could always be found,
But for all of the beauty of that lonely, pink rose,
Where it stands now - nobody knows.

Stacia Glenn

Untitled

I live in the country where my heart feels it home.
Everyone smiles and waves, we know we're not alone.
I sit up at night and listen to the rain,
You can feel your heart beating silent like a steady flame.
At home inside I don't have a worry,
Until I unlock the door, everything is mad and in a hurry
It's sad when you think how much has changed from past,
Now everyone locks their doors because we're afraid of other peoples outcasts.
Life is full of trials and tests,
Yet few still pass even when they do their best.
Things have there way of going up and down,
It's a real hard thing to stay above water so you won't drown.
Most people think the world is in a crisis stage,
But if we don't take it upon ourselves matter won't change.

Leslie Young

Childhood Dreams

When we were small children and talked of what we would be,
Everyone was uncertain, everyone but me.
The other kids spoke of doctors, lawyers, firemen, and teachers,
Movie stars, singers, and preachers,
Ball players, nurses, and cops,
No matter what the job they would all be tops.
There was one occupation we all played with lots of joy.
We had our greatest fun being a cowboy.
My playmates have grown up and made their dreams come true.
I have grown up, too, but I haven't done what I planned to do.
I have a decent job, two wonderful kids, and a perfect wife.
There is just one thing missing or I would have a perfect life.
It won't take fame or fortune to make my dream come true.
I just want to be a cowboy, that's all I want to do.

Randel M. Lee

One

Looking into your eyes is like looking into a mirror
Everything becomes 100% clearer.

You looking at me, me looking at you
I see me inside of you.

Seeing the pain inside of you, I feel the pain inside of me
When two souls become one, that is the way it should be!

Looking into your eyes - I see me inside of you
We have now become one, we are no longer two.

Simone L. Wilde

Mind Of A Child

I was dancing on the skirts of a dream
Everything meant nothing to me
Clumsy, with insecurity, stumbling into a wall
With the mind of a child
Yearning to experience it all

With fork in hand before the feast
Across the table sat the beast
Also too lost in a misty dream
Without a clue of what was happening to me
A mind too distant from his sparkling eyes
To experience reality held inside
For I am but a child, but when gone from this night
Wisdom and maturity will diffuse my spite.

Michael Everett McGalin

Silent Splendor

The breath of God carefully kissed
Everything with a frozen mist.
The world now quiet with reverence,
Sounds of silence fill the air.
The atmosphere so serene,
Chilled splendor everywhere.

The only thing heard
Was the chirp of a bird,
Or the crackle of a limb.
It chills my spine,
Yet warms my soul,
I have truly been with Him.

Captivated by the beauty of my Master's art
I felt His touch upon my heart.
Be still my soul,
I can hardly behold
Such beauty You unfold.

Shirley H. Ketner

A Daisy And A Rose

A daisy and a rose, are really quite the same.
Except for color, shape, and feel, and also for their name.
They both grow in a garden, needing light, time, and care.
Just the sun, some water, and they also need some air.
In the garden of life, they bloom and grow.
Without feelings of hatred and woe.
Roses and daisies live together.
In gardens young and old.
Some conservative, some dependent,
and some that break the mold.
The world is like a garden, and people are the flowers.
But unlike the daisies and roses.
Humans don't get along.
What difference does it make what color I am.
Why can we not become friends.
Learn from the flowers and change the world, make a better life for each boy and girl.
Could this be the path that we chose...
Why can't we be like a daisy and rose?

Megan Murphy

Memory

Raindrops of pain
Fall from a darkened sky
I remember your touch
Like the kiss of a butterfly

A colorful Horizon
A tear slides down my face
The beauty of your smile
I long for your embrace

A waterfall of memories
Appear before my eyes
My heart says "please believe it's real"
My mind says "It's all lies"

Your memory can carry me
Like an eagle into flight
But while I hide in fantasy
I'm all alone each night.

Mellonie A. Grigg

November's Child

I am a tree that has blown away
except for its skeleton;
bones to heavy to be moved by the wind:

And you are the wind with cold display
of rushing red sandstorms;
leaving dust from bones once thought to mend.

Terri L. Bilbo

For Lenny

As I walked out of the bar last night. The snow was falling, covering all in white. The city streets were so quiet and still, I alone witnessed the splendor and thrill. The glow from the street lamp made everything shine, I was captured there by a moment in time. It took me back to a night from the past. When we swore our love would forever last. My heart was so saddened without you here, As I stood there alone, fighting back tears. My mind was a whirl, like the flakes coming down, Sweet memories of you, just dancing around. I looked up at the sky, stars not in sight. And prayed to the angels to make every thing right. For one beautiful moment, you were right there, Laughing and smiling, shaking snow from your hair. You gently wiped away the tears from my face And said, "Go home Lynnsie, to our special place." The warmth from the liquor, the new fallen snow, Made you seem so real, I hated to go. Then I was home, climbing safe in my bed, Thoughts of your kiss goodnight filled my head. All I could do was smile and say, "Goodnight my love, forever I'll stay!

Lynne M. Crooks

Rain

Rain
falls gently
to the ground
making a splashing
sound as it hits the
already wet pavement,
Rain falls pouring hard
and soaking the entire ground
making people sad and depressed
children wanting to go outside and
play, but parents are not letting them
because they will splash in the mud and
get incredibly soaked only to have the
excitement of coming back inside to soak,
and dirty the carpet, but eventually the
rain will stop and the sun will come out
again making rainbows for the same
children and people to gaze at
proudly, only to think about
how sad things can turn out happy

Melissa Leigh Garrett

No Strikes Here!!

As the sun comes up over the track.
Fans crowd in; racing is back.

There's drivers to meet; autographs to get.
These autographs are free;
For these you don't have to pay a fee.

No salary caps to settle here;
Just the roar of engines and thousands of cheers.

Some people want baseball back.
Over bats and balls; I'll take a Nascar track.

Susan Reeder

Pointless

I pondered the meaning of life one day
Far in the crevasses of my mind

Trying to find the treasures of happiness
Chasing fulfillment under the sun

What is life that it is worth living
pointless and with no direction

Seeking meaning to my existence
Finding only toil and weariness

A pit stop in the cosmos
soon forgotten and gone

Linda Rodrigues

How Do You Tell Someone You Love Them?

How do you tell someone you love them without scaring? Without fearing what they'll say? How do you communicate your feelings without constantly saying "I'll wait 'til the next day?"

How do you tell someone "My heart beats faster when I'm near you. Gazing into your eyes makes me weak at the knees. I can't stop thinking about you. Ever since I first saw you, I couldn't believe the exquisite aroma, the beauty, the style, the grace. You were flawless. When God created you, it's as if Michelangelo's soul controlled his hand. If you were a painting you'd be a masterpiece."

I often find myself anxiously awaiting to see you, as a child awaits to open gifts at Christmas. My love is straight from the heart, it melts down to my soul, and sets it on fire when I'm near you. This burning flame within me is tearing me apart. I need you by my side for my life to be complete. Society makes us believe life is all about power, prestige, and money. However, the true meaning of life is Love. It's the love you share together with that special person, the happiness you create, being there for each other, and loving each other unconditionally for the rest of your lives. That's true love. It's telling someone "If I should leave this earth, and move on to a higher level, all the angels I'm about to see will not compare to the angel I'm leaving behind.

What I'm trying to say is: I love you with all my heart.

Markus Harvey

Epiphany

Time expelled,
Feelings repelled as a poker in the heart
Fear of losing the one thing you love.

Anxiety approaches as the feeling surmounts
Fatigued of company constantly kept.
Estranged from continuous exposure,
Need for detached time, or wept.

Marrow of life before your eyes,
Discerning in a moment your life's path.
The wake of anguish and despair gurgling by
Such as water over the brink of falls.

And potent waves of repose purify and refine
Spirit and essence of life.

Timothy R. Brophy

Thanks

Thanks to those who encouraged me,
For they gave me the strength to continue on.

And even to those who doubted me,
For they gave me the resolve to prove them wrong.

Terry B. Reichenbach

Fear

Faceless shadow, you haunt me in the night,
Fill dawn's somber hours with fright.

A presence just beyond my shoulder I see,
When I turn, there's no one here but me.

Standing upon a threshold I cannot comprehend,
The beginning, the end, of man.

So tiny I feel, so fragile and alone,
Easily compromised and undone.

Oh, my brothers, part of me wishes to stay as we are;
The higher, to fly to our star.

For so I have loved you, I must move on.
In parting, may we be strong.

Piece of a giant kaleidoscope, a fragment of glass,
I mirror a time in space, already past.

Beloved, that I could bring you with me;
Yet such is not our destiny.

So I fear and cry for the flotsam left behind;
Other selves, a transient mind.

Myself and selves are reflections in a stream;
Life on earth, an ephemeral dream.

Sarah Steadman

Forget You

Tears form in my eyes,
Filling my heart with lies.
I try to forget you, to move on,
Knowing your love will not last long.
Remembering your laugh and smile,
My love for you will last a mile.
Seeing your moves in every man,
Feeling no one will make me feel as special as you did.
Dreams I see you in every night.
Hoping this is the light.
Forget you I will not,
For I love you a lot.
Forget you, I will not.

Windy Hnat

The Retarded Child

God created us one and all in His infinite plan
First He made this big wide world, then He created man.
He designed each a little different, some black, white
and other colors too.
It does not matter the pattern for each has the
same goal in view.

He supplied us all with plenty; a healthy body, soul and mind
To meet our every need with only humility to find
So to make the task much easier which might be hard otherwise.
He made the retarded child with beauty in disguise.

You'll never ever find them main speaker in a hall.
Seldom will you see them in society at all
For their lives are pure and simple and guarded from above.
What they lock in knowledge is substituted with love.

We will never understand them no matter where they roam.
Like the stars that light up the heavens they seem
to radiate a home.
So when your life seems such a burden you know not what to do.
Clasp the hand of a retarded child and he, with God,
will see you through.

Mary H. Moody

"Surging Love"

Surging life is here, my memory holds it all
Flames in Dublin; a lane to Chapelizod, love for
this family "Caulfields" all!
Then now another "life"; a cruel village and schoolmaster,
the boys who throw stones; but friendship! With sweet girls too!!
Wait!! But it's Scotland now, like an opening flower
Life brings love — and through a man who loves God and His Son
Our lives are joined and we help each other then he clasps our first
Born in his arms — and then our "next" a girl!!
Now my heart reaches out to this world as I
and — we enter deeper and deeper — waves of
feeling reach out to it all and we wonder??
Love or hate — kindness or cruelty —?
My friend of childhood? Jesus helps me through!!!
Oh United States of America!
send out your rays of love: - not cruelty —
Join the rhythm of blossoming life —
And spread it around.........
And down the drain with brandy and cigarette smoke!
I love you all!!! Men, women, and children best of all!!!

Mary Lambert

A Life Expended

Candles glow in dead of night
Fleeting thoughts before daylight.
Inchoate visions of what might have been,
More paths to choose, more life to spend.

Tentative feints toward elusive goals,
Adjust, refine, continued toils.
Moves along the road of life
Some lessons easy, some learned twice.

See the fruits of decisions past
Watch the progeny develop fast.
Did the tone I set confound the pace
Mix the issues, confuse the race?

Am I the one to emulate?
Say "follow me and don't be late"
Or did I stray from nurturing
To squelch their souls, to still their ring?

How can one really know
If the course is right, too fast, too slow?
Will something solid or the lack
Be perceived as built when looking back?

Roger L. Markle

Return to Forever

Days
Floating round the bend
Through the rainbows end
Return to forever

Nights
Ring around the moon ... ending all to soon
Return to forever

When we reach the autumns bend
We will wish we were friends again
Laughing in the face of time
If only we grew now as we did then

Clouds
Bellow across the sky
Changing as they fly
Go back
Return to forever

Waves
Rush to touch the shore ... once and never more
Return to forever

Melinda Q. Hernandez

To Each His Own Time

We, human, are travelers of Earth -
floating through what we call time,
in a place we call space,
as a species named mankind.
Is a small child fascinated
when he watches the millennium turn?
Does he know we must all die
and that man has much to learn?
That he is a lone candle
in a brilliant mass of flames
slowly climbing toward a destiny
that he himself can only name?
But you yourself once were him:
unknowing, naive, facing life without care -
grinning silently at his toy,
Not foreseeing the burdens he will bear.
Yet, he will seek his place in time
and know he never is alone,
through the simple love we give him
and a place he can call home.

Spring M. Berman

The Ocean and the Sunset

I love the wind as it blows, the water of the ocean as it flows. The gleaming stars, white yet bright, lights up the sky like a flashlight. It makes me feel free and calm, as I pick up a sandy sea shell I lay on my palm. In which the sunset glares. The beautiful ocean full of life, what a beautiful sight. The gentle wind pressing gently against my skin, quiet; not even the sound of a drop of a pin, just the echo of the ocean's talk as I walk, and as I explore more and the sunset's roar. As the sun leaves, reddish-orange and blue, a dream come true. The beautiful ocean and sunset forever in my mind, the thought of it is so very kind.

Sandra Molthop

human labyrinth

How subtle the wind changes
fluently to different visions
And makes me melt to a
soft flowing maddening puddle of
never ending Lust and sweet Pain
My own mirage spins a net shades me
from the truth.
I give in
Too weak to resist.

Solitude is my companion
disguised as a friend
Knowing Her devastating power i love Her still
And kiss Her softly on the lips.

Sacha Wamsteker

Darkness

I sat in my room feeling alone,
Feeling the broken pieces of my heart
Drop down into the emptiness of my soul
I knew then that the dreams which filled
My head were never going to come true
But still, I longed for him to be mine and
Only mine, to cherish and hold forever
Every time a piece of my heart falls, I
Go further and further into the unknown,
Where no one can reach me.

Katie Piper

Autumn

Apples to be pressed into cider, gathered from the ground.
Fodder in the field, with its ears turned down.

Fowl flocking for the South migrating journey.
Grapes, of frosted vineyards, harvested for juice, wine, and jelly.

Restless, Scattered, Fallen leaves of red and gold.
The O' Man-in-the-Moon appears icy cold.

Pumpkins and Squash surround shocks of fodder.
Squirrels and Chipmunks, with nuts, scurry and scamper.

Bats above our heads, screech and glide.
Black, green eyed, cats arch their backs, and run to hide.

Whoo!, Whoo!, Owls' restful day came to end.
Witches on brooms, across the sky descend.

Ghosts casting white shadows, Boo! Boo!
Goblins are demanding past debts due.

TRICK - OR - TREAT
Instant collection, or a prank on you.

JACK-O-LANTERN guard secretly spying.
Turns into Pumpkin Pie for Thanksgiving.

Linda L. Busse

Getting Older

You know you're getting older when...
Folks have to repeat themselves over and over again
When every move you make causes you hurt
And after every meal you have prunes for dessert!

You know you're getting older when...
You sit down to watch the news and then
Next thing you know it's half past eight
You'll be sorry tomorrow for staying up so late!

You know you're getting older when...
You need the tonic but not the gin
A pile of covers you sleep underneath
And in a cup you keep your teeth!

It's hard on you to get older when...
Everyone around you is young and thin
You'll never understand the things they like
And you wish you could when they say 'take a hike'!

Ruth McCumber

Down the Stream

I heard your voice Echo through the reeds
Foot-steps galloping the dry leaves as the
grass paved your way. I kept waiting.

Watching pebbles and sticks rolling down the
Cascades of the Riyabe river, I saw your shadow
floating on the water as you carried the pot
on your head and a calabash in your hand.

I was overwhelmed with that spark of love
that burst and filled my heart
I felt your scent come through the wind then
I saw your image in the dream as you gently
gave me a drink from the calabash.

In a moment you dashed my way leaving me lonely
and anxiously waiting in the cold night breezes
hoping for another opportunity to meet me by this
river where I first met you.

Our fortune moments lingered fresh, fresh in my
mind as memories carried me through the hectic
night. The waters of Riyabe river snatching my
loneliness as I walked through the silent night.

Samson R. Ondigi

September Wedding

It isn't difficult, you know
For Dad and me to remember
That you and Bill took wedding vows
On the 14th of September.

You were the last of our offspring
To happily say, "I do" —
To tie the knot in church that day
And pledge your love so true!

Your brother, Greg, and his wife, Susan
Chose a winter wedding,
And Tom took Nancy for his bride
With a very early June setting.

So it matters not just when you married,
Whether summer, winter or fall,
You each must know that Dad and I
Wish happiness for you all!

And, as I said, it's rather easy
For all of us to remember —
That you and Bill did pledge your troth
In beautiful September!

Marjorie W. Smiley

A Birth Mother's Victory

When you think of me son, please do it with a smile,
For I am the woman who went that extra mile.

To ensure your future, the pain was so great,
But I'd do it again my Love, for both our sakes.

I am the woman who went to war, I won my love,
You now have open doors.

I am the woman who gave you life,
your future to me was worth the fight.

The fearful uncertainties have now all diminished,
and a future of opportunities have now been replenished.

I am the woman who thinks life is worth living,
for you my son, I had to keep on giving.

I am the woman who smiles through her tears,
For I know now my Love, you'll have fruitful years.

Kimberley L. Flores

On A Cloudy Day

A cloudy day can bring joy to your heart
For it holds the rain
that helps the flowers start
And behind each could
The sun hangs true
And it will shine brightly
For me and you

A cloudy day can bring peace to your mind
For it's there your eyes drift
When a gray sky's behind
And you know so soon
That the suns bright rays
Will bring joy and happiness
In your path this day
For tho clouds dim the light
Of a brand new day
Standing right behind
Is God's love displayed

Shirley R. King

God's Precious Flowers

Look carefully at the flowers in the earth
For it wasn't so long ago it was their time of birth.
Their petals are delicate, soft and bright,
With a unique, special way that is a delight.
They bend and they twist with unusual turn.
But if you look closely you can learn.
They have senses all of their own,
With a beauty to give that was sown
This beauty came right from God's
Garden on top of the hill,
That was done by gentle hands when he would till
The soil is dark, rich and lush,
So please stop a minute before you touch.
Try not to hurry to cut down the flowers when you mow,
Instead listen to God's word on how plants grow.

Katherine Donahue

Alone

A song agonies with the joy of it's days.
For it's days shall be remember
Like the lightening beneath the moon
In search for it's destiny.

The day resting it's shadows
For its' shadows will not be lived
And neither shall be the same day
Like minutes on the hour
Being left in the depths of times.

The light has arisen
Though it shall not be observed
Like the strange voice isn't heard
And slowly dies the image
Fading the silhouette like a thunder in it's fervor.

The skin, the lover, the unfound kiss
Shall also go;
As everything disappears
Like the stare which searched
Gaining nothing to hold.

Manuel A. Galvez

The Love I Have For You

The love I have for you is strong
For I've loved you for so long although you may not know it,
Because I never show it
But I have hope that one day,
You will find a way, to love me as much as I love you
In all you do and say

The love I have for you is great
But no longer will I sit and wait
For there are many fish in the sea, who are waiting just for me
I will not sit around all day
And hope that you will find a way
To love me as much as I love you
For the feelings has gone away

The love I have for you is gone it left no marks to carry on
I've waste my love on someone wrong
You made me wait just too, too, long
The hope I had will not return
It shattered one day and I let it burn
My thoughts will not go back to you for now it is too late
The love that I once had for you has gone and turned to hate

Lorena Villarreal

The King's Daughter

A child was born of royal birth, yet this she did not know,
For many years her world was dark; she wandered to and fro.
Searching blindly, cold and scared, she went about her days,
Tears and fears and life's regrets companions on the way.
Until that precious moment when the King himself appeared,
He whispered gently in her ear and said,
"You are my child, my dear!"
You see, my son, died for you, that you might be reborn,
Removed from worldly tragedies and tossed upon life's storm.
And in your place he stood for you, a crown of thorns he wore,
The sins of man, a cross of wood, and all your tears he bore.
So come into the kingdom child, into the light of love,
Put on the robes of royalty, my gift from up above,
And live your life as heir, my dear, for all eternity,
Where Christ, my son, your savior,
Waits with open arms for thee.

Mary Elizabeth Davis

Bikes

Ticker-tape parades are made for cars and public folks, but life for me, the loving done, comes for riding two-wheeled spokes!

Flying by at night like bats, flickered-flying traffic lights, gone thru in a trice you know, the two-wheeled way-ward gizmo go!

Daytime less to speed, dependant on your need (driving calmly is outdated) but pedestrians warn "drive sedate, not sedated."

Coming down to pass, the pack no more a mass, the clipped pedal-foot spindle blurs (hurry hur, hurry hur).

Spokes in sunlight gleam and run, click/clack change, the gearing done, leaning far to take the turn, no front brake now rubber burn!

Coming on a lone postal man, ten of bikes circled round, wagon trains this Indian done! Pedal on, pedal on!

Shock not (worry don't) normal cars, gridlocks got their goat, cutting through, tiny lanes, ending, you can gloat!

There is no end to pack or one, tearing on from town to town, riding up the city down.

Stephen H. Kidder

Untitled

She sits and she waits.
For someone
Someone to break through the invisible wall
The barrier,
The wall she puts around her heart.
So no one can hurt her.
Like a forest whose trees block
Any tendril of sunlight that might
Dare to creep through their leaves.
Killing the flower underneath.
Her emotions well up inside.
But cannot escape through the wall.
Killing her heart.
Underneath

Sarah E. Curl

"HIV," Hope Is Victory

The HIV virus is the contagious seed;
For it causes AIDS the deadly disease;
Keep the faith, hope; and always pray;
That the cure will be found, as we speak today;
Like a forest fire, it has spread all over the place;
And it is found in most of the world today;
Hope pray, and keep the faith that we all live another day;
Hope is victory to cure all of us;

Luis Ramon Castro

To Seek Happiness

To seek beyond tomorrow
  for that happiness and joy,
For all you need to really do
  is tear
    down
      all those
        walls,
Reach inside, open up your heart
  and start believing in yourself.
So start your life anew
  and believing in all you do;
Stretch out your hand to the needy ones
  your reward will be greater still.
So believe it from the start
  whether morning, eve or night
that you worthy
  and have the right
  For HAPPINESS in ALL its Light!!!

Patricia Eisenhauer

Precious Hope

Dare I hope,
For that which is beyond my scope?
What does it mean?
Grasping with faith toward the unseen;
Out of the depth of misery's gain;
Reaching with expectation for the unfeigned hand;
Thereby loosening degradation's debilitating chain,
Placing the mortal body's triumph in the realm of reality;
"But Soul, 'where stand you, in your quest for immortality?"

Muriel G. Singleton

"Knocked Down But Not Out"

They thought they had gotten me, so you see
For them the victory had been so easy—
But I stood my ground and looked above, for I heard
"You're knocked down, but not out with my love"
So I dried my tears and stayed on the job
I discarded my faults and fears with the strength above,
So when people hurt you as they will
Remember it's okay to be knocked down but not out —
For you will feel the love of God without a doubt.
So as you journey through this world and
you're knocked down but not out
Remember to stay on the task as they will see
There's a greater force than you and me.

Sylvia Morgan

Winter

I am filled with great despair,
For this cold winter air,
Swirling around me,
Whipping in my face like the sting of a bee,
My feet feeling heavy with the burden of the cold,
Those before me must have been bold,
For now I collapse in the snow,
Through my hair the icy wind does blow,
And I pray,
That live through this judgment day,
And if I do, I swear
That in my heart I will always wear,
This feeling like I have done wrong,
But I'll always know that I have been strong,
All along, yet I know,
That I have failed, for,
Here I am lying in the cold snow.

Radwa Penny

"Indolence Knowledge"

Inside dangers are growing
for us to deal with, but no, we
can't because it will become too
mammoth to be solved.
The truth lies within our
hearts to heal the wicked illnesses
of humanity. After all, we are enjoying
ourselves today, if we start now,
we can enjoy the earth tomorrow as well.
People alone and could I think
can be in touch with themselves
more than people who think of
themselves as "Great People".
Conceitedness will never work.

Mekesia Bartley-Brown

My Fortune In Having A Friend In You

Friends, you know, are so far and few between;
For you are more than fortunate should fate bring at least
one your way;
Whether we laugh, or whether we cry;
I know my friend in life you will always be.

When days of life turn dark and ever so grim;
Wondering maybe, just how will the once-silver lining ever
shine once again;
How could you know of my days like these?
Somehow, you do and always come through.

Make no excuses to give up; or simply call it quits;
Tomorrow will be better, just wait and see;
Being more than fortunate having you as my friend;
How do you know of my days like these?

Thank you for the friendship you have given me;
For your thoughtful and caring ways from your heart
you have given to me and mine.

Lois E. Hill

Forever In Our Hearts

Will you love me
forever?
Will you care about me
forever?
How do you feel about me,
are you more than just a friend?
Someone to be with until the end

Between the desire and the passion
between each tick of the clock
Life is very long
Will we have the time to live it
together?

These have been the best years of my life
and I want you to know
we'll always be together
forever in our hearts

Ronald A. Busse

Don't Promise....

Don't promise me your heart
for it won't ever be fully mine
Don't promise me tomorrow
if you won't be here tonite
Don't promise me the world
for it's too hard
Don't promise me forever
for you don't know when the end would come.

Michelle Toledo

Summer

Finally summer vacation is here,
Forget stupid locker combinations,
The humid sunny days are O' so near,
Now we will have a super vacation.

Notebooks with papers falling everywhere,
You can wear any clothes you desire,
Now no more worrying about my hair,
We can go camping and build a big fire.

Murchison school will wait till next autumn,
Eating round cookies and ice cream galore,
All I will do is sit on my bottom,
Cool swimming and so much, much, much more.

The sparkling pool
Is extremely cool.

Melissa Sewell

"Continues"

Fallen goals, misplaced dreams
forgetting where you came from
forgetting what you mean.
People come and people go
so many stones on the beach to throw.
Seasons change and lovers leave
but it continues.
Trying to forget faces in the sand
leaving yourself behind in your land.
Driving all night without the headlights on
a dark country road where everything's gone.
There's a stumbling block in the middle of the road
Keep on going, it continues,
Nobody cares if you stay or you go
so many stones on the beach to throw.
You can stay behind or run with the pack
the decisions for you
you can choose to stay back.
Because it continues
until you stop it.

T. Jay Earley

A River In All Directions

The Past: The beginning or the end? Was. No more. Every
fraction of time anticipated, counted, forgotten,
looked back on.

The Present: Now, measured to the very second.
Recreating itself every time.
What was the present is now the past.
Is there a present?

The Future: Flowing into the past. A river of time, never a
certain place, always moving. Forgotten yet remembered.
Space: Endlessness, intertwining with time. Universes in whatever
possible belief and more. Are we the only ones? Not known and
never will be.
Eternity: Forever, everlasting, and always will be. Do the confines
of time conceal it? Always a future, past, or present,
forgotten but recalled.
Time: A winding, uneven, never ending river. The basis of creation.
Secrets unfolding as well as misleading. Still the same every
time, flowing like a river.

Kristina Orosz

Lord I Thank You

Jesus gave His life so that we might be
free. He died on the cross because He
truly loves you and me. He took harsh words
from people who didn't know Him at all
So that He could be here whenever we
call. His love is unconditional He's there
till the end. He's our greatest confidant
and our closest friend. He answers prayers
and perform miracles everyday. All
we have to do is walking in the Godly way.
With faith in one hand and the other in love
He's truly a blessing from up above.
One day soon He will prevail. God
can do anything, but fail. Lord? I
thank you for loving, and forgiving
me irregardless to all the wrong that
I've done, and for me sacrificing
You only son Jesus Christ.

LaShonda Willis-Burton

Impossible Dream

No government to rule me, no enemies for my thoughts,
Freeing my illiterate mind
No need for money, more room in my pocket without my wallet
I left it on the sidewalk behind
No conflicts in other countries for us to butt into
Freeing our soiled and bloodstained hands
No guns, no knives, assault weapons of any kind
Returning to youth the yearning for truth
And knowledge....
So hard to find

Kenn Phillips

Happy Mother's Day

Sometimes you think she's your best
friend and at times your worst enemy.
But a wonderful person is all your mother
can be expected to be.
You may not like it when she tells you no,
But mother knows best as you all too
well know.
She's a wonderful person who loves you so much.
She'll always be there to give a gentle touch.
She's loving and caring and always
will be.
A mother is someone special to me.
God has blessed me with a mother
who is number one.
The love my mother has for me it
cannot be undone.
My mother is very special to me,
and I'd just like to say,
I love you mama, and always will,
Happy Mother's Day!

Stacey R. Thomas

Man

You are a counterpart to all
Friendly, knowing of this land
But under the land, in the sea you know none
Alone are you, Man
You see murky water and dying animals
Of these things you have knowledge not
This is of your doing and you are the cause of this
Man, help your home survive
For it like you needs air, water
For it like you is alive

Jennifer Kelley

Friends

Friends are special, friends are kind
Friends are excellent, especially mine.
That's why I'm glad that you're my friend,
And I'll be your's until the end.
Through fights and laughter,
I'll be with you forever after.
To see you smile,
I'd walk a mile,
But I don't have to 'Cause you're always there,
And you do what friends do best, which is share, share, share.
You share your happiness, you share your glee,
You share your joy, and you share it with me,
But the top reason friends are special to me,
Is that you are my friend, now do you see?

Shannon Becker

Don't Grow Up Too Fast

When I was about the age of ten
Friends just seemed to roll right in.
But in a few year, things weren't the same
They seemed very fast to forget my name.
I set my goal, what I wanted to do
And I had to see I followed them through.
Dope was floating and the hang over blues
So my friends dropped down to only a few.
The world was spinning, things going so fast
Girls getting married, but few would last.
Some having babies, they were having a ball
Trying to be popular, with a big down fall.
I really looked around, do I like what I see
I can truthfully say, I'm glad that's not me.
Marriage is beautiful and babies are too
But right now, I have my school.
I'll need that knowledge when I grow up
Cause I've got my plans for a lot of good stuff.
Oh, I want a family when the right time comes
But right at the present, I've got lots to learn.

Virginia R. Harrison

Rainbow

My love for you is dying now,
from burning flames, to cold desire.
Those burning flames - could go on higher,
but you choose the cold desire.

For every end, there is a new beginning,
and after every rainbow, there is a sunny sky.
But I feel, that I'm winning,
and after long rough road: "I still could reach the sky."

The night grows cold, and I still love you.
But deep down, in my heart, I know you'll not return!
I'll write you songs, be in my dreams.
You met a dreamer, from the east.

Again the sun will shine, for many
but, if tomorrow comes to late: "Don't ask me why!"
If we lose somehow, remember - just reach out...
and touch, that precious rainbow, in the sky.

Silvana Krculic

Weeping Rachel

Oh weeping Rach'l, lamentable ship,
E'er shall you curse the day you left
The maudlin ports of where you birthed
The crying sons whose lives do sift
Through hourglass hole; of ocean wide,
Where do these sons of Ad'm now reside?

Michelle Lynn Muenzler

The Beginning

They stared eye to eye, as her tears begun to brim from her eyes, seeing that she has hurt, the only man she loved. So she puts her hand down, and says the words of false truth, as she speaks her heart pounds, and feels to full of pain as she tells him that it's over. He sobs and she holds him close. She lifts his head and stares into the deep pools that were once full of love, but is now empty. She tilts her head and kisses him gently, then fiercely, there tongues battle and there souls sore, and become one. The kiss is ended both left with a fast heartbeat, they hug for one last time, and he whispers in her ear, bye. Knowing those will be his last words. The words hit her hard as she turned and left without looking back, and all that is left is there souls laughing, because there souls had become one in that kiss and for that last word he said was only the beginning of there whole lives together.

Merida Deynes

A Day in the Life of a Little Boy

He peddles papers down Pleasant View Lane
From house to house, in the soft falling rain,
Wishing he had just one more candy cane.
Splash! Through a mud puddle he calmly walks,
And then trudges off with wet shoes and socks.
Finally, he reaches the last mail box.
Heading homeward, he stops so suddenly
To boast, "I'm a brave captain on a ship at sea",
As he waves a small branch which fell from a tree.
Moving on, he becomes a private eye
Who is now on a mission of "do or die."
Seizing a stop sign .... he captures the spy.
After he's at home and he has been fed,
It is T.V. time, then to riding "Big Red,"
Where he's tall in the saddle till Mom calls "Bed!"

Tim O. Fugleberg

If I Had A Ship

If I had a ship, I'd sail away
From my troubles and woes
No special direction, I'd head out
And go where my ship goes

If I had a ship
Then I'd be
So close to God
Upon his sea

If I had a ship, I'd sail away
There will come a time
That my ship will come, then I will know
A life that is sublime

Vera Mundt

Metamorphosis Of A Butterfly

Trapped inside I hide
from all the world
Isolated I become more confidential waiting for
the day to come out
Now I fear when I flutter will you
Capture me, and put me in a bottle for all
the world to see
While I die will I still be pretty
.... for all the world to see

Shammara Williams

A Refugee's Prayer

The ocean is tainted with blood
From refugees who dare to cross
On their make shift wooden coffins
Not looking back at the family they have lost

Little children, mothers, and fathers
Have all drowned in that big blue sea
Just because of one man
Who doesn't believe that people should be free

Castro opens the door to freedom
Go! If you can cross that big open sea
If you want freedom so much
Risk your lives if you don't want me

So the ocean awaits those who suffer
Who would rather die than stay their
People who are starving, who have nothing
They pray to God that the ocean will be fair

They set sail when the winds are blowing our way
They follow the stars
Sometimes we take freedom for granted
But refugees have the scars

Peggy Rodgers

True Love

From the sunken sun to the rising moon,
from the breaking day to the midday moon,
from the infinite sky and the clouds high above,
to the depths of the sea I proclaim my love.
From the ground that I walk on to the
air that I need, from blossoming flower
to unplanted seed.
From passing days to changing seasons,
there are so many different reasons, why
between our hearts stands a love, that's
stronger than gravity's pull, and with
true love for you, my heart is eternally full.

Rachel Condon

The Obscurity of Demise

Stealing the soul
from the fire of life,
I rage though out the thoughts
of those ignorant
to the sins
in which we all commit.

Many try to escape the fear
that dwells
in the heart of us all.
And this inquietude that we all cower to
has only one name. Death.

From this cessation we, as mortals, continually try to dodge.
Yet inevitably collide with.
Thrusting our worthless
Spirits
upon a new world,
in which to its reality
we are nothing but
mere
virgins.

Rosemary D. Gerace

Where Am I?

Do you really know where you are?
From what you want to achieve
are you that far?
Could you sit here and tell me just that?
Or would you sit and wonder where am I at?
I am totally lost in a world of dreams,
Or just don't know where I
am at least it seems.
To be truthful I have not been united with my mind,
I am to believe that it is it that I shall find.
It's hard living in a world where there is no one but me,
Seems that everyone is just
too damn blind to see, I feel as if I am in a deep
sleep and can not be awakened,
If you think I am a nobody
I'm letting you know you're mistaking.
I am still sitting here with a sad face and a painful sigh,
But the thought that keeps crossing
my mind is "where in the hell am I?"

Tamia M. Camper

"Let Go"

When a friend seems to be drifting
further and further away - keep holding
her by the memories of each lasting day.
Her preference and her mind tell
her not to go but her own heart has a
yearning deep down in her soul.
All the time this friend has spent
with you is now being shared two by two by two.
Soon the view of your friend has faded
and you must learn to let her go. Not because
you believe you should, but like your friend,
your heart tells you so.

Kim Siller

America Mother of the World

America mother of the world on the people's front,
Getting up, and strong, working hard, making money a lot,
Investing in business, getting rich, and rich.
Computer technology, air force, and the best army, all over the world,
Peace by talking, or peace by the force, take it, or leave it,
It's order from Washington U.S.A. mother of the world.
God, merciful has given them the power to save the best of the world,
God has chose Washington to give all the world "order." For peace
and liberty, no more slavery and no one dictator, no more Fascists,
Hitler or stalinism. Order, order from Washington U.S.A. mother of
the world. Long live America, I am proud to be. This is America, for
you and me. America is for all, racial status, all colors,
and Nationalities, but there is not space for terrorists, they'll be
caught shortly alive or dead, there is no escape. FBI and CIA,
they are not sleeping, but watching day and night. It's their duty,
they are proud to serve the country they love, they are patriots, they
don't fear life. Out terrorists, out from America, There's no space
you, don't even try the U.S.A. We'll catch you, you'll be sorry
for being born and terrorizing American cities. You'll be punished.
You're going to pay with your life.

Pal Imeri

Helen

Losing a wife is a strange and private thing.
Grief and regret return, not in the night,
but in reflected color from a glass of wine
in the pale splendor of an autumn afternoon
companion to the soft October light.

Mark T. Sheehan

The Rat

There once was a sewer that sheltered a rat.
He sat in his house, ate and grew fat.
He said, "I like food
When I sit in the nude."
Now what kind of rat thinks like that?

Nicole Stephan

Halloween

Halloween night, is such a fright.
Ghosts, goblins, witches,
and Frankenstein with stitches.
A yellow moon and autumn leaves,
will make anyone queeze.
High on a hill is a haunted house,
rumor to have killed many a louse.
As I approached it's big door,
I thought I heard the sound of a ghost snore!
As it screeched open and I walked in,
I prayed to God to forgive my sins.
Suddenly, I heard a noise a far,
I thought I saw a ghost with a cigar.
As I wiped my eyes to look again,
it turned out to be a fountain pen.
Nevertheless, I was really afraid,
when I turned around I thought I saw a headless maid.
I ran to the window, threw up the sash,
and then began a mad dash.
I know I will always remember this night,
As a Halloween of fun, but full of fright!

Nicole King

Arcadian Rhythm

One rising slightly higher.
Gifted with the infinite view.
A small white peak on the horizon
Melted in tan matting of the distant isle.
Precocious porcupines play with fire.
Scorching and clipping to mold unique virtues.
Glowing tops that no longer spin.
Trustfully grasp the gentle waves.
Baby barnacles bathe in the mist.
Clustered together in tenuous masses.
The force of many shields the strength of one.
Engulfing the wispy locks that flutter out of sync.
Is this a slow waltz or a tantalizing tango?
The crescendo rises.
A white spray hurls onto my fingertips.
Luring me to join the dance.
I step forward then back.
Retreating toward the summit.
I meet the gaze of the tallest pine.

Shoshanna Zucker

Too Young

Starting life so young,
giving birth to a baby.
Realize life for you has only just begun.
Now you rely on your
Family and friends to
help pull you through
but everyone knows, all
the fault belongs to you.
So my sister a piece of advice

from me to you, nobody knows
what life will bring, but just
remember to follow your dreams!!

Monica Martinez

"A Father"

A father is there from the very start
Giving love and discipline so you'll never part,
A father is there when you lean to walk
As well as being there when you start to talk.

A father is there when your skin, your knee
So often the pain he sees you smile with glee,
A father has many qualities you can see
Take for instance, his got me.

A father has good days, as all of us do
But watch out for the bad one, they come to,
A father is a blessing from God above
He holds you tight and gives you love.

A fathers love has a very special touch
It makes you feel safe and means so much,
A fathers little girl am I from the start
So nothing you do or say will tear is apart.

A father is special an one of a kind
So this is for Daddy and I'm glad you're mine.

Marie Chastain

Bittersweet Love

The pain runs deep. Gripping, tearing, gnawing away at every shred of logic's delicate strands. I lie awake, alone in the dark, waiting for a sign. A sign of genesis, a new beginning. That things will be alright, that I will find the life I recognize, the warm touch ... human flesh... not my own. I gaze deep into eyes of brown, longing, needing, wanting the touch... caress... laughter and love. As I spend another long, lonely, night staring into the emptiness of my soul, I wonder... maybe tomorrow....

William R. Culver Jr.

Into My Heart

I stare back to the places I have been.
Go where I don't know then to know myself.
To lose my problems that had to be dealt with,
I was sure that I could endure.
The mounting of life upon me,
But you can't see it built up inside
I never show the hurt or never the envy.
During this week.
Seeing all the meek.
More of me to open,
To dig deeper into my heart,
To let it all out hold on.
I used to have doubts.
The Lord sought.
His sheep from night to dawn.
This week I think he found he was looking for,
And I found the door.
My life has a new chapter.
My spirit is now better.
To end this with a smile I will try.

Nae Soundara

Untitled

The words I cried down the canyon
  had no meaning, yesterday;
But suddenly, today, they slapped me hard
  as an ocean tide moving in
  crushing against some rocks.
They echo in my memory, every now and then
  reminding me of their existence
While only marking a time limit like clocks.

Patti Jo Maki

Time Heals All Wounds

With time comes patience
God Almighty's great graciousness
With time comes healing
His effects keep me reeling
Whoever said that you're immune
Take a look at me, you'll see no wounds
Changing course can be a difficult thing
I know 'cause I've see...

His handiwork can make a weak man strong
Put your faith in him and it won't be long
Before you see a change in the ways
That used to get you through those days
You'll finally say to the man above
Thank you Lord, it's you I love

As time moves on, I see the light
From his graciousness I've found new sight
I've learned to live one day at a time
And place my faith in Father Time

Karen Sullivan

"Peace" Of Mind

After a hot summer day as the sun
Goes to sleep, a little blue bird sits
Without even a peep, he is so lonely and
He is so sad, for he thinks, is there any
Place left in this cruel desperate world.
Is there anything we can do or anything
We can say to help our world
Overcome this journey. This journey of
Hatred, this journey of crime, its overpowering
Our journey of pride. Pray he says to
Himself. Pray, for God is listening to our
Desperate cries, to heal our world. Give it
Love, give it seeds to sprout new beginnings
For the people in need. But most of all
Lets fear no more. Lets give our world what
It deserves and desperately needs, "Peace".
What a beautiful thing.

Mandy Durnan

Golf

Here I am, a seventy year old—-
Going out for that golf game——
And let's see, what's my name?
One wood, three wood, seven iron, or putter
Oh Dear! I can't decide between oleo and butter!
See that flag down there behind the tree!
Tee Off, keep your head down,
Watch the ball and don't forget your tee——
See the traffic over there? Don't hit a car!
WOW! Maybe I'd be better off in a bar!
Well, Dear God, I'm out here now—-
The fresh air is wonderful, that I will allow
Be patient, dear friend of old—-
I'm just six strokes from the hole!!!

Margaret E. Koester

Earth

The child lies in a puddle of blood.
His pain drenches the sphere.
North, South, East, West
Ocean blues bleed scarlet.
The universe watches in horrific amusement
at Normandy, Hiroshima, Birmingham, Baghdad.
The unending terror spreads from this child,
Earth.

Melissa A. Howard

Happiness

Happiness is when you make someone else feel
good inside by lending a helping hand.
Happiness is when you walk through a meadow
early in the morning and see the sun rising over
the horizon.

Happiness is when friends come together just to
spend a little quality time with each other.

Happiness is also when you put someone
else's feelings and needs before your own to make
someone else feel good and loved inside.

Happiness is when parents see their baby for
the first time,
One of the most important of all the other
kinds of happiness, is when you make a
difference in the world, or in the life of
someone else. And you also better yourself
for you sake and for the sake of others
around you!

Krissy O'Hawk

Goodbyes

What are goodbyes...
Goodbyes are when someone says "Goodbye"
for a day, week, month, year, or eternity.
When are goodbyes...
Anytime and any place. Day or night.
Summer or Spring, or even in between.
Goodbyes are everywhere. When best friends
part, when a daughter leaves, or when a loved one goes to heaven.
Some people don't like goodbye. I don't do you?
What are goodbyes? Goodbyes are sometimes
forever and sometimes not, but a person always
leaves and says the word "Goodbye" and with that. . .
Goodbye

Tammy Fields

The Turtle With A Big Shell!

Once there lived a turtle named Lumpy. He
got his name from his shell, it was so big and
bumpy! He could barely move but yet he wasn't
very smooth. All the animals called him names and
played mean tricky games. He would walk alone
and let out these tiny moans:
Oh how, oh how, oh how could it be, why did
God pick little oh me!
I'm walking and walking and everyone's
talking.
Look, oh look, oh look at that back if it was
food it would be a great big oh snack!
If I had a wish I would want to be a
fish and swim with glee! Then they would not go
He! He! at nice little me. Oh well, God made me
the way he wanted me to be. I'm one of a kind
that no one can find.
Even though I walk alone, step by step I
let out a moan. I must be I even till I die!

Matt Perry

Cars

Yellow bomber
I have a yellow bomber parked in my yard.
I call it my banana and its hardly even marred
Its jacked in the rear and peels like a charm.
I wash it and clean it and cruise around town.
When people look, I never get a frown.
I rebuilt it with a super charged kit,
and when I hit the gas man do I split.

Shane Shelton

Man-Giant

Stand on tip-toe,
Graze the summit with outstretched hands!
Run across flower-tops,
Leap over glaciers
Like so many cracks in a sidewalk,
Man-Giant!

Let your steps be light
As sun-rays touching the foot-hills,
Brightening the dawns of your days,
Illuminating your senses!

Slip on the shale slopes,
But don't go mad
Crashing with the flat stones
To the bottom.

Get up and walk, Man-Giant!
More careful and more beautiful -
For the pinnacles are but a place
To put your feet
And the sky is your domain.

Marika Martin

Last Words

As you walk along the ocean,
Hand in hand, you and he,
The sun is slowly setting past the horizon of the sea.
You stop, and face him, to look into his eyes.
Instantly you are mesmerized by his crystal clear, blue skies.
You wonder if he loves you, but, do not dare to ask,
Knowing that if you do,
Your time together will surely pass.
You continue your walk on the sandy beach.
You want to know him better.
He is too distant, out of reach.
Does he regret something of his past?
Visions fill your mind. Accept he will not talk about it.
No answers will you find.
Just being close to him, for you, is enough love.
Suddenly he transforms and away flies a beautiful dove.
What has just happened? Where has he gone?
A voice silently says "Goodbye, my true love, farewell, so long!"

Kristy L. Briggs

Two Feather

An indian brave of long ago
hangs on my wall at home
with his piercing eyes and strong
firm chin I'll never be alone

I wonder if he were alive today what
his feelings and thoughts would be
I can only imagine the stories he might
relate if he could talk to you and me

I know he's just a painting that
hangs on my wall at home but
with his piercing eyes and strong
firm chin I'll never be alone

He will be there for me in every month
and in every kind of weather this
handsome rugged brown skinned brave
that I have named Two Feather

Mitzi Gorden

"Things of Life"

Life is many things;
Happiness to be enjoyed, wrongs to be righted,
Help to be lended,
Love to be given,
Children to be understood,
Words to be listened,
Goals to be reached,
Mistakes to be made, People to be forgiven;
All to give freedom.

Without freedom;
People shall not be forgive, Mistakes shall not be made,
Goals shall not be reached,
Words shall not be listened,
Children shall not be understood,
Love shall not be given,
Help shall not be lended,
Wrongs shall not be righted, Happiness shall not be enjoyed;
And life is lost.

But all is forgiven and love is there.

Katie Hoefs

"Hard Times"

Hard times, I'm on the streets again,
Hard times, here's where my heartaches begin,
Hard times, I ain't got a dime, hard times!

Well I guess I'm pretty lucky,
I don't pay no income tax,
I have a brand new cardboard box, that's home,
and the shirt, that's on my back!

Well you say, you wished I'd disappear,
get off the streets, quit bummin' a round,
But then you snicker, when I ask for more,
you'd rather kick me, when I'm down!

I'm gonna pick myself up, dust myself off,
turn over, a brand new leaf,
I'm gonna get a job, buy a house,
please don't wake me, from this dream!

Hard times, I'm on the streets again,
Hard times, here's where my heartaches begin,
Hard times, I ain't got a dime, hard times!

Rick Allen

White Soldiers

Gentle is the snow that falls upon the hard ground.
Harmless, airless mass of white it deceives the stolid mound.

With its icy army, its numbers do increase;
By morn the earth is covered and has to admit defeat;
For where it had its frozen turf is now completely bleached.

The tiny limbs break with acquiesce, the pines drop lowly down.
The maples, elms, and mighty oaks can only hold their ground.

Despite the complete compelling slaughter,
a new landscape has been born;
for what was brown and old and tattered,
is now fresh, white tipped in orange.

The shadows that were hidden, can now be clearly seen;
as the sun rises to show the land, so stark and virgin clean.

Oh, the overwhelming beauty of water froze to ice!
How quickly can it take the darkness
and turn it into light.

White soldiers-hurry,
come again, and quell the spell of night.
Gather gray clouds of hidden arrows
and smother the black with white.

Kimberly Kann Thompson

Moments

A smile that echoes from the heart
Has a beauty brushed with stardust —
To receive one, and then of course to give one,
Remains as always, a most definite must.

Having a friend, while thus being a friend,
Intertwines into magical splendor,
Weaving a spell both of peace and of joy,
Blending a balance no other could render.

Laughter adds its varied treasures
With special virtues to convey.
Knowing quite well that no one can ignore,
such great hidden values, it has to portray.

Love proves an awesome difference
Through its constant total caring,
It's just people loving people,
That becomes a miracle through sharing.

Moments so captured by kindness
Gently enhanced by a touch of concern.
Aware of just how truly incredible,
This marvel of love all may learn.

Joana L. Soule

"Let There Be Life"

The most wonderful man that I've known in my life,
has asked me today to be his sweet wife;
Our future's upon us, so bright and so clear,
as our love just grows stronger with each passing year;
Home is our haven from life's bitter woes,
we know we've truly been blessed as our little ones grow;
If the world could all feel the love that we share,
there'd be no fighting, no hunger, no strife anywhere;
For this was his goal, for each man and wife,
when God said unto us, "Let There Be Life."

Sheila Santee

My Lover's Hands

My lover's hands
Have felt the pain of losing a dream
Were bruised with emptiness and, of hope, washed clean
My lover's hands
Have reached toward the midnight sky
Spreading like wings, but unable to fly
Yet, my burdens collapse upon their touch
And, in their embrace, my cries are hushed
My lover's hands, after all they have been through
Possess me in a love that has remained true.

My lover's hands
Come to me each day, faithfully
Are familiar and, yet, still a mystery
My lover's hands
Are forgiving and gently strong
Never surrendering when all goes wrong
They bleed with the tears of my joy and sorrow
And fight back the fears of each day's tomorrow
My lover's hands will never reach and not find me here
For my love is for my lover's hands to share.

Louis Riehm

Untitled

Wishing for you:
Enough health to be independent;
Enough challenges to grow;
Enough love to fill your heart;
Enough faith to fill your soul.

Marcia T. Bruce

Diver and Starfish

There is a diver under the sea,
He admires a starfish - that starfish is me,
He visits the starfish everyday
Diving in the ocean bay.
His admiration grows to more
as he sees the starfish on the ocean floor.
He loves the starfish, and she returns
the feeling which greatly, steadily burns.
Until one day, the diver gains
the tools of a fisherman, the ocean's pains,
suddenly the starfish is an enemy of the diver
turned fisherman, the person she loved.
He mutilates the starfish, cuts her in two,
deep in the ocean, the ocean that's blue.
The diver believes that defeat is his goal,
but he is wrong; soon the starfish is whole.

Martina Villarreal

The Kiss

As he was leaving for the day
He blew a kiss to me

I caught the kiss and held it tightly
Then slipped it into the pocket of my apron

It was there for most of the day
Until I put my hand in my pocket

And there it was - the kiss that he blew to me
And which I caught and held tightly

I could feel its warmth and tenderness
With which it was given.....

When he returned that night
I held the kiss in my hand

And when he came close to me
I put the kiss against his cheek

He smiled knowing what he felt

The next morning as he was leaving
I blew a kiss to him

I watched as he caught it and put it in
His pocket to keep throughout the day

As I had done.....

Lois Grossmann

Gifts of Love

A man once gave his life for me.
He blinded himself so I could see.
He broke his legs so I could walk.
He cut out his tongue so I could talk.
He broke his nose so I could smell.
He fractured his lungs so I could yell.
He cut off his ears so I could hear
He gave me his hand to wipe my tears.
He gave me his mind so I could learn.
He stepped out of line and gave me a turn.
He gave me his last breath so I could breathe.
He gave me his shoes to wear on my feet.
He gave me his heart so I could love.
He opened his wounds and gave me blood.
He pulled his muscles so I could be strong.
He told me I was right when I was wrong.
He gave me the ability to understand.
When I was lost he held my hand.
For me to live, he was crucified.
That man's name is Jesus Christ.

Mary Henry

Untitled

They say that science is a blast
but this I do not agree
I hope this class goes by fast
so there I will not be

Janelle Maplesden

The Seaman

There once was a skipper coming from the east.
He came from Nantucket the land of the beast.
He dressed in rundown rags, but he had bags
under his eyes with purple circles shaking
his head as he were undertaking
a big risk with his boat.
He smelled like a dirty goat.
That had been lying in the dung
and had been dying in the sun.
He was certainly not an excellent fellow
because he was so droll and bellowed
out everything he said and did,
but he took quite a bid.
By sailing from Nantucket
in a big rundown bucket.
When his vessel sank he was the plank
into the cold Atlantic Ocean,
But he still felt the sea motion.

Natalie Virissimo

The Benefactor

Jesus Christ, Messiah these names he was given
He died so all our sins could be forgiven
What thanks is given to he who sacrificed all
We celebrate the day of his birth and his fall

Miracles he performed for all to see
Made lame men walk and blind men see
Some called him a prophet, and others a fake
To prove his sayings they crucified him on a stake

Born of woman untouched by man
No hate in his heart but carried peace in his hand
To this man we all are indebted, and his price is kind
One day a week you worship at his shrine.

Leonard F. Hildreth

The Meeting

We sat in the garden, He and I.
He dried my tears and said, "Don't cry".
He said, "Your fears, leave here with Me."
"I AM here to comfort thee."

A Garden of Beauty ever so rare,
I felt the presence of Angels there,
A radiance no human could ever bare,
For some reason, He brought me there.

Water Pure, yet, Crimson gently flowed.
My past, present, the future He then showed,
We sat, we talked, my life you see,
With out stretched arms, He set me free.

"Go back, it's not your time," He said.
"You should be with the Living, not the Dead".
I begged to stay there which His Grace,
Such love and warmth, found in no other place.

But, gently I floated on Angel's wings,
As harps and bells and voices sings,
Until one day the Rapture rings,
Into the fold His Lamb, He brings.

Sandra Evelyn Thompson

Surfing

His soul stands at the shore
He enters the deep
Not alone, He is prey
As he tests the depth for boundary
Facing distant heaven
You can hear crystal clear interlude calling to you
Challenging daily highs and lows
Misleading vantage point
Generation of youth acquiring tastes for
Fresh air, illuminating light, and massive waterfront face

Mia Michelle Schlinger

God's Love for Me

Jesus is a friend who sticketh closer than a brother,
He has more love for you, than does your dear sweet mother.
He showed this love for us one day on calvary.
That is where he died for you and me.
We think dear Dad loves us
But Christ loves us so much more.
He proved his love for us, just by the stripes that he bore.
He walks with me on the mountain top
and carries me through the valley
I am so glad to know that I can call him father.
He loves us, oh so much.
You ask me how I know
Just by the scars inside his hands
through which the spikes were drove.

Kathie Estes

Reflections on an Armadillo Crossing a Texas Highway

What is this urge in the armadillo that
He has to see the world
And risk his life in the endeavor?

Did this same urge push man over sea
And mountain and even to the moon?

Are we, then, not born of the same dust,
Propelled by the same drives?

The armadillo eats and drinks and mates —
And perhaps loves — or will
In some distant time when armadillos reach the moon.

Norma Ware

September

Today I saw a hummingbird
He left no sound to be heard.
Beating his wings rapidly,
Searching for nectar with the bumblebee.

I also saw a butterfly,
Gracefully he fluttered by,
A beautiful swallowtail was he,
Landing on the flowers merrily.

The flowers give a beckoning wave.
It's a day like this I want to save.
Coaxing the butterfly's, birds, and bees,
To sip their nectar in the breeze.

September is a month of beauty,
Offering color is its duty.
Contently I observe the display,
To relive the memory on a rainy day.

Kathy Kays

The Problem with Jonathan Swift

In reading verse and prose by Sw— I find,
He loves to slander all of womankind.
He thinks himself so clever as it's sung,
He can enjoy the "....Tulips rais'd from Dung."

Well Dean, I'm sure you'd be surprised to know
I have no stink, no stench, nor moldy toe;
And while my breast's no sixteen feet in height,
I find your works offensive and you might

Begin to see the problem with your rhyme.
You really give no morals to mankind.
For all men find is humor in your verse
That always makes the women look much worse.

A liberated woman I might be,
An unforgiving wench, but I can see
The ugliness of women you create—
Excuses of redemption come too late.

As women we are through with this whole mess,
Your filthy stories and your rude address,
And now that we can teach an English class,
We'll find amusement proving you're the ass.

Kim Koeppen

The Perfect Nerd

There he was, the perfect nerd.
He never spoke a single word.

Humiliation in his head.
Sometimes wishing he were dead.

Often dissed and thrown aside;
An outcast in his social life.

But when he dreamt, he dreamt so dear
Of things he wished that he could hear.

People saying "hi" to him,
Or even saying "good-bye" to him.

He wakes-up lonely as can be.
They think his life is worry free.

Nancy Dupree

"My Papa"

My Papa was funny and kind hearted,
He use to give us candy,
It made him happy,
You could tell by the twinkle in his eye.
One day they told us he had cancer.
It was a long, painful, fight but,
On the morn of January fourteenth,
My Papa left us,
Everyone was sad,
He had took with him a piece of our hearts.
I was very lucky to know my great-grandpa,
Many people do not.
I still miss my papa a lot,
Although it's been many months
Sometimes I talk to him at night.
I'll always remember my papa,
And the happiness he brought.

Kelly McGrew

Valley of the Shadows

He will go with me thru the valley of the shadows.
He will lead me where the gentle waters flow.
He will take me thru the green and velvet pastures.
I can trust him to lead me right, I know.

He will be with me in the good times and the hard times.
He is watching and he knows right where I am.
He'll go with me thru the valley of the shadows
He's my shepherd and I'm his little lamb.

When I am weary I can lay down my head
The Lord and His Angels are there by my bed.
If I something should happen
I never need fear, he will go with me thru the valley
My saviour so dear.

He will go with me thru the valley of the shadows
He is with me every night and everyday.
He leads me by the still and peaceful waters.
I can trust him to lead me all the way.

Marian L. Dunham

The Heart of a Goop/Goof

A GOOP is a man who's in love with a girl;
He won't tell her so, or give her a whirl.
A GOOF is a golfer who has lost his spirit;
Feels crushed and worthless—without merit.

Ferdinand's morbid, brooding, and unfit for life
Can this GOOF ever cure his deplorable slice?
His dearest friend, BARBARA thinks he's a GOOP;
And that this - "Flub Dub" should be put in a Coop.

Ferdinand went to visit a glitzy Hotel Resort;
Here, he found Goofy Golfers of every sort.
He hoped to learn the secret of a truly great Shot;
If he'd stay in his right mind-He'd hit it a lot!

Ferdinand became the Champion of this glitzy Place;
But it was really Barbara- He wanted to face.
Now that all the problems have been worked out,
Let's see what this love affair is all about.

Here's good o'le Ferdinand - Down on his knees;
Saying, "I love you Barbara - Marry ma please."
The reason I am asking - I'm no longer a GOOF;
Barbara's reply, "I'll do it" You've given me Proof!

C. Jay McWilliams

What Is A Man

A man is a creature made by God.
He works very hard, he tills the sod.
A good man is someone to love and hold
To honor and cherish as you both grow old.

He is someone to talk and listen to
His wants and needs are important to you
He makes life rich and always worth living
He is honest, loving and very giving.

A good man is special, hard to find
Another of his virtues, he is very kind.
Tall and handsome, witty and warm
All who know him succumb to his charm.

I prayed to God to send me this man,
I have found him now and will do all I can
To make him happy as we go through life
I hope someday I will be his wife.

Laretta F. Gibbs

Eye Of The Storm

Gaze through my eyes, look past the rain
Hear with my ears these cries of pain
Feel with my hands the ravaged child
Hold with my heart a world gone wild

Be strong although your spirits torn
Find comfort in a new world born
My blood was shed so that you live
Eternal life to you I'll give

So bear the cross, extend it high
Look to the Heavens, past the sky
The clouds will part, the storm will end
These times of chaos I shall mend

Be strong my child, keep faith in me
Rewarded efforts you shall see
Walk through this world a soldier bold
Know in my palms your soul I hold

For like a thief I shall appear
To wipe out hatred, lust and fear
I shall not give what you can't bear
Search deep your heart and I'll be there

Marilyn Yohe

The Waif

The little waif, head bowed in shame
Heart broken for she had no name
Abandoned, for perfect, she was not
Left on a doorstep, to be forgot
With raven curls, and blue-green eyes
A kind of sadness, to alert the wise
The years showed in her face
Searching, hoping for a home, a place
The crowd passed by, never taking notice
The little waif, drinking the cherry soda
For hours she sat, clutching a worn bear
Now it was dark and she was scared
With no home and no warm bed
Newspaper she used, to cover her head
Never once complaining, not making a sound
Limply her body, slumped to the ground
As the night grew cold, icicles formed
The waif would be found, dead in the morn
In Potters field, a grave, a mound
For a home, finally, the waif had found

Judith Ann Buchanan

Final Moment

I was dreading this final moment. Where times stands still and my heart sounds in my ears.

I wonder what are you thinking and why your eyes turn away when I speak.

It seems you cannot look at my emotion. At the volume of misery coming from my speech.

But, then I think, am I miserable because I am without you... or because I do not like to lose.

The moment ends, you walk away. I think we will never pass this way together again.

That seems to hurt even more. I want to call after you and say I hope you find happiness and love.

But, I am mute. Powerless, in a war against my own tongue. Maybe that is why we are not together. Our silence was never broken.

We never developed our own language of love. We are both blind, deaf and dumb.

Leslie Perry

What Are Little Boys Made Of?

What are little boys made of?
Hearts - courageous and strong:
They often miss the dinner gong
as with a toy sword and a little red wagon
they go out to slay a fearful dragon.
Boys are imaginative:
With an empty box they'll play for hours.
It's a castle in Mexico or Spain
or a refuge from foes in the lane.
That box has magical powers.
Boys are trusting:
If you are late returning home
from a meeting or other place,
a boy will lift a trusting face
and say, "Mom, I knew you'd come!"
Best of all - boys are loving:
You don't have to plea,
they'll give you a hug for free.
And, boys have the art of
capturing your heart!

Ruth Calkins

Where Did They Go

Friends that are friends forever
Help each other through every endeavor
Where did they go

Mommies and Daddies that cared a lot
Helped their children in a tight spot
Where did they go

Teachers who really wanted to teach
Helped even those out of reach
Where did they go

People that had some respect
That their parents upbringing would reflect
Where did they go

A gentle man to ask you hand
Not for a drink or a one night stand
Where did they go

Where did all the innocence go
Is it there but not to show

People that embraced each other with love
People like the ones I listed above
Where did they go

Magee

Her Smile

She smiled at me, and I smiled back
Her brown eyes twinkled and made me relax
She said Hello softly as she stared at my frame
And reached out her hand to ask my name

I reached out blindly to shake her hand
Lost in her eyes barely able to stand
She was a beauty with hair like fine silk
I could tell by her touch she might be too much

We sat and talked until it was late
What a good time in fact it was great
We danced and drank and parted that night
I left wondering why it felt so right

Months went by before I saw her again
It picked right up where it had began
Now we are friends and talk once in a while
I'll always look forward to seeing her smile

Webb McDowell

Mother

She caresses my hand with love,
Her eyes look yonder with patients,
For thy hidden heart deep within, past her soul
and beneath her skin.
God's love is unto thee, forever until eternity,
The Mother the keeper, comforter of thy
weeper. Blessed woman from whom I come,
she gives help to many not just some.
She who lacks evil is to be called upon by
thy name of thy mother, thy keeper and
thy comforter of thy weeper,
For Her love of which caresses my hand,
beats thy number of thy grains of sand.

Michelle McCarthy

The End

The woman lay in her bed,
Her face wrinkled from years of sun.
She said her prayers.
Knowing each could be her last one.

Her husband stayed beside her.
So many years they'd had together.
She didn't want them to end,
Yet she knew that soon Jesus would come and get her.

She'd lived her life
With decency and pride,
But now the pearly gates
Were opening wide

She squeezed the
Old man's hand,
And said, "I love you
Much more than I truly think I can."

He smiled at his wife,
Hoping the end wasn't nigh.
He kissed her lips as
He felt her die.

Sandra D. Sperry

Love

Love wears a golden gown.
Her feathers are soft and delicate.
Her eyes are as blue as the bluest skies,
And twinkle like the stars of night.
Her cheeks are as red as the roses in spring.
Her skin is as fair as the first winter's snow.
Her hair is blond and touched with golden streaks.
It is long and flowing, like the river,
Beside which she stands.
Her words have as much power
As all the strongest men that ever lived.
Her voice rings with a joy heard around the world.
Her heart is the diamond in a land of evil.
Her soul - innocence in a time of danger.
She is the fairest of beauty;
The purest of soul,
The kindest of mind,
The loveliest of heart.
Love is an angel floating overhead.
Nothing can harm her.

Michele McCue

Skeletons

Skeletons in your closet,
Hear the rustle of their bones,
You thought you could forget them,
Then you find yourself alone.

Jackie Johnson

My Mom

She walks her path with elegance, beauty and integrity.
Her head held proudly, her voice, as soft and pure as the quality she bares.
The strength and courage of man, yet the wisdom and essence of woman.
She is a monument among those who know her, and a queen to all who love her.
A gift of life and priceless fortune.
The brace upon our backs, and the crutch beneath our arms.
A life of dedication, devotion and undying love has earned her the title of "Mom".
Our love, her love. Our burden, her joy.
She is the hands that feel our needs.
She is the voice that soothes our hearts.
She is the ears that comfort our cries, and the eyes that absorb their tears.
She's my love, my life, my "Mom".

Thomas J. Fortunato

Untitled

Oh my love is lovelier that the summer air,
Her lips, her eyes, her hair so fair,
Her face, her breast — forget the rest
I am obsessed by her God damned breast.

I really shouldn't think like this
My soul is gonna go amiss.
I know it really isn't right
Should write poetry and pine all night.

But it's all her fault
She belongs in a vault.
With breasts like those
My thoughts transpose
From lollipops and roses
And just rubbing noses
To Lucifer's fire
And voluptuous desire.

There is simply no rest
When one's obsessed by a breast.

Leonard A. Robusto

Third World Hunger

"Could I have just a bite?" she hopefully asked.
Her little brown body shivered.
But the stone-faced woman shook her head.
"There's only enough for the baby."
The nine-year old searched
The filth-strewn street,
For a discarded scrap, or a bug.
"Go out like your sister," the woman said.
"And bring back the money to me."
"Do I have to, Mama?" the wife asked,
Fear in her great, dark eyes.
The woman turned, before she replied.
"You do, if you want to eat."
The ragged child reached the corner,
As the pale-skinned tourist walked by.
"Hello, Mister!" she desperately cried.
"You want to have a good time?"

Leta Mae Poe

Untitled

Claim the body
He's no son of mine,
White tie, Blue tie
Walk on by

Do I know this man?
Do I owe him my riches
A life of quality
His life lacks all power
No mourning, a meaning
I can hear his soul screaming.

Do I owe him my lungs now?
A life of breathing
From the depth of my body
I can't feel what he's feeling
I ignored his life
His existence, his meaning.
The street where he lives dirty sidewalk grave
Homeless inequality his debts are all paid.

Stephanie Leshan

Blind

Hey, drug, can't you see-she's addicted to you
Hey possession, can't you see-there's a leash around your neck?
Hey, replica, can't you see-she turns you mind into hers
You're so blind it makes me sick.

You were attached to her
and I tried to pull you away
but she pushed me away through you
and I found myself in despair.

Hey, malleable, can't you see-your weakness has broken me?
Hey, ruiner, can't you see-there are shattered fragments strewn across the ground?
Hey copycat, can't you see you're carrying on the tradition?
You're so blind it makes me sick.

Jessica Zarkowsky

Morning Gaze

[Beneath her hat of sunflower and straw
(Hidden by a shadow from whence it draws),
A spotting of freckles plays to and fro,
Gently cupped by waves of gold.]

Softly spring flows 'round her body to rare,
And the green thin blades cradle her there;
Arms outstretched under the morning sun,
Her fingers comb the sod wetted by dawn.

As idle Time runs gadding along,
And the redpoll finch pipes his sing,
A wayward trav'ler happens into view—
A cott'ny puff 'gainst a field of royal blue.

Through the skies her eyes give chase,
And slowly a smile envelops her face;
For to follow the figure is to find mellow,
The harsh reality 'neath her sundress yellow.

To her lips a rings of petals she lifts,
The flaccid stem of a dandelion eclipsed;
And like an April's breeze lightly unrolls,
She nods her eyes and softly blows.

John Cacciatore

The Old Tree

All these years I've swayed and swayed,
high in the air while planted in the ground.
I've watched my leaves come and go, my
trunk grows rounder as I get taller,
the birds like to set and live on my limbs.
And in the fall when my leaves go to the ground little
ones rake them up and jump in them all day long.
Now the bigger ones have come
with their machines, they have hurt me,
and now I'm laying on the ground,
it doesn't hurt much, but they are taking
my limbs away, for their flames in their homes.
I've seen it happen to other trees,
but I never thought it would happen to me.

Nathan Wills

'The One That Got Away'

His hair was the color of a bright yellow neon light.
His body was warm on those cold winter nights.

When he opened his mouth his words would flow, they
meant something deep.
When I closed my eyes, he'd come to me in my sleep.

he brought my spirits up, and never put me down.
Every time I'd turn, he'd always be around.

When he would laugh and toss his head back.
It was then I knew why I had found him so attractive

But now that he's gone the memories will fade.
And I always remember as the one that got away.

Melissa Maylath

Pain

He stands silent, with eyes aflame,
his disease inside him without a name.
No cure for the illness that stays locked inside,
He just keeps searching for the eternal high.
The gnawing and eating away at his life,
too late to heal, too late to fight.
The love kept muffled by his agonizing pain,
is gone for the giving, all in vain. No more mourning,
no more tears, the disease can't touch me or bring back the fears.
He tries to be normal and forget the past, but the scars are too deep,
and forever will last. Ignoring his problem seems to be best;
then we can pretend to be happy and blessed. The disease brings the
hatred and pain to the heart. It doesn't kill you, just tears you
apart. His disease is so common, it happens every day;
and he wonders what happened, what went astray?
If he could see the cancer eating away his brain-
the black hole of life would bring back the rain.
He's loved yet hated, he's blind to the pain,
he's proud, full of spirit, his morale does not wain. Goodbye Old Man,
bring in the new- his cancer has overtaken, the Old Man is through.

Karen Ellis

Dreams

At night I dream about him
his life that seems so dim
when he was little
he had a twinkle in his eye
It was the kind that made you want to cry
He was so sweet and cute
he made you want to put your life on mute
But now he wants to ruin other's lives
all of which are in sight
He joined a harsh gang
as we hear the guns go "bang"
And as for his family, he doesn't care
I think that this is really a nightmare.

Nicole Rossman

Dog House Observatory

There exist a dog who yips at balls of light
His eyes turned upward into the night
He tastes the wind the creek
Where turtles sleep extended
A meteor moves across the dazzling sky
The dog's ears stand up his rest upended
He barks and yips and makes a sigh and once more
Sits back down and sticks his nose out of his little wooden door
But the turtles sleep with their arms outreaching
A mystery before and after dogs or men
Before us even if and when
All the seas by a rock are shattered
And all the land is rolled beneath the mantle
They drift with their heads tucked in
Past the shoreless ocean
Beyond the leeward heavens.

Reynard Jay Wellman

The Dream

His eyes show of happiness and of love,
His lips so sensuous he must have been sent from
heaven above.
Now I wish to have his heart,
to have him notice me would be a start.
Can I have him No, not today,
when may I have him, maybe someday.
Today I see him he leaves me with a kiss,
a sweet sensational tingle oh what bliss.
Oh how real it all seemed,
but it was all just a dream.
I hope someday I can meet him,
so my life can really begin.
Life would be so heavenly,
If my dream became a memory.

Marlene M. Fuerst

The King's Sojourner

I travel a road trodden by the King,
His royal highway through a desperate land.
I search for the signs that he's gone on before me,
And my only strength comes from his Almighty hand.
The road is quite narrow, the travelers few.
But we carry the banner of his most holy name.
The journey is long, yet we march onward singing,
As the weary band cries out his glorious fame.
The word of the Lord is most faithful and sure,
He shows the true pathway to all who would go.
His hope is within us and his love is our charter,
For we're strangers and aliens and we're on our way home.
Our vision, our voyage, all lead to his house,
Through valleys and highlands, by faith, not by sight...
For faith isn't faith when you see where you're going,
Yet I'll sing of his mercies and I'll walk in his light.
I'll walk out his promise for I know whom I trust,
Trav'ling mile after mile, by night and by day.
I've never seen heaven, but my home's where my heart is,
For my king is my refuge and he's leading my way.

Marti Fuller

The Problem

There is a problem
A very "BIG" problem
I don't understand the problem
But, there is a problem

The problem is I have a problem
The biggest problem I've had is this problem
Only if I knew what is my problem
Maybe there is an answer to my problem

Sandra Dee

Untitled

He reached out his hand to you one year ago today
His strong arms helped carry you as you went along your way.

And at the end we told you because we wanted you to know
"Daddy we all love you, and it's okay to go."

And I'm sure you turned to look at us as we sadly said goodbye
And wished that you could tell us hey. I've made it — please don't cry.

We know that there's a special place for people like you, Dad
Jesus picked it just for you — it's the best one that he had.

Life is very different now because you are not here
But the memories that we hold of you keep you very near.

Heaven is your home now so we can only pray
That it's everything you'd hoped for and that you want to stay.

Only time can heal the pain of losing a man so dear
Oh Jesus keep him safe with you, keep him ever near.

Sally Balsmann

My Father

I remember my Father, for all that he gave
his wisdom, his humor, these memories I save

I remember my Father, a man of his word
soft spoken at times, but always heard

I remember my Father, capable and strong
with caring and kindness carried along

I remember my Father, in the funniest ways
a tickle of the senses recaptures those days

I remember my Father, respected ... revered
with honest convictions not easily steered

I remember my Father, a handsome "gent"
with Love in his eyes and merriment

I remember my Father, whenever I see
that I've done my best to be all I can be.....

Susan M. Zammikiel

Fortune Favors the Bold

Fortune, it is said, unambiguously favors the bold,
History tells us that this truth was ever so...
Millennia ago Hellenistic merchant-adventurers came,
Tacking ashore across the frothing white sea-foam,
To far-distant Taprobane, seeking spice, laden with gold...
As the ages passed, the ambitions of the bold only grow,
Yet amid all times changes, one thing has ever remained the same,
For to whatever light-years distant alien shore we may roam,
We, no more than Ulysses, can escape Woman's entrancing hold,
The how and why of this we seem fated never to know,
Oh, whether Her attraction be a sputtering candle, or a raging flame,
She is the final word, for away from Her, we can never be home,
Thus it shall ever be across the ages as the Universe does unfold,
Therefore my lady, I boldly ask that upon me your favor you bestow!

Michael P. Byron

Your Name

I love to say your name,
I can say it everyday,
When I say your name it brings
  smiles to my face,
Your name reminds me of beautiful
  spring days
I love to say your name

Melanie Albaladejo

January

That month of great despair
Holds within her, nothing
And gives with equal, nothingness.
She cradles me inside her cold,
  dark bosom
And depress my soul beyond my
  total endurance.
She has no compassion from start to end
And revel inside her evilness.
She is the wackiest of the 12 siblings
And exist just to be intolerable
Because she enjoys every second of it.
Though she takes pleasure in being the
  first sibling,
Her main love is just to be the cruelest month.

Melvin L. Jones

Mrs. McDermot

Two years tied to a relationship
Hope, pray - silently. Inside womb, it does not grow
Another two years, sit and wait - alone
The womb - empty, frozen, gray
In the white and steel cold box
He says, "Yes, yes you are". Womb now warm with embryo
Child inside child, it kicks, feeds from umbilical cord
Womb expands, it moves, it grows
Two trimesters - fetus, three trimesters - baby
Heart, fingers, toes - life. The journey begins
Baby is cut from mother
child of time
Nine long, miserable months
Womb is cold again, ready for life
Baby cries
Mrs. McDermot dies
child of time -
survives.

Tobi Perl

Moonbathing

A visit from a muse while drinking in my hot tub
  Hot and thrusting
    Liquid surges
  Wet and throbbing
    Ancient urges

  Submerge my body in the pool
  Bare my breasts to breeze cool

  Timeless ritual of delight
  Gaze into the star pricked night

  Pagan nymph
    Drenched with desire
  Volcanic passion
    Blood on fire

  Inhibitions burn away
  Erotic fantasies come play

  Lick the last of Irish cream
    Solitude
    Lost in dream

Valerie Davison

"Unanswerable Plight"

Shameful surroundings of the unwanted night,
I whisper to God, if what I'm doing is alright!
I wait for an answer, but there's no reply.
I guess He's on a trip, who's tending the sky?

Mike Keas

Abusive Relationship

I thought I loved you,
how could that be?
When all you ever do is hurt me.

I sometimes wish that you
would never care,
It's always just temporary like
mist in the air.

I try to hate you, I really do try,
Those flowers you send me they always do die.

But who really cares, you
send me more,
Then we're make believe happy
just as before.

Sommer L. Berg

Confused About Love

If confused, can you live your life to the fullest?
How do you know if commitment is the key to happiness?
They say you cant buy love and love is happiness.
Well how are you to be happy if you cant purchase love
Anywhere and you cant find it anywhere either?
Is love an obsession or a feeling of warmth?
Is love a desire or just something to keep you occupied?
They say there's somebody for everybody,
Then how come those people seem to be lovely and lost
Since love is essential, why is it that you can't buy it?
If love is so wonderful, why cant everyone experience
It to the fullest?
Feelings are like a maze, you don't know which
Direction you're going toward or which direction
You'll end up in.

LaTrina Nowden

Pain

How I really love the rain;
How I cannot feel the pain;

Of others who don't seem to see;
All of the hurt inside of me;

On sunny days when I can go outside;
I just seem to want to hide;

When others tease or laugh at me;
I feel like a bird living in the sea;

Or like a fish in the middle of the sky;
I just want to lie down and cry;

I feel like something from outer - space;
All mixed up and out of place.

Shannon Spry

Our Old House

How many children have played in your halls?
How many children have bawled and squalled?

How many people have laughed and cried? Born
And died? How many people in a century and a half?

A castle of comfort, a shelter and retreat, a
Feeling of contentment. A sense of relief.

Built by carpenters of old and masons with pride.
A creation of art. A home with a heart.

Still proud standing by restoration of
Encounter all those like us whose now the owner.

By replacement and repair we have left this house
A majestic wonder. A strength of resolve to be eternal.

Jimmie G. Daniel

The Savee

Rummaging through the river of dread
How I want to reach out
Am I the only one who can see it
Is all else blind
I see it, there it is
The cliffs of doom over the fall of death
Forever flowing toward it
Nothing can help me now
No screams for mercy
No cries for help are heard now
The edge is here
I flow over it like a limp fragment
Then as all is given up from out of no where
A soft branch of amnesty glides out
All in a gentle breeze
It stops my fall suddenly, mystically
What luck for its sturdiness
All of this and not even a thank you
From my unspoken lips.

Terina Clark

The Storm

My heart was beating in my chest.
How I wished that I could rest.
The storm would soon be thundering near.
I trembled as lightning appeared.

I rapped tightly 'round me my heavy cloak.
Waves violently shook the boat.
Pouring water washed on deck.
Hail hit the back of my neck.

The captain shouted to the crew,
"Secure the ship!" as the wind blew.
I wondered then if I would die
Or make it to America alive.

Finally the sky began to clear,
And a sweetness filled the air.
The sun slowly began to rise.
The dream of freedom had survived!

Katie Hosack

Untitled

I used to want to die but that fads passed by
how I'm just a plain 15 years old girl
living in this fast lane world
While looking in my school boards text
it says simply don't dare teach them of sex
but I've learned the hard way
without any one to sway, my curiosities of today.
And now I think back and wonder
how this gave me such a dreadful summer
how could one little rope
ruin my destined fate
I remember all sexual dreams
that did not come close to my frantic screams
on that night I lain so quiet
no one knew the feeling in which I felt
my head felt like a jumbled riot and I just wanted some help.
To tell the truth is right of course
but who would believe I tried to fight him off
So I'll keep this in my heart and hopefully someday start.
to forget the darkness that will forever be a part of me.

Maria Wormack

Baying at the Moon

The hounds are baying at the opal moon again,
Howling a primal aria of anguish and despair.
Piercing wails weaving an eerie, restless chorus
That crescendos, then vanishes, into the ebony sky.
They beckon others to join their somber verses
Of dust-covered hopes and stolen dreams of days gone by.

Their weary bodies outstretched, like desperate hands,
Basking in the silvery slivers of mystic moonlight.
As the oblivious lay their emptied heads down
And float with light hearts along the sea of slumber,
I cannot let myself drift off with false comfort
For I have woeful ballads that have remained unsung.

Like the hounds, I do not know a gentle night's sleep
Though I have lived illusions of content and peace
During a mad tempest hurled from another's bane.
Harvesting strength, I climb the steep grassy altar
Where the hounds sit with fiery eyes, revealing their souls
To those kindred hearts who understand their lyrics.

Head high-I bayed with them, a soprano melody
That seized the moon's ear, even if for a moment.

Pamella A. Cunningham

My Soul

The room is bright, my eyes adjust, he's there the man with no name.
His eyes meet mine, deeply searching, the eyes so gentle and tame.
Darkness has come, I climb the wall, but his eyes have touched my soul.
Take a deep breath, and concentrate, erase his image... let go.
The moon is full, I walk alone, it's peaceful all are in bed.
The stars glisten, as I gaze up, his voice echoes in my head.
If only, I could touch a star, to caress it in my hand...
The secrets, of his universe, would unfold like grains of sand.
I lay down in the crisp, cool snow, far, from the eye of the storm.
The snowflakes fall onto my face, my body now feels so warm.
The snow is swirling around me, hear my heartbeat in my chest.
Tiny angels, fall from heaven, his name whispered on their breath.
The night is still, I'll try to sleep, the shadows dance from the fire.
My spirit sparks, like the embers, my body burns with desire.
A new day dawns, we meet once more, his eyes meet mine. I must go.
I turn away, afraid he'll see, this man, has stolen my soul.

Terri Schwalbe

Scene While Walking with a Student to the Nurse

Four birds bent to drink dirty water in a swallow concrete ridge.
Heads and seeking beaks were parallel to concrete - awkward -
thirsting to be quenched from the parched drought we were enmeshed in.
As the child and I walked by, the thirsting birds did not turn to fly.
"Look I whispered", slowing down our pace - hands locked, fingers
entwined - we stood in place - our presence there ignored.
Thirst had delayed their caution - but we stood silent anyway -
humbled by their thirst, awed by their instinct for survival.
Then, satisfied, thirst quenched, the four birds swung aloft:
their wings a whrump - whrump of sound - arched wings spread wide -
feet tucked - we watched them glide, and tilt, and circle overhead.
Then they were shadows on the hot-heat sky - and, in too brief a time
they all were out of sight.
In silence we walked to the place they'd stopped to drink:
looked down, as one, and saw a shallow pencil-line of moisture
being swallowed by the sun.
We walked on in silence - for our thoughts were one.
A child and I had shared unwritten knowledge - universal awareness
of a "need." We had had a temporary glimpse of all life-forms unity.

Kathleen Elliott-Gilroy

The Raging Moment

How blind the passion of a lost night
How strong the rage of a wandering light
Where is the brink of your insanity
Where is the path of reckless vanity
Do not despair to every waking moment
Do not lose sight of this aching torment
It will come to haunt the soulless eyes
It will come to whisper forgotten lies
Listen for the hope that cries out
Listen for the lone, the rising doubt
Oh it may signal a silence too late
Oh it may ring forth a protest to fate
Did the end begin the circle here
Did time wrestle truth to fear
Pray the agony outlast the day
Pray those now lost fight the way
Who sought the blood upon your hand
Who stifled the scream of a soundless land
If only vision came before sight
If only morality could overcome might

Sherry Robson

Night Sounds

High upon my rooftop
sitting quietly,

I hear the sounds of nighttime
echo softly through the trees.

Crickets play in unison a haunting
melody,

Din and patter of the traffic
plays night rhapsody.

In the distance, I can hear a
haunting whistle blow

And overhead yet far away an
airplane lulls my soul.

I cannot help but feel that
all these sounds combined

Join the sound of heartbeats
to play night symphony entwined.

Barbara A. Opyt

A Stocker's Day

I rush through the door to the clock,
punch in to be ready to stock,
head back to Receiving for a gun,
then to my back stock I so run!

While rushed through the aisles I pass,
I quickly look around, letting gas.
Then off to my aisle — Number Three —
That's where Mike expects me to be.

I hurriedly move my behind —
Customer Service waits on the line.
I take the call with a SMILE,
then someone jerks me to another aisle!

No matter how hard I work myself,
there will always be unfaced shelf.
So I just bee-bop along the way,
too SOON comes the end of the day.

Stanley Aurthor Marquette

The Rule Book

MAN, everywhere, has a perception of a Power greater than himself, and
he calls this Power, GOD, or ALLAH, or other diverse names.
MAN makes rules for this God as to how he should rule the universe,
and then makes rules for his own conduct. He calls the first the
Bible and the second the law.
MAN accepts the notion of a Deity that created the black man, the
white man, the brown man. The Rule Book says all must love one
another despite physical differences, religious creeds, or
language variances.
MAN then proceeds to kill those who are different. If he does not kill
them with weapons, he does it more slowly and cruelly through
neglect and indifference.
He lets them starve or be killed by maniacal leaders within
their own domain.
MAN wonders at times if he will be punished by God for such
indifference. Then, this thought leads to a troublesome doubt
about the omnipotence of God, and he becomes frightened by such
inner thoughts.
MAN — a thinking animal — may wonder at times if God may have his own
Rule Book.

Lyle K. Williams

Missing

Our loved one, our little child.
One of God's own, meek and mild.
Loved and cherished for all their days.
Known and nurtured of all their ways.

Considered missing, now their gone
No matter where their at, they're alone
Maybe they're hurt or maybe they're sad.
Because they miss their mom and Dad.

Missing a terrible word to hear.
So many times in just one year,
Babies, teens and small children too.
Missing, making everyone blue.

Missing but sometimes found.
Not hurt weary and glad to be around,
People who love and care so much,
Moms, dads and kin whose heart they touch.

Eula Howard

My First and Only Love

He loved me,
He left me,
He treated me like dirt.
It was all talk right till the end.
I fell for his lies, like putty in his hands.
It meant nothing to him, nothing at all.
A mere four letter word that changed my life.
Can we still be friends? Yea only in my dreams.
Now he's out there scouting the town for some new girl to make putty
again.
He will tell her he cares, but in reality he never will.
He is gone now and that is a fact, one I will have to face.
It hurts to look truth in the eyes, but it's something I will have to
do.
I would hold on forever but the rope is already frayed, I need to
start over from the end.
He's already found his new string and he's climbing higher still.
Maybe he will slip and fall back on me but I will tie the not to stop
him.
He will fall in love someday and my name will be an old memory if that.
But in my heart I will hold his name forever.
As my first and only love.

Maggy McKinlay

One More...

One little promise never fulfilled,
One white lie was told,
One more day in solitude
No one there to hold

One more chance to say "I love you"
One more chance to press your sweat lips to mine,
One more chance is all I ask for,
One more chance for you to be mine

One more look into your eyes,
One more smile that's meant for me,
One more time to hold you in my arms,
One more chance is all I need.

One more time to say you're mine,
One more time to have your heart,
One more time to hold you close,
One more time for a new start.

One little promise was never fulfilled,
then one white lie was told,
now there's too many days in solitude,
and you're not there for me to hold.

Heather Winstead

One Man's... Another Man's...

On a cool summer night, only the crickets can be heard.
Everything seems peaceful in the world, but somewhere countries are
at war, and somewhere there is some one being killed.
It's funny how one man's silence can be another man's noise

A country tries to stay neutral, and claims that it is.
Yet, it sells arms to one of the fighting countries.
It is strange how one man's peace is another man's war.

Athletes all over the world trying to break records set by someone else.
They want to swim faster, jump higher, and score more points than
their predecessor.
It's funny how one man's victory is another man's defeat.

People without money wishing they had it, thinking they would be happy.
People with money wishing they could just be happy.
It is strange how one man's wealth is another man's poverty.

There are many different religions in the world and all trust their belief.
There are a lot of atheists in the world and all believe in evolution.
It's funny how one man's heaven is another man's hell.

Timothy Eric Thompson

One In A Million

I'm only one face in the massive crowd,
only one heart screaming out loud.
Everyone loves me, so that's what they say,
everyone loves me, just not today.
My heart is bleeding but I can't make it stop,
the pain is so great, but I think they forgot.
Love is so very dear to me,
they want me to do right, but why can't they see?
I try and I try but to no avail,
nothing works and I feel like I've failed.
I wish they could remember just for one day,
the pain that they felt on a cold dreary day.
The pain goes through you like the wind does the trees.
and you're left there crying 'til you no longer see.
One little face in the massive crowd,
drenched with tears and screaming out loud.

Jeannelle M. Launey

"The Memory of Love to Continue"

The big red rose shines through the clear blood drop from my heart,
A passion so deep as the petal that guides you through a dream of love.
The eyes full of light and trust
His love wonders through my soul,
The trees blow like my hair against his face,
A memory kept so fulfilled.
The flowers bloom as I walk down the path.
The time fades on and we are so close as friends.
The memory is kept like an album full of smiles and tears,
But the heart is left with one question,
Does love really conquer all?

Merry O'Brien

Mystery

Ancient church buzzing with conversations when
12 young musicians file in and applause replaces talking.
The Concertmaster sounds 440 hertz and the tuning begins.
Why do I smile in anticipation?

A determined stride echoes down the side aisle revealing
the very young Conductor who turns and bows.
Lifting his baton to the musicians, his intensity
flows from the podium around them
and draws the audience to attention.

Suddenly the baton springs into action
(like a cat impaling a mouse) and the Andante is engaged!

At this point I am fascinated by
the energy, precision and control of the "kid"
with the baton for certainly he understands the
genius of the score and draws from the players
their own understanding in a seamless piece of work.

(Why is it that I,
with so little understanding,
find my eyes
filled with tears?)

A. Ross Cash

Love Is A Gemstone

Today I found a prize in the rough
A beautiful thought - love is a Gemstone.
It's up to me to cut and polish this stone
And in my heart give it a good home.
Yes, Love Is A Gemstone.

The first step is to cut and smooth the top,
That's for my dear loving mate.
And around it each cut is for our family and friends,
They're very dear - ace high they all rate.
Yes, Love Is A Gemstone.

Next comes all the facets that are underneath,
They each involve my character reflections.
Each one will take time and careful thought
And much polishing, and some corrections.
Yes, Love Is A Gemstone.

There's humility, respect, laughter, congeniality -
To work on each everyday is my aim;
Tenderness, tolerance, cooperation, compassion,
And all the rest, oh, - it's a lifetime game!
Yes, Love Is A Gemstone.

Katie M. Jessen

What Is Not to See

A horse's mane, as it flies as he runs.
A bird in song, flying in the sun.
A field of sunflowers bobbing in the wind,
An owl in the night, as he takes flight.
As I sit by my window looking out.
All this and more when you are
blind and sight no more,
What is, Not to see?

Margaret E. Woodard

Untitled

All the world has never yet seen
A bond more durable, lasting, or free;
A love that surpasses all other ties
A joy that exceeds all other highs;
Comfort and affection in endless supply
Trust and loyalty that no one can deny;
Caring emotions running free and wild
In this the bond of mother and child.

Susan Armstrong

The Shining Star

The wise men came from the orient.
A brilliant star was overhead and
They would seek the Savior where
The star would come to rest.

They wondered how their gold and jewels
Would adorn the new-born king but what
An awesome sight to see they found
The King of Kings!!!

The star soon rested near his head
And what a wondrous sight...
'Twas better than their gold or jewels
And had a far more brilliant light.

They bowed down and adored the child
And brought him gold and myrrh
But their gifts were paled by the
Brilliant light of the precious
Shining star.

Librada C. Baldazo

River Of Life

A tributary to the Ocean of Death, none can stop its flow -
A captain unable to navigate his ship,
Tossed upon the currents,
Encounters unspeakable miseries,
But he cannot avoid them and time is his enemy,
For he spends so much battling these adversities,
He has none left to spend on gainful pursuits.
He still marvels at the wondrous things that could be his -
If only he could navigate his ship within reach of them.

Another captain, a seasoned navigator,
Travels down this river encountering miseries.
He quickly steers his ship away,
While all the treasures he comes upon are collected
In the ship's hold and are his to keep.

When finally the River of Life
Empties into the Ocean of Death
Which of these navigators will be you?

A. Fitzwater

Somewhere

Somewhere,
A child cries,
And an old person looks through solemn eyes.
But, this world still carries on
Somewhere,
A child is born,
And another loved one passes on.
Still time passes on.
Somewhere,
Loved has turned to hate,
And someone's hate has caused pain.
Still life goes on.
Somewhere else,
There is a place where people care.
Someone to love a crying child.
Someone to make the elderly smile
Everyone to love a new born
And death would be no more
Somewhere else,
It exists only in my dreams

Karen Shupe

Things I Remember

A picnic beside a babbling brook
A cozy fire and a mystery book
Noise, dogs toys and faded blue jeans
swinging jazz and blues from New Orleans
Chocolate ice cream on a lazy
summer afternoon
Halloween night with visions of pumpkins,
goblins and a witch on a broom

Cold wintry nights with snow all around
Squirrels are scrambling to find
food on the ground.
Boys acting silly and wanting to carry our books
But we stuck out our tongues and gave them awful looks
Slumber parties, girl scout meetings and hours on the telephone
Trying to fix dinner, finish homework
Before our parents came home
These are some of the things that I miss.

Marva J. Caston

The Ballad of a Song and Dance Man

A little laughter and the day begins;
A dance to the music of the breeze
Rustling leaves in Tulip trees
Brings shortened breath,
Sweet delicious pain.

A song without words,
To speed the hours of the day,
Is sung in the turmoil of my mind.

Who makes the breezes stir?
Who plays music on the leaves?
Who causes pain that doesn't hurt?
Who sings the song I alone can hear?

Am I a fool who hastens through the hours
To some dreamed of destination
I seem to recognize
With joy
In tiny bits of laughter
And little children's voices?

Peter G. Connell

In Memory of My Mother

A Mom is a friend like no other to be found. And there's a day you will face when she isn't around. My day came on January 18, 1992, a day when I felt like my life was through.

I held you in my arms before you had died, trying to say my last good-byes. I kept thinking you would pull through, for your were so strong, but it turned out to be, I was wrong. I wish for once I could've been right, and you would have continued to fight. But you were too tired and had to move on, so God stepped in and took my mom. He took you to a place which is more beautiful to see. A place where you can look down on me.

So take my hand and be my guide. Stay right near me, by my side. Help me out when things get bad, make me smile when I'm feeling sad. Wipe the tears that fall from my eyes, but understand why I need to cry. For so many hearts have been broken, so many words left unspoken.
I miss you mom, I love you too.
Someday I will be back with you.

Lisa Cross

Reflections of a Young Black Woman

Inspired by a vision, a vision to succeed,
A desire to move on, a desire to fulfill a need.

We look back on the past with sadness and understanding,
A time of great struggle moved to a new beginning.

We look at the present with a bit of dismay,
For all the efforts of the past have been wasted away.

We look forward to the future with hope and new direction,
A deep respect for our heritage steeped in tradition.

Found, within the hearts of survivors, but not deep in their minds,
The young, our future, have found this treasure hard to find.

The struggle has continued, the fight rages on,
The struggle for equality, against racism, not yet done.

The spirit of this fight is found within all,
Within all who reach for better, all who hear the call.

The struggle cast all fear and doubt aside
Success is our goal, met only with black pride.

Sabrina Gates

Cigarette Butts

A single cigarette butt falls to the gray pavement TAP.
A few are laid against an ashen tray TAP TAP TAP.
People
tapping away -
TAP TAP TAP TAP TAP TAP TAP TAP TAP TAP TAP
Until a trail is left.
Some people do not care.
"Do Do lee Da Da da Deeeeeeee!" They sing.
Happy and Gleeful,
Until,
They,
Like the cigarettes
fall
to
the pavement.

Michelle Garrett

Beauty

Mounded golden pumpkins!
Gentle cricket melodies!
Cool winds stir multicolored foliage.
A distance thrush call echoes.
Pensiveness lulls restless hearts.

Regina Veale

Rhymed Poetry Interior

Well I been down a long time, I need
A good joint to ease my mind
Please come by a give me one and I'll
Be your best friend till the end.
Don't listen to the law they just
Want to call you a sissy straight
cut square.
Please don't rat on me are I'll cut your
Finger off to prove you love me.
Just think before you talk because it's
No one's personal actual charge.
If I go down I'll surely find you my dear man
women are smarter then to turn me
in are they know they can't sleep
with me if they did that ever again.
so please keep a low profile so the law
Don't do a follow up and see you with me.

Patrick Prue

Reflections

I have a Lord who's promised me,
A good life here on earth and into eternity.
He's taught me many ways to be confident, faithful,
and sincere in everything I do.

With willingness, I try real hard
to accomplish each and every task.

He helps me to be thoughtful and caring-
toward my fellow man;

To listen and to understand.

There's hardly anything I tend to pursue
that I haven't had his helping hand,
To be sensitive to his command.
My creativeness and talents
He's given to me to explore.

It's exciting to enter through each and every door
That's opened up for us to share;
He's our foundation and example of loving care.

His steadfast guidance, day by day has helped me to find -

The patience and the art of coping
With the many problems faced by all mankind.

Phyllis M. Bonney

Hero

From the moment you were born
a hero lied in you.
If someone was in danger
you'd know just what to do.

I have no fear of the world today
so I just let things be
because I know always that my
hero would rescue me.

I won't take advantage, but I'll ask
for a little help
only when I've tried to do it
all by myself.

If I can't accomplish what I did begin
I know my hero would help me from within.

So whenever you're in danger
just look down below
and you will see you're one
and only HERO

Monisha Mann

Canadian Mountain Majesty

The whispering wind, a babbling brook
A hummingbird at the Columbine
Waterfalls, forests and peaks upon which to look
All of this and more is yours to find

The lure of a trail to a hidden mountain lake
An elk ahead slipping through the fen
The scents, the sounds, the sight of nature the soul to sate
This you will see and feel, bring within your ken

Smell the cedar and the pine, see the meadow, its wandering stream
A rustling martin a whistling marmot, a screaming eagle to behold
Snow on the mountaintop, sky blue, scudding clouds as if
in a dream
With each stroll you take, this and more will surely unfold

Descending like a mist, a sense of well-being
The mind drifts, worries fade from another time
God's creations so uplifting, doubts, cares, problems sent fleeing
Serenity, peace, solitude set in as you unwind

The grandeur of the peaks, stark, lonely, fill you with awe
The views, the vistas, the scenery so great
Mind, body and soul meld in harmony to this wondrous call
The majesty of these mountains no longer can wait

Philip C. Furber

Alone Pine Canyon

A basaltic dike guards my canyon
A hundred faces peer from the wall
I drink my coffee and think of you

Is it you that I want
Or what you represent?
The stone faces do not answer

The wind whistles at one end of my canyon
It takes some time before it reaches me
Strange, to hear wind long before you feel it

The flies are buzzing
They smelled the water when I made my coffee
The wind clears them away, but not those thoughts of you

It's beautiful here
Not peaceful, but wild and dynamic
I love it here, but something — someone is missing.

Clear my thoughts pine canyon
You're different than the one in my dreams
You're real.

Norma Susan Heidger

Grandpa's Boy

Chubby cheeks, stubby fingers
A "jack-o-lantern" smile
A "too many cookies" tummy-
And a "grandpa" hair cut...
Where is my "little man"
who seemingly only yesterday
wore these winsome traits?
Where is the short little person sitting on my knee
patting my face and telling me stories?
He has all too quickly
gone from this
to a grown and wonderful young man
But wait, what's that I see?
That little twinkle in his eye returns
"What are you up to now?"

Wendy Marie Brandenburg

Untitled

Snookie wookie wanted cookie
Cookie wanted snookie wookie
Snookie wookie get cookie
Now snookie wookie's gone.

Michelle N. Wiksen

"My Eyes"

I wish I had green eyes
A light emerald green,
Not grass green or sea green
or anything that comes between
Just a light emerald green
With thick, black lashes
that touch the lens of my glasses
Every time I blink, "the guys" hearts would sink
I know I shouldn't pout just because they didn't ask me out
Oh, here comes Jemel. Will he say, "Hi," or just pass me by?
Did you know you have pretty eyes?
Is he serious? Can this be?
You have pretty eyes. Talk to you later.
He talked to me.
Yipee! But now I have to start over
I love my beautiful brown eyes
They're dark, not too dark to be black
Just dark brown with thick black lashes
That look like I'm wearing false ones
They almost touch the lens of my glasses...

Shamica D. Belo

The Boy I Knew

The boy I knew had big blue eyes;
A little boy who brings tears to my eyes.

The boy I knew had wavy blond hair;
A Little boy who liked so much to share.

A boy who liked to play with his friends at school;
A smart little boy who liked his teacher too.

A shy little boy, like a puppy, as cute as could be;
A boy who was only three.

The little boy who was so shy;
Was a little boy I used to kiss good-bye.

A little boy I loved so much;
Would sit on my lap and hug-a-bunch.

That little boy is resting right now;
He's an angel in heaven, whispering no sound.

Susan M. Andre'

Memories

Memories are made of this,
A little tots arms reaching
out for a hug and kiss.
A husbands love, a wife's embrace,
A little tiny boy's broken shoe lace.
A glimpse of Mama baking bread,
A little bitty girl all snuggled in bed.
A christmas tree, a Birthday cake,
Last years vacation down by the lake.
So many things over the years,
Some brought laughter some brought tears.
A daddy holding his little boy's hand,
The shiny gold of a wedding band.
An old couple strolling down the lane,
Both bent over with age and pain.
They stop midway and exchange a kiss,
Ah yes, memories are all made of this.

Thelma Jeffers

"Do You See Me?"

Look into my eyes, what do you see?
A look of longing, an everlasting plea.
I look for an answer, but nobody's there.
Are you even listening, do you really care?
I sit and gaze at ceilings, and windows all around.
I can see the sky, the earth, things growing from the ground.
I do not know the colors, or understand the smells.
I see you walk the hallway, and I hope you come my way.
Just hold my hand, and speak kind words.
Tell me what you see.
Rain drops that fall, the color of the sun.
Birds in the trees and the music they sing.
Remember, I'm still in here.
Do you see me?

Jean Hamilton

Mystery

A glass sky, a pillow moon
  A majestic earthly hue.
The beauty enhanced by light and eye
  In earth's panoramic flume.

The sun subsides in western skies,
  Its golden rays echo upon the clouds,
And beauty dies as darkness comes.

Darkness, the nothingness of mankind
  The void, the stillness, the blindness, the lack of loveliness.

God created man and the universe,
  Who created darkness? Who created space?
Who created nothing?

Robert E. Brown

Vicious Stars

Deep in the black of her eyes she kept
A man with squinty eyes.
Glancing at her with his hands in his pockets,
He's got her right where she stays.

In her eyes you can see her life walking by.

She makes excuses for wings on her feet;
Feathers litter the floor.
Sparkles, and angels, and shapes in the clouds,
She won't need them anymore.

In her eyes you can see her kiss them goodbye.

Walls rush to meet her, red all around;
Her skin paints the colors of night.
Squinty eyes gleaming with humor and power—
Two vicious stars in her sky.

In her eyes you can see her wish them away.

In her eyes
You can see her life
Running by . . .

Bye . . .
Bye . . . . . . bye.

Katherine Elizabeth Cameron

The Horse And I

The horse
Gallops across the fields,
When the sun rises,
Over the sparkling fields of wheat,
Carrying me back home.

Kelley C. Walker

A Gift for My Father

Gently washing the wood curves
- a man's face -
I caress the memories.

The eyes stare at me;
it is only a pipe,
but it had been yours -
a gift for my father.
I chose it with care...

But you left it behind,
along with 16 years of discarded furniture,
gifts, hopes, dreams and love...
and the face I washed held no tears:
but mine did, Daddy;
mine did.

Trisha Barry

Rain

As I walk outside amongst the rain
A mixture of my thoughts and pain
I try to drown out all my sorrow
And search for ways to make it a better tomorrow
I'm a little confused about these things I feel
I hope that soon, I can get through this ordeal
This feeling of frustrations completely new
I'm trying to figure out what I feel for you
The comforting rain beats down against my face
And as I try to look beyond this place,
I find that, my answer, I am not going to see
Now, I wonder, what's a matter with me?
I am no better off then before
I just can't seem to reach the core
I search for a reason and start to complain
As I walk outside amongst the rain.

Jennifer Hunt

Morning Glory

This morning I watched a flower -
  A morning glory.
The flower was so beautiful
  It opens with the dawn.
Such a beautiful time -
Such a beautiful flower.
  When the light gets too strong -
For the pretty little flower
  It closes up.
Like a chastised child.
  When the world gets too much
For me to take. I want to be this flower.
  To close up
And come out new and beautiful
  Like the dawn it welcomes.
This morning I watched a flower -
  A morning glory.
New and beautiful - just like the dawn.

Rachel King

A Child

A child is part of our body and soul.
A child is someone we point toward a goal.
A child always seeks attention and love.
A child is a gift from One, up above.
A child will not always do as he's (she's) told.
He wants his own way and acts plenty bold.
He'll argue and fight and get us upset
And then act so sweet, it's us who will fret.
A child we'll promise to guide life through.
A child, what's a child? It's what we were too.

Virginia A. McHugh

A Place I Call My Own

There is a place I know,
a place I call my own.

Other places are full of voice,
the tapping of feet,and other strange noises.

But my place is peaceful,
and truly divine.
With only the sounds of nature behind.

No one can enter this place of mine,
the place that is peaceful and truly divine.

In my place there is no violence,
not noisy and not plain silence.

And now I have told you of
this place of mine. You might ask me,
"where is this place that is truly divine?"

But you will never see,
because it is only in my dreams.

Kristen Kuebli

The Coffee Beanery Cafe!

A coffee house, a quaint spot to be,
A place to speed rest, a place to hear rhymes.

To be the offender, not the off sender,
Picking poems to fit all, can be no small task.

A poet is the only one, that can pick and find his way.
The listener is for listening, for phrases bent anew.

With no copy, nor creating a stir,
At some later date words heard here,
Will someday return.

I being sober and somewhat confined,
Try only to commentate a line.
Only to be given a chance, to soar to my peak.

I fear if I stumble or stammer,
That they not point me toward the gate.

On stage faced by unbiased strangers, that is all I see.
Confidence, courage is my reward,
And I love the stares that quiz my soul.

I am finished, I am done, none have come,
some have learned, my words have been documented.
They rest in their veins, none have fallen barren away!

Walter Tomalis

Dream

I see you, passing in the night
A place where my dreams take slight

With you, I am for a short span
in time only to wake to
find you're not really mine

Even though I return each and every night,
to be by your side in the dreams bright light.

The fun we have
The closeness we shares
Always makes me glad, to know you'll always be there,

And, for you I feel,
A love so real,
So the passing of time you are only mine

And someday soon you'll see that we
will share a moment of Reality!

Rosanna Stookey

"Face of a Mirror"

Look at me, I'm over here and exact,
a point of reference and natural fact.

Believe me, I have no misconceptions to guess or assume,
no fear of reprisal from which I'm immune.

You may smash or splinter me, but I'll still reflect reality.

I answer questions of personal vanity, or can lead your mind into insanity.
Whatever I see, I swallow rapidly and clean,
no matter what the color of rhyme or scheme.

I have no opinions, unmoved by love or dislike,
innocence or guilt, I see both alike.

When people look too deeply into me, they may not like what they see,
because I return to them themselves,
the eye of self inspection that reflects depth and detail.

I am not a rational respecter of persons,
or a logical escape for diversion.

Most of the time I meditate on the opposite wall,
reviewing spots, speckles, pits and falls.

Yes from where I stand the world is much clearer,
Because it cannot lie in the face of a mirror.

J. Symlar

Seeking Freedom

High above the eagle soars on delicate wings of steel
A pure and total freedom which man will never feel
Sweeping wings upon the wind his rhythm ebbs and flows
As eeriness of his plaintive song breaks the quite days repose
A fierce and mighty hunter the noble eagle reigns
A symphony of natures movements, a master of his domains
Slowly drifting from mountain peaks to fertile valleys far below
Where ribboned rivers twist and dance and fragrant forest grow
A creature of simplicity, wings the eagle bold and proud
Soaring to apex of infinity amidst a magical silver cloud
Curiously seeking new horizons where warm virgin breezes blow
Soars the eagle in total freedom, which man will never know

Paulette Verroca

Love Is

Love is sometimes like
a rose it blooms so beautiful.
And some loves dies so fast.
But true love endures to the end.
Love beginnings is like a raging storm with
passion. A kiss on a summer night.
Soft rain. Two hearts beating
as one. A tender touch, looking into
each other's eyes and touching their
soul. Feeling what the other feels.
Pain, love, joy. Love is a caring
feeling unselfish and giving.
Sometimes you have to give something
up for the one you love.
Love is saying you are sorry
when you are wrong. Even when the
one you love passes on. You can
still feel that love and keep the
memory alive every time you see a
rose in bloom or hear the soft rain.

Lois Burch

A Cry For Her Heart

She led a wonderful life, for seven kids to care,
A smile she held so fair.
Everyday to her was called bright,
She shared with everyone her light.

Later she had grandchildren and lived alone,
No husband to care for, children grown.
Still active with everyone and everything,
Her life has just begun; her heart to sing,

Then a windy, sunny day, traveling to see her family her way.
It was but the last few hours till her end-
She didn't know; our hearts couldn't mend.

Sundown now, glowing with light,
Back home she traveled into the night.
But now her life taken by a car- she has floated oh so far.

The next week our tears flowed.
Why must she leave and go?
We don't believe life is fair, it is too much for all of us to bear.

Days and days have gone by- our tears have gone, but still a cry.
A cry for her smile, a cry for her heart.
Why must He have to end it and break us apart?

Nicole M. O'Donnell

Behold His Glory

Behold His glory....
A still small voice, like that of a child,
A gentle whisper, a toothless smile,
Sunrise bursting across the sky,
The glimmer of joy in a loved ones eye.

The patter of rain on an old tin roof,
The laughter of mother with kids underfoot.
The silence of snow that covers the earth,
The cry of a new born just after birth.

The scent of a rose, the velvet of violets,
Cottonwoods speaking in voices most quiet.
The Lord's very presence is revealed everywhere.
We're made more like Him by beholding Him there.

Lord, open my eyes. Make us pure, make us holy.
Lord, open our hearts. May we
Behold Your Glory....

Susan Gaston

A Single Tear

As the pages of life turned
A tear appeared, marking the lessons learned...
A single tear of sadness and despair.

Each page left the writer desolate.

This "Book of Life" has not been published
Instead it has only been forgotten.

A book of one's life from beginning to end.

One of dreams abandoned,
Hopes turned to a misty haze

Oh, how sad it was to read from this "Book of Life."
The pages unfolded a dream never to be reality,
With only a single tear to honor the author.

I know, for I was the writer...
The solitary tear belonged to me,
But I am on more and my life has been forgotten!

Lori Sheppard

Hand By Hand By Sta. Drew Sta.

A thousand years them a steal from we
A thousand years in a captivity

All we wanted was peace and harmony
but they put us in a slavery.
We are not content with the world today
"We want more fu we family."

A thousand years of slavery my
grand parents paid the price already.
So let we feel the freedom
Just let us be free
All we ever wanted was peace and harmony.

A thousand years them a steal from we
A thousand years in a captivity

We should come together walk hand by hand
Learn to trust your brothers, teach them right from wrong.
Hand by hand together.
Together we grow strong.

A thousand years them a steal from we.
A thousand years in a captivity.

A. Hercules

A Time for Life

A time to live, a time to die.
A time to sing, a time to cry.
A time of sorrow, a time to pain.
A time to heal, a time to live again.
A time of joy, a time of happiness.
A time of peace, a time of gladness.
A time of faith, a time of pureness.
A time of love, and a time for goodness.
A time to be free and fly like a bird, to
live to the fullest in this crazy world.
Where you are going its
either heaven or hell
and one is not very funny.

Katrina Bailey

Andrew's Dream

In a cemetery in Eastern Kentucky
A two-year old took leaves from a tree
and pushed them to the mouth of the little lamb.
Is this what Jesus meant when he said,
"Feed my lambs?"
Of course not.
This was a stone lamb, on a child's headstone.
It never lived.
But in the mind of two-year-old perhaps it would.
If he could get it to eat these leaves.

Jeannette Carr

The Passing Years

Life passes by so fast, Lord, I know I'm sure to miss
A vital part, unless you keep reminding me of this.
There's so much that I want to do; a lot I've left undone;
So many plans discarded and a few I've not begun.

Life passes by so fast, Lord, how often I've been told;
It's faster yet around the time that we are growing old.
Teach me to lean upon your arm when pain and sickness strike;
To tell the facts from fantasies that sometimes look alike.

Life passes by so fast, Lord, the days, the months, the years.
Lord, keep a smile upon my lips and blot away the tears.
So let the days grow shorter; the darkest shadows part
And please put wrinkles on my face, but never on my heart

Mary E. Means

If Ever

If ever you need a helping hand,
A warming heart, in seashore's cold sand,
You can honestly know I'll be there.
You can honestly know I do care
If your heart takes a crumbling fall,
You can count on me, I'll catch it all.
If ever your dreams come to a desperate end,
I'll be there to make them start again.
When your sitting in a corner
all lonely with fear,
And you need someone to be near,
Just call on the phone and you will see
I'll lend you a shoulder,
you can cry on me.
Now in your heart, you know it's true,
I am a friend
And will never abandon you!

Tina Laczny

Inspiration

Fronds of lilies, aspens white
A weeping wind, vibrant sunlight
All too soon, yet far away
See many times before the day
To wish, to dream, to hope, to feel
The sands of time, an eternal seal
The words of love I find so dear
My soul desires, shed no tear
Wilting grasses, fading green
Quite a wonder to be seen
Mind and body meld as one
Curses gone, no evil done
Meditation, gravitate
Feel our earth, do not hate
Embrace the sands before they've washed
Away to sea, before they're lost
Lay in grasses calm and cool
Trees that sway as nature's tool
Forgive our sins, though we've done wrong
And may all sing a universal song.

Lorien Reid

The Gift

The greatest gift
a woman could receive
has been given to me.
An understanding, gentle man,
who has instilled in me such confidence
I have never had.
I feel whole,
he loves me
for what I really am.
He has given me the right
to be the person I want to be.
He gives so much of himself and
yet asks so little in return.
I love him.
To whomever it be
gave this love to me,
thank you for allowing me
to touch the life of one
so beautiful.

L. Christine Evan

Time To Move On

I've seen enough to let me know
About this phase of life
And now with wisdom gained from experience
It's time to move on

So much to see and learn
So many people to meet
Lives to touch, hands to hold
Hugs to be given, smiles to be shared
It's time to move on

We pass through many doors in life
Each one holds a story
An experience to be shared
A purpose, a challenge

Knowledge to be gained
And turned into wisdom

Sometimes we become stuck
Trapped in a situation
And wither away
Instead of realizing
It's time to move on

Toni Henkel

Control Z

Playing with fate
Adding, deleting files... Whoa - control Z!!!
Look at what it does. Screen goes crazy.
Flirting with fate. Delete too much you'll
Be ruined - add too much life's too
Complex. Gotta find the balance
Ups - downs; use the Mouse

How 'bout the keyboard.
Don't like either - voice
Activated "Computer...."
Maybe not now - maybe soon -
Maybe not - maybe - maybe -
Maybe sounds too much like
Mayday - mayday - mayday -
Going down -
Need assistance

Maybe maybe I'm Moron -
Need assistance.

Watch those function keys.
Control Z - it'll getcha
Every time. D - for delete.

Randall O'Neill

Sail Boat

A sail boat
Adrift, adrift, adrift...on the bay
Rising, falling with each gentle swell
Adrift, adrift, adrift...abandoned on the bay
No sails to set, no tiller to man, no anchor to deploy
Adrift, adrift, adrift...crippled on the bay
At the mercy of the wind, waves, current, and tide
Adrift, adrift, adrift...controlled by the bay
The wind shifts and gusts, waves rise, temperature falls
Adrift, adrift, adrift...swept away by the bay
No safe harbor to be reached
Adrift, adrift, adrift...abandoned by the bay
Dashed upon the rocks on the leeward shore
Floundering, floundering, floundering...upon the rocks
Broken, battered, wrecked in violent solitude
Never...to sail...again...

Richard K. Lloyd

"The Kisses of an Angel"

To my father who knows that death is near to come and is afraid and in pain because of his unfaithful wife:

"As she is as cold as ice with you, you are calling for love, you are begging for a kiss. You called all your daughters and you want to see them all together around you very soon. I am sure that they all want to be with you and fulfill your wish!

I am the one who is far away from you. However, Father, I am telling you that I share your pain because I have great love for you. I am sending you all the kisses that you wish and I will be there the day you want all your daughters around you.

I pray for you and I will tell you a secret: Do not fear Father and have faith, courage and hope, because I was told that an Angel will soon come to you and that she will take away all your fears and pain; I was told that she will help and comfort you better that nobody around you, better that I would like to (and God knows how much I love you!),

Because she will give you the 'Kisses of an Angel!'"

Nicole Mefret

Faith

Here I go again down that lonely path
afraid to feel the true beat of my heart
afraid just to stop and scream and breath
afraid to say, hey....God!, can this be real

Here I go again down that rugged road
He knows that I am praying with my heart and soul
He knows that at times like these, it's a cancer
He knows that at times like these, he's the only answer

Here I go again down that twisting lane
showing in all forms that I am in pain
showing in all forms that I can't go on
saying to him, hey... God!, must I moan and groan?

Here I go again up that familiar hill
Yes! He rescued me again, and it's a thrill
He carried me again, and it's a relief
He has tested that faith of mine again
But!!, he knows no one can take away my belief

Patricia A. Hosten

'Twas God

What makes the buds come on the trees
After a cold and winter freeze
What makes a crocus bloom in snow
I have the answer—yes, I know—'twas God!
What makes a salmon swim up stream
To satisfy a fisherman's dream!
What makes a bird, with all its grace.
Come back to nest in the same old place—'twas God!
What makes a cloud fill up and burst
When nature feels its need of thirst,
What makes a plant from a tiny seed,
Grow into a giant redwood tree—'twas God!
What makes the day and warm sunlight
The moon and stars that shine at night
What makes the mammals in the giant seas
And all the animals plus you —and me—'twas God!
Who or what made these things and —all—mankind
'Twas made by one —with a brilliant mind!
All life is from this earthly Sod
Who gave this love, no doubt—'twas God!

Lauretta Dandy

Untitled

I can't believe we're together like this
after all the hopes I went through,
all the wishings and wantings and wonderings I felt.
All the dreams that I dreamt about you.

Now that we're together
in the way I've wanted so long
my body tells me it should always be
my mind tells me it won't be long,

Before time comes along and steals you away
to places that I'll never go
to feelings and dealings that won't bring to mind
the way we felt so long ago.

So when time sends Spring to your door again,
when new life and growth have begun,
remember me as the seedling.
I'll remember you as the sun.

Valerie Gould

Rotation

Beautiful babies, lively children, and concerned adults;
all go through constant change.

Innate patterns that parents stamp on their
offspring are nearly impossible to wipe out.

Everyone goes through its life cycle in spite of
the eternal quest for a fountain of youth.

This constant repetition that can be counted on,
is so very wonderful to observe.

We can count ourselves as lucky, truly
lucky to be able to look around and
see this constancy surrounding us.

Rita P. Kriesberg

Daughter Mine

How quickly you have grown, my dear
All gone the days when you were small
How quickly time has flown, my love
Summer, winter, spring and fall

If we could just return, my child
To days you sat upon my knee
Oh, how my heart yearns, my darling
Your beguiling smile again to see

But you are now a wife, dear one
No longer mine to cuddle tight
You have a brand new life, daughter
Love him, but keep me in your sight

It may not always show, dear girl
The love I hold so deep within
But you know it is always there, beloved
Will always be - has always been

Lila Wiegert

Just As You And I

A Frightened flower caught within
a raging storm bent down its head
It drooped in anguish and
I thought surely morning would find it dead
but when the sun came out in the early morning
it raised its head,
its petals half torn with pain.
and wouldn't you know,
its fragrance was so much sweeter from the rain.

Roberta Stroup

AIDS

It's spreading quickly
all over the land,
It's being passed
from woman to man
AIDS isn't just going to go away
just like that.
It creeps in slowly and
crawls around like a cat
You can be careful, but you can't be sure
Because if you catch it
You know there's no cure
learn all you can about AIDS
From a text
so you will know to practice
safe sex

Tiffani Alston

Twilight of the Gods

The day is upon us
all that is seen and unseen
comes together in glamorous thought
just as the Shaman promised
the clouds and the Gods debate
the acts which our inner evil caused
to bring ourselves to this fateful night
and as the ground breaks open
to reveal Hades
in all its empty splendor
we are thrown into purgatory
and Ragnarok begins

Michael Magdaleno

Thoughtfall

Gracefully, thoughts fall upon the desolate road,
All ties to habitation are released.
Essentials endure the pavement of heat.
Dispensable unwillingly tiptoe.

Desired attention granted to some.
Solefully done, the task proves difficult.
Savor the yellows, oranges, and reds.
Brittle brown will soon triumph.

Religiously, meet with them; gather as many.
Consume in them, bathe in them soothing anticipation.
Some disintegrate. Others clinging to rejuvenate.

Suddenly, all of them panic-whirling out of control.
I seek for the origin only to find a glimpse of
your distant eyes
In the rearview mirror.

Pam Stevens

Power

Billions of galaxies
All with millions of suns, moons and planets
hurdling through space
dashing farther and farther out into nothingness
unfurling like a carpet
into the endless emptiness

Here on earth
men seek prestige,
They yearn for wealth,
They pursue possessions,
They vie for position
Often trading their souls for power
Power over what?
A grain of dust.

Virginia Englehart

Sonnet 38

By all the saints this poetess would swear
Allegiance to your love and would decree
To all the earth and heaven's skies declare
A joy and hope that all the world would see
My soul ablaze with longing for your love
Creates a phrase inspired by heaven's hand
The song, the gift, the will of Him above
May grant to us a glimpse of what is planned
An instrumentalist to some degree
The song you play embedding in my soul
With melodies that grasp so easily
So simply fuel my heart with tender coal
The violin, the trumpet - ev'ry part
Sings out the melody within the heart.

Rebecca Benedict

"Penny"

It happened at the dark of night.
Along came head lights that shined so bright.
Who would have known about our little tike.
All she wanted was to take a ride on her bike.
There was no time, not any,
Now there Lyes our Penny.
It was a sight I couldn't believe.
I yelled for my husband Steve.
There she lie under the Wheel.
Just across from the old Mill.
The man looked like a punk.
As it turns out he was only drunk.
Just because he had one to many
We no longer have our little Penny.
Now that she lay under ground.
I see that man still out and around.
Going in and out of the bar
And he still has the nerve to climb into a car.
I only ask in someway.
To hold my Penny just one more day.

Vicki L. Carney

Altered

Me and my ego
altered walk-together along
the white, burning sand when my:
ego altered questions my altered (being
and I being) me altered wish
death upon my ego unaltered and
Me and my ego
altered walk together along the beach we
laugh aloud though only I (and
as I lose) my altered state as
also my ego we; well we suddenly
become just
me (and) my ego
Laughing We United
Solemnly We Depart.

Kathryn Gracen Cook

Thoughts

Here I sit,
alone with my thoughts.
Sometimes they drive me crazy.

All I want,
is to have you hold me in your arms.

Whisper I love you,
everything will be alright,
if we believe.

God, I love you!

Marlene DeLeon

"I've Got a New Mind but, I've Got the Same Old Broken Heart"

My old heart still aches for you in the middle of the night.
Although my new mind tells me that everything is gonna be alright.
My old mind used to be controlled by my old heart. But, now my new
mind controls that same old broken heart. "I've got a new mind,
but I've got the same old broken heart" if I still had my old mind
I guess I wouldn't know what to do. Because like my old broken heart
My old mind loved you too. They're partners and they thought the
same. But, now my new mind rarely mentions your name. Whatever my
old heart would tell my old mind to do it would do it. There was
no sanity for my old mind; and no need to pursue it. My old mind
had a mind to forget you. But my old broken heart had a
mind to forever love you. "I've got a new mind, but the same old
broken heart" That old mind could no longer live with that old
broken heart. My old broken heart will forever beat for you.
But only if, and when my new mind tells it to. "I've got a new mind
but the same old broken heart"

MaryLee Graham

Our Graduation

Well this is it, this is our day.
Although, there is another that was special to me
it was the day I realized we were related
and a new found friendship began to be.

It feels like only yesterday; we met and we laughed
and there's so much that I wish to say
the hardest part is where to begin to tell you
knowing you're my cousin, I wouldn't have it any other way

In a semester period of time, we shared some great moments
and all the kindness you addressed towards me
is greatly appreciated, just one problem lies
if I only knew how to begin to "thank" thee.

I pray that you get the best out of life
I hope that all your life - long goals are achieved
Always remember there's nothing in this world
you can't overcome if you'll always believe

I wanted to give you something special,
Something that will never lack Communication
it's a gift that I wrote just for you
a way of saying "Hat's off" to our Graduation!

Kathy K. Padilla

A Lost Soul

On that stormy night when my wife gave up the fight and she died
I became so lonely. I began to fight I know longer could see the light.
All my Sunday learning was not in sight

So I began to drink and I sat on that bar stool
Until I could drink no more.

And I fell to the bar room floor and as I lay there on the floor,
My mind began to score, and I dreamed I was on a hell bound train

And the devil was at the wheel. People were crying and screaming why
And the devil said you made your choice and now you die.

All I could think was why! Why! Why!
I was so scared I awoke in fright
And little by little I saw some light.

And then I saw I was in hell and earned my place in this cell.

And on bended knees I cried! You mothers hear
My pleas. Teach your sons well don't let them go
To hell and spend there lives in a cell.

A lost soul I'm dreamed to be, because the devil owns my soul.
And I'll spend my life here in hell.
I have no hope. I have a cell.

By Jerry Holly, an inmate here in hell. A lost soul in a cell.

Holly

The Painted Lady

Pretty, painted lady;
Always at your post
Making a living for your baby.
But at what cost?

I watch you everyday
As I go to and fro.
I watch them, with a smirk, pay
For your services and show.

You always have a painted smile,
But inside is it a frown?
I'd never know until I walked your mile,
My pretty, little clown.

Pretty, painted lady;
Always searching for more.
Live for your baby,
But never hear them call you "whore."

Shannon Schultz

Thoughts

I think a lot about the blessings God brings, those thoughts always cause me to sing. A wonderful hymn, just praising your name.

God gave me an angel so long ago, with a heart full of thanks and love I watched him grow. I called him Stephen, he's a gift of your hands, now he has grown into a wonderful man.

When angels grow up we must let them fly, that's what mine did way up to the sky. Now he serves his country in a far away land, this angel of mine, this wonderful man.

You sent him to me on this earth below, to teach him about the things he aught to know. I tried very hard to do a good job, some times praying through my sobs.

He was such a good angel all his growing up years, until one day the world touched him and brought all the tears.

You were there in the beginning, you're here for me now, that's why I keep asking Lord why? And Lord how? You know what I ask, and your answer will come, if only I have the patience to wait with a song.

Susan Paula Watkins

The Journey

I've traveled near and I've traveled far
Always in pursuit of my shining star
The months had passed as did the year's
And with them grew my doubt's and fears
Then came the day when my weathered
  bones could no longer roam
That I set out on my journey home
  As I approached the home of which
  I was born
Tears ran from this face so old and worn
I looked up to the sky's so close not far
And there I found my shining star

Sabino M. DeCrescenzo

JFK

He stands tall
America's dreams soaring on his every heartbeat
higher and higher they reach
Anything is possible
suddenly, they are falling
they hit the ground
shattering
Leaving only pieces of broken dreams
unable to be fitted together
And an empty place
that never again can be
completely filled.

K. Stelmach

Always Remember

They stared painfully into the enemy's eyes, while we waited.
Always Remember.
They climbed mountains with loads too heavy to bear, while we waited.
Always Remember.
They lived in conditions no man would ever live in, while we waited.
Always Remember.
They crossed the seas and bombed the land, while we waited.
Always Remember.
The lost their lives, lives given for us, while we waited.
Always Remember.
Now. As we watch their graves, we think it's over.
Always Remember.

Molly Katharine Martin

Sarah

I want only to keep her.
Always to smell her sweet skin
to stroke her soft hair
to glorify in her smile.
No talk of butterflies that are released
with the futile hope of their return.
I want to close her in my fist
until her wings are crushed.
To keep her from the journey
she's preparing for.
Each day she readies herself more
to travel bright paths
or dark tunnels.
And I will open my hand and watch
because I love her.
My daughter

Maria G. Norris

"Who Am I?"

Who am I?
Am I a lonely, confused girl?
Or am I a smart, boisterous girl?
Do I try too hard to impress others?

Who am I?
Am I the loudmouth, boy-crazy Lynda?
Or am I the shy, quiet, intelligent Lynda?
Am I the actress or the poet?

How does one answer these questions?
Do I think before I answer them?
Or do I give the first answer I think of?
How can I find out who I am?

How can I tell I'll be there for him?
Do I just give him hints?
Do I say it in a letter?
Or do I wait until we meet again?
Who am I?

Lynda Durante, age 13

Love

The path of life that God lays out
is a confusing road there is no doubt,
but God is fair, loving and kind
with the loss of one life another you find.
Losing a loved one causes much pain,
but with a new life, happiness you gain.
Pain and joy come together as one
The love resulting shines with the sun.

Kate Lanigan

Upon the White Rose

Upon the White Rose one does lie,
a time to live a time to die,
for I must live my life you see,
for no one dies this life but me.

Leon E. Miller

Wanting

To be ever wanting...
amid a feast of delights
only to be consumed again and again by an unending hunger
and once more left on the mind's desert...
a barren land of no temperance.
to be ever hung from invisible strings...
puppets performing acts
compelled by some covetous force
to want ... and think of need.

YES...
but what other playing would you have
what better measure could you find
to know...feel...suck...lust...one life.

Michael Justin Ippolito

Loneliness

How many lonely people are there,
Amidst the crowd of many?
Having everything we could possibly want,
Still....
we are lonely.
We love
and are loved
Yet that emptiness still prevails.
Who cares that we are here
among the millions?
And yet there are so many who care
As a tear of loneliness
slides
down
my
cheek
I think of the one I love and loves me.
At last I can return to this reality
and go on....

Pamela McClellan

Youth

A drifting island of innocence
amidst the swirling tumult of reality.
A haven from the sea of sinners.
The burning envy of the wise.

Precious golden nectar
possessed by the cursed flower of life.
Tempting the remorseful souls
of waning generations.

Shadows of the moment
creeping towards definition.
Drawn by the eternal tides of fate.
Flirting with the shores of the future.

A humble fortress of bliss
sheltered in the depths of ignorance and love.
Radiant with the light of joy.
Obscured by the ebony shroud of age.

A sacred time never appreciated...
until too late.

Kathleen M. Canal

Feel

I'm trying to live my life
Among the beings of my own kind
Everything suspended in time
God only knows what's on my mind

Here I am here I stand
The spotlight shines 'cause it's in demand
The time I spent in your padded cell
Wasn't worth what you put me through this living hell

It took a thousand days
A thousand lives a thousand ways
The nature of the beast
I gotta take time to rest in peace

I took a walk with me
I say 'Hi' to all I meet
They shake their heads and sigh
I walk on as I roll my eyes

There I go again and again
Time passing by and by my friend
I could never show you just a-what is real
You decided in your mind just how to feel

Todd Hippie Terrebonne

She Is...

She is
an angel from paradise,
an old soul who has experienced many things,
in her journey through eternity,
now residing in the body
of a beautiful, vivacious woman.

A woman with the wisdom of the ages
in her mystical, almond-shaped vibrant eyes.
A woman with an elegant well-defined nose
and sensuous full lips.

Truly, a masterful work of art
by the creator of all things,
who is love, joy, light, sound and is-ness,
the nameless power of the universe.
Her body is the temple of the "all-in-all,"
which shines within her,
divinity manifesting itself in human form.

Therefore, she is...love.
She can be nothing else,
but her true essence.

Philip Ingrasciotta

Guarding Angel

At night when my eyes are closed in sleep,
An angel of mercy watches over me.

To protect and keep me safe until the light of morning breaks.

And then when I rise out of Bed;
I want to always remember with bowed head,
To say thank you Lord in keeping me safe;
That you let no harm come near my bed
You let me on a soft pillow rest my head.

And then you let me open my eyes.
I looked around and then did realize
That the sun through my window had just begun to shine.

It made me leave my worries behind;
Got new strength for the day
To do the things that might come my way.

Polly Boy

The Dawning

I find it hard, choking
An emotion sucked away by a nighttime of denial
Quelling excitement encased by nerves and fear
While blocked by my new friend
The friend who took your place long ago
Before the mechanisms of reality set forth
Their evil plots of progress
Seeing far into the future,
A soul cried against the slipping sands of time
And was silenced by the self-defense of human ways
For now, backed by hardened metal,
I coldly turn away
The faucets have been tightened
And the ever-going activity numbs all thought
Until that day when dawning slowly comes
And the hurt of unspoken words can no longer be denied

Tracy Karas

He Walks By

A stillness is in the air
an expectancy, a feeling, he will arrive soon
this, you know, though no one has told you.
all because he will soon walk by.

He walks by and I forgot
What I was saying,
What I was doing,
Where I was going,
All because he walked by.

You feel his presence across a room
a glance, all yours, though others are around.
a wanting, a longing, a need!
All because he walks by.

Take my hand and hold it.
Age and time have no meaning,
just this warm trembly glow inside
Take my hand and keep it, as you walk by

Patsy R. Humphries

Washington, D.C.

At the Washington Monument,
An intellectual kid to his older brother,
"If brains were dynamite,
You couldn't blow your nose!"
Kites flying, greasy hamburgers,
High taxes!
And a street person,
"Can you spare some change?"
I just fed the pigeons!
Saw one pigeon and two squirrels
On the way to the Vietnam Memorial.
An old black man,
"Please help me get a hot dog!
I need twenty cents!"
I gave him a quarter!

Johnny Rogers, Jr.

November Day

The brilliant skies have turned to gray,
and Autumn leaves are swept away.
Fond memories linger in my mind
of trusting friends, who were so kind.
The chilling winds have promised snow,
to flock the trees from tip to toe.
A Blue Jay calls from a nearby tree,
I believe inside, he calls to me.
I thank you God in every way,
for a beautiful gray November Day.

Maxine L. Sproull

A Remembrance

As a definite sun shines upon a colorfast rainbow
An old man sitting by the waterside has grown tired
The wise one with the never ending formality
Shall retain his just significance
And a glorious existence has just been acquired
The good fellow remembers his days past
Then smiles at the sunshine as if a brief moment gone by
The essence of life has advanced ever so fast
And so, the end draws to its final conclusion
While a teardrop falls from the sky
Life clings to a flower, - birds praise by the hour
And an old man salutes his ultimate goodbye...

Robert Lee Elliott II

Prosperity Of Man

Spotted sky across a domain
An unostentatious remain soars the spirit within thee
A dormant heart creates an initiative for an
Unbridled flight. The midnight solidarity partakes
In the relentless meeting of an impartial deed
A new meaning, a desperate soul rides the wings
Of dimension far from what reality can touch
A touch of death from waxed wings leaves
The mind with nothing but the touch of death from touching
The prosperity of man.

Khrystina Mayhew

Total Recall

If there's new growth on a brown, old tree
And a rosebush, dry, becomes new green
And heart-shaped leaves from potatoes grow
And after a shower a rainbow is seen,
Then let us recall, there's a God to guide us
And He gave His Son to prove His Word.
So, if our loved one's no longer beside us,
Keep in mind ..... the new green leaves .....
The scent of the rose ..... and the rainbow you see .....
And the promise He made to you and to me.
Just say to yourself that God is good;
He shows us in Spring, clear as anyone could
That the rose is reborn and the tree is, too.
If the heart-shaped leaves begin to renew
And the rainbow is there with His promise, true,
Then isn't it clear to all who can see?
The Lord's making plans for you and for me.

Marian Bruce

Dear Mama

I finally understand after nineteen years;
And after I've cried over a million tears,
That you must have suffered a lot of pain
  and strife;
So that is why you ended your life-
  And I often wonder why;
You left me all alone in this cruel
  world to survive?
And you don't even know that you left my
  heart broken;
Many things I've wanted to say to you
  are now left unspoken,
So after all these years;
It's time to dry my tears,
And I must go with my life;
Now I can finally say goodbye.

P. J. McGahan

"Betty Joe"

I went down to the border just across in old Mexico,
And all I could think of was that sweet girl name "Betty Joe,"
Then I traveled back to Austin,
On my way to San Paid Roe,
All I could think of was that sweet girl name "Betty Joe".

I thought I would visit some of the night spots in old Mexico,
Every time I went in a night spot, all I could think of,
Was that sweet girl name "Betty Joe,"
Yes, I like those night spots in old Mexico.

But theirs never been a girl that touch me so,
Like that sweet, sweet girl name "Betty Joe",
I love them both "Betty Joe" and old Mexico.

Lem Poteete, Jr.

Imaginary Trip

Classic Chevrolet Coupe, running boards
and all, was parked in our backyard.

Safe as could be for our imaginary trip.
The battery was removed and put indoors.

Planning a trip to the apple orchard, my
brother and I, tossed a basket into the car.

Off we went imitating sounds of the engine
and rotating the steering wheel many turns.

Screeching the brakes and coming to a stop,
it was AW Root Beer time.

Moving on we reached the orchard, it was
really our neighbors yard.

Filling our basket with many apples,
thanking our neighbor again and again.

Beginning our trip back home, already
wishing for Apple pie.

Pat Bordner

Till Death Do Us Part

Nights like these when all is dark and silent,
and anything would turn to ashes in my arms
are when I get lost in nights long gone,
when I was so high I thought your face
was the sun and we kissed once half way
over the bridge and I know, no one's
gonna stop the car to dance slow with me again.

Rebecca Waldhart

Change

When autumn leaves replace the summer's gay,
And blossoms sleep beneath the frozen ground,
You're sweet soft voice did pass my way
To bring me nothing but joy in each sound.
But time has defaced our love's silent plea,
The windmills of my mind are cursing far.
For in every web no spider lets free,
The tangled fly which only leaves a scar.
Time has passed and our lives have nothing seen,
But endless walks, the lonesome memory.
Who can survive in a world full of dreams,
Even with hopeful joys we just might see.
In all remember the sweet love displaced,
For the love we proclaimed cannot be replaced.

Michelle Mrkva

INEEDAHUG

When hours are slow
And days are long
And nights seem never-ending —

That's when my heart is missing you — Ineedahug.

When thoughts of you
Fill all my hours
And duties come between us —

That's when my arms are missing you — Ineedahug.

When day is gone
And evening comes
And moon and stars are glowing —
That's when my heart is loving you — Ineedakiss.
INEEDAKISS

Marjorie M. Miller

Dedicated Kindness

At the edge of the lake in the dawn
and dusk of everyday the white haired
man feeds the ducks and geese as they fly
in and out and go on their way.

He loves these birds and their funny
ways and knows if he feeds them faithfully
then they will stay.

He's standing in the midst of them,
throwing out bread and corn.
The water on the lake sometimes so calm,
reflecting the Man and his birds, peacefully,
together, as if they are harmoniously one.

The birds are eating and quacking and
getting frisky and running around, and they
know and believe that this white haired man
will never do them any harm.

The man knows, through his
kind deeds, that throughout the seasons,
the birds will remain, and he will be pleased.

Shirley N. Colbert

Morning

In the magic hour that falls between the waning of the night
And earliest dawn,
We launch canoe upon the waters of the lake.
Still covered snugly with her comforters of misty fog
She sleeps.
Nor does the stir even when her privacy is thus invaded.
We kneel transfigured as in a moist primordial womb;
Our dim visages converse in whispers.
We dip our paddles stealthily, not wishing to awaken,
And drift and listen, waiting to be born into the day.

Much later, so it seems, lake throws her coverlets aside
And stretches 'neath the sun.
We know the time has come for other things.
And as we bring canoe with rapid paddles to the shore,
A heron, standing on one leg among the reeds
Lifts on startled wings
And flies away.

Suzanne Peterson

Wishing

I wish we could live in peace.
I wish we could live without pollution.
I wish the rain forests weren't being destroyed.
I wish I could stop wishing.

Lucy Baier

I Didn't Know Daddies Cried

You were the dream that filled my heart
And even though I tried
I could not keep you with me
I didn't know Daddies cried

You were my inspiration
But with you my courage died
And my little girl looked up at me
And said "I didn't know Daddies cried."

I touched your cheek for the last time
And the tears fell as I sighed
My little girl looked up at me
And said "I didn't know Daddies cried."

Without you days are empty
Like the ocean deep and wide
And my little girl looks up at me
And says "I didn't know Daddies cried"

I face each new tomorrow
With my little girl by my side
With tender looks she says to me
I didn't know Daddies cried.

Margaret V. Herbert

His Life

He wakes and steps from his card board box,
and gives himself a hearty stretch.
A cool breeze whizzes through the air
and sends a chill up his spine.
He zips up his faded blue denim jacket
and watches rain drops stain his dirty old shoes.
Walking down the crowded Boston streets,
his eyes come across a half eaten slice of pizza.
Looking around to see if anyone's looking
he steals the crusty, old pizza
from a herd of starved red ants.
He finishes and says to himself "Time to get to work"
He pulls out an empty Dunkin' Donuts cup from his pocket
and slowly walks over to an empty bench.
He patiently awaits for sorry souls to spare
a few pennies.

Keri Smith

Goodbye

He had been drinking
And he wasn't thinking
He thought he could get home,
Now she is all alone.

His unborn child,
Who's father he will never see,
and his life,
will forever be lonely.

He had a family, a job, and a great life,
Yet he risked it all that horrible night.
He risked it all for one lousy high,
She never had the chance to say Goodbye.

Katy Larsen

Autumn

Nature is playing its tune
and making its art.
The leaves are changing color
and it is the start.
Fall is here and the trees
will soon be dying.
The animals are scattering about
and the forest is crying.

Julie Ernst

Hurt Again

As you lead me on
and held me tight
you remind me of morning dawn.
I thought you were Mr. Right.
You told me you loved me
and wanted me to hold.
I would keep the key and you the locket
we were brighter than gold.
But soon enough you didn't care.
You, looked, but turned around
acting as if I wasn't there.
Knowing your love can't be found.
I asked how long will this last?
You replied with a simple - I'm confused.
I guess all your love is now in the past,
and you took all my love away - leaving me abused.

Y'vonne J. Meyer

Untitled

Friendship is a special word that lingers in the mind
And helps us to remember all the joys within our time
The joys that make meeting special
The joys of a special night
The feelings of warmth and tenderness
And the thought that maybe it's right
To keep life alive between two people
To treasure and to expand
The few hours we have together without even holding hands
But happiness isn't just touching
It's a sharing and being aware of the times that could
be spent together
In a life that isn't always fair
But if you think it is possible
And possibility is in the mind
Then the feelings will grow and be nurtured
Until the days run away with the time.

Judy Jagerman

Woman And Me

The sun rose from the west,
and her brilliance was noticed by him.
The sun was blind,
and she shone her light on an outcast.
She approached slowly
and her warmth enveloped him.
He smiled
and whispered, "Thank you God."
The wind danced,
and subconscious drums played her music.
His mind disconnected,
a pathetic should plucked an inaudible chord.
She was interested,
and let I'm spoke.
He blinked,
the gold had been replaced by platinum
Flesh.
She said "Hi!"
He said... 'woman and me'.|

Miguel Llinas, Jr.

Hate

Hate is the color black
It feels like a knife going into your back
And looks like your worst nightmare.
It smells like a dead corpse
It taste like a bowl of spoiled milk
It sounds like the quit night.

Jennifer Simek

Life's Puzzlement

why is it that people who don't know Christ
And His teachings-don't want to?
If they only knew His teachings
Are their answer to life!

Why won't they try to make sense
of His love for them?
It's all in the New Testament books
of the Bible. Take time to read.

I know what the teachings are-
These sayings of Jesus, the Christ.
Who wants only good for all of us;
If we'd follow His wise advice.

Let me assure you, the answers are there,
and not in wild seeds that are sown;
To find so called happiness and usefulness,
We need to leave wrong things alone!

If you want to find better days;
Read, think, pray in response to Him.
Stop trying the unreal assurances
That you have the answer to life.

S. Ramelle McDonald

When He Asks Me, I Do!

Son of light, I do ignite to dream
and hope brighter thoughts than your rays.
Survive trees of emerald green,
receive the whispered screams of
my lovers dreams.
Grass of plunder, I travel on thee,
to implore my lovers exclamation.
Fairest sky of white and blue,
when he asks me, I do!

Clouds of fluff, reality soon will
be my fondest dreams come true.
Moon of messages, in my darkest
hours, I still hold to the
brightest, noblest light.

Sherrie Anne Rogers

"Shells"

(Dedicated to Bryan for faith and footprints in the sand.)
And I depart again, from the sea of troubles
To anchor myself on the beach of self
A beach which prides itself upon having too many selves
All being unique and collectible and lost.

And I stand watching the waves of uncertainty
Wash away the grains of soul, sweeping
Them away in glittering shards, yet leaving
One lone abalone, the only pearl of personality left

And I stare at the moon - the entire world and wonder
How it will control those crashing waves,
The relentless erosion leading to miles of nothing
As it brings the abalone hurling into the cliffs of doom.

And I know the way the sun, in its intimacy
Will bring another relentless, self-knowledgeable day
Though it won't allow sleep or recuperation, will bring
Another perfect ONE, a new facet of the alternate abalone.

Another life has begun...

Michelle Mandelbaum

Canawlin' Along On The Old C And O

We'd watched all those cruises they show on TV,
And I said, "Why not book a snug cabin for two
On some tropic Love Boat and then blissfully
We'd sail off together into the blue.
But finally we decided that we'd rather go
Just floating along on the old C and O.

Why not try Polynesia? You'd put on a grass skirt
And do one of those hulas that drive me out of my head;
We'd lie on the beach where we'd cuddle and flirt
There under the palms until ready for bed.
But finally we decided that we'd rather go
Just canawlin' along on the old C and O.

We knew the Rive Gauche in our green salad days,
And Brussels and Rome and the Norwegian fjords,
Back when there was time to sit quiet and gaze,
Before the mad rush of the loud tourist hordes.
But now on the barge, I hold you near me,
We watch the sleek mules and admire their sheen,
And I whisper, "Can't imagine more bliss here below
Than canawlin' with you on the old C and O!

John Lacey Brown

I Heard Her Voice As She Called My Name

I heard her voice as she called my name,
And I saw her hand as she beckoned to me.
Then quietly I listened as I heard the words
"I'm the little girl you used to be."
At the words she spoke, the memories returned
Of a laughing, carefree, bubbling girl.
Vaguely I realized that girl had gone,
Existing blindly in a lonely world.
But maybe a part of her had stayed behind
To welcome me when at last I returned.
Maybe she had stayed to pick up the pieces
And listen to what I, the wanderer, had learned.
The little girl kept calling my name,
Ready at last to comfort me.
But try as I might, I could not return
To the little girl I used to be.

Melody Brann

When a Star Dies

I look up at the sky
And I see a star die
It falls out of the sky
And no one even stops to ask why
Stars die just like people everyday
Only in a different way
They both just cease to exist and fade away
They don't seem to be able to stay
For all of our days
New ones come and old ones go
And there is no reason it is just so
And that is why stars must die
Instead of always flying high
And you my friend are my star
And that is why you had to die
And at least now I know why
You had to die
When you could have flown
Oh so high

Tracy Krise

The Brook

The babbling brook is like the blue sky.
It's like a blue eye.
The brook is like a blue ribbon,
It's not at all timid.
It flies like a flock of blue birds.
It doesn't fit words!

Karen Nowicki

This Old World

This old world is filled with crime and hatred
And I want to lend a helping hand
But I've got problems of my own
And no one seems to understand.

If I don't help, tell me who will
There are millions of people on the street,
who haven't had a home cooked meal.

We need to come together and rise up as a whole,
or there will be no one left, able to grow old.

The killing and stealing has got to stop
If we work together, we can come up on top
This old world will be doomed, if nothing is done now
No one is willing to look for the answer,
but everyone wants to know how.
This old world doesn't have many values installed
And like humpty-dumpty, this world will have a great fall.

This old world has become a dangerous place to be
If things are going to change it has to start with you and me.

Patricia Jones

My Lost True Love

He was that one special guy every girl dreamt of
And I was the one lucky girl who his love he shared
He was quiet yet sympathetic, and best of all the only
one who really cared.
The last memory I'll ever have of my true love.
It was cold out, yet deep inside I still felt the
warm tingle throughout my spine as I held his hand firm.
As many people approached the room I knew their hearts were
filled with love, and then to watch our little one squirm.
A silent tear ran down my cheek, a total stranger began
to speak.
A man in black helped to my seat, I tried to look back quick
and often.
The last look I took was painful yet special.
It was then they closed the coffin.

Valerie R. Rael

The Vacant Chair

Across from me sits a vacant chair,
And in memories I can see
Of one whom I loved so much
And meant so much to me.

I can still visualize him sitting there
With his bible in his hands
As he read and studied the word of God,
Of a far away better land.

Oh, the expression of joy, love and peace
That shined upon his face
Helped me to study more about
The great amazing grace.

Now I too have joy, love and peace
With the holy spirit I am filled,
What a day it shall be when we all together again can be
In that great beautiful city on the hill.

Stella M. Coffey

Autumn

I sat in my forest so green and vibrant
and it was sensed that something was displaced
The smell of change brushed my senses
sunlight through the trees fell upon the ground like lace

A chill - the finger of death ran down my spine
the forest chanted in the steady breeze
As I sat in wonder of the coming change
I knew it was an answer that man couldn't see

I felt something graze my hair
it swayed gently to the ground
A leaf - golden with stains of red swirled through it like blood
to death my forest was bound

More and more leaves rocked to the ground
they wove a blanket for the earth
I longed to speak - but was hushed by the wind
and I left my forest to change, awaiting the beauteous birth

Sharon Rolirad

O'er an Empty Cup

I sit here perplexed o'er this aloneness, prevalent
And know not why passing time was so wasteful spent;
When to but lift welcome hand I could reach, touch
Those who gathered close and loved, loved so very much.

And friends who called, near every night
To say hello, to dine, to know we were all right.
Those people passing by my window, who are they?
Some are happy—sad; some too have gone away.

The crippled man, the bearded one, the one who leers
And reflects the hardness of long relentless years.
They all hurry! Why? Do they realize or know
That they rush by friendless, brothers enmeshed in woe.

Why do I not return, why not go to see?
Yes, I must leave now; surely it will be
as it was before, they will be there still.
Hurry! Hurry! They'll be home — I know they will.

But listen, what tiny voice says, "Don't go!"
You cannot, you dare not; for you know
That when you return to capture what is gone
It will be night again, shrouding this flash of dawn.

Richard Floyd Dickens

Power

If massive mountains shook their sides
and laughed,
And spat upon the earth in fiendish glee;
If savage waters sprang from ocean
depths,
And sucked away the land into the sea;

If winds in frenzied rapture tore the
world,
From the end to end and scattered gusty
death,
if crimson streaks of sun-set, lit with
fire,
Were used to heat their devastating
breath;

How then would man in self-defence engage,
And quell the rage of madden'd might
untold?
Think, little man, how mighty you are not,
Think of the force by greater Power,
controll'd.

Kenneth B. Low

Spring Lamb

Sheep are cheap to keep,
And little lambs don't need prams
Or baby toys to play with.
They grow and gambol in the fields
While we make tools to slay with:
Butcher in his carnal store,
Apron striped and boatered,
Proudly sells his legs of lamb
To ladies who have motored in from happy homes
To buy their Sunday dinners,
Which mother cooks while children play,
And dad picks next week's winner.
Oh, what contentment fills the scene
As mother serves each course,
For everyone it's Sunday lunch,
For little lambs................mint sauce!

Michael Lev

Poet's Grave

When we're both dead
And lying side by side
In our little dirt bed
A tuft of grass our only divide
When our skin is shed
And our bones are dried,
Upon the ground above my head
Long after we both have died
I know a little boy will tread,
Hair mussed up and shoes untied
He'll glance at the stone above my head,
In the still countryside
He'll squint at what once read
"Long ago this man died
"He'd a poem in his head,
"He'd a pen at his side
"But now it's cold and he is dead
"But before this man died
"Two words he said,

"I tried."

Trey Gemmell

Oh! Sister

Oh sister, sister I can't help but shake my head.
And Mama would roll over and be dead again
If she could see you now all drained with nothing gained.
I know she's up there with God watching her baby evaporate from the smoke of crack cocaine.
Looking on we feel your shame, see the blame and share your pain.
To help you I offer my advice in hopes of saving your wasted life.
What's up with you sister leaving your kids for the love of drugs and misfit men? Put up your dukes I'm calling you out!
I wanna know what your stuff's all about.
What'd you mean you're tired and weak and all you need is a lifetime retreat? Pick yourself up, pull yourself out!
Straighten up and listen and stop yourself from kissing the pipe!
Get off the hype and the misfit men whose messing up your life.
You're stronger than you think in more ways than one.
Life ain't no practice, it's more than having fun.
Remember who you are a queen.a star. Stop being a has been or wannabe
and pull yourself up by the bootstring! Oh sister!
Clean up your act and get your kids back! Raised them yourself!
Show them their special and you've got something left of yourself!.

Mary Can

Mother Moon

When night in all her splendor stalks the fields
And man and beast beneath her blanket shields,
Like some kind God from famed Olympus' height
Who tends his flocks and rules with tender might,
Then o'er the hills I rove to eulogize
The golden mistress of the midnight skies.
Who, likes a beacon, tinges somber earth
With that same hue which shone at Jesus' birth.
Her face with incandescent glow beholds
The earth in safety wrapped in slumber's folds.
Then, pleased and satisfied that all is well,
For all are resting deep since curfew's knell,
She pulls her cloudy cover o'er her head
And slumbers on till morrow's day is fled.

John Bayer

Rascals in the Reeds

We sneak into the murky mud
and meadow meanders
of the wilderness creek,
—like rascals in the reeds.

What mischief this: Seeking to know the wiley ways
of a wild waterway.

For a wilderness creek is a fierce fabric of cattails,
water lilies, lily pads, reeds and glistening grass.
But more, it is the deviously dim din of life heard of,
but not yet experienced.

We pass as a transient thread, feeling the fabric's freedom.
It is us. — We are it.

Departing, we are transformed by mysterious messages:
Images of wildlife, and
—Life Wild—
instilled by sharp whispers, whittled into our souls.

Our roguish, roving spirit thus made alive,
this earthy place will remain embedded in us,
and we, in it ...

Rascals in the Reeds.

Randall W. Peters

Life in the Fast Lane!

Here I sit tried and condemned,
and my only crime is of loving a man.
He was found guilty and whisked away.
So here I sit all alone day after day.

Domestic life can certainly be a bore.
But, iron bars and prison walls surely lay in store.
when motorcycles, loose women, drugs, and booze,
loom upon the horizon of the life that you choose.

Life in the fast lane is exciting and fun!
Until the jury says "guilty" and your sentence has begun.
How often do those who are guilty of the crime,
think about the sentence lived by the family left behind?

It is true, prison walls and seclusion we do not see.
But after all is said and done, are we really free?
A life of loneliness without a loved one day after day,
in time can be one hell of a price to pay.

So, if life in the fast lane beckons its fun - loving head.
Pause, for a moment, before astray you're led.
Think of your loved ones you're leaving behind,
to serve their own sentence to society for your crime!

Karen M. Cole

Shattered Minds

Yesterday I walked through hell
and my soul was slashed to pieces.
I came upon a hall of mirrors, left with
a hundred reflections of myself to confront,
and my mind was shattered.
The echoes of my screams
break the silvery glass
and my life falls apart -
(just to go along for the ride).
All that's left are
the king's horses and king's men
and as they look around
they wonder where to begin.
As they hear the sobs of hundreds
of others, they look into the thousand
pieces of glass.
And their cries echo as their minds shatter,
and then silence falls - no more victims
to pick up the pieces of life.

Jaime Lambert

Hungering Hearts

Some hearts go hungering thru the world,
And never find the love they seek,
Some lips with pride or scorn are curled.
To hide the pain they may not speak.
The eyes may flash, the mouth may smile-
And yet beneath them all the while,
The hungering heart is pining still.

For them does life's dull desert hold,
No fountain's shade, no gardens fair,
Nor gush of waters, clear and cold,
But sandy reaches wide band bare.
The foot may fail; the soul may faint,
And weigh to earth the weary frame.
Yet still they make no weak complaint,
And speak no word of grief or blame.

O, eager eyes, which gaze afar; O, arms which clasp the empty air,
Not all unmasked your sorrows are; all unpitied your despair.
Smile, patient lips, so proudly dumb-have faith.
Before life's tent is furled; your recompense shall come,
O, hearts that hunger through the world.

Viviane Klein

What Would You Take For Me Papa

What would you take for me, Papa, if somebody wanted to buy,
And offered you bright shining dollars and piled them up,
high as the sky;
The say you are good at a bargain,
Come tell me as true as can be,
If I could be put on the market,
What would you take, what would you take for me.

What would you take, what would you take, Papa,
Tell me what price, I would be;
What would you take, what would you take, Papa,
Now what would you take for me.

Sometime when you say I am naughty, I don't think I ask very much,
But then when I hug and kiss you, you call me your darling and such;
And so I would like to ask you,
to find out my price, don't you see,
If somebody wanted to buy me, what would you take for me.

I don't think Mama would miss me, I'm so much in her way,
Except when she wanted to kiss me, at night,
When we kneel down to pray;
But just say she is willing, come tell me as true as can be,
If I should be put on the market, what would you take for me.

Virgie H. Hayden

Sweet, Gentle Death

I went forward too early, eagerly to meet death —
And once met I cannot draw back.
I let death envelope me like a great black cloak,
Shutting out all sight, all light.
It warmed me and comforted me like nothing before.
Oh gently, now gently I'll go.
So come, sweet, sweet, death
Lead me by the hand,
Cloud out all that surrounds me...
Lest by some chance, I would slip back and wake again.

Linda Pittinger

"Differences"

Differences, each being considers the other weird,
And ones home is right "here", but where is "here"?
Is it "here" to me and there to the other?
Which is which? and who is the stranger?
Is "here" what we call home?
But then again "here" has existed since the age of stone.
So, does "here" ever change?
And move on from stage to stage,
Does it always stay the same?
Or is "here" just another name?
A name for something we know not how to explain.
Differences, why in the would do they exist?
Differences, they have caused so many to hate and detest.
So many in this world have died and suffered,
Only because they differed.
All because each wants to lead,
Not only his, but even others "here."
If only "here" existed everywhere,
It would be much more fair,
But I suppose that only happens in fairy tales.

Nawar W. Shora

Untitled

Love is a rare, once in a life time gift
And only the lucky know who to share it with
Only the lovers know life's lighter side
That our differences are not to hide
Everything in harmony, in perfect sync
Ironed out perfectly, without a kink
Not to rush, the fortunate know
Give it time to bloom, to grow
Of true love, the one to last 'til the end
Is when you're my lover, as well as my friend.

Michele Miller

My Special Christmas Angel

We sing of them in ballads and carols
And place atop our Christmas trees,
But none will e'er be the same to me
As the one I can no longer see.

Hair of gold, eyes wide and true,
Her smile filled with girlish delight.
I'll always remember her hug that night,
"I love you; I'll see everything's all right."

This Christmas, by heaven, she's been kissed:
  somehow I feel she knows—
  how much she's loved
  how sorely she's missed:
  And it'll always be so,
For she's my special Christmas angel above!

Libbyrose D. Clark

Untitled

If I had the strength in me,
and promises I could believe,
If I had never been deceived,
I think I could walk with
My head held high, never be hurt and never cry.
And I wish that I could be that strong
Find some where to finally belong -

But there's been too much pain,
and my soul has many scars.
I've given up on wishing scars.

Inside,
I've grown so numb and cold.

So many secrets have been told.
I think too much of who I am
has already been Sold.

Marie Light

Thoughts

May your thoughts cross mine
And reminisce of past times

Thinking of all the time we've spent together
And how we endured all kinds of weather

The thoughts of us in sunshine and rain
Sometimes in great ecstasy sometimes in pain

When I try to remember some who is a true friend
My thoughts are of you again and again

Thoughts of how our eyes shut out the world
Two people entwined in a maze of a curl

Thoughts of how we loved and shared
To each other our inner soul we bared

Now may your thoughts cross mine and reminisce of past times
Thoughts are precious jewels that crosses space and time

Thoughts are so refreshing and divine
Please let these thoughts last a lifetime

Now may your thoughts cross mine
And reminisce of past times

Shirley Mack

The Long Shadows of Late Day

I see the reckless ivy kisses on the trail
and see them too thrown high upon the wall
to fall in pointly tresses
like the green hair of a Wildwood Princess.
My waffle soles flatten all the kinks in fallen Maple leaves
and make me think of passages,
of time,
the mulchy ripener of life.
Perhaps, the woody message 'tis true,
that none of it is wasted,
just packed down,
treaded upon, pressured
into solid wisdom that rises
in the long shadows of late day.

Linda Ross Swanson

Never Tomorrow

Never tomorrow for time is fleeting and tomorrow too distant.
Live for the moment, life offers no guarantees, no second chances.
Cherish each memory, for they our the scripts of our lifetime and
each is special to us.
Love every minute, for love is the elixir of life and is as fleeting
as time.

Joe Fiorillo

The Little Smile

There was a little girl who was only two
and she knew what to do.
For she was only home for awhile
she always kept her little smile.
She would help her mother brush her hair
for she knew she really cared.
She would help her with the dishes
and gave her mother big kisses.
For she was only home for awhile,
she always kept her little smile
Until one day she went away
and there she will always stay.
For she was only home for a little while
and now she has lost that little smile.

Norma Hemminger

In Awe

The longest days in all the world
and skies filled with tranquil blue light.
In such awe of natural beauty and wonder
I'm thankful there is no summer night.

The mountains are awesome to see
and hold the most wondrous view,
You think they will never be more magnificent
Till you see them covered with fall's golden hue.

They tell me - winter is on its way
and I should be ready for the boredom and strife,
But the silent murmuring inside me says
I've searched and I've found... this is the life.

Winter may hold a great surprise
With its dark and endless night,
But the melody of Alaska's song
will sustain us all till Summer's Light.

Victoria Clamon

Harvest Meadows

Harvest Meadows full of sweet honey for the bees
And someone aware of these things in a field across a city
In a cloud of disillusion an array of metaphorical
Plastic people in a cohesive group entertaining each other
How merely pegialent we are belonging to ourselves
And never reminiscing our birth at harvest time in the meadow

Terry O. Connor

Love Is A Drug...

Your love is so addicting,
and sometimes contradicting.

It fiddles with my mind and plays with my heart.
Sometimes I feel we couldn't be more apart.

Our hearts fit together at times,
but they never go together like a rhyme.

It sometimes controls my life,
then it always seems to turn around
and stab me in the heart with a knife.

At times you give me a lot,
other times you seem to think that
my love can be bought.

Our memories together are forever
etched inside my heart,
in hopes that we will never again part.

Vicki Stevens

The Angel in White

An angel in white stood by my side
and soothed my troubled mind,
With a gentle touch of her silk soft hand
my heart did rest in that painless land.

Yes, an angel in white stood by my side
with touch of a silk soft hand
she made me feel as in days long past,
there's life, there's hope, ...you'll win at last.

So remembering still that silk soft hand,
of the angel so lovely and fair,
I'll gather my will, my strength... and dare
to walk with head held high and face what ere is there.

My life I owe to that angel in white
with the touch of a silk soft hand.
Somewhere above like a pure white dove
awaits a crown so bright, made not by the hand of man.

For the angel in white with a heart full of love,
and the touch of a silk soft hand.

Ray J. Snelson

To My Cousin, The Runner

The sun rises in the early morning
And the breath of a runner hits the air
The sun sets at the close of the day
And the heart of that same runner is still there

The cheer of the stadium crowd rings loud
As the runner steps up to the blocks
The scream of that internal voice grows stronger
As the runner fights against the clock

Sometimes the runner feels alone
Perhaps this is a race the runner cannot win
But the long track ahead is nothing
Compared to the joy the runner feels at the end

The vision, the drive, and the burning desire
Are dynamic forces the runner is under
The pain, the fear, and the heartache each race brings
Are forces that can't stop the runner

As the sun rises in the early morning
And the breath of a runner hits the air
As the sun sets at the close of the day
The heart of that same runner is still there!

Marlina L. Lewis

You Are

You're the teddy bear in my arms when I rise to wake,
and the first fresh breath of air that I take.
You're the warm rays of the sun that caress my skin,
and what keeps my heart from beating within.
You're the breeze that blows through my long blonde hair,
and the feeling I get from the silky clothes that I wear.
You're the clouds that play in the romantic blue sky,
and the fields of green grass in which I lie.
You're the little white bubbles in my hot bubble bath,
and the nighty night blankets that around me I wrap.
You're the silver moonlight which through my window it shines,
and the one thing that constantly weighs on my mind.
You're the special one that God sent from above,
and from you I've learned the true meaning of LOVE.

Krista Leigh Taylor

Love

Love doesn't come from the mind
like most things do.
It comes from the heart,
that shows it's really true!

Stefanie Nichole Wampler

I Am Serving God

God, You're the Master, the Way,
and the light
So, I'd like to please you
by doing things right
When I see a man
or a woman in need
An effort I'll make
to do a kind deed
Your only son whose life you gave
Pardoned my sins my soul to save
To worship and praise you by lifting my voice
In song or in prayer I've made it my choice
The idea of heaven
some choose to ignore
While earthly pleasures
they explore
Everlasting pleasure
to me is quite clear
It's obtained in your kingdom,
not while we're here.

Renee Norris

Freedom, You Never Told Me

By the heat of the August sun
And the light of its full moon,
I had my first affair with freedom...
But it was over all too soon.

How totally naive of me
To believe without a doubt
That memories of you could keep me high...
Now remains the final bout.

The restless nights, nightmarish dreams.
You're beckoning me again
Out of my prison, into your lap.
Freedom, you never told me...
'There is no turning back!'

Jean E. Trujillo

My Time of Day

When long shadows creep o'er the meadow,
And the sun slowly sinks in the West,
When the gentle breeze touches the tree tops,
That's the time of the day I love best.

When the birds have silenced their singing,
And a hush falls over each tree,
When I see the last ray of sunset,
I know that evenings are made for me.

When fire-flies wake from their sleeping,
And the moon above starts to shine,
When I see the first star of Heaven,
I know that the evenings are mine.

All through the day I have troubles and worries,
And it looks like they're here to stay,
But when I see the calm peaceful evening,
Then they all seem to fade away.
Yes, evening is my time of day.

M. Helen Stacy

"Beauty"

By the willow's sudden sweeping bend
  And the thorn's own flesh newly undone,
Nature's sweetness she would send
  O E'er didst love see such a one.

The softest pod in hazeled brown
  'Tween rubied fruit bound in run,
Her heart's visage free from frown
  O E'er didst love see such a one.

Her sacred crown circles silky coal
  The haven of her husband and son,
A fragrant dew for the purple stole
  O E'er didst love see such a one.

In the solemn mist of the casted mourn
  Where the day's past voice speaketh non,
Her winnowed song comes to mend all scorn
  O E'er didst love see such a one.

A sun's cast ceasing, her bow is her shade
  Herself she drapes, a plant gently spun,
The moonlight spilt, her creamed lashes fade
  O E'er didst love see such a one.

Joseph Griesedieck

Reminiscing

The comfort of the swing
and the wind blowing upon my face
Brought back all the memories.

I overlook the playground where I once played.
Every part has a certain role;
Every piece has its own story.
I sit here now
and watch the young ones play.
My life is going by fast-
like the swing.
I wonder when I'm an adult with children of my own,
Will everything still be here?

I come back to reality
And wish I hadn't taken things for granted.
The swings are slowing now
The wind isn't as strong.
It's time to give up the swing
For someone else must take my place.

Jessica Burns

Homeless

Their homes are made of cardboard,
  and their blankets from the Sunday Times.
Their food's from the Salvation Army,
  and they'll work for nickels and dimes.
In today's mixed up society,
  we all must play a part.
And everything these people own,
  will fit in a shopping cart.
We call these people homeless,
  You see them from coast to coast.
To some it's very degrading,
  but it's a way of life for most.
It doesn't matter where you come from,
  you can't pass or fail a test.
Just a wrong turn here, some bad luck there,
  and you'll end up like the rest.
So, let's try to be more understanding,
  and help out those we can.
Let's thank God for what we have,
  and don't forget to say 'Amen'.

John Gordon

Entropy

I sit in the heat of a summer night
And think of things that might have been.
Of things that grew from nothingness
With high expectations and cheerful song.
And I think of the hopes and the careful plans
And all of the things I've done that were wrong.
And I wonder why, in the dark of the night,
My creations have faltered in flight.

Are hope and optimistic dreams
Of what we might have someday been,
Ultimately and beyond our control
Doomed from the start by entropy?

Press onward to eternity.
Come back and try again.
What good will it do to try it anew
If entropy will win.

Maybe the answer is not in the end
But where the journey went,
That it's not in the distance of the trip
But the height of its ascent.

William F. Pustarfi

Turn To Jesus

A woman cries that she's been raped
And thinks that no one hears
A man was shot by a drive by
And think that no one sees his fears
A mother's child was killed today
And think's no one hears her cry
A father is hospitalized for drug overdose
And think's no one really cares, why?

All these news lines goes on while we think we know why
In the meantime, victims don't know if to live or die
We all forget when situations come around
To seek that one person that won't let you down
This person will have your situations to build you
So, in your life, you will know how and what to do
Putting your life in mankind's hand
You'll remain puzzled and will not know where to stand

But, giving your situation to Jesus Christ
He will give peace of mind and true advise
All you have to do is humble yourself and pray
Will you seek him? Will you turn to Jesus today?

Shelita Williams

"Holding My Hand"

Ever since the day of my birth
And throughout my young life on earth
There was a strong woman
To guide me, holding my hand
She has stood firmly by my side
Comforting me those nights I cried
Enigmas I now understand
Because she was there holding my hand
She chased away the monsters that go "bump" in the night
She kissed my bruises and made them "all right"
Working toward the future that I have planned
She is ushering me, holding my hand
There to help me with loads of advice
Like "think before you speak" and "always think twice"
Together walking through the white sand
My mother is still holding my hand!

Melissa Hunger

I Am Here

Of you and I there is no more
And thus, In trying to hold on,
I come to this place, most visited by:
Us. I am here.
The sands are warm beneath my feet.
The summer grass smells softly sweet.
And I am here —
Here in the velvet blackness of midnight
Blue stars are shivering in the distance
The moon is full and bright.
The surface of the lake is gently rippled,
as though a hundred shipping stones had just left its banks.
And I am here.
The moon is sparkling across the water
like a queens crown of a thousand years ago
And as the breeze from the valley below
whispers across my face
My thoughts turn to you, where are you?
And suddenly, the night is shattered by the loudness of
It's silence.

T. C. Parker

The World Today

I'm walking down a lonely street.
And to myself I can no longer keep.
What I think and what I feel.
The nightmare I had that did turn real.
A world filled with sadness and remorse.
Always using violence and unnecessary force.
A place of crime and cruelty.
A place no one wants to be.
There's people out there
without food or a home.
Only the deserted
streets where they may roam.
Night has fallen and eerie are the streets.
And I'm afraid of the danger I might meet.
Why is the world the way it is.
I often ask myself this.
For what seemed like
a dream is reality.
The world isn't the
place I thought it to be.

Vicki Delucia

"Try Telling that to My Heart"

You said I'd be better off without him,
And to our own separate ways we should part.
you said I deserved someone more worthy of me.
But try telling that to my heart.

You said that I'd get over Him, Quickly.
Plans he'd make to try and see me, you'd thwart
you said all of this was in my best interest.
But try telling that to my heart.

You said it wasn't really love I felt for him,
But only and infatuation in part.
That I was only in love with the idea of being in love
But Try Telling That To my Heart.

You said that together we'd start a new life,
sharing a love that would never grow tart.
you said remaining with Him would be gross mistake.
But Try Telling That To my Heart.

So I tried it your way; and its been five years now,
I feel no more for you than I did from the start.
you say the material gain should make up for love lost.
But Try Telling That To my Heart.

Sandra E. Womack

Love Dirge

A blackened sun darts in the clouds above
and waits to pounce upon me.
And black roses grow in the black garden
and fear or love gives them teeth.
The garden's grass breaks in the cold black wind;
the wind carries grey-black leaves.
The sun bakes, bakes black, and moves closer,
and the earth burns black and heaves.
There is no limit, the sun comes closer
and it burns the morning dew.
Black smoke rises from the dead Mother Earth,
and it's all because of you.

Noel Gotthard

Beth

Child of my youth born from flesh of strength
And whispering promises of rose gardens
I will swathe you in sweet williams and watch you climb the vines of a sweet pea
While beacon lights guide your way into the fourth season of life
Eagerly, you climbed until a thorn pricked you in the season of life.
I picked up your fragile body as I felt piercing pains within my innermost chambers.
A cloak of doom fell upon me as I knew no longer protect you
From the ravishing evil of pain.
I sat to wait beside your still form in world of whiteness.
I no longer had strength of youth and promises of rose gardens for you
As the darkness of death hovered near.
I felt as if traitor of my own flesh, when suddenly I saw a light
And visions of sweet williams swathed you.
I drew not from strength of flesh but from my inner chambers
And sat to wait in a vision of a rose garden.

Linda McKee

A Whale's Fate

And what will be Willy's fate?
And who will there be to care
That once he roamed the oceans great
Only to feed man's great snare?

And what will happen to Willy now
That his family and freedom are gone?
Will some soul come forward and vow
Willy won't die an entertaining pawn?

With a skin disease and teeth going bad
Willy's eyes still see mankind's sorry plight.
That we touch and cannot feel is so sad,
And keeping wild things prisoner only makes Willy right.

Yet Willy and mankind can still free one another.
Let Willy swim free; let man and beast become brothers.

Jill K. Quick

While

Time is the establishment that man cannot live without
and yet desires earnestly to.
Everything, on Earth and in space,
runs to the precision of time, while,
all the while, man and his counterparts
are trying to conquer it.
Not realizing, nor accepting the fact that
time must take its toll, on everything
in order to meet itself in the end
For after all, if everything must run according to time,
mustn't time itself.

Tessa E. Martin

Precious Moments

It all happened so quickly, right from the start
And within a few weeks we exchanged our hearts.
Never did I dream that I would find a love so true
But all that changed the day I met you.

You made me laugh, and you made me smile
How did we know it would last just awhile?
Death came and took you away from me,
I guess it wasn't time for you and I to be.

Now that you are gone I feel so lost inside,
Friends tell me to let go and move on; I tried,
But a part of me has gone to Heaven with you,
And you're in my thoughts with everything I do.

I guess now, it's time to say goodbye,
But I'll never let go of our precious moments;
I won't even try.

Lisa Bazzo

War and Power

I still wonder if there are Gods
and wonder if we learnt from wars!

Why did Sadam crush through Kuwaitians
and then Bush opted for military solutions!

Allied forces bombed like arcade games
but no one counted the number of deads!

TV showed the accuracy of bombs
but I could smell the human flesh from tanks!

One allied soldier buried with honors
and thousands of Iraqis in makeshift groves!

Why did Sadam do what he did
and then allies dealt with Iraq's lead!

Is this 'war equals jobs' as Baker says
or it is 'the new world order' as Bush declares!

To me, the key lies in the 'Power in hands'
which makes you blind when dealing with lands!

N. G. Humbad

"Wondering"

I often look over the ocean
And wonder what's hidden from view
As I think how pleasant it might be
If I could cross that ocean too.

The wonders God created
Are scattered near and far
And I love to think about them
Hoping to be right where they are.

They say that there is no place like home
And on this I must agree
But before I accept this fact for good
There's some place I'd like to see.

So here's to the future
And if my dreams come true
I'll witness some of these wonders
And describe them all to you!

Norman Van Horne

Those Of Us You Left Behind

We still think of you quite often,
and wonder where you are.
And what you would be doing right now,
if you were not among the stars.
We wonder what you'd look like,
and how tall you'd really be.
Would your hair be long, would your ear be
pierced, or would you just be short like me?
We just can't forget you
no matter how hard we try.
Sometimes I feel so alone, all I
can do is just sit and cry.
We wonder where you are tonight
and we wish that you could say.
We wish that we could hold you
tight but you're too far away.
Even though you're gone, we know
you're happy where you are.
But we still can't help but think
of you each time we see a star.

Lori Mohler

Alone in a Cave

While cowering in the corner of a gigantic cave
And wondering who I'd be if I were brave,
Could I find a way out?
Might I search bravely about
To seek a place of refuge.

The shadows on the walls,
The wailing of their calls,
I couldn't comprehend their sorrow.
For them, I guess, their cries of distress
Will not be healed by tomorrow.

As I sit all alone in a cave full of fear,
Wondering for the first time
How did I ever get here?
Why is this cave that I know, oh so well,
Come to be my own private hell?

Tobey Robinson

If It Were Only So

I see the stars so far away-
and yet so very bright.
They light up the night sky-
like so many shimmering crystals
against a black background.

As the night fades into day,
I see my world.
A world that has no hunger
and cries in the night.
A world that cares,
a world that shares.

In my world, my most perfect world,
distrust and fear are gone.
We shelter our poor, and care for our sick.
A world where we ask:
How can I help?
And not, how much will it cost?

For in my world, is a world of love.
My most perfect world.
Oh! If it were only so.

Sidney Wechter

"Life's Road"

If the road you are traveling is rough,
And your burden so heavy is.
You can smooth the way, lighten the load,
If you will remember this.
There are never days so dreary and dark,
But what there comes a light.
A new vision of God, if you will,
Only hold fast to what's right.
There's nothing much we can do.
About the weather so wild.
But you can create sunshine inside,
By just a great big smile.
Though your body may be battered,
Or scarred with disease.
Every handicap can be overcome, if,
Life is worth living you believe.

Violet Marie Prater

They're Gone

The Dr. says "you're pregnant",
and your friends say "Don't you look sweet"?
So as your body grows and grows
you can't even see your feet.

They're gone..

Breast feeding, spitting up,
being awaken at two,
Tons and tons of diapers,
and running to the potty chair too.

They're gone...

Tea parties, the first day of school
and clothes all over the floor,
Children running in and out continually slamming the door.

They're gone....

Baseball games, field trips and every local dance,
Grade point average, class rings and the first big romance.

They're gone.....

Being there, guiding them, and trying hard to understand,
And always be willing to help with loving hands,

Before they're gone......

Sharon Jenkins-Garland

"I Was Old Glory"

I was old glory, my stars and stripes displayed
around the world with pride.

I was old glory, my staff has become my cross
from which my shining stars and crimson colors
must now hide.

I was a symbol for the brave, and all who would
be free.

I was carried into battle over land and over
sea, I displayed my colors well, by the ones
who fought and fell.

Now the bugle is silent no more for me to hear,
for my stars are now dim and my colors faded
away, my nation no longer holds me dear.

I was old glory, by the dawns early light
no more to be.

For I was laid to rest by those who have lost
their pride in me.

Robert L. Stowe

In Love

When you're in love, the stars are bright,
and your heart is light.

When you're in love, you feel so good,
dancing on air you wish you could.

When you're in love, you wear a smile.
peace reigns within you, all the while.

You look at the sky and wonder why,
you feel you could fly,

Right into eternity, where you then could see,
what's happening to me.

You're in love a voice said from above.

Now pick up your heart and join the other part,
that caused this feeling in you from the start.

Treat her gently with kindness galore,
never to be removed from your heart or your door.

True love will last forever,
if you show sincere endeavor.

Love in your heart for God and man will never depart,
if through life you do your part.

John L. Becker

A Friend All Along

The qualities I look for in a lover so dear
are really quite basic and reflective like a mirror.

A sense of humor from deep within
would definitely open up my heart for you to come right in.

Looking at life with a lighter side with laughter
would rate you high on my scale as a good factor.

Pleasing to look at would certainly be nice.
Looking for goodness inside, that's really my best advice.

Someone that cares and can talk openly to me,
now that's rare quality you don't always see.

Do you see what I'm describing isn't a trend?
Yes, it's the true qualities of a dear, honest friend.

Terry Mjelleli

For Robert Lowell

Voyager, the veering and sea-circling
Are recharted at Dunbarton mooring,
Portage place of proud ancestral pilings.
Beneath those crumbling rows of unraked stone,
Rigging and root merge, and tough-tangled, run
Coursing salt-ward through timeless catacombs.

Now nearer the heaven-hung horizon,
A kinder sea hushes earthling oar sounds;
The quiver of your wood wanting the wave,
The quaver of your soul still seeking shore.
Calm couple-closes the dichotomy,
Opening, freeing, new vision, new voice.

Untethered, you encompass - a sky-sloop
Circling, sailing full in sweet blue-brimmed winds
That transcend the old odyssey turmoil.
But when your healing song tilts in world-turn,
The earth blooms and begins again barefoot.
You, and earth, are younger than when you came.

Marguerite Heltemes

The Dancer

Beautiful, graceful
Are what comes to mind
As she dances through the trees
She is lovely and kind
She speaks of only love and kindness
Her heart is gentle and pure
Seeing her smile is a broken heart's cure
She moves softly
Without making a sound
And when you see her
Peace is what you have found
She is friends with all
And her beauty really shines
When she has a new friend
The kind that love finds
We all want to be her
As she glides through the air
We want to be in her magical world
We want to be right there

Sarah Lynn Utso

My Father

A strong man my father,
arms with muscles and hands filled with strength.

A happy man my father,
tall, dark hair and eyes that light up when he speaks.

A witty man my father,
makes jokes about politics and talks sports.

A clever man my father,
understanding my every thought even though I don't.

A kind man my father,
filled with love for his children.

A giving man my father,
giving more than he will ever receive.

A respectful man my father,
who this daughter will always remember for the rest of her days.

Nina Genco

Dreams To Find

The long shadows have now all fallen away
As evening fades into the darkness of night.
The mind will slowly trace the many dreams
That the hungry soul will not let one forget.

Storm clouds may gather above the decisions one has made
And lightning will charge the broken channels of the mind.
While the cold and bitter winds of sorrow and regret
Filled with snow flakes of tears fill the dreamers eyes.

It can be strange and lonely world if we so choose
While crossing the wide plains of the dreamers mind.
Where a man can ride for many troubled days
And no one will ever ask for the dreamers name.

There is always the promise of a bright new morning
If one would but search for the answer in their prayers.
For like the warm and gentle rain that sweeps the plains
His precious love will always be waiting for us there.

J. J. Staker

"I Really Care"

There is so much I can say
As I go along life's way
  I've loved you with an everlasting love
  As our Savior has above
Don't you worry; don't you fret...
your journey's not over yet
  Be content and be serene
  There is much more to be seen
Take each day as though your last
Forgetting everything in the past
  I'll be with you throughout the day
  In your heart is where I'll stay
Call on me and I'll be there
'Cause you know "I really care"

Maryann Ringwood

The Immortal Me

Days slip away like the waves on the shore
  As I move toward eternity

Striving for tomorrow —
  Reaching beyond the present

Uplifted eyes light the search for the future
  I see my destiny

The lines of wisdom embrace me
  Creating fullness within

Worries cast up - to far to see
  The inspiration for a lifetime

Tracy E. Milanese

Loving

Loving you is not as easy
as I once thought it to be.
You are you and I am me.
Together what else could we be?

Loving me was not what you expected
When you searched to your very core.
There's a weariness in your eyes now
Where there used to be so much more.

Loving you is more complicated
and involves much more than I was ever told.
Love, they said, is the greatest gift.
It is worth more than gold.

But they did not tell me of love dying
or of it fading nice and slow.
They did not tell me that as you love
you must also learn to let go.

Melanie Mitchell

Seaside Avenue

The swimsuit is tacky with sand and damp
as I pull it on
in the dark of the back bedroom
foot sticking to cold linoleum floor
skin pulling, shuddering at the touch.

Chilled, I step through shadowed rooms
to the light, to the pungent air outside
and sink blissfully
into soft mounds of sand.

I will embrace the salt spray later
But now, I yield
to the sun's enticing warmth.

Marie Seifert

City Of Hope

Time seems to slip, through my fingers, like sand.
As I walk through this life, that's a dessert waist land.

I turn to my left, and I turn to my right.
But, all that I see, is destruction and plight.

I walk down my path, and the people I see,
have lost hope for our World, and any tranquility.

But, there must be an answer.
There must be a way, to gain back our dreams,
that once lit the way.

But, if we give up all hope, for our World to be healed.
We'll never reap happiness, in this lost, barren field.

So, wipe the dust, quickly, from your dark, clouded eyes,
and re-build what is lost, for the ultimate prize.

For that prize is new hope, in a city of peace.
Our sorrow then ceases, and our joy will increase.

Robert J. Mortenson

The 4 Seasons

A lonely day I seldom see
As I watch the seasons come and go
And each one is a beauty in its own way
I enjoyed winters, and spring is once again
And I watch the flowers burst to bloom
And the clouds gather to water them with
Their soft rain and morning dew. I watch children at play
And as time passes and summer passes too
It's almost time for fall
Which shortens our days and the leaves begin to fall
And they turn to yellow and brown
As you walk they rustle under your feet
And soon a light frost covers them all
And once again winter begins
And snow blankets roofs and covers all
And children again with snow hats and sleds
they are at play and they have a happy time
And flowers and grass and trees sleep under
A blanket of snow and I am preparing for another spring
The seasons were made for us to embrace and enjoy.

Mary Robbins

My Grown-Up Child

Ah... my grown up child,
As I watch you leave your childhood
  home with me,
I wonder if the fabric of our life together
  will hold you adequately?
Will the love and faith I worked with,
  tie up unraveled ends,
When life's travails and heartbreaks tear
  the fibers now and then?
Ah... my grown up child,
Take the tapestry we've made,
Keep it always near your heart,
  and do not be afraid.

Merrianne Dyer

"Time"

There is a time for love and tears,
and there is a time to look back on past years.
There is a time for the caring of friends,
and there is a time to grieve for lost ones.
There is a time for happiness and hope,
and there is a time to learn to cope.
But most of all, and you shouldn't forget,
the time you had when you first met.

Terris Renfro

Roller Coaster

Slowly shoving me higher and higher,
As I wonder what I will find.
Holding back my breath,
As thoughts whirl out of my mind.
Blind to what is before me,
Letting my fears collide,
With a tiny pinch of excitement,
All bottled up inside.
But lasting only a moment,
For now the curtains have been drawn,
My thoughts die with each second,
For I...am..going..on..

Down as the blurs surround me,
The world is a spinning top.
Feeling as if I'd plunge into the ground,
Never a second to stop.
As I approach what I once saw as life,
My thoughts are crystal-clear.
Knowing in the deepest part of my heart,
My world is truly up there.

Jennifer Cheng

The Mother

"Poor Mom", they said in loud pitched tone
As if she were not there.
"What on earth will do with her?"
She moved not in her chair.

"It's such a trial, every plan revolves
Upon where will mother go."
The wrinkled face stayed expressionless
The grey head was bowed low.

The old woman rose from her chair
Faced her children standing there.
"You know my dears, I've thought for some time
To burden you is not quite fair."

She smiled, her tired face lit up.
"I'd like to go today
Where other old people like me
Are not always in the way.

Now I must go and pack my things.
Oh yes, I can my dears."
She turned and slowly walked away.
But not before I saw her tears.

Mary Menser

Untitled

The moon shines,
  as my soul wanders freely through space.
Clouds drift all around me,
  carrying me to my hidden destinies,
Time is forgotten,
  now that my mind has been taken over.
Some creature of the devil,
  he's tearing at my skin.
Acid pours from the sky,
  deteriorating my flesh to the bone.
I'm lost,
  gone forever.

Krystal Mitchell

"The Love Of All"

She unfolds her red silk in the mourning.
As she stretches herself to the wide open sky her emerald leaves start to droop. She sicks them up with delicate care
as she opens her beautiful eyes we se a tear.

And why shouldn't she cry?
she sees a couple walking by.

And wishes she could be loved by just one.
Just one with how filled with the golden sun.

And eyes painted by the deep blue ocean
His heart filled with so much emotion.

Suddenly, a young man stoops down to touch her,
emerald stem with a delicate soft whisper.

A drop of ruby blood falls to the ground seeing that she had pricked Him with one of her thorns
She cried with a cold thrust in heart but tried not to make a sound

A single tear full on his bloody skim sealing it with a kiss.
With pure amazement he crunched his fist.

He gently picked her up with loving care and kissed her with his soft lips avoiding her thorns.
Now dear rose you will be the love of all and mourn no more.

Jamie Michelle Russo

The Dreamer

The dreamer wishes upon the first star
as the dragon dances in the distance far
The moon creeps upon the sky each night
While the dreamer wonders why and looks to the starlight

The moonlight shadow dances free
as the dreamer realizes he is me
I am the dreamer of all worlds as one
I am the only who worships the sun

I am the bird who cries so loud
I am the eagle who soars to the clouds
I am the fear that lurks within
I am the child who has no sin

I am as free as the ocean waves
I am also the King of the slaves
for I am the dreamer who will always be
and the dreamer will always know that he is me.

Michelle Lathrop

As A Friend To A Rose

A true friend is like a beautiful rose,
As the petals blossom - the friend will grow.

A rose comes casually into this world,
Just as a friend does - mid the busy whirl.
The petals develop into reds and in whites,
Into colors of friendship - that help one in strife.
And once in a while a rose may perish and die,
Just as a friendship - when saying 'good-bye.'
But spring will renew the rose and the love,
Of a true friendship - blessed from above.
Each grows and each wilts as the days go by,
But each will return - if love is nearby.
A rose, like a friend, must often be checked,
To be sure both are receiving - love and respect.
The beauty of a rose is more than one can say,
The same as a friendship - if true in every way.

Because a true friendship is like the life of a rose,
As the flower blossoms - the friendship grows.

Kristina M. Larsen

So Great a Gift

So great a gift was never given
As the precious gift that came from heaven.
It was not found 'neath a glittering Christmas tree,
But in a lowly stable, in a land beyond the sea.

So great a gift, yet no shinning ribbon with lovely bows,
Just a little bundle wrapped in swaddling clothes.
Yet no greater love has never been shown
No greater gift has ever been known.

So great a gift, no amount of money can ever buy
Yet was so freely given by the father on high.
The Son of God, our saviour true
So great a gift to me and you.

So great a gift was this tiny babe
Who slept so peacefully on his bed of hay.
That thru him all mankind might know
Pardon from sin, because He loved us so.

Ruby Baugh

A Storm at Dusk

My niece examined her insect menagerie
as the red wind of dusk ruffled the mottled,
mad, Van Goghish, sunflower swirls of her dress.

Birds softly twittered in September fields,
tree shadows slowed to an earthworm's crawl
while ants, crickets and beetles were bottled.

Dark dialogues of thunder woke the nest,
crooked fingers of lightning clawed the west,
the horizons closed in, masked in rainy mist.

But she ignored the grumbling storm, gazing
in studious worship at her lifeless darlings,
counting, qualifying like a seasoned scientist.

My wrinkled arm wrapped around her thin waist.
Our faces engaged: blue ice filled her eyes.
"You seem so serious today, my dear,"

I said, as the sky groaned in grey sunset
and summer drew a sickly shallow breath.
She sighed and said, "As serious as death."

M. C. Guimond

"Our Love"

Just take me in your arms and hold me
As the rest of the world may scold me;
Just be the only one who sees my truth,
And looks beyond my seeming youth.
Just hold my hand in yours with care;
Let me know you'll always be there;
Just smile at we when life gets tough;
Let me lean on you when the waters get too rough;
Just walk with me as the stars shine above;
Let me feel the strength of our love;
Just hear me when I share my fears
And be there, please, to wipe away my tears;
Just laugh with me in times of gladness
And cry with me in sadness;
Just be the man I know you to be,
And God will take care of you and me.

Mary C. Patanella

Myself

I am what I am and what
I will always be and have been.

Rosa Fagiolino

The Blizzard

Calm dissipates into a ferocious storm
As the snow falls heavily, the silent anger lies buried
Beneath the perfect blankets of accumulation.

The world outside is silent and pure;
There are no signs of footstep, interruptions or intrusions.
Children inside laughing; thoughts of sleds, snowmen, fill their heads
As they put on snowpants, boots and gloves
Anxiety and anticipation enter
Their parents breaking the silence and beauty of nature's snowfall.
Fighting, clawing and staking their claim;
Neglecting their innocent children and the impacted shame.
Violence takes over and one thing's for sure
When the ground peeks through and regains its visibility
The scars will be irreversible;
Nature cannot undo the tragedy that has overcome the angry family.
The snow will eventually melt
But the traces of the blizzard will lie dormant on the property
Forever.

Sandi Cohen

Natural Beauty

There is a quiet in the air
as the soul finds peace amongst itself.
Despite the heavy blanketing of the humidity
it still finds a way
to let all the troubles, pressures, and worries slip away
so that it may be free to fly
not suffocate in it's own sorrow.
The depression released to bring the happiness
of a bright, cool, sunny day into the open.
Something to stay with it
for many seasons yet to come.
To carry it through all the up hills
and roll with the down hills.
Through the opening of the flowers
to the closing of the petals.
A natural beauty that can never be completely defeated
as a beauty is not skin deep
but within itself as the soul is.
My soul is beautiful
therefore so am I.

Stacy Katz

When Steps Are Not As Swift

My steps are not as light and swift
As they were just one year ago,
But each step is a priceless gift
That keeps me moving to and fro.

My hands are not as apt and strong,
They sometimes tremble as in fright,
And simple chores take twice as long
Although I try with all my might.

My brain is oft times in a spin
Sometimes it hardly works at all,
My patience frequently grows thin
When someone's name I can't recall.

Oh yes, I know I'm growing old
But I've yet treasures by the score,
With friends worth twice their weight in Gold,
I've riches rare and so much more.

Ocie Tackett Lay

Footprints On My Heart

The moon shone bright above us
as we walked along the sand
I had not a care in the world
when I held onto her hand.

We sat and built a castle
that soon would wash away
we shared our dreams as Lovers do
as upon the sand we lay.

It all seemed so easy then
the problems we faced were few
we never thought of loneliness
for we knew our love was true.

But then there came the bitter storms
our castle began to fall
and watching our dreams wash out to sea
was the hardest part of all.

And now the beach is a memory
if I had known it from the start
I wouldn't have let my summer love
leave FOOTPRINTS ON MY HEART.

Kenneth D. Clark

Untitled

Alone he set sail on an endless sea
Assured to be the master of his fate.
The storm on the horizon was sure to be;
Confidence, his companion and first mate.
The sky blackened, the winds began to wail;
The angry sea was his relentless foe.
The storm came, as a thief, and took his sail;
Abandoned by Confidence, replaced by Woe.
Hope came and asked, "Why must you sail alone?"
Fear had seized his heart with his shattered pride.
With his tiny ship, he was tossed and thrown;
Wearily falling to his knees he cried.
And there in the distance, a glow burned bright;
Alas, Hope had shown him a guiding light.

Lori Mills

Fun

Now great grandsons I have three.
At Easter time a one year old visited me.
I colored for him his first Easter Eggs
He had an egg hunt on his chubby little legs.
I rented a high chair and a crib.
I got a two-handled cup and a baby bib.
Bought bottles and bottles of baby food
Got huggies and wipes and powered him good.
I even took him to the zoo.
Showed him the turtle, giraffe and other animals, too.
He laughed and hugged and slept and cried.
I kept his crib by my bedside.
In the years to come
He won't remember any of this or me.
But 80 year old great gram and Colton had a spree.

Lois Belcher

Learning To Forget

The days seem long, and so very lonely.
No one to love, no one to hate.
But yet you still feel for him.
In your past, but still in your mind.
Learning to forget the past times,
And going with the winds of change.

Kelly Smith

Watching

I huddle on the mountain and gaze through the winter air,
At the shining stars and golden moon perched in the heavens there.
And I wonder at their agelessness, so changeless o'er the years,
Then, as silver as the sparkling stars, fall my own unhindered tears.

Wispy tendrils of pearly cloud blanket the stars in their homes on high
Sometimes stirred by the moons soft breath
As she reigns as queen of the sky
A cold, gentle wind whispers through the trees
Singing soft, deceitful lies
Whilst dry, cracking leaves swirl on an icy breeze
That resounds with their hollow sighs.

The silence echoes mournfully throughout the winter night,
The stars are cold and heartless as they shed their silver light.
The moon dances in the darkness, and passes me, unaware,
Of my shivering silhouette crouching in the darkness there.

Kristina Breeding

Untitled

To be free to sing with all my heart
At the top of my soul with each day's start
To show all my love of song...
It's been far too long!

If God would only grant this dream.
Out of reach it, forever seems.
Life would be endlessly fulfilled.
No longer would my voice be stilled.

I'd sing until He calls me to
His eternal home...but He'll wait 'til I'm through.

Marie A. Wicks

Not Only Was I Blind But Mentally, Visually and Spiritually

Paranoid, about being held back.
At times I thought I was sinking.
I fooled myself into thinking I
am better off being alone with
only the companionship of my son.
I realize that there is a lot more
to be and do out there in the
world. I am happy to
be out there busy being me.
Now, I don't have to flee. I am
thinking about sailing the sea.
Now I smell the flowers
and the trees I am still
out there being me.

Saundra R. Patt

Optimism

The party is over,
And I'm the only guest still here;
I want to cry;
But I don't dare shed a tear;
I want to scream
But I doubt anyone would hear;
Someone once told me that the end is near.

I refuse to believe that cause I know it's not true,
As long as the grass is still green and the sky's still blue

Lorisa Robinson

In the Name of Progress

Imagine the Old West,
Attracting foreigners on a quest.

Changing the land in the name of progress,
Will they ever be satisfied? Will they ever rest?

In the desolate prairie, through the shimmering heat,
Where two iron, silver lines meet.

In the distance a huge, black shape appears,
The Indians and animals frightened, draw back in fear!

The iron thing bellows black clouds and moves too fast,
The white man calls this progress at last.

The Indians cry out in hate,
Is this become their dying fate?

And what of the human race,
Why are so many innocent ones crushed in the pace?

Michael Lutz

"Awe Struck"

This garret is frozen stiff like Walt Disney
-awaiting a second chance-
It's ebbed, reckoned and ransacked with mockery.
Only this good size UPS corrugated confinement remains.
It too is inching itself apathetically out the door.

Inside it are duel-masks cushioned in pink scraps of styrofoam foaming
-this cardboard content is flooded with vengeance-
One tuft-veil was excavated from a grinding mudslide quickness,
The other cloak without eyes was saved from a seaweed strangler's drowning.
It's an earthquake family tree uprooted high on the Richter scale.

Now the family album is in storage with mothball seasoned mugs
-and tears adhering to its stuck aged pages-
Outside this room the word is out, cold and branding.
This ready to go shipment of accusations, lies, tips the scale awkwardly.
A dead weight not in balance with its genuineness.

All these recollections are now taunted, twisted and forebodingly animated.
-a feast for beasts and not for beauty-
They're Kafka marks of metamorphosis children with scaling wings
And incognito scratches ripping open the heart's nucleus.
Red is the under the surface running over hue.

Paul Fortin

God's Starry Night

Out in the country, on a warm summer night
Away from the city, and all its bright light.
I looked at God's creation in the heavens above
And, suddenly, I felt so wrapped in His love.

I saw millions and millions of stars light the sky
Meteors falling fast from ever so high.
Formed by the stars, I saw a bell, teapot, snake and a cross
Then, suddenly, a satellite came twinkling across.

Through telescope eyes, precious sights I could see
And somehow I knew God had really touched me,
I wanted to stay, and worship God all night
I really wanted to stay, and not say goodnight.

I felt the hug of God, a friend prayed I would feel.
I knew deep in my heart that God is so very real.
My love for Him grows more abundantly each day.
Please, God, continue to show me your way.

Wilma Eastridge

Home At Last

Could it be? You are coming
Back from war, coming home.
The neighbors will plan a big surprise;
And old Rusty will wag his delight.
But wait! You are crying,
He is coming — is he not?
Yes, he is coming, but not the way we knew him best.
Quick! Pack his things.
We must not let his memory linger here.
The heartbreak, the sadness, the love that is lost
Now lies far away in a wooden box —
On his way home?

Patricia Dorazio

Just Because I'm Thinking of You

Sitting here thinking of you, brings
Back sweet memory of times that we shared together.
Of loving each other, in a very special
Way that need not to be said but
To be love in a tender and devote way.

Just because I'm thinking of you
With the though of all the things that we can do.
With how much I miss you, full your
Heart with joy that I'll give my all
To say on this day in a very special way
I love you in all that you do of how
You made my dream come true. . .
To have met a woman as beautiful
As you. With a smile that is as pretty
As the sunrise.
You full my heart with romance which
Has given me this chance to express my feelings
Of how I feel about you. Is like a number one best
seller romantic novel that has no ending just that I'm your
King and you're my Queen.

Kenneth Cobb

Life for a Life

A time of morning he met his fate.
Banging was his life, it was all he could take.
His life was short 20 years was all. Six bullets
in the head is how he took his fall. To him it
was worth it a little coke in his nose. They found
in his pocket him and his homeboys in a pose.
He knew life was hard, but he didn't care.
A woman and 2 kids is what he left there. Yet
towards the end it all came clear, that this man's
death was coming near. Now the mornings over and he is
gone. No one said what was done was wrong, but two
nights before the summers start, 4 bullets went out
into one man's heart. He had no chance, he couldn't
avoid it. His fate was sealed with just one bullet
He messed with the strongest of them all.
Yet they know someday they're all gonna fall.

Mishell Bergstrom

Dad's Place

A good father is rare to find to this I can attest
Because you see, for 44 years I had the very best
He sheltered me, protected me, from the very start
You see my dad was blessed by God with a very good heart
At times I felt sad and a bit rejected
Now that he is gone I know I only was protected
He seldom talked, but when he did his words were like a dove
You stood stark still and stared in eyes that were filled with love
Until the end the smile and joy never left his face and
I thank God now everyday he left me at Dad's place!!

Sylvia Johnson-Lee

Lily of Light

It stands alone in a desert,
Barren of all life;
Brown grass all around,
Winds blowing.
So tall, green,
Strong, yet bending with each breath of wind,
As a reed;
The lily.
Its purity of flower
Glistens in the light.
The cross, its only cane,
Gives strength where it stands,
Supporting
Against the fiercest cold,
Alone,
Yet not alone.
As, not cold, but warm and glowing
From the light
Of the cross.

Nancy Broczkowski

Mark In Time

As we share our life adventures we pass many points,
Be they challenges or obstacles they still come.
Able to share this life adds strength to our hearts,
With strength is power to hurdle obstacles with joy.
For my steps that you've shared I will always be in debt
For the light that you held to brighten the darkness.
Sunshine that came without regard to time or place.
A gift of the heart is so treasured,
Jewel too great to price but sought after by all.
For being my ruby, my emerald, my diamond,
A world of thanks is for you and for being in my life.
My gift is what I am and what I will be,
As my heart holds its warmth for you and all you are.
When clouds rest on your horizon may I be your shelter.
As days run in to years, years turn to decades
May our love share our mark in time.

Michael C. Heltemes

Untitled

Gardens, pottery and I wish my sense of smell remembered more.
Because I know spots would awaken that had only you
Full of life and dignity coming out in every angle;
The most beautiful deep very here, simultaneously there
Eyes that took me too long to notice
But now I remember; and now nowhere to look for them
Hits me with the resentment they say comes always late.
Then, they say too much, but they are abundant and
You are gone.
Ocean, zucchini, oatmeal with milk and sugar in warm brown bowls
Birdfeeder-and the birds that must miss you more than capacity allows.
Grapefruit, jewelry, and a voice too everything to write about
Voice goes with hands. And they poke the most at me
Since your hands were the first things I remember
And the last things I felt some sort of goodbye from.

Rachel L. Mears

Whale Styx

As plumes are sprouted into sky
And men with antic glee
Watch wakes, hone knives, reel ropes, pull oars,
Rouse water heaps from sea,

Whale swells, seethes, wails, shifts, swoops, snubs ropes.
Whalemen yowl, row, heave round, curse.
Whale lost; men saved - merely
Their wrack with Charon they rehearse.

Thomas J. N. Juko

"Mother"

Here's a special wish just for you, Mother
Because like you there is no other.
This is specially for your special day,
Although we continue to love you everyday.

The calendar recognizes you once a year,
But with your children you have nothing to fear.
The six of us acknowledge you everyday
Because we love you more than we can say.

You have helped us grow up to be what we are
And that makes you extra special by far.
You have always been there for all of us
And never doubted us or made a fuss.

On this day we wish you Happy Mother's Day
And will always love you in our special way.
Not only this day do we send all of our love,
But each day throughout the year we share your love.

Lori J. Sorensen

The Desert

Why does that place haunt me so?
Because of my youth .. the passions that flowed?

The golden dunes and whispering sand;
The purple mountains that go hand in hand.

They call me constantly no matter where I go;
Their whispers they beckon me ..
I can't escape.. the memories won't depart!
... It's beauty taunts me so!

When I was young I would gaze at the mountains
I wanted to climb; I wanted to run.

Now the mountains I have climbed, have changed me
My roots somehow I can't deny.

Maturity has engulfed me..
But the desert night sky still taunts me...

Julie Moffat

The Only One

Come unto me my little one.
Because the race is almost run.
If you love the Lord you have won.
He helps you up when you are down.
And guides you along the way.

Just put your trust in him and he won't let your down.
I pray for you both night and day.
That you won't let me down.

I trust the Lord will bring you back all safe and sound.
For I know you can't hardly get around.
That's why I want to be around to help you up.
In every way and never let you down.
True love is hard to find.
But I would be around until the Lord called me home.
And the race we would have won.
You are the only one.

Oneta Hasley

Mail Slot

When you open the door to the mail slot,
and you drop your letters in.
Do you re-open the door to see that they're gone,
and properly fell in the bin?
Do you really expect them to still be there
Hanging on for dear life to the door?
Or don't you know they fell all the way in,
As they've done every time before?

Patty White

The Love of my Life

You've been patient and I thank you a lot,
Because very few people seem to have what we've got.

It took a long time to really be sure,
But I am the ailment and you are my cure.

Love without you is a life without love,
Like living on earth without the heavens above.

Love without you is like a day without time,
A million years pass and the sun never shines,

My love for you can hardly be told
It's something you feel, but you can't ever hold.

Among all the words, what I'm trying to say,
Is I love only you in that every special way.

Kevin J. Gandy

Love

Our love is heaven sent. Nothing could tear us apart why?
Because we love each other and no one can come between us
or tell us that we are wrong
we don't have to listen to what people tell us;
or do what they tell us to do
we have to listen to what our heart
tells us and follow it until it stops
with the right person and that
person is you that's why I'm with
you and I want to be with you forever!

Leticia Miranda

Death

Death is a part of us now
Because you no longer live
And I feel I don't either.
I could tell you anything
And you would always listen.
You knew when I was in trouble
Even before I did.
You could feel my pain
Even before I could
You understood me
When nobody else did.
When I was confused or down
You helped me understand and brought me up.
Even though you are gone and away,
I still talk to you
And tell you everything.
I only hope, that you still listen.

Katherine Mosen

Those Three Little Words

Those three little words I have
been waiting to hear, for what seems
like forever, my one and only dear.
When you walk by, all I can do is
stare, into your big, brown eyes, I
can only glare. My friends catch
you looking over here, and I'm
still waiting for those three
little words for my ears to hear.
I can see you looking at my light
brown hair, just say those words
that bring music to my ear, you know, those
three little words I'm dying to hear.
Come darling, come over here,
what did you say? Finally, three little
words, I thought I might never hear.

Natalie Rhodes

In Memory

For more years than I can remember, Saturdays
began with a weekly call from Mom and Dad.
One phone call, out of sequence, Mom whispers only my
name, and I learn in seconds what I could never prepare
for in decades, that death strikes without warning.

My throat, neck, jaws ache with submerged sorrow
as I start the long journey in grief to their house.
In the next few days, I learn about my father - that he
mentored men I did not know in integrity, that he
liked hamburgers and bologna and I would have guessed
mashed potatoes and gravy.

Daily I mourn his death. I look for him in family pictures,
run my hand over the smooth surface of the child's rocker
he restored, as if in this gentle movement I can call him back.
Nightly I dream him alive, dozing in his chair, solving problems.
I have always listened to him not because he had all the answers
but because he had a way of thinking that led to them.

I wait as one who sits at early dawn immersed in a fog
so thick there is no other side, slowly watching outlines
emerge until the sun burns through.

Marilyn Campbell Scala

Believe In Love

Believe in love, those words once said to me.
Believe in it's power, to make you who you want to be.

Believe in heartache, even if it's tears you've cried.
Believe in healing, and know the hurt will subside.

Believe in the emotion, that every heart can feel.
Believe in time, all your wounds it shall heal.

Believe in the dream, that we want to come true.
Believe in the love, that someone will feel for you.

Even though our heart may be broken and sadness
is all we feel. All we
need is time for our wounds to heal.

And even though you may have been
hurt in the past; believe in the love
that will forever last.

Vanessa Arnold

D-Day, 6th of June; Fifty Years Later

White crosses, thousands, all in a row; how still.
Beneath them, young men who never grew old.
Heroes; some say, who died so that others could live in freedom.
Look closely at these crosses and listen to the voices of all these
young men.
I died so that you might live in a free world.
I died so that you could do greater things with your lives.

I died so that this earth could be a better place for you and your
children, so that peace, love and respect for each other as brothers
would rein.

I gave you the rest of my life so that you could build a peaceful
world. Each man living their lives for good; enjoying all the good
things life has to offer.

I gave you the most precious gift I had; I gave you my life, my future.

Oh, if only we could rise up from this place where we have laid so
long; we could show you what life should be like.

All of us here, could show you what life really means.

Rita Rudolph

Home

Along the grassy plains
Beside the dirt road
Up on the cliff
Toward the oceans arose

Past time had left
By the time the sun was down
for there was no way home

Against the curtain of blackness
Into the darkness of night it was then
I found my way home.

Megan Lech

The Importance Of High Expectations

What makes individuals strive to excel
Besides self-motivation, it's easy to tell
When another expects the highest of standards
Suddenly it's contagious: the brightest of lanterns
That stream of light beckons
No's can't be reckoned
Achievement becomes natural
Successes start a whirl!
So as competition and self-esteem
Are debated, as is the role of the team
Don't lose sight of the critical key
Expect the best and it will be.

Wanda A. Wallace

Behind the Mask

A woman's smile masks a child's silent cries.
Betrayed innocence is hidden behind a forced grin.
No one notices the pain in her eyes —
The pain caused by one man's secret sin.

Every night her mind replays the events.
The agony, guilt, and shame wash over her once more,
And she hears his voice tauntingly say,
"I love you" as he steals her childhood.

In the morning her mask is once more donned,
As she tries to wash away the feel of his touch.
While she prepares to face the day she prays
No one sees her dignity is lost.

Melissa Gilbertson

Country Boy

Well a country boy in the
big city blues, becomes confused and abused
and accused of a crime committed, Man
you've got to get with it, and quit that
Mansion on that hill. Where you got you're last
prescription filled. So forget that mess and bring
out the best the big daddy D so come on
roll with me as I make this all come easily
Because I don't roll a cadillac I roll an
olds. Forty four deuce So I can get
loose. So take that noose from around your
neck because you was about to hang with
all do respect. Just because of the type
of intellect you posses. So when I'm
on the Job I never take a recess. I just smoke
the suckers ass and clean up that
mess. Because I'm not just a rapper
I am an artist. A creator in the making and someday this
all will be taken.

Darrell

The Color Of My Brain

I acknowledge your eyes looking, but not seeing me
Black, female over two years of age, independent and demanding.

I know the sound of your voice edged with fear
of imagined hurts.

I see your hands moving to guard your life flow
rushing inside, putting distant spaces between us.

I smell your fear hanging like rain clouds
separating spectators and performers.

I acknowledge my anger unspoken, but always there
in anticipation of another hurt, added to memories past.

The sun kissed many in the land of our ancestors,
giving some a different hue, immediately identifiable.

The real difference between us in not the darkness
of my skin, a life factor demonstrated in many places, but the
color of my brain.

Luvenia Pinson

Gray

On a surface level life is easy
black or white, yes or no
all figurative, no literal, clear cut -
yet moving to a realm
where there are no clear cut answers
when it applies to you.
A realm fading to fuzzy grays
unyielding absolutes becoming uncertain truths
where the heart overrides the mind.
and feelings override fact.
Surface level is easy but
Life doesn't begin until one is forced to
probe deeper
And discover the truth is not always an
an absolute, but rather a vacillating door
to be entered
when there is nowhere else to go.

Susan S. Leggett

Obsession

No need to call his name
Blackness reminds me of him
At night it draws me...
Come lay on my side walk
Forgive in my bedroom
I'd give all of me for exchange of you....

Not a feeling, just a touch
Isn't that the way you view it?
I can't see past your shutters
Although I dream to shatter and break them.....
But you, I wait to devour, Left always in my body
Only a night in yours....

My eyes bleed for you....for you to notice
My flesh is of value to you but nothing more
In time my desire grows
from hunger to psychotic rage.
Your blood is mine to spill as, Soon as day has fallen
Against your cold, still life I lay, naked in my fear....
Your purple, bruised lips are open, but not to speak to me,
as if you did before.

Salina Riggins

Descent Of Joy

The reds, the blues, the greens and the yellows
blend together across the sky.
As I gaze upon its beauty
I become entranced with enchantment and glory.
And deep within its depths with silent symphony
it seems to me that angels dance and sing
around a silver pole.
As they dance and sing
they toss their wands away
to let them fall wherever they may.
And they dance on
until the colors fade.
Suddenly they are gone
into the silent Night.

Marjorie Boynton Spencer

Hands of Time

My child's hand...so softly plump, pink and pure
Blindly curling, pulling me always near
Soon freckled, dirty and scratched
Stretching often now for something new, yet near
Thankfully, she's not quite clear

I touched your cheek...I held your hand
Too soon, so soon these moments change with time
Long, tapered, graceful fingers now
So like your fathers, not like mine
Butterfly wings touching, lighting all the time
A flirt, you and he...but still I see a little of me

Soon a mother this child of mine
Hands not quite so soft and pink, as now I see
Yet strong, sure and quick, as they'll surely need to be
Oh how my heart aches...alas, she's so far away from me

My own now lay quiet, old and chaffed by time...so empty now
Oh, my dear sweet child, how I wish your were near
To repeat and share with me, all the wondrous things yet to be
Your child's innocent touch is so forever dear
Yet sadly...so shortly here

Lyn M. Graham

The Sphinx

The rising sun dries the mixture of stone and clay
Block upon block my existence is created
My infant body awakes at the start of the day
As I crawl on all fours, my creators are elated

The sun reaches its highest point in the sky
The heat is intense, but it's my time in the sun
Though I'm walking on two, sometimes I fly
Sometimes I look for shade, but in a desert there's none

The dusk will come and I'll walk on three
The sun will set, my life will be history
The sands of time will show me no mercy
Will my life make an impact, or just a mystery

K. R. Maury Jr.

America Is My Home

America is my home...
Between the people there's
A bridge of brotherhood,
like a dome....
In this land, these are
the ones I stretch my hand......
for every man is my brother,
Irregardless of race, creed or color....,

Robert Reese Jr.

Humanity

Many people say that to restore justice, peace, and humanity,
Blood must be shed;
Tears must flow from the eyes of the innocent,
And lives must be ruined—and lost.
Leaders of our so-called great nations say that to
Restore democracy,
We must be forceful;
We must be strong,
And we must be courageous—
In essence, we must be fools.
How many people must lose their lives before we
Become sane enough to become humane—
To make an eternal world peace?

Narin Wongngamnit

Twilight Indian Summer...

It has been many seasons since the spirits nourished the tribal lands,
bountiful were the buffalo that diminished to half,
still, healing continues to flow from our medicine man,
though they call us engine, we remain steadfast.

Days of old and great chiefs, warriors miss so much,
in lighthearted tenderness I watched when young
as pale face bargained with firewater promises and such,
offering gifts of woven cloth while speaking with a forked tongue.

Forged were treaties of peace, never is the cavaliers vendetta to
cease, as smoke signals warn, soldiers approach the east,
the rhythmic sounds of drums echo war
wringing rebellion to the blue coats sword.

Many are the war colors painted upon the young braves face,
just look how those white devils massacred our race,
on the battlefield, even siblings take aim with arrows and bow
awaiting a journey into the great tepee beyond the rainbow.

Is the painstaking end of this tribesman soon to come?
bringing all braves into the spiritual realm, as did Geronimo,
the trust of hunger no longer allows my pony to run
warning future indian nations by the tell I have told.

Kevin Fisher

Lovers Cry

As life leads on we wished it was tomorrow
Bowing my head in a bit of sorrow.
Looking in your eyes, I feel the love
Like having a wedding, with a few morning doves.

Babe we know how life is now
But once we are together, we'll move out of town.
Love they say is like a game
Up and down in a bit of shame.

Parents look at the different side of view
Once its all over, it'll be brand new.
With our hearts, strong and filled
We'll make it last with power and will.

Yes, babe, I know its a "lovers cry"
But open up more freely, don't be shy.
Take it for granted; the love we have
Don't turn away and make me sad.

Please keep your head up with some pride
Don't turn your back from love and hide.
Thank you babe for hanging in tight
Won't be long before its right.

Mary Soucy

Only One

Rewind back to where I was my heart is standing still
Boxes stacked surround me with my memories they're filled
I walk and talk and say nothing colors shooting from my mouth
Where stars will go I'll follow and my feet will lead me south
Stylish is not my manner I've never been a fool
Sitting on a cloud-made chair I stand upon my stool
I have been known for tripping yes and falling on my face
But smells of color changed me and my head is wreathed in lace
Of smoke is made my halo though no angel wings have I
I live off grass and rubbing alcohol I'm forward though I'm shy
Green is my equilibrium yellow is my mind purple is my angel dust
I say again no angel am I
Flying I have never done swimming in the sand
Look at me I'm only one
I wonder if God has a rock and roll band

Xavier Alexander Robertson

A World Gone Mad

The silence of the night
Broken up by men in white
Laughing and sneering on horses
Cruel, evil, heartless men holding torches
A black boy alone and unknowing
Of these white ghost, where were they going
Thinking whites are the superior race
But they are shaming there own with disgrace
They beat people, scare people, kill them too
Hitler did the same because they were Jews
Everyone is different no one the same
There is not only one race someone can blame
To make this world a beautiful place
One should look in the heart and past the face
Equal is what every man should be
Our Constitution states mankind must be free

Maegen Elizabeth Philbin

Illusion of Reality

Split in the Divan of his conscience!
Bruised by the hours of hard labor!
Elevate in immortal flight the worker!
His mental feather!
To travel the hidden world of illusion!...
Ah! The parchment of silence and unhappiness unfold!
And the river of his thought flows free and old!
Dragging down sweet memoirs!
And the worker observes his hardened hands!
Consequence of so many books he has written!
In walls of concrete!
And with a smile!
That shines the dark cubicle where he lays upon!
He elevates a prayer!
That flutters with a thousand swans in flames!
Through the circumference of the earth!

Mario C. Zilleruelo

Killer Bees

Bees, Bees, Killer Bees — They're comin' from the South;
Bees, Bees, Killer Bees — They're comin' to your House;
Bees, Bees, Killer Bees — The worker bee comes First;
Bees, Bees, Killer Bees — They swarm around and Hurt!;
Bees, Bees, Killer Bees — A Scientific Blunder;
Bees, Bees, Killer Bees — They're not afraid of Thunder;
Bees, Bees, Killer Bees — Watch out, and quickly find some Cover;
Bees, Bees, Killer Beesssssssssssssssssssss!

A. J. Eldridge

Life And Death

And then an innocent cry of baby girl
Bursts from its warm home. Its cry is small and shrill,
So shrill that it could break a glass

When cleaned and handed to its mother,
The mother smiles and says that her child will be a singer,
will grow to be beautiful, wise, and cunning
the mother says with a glowing feeling

The baby smiles at this remark for it would be nice to be singer.
And finally the mother greets her young with a
warm fulfilling smile,
"This world was made for you my dear and this is not a lie

So days went on and years seemed like minutes
as mother once had said "The years, will go by quickly so enjoy
it while you can."
Before long the little girl became a
singer with the voice of a lark which
matched her beautiful ways.
And in the end her heart was still with her
mothers, for death had come for the beautiful singer and her mother

Linh-Nhi Trantien

Camelot Remembered

It was a long time ago,
But I could still remember
The lush green hills of Camelot
In the months before November.

The sunny days and starlit nights,
And the bloody gore of tavern fights,
In the months before November.

November was a month of death.
The sound of stifled people's breath
Was more than I could handle.

The warriors died and still they fought
To save the freedom of Camelot.

King Arthur's name was dragged through dust
There were no more tales of love and lust.

Now Camelot is dead and gone,
It was along time ago, but I could still
remember.

Katrina D. Smith

Party

I went to a party, mom, I knew I shouldn't have gone.
But I went against your word, mom,
And now I pay the price.

I didn't drink and drive, mom,
I drank soda instead.
I felt really proud, mom, you said I would.

I didn't drink and drive, mom,
I did the right thing, mom, you're always right.
The party is finally ending, mom.

I knew I'd get home in one piece,
Because of the way you raised me so responsible and neat.

As I started to drive away, mom,
But as I pulled into the road,
The other car didn't see me coming, mom, and hit me like a load.

As I lie here dying, mom,
I hear the policeman say,
The other guy was drinking, mom, and I'm the one who'll pay.

Mia Pritchard

The Light

The sun is out, it casts orange rays over the trees outside.
But I wouldn't know, the room is dark, it is always dark.
The curtains are open but the light is a stranger to the window.
The window is clear but the light does not lighten the carpet.
It does not spill over the dark walls like bright paint.
The room is dark as night, but it is day. I want to let the light in.
I want to let the illuminating glow cover me and fill me with happiness
I want the darkness to fade. Maybe if I open the curtains a bit more
the light will peak through. Maybe it will twinkle on my face like
a prism, and make the room glow with light. Maybe the brightness will
take away the shadows, the loneliness, the fear. I can't reach the
window though, not yet. But soon, soon I will reach the window,
I will invite in, the warmth, the joy, the life. I'm getting closer,
soon I will be out of the dark, and I will have beaten the blackness.
Yes, maybe, just maybe, I'll beat it. I may reach the clear glass in
time, and the light will come in.

Lisa P. Tuters

Distance

The distance between us is not that far
But in our hearts we've miles apart;
I long to hold you in my arms, and comfort
you when it storms:
Reality is hard for us to see:
But one day soon, I will be free:
Even though my choice was wrong:
I ask you please please, be strong:
You are the light, the light
of my life: and one day soon
Betray me not put up
A strong fight, and continue
to guide me to the light:
Hopefully upon my release
well have a fresh start:
I write this poem straight from my heart:
Treasure me in your heart,
let no one or no man tare us apart:

Robert D. Lewis

My Father, My Friend

My father, my friend, has passed away,
But I know that I'll see him again someday.
For when the Rapture comes, we'll meet in the air,
And live life eternal in our home over there.

My father, my friend, was a man who cared,
And I can remember the good times we shared.
It's those precious memories I've cherished the best,
Since the day the Lord called him from labor to rest.

My father, my friend, was a very good man,
Who'd do for others all that he can.
Although gone, he'll continue to be,
My father, my friend, a precious memory to me.

Lois T. Tibbs

I Live For Loving You

The world could crumble around me, and the sky come falling down,
But as long as you are by my side, my face won't bear a frown.

I could lose all my possessions, and everything I own,
But as long as I have you, no sadness will be shown.

I could die tomorrow, and my time on Earth would be through,
But life would be well worth it, because I lived for loving you.

Stacie Salipek

When Loneliness Becomes Your Only Love

As the sun shines through my bedroom window, I lie awake hoping
each time my body could be filled with the warmth and brightness as the sun.

I walk along the beach looking so desperately at the waves, wishing
I too could be so free to leave this dark cold place called life. Not having
to feel so confined to the responsibilities that is expected of me.

I look up to the sky, enviously wishing I too had wings like a bird.
To be born with such freedom. To feel as the whole world is my kingdom.

How I hope my heart to burn as hot as a raging fire.
To have a man see the real beauty in me and not the surface.
To feel the true passion of a man's arms embracing me ever so tightly.

To have a man so deeply desiring and wanting my love.
To make love in the way true love-making is suppose to be.
To be adored and treasured as faithfully as I would.

Will someday this world of emptiness become non-existent?
Will this world I live in become worth living for?
Will I find a man strong enough, willing enough, to break down this
lonely world I live sleeplessly throughout the days of my life?
Or will this loneliness become the "marriage" I'm destitute for.

When loneliness becomes your only love.

Lucila Cordova

Reflections

Why must one look at himself through the eyes of another?
Are we afraid to show the inner beauty one has to offer?
The heart must fear that the element of rejection should arise.
A mirror is but one dimensional in perspective and does not always tell all...
But we do resist that simple pane of glass, afraid to behold an image of truth?
Do we love the sanctity of the soul for what it is; or do we live for
for the love of others and their harsh criticisms?

Each day is your own, and a reflection of you. Make of it what you will.
Do not try to impress upon the images of others, for it wastes the
purpose of life itself.
Live life, and take each day as if it were but the last grains of
sand slipping further away.
Don't waste any time.

Each day is your own, and a reflection of you. Only you behold its outcome.
Make of it what you will.

Marysusan Villa

One Kiss

One kiss and the heat between us was more intense than the fiery breath of a mighty dragon solemnly guarding his beloved treasure, beneath the luminescent moon which gently casts its light upon the priceless gold and gems that sparkle brilliantly as does the fire in your eyes as I lay my hands upon your skin, softer than the finest silk, perfectly spun for an enchanted princess about to be joined forever, with her dream, in the royal courtyard, to the triumphant sound of the majestic drums echoing loudly as does the beat of your heart as I rest my head upon your chest and fall into supreme happiness, an eternity, like the journey of light from the ancient stars above, so many distant miles away, yet as magnificent as the day they were born into the universe to watch over and protect, as I have sworn to do for you, for my love is as broad as the great sky above and growing with every passing day. Now as the sun rises in early mourn and warms the frozen surface of the land, your touch sets my heart a flame, for when we make love it's more explosive than the mightiest volcanoes erupting with enough force to violently shake the core of the earth and sing the clouds above, simultaneously evaporating them into the atmosphere as does each breath we expel as we lay exhausted, completely fulfilled, and all the while remembering it all began with a kiss.

Scott Curtis

Grandfather

He had known her from the start
A baby girl, a most precious
possession in all of the world.
He never thought to be loved like this,
she was his world as he was hers,
always there wanting to please him with
all she did...
To make him laugh when she was happy,
and to make him cry when she was sad.
One day her world was shattered
When daddy told her he was dead.
She didn't shed a tear
but held her head high as she
lay a Red Rose on his coffin.
She looked at daddy
and wondered why he was crying.
She didn't understand,
until later in her life
and she now wishes to God that the
day had never happened.

Tammy Lynn Roop

Untitled

A child young, fragile from innocence
only to be betrayed by his loved ones
Taught that an open mind and a free heart
will make his dreams a
Reality
All along forgetting to mention the
Man in the Iron Mask
who will kill the Dreams
for his high
of watching a child killed
from the inside out
Tearing any chance for a Normal life
Always to be chased by the
Man in the Iron Mask
Always never ending the chase
goes on forever
Till the last Bleak Black moment before
The Death

Digger Rasmussen

Untitled

If I were a hundred years old today
Or even ninety-five
I'd consider it quite an accomplishment
To be so well and alive

I'd think I had done things correctly
And minded my P's and Q's
Why else would I be so privileged
And never my faculties lose

I would think I could draw some conclusions
Of what living is all about
The ceaseless striving for power
At this end seems senseless - without doubt

I would think that I had the right
To mete out a fashion to live
And my advice to posterity is
Hurt no one - learn how to forgive

And last, I'd embrace all my loved ones
And hope that my being contain
For them - a great inspiration
Then my life would have not been in vain.

Bernice Targ

Questions

Do you dare to dream the dreams, that only geniuses dreamt?
Do you wonder when you walk, as to where and when you went?
Do you think before you talk, about the tall tales that you'll tell?
Or do you see the smiles that stars bring, as they shine above so well?

Have you heard the harmony of the hills, as an orchestra plays quite near?
Have your toes grazed in the gentle grass, where the ground lets it grow so new?
Have you tasted the tantalizing nectar, only treasured treats will bring?
Or have you laughed aloud when you're alone, just to live the love you need?

Can you say that you've been fair in life, willing to forgive and forget?
Can you say you'd be breathless, as a breeze blows gently by?
Can you say that nature's nurturing way, makes you feel so nice and new?
And can you say your spirited soul, has soared above the sky so long ago? Alas, I can.

Matthew S. Taylor

The Pilot

I flew facing the wind that one last time.
As the beast's breath carried fire and ash, I soared and waited
For the moon to turn, and blood dripped from the sky.
It scared me, so I turned away. I reach for serenity
And called for it to float me across that vast realm of emptiness.
So alone, suspended in blue above a white carpet of soft billowy
Snow, and the earth so far below.
So far below, I was not a part of it. And the falcon master
Loosed his tether and he soared.

A sharp eye for raw meat and movement on the ground below, he circles,
then drops a thousand feet. Straight on target his talons pierce
flesh and he carries it to his master. He is Tethered and hooded and
rewarded with a piece of meat and the Blood of his enemy.

I circled and dropped a thousand feet piercing white snow. Many
movements within my scope, I found my target and locked on. Seven
trumpets and seven seals, the wind was stopped. Held back at the four
corners and sucked from the middle. Whiteness and brightness but, no
golden city. I pulled and climbed, trying to soar. But, my wings
were melting, My tether being pulled in. I was hooded and rewarded
with the Blood of my enemy, never loosed to soar again.

Paula Hinton

Cardiff by the Sea

To collect special stones and gems of simple beauty to perceive
A crystal to have positive energy, if one truly believes.
To give you special strength of the ancient gods
To sooth the beast, this unrighteous cancer disease.
Next to have the heart stone of Quartz to rejuvenate and calm your inner being.

I took these gems to the Pacific to cleanse them in the ocean breeze,
To say my prayers for you, Paula, for God to hear my plea.
As I cleansed your gems, at Cardiff by the Sea, I left one crystal
in the pebbles upon the beach to bring your strength from these waters of majesty.
The other crystal I sent to you to transmit this healing power to thee.

These stones from the beach were shaped by the salted waters of life
in endless movement of the currents of Poseidon's decree.
May these ancient weathered stones bring you comfort in your time of need.
Upon my journey home, in twilight, to march through mountain pass, in
glimmer of velvet green of Spring, to purify these stones and gems in
my hand for you to embrace in gentle plea.

Let the forces of Mother Nature be a comrade at your side
To relieve this relentless, unforgiving pain that you receive.
May these healing stones and my prayers be a comfort to thee,
Upon my solemn venture to Cardiff by the Sea.

Michael Paul Corman

A Prayer for Our Little People

Bless their little hearts, Oh Lord,
Our little people of today,
So innocent and unmarred by evil,
May they follow Thy paven way.

Strengthen their happy little bodies,
As they skip and run and go
Into their world of fantasy,
That knows not fear or woe.

Broaden their little minds, dear Father,
As they travel through the lands,
Lead them safely here and yonder,
Protect them from evil hands.

Then when finally comes tomorrow,
And our little people are no longer small,
Oh make them fitted to man their guns,
To conquer, if must, the great, the tall!

Let them march stately, with chin up high,
Prepared for the sunshine and shower.
And may the prayers from our lips today,
Be a pillow for them tomorrow.

Hannah G. Hutchins

Untitled

When we started out as bride and groom
Our love more than filled the room
As time progressed and we grew
Our love for each other, we both knew
Now, as we start one more year
I don't know how to express myself to you, my dear
I hope we become the closest of friends
Yet that's not where I want it to end
I want our life full of love and happiness
Our Golden Years, I don't want to miss
I hope we are together for the rest of our days
And learn to accept the other one's ways.

Amy L. Ross

Ode to Edgar

Tears and pain
Pain and tears
How can I allay my fears
Of not seeing your face anymore
Of not seeing you walk in the door

Your smile, your hello and your cheerfulness
Will be sadly missed by all of us
Your handsome face, your gentleness
This face we can no longer caress

Time cannot erase your gentle face
And that magic touch
On everyone you met
This is a man who one and all
Can never in this life ever forget.

Edna Cott

Respite

And so he starts the lonely trek
Past empty chairs, and half dim halls
The sound of applause still ringing in his ears.
A sudden stop, a quick glance
Upon the stage of his life,
And then a smile of content.
The actor is pleased
"It has been a good year..."

Anna Viray

The Search

Greetings from the corner room of the corner building,
on the corner of the couch, at the edge of my seat
Staring into the eyes of a woman who is a stranger
and who is my sister - both and neither -
at the same time.

I look longingly into her eyes and seek to know
what I already know.
Sometimes I wonder, the harder I look,
am I looking for her, or
am I looking for me?

Grace Dadoyan

The Song of the Manic-Depressed

To live a life in uncertainty, emotions flying high and low,
On which plateau I'll find myself each day, I really do not know.

Will I feel rage at an unknown adversary, a phantom foe,
Or will I be on depression's edge and just as low as I can go?

To soar with the eagles or crawl with the slugs are feelings I know well,
But at which level I will find myself is impossible to tell.

Life is so difficult; it's so hard to make myself trudge on,
When all I want is this excruciating pain to be gone.

This illness is sometimes more than a body can endure,
Because often much of my life is nothing but a blur.

Maybe one day my mind will be whole and think as others do;
Well, I know it will be in Heaven because God's Word is true.

One day I will not cry and hurt inside, as I often do;
One day I will not feel the rage and my heart will not feel blue.

I long for that day with all my heart, mind and soul,
That day, when my life will finally be made whole.

David A. Taylor

No Dust on the Cross

Though buried deep by ages long past,
Once despised by all but a few,
I can never forget the burden it bore
Or the debt that was finally due.

It is secreted away from contemptuous minds
Whose lies flow on every breath,
As they seek to deny the one who hung there
And the sins that were cancelled by death.

But deceitful words and treacherous acts
Corrupt not this pillar of old,
The fact that it held the dear Lamb of God
Increases its value tenfold.

Even the feared, obscene ravages of time
Have no power to change gold into dross,
So, wherever it rests, I'll always believe
That there is no dust on the cross!

Jo Ann Walker

Dream Expert

One starves to bring ecstasy to the nose
One curses constantly to be captivated by the rose
Dreaming wildly to release the pain
Looking vividly at woman in vain
Admitting the pain is to become the beast
Pitilessly cooked for the feast
So do all these wonderful things with a silent tongue
A straight stance
Still as a cocked arrow
Dry as men
Giving up life as if it were a weekend fling

Fitz Weiss

"This Is A Beautiful World"

This world is beautiful, if sin was out.
One day sin will be gone there is no doubt.
The people are lovely,
The children are beautiful, and the
Flowers are lovely and they smell so sweet.
They make my heart almost skip a beat.
When you see a bride and groom happy in love
It makes you know there is a God above
How could anyone want to harm an
Animal or a child?
I hope people will get more tame.
And not be so wild.
The Lord made these beautiful people,
And also this beautiful World.
This world is more beautiful, than
Precious jewels and pearls.

Edith Howard

Old

My darling child don't be scared
One day you too will turn gray haired,

Little one don't be afraid,
For that's the way we all were made,

To grow older each and every day,
Is life's one and only way.
I would go back to childhood,
If only wishing would and could,

Please don't worry, there's nothing to fear,
Although your time does grow near.

Dear sweet child please be bold,
Because one day we all grow old,

Colleen Waller

And You Need Him

One little kiss and your heart starts to dance.
One little touch, you can feel the romance.
One little moment, a precious hug.
And then you know you need him like a drug.

The drug gives you happiness, a word undefined.
The drug can make you cry, but you never mind.
The drug always will you pursue.
And then you realize you need him to need you.

When he needs you, you know he will stay.
When he needs you, it's not a game just to play.
When he needs you, anything can go.
And then you wonder if you need him more than you know.

Amy Schafer

Untitled

When things seem to be hopeless and far away
One tends to grumble and blame the world
But where is that "Eye Of the Mind"
The one thing capable of getting us to understand.

It took many years for me to understand that it was not me
But circumstances which had made me doubt my ability to cope.
How simple it would have been to trust to that "eye" to
Realize that a light sometimes does not shine if we do not see.

Trials and tribulations often come unexpectedly but,
If one realizes that the "eye of the mind" is really
The imagination which opens the mind and finds a way.
Whenever we are distraught and need help, check yours
And you will see that everything can be understood in time.

Alice R. Lafleur

Dear Heart

When loving hearts collide there is no reasoning,
Only the magic of the impact.
Joyful and triumphant,
Giddy in delight of enduring the shock,
We the separate, we who long to connect,
Believe in the dream that two hearts can be one.
The sweet intensity of our collision
Makes us believe.

That divine dream carries our heart through time,
Pulsating to its own tempo and rhythm,
Enabling us to endure, together.

And when we forsake the other,
The impact still boasts of magic.
But the intensity is no longer sweet,
For the wrenching of hearts is agony.
And the only solace we can expect
Is in the sublime memory of the magic and the dream.

So dear heart grieve not.
Rejoice. Rejoice in your wisdom not to reason,
But to collide.

Charlotte Anderson O'Brien

Others

When there's no one to say "I love you"
or even seem to care.
When your spirits hit the bottom,
remember, Jesus is there.
When the world seems to have forgotten you
and you wish somebody cared,
Remember there are others also
for whom Jesus cares.
Others low in spirit, sinking in despair.
Others also thinking, no one cares.
Do you have a little love,
enough to spread around?
Jesus will bless you
if you spread your love around.

Edna Strahm

A Step Behind You

If you ever need a hand to grasp,
or feel you're in the dark, put a hand
behind you I'm there, I bear the scars,
I'm here always behind you to catch you
when you fall.
If you start to stumble or come to a barricading
wall, I'm here a step behind you to
catch you when you fall, I'm there I bear
the scars. To watch you, and to comfort, and
to just go on.

Elizabeth A. Summerhays

Untitled

Our oceans are full of pollution,
Our children one full disease,
they say that there is no
solution, and too tell you the truth I agree.

The animals are all gone now,
They were killed off by poachers
and thieves, some day my children
will ask me why there are no
more to see? and I'll tell them
with the saddest face, It's
because of us - the human race.

James Hanberry III

Unconditional Love

Maybe I ran when I should have walked
Or held it inside when I should have talked
I might have quit when I should have tried
Or maybe I laughed when I should have cried

Some days are filled with indecision
Some times I don't know what's right or wrong
But I'm certain that as long as we're together
Whatever turn I take, I'm not alone

Maybe I left when I should have stayed
Or maybe I cursed when I should have prayed
And there are days I wish I could live over
The times I treated you like some one else

And through it all you always understand me
When I don't even understand myself
But I'll always try to get it right with you

Brenda Lee Souder

Is Different Better, Or Just Different

Is different better
Or just different?
If we sang the same song,
You your way and I mine,
Is yours better, or is mine?

Is different better
Or just different
If I sang your rendition and you honored mine,
Would the better of the two
Be yours by me, or mine by you?

In what categories would we fall
And what names would we be called?
Certainly my supporters would favor me,
And yours you, don't you agree?

Come;
Tell me how do you really feel?

Do you have the answer I seek
That makes us so unique?
And is your answer better than mine?
Or just different?

Eugene Chico Waters

Heart and Soul

Does anyone on earth see my soul
or someone here know the fears I hold
Will mankind care if I do or die
and do they know, truth or lie?

Can I trust that man really cares
what is really honest or fair
Is there belief in the commandments God hath bestowed
And will my countenance grow old or cold?

My heart holds many aches untold
for many lives that I couldn't mold
I know what it is I feel inside
And find those feelings hard to hide.

Both love and pain are held within
and deep repentance for my sins
A love for God that knows no bounds
it peals in my soul, 'round and 'round.

Here I am in confusion, again today
wondering what more it is I can say
To those whose lives I've guarded so much
to those whose hearts I may have touched.

Catherine Tetrault

In the World of Living

It's too dark to see this beautiful landscape of imagination,
Or this colorful horizon of imagery working so hard to be beautiful.
Why is this light shinning so brightly?
So brightly that I have to close my eyes just to feel the color of its gleaming emotion.

I can see-
There's just enough light-
I can see-
But I don't want to see...
The thin dark allies, and bright open streets of hideousness
In the world of living.

Jessy Hinton-Scott

A Winter Miracle

We took a long, long ride in a one horse open sleigh;
Our eyes opened wide with awe at the sights of this day.
The bells upon the horse were so merrily a-jingling;
We sat on the seat; and in the cold, we were a-tingling.

People sliding their skis, passed upon the long white road,
Pushed with their ski-poles to glide easier with their load.
They heard the bells jingling; they stopped along the side.
We waved and smiled to each other and continued with our ride.

We saw tall Christmas trees, mantled with sparkling white;
The snow covered beaver dams, such a marvelous delight.
The many animal tracks along the bright unblemished snow,
Criss-crossed the openings; down to the water they must go.

We watched for the animals; we knew we saw their tracks!
They stayed hidden; we never saw them; alas and alack!
Glorious smells of the trees, wafted upon the clear air.
Winter birds' lilting songs, came to us from everywhere.

The azure blue sky above; the snow sparkling radiant hues;
God blessed us, he presented to us, various beautiful views.
He gave to us these Miracles; all these wonderful scenes;
We marveled at His many works, we hold Him in high esteem.

Ada Stein

Our Generation

Our generation
Our fathers' heirs,
We now inherit what they once called theirs.
The Crime, the Poverty,
The Guilt, the Hate;
But is it too late to recreate?
A time existing long ago
When our fathers made the things we now know as home.
Our generation
Our fathers' heirs,
We must now fix what they once called theirs.
The Crime, the Poverty,
The Guilt, the Hate;
But is it too late to recreate?
A people just like you and me,
Who tried to help the world so destructively.
Our generation
Our fathers' gem,
We have no choice,
We are now them.

Hedy Henderson-Favara

Fear

Fear not of what you see.
Fear not of what you hear.
Fear only of what may be.
Fear only of what is there,

Stacy Lytle

Since Mother is Gone

While mother lived, she was so sweet, and always was so kind
Our home was always nice and neat, and cooking was so fine
But then there came that awful thing, of which there was no cure
And took my mother to that other land, which is heaven I'm quite sure

Although I could hardly bear, to see my mother die
I knew that she'd be happier there, in her mansion there on high
Now since that day has been four years, since she has gone away
Sometimes my eyes will fill with tears, for mother's gone to stay

Though dad does try to be so brave, his hair is turning gray
He tries to hold up from the grave, but he's fading fast away
It's been so sad and lonely, since mother's gone to stay
No one can ease the burning heart, since she died that lonesome day

While I'm at work I make it fine, and never have a sigh
But I can't help but pine at night, no matter how I try
While mother lived, I was always glad to see the sun go down
But since she's gone at night it's sad, with sorrows hanging round

James W. Fox

Conception

And now there is light,
Part like the Red Sea did the clouds which obscure sight,
Raising the curtain to a drama entitled life,
What was venom is now honey,
Banished are the fears that steal words from the tongue,
Expression dominating the perils of hush,
What once antagonized now gratifies,
Behold this man, emerging majestically from the cocoon of immaturity,
Presence of mind ousting the clutches of naivete,
Apprehension is now anticipation,
Born is a man who wanders among fledging forests of possibility and
hope,
Inevitably lost to the limits of time is a child who planted the seeds,
And life begins,
Again.

Heath Harper

Untitled

A dream of all there is to come
passes me by-
Haunts me like a shadow in the night.
Search through the void, the darkness of my mind
to find
a future so close, yet ever beyond reach.
with flailing arms I attempt to grasp
some weakened sense of reality,
but if, in my search, I find
something I'm unable to hold
should I let it go? Lead it home?
Or take its life as it took mine.
Or leave it be, lost and scared -
Alone-
On the road to my dreams;
To cry itself to sleep at night,
And never feel the dream of light
that shines so far away from me.
My future holds no dreams.

April Homich

Prince

Your eyes are like the eyes of a dragon, burning beneath my soul,
peering through my windows of sight;
demanding to take full control.

Your moves are those of a lion, swift, smooth, and definite,
accompanied by the touch of your finger tips that drive
beneath my flesh.

You are a man of magnitude; wrapped in a wall of stone.
While your eyes are like the lights of a light house
guiding the lost ship home.

So be the man that you are, the ship is always at sea.
Shine your light long and bright, and shine your beam on me.

Raise your arms and embrace me, tearing down the wall;
for your eyes are the eyes of the light house that guided
the little ship home.

Diane Pope Waller

The Hare And The Tortoise

Said the hare to the tortoise, one fine summer day,
"People are like us, in a strange sort of way.
They're in a tough race, every day of their life,
Some a hare's pace, some a tortoise's strife.
If people just live one day at a time
Their own road of life wouldn't seem such a climb.
For they're either looking back and remembering the tears,
Or they're looking ahead and planning the years.
Life wouldn't be so complicated, I'm sure,
If these people would find a sure just cure."
The tortoise looked up from his heavy brown shell,
And uttered a cure that solved it quite well,
"If people only listen to God and His Son,
Then the race of life would never be roughly run,
For each and everyone one has a job that can be done,
In the name of God, the Father, and Jesus, His Son."

Cheryl Skinner

Suicide

The taking of your life is depressingly sad,
People do it although it is bad.
We acknowledge this and know its true
Yet we do nothing to see it through.
The life of a youth is full of sorrow
For them they think there is no tomorrow;
But there is hope, they don't realize,
For they are just children in some people's eyes.
They have lives of their own
But they feel so alone.
Their hopes and dreams have flashed right by,
They feel hopeless; they want to die.
A gun is raised up to their head,
And before they know it, they'll surely be dead.

Amy Nix

The Blinded Sight

What is it like to see with your ears?
or not to know when someone is near.
To feel trapped in darkness and no way out.
The need to cry, and scream, and shout.
Rage running through your skin.
Wanting to be let out and not stuck in.
The terror that's deep within your soul.
The fright of someone letting you go.
Did you know that sight is worth gold?
I'm not sure, but that's what I've been told.

Amy Shaw

"Self Discovery"

I was on the most important
Photography assignment of my life -
Doing a self portrait.
I sat in the meadow,
Weighing, and discarding, thoughts and ideas.
Then I saw the delicate blossom -
Standing alone, completely segregated
from the other flowers.
It was a dandelion.
gently placed
Near a patch of wild daisies.
It was an ugly blossom,
  in appearance.
But in appearance only.
At that precise moment, I knew.
I knew I was that dandelion -
Alone;
Alone but standing Tall and Proud.

Candace Sluder

Daddy's Tapestry

Threads woven into the tapestry of a little daughter's life
Placed there by a loving father as a shield from sin and strife.
Threads of wit and love and laughter gently woven through
  the years,
Beautiful strands of understanding which would shield her
  from the tears.
Never tiring and ever patient he continued in the task
And his little girl up knowing all she had to do was ask.
Oh, she took his work for granted many steps along the way
Never knowing that this tapestry would serve her well one day.
She thought his work was finished when she became a wife
Only to discover it would continue throughout her life.
"Daddy, show me now the colors and the pattern that you made
So that I can give my children the same comfort, care and aid."
As he wrapped her in the tapestry she then began to see
That his handiwork wasn't just for this life but for eternity.

Elaine Pullins Winsor

"Oh Just Tell Me"

There was a man, in the hall of fame.
Playing football, was his game.
Famous far, and famous wide.
With everything, just at his side.

Two little children, and a beautiful wife.
Yet went to a store, and buy him a knife.
Then the lady stop living, Oh! She is dead.
So he rode in a bronco, with a gun to his head.

Then the cops did follow, wherever he roam.
But ended his journey, back to his home.
Now and safe and secluded, behind the bar.
What is the faith of this superstar?

Celestine Assoon

"Blessed"

Glancing at the paper's front page,
Reading, the headlines speak of rest,
Thinking of the world's darkest age.
Wondering what possibly is left.
Sadly enough, though, some are caged.
Then starting to realize what was kept-
Service to God, so sorely gauged
In safe, warm, sheets the long night spent.
Waking up and feeling outraged that
Some sleep outside in what debris lent.

Ashley Hydrick

Phantoms

One might think you are a coat of armor the way you cover me
Playing video tapes of pained memories night and day and inside
and outside haunting cycles of the past that over shadow the
present.
Enslaving the invisible multitudes of lurking skeletons
crouched in the dark corners of one's mind
casting suspicious shadows magnified
the counterfeit creatures, deceptive beasts and imprisoned terror
that masque as a resemblance of reality
disguised and distorted as truth
a taunting marathon attacking then retreating
but never leaving
'til death do us part
paralyzing the veteran
who defends and holds on to what once was reality

Cathlyn A. Troyer

Tribute to Mary Ann

Casing mail with accuracy and speed
Pleasing carriers and customers there is a need
To this management would add, "Indeed! Indeed!"
Customer satisfaction is like planting a seed

However, now the anxiously awaited time has come
To leave our Eaton Rapids Post Office and run
Go home, my friend, and everyday relax
No more to unload those heavy sacks

Unloading is certainly enough to break our backs
To that old alarm clock, you can now take an ax
That 4:00 A.M. hour will now be for us
As you stay home planning tours by bus

We will be certain to miss you with much envy
That precious time being spent with friends and family
Remembering postcards of men you couldn't resist
Without your laugh and humor, how will we exist?

Good luck and God Bless You, my friend
Into a world of retirement we will send
Back into the hands of loving family
With happiness forever for all to see

Joyce Coats

The Boy

See the boy standing at the door,
Pray for him as he leaves for war.
Going places that are unknown,
When he walks out the door he's on his own.

See the boy with the gun by his side,
Crying as he watches another friend die.
Whispering orders that are passed down,
Stay low, but watch for traps in the ground.

See the boy running through the fields so fast,
His every thought and breath could be his last.
Here comes the chopper to pick him up,
This boy deserves a medal and to be wished good luck.

This place that holds young men dying,
This place that leaves families crying.
This place where boys were sent by Uncle Sam,
This place is known as North and South Vietnam.

Debbie Lloyd

Sidewalk

Enmeshing myself into this city's streets,
Pressing my face against the grainy walk
My eyelashes softly caressing pebbles and sand,
Eyes absorbing the texture
of what life must be like here.
Fingers feel the grains, ingrained,
make patterns on palms,
leave behind memories
of a life I couldn't live,
except through your eyes
and I can only remember
by the patterns of the grains
Laying silently on the sidewalk
where you walk everyday,
on your way to a life
I couldn't live

Erin Bradshaw

Blue Dream

Smiling eyes, a soft, hazel brown
  Pulling, tugging, grasping to find their message
What is it about the gentle rise and fall of their
  light that leads men to love, to live, to die?
Quiet eyes, puzzled by a frown.
  How could one feel anger under their gaze?
The feel of soft caresses are carried floating
  across my mind.
Brought to me by the siren of my soul.
Crying eyes, love song sun, now weep in solitude.
  straining, praying, failing to hold together a dying dream.
Emotion stays unchecked by the white lie "always".
Knowing eyes, dulled by the truths of reality
  The light is rekindled by a newfound star
  Leaving another trailing a blue dream as it
  falls slowly from sight.

Arnold E. Johnson IV

One-Of-A-Kind

So many beautiful thoughts of you in my dreams
Puts me in heaven, or though it seems.

An endless place to coral thoughts of you
Of which I hope to fill, before the night is through.

So as I lay in bed with these thoughts of you in my mind
I begin to smile and realize you are one-of-a-kind.

The expressions of laughter, sweetness, and love in your smile
Makes me forget about my problems, if only for a little while.

So let me take this time to pay thanks for all you do
Listen real close and you'll hear the words, "I love you."

Each night I thank God you are mine,
Because you are definitely, one-of-a-kind.

For 20 years you've been my lover and best friend
And in my heart I know we'll be together until the end.

So place a soft kiss upon my lips as you look deep into my eyes
To bring the hidden tender side of me out of deep disguise.

Locked in my heart is all my love for you to find,
Because you are definitely my, one-of-a-kind.

Jeff Foster

Stop - Smell the Flowers

The sun is rising and a new day is upon us.

A new day with demands, concerns about yesterday
questions about tomorrow

Another day of giving of ourselves to others
Nourishing their souls while giving little regard
To our own needs for nourishment, love, and care
Pulling from the depths of our souls
Trying to be everything to everyone.
Exhausting our bodies and our beings
Shutting out our own need for closeness,
Friendship and love, allowing our well to reach
Its depths until there is no more to give,
or until we become empty shells

When will we realize that we need to
stop and smell the flowers
Or their beauty will not be ours to behold
but that of the one who places them on our grave

Carole Dowds

From the Heart

Into my life you came
Quickly and unexpectedly
But step by step we grew closer
And now you are a part of me.
I thought I knew what love was all about
But you showed me things I'd never seen before
You gave me hopes and dreams for the future
Now I find myself always needing you more.
Every day you make my life worth living
You help me through things that I couldn't go through alone
There was a time when I would have been afraid of this commitment
But now I couldn't make it if you were gone.
I look forward to each new day
Knowing that you will be here to take care of me
And knowing that no matter what happens
We will be together for all eternity.

Jennifer Plylar

Untitled

Young and foolish,
reckless and bold.

I didn't care
what the future would hold.

"The years will pass so fast."
I was told.

I wasn't worried, I thought I'd
never grow old.

Selfish and self-centered
I lived a life of full of fun.
"I won't be sorry," I thought, when my life is done.
Now the time has swiftly passed me by.
It won't be long, before I too will die.

How can I warn the youth of today.
Don't let your tomorrows just slip away.

Cherish each day, and those you hold dear.
Your family and friends, always keep them near.

Then when you come to the end of your years,
you'll have beautiful memories.
Instead of sad, lonely tears.

Domenica Puzzuoli

Right or Wrong, Black or White

Black or white,
Red or yellow.
What's the big fight?
It doesn't matter, your color.

You know not to,
Judge a book by its cover.
No one has the right, old or new.
God is the one who has the right to govern.

Everyone thought Hitler was bad,
Killing people because of his looks or religion.
Look at your own lass or lad,
It's not their decision.

Some call black people niggers,
I think not!
Anyone who goes around causing trouble, I think, is a nigger.
Those people in hell, they will rot!

An opinion is right to own,
But it doesn't mean it's right.
I think this poem has shown,
Why the fight, everyone has the right.

Jessica Mazon

Remember

I'll always remember you, if you always remember me.
Remember our love and it well always be.
Remember the good things and God help us the bad times.
No matter how bad things get, always remember the love we shared,
Think of me daily, for I will of you.
Never forget the smell of my hair, the way I walked, my sweet smiles.
In your old age let your memory go but don't let me go.
So sorry we didn't have a chance to grow old together
Young love dies so young.

Christen Lippincott

Funny I Say

Off to market I ventured one day
Remembering my grocery list halfway
Returning I parked in the driveway
As I locked all the doors
I momentarily froze
Watching the keys dangling at bay
My face beaded with sweat in the brisk of the day
As I searched high and low, to open it someway
I smiled big and wide
As my embarrassment I tried to hide
Only to discover much to my dismay
The back doors had been left open this day
Oh well! What can I say!

Angela L. Bunch

I Imagine

Can I imagine being black?
Racist people talking behind my back—
I don't know why they think they're great,
When people of color they can't tolerate.
If I think too long, it makes me feel bad.
They've no right to make me feel sad.
God made all people,
They come in all colors;
But color shouldn't matter
If we love one another.

Jessica Rankin

My Love...

Is the misty dew on morning clover
remembrance of a kiss from a long lost lover
It is shames resolve in embarrassments shadow
a stream running silent past a slumped over willow

It's the innocence of youth through ageless eyes
the heartbeat of sorrow when someone dies
It's the giddy excitement of Christmas snow
it's eyes welled with tears too happy to flow

It's a sigh escaping parted lips
for a view of the sun
beyond a plateau or cliff

It's the drive that moves me
a "Silent Quest"——
It's all that I hold dear, in truth
PRICELESS...

Faye A. McBride

Sugar Maple Cove

Content in this quietude,
Removed from the rush of metropolitan hustle,
At peace in this solitude,
Engaged contemplatively with bird, breeze, tree, and mussel,
Sparsely set leaves tickled by whispering winds rustily rustle.

The rain off and on all day long has been;
The lake has seeped up the shore's earthy shin.
The sad smoky sky signals sweating storms;
Wisps arrange the clouds in beatific forms.
A harmony of mind and nature dances dreamily and conforms;

This is how heaven might be imagined to be:
Peace, cool, calm-like a cloud on the sea:
Tranquilly floating and gently divine,
A place where time travels in grace and ease;
A space where the soul is warmed by the most elegant wine;
There, kind words and thoughts between all pass
Like sugar maple leaves asleep on the grass
Sleeping gracefully in this cove fit for a queen. . .
Peace, cool, calm. . .
Sugar maple ravine, sugar maple ravine.

John F. Bolinger

The Room

Daggers of a foreign light,
Resolutely penetrate entangled recesses.
Previously untrodden paths stand disclosed.

Stealthily the Fortress dissolves —
Amidst this company.
Whence walls removed
Can self sustain; or does
Greater darkness find it's way.

Ann S. Wichman

"The Soap Opera Extravaganza"

If in this life you discover that you are one of the "Young and Restless" and you're sitting on the "Edge of Night" and "As the World Turns" you are constantly complaining about "All My Children" and are more concerned about "Ryan's Hope" than that of your own. Then you are on the way to "General Hospital" by way of "Dallas."

If Jesus is not your "Guiding Light" then you need not "Search For Tomorrow". Because you have only "One Life To Live" and you will never see "Another World", for so will be the "Days of Our Life."

Elder C. L. Barnes

Gift from the Prairie

The pasque-flower's lavender wisps
rise to herald the coming of Spring.

Leadplants and coneflowers strain heavenward,
accenting Summer's green mantle of grass.

The coneflowers' burnt-brown heads stand stiff
straight in the wind,

Autumn sentinels to the bluestems and gramas
waving farewell to the migrating millions.

As the plaintive calls fade away,
Winter snows settle in around
the dried and resting herbs,
slowing, sheltering the tiny buds, until

Touched by warm spring radiance, they
awaken,
renewed,
replenished.

As our faith that God is with us
in this place and everywhere.

Jean Ann Robinson

Rise Up

Rise up above thine own desire,
Rise up, far greater things aspire.
When things go wrong, hurt the quick,
Rise up, and in the battle thick,
You'll sear and scar, but then you'll stick:
Rise up, head high, your heart's afire.

Rise up, heed not the cynic's ban,
Rise up, and be a greater man:
The torch you carry flames on high,
It's radiant beams hear not the sigh
Of wind, and storm, or passers-by:
Rise up, aflame, I know you can.

Rise up, and greater things and deeds,
Rise up with you, inspires, exceeds,
To do a turn that speaks, achieves,
Thy soul won freedom, lives and breathes,
And all mankind, ye, priest and thieves,
Rise up with you, you're what man needs.

James Arthur Roche

Sense of Awareness

Imagine ....
Rolling fog on a wet London Street
Soft floating snow on an Aspen mountain peak
Warm sun in Cali bakes the concrete
Waves crash on a tropical island retreat
Senses run free.... reaching their full potential
Soothing, tasteful,as it tames the intellectual
Burning orange skyline, leaves the mind, in peace
A sense of relief .... or release
Comfortable as a hot night under cool sheets
Sights so simple, as a dimple, on a young child's face
Smiling gaze, easily the innocent are amazed .....
From a shaggy carpet under bare feet
Another soul sprouts and blossoms from a single seed

Jeffery A. Chavez

Ethical Morals

Square as a triangle
Round as a diamond, simple as a labyrinth
Less active than a lucid pond
Cooler than hell
I stand.....

Staring into the end of time
Holding death's hand
I stand.....

Being timid as a lion
Everything's different, lavender sand?
But still, I stand.....

With the blood red sky above me
And under.... the black land
I stand.....

Temptations watching ... waiting.
Surrounding me, a grim band
Firm I stand.

Conspiracies!
Monstrous, powerful discrepancies
Facing the worst, I will always stand.

Heather R. Jones

The German Shepherd

The German Shepherd,
Runs through the still,
Cold,
Darkness.
Chasing the criminal that robbed its owner.
Unaware of the dangers that lies ahead.

The criminal reaches a dead end,
Turns around,
And sees the angry dog.

The dog leaps at the criminal,
Knocking him on the ground,
Biting him,
Ripping his flesh.
Killing him.
Leaving nothing but flesh and bones.

After its kill,
It goes back to its owner.
Licks the face,
And whimpers.
Knowing that the person will never harm its owner again.

Elisha Ouano

Joan of Arc

At thirteen I saw it, the light of God;
Saint Michael, saint Catherine and saint Margaret came
To tell me to leave and perform a great task.
'Tis three years later, I've tried to run away;
The Dauphin I see, before I must save France.
They think me a witch for seeing the light.
I cut off my hair so I would look male,
Wore suits made of armor, a helmet of steel
Fought with my two brothers, Jean and Pierre,
With my friends Vignolles and Alenion,
Wounded many a time. Our ruler deceived us.
They would not help, I was tied as a witch.
They burnt me at stake, but my heart still beats.

Joanne Alexandrea Peroo

Untitled

At last—the south wind, cloaked in clouds that stream,
Sad-colored, between the splendors of sun a flowers,
Like thoughts whose course—from far horizons of doubt
To more remote resolution—dazedly
Parts truth from joy.

The young tress, swaying supply nightward, seem
Dancers that lean aback from a too close
Embrace, and those in blossom sigh away
Petals which play—float—fall with grace perverse
As heartless words'.

From gray, hushed heights the laughing rush of rain
Beats in the strained, expectant ear of earth,
So each note stirs to hope the sleeping seeds
Of summer and spreads rich darkness on the sod,
Like startled blood—

Till loosed in answer from the listening heart,
Out of its dark delight and coiled suspense,
Drifts dreamy scent between the nests and buds,
Winged with bright dust of snowdrops and tragic promise
Of unborn roses.

David Barraz

Goodbyes

I don't know why, but even though we
said goodbye everything I do just keeps reminding
me of you.
I didn't want our relationship to end, but
as everybody says all good things must sometime
come to an end.
You were always such a puzzle to me. I
don't even know how it ever came to be.
I know neither of us meant to hurt one
another, because our love was so strong and even though
we're not together now our love is still so very strong.
Everybody says that there are other fish in the
sea, but you were the only fish that ever
meant anything to me.
I don't know how it comes to be, that all
bad things always happen to me.
No matter how hard I try, I can't help
but sit and cry.
There is not much I can say, but one
thing is for sure you were with me most of the way.

Julie Culp

The Flight

My sister sat,
Sat in that chair most of the night,
Thinking that her vigil,
Would keep Mama's soul from taking flight.

She sat in that chair thinking,
That if she did not fall asleep,
Old Square Toes would not have a chance,
Into Mama's room to creep.

In that chair, she sat thinking,
That if she could just stay awake,
There would be no way for Old Square Toes,
Mama's soul to take.

But in the stillness of the night,
Mama came to her and said, "I'm alright,
Go to sleep now because God has taken me by the hand,
And we are leaving to travel to the Promised Land."

The peace of God descended upon my sister,
As she sat in that chair.
She finally fell asleep,
Knowing that Mama was in the Master's care.

Barbara Ann Washington-Smalling

Little Loggerhead, Planted Deep In The Sand

Mother's journey, working her way toward the beach
Searching for the protective spot, her flippers
Dig deep into the sand, cutting a path like a canal.
Like a backhoe she begins her nest, reaching deep into the sand
To protect her little loves, her survivors.
Planted deep in the sand they wait, packed together.
Their day nears as the eggs begin to crack,
Three more days submerged beneath the sand, gaining strength.

Glowing brightly in the sky the moon illuminates the beach
Like a street light, to guide the little flippers to the sea.

The time arrives and the little loggerheads emerge.
Digging their way out of the safety and security of their home
They begin the first of many journeys.
A small army paddles its way toward the water.
Guided by the moon, they are hopeful of success.
Through thick sand, across the shell bank covered with salty foam
Like little mail carries they are unyielding
Stopping just moments for their second wind, they trudge on
Awaiting that first taste of salt water
So they can fly through the sea like birds.

Julie A. Cook

"Stars On Your Nose"

You sit on the porch, your thoughts start to wander
Searching your mind for times that seemed fonder.
That sun's on the horizon ... a pale golden light
Creeping so softly, to slow down the night.
In a blink of an eye or a twitch of your toes
the dark ... the silence ...
The Stars On Your Nose!

Noises from the forest ... the crickets ... the owl,
darting bat wings the she-wolf's howl.
Crackling embers, the warmth of the fire.
Wrapped in a quilt .. country smells you admire.
The wind breaks the silence, whispering as it blows
to the pinetops ... to the mountains ...
The Stars On Your Nose:

Strumming the guitar, hum a peaceful tune
echoing through the valley, bouncing off the moon.
Stepping off the porch, wet grass at your feet,
gazing at the heavens, a Falling Star Treat.
Back in your rocker, your eyes start to close,
You drift into slumber ... With Stars On Your Nose!

Christopher J. Marsar

A Silhouette

The dawn will come when there will be no one left to
See the sun rise or the moon glow.
Birds will sing no more,
For the devils of the earth have plagued them with disease.
The sounds of life echo through the wind amongst the dust.
The waters that were once blue with happiness,
Are now blackened by the clouds deadly tears.
Tropical forests of life will flourish no more,
For there are only whispers of it being.
The stars no longer shine upon the earth,
For they are ashamed of what the devils have done.
The laughter of an innocent babe will no longer be heard,
But in the memories of a dead planet.
Far to the west on a desert mountain
Stands a silhouette of a wolf
He howls the song of betrayal that carries on for eternity.

Joni Jovani

Do You Know Who I Am?

I'm some what confused, "Do you know who I am?
Seems to be lost, can you help me please, ma'am?
I, I, have no idea, what I'm doing here,
Don't know where I'm going, or how to get there.
I must have a family and someplace to stay,
Right now, I don't know the time or the day.
Can you please help me, find way back home?
Oh, how long have I been walking, how long did I roam?
Lord, Lord, please help me to find my way,
Let this kind lady know, who I am today.
I don't understand what is happening to me,
Sometimes I'm so mixed up, I feel like I'm crazy,
Miss do you know my name, do you know who I am?
You say you are my daughter, why, thank you ma'am
Lord, I hope this lady knows what she's talking about.
Lord, I putting my trust in you, and you, I don't doubt.

Catherine Moseley

Maude

I'll tell you a story you won't like to hear,
Sent home from the hospital to live less than a year.
Staring death in the face, time comes near.
Talking of old times, and faces held dear.
Pain so severe, hard to endure,
Fooled everyone didn't shed a tear.
People coming and going from my house
To feed me and bathe me, making me grouse.
Sleeping a lot, growing weaker and weaker
My mind still strong - looking for my keeper.
Family looks on with avarice eyes.
To hell with Mama, can't wait till she dies.
Hold me and kiss me, that's all that I asked.
For us it was easy, her kids unforgiving the past.
Able to joke right to the end.
Unforgettable spirit, I was glad to call friend.

Cherie Manion

Coming True

At night I sleep and then she comes,
She comes to hold, to caress, to love
But when the new day lights, she is gone,
for she is only a dream.

The next night I sleep and there she is,
the love is back to see, to feel, to enjoy
But the new day dawns and it ends,
for she is only in a dream.

The third night comes and I lie down to rest,
she is here, with me, becoming apart of me.
The day begins to break and a tear forms in my eye,
for she is only in my dream.

Another night darkens and she comes to me,
She captivates me with her smile, her touch, her eyes
She is the only one for me, but the night is over,
for she is my dream.

The night comes again and again and again,
each night she is there.
She will always love me, hold me, be with me.
The morning comes and she is there. For she is no longer just a dream.

John Baxter

Abortion

I'm the creature that is forming inside my mommy,
She doesn't know about me yet, but she will very soon.

I'm one month old now and I heard a heartbeat inside me,
I'm so happy, I can't wait until my mommy finds out about me.

I'm two months old now and my hands are forming and my feet
are getting shape, I can't open my eyes yet, so I'll just rest inside
my mommy.
I'm three months old now and my mommy is noticing that she
is changing and has become very ill.

Today, my mommy went to the doctor and has found out about me.
I can feel her crying out in loud sobs. I wonder why? Shouldn't
she be happy that a new life, a new soul, a miracle is happening
inside her?

I'm four months old now and mommy has told my daddy about me,
He said he would stay by her side.

I'm five months old now and my daddy has left me and my mommy all
alone, he said he had changed his mind and didn't want to deal
with me.

The time has come now when I will see the world and I'll get to
see my mommy. But something is going wrong. What are they
doing?
I knew then that my mommy didn't want me either. That day I died
and someone else was saved.

Angela D. Norris

Married Bliss

She gets up in the morning with a smile on her face.
She goes to the breakfast table, where she says grace.
She gets the kids all dressed and ready for school,
And my clean shirt for work hangs on the back of the stool.

She greets me at night, with a hug and a kiss,
And that's what I call married bliss.
Sixty years of married bliss —
And to think, it all started with one little kiss.

We've had years that were good.
We've had years that were bad.
We've had years we were glad.
We've had years we were sad.

But we walked hand in hand;
We never looked back;
And I still love the woman
That I once called ... "Hess."

John T. Loague

Madam of the Night

One lady is gowned in white and jeweled in gray.
she is like the stars, but she shines in a bigger way.
Like a skirt; she wears the darkened night.
She always seems so sad and lonely, so mysterious.
She is always by herself.
Even though, her beauty is admired by the stars,
Whom carries her spacious dress,
As if she were their queen and they were her heirs,
And so proud of their inheritance.
They call her Madam Moon.

Amber Greenhoe

Out of Love

My violet is in bloom.
She must tell me the secret of her
coming to growth in August.

How beautiful she is—coming from Yahweh's hand.
Jesus, you chose a lily to reveal God' care,
as Matthew narrates for us:
'See the lilies of the field:
they neither spin nor weave, yet
not even Solomon and all his glory
was arrayed as one of these'

Then why do you doubt? Could I care less?
Would a mother forget her baby?
Even so, I will never forget you;
you are mine.

Creative Spirit, when my mind starts to wander on a tangent,
let me remember: I am yours. I am precious to you no
matter the task. Sanctify everything by love.
Out of love, be at one another's service.
Amen.

Jean McNeil

Ode to Inky

There once was a cat named Inky.
She once was long and slinky,
She walked into our home one day
And never since has gone away.
When she's hungry, then she bites
And with her tail she often fights.
She mounts her chair as if the queen
Now don't you push, she'll get quite mean!
Now when she runs you hear tromp-tromp.
And when she jumps, of course, ker-plomp.
She loves to cuddle night and day
And don't you dare push away!
And if you're reading you'll be surprised
To find your reading jeopardized
She'll purr and purr 'til she can purr no more,
Then walk away to say you're a bore.
She's now rolly-polly and rather quite fat,
But remember that: I love my cat!!!

Jennifer L. Allendorfer

Someone I Love

There is a person I really love,
She reminds me of a turtle dove.
She was a teacher, friend, and aunt to me.

But now she can't take a walk,
or stay up late at night and talk.
She loved every star,
And she loved to teach,
But now she is afar.

She loved rainbows and butterflies
The stars remind me of the twinkle in her eyes
But now she lies six feet under,
Without a worry of making a blunder.

Now two long years have passed right by,
And sometimes I still sit down and cry.
Soon I will get over it,
But still miss her every bit.

Abby Blessman

Mom

Our Mom had to go.
She slipped away.
It was very hot.
When she left that day.
I know that's the price for life we all have to pay.
Our hearts were broken because she couldn't stay.
Our eyes filled with tears cause she passed away.
Our lives are not over, and they had not end.
For if we had to choose a Mom, we would choose her again.
So remember now as the days end.
That she love us now, as she had loved us then.
You'll never know, until she's gone.
She was the only one, that you could really rely on.
Who stuck by you through thick and thin.
And her understanding had no end.
And as you had laid your head upon her knees.
As she stroked your hair, your mind and heart felt at ease.
So be Loving and caring to her my friends.
For you see.
When a mother dies her love never ends.

Dorothy Delaware

"Apple Pie"

Susy had a pony, she called it "Apple Pie."
She would give it an apple when she was passing by.
That pony was an ornery one, it was rotten to the core.
No matter how many apples that it got,
  it always wanted more.

It made no difference what the pony did,
Susy took it with a grin.
Sometimes it would run real fast to a big
  mud hole, then stop and throw her in.

Susy is a young lady now and the
  pony has grown old.
It spends a lot of time in the barn when
  the weather outside is cold.
But some things never change that much,
  and maybe we shouldn't try.
That old pony still likes it's apples and
  Susy still likes her "Apple Pie."

Harley Allen

Mother

She's the one who gave me life;
She's the one who gave me dreams;
She's probably thinking right now,
"Is she happy? Does she love me?"
Maybe if I wish on a falling star,
I'll be able to answer those questions for her one day.
Maybe.

Erika Risley

Trusting Hearts

Eyes open to sunlight
Shining over your mind
Staring at enchantment
Trusting vibes
Compelled to touch
A flavor of lemonade
Relaxed and laid back
Nourishment, with no pretends
A feeling of commitment that never ends
Never questioning moments
Always prepared to give
No matter what the circumstance
You're always near.

Deborah Brown-Richardson

Untitled

Wild and free some believe you to be.
Shy and distant you are with others.
What is your true self you may wonder.
Are you someone whose lost,
  or just trying to discover the man within.
Your feelings are hard to share with others.
Hiding your emotions in silence,
  has been your greatest achievement.
In so doing,
  you have forgotten to share your thoughts and dreams.
Allowing a war to break out in your own body and mind.
You've searched for someone to listen and understand.
Be assured you have found that person in me.
There is only one question to ask,
  "How can I reach you?"
Is it with an open heart
  or silent touch.
Have faith in yourself and me.
And with this new trust,
  the man within shall be free.

Judith Carreiro

I Am

I am the sound of the ocean
singing its lullaby late in the night

A tree dressed in the colors of autumn
of this I am the sight

I am the smell of the pungent aroma
escaping the fireplace

Nectars which blend to sweeten the honey
of this I am the taste

Mother nature to the senses has universal appeal
and her touch I'd like to believe
of this I am the feel

Cynthia L. Colvin

Where Are My Children

Have you seen anywhere, a dear girl and a boy, with a much younger sister, aged four?
It was only today that barefoot and brown, they played by my kitchen door. It was only today, or maybe a year...it couldn't be twenty I know,
They were calling me to come out and play, now they've grown up and wandered away.

If by chance you should hear of a girl and a boy, and their small winsome sister aged four,
Please tell them, I pray, that to see them again, I'd gladly stay hungry and poor.
Somewhere, I'm sure, they must stop and reflect, and wish they were children again.
Oh, to be wanted and with them once more the way they were back then!

There is no task that would keep me away, Could I just hear my children call me to play,

Where are my children? I've got time...today.

Irene M. Cash

Untitled

Go ahead and dream,
Reality will only crush whatever it is you want
Go ahead and cry.
People will only laugh as they go by.
Go ahead and be yourself.
Society will criticize you for your honesty.
Go ahead and sit in the corner.
  No one will bother you.

Heather Sarkissian

The Race

Hurt, alone and scared,
Sitting through a life of trials and errors.
Who is there to hold the ties,
That bond the human creatures to their lives?
Questions with no answers,
Rugged faces, dry and haggard.
Who is there to hold the ties,
Feed them and poison them with their lies?
Starts, with no stops,
Beginnings, with no ends.
Running from what is not there,
Being chased by thin air.
Where to go?
No one knows.
So every one will run,
Like a race never won.

Ericka Rae Hill

Autumn

Winds roar like a train
Skies hard slate blue
Leaves of red, yellow, orange
In a funnel explode like fireworks

Above the evergreens
Silent and watching
Dark then light clouds float overhead
Like giant figure balloons

Drifting above a parade
Blending and separating
Keeping their pale towards an invisible
Finish line

A chill down the neck, chap of the skin
And a flash of warmth when the sun performs
Its small part on the stage
In the sky

In this short
But most beautiful play
Of seasons we know as
Autumn

Alfred J. Texeira, Jr.

Timeless Beauty

The ocean with it's heavy roar
Slammed into the beaches door,
And left it's mark for each of us
To view this beauty we love so much.

I walked along this beach one day,
And gathered sea shells on my way.
Footprints in the sand I found
Led me to a higher ground.

Now I look below and see
My first glimpse of a foaming sea.
Rocks being washed by the ocean's hand;
Footprints gone that were made by man.

So, watch the sea gulls in their flight;
Their wings come to rest at night.
This is nature, strong and pure,
It's timeless beauty for all to endure.

Dolly L. Porter

LOOKOUT

Metal floats shuddering down water
Smashing black swells, imprinting in the sea
A glowing froth. Rise again, bad lover.
Ship and see engage in tortuous fond
Embrace! Follow, sonnar-gifted porpoise
Caress the angry bow, so both exude
Trails of sparkling iridescence blinding.
Stay night, daylight turns the sea substantial;
The waves will calm and our clumsy freighter
Will slower and higher ride dead water,
All passion wearied.

Barry Bartle

Elements of a Journey

Rich lodes,
Smelted, smoothed, shaped
Into brownstone skin and carbon curls
Framed tenderly by swirling white lace
She gathers as her legs submerge
And she wades daringly into the depths
Gliding past the blur of bobbing gazers
On sturdy rafts and driftwood
Absorbing their smiles, tears, envious stares
While fixing her shimmering cafe eyes
On the navigator of her novice craft
Who waits fidgeting, feverish
Palm extended proudly
Grasping her approaching glow
Other hand loosening ties
To sail from her shore
On northerly gales and breezes

Daniel Kaufman

The Hollow

Enter the hollow
Smiling lips kiss your face
Welcome
White is blind
Your eyes are open but you can only see what is not there
Painful emptiness followed by suffocated silence
Your eyes are closed and you can only imagine what is not there
Black is blind
Good-bye
Salty tears kiss your face
Enter the hollow

Dara Frank

"Life in the Fast Lane"

Friday night it's time to get high
Smoke and drink a little of this and you'll really fly
Hop into the car lets go for a ride
tell your mom your going to show she'll never know
you've lied.
Speeding down the road doing seventy-four
that ain't fast enough I want more
there's head lights ahead were there not suppose to be
there blinding you now oh God I can't see
you turn a sharp left the other can missed you
praise the Lord I thought we were through
I can't believe it's true
Oh know I can't see the night is so dark
We'll have to go on
We'll stop later to part
they never saw the drop off ahead
all found the next day were dead
Oh God
I didn't want to die
Please God forgive me, I didn't mean to get this high.

Ellen M. Anderson

Just One Hit

A man with rocks came to me and said
Smoke some of these, it'll do your head.

O.K., I can smoke just one, give me the pipe and I'll have some fun.

I lit the pipe up with a blaze, just one hit started the craze.

Mr. Mr., what rush, I said, give me one more, it's good for my head.

That rock turned to 3 or 4, there went my tools and I needed more.

Next went my guns, then my truck, it's not hell, it just my luck.

What do I get for $50, tell me man
I'll be back, you know, fast as I can.

Now it's hard for me to understand all this geekin'
And friends won't help and they're not speakin'.

Crawlin' on my knees around a motel room
I know I dropped a rock and I pray to find it soon.

I wake up to pounding on the door
It's the manager, I must leave, it's almost 4.

Now it's hard to leave without my truck
I've lost everything and now I'm stuck.

Is life worth living, is the thought in my head
Started with just one hit, now I wish I was dead.

Let this be a lesson for family and son—
Don't take a hit, not even one.

John E. Phillips

Covet

An immense yearning for the one I love
Smothers my ordinary thoughts
A kiss on the belly a rub on my thigh
Are craved when we are apart

Your beautiful skin a heavenly mystery
Brings ecstasy to my being
Your arms a perfect fit; your words so secure
Melt away my common sense

Come forth my love come forth I pray
Your aroma will fulfill my day
An extra treat to lie on your breast
Soothes my woes away

I suffer long when your presence is gone
My desire hard to appease
The love we share an original art
Helps place my longings at ease

Amy C. Watson

"Head Games"

The night has settled in. The streets are so calm its almost scary. I am already looking towards the next day, knowing It's still clicks of the clock down the road. Never the less, the anticipation is great, partly due to my brief glancing at surroundings and realizing that past mistakes are now history. Still even after arriving at that mark, one cannot help the sick feeling that is followed closely by sheer confusion. Fitting firmly in the self-help category, choices both small and big dominate the everyday agenda. So many things have become daily routines, such As searching for an inner direction and the constant retreating of everyone and everything around, till the goings-on inside my head are blurred - unfocused. I am dared to take "The road not taken" which hopefully, will make the ultimate difference.

Irvin J. Green

Untitled

It lay on the road,
so cold,
so alone.
It never did any harm;
it was so innocent.
Man and his technology;
it's the creatures that suffer;
the innocent.
Don't chase the rocks on the street, kitten.
Don't chase the cars, puppies.
Deer, don't cross the roads at night.
Be careful little rabbit, raccoon, squirrel,
frog, gopher, bird...
These men just keep building;
they don't think;
they don't care.
Now that little kitten...
is dead.

Debbie Gilbertson

"A Frightened Child Was I"

There I saw him lying in a crypt dead.
So confused, I was, they all said.
But I'll admit to the truth instead.
I was afraid for myself.
If what happened to him
Could happen to another
To my mom or my brother.
I was so scared,
A tear rolled down my eye:
A frightened child was I

A demon attacked me there in my sleep.
It gave me dreadful visions of what was to be.
There I was so desperate and alone
Lost of love and far from home
Then the demon let out a frightful sigh
A frightened child was I

Jase Parsons

"To Watch An Autumn Evening"

Autumn winds are sweeping,
so dry and hollow, they must be weeping
A faint, sweet scent blows about
The fiery burning of leaves no doubt
A sinking red sun, sinking below the
crisping earth, no raging heat but
blooming coldness,a worthy new birth
I ponder to glimpse at this beautiful
sight so does everyone deserve this right
But soon Autumn too will
fade away and then I'll watch
a winter day.....

April Daley

Driving Through the City

Sitting in the monotonous,
ragged street corners,
they wait.
They are hungry, They are tired, they are
desperate. Hands extend.
You say, " Maybe next time...
no not today." And turn your head the other way.

Charon Nicole Muchison

Our Love

What is this love we share?

Two people loving, caring and growing,
so full of passion hearts overflowing;

Lives intertwined, never ending, while
together standing tall, strong like the
oak, yet bending;

Promises made to share earthly tomorrows,
while treasuring life's pleasures,
struggles, and sorrows.

What do we feel in moments serene?

Our joy, laughter, comfort and tears,
lingering and warming us throughout the years.

Would we ever think to part from our love?

Alas, how our hearts would break like a
chasm so wide and deep parting makes;

Let us think of our resolve, so sure and
complete, pledged to each other now and for
eternity.

Eileen L. Jurak

On Being "In"

All men are devils!
So I hear in the screeching
Of my smoking heels, grinding
In the fiery gravel, at the gates of hell,
As I fought, resisting
Belial's hairy hands, dragging me, "In."

All men are angels!
So I heard in the hissing
of my hot breath, condensing
On the cold, pearled gates of Heaven,
As I pushed; then pounding,
Fell to my knees, begging, any way "In."

All men are human!
So I heard in the roaring
Of the wild wind, winging
My scarred soul homeward,
To learn humanity's true teaching,
While warm Mother Earth WELCOMED me - - - "IN."

Adelaide M. McCready

"Our Father"

Live crime was performed so rampantly all around us every day
So I tried to rid me and my family, of this very dangerous play
By calling on our law of our land, just simply asking for a hand
Our law instead has a stinking jagged edge, so I saw and I said
So with a passion what's become of them, they all want me dead
Now help is an evil word, that has become haunting to me
Because justice is blind, but insist it will always see me
And death has approached me more than one hundred times
By strangers in the way, and my so called friends of mine
Shiny badges of honor is disgraced, it's place a filthy bed
Some men who wear them lay with thugs, to try and make me dead
It's with no cause my life they want, so desperately to stop
Oh why give them a loaded gun and respect, and call them a cop
Now my safe refuge, is faith in the highest of all power
So I know that all their attempts, will continue to be sour
Because I believe in my friend, who absolutely made everything
From all the evil's that lurks, to the birds that softly sing
And he's mightier than any man, and anything man can dream, so,
Public servants, you turned your head, or chose not to bother
So I am being protected, by my Lord, God, and all, Our Father.

Fred E. Robinson Jr.

Untitled

An escape from the secure world I lived in, there you stood
So innocently sinful it was -
When our worlds combined, as fantasy become hell.
Distance in our lives destroyed my being -
Torn apart into wounds you created to nourish yourself.
Let me go -
So I may be free
Stop feeding off of me - for there is nothing left.
I must not hide again so I can end the pain of
a past filled with sorrow and suffering.
My wounds are fresh, and scars remain -
They will stay with me forever -
for all to notice.
I am myself because of you.
You have made me what I am.
I will lie in your bed of thorns that once were roses,
and I will not feel a single feeling -
and I will think of you.

Angela L. Spero

Sisters and Brothers

The world is full of woe and strife,
so many kids carry a knife; because
they have no respect for life.

The reason started from taking drugs,
it changed kids to a bunch of thugs.

Instead of filling you with love and hope,
it turned you from being smart to a dope.

We are all sisters and brothers,
there is now and ever will be no others.

I want to be your big sister dear,
and chase away all your fear.

Listen to me for I have heard,
their is no future in being a nerd.

Life can be sweet you shall see,
if you take my advice you'll be free.

You don't need to take drugs and booze,
if you want to be happy, wake up from your snooze.

Let's all go back to loving one another,
Because I'm your sister and your my brother;
We all originated from the same Mother.

Catherine A. Scarelli

Cry of the Paper Doll

I've been torn apart and put back together
So many times I can not remember.
If only they knew what goes on in the mind
Of a paper doll. This my cry unto you,
The cry of the paper doll.

I have a heart like no other doll. I need
A strong, loving heart so that I may survive
The rippings and tapings. My heart cries out
In pain when no one cares; my heart rejoices
When someone does care. Please listen to
My cries, the cries of a paper doll.

Please listen to my pleas. I do not want to
Go through the terrible rippings and tapings
Any longer. All I have ever wanted is for
Someone to love me, to cherish me. Please
Listen to my cries, the cries of a paper doll.

Christina George

In a Pinch

All tied up...
So natural within the box—the territory he claims in a clutch;

Two rosters can both smell victory...
All upon his shoulders...His only chance to shine—
To end it here and now..Will he be hero or goat?

No curve too smooth, no heat too strong
Bolts across the foul skies...

He knows his pitch; there it is!

A smile. A strut. A group huddle. A big win.

A happy fan who sat in center field holds the prize.

Christine M. Dick

The Red Bird

I heard a chorus from above,
So sweet and tender was the note,
My heart beat with the song of love,
The rhythm moved as if afloat.

High in the tree against the blue,
Stood a beautiful Red Bird in song,
Beneath lay a sheet of glittering dew,
Nature's labor of the whole night long.

How happy he seemed with his crest of red,
Fluttering his wings in the air,
Blessing the oak whose leaves it had shed,
The day breaking early for all to share.

Through life's struggles man cannot see
Our world has beauty and joys unheard,
Sharing nature's simplicity,
With the song of the Red Bird.

Bettie Soukup

Howling Wind

Young person: How come you reject my friend?
Some call him death at best,
Others call him eternal rest.
I call him Howling Wind.

You say that you don't like Howling Wind,
Because he's too grim,
Lacking in personality, vigor, and vim;
A consort of the older age groups, you pretend.

Please don't deny Howling Wind.
He fits in with all age groups, you'll see —
Cunningly able to embrace those of all ages despite their plea.
Yes, do meet my friend. He has peace to extend.

I, myself, once denied Howling Wind,
Not even considering his advances,
Now I'm much older, having experienced many of life's circumstances,
And as timely disillusionment sets in, Howling Wind
may yet become my best friend.

Clayton Mitchell

Beauty of the Night

The pale moonbeams ripple as they fall upon a pond,
They dance on light feet over the silvery casted trees,
The lily pads sit under the natural spotlight of the moon,
As the gentle current carries them silently along their path,
The leaves shift in the cool breeze,
The crickets' chorus fill the night air,
A bird takes to the air carrying the beautiful messages of night,
The stars glimmer in the pitch black sky,
And shine love down on the peaceful setting.

Emily Gaukler

Fancy Free

It has long been a fancy of mine to compose some compelling verse -
Some melodic words to woo this world with mesmerizing mirth
With lilting cadence; a subtle mix of teasing, tantalizing grace
To beguile a smile, a laugh, a grin from all the human race -
To reach the child within us with an oft recurring pleasure
To tap-toe to a beat of enticing, undulating measure
Sadly it has become apparent and a most appalling fact
that igniting words explosively is a talent that I lack.
My angel wings ne'er brush my words with golden, shining gleaming
Without the magic of their touch the words can have no meaning.
My fancy dies within me and its going leaves me free.
Versifying is for others, rhythmic lines are not for me.

Helen B. Welcker

Hindsight/Foresight

Many days have past, and years have gone,
Some things gone well, and some gone wrong.
Like a pages of books, you've already read,
You can't turn back, you must go ahead.

Look not on the past, nor woe your mistakes,
The world will continue, you must keep your faith.
Try to ignore, what you cannot control,
Make plans for your future, set realistic goals.

Be kindly and helpful, to every one that you can,
Trust in your instincts, be your own man.
Don't expect anyone, to give you the answers,
For life is a puzzle, it's pieces are chances.

Reflect in the things, over the years, I have said,
I've passed on to you, all the thoughts in my head.
Your special to me, in so many ways,
So cherish our time, throughout all of our days.

Frank W. Flynn

Oh, Well.....

It finally happened.
Someone besides yourself
made me smile.
I've been sad for a long time
remembering and trying to forget.
I know you were hoping
that I would wait for you to get a divorce
leaving me to rely on love and memories
to make it through the night.
Well, you left me along for too long
and, now, someone else has made me smile.

Diane J. Morey

Trust

"Trust no one and suspect everyone"
someone told me one day
pull the knife from my back
where do we go from here, which way.

Trust is hard to achieve once broken
lied to, cheated on, why do it.
Where will we end up if we can't trust
the light in my head has been lit

We will go nowhere as long as we lie
learn to love and be honest with each other
Then maybe we will survive
till then look for another.

Barbara Ries

Something For You

I want to give something
Something new and special too
I want to give you something
That will mean something to you
I don't want to give you flowers they wilt and die
I want to give you something
that will stay with you, till the end of time
I want to give you something
That will last through the years
I want to give you something
That would calm all your fears
The only thing I could think of,
That comes close to this is my heart
And you already hold the key.

Belkis Perez

Mystery Love Story

There are love stories about a wife, husband and
sometimes about a mistress or lover.
But my 'Love Story' is not about these at all,
as you will soon discover.

I have a love that started, and matured, when I
was but a young man in my teens.
It is a growing love that has endured, for this
love of mine is as great as any that you've seen.

If it is not a mistress, lover, husband or wife,
you might ask, who is this love of your life?
Before I answer your question direct, first
give me a moment to reflect—

Beauty, kindness, generosity, knowledge and love,
this love of my life has, and shares, all of the above.
However, with all of these virtues, I will not say
that my loves not without flaw, but 'surprise'
the love of my life is — My Mother In Law.

Donnell R. Bryant

Goodbye

It hurts to say goodbye,
Sometimes I wonder why it has been said.
There's no way to figure it out
Every time it's always the same kind of pain.

Knowing you'll never come back again
Makes me want to scream and shout.
I don't, because of soothing memories I have been fed.
Sometimes thinking those memories makes me cry.

I know more tears will be shed,
Memories never leave you.
Unlike eyes, puffy and red,
There's nothing anyone can do.
All I ask is for you to remember as if it were yesterday,
Please don't forget about,
The time we spent everyday.
And don't begin to doubt.

The memory will never be dead
The memory of you walking to my house, up the lane.

Angela Cutright

Steps In Time

A time to dream, a time to dance
Sometimes you need to take a chance
A time to be young, a time to grow
Sometimes you are high and others low
A time to rejoice, a time to be sad
Sometimes to dance can make you glad
A time to look forward, a time to look behind
Sometimes you don't know what you will find
A time to talk, a time to sing
Sometimes life is filled with wondrous things
A time to hurt, a time to care
Sometimes it is easier if you share
A time to be alone, a time to give
It's through these steps in time that we live.

Carol Pochron

Life

What will the future bring,
Sorrow, grief, or cause to sing?
Will our days be sunny and bright,
Always with peace and joy in sight?
Our journey on this earth may be short;
Only God knows things of that sort.
So, what ever time is given to you and me,
Let our hearts rejoice and our eyes open to see,
The precious beauty of life in every face, color, and smile.
Even those times filled with fear and doubt, stop and listen awhile
Let us always reach out to touch, feel and be taught,
Then our lives will never be in vain or for naught.
Those memories we've left behind, will surely be,
Precious and true to those touched by you and by me.
For we lived our lives, not for ourselves, but others,
They, too, were God's children, our sisters and brothers.

Glenna M. Cika

Come, Preacher Man

Come, preacher man, you say you'll save our
souls.
come, Preacher man, we'll listen to your
tales
Yet, preacher man, you know not who we
are.
You've made a promise, preacher man, but was it
yours to make?
How do you know, preacher man, that our souls
should be saved?
You know us note, preacher man, and a promise
is nothing
From a man who knows not your name,
we know.
but come, preacher man, we'll listen to your
dreams
come, preacher man, listen to our
truths.
come, preacher man, let us save your
soul.

Elizabeth Linhoss

Untitled

A second chance was given, but was that what it seems?
Things still aren't as they should, like in hopes and dreams
It really wasn't a chance, I guess it was an excuse
for all the silly nonsense talk, but not quite verbal abuse
Why it still goes on, is kind of hard to explain
Nothing serious wanted, so what do I hope to gain?
When that question can be answered, life should fall in place
I hope it works like that, I need a sincere embrace.

Fiona Hood

Sounds of a Noisy Classroom...

I hear sounds of a noisy classroom.
sound of flipping of pages,
sounds of muffled voices,
complaining and groaning of people with unwanted work.
the beat of MAGIC FM,
laughter in the back of the room,
pencils less than busy at work,
and snapping of binders
with a snap from mine,
feet shuffle,
and I hear the hall bustle,
soon sound is rather silent,
then the teacher's voice begins.

Jessa K. Lynni

Are You Coming Home

I can see Her,
Standing in the garden
With flowers all around
I start to hear the sound
Of the Sun rising from beneath the Horizon.

Slowly and Majestically hovering,
The sun provides an abundance of light
With flowers all around
I start to hear the sound
Of your lovely voice bringing forth heavenly delight.

But you say, "that you want to stay there"
And you say, "that you want to be alone"
So I respond by saying, "that I really Care"
And I respond by saying, "that I wish you would come back home."

Gregory Scott Salzer

Resurrection

High in the heavens above the sepulchre Rock
stands a star of remembrance high sublime swayed in the
centre of the sky, it dwells the everybody welfare.!
And awaited to love, astray, it slid thru the rock away.
God's angels have rolled the deaths stole away
Alleluia he is Jesus! He is not there any more.
By the mighty force of Hranusdre, the sepulchre
Trembled on the occasion unique and divine:
The whole earth was shakes by the intervention of the star of Ur.
The white lad was an angel sent by God rare
Occasions to certify the great miracle of changing
The bread and wine. Bread color of life - the wine
color of blood and love!
Jesus compelled Uranus to dwell our earth from on high.
Cherubin and Seraphin laided the Red-Rocking fire
from heaven where they were coming down. The saint prophets
adored and prayed while the Principalities sent aromas of roses
and flowers. Adorned by the Cherub in our iquited warm night,
Surround by the Zephyr-Breeze of the Sepulchre Requiem night.
Lux Stellae lucet in tenebris! Beatitudiuem perfrui. Deo gratias

Alan J. De Fiori

Untitled

Think of the sun shining upon us as if it were a spotlight allowing the world to admire our love.
Think of the wind as whispering soft songs surrounding us with warmth and a sentimental feeling of love.
Think of snow as crystals dancing their way to the ground.
Think of thunder as an ovation from the angels commending us.
Lightning is a shock given to my heart making it forever beat for you.
Think of the rain as tiny diamonds falling from the sky or as tears when it's once again time to say goodbye.

Diane M. Flynn

Lost Treasure

What is this sad and sorry sight that meets my eyes -
Stark blackened arms that reach up to the skies -
All the beauty and life that was nature's greenery
Delighting us all with God's wondrous scenery -
Lost forever in one tragic night -
How she must weep for such lost delight,
Her handiwork gone her wild life in flight.
Can we afford such treasure to squander -
Nature's wonderland where all may wander
Solving our problems in solitary meditation
All the tensions and troubles of our civilization
Fade away in sweet content -
Ah! nature has a way of healing all sorrows.
Let us take good care to preserve her tomorrows.

Joan Lack

God's Testament to Time

A trail leads gently upward across the alpine glow.
Statuesque, the towering spire enhances realms below.
Conquest bound, a zealous man ascends the vast incline.
Up God's Majestic Mountain — His Testament To Time

Pristine snow smoothly covers meadows, woods and all
And nature in a wondrous way reveals her waterfall.
Tinkling sounds of crystals splashing down a broken stream
Rouse pleasant feelings in his soul as he emerges on the scene.

A circling path winds slowly from above the church of snow.
Statuesque, the shimmering peak transcends the view below.
Homeward bound, a lofty eagle descends from valiant climb.
Down God's Majestic Mountain — His Testament To Time

A quiet breeze blows softly as it sings a peaceful song.
It cools the evening mildly and gently pushes clouds along.
Evening mist, curves that twist and rugged cliffs move by.
Then, timberline emerges on the journey from the sky.

Tranquility is savored here like the taste of a vintage wine.
The eagle settles quietly within its nest sublime.
The man rests peacefully in his tent contented with his climb.
On God's Majestic Mountain — His Testament To Time

Donald L. Hendershot

The Light Of Love

Love is a character that stays inside of us...
Stays until that special person comes along
Known only as a friend, but love can find a way.
The power of love can change thoughts.
Like a switch to the light...
It can turn on emotions with a click...
You travel in the dark,
Not knowing where you are, or where you are going.
Suddenly, love turns the dark into light,
You find your way...
Just a click can send two hearts flying
Hoping to find their way through this crazy world...
Knowing it will be much easier in the light of love.

Charlie Michele Walls

Froggies

Froggies are really cute.
They skip, hop and jump to boot.
If you have one, treat him kind.
He'll delight your senses and blow your mind.
Just feed him some water and two bugs.
Let him sleep and give him hugs.
All he needs is a little food.
Never take him to the zoo.

David J. Seigle

Busy Autumn

When October's cool days
Steal away summer's haze,
Fall bursts forth in living hues
And cut grass is drenched in rainy dues.
The penetrating aroma of cotton open
Signals Grandpa - it's time!
"Time?" - You say to rake and bale the hay,
Drag a sack, bend the back, and fill the rack.

Pumpkins of fireball orange
Sparkle in the dazzling sun;
While Jack-o-lanterns expect to be made
In the evening shade.
Sorghum nods in the late breeze
Waiting to be stripped and squeezed.
Molassie time is always a joy
Even when Dad was a boy.

Routine farm chores may abound,
But the anxious call of nature does sound.
Crows in the corn scream scorn
While geese open their mouth for the South.

Jimmie Nell Inmon

The Thief

It snuck up like a thief during the night,
stealing God's precious gift, the gift of life.
Like the thief it doesn't know who it might affect.
The selfish way of nature's knife,
cutting into lives no longer so bright.

Don't you know the seed lies dormant within?
Just waiting for its signal to sprout like
a flower in Spring, only to begin
by spreading death, a life's final hike.
You cannot escape its spreading therein.

Conquering all, similar to that of
a spider, prey trapped in its lucid web.
In time your dignity is depleted,
however, one must first feel defeated.

Donna McEntire

Voices From The Land

Sister, sister don't you know?

I have traveled through deep dirty muddy waters,
stood waiting for you in the moonlight,
and was trampled by endless feet.

In these dirty clothes to find you, and to tell you, to strive,
and strive on.

There were many roadblocks in my way and ignorance,
oh, oh so much

It almost suffocated my soul.
But, I kept moving, despite all that
You sister, me sister, we are all sisters.

And I want you to know, to come, join me on my quest,
Take this hand, that longs to hold you,
embrace you and nurture you.

Let me be that beckon of light that wants to share the love you
never had.
I am awaiting...., I am embracing....,

All of you across this land
Let the circle never be broken again, come in and stand.

Felicia D. Jones

Can You Hear

The loneliness that surrounds you
storms about me as pouring rain;
My heart beats with a rhythm
of forlorn and disdain.

I swear! I've felt it bleeding:
No one will ever know
the depth of our pain;
I want to put my arms around you
and make the sun shine again.

Mine eyes they have shed a pool full of tears;
Won't you help me
make these feelings disappear?
I'm afraid for you, my darling;
I hope you can hear!

I treasure each stolen moment
every time that you are near;
I love you more than ever with each passing year.

To you, I surrender all my hopes to endear;
I love you more than ever—
I hope, this is clear.

Carolyn Hartnett

Celluloid Romance

Apricot light trickles over the table,
Strokes crispy lineny napkins, kisses fluted glasses,
Shimmers off sterling, settles on china. Deft, able.
His fingertips seek hers. A moment passes,
Breathless. Silent. Their eyes meet,
Lock in an "always" embrace. Seconds,
Minutes, all is still. Hearts seem to beat
Audibly. He hesitates, hoping. Her glance beckons.

"Cut! Who wrote this shit! Throw
Some powder on the ingenue. Her face
Looks like a peeled grape. You, Valentino,
You look like you're smelling toxic waste."

Apricot light curdles, linen withers. Crystal shows
A fine dust. Offstage, the understudy picks her nose.

Ann Watson

The Man with the Cane

The man with the cane
Struck a note of fear
In many a child when he came near.

He walked with a limp,
He didn't stand tall
His body was bent his head was bald.

But he was a man
Of beauty within, of strength and courage
Found in few men.

When the great storm came,
He gave the word.
"Get under your desks!"
Their prayers were heard.

You may not agree
With the way that he ran
The old school with his iron hand,
But our lives are all fuller
With knowledge we gained
From knowing this great man,
The man with the cane.

Mildred Hardy

Friends

Friends
Such a simple term
For such a complicated thing
Friendship
Another simple term for
The relationship two people share
Such simple term to understand
But do we really understand
This bond between two people that should never be broken
Or are we just stumbling along the path of life
Improvising as we go along
These terms we call simple
Do we misjudge their true value?
Do we take for granted these terms so precious and unique?
Two people together bonded by a love so strong
Stretching on to the fullest extent of all friendships
Though the path of friendship is sometimes lit ablaze
These terms of friendship, so powerful can be rendered
Put out by the love we so often take for granted

Cheryl Cottrell

Dancing Shadows

I laid sound asleep on the ground — a slight smile upon my lips.
Suddenly I heard a loud close whistle go off,
I opened my eyes in haste then heard my motor-pool sergeant yell out..
"Everyone to the perimeter, a night assault is expected!"
Everyone jumped-up, grabbed their equipment and scrambled toward the
perimeter.
Suddenly a flare was shot-up into the dark sky — brilliantly it lighted-up the whole area around the perimeter.
As I'm running I see the flare in its brilliant beauty.
I quickly stop and gaze in fascination.
A second later I hear a familiar voice yell out to jump into the darkness and take cover from the light!
I quickly jump into the darkness of the night and see the bushes and shadows around the area dancing in the dark.

George Bielma

Musical Soul - O

Do you know the words to life's song -
Sung by the artist it chose to belong?
Deeply expressing it's graceful flow,
Like Angelic voices heard long ago
harmony is balancing the notes you are dealt,
Soprano's height soars above Orion's Belt
Echoing melodies of heavenly grace.
The songs of the soul wrapped in fine lace.
Words of wisdom, kindness and love,
Are the keys to lead your soul Above.
Listen carefully for the musical distance,
It will change your lyrics that very instant.
The soul's solo of musical bliss,
Is the heart's beat that can't be missed.

Dianna Lea Goodman

Thank You God!!

Thank you God for my baby boy,
Thank you God for my pride and joy.
I prayed for a baby I can love and hold,
and know he's a cute two year old.
Every night I lay down and pray,
and ask you to keep him safe day to day.
I thank you for giving me the love of my life,
and now I'm a mother and a wife.
I pray thing turn out fine through out the years,
I now there will be good times and hard
times and we'll shade a few tears.

Gina Lindgren

This Spirit

This Spirit is king of universe, man's only way out.
Superior in a field no man could ever surmount.
This Spirit is a part of you and me.
A part of everything, everybody,
Look around, you will see,
Life does not stop with human beings.
This Spirit gets tired, is that so hard to believe?
Especially since Spirit controls entire universe...
Has compassion for all humanity.
This Spirit is dissatisfied with wretchedness,
Soon coming down, taking good back.
Nuclear weapons will not mean a thing,
When the Almighty comes back to reign!
This Spirit is a struggler, never gets depressed,
Even with all the sinfulness of human creations,
Some are a mess. This Spirit ranks top of the charts,
In a unique fields. A winner. This Spirit will
Achieve all goals. Man will not.

Dawana G. Smith

Game or a Frame

From opposite corners of the house we came;
Surprised by each others presence, stilled we became.

Briefly advancing as if in a game
Reality hit this could be a frame.

Scamper if you must, I'll not look for fame,
So quickly into the house chuckling I came.

From the window revealed this was to be a frame,
For around the corner four stinkers remain.

They scampered and frolicked with such playful glee,
Thank God for your spirit that helped me to flee.
Thank God for the skunks that didn't get me.

Joan E. Maciel

Father Neptune

Father Neptune was bearded, you see; law of the universe, he knew to a "T". What is his, he keeps in the deep; from prying eyes, theirs that seek his temper, or so I've been told; went to the old school, the one of old. Learned from the Maker, at beginning of time; traits and customs — the rules, his line. Picture this - Father Neptune's regime; my way of thinking, my highest esteem. Was the ultimate of all the myths; ruling it all with a three pronged stick. The seas the cover most of these lands; was his to rule, with a wave of his hand. From the depths of the ocean, to this side of Hell; stories of "old" salts, they had to tell. Most everywhere you look, you'll find the briny deep; wreckage of ships, where mermaids sleep. Most fishes we know, call it their home; over, under which, the seafarer's roam. Frivolous tales of the Bermuda triangle; realms of sanity, ours to untangle. The sea, a real and most relaxing place; but when aroused, there's scowl on her face. A sip of water, not mine for drinking; the salty intake, starts my stomach to shrinking. The treasures lost, but for his keeping; skin divers dive, their's be the seeking. The waves that fall on islands and shores; from the beginning of time or last evermore. A real clean environment, a fine solution; till factories came around, with their pollution. Bodies of water, be it ocean or sea; springs, wells, lake — rivers you see. The Lord over all of the H20; from a glass of water to fathoms below. So do not rile, he's not hard to wake; proceed with caution, the route to take. A loveable old man, his home is the sea; lives in his comfort, BEST LET HIM BE.

Charles R. Connor

You and I

Bless me Lord oh how I've sinned,
take the mess I've got myself in.
I can't bare the pain as its driving me insane
"Oh Lord please help."
Now its lonely deep in an out,
an all the fear has come about,
oh Lord how shall I feel
for time has come for this appeal.
Shall I be strong deep in an out
or kindle like a mouse.
No Lord I shall be strong,
an face this cruel world where I belong.
Whatever happens deep in an out
I know you will be there when I get out.
There's only on thing that walks in my life
An oh Lord that's you and I.

Janice Deal

Cage of Rose Petals

Life in itself, a contradiction to living
Take what you're given, they'll take what you're giving

Best thieves are our rulers, we are but slaves.
The only free house ever built was a cave.

Organization, where we are all lost
Inked in green, it has value but much greater cost

The smile we see is no more than a sneer
We got here from there, can't get there from here.

While holding the torch, she bends down to restrain us
In a cage of rose petals, she traps and detains us

Joe Ernst

Entering the Tunnel Of Darkness

Closing your eyes to the dark imagination of reality - the first step taken is by the one who has been mistaken with an identity of a foe, but not everyday average Joe.
Thoughts are flowing is darkness true, once you enter theirs no one but you; facing walls you can never walk thru. You are the first to enter because you cannot hinder the tracks that lay in front of you. Once a puzzle in your mind, but now the facts of time, short talks, walks, and thoughts, are now all behind. As the long hauls began to unwind, the dark walls go into divine. Opening your eyes, you will find believing in Christ puts the darkness aside with love, trust, and faith for your kind.

Bruce Hammond

Strike of '94

Debris in front, rubble inside, roofs to be replaced
tell of the night that lightening struck.
Awakened by the sound of jangling panes of glass, I asked,
"What was that?" told by Claude investigating,
"Your light fixture is down, ruined, lightening struck."

Almost immediately upon my returning to bed
Claude shouted, "Get up, our house is on fire."
Running to the doorway firemen met me saying,
"Keep on coming' don't turn back. Your house is on fire."
We both, led to the safety of their truck
walked barefoot in the rain, clad in nightclothes.

Months later occupants of six townhouse units wait,
wait from varying locations to return to our homes,
to normal living. Sometimes impatient, we grumble.
dwell on inconveniences, forget blessings.
No injuries occurred. No lives were lost.

Bethel Sykora

The Beauty Of Flowers

Flowers are like a friendly smile
That brightens up the day
They form, at least a little while,
A beautiful bouquet.

Red, pink, and white and sometimes blue
The colors are so bright
Yellow and green all seem so new
In the warm and bright sunlight.

Carnations, roses, violets too
Lilacs and marigold
Since colors vary as they do
They're pretty to behold.

What would life be without the blooms?
Quite dull, it's safe to say
In the garden or in our rooms
They seem to light the way.

Can there be one among us all
Who doesn't like to see
A lovely flower, short or tall,
Blooming for you and me?

Alice Pugnier

Imprisoned Within

I'm so lonely
that every night, I sit in my window
looking out into the desolate streets of Paris
waiting, hoping
that someone will notice.

I sit and watch
as days, weeks, and months go by
Still waiting to be rescued
from these layered walls
which imprison me inside.

Does anyone really know
that I exist?
or am I just a ghost
who wonders through the towering halls
searching for happiness.

I cry out a name
but no one answers.
then turn slowly towards my window
waiting, hoping
that someone will notice.

Darian Childers

Memories

I have memories of you and me
that tumble inside my head.
They remind me of the way we used to be,
and the things that we once said.

They remind me that no one has ever made me
believe so strong —
Now you've left me with just my memories
to wonder where our love went wrong.

They remind me of how you broke my heart and fooled my brain,
maybe you're just the hurting kind.
But I can't take anymore of this pain,
I've got to get you off my mind.

Except I don't want to let you go,
all these memories stand in the way.
They confuse me, but they let me know that
I've never needed anyone like I need you today.

Jackie Schroeder

Untitled

The sky was Brown and dim as fear
that hovered in their souls with tears
got smothered.

The children came out in the streets to play
as the men that put their guns away
got brothered

Black and white stood to fight
to protect red, white and blue.

Realization hit them hard
As the fear in all eyes shined through.

The bomb, they sent them smoking while
the radiation seemed to smile. Forever,
was what it took to make their
world a place to live together.

No one was afraid to die.
No one felt alone.

They sang and danced as all was one
and America became a Home.

Holly Reindl

Life in a Strange Land

Like strangers in a strange land
that is fraught with dangers
at every turn, we struggle
to live and to love each other
as long as we can.

Why should it be so,
to hear everyday of another demise?
Why can't they learn to settle discord?
All around me they fall, unable
to pick up the pieces when finally they stand.

Possibly selfishness carries the blame.
Maybe unwilling to bend or to see,
they quickly give up the wonderful fight.
Too easy, it seems and frightful,
to even abandon the children.

These words are unfair? I don't care.
I'll just keep on working, talking and listening,
encouraging, playing, courting, participating.
I plan to hold on to my wife and my family
in this strange new land.

Fernando Crotte

Neapolitan Life

I live a life of many flavors;
That is, I like to do many things.
Why waste all my time and energy on one interest
when there are so many new discoveries to find
and intelligent minds to listen to.
And sometimes
open minds that listen to my philosophies,
and engage in conversations little known to most.
And quiet times
When I look at the stars
and feel the love of GOD in my soul.
And times when I lay my head to sleep
and dream
that someday
all will live
a NEAPOLITAN LIFE.

Gina M. Binkley

Untitled

Black is the heart that does not love,
That only feels hate and disgrace.
Blue is the heart without reasons to love
As the tears roll down my face.
Green is the heart full of envy
That longs for a precious one's healing.
Yellow is the heart with no courage
To express what it is feeling.
Red is the heart completely in love,
A burning and longing flame.
White is the pure heart that hasn't felt love
And with it all the pain.
The rainbow of emotions the human heart can feel
All lead up to gray.
When love is lost and we are gone
All the colors fade away.

Cathy Horniak

"Different But The Same"

When will people realize
  that sooner or later everyone dies?
No matter your colors, religion, creed-
Whether you're noble of thought or deed.
Whatever your beliefs, whatever your race,
We all end up in the same old place.

When will people realize
  that sooner or later each of us dies?
Why aren't we learning, why aren't we seeing
  that each one of us is a human being?
Don't we notice, don't we care,
  that for all of us life's often unfair!?
We're born the same way, we feel the same,
And we've all got to play by the rules
  of the game.

When will each of us realize -
Sooner or later everyone dies!

Adrienne Pizzolante

Gee

This word always comes with the sweetest of grins
That warms my soul from my toes to my chin.
The word is gentle and warm as can be,
It's filled with innocence and sincerity.
No linguist can translate, no dictionary define;
This word she'll forget in a matter of time.
So happy, soft, loving, and bold,
"Gee" comes from my baby, who is six months old.

Soon this word we'll no longer hear
And from her mind, it will disappear.
But nothing can ever remove or erase,
The closeness and love—not even a trace!
Daddy and I will hold it tight
With every sunrise, each kiss good night.
No word could better express to me
The most special love, which I call, "Gee."

Dawn-Michelle VanderMeer

Puddles

Places you'll find thrown rocks and tossed sticks,
Tadpoles and earthworms, tin cans and bricks,
Little boys, boots and little toy trucks,
Small flapping birds and cacophonous ducks.
A seasonal nuisance, there isn't a doubt,
But then, what is Spring without
Puddles.

Diana M. Ingraham

"Man and His World"

If Man would give unto his peers
That which he seeks, for his very own;
His world could then be shed of fears
And not be timid, of what is unknown!

All of his offspring, that are yet to come.
Would greet a life, of peace and bliss.
They would bask not in darkness, but in the sun,
What greater future, could he leave than this.

Lay aside his thoughts of strength and gain,
And give of his efforts to aid those in need
Look upon all mankind to ease their pain
And with open heart the hungry feed!

Let not race nor creed bedim his eyes,
Let reason, conquer all of his hate
Let him leave a legacy just and wise
This could change his world and in truth its fate

Hector R. Cataldi

"The Destiny of Life"

A walk through the trees
that would be nice,

To smell the smells that smell
like sugar and spice,

To walk through a garden sure
that's for me,

To smell the beautiful flowers or
even a small tree,
To walk through a field I am
filled with excitement,

To touch the soft cotton or
swing from a tree or even camp in a tent

To climb a mountain what an adventure,

To climb the rocks my
goal for the top,

But I walk through a desert
I walk forever in my desert
so vast I go nowhere only to
grow old very fast.

Candace Miller

Letter to My Wife

I do not have to tell you
that you are my only love....
How can I express my thanks for all that you have given me...
My mind cannot express what is in my heart, my darling
How can I say thank you
for so much happiness, for four wonderful children..
For all the loving memories..
For every deed and word..
For each whisper in my ear.
For every breath upon my cheek..
For all the many ways that you have been so dear to me..
For the many years of happiness that I have had with you..
How can I say thank you..
For the faith that you have in me..
For that faith that made me
attain the goals in life that I have attained..
For taking care of me in sickness and in health..
For the joy of being with you..
For taking care of me since I have been paralyzed..
My darling with all my heart I say thank you..

Ted Johnsa

Have I Told You Lately

Have I told you lately how much I care for you
That you've been the one to turn those dark sky's into blue

Though I don't always show it I'd like to say I love you
And know that I'll always do anything for you

And I see quite frequently tears falling from your eyes
Just like a flower needs water or otherwise it dies

And that what you are, a flower and I'm your sun
And no one can compare, no there never could be another one
I'm letting you know how I'm proud to be your son

And have I thanked you lately for bringing me to this place
cause if it wasn't for you
I'd be born to a different family, a different face

And I'm saying this now I'll never fade away
There's going to be no more, have I's cause my lately starts today!

Andrew Mitchell

"Southern Belle"

The picture of true southern beauty and grace
That's what I see in your lovely face.
From the fragile look of your fine porcelain kin
To the ever so slightly haughty tilt of your chin
Everything about you whispers softly "Southern Belle"
Like some subtle secret that you just have to tell.
You carry that grace about you like a warm shawl
To be admired from afar by any and all.
Each gesture from your hands, like doves set a flutter
Just causes me to take pause, my thoughts to stutter.
I cannot help but be confounded by the grace I see
And just a little bit blinded by the glowing beauty
With your head held high, eyes set above the crowd
You appear to all who watch, regal and proud
Just like the ladies of your heritage, of your proud past.
You'll be a lady, a true southern belle, to the last.
When old age steals upon you and your shoulders bow
People will look at you and will still know
That lady is a true southern belle through and through
They will see the same things I see in you.

Angela Mounts

She Was There

Surely, with a gentle but glorious sound from their trumpets,
the Angels must have announced Her coming; they were not seen.

Surely, without touching Her exquisite hands, the Saints and
Apostles must have ushered Her in; they were not seen.

The maple and the dogwood were made aware; they were still.
The wind and rain were alerted; they were still.

Positively, the setting Sun was only a reflection of the blended
hues of red, orange, yellow, and gold Her clothing radiated;
She was there!

Positively, Her eyes sparkled more than the clear blue sky;
Her modest garment was composed of an elegant substance not
identified to man; Her majestic mantle was held out as a protective
shield; Her appearance called forth peace and joy.

The magnificence of Her beauty was breathtaking splendor.
She was there!

Dorothea M. Smith

The Sunset's Soul

The sunset rises,
The birds all sing,
You're at the ocean front
You hear the boat bells ring.
You see the sea gulls
at the shore,
You just stare ... look ....
amaze and adore.
You see the water touch the sand,
It's just like a soul has touched your hand.
at the right time the sunset must go down,
So it can touch a soul that you have found.

Elizabeth A. Giannini

God's Gifts

The smell of fresh mowed grass.
The breeze against my face.
I hear my children laughing.
And see the smiles across their face.
Their dad has one child under each arm.
And grass clippings covers all three.
The twinkle from his eyes lights up the day.
How could I be so lucky?
How could I be so blessed?
You given so much to me.
Your love has been so free.
You ask nothing of me in return.
I lift up my eyes to the heavens.
For a moment of prayerful thanks.

Becky Villanova

Fall Melody

Autumn has come to the valley...
The breeze is cool with the promise of coming winter.
The night comes much more quickly now.
Autumn brings with it a feeling of completion, an end, a harvest.
A time of satisfaction at the years accomplishments...
Life's accomplishment.

Her body moves much more slowly now.
The eyes are dimming of life, but twinkle brightly
At memories of love and family.
There is a slight feeling of remorse upon reaching the autumn
of life. But a sense of pride at seasons will spent.

Autumn has come to the valley...
The leaves have changed to brilliant colors,
The cool breeze carries them ever so gently to the ground

Cheryl Sanders

Old 99

'Tis the old road now, its use surpassed.
The cars are few but nothing lasts
In these hurried times, our fates are cast.
But by the wayside the oleanders are blooming.

In the olden days when the road was new
They were planted there to brighten the view
For the travelers passing the long valley through.
By the wayside the oleanders were blooming.

Today as I drove the old road again
For the modern travelers I felt some pain.
They drive the freeway staying in their lanes
Never knowing - the oleanders are blooming.

Betty James Sexton Williams

The Problem that Shouldn't Be!

Yes, Martin Luther King Jr. did lots
The Civil Rights Bill was signed
But that doesn't mean the problem is gone
People still hate others of different race or colors
The problem won't just go away
We have to help and fight for others rights
Nobody is different on the inside, only on the out
So someone may not be exactly like you
Does that give you the right to go out and shoot them?
Why can't people look deeper,
Deeper into the inside
Yes, you are entitled to your own opinion
But when you make your choice
Think of the people who's family members
Have been shot or hurt because of
Something they can't control
You'll not only be hurting them, you'll be hurting yourself
And the entire world, too.
THINK before you choose.

Janis Nava

Be Still, It's Not So Bad

Today, wasn't any different then usual, at least I thought!
The coffee tasted the same this morning, my shoes fit as
perfectly as they did two years ago, when I purchased them.
I walked into this same office as I did the day before.
What has changed?

Nothing working! complaints! and more complaints from everyone.
I need this, this isn't working, my printer is broken, I can't
use my PC. Too much commotion, noise everywhere, where was
my warning! What changed these same sane people from yesterday?

Life's trails and tribulations comes in many different forms,
today mine came full force in verbal abuse from employees.
Didn't that darn printer work yesterday? And what happen to that four
thousand dollar PC? Why is everything spinning around in my head?

Get a grip, it's impossible! There's problems everywhere! Run this
way, run that way. Make things work fast, before more complaints
come. Who will be the next thorn in my side today?

Oh, it's five O'clock, time to go home. This is the same office,
same clock, my same desk, but I don't hear any noise. Where's
the complaints, the noise. Be still, it's not so bad!

Joyce B. Williams

In the Stillness of the Night

In the stillness of the night,
The cry of an owl can be heard.
In the stillness of the night,
The howling of dogs fill the air.
In the stillness of the night,
The autumn leaves falls gently to the ground.
In the stillness of the night,
The winter wind blows harshly against objects.
In the stillness of the night,
The spring rain bathes the grass.
In the stillness of the night,
The summer winds blow softly.
In the stillness of the night,
The voice of silence is heard.

Farrell Bennett

Rider

A relic from the past,
the die has been cast.
Refusing to let the sculptor of society
chip away the rough edges.
A biker, unwilling to give up
the look for the comfort,
everyone(?) else rides in.
A seat worn, dust from many roads in the eyes.
Sounds so close, like the elements —
earth, wind; old friends.
Too young in spirit
and close to the fire
to let die the flames.

Deborah Laursen May

Sunrise

As the fire engulfs the sky,
The embers of night begin to die.

Through the trees, light creates a patchwork,
Beneath the clouds, shadows still lurk.

The birds above begin their song,
The dawn of awakening will not be long.

The sun caresses the earth in her embrace,
Each blade of grass becomes a shining thread of lace.

Trees and flowers stretch toward the light,
Shaking away the last vestiges of night.

The dawn on a new day shows bright and clear,
The moon and stars will wait patiently near.

Jennifer Lyn DeShields

Smiling Faces

As I look around my living room I'm really proud to see
the faces of the ones I love all stirring back at me
In frames of Gold and Wood they smile as though they'd like to say
Hi mom, Hi pop we love you both and a letters on the way
Don't worry, we're adults you know, no more the little ones
That needed help to comb our hair and put our slippers on
Who got so sad when things went wrong or got hurt in the park
And cried out please don't turn them off I cant sleep in the dark
You put up with so many things, the fights the noise the screams
The broken dishes, notes from school among other things

But still you seem to long for us to be back there again
And know that we're all safe and that you're there to tuck us in
It started out because you two knew nothing more than love
Could stir the peace that we all have that comes down from above
The love that gives us peace of mind and permeates our air
And makes us proud to be alive and know that others care.

How-ever could I doubt, I ask, our love they won't forget
As others say their children have. when old age they had met

No in these faces smiles are grand, a truly happy lot
Of Hayes 1,2,3,4,5, No way have they forgot

Earline Hayes

Dreams Of Death

Dreams falling, twirling to the ground,
the deep feeling of awe touches you.
You feel the awe and it kills you,
You remember the feeling of the Dreams of Death
Your dream steals your soul but never reveals it.
You try to take the dream back, but it wants your soul,
Suddenly the dream lets go, Your soul drifts back to
your body, Your soul awakens. It is alive, but what
will the dream do next?

Alison Payne

Look At What Is Lost!

I am lost in a dark forest,
the forest being my thoughts.
Trust is lost in a community of lies,
the lies must stop if any progress is to be made.
Hope is lost on top of a steep mountain,
the mountain is made up of bitter and narrow-minded people.
Equality is lost in a population of bigots,
the bigots are causing us to fight each other instead of the
problems we face.
Love is lost in countries at war,
the wars sever the bonds of the human race.
Peace is lost in a world of hate,
the hate makes us fight instead of joining forces.
Life is lost in a planet of violence,
the results of this violence should be inconceivable to all.
My intellect is lost in a sea of questions,
the questions all begin with "Why...?

Jennifer Molby

Winter

The cold wind howls in the darkness of night
The frosted ground glows in the pale moonlight
Snowflakes fall and dance, to the wind they keep time
Speckles in the moonbeams, they sparkle and shine

Animals camper and forage the snow
For tidbits of foliage to make hunger go
Two rabbits frolic in the cold, frozen mist
As a deer senses foe and nervously shifts

A lone wolf's howl echoes through the dark
The timid woodland creatures, they quickly depart
Each finding shelter under branches and in holes
To escape from the predator and chilled, biting cold

All slumber cozy now save for the wolf
Still stalking about upon sleek, tender foot
And the man that has curiously witnessed all this
Lamenting the fate of the vanishing forest.

Darrin Mason

Changing Seasons

Think of summer time's beautiful days.
The glow of the suns hot, shiny rays.
The children out playing, the birds singing.
You can hear the faint sounds of the church bells ringing.
The flowers in bloom are a pretty sight.
Hear the soft winds blow all through the night.
Then fall will come and leaves will turn.
The nights become chilly, more stiff, more stern.
The flowers close up, so soon they die.
South is the direction the birds will fly.
Not far behind comes winter, how cold.
You want to stay in doors, put everything on hold.
The snow buries the grass, lightly whitens the trees.
Coldness enters our bodies, and in our mind, spring is all we see.

Christina Crandall

California Sundown

The ocean swallows up the sun.
The day is done and night has begun.
Sailboats go to shore,
But the passengers want more.
The stars twinkle above in the slightly dark sky,
And you feel as if you could fly.
So many wondrous things are happening.
Only if time didn't pass by so quickly,
You could hold this memory forever in your heart.

Crystal Young

The Visitor

I watch the wide expanse of rolling surf.
The grayish-blue waves come crashing in,
each on top of the other.
The wet sand shifts as the white foam pulls back everything
it's given, except a stolen shell.

The crash and roar of the sea are ancient.
I am comforted by the sea-spray that has been here so long.
I stand and breathe deeply, letting the air seep through my pores.
Overhead, I hear the sea gull's raucous laughter,
and wonder if,
they laugh at my thoughts.
The wind whips the sand against my legs;
I ignore the sting as I stare, mesmerized
by the continuous give and take of the surf.

As it grows dark, I turn to leave
and the sea grass sways softly, as though to wave
good-bye
knowing I will be gone awhile.

Jill M. Shope

Tranquility

Upon a tree limb was perched a sparrow
The ground still wet with misty dew
Down the lane I could see her runnin'
The sunlight shinin' through her hair
Takes me back to the days when I was seven,
Not a worry not a care
The smell of coffee from the kitchen
I think I'll have a cup or two
Grandpa is on the porch, a-rockin'
In that squeaky rockin' chair
Every morning that's where you'll find him,
Whistlin' while he whittles away
The dogs are runnin', barkin', jumpin'
And the smell of the new mown hay
Peace, tranquility, no one rushin'
Country livin's here to stay

Helen Brown Dunlap

The Face in the Mirror

There's a face in the mirror looking back at me
The hands of time have carved it, it's so easy to see
The face can tell the stories of what used to be
The lines show the wisdom the years gave to me

The face in the mirror, it knows me so well
It scares me to think of the stories it could tell
There's happiness and laughter, there's been misery and pain
And if the clock could be turned back I'd do it all again

Of the many roads I've traveled some put me to the test
But, there's been peace and joy so I know I've been blessed
The many trails we walk in life will go down in history
The lines are etched forever, so are the memories

Geri Caplena

Winds

The winds are soft around my body
The leaves of the tree give a soft whisper
The soft music all around me
Take away this wall from me
Give me the winds, the whisper of the trees, and all
the soft music around me
Open my eyes, my heart and let me be free
Free from this wall all around me.
Let me love once more,
Let my body be free.

Delores Decker

The Time Traveler

Out of the corridors of time, drifting aimlessly,
the haunting echoes of the past beckon to today.
Who listens to their tales?

Long hallways covered with runes, written from another age;
tell stories of laughter and dancing,
sparkling gaily as dancers in gilded costumes
weave their fluttering satin ribbons in and out
of the flower strewn streets.

Down the ancient gallery, empty now with gaping ceilings,
the time traveler marches on.
Who sees the aged portraits of the past?

Landscapes of serene pools, with long - haired ladies weaving daisy
wreaths,
gossamer clouds floating above,
lovers wading hand - in - hand in the trickling stream,
as ferns watch with sleepy drooping fronds.

Thunder rolls!
Season pass and eons are but an instant.
Time flows perpetually down the universe.
The gong resounds, and out of the corridors of time,
the echoes of the past...

Barbara S. Arnold

Indian Summer Remembered

Waking to cool, crisp mornings
the heavy dew sparkling like diamonds
on the dying grass
The sun is a brilliant yellow ball
in the cloudless, turquoise sky
Nature is starting her lazy trek into winter
Leaves beginning to show off vivid colors
fiery red, bright orange and yellow,
deep rust and shades of purple
Milkweed pods burst
tossing their feathery seeds to the breeze
Above, flocks of Canada geese
start their V-shape flight
to the South for the winter
honking as they pass overhead
It's time to relax and enjoy
the warm, hazy days that will soon be gone
as the season changes once again, too soon!

Amy Howard

Hope for All Time

Of the times too numerous in its life here on earth,
the Hope of humanity has been challenged since birth.

For brutality and destruction often have reigned,
and yet, through the Ages, Hope has remained.

Perhaps, it's our innate spirit to forgive and seek good,
but, whatever the reason, Hope survived and has stood.

Its survival seems so natural throughout all the Ages,
and, yet, what if all Hope had succumbed to the rages.

The intrinsic growth of humanity would surely decline,
with evil filling the void and the world less sublime.

Any hope in preserving Hope is simply unimaginable,
and its loss for all time would be so unforgivable.

So the message to humanity forever and ever is,
only through our own hope can there be Hope for all time.

Bernard J. Trescavage

She Shines

How can I speak of such a tragedy?
The "hows" and "whys" are sure to come

The anger, the guilt
The depression and self doubt

Will not be welcome.

She is to me as a luminous star on a crystal clear night
Her shining gives me hope and inspiration

During times of discord;

When my life is like a pathless desert
and the endless hot days and cold nights
make me question meaning

Now it becomes clear - I must go out at night alone
God has set her on high to guide us, the aimless wanderers,

To the path.

And there, when I look up into the bitter cold night

I see her There!

She lives!
She loves!
She guides...

She shines.

Joel P. Rooney

The Sailors

The land they sought now in the mist lay hidden.
The land that was for all intents forbidden.
Why are you sailors just tempting the sea?
Just tempting a fury that can sometimes be.

What treasures await in the land that you seek?
The call to adventure, the bold and the meek.
Are lands that you seek so rich and so fair?
Rewards just there waiting for you to lay bare?

Sometimes mighty sailor, so stormy the sea.
The risk and the danger, don't you care to see?
Some day mighty sailor, reward you will find.
Make do for the sorrow you have left behind.

Carlos C. Magallanes

Seasons

As the seasons change all around.
The leaves fall swiftly to the ground.
Soon the snow begins to come.
The songs of Christmas are softly hummed.
As the snow begins to melt.
The fresh cut green grass will soon be smelt.
Flowers begin to bloom.
Smell of spring becomes the room.
When days become long and hot.
Joyess days of summer are soon forgot.
As the days drift slowly by.
Sometimes it makes me want to cry.
To see the beauty of it all.
When the seasons change from Spring to Fall.

Angelia D. Cole

"The Ride of Life"

Falling and fluttering to the ground,
the leaves nestle on the warm earth.
Without a care, without a worry, without a memory,
they let nature take its course.
Peaceful form of life, beautiful form of life, envious form of life.
Why can't I be a leaf?
Why can't I fall helplessly, tranquilly, into nature's gentle grasp.
Green, red, brown, yellow, orange, all diverse yet all together.
Peacefully living together with their own unique qualities.
Why can't people behave like leaves?
Why can't we learn from their positive example?
Floating, riding on air, enjoying the ride of life.
leaves know how to live better than human beings.
A peaceful inner envelope, a loving inner instinct.
Why can't people learn from leaves?
Why are they ignored, taken for granted?
A simple leaf has more wisdom of life,
than our most recent ivy league graduate.
It sounds so easy, it sounds too easy.
Just listen to the flutter of the leaves,
listen to the flutter of the leaves.

Dawn M. Volker

Reflections with the Holy Child

O Radiance, encased in human flesh so small,
the light from you pervades my soul and
warms me from within.

Your form looks tiny as I watch your arms and
legs move gracefully upon the manger straw.

Beautiful being and earth's delight, you are
so astonishing to behold! My eyes cannot
take in your utter vision.

O Holy Innocence, my stains of sin will not
become you. How is it that you've entered
into such a destiny for me?

And yet you lie there quietly content. I hear
the gentle breaths you take, and with them
I inhale my own eternity.

Ann K. Gecelosky

Yearning To Be Free

I want to be
The me I was meant to be,
The me that is bursting inside of me,
Yearning to be free.

Through life's toil and strife.
I will continue on my path,
Facing the enemy's wrath,
Conquering all obstacles before me.

Some days the burden seems too heavy,
Much more than I can carry.
The tears flow from within my soul
And I long to one day be whole.

The pain and sorrow seem more than I can bear.
Yet, deep inside, I know that somewhere
Someone truly cares out there
And I am surrounded by the love of God, so fair.

And then I truly can see
That in God's plan, I am meant to be
The me that is bursting inside of me,
Yearning to be free.

Eileen Smith

Dreams

Webster states a dream is a fond hope.
The meaning of fond is cherished.
Cherished is to hold dear, to cling to, nurture.
The definition of nurture is training, rearing,
to feed, to educate.
As one may construe, a simple word, dream can become
the explanation of a sentiment, which is a
complex combination of feelings and opinions.
Feeling is the ability to experience physical
sensations through emotions.
Opinion is a formal expert judgment.
As an expert, one must deduce that the definition of
dream is much larger than the five letter word
it denotes.
To conclude, Keesha you are the woman of my dreams.

Eric K. Tondera

Corruption

Darkness hides and silence speaks
The night is hushed and blind.
The nocturne see; the true-heart cringed
The city's black with grime.

Hence is born an evil form
clothed in midnight fire
A mate to greed which hungers heart
from dusk to dawn it burns.

And, in the end alone will stand
The charred man stone and still.
What right has won what wrong
has done?
He breathes its will — corruption.

Diana Bogan

My Little Blue Bowl

As I wash and dry my little blue bowl,
The one I used to fuss about you breaking.
The smallest one of the set of four,
a long ago Christmas gift you gave
my soul.
So many good things I stirred together
as I was creating.
Cakes, cookies and spaghetti salad,
serving mashed potatoes, dressing, gravy,
the special holiday fruit salad,
like a happy, magic troll.
The years have passed, they safely moved
across the country from
where the cold snow blows,
to the constant sunshine of God's making.
Wonderful, how the long stored memories of all
those years come to me just because tonight
I ate cereal from my little blue bowl.

Janice M. Calandri

Sunshine In The Rain

Even though there may be sorrow and pain
Somewhere there is sunshine in the rain.
That may be hard to realize
Because we only see the grey skies.
Instead, how wondrous a rainbow above
Is to see and share with those we love.
The friends, family, and caring wife
Are the greatest treasures in man's life.
So don't let those black clouds bother you
Look at everything through a rosy hue.
And always remember this refrain
Somewhere there is sunshine in the rain.

Hardy Reese

Hebron Massacre/Argentina Bombing

The path of terror never deviates.
The pain of terror never alleviates.
Current political arguments do not persuade
And memories of past massacres do not fade.
This in itself is another phase
Of an attitude problem in the Middle East maze.

There is a definite character deformity
When anger and violence reaches such enormity.
Be it in Hebron, Rwanda or the United States
The decay of the goodness of humanity's soul
Is in a threatening non-objective state.

Mankind's inability to forgive perpetuates a militancy
To only be relived. Time to get off the never ending binge
Of pathetic unproductive revenge. Instead of attacking
Each other, attack the vicious disease. The mental illness
Addiction of: terrorism, reprisals, threats, power struggles,
Tease, never ending, mind bending, paranoid discrepancies.

Peace cannot be determined by a couple of hand shakes
If the hearts are false and the smiles are fake.
We have to address the hate.

Barbara Bloom

Untitled

Tucked inside a little one
The perfect place to hide
This feeling of emotion that she holds inside
Deprived of all her freedom
On this ship of death
The sea will meet her fortune
This soul so pure and fresh
Some tell me it is hell on earth
And I think it is true
That these people are tortured from birth
Their life is never new tears roll down her face
Her heart forever scarred
For she never found her place
In a world completely barred
For there is only one threshold
For the people of this trade
Their bodies will run cold
With the death the other has made
So come and meet your last breath
The ocean shall end this test.

Benjamin Johnson

Take My Hand

Take my hand, walk with me, through the years, through the
sunshine,
the rain, and the tears. Hold on tight, don't let go, for I love
you so, Take my hand, walk with me, through the years.

Take my hand, cling to me, don't let go, and forever, I want you, to
know. That you'll always be, something special to me, take my hand,
cling to me, don't let go,

Take my hand, as our fingers entwine, lay your body so warm next to
mine. Come as gently to me as this moment can be, take my hand, as
our fingers entwine.

Take my hand, in the winter of life, when my hands are all wrinkled
and old. When these bones of mine, have been ravished by time, in
the winter of life take my hand,

Take my hand, as I lay down to rest, and I never awaken again, as
you walk with me, through the pages of life when I stumble and fall,
take my hand

I will always be here, to hold on, to your hand. A bond that's much
stronger than gold, when the burdens of life you can no longer
stand, reach out for me, take my hand.

George Dry Jr.

Magic Words

"Of all sad words of tongue and pen
The saddest are these - "It might have been".
All of us know that fact is true
But the happiest words are "I love you."

These words will lift you out of the dumps,
Let you face the world and take your lumps,
They can change a frown into a smile
And make you know that life's worth while.

Whether said by parent, spouse or friend,
By child or neighbor, there's just no end
To what can happen in a moment or two
When we hear the magic "I love you".

Ann Saylor Mullins

Look on the Bright Side of Life

When life takes a turn and you feel all alone.
The sky is the darkest just before the dawn.
Stand real tall, keep your chin off the ground.
You will see the sky and the beauty all around.
Let in a little sunshine, don't sit in the dark.
Keep your eye on the ball, hit it out of the park.
Life is not about winning, it is about trying,
Just put a smile on your face instead of crying.
Don't just wade through life and grow old,
So while you are wading, baby, pan for gold.
Remember, this is the day the Lord hath made.
If life deals you lemons, then make a lemonade.
Let time pass and your heavy heart will sing.
After the winter, God always sends the spring.

Brenda C. Harris

Poesy in the Garden: A Victorian Posy of Hope

When Despair seems heir to every morrow,
The soul seems silent, strange, lotus hollow.
Yet, Snowdrops— hope's stoic knights— meet sorrow,
Leading pink tulip dreams you may borrow:
Herald hopes of happy years to follow.

And if peace eludes you, still persevere.
Bloom with plum tree courage through care and fear.
Through bleak ruin, iris rainbow colors peer:
Valor, faith, wisdom, and this promised cheer—
My blue violet fealty through life's most drear.

May sorrow's purple rose seem more rosy,
When you receive this odd paper posy.

Ilana Zanger

"Night Sounds"

Neon lights flashing in the night,
The sound of cars in the streets,
Horns sounding; Sirens wailing far off,
Searching, endlessly searching for someone to rescue.

Cats screaming and hissing in dark alleys,
Fighting for food mingled with trash,
A bone, a piece of meat,
Anything to fill empty crying stomachs.
A lonely child crying for his mother
In the cold empty night.
And no one is there.

Arthur A. La Chiusa Jr.

The Star of David

The star of man and the star of pride.
The star that held their fears inside,
For years they hid while others died.
Their tears were silent and wrapped inside.
Believe this: They are not cowards,
And never were.
Because of them traditions still breathe,
To live and grow in other minds and hearts.
The ones who died,
They put thoughts in our heads and made us think.
The killer,
He was a master, but what he did was
Wrong.
It is not color, nor is it race,
It is what is hidden behind your face.

Jolene Jimenez

Untitled

It's dusk out, the sun is getting low.
The stillness is only broken, by the sound
in the far distant of a bob cat calling for it's mate.
A sound that once would have frighten me,
except for the safety of your arms in which I lay.
The wind blowing, softly a cool breeze, through the window;
along with the sweet smell of night blooming jasmine,
fill the air, in your arms, I feel the warmth of your body;
along with the smell of your manhood
and I know how deeply I'm loved by you.
As you turn and hold me, in your strong but gentle arms.
Until the morning light comes forth and brings a new day.
A day that brings hope and faith, that this love
will get stronger and stronger as time goes on.

Darlene W. Cox

Untitled

A story of an Ancient Goddess seen yesterday.
The story told of her running away -
Running, running until the end of the day -
Then, only at night, would she play -
Playing the games of other one's worries -
Trying to stay locked in their memories -
Pictures of naked people committing suicide -
Hanging themselves, or swallowing the tide -
No matter what they do - they cannot hide.
Even if their spirits should collide -
They will have to abide by me -
Ruler of the sea - old and cold -
Brave and bold - I haven't sold -
The diamonds engulfed in gold -
No silver for her - she is not worthy
Of an award - kill her with your
Honorary sword - let your men begin the war -
They shall go south -
To find 50,000 bullets glide into their mouth!

David Fancher

To Be a Frog

O what a night to be a frog,
The rains have come and washed away all the smog,
The earth is covered with a clinging shifting fog,
And the moon sits high a top a dark and cloudy sky,
While most other creatures sit at home and wonder why,
On a night like this a frog is gay and sharp and fly,
It may not mean much if you were born a man or dog,
But on behalf of other Rana Pipiens and I,
There couldn't be a better night to be alive!

Bernard B. Anderson

For Jimmie

I can't remember the day we met.
The time, the circumstances I forget.
It was twenty-three years ago, I know.
you were a baby; I watched you grow.
That our friendship developed, I'll never regret.

You had your friends, your life went on.
I got married, so I was gone.
The ones you befriended
Left. My marriage ended.
Leaving us both all alone.

We met again after many years.
Our lives had changed and filled with fears.
You became my best friend,
And then in the end,
We shared with each other our tears.

Our friendship grew and changed to love
With blessings from Jesus up above
As I live my life through
In love with just you,
My heart soars on the wings of a dove.

Carol Caves

"The Unfortunate One"

Just as I stepped out of Jerry's saloon
the time was nearing the afternoon,

Later that day, I was told by someone,
somebody wanted to draw with their gun.

So as I stepped out of Jerry's saloon,
Somebody was to meet their Fate or Doom.

He was told that I was the one,
So he stepped out and said "Pull with your guns."

And as he winked, I stood as still as a brick,
We were looking at each other as if we were sick.

So he started to pull so bristol,
I had already shot from my newly made pistol.

And just as I had shot from my guns,
He turned around and I shot his buns.

He was scuffing around like a headless dog,
And as he got up, he screamed like a hot-hoofed hog.

Then after I had put away my gun,
I thought to myself he was "The Unfortunate One."

Poul Moran

The Trees

As we look upon the beauty of fall.
The trees show their colors to all.
So proud they stand, so very bold,
Leaves of red, yellow and gold.

Alas, the winter wind doth blow,
And all to soon they're covered with snow.
Still they stand, barren against the cold.
Daring the saplings to call them old.

Through storms that rage with winter winds.
They stand undaunted, with sturdy limbs.
All through the winter they will survive,
And in the spring, burst forth alive.

Whether growing or fallen or somewhere between,
The trees give values to things unseen.
The trees God made for all mankind.
Will last forever...till the end of time.

Jean Benson

Happy House

Happy house, happy house the place we occupy
The walls they laughs, the floors they smiles
In here I'd Gladly die

No house can be a happy place, when all seems
Sad with Gloom
But, sunshine lives in our house and hope in
Every room

The lived-in look is evident, who cares we'd
show you through
Cause we're proud of Happy house, although
It's not so New

Visit us anytime you'll come again I bet
Cause Happy House has Family Love the Best
That you can get.

Janette J. Singleton

"A Summer Day"

Close my eyes letting the bright yellow sun nurture me with
the warmth of its light,
The rays slowly penetrating every cell in my skin
caressing me to relaxation,
Feeling the cool gentle breeze that brushes through my brown hair,
Welcoming the different aromas of the flowers that
graciously stands with its vibrant colors,
Receiving the harmonizing tunes that echoes from the
mysterious birds that is lost within the leaves of the tall tree,
Hundreds of green strands massaging and soothing my feet,
A feeling so unique that it goes deep into my soul,
Taking me to a place of tranquility and beauty,
Captivated by natures masterpiece that comes within the
Summer days.

Gloria Quinones

The Other Side

If you listen closely you will hear
The whispering wind without fear
Watch upon the rustling leaves
Feel the pain as it relieves
As you sit and wonder
You will soon realize
You're deep in thoughts
As you look upon the beautiness of the sky
Then you will wonder why
Time passes on
You watch and wait
You will get a strong feeling of fate
Express your feelings
Feel the breeze
Then watch and see
And you will feel free
The feeling of hurt will go away
But the feeling of confidence will stay
You'll fight your way through all your pain
And happiness you will regain

Beth Randy Lauer

A Tear Will Be Our Token

The wind rose up from the great plains, as the Buffalo made it's pass.
The hunter with his arrow straight, takes what he needs from the mass.
The white storm from the east took everything it could,
It took the food from the mouth of the Native, it even took the wood.
A trail was made to find peace of mind, for the Body and the Soul.
Lives were lost but not forgotten as the stories Do Unfold.
Little Big Horn, Wounded Knee and An Apache that could not be broken,
These are the things our history holds.
And A Tear Will Be Our Token.

Thunder Bear Talking (Eugene A. Vasquez)

My Peace Poem

If I could write a song
The words would express my longing for peace
A peaceful world where children can laugh
with strangers and no harm would be done
A world where you and I whom were enemies can now hold hands

Aren't we all humans?
Don't we all laugh at joyful moments and cry at painful times?
Don't we all bleed blood when wounded?
Aren't we all humans with the same goal?
To live, to learn, to love, and to be loved?
Then why are we killing ourselves with weapons made by our own hands?
The hands that should be hugging our children rather than waging war.

If I could write a song
My song would have the call of a dove
The children's laughter in the evening sun
The melody of happiness at sunrise and sleepiness at sunset
And the warmth of the spring air warming our blood
and not the flames of the village war.

Hang Nguyen

Earthquake

It was a quiet night,
The world sank to retire.
Our Mother Earth suddenly raged abnormally,
She shook off things on her body.

Buildings were crashed, lives ended unexpectedly,
The beautiful earth turned out as an ugly lady,
People couldn't wait to see the dawn, then died immediately,
Tears pouring on muddy faces, the alive ones cried despairingly.

Families worked a life time to accumulate the small properties,
But now they have been destroyed absolutely,
It will take years to rebuild the whole communities.
What a disaster, residents have faced the ruinous city.

Why our Mother Earth showed such unkind nature,
To torture her children and destroy the innocent creatures?
Is she an unsophisticated woman,
Or an unaccountable layman?

We can fly to the moon and other cosmic places,
We can repair broken machines in space;
We can put things in logical order,
I hope someday we can tame the Mother Earth's bad temper.

Diana M. P. Chang

The Noble Woman

With her head held high on a summer's day,
The young girl walked by the men baling hay.
She was proper and did not associate with common men,
Forbidden the chance, so she studied in the den.
She was raised well and respected in town,
Not the kind of girl who would accept a frown.
She was well bred and noble straight to the core,
But her life, she mused, was quite a bore.
At her parent's wish, she married young.
Her husband was rich so her life style was not strung.
For the first time her head hung low, she was not glad.
This was not what she wanted in life; her heart was sad.
On a cool summer's morn, her husband died.
She rejoiced the fact, for she was no longer tied.
She moved to the city to start a new life!
And soon became a poor man's wife.
Her new life was happy, but not for long;
She died giving birth to her daughter, Angel Song.

Jane Wilson Chasse

The Magician

I never thought I wanted to be magician until this very day,
Then I could utter a single word to make everything O-Kay.

Life wouldn't be so hard, in fact, it could be something you might find quite fond,
The beautiful part is all I would ever have to do is just wave the magic wand.

Say "Goodbye" to all the toils, "So long" to all the strife,
Yes, If I were a magician, we would all have a perfect life.

Now, I know nothing is that simple and it never will be,
But it doesn't hurt to wish or dream just to be trouble free.

I don't own a wand, a top hat, or a coat with any kind of tail,
But what I do have to offer is friendship that will not fail.

Well, my friend, the only magic that I can really do,
Is to say I am someone who will always look out for you.

Though I am not a magician, please do not despair,
Just glance behind or beside you and I will always be there.

You see, magicians are just plain human in the very end.
And all the magic in the world cannot compare to a friend.

Julie Zimmerman

A Tribute To Dr. William Gahl M.D.

Seven years ago, I never thought the future would come for me.
Then I was told, that there was someone who could help,
and once again allow me to see.
This man must have been an angel from above.
Who changed my life, through your care and love.
I've never know anyone like you, who cares so much in your
words and gentle touch.
Whenever the time came to see you again, my eyes lit up
because you helped me so much.
You allowed me to not only regain my sight.
But now I can see life, in a different light.
The gratitude I have for you is very clear, and those in
the future will know what a great man you are, just by the
shed of my tear.
There is not much more I can say, to thank you, for all you've done.
But the thanks and gratitude I have for you could only be
appreciated by such a few.

Deanna Lynn Potts

Go Beyond

The nervous balls of sweat glisten in the light,
Then, like a race, they dash down leaving a moist trail
Each eye pierces her stability, oozing out familiarity
The bright light is upon her, so let the dissection begin.

The wood creeks with every shift of fear
A permanent imprint:embedded in the carpet
Left over right, right over left, continuous
The anesthesia has begun to slowly take effect.

The tingling sensation of pain by the leather snake
Metal tears open her soft, smooth flesh
Five, red reminders sting her face
Always last, in back, or never given a chance.

She is the Asian, she is the black, she is the Native American,
She is the minority, but...

She is also the human.

Joshua Michael Russell

The Golden Rule To Be "Cool"

If you really want to be cool
Then play it smart and
Stay in school

Is it easy?
Of course not
You have to work
If you want to be hot

You say you like to work with your hands
Great, I think that's really grand
And you, you want to learn to develop and plan
Then go ahead and do it, you can, you really can

You need to learn
How to chill out
But, you don't want to learn
To be a school drop-out

So, be sure you learn this Golden Rule
Learn to read
Stay in school
And when you graduate
You'll be really cool

Anne Dalrymple Runyan

Excerpts From A Lovers Diary

Thursday: The dirt road, our hands trembling
Then, the mountain green and warm
I said forever - you said always
On the blanket our bellies, my desire and ... your eyes
I want to stay.

Sunday: The pavement, the robin singing
Then, the house old and silent
I said forever and you ... you were not there
By the mailbox the cat, my agony and ... your eyes
I want to cry

Dunnia Burnham

"Waiting"

I waited a long time, and then I was born.
Then waited for clothes, my brother had worn.
All through my childhood, come early or late
For one reason or other, I just had to wait.
I waited to grow, and learn about Life,
Then waited again to find me a wife.
Our first child was born, I waited again.
He arrived two weeks late - I just couldn't win.
I've lived a full life, and now I am old.
My summers too hot, my winters too cold.
My body grows weary, my mind grows dim.
I'm waiting for God to come take me in.
He came last night about half past eight,
And left me standing at the Pearly Gate.
But, alas, the gates are closed for the day.
Be patient, old man, and don't go away,
Tomorrow morning we open at eight.
Sorry, my friend, you'll just have to wait.

Hobert F. Herpin

Summerend

A whisper of wind shakes the shadows into night.
The crickets catch its song and carry it to earth.
A firefly revisits gentler remnants of a day
gratefully retreating
from a moment hopefully suspended
in an eternity of quiet cricket-song and stars.

Donna McHenry

The Poet Is Dead

The song is gone. The poet is dead.
There are no more songs in my heart.
No more poems in my head.
I use to wear a smile upon my
face, but now the smile has lost its place.
Where there use to be love and
happiness, now I can find only emptiness.
Oh.... how I long for the days when
my heart use to sing. But now, the
melody is gone. It has felt death's sting.
Maybe some day, the song will
come back to my heart. But, I'll need
some help. So tell me, where do I start?

Carolynn J. Corbin

America

There are people on the corners, wanting money for some food
There are people on the corners, wanting money to be screwed.

There are murders and rapes in each and every state
There are people in this country, filled with only hate.

There are women being beaten, every fifteen seconds to be exact
There are babies in this country, hopelessly addicted to crack.

There are people being killed, by weapons we call guns
There are people on the street, who happen to be bums.

There are people in this country who cannot read or write
There are people in this country who have lost their hearing, voice, and sight.

There are people in our government who are being bought
There are wars in our time that we should not have fought.

There is a deadly disease going around the states, AIDS being the name for it
So if this is the land of opportunity, I say one word, BULLSHIT.

America, God has not shed it's light on thee
For if he has, there has been too much death and destruction for me.

So people, if America is where it's at
I think we had better clean up our act... Soon.

Brendan Liszanckie

Love

Various feelings meander about
There are too many present to be sure
Confusion hangs like a dense fog
One wonders what the other thinks
Each hoping their thoughts are alike

Though it is rarely discussed
It is subconsciously ever lurking
Abundant advice is shared by all
Unsure of what to believe as the truth
Unworthiness and regret go hand in hand

One emotion simply breeds another
Yet, the facts remain untold
The stakes appear to be high
Rejection, seemingly the ultimate fear
A long process of contemplation begins

He said, she said the game gets under way
The outcome is inevitably mysterious
Tensions and blood race upward
Eventually a result emerges
Finally the realization of love surfaces

Brandy Korpics

Will There Ever Be Another

Throughout the annals of history, across the corridors of time,
there has only been one, but is that really a crime?

For those who have the pleasure to know; this one was
unique, as the books of history shall surely show.

Individual of thought, and sincere in desire, a giant of
intellect whose words could inspire.

Honest and strong like a king on his throne, this lion
roared loudest defending his home.

The stars in his eyes, the earth at his feet, if it could be
done he'd do it, he would not accept defeat.

Will there ever be another, like this mighty warrior king?
Will god create another, of which family legends will sing?

Will there ever be another who means so much to so many?
Will you offer the shirt off your back, or your very last penny?

In our lifetime I don't think there will ever be another,
such a husband and father and true loving brother.

Our lives must continue, we must move towards the light, we
will never forget you, but we will say good night.

We'll see you real soon, on the other side of this life,
In the kingdom of joy, which is free from all strife.

Gregory A. Nelson

Untitled

In this heavenly bliss
There is something wonderful amiss
To endure what I will surely miss
I seal this moment with a kiss

Through the mist there comes a light
Emitted from a sun that glows so bright
As I perceived such a sight
Thoughts of you come forth from the night

On satin sheets your body lies
With a hint of mystic in your eyes
If only I could penetrate your desires
We would complete the ties

From the still of the night
I awake to the morning light
With such feeling of delight
Knowing that you will soon be in my sight

John B. Gilbert

My Gift

Beyond the blue eyes and stringy hair
There lies a glowing soul,
For this gift which has been brought to you
Is for only you to hold.
In it lies a special power
Which no one can define,
It must be a special love
because it's yours and mine.
Even though we're far apart
My love will carry on,
Endless I will hold you tight
Though I know your gone.
For my loves my gift to you
And I hope you will agree,
That all the love you've ever needed
Lies inside of me.

Jennifer Pingley

Loved

(Dedicated to my grandmother)
There was this man who is Loved very much,
who was so brave, but sensitive,
so cute, but tough that he could never be Loved enough.
He was a son of a loving mother,
And in our hearts there could be no other.
Now you see he was loved a lot.
By all the people who haven't forgot.
We still pray for him each day,
And in our hearts he'll always stay.
God took you home to be with him,
but we still miss you. We love you Tim.

Crystal A. Place

No Visit Tonight

It's Thursday night and half past eight,
There'll be no visitors cause it's too late.
I waited and waited but all in vain:
Deep inside I can feel a pain.

I told myself "yes they'll be here,"
"They're on their way, they're probably near."
But the hour passed and they didn't come;
I felt so alone, I prayed some.

I guess I hurt easy, for this hurt a lot;
But as I was thinking, I knew I forgot,
My sweetheart was working, she couldn't come,
Now I feel stupid and kind of dumb.

My parents are quite busy and are the best
They couldn't come, they need their rest.
My brothers and sisters, I expected tonight
They couldn't come but still we're tight.

With all this in mind I came to a conclusion,
It's not my sweetheart or my family I'm losin'
But rather the sadness I had at eight,
So for future visits, I'll gladly wait.

Gregory Blessinger

Let It Be Me

Another night alone, you're in my dreams
there's an emptiness in me, but if it all falls apart
I will know deep in my heart
you were the treasure that I longed to find -
Something I hoped to have forever.

To hear you speak my name, to see you search my eyes
to feel you touch my hand would more than satisfy
Now I can only dream of being all you need
I can only try to be the reason why
you think about today and forget about the past

I bless the day I found you, I want to stay around you
and so I beg you - never leave me lonely
and promise that you'll always
let it be me

It's too much to expect, but it's not too much to ask

Anita J. Shouse

Life's Special Gifts

Have you smelled a fresh new baby
or been warmed by the summer sun...
or maybe played with a frolicking puppy,
while walking by the ocean when the day is done.
Oh yes, there are many wonderful things to do
that can prove what a special gift life is to you.

Laraine F. Palumbo

True Friends

Who would have thought...
These two strangers are now friends.
The ones who knew of each other yet never seemed to care.
The ones who had totally different lives
now have to many thoughts to compare.
They are alike in so many ways
and grow closer with each passing day.
With heart and soul and mind
these two have only their dreams to find.
No one can understand their friendship but them.
But then again...
Who would have thought these two would ever be friends.

Bessie Webb

The Sisters

There are two whose beauty and intelligence is immeasurable.
They are a pair as intricate in form and grace as the
animals of mythical time.
On their hands, only a ring graces their fingers.
They have a beauty no man can resist.
They are together, always, like the gemini twins.
This is who you would think they were if they just came in.
There sisters fair were never matched.
Even as others persisted they couldn't match the sisters
with the eyes of golden brown.

Geoffrey Miller

Parents

My Mom and Dad are like angels, sent from up above,
They are always there to share, their sweet and
precious love.
They guide me through life, always standing by my side,
And from their many hours of helping me, I know I
have nothing to hide.
My parents, they are simply the perfect role-models for me,
Just by watching them I know they are everything
that I want to be.
They are forgiving and patient, and really just more
than words can say,
I look up to them more and more, with every
passing day.
They've helped me with my problems, they've always
been there to comfort me when I was sad,
They have always been there to point out my
good qualities, and to show me what I had.
To this day, and forever more I will be thankful, that's true,
But now it's my turn to say the three words
that you are famous for, "I Love You."

Annemarie DeClark

TV News Censored

Raised on rules and status quo. I've witnessed
things I didn't know. How well we treat
those we detest, with fame and fortune,
send our best. These hawks who prey
on gentle folk now light our lives with
nightly jokes. We sit and watch now,
so serene, while death keeps surfacing
on our screen. Carnage, blood, flesh and
fire a fascination truly dire. It feeds
the senses and starves the soul,
poisons the one and dooms the whole.
But what's the harm yah where's the
rub this thirst for mayhem, lack
of love. Were rushing head long around
the bend just ask the devil you'll
see him then.

Gregory "Mr. Positive" Balteff

Shadows on the Wall

Shadows on the wall
They move left and right,
Yet they don't move at all,
When day turns to night.

Is life so quick and easy to fade?
Or do we last, years from when we were made?

My friends are all shadows,
Like you and me.
Some of my friends' shadows have ceased to be.

Can you trick a shadow,
By turning on an light?
Can you trick life,
Pretend it's not yet night?

We can fight to change our fate;
We can fight until it's too late.

We struggle to keep the light burning bright,
But sooner or later it will be night.
What's the use? For through it all,
We are still just shadows on the wall.

Angela S. T. Sprague

Evening Love

Sure I see the wrinkles, and lines upon your skin.
They only show that time has passed, now I look more within.
They show the years of happiness, that you have given me.
Of all the moments we have shared and all those, yet to be.
When we are walking, hand in hand, I see a bruise or two.
I think of all the work you've done, those little things, "say you."
With pleasure I remember, most days, in all these years.
The cards, the gifts, the smiles you give, all bring me happy tears.
The music, that we love so much, may be from yesterday.
Yet time stands still, for both of us, when all those old songs play.
Now as the evening shadows fall, we hold each other tight.
"Oh", to be as youthful, as we were, on that first night.

John Kinser Hall

The Witch Trial

He was quaking and shaking in his bed,
They pushed me over, I touched his head.
He was stilled and I knew he would live,
Yet, I knew the verdict they would give.

I couldn't float, I wouldn't drown.
I swam to shore and saw them frown.
"Guilty! Guilty!" were their cries.
Hate looked at me through their eyes.

"Hurry, hurry! Build up the fire!"
I watched the flames leap higher and higher.
"Please God save me from this death!"
"Give me one more day and one more breath!"

Jenny Kaczmarowski

Last Night

When you sleep you see visions
They run through your head
Mine aren't sugarplums
They're visions of death.
I see a preacher who speaks from the book.
I see a group of people with a very sad look.
I see a stone which is marked with a name.
I can't read it out it's not very plain.
I wake up in sweat the name was mine.
I gasp, I choke, I yell it's not right.
For death reached me in my dreams last night.

Aaron Long

"The Other Side"

People say that love is great.
They say it's the most wonderful thing that can ever happen to you.
I have a different view on love.
Love hurt me, love broke my heart,
Love made me crazy and upset.
People throw the word 'love' around like it's meaningless.
To me, love is a gift.
If you have the strength, you can love anyone.
I used to have that strength, I used to be able to love anyone.
Then he threw my love back in my face.
I kept giving my love to him, so much love.
He obviously did not want it.
I was stubborn and wouldn't give up.
I never stopped loving him; I still do love him.
Now I'm afraid that when the right person comes along,
I will have given all the love in my heart to that first love
and there won't be any love left
To give the person who really deserves.
Love has hurt me more than anyone will never know.
Love has killed me.

Erica Mutchnick

Shadows Remembered

I hear them whispering in the night; the shadows remembered.
They tell the tales of the past now visions surrendered.

Hovering above, they dance about unveiling former choices.
Representatives of experience all with unique voices.

Regret speaks loudly. He towers over all. He tells of what
if or might have been had made I a different call.

Satisfaction wears a smile. She knows what's done is right.
She tends to happiness of yesterday; never ponders: "what might!"

Hope contends to keep alive past dreams not yet achieved.
Willing forth positive goals to assume they are believed.

Stress engulfs excitement igniting fear inside.
Worries ruled by insecurity: that's how they work to abide.

A single scent, a certain sound triggers memories rendered.
Often do I lay awake longing for shadows remembered.

Becky Bowers

Read the Book Instead of Just Looking at the Cover

When people look at us
they think what a disgrace,
All these men, women and children
discrediting the human race.

Why did they do these crimes?
Why did they do what they did?

What was on there minds
As they was growing up from being a kid.

I do have to say
that not everyone locked up is wrong,

Some was misjudged
And some just wanted to belong.

Its hard growing up
When there is know one to show you what to do,

And before you realize it
Everything's up to you.
So from know on
please try to understand,

that we are all entitled to mistakes
every women, child and man.

Christopher A. Foster

I Don't Know Why...

I don't know why I love you so,
Things like that just happen you know.
It's funny how it came to pass,
I prayed that we would forever last.
It's like a bird up in the sky,
Flying free and flying high.
I don't know why I love you so,
I guess it's something I'll never know.
A love that's sweet and a love that's strong,
It should last your whole life long.
Love is one of the strongest things,
That makes you want to dance and sing.
I don't know why I love you so,
Things like that just happen you know.

Devan Porter

The Long Walk

As we walk down the lonely road, I look at you,
think of what you've told. You say that your love
for me is forever, a love that nothing or no one
can sever. The birds above sing softly their song.
You assure me that nothing will ever go wrong.

Now you're gone, far away from me, sailing over
some far and distant sea. You can never come back,
that much is true, but nothing can stop me
from going to you.

I dream every night of you; your eyes, your lips, your touch.
You who loved me just enough, but never too much.
You've passed away and I'll see you soon.
I'm going to take a long walk, 'neath the harvest moon.

Angela Livermore

Love Never Ends

Walking down the path in the sun of the day
thinking of how I'll miss this place. It is sad to
say good-bye to all my friends and the love
of my life, for love never ends.
It is true I will always have the memories
of my friends and the funny things, for love never ends.
Walking down the path in the sun of the day
a bird sings to me a tune, and it says,
"Friends are forever and some things
aren't, but you shall always have a place in
my heart, for love never ends."
Walking down the path in the sun of the day
a bird whispers to me my name, it makes
me think of all the things I'm going to miss.
The nice sunny days and my very first kiss
and all the roses I have received makes me
feel very lucky. To the bird that helped me
and all my friends. I dedicate this poem,
for love never ends.

Bobbie Slocum

Wedding Day

Who is this that walks beside me?
This beauty in ivory lace and cameo.
Is this the babe I held, wrinkled red,
so many years ago?
Is this the child I nourished
With love and patience
Who came to me in times of need
And never was turned away.
Who came to me in womanhood today,
beautiful with grace.
And asked a blessing for this time and place.
Oh, such a feeling of joy and pride, for this my child,
Today a bride.

Joan Hansen

Empty Soul

My heart is pumping with spite
This body is woven in dim light
I have been driven into the darker side
Non-religion
This endless pit holds my human life
Every thought that arouses in my head
I am called to bring upon it grief with pain
I cannot see no turning back
Depression has made me its everlasting catch
Forever inside me this will live on
I crave it so much
Like the pervert falls in love with master-bation
My soul within it will never die
My body it someday will
Can't you see I'm already dead inside
Myself somehow I managed to kill

Dawntrell Emanuel

One Two Flea

One little flea said to another
This dog stinks, let's find us another
The second flea said, don't be too hasty
He's not all that bad, I think he's kind a tasty

Tasty or not, I've had it mister
I'm going over and check out his sister
With a couple of skips and a hop or two
He did just what he said he would do.

He got settled in so nice and so warm
Then Lo and Behold, it started to storm
The lightning flashed, the rain came down
The flea was furious, he thought he would drown.

That dizzy dog gives me a pain
Don't know enough to get out of the rain
Her B O is so bad, she's starting to reek
I'm starving to death, I haven't eaten in a week

It's so-long suckers I've bought a dog of my own
It's a Wal-Mart model, I ordered it by phone
It came special delivery, and boy was I huffed
I knew it would be nice, I didn't know it would be stuffed.

Cecil Powers

"Letting Go"

As I sit in this place
this place without a face.

I daydream about days to come
filled with freedom, blue skies and sun.

Life without drugs and alcohol it will before me.
For the addictions are now ready to set me free.

My higher power called God has given me inner strength.
It takes me through the pains of any length.

My sobriety allows me to be anything I want to be
It sets me free so that I can be me!

Jamie Papa

Untitled

He's an angel sent to me, to be my guide, my
one true friend, in whom I can confide. He's my
every perfect vision of a dream come so very
true, he's by my side no matter what I go
through. Yes, he's an angel sent to me, and we
will never part, simply because this angel
lives within my heart.

Kristin Shore

Spider's Web

How could I know that I would miss you
Those nightly visits so subtle
An hour either way
That brought me softly
Lest I interrupt the beauty of your work
So intricate in lace perfection
As if angelic threads of gossamer
Were heaven sent
And days were measured
From dawn's disappearance
'Til night shades beckoned your automation
Was your season's time completed
And was the storm God's sign to you
It took so long for me to know
That ugly is what we each perceive
And in our clouded vision
We miss the beauty that God Himself created

Betty B. Kirsch

A Fathers Lament

We're all born into Gethsemane,
A garden black with dark despair.
And we're convinced by paid believers
That our only hope walked there.

But, hope, like darkness on that night,
Was not reflected in Christ's eyes.
His veretic death not death at all,
His truthful life, a lie.

And, as proof there are the children.
Who, with his loving imprimatur,
Endure sickness, death and sorrow
Although quite innocent and pure.

No, death brings but little sorrow
To Gods that cannot die.
or to Gods with hearts unfeeling
Who'll sit and watch a father cry.

Sepulchres hold but mortal men,
The divine they all go free.
Pillories hold but flesh and blood,
Sighted men too blind to see.

Jeffrey Andrews

Reputation

There IS one thing that's yours alone,
And it's up to you to guard it.
That thing's your reputation—
Be sure you haven't marred it:

When someone asks, "Do you know him?"
And you respond, "Of course,"
Your curiosity's aroused—
Why? What thoughts are yours?

Are you visualizing someone
Who is pure as driven snow?
Or is his reputation showing—
Painting pictures base and low?

What's YOUR opinion of yourself?
Could you safely pass the test?
If ever your name's mentioned,
Would you feel you've done your best?

It's not too late to ponder
On correcting your mistakes.
If your reputation's tarnished,
Polish it—for goodness' sake:

Mary Burger

South Africa

South Africa, the beauty of the people, the landscape so green, the sun so yellow, the blood not spared but dispersed throughout the land

South Africa, ruled not by the people by the structures of wrong doers, elements of hate, power so inhumane that the cries of our people produces rivers unconditional

South Africa, where apartheid existed, no means of escape, where wells, unclean waters are the route to survival

South Africa, the people, beaten to death, shot, wounded, by the adversaries of their tribes

South Africa, killings amongst ourselves, provoked by our enemies who observe as they produce more violence against the people

South Africa, disease stricken, incurable, inflicted on our people for experiments, so sad the acceptance of something so cruel, an injection of death

South Africa, a place where reality unfolds and no one seems to care but those that feel the pain and agonies of the people

South Africa, blessed are they who promote peace and love and have

"faith" in our most high God

"With this faith we will be able to hew out of the mountain of despair a stone of hope"

Evonne Moye

Untitled

A youngster who just starts to grow,
A seed among the flowers,
The world will come to reap and sow,
And waste away the hours.

How senseless is this child we see,
So helpless in his flight,
So lonely, scarred in infancy,
A stranger in the night.

Forever searching, seeking, peace,
This tortured, gentle child,
And will the horrors never cease?
In a world so fierce and wild?

He laughs and plays with other tots
In a vision of childish dreams,
Lost in a world of forget-me-nots,
It is not what it seems.

For all that life is really worth,
Until the very end,
He'll seek to find his truest birth,
He'll seek to find a friend.

Karen Plumley

"Star Gazer"

Oh radiant diamond in the sky,
Descend your beam unto my eye,
And I shall bounce it back to you,
So we might share each other's view.

And after solemn vows are made,
Our inner secrets we shall trade,
So each might gain the other's trust,
As distant allies justly must.

Then as ripples in a lake,
Our mirror image we will break,
And send our beams to search in vain,
'Til e'er they chance to meet again.

Perry White

The Storm

In the distance the clouds rolled in,
darkening the day.
Suddenly the sky began to spin,
and the trees began to sway.
One small drop fell from the clouds,
followed by another.
Then came a great downpour,
following the thunder.
The storm raged on throughout the day,
and long into the night.
'Til finally it faded away,
and the clouds let in sunlight.

Kristen Bradshaw

Letting Go

As leaves depart reluctantly,
bidding farewell in twirling motion,
soon desiccated, scattered wild,
whimsically by the storms,
so my thoughts, beliefs and dreams
tear loose with pain—
once part of me.

Stripped naked, robbed
of yellow, orange, red, and brown
stands garbless contour
simple, plain—
and, like a tree, I gather strength
in loss and solitude—
now part of me.

Martha Dunnebier-Fraunberger

America

America is great, everyone's free because along time ago, we made a plea.

Because of our colonies unanimous attendance, we gained our freedom and independence.

The civil war it lasted four years, it was a time of blood guts, and fears.

Then there was the Vietnam war and no-one wanted anymore.

We take for granted what we have now, which back then they would not allow

So please help out and lend a hand to the country I call "The promised land"

There is a hole in the ozone our landfills are filing and polluting the oceans our animals its killing.

Reduce, reuse, and recycle are important things to do, because one day pollution may kill you too!!

We have to help America that's all there is to it because no one else is going to do it.

So reach out now and take a stand with what's left of our promised land

Pick up the garbage on the street, instead of kicking around with your feet.

It may not be perfect to the naked eye, but its perfect to me and that's no lie

So this is the end of my American story, we fought for our freedom and our all-mighty glory.

Ashley McDow

Nippersink

On the bank of Little River,
A short walk north of Desota Falls,
Stands an edifice, tall and rustic,
Beckoning pilgrims: come one, come all.

Here, there are no stained glass windows,
Neither are there polished floors;
Fancy carpets are not found here,
No security locks on the doors.

Sit before the oversize fire place;
Sample the food at its tasty best.
Why would one want to go there,
Kick off the shoes, and take a rest?

Many strangers have been there,
Overnight guests or a long week end;
No stranger has ever left there,
But been converted into a friend.

Plan a trip up to Mentone,
Follow down the river's brink
Until you come to this charming mansion
Fondly known as Nippersink.

Thelton L. Eubanks

Anniversary Dearest Dream

40 years married
5 children carried
Happy sad tears when mad
Faith, trust in God and ourselves
Have carried us through
How about 50 more
God keep us

Peccy Ann Campbell Evans

Untitled

A gush of wind
A beat of the heart
Will never keep the two of us apart.
The sound of your breath
Your whispers to my ear
Will always keep us close and near
The softness of your smile
The feel of your skin
In my heart you will always be within.

Pamela Mellem

Poem

I won't to fly like a bird
a bird that has high wings
that will take me to a place where
I can see the Ocean from far beyond.

And when I get to that point above
the world I wont to go to the highest
Mountain above the sea to see the
big whales beneath the sea and
all the sea monsters and everything
that lives beneath the ocean.

For their is a purpose for everything
that lives beneath the sea
and on dry land and when I return
back to my next I would be the
wisest bird that ever lived.

Rebecca Holloman

Tomorrow

Tomorrow's dawn,
a brand new day.
Yesterday's fears,
fade away.
Lives enriched,
from lessons learned.
A story unfolds;
the pages turned.
Dreams held tight,
near the heart.
Hope for tomorrow's,
encouraging start.
Memories embedded,
from yesterday.
For tomorrow's dawn,
a brand new day.

Mary Richardson

The Illusion of Love

Love is an illusion
it comes on the
Wings of a dove
and leaves on the
tip of a sword

Kathy Masters

Insanity

The mad who are sad
May be bad in battle
For they tattle as they rattle
Along their way.
Waiting for the day
When they can say
That all is not lost,
And the cost is some frost
Marking their hair
From past affairs.

Mark Anthony Burbano

I Love You

Thoughts of you flutter my mind
A constant rapture of love
Impeccably paired you and I
We shall always be together as one
A new light has shone upon both of us
Unlike any other before
With each dawning day
You dwell in my heart
I know that it is you I adore
As time passes on
What more can I say
To inform you of how that I feel
A million and one times over again
I love you
I love you for real...

Lori Tubello-Cassinari

First Love

Her heart bursts open,
A crimson, red, rose,
Her body trembles at his touch,
Her lips find sweetness with his only,
She will never wash where he touched.
A word and she crumbles to powder,
Her resolve thrown to the winds,
She will lay in his arms forever,
By the light of a silvery moon.

Kristin L. Hiatt

Transcendental Time

The future is just moments away
a curtain hides the view.
Subtle silence and my heart awakens
fanciful, anew.
The past was just minutes ago
the curtain torn in two.
A disenchanted heart again broken
tears that follow through.
The future and past now have met
everything left exposed.
The sorrow and loneliness with me yet
another curtain has arose...

Jacquelyn M. Strawn

"Pumpkin Pumpkin"

Pumpkin, Pumpkin,
Look at me.
Pumpkin, Pumpkin,
Come out and see.
Pumpkin, Pumpkin,
In a tree.
Pumpkin, Pumpkin
Cute as me.

Lauren Cash

The Dream

Last night I had a dream.
A dream of forgiveness,
and a dream of hate.
Of coming to terms
Of realizing the past
Of raking the ashes
and finding the cause.

The ashes were your body
because I killed you in my mind
all those years ago,
so I could be free.

But you raped my body
and abused my mind.
I may forgive you,
but I will always hate you.

Last night I had a dream.
I raked the ashes
and let them blow away.

Kate Emmett

the mask

A piece of invaluable material
used as a shield for protection
a wall to hide behind
a strong and powerful weapon
strong enough to shelter the
deepest emotions
powerful enough to shun the
softest touch
deadly enough to ruin the
most reputable character.
The smallest flaw can be tragic;
just big enough for a ray of light
just small enough to go undetected
only to be conquered by
the unstoppable hand of time
the unforgettable touch of love
the undeniable presence of truth.

Kerrie Ann Tinelli

Ray Charles - Diet Pepsi Cola

Hi Ray,
A few lines just to say,
That on that faithful day,
When the postman came my way,
He delivered a package
Just in time,
To make me change
My funny mind.
He changed my taste,
But, not in haste,
So, now I know
It wasn't a waste
When you said that famous line
"You got the right one baby"
Un - Huh!

Joyce Branch

Untitled

I am here
But I am not seen
I am not here
And I am not seen
I am talking
But I am not heard
I am loneliness

Synona Culbertson

Attitude Checks

Age is just an attitude
A friend once said to me.
As I moved slowly down the walk
Not far from eighty-three.

My attitude may be quiet young
While I am growing old.
Many a mile I've traveled here
And seen the years unfold.

God promised not an attitude
But shelter in the storm.
The psalmist said three score and ten
Would really be the norm.

If by strength you reach four score
Just keep in mind this thought.
Check your attitude, my friend
And see what age hath wrought.

Mary Lou Hinson

A Lie

A story is better left untold,
A heart of a women to which.
Misfortune was sold.

Lies a devil in man soul,
The illness of grief,
A pain spread much too slow.

To much pain, to much lie,
The devil's always seeking,
Murder a women soul and mind.

But love become guilt and anger,
Flaunting breeze across the moors,
Satanic plain is an the move.

Hazardous places, hazardous plans,
Behind the shadow darkly plans,
Seeking and killing the devil's eye

Paulo Ortiz Luis

Untitled

I cannot tell
a lie.
My heart pours
for knowledge.
My soul pours
for you.
I cannot help it
It wasn't asked
of me.
Remember,
I still care
And all the times
we shared.
Think of me and
you will be...
happy and
forever free.

Stefani Salzman

Clockwork

Kids believe—
It's Christmas eve.
Children play—
It's Christmas day.
Siblings fight—
It's Christmas night.

Maryann Westhoff

Mothers Day

You are a mother,
a mother of two.
This day is dedicated from us to you.
We would like to tell you how
much we care, because you are our
mother and always there.
This day probably means more
to us than you,
because we love you and
were very proud of you.
You work all day and then come
home to us.
We would like to share with
you, what you've shared with us,

Lyndsey A. Holliday

Aurora

Again her light borns
a new day
Waking songs in birds
while the wind whispers
gently the secrets of
a new day

Again her light unveils
every color in the field of life
opening the most delicate bloom
she lifts the saddest heart
and sails it on a stream of sunlight
of new love

Again the sun sets
beckoning the shroud of darkness
only to illuminate a bed of stars
sparkling in the solemnness
in the close of another day
of yet a new dawn

Kris Murakami

Hoping For You

A dark shadow
a reflection of you
a drop of mist
like a drop of dew
that sits upon
my moonlit face
staring into darkness
into an empty space
looking into my heart
I can't see any light
nothing but darkness
so empty, like night
no stars, or hope
just a place for you
knowing you don't love me
but I love you, I do
I love you so deeply
so deep down inside
I'll be waiting here for you
and in the darkness I'll hide

Johanna Turpin

Invitation

Dive into the darkness;
Plunge into the pain;
Feel the fright, that seizes night,
breeding in my brain.

Sarita Lopez

"Fire"

Your arms
A ring of fire
Encircled around me
No where to run
No place to hide
Emotions
Flowing in me
Caught
In a love trap
Of fire
Don't know what to do
Do I stay
To get burned
Or do I run
And get burned
Even worse

Sarah Ebbett

Tears of a Dove

Beneath lowly clouds
A silence is loud...

I'm lost, I'm found
I'm the music, No sound...

A void going round
It's lull unfound...

An illusive quest
putting hearts to the test.

Such emptiness sought
So valiantly fought...

An evasive intrusion
from a depressive illusion.

An enigma that hounds
No echo, No bounds...

Transcending above
through tears of a dove.

Kim Lorraine Boehm

"Little Girl Lost"

Wet, shiny,
a tear rolls down her face.
Pain, depression,
no happiness to take its place.

Steel, razor sharp,
her faith is in the knife.
No more suffering,
she wants to end her life.

Slow endeavor,
the slitting of her soft wrist.
Hot, sticky blood,
flows as she makes a fist.

Stone cold expression,
no more tears to cry.
Gentle winds blow her blonde hair,
as she silently waits to die.

Tired, sluggish,
she draws her last breath.
Dark, tranquil,
death...

Rebekka Osheim

Dreams

A dream is a dream
A thought to be.
Work for that dream
And success you'll see.

That dream is yours
And yours to keep
One little step is
like a giant leap.

Work for your dream
and reach for your goal.
The higher you get
The better your role.

Dreams are dreams
Can be any kind.
For fill your dream and
And take no step behind.

Keryn Rossini

Time

A time to sow or reap;
A time to work or sleep;
A time to laugh or weep;
A time to plumb the deep
Thoughts of birth or death.
A time to always keep
The memories of life, a heap
Upon the heart before we leap
The chasm, so steep, called death.

Louise T. Johnson

Trees

Red, Green, Yellow, or Orange
A tree is a living thing
It provides us with Oxygen
One day a match is lit
The fire spreads quickly
Animals homes are ruined
The air is polluted
Animals lay dead
At the end a century is lost
All because of a match

Sarah Ward

Dusk to Dawn

A breath of honesty
A whisper in the night,
Peace and Tranquility
Silhouettes in the moonlight.

A fragrance of sweet perfume
Lingering on a pillow,
Light from a candle in loom
Music plays soft and mellow.

A touch from a hand so tender
A warm and soothing caress,
As a prayer for love is answered
A soul is graciously blessed.

A rain falling in the distance
Sighs too soft to hear,
As Embers glow warmly in the fireplace
Dawn is closing near.

Paul Vaughn Brown

A Child's Cry

You see before you
A woman grown
But a small child
Lives within; crying
"Please love me—
Think I'm special"
Her life is almost done
And yet it's not begun
When will she be free
To grow up, happily
And truly be-
The woman grown, before you

Susan Greiner

Escape

Escape into a world,
A world of your own.
Where all life flies freely.
And the silence,
screams out a freedom.
A freedom from everything.
Free your mind.
From the world as we know it.
Escape,
escape into a world,
a world as we should know it.

Mistie Bauerly

My Grandmother

I wish I knew how you feel now,
About you and I.
But I love you with all my heart,
For reasons only I know why.

I can never show you this poem,
I can never tell a soul.
I didn't try to make you stay,
I just let destiny take its toll.

I dream about you every night,
You're in my every thought.
I wish you were still here with us,
But I guess your what god sought.

You put a sparkle in my life,
Your picture is my treasure.
You lived life to its fullest.
And enjoyed all of its pleasures.

I wish I had your pretty smile,
I wish I had your dignity.
I wish I had your patience,
But I guess I'll just be me.

Kelli O'Brien

Paint Me A Sunset

Paint me a sunset
  across the skies,
With lots of colors
  to please my eyes.

Splash on shades
  of red, orange and blue,
Sketch wispy clouds
  and tall mountains too.

Draw in a clear lake
  to reflect all of this,
Then paint me a friend
  to share it all with.

Malia A. Haberman-Sperry

Stay True

Words can never be unsaid,
Actions can't be rewound.
Painful mistakes leave ugly scars,
So is what I've found.
I understand what you say,
But be sure it's what you feel.
Despite what you think you know,
Scars don't ever heal.

Samantha Sansevere

I Moved Today

I moved today
After only 38 years
I moved today
Leaving behind all that I held dear
He's gone somewhere-up there
Beyond my reach-my touch
He left me behind to grope-to adjust
To survive in a world of cocycles
Where life moves on in doubles
A shiny new home
Where I'll live all alone
With many new friends
A new life begins
It was grey-but
I moved today

Rita Bradley

Does Anyone Really Care?

It's wisdom and courage
against love and hate.
Some people are so dumb
they walk right into the gate
No one knows why,
no one really cares, but
someone has to stop it, or
are there too many fears?
We ask ourselves why,
and just keep on doing it, someone
has to stop it before we all run it.
The world, the earth, the
children, the air, we have to
stop it now, but does anyone
really care?

Katherine R. Stuva

You Made Them All

You made them all, dear Father;
All creatures on this earth!
I love them all, dear Father -
Each thing you've given birth;
The birds, the animals and trees,
Each flower and each plant;
And you, dear Father, they do please.
So in your love please grant
That we will show them kindness
As we trod upon earth's way.
Please take away all blindness -
May understanding stay
Deep down within our longing souls
That we will know you more
By what you have created,
And in our hearts please store
Compassion for the ignorant,
The wayward sinners who
Have lost their way upon life's road:
Help us lead them to you.

Natalie Leonesio

Faces

Look at their faces,
All different yet the same
But still so different
we all need a name.

Look at their faces,
Look at their brow
This one wears a grin,
This one wears a scowl.

So when you meet someone new.
Try and remember their name
Because look at their faces
All different yet the same

Randol P. Hill

Off The Shelf

I am not a crystal glass
all finely etched and believed
a pretty little thing
serving no real purpose
except that of ornamentation

Life would not let me
sit upon its shelf
polished and all protected
so if in my living
I have chipped away
a few of my edges
and made the smooth places rough
and the rough places smooth
then I know at least
I've held life's measure
not spilled it out
nor cracked beneath its volume

No I am not a crystal glass

Patricia A. Kabore

Somewhere

As the tide rolls in
And gently kisses the shore,
Somewhere a woman is beaten,
By a man above the law.

As the sun goes down
Leaving behind a starry night,
Somewhere a child, abused,
Cowers in fright.

While the crickets chirp
Their sad love song,
Somewhere a mother wonders,
"Where did I go wrong?"

While the pale moonlight
Cascades against the waves,
Somewhere a child sits hungry,
When bread is all he craves.

As the night air settles
The nerves of the day,
Somewhere a mother tucks her child in,
And kisses his fears away.

Lisa M. Pelletier

Untitled

I don't remember when
All I do remember's friend.
You've been always there to listen
No matter where or when.
We may not see each other
For time does go too fast.
But when we meet one another
We know the friendship's last.
We've shared a closer moment
In past times long ago.
Passion peaked without a comment
For our own vows stronger though.
For I don't remember when
All I do remember's friend.

Krystene R. Towne

To Damon...

When I look into your eyes
All I see is love
We seem to fit together
Like a hand inside a glove
When you hold my hand in yours
All my worries disappear
'Cause I know that if I need you
You're going to be there
When you gently kiss my lips
All my anger melts away
All I think about is you
And all the things I want to say
It doesn't matter any more
You know now how I feel
All that's left for me to do
Is pray your love for me is real.

Lori Laquidara

Deep In Thought

Here I sit deep in thought,
All of my feelings may never be bought,
All I do is hurt and cry,
when all I want to do is die.
I am constantly being told,
I act like a kid,
When all my emotions try to be hid,
I sit and drink my life away,
Hoping, I could change my life someday.

Tina Aleasha Covan

Coffee

Today I spilled my coffee—
All over the floor,
And on my blouse.
I knew today would be bad
And we would fight.
You think everything is fine.
I disagree.
You moved into my home
And said we would become closer—
We did not.
I drink my coffee alone now
And remember your sweet kisses
So long ago.
The kisses have been replaced
With bitter words.
It is time
For you to go.

Kelly Suzanne Rimer

Childhood Dreams

I remember those childhood days
all sunny and bright
Those warm summer breezes and
winters snowy and white

Dreaming those special dreams
all filled with fairy tales
Meeting the King and the Queen
for lunch and cocktails

How special I thought I once was
in those carefree days
Dreams which shattered in pieces
in many different ways

Riaz Sayeed

Free

Young, carefree
always smiling no matter
what happened to me.

Dancing through life
loving everybody that
I see.

Happy, singing
life was full of
joy and ecstasy.

No barriers, no colors
life was safe
in my world.

Why do they have to change
Why do we let them
Why can't I remember
how to be so free.

Youth, freedom
I now wish that
I was young.

Rick Bennett

Love Light

Will I find the path
Am I in the dark alone
Is it only a chosen few
The light has truly known

It's the light of love
Can I ever find the way
Will someone love me
Without drifting astray

Warmth from the light
Would keep me safe
The glow will protect my heart
But only if I have faith

Can someone show me the path
Walk with me to the light of love
Does this light really exist
Or is it something only dreamed of

Kim Jones

Mothers

They are the ones who
love you
They are the ones who
cry for you
They will love you
forever.

Slugger Priest

A Dream Unfolding

Begun in joy,
An awakening of adventure,
A dream unfolding.

Begun in fear,
An anxiety of inadequacy,
A dream unrealized.

Begun in faith,
A trust of experience,
A dream undefined.

Begun in loss,
An abandonment of choice,
A dream unrelenting.

Begun in love,
A fulfillment of desire,
A dream undertaken.

Nancy Klaffky

Separate Lives

Raw sore, open.
An itch below the surface -
indication of something wrong.
Peace patched together
from the scars
of screams.
A house; together
yet separate,
Nullifying childhood dreams.

Tracy Causey-Jeffery

The Price Of Freedom

I gazed for miles
And all I could see,
The vastness of the ocean
Lurking at me.

I pondered if I would make it
To the "Land of the Free".
Some tried and succeeded
And some were lost to the sea.

But those "Lost" also made it
Because now, they too are "free".

Maria Kosar Mills

Dreams

When all your dreams fall through;
And all your faith is gone.

It's hard to understand;
Just what you've done wrong.

When long hard fights are lost;
And triumph fails to come.

What's left for us to do;
But watch what won't come true.

Sharon A. Thomas

Poetry

A world left untouched,
A sky, still blue.
It brings out feelings,
Fresh and unseen
Paint on picture,
Song on sheet.
Poem is there,
Still clean, still neat.

Sarah Talbert

Rainy Day Down On The Farm

Harvest moon
  And autumn rain;
Pastures green
  And golden grain.

Falling leaves
  And apples red;
Faded barn
  And leaning shed.

Thistles brown
  And yellow mums;
Clustered grapes
  And purple plums.

Harvest waits
  For sunny day;
Farmers rest
  And children play.

Summer's gone,
  The mercury drops;
Hearts rejoice
  For bumper crops!

Julius K. Strand

Linger, Summer

Breath a warm air, oh, South wind,
And chase away the frost.
Gently calm the North wind,
E'er all of summer's lost.

Whisper to the birds on wing,
Linger yet awhile.
Then you can fly together
Along that southern mile.

Weave softly through the morning mist,
And catch a silver thread.
Tie each leaflet to its stem,
E'er this sweet summer's dead.

Southwind round the harvest moon,
Softly warm the night.
Cradle all the restless hearts
Until morning's rosy light.

Shine on one more day of summer,
In this, too soon, September,
A day to dream of in our winter sleep,
A day we can remember.

Marjorie Yeoward

Firstborn

I view my life on pages
and know one day you will be
without my heart to shield you
from all that I have seen.
I pictured life so differently then
when innocence was golden.
The grass was evergreen.
The sky, a shadowy blue.
Nights were clear and starry,
each day was new.
I weep for you child,
one day you will grow.
Reality will come for you
and you will know, as I know.
Years can never be retrieved.
Only memories will we have then.
We will pray for the days
when innocence was golden.

Mala S. Crass-Lowe

You

Whenever I feel lost,
And don't feel like going on;
Whenever I feel lonely,
All I do is think upon...

When no one understands,
And all they do is scorn;
When they beat up against
These defenses so worn...

When all I want to do
Is just disappear;
When things seem hopeless,
Whose voice do I hear...

Whenever I am hurt,
And my heart's been left in tatters;
Against these mighty walls I've built
The thought of you still batters...

When I'm ready to give up,
And don't know what to do;
Constantly my heart cries out,
My heart cries out for....You.

Shoshana Bauminger

Untitled

In winter silence I sit by the fire
And enjoy myself for about an hour.
Yay, yay, yay
I have come to stay
In sparkling light -
No more than just that.
Now it is time for you and me
To see through my eyes;
Please tell me what you see.
I hope you see a star in the sky -
And you learned that just from me.

Amanda Lesher

Untitled

I, looked, upon the waters glow,
And faces that I see,
Are faces, from the years, now gone,
Who made life good for me.

I think about the happy times,
That filled some special room,
But I try not, think, about the tears,
That turned it into gloom.

I leave my quiet thinking place,
The sun now, sinking, low,
And try to be a happy face,
For someone's future glow.

If I could only change the world,
My biggest change would be,
That all, could, find, a special place,
And share, this, calm, with me.

Patricia Leach

Poet?

I long for the life
of a poet,
a poet's life indeed.
If only the life
of a poet
was not a life of need.

W. H. Terrell

Bed Of Dreams

I see him coming
And feel his presence.
I look into his dark eyes
And feel not afraid
For hidden deep within
Is the secret to love and compassion.
I take his hand and together
We walk through the clouds.
We had been separated too long,
But now we are as one.
He puts his arm around me
And I feel his power and strength.
His lips meet mine
For what seems an eternity.
I know what he wants
And am willing to give it all.
I am to be his mistress
For all eternity
And shall slumber forever
In his bed of dreams.

Yvonne D. Dunson

All That Matters

I am no Hemingway
And I am no Shakespeare
Nor live by the Art of War
Nor die in vain or fear
I am no Plato, or Homer
I deal in fact, not friction
I follow the Truth, and the Way
I follow the Holy Direction
Which points me to a place
Where I'm part of God's connection
I eat the bread of life
I drink the living waters
And then I'm one with God
And that is all that matters
And that is all that matters

Leo Napoli

Your Special Friend

I found somebody special today,
And I want for them to know,
That when I find someone like you,
It's hard to let them go.

I'm glad we had the chance to meet,
And hope we meet again,
But If you we have just that one time,
It would last until life ends.

I know you haven't known me long,
But things have just begun,
If we try, and do things right,
We'll be more than just friends
And every letter that I write
Will end, love,
  Your Special Friend.

Shawn Schultz

Untitled

For no one in the world
shall ever stand by you,
hope for you,
nor believe in you
more than I.
I love you -
I am your friend.

Laurie Meech Mast

Hearts And Kisses

Hearts and kisses are love
Sharing and caring is too.
But your the one who does
All these things so the worlds
Wishes can come true.

Kallie Seier

Untitled

Still waters run deep -
  And if we let our minds wonder, -
    out of control, -
We can have anything and
  so much more.

The waters are deep,
  as is our mind.
We can wade in the water
  or drown in time.

As surely as the tide comes in,
  so will our destiny,
Sink or swim -
  we all want to be free.

A. Publicover

Birthday Wish List

You ask me what I want for my birthday
and it's really hard to say,
for you give me all I really need
each and every day.

I can ask for the sunshine
and you let it shine with your smile,
so even when it rains
I have the radiance of you inside.

I could ask for blue skies
and you provide that too,
for it's in the serenity of your eyes
there's nothing more you need to do.

I could ask for peace and security
and distance between all harm.
But you make me feel so at rest
every time I am in your arms.

But as for material objects
I don't know what would compare.
Your love is special enough for me
So to ask just doesn't seem fair.

Tina M. Baker

Untitled

You locked the evils in
And left me astray
When will it be the next day
For I have seen
What you fear
I know your desires
How are you going
To put out my fires
Dreams of death
When will I breath
My last breathe.

Michelle Downs

Love

Your face stays before me
And love blooms in my heart
I am content.

How can I tell you
What you mean to me?
I am at loss for words.

But heaven is here on earth
With you in my mind
And in the space behind my eyes.
You stay forever.

When we are here no longer
And but a memory
Love will remain—

In the air,
Between the parallels of the universe
Older than mankind—-
Like magic.

Love will never die
Love is eternal.
Mine. Yours. Ours.

Tanya L. Ladika

Untitled

By these young men
And many more
For country's sake
And even yours.

So write again
And bare to all
Your twisted soul
For pity's sake.

But write on more
Of my fair wall
Of ghosts of grey
Of Southern stance.

The cost to pay
Was much to bear
For freedom's sake
And even yours.

J. I. Williams III

Purple Berries

What are they so ripe
  and mellow
tempting the eyes to ask?
  Once were greenish
or a shade yellow,
  Now to ripen...
  A such easy task.
Not edible unless you
  wish to fly
far from this garden
  and from my eye.
Just purple berries delighting
  our vision
hanging from a tree
  in such precision.

Sarah Ayers

Loneliness

I was married at home in California
And moved to Iowa, so far apart.
I couldn't see my parents often
And loneliness nibbled at my heart.

When our firstborn came along
My heart was filled with delight,
But my parents couldn't see him.
From my heart loneliness took a bite.

The years have taken their toll—-
My husband's parents are gone.
Mine too have passed away
And loneliness nibbles fast and long.

Now when we are alone on Sundays
Sometimes it pierces like a dart
As loneliness takes over
And eats away at my heart.

Someday, when the Lord calls me
And from this earth I will part,
That will be the time loneliness
No longer will nibble at my heart.

Nadine Wolter

"Lasting Love"

The ships are sailing out sea
 and on board is our love
The huge waves crash onto the beach
 sending messages from above
Telling us that what we have
 should last forever after
We should never overlook
 the good times and the laughter
The days are so much longer
 when we spend time apart
But I'll always have you with me
 if only in my heart
I wonder if my love for you
 will ever fade away
Will this pain inside die down
 with each new passing day
Whatever prevails, I want you to know
 I will love you until the end
For you are very near to me
 much more than just a friend.

Nicki Mord

My Stone Ship

I built a ship of tiny stones,
And placed it in the moat.
But only a fool could ever think,
A ship of stones could float.

I loved you with such a passion,
I loved you with all my heart.
I'll love you until the ending,
Because I loved you from the start.

You've never seen me praying,
You've never heard me weep.
You've never seen me crying,
When I tried so hard to sleep.

One time, just once, you kissed me,
I can't forget that day.
For when I looked into your eyes,
My stone ship sailed away.

William D. Tate

Jim

Six years he stayed at home with me
And played with toy and tool
Waved good-bye reluctantly
Today he went to school.

I wonder if he'll mind his ways
And learn to keep the rule
As mother's always have and will
When sonny goes to school.

I hope the path he starts today
Will light eternal fire
Of thirst for knowledge in his soul
Wipe out all base desire.

Attune his mind to higher things
Teach him to champion right
To cherish justice over all
And freedom over might.

Mallie Booe' Page

Observation

So we're growing old
 and really can't win.
Instead of plucking our eyebrows,
 we pluck our chin.

We may have hot flashes,
 but still
Its nothing we can't fix
 with a hormone pill.

But we're still women
 and statistics will tell
We outlive the men
 so why sit and wail!

Josephine Duncan

Temporary Love

As I lay here
and recap our day,
I feel an unexplainable
difference of heart.

It is as though, my heart is sore-
injured- in a hatred way...

Scary, this emotion-but
I'm trying to remain calm-
to not give in and cry...

because that is what I
want to do...

It seems that my happiness
is always temporary!

Lorraine Pitre Raham

April's Changing Face

Petals
Of dogwoods,
Over shorn lawns,
Scattered like strangers -
Aging and changing
Too-much, too-soon
April's pert
Proud face ...

Margaret S. McKenzie

"Forever Yours"

I walked among the stars tonight
and saw you standing there
Your wistful eyes with beauty bright
Beneath your glowing hair
You were so perfect, so divine
But you were human too
Because I took your hand in mine
And whispered love to you
We lingered through the hours long
and leaned against the sky
While in the magic of a song
Our dreams went drifting by
I kissed your lovely lips and then
I promised with my heart
I would return to you again
and we would never part
And though the stars may disappear
An' I may walk alone
I shall be yours forever, dear
Forever, dear, your own

William J. Collins II

Storm Warning

How we desecrate our Mother Earth,
and scarcely blink an eye.
Burn and cut her very flesh,
and expect she sit passively by.
But one day soon our Mother Earth,
will take things into hand.
And the cataclysm that follows,
will mark the end of man.
Lighting raining from above,
Fire spewing from below.
Waking the children,
that must now say goodbye,
before ever saying hello.

Michael DeMartin

My View

If writers can write
And singers can sing.
Then life is a miracle
in which you receive everything.

The drinkers get drunk
and the stoners get stoned.
Reality is around the corner
and I don't know how to go.

The powerful are powerless.
The dead lifeless.
There are no maps no signs.
I am lost!!

Change is a chance,
While security is a dream.
Temptation is close and
innocence remains far behind.

If writers can write
and singers sing.
Then life can be a miracle
in which you receive nothing.

Phillip J. Carson

Mind

The world passes beneath our feet,
And slips through our fingers timelessly.
A day, merely a drop of rain,
In a great April shower.
The light of day, only a second,
Though moonlight can last eternity.

The earth whirls endlessly,
Like many whirling minds,
And every aching heart.
The fingers of time reach out,
Yet grab hold of nothing.
Life is only so long,
But yet, it is so long.

Stacie MacArthur

Requiem for a Friend

I say the words I used to say,
And tell the tales,
I used to tell—
But the echo of my voice
Cuts against my face—
Like a cold, wet sheet—
Flapping—
In an ice-making wind,

My words have no place to go—
Since—
You are gone.

Vivian Volk

Tears

Life has its ups and downs,
and that fluctuating tendency
can play havoc with emotions
causing at times a tear to fall.

Sometimes a fleeting memory
can be enough to send
the heart and mind into
a sullen and tearful mood.

Injustices from the past
weigh heavily on the soul,
wanting to change the situation
but unable to - produce a tear.

Absence of a special someone,
not necessarily for eternity
may feel unbearable, and
in the loneliness a tear may appear.

There will never be a time
when tears will cease -
they are a part of our existence
waiting to roll down a cheek.

Ruthe M. Dusette

Art

Art is any time
I stop and look

At mist rising
From the river
On a cold sunny morning

Or when someone
Saves it
Until I get there

Karen Vincent

Absent Love

Between the stroke of midnight
And the first faint streaks of dawn
I live again within your arms
And can't believe you're gone

The weary months that lie ahead
Will crush my lonely heart
Unless, in fancy, we can meet
Within a world apart.

Scarcely awake I can recall
Forgotten things I meant to say
To prove to you how much I loved
Before you went away.

Fragrances of tweed and pipe
Into my fancy creep
And with my cheek against your cheek
I drift at last to sleep

Patricia Elmore Dunlap

World Gone Mad

The world it seems is crumbling
and there's nothing we can do,
The midnight sky is distant
and the light is out of view;
A dawning of a new day
- one which may not come,
Brings hopefulness to others
and yet disparity to some;
The world is out of focus
- a madness with no end,
A place with little healing
- a wound that will not mend.

Joe Alvear

Only Try

If there are goals you wish to reach
And they seem so very high
Do not give up, they can be met
But, you will have to try

There will be times when it might seem
Good fortune has passed you by
Do not despair, you can succeed
Though you will have to try

Some have failed to reach their goal
And then they wonder why
Yet I suspect that it could be
Because they did not try

Do not let this be your fate
Nor let your ambitions die
For success, remember, depends upon
Just how hard you care to try

Ruth H. Clark

Reincarnation

We create our place
In time and space
So that we might mortal be

We play our part
With mind and heart
Until death brings us immortality

Again

Robert W. Krupa

Homeward Bound

The old man sits upon his chair-
And though he doesn't have much care,
He sits and looks into the sky.
And wonders when he'll ever die!

He's lived a life with rich reward,
He's run the race, and how he's scored!
The path he trod from day to day.
He never failed to ever stray!

He loved his native country land.
He loved the one's who came around.
He always had a smiling face.
And always offered love with grace!

He won respect from young and old,
But now his home on earth is sold!
He's left the bitter fight of life.
He's "Homeward Bound" where
There's no strife!

Roger A. Hutcheson

New Friends

I've discovered a truly good friend,
And though she's not out of my past —
I feel I've known her forever
And that the bond will always last.

We were drawn together in sorrow.
Best friends we both had lost.
It seemed to make us realize
What loving sometimes can cost.

So now we look to each other,
For a smile, support, a kind word —
But even when there is silence
The unspoken seems to be heard.

We have an understanding,
No words do we need to say —
Somehow we know in our hearts and souls
We can handle what life sends our way.

We know we can rise above it,
As friends we can see it through —
For together we have become much stronger
Even though our friendship is new.

Mary C. Wilks

Where?

From where came the flowers
and trees, all the birds and bees.
The oceans and sand, all the
animals and man?
Did we descend from evolution
Through the decades, or were we
from a higher spirit made.
From a spirit no one has seen,
but each life does gleam. The
beauty that evolution could not
bring, or from an ape come a human being.
From where came creation of life
as we know it today? From God above
is the only way.
For the beauty is so great to see,
and only a higher spirit like God
can create things so great as you and me.

Rhonda L. Hunter

Love Is Blind

People who love are blind
And what is in their mind
Combines together so
they will love forever
Only those who see color
do not love each other
Love is freedom of the kiss
like angels in the mist
Blindness in a person's sorrow
will bring love tomorrow
So when there is love in the mind
love shall always be blind

Liz Rodriguez

Who Will Think Of You

Think of me often,
and when you do,
I will think of you,
and you and you.
Think of me sometimes,
and when you do,
I will think of you,
and you, and you.
Think of me never,
and when you do,
who will think of you,
and you, and you.

Mary Ann Mason

"Tribute to Our Country"

In the springtime when the flowers bloom
And winter is gone with all its gloom
We laugh and play out in the sun
And over hill and dale we run
Oh, who could have a better time
Than we who live upon this clime.
In this land of ours
Where no man cowers
Or begs for mercy to a man with power

Raul N. Martinez

My Lost Son

I wish I could have seen your face,
And you had seen mine, too.
I desperately wanted to say the words,
"I will, forever, love you."

I felt you moving in my womb,
So dearly close to my heart.
I wanted to see you grow and thrive,
But, I was denied that part.

Now I wonder what it's like,
To hear, "I love you, Mother."
Maybe, someday, somehow, someway,
I'll hear it from another.

Virginia C. McCoy

Diary

Another day, another fight
Another story into the book of life...
Another challenge, another fall
Another reason not to give up...

Another night, another moon...
Another sleep, will end up soon
Another star, another wish...
Another dream... you... and me...

Linette Mattei

Knowing

I know I shall never see,
Anything as christs life in me.
I will never be the same,
Since into my life you came,
Who has quickened my spirit,
And raised me up from death.
And is closer than my breath,
Who in every way,
In my life, His wonders you display.
The working of your ways,
In whom I put my trust,
And for others to see,
His light in me.
In Him I am complete,
Whom the enemy can't defeat,
He's the day star risen in me,
Now in Him in maturity,
I know I shall never see,
Anything as Christ's life in me,
Or anything else I'd rather be than part of
His body.

Naomi R. Huston

Love Sick

Words that cannot be spoken
are fought back, yet
they struggle to be heard;
your throat hurts.

Your heart beats violently
inside your chest making
breathing nearly impossible;
your lungs hurt.

Lips, eager to be tasted
strain against your teeth
until they almost bleed;
your mouth hurts.

Arms, breasts, stomach, groin, thighs
ache from the urge to touch
and be touched;
your body hurts.

I thought I was falling in love
with you.
Thank God, it was only
the flu!

Scarlett V. Finney

Heartspeak

Promises made with words that
are spoken
with good intentions that they
never be broken.
But alas, we are human
with feelings we hide,
that come to the surface when
we do not abide
by words that are spoken by our
hearts through our minds,
by a love that controls us,
holds us and binds
the love we hold dearer
than I'll ever tell;
and that's you love, my true love,
in love with I fell.

Robin Tena

Yesterday

A stranger asked me yesterday:
Are you looking for something,
or perhaps somebody?
Your eyes are so blue! May I ask?

Oh yes, I am looking for something,
but I can not find it anymore.
I am looking for yesterday!
I did not say all I wanted to,
much was left undone.

But the moon came up
and died yesterday...

Magdalena L. Janoska

Dawn

A faint light heralds the break of day,
as angels sweep the night away.
A small breeze stirs the leaves
as it tiptoes thru the trees.
A bird chirps and starts to sing,
then the alarm clock starts to ring.
I linger, stretch and yawn,
then I rise to meet the dawn.
It lightens to a rosy glow
and circles the earth like a bright halo.
I bow my head and start to pray,
"Thank you, Lord, for this lovely day.

Wilma Wohler

"Forever Lovers"

Problems in life pass by
As clouds streaking the sky,
Peaks of mountains - Afar
Touch lovers "as we are,"
Passion lies within us
Wild as the forest.

In the rapids midst - alone
Stands our lives stepping stone,
Spirits move swift in streams
Likewise, you too, in my dreams,
Emotions rise up - and fall
With the Hearts....
....Eternal call
of Forever Lovers.

Ryan Lee Shipley

"Happy 10th, Jule!"

Ten years ago this very day
(As rare a day can be)
A gift from God came down our way
For all the world to see.

And what a gift it was, indeed.
(As great a gift can be)
A living gem; a tiny bead.
About the size, a pea.

And over time this bead has grown
Into a precious pearl,
As pure and cultured as one's known:
Our one and only girl.

And "one and only" is the way
The world must view this thing...
For never will you see the day
Such pearls exist, a string.

Richard P. Barnitt

The Streets

They wander the streets
as everyone stares
No home of their own
But nobody cares.

Groping for life
and hope in the dense
Wandering blindly in darkness
for change to commence.

Confusion and wishing
for fate is their route
As we prosper - they die
The fire is put out.

I give you a match
to relight the flame
To comfort and guide them
and cover their shame;

To give them a chance
to give them a hand
To thrive in this country
America - our land.

Kristin Lie

Forgotten

I sit and ponder,
as my thoughts grow fonder.
What we used to be,
you and me...

Immortal devotion,
deep as the ocean.
Murmuring affection,
beyond dissection.

Passionate fate,
love not hate.
Once potent lust,
now dreams covered with dust.

Elated dreams,
overwhelming scenes.
I pray you will find,
you've left me behind.

Spenser Villwock

"Foxx"

(Dedicated to Kathy Smith)

The glance of a foxx
as she walks by;
Twin clear pools of liquid light.
Concealed in her nature
is something sly;
Borne in the dreams
I dream at night.
I thought I would,
I thought I could.
Reveal the dreams I dream,
It's something good,
That's understood.
But...
Are her dreams what mine seem?

William George Vine

Peaceful Resolution

A peaceful resolution
as the stars shine,
and the moon sings
to its sister
the sun.
And in the beginning
there was falling rain,
but in these days of spring
the sweetest song
of love
has begun.
In the days of renaissance,
no courtship
has ever measured
to this endless
peaceful resolution.

Stephenie I. Wasche

By The Light Of A Tainted Moon

The haunting sound of whales' songs
As they seek to flee their doom.
The frantic cries of oil-slicked birds
By the light of a tainted moon.

The pillage of earth's forests
To assuage man's awesome greed.
The pollution of worlds' oceans
In the name of progress's need.

This world in which we make our home
This land that claims our birth .
By greed we are destroying
As we kill this planet—earth!

M. H. Wesson

The Perfect Face

Wide innocent eyes
As yet untouched
by the world's sorrows
Set beneath gracefully
Arched eyebrows on a
Forehead free from
The tension of life
A button nose between
Smooth cheeks tinged with
Just the right amount of peach
Nestled at the bottom,
A small rosebud mouth,
Curved in a smile
The perfect face...
A child's face.

Rachel Lilly

Dark Inside

The pain continues to grow,
but no one will ever know,.
Never sharing how I feel,
It's too scary to reveal.
The shadows are my hiding place,
Not having to show my disgrace.
My smile covers the pain,
But doesn't stop the inside rain.
No one will ever understand,
I am truly in my own land.
It will never end,
I am my only real friend.

Sheila Sarhangi

Ward of the Court

There was a little boy.
At first I didn't know his name.
I didn't know his people
Or from where he really came;
But he was sick and dying
In a hospital bed
and all alone—-
Or so the doctor said.
It was my job to tell him
That he would soon be gone.
You cannot tell an eight year old
That on the telephone.
I stayed with him
Through the long, dying night.
I don't remember all I said
As I held him in my arms;
But he was conscious
And he smiled at me.
After a while he was dead.

Wilda V. Gretzinger

A Summer Sunset

As I stand watching for the moon,
At the end of the long afternoon,
I see it faraway,
It is so beautiful,
I wish it would stay.
With its golden colors so very bright,
I know that soon to come, is the night.
It is the sunset that I have waited for,
During this summer and forever more.

Kimberly Sullivan

Dear Lord

Be in every move I make
Be in every step I take
Be in every word I write
And help me do the thing that's right
Amen

Sarah Strack

The Tree

Oh, what a desolate world this
beautiful country would be.
If God had made all the land
and forgot the majestic tree.

All the lakes with its rippling
white caps to adore.
Would be nothing of such beauty
If there was no tree ashore.

And the bleakness of all the land
without a tree He'd made.
With all the children in the sunshine
just sitting there — no shade.

I can remember the mighty laughter
when we kids climbed a tree.
And, I can remember the tiny hurt
when we skinned the naked knee.

I've watched the leafy branches
sway back and forth and nod.
Knowing that the cool and gentle breezes
Just could be the breath of God.

Lloyd W. Mallow

Through the Years

Your eyes are the most
beautiful I have ever seen
You are the only vision
I see in my dreams
You lift my soul
When I am down
When I am weary
You always seem to be around
The same to you
I wish to give
As I look to you
For my reason to live
So if I can ease your worries
Or wipe away the tears
It would be my pleasure
To be with you through the years

J. J. Campbell

Fields Of Doom

He made them all for us to love
because He loves them so
but we all seem so self-important,
can't be bothered so.
Still, they live on to grow and bloom
all loved by one another
and we all hate to live in fear
but cannot stand each other.

And yet some day we'll be together
hating where we're at
and they'll still be here many years
doing what we could not.
Then in the end He'll gather them
to keep their fragrant beauty
and we, still in our fields of doom
no fragrance, much less beauty.

Joseph A. Tobia

"Just a Thought of You"

Now we wait in quiet,
because we wait together.
I am sure that I'll speak to
you; and you will hear.
Accept my confidence,
for it is yours. Our minds
are joined, we wait with one
intent; "to hear our love
answer to the call"; to let
our thoughts be still and
find its peace. To hear our
love speak to us of what we are;
and to reveal what it means
to us when we are finally
together again.

Timothy C. Davis

Untitled

Yellow was the moon
blue was my heart
cold was the night
who's darkness will forever
remain as a veil against
the sun for on this night
I fell as I have never fallen before
so new yet so old
and as we make our vowels
we break our vowels and the
yellow moon rise's again

G. J. Steatean, Jr.

Miles to Go Before I Sleep

I was different,
Before you left me.
Now, can I go on?
Yes, because I have to.

I was put on this earth,
For what reason I don't know yet.
I'm still very young,
The road of life is still very long.

Right now I'm running down the path,
How many times have I fallen?
I don't know,
But I'm sure I'll fall some more.

I just have to look ahead,
Not at when and where I'm going to fall,
But at how every time I fall,
I get right back up and feel stronger.

I run down the path the older I get,
Faster and faster I go each day.
But I will keep going because,
I still have miles to go before I sleep.

Nicole Carrier

Before Me

Notice
Believe in
Understand
Take hold of
Yourself before me.

Express
Release
Relate to
Learn to love
Yourself before me.

Be creative
Take time to explore
Be a part of each day
In your own life before mine.

Lisa L. Griffith

"Wish You Were Here"

Tiny island,
Below the equator,
Far from the buzzing of all elevators,
Small beach,
Civilization out of reach,
Nothing but the sand, the water,
Maybe even a few otter,
A letter in your hand as you
walk through the sand,
You set a stamp down,
Wishing you were back in town,
"Wish you were here"
Walking back to your bungalow,
You wish you had somewhere
else to go,
You walk back to the beach,
Not a fragment of speech has
been spoken from you today,
You decide to say something anyway,
"Wish you were here"

Sharon Shy

Colors

Apples are red
Berries are blue
Tress are green
Cats are black
Dogs are brown
Foxes are orange
Flowers are pink
And you I ask
What color are you?

Kira Zamora

Eternal Love

Eternal love is the time lapse
between a death and a life.
Nothing can feel as good
as the eternal love
of the ones deceased
and the recently born.
Though you may feel sadness
for the loss of a loved one,
soon something will come
and help heal the pain.
This will be the love
of someone new.
But either way, new or old,
eternal love remains with both.

Jaclyn DeZell

Cherry Wine

The darkness is merely a short sorrow
Between the aging, setting sun,
And the new dawn of tomorrow.
Please don't cry my son.

The hand of God shall make thy bed.
You shall awake soon my child
In the realm, I said,
Of the wonderful and wild.

But, while here, do not weep,
Thy cup runneth over.
I say to you, the sheep,
Drink to the very fullness of life.

Only once shalt thou sup.
Do not spew the wine
Of life from thy mouth.
All people from the cup
Of life do dine.
But only a few do discover
The wonderful cherry flavor
Of the grape wine of life.

Randy Overbeck

Untitled

In a darkened room
Beyond God's fate
Lies the wounded
And the dead.

The love that they
Lost would forever
Be in their hearts
And souls but the
Ones that they loved
Were killed forever
In their minds.

Torie Middleton

A Dying Man

A dying man
Breathing his last,
washing away,
he cries for help,
Searching...
For one that cares
Searching...
For one who will carry.
His dying body,
his dying soul.
He turns to a sage,
a wise man,
a scholar.
He finds no peace,
in the wisdom,
of the world.
He turns to a book,
to the Son of God.
His body dies;
his soul lives on.

Wendy Leavitt

The Sounds Of Spring

The sounds of spring
bring us the bees, and
the bees bring us honey.

The sounds of spring
bring us flowers and
the flowers give us
wonderful smells.

The sounds of spring
bring us beautiful rainbows,
which lights up the
sky with lots of colors.

The sounds of spring
bring us friends,
which is better
when we are together!

Jennifer McSwiggan

Remember This

Those special things that life
brings the wonders and Joys
of dreams to come.
Their is always a chance
you're young. You have plenty
of time to for see your
future that comes.
Hold on to what you have
and give thanks to God.
Life isn't easy it has its
ups and downs. But no one
drowns if they can swim
I know you can float
and those things that you
have wanted will be yours
have faith I do.

Madeline Nerys

A Lover's Pray

Right now I feel like a pauper,
Asking fun the must precious things on
Earth; your heart.
Some paupers become rich with wealth
Some with the love of another,
Let me have the love of another.

Sidney Hanna

My Mending Heart

I'm thrown in a box,
broken and alone in the dark
like a child's discarded toy.

There's no way out.

But you lift my box,
shake it,
and hear me rattling around.

You lift off the cover,
and I look up at you from the bottom,
blinking into the brightness.

You, smiling, reach down
and gently pick up my pieces,
rescuing me from my prison,
and you put me back together.

Tracey A. Cotignola

Only A Rose

It's only a rose
but I watched it grow
and as the tears rolled down my cheek
I thought of you
it's only a rose
but I watched it bloom
and as the tears rolled down my cheek
I heard you say I love you
it's only a rose
but I watched it die
I never got to say goodbye
and if I could
I wouldn't want to
because you know how much I love you
it's only a rose
but every night I cried myself to sleep
as the pillows caught the tears I weep
I love you so much
even though....
it's only a rose

Jennieve Brummel

Bereft

My heart wasn't glass
But it broke
When they told me
You had gone.

After crying
I endeavored
To pick up the pieces
And go on.

And every year
I remember that lost feeling -
Something sad reopens
After so long.

I can see you
In my mind again -
Not your old, vibrant self
But tired and wan.

And I know where you are now
There's no sickness nor heartache,
In that realm yon.
Plead for me; for I must see you again.

Sharon Rice

"Pain"

Some people say it will get better,
But my question is when,
when will things get better;
It's gone on for so long,
when will the pain and suffering end;
When will the jokes and rude
comments end;
Don't they realize how badly it hurts
when they say those things,
Or do they even care;
Why can't they just leave me alone,
so the pain can go away?!

Michalyne Lackey

Just a Thought!

I do not think of my destined place,
But of my destiny.
I do not wonder why I'm here,
But why I came to be.

This moment is the present,
Though now it is the past.
Each moment should be cherished,
For a moment does not last.

I live my life today,
As if tomorrow will not come.
I want to live life blissfully,
So sadness shall I shun.

Love is my defender,
For it rarely deals in Pain.
To passion I surrender,
And serenity I gain.

The sun rises just to set,
So it may rise again.
And like the sun it warms the soul,
Is the closeness of a friend.

Suzanne G. Kelch-Gear

Untitled

I'm pulling myself up
But slowly falling down.
I've been there before
And I left with a frown.
I can't face it again,
It hurt me so much.
I cry when I remember
I miss his soothing touch.
Now I fear I love again.
And I just can't turn away
For the sincerity in his voice,
Makes me want to stay.
Another man has entered my life,
He's trying to win my heart.
I don't want to hurt again.
This is tearing me apart.
I can't face this alone.
I need guidance from above.
I have to face the truth.
I'm falling in love.

Tanya Marie Almeida

The Flame

Smiles within the embers,
of our burning fire of love.
Once fierce, flaming reality,
it is now but ashes.

Tom Tabor

"Home"

Life goes on and time follows...
but the darkness never shadows.
The light of a child...
is very precious in many ways.
Hearts mend at the sight of a tear....
but the cries are not of sorrow.

The smell of nature...
brings back lost time memories,
which only time could hold.

The bridges stay strong....
as you make a path to follow,
but the water never fades.
But if the bridge would ever break.
there will always be my
"Home"

Kristy L. Duplantis

The Soldier

A war of wars has begun
But...there is only the soldier
A cannon fires
The soldier is still standing
A tank is rolling across the sand
It rolled across the soldiers shadow
The enemy conjures a ground attack
The soldier lies behind a bush
The enemy is closing in
Firing all the while
The enemy runs past the soldier
How is it the soldier is not seen?
The entire army has run into oneness

Raign Kyanthony

The Love Letter

I never wrote a love letter,
but this letter is for you.
And it is written with love in mind;
I hope you feel it too...

Dear Friend,

You've come to mean so much to me,
so very much indeed;
familiar friends we can remain,
or move to intimacy.

But I must warn you,
you must take heed,
that I abstain from sex;
Unless I'm married to you, Dear friend,
the thought we can't caress.

And so, my friend,
know that I love you;
but I, also, love me too.
And since I believe
that my maker I'll meet,
then I must wait until the I Do's

Yetta N. Armstrong

Untitled

My heart is like a rose,
tender and full of love.
But you can not come too close,
because I will close up on you.
For my feelings run deep
and there's no time to weep,
for someone who doesn't care.

Rebecca L. Blevins

The Real Us

I am the girl whom everyone knows
but what nobody knows
is that I'm not as brave as I seem
Inside, I'm scared and confused
by everything that awaits me
We are not all what we seem
So sure and confident
but there are few of us
that will admit
that it is all
just a cover
And reveal our true selves
No fakes, no masks
Take the time to notice
the real us.

Jessica Ames

Life

Life is so short
  but yet so dear.
A new dawning day
  comes with every new year.

Time flies on
  when you're having fun.
Until you are left
  with everything done.

So treasure the
  memories of each day.
For they will slowly
  fade away.

Stacey Rhoads

The Dragon in the Clouds

I can see you,
but you're blind.
I can hear you,
but you're deaf.
I can feel you,
but you're dead.
I can pretend,
but you're an adult.

Do you believe?
In what?
Love.
What kind of love?
The simple kind.
I don't understand.
Do you have a heart?
Of course I do.
Then you understand.

Michelle Birkenstock

Untitled

Possessed by your passion
Captivated by your beauty
Absorbed with desire, exalted
the rapture of love is ours
hypnotized by your gaze
lost in primitive sexual want
care for my heart forever
it is all I have to offer
skin so soft, love in a mist
Soon to be coupled, impassioned
fervor of venery

Vince Dudley

Untitled

Through glades of green
By waters serene,
His hand, it leadeth thee,

Neath skies of blue,
With faith that is true,
His hand, it leadeth thee,

Though clouds of gray,
May darken your day,
His hand, it leadeth thee,

With his love so sublime.
In the newness of time.
His hand, it leadeth thee,

When life is no more,
And we reach that far shore,
His hand, it leadeth thee,

William J. Seman

ALCATRAZ

Driven
By years of genocide
The American Indian
Emerges from his own
  shadow
And braving the currents
Of a fog-filled night
Captures the pelican
  island
For all that it symbolizes
In its isolation
In its suppression
In its freedom

Philip Hackett

Love

A place that you
can always come...
The endearing way you
gaze at someone...
A warmth you feel
deep in your heart...
The awesome surprise of
cupids romantic dart...
A memorable party of
constant celebration...
The quiet, exciting corner of
your imagination...
A feeling of promise
and being complete...
The absence of loneliness
and passed defeat...
A passionate song sent
from up above...
The undoubted true
meaning of love....

Mary Kakuk

Time

Is here to stay.
Can never go away.
Is always there.
Is fast or slow.
Is on the go.
Is a gift from God.
Time is everywhere.
Time is now.

Jomel Bobbitt-Thomas

Nightmare

Completely dark and soundless
Can't breathe he'll hear
Sit down in a corner with
My loyal companion, fear

He's always there watching
He knows right where I sit
Looking deep into my soul
As if the room were lit

No, he's coming closer
Touching me so cold
A light comes on, it's over
My mom is there to hold

Surely Vanderstaay

Great Lady

Aristocratic,
charismatic,
loved by all for her
dignity and grace.

Icon of an era,
the brightest of stars,
first lady of ours
in Camelot.

Courageous, the best
of us - America -
in spite of what
it took from her.

Horses and books,
a walk in the park,
envied by some
her wealth and looks.

Mother, grandmother,
family first, last
to be seen by lovely
Jacqueline.

Jamie DiMatteo

Children

Children of love
children of hate.
Will we know the difference
before its to late.

(W)here are the children
we gave birth to out of fear.
Arms reach(ing) out
to hurt or caress.
Are these the children
we nurtured at our breast
that turn away
to plot and destroy?

Mothers and fathers
across the land,
weep for the child
you hold in your hand.

Rowena D. Morris

Untitled

Our dear old flag
Red, white and blue
Flies toward the sky
And it flies for me and you.

Zelda Lawrence

Relating

Conversations, intonations
clearly come to mind.
Degradations, true confessions
never quite defined.

Infatuations, situations
set our minds to whirl.
Allegations, instigations
reflexed, as to hurl.

Confabulations, confirmations
enter into play.
Conflagration, ruination
sweeps them right away.

Alienation, machination
rips the seam of life.
Maculation, saturation
stains with drops of strife.

Observations, interrelations
given to release.
Intersections, pacifications
tour guides into peace.

Peter N. Crepeau

Children

Father and Mother
Closeness and love
Bonding together
Sent from above.
Growing each day
The time passes fast
Tugging each second
How long can you last.
They jabber and crawl
Everything is a mess
One's starting to bawl!
I'll have to confess
That I'm losing my nerve
I'm changing my mind
And rounding the curve
I realize I'm blind...
In the love of my children
I'll stay calm and cool
And try to remember
They'll soon be in school.

Molly K. LeCroy

Dark Days

Dark days,
  clouded vision.
Things pressing in,
  nothing clear and bright.
Survival ruling living,
  hazy/powerful pressures.
Light spirit weighted,
  free will lost under cares.
Someday will it ease?
  or stay lost and denied?
Its absence noted, mourned,
  like a passing rosy dawn.
Will lightness/freedom return?
  let me soar, transcend?
Has the world really darkened?
  or has my vision clouded?
Did the dark forces win?
  or did I just give in?

Mike Pearce

Outside Looking In

The reality of life
Comes hard to some
Early or late in life
It still will come.
The tongues- They crucify
The young and the old
The weak will not make it
BUT- Watch out for the bold.
For years the evil tries
Everything they can
The weak will join sides
To form a stronger band.
This band-This group-This society
Get's larger day by day
The bold will withstand
Dear Lord -Let us Pray!
The gates will open
The BOLD will walk in
The WEAK stand
OUTSIDE LOOKING IN!

Lisa Goodin Palmer

Itself

Cold
Constant
Confusing
Controlling
Asphyxiating
Debilitating
Paralysing
Nauseating
Guttural
Desperate
Shivering
Deathly
Darkly
Numbing
New baby soon and no job

Ward B. Welch

Poems On Paper

Smooth tubular plastic
Containing blue blood stain,
The smells of inky emotion,
Tainting the bleached pulp
With the essence of a poet.

Suzette Shelanskey

The Graduate

The thousands that we spent so he
  could soak up all that knowledge,

That was absolutely obsolete before
  he left the college,

We're very proud of him, he pays us
  rent you see.

He gets his money flipping burgers
  down at "Micky's D's."

Mike Stephenson

Psalm One

That man is blessed who never takes
Counsel from wicked men,
Who goes not down the sinner's road,
Nor in the scoffer's den;

Instead he loves the law of God
And makes it his delight,
And on this law he meditates
Both by day and night.

So like a tree that flourishes
When planted by a stream,
Which bears its fruit when it is due,
Whose leaves retain their gleam,

He prospers well in all he does.
The wicked are not so:
They are like chaff the wind controls
And carries to and fro.

When judgement comes they shall not stand
Assembled with the just.
God knows the life the righteous lead,
The wicked end in dust.

Sewell T. Jemmott

AIDS

Slowly torture my insides.
Crawl never out.
Kill me slowly,
more than needed.
It hurts to think
more than to feel.
The true pain is in my head
beating in my heart,
only to explode and wither
into the world of pain,
never able to be "well"
or to be "normal"
Because of a careless
mistake!

Nimai Rivet

I Do Believe

I do believe that God above
Created you for me to love.
He picked you out of all the rest
because he knew I loved you best.
If I die and you're not there,
I'll wait for you at the golden stairs.
If you're not there by Sabbath
day, I'll know you went the other way.
To prove to you my love is true,
I'll go to hell to be with you.

Nikki Knutson

For Grandpa

My time is close, the choice is clear
Do I linger and tarry here?
Or do I let my spirit fly
to look for you in the Heavenly sky?
My body is old and frail and tired
And yet my mind is still yet fired
by all that I have left undone
and all the life that's left to come
My time is over, the choice is clear
It is His choice for me to leave here
Do not cry when I have gone;
It is my time to travel on.

Sandra Weeks

The Barn

As the crimson Fingers of the sun
creep slowly over the horizon
a rooster calls out
his ever vigilant song

Crows gather
among the thorn bushes
and tall grass
where once chickens fed

A broken fence
staggers off into the distance
like a drunken man
trying to get home

The charred and sagging frame
stands as an old man
remembering
a long forgotten youth

Paul Granick

Cry of the Locust

Cry of the locust,
Crooning out at dawn;
Swarms near the beehive,
Buzzing in a lawn.

Thunder in the distance,
the rain will sometime pour
and in the dark green jungle
you'll hear a lion roar.

But in the city streets
the foghorn merely mourns
at the church the organ plays,
entertains and adorns.

As Grandma churns the butter,
the swishing of the curds
turns into the sound of music
accompanied by the birds.

Olivia Hulsey

"Loneliness"

Shadows cast upon a wall,
Crystal clear turned black,
Catch her not should she fall,
Nor help to bring her back.

Stealing hope so deep within,
None could cast it out,
Emptiness could only win,
And leave her so in doubt.

Mandy Oliver

Passages Of Live

Sing the meadow
Dance in the vast wilderness
Run in the deep woods
Walk through the misty night air
Feel the breeze while it's here.

Glide through the harsh wind
It is very worthwhile
Sail on the ocean
Walk on the beautiful isle
Ride through the tunnel of death.

Kevin M. Barnes

The Madness Of Love

What madness is this,
Dear heart of mine,
That you should be so brave?
You offered your self
You gave from your soul
Like the ocean offers the wave.

What madness is this,
Oh vulnerable one,
That you should change your ways?
You let enter in
A bit of sweet love
Like the sun enters its rays.

What madness is this,
Sweet holder of Love,
That you should be strong?
He took you with desire
Like the bee takes the flower
Surely loving him cannot be wrong!

Mary Lou Vasquez

Who Is Responsible

Who is responsible for
death before death.
Who is responsible for
the death of a wild flower.
Who is responsible for
lustful desires.
Who is responsible for
naked, empty days.
Who is responsible for
naked, empty nights.
Who is responsible for
flames to burn a man.
Who is responsible for
aimless drifting.
Who is responsible for
an empty box left behind.

Sati Mohan Das

Beyond Love

I look at your eyes and see
Deep within-like we can see
The ocean from here until than...

Your dreams my little one are
As much mine-we cherish each
One with more to come...

Forever is just a word but your
Touch holds me near-with my
Heart only for you my dear...

Your beauty is beyond words
I know, however I treasure
Our moments to explore the untold...

Our love is not understood by
Some despite all we have said
And done-this is their loss
And we shall forever hold on
And be strong...

Rebecca Altringer

Vietnam American's Unsung Heroes

Sent so far away from home,
Defending a land yet unknown.
For freedom's cause;
No bells would ring,
No praise for our heroes
Would we sing.
Pain, horror and bleak despair,
Blood curdling yells filled the air;
Sacrifices were willingly made
Oh! So dearly have they paid.
Yet - no bells began to ring,
No praise for our heroes
Did we sing;
Our shame and sorrow
Should always be
Not thanking them properly.
We have learned its not too late,
And no longer should we wait,
For our Nation's bells to ring,
For our heroes praise to sing.

Madeline L. Denson

Magic

Mankind's Magic
describes a circle,
it arcs the future
and joins us, in webs of light.
It never ceases.
It increases us.

Nature's Magic
is a snowflake,
a leaf shouting color,
blazing sun...moonlight breezes.
It never ceases.
It releases us.

Linda Jones

Shattered

Agony.
Despair.
The prize was mine,
but I've
Fallen.
Wrenched from me,
my heart knows
no joy.
Twisted and
Mutilated beyond
recognition.
I am
alone.
I speak to
no one.
Fractured
hope,
Shattered
trust.

Kelly Cluney

When You Gotta Grow!

Long ago I wore a dress
The size denoted with an "S"
In a while, not on a whim
I thought it best to buy an "M"
Lately, how I hate to tell
I have really gone to "L"

Lois Blackwood

Sweet Dreams

Little one when you sleep
Do you dream?
Of death?
Of goblins?
Come into my World of Dream,
Welcome!
Picture a graveyard
Alone at night.
You are full of fright.
No one is in sight.
No light.
Only hate.
It's too late.
face the music.
Not fun,
Is it little one?
Bite your tongue.
It's okay to cry — but if you lie,
You're gonna die.
Sweet dreams, little one!

Tegan E. Pabst

When You're In Love

When you're in love but that person
doesn't know. All you can do is hope
the storm doesn't blow.

When your heart is torn and your
so confused. All you can do is hide
your blues.

When there's such a deep
attraction. All you can do is keep
from showing your actions.

When you want so much with this
person. How do you let him know
without knowing his version.

When he's always on your mind.
How would it be, if it were him and me.

How does a person deal with
feelings like this. Or is it all
just a wish. Its so hard not to
say. I wish there was same
kind of way.
When your in love....

Kathleen Thompson

Untitled

Hey, you with the baggy pants on,
Don't shoot your brothers.
Don't make your parents moan.
Give the something good to think on.

Let the baggy pants go.
Turn your cap around.
And
Turn your life around.
You don't want to be no clown.
You are manhood bound
Don't let drugs turn you around.
Put those life-destroying drugs down.

God gave you the gift of manhood,
Use your gift for all that's good.
You'll be proud my Son;
When the good race you have run.

Ruth Luckett

Tear Drops

Past my nose
down my cheek
it drips
further and further
each time
I weep.

Regardless if its
big or small
the pain
just gets worse
every time they fall.

With every little drip
that falls down my face
it has another memory of him
that I just can not replace.

All the little drops
that came out of my eyes
makes me realize
the feelings I have
for that special guy.

Letha Elliott

To a Very Special Mother!

My love for you grows in special ways;
Each day is a blessed Mother's Day!
You have taught and protected me well,
About God's love and the devil's Hell.
I will not tarnish your holy crown;
I promise never to let you down!
God's heavenly grace and love acquired,
You live as a saint. That I admire!
Each day grows for you in blessed ways;
My heart sings "Have a super Mon's Day!"

Robert T. Anderson

Song of Serenity

Harps within your mind
Elation within your soul
Love within your heart
Peace to keep you warm

Surrender to your weakness
Open up to what abounds
Serenity within you, maybe yet,
but will be found,

Angels of God are always listening
Speak freely from your soul
Keep faith, always believe and
serenity will unfold.

Lina Rueda

Soaring

Soaring, soaring into space,
Endless flight,
Endless pace,
where will go,
what will we see,
Eons go by,
Light years flash,
Time stands still
As we soar,
Always, always
reaching for more.

Marilyn R. Schwab

"Hearts Cry"

Do we have to say good-bye,
even if our love was a lie.
or should we let it be
only because hearts cry,
You can say what you will
And do what you do
After all, I may miss you,
How, I'll miss you,
Though I ask myself, was it me.
Who really set you free
under the soft dripping rain
to wash away the pain.
of all the hurt and sorrow
for a wonderful tomorrow
was it meant to be this way
of these good-byes.
So many hearts cry... So many.....

D. D. Lehman

Something

Something I did not hear,
even with you near.
Something I did not feel,
even when it was real.
Something I should have known,
but didn't and was left unknown.
Something I did not see,
even when I hoped and prayed.
Something I did not see,
even when it when it was to be.
Something.....

Laura Meckle

The Soul; The Tree

The soul is like a tree
ever growing until maturity
starting from a seed
watered and nurtured it will sprout
new leaves begin, new branches form
if left alone
its width will grow round
if left alone
its leaves will become countless
if left alone
it will reach high in the sky
able to withstand all weather
it can be knocked over
it can be wilted
it can be frozen
it can be burned up
it can be cut down

It can last a lifetime

Rhonda Venema

Doctor

Here's to you Doctor,
For all your hard night's,
For all your hard days,
Working is quite inspirational,
But having fun is exhilarating,
We all need to get out,
And smell the fresh open air,
Feel our toes in the warm sand,
The breeze blowing in our hair,
Let's take a moment,
And do this together.

Myrel Schlaffer

A Child's World

It is a place where
everyone once lived,
a place of happy times,
and sometimes sad.

This place knows
no race or color
nor doesn't know the
meaning of violence.

'Cause you see this place
we all have known it is
a child's world

In this place the children
they laugh and play.
And they sometimes
think of this place passing by.

Lisa Gonzalez

Poetry Is

Poetry is song
Expressed in tone and rhyme
A message short or long
Carried in the media of time

Poetry is music
Of hovering souls above
Who search for those minds alike
In thoughts of love.

Poetry is feeling
Expressing joy, despair.
In living with all humans,
Who find there's love and care

Poetry is joy
When all of life is spent
In love and peace of mind
Then souls are content.

Poetry is thoughts
Of love, joy, strife and tears
Within the souls
Of those immortals whose ears will hear.

Marie Saint

The Answer

As I glanced across the room, my
eyes fixed upon her face —

Was she bewildered?
Confused!
Lost in thoughts —

Her face remained motionless;
No smile, no frown
Blank

Feverishly searching the room
my eyes caught my own reflection
in the mirror

I wondered — no more

Karen Kaptur Jasnoch

Spend Times Change

Bone and flesh common sense
Remnants wondrous purchase,
Revolving times change -
Paid efflorescence.

William Ellison

Dwelling On

Abruptly we turn,
Eyes lock and isolate;
Freezing an impression
Lifting out the moment
Sealing it inside our minds.

We court attention;
Over time and proximity,
Over inhibitions
Over limitations
We seek the other.

Subtle surprises
Of personalities revealed;
Enlargement of perspectives,
A filling out of personas;
We shade in each other.

Visions and fantasies promote growth,
Of a desire for presence
As nights bring images
And thoughts of a name
As we dwell on each other.

Lawrence Michael Dickson

Snow Flakes

Downy flakes
Fall outside my window
Each white crystal
Reminds me of
My childhood
Reminds me of
How much I miss
Snowmen, and
Snowball fights
And the innocence
Of that time.
They used to be
Toys from above
Now they are
Slick roads and
Car accidents
And I wonder
Why did it all
Have to change?

Pamela Tarnecki

Sowing Season

Without knowing, I bleed you
Feed you vengeful gazes
Soak in your shadowy pond of fears
Bite your outstretched hands
Find vengeance, then burrow in sand
Shamed, docile as a morbid cow
Waiting for the next refrain
To start the cycle, once again
An endless pattern like crazy-quilted
bed covers
Weeding our garden of confusion
I mix sand and water
and watch the soil
sink to the
bottom
of the
cesspool.

Mary L. Perchik

"Dirty Dishes"

Centuries away.
Feeling alone tonight.
Knowing that yesterday
was all the same.
How many more days until tomorrow?
It's cold outside.
This rage engulfs like a tsunami.
Drowning those who refuse to retreat
I feel the rain pelting down on me.
I feel the pain inside.
Suffocating, reasons why, unclear.
Way beyond the land of morality.
Receding footsteps.
You don't understand me.
In your quest to find yourself.
You don't know me.
Though you say you do.
Oh well.
That's too bad, no one's keeping you.

Vera Finney

Untitled

For a moment I have returned to a
Feeling I thought lost
Inner peace again has touched me
Even though I have not sought
In feels so good the calmness
Feelings flowing like wine
Time is still moving though I've
lost all sense of time
I'm sitting in a building, yet
I'm not staying there
I seem to be traveling
And to be every where
All seems right with life
Like nothing is wrong
This moment comes so rarely
And then it is gone
Yet while it is here
I'm in touch with it all
And I sit and I listen
As my name is being called

Paul Ellison

Climbing Lover's Hill

Climbing Lover's Hill
Fighting for every breath
Searching for a love so real
It will last 'til death

I fight my way to the summit
To find nothing there
I turn around and plummet
Through the cloudy air

As I fall through empty space
I glance up and see
A beauty found on no other face
I knew she was meant for me

I visioned myself flying
Of flying to my beauty
But I continued to fall; crying
Falling very lonely

I feel screaming not a sound
Fell fast as one can
Then I hit the ground
And died a lonely man

Ross Kindler

December 24th

Quickly now-dashing through shadows
Find just the right house
Just the right family
Red Suit-White beard
Sack thrown over his shoulder
to conceal his tools of trade
Here! Now! This door, this house!
Inside easily
Nobody noticed
Opening the bag-
Family sleeping-
Remove axe, remove knife
Sinister smile, small laugh of evil-
"Yes Virginia, there is a Santa Claus."

Tina Marie Sneed

Thinking Of You

As a thought of you
Flash across my mind
All the memories of you
Came rushing back.
I remembered when we first met;
I remembered the tender words
You spoke;
And the sweet smile you had.
I can't seem to forget you;
Your smile, your face, your unique self.
And today, I realized
How much I miss you.
Without you,
The days seem to go on forever.
But then I think of you
And all that we've shared,
And somehow I feel
Just a little close to you.

Youa Alyssa Lee

Untitled

When it hits people will cry
for all the lives that had to die,
children weep at the show and
wonder why the people have to go

Which way to go, which way to turn
people in this world will never know,
they cannot call one place home cause
forever they may roam.

Richelle Bukovitz

My Prayer

For peace of mind,
for blessings kind,
Dear Lord, I give you thanks.
for solitude,
for attitude,
And patience loving kind.
Help me to learn
to have concern
and pause to say
I care.
My busy pace
Leaves not much time
to linger, to chat or to laugh.
So slow me, calm me
and most of all make me aware
that I was placed here
to help others to share.
Teach me, oh Lord, to care.

Shirley F. Cole

One True

To you and only you.
For eyes of innocence
with your happiness,
to what. Why else.
They say him,
With pleasureful
thinking on a mind.
To bounds unbroken
yet nevermore,
Flesh and blood is
all apart.
Deceivement is all
around.
Trust is unknown,
For true love is never
found.

Sarah Forrest

Glory

Somewhere I dream of glory.
For fighting this great war.
For living and for dying,
So my country's name could soar.
For freedom of the people.
For freedom, Black or White.
But still the people will not stop.
They always seem to fight.

Renata Dantzler

"Broken Glasses"

A dream coming along
For hope,
Wishes,
Desires.
All smashed to bits
Feet trampling all over it
Like panic stricken people.
Broken glasses,
Comparing as broken
Dreams.
Bits and pieces everywhere.
Just replace with
Another new window.
But you just can't replace
Dreams...

Trisha Jane Lessard

I Know Not What I Do

Forgive me Lord
For I know not what I do.
My life seems so empty and blue.
I never had the chance to choose
between the two.
All my life I've wanted this.
Now I don't know what to do.
Help me please,
I'm on my knees.
I've made all the wrong choices
in life,
Or so it seems,
Now it's time to see
What the future holds for me.
I need your help,
So save me please.
For I know not what I do.

Lee Keim

Today I'm Free

I follow the path God has laid me.
For three years I've been cancer-free.
It seemed like a big emotional wall,
But surgery and treatment became my all.

I endured the radiation day after day
Leaving me too tired to think of play.
I let God and the doctors lead the way
To the renewed health I enjoy today.

Oftentimes cancer can lead to sorrow.
A positive attitude eases each tomorrow.
Eat all the foods that you love so much,
Rely on your doctor's HEALING TOUCH.

These past three years seem so brief
Because I never dwelt on cancer's grief.
Today I'm a healthy living new me.
Because God chose me to be cancer-free!!!

Winnie E. Rogers

Forget Him

Forget his name, forget his face.
Forget his kiss and warm embrace.
Forget his love you once knew.
Remember now there is someone new.

Forget the love that you once shared.
Forget the fact that you once cared.
Forget the times you spent together,
Remember now his gone forever.

Forget the times he use to phone.
Forget the nights you were alone.
Forget he was you whole wide world
Remember now you're not his girl.

Forget the times he held your hand,
Forget the sweet times if you can.
Forget the times you played the fool.
Remember to keep this as a rule.

Tammy Capes

Aubade

Serene is the image of the open sea
free soaring flight
of wordspray and water
calm sighs
contained in her smile

She dreams
unceasingly
in the distance
of the sea waves
softly caressing
the beach
She dreams

In the unending vastness
the real is etched
images never possessed
like the white laughter
of the children of the mother sea

Marie-Ange Somdah

Antiphon

In the bushes.
Sharp beak noises.
Marbles striking together
In a boy's pocket.

Richard Miller

Flowers

Exquisite petals of color
Fragrances of delight
Blooming fields of flowers
Surrounded by buzzing bees
Roses, daisies, and petunia's
Ravishing array of flowers

Rebecca Rogers

"The River"

In the fastness of the Rockies,
From a quiet little lake,
Starts a tumbling little brooklet,
And a wayward course it takes.

Down the mountain steep and rugged,
O'er rocks and boulders there;
Swiftly rushing; angry, snarling,
Like a tiger in its lair.

Flowing now through rocky gorges,
Perpendicular and tall;
Where the river, black and silent,
Mirrors back the stately wall.

Wide and deep and ever swelling,
By the giving little streams;
Flowing onward to the ocean
To the Mecca of its dreams.

Martha Dodson

Unfair Fate

You can go through life,
From one love to the next.
But you'll never know who's
the worst or the best.
There's one chance in a trillion,
You'll find your true love.
So many places to look;
Below and above.
Very few people find their
true mate.
But were all in the hands of
something called fate.

Jennifer Malak

The Circle

Memories long forgotten
frozen still in time
come flooding back to taunt me
and fill the voids within my mind.

Promises made so long ago
vows left incomplete.
One hundred lifetimes aren't enough
For all our love to keep.

Each time our life's song ended
our souls must move apart
but as the dark descended
we each await the start

of life's new beginning
to learn our lessons new
and when the class is over
I begin my search for you.

Our souls were fused together
in creation's fiery heat
and back together we always come
the circle is complete.

Mike Brown

Evening Shadows

In the setting of the sun,
gather evening shadows.
Over children having fun,
above lakes and meadows.

Over boats in the bay,
men relaxing happily.
Stopping sunlight's final rays,
they are playing, grappling.

Gently blown by the breeze,
they are now settling.
In the Oaks' waving leaves,
over neighbors' prattling.

Some are caught upon the walls,
Others in the trees,
As the girl in bright lit hall,
from her lover flees.

So let the wind caress your face,
look upon the sea.
It is time we learned to base,
Our lives on harmony.

Oleg Stolyar

Untitled

Sitting by the fire,
gazing into space;
In each flickering shadow
I see your smiling face;
I dream of moments of ecstasy
and all your enchanting charms,
But I'm alone by the fire...
without your loving arms.

Velma F. Storm

Your Heavy Eyes

Your heavy eyes,
Gentle inside,
Have the gift to listen -
To our fears or tears.
And our eyes seem to glisten
With reverence.

I know I can tell you
My point of view.
You do not criticize,
Or close your eyes.
You listen to even our joys -
For that Dad - I thank you,
And I'm glad you say
I have your eyes.

Natalie K. Stewart

Gone

You pack your bags
Get on a train. Don't know
Were your going but your
Tired of the pain. One thing
On you mind was getting
Away as far as you can
This ain't no game. Your
Never going back to the
Hurt and the pain. Once
Your gone your gone for
Good. Don't bother looking
For me. I'm gone

Lerri Vega

Give Me A Horse I Can Ride

I'm telling everyone I know,
Give me a horse I can ride,
For when I'm very old and gray,
My horse Ned is there to stay.

Give me a horse I can ride I say,
Give me a horse I can ride,
When legs are weak, they have no pride,
Give me a horse I can ride.

With my horse I'll tell him come,
He will take me home,
I'll be clutching to his side,
I'll not be alone.

When my steps begins to slow,
And no other love I know,
On a journey I must go,
Give me a horse I can ride.

When my doctor says I'm ill,
And my lawyer writes a will,
And my heart is beating still,
Give me a horse I can ride.

Miriam A. Trowers

Yellow

Yellow is like the bright sunshine
gleaming through a window on a hot
summer day.
Yellow reminds me of you, bright
and always standing out in a crowd.
Yellow reminds me of happy times
we've had together.
Yellow is a color that is a million
miles away in some far off place.
Yellow is the song that reminds
me of you when we were in love.
I wish that we could still
be yellow together for ever in time

I love you!

Linda Sivola

Lost

Catching a
glimpse from
afar
The smile
Only a
glance
Then gone
forever
Abandoned
Caressing
the mind
Concealing
all feeling
Dividing the soul
Waiting for a moment
A single
solitary
moment
To say
Goodbye

Stacie Thompson

Gifts from the Sea

Beauty by the sea
glistening sun on the
waves and sand
Sea shells brought in
by God's own hand
Footprints left by your
fellow man
Sun setting over the
waves and sand
Cool night breezes felt
by one's own hand
Moonlight glistening
on sea and sand
Once again to be enjoyed
by your fellow man
Oh! What beauty by
the sea and sand -

Shirley Tucker

Ode to Ed

Deity of dreary
God of gloom
Lure me into your secret room

Emperor of eerie
Martyr of madness
Bring me more of your inner sadness

Pilot of panic
Creator of craze
Lead me through your mental maze

Director of death
Sultan of screams
Change my nightmares my tranquil dreams

Sorcerer of sinister
Wizard of words
Fabricate evil in ebony birds

Master of mystery
Father of fiction
Satisfy my zealous addition

Sara Sowers

Masks Of Life

Wearing faces like masks,
going through life's daily tasks.
The masks are to hide,
you're not safe outside.
You've been betrayed and intimidated,
abused, afraid, and manipulated.
Suicide, once a consideration,
daily trials and tribulations.
Writing to escape.
With words you don't get raped.
From words you can't hide,
you go along for the ride.
Yourself you can be,
rhyming words and melody.
Still, no one knows;
it's all tied up in pretty bows.
Just thoughts you ponder,
heading towards that great blue yonder.
Hour by hour, you find a way,
to face just one more day.

Shalene Matthew

Fall Fun

Yellow, Red And
Golden Brown,
Changing Colors
Falling Down.
Leaves Are Gathered,
Piled High.
Crackling Sounds
Of Crisp And Dry.
Work And Play
Both Are True.
Windy Air,
Sky So Blue.
Running, Jumping,
Lots Of Laughter.
Plenty Of Hot Chocolate
After.

Regina A. Nelson

An Ode to Goldie

April 1977 - April 29, 1994
Goldie a beautiful friend,
more than a cat-
Loved adored no end.
Yellow gold and perfect marking
I see you in my dreams, I
feel your presence on my bed.
I see you in everything I
can't believe you are dead.
You followed me no matter.
Where my path lead.
Over the garden path
To bed with me to take a nap.
When young you and I lay on the couch,
no one bothered us for we would have
been a couple of grouches forever,
farewell dear friend,
as my heart slowly mends.

Mary B. Fulton

"I Wonder"

Wonder, why you said
Goodbye.
Wonder why you made
Me cry,
Wonder if we'll meet
Again
Wonder where or when!

Wonder if you'll hold
Me tight.
Just like you did
the other night
Wonder why you didn't stay
Here in my arm's
Just like today
"Wondering"

Opal Hopps

"Untitled"

Love is a feeling,
found in your heart.
Love keeps two people together,
never apart.
When two people meet each other,
and love is found.
They stay together forever.
Their hearts are bound.

Josie Collorafi

Rose and Sun

There are many roses,
grown in the sun.
All have thorns,
all, but one.

This single rose,
filled with grace,
discovers the dew,
leaving a trace.

The rose is alone,
as it slowly settles.
And so is destined,
to lose its petals.

Only the sun,
with its magic rays,
can heal the rose,
on its last days.

If you are wondering,
Can this be true?
Believe the rose is me,
and the sun is you.

Sharilynn Wrezinski

A Mother's Day

Red is the tulip that
grows in the spring,
Red is the ruby in my
mother's ring,
Red is the rose that
blooms in May that we
give our Mothers on
Mother's Day,
Red is the ink on the
note that my sister and
I sat down and wrote,
Red is the color of my heart,
For I know my mother
and I will never part!

Tia Brown

Violence No More

The crime in the streets
grows more every day.
We could end all the pain
if we could just find a way.
A way to stop violence
and a way to stop grief,
but what we need are more people
to just share that belief.
The belief that in everyone,
which is deep down inside,
is the strength, love and anger
to face this challenge with pride.
So up on our feet
and let's walk through the door,
for we'll stand for the violence
and for the fear no more.
With every ones help
and with the Lord on our side,
life will not be perfect
but we can take it in stride.

Robin J. Havens

...And Life Goes On

The greatest bloom upon this earth
Has always been a rose.
But the greatest bloom I've come upon
Just grows... and grows... and grows.

It started out as a little bud,
A miracle I'd say,
And blossomed into a perfect bloom
Day.... by day.... by day.

...And now the stems are branching out
With perfect little flowers,
And we sit back and watch them
For hours.... and hours..... and hours.

I wish we could delay
And preserve that perfect flower
But God has other plans
By hour... by hour... by hour.

Rose A. Gindlesperger

Love

Never in my life,
have I loved someone so
with my heart, mind, and soul
Love is great many splendid
things: feelings, emotion
passion and trust
Honesty, sharing, and compromise
are all part of love too.
To love somebody is to be
a part of them.
Weep together
Rejoice together
See through one another's eyes
Love is strong
Hate can be stranger
Follow my advice
and love will conquer all

Mona Lotfallah

My Eyes

I saw his eyes
He caught my glance
He turned away
He had no chance.

I saw his eyes
I stopped to wonder
His face was lined
Who stole his thunder.

I saw his eyes
His time near end
Alone and scared
He couldn't mend.

I saw his eyes
I reached to touch
The face I felt
Was nothing much.

I saw his eyes
The mirror was cold
It didn't matter
We all grow old.

Nancy Shoaf Kupcik

The Healing Solo

He upon the shore.
He looked across the sea.
He knew what could not be known.
He lifted voice and bended knee.

The song rose light, rose free.
It knew no real form.
It soared with aching sweetness.
And floated on past morn.

The wind seized upon the lyric.
The sun warmed its lilt.
The man turned toward home.
Freed, healed from guilt.

Mary T. Keating

God Made Me

He made the trees for all to see.
He loves me.
He let's me be me.

He made you and the ocean blue for all
to view.
He loves you too.
He lets you do what you want to do.

And he made it all with a speck of
dust, which some day we will return to.

Loretta Pryor

Own Little World

He hears of her pain
He sees of her hurt
And he knows
That he is the cause
Yet he still lives on
In his own little world
And he watches
As she cries
Her last tear.

Robyn A. Davenport

A Mighty Oak Has Fallen

Like a mighty Oak
He stood straight and tall
Branching out his love
For us all.

His courage was a tough
as an old oak bark
and his Faith as strong
as Noah's Ark

He shaded us with
his leaves of love
with a song as sweet
as a turtle dove's.

His roots were strong
to hold the tree
From the winds of life
For you and me.

Now when I look
at an old oak tree
I'll always remember
what he meant to me

Robert H. Elliott

The Last Action (Part One)

I feel the heat, and
Hear the agonizing screams
Of my parents' deaths
As I watch my house burn.
I ponder on what to do.
Part of me is screaming,
"Go call the fire department."
I block out that voice
And listen to the other.
I brush away the single tear,
Throw the book of matches away,
And start to walk.

Misti Holcomb

The Dream

I held her in my arms,
Her blood was on my hands,
It covered my white shirt,
And stained the warm, bright sands.

It turned it all a red,
Darker than I have ever seen.
It was the red of Death,
I heard it in her scream.

In her eyes there was a pain,
That I will never forget.
It was the last thing that I saw
Of my beloved pet.

Rebecca Schmidt

A Chid Is A Blessing

Her faith filled your spirit,
Her loves has made you whole.
The warmth within her womb,
Gave you the breath of life.

She cradled you in her wanting arms,
As your eyes crept gently open.
Her presence brought you peace on earth,
As her smiled warmed your soul.

Welcome to this world my child,
You were heaven sent.
Your eyes gleam with hopes and dreams,
And your smile steals all hearts.

Fear not for God will protect you,
Your mother will bless you with love.
Life will certainly test you,
But your faith will keep you up.

A beautiful boy you are indeed,
I love you more than words.
My wish one day is that I may bare,
A child as wonderful as you.

Stephanie Tappen

Ode to a Mechanic's Wife

If I go first, and you remain;
Here is what we'll do.
I'll wait for you on heavens road;
Till you come traveling through.
You'll know it's me I'm sure of that;
Though I am weak or pale.
Just take my hand, and you will see;
The grease beneath my nail.

Robert L. Matthews

In Memory of Grandpa John

Even though
He's dead and gone
A lot of special memories
Will linger on.

I can still hear his voice
Saying "Tricky,"
I need up "Tricky."
His voice tells me to be strong
For he will again
Laugh with me some day.

I hear his voice saying
"Tricky", be strong
Either if that road be
Short or long.
Just remember I love you "Tricky,"
And one Glorious day,
I will again hold your hand.

Kristy Yoder

Sand

I am everywhere,
hidden at the tips.

I am small,
but make mountains.

I can't be destroyed,
only removed.

I am stronger than the wind,
but can be moved with a hand.

The oceans worships me,
while man tramples me.

Everything comes from me,
and everything returns to me.

I hurt no one,
yet make hatred.

I bring forth life,
yet cause death.

Jeff Derenthal

Scented Flowers

Amidst the sylvan bowers
Hide scented stealthy flowers,
Always searched by languored eyes
And nourished by ceaseless cries.

Was it ever meant
To mourn the scent
The seasoned breeze
Has brought?
Spring comes to please
And quickly leaves
When such a scent
Is sought!

Louie Petronijevic

Our Flag

There's a flag way up
there, flying in the air
its colors are red, white,
and blue
it reminds us of the people
who made this country free

Laura C. Cross

At Midday

Hands reach out for me
high above the clouds
I can't grab them
for I am far away
laying on a bench
Looking up at the sky
hands signal to me desperately
as if speaking
I can't understand what they're saying
the suns gets in my eyes
as if to blind me
I look away and when I look again
they're gone
I am left alone with the wind
no clouds, no hands, no sun
I get up and walk away

Sonsiris Tamayo

Christmas

Christ is born;
Holy is this nigh.
Right in Bethlehem
Is born the Savior.
Star shines
The way for the wisemen.
Many gifts are brought
As presents for the
Savior, God's son.

Tina Jo Niess

"Oh, Jackie O! Oh, Jackie O!"

Oh, Jackie O! Oh, Jackie O!
How greatly she will be
Missed!
Oh, Jackie O! Oh, Jackie O!
A lady full of beauty and grace!
Oh, Jackie! Oh, Jackie O!
Oh, what a great lady she was for
All of us to admire!
Everyone was in love with Jackie O!
How greatly she will be missed!
Oh, Jackie O! Oh, Jackie O!
If the mirror could talked, it would
Say, "Oh, Jackie O! Oh, Jackie O!
She's the fairest of them all!
Sweet Jackie O, Sweet Jackie O!
She went to be with our Lord
May 19, 1994! Them on May 23, 1994
Sweet Jackie O was put to rest!
Oh, Jackie O! Oh, Jackie O!
How greatly she will be missed!

Theresa M. Boyd

Love Lorn

If I could only tell you,
How I feel inside;
I am too shy to face you.
So all I do is hide.
Each day I think of you,
Standing by my side
My fears, my hopes and dreams
In you I would confide
So I'm simply saying,
What I know is true;
I love you my darling,
but there is nothing I can do.

Jason Waters

Whirl

You've never felt
how I'm feeling

Now. My body rises,
writhes in emotional

Agony. Pain of my
lost memory haunts

Me. To be free and
young again, I

Desire. A child fights
to get out, to

Live. I keep her
locked away

Inside. Escaping reality,
dreaming of

Happiness. I cry for
freedom to hear my

Voice. My voice is
withering

Away.

Ryan LeVasseur

Martin Luther King

I am tired of war and conflict,
I am tired of violence.
For I seek a joined nation,
with a bit of common sense.

I shall never fall to weakness,
never answer riot's call,
and never knowingly hurt anyone,
but will shalt my hopes to all.

I do not speak for those who think,
that peace will come by death,
but those who shalt for brotherhood,
with everlasting breath.

I have fulfilled my place in life,
I have withheld my stance,
and I would speak the same again,
if I but had the chance.

I shall never be forgotten,
my brothers black and white will sing,
The father of peace in our nation,
was Martin Luther King.

Ron Palmer

The Realist

It isn't my concern
I don't care what you feel
Blackness, total blackness
Just shut your mouth now dear

I have been listening
To your endless thought stream
Is it your conclusion
That life is like a dream

Open your eyes now dear
And face the things I see
Your beautiful picture
Is dust beneath my feet.

Kathleen Matus

A Gift For A Star

What shall I give him?
I asked my heart.
Give him me, but
not in part.

How shall I love him?
I asked my soul.
Love him from me;
let his creation behold.

Oh! how shall I praise him?
I asked my mind.
Be his praises from me;
Leave nothing behind.

Of me, what shall I yield?
I asked my might.
Yield all of me with love
and all the above.

A gift for star

Merry Christmas
And
Good night

Ruby Taylor

"When I..."

When I am alone,
  I can think of only you.
When I am upset,
  I just picture your smile.
When I need love,
  I just wish you were here.
When the day grows dark,
  I imagine you beside me.
When I need to be held,
  I practically fell your touch.
When I dream at night,
  I dream of us together.
But when I think you're there,
  I realize we're miles apart.

Rebecca Brotzman

Endless Love

With all my heart I love you.
I cannot say how much for
there is no limit.
There are no boundaries to
which I am restricted to.
With miles between us each day,
I hope you remember our
times together.
A loving moment shared as our lips
touched to mark our new beginning.
Our destiny was to be together.
Star crossed lovers that crossed
at a perfect moment in time.
That time, has only brought
us closer.
With all our love, we can
find the strength and understanding
to move forward, together, hand in
hand, to last forever and always.

Robbyn M. Clark

Hormones

My life is Black.
I cannot see
Only can I choke
On the sea of tears
I am drowning in

I see the light
So bold. So beautiful.
I am so strong,
And so powerful
I can do anything!

I'm so confused
I don't understand
Why? Why?

Ahhhh!
I can't stand it anymore.
Enough!

Jessica L. Hill

Why Do I Love Nature?

Why do I love nature?
I cannot tell you why;
I only know my feelings
For the sun and moon and sky.

I look at things around me
Like the beauty and the space;
They show God's love and power,
And his unending grace.

When things close in around me,
And I am pressed within,
I need to look into Jesus,
Who freed me from my sin,

He'll give me peace and comfort,
And I'll never walk alone;
He'll be there close beside me,
Wherever I may roam.

Ruth E. Bell

Final Anthem

Tears fall with the rain outside.
I can't seem to find the sun.
Happiness, where do you hide?
From all my sorrow, I run.

But pain still embraces me.
Unanswered remain my prayers.
I long so much to be free;
Of this... my life... my nightmare.

Now I'm weary from trying.
I hope peace awaits demise.
The tears dry from the crying.
I finally close my eyes.

Rebecca Lynn Rzeszut

Childhood

Ice cream simple
sweet tasting fairyland
dripping,
melting,
disappearing
too soon!

Ralph B. King

Solitude

My toes sink gently into pristine sand.
I wander along the pale cream strand.
Eagerly my nostrils drink in the ocean smells,
And eyes feast as each wave looms and swells,
Then crashes, frothy, on the wet brown beach.
Bubbly waters race till my feet they reach.
Tiny line prints catch my eye and proclaim
The sandpiper too treads this lonely domain.
Silently i retreat, leave that small thing,
To rule the secluded stretch, the unchallenged king.

Irene M. Delaney

Drippings

Amongst the shades of the great oak stood a man in darkened robes.
Rings of gold and of silver donning pale lobes.
Thick, black hair violently whipping in the wind.
Life of Gaia; Mother Earth, coming to an end.

Beneath him lie the piles of the rotting corpses; death.
Inhaling, breathing in, and cumming on the flesh.
Make a mockery of the leaf falling on the brow.
Orgasmic pollination from the hereafter 'till now.
Menstruating toxic fluid, push it all away.
Feeding poison to the blood, the man who stands, betrayed.
What will it take, for you and I, to plug the knowledge in?
Plasma goading from his lip, falling off his chin.

Retard the image of the green, enlightened sun, feeling fresh
With lemon water squeezing bubble gum.
Reaching for the stars, he falls upon his knees.
Crying for his mother's pain and weeping for the trees.

Becoming one with dirt and twig nothing more to chart...
Fade away with little things, the atom and the art.

Adam Anderson

Pain

Sometimes when life's too hard to deal with
I want to run and hide, find a safe place
There is no where to go, Nowhere safe to hide,
life can be so cruel at times,
It can even be unfair, It always hurts.
What is my purpose on this earth.
My life has been filled with only pain.
What did I ever do, to deserve all this?
I only wanted love and happiness
I came very close but I now know
it was not meant to be for me
So I can no longer dream of it
I will never try for it again
Now my goals will be to never hurt again
To never let anyone close to me
To just survive in this cruel world
That's all I want then I'll be safe
Safe from all the pain, I've always had
Love is wrong for me, I give to much
I receive to little for my needs, why me?

Dena Bradford

Fear Not!

The path I took was dense and dark.
Fear not! The sun does shine.
The thoughts I had were never heard.
Fear not! The bells still chime.
My feelings strong were trapped inside.
Fear not! I beauty find
In tree and beast and man and God.
Fear not! For faith is mine.

Kristin Lee Cameron

Goodbye

As I sit here about to die
I want you to hear my last cry.
Time is precious and life is a thing of the past.
My life flashes before my eyes.
I feel death coming fast.
I start to appreciate simple things,
such as sand on beaches.
Water in the sea, even the birds and their trees.
I start to think of the good old days
and when I was younger with my childish ways.
But then I realize I'll never see another night,
or wake up and see the morning skies.
Then death comes and flies by.
And with this I close my eyes and die.

Jennifer Pratt

Up, Up And Away

It was the day of my big birthday party.
I was blowing up colored balloons
to hang around the room.
As I was blowing up the last red balloon,
there was a whoosh of air!
Suddenly I found myself inside the balloon.
I floated up and out an open window.
The gentle breeze carried me off.
I was up in the deep blue sky among the clouds.
I was happy and then I was scared,
because I did not know how long the air
was going to last in the balloon.
The clouds were as beautiful as roses
with rain drops on them.
The wind became softer.
I landed back in my room

Dani Elaine Parker

Woman

I was not born from Adam's head to lead or rule
I was not born from Adam's foot to be trampled or ridiculed
I was born from Adam's rib to walk by man's side
This is my spirit, this is my cry

Through my body, I bore you children, you love and praise
I bring you joy and pleasure, and your children I raise
I am sweet brown honey, dark molasses, and cocoa butter rum
I am your mother, your lover, your friend, and sometimes the only light
when there is no sun

I am a sweet smelling rose when my man treats me with care
My thorns only prick you when you bring me despair
I am calm blue seas, autumn leaves and cool winter winds
I am birds singing, flowers blooming when spring begins
I am snowed-capped mountains, the mating season for creatures to give birth
I am the early morning dew, they call me mother earth

Love me, respect me and together we will stand
I am Woman, God's loving gift to man

Charli Holmes

Me

I may not be pretty enough
For a prom queen,
Or very good to play soccer,
For I'm different,
I'm the outsider,
But writing is my life,
As this poem is.

Starr Kreling-Taylor

"All Alone"

Taking a walk on the beach one day,
I watched the sea gulls as they play.
I stopped to sift the sand so white,
Through my fingers, as the day turned night.
The roaring sounds of the ocean tide,
Covered the feelings I had hidden inside.
All seemed better for a time,
While the world there around me became mine.
As I turned my back to the sea,
I knew I was leaving my thoughts so free.
And again tomorrow there will be
Just another day - just me.

JoAnn Viscomi

Hospital Angel

Hospital angel, dressed in white.
I watched you make your rounds this night.
You approached, I was going to ask,
"Why do you work this unpleasant task?
Your hours are wretched, your perks too few.
You're underpaid for what you do."
She gave me a look of great surprise.
"Why you haven't even closed your eyes!
We have pills that will relieve your pain.
I'll get one for you sir, once again."
I thanked her again through bitter tears.
I've grown cynical over the years.
There are many of us, born to serve
And we seldom get what we deserve.
Hospital angel, dressed in white.
God bless you on your rounds this night!

Henry Mattia

"A Glimpse Of Heaven"

David, how happy I'll be when you enter My gate!
I will be there waiting with a smile on My face. We shall embrace.
I will take thee by thy hand, and show thee thy promised land.
First, we will walk on the path to thy Father's Throne.
He will be there waiting to see you; His very own.
As we kneel before Our Father, He will place on your
head a crown of gold.
He will give thee gifts for you to unfold.
You will open the first and out will come dignity.
It will be for you to possess for all eternity.
You will open the second and out will come peace, joy and
laughter;
another eternal gift from thy Master.
You will open the third and out will come perfected love.
You will stand amazed, as you gaze.
For this was your love, once broken, mended from above.
You will receive many more gifts that I will leave as a surprise.
After you open them all, we will rise.
Your Father's eyes will be dry; no more does He cry.
For then David, Our Father will finally have what
He longed for, you my brother; His prize!

David J. Linsalata

A Street Called Life

I was born screaming, and yelling,
On a road called life.
with my father Lathan, and my mother Jessie, his wife.
I was their first girl baby, and they loved me well,
And aren't all babies expected to yell?
They taught me to laugh, to love and adore.
And that the road of life had match to explore.
We found gods love there
With all its joys and strife.
We learned how to endure on a Street called life.

Edith Lewis

A Martyr Inside

I will fast until I no longer howl for sustenance; my hunger.
I will break the unbreakable chain; my soul.
I will be empty with everything and full of nothing; my drive.
I will sense the presence of the ultimate form of control;
my obsession.
I will dismiss the watchful eye over time; my patience.
I will be free of breath too spoiled by pain; my passion.
I will gain security through a force of immeasurable dominance;
my life.
I will acknowledge the truth and make no mistake in recognizing
fate; my mind.
I will deliver a guarantee of resurgence of life being
indefensible; my promise.
I will be inextricably intertwined with immortality; my death.
I will not fear, I will not take pleasure; my nirvana.
I will be complete; my journey.

Inger P. Brinck

The Most Of Love

If I don't look back
I will miss something
I ask myself

What is it that I will miss?
I ponder this question for many years
one day it comes to me
What I will miss is the person
whom I love the most

But, again I ask myself
Why did it take so long to find the answer?
And then my heart shows me.

Brandon J. Belveal

I Will Remember Autumn Leaves Dancing

I will remember you dancing over trees In the breeze you were
dancing.
I will remember the red, orange, and yellow colors of you.

I will remember you dancing on a Autumn day, and how you
flipped over
and over again.

I will remember you dancing, the falling to the ground, and blowing
away in the wind again.

I will remember you dancing, you just a little leaf falling and
dancing from such a big tree, and you such a little leaf.

Jennifer Peters

Stalker

Like shadows in the dark you haunt me in the night
I wonder just who you are there's just no end in sight
The breath you breathe so familiar on my telephone line
The things you do are all a game it's main attack is my mind

I look in my rear-view mirror to make sure that you're not there
But it seems with every step I take your ghost is everywhere
I try to find a place to hide so I'll be left alone
But there's just no way that I can hide as long as you have your phone
One question keeps running through my mind why must you do these
things to me
Did I hurt you in some way is that what it could possibly be
Or are you filled with hatred does it fill your very soul
And you think by hurting me you will somehow be made whole
Or is it that your love for me is something you must hide
Are the feelings hard for you does it tear you up inside
If you would only tell me I would try to find a way
To understand the things you do and the wicked game you play
If you could only hear my plea and listen with your heart
Please stop the things you do to me your tearing me apart

Brenda Rohrer

Untitled

I work hard,
I work long,
I am doing my best,
I haven't lost my faith,
I have been able to deal with my condition of cancer.
Some people have already prejudged my mental, physical,
and emotional
conditions as the end.
But, I have accepted the reality to go on and do my utmost.
In my mind, we all must accept death.

Daniel M. Pruski

A Slow Change

The glistening snow,
Icicles hanging off your toes.
Shivering in the sheets,
Caroling in the streets.
Freezing in every room,
Hoping spring will come soon.
A beautiful white blanket covering the ground,
Slipping and falling face down.
Watching the sky turn gray,
Wishing for a sunny day.
Then one day the sun peeks through,
And the sky begins to turn blue.
The snow has begun to melt away,
Revealing that spring is on its way.

Jo Dell Smith

I'm Still Loving You Now

Then the night exploded with the fear
I'd been running from,
We were finally embraced - face to face.

We are right where we want to be
The picture that we're painting
When I close my eyes I see

That the night will live forever
Our first time to be together
Both belonging to another
But, yet longing to be lovers

There were all those nights you couldn't sleep
You'd been waiting for that someone special
Baby - I'm the only thing truly meant to be

All the nights we've spent together
The way you call my name
This lustful spell you've cast
Only time can make it last

I chose to be your wife and to love you
the rest of my life.

I'm forever or just whenever.

Amy Suzanne Carter

"Turning Back the Clock"

If I could turn back, I'd change all the mistakes,
I'd change a lot — especially the heartaches.
I'd take back losing you,
I'd take back being sad,
I'd take back never knowing
What I really could have had.
Why don't you realized how much I still care?
Even if I could change the clock,
I'd still be there.
So why don't you understand that through the future
and from the past,
The love I have for you will forever last?

Candi Kendrick

If I Could Give the World a Gift...

If I could give the world a gift
I'd make it a special one.

It wouldn't be wrapped in paper or string
and it wouldn't cost a ton.

It would be very unique, kind, and dear,
Something everyone would want to be near.

I could plant a seed and watch it grow,
and I'd tingle inside because I would know.

That without me this tree wouldn't tower above
for all of the world to see and to love.

Becca Silva

The Gift of Memory

Without the God's gift of memory who or what would I be?
I'd not be very much—do you not agree?
If I had a name I'd forget it, had a house I knew not where.
If I had clothes and didn't wear them, I'd not know enough to care.

If I had food I'd not even know where to put it
Furniture? I'd not know how to lay or sit.
If I had an appointment, get there wrong day and also late?
Gee! I'd forgotten the appointment, so no fret of time and date

I'd not know of a smile or what caused a tear
Not know of my true feelings- happiness or a fear
And what about a baby? Would I know of its coo?
No worry, cause making one I'd know not how to do.

Without knowing about yesterday would tomorrow even be?
No remembrance of parents, events, could I ever hear or see?
If there were no memory for me I'd be the only one —
or would I?

Betty Southwick

The Echo

Empty, hollow heavens echo
Idle, hollow cries.
Man beneath them longs to live.
Man beneath them slowly dies.

Who am I to follow what cannot be understood?
Who am I to understand what no one ever could?

Should I just sit and wait my fate beneath the darkening sky
To eventually deteriorate and ultimately die?
Or should I fight and work and pain to reach some high plateau
To suddenly capitulate with nowhere left to go?

Either way I'm doomed as all before and after are
To ponder Man's existence on this lonely, blue-green star;
To one day wake to certain death, my brief existence quickly lost
Inside this endless churning cycle to which I've careless been
tossed

Man within it longs to live.
Man within it slowly dies.
Empty, hollow heavens echo
Idle, hollow cries.

Alan J. Sachs

Gossip

Gossip is like wild fire that cannot quench.
Like introvert water of dams seethed through tiny cracks.
Burst forth, wash away friends, inflict incurable wounds.
Whisper to erring ears driven by wrestles wind.
Saturates, satisfied curious meddlers.
Like uncontrolled fire, burn to homes,
reiterates and distorts into immortality,
leaving its owners exacerbate.

George Green Alexander

"Delicate Flower"

The Queen of the earth, the mother of me
If not for you where would we be
I cherish your mind as well as your beauty
Won't neglect you I'll protect you cause that's my duty
Inspiration, love, wit and charm
A woman with these gifts I could never harm
I need your guidance, your wisdom and understanding
Because being Black in this world is so demanding
I put you on a pedestal, that's where you belong
You're the love of my life and you spur me on
I'm physically strong, you have more mental power
I'll love you forever my delicate flower

Brian G. Randall

The Hard Way

I learned the hard way
if something wrong should happen to me
I could be tortured for a lifetime.
I learned never trust men,
no matter how much a friend or enemy he is,
Now my life is a total mess,
all because of childhood memories,
I think I should have fought
when I had the chance.

Angela L. Wonder

By Day and Day

It has been a long time, my friend, and though you cannot decide
If the tingle in your heart is genuine, or a thing to hide.

You haunt my days and nights alike and drive me wild with rage
But still you dare talk to me or write me on your page.

Precious time with pals is oh so dear, too rare at any cost
Though time for us seems questionable, and much of it is lost.

Could be your preference is solitary, I'll wager you're a mysterious dabbler of sorts
And lame excuses are evident, though lost time cannot be bought.

My weekly score you aim to keep, faithfully, yet concealed
While the moment begs an encounter, though emotions may be revealed.

You're a wonder and a puzzlement, what a painful shame my friend
When love cast on hesitation equals hearts that may not mend.

I wish you well in all of life, may you never voice one small nay
On the premise that a beautiful dream melts away, by day, by day and day.

Betty Streeter Lanier

Eyes of Gray

(In loving memory of Donald G. Koehler)
I'll never forget your compassionate ways,
The times we talked and cried for days.

I hate the thought of losing you,
But your time is up there is nothing I can do.

I tried and tried and did my best,
The doctors all say it's your time to rest.

Memories of love and laughter reek through our home
Without your love I can't help feeling alone.
I want to reach out to touch your gentle face,
This is only an illusion I've stated my case.

Thank you for all the special times we shared,
Especially for the reassurance of knowing you cared.

I'll always remember your piercing eyes of gray,
The way that you stared at me late in May.

Debra L. Vega

Love

Love is something, we each should share
  If you don't have it, could lead to despair
Love is that, which comes from the heart
  And as it grows, you'll sing like a lark

Love is what, makes the world go around
  And if you have it, you could be sound
Love is not, just for the young
  But older folks can share the fun

Love is true, when a man takes a wife
  And usually lasts, throughout their life
Love is blind, so many will say
  But I can tell you, its the only way

Love can take you, many a mile
  And always be there, with a smile
Love can usually, fill a room
  Especially when, its in full bloom

Love is that, which will never die
  And sometimes taken with a sigh
Love will help, when you are blue
  So keep on loving, it's the thing to do.

Harold F. Gregg Jr.

Between Us

You will always be my man,
I'll cherish our moments all that I can.

Although you will never be mine,
To me you will always be one of a kind.

You are more than just a friend,
I will love you dearly until the end.

You're kind, wonderful, and warm,
and I pray that I can weather this storm.

I will always believe in you,
because our relationship will always feel fresh and new.

As we love each other through the years,
let it not be any tears.

Carolyn Hall

Canyon Glow

A thousand stars that shine so bright
Illuminate this crisp clear night
A coyotes howl the only sound
Inside the canyon echoes abound

A blanket of frost clings to the trees
Sensing there's danger, a mule deer flees
Across the horizon bright golden rays
Go filtering through this colorful maze

Towering spires embrace the blue skies
A rainbow of color awakens your eyes
Steep canyon walls glittering with snow
As afternoon shadows slowly now grow

Simple but unique is nature's design
Continually shaped by the passing of time
As evening draws near, witness a change
From purple to mauve the colors now range

Erosive forces are transforming this land
Each day creating a new scene so grand
This rock amphitheater that nature displays
Leaves an impression the mind still replays.

John Maysuch

For Nita

Golden rays of sunlight descend upon her hair,
Illuminates her beauty, her aspect is so fair
Sunlight caresses her shoulders, rubs against her knees
Warmth; radiating through her reflecting back to me.
Her touch soothes the fire, which rages within my soul
Urging response to her passion - in like respect, in whole,
Pleasant, the memories linger, untarnished through time
Of days when we were young and love was so sublime.

But now the days continue, she's no longer at my side.
And with other women, my heart's unable to abide.
As the fresh rose plucked from the bush begins to wither,
I too "have seen the moment of my greatness flicker."
Constant were we then, as the incessant dance of waves and shore
Nita, the harmony that we shared I desire once more.
For what is knowledge without wisdom or passion without love,
Listen intently, the answer is flowing from above.

Barrington H. Bowser, Jr.

I'm A Nobody

I walk the streets all day and night.
I'm a nobody.
I ask people for quarters, dimes and dollars.
I'm a nobody.
I wear the same clothes everyday.
I'm a nobody.
I go to churches that serve food.
I'm a nobody.
I carry two shopping bags everyday.
I'm a nobody.
I only sleep two or three hours a day.
I'm a nobody.
I have some family somewhere.
I'm a nobody.
I talk to myself a lot.
I'm a nobody.
I did this to myself.
I'm a nobody.
When I pass no one will know.
I'm a nobody.

Gloria Peoples

Untitled

It's incredible how you make me feel
I'm always happy and it's because of you
And my feelings for you are so very real
You make me feel so good
When you do the things you do
How do I thank you for your thoughtfulness
How do I thank you for making me feel so good
How do I thank you for making me feel wanted
By loving you with caring feelings
By loving you with passion and understanding
By loving you forever and a day
Because it's incredible how you make me feel

Dave Gibb

Inner Feelings

Inside I feel sad and confused.
I'm always mad and never amused.
On the outside I may look happy and free.
But that's what I want everyone to think and see.
I sometimes wish I can lie down and die
Instead I lay alone and cry.
I close my eyes and think of tomorrow.
And new ways to hide my sorrow.

Jessica Lauro

The Message

Respondanswermeyoudon'ttalkbackapparently,
I'm not alive. Pieces of paper and telephones,
The only way we see each other through the window of a storm
I'm frustrated and maybe you're indifferent
I don't know what's wrong! I wish I did, but I don't !
Can you lift a finger, are you paraplegic, or do you just not care?
Help me! I can't do it alone! Meet me half way because I can't go any further
Sometimes, I wish you'd cut me off and leave me before I leave you
(If and when I get the courage)
Call me! I call you! Do what I do for you or damn you!
I've almost killed myself (I don't know how many times) over you
Understand my pain? No you don't
Nothing, nothing for a whole damned month
I like to pretend that you care about me (how am I to know?)
If you do, sorry. If you don't, no shock effect here
Bitter? You bet I'm bitter! What's wrong with us? Why aren't we like others?
Is there a problem here, I think so. (Is all said and done)
Wish I had the courage to say goodbye (I dream about breaking your heart)
You've broken mine every minute of every day.
(I don't want you. I despise you.)

Arthur Baker

"There's a Mountain"

There's a mountain as I'm sure you know.
I'm on my way up if I get lost I hope you'll show.
A hint of the way to the top.
Like the one I admire I won't ever stop.

For without trying I will be nothing.
On my heart strings regret will be tugging.
Some will succeed and none shall fail.
Think of the hope your grandchild you will tell.

There's a mountain and it's so beautiful Mother Earth's Fountain.
To appreciate its beauty will forever be my duty.

There's a mountain its name is king.
It doesn't know it but it will forever be.
Precious and bigger than life.
Where baby eagles fly over its mighty high.

And I pray that I shall be like the man.
Who gives the more precious than gold
Gift of music to his fans.

What is his name? Like you need to be told.
What is his fame? His heart of gold!
There's a mountain and it is so beautiful.

Donna L. Saulsberry

To My Husband With Thanks

Thank you for removing the box that I tripped upon every day,
I'm scarred up to my hocks from the box that was a pox in every way.

It sat there right in the middle just waiting for me to come by,
And I never disappointed it as head over heels I would fly.

I raged and screamed and I swore that box would be my end,
Even the clothes I wore were torn from rend to rend.

But, lo and behold, there came a day that ne'er would I forget,
That box was gone and nevermore angry would I get.

So dear Sir, I thank you much for taking from my day,
Those screams of anguish and such 'cause that darned box was in my way.

Dolores Amberg

"Tired Of..."

I'm tired of worrying about what people say
I'm tired of trying to be perfect each day

I'm tired of arguing whose wrong or whose right
I'm tired of days who won't accept nights

I'm tired of all trying to be one and the same
I'm tired of hatred and violence and shame

I'm tired of people who won't put forth effort
I'm tired of people who won't lend support

I'm tired of people who think they are better
I'm tired of people who won't answer a letter

I'm tired of people who won't follow rules
I'm tired of people who think destruction is cool

I'm tired of people who are constantly critical
I'm tired of them being so hypocritical

If anyone thinks I am judging unfairly
Or that I'm not seeing the world very clearly

That I'm only looking for someone to blame
And think I, myself, am the cause of no pain

That is not true as I must now tell
For sometimes I even get tired of myself

April Reitz

Untitled

As a child, I looked out at the sea,
Imagining how my life would be.
While the birds flew, so free,
I thought that's how it would be for me.

Then my life got turned upside down,
Year after year with only a frown.
Stumbling through life without a sound,
Until, finally my life got turned around.

What as a child, I used to fear,
Now as a man seems all so clear.
Once again birds singing is music to my ear,
But now their message is one I can hear.

Chris Cox

An "Oreo" Love

My vanilla coconut custard pie tasted of
impressionable sweetness, suffering sensitivity, and naive endearment.

My glazed chocolate swirl cake tasted of
a darkening smoothness, a strong rich flavor, and a sensuous spirit.

My pie promised me eternity.
My cake whispered, "In due time."
My custard pie pleaded for acceptance.
My chocolate cake demanded commitment.
Society said having my coconut custard pie was a sin.
Tradition said my glazed chocolate swirl cake is best for me.
Friends said different tastes are allowed.
My choice was an "Oreo" Love.

Belinda Gilmore

Loneliness

Loneliness is...
Losing my best friend.
Being all alone on Christmas Eve.
Seeing a child emotionally abused.
Watching a helpless animal die.
Living in a world of anger and hatred.
Calling someone for help and no one answers.
Dying with nobody there to say goodbye.

Elaine Guillozet

Old Man Higgins

He laid there
In a box of warm streams,
Exposed.
His control gone,
Only his brain functioned
And this only in thought.
A world of machines and fear
Dictated his pathetic life.

Reality hits, but the dream is still there.
The dream of disbelief.
No movement, no sound,
Came from his forlorn body.
Only helplessness, dependence.

They came dressed in white
And he tried to communicate, but no one knew.
Instead, their words were routine.
Their actions, mechanical.
There was no understanding.

He cried, but no one saw.
He died, and no one cared.

Jennifer Sullivan

Life

In a world of hate and love, who can survive alone
In a country of drugs and violence
In a planet which an air of starvation surrounds
A place where spring means rebirth and fall shows death
With relationships of happiness and heartaches, truth and lies
What has happened to this world with anger and madness fills the rooms
With hard beginnings and even harder ends
Where time can mean everything and nothing
What kind of person would want to live in this world
A person of madness and disappointment
The human being who is out to kill or be killed
A man of which is feared but yet fears himself
In a period of confusion, where people don't know between right and wrong
Is there time for change or a chance for revolution
Only time will know what is to come of this world

Dena Rickertsen

My Sister

With your life so hectic and busy,
In a hurry and such a tizzy.

Now with many years gone past,
Your youngest one, gone at last.

Your time before, was not to share,
As we grow old, you say you care.

Our beloved Mother, now gone away,
Just what is there left to say?

To turn back time, there is no way
Past mistakes we must pay with each new day.

Life is to learn and to live,
Love is to learn and to give.

From all of life's heartaches and pains,
Strength and courage, I do gain.

Friendship and sister, is what you ask?
For me my friend, it's not a task,
Always was there, you just needed to ask

Dolly Colbert

Untitled

Pale
in a nation of color.
Blamed
in a time of chaos.

It doesn't seem to matter my Grandfather fled
from Italy.
I am still held responsible for the mistakes of my color
before he was born.

I have no club
no dance, no song.
I am not allowed to be proud
of my past.

Can I not sing along?
Can I not dance in the fire of brotherhood?
Can I not preach my power
or hang my flag?

This is my generation
I refuse to live
ashamed
of a crime unknown to me.

Ashley M. Wilkinson

The Best Friend

You're as great as great can be,
in every way I see
Your twinkling eyes,
a smile that never dies.
You're like a dream come true,
I'll never be lonely with a best friend like you!

You're always willing to lend a hand,
when I need help or just don't understand.
I can always count on you,
to make me laugh when I am blue.
Sometimes we try to hide,
all our feelings inside.
But I want you to know,
even though it doesn't usually show
I'll always be there for you,
no matter what you say or what you do.
I hope our friendship will last,
and never become a thing of the past!

Jessika Moon

Forever Friends

Your hand reached out to me
In friendship long ago
A warm handshake
Melted our different worlds
You gave me insight
As we explored our youth
Constantly overwhelmed by our
Never ending list of things in common
We gave each other strength
To endure the challenges ahead
Friends walk side by side in life
But there are moments, special moments
When they stop to embrace
Upholding each other in love
Knowing that there is a loyalty long lasting
And a bond unbreakable
That though our lives be separate
We shall be forever friends

Desiree Hopkins

BELOVED DENNY

Though I know you are at peace
In God's Kingdom in heaven,
As I kneel at your grave site,
The tears in my heart, in my soul, overwhelm me.
Oh, If only we could see you again,
If only we could once again
Tell you how much we all love you, how much we miss you.

You are always in our hearts, dearest beloved Denny,
We will forever remember
Your sweetness, your compassion,
Your love of people and life,
Your hand always outstretched
To help the troubled and the weary,
To comfort the sick and help the handicapped.

It is no wonder God called your name
On that day we said good-bye,
For He, too, loved and needed you,
In His heavenly home on high.

Sleep in peace, my dearest beloved son,
Forever loved, forever mourned.

Eva J. Dolin

Untitled

Holy Provider, blessed is your name:
In good and in bad times you are ever the same.
You watch o'er your children; fill them with love,
To do your will, God, as it's done above.
Angels of mercy come by your will
To sanctify those who do your will.
By your kindness we come to our knees;
We share your love, Lord; it's you who we please.
We share your message, your word of hope,
To every soul, Lord, world wide is its scope.
You are our comfort, dry the tears which we weep;
Bandage the wounds, Lord, give rest to the weak.
In New Jerusalem this song I will sing;
(with angels in chorus) "Death, where is your sting?"
Led through the gates of pearls, we'll be blessed
With unending Peace and heartfelt happiness!
Thank you, dear Father, for all you have done.
Yes, I will praise you, as will daughters and sons;
You are the First, and you are the last;
This faith I cling to, with you, doubly fast.

Jon Ragsdale

Tell Me If...

Tell me if in the cricket's echoing night song
In mother nature's bosom she doesn't belong,
From outstretched arms a stoic heart bleats
In hushed silence, furtive prayers she speaks.

"Out! Out! oh misery and end
the pain that tears me from within."

The night bird cries out across the sky
Chilling the soul that begs to cry.
"Settle the score!" and from whence daylight appears
in one shining moment courage drives away fear.
The swiftness of darkness settle fast
Bades well to future light quickened past.
Once again the sun's streaking rays upon the land
give birth to a vision humble, strong and grand.

Alexandra F. Lamb

A Child In My Place

Far away, inside of me, there lives a little boy
In my brain, safe from the pain, among the laughter and the joy.
He comes along, all timing wrong, he follows no known plan
He laughs aloud and jumps about when I ought to be a man.
There have been times when goodness dies and serious is king
Then he comes in and makes me grin. He brightens everything.
You probably have been with me when he comes out to play
In supermarket check out lines, or a movie matinee.
The things he does, to you or I, seem totally absurd.
He speaks to things that are not there, or creates a brand new word.
When he's not here he takes a ride out to some fiery star
Or ocean deeps and pirate keeps in his Inviso-Supercar.
He sends to me what he can see, for he knows I cannot go
It would be fatal to us both with no one to run the show.
But I can't go and leave him here, a child in my place
He'd prob'ly go do something dumb, like save the human race.
I'd like to go but I will wait, I was born so I will die
He has a seat reserved for me, then together we will fly.
But if we're out, for help you shout, at your side we both shall be
But who's heart and hands and helpfulness I cannot guarantee.

Clay Lloyd

Special Thoughts And Wishes

You were such a sweet kid.
In our hearts you'll always stay.
Wish we could see you, especially this day.
And we'll remember you, too.

My lips cannot tell how we miss her.
Special thoughts are being sent by everyone, who loves you.
On my mind I can not say,
In a home that is lonesome to day.

We think of you always, cousin.
The pain is so clear.
The family will never be the same,
With out you here.

The day God called you home.
A part of us went to.
We live day by day.
Not knowing what to do, without you.

I never knew her in life.
Take her in your arms, dear Lord.
And ever let her be, messenger of love.
Between our hearts and thee.

Evelyn T. Tallman

Lovers Reunion

Just to let you know how you've been missed
In our time apart, I've never been kissed
Not knowing whether you're happy or sad
I've hated, yes I've been very mad
But deep within I knew one day
I would have the chance to say
First, I'm sorry for what I've done
But life is funny like a hot cross bun
I can't condone what I did
But in the auction I didn't know how to bid
I came direct and from the heart
From the beginning, our love was the ultimate art
But even though time has gone by
I'm still learning the ability to fly
To soar with you away from this planet
Our love is solid as a rock called granite
And even though we had to live on
Our love still has the ability to spawn

Joseph Hester

Hot Stove, Cold Coffee

Early in the morning I feel the warmth of that good old hot stove. In the kitchen near the window warms up the room and my body, and it feels just great I'm always in a hurry to taste the coffee that sits on the stove when I tasted the coffee, it was cold. Cause it was old, when you touched my cold cup of coffee it some how became warm. I felt the warmth when the coffee touched my lips. And as it went down my throat, I felt the warmth in my tummy, in my tummy, tum, tum; sure is a great feeling after you contribute to my morning with such a great warm touch, touch that turns my cold, cold coffee to warm coffee warm coffee. Early every morning, I feel the warmth of that good old hot stove in the kitchen near the window it warms up the room and my body, and it feels just great, and it feels just great. "Hot Stove Cold Coffee!"

Donald Earl Hardy

Imagination

I was looking in the sky one day,
In the meadow, in the grass is where I lay.
Next thing I know I'm not there anymore,
I'm in the mountains, near the edge and I
watch the eagles soar.
I take a step, into the snow,
Where I am? I don't really know.
I turn around, leap into space,
Then look up and see my brother's face.
I am there no more, but until next time
you'll see,
We'll be in space waiting, my imagination
and me.

Carolyn Curtis

Lady Alone

An old lady cried the tears of pain
in the old country nursing home.
It wasn't the pain of old age, my friend,
she felt the sorrow of being alone.

She had spent many years hoping in vain that
she would once again see her dear son
and wondered if her daughter would come
before the holiday season was done.

She waited and waited all through the years
for one visit, a card, or a call.
But always, her hopes were dashed away,
they forgot her, one and all.

The little old lady with much hope in her heart
awoke to a presence she had always known.
The image of Jesus with His arms outstretched
had come to take her home.

Carol Bednar

In the Fall of the Snowflake

In the fall of the snowflake and flickering flame
Of the fire and candle on frosted white pane,
In the soft silver glow of the tinsel projecting
In myriad points the tree lights reflecting,
In the song of the carollers passing at night
And the thought of the Christchild is swaddling clothes white
Lying there still 'neath the radiant star
Guiding the shepherds and wisemen afar,
Filling each symbol of Thee with the story
Thy peace shall reign, Thy love and Thy glory!

Ivy K. Stott

Angels Meeting In The Air

Last night a meeting was called to order,
In the sky were millions of falling stars,
Sailing across the heavens in every direction.
Were they searching for special people from afar?

God's wonderful little messengers,
All adorned in glimmering white;
Flitting across the sky like little scavengers,
Seeking a chosen one to shed a little light.

So little time left to claim,
So God must come upon the scene;
With multitudes of his special angels,
To open their eyes so God himself, can be seen.

Angels meeting in the air,
Seeking those God sent them to find;
With all his love and his care,
God's angels will change their heart and their mind.

Glenda Dennis

Fair Maiden

Fair maiden dancing in the fields, thy dress floating
in the soft breath of air. Thy beauty is deep within
my soul, I hope you will take notice and stare. For
here I am, a broken hearted man seeking for someone
to love. To give me comfort and ease, to cool me from
my heat. Fair maiden, only if you knew what manner of
man that I am. For in my breath is love eternal, if
only you would try to understand. Will you play me for
a fool, to trap me in thy webs. Will you play the shrew,
to split my heart in two. For many women have done this
to me, but now I have come of age. So now I will watch
thee, and listen to thy breath. For this I know, that
many women hold the kiss of life or death.

Frank J. Florio

Creation

The lonely call of the whippoorwill,
In the soft dark of the evening.
The song so sad, fell on my heart
As I sat in the summer eve so still.

Why does his song seem so sad to me?
When the mockingbird sings so merrily,
The bee's hum their tune, as the flowers they find,
God makes them so, and the sunshine.

The rain falling softy, touches grass and trees,
The coolness of the summer breeze.
Then I hear a soft step, come close to me.
As I strain my eyes, in the darkness to see.

My heart take a leap. 'tis him I see
My love, my companion, my friend to me.
He sits down close, and hold, my hand,
God created his likeness into man.

Eloise N. Callin

Life's Legacy

When life is done, and I am called to sail the endless sea;
  Let those I've met along the way think only this of me.
That I have brought some happiness into a lonely place,
  Or made a smiling countenance replace a tear-stained face.
May words I've spoken cheerfully help ease a lonely heart,
  And that I gave encouragement to forge a brand new start.
Have them say I wore a smile while others wore a frown,
  That hope I gave sustained them when troubles had them down.
If I can say I've given of myself mile after mile,
  Then I can feel my time on earth has really been worthwhile.

Evalyn Phelps

To Live in the Sunshine

To live in the sunshine
In the warmth of the day,
Loving and helping all people
For this is God's way;
This is how I picture doing God's will
In my mind's eye;
The bright warm sun, the deep blue sky,
The fall colors and leaves on the ground,
Walking in a meadow, the sun all around.
And in the winter when the snow covers the earth
And the trees are laid bare,
With God as the center, the sun is still there.
And when I lie dreaming
And picture these scenes one by one,
How I long for the day
That I can live in the sunshine,
With God as the sun.

John Edward Cotter

Thoughts

Deep inside oneself there is a passion, a life. If we are all
individuals why do we try to fit in? Why is there a great need
for acceptance? Is being who we are, or the desire
for what one can be wrong? If we all live up to what
everyone wants us to be, how can we say that we are people?
We do not choose our names they are given to us.

Are we "normal," is normal right? What gives us the right to
say what is right and what is wrong? When it comes time to
die how many of us can say I have lived my life?
We (meaning humans) have been dying since the day we were
born, but
most have not begun to live. What gives us the right to
judge, we are all going to die someday, shouldn't we try to be
remembered? Or does anything I've written matter
in this vast world, life, universe? Can you tell me?
Do you agree?

Anna Shaw

A Poet's World

Is an endless story of cosmic tales of creation, of discovery
Influenced by perception as imagery from ideas, theories, beliefs,
Some truths learned through real life experiences not only by
Trial and error but by habits as well.

The screening process related to basic senses used by systems
From absorption, digestion, interpretation ends in feedback.
Electrical forces negative or positive out of think power' flow
Into the "Universal Seat of Ideas."

Awareness by way of heartfelt qualities evolve into handless—
Will, mind, respect for, appreciation of are unmeasurable.
The focal point is in finding words. Later communicate with
World vision to sense an idea of freedom.

A poet's world transcends natural barriers as space, color, time,
And may disagree with present laws merely to bring a fresh view
Of the old or give birth to the new while civilization after
Civilization remains (unchanged) a slow process of learning.

All things are suspending from degree and continuing existence is
In the state of becoming.

Eunice M. Franklin

Leibniz Looking On

I know these monads,
Informing judgment to direct desire.
Wise ones, seeking real goods,
Where pleasure and perfection
Wear one coat.
These are my proofs:
Their broken stones fall true
Toward the center of the Earth.
There it is made one piece,
And fire of joy warms all when
Virtue pays.
(The writer's virtue flowers when subject
and predicate copulate to conceive truth.)
Searchers already, workers with words,
Study to search again
Lights up this place.
Not Voltaire's Doctor but these are mine —
Making concerted effort in the realm of grace.

Betse Judd Miller

The Secrets of the Night

Dark is the sky that hides the secrets of the night,
insane is your mind as your overcome with terror and fright.
A cold hand falls on your shoulder and your voice is taken by fear,
you look into the eyes of your attacker and your eyes begin to tear.
You can't move, you can't shout, you can't see,
the only feeling left is the need to be free.
Bang goes the gun and slash goes the knife
either weapon could take your life.
In this heartless world with violence abound,
in your last threatening moments these are the sounds.
You feel like a prisoner with so much left to say,
but the world falls silent as your life is taken away.
Wait! This isn't how it's supposed to be; this isn't
how it's supposed to end,
I'm telling you now, we've got to stop this my friends.
If we all took the time to think of how it should be,
then we could live in peace and we all could be free
Then the secrets of the night will be unveiled,
and the good in all people shall prevail.

Jenn Szczytkowski

Spring Conquest At Frontier

Million miles out of the frontier turn to spring.
Inside the deserted city thousands of men and horses
keep on racing.
Rays of setting sun reflect tiltingly through layers of cloud,
Tears dampen front flap of the warrior's clothing.

Helen H. Chien

The Threads

Friendships, to me, are like fine silk threads
intermingling, yet each thread different in design
and content, forming patterns invisible to the naked
eye and yet, so clear and crystal bright to the soul.
One thread is as important in itself as the mass to
keep the pattern alive and glowing.
My pattern is so colorful and full of life!!
My fellow threads are of so rare a quality,
both mystifying and divine in structure!!
If it were in my powers I would demolish that force
which so crudely sets its strength to ripping
and tearing the pattern apart destroying the beauty
and joy, leaving the ends frayed and the pattern empty
and incomplete to stagger in the breezes of time, always
looking, seeking the missing threads.

Demian Noone

Companionship's Bliss in the Perpetual "Present"

The perpetual "present"
Is exceedingly pleasant
With the people you like the most "!"
Discreetly confiding;
Or, quite peacefully riding
Along a forgotten coast (!)

The gloaming's followed by the long night
Enlivened by entrancing moonlight ("!")

Wherever one gazes;
A goddess amazes
Much like the majestic dawn "(`!')"
Sagacity settles,
Like lavender petals
Upon a luxuriant lawn "(!)"

Harvey Corales

The Passion

A wild fire burning on a hot summer's eve. That's how my love is for you and it just won't leave. Burning on a passion that seems too much to bare. Heating everything on earth and all that's in the air.

The passion is so hot that all the rivers are running dry. The people that are too weak to bare it can do nothing but try. The touch of your body makes the passion grow stronger. And it does nothing but intensify the heat making it last longer.

The oceans are running dry and pretty soon nothing will be left but the stars and the moon. With all this heat in the air nothing much will survive. Except for the two of us nothing else will be alive.

The passion that started out as a little spark. Grew into a fire that lit up the dark. We have killed a whole civilized planet that was once called earth. So now I guess it's up to you to plant seed and for me to give birth.

Grace Patton

What Makes A Grandma Special?

What makes a grandma special?
Is it her tender love and care?
Like a simple loving smile
That lets you know she's always there.

What makes a grandma special?
Why there's so many things to name;
Perhaps, the biggest one of all,
Is all the love and joy she brings.

For a grandma is a sacred gift
Given by God's own hand
To put that sparkle in a little child's eye
And guide them through their childhood land.

But although she's as soft as lace,
And has a temper mild,
It's granny who'll fight the biggest man
To protect her beloved grand child!

So here's a note to Grandma,
Just to let her know
How much she really means to us,
And that we love her so.

Charles R. Taylor Jr.

Untitled

What is life?
Is it something that just takes up space?
Who really knows?
Life to me is the sky.
I am the beautiful light blue.
When the clouds invade the blue,
problems come into sight.
The clouds collide and start
to fight over which problem is bigger.
The biggest problem is that there are too many clouds
invading the beautiful light blue.

Ami R. Drogo

Knockin' on Heaven's Door

The pain to see a loved one go
is really hard to ever show.
You love them more than words can say
that's why it's hard to find the way
to say how much you love them.

Knowing you'll never be with them again
brings tear drops to your eyes
you walk around in deep disguise trying
not to show how much you love them.

No pain in their eyes
no pain on their face.
Going away to a faraway place
where Jesus awaits them as they
knock on heavens door.

Heather Hutton

For Someone Special

I guess the best thing for me to do,
Is say how I truly feel about you,
I've tried to get it through your mind,
But I couldn't ever seem to find,
The words to say just how I feel,
'Cause my words to you are fake not real,
I need you deep inside my heart,
I wish we'd never have to part,
I'll miss you and your sweet affection,
I'm glad you dealt with my imperfection,
Now I must go on with life,
I feel held down, my heart cut with a knife,
I have many things to say and do
The easiest for me is I Love You!

Alishia M. Cox

Clitter Clatters

Pull up the recipe for cookie batter
It calls for sugar, eggs and butter,
A mixing bowl perhaps a wooden spoon,
Be careful now the table's beginning to clutter,
Clitter clatter,
Mix the batter,
We will have dough to roll out soon
And to cut with cookie cutters,
A diamond, square, star and moon,
Pop 'em in the oven,
Till there golden brown,
Count 'em there's a couple dozen,
Now let's spread them
Throughout the town.

Jamie Rex

My Ocean Breeze

As soothing as an ocean breeze on a hot summers eve
Is the tranquil effect of you gently kissing me
The rising sun warms the earth's crust
A smile from you reassures me of your trust
As we strive together to make our union last
Never forget that if we fall to keep our commitment to be as one
What really would we have done?
To start out building a loving home
Then fall apart and have to dwell alone; oh, yes, its common
And most consider it the thing to do, but in reality
We have become a statistic that means "we're through"
The thought of sharing my life with you, is so appealing to me
But, face the truth and really see
I'm not a millionaire and will never be
I'm not going to take you around to the seven seas
Nor will our life be one big shopping spree
So if you want to know and experience the meaning of true love
Enduring the tribulation of trying to stay, as two turtle doves
Then be my ocean breeze, my morning sun
Let us become one.

Danny Moore, Jr.

A Conclusion

Precious and something to be cherished
Is true lasting friendship,
Shedding upon our lives
A radiance that survives,
Reflecting recollection through the years,
To souls delight
Of a ne'er forgotten memory:
Heart's joy - when suddenly aware
Of an endearing symbol on high
The all encompassing beauty of
The rainbow in the sky!

Clara Magnussen

Untitled

His left was a piston that cut like a razor
It finished off Liston, Foreman and Frazier
He caught Frazier's left and they thought he was out
But he willed himself up and he finished the bout
Then Foreman got Frazier and left him for dead
And he'd wipe out Muhammad or that's what they said
Well, he cancelled the dance 'cause the night was so hot
He lay on the ropes and took Foreman's best shot
And Ali played George like a fish on a line
And delivered the knockout one round before nine
Last time in Las Vegas he lost to the jinx
But later he worked a sweet number on Spinks
He threw combinations and put them together
So fast they were only a blurring of leather
They said he was through when he lost his last fight
So what does he do but dance all through the night
Some fighters caught him, even some made him fall,
But he always got up and outlasted them all
He defied probability, logic and time
And won back the title ten years from his prime

Jeff Nasser

I Will Love You

As long as there is breath in me,
I will love you. As long as my heart beats true,
I will love you. As long as my mouth can speak,
I will love you. As long as my limbs can move,
I will love you. When I'm laying on my death bed,
I will love you. When I'm being lowered to the ground,
I will love you. When you love someone new,
I will still be in love with you.

Angie Oster

Summer Romance

It bloomed in spring, just as do the flowers.
It flourished into a beautiful, wonderful, unexpected love,
just as spring turns to summer.
So sweet but ever so slowly.
This unique in itself, not an original beach romance but country love.
Two together, running hand in hand through the warm wind, up a hill.
With the smell of flowers, the warm sun upon their faces
and the chirp of birds surrounding them.
This vision of love takes their minds
and leaves them behind free of cares.
What will happen up on the hill in the summertime breeze?
No one knows? Maybe a kiss, a word?
Maybe he will grab his summer love,
hold her close and kiss her in the summer sun,
with the sweet air gently blowing through their hair.
This summer scene will continue until the sun sets on the country,
full of sweet air that in itself is full of love.

Joy De Voe

Life Is A Rose

I gaze out the window and see a rose,
It flourishes from the rain and the sun,
Its beauty beyond the sight of those,
Who see not and pass on the run.
A rose is like life in its infinite birth,
It's born in innocence and ignorance of girth.
Life is a treasure we hold in our hands,
Like a rose in its beauty ever essence it stands.
For us to see, admire and to love,
Smell and observe as the flight of a dove,
Ask not for praise for the life you have born,
Nor for pity for the times you've been torn,
To expel your anger you held in your heart;
For life's burdens are great and do not depart.
Of the rose in our midst, may we pause in our life,
Give love and understanding, to its hardships and strife.
Life is a rose of the seeds we have sown,
And the acts of our live's, are like petals wind blown.
To the winds goes the days of our lives here on earth,
To death we go, as to life we give birth.

Doris Needles

When Night Arrives

When night arrives,
It gets dark in the skies,
and the night creatures rome,
while I'm safe in my home.

When night arrives,
the dark floods my eyes,
the moon comes out,
and stars scattered about.

When night arrives,
you can sometimes hear cries,
the moon and stars give what light they can,
for a poor, lost, and lonely man.

When night arrives,
sunlight dies,
the sun goes down and out of sight,
so now you may no longer see light.

When night arrives,
the stars act like spies,
peeping out like little eyes,
and that's what happens when night arrives

Joe Dwyer

The Shock

Someday, the shock will come.
It has a force stronger than all men as one
It will release its anger
With a power so great, it will be invincible.

It comes and goes just like that
And leaves a turmoil in its tracks
Treasures and gold scattered about
Lifeless innocence lying on its back.

Then a rhythm will shake the earths surface
And destroy everything but itself.
The shock will kill all human life.
Everything bad and even the good.

The human race will be gone forever
Lifetimes of hopes will be forgotten
Many dreams will never be fulfilled
So many good people never to be remembered.

Sometimes, I wonder what I'll do
If the shock will come for me.
It often scares me when I'm alone at night,
That it's heading for us with all its might.

Crystal Carpino

"Loneliness Is Forever"

Loneliness is forever
It is like a lost soul
Crying out in the night
Crying for a soft touch
Or gentle smile to delight.

Crying for someone to care
someone to come and dare
steal this deep dark loneliness away
someone to brighten just a moment of the day

Loneliness is the endless depths of despair
deep and dark and endless days with no one to care
Loneliness is forever.

Donna L. Cole

The Travel Clock

Beginning as a compact black box, the partitive article discloses.
It is now a three-sided object, two of the sides ebony
 in color, shiny, and smooth.
However it is the other side that is impressive.
It once told a story of time, a story of constant rush and stress.
Hidden behind its crystalline facade of glass, the
 clock is no longer functional.
The small hands, once marching around in their unchanged pattern
Have ceased in their ritual motion.
Surrounded by a frame of gold, the dock was once a portrait of time.
However, the timekeepers seem to have forgotten about
 their once-frequent voyage
Around the orbit of numbers that never budged;
Yet stood fast as the timekeepers trudged by,
Minute after minute, hour after hour, day after day, year after year.
Maybe someday they will be reminded of their long-forgotten
journey
And begin counting again with their repetitive footsteps
 through time.

Brooke Perrault

"Love"

Love is something we all cherish.
It is one of life's greatest treasures.
If you have never loved someone, you
have never really lived life to it's
fullest. If you have loved, you have
felt the greatest feeling ever. The few
people who do find true love, are truly the lucky ones.
Love is a two way street though
just like everything else in life. It can
be heaven or it can be hell. It can
make a life or it can take a life.
Love is not something you can put into
words, because their are no words that
could ever mean enough, or explain it.
Love comes from the heart and soul, not
the mind or body. It is a gift we have been
given, but it is a gift that we take advantage of everyday.
Maybe someday we will be able to harness
the love that is inside of all of us.
When that day comes is when this will be a perfect world.

Joe Campbell

Seasons Of My Walk

My Lord calls, "Come away My Beloved",
It is Spring"!
Ah, joyous spring finally comes.
I am watered by your Spirit.
Saturated in your love.
My branches become heavy with bud.
Comes the summer
and I am warmed by your love.
I am in bloom, soon to bear fruit.
The South Wind carries my fragrance afar.
Many come to eat of my branches.
Fall beckons.
My branches weary, my fruit has been given.
The time of pruning is here.
The North Wind awakens.
And Winter has come to my garden.
I wait once again for my Lord to whisper,
My beloved, the winter is over,
'tis the season for singing,
it is Spring.

Dolores Niedzielski

Laughter

Laughter...That feeling inside you
It keeps you from going down beyond reach
It makes you happy - even when you think you aren't
It makes you smile when you have nothing to smile about
It gives you an air of confidence
It makes you feel like you can do anything
I believe God gave you this gift when all you have left is your faith
Laughter...There is nothing else like it!

Dawn Walsh

Untitled

Love is a feeling that conquers all
no love is perfect - but neither is life
it gets you high, but for only the great fall -
a wound to your heart that cuts like a knife

You doubt if you may ever love again
as time goes by, the pain faintly fades away
you keep your true feelings smothered in
because forever scarred your heart will stay

Chris Stansell

Autumn

Throwing the days into the light,
One never knows the harmony of sunshine
Until the everlasting moments of memory
Have eluded the mind in order to find
The passion.

Kevin Castillo

These Precious Little Ones

Some are black, some are white,
It makes no difference, they're all precious in His sight
These dear little children, created by God
May someday, rule a nation, even right here, on our own sod
Just looking at these tiny faces, so filled with delight
Not a worry in the world, when it seems, all is going right
But we must be watchful, and take heed of how we talk
Because it's after us, that they are patterned, for the way they will walk
Sometimes we think, Oh they're too small to pick up our habit
But those ever searching eyes, are as quick, as a rabbit
We must live our lives, in God's Holy way
So when they see us, they'll see only good, and they will not stray
I believe in the statement, "Spare the rod and spoil the child."
Even though some may think that this is out of style
If you bring up a child, in the right way they should go
They will grow to be responsible adults, and good will, they will surely sow.

Hazel E. Connor

The Sun

It is the prosperity of our lives;
it serves many purposes in creation;
it is the sun.

Without the sun, people would perish;
and with it, there is a world of phenomenon.
The sun is essential to our lives.

We have delicate possession that is unperceived to many humans.
The aurora of dawn;
the dusk of darkness.

The sun is the founder of life,
producing vitality for trees.
Trees producing vitality for humans.

The venture of our future is in it's hands.
We are able to perceive the future with it's light.
It presents us visibility.

It is the heat perception;
rejoicing pervades the atmosphere;
people progress sufficiently.

The on bringing of a new day,
makes us want to stay forever!

Alpa Patel

No Contest

Like distant thunder whipped and frapped by wind,
it swallows up the rocks where I'd been.

Its milky foam surges...
my heart takes flight;
But sight and sound consume my senses
as time stands still in endless movement,
and perpetual power and static strength collide.

I watch the sea create her chiselled sculpture,
and contemplate her work not yet complete,
it's no contest between the rock and sea,
There... lies the evidence at my feet.

Deborah Chapin

Peace

Peace is the signal that sends out many vibes.
It takes a soul of words to feel them to believe.
Peace is away to express feelings
about violence and life in your hands.
Peace flows through many souls but many pass them by.
Love is away to express
peace to let it flow to the many missing
pieces of the puzzle.
Peace fills the past that has been forgotten
and the way in which they had been taught.
Peace is away of mischief that leads to the soul.

Amy Schilpp

Little Boys

Little boys can be fun
It takes two "No's" to get things done
They can find a special way into your heart
Usually from the start

Boys are made of adventure and wonder
They can storm through a room just like thunder
They can be joyful, happy and sad
Deep down they want to be just like Dad

They have their dreams and fears
They sometimes have many tears
They need their moms in which to share
All the things they cannot bear

The growing years can be rough
But little boys are really tough
They grow into little men
Then all you can do is remember when

Barbara Poppen

Ice Cubes

Fire...

Ask me to describe fire...

All right I shall.

It is death.

It burns beyond the skin of your children.
It tortures the mind with the agony of concrete
being uncurled, and ripped away from the skin of the human that
it clings to like a vine in the ripe Amazon.

Fire is like hate-

Unfurled without passion, yet lashing out with the impetuousness
of youth incarnate in an effort to absorb the very nature of your soul.

It sucks everything out of you!

Your breath!
Your conscience!
Your jokeable mortality!
Your family!
And when it's done...

Ice cubes...

Lot's of them.

Frank Aprile

Friends

They are forever and more
They are my second family
They share my secrets
They know my sorrows and joys
I love them, dearly!
They are my friends

Leonedia Moreland

The Tree of Life

I planted a little tree many years ago.
It was just like a child as it started to grow.
In the winter I wrapped it so it wouldn't get cold
And in the summer gave it water, as I was told.
Then the years passed by and it grew straight and tall
Until it no longer needed the care as it did when small.
Today as I sit under the shade of its arms,
I am now the child intrigued by its charms.
The wind blows the leaves and puts me to sleep
In a world where I dream of the secrets we keep.

James B. Allis

Untitled

She saw the gentle flower
It was sitting in the sand
Alone but strong and on its own
She didn't understand

She cupped it in her loving palm
She kissed it, held it, and loved it so
She gave it water, light, and lots of calm
Then she smiled and turned to go

Her intentions were good, her love was real
The flower grew to find more than it thought it could feel
But when she left, the flower stood alone
Alone without the light that had previously shown

She went back home, just passing through
The flower went back to what it formerly knew
But a change had occurred and things weren't the same
The contentment of old was now a foreign game

Bob Williams

A Nightmare

It came out of nowhere.
It was tearing him apart.
It was tearing us all apart.
It was something the kids don't understand.
It went away.

It has come back.
It is tearing him apart.
It is tearing us all apart.
It is the reason our future is so unclear.
It is painful and demanding.
It is all consuming.
It is CANCER.

Constance Johnsen

Why

I lay in bed and wonder why
It was you He picked to die
I always thought you would be near
Doesn't He know we need you here
I need your guidance and your love
But how can I get it when your so far above
I miss your touch, your voice, your smile
Since I've seen it has been such a while
So many times I sit and cry
Remembering my tears you use to dry
I think back with fond memories of you
And wonder if you think of me too
And when my turn comes will you be there
Will you know its me and will you still care
These thoughts come like one big wave
Knocking me down while I try to stay brave
To my questions I get no reply
But why did He pick my dad to die

Candice Pendergrass

The Unwritten Poem

There is a poem inside I can not find.
It will lead me around like the blind.
The words are there, but they shuttle,
But all come at once, as in a huddle.

I search my mind, to find the meaning,
Hoping to find those that are beaming.
Ready to jump upon the page,
And let them flow free, from the cage.

Caged up inside and ready to leap,
Only to find they aren't there for keeps.
Write them down or lose them fast,
You'll never find them from the past.

It's there today, to have and to hold,
Many stories of the past that I've been told.
I'll find the poem and write it down,
And on the pages will be bound.

Anna L. Fellenstein, Swackhammer

The Tear

The tear is its name
It's a single drop let of moisture
That says many things

It tells people without words
That down deep in your heart
It hurts

A sign of sincerity
A sign of pride
A sign of happiness that you can not hide

Its a signal to the Almighty above
That you are still capable of giving Love.

Jerald W. Tollison

Life

Life live it fully, life live it free
It's free as the windstorm
Full of mystery

Life is a spirit, Life is such a thrill
Live it with conviction
Live it with a will

Find a reason
And just live your life
Find a reason
And just live your life

Life is just like fire, life will never die
It is the soul eternal
So keep on reaching for the sky

Find a reason
And just live your life
Find a reason
And just live your life

Carrie Rice Suter

Untitled

A dream is a personal thing,
It's elusive and quick like a gossamer wing,
Maybe subtle or tragic but always it's magic
Mans' mind taking time out to sing.

All dreams hold a message for you,
They're telling you something your mind wants to do.
They remember the past, or want something to last,
Or they ask you to try something new.

David L. Doyle

Memories Of Our Son

Our eyes burn as they swell with tears.
It's hard to believe it's been three years.
Time has a way of standing still,
We keep on going, we have to, we will.
Beautiful memories of you keep us strong,
Mention of your name sounds like a song.
Bright eyes so pretty and a smile so sweet,
So many good qualities, you were hard to beat.
You may be gone but you're with us still,
By the sun that rises and the warmth we feel.
In the flowers that bloom,
By the rise of a full moon,
Rain that falls soft in early spring,
Birds that serenade us as they sing.
God's creations and the seasons that pass,
Are heartfelt reminders of your life that will last.
We'll miss you forever this is true,
Our memories of love will be of you.

Carol Sharp

Liberated Woman

It's not Me who's wrong...
It's just that I can't fix the kitchen sink!
And the landlord said he'd be over
But he hasn't called.
And it rained last night
And my dreams left me cold.

So I bought myself a "self-help" book...
In self-defense
Which told "how to do it yourself."
So I did, and that's supposed to mean
My self-esteem has climbed another step!

It's not that life's so hard...
It's just not easy living a hard life...
But my soft-skinned boy just smiled at me,
So I guess it's all worthwhile.

Oh, I'm not complaining...
It's just that I fear
The insanity of the world might rub off on me.
So I'll toss a coin between anxiety and depression
And choose to go out dancing!

Elaine Starrett

Who Am I?

I like music, exercising and cooking, but I love yard sales
it's my Saturday morning recreation with my mom
journeying through a trove of treasures

I visit many unique places, discovering a library of books
10 cents, 25 cents, hundreds of children's books last year alone
building adventures on classroom shelves

I've unearthed rainbow wedges of petrified wood, wagon wheels,
even an etched copper map of the Arizona territory
mining collectibles and antiques usable in yard and home

I'm like a jeweler sorting diamonds from a pile of glass
eventually though, I can find just about anything, or it finds me
taking joy in each of life's sparkling moments

I'm just an explorer, a builder, and a collector
I like writing, gardening, swimming and eating, but
I love yard sales

Diann Wenger Knipp

Black Rose

Their eyes are closed,
It's not a doze so why don't they decompose,
They seem to have lied,
But it's not what I chose,
They seem to have died,
But it's not what I chose.

In the hearts and souls of those.
I suppose will grow a black rose,
They seem to have risen,
But it's not what I chose,
What's wrong with them, don't they listen,
It's not what I chose.

And still the black rose grows,
And still the living put on their everyday shows,
Don't blame me for the blood shed,
It's not what I chose,
It may be my fault they're dead,
But it's not what I chose.

Erik Schmidt

Romance

A romantic night is not a movie,
It's not partying somewhere groovy,
Romance is on a ship with bare moonlight
White wine and music so light
Romance is the wind playing with her hair
Romance is a gentle kiss showing that he cares
A romantic night can be filled with rain
With so much passion causing you pain
Romance can be his hand in yours
Or at the end of the night him opening a door
Romance is an event that leads to true love
Romance is goodnight with a kiss and hug.

Bobbie Blakely

Slow Down and Look

Slow down, my friend, the old man said, you're going much too fast.
It's time to look, and think about,
The present, some, the future, more,
But most of all, the past

You're in the middle, of your life,
The same amount to go.
Don't waste these years, in passing by,
The things that we love so.

You raced right thru your younger years,
You lived each day so fast,
As if each day of your young life,
Were going to be your last.

Take time, my friend, and look about,
Look down, around, above.
Take time, my friend, take a good look,
At all the things you love.

Don't waste the second half, my friend,
Don't throw this part away.
Take time, my friend, to look around,
This could be your last day.

Earl Van Winkle

Tahoma

O great mountain, cold and high,
The crest of your peak reaches the sky,
Thy magnificence unrivaled,
Thy beauty untouched,
O Rainier! Rainier! I love you so much.

Matthew S. Selin

Sisters

It must be wonderful to have a sister.
I've always wished I did.
To have someone share life's ups and downs.
Forever, since a kid.
I'll never have a sister. This can never be.
But it makes me very happy and I pray will ever be
That my daughters have each other.
How wonderful that must be!
Thank you Lord.

H. Vivian Beck

Untitled

I'm losing sense of sanity
I've hit my ruination
Can't hold on to this hell on earth
Goin' down an inclination
I'm on a one way road to the end
In an endless search to find a true friend
I've lost my head, I've lost my mind
Don't know where to look, guess I'll never find
 the true meaning of life
 (could end it with a knife)
 the true meaning of death
 (take my last breath)
And I'm gone, and I'm gone - won't take long
But what if something went wrong?
Then I'll be stuck here forever
Stuck in a permanent dither
In this world I call my home
In this world - I'm all alone

Heather Silston

Looking for Someone to Call My Own

Looking for someone to call my own,
I've searched in vein and have been looking for so long,
For someone to fill the emptiness in my soul,
and promise never to leave me till we both grow old.
I dream of fields covered with flowers where lovers go to lay,
Just holding each other close and feeling the warmth and love all day.
To look into the eyes of the one I love
And feel the love I give being returned, is a gift from up above.
To sit by a fire on a cold winter night,
And have someone to hold me and
tell me everything is going to be alright.
To hear the words I love you each and everyday,
And feel the calmness in my soul and know that it is here to stay.
All the long lonely nights I've spent alone,
Would be worth it, if I could only find someone to call my own.

Jackie Malone

The Holocaust

What is this I see before my eyes
Jews waving and saying goodbye
As they see their family taken away from them
just before the day starts to dim.
Hitler orders soldier to kill them all
When he sits there laughing and having a ball
Jews sit and wait to see if they will be the next one
that soldiers will kill for fun.
Why did they all have to die
nobody got to say goodbye.
Hitler should pay
for all the lives he took away.
Nobody will forget those days

Jennifer Jefferys

Missing!

Where is my shadow that talks to me that gleams.
I wonder who took her, the stingy the mean.
One had said she dislike my shadow, how rude how mean.
The next minute you know its all her gleam.
That talks, that visits how terrible it seems.
I wonder when it will be,
when my sunshine and gleaming comes back to me.

Jovan McClinton

Cheated Holiday

Dear God it's almost Christmas, but the spirit isn't strong.
I've tried to make the best of things, but somewhere I went wrong.

I don't have any presents for my little boy this year.
The time is passing faster, and the day will soon be here.

He has long awaited Santa Claus and all the newest toys.
He has many Christmas wishes - like all the girls and boys.

But this year mommy has a wish - I hope you'll answer me.
I want him to have happiness and a pretty Christmas tree.

I want him to enjoy the songs and play out in the snow,
And there's a little something that I'd like him to know.

His mommy has a love for him that fills her heart with joy.
She'd like to give him everything - he's such a special boy.
And although she cannot give him all the things he wishes for.
She has a lasting love for him that someday will mean more.

And lastly, Lord, I pray that soon success will come my way,
So my son will never have another cheated holiday.

Carol A. Borden

The Definition of a Real Good Friend

(Dedicated to Jessica McKnight, Jennifer Cheslock,
Jenny Wheeler, Matt Chirazio, Kimberaly Berger,
Kim Summers and Jason Horwitz)

Someone who cares and likes to play,
Someone who cares and plays with you all day.
Someone who plays and plays with you alone,
Someone who cares and talks to you on the phone.
Someone who has a lot of fun with you,
Someone who likes to do the things you do.
Someone who knows what you're thinking,
Someone who would help you if you were sinking.
Someone who is honest to you,
Someone who thinks about your feelings too.
Someone who will go with you to the end,
That's my definition of a real good friend.

Jamie Horwitz

Tim, Jim And The Bay

There was a little boy whose name was simply Jim.
Jim had a cute twin brother whose name was simply Tim.
They went walking, walking, walking on a warm and sunny day,
When they soon did come upon a horse that was a bay.

At first they were quite startled, as startled as startled can be.
Then they both did holler out, "That horse looks just like me!".
They realized what had happened. It was dreadful, yes, indeed,
For Tim and Jim had each become a handsome, sleek bay steed.

Before long they both did learn 'twas a great honor to be a steed.
And although they both were quite surprised,
They learned to be happy indeed.

So that is the story of Tim and of his brother Jim.
They were fond of their adventure,
The two horses Jim and Tim.

Elizabeth Ivester

"No Phone Needed"

You don't need a phone to call Jesus
Just a simple thing that's called prayer,
and he's never out when you call him,
Because he's always there!

You don't need a number to call Jesus
His name you just have to say.
You'll never get a busy signed.
He will answer night and day.

He won't hang up when you call him,
Your needs he will always share
You can talk as long as you want to
He will always listen and care!

And, even though it's long distance
There's no charge and you won't get a bill,
And, he's never too busy to answer,
So, call him whenever you will.

No, you don't need a phone to call Jesus
His prayer-line is open to all.
Just say his name and he'll answer
No matter how often you call!

Eva Lee Dykes

Lost

Another love lost, another love gone:
Just as the day done I know another love will come.
But the love I lost I will never regain
Oh how could I had been a fool to think our love
would endure so much hardship and pain,
Now I see that I was wrong because my love is gone.
I heard today on the new's that a friend
Of mine got shot by another friend
Now he is going to do time why?
One in jail dying of time and the other one in the ground.
Say brother before you get foolish
Thoughts in your mind think, can you do the time.
If not, you better think right before you get
Ready to fight cause that bad thought will get your
Bad ass lock up every time. So think right tonight
And you make around to see the sunlight.
I heard today on T.V. new two friend's of mine won't be around.

Bernice Rush

Direction

How softly blow the winds of time,
Just as the waters of change lap at my feet,
In my lazy life I sit and wait,
While my mind roars ... "Now".

On a cushioned chair or a wind-swept isle,
It matters not for in each place and time,
Each tree weeps its own brown tears,
As the winter comes.

What peculiar punishment is this God gives earth each year
For a crime I know not what,
As I stand, sit or float,
On whichever land or sea I am.

As the seasons turn and I walk in some unknown line,
Is it destiny moving me to what seems like nowhere,
I do not know even as I ponder,
Ever watchful for my place.

Must I decide my fate,
For I have no knowledge which path to take
Lost in the present,
Searching to find ... direction.

Christopher Graham Martin

"Satan's Crack-Crew"

We're Satan's Crack-Crew, now, what you wanna do?!
Just give up that dime and we'll blow your mind!

We got a sho-nuff high, that'll take you to the moon
Make your body quiva, make your mind swoon!

As quick as a flick of a bic, it'll turn you into dirt
Have you takin' folks off, like a dirty shirt!

This stuff's hi-powa, it'll blow your lid
Make you steal an' kill, yea, abuse your kid!

It's a top-shelf hooka, make you sell your hide
Make you "dis" your momma, commit suicide!

This stuff's no racist hey, it loves you all
From Black thru white, be you short or tall!

DOESN'T MATTA WHO IT HOOK
BE A JUDGE OR A CROOK!!!

If you're tired of livin'
Or you wanna be in jail
Then let us make a sell
And we'll see you in HELL!!

'Cause we're Satan's Crack-Crew
We'll end it all for you!!!!!

David L. Moss

Just Like....

Just like the wind, I would like to travel the world.
Just like the clouds, I love to twist and curl.
Just like the sun, I can make your day shine.
Just like the snow, I can cool off your mind.

Just like a branch, I can hang upside down.
Just like a tree, I can have a smile or a frown.
Just like a leaf, I can crumble and fall.
Just like a tree, I want to stand tall.

Just like a puppy, I am cuddly and sweet.
Just like a pony, I trot with my feet.
Just like a kitten, I slurp the milk in my mouth.
Just like a bird, I yearn to go south.

Just like a car, I could break down.
Just like a plane, I can spin around.
Just like a truck, I can carry a load.
Just like a bus, I travel the hard road.

Just like you, I want to go home.
Just like you, I stand all alone.
Just like you, I have nightmares and dreams.
Just like you, I know life is not all it seems.

Josie Landin Aleman

Untitled

Why you have left, I have no clue
Just one more chance
And I'd tell you I loved you
The last thing you said, was sweet "goodbye"
Now that you're gone, I can't help but cry
Why God chose you, only he knows
For what she says and does,
Always goes you were the hero
That I once knew, people so caring
They're very few
I can't remember a time, when you weren't there
You knew all my faults, yet you still seemed to care.
Now all I can do is reminisce those memories of gold
And all the things I wish I'd said, now go untold.

Amy Nolan

Forgotten By The Memories

He gave me the roses
Just two,
He gave me the kiss
That magical morning.

He gave me the romance
I believed, was true.
He gave me the happiness
Cracked my unbearable loneliness.
He gave me the beauty
Could be seen in my eyes, so easily.
He gave me the attention,
but I was only asking for his affection.

And that very night,
He gave me the tears, released by my own fears.
Then I stopped,
Led, the red roses, slip through my fingers,
Hitting the floor with my angry tears
Which were forgotten by the memories.

Elsa E. Aslan

Kids

If we care about tomorrow, we must care about today.
Kids are waiting anxiously for what we have to say.
So you hug 'em, scold 'em, praise them
To help them along the way.
If we care about tomorrow, we must care about kids today.

Kids are baffled by technology, they worry about their peers.
Excitement over sociology can sometimes bring them tears,
Fashions, friends, future goals are always on their minds.
We must advise from our souls that there's choices of many kinds.

Broken homes, broken hearts all seem to interfere.
But reading, writing and arithmetic must somehow be clear.
Textbooks, homework, sporting events are usually just fine.
But promotion, retention..... pass/fail must be the bottom line!!!

Oh yes, we care about tomorrow, so we'll handle it today.
We'll hug them, scold them, praise them......
and we'll help kids along the way.

Doris T. Lucas

Blue Eyes

I fell in love
last autumn
with a pair of blue eyes.
I know a lot about blue. It is my favorite color.
These eyes were deeper than a robin's egg blue,
yet not so deep as the true sapphire is blue.
There is a color described as cerulean.
That is the color of blue that I mean.
And the beautiful soul behind the eyes—
His name is Jon.

Carol Kieda

The Snap

I heard a snap,
It was a mouse in a trap.
He was covered in blood,
My mom threw him out with a thud.
I looked the next day
He was shriveled up and gray,
That was the end of that mouse,
But we'll catch plenty more in this house.

Jason Morrison

They Could Only Tell Lies

She stood in the crowd holding him near,
Laughing at my sadness and my fear.

She held him close while I was so far,
I felt alone trying to shine, like an only star.

I stared at their faces and could not believe,
All the lies about love they had me conceive.

The past years I remember being the only one,
Watching, instead of being apart of the fun.

Why they put me through these lies, I do not know,
They just went on with the act till it started to show.

Now I must move on, with these tears of goodbye's,
For the mother and brother who could only tell lies.

Jessica Levine

Untitled

Upon the scorching sand
Lay sorely wounded man
Torn by beast and racked with pain.

With burning lips he prayed
Oh God, what have I done to warrant this such pain
Take this life of mine, it nothing means to me.

God in this wisdom, infinite, did heed the pleas
And in His hand took life and soul of tortured man

A happy marriage feast draws to joyful end
As guests depart and newly wedded hosts
Bid them happy on their way.

Soon in the marriage bed the newly wedded pair
Is gladly watched by God who then decrees conception.
And at that moment, ecstatic
Instills the soul of him lying dead on burning sand.
Now by plan of God mysterious
Invests a new conceived' child with another's soul -
by Hand of God.

James Smith Jr.

"All I Ask"

I look out the window the wind is blowing the
leaves back and forth
The mistletoe on our tree is bending and it's
pointing north could this mean that Santa is on his way.
When I kneel down and I begin to pray I
ask for these simple things on Christmas day
I don't need a new bike
I want some shoes made by Nike
I don't need a basket ball
I want a coat for the fall
I don't want toys made by Fox and Gayble
I want food to be on our table
I don't want a car made of rubber
I want some clothes for my little brother
I don't want toy guns to play cops and robbers
I want a job for my father
I don't want my mother to clean other people's homes
I want her to be queen of her own throne.

Harry L. Kitt, Jr.

Loneliness

There are times in each of our lives
Those times when nothing seems to go right
And we wish someone was there to care.

We feel the need to share our thoughts
But when we turn around and look
There are times when no one else is there...

James E. Bishop

Dolphin

The dolphin swims, the dolphin dives
Let's thank God we are all alive
And when the dolphin comes to the surface,
Just like us, it has a purpose.

But when the dolphin always swims
He never does it on a whim,
He does that because he has to
He does what he does to get him through.

The sharks are out there, as you know
But the dolphin can deliver a lethal blow
As long as you think of them in your mind
Life will be good and life will be kind.

Above the ocean the sea gulls sing
But did they ever give you a diamond ring?
They fly just like they were kings
And they don't even know the pleasure they bring.

And so, my dear, I've written this through
I do wish I could be with you.
You are like a dolphin and also a dove
My thoughts are with you, my heart's full of love.

Elliott B. Elfrink Jr.

The Rain God

From a distance, the rain in this county is God
letting down her straight long hair
to trail along the ground.
I can see her coming, her head tilted
as she combs out the morning dew.
Her body is as naked as the land.
She kisses the crops softly on the mouth,
and leaves them reaching for one more or two.

I remember standing in the rain, and you were there
wet as I was, last summer in Davis Square.
I will never forget the feeling of your free hand
on my body, or how your clothing clung to my desire.
When I hear the rain now, I think of you—
I want to drink from your mouth.
Pour over me, touch me everywhere
and let me drown and drown and drown.

Henry Hudepohl

Forest Treasures

Deep within the redwood forest
Lies the heart of God and man.
If you look and find it's treasures,
You behold the secret land.

Take the path along the river
Walking deep within the woods,
And your heart becomes enlightened
To God's special works of good.

Sunlight shadow's dance through treetops
As you walk along the way.
Wildwood flowers gently blooming
What a wondrous glorious day?

The enchantment that enfolds you
And the reverence of the land,
Seem to touch you with it's magic
And the love of God's own hand

Bettye Lopp

Dreams

Dreams float in and dreams are shaken
Like a butterfly forsaken -
They flit away on wings of gold
The dreams have gone to leave only cold.
Mem'ries dance in the labyrinth of sleep
As shadows thru misty tunnels creep
Look, there! A glimpse of fluttering gossamer wings,
A wafting bittersweet aroma of forgotten things.
A silken touch - remembrance of love since past
Or was it something else? It was gone so fast...
Waking brings gentle stirrings of dawn
But the dream is lost - all memory gone.

Jill R. Witte

Nature's Colors

All nature's colors are beautiful,
like a rainbow after a spring rain.
Yellow is the sun,
splashing its warm rays onto the earth.
Red opens like a rose,
twinkling on a warm spring morning.
Blue splashes like the cool water,
from a glistening waterfall,
White floats within an enormous fluffy cloud,
sailing in the breezy sky.
Green glows from the sweet grass,
swaying in the air.
Pink blooms as an apple blossom,
Spreading out its beautiful color.
Orange springs from the sun when it sets.
Making the last bright and soothing colors of day.
The colors of nature have the ability to spring
a beautiful day forth,
glowing bright colors all around and to end a day with
beautiful colors,
To say good night to the earth.

Amber Havermann

Our Paula Jean

An angel came to live with us a year ago today,
Like a star that lights the heavens she sparkled in every way.
Our baby is asleep now, in a soft sweet smelling bed.
Sweet peas of white and blue, with tiny rose buds for her head.
Oh God, speak softly to her, and make her dream happy dreams,
And let the sun tan her lightly, with their faintest beams.
She came to us and filled our home with all the happy things
That little girls with bright red hair and blue eyes always brings
Her tiny cry and laughter that filled each and every room,
Remains only in a memory and in each flower that's in bloom
We knew she was to stay awhile, but time was much too short.
With Blessed Mother, whose birthday she shares, in
her flower garden she lies
Oh, Paula Jean, our baby, our love, how happy you made our lives.

June EmmaLee Voight

The Rose Petal

The rose petal falls lightly to the ground;
just as the dancer lands upon her feet with much
skill and grace.
The brilliant red rose petal is just as the
dancers scarlet red costume
The dying rose petal falls to the ground just
as the discarded costume of the dancer falls to
the floor after her last performance.

Alberta Edson

The Germ of War

Tension rides on passion divided.
Like a tempest that drives the sea
It churns deep the abyss and rises
Uncoiled and true, yet strident.

Beneath the eyes of a warrior's soul
Civilization is made, unmade, and made anew.
From the chalice of want desire does flow
And from it spills need, good motives left eschew.

Validate the cause by sleight of hand,
Touch the fears common to man;
Add warmth to your fallacious speech
And cultivate ears receptive to teach.

Fertile is the soil of the malcontent,
Insatiable are their fears that roam;
Rest they find in those who are fraudulent,
In whom bigotry strikes home.

Garry Stockdale

Background Noise

Traffic at a distance rolling
like rushing water in
a continuous flow broken
by a chuckhole strategically placed for effect

Rock music through the walls
with an ever changing beat
ritualistic paganism with
volume fluctuations not for a queasy stomach

Women practicing the art of conversation while
a child plays close at hand
punctuated with nervous laughter attempting
to find meaning

Rain hitting the window
drops splitting through the screen leaving
their signatures on the floor washing
away the days mementos in preparation for tomorrow

Fire crackling along the frame
the roof collapsing crashing down
pedestrian muted silence while a sirens wail
strikes home the mortality of those tomorrows lost

Andrew J. Averman

Branded

I feel the black coal my grandfather mined burnt into my face
like the identification numbers from a concentration camp
While the ticker of history wraps like a snake around my
neck and pulls me from my familiar home.
What is this sickness?
A nurse shrieks the orders while the Surgeon carves out my
self.
They give me the diagnosis.
A baby boy.
Judgement Day falls on Monday in an Eagle Talon with
Camus.
god has decided on my friend
and she has decided on me
Run a test on me in the innocuous school cell, devoid of life,
and pronounce me man and accountant.
Oh, to flee now
Dependents and dependency
Expectations and expectancy
And sail to Montana.

Amy Lorenzo

Untitled

Beads of sweat form on my flesh
like the night before when
our souls were intermeshed
two lovers free in spirit
Dancing is eternity
Immortalized forever in a memory
Escaping today's pain in the dim of the night
And so now their off for a mystical flight
the time has come for them to be together
to be captured in a fragment of
the spirit world forever together

Jhone Hayden

"Portrait Of A Dream"

I met you in a dream I think
lined with silver stars.
We lived in a palace on a cloud
happy in each other's arms.
We laughed in the sun with angel children,
and the moon sang to us at night.
We loved one another in darkness,
we danced together in light.
Our hands locked as we slid down the rainbow
Our lips met as we strolled in the rain.
A heavenly realm of happiness
shielded from any pain.
I awoke with a smile this morning
as my teary eyes began to gleam.
Reality may never allow you -
But we will always share the dream.

Elizabeth Ann Garrity

Future Revival

Followers faithful required to lead.
Listen all ye Lamentations cry
frustrated feeling anoints each eye.
Suffering can still Salvation breed.
Needy of neighbors sublime and certain of creed.
Deviants hallow Apostasy's poignant lie
stricken communities Evil intends to try.
Cruel Forgiveness makes dogwood bleed.
Sovereign spirits, delightful praise copious.
Peace does unite souls together invincible
Hope dances freely with motion like Exodus.
Penitence fastens Our covenant durable
Heaven is truly man's dwelling indigenous.
Natural Majesty, naught are so honorable.

Cheryl L. Kotula

"Gods Little Angels"

There is a special place in heaven don't you see, the blessed little children God calls home to be, His special little angels through out eternity. They filled our heart with joy and love for all the world to see, but something happens and the world sees them no more because the child knocks on Gods door. Jesus softly touches the child and takes Him home never more to be lonely or alone. So Jesus loves the children and loves them tenderly. Gods always in the valley, and always in the sea, no matter when I need Him He always comforts me. The lights in heaven are very bright shining in the night. If you've ever lost a child let them live in your memory being ever grateful for just an opportunity of loving little children that belong to God don't you see. Their only lent from heaven for just a little while only just to love, but we have to let go somehow. Oh mom and Dad I love you and oh so tenderly but Jesus has a home just for me.

Barbara Stone

Say You Love Me

I love you, that's all I want to hear, say you care about how I'm living
What I'm thinking, what I'm dreaming
You don't hold me like a father should, nothing is understood
You come and go like the seasons, you leave without any reasons
What did I do to make you go away, you can't hear a word I say
I'm your blood, we should have a tie, what if one of us were to die?
So many things left unsaid, like our relationship, my heart is dead
Don't you wonder why I've never called you daddy?
Just say you love me, it'd make me so happy
Where are you, where is your head? Don't you wonder if I'm fed?
I have so many questions, I have so much pain
Sometimes I can't function, and it's you I blame
I'm trying my best to live without you
Sometimes I feel like dying, but what good would that do?
I continue to struggle, unsupported
I wish I had your love that you have aborted
Daddy, say you love me
Daddy, say you love me
Because I love you, please hold me

Arletha M. Brewer

Loner

Lonely is the life I lead,
Lonely I can only be.
On my own is how I must see,
for if only to please that of me.
A loner I am.
All by myself, my "Life goes on"
Others may see
But, will never understand me.
I'm not to be classified as a
stereotype. To be limited to the world
for the one within will only be
misunderstood by those who misunderstand.
Don't try to know the real me, for
you can never see, that of which I shall be.
A loner is my life, not of thee, but I only be.
I'm here for you to see
But, you can never understand
the real me!

Bobbie Sue Bertloff

A Cry in the Night

A cry in the night...
lonely, scared, blowing on the wind,
increasingly louder, screaming, terrifying,
all around you, pulsing, beating.
Its coming,
threatening, destroying—
no where to run.
Desperately searching, finding no answers.

A cry in the night,
ebbing, fading,
all around you,
softer, softly,
quietly, flowing,
deafening silence.

A cry in the night,
what is it?
A cry from a child.
"Won't you help me?"
In the end
there's only silence.

Cassandra Fengel

Moe and Bo

Now here's a real sad story, that happened
Long ago, bout' a country boy, from way
Down south, that all the folks called moe.
Now moe was big, but not to smart, but
Home folks say he had a heart. Was said
He "Hatched" in tennessee, and never lernt'
Bout' birds and bees.
He roamed the woods with his dog bo,
Cause bo had lots more sense then moe.
Town folks said was such a shame, that
Poor moe's folks was both insane.
Moe had no lick of sense at all, an' neather
Did his maw and paw.
But moe and bo was happy, as happy as could be,
They was happy as fat pigs in slop, way
Down in tennessee.
Sad thing happened, don't you know, down at
That ol'water hole... Moe slipped and grinned
But couldn't swim, and neither could poor bo.
And to this day, they both still lay, in that ol'water hole.

Annette Venable

Bold And Beautiful, Dignified And Knowledgeable

She was bold and beautiful
looking dignified and knowledgeable
standing straight and tall
standing high above them all
she said I mustn't frown
or keep myself down
but to think high
having my thoughts reach to the sky
Her smile was full of love and happiness
But I never told anyone about this
Now whenever I'm not feeling too great
When it makes me almost filled with hate
I think of the bold, beautiful,
dignified, and knowledgeable woman
keeping my thoughts high
very high to the sky

Brianne Lauren Barbour

Let Us Go to the Other Side

There is a storm raging on the sea
Lord, can you see the fear in me?
Be still my child do not fear the storm
I am with you, don't be weary and worn,
You want to stop right here and now,
But my child you must face the bow
Right into the very heart of it
and keep going across, don't quit.
Let us go to the other side and you will see
That facing your storm has set you free.
Meeting it head on, going through all the way
The victory is your's, you've survived the day.
Jesus let us go to the other side
On a sea of victory a mile wide
Jesus and me a team that can't be beat
Thank you, Lord, for victory that is sweet.
Let us go to the other side
For ours is a victory ride
The storm may rage on and on
But the battle has been won.

Evonne Walsted

"Brown Eyes"

I watch those Brown eyes as they stop and stare. So confused, so lost, so unaware. Of the people around them who really care.

They are looking for something a person, a place. Something that seems lost to the human race.

It's as if they can see it but touch it dare not. For it may not be what they really sought.

They are in a place all alone somewhere between heaven and home!

What can it be? This thing that they see, a touch of a hand or a warm summer breeze.

I know what it is. What it has to be! This strange thing that Brown eyes sees.

It's called a Dream!

Christine Marie Beeson

Love

What is this word?
LOVE.
Will someone please tell me?
Is it a strong feeling or is it weak?
Can you find it in a can or a box?
Does it taste sweet, bitter or sour?
Can you lose it?
Can it be destroyed or damaged?
Does everyone have love or only certain people?
Can it be caught or bought?
Or does love find you?
Please someone explain this thing called love.

Damita Lea Aliff

Love

If we love our neighbor and treat them kind
Love in the world is what we will find
We will be blessed with everything good
Because loving is great but, that's understood
Love is the key to our success
Because presently I think this world is a mess
Love is the energy that we should supply
To our poor helpless children, before they all die
Love is the answer to bring us all together
Try loving yourself, no matter whatever
We must feel this love so deep inside
To find true happiness and be our own guide

Bettie Blossom

Love Conquer's All

When we fall,
Love is a cushion that break's our fall.
Love chooses no race.
Because love is full of grace.
Love is merciful and not divided.
Love is always united.
Love is a candle in the world today.
If all would use it we could bring light in our day.
Now you see that the light is love.
And darkness that is all around us
Will be crushed with a thing called LOVE.

John W. Carpenter

Love Is

Love is something special to me and it comes from the heart.
Love is something grand you see, but not when your split apart.

Love is something that can't go wrong when you know that you belong.
Love is like that wind that whispers in your ear,
"I love you," softly, "my dear!"

Love is like that roaring thunder and that rain.
Love is also like that rainbow that takes away all the pain.

Love is like that gentle tear that falls down your cheek.
Love is like that telephone call you've been waiting for all week.

Love is something indescribable and hard to understand or comprehend.
Love is very hard and very difficult but easy to begin!

Clarissa Ramirez

The Marble Trees

From the marble trees are the leaves of names whispered by the loved who feel your faces like the blind.
They rub you with the color of bronze to help them believe that you will stay young forever.
In order of death you are carved in formation polished like your pride which shows in every letter of your mangled bodies.
Do not wait for the insanity of explanations from heathens as to why you died in vain.
Even now you duck behind the shadows of the marble trees to find comfort in a world you can't escape.
Do you see the guards the government sent to protect you decades too late?
Reach from the jungle your troubled hands and embrace your youth that knew it was better to be alive.
Let your lungs blow out the candle of fear and see that your bravery turned cowards into heroes.
Your names will be forever praised on the mirror of time by soldiers unborn,
and they will one day find their peace in the swaying of the marble trees...

Brandon Foley

Untitled

Honey, I love you, honest I do.
Love's deep, in my soul, love that is true.
My heart starts to patter. My heart skips a beat.
Body just tingles from head to my feet.
Passions, Unlimited!! Waiting to burst.
Only you, my darling, can ever quench that thirst.
I think of you constant. Morning to noon.
Waiting so patient. You'll be home real soon.
Passionately, wantingly, when you're not here, babe.
I dream of loving you in so many ways!
Of passing the time embraced in your arms.
Whispering sweet nothings; using all of my charms.
As we lay together, I look in your eyes
How beautifully intelligent and cunningly wise
Much sweeter than honey, as delicate as a rose.
Softer than midnight, gentle as a doe.
Lips to entice me. A smile that could kill.
Your sweet juices fill me. TILT!!! What a thrill!

Gay M. Chan

Untitled

There is beauty in all sorrow,
There is laughter through the pain,
And the end of each tomorrow
Brings sunshine through the rain.

Stephanie Ott

Untitled

The shadow of the clouds hangs over us,
low and glum,
After the deadly storm that struck upon
An innocent one.
Rain still showers over the hills of
Sadness and pain,
It seems to linger there quietly, and forever
Will remain.
As time passes on the rain
May clear,
But in some hearts it will not be forgotten, and the one
Who was lost will always be there.

Alyssa Friebel

A Flight

Fly to your Destiny oh Spirit of Man
lowly creatures as we are acceptable in God's Sight.
Who are we but God's chosen to do with as He pleases.
Kindled in the fire of the spirit and refined as pure Gold.

Why does man question his authenticity when God has revealed it so? That man is what he appears to be and God Himself the invisible but visible truth. God is showing his Handiwork! He makes us, bends us, and gives us of Himself. Who are you to ask what His eternal plans are, the day of His coming and Day of Judgment?

What is my compensation for abiding by the rules and playing the game? The Psalmist and the Prophet have said; For He has made us and not we ourselves. Play your part as it as been apportioned to you. Reach for the stars and land on them like a great eagle flies to the mountain tops. Fix your eyes on the prize. There you will receive God's peace... and as you look through window of life a mirror will reflect your image and the wonder of God.

Fly to your Destiny oh Spirit of Man
lowly creatures as we are acceptable in God's Sight.

Jerald Morris

Ode To Mathematics

Numbers, letters, and arithmetic
Make no sense when beat by a mental stick
Quadratics, equations, and raticands
Ordinates, integers, and dividends
Inequalities with division, domains of relation
It has to be the weirdest thing in the nation
Year after year and day after day
Mathematics is never done the same way
After learning real numbers, it's just not enough
Then they give you imaginary of all the strange stuff
Just what is the point, oh I'll never know
I guess I'll take Greek so my English won't show.

Ann Gandy

My Love

Have you ever loved someone that didn't love you back,
my love is not a joke it is not an act.

My love for you is like the purest of gold,
not to be cheapened and never withhold.
To say this is not true would be a lie amongst lies,
hidden away in a dark deep disguise.

I tell you my love that this is all true,
whenever I see you my mind has no clue!

Corinna Guerrero

Thanksgiving Day

If having a day for Thanksgiving
  Makes all of us more aware
Of the blessings we have as a nation
  In this beautiful land that we share,
If it draws friends and families together
  And shows us how much we care,
If it makes us more willing to answer
  The call for love everywhere —
Then, having a day for Thanksgiving
  In itself is an answer to prayer.

As Americans observe Thanksgiving
  The Pilgrim tradition holds sway.
We relish turkey and pumpkin pie —
  Feasting keynotes the day.
But undergirding all of this
  It's awesome when we stay
Mindful that our heritage
  Highlights the need to pray
By setting aside at harvest time
  A special Thanksgiving Day.

Emily M. Landstrom

Mi Vida Oscoro

I see visions before me
Making me remember happier times
Causing me to sadden.

I feel so lost without your hands to keep me on track
Following you gladly.

I need your smile to light my way
Or I am surrounded by darkness.

I need your love to protect and warm me
Or I am vulnerable and frigid.

I need your voice to remind me I am loved
Or I am in despair.
Most of all I need to know you are
And always will be there
Or I have no reason for living.

You are my heart, soul, breath - my life.
When you leave my world's door shuts
And I am locked inside.

Angela Hunt

"Thoughts"

I am not going to say that I don't want too much out of life.
Materialistic, I am not.
Recognition, I do want.
There is nothing wrong with reaching for the top.

Ten years from now...where will I be?
In Italy, sipping some wine.
Perhaps, making effective relations with individuals.
Is it possible that one of my clients becomes a secret admirer?

I must snap out of my daydreaming!
My professor is handing out a survey.
Well... Isn't this something?
The first question wants me to describe myself in twenty five
words or less...
Now, what shall I say?

Janet M. Suarez

A Flower of Friendships

When my last day on earth I share with you.
May my casket be adorned with a flower or two.

For in death my feet will be laying still,
No longer to pick a flower growing on a hill.

No longer will my hand caress the petals on a rose,
Nor smell the dandelions my grand child holds up to my nose.

No longer will my eyes be hold beautiful arrays.
Or will I smell their sweet fragrance like in my yesterdays.

One last flower to share together my friend,
And I shall be waiting beyond death,
For when we shall meet again.

Grace A. Carlson

Love Is Forever

Love is forever, forever we are
Maybe we'll dine under the big white star
I love you in May, I love you in June
I love you every morning and every afternoon
Love is forever, forever we are
Maybe the sky fell in a sea of tar
I love you in, I love you out
I love you when we're both about
Love is forever, forever we are
Maybe we'll drive away in a brand new car
I love you now, I love you then
I love you when the world will end
Love is forever, forever we are
Come and let's dine under the big white star.

Chenika Alexander

Untitled

We shared a wonderful life
Me and Phyllis, my darling wife

15 years of wedded bliss
Could we want, we asked, for more than this?

Then one day she became quite ill
The diagnosis was a bitter pill

Tests revealed that she had cancer
Her doctors searched for an answer

The months that followed, to be sure
Were unbearable; they could find no cure

So together we would not grow old
Her illness was terminal we were told

She was taken from me one July day
To express my feelings, there is no way

Her absence leaves me terribly sad
I truly miss the life we had

This precious woman I loved so dearly
My life goes on, but oh, just barely

But Phyllis, when my life on earth is through
I hope to spend eternity with you

Jack J. Coppola

Tree Women

Tree women dance in the wind.
They are adorned in rose, plum, and silver.
They toss their colored scarves into the breeze.
They spread their fantastic colors
For every being to see.

Rosa Ursetta

"Halloween"

Scary, hairy halloween
Meanest things I've ever seen
Come out at me in the dark
Makes me quake and clutch my heart
Behind each bush there's an eerie sound
Rats, black cats and spiders around
Headless horsemen come riding by
Bats come darting out of the sky
A witch floats by on her broom
Casting a shadow on the big, yellow moon
The moon drifts behind a cold, dark cloud
Something goes "hiss" then squawks real loud
Monsters & goblins chase in the dark
I hear a shrill voice warning "hark! hark!"
Nothing but terror and hearts that flutter
Makes you want to hold on to each other
It feels just like a scary dream
I try to wake before I scream
Oh! how I wish that I was home
And halloween was past and gone

Eilene Meadors

No Reason

In fifteen years this is all I've obtained,
meaningless pieces of life to frame.
If to be in the same circumstance,
as fifteen more finishes their dance.
With time again in endless motion,
bring reason to our failed experiments.
Through the shadowing passages we drift,
what's to remember of our deeds.
Natures anguish holds starving,
as do the candles' flame.
Reason with the darkness that falls,
cry not for yonder light.
Thoughtless dreams of yesterday,
bring forth new insight.

Daniel Laird Jeffers

"Memories"

Memories of marriage fill a woman's heart
Memories of a love that was never torn apart
Memories of a father remains for five girls
Memories of a childhood full of pink dresses and
hair with curls
Memories of a grand father remain for those like me
Memories of the man that I loved faith fully
Memories are all we have now that he is gone
Memories of a man who woke up at dawn
Memories of his strength and his very gentle way
Memories of the man who is in our hearts today.

Andrea Nichole Poole

Illusion

Bits and pieces just fall into place.
Memories of happy times we left without a trace.
And if I try, I know inside, I still can see your face,
smiling down on me,
bringing security.

But it's all so surreal,
and I'm not sure about the things I used to feel.
So, now I must conceal
all that cannot be.
all the insecurity,
of loving you.

Debbie K. Drake

Friends are Forever

As we come upon another year, plenty of
memories with many a tear.
The friendship we've shared get stronger
each year,
Always understanding and always near.
The laughs we've had, the time we've cried,
too many to count, nothing to hide.
To give and receive is what a friendship make,
Always we give and never we take.
As another day passes, a thought to keep,

Friends Are Forever
Forever We Reap
Always,

Carolyn Wallace

You and I Together

Not a day will pass that I won't think of you.
Miles cover the ground I've walked
But I'll only remember ground-travelled with you
If words could say just how I feel
For them I would trade my every meal.
So deep inside you'll always know
where you can turn to
It will tell you just how special "we" are
Not just"you"
Not just "me"
It is "we"
Hand in hand
"we" walk
"we" talk
"we" share
"we" give
"we" you and I Love

Crystal Tanner

Mind's Fate

Growth is to ascend, rise above the depths
Mind expands with time direction is the test

Conscience it is fragile pictures etched in stone
Some do last a lifetime many change in tone

Much affects the masses morals the dilemma
Options traverse time, differs each life's schema

What difference can one make? Universe so vast
Mi-nute a single thought, yet gaze into the past...

History unto present self and indignation
Material obsessions a world of degradation

What of all the others? A struggle to survive
A race, a creed, a color unchosen tossed aside

Each conscience is a universe pauper unto potentate
Goodness or iniquity? In this, lies all man's fate.

David Anthony Garcia

The Journey

Death is like harmful song
Never caring if its lyrics are wrong.
It takes away the ones you love
Quick in flight like a mourning dove.
Hoping, yet dreading the day that we must face
That strange and wonderful place,
Death is like a harmful song
That lasts eternally long.

Beth Jones

My Fortress

Simply a secluded place I call
mine
A place to sit and think among the
pine
A place to hear the trees whisper and
sing
Almost as peaceful as the church bell's
ring
In spring a green mist sleeps with hope,
not doubt
In summer everything is alive
and about
In autumn my place is informal and
welcoming
In winter the surroundings are peaceful and
tranquilizing
All these things are what compose
My Fortress.

Cheryl Lynn Tepsa

Yesterdays

The unforgettable moments of all the yesterdays
moments filled with happiness
moments filled with so much joy and love
moments of a beautiful relationship yesterdays
moments of the good times
if only those yesterday memories could come alive always
maybe my love there will be another moment in time
to bring your memory alive within
yesterday moments year after year

Gerri L. Brickle

Gift of Night

As night sleeps through the starlit sky,
Moonbeams carry God's love from up high.
You can hear angels breath a warm sigh,
And see heaven through all nature's tie.

Small clouds are sleeping, they're all tucked in bed,
From dreamytime tales that raindrops read.
Mother Earth rocks trees, with something she said.
Animals all slumber, without much dread.

As dreams approach your mind to recall
The peace you can find in this comforting lull,
Let slumber take over, on you befall,
As God's arms cradle you all.

Judith T. Shelton Tilman

"Summer's Night Sky"

I stared into the sky tonight,
Moonless night, the stars so bright!
To the south, summer constellations there,
Sagittarius, scorpio, though I can't tell just where.
To the west, a lonely evening star,
Bright sentinel, shining so near, so far!
Back north, big dipper, and yes, little too,
And the big "W" of Cassiopia comes into view.
Then overhead and slightly to the east,
The milky way, dimmer, yet awesome at the very least!
Just a few special moments on a cool summer's night,
Those myriad stars, a loving God's delight!

Garry Hinkle

Dream Escape

I often find myself drifting away
more and more so each day
I could be dancing in a field of flowers
or sailing on an emerald bay

Wherever I am, I always feel free
Always content on just being me
No angry faces screaming unkind words
No tears that leave me unable to see

This other world is a sacred place
People have love for the entire human race
Where the birds always sing and the sun always shines
Where the past is gone without a trace

When reality captures back my mind
I am again ready to seek and find
The world made up of treasured dreams
The world that keeps me alive inside

Deidre Maturo

Old Glory

I see you fly,
More now that there is a war going on.
I know that you have seen many wars,
and I hope that there won't be many more.
I hope that we will fly you all the time,
Not just when there is a war.
I hope we will make you proud so I say this,
"fly old glory fly"
Forever more in times of peace
as well as times of war,
fly old glory fly forever more.

Debbie Knight

"It"

In reality it is valuable
More powerful than any
visible existence
It separates class,
It augmentates itself,
It is known for it's greed
to a race called human
It can obtain any form of pleasure
whether it be human flesh to destruction of
the world by means of arms
It is worshiped by those who have not
and wasted by those who have too much
Evidence of its popularity
is shown in every corner of the
world, in any colour, shape, or form
A necessity maybe, a friend it is not
It never lasts for long as wonderful, as it
may sound, it saddens my heart
for the one thing it could not get is the love
that I have for you.

Doug Anthony Gardiner

Rainbow

I am a rainbow
My life is full of color and brightness
My colors are red, purple, pink and yellow
Red is for love
Purple is for trust
Pink stands for peace
Yellow stands for anything and everything
you wish for.

Cassie Brown

The Time Is Now

Grandfather's hands hold no promise of
moving forward in time.

Time has no tomorrow—only the anticipation
of future events which have been generated
within the mind.

Yesterday is gone—leaving only an undiluted
recollection of memories—a thought process
which has been stored until the hands of time
cease to move.

This very moment is the only time we will know
to be exact.
And NOW, this moment has passed more rapidly than
the breathe we have just drawn.

Donna L. Murphy

Eyes Of Leticia Mendez

My beloved Leticia,
My beloved flower of Quetzal.

In the dance of youth I found you
Oh! And how time hits me.
I am always hurting.
I do not comprehend.
All I know is that I love you.
Blindly I love you.
I do not care, if you bring me suffering.

Green is the color of life,
Green is the color of your eyes.
You will always live in my heart,
Even though you are far
You are always near,
In my suffering,
in my laughter

My beloved flower of Quetzal.
I love you.
Never will I,
Forget you.

Alexander Ocampo

My Morning Walk

I left the house at six on the nose
my body awake from my head to my toes,
For a brisk walk and a talk with God
asking for peace both here and abroad.
It's a wonderful feeling, invigorating,
hearing the birds sing and meditating.
From family and friends my thoughts always stray
when seeing the new leaves in the breeze gently sway.
When I pass the church, the sun on the window reflected,
makes my heart remember the friends I've neglected.
So, dear God, please give me the strength to continue to walk,
and I know you are listening to me as I talk.
I thank you for all you have given,
but thank you most for the life I am living.

Geraldine Page Bess

The Diamond

One immortal tear
shed for the sorrow of love long separated from love
shed for the joy of loves together at last
gathering light
turning the light into fiery flashes of love
given back to my eyes.

Martha M. Pope

The Bunny

Deep down in my heart, I feel this pain,
my bunny died and I can't explain.
For so long he's been around,
now suddenly I have to do without.
My dog is happy, he finally won,
he's got him now, and the bunny is gone.
Forgive him now, I have to do,
how can I, for it was cruel.
Life unfair, I feel the change,
once more, things will never be the same.
My children ask what they have done,
there friend has been taken from them now.
So bad we'll feel for a long long time,
till we can look back on him and smile.

Elke Mullins

The Grass

Alone lying on the grass, sharing stories of our past
My ears soak up all thy fantasies
Clouds dancing above our heads, finding between us our common
threads.
Staring together into starry seas, I feel thee cuddle up next to me.
My hands slowly move from their place to trace the soft curves of
thy face. Tender passion slowly starts to bloom. My lips touch
thy sweet smooth skin, ye gazing eyes pull me in, like rain falling
in the afternoon. Our secrets shared b'neath a silent moon. Beauty
melting on my fingertips. I move again to caress thy lips.
Thy streams of hair across my chest, shining, reflecting starlight's
tricks. I lie so still in heaven's rest, my arms embracing the ripest
breasts.
If time could freeze solid to a block of ice, 'tis this moment I
would suffice, that I may save it and let it melt, an intimacy that
I should spend then after freeze it, and enjoy this moment forever
again.

Christopher Biemeck

The Lie

They were sitting on their pedestals, although their feet were clay;
My eyes beheld their perfection, no faults within them, lay.

I gave unto them, one by one, my utmost admiration,
While they were casting pearls, fraught with devastation.

Be careful of the glittering gold, they let run thru' their fingers,
It might just be a pot of "Bold," with aftermath that lingers.

So houses built upon the sand, and lined with many windows,
From without, 'tis spotless, but within, not splendid.

If the rose that you are holding, crumbles in your hand,
The perfect thing of beauty, now scattered in the sand;

The pedestals, will, likewise, fall unto the ground,
Adoration, becomes bewildered, and thorns, replace the crown.

Ann Riggle

Mother At 80

She knows too well how age can disappoint the lovely dreams
of youth.
How once bright and delicate beauty has faded in the mirror
of truth.
The unfulfilled yearnings of so long ago are now mere
memories tucked into the corner of her mind.
And, as she reflects on how quickly life has passed her by,
it's clear that fate has not always been kind.
She's tired of fighting with the emotions of inner strife,
and hopes death will be a soft whisper as she nears the
end of her life.

Hanne Hartmann-Phipps

"My Grandpa"

He's a person who I'll never forget,
my grandpa.
He'd tell you about his past,
And you'd sit and listen as he talked.
But now he's gone so I have to move on.
Because that's what he'd want me to do.
God, I miss him so.
But it was his time to go.
So I have to wipe away the tears,
And sit back and remember the years,
That I spent with my grandpa.
I wish I could see him once more,
Just to say hi grandpa, how are you?
But I know I'll see him again in a better place.
So until then I'll have to keep on missing him,
my grandpa.

Amie Ludwig

The Man I Wish I Had Known

One bright and sunny day
My grandpa quietly slipped away.

I often look up at the sky above
I hear my dad's voice talk of him with love.

Sometimes I think I see him in the clouds
I imagine that I hear him speak out loud.

I was not born when he was on this earth
It was two years from his death until my birth.

A hard-working and respected man he had been
Mostly serious with no nonsense, without a grin.

He was tall and slender with a slightly gruff voice
With soil under his nails, he was a farmer by choice.

When he was old and his hair was white
He had a stroke which stole his will and might.

After several months of a deep, dark sleep
God took him to heaven and left others to weep.

My parents keep his memory alive for my brother, sister, and me
They help us know how wonderful and loving he used to be.

Connie Call Sanders

"Dear World"

You have been cruel to me
My heart bleeds in many different ways.
An undesirous seed unready to ripe.
The chains of death hold me in captivity,
and the innocent victim walks shallow in
the depth of thy shadow.
The agony my body quivers into a hot sea
of uncertainty.
Too many times I have failed and too many
times I shall fail once more.
Loneliness runs through my steamy veins
like a hungry wolf.
Seas and seas I have cried for thee,
I drowned many a time.
Why do I deserve this monopolized life?
World, you're an unthoughtful creature,
and you make me be whatever your
unforgettable horrifications may be.

Deanna K. Lucas

Mary Ann

Mary Ann, Mary Ann, how sweet is thy name;
My heart is a flutter - I hope yours is the same.

Since I have met you - I haven't been the same;
I believe if I don't see you soon - I will go insane.

Now - what a state and a terrible condition;
My heart plays a tune - a sweet rendition.

Every day that passes by;
My feelings for you are so high.

O! Mary Ann, you completely fill up my senses'
All day long the thought of you is unrelentless.

To hear you laugh and be happy is all that matters;
You make all my fears and worries totally scatter.

To see that wonderful smile brings me great joy;
And that cute little curl of your lip is so coy!

To be with you all the day long is such pleasure;
The fond memories of these days I will always treasure.

The very touch of you is so divine.
All I can think of will you be mine?
this Valentine!

David Snapka

"The Same Old Nothing"

Lonely tears are falling while you're still here
My heart sees the future
It allows me to feel on coming pain
You'll be gone soon
How am I supposed to live without you?
Possibly you'll come back, and that's why I'm still here
A simple muscle movement can wipe me away forever
Black is my favorite color
I wish to see it more often
That's why I watch you from behind closed eyes
And why I stay behind closed doors
is none of your business
Who knew life could hurt so much?
It is that, or just constantly depressed me?
I'd use a syringe to suck out imbalances
rather than to put them in
You don't and won't ever understand me
But it worth feeling the way I do
It's funny the looks I can get from you

Jennifer Korolchuk

In Remembrance of My Loving Mom

I never got the chance to say good-bye to you.
My innocent tears cried.
Breaking my heart that you're not here.
Never to come home again.
Never to smile or to weep with me.

I watched my precious sisters and brother leave
to be cared for by another family.
I see them occasionally, but the strong bond's gone.
We're not growing together to share our smiles or tears.

I always wanted to blame you for everything.
All I could think of was to cry for home-sweet-home.
But I knew you would want me to be strong.
Get through the tough times and go on with the future.

There are some shades of doubt but you will always be my shield.
I know that you're there following and protecting my shadow.
Guiding me through with your hope, love and faith.

You're Mom who will always be in my heart
and it's never a good-bye to you.

Emilie J. Butler

Poem of Passion

The passionate sound of our
nighttime lovemaking echoes into the
morning sun. Our passionate sweat
becomes the morning dew on the
flower petals of life and may we
join together night after night after night.

Christopher Stile

Missing You

Since you've been gone away from me
my life's not what it used to be

The space you filled is empty now
If it can be refilled I know not how

I wrote this poem to help you see
how much you really mean to me

There's others here to help me through
But they'll never be anything like you

I miss you Summer, with all my heart
Just promise me we'll never totally part,
for that would truly break my heart

Keep in touch through all the years
through the laughter and the tears

You'll be my very best friend
Separated yet together to the very end.

Andria Lyn Ross

Elizabeth Ann

You're my precious little granddaughter that I never got to hold.
My love for you will last through the years, as I grow very old.
You caused a big commotion, Dear,
And I wish you still were here.
I watched as Mommy first touched you, with tears of wonder and
love in her eye
And I only wish I could have held you before you had to die.
Why God took you, we will never know;
I love you and wish you didn't have to go.
I cried so much when you went away,
And I thank you for your fight to stay.
And since you're up in heaven, look down on Mom and Dad
And guide them in a happy life like they wanted you to have.

Eleanor M. Graham

The War

I made one mistake, now I'm trapped in a war.
My mind against body like waves on the shore.
I'm 20 years old with so much to give,
But I have the AIDS virus with six months to live.

There in the darkness, just beyond my grasp,
Lies my hopes, my dreams, my memories past.
There in the distance too far to see,
Lies what's to come and places to be.

A deep, dark tunnel an ending love;
Memories fade as daylight comes.
Promises were broken as though nothing was said,
While hopes are destroyed, and heart-aches are fed.

Trembling with fear, I wake in the night
The tunnel is shrinking and has lost all it's light.
The monster is winning, I feel his breath on my face,
It's the end of the war, It's the end of the race.

Brenda D. Yurow

Voice of the Angel

I'm your guardian angel, I'm here to assist.
My purpose is helping you want to exist.

The bridge of reality, all must cross.
The death of an artist is everyone's loss.

You're filled with sadness, I know the pain.
Controlling the sadness will be your gain.

Life is hard, but can also be sweet.
Inner strength will bring to the pain, defeat.

The love and laughter that you bring to all
Destiny has brought you to make your call.

Confusion demanding that you make a choice.
Don't want to hear it! Go away little voice.

My door always open so we that we can talk.
Down the road of confusion, together we'll walk.

Pain from the past is still in existence.
You can overcome the pain with great persistence.

Be brave, be strong, for you are the boss.
The world is not ready for such a great loss.

Jeanette Trauth

Alone

I was tired of being alone I needed someone to be with
My thoughts landed upon Joy so I picked up the phone
and dialed Joy's home.
Her phone rang and rang I was so eager to hear her voice
so I could tell her I was tired of being alone.

Then my call was answered my heart fluttered with joy
Until I heard
"This is Joy I'm not home"

I hung up the phone and almost started to weep
I was still so tired of being alone

So I picked up the phone and dialed Brenda's number to
to let her know that I was home alone

Brenda's phone rang and rang but I received no answer
so I hung up the phone and thought to myself
Man I am tired of being alone.

Ernest Richard Foster

Image of Doubt

The night was growing darker,
My unanswered dream still longing to come true,
My wishful thinking
I'd soon be close to you.
If aware of the idea,
Lord knows what you'd say-
Your feelings are the same,
Or laugh and head the other way.
Every thought that passes my mind throughout the year
Only entails the feelings I want you near.
I sat there hopelessly waiting
For the moment you'd walk through my door.
When the awkward feeling mutual
Neither one of us knowing what to say.
One of us knew but wasn't revealing.
I wish I could tell you
How long I've cared and how much I love you.
As a river continues to flow,
My imagination continues to run wild,
As does my love continue for you.

Becky Weir

Taken By Storm

The darkened billows roll over me eclipsing
  my very soul,
Black sulking waves crash on every side.
I am tossed—lost—out of control.
My small vessel is thrown—hurled by the unceasing tide.
The lamented wind seduces away my hope;
The echoing thunder gnaws at my flesh;
I give in—cannot think or cope.
My last sight— lightning dancing the dance of death.

I am awakened by the gentle nudgings of harmony and peace,
The balance of my being has returned full sway.
No hint of the storm, the pain has ceased;
My Captain's voice breaks the silence, "Anchors away."
My soul leaves the vessel and soars into the unknown,
Here no storm rages—here the light eternally reigns.
No more flesh, no more blood, no more bone!
Peace is the body in the Captain's domain.

Drew Taylor

More Than Yesterday Less Than Tomorrow

Friend, I'm not a prophet, mystic, nor seer,
  My wealth is not in riches the world considers dear.
  Witness am I, treasure I see,
  Love is truth, and truth will set you free.
More than yesterday, less than tomorrow,
Love is the key to life, in eternity.
More than yesterday, less than tomorrow,
Love will always be blessed and heavenly.
More than yesterday, less than tomorrow,
Love and live each day life's joy and sorrow.
On that final day, love will lead the way,
To more than yesterday, less than tomorrow.

Durbin H. Downey

Brush Strokes

The canvas is huge, seemingly endless,
Naked blank beginning broken by life's first cry
The brush comes alive, the pallet bursts with colors,
The meshing, the building, the living begins.

Brush strokes, not missing a beat, filling in every space
Vibrant reds, yellows, oranges remember happy times, good times,
Greys, browns and blacks recall moments of despair,
Blues, greens, and purples fill in the many emotions of life.

The canvas fills up with memories, day by day
Edging toward the end, again blank, coming round full circle
No one knows when the brush will declare the canvas finished
and it will move to that dark unknown.
I watched twice as your brush strayed into that darkness
As I witnessed that "brush with death"
But each time you fought your way back onto the canvas
And I cried as I heard your words,
"I couldn't leave you. I didn't have a chance to say goodbye."

Bernice Epstein

Alone

I am drowning in the sorrows and cries that haunt me.
Nobody can hear me, nobody cares to listen.
My clothes hide me and protect me from the waves.
But as the waves hit harder and harder
the more my clothes weaken.
So the more weaker I get.
The waves don't take me with them
I am only an obstacle.
I am alone
there is no one else to experience
the waves, the weakness, and the sorrow.

Deanna Doyle

Do You Believe in a Heaven?

Please, Believe in Me First

Oh my child, I know you're not ready
  Neither am I...and I've never been
So I just cannot let you come into this world
  So,...I'll send you there
    I'll send you where...
....Where angels such as you splash splendid ways
    not to decay but to absently play
    not to destroy
      or to employ
        the absent follow
        the absolute swallow
    of choice not yours
  But a voice all yours
    for all us on the planets
      to lush fruit—fully hear
        in our dreams.
In our dreams
  And in your wake
I'll be joining you soon.

Alexander Nishimura Jr.

Helen

Oh! Helen town of mystic with your German red rooftops
Nestled in the mountain tops on high.
Winding roads lead to your body
That brings vacationers from all over the world.
The Chattahoochee River runs through your veins.
Like blood rushing through a human heart.
The town is cradled in your bosom as a child is to its mother.
Your soul is the towns people always friendly, always courteous.
Oh! Helen town of mystic
The horse drawn carriages line your streets
So do beautiful flowers that reach for the sun
Vacationers are here from all over the world. Hear the laughter.
See the smiles. Smell the aroma of fresh baked goods.
Open cafes line the mighty Chattahoochee River.
Where tubers ride the mighty white water.
Laughter fills the river. As gladness fills your heart.
People enjoying themselves like God intended
Oh! Helen town of mystic God would be proud of you!
The joy you bring to people the laughter in their hearts.
A day to remember for we are all God's Children.

Ann Brown Hurlburt

Prisoner of Love

Hold me close, hold me tight
Never leave from my sight.
I was slow to say these words
For now we are separate and hurt.
Cells so plain and bars of steel.
Tears roll from my eyes for pain they feel.
I try to reach for you but my hand is blocked
By glass, reality, and clocks that don't stop.
All I can do is wait for the time to come
When we are reunited again and become one.
So many things yet to be discovered.
So much pain we have to recover.
I have faith in all we do.
For I now know there's nothing we can't get through.
Love is now putting us to the test.
I just ask you, keep holding on to me and
Love me, for God will do the rest.

Jazman Lopez

Being a True Friend

Lord, please help me to be a loyal friend,
Never to criticize just to comprehend,
A friend that is a friend in deed,
Never forgetting the worlds ceaseless need,
Please give me one day at a time,
Keeping me in stride with that will of Thine,
Perhaps as days come and go,
You will teach me specially to know,
The road to you some poor lost souls to show,
Peace, goodwill, friendship to bestow,
Lend to everyone a helping hand,
Teach them to pray and understand,
To strive for the best against great odds,
Never to give up, to see the silver lining through dark clouds,
Help me not to ask for love, but to give it and be kind,
To be able to cope with hardships everywhere that I find,
Let me be a volunteer and do the work you want me to do,
To seek, to find what in life is true,
Please reveal to me my life's destiny,
Thank you for letting me be the friend you want me to be.

Georgia Gloria Hamil

"Bull Rider"

When you were born.
No one knew you would be taken by a horn.
You rodeoed from east to west.
Also ridden with the best.
There was a battle with Red Rock.
No doubt you had to be a tough jock.
You won four out of seven.
We all know you rest in heaven.
In Cheyenne you took your draw.
Who knew it would be your final call.
After all was said.
They pronounced you dead.
You've reached many goals.
Forever you'll be in our hearts and souls.

Amy Eaton

"Now That I'm All Alone"

Now that I'm all alone,
No one seems to telephone.

Because I must admit,
I never was a big hit.

And when I stop and think,
I didn't dance or go to a skating rink.

Didn't play cards so very hot,
But with my man I meant a lot.

Seems only yesterday he called me dear,
And I felt mighty great when he was near.

So I look at it this old way,
He's just gone for a single day.

We loved each other with all our might,
And I remember that by day and night.

Still I hear those words so fine,
Now that I'm alone you still are mine.

As I close my eyes for a night of sleep,
I try not to break down and weep.

But just look up to God and pray dear,
Now that I'm all alone you'll still be near.

Elizabeth Standt

Hiding

I found myself a hiding place tonight.

It is covered with the warmth of love.
Not a soul can see me and I wander my eyes
to take in glorious visions.
It's quiet in the darkness.
I see a moth twirling her body in time with
airy motion as though a dancer in flight.
The stars wink down at me for they know—-
I can hear cricket sounds.
So peaceful- so calm.
I can barely contain myself and let out a sigh..
Now I am found and once more return to unfantasy.

Francesca Mantione

Visions

I thought of you,
not only in this eve,
but on countless ones before.
It was only last night that you
come to visit me in a dream.
You stood there, like a mighty oak.
Straight, and tall, and strong.
You gazed into my eyes,
yet said not a word.
I was certain you could see into my soul,
and knew every thought.
My heart pounded fiercely,
as I reached out to you.
I stroked your hand with mine.
Then ever so gently,
I touched your cheek with my warm wanting lips.
You smiled,
and in that very moment,
I knew perfection.

Elizabeth Steinhilber

"The Lake that Sparkles like Diamonds"

There are water gems that sparkle and shine —
not the kind of gems you wear.
There are moments divine that are cherished for life
and you'll find them invariably rare.

There's a blue lake that sparkles like diamonds
where fir trees thrust upward in green
Against huge boulders with patches of snow
where rocks majestically lean.

Such beauty is stored in the memory
where later can be brought to mind.
'Tis food for the soul and worth more than gold
for it's a treasure that's hard to find.

Bess Huber

A Pearl

Nature sometimes has a way
Of turning plainess and ordinary
Into beauty sometimes quite extraordinary.

Out of a most unlikely place
Comes wonders this world to grace.

An ugly larva belies
The beauty of its issue; a butterfly.

The rough, unlikely oyster, in time produces
A glowing pearl, with all the pleasure it educes.

But the most wondrous thing of all to me
Is that I could be part of bringing forth
A gem, a beauty...My Stephanie.

Dom A. Apikos

Field of My Dreams

I walked into the vacant field -
Not thinking of what it might yield,
First I noticed someone else had tread the open path.
So I slowed down, rather than too fast!
Noticing a new vicious seed - it had to be the devil.

It took time to gather my thoughts and remain civil,
The beauty of flowers stood strong and tall
Amazed and wondered if there was someone I should call?
As my hand reached for the flower -
The stem bent over and my dream seemed like on hour.

Having stood in silence so still -
Gave me thoughts, "Maybe I will."
My clothes were tattered and torn
Yet you left me time to scorn.
Tired, bare, sore feet told me it was almost defeat.

There were acres and acres to trod -
Then I caught my first glimpse of God,
Finding my way out gave me plenty to think about.
After wondering down to one of the streams
I was welcomed to the "Field Of My Dreams."

Hilda Sumwalt

Mastered By Evil, She Mastered Their Souls

She forgot, she forgave. Nothing dulled her vision,
nothing dulled her thoughts. She adopted another,
she betrayed me. She helped her hurt me,
she helped her lie, buy pretending the forbidden
was beyond the sky. I believed her,
I trusted her thoughts, until she broke my soul, my life, my thoughts!
I can't forgive her, I can't forget, I hate her,
I won't trust another to defy me the right to grow.
Why can't they see it, how can they let go?
What makes them trust another, who is veiled with the unshown?
Why can't they see the real her, what mastered there souls?
Who killed my family, who let go? I do not remain here, I did not let go? She shall not remain here, to leave the unknown,
because with darkness betrayal comes slow? I loved you mother,
what made you forgive her and forget me?

Fiona Garrison

The Wall

At first just an empty space,
now black marble so many names.
Friends and family lovers too.
They died for our freedom,
Yeah for me and you.
They didn't ask why,
just went to a distant land to fight and die.
Families cry for the ones that are lost.
Don't ever forget what they did,
they paid the highest price.
If it wasn't for them
There would be no you or me.
Survivors come back, some stand tall.
Others are spit on call them the clowns.
Emotional price just to high,
they took their own lives, now it's goodbye.

John Hacker

Tales of a Deadbeat Sergeant

In the beginning I loved him.
Now, I'm not so sure.
Korea has come between us,
like many tours before.
He is defending some foreign country,
while I'm home manning the fort!

His life has always been an adventure,
but he is denying life's precious joys!
The giggles and laughter of a child —
he doesn't acknowledge he has a little boy!

I read to him his daddy's letters,
the photos he adores.
And tell him his father is a hero,
a soldier who died in the war.
He will never know his father ignored him
in favor of women and war...

Now, I realize I must leave him,
for love, life and the sake of my little boy.
In the end I will always love him,
after all, he did give me one of life's precious joys!

Dawn Serna

The Window

Picture a window, what do you see?
Now picture yourself... are you out there,
or in here? are you? or are you me.
Now again the window. What do you see?
you see the draperies with every detail
or a stark, plain frame the paint peeling
Again the window what do you see...
are you you or are you me?
Sometimes when I look through the window
I see what's inside, outside can never be
Other times I see people, they never see me.
look out my window, what do you see?
Do you see you or do you see me.
Can you see through another man's eyes?
look again towards the window, do you dare to see?
Forget what you know, forget what you see!!!
Each person lives a life separate and unique
See through my eyes, can you see me?
Picture a window, what do you see?
If you see yourself, you can't see me

Elizabeth Anne Fawcett

A Moving Experience

"This house is too big", we often say,
Now that our kids are grown and gone away—
Save one, who in our hearts will always stay.

Too many windows to wash and rooms to clean,
Too much grass to mow and garden to grow.
Too many leaves to rake before all the snow!

But it will not be easy
  to leave the house
  where our kids grew up
  —and we grew old!

Eleanor Vought

Il Neige

It comes in the night,
Silently swirling, twisting and turning
Dancing and prancing and playing about
Touching the earth, without a sound,
Yet softly and subtly,
It fills up the ground.

Kathy Panza

"The Snap of Your Finger"

God, I thought we met this November
Now you say it was last September.

Time flies by with joy and sadness
As we careen through life in fogs of madness
Following a path and finding a role
To gain inner peace and achieve our goal.

So few are able to reach their peak
Or gain the insight that they seek.
Yet some make the grade and do great things
While the rest just flutter in the wings.

Which ever way one opts to go
Enjoy the ride, 'cause who's to know
The perfect plan to spend one's time.
It goes too fast, and as we climb
We lose the power to just love life
And end up moaning about our strife.

Evelyn Schaffhauser

Daughter Loss

Who! Is this daughter? I gave birth to;
Nursed, nurtured, and protected.
I thought, I knew her well!
And had here everlasting love.
To my amazement; I found I failed.
Now, I wonder, if I failed her sisters and brothers too.
I feel, this emptiness in my heart;
And regret; I didn't know;
A real mother, I couldn't be to this lost one.
To admit failure, and say "I'm sorry", may not be enough.
How does one mend the ways of the past?
Feeling unsure this can be done;
I never claimed, to be perfect in my ways.
Am sure an error; I still will make;
Before my days are numbers, and am laid to rest.
Will! This lost one be found? Or will the rest be lost too?

Beverly Dobias

Now that I Can Pray

Now before, I lay me down, for a long awaited rest;

I believe in a life above this world of yoke, I fantasize
of candy colored hearts of love, that are even more
scarlet than a dream, true love, and no pain, of truth and happiness

I will pray, for the past, and present;
For the many deeds I deserve, and for when I didn't serve;

My God is first; my family next,

For my wits, and nerves, I will pray for Salvation, that the
The Beauty, and my family's love is here to stay;

That I can, and will share more, and more as much as I can;
For a bountiful harvest, and belief, that I can survive my fears;

With a Heart of Stone that I do so in Cheer, and continue...
believe in my prayer that I have made, a foundation, that
will uphold my family from, fable in life that they will not
falter, and continue to love even in spite; if

All of these things seem to go hand, and hand, even down their
road of world possessions, remember that a prayer now
Seems to harvest, a heart full of God, and love, that begins,
Even now...

Dennis Lee Maxberry

Bike Ride

I followed you home last night.
Tires flat; limping down the highway.
Watching my speed so as not to be seen.
Stopping occasionally...
You knew I was behind, you didn't look back
I wasn't where you wanted.

Matthew William Becker

Let the Children Speak

Unfamiliar sounds I hear
Of cries calling out to me
And I know not what to do
I feel the blanket of death smothering its victims
And I see the mournful souls left behind
Their echoes haunt the memories of yesterday
And shall live in the thoughts of tomorrow
We must escape this genocide
We must find freedom
And take hold of what we believe
Set our feet on the path that leads to life
The innocence of the lamb has been swept in the rain
And what is left is cold and mysterious to the mind
Will we ever know what it is like to laugh?
Only time will tell.

Allison McClure

Live Life

A fleeting glimpse we have of life.
Of family, friends and foes alike.
Of happy moments and those of strife.
Can't slow down life try as we might.

To some it seems that life's unfair.
Troubles and pain they've had their share.
Observing others without a care.
Why me? They ask, lost in despair.

While others revel in everyday.
Eager to joust what comes their way.
They don't complain, that doesn't help.
They have acquired true sense of self.

We plan our futures, we set our goals.
Designs that really appear quite bold.
For, you see...
No time is given at our behest.
We're here one moment and gone the next.

Eddie Pabon

The Real Me

I am the Master of the art
of hiding the real me in my heart
When you look upon my face
of the true me there's not a trace
The person I am, others must not see
for I fear they wouldn't like the real me
So I wear a mask, held in place
by all those fears, I can not face
It's what I think others want to see
that I try very hard to be
Sometimes I wish it would end
when I no longer need to pretend
To remove the mask, put it on a shelf
and for once be my own true self
And it's when I'm alone I cry
for the real me that I deny

Alice Smith

Untitled

I have a friend who is in need
of love attention and self esteem
I have a friend who means a lot
who shares, and cares and tells me a lot
I have a friend who is very possessive
She wants to be the only one with me
I have a friend who is the best
except when she's depressed
I have a friend who think she's
ugly and fat, no self esteem I know for a fact.
I have a friend who wants to die
And so she makes me want to cry
I have a friend, so what can I do except say
I love you

Caroline Barber

For You......

I have written so many poems, stories and letters for you,
of our time together, but this one stands alone.
I love you... for what we are and for what we hold...
Know in your soul
that each night when I close my eyes,
I thank God for the years with you.
I love you... for what you give... for all of the sweet, melancholy
memories... I love you for your caring and protectiveness...
I love you because you always touch me.
I love you... because of those eyes, because they look
at me so many, many times... and I love those eyes because
they cried for me.
I love you...because you share your life with me.
I love you...for your pride, your confidence and
your inner strength.
I love you...for those words of yours...
Will you promise to love me...
Tharco, you are my life...my only true love.
I love you...
because you let me go.

Caroline Anne Kelly

Being Lazy on a Warm Afternoon

The cats and dogs recline on cool concrete
Of patio, or lay upon the floor,
And no one has the energy to greet
The couple selling Jesus door to door.

While palm trees' idle chatter fills the room,
I raise a hand to brush away a fly.
Gardenias fill the air with sweet perfume
While birds and bees rehearse a lullaby.

I feel a gentle breeze caress my face
And send its tendrils lightly down my arms,
Yet sunshine holds me fast in its embrace
As I surrender wholly to its charms.

Let others glorify the harvest moon,
I love a lazy summer afternoon.

Joy Ayala

Laws For Liquid In A Liquid

Brownian Motion:
Surface tension holds two drops together, and they cannot
part.

Human Emotion:
Surface tension holds two drips together, and they cannot part.

Joan Blake

Beach Lunatic

Back amidst the trash can skies
of present time Babylon
waitin' for the star of Broadway to rise
a streetlight angel touched me on the right shoulder
didn't know whether it was just bein' friendly
or was she trying to tell me
she wanted to forge a new universe
in the beach breeziness of night

This veritable orgasm of wistful dreambrain ideas
this inane wandering of void mindwords
tho desultory and infinitely
discursive
are the dreams of a spirit come forth
out of inertia
I don't consider myself a poet in any
"institutionalized" sense of the word
I am more like a beach lunatic
throwing out visions

Albert Estiamba Jr.

Shadows

I live in a shadow, where no one sees me, I follow the sparks,
Of stars in their flight, I look at you, you cannot see me,
I only come out in the cover of night,
The things that I learn, all about you, I carefully say what I'm
Afraid to write,
I follow the seasons, in the winter to summer, I look up and see
the wild geese in flight,
I feel the crispness, and the silence of autumn,
The colors are wild bright red, yellow and gold,
I feel the steel breeze of winter, it's coming on,
Fast, so windy and cold,
The mountain trails will soon be covered,
With a cover of snow, the seasons grow old,
And I grow tired and want to go where,
The hot desert winds would chase away the cold,
I live in the shadows, where you won't find me,
I have my blanket of life to keep back the cold,
I look forward, I don't look behind me,
For everything's gone, when you get so very old....

Donald "Jerry" Coutts

Another Birthday

What care I for the many pages
of the many calendars I have seen?

I feel young!

I wake to the glow of the morning sun;
I tingle to the sadness of the evening breeze;
I even greet the lonely night...

I get drunk with the smells of the grass;
With spring blossoms on the fruit trees...
I am overwhelmed at the beauty and short life of my rose bush...
The sting of its thorns says "I'm alive!."

I love to walk in the rain,
and feel the raindrops on my face...
and the sting of the winter frost
makes my blood warm and alive.

I am aware of the life that is around me
and I have a need to do something about it...

I thrill to the love of the young for I had loves of my own.

I feel... I think... I hurt...
I laugh... I cry... I dream

My heart wants to sing I'm alive - that's the thing...

Edith Beck

Untitled

When the lightning strikes
And the demons howl...
When the vampires continue
Their endless prowl...

I'll be there...

Kelli Diane King

A Young Man And His Guitar

Is this the way of the old men
of the mountains?

No modern electronic obstacles to
chase away the songs from their heads -

They built a fire, sit on the hearth -
take guitar in hand - and let it flow -

From the heart, soul, - and mind - through
the instruments of God - their fingers.

The gifts of the Almighty come in many ways -
He gives us music in our hearts -

To show the world what words alone cannot -
— peace, love, contentment, beauty - a REASON.

Thank you, son ——

Carol A. Barry

Untitled

There is a picture in my mind
of the place I would love to be

Of tall majestic mountains penetrating
cotton balls of clouds against a
Backdrop of azure skies

And looking way below and beyond
blankets of green brown and yellow
Of hills valleys lakes and rivers
all scattered at my feet

Away from destruction
away from pollution, away from masquerades
There's a place I'd love to be - a place
of peace and tranquility
A place where I can be free and just
Be me

Cheryl Gittens

Ode to Brooklyn

B for Brotherhood - a feature divine 'tis the light
of the world, the hope of our time.

R Religion - our churches inspire the symbol of
freedom - humanity's desire.

O Opportunity to work, to earn; all progressing,
those willing to learn

O Opportunity again makes a call with freedom to
worship, equal to all.

K for the Keynote of this score, echoes all freemen
this world o'er.

L for our Library, museum and college, from out
these portals flows all worldly knowledge.

Y for our Youth, all fine, stalwart, and grand; all
ours to acclaim, the best in the land.

N for our Neighbors, north, south, east and west,
all striving for good, but our stride — the best.

Jules Chalif

Untitled

I always wanted to spend lots
of time with him

Taking walks
Listening to his thoughts and dreams
Laughing together
and most of all, hearing those three words

Or just to feel his arms wrap
around me would mean so much

For this is how I use to feel,
presently those words are dark

Like a dark hole that will
never become light again

The coldness is his heart
has driven me so far away
I feel angered every time I see him
Even though I'm angered I'm also sad

Feeling the tears run down my face
I think to myself...
All I wanted was a father

Heather Mastrangelo

Trust and Regret

Was it love at first sight; or was it just out of spite?
Oh, it was so much pain; and I know it was all in vain.
Oh, God, save me from this mess; I have the right to my happiness.
I'm dying of suffocation; and I'm moist with perspiration.
Regretting all the times I've forgiven you;
now that I'm upset, sad, and blue.
I knew it wouldn't last; but it's all in the past.
Looking into you tempting eyes; thinking of all your cruel lies.
Crying on my pillow; like a weeping willow.
Starving to get away; but I know you will make me stay.
Remembering the times we were lovers;
but now were fighting over the covers.
There's no magic left in our love;
and I know this is a sign from heaven above.
I'm sorry if I made you mad; but you made me very sad.

Jennifer Jacobson

Silent Screams and Hollow Tears....

Little girl, with pigtails, gold;
Oh' what horrors you behold!
As day goes, screaming, into night
Oh' how your soul is filled by fright!
And as the stars are hung, anew,
You fear that he will come for you!
You see his shadow on the wall;
You hear his footsteps in the hall!
And as the tears swell in your eyes,
You know that no one hears your cries!
For, although, you fight to set them free,
Within your mind, they form a sea,
Of raging waters, absolute;
And your sanity, pollute;
And, on this earth, no place is found,
Where love and joy and hope abound!
For all these things must take their leave,
When little children can't believe,
That hope is real and love is true,
And red is just another hue!

Jenny Mojica

"A Friend Is Always There For You"

A friend is like a gold mine, a treasure hard to find
Old or new, they're rare and few
A friend is always there for you
They're always there to love and care, and help you through the day
They understand your every mood, in each and every way
Forgiveness is their greatest gift, and understanding too
Acceptance of the good and bad, that lives inside of you
Through all the many ups and downs, they're there to cry or there to clown
A friend is always there for you, through thick-and-thin and laughter too
For they bring out the best in you, to teach you how to love them too
To teach you how to be a friend, when to break and when to bend
To teach you how to give, as well as to receive,
Brings love and joy, and hope, you never could conceive
For friendship is a two-way street, that we must travel 'fore we meet
A friend is always there for you, to the very end-it's true

Darlene Luker

The Children of the Sea

Each child's ashes thrown upon the waters become like the waves—-
individuals never the same; always there—.

The active child is the stormy; never-ending wave.
A photographers wish—.

On the calm days it is the shy child playing.
The waves, little laps on the rocks, barely reaching the shores,
a divers dream—.

The precocious child. The sleeper wave.
Peek-a-boo! Here I am! Watch-out I'll get you; forever playing tricks.
Finding other children to play with,
not meaning to keep them; just someone to play with—.

The babies— rock forever to the smooth easy motion of the sea.
The ocean sounds become the singing of a mother; always for them—.

Children of the sea—look and you will find them; each wave is different.
As different as the faces of the children in a crowd,
Waves dancing, playing. Some resting; always there—.

But it is not the tears of the children that continuously
fill the oceans—.

It is the tears of the ones left on the shore; they don't know—.

The children of the sea are home.......

Jeanette Kaufman

School

It's the first day of school, I'm scared and I don't know what to do.
I'm having trouble finding my class, the bell has rang, I've gotta
move fast.
The teacher seemed to be real nice, instead I had to make a sacrifice.
I had to sit next to a total geek, she wasn't that bad, so I did speak.
At the end of class, she bugged me to death, I ran and I was out of
sight. I stopped and took a deep breath, then I proceeded to class.
I said this class is hard, I'll fall behind.
The subject I hated most is ....MATH, I thought, oh my God, what a task.
The bell rang, time to go, I asked myself, why is this day going so slow.
Lunch was pretty GROSS, they served grilled cheese on burnt toast.
The day is ending, my parents will think I'm making a new beginning.
One last thing to do, before I leave this never ending day of school.
Stop at my locker to get my books, take a last glimpse at my
beautiful looks.
I know I succeeded, I tried my best !!!
FINALLY, THE DAY IS OVER...YES...YES

Brittney Nicole Barnes

A Walk Along The Beach

Of all the places within my reach
I choose to walk along the beach.
While ocean waves wash into shore,
I have to walk, I yearn for more.
An old straw hat upon my head
Miles of beach I've yet to tread.
Carrying a bucket in my hand,
I gather sea shells from the sand.
Under my feet, the sand feels light;
I hop, I skip, I jump, I might.
Summer rays so strong shoot down
They turn my skin a toasty brown.
Sea gulls weep their lonesome cry
With wings stretched wide across the sky.
Out to sea the ocean goes
Leaving wet, my feet, my toes.
When summer days come to a cease
I feel no worry, I'm at peace
As long as waves rush to the shore
I'll be back forever more.

Sally Kernstine

The Garage

Boxes, nails,
Old lunch pails,
Leather gloves, welcome mats,
China cups, baseball hats,
Suspenders, roofing tar,
Buttons, homemade vinegar.
An old Mustang up on blocks,
Broken combination locks.
Old t-shirts, lacy rugs,
Dried flowers, coffee mugs.
Pots, pans,
Trashy books, aluminum cans.
Jewelry, slippers,
Candles and yard clippers.
Tied all together with a whole lot of string
And all my friends ask "What is this
thing?"
It is a wonderful, splenderific,
Ganoopalabigamick.
"What does it do?"
This, I cannot answer for you.

Elisabeth Anne Jones

Deep Inside

In my sleep
I cry inside
No one hears me
In my heart
I know my love
Will not be lost
But now the candle is burning out
The door is closing
On the love I once felt
He feels no more for me
I have no more feelings
Does my mind reject happiness
That I once knew of
Or does it only accept pain
Or the feeling or being alone
I smell fear
Fear of the unknown

Nicole Androsky

My Heart Has A Voice

My heart has a voice. It cries for all those who are lost
on the battlefields of the streets in our cities. It
cries for all the children in this world who go hungry and
unclothed. And for the elderly who's past we forgot.

My heart has a voice. It breaks at the sight of violence
among the people of this earth and for the mother who
watches her child graduate to gangs, only to bury him in a
cemetery of lost youths.

My heart has a voice. It bleeds of anger for those who
are blinded by racism and ignorance and for a system of
justice that cares more for the criminal than that of the
victim.

My heart has a voice. It dies slowly with each passing
day. Before this voice goes silent it wants to feel a
different voice. It wants to hear a symphony. A symphony
of hope, of peace, of charity and of love.

My heart has a voice. Does your heart have a voice?
listen to the voice in your heart, hear the symphony, make
it sing. With our voices and by the grace of God it can
be done.

Carol S. Triplett

Angel White Snow

Once on the snowy river bank. A bird in search of food reminded me
of an old armored tank. From the mountains the stream flowed into a
long bubbly brook. It wound and wound into a little nook.
My eyes laughed, and my heart was full of glee.
I saw the funniest sight as I crouched on one knee.
Two squirrels I saw chasing each other to and fro, they whipped
and they whirled and they played in the snow.
Then behind me I heard a crunch of the snow. I turned behind me to see
my two puppies, Chloe and Sara Lee. Sara came running right up I
giggled when I saw this cute pup. For nose the color you know, was now
angel white from the new fallen snow. She licked my hand and left to play, then
Chloe came up and decided to stay. It was growing dark and the sun was to set.
So I headed for home with my two Little pets. Everything was so quiet.
Everything so low. As I saw, fall from the sky more angel white snow.

Jill Rupley

To Be Your Life's Joy

To Be With You, To Be Your Life's Joy;
I would become the sea flowing high and low to bring my sweet nectar
to quench your thirst.
I would be the Sun, shining bright, as warm as a hearth to warm your
heart.
I would as the Puppy, always waiting for you, wagging my tail in love.
I would be the Salt adding flavor to your meals, providing the
sustenance to sustain your beauty.

To Be Your Friend;
I would become the Eagle, soaring high, lifting your spirits into the
heavens.
I would be the Warrior, protecting my Princess from the cruel world
destined to do you harm.
I would be the Wolf, howling in the moonlight with the night drifting
your sweet scent, flooding my nostrils.
I would live as a Poor Man, to give you your inner most desires.

To Love You;
I will find the highest mountain, building a majestic castle, to
honor you.
I will find flowers whose beauty is surpassed only by your own, to
shower you.
I will create diamonds from your tears, for nothing as pristine as
you should cry.
I will be as I am now, Loving you always.

Alix A. Bien-Aime

Broken Dreams

There were once bands of gold on our fingers
With hopes of happy days
But the shiny gold is gone now
With them our dreams have faded away

Tears have replaced laughter
Trust a thing of the past
Were we so foolish to think
This love would always last

Too many cruel things were said
Too much pain has gone by
Maybe this fairy tale love of ours
Has faded away and died

The flames of passion have subsided
The embers have burn out
Lives once filled with certainty
Are now smothered by doubts

Those little bands of gold have tarnished
Because of our hurtful ways
Those bands of gold we held so dear
Put now on a shelf to fade away

Brenda F. Crum

Untitled

You are a picture of life and love
With colors bright and strong
Parts of you are rough and smooth,
Yet you are living and loving,

You are my pictures, as I try to discover
I seem to be collecting up many
new thoughts & sounds,

Only memories of how things were,
looking at our pictures of us
That only seems to be collecting up dust.

Someday I hope to be placed by your side,
to feel the love that once was inside.
Yet I want you to feel it too...
Just maybe someday....
there will be me and you...

Jennifer Ginther

A Poem For Dawn

You looked at me when you were born,
with eyes so clear and bright.
I could not wait to take you home
and tuck you in at night.

Your eyes so blue, so innocent.
I gave you my love and devotion.
I'd never felt such tenderness.
My heart was filled with emotion.

Your first night home was precious to me.
I held you close and cried
I thought of the way you'd marry someday,
and would have to leave my side.

"You're silly!" You say, and smile so sweet.
"Oh, mother I love you so!"
"I can't believe you cried like that."
"You know I'll never go!"

You looked at him as you walked down the aisle.
Your eyes so clear and bright.
He could not wait to take you home,
His lovely bride in white!

Donna Skelton

The Eulogy of Mom

Her name was Filomena...
Though a human being, her efforts were always superior;
Though of simple life, of common birth,
She was a lady of truly...royal birth.

She had no imperfection, or distortion of mind,
As her eyes and ears were always closed...
From the evils of mankind.
Through turbulent insurgency, from the storms of the imbalance of life,
She was the one, whose boat was always on an even keel.

Though her struggles were for all, she knew her life would benefit others,
As this was her wish, she continued on her way,
To the benefit only of others,... that took her way for granted.

Though on her deathbed she knew, she asked, with shortness of breath,
"Why was I always the one...?" to help continue her life,
The life of little worth, on the behalf of mankind.

As I gazed upon the weakened face, to answer truly,
This mortal of noble birth, in the most humble way,
I tried to say, 'twas nothing... as you will always be .....our mom.

Jim DiGregorio

Friends Depart

Together forever, is what we dream
Though we imagine what the end might seem

But that's then, this is now
No worries, no fears all we wonder is how?

How could we ever stand to say good-bye?
Wetting the truth with the tears we'll cry

Slowly the final laugh draws near
Questioned by the silence we soon shall hear

Remembering the old times when, it was safe to smile
But the memories can fade after awhile

In all directions we shall part
Sending you all love from the bottom of my heart

Time. If only we had more
Regrettably and unwillingly we shut the door

Only to open it again to find new times to be faced
Though the feelings we shared can never be replaced

Friends are a life's treasure
Pain, tears, love, hope and pleasure

Well, now it's time to say the final adieu
Remember, I will always think of you

Jessica Zajicek

Because Our Love is Strong

Though we're far away I know she can hear me.
Though we're separate, love knows no boundaries.
I can still stand tall. For our love can conquer all.

I light this candle to symbolize our love together
and if the warm flame dies, our love will survive
because it is so strong.
And if the cold winter wind blows out
the fire of our love
The heat from that same flame will start again
because our love is strong.

I still think of her and I know she thinks of me
Though she had to go, I wished she wouldn't leave
I know she will return, for our love still burns

Chris Tyner

"Memory From The Past"

At daybreak they'd crank up the engine.
Thought this child "It's a powerful THING!"
I can still hear the slap of the belt,
Driving that big old threshing machine.

It seemed like a modern miracle,
Forks of wheat swallowed up by the THING,
Then I'd walk around to the other side
And see hard, shiny kernels of grain.

The sun was hot, farmers sweated a lot,
Then someone would yell, "Water!"
Heavy bucket I'd carry from the back yard well
And the men would sip and rest a spell.

Then, little was known 'bout germs and such
Guess God was close to the land;
'Cause none of those farmers ever got sick
Drinking water from the same tin can.

Anne J. Pierre

"So This Is Love"

As I lay beside your sleeping body so warm and tender, my
Thoughts do wander. As I turn to watch you sleep, mmmmm...
In total splendor. So calm is the face that I adore, your
Thoughtfulness overcomes you my heart does pound, my body
Does tremble with wanting desire. "So this is Love" so hot and
Lusty I feel on fire. Joy, happiness, and unbelievable
Giddiness is combined, it rushes thru me with a quickness.
From the pit of my stomach it rotates thru out. As I look at
You, this is what love is about! When we touch I soar like a
White virgin dove. Higher and higher you take me. So deep is
My love for you. Please take my soul for I will follow, take
My heart for I will be true, take my body for I will obey,
Take my love so we can be one. "So this is love" my sun rises
In your eyes and sets in your smile. I believe in you and I
Will give what you want and what you need. As I spread my
Wings to fly I ask of you to come, come and feed me your
Love, for I hunger you. My doors are open never to close, my
God, "So this is love" for you are my love, my joy, my
Happiness, and my heaven!

Francesca Cosentino

Untitled

Oh, what grave silence as it fills the night.
Thoughts enter my mind and nothing is ever clear.
I wonder why, on many nights alone
Am I real, am I here?
Mistakes I've made, and oh so dear.
I've been lucky, there's a reason I'm here.
I feel lonely, yet secure.
Because I know who I am, and no one can ever change that.
Long nights and short days,
I live one more day longer.
Hoping to find an answer one day.
What is real and what is not?
What is day what is night?
Days are filled with sunshine,
And nights filled with darkness.
Who is lurking in the darkness?
No one but my thoughts.
What is real and what is not?
One day I'll have an answer
To a question I forgot.

Gracie R. Fjeldal

Untitled

Cold rain plummets
Through the warm, dense, mountain forests.
Mist ascends from the ground
To the grey abyss above.
Dilapidated ag structures stand lazily,
Grim, amongst the atmosphere.
An old cemetery sleeps quietly across the way.
As the air hangs cold and damp upon the countryside,
Despair yet peace mingle
So one may find comfort.

Daniel A. Lagacy

My Story

We've been together for nine years,
Through them I've cried a million tears.
The man I love with all my heart,
Is slowly tearing my world apart.

At first I felt his love was true,
But after her I just never knew.
It was very hard to get it together.
Somehow I needed us to last forever.

He'll never know just what he means to me.
It's killing me to think of setting him free.
When I sit alone in the middle of the night,
I know I can't quit, I've still got to fight.

I'm told once again he's been cheating.
It's hard to take, worse than a beating.
Once again he's denied the cruel accusation.
I'd like to escape this painful situation.

But I most continue this acting quest,
For if I don't, I'll never rest.
I pray what I find the truth to be
Won't tear me apart, I can't set him free!

Charlene Curley

The Wedding

Today, Tomorrow and Always

Today, we promise to love, honor, and cherish.
Through thick and thin, Our love shall not perish.

Tomorrow, we share, we take and we give.
Our sorrows and joys, as long as we live.

Always, our hearts shall be as one,
Hearts joined in love, shall never be undone.

To those who came from far and near,
We thank you for your presence here.
And may God bless you, this we pray,
As he has us, this wedding day.

Connie M. Dearolf

Luscious Red Rose

Luscious red rose how sweet and tender are
thy subtle lips of passion. Are thy lips
like soft whispers of a dove. Or are thy fleshborn
petals full of love. Thy will open up and
peer at the blue skies above. And thy strong
stem will pose in the path of love. Thy
is subtle thy is sweet. Thy drinks nectar
beneath my feet. We are one as one can be.
Oh luscious red rose will you comfort me.

Courtney McElroy

Despair

When your heart cries out in deep despair,
'Til you can't find comfort anywhere;
You've searched through valley's dreary,
And now your spirit feels so weary.

You hide yourself-with foolish pride
The world don't care how hard you cried.
They never grumble when you call-
They never see you when you fall.

Sometimes you feel so alone
You wonder how you can go on.
Then God sends comfort from above,
And gently lifts you...with his love.

On wings of prayer - He heard your plea,
Unbound your spirit - set you free.
Your heart so broken by despair
He heals with all His love and care

And on the mountain once again
He hears you singing praise to Him.
We find He's only a prayer away,
Answering every time we pray!

Ida M. Lee

"Prayer of Forgiveness"

Forgive me Father, for I have sinned,
Time and time and time again.
I know what's right, and I know what's wrong,
But Lord! It's so hard to carry on.
My feelings hiding deep within,
Of hurting you, day out and day in.
My love for you, I know that's true,
Needing you now, telling me what to do.
This world has gone crazy running wild and free,
But I don't want it in my life just you leading me.
I'll do anything I can to make it up to you,
Proving Lord! that you can count on me too.
I'm walking each day, with you by my side,
Throwing out the bad, then I'll have nothing to hide.
Now I lay me down to sleep, but most of all I'll know,
That my soul you will keep.
Amen.

Charlotte Jinks

Respect

The world is gettin' worse and worse,
Times are hard and jobs are few,
This I was thinkin' while stradling my horse,
Find a solution is what I need to do,
The answer came to me while fixin' fence,
Return kindness for rudeness,
And have more church picnics,
Practice the golden rule and do no less,
More rodeos and family camping trips,
Let the older teach the younger,
And show 'em al their tricks,
Still I have to wonder,
What is the world really lackin'
And here is what I came back with,
RESPECT, that's what we lack havin',
Without it we're all left in a fix,
Respect your neighbor OF COURSE,
And they in turn respect you,
'Cause the world's gettin' worse and worse,
And times are hard and jobs are few.

Chris Pembelton

A Mother's Emotion

What other emotion can quite compare
To a mother caressing her baby's soft hair
Or her loving eyes when their eyes meet
As she gently helps him rise to his feet
Her never ceasing care given day after day
Binding him to her in a spiritual way
As she often calls upon the Lord above
To help guide her in her blinding love
For this human being whom she created
That perpetually leaves her feeling elated
As she watched his young body grow
Into a man who will always know
Her enduring love and complete devotion
Fraught with years of a mother's emotion.

Audrey A. De Cook

A Perfect Dream

I slept in the garden last night
To awaken to sheer delight

Good morning, in flower language said the rose
I smiled as a kiss was placed upon my nose

Sunflowers were braced against the sky
As if to shield me should the sun cry

Poised against the earth with ease
Were those gentle little sweet peas

I saw stretching, those great creations
A graceful row of lovely carnations

While strolling by a patch of bluebells
I marvelled at the story I would tell

And catching my breath in a moment of thrill
Just behind me were beautiful daffodils

As I made a path out I felt rather silly
When I almost tread upon a lily

I wish I could remain all day
Witnessing nature's dramatic play

Leaving the garden with sheer delight
I am glad that I slept there last night

Bettye Ludy Holland

"The Best"

She stood alone, outside from the rest,
to better herself to become the best.
Day and night she worked, for she
was determined not to fail but only to succeed.
No matter what it would be there
was nothing she wouldn't work for.
She was the one who would give that extra
effort that no one else would give,
because she knew it would better herself and the
way she lived. Though no one really
noticed her, she didn't care, for she
wasn't bothered by what people thought,
in her mind she knew that all the effort
she put forth would someday bring her
out on top. As the days went on and
the years went by, she gave up a lot
of things and as her life came to an
end she still stood alone outside from
the rest, not unknown, but, as the
girl who was the best.

Janina Perna

A Poet's Dream

I wish to inspire with poetry;
To contribute enjoyment to society.
Touching hearts with words so sweet
Would be a goal I'd like to meet.

I long to express the way I feel,
To share my love so dear and real.
I hope to bring beauty to a dreary life
Allowing my reader freedom from strife.

I'll share my heart's joy and gladness
To lessen your pain and sadness.
I'll write of the sun's warmth, the blueness of sky.
The elegance of an eagle soaring so high.

I'll write of the peacefulness beyond the city.
Where trees are greener and flowers are pretty.
Of farms and fields that lay for miles
Clean country air wholesome smiles.

I'll write of events as they occur.
And sometimes from memory, of the way things were.
But, moreover, I'll write of life's beautiful things
And sit back in contentment at the joy that it brings.

Debi Craig

The Reality Of Prejudice

Prejudice is seen each and everyday,
  To experience it causes the mind to wonder;
How can we be so ignorant and selfish
  To oversee others' feelings down under?

The qualities which make us unique
  Are different in their own ways;
Color, nationality and sex define our character
  Which can be lessened in the things we do and say.

I don't understand why it seems so visible!
  To hear such remarks is degrading;
We must appreciate everyone for who they are
  Or people's characters will soon be fading.

When you meet an enemy face to face.
  Conceal what you would say, don't fight;
Those hidden few words which remain inside
  Shall hopefully change your mind to right.

Jennifer Barr

Integrity

Life has a purpose for you and me
To find that hidden talent that has been decreed
By souls immortal to the tune up above
Whether it be the spirit of truth or the voice of love
By coming through to the mind in an inspired message
From all minds who have lived through past ages
They have recorded in words and symbols and tunes
Throughout decades of many past moons
The need for us humans to rise to the call
Above animal instincts and yet most of all
Not succumb to endless years of semantics
Fouling all souls with their corruptive gimmicks
Negative phrases meaning the affirmative
Reversed translations denying the negatives
Voting yes to mean no or voting no to mean go
Yes you and I have seen it at the polls
We are the generation of chattering fools
Who keep men from understanding the rules
Of how to succeed honestly in a task
And love what they are doing without the use of a flask

Jean Sublett

Dame Du Ciel

Ms. Dickinson owed her own brand of martyrdom
To Francois Villon who saw "light"—at night
She—too—was the poor-neglected waif of Love
"Le pauvre Emily"—achieved greatness in Art

All the themes of 15th Century France—Invade
Her Poetry—"Death—Fate—the Martyred-Lover"
"La Belle Dame Sans Merci"—"Virgin and Harlot"
"Secret Love" amid the Vanity of Earthly liaisons

Dickinson as Villon—escaped Time into Eternity
"Immortality" came to them in prostration—alas
Before the "Lady of Heaven—Dame Du Ciel"—She
Poetess—"your humble Christian—among your elect"

Images and Ideas—Miss Emily embraced by 1858
Fashioned and forged one thousand poems by 1865
Eternal Bride indeed survived The Seven Year Itch
Of Samuel Bowles—in "White"—"Empress of the Sky"

"Title divine—is mine!—The Wife—without the
Sign!—Empress of Calvary!—Betrothed—Born—
Bridalled—Shrouded—'My Husband'"—S's & B's
Poem 1072—folded—1862—sent to Samuel Bowles.

Bill Arnold

Wedding Day

Upon this altar, I take my stand
To give my heart and receive a gold band;
With God as my witness, I testify
To love this one 'til the day I die.

With this ring, I thee wed,
That tender voice beside me said;
Then all our love, we did bestow
Upon each other while knelt so low.

The arrogant groom and the blushing bride
Depart the altar glowing with pride,
Filling with love is my swelling heart,
Beating, repeating...'till death do us part.

Denise Hemmerich

To You

From far and near the voices call
To heed the words unspoken to all,
For there is no justice within this place
Just the smiles and lies behind a pretty face.
Thou know not the chorus until it is heard,
This I know from those hurtful, loving words.
They have no meaning when uttered in shame
No one knows from where these blinds have came,
Or why they blend the colors of disdain,
That tastefully reveal those tender shades of pain.
But if you look you shall surely find
Those hidden stakes within my mind.
And if you wish to live the truth
You will surely unwind it within your youth.
So while you laugh and maintain your cage,
Don't forget to turn the page
And journey down your road to rage.
Life is not clear, life is not true
With God and lies, keep your life to you.

Derrick A. McDade

Legacy

Protectively, I took your hand,
To help you find the way.
To inward peace and happiness
Lest by yourself you stray.

I pointed out the pitfalls -
Along life's road you'd find
And how you could avoid them,
Through experiences of mine.

At length you then were anxious,
To walk without my aid -
Thinking you knew what was best,
For your specific age.

My heart cried out, "you're much too young"
To try and fly your wings,
But only "echo," did I hear -
"Mom cut the apron strings."

Ellen Beckstrom

Planted in God's Hills

I was not quite twelve, when I gave my life
To Jesus and I heard Him say,
"I want to use you to reach lost souls."
And I surrendered to Him that day.

It's been many years since I answered His call
And my desire grows stronger and still...
Do I find myself on the mission field?
No, I'm planted in God's hills.

My heart still yearns for the city
Where greater would be the thrill
Of planting God's word and being used by Him
But I'm planted in God's hills.

Oh, why am I in the country, Oh Lord
Where distance is great... and the bills
Keep me at home where I'd rather not be?
Oh, I'm planted in God's hills.

What makes me think I can't be used by Him
If I earnestly seek His will?
Yes, I'll write more letters and increase my prayers.
For I'm planted in God's hills!

Joanne Jurjens

"In The Earliest Day"

In the early morning - I have time with me,
To know my mind and concentrate on goals, I
set, and how I want my life to be.

In the early morning - I have time to think
an active plan - of new programming toward
the true self - that's me!

Undisturbed by the ringing of the phone - where
alone with my thoughts and life long dreams.
I can be free.

To set the pace, toward a new direction and
The places I want to go to learn in this
early time of day - the steps I need to take and so

In the earliest day - my mind focused on my goals
will stay - with concentrated thought I hold
by an act-of-will, unswayed, I will complete all of my day.

Though my mind sometimes wander - I must
bring it back on course - to focus continuously deep,
concentrated thoughts - soon my goals
Will become a reality - though my use of the earliest day

Jeanette Chambers

"Baby Of Mine"

This baby of mine, I cradle in my arms;
to love and hold and keep from all harm.
My baby, to my heart, is very dear. I wish to keep him oh, so near.
He'll play with his toes and make cooing sounds.
He grows and learns with leaps and bounds.
I'll hear the pitter-patter of chubby,
soft toes and always remember his cute, pug nose.
Time will pass on and he'll grow even bigger.
He'll love "Winnie the Pooh" but most of all "Tigger!"
He's my little boy learning life's games,
all he does being innocent, bearing no shame.
He plays with his blocks and builds so tall.
He looks with amazement and the wonder of it all.
He sees the world in his own little way.
I want him young forever in my warm arms to stay.
I know he must have space to grow, play and learn.
When mature he'll move on his adventure to yearn.
But while he's small, I'll cherish the days; his sweet,
tender face and flawless ways. God, bless him and keep him in your
loving care. I thank you, too, for sending me baby's love to share.

Angela G. Smith

Stolen Love

To have to hold,
To love and to cherish,
I give you my heart.

For moments you hold it
Gently in your hands,
As crystal, afraid it will break.

Time passes, and in your eyes
It turns to stone,
And is carelessly tossed aside.

Sometimes, though, when the moment is right,
Again you hold and caress it,
And continue loving me.

More often, the crystal fades to stone
And is set aside. Still,
You choose to keep it as your own.

I cannot ask for it back,
Only you can return it to me.
Yet you still hold on .... forever.

Barbara A. Stevens

Memories Make it Fonder

You are everything I want - or need
To make my life fulfilled,
It quiets the longing of my soul
And gives me such a thrill.

You say the words of loving kindness
I have longed from you to hear,
And everything you say, and do,
Makes you, to me, more dear.

I love to hear your happy voice
And look upon your smiling face,
Then I gaze down deep into your eyes
And know we have found our perfect place.

To have you right back here in my arms
And lay beside you in the night,
I wonder if I am only dreaming
Then I awake to see the light.

I fondly remembered you all these years
Of us laughing and loving together,
And now I look at you through happy tears
Just look at us now - I pray, forever!

Frances W. Pollard

Silent Benediction

The winds have stilled o'er the desert lands
to return to the source of their birth.
Mesquite and tumbleweeds are now at rest
and palm fronds, burnished by the sun,
lay on the sandy earth, broken in places
by boulders, massive in girth.

The yucca, a matriarch, so stately stands,
displaying the gold-tipped silver of her blooms
defying the laws of the desert lands.

Held high in the sky are the fleecy clouds
drifting to cast the long shadows of the
small cacti, when mirrored in the human eye,
are like sheep, content to graze,
secure from predators by the watchful gaze
of the giant saguaro cacti, standing steadfast
at stations on the valley's barren floor.

At day's end, a magenta light will spread
across the desert lands to herald the coming
of night and the silence that carries within
strange and distant sounds.

Barbara Reykalin

Angels

I look out my window everyday
to see angels flying every which way.
Their sweet, beautiful creatures,
with lots of gorgeous features.
The men are so handsome;
very muscular and extravagant.
And the women are perfect,
with the gifts God sent.
They have wings of feathers,
and gowns of silk.
All angels are warm and caring,
and have hearts of gold.
For I have seen angels and I honestly know,
their true love can never be sold.

Eva Oleksy

So Now What

We've gone from African to Jungle Bunny
to Spear Chunker to Nigger
It didn't matter if we were smaller or bigger
We've gone from rebellions to sit-ins
to peaceful demonstrations
It didn't matter we were considered less than graceful
We've gone from Colored to Negro
to Afro-American to Black
It didn't matter we still had to go to the back
We've gone from walk-outs to walk-ins
to riots and civil revolutions
It didn't matter there was still no solution
We've gone from Sister or Brother
to Homeboy or Girlfriend
It doesn't matter—we're mistreated the same in the end
We've asked for peace and equality
and economic freedom
It doesn't matter—we still get racism
So now what . . .

Carol Williams Glasco

Untitled

Pretty poems people write for people
Other peoples poems are beautiful
Many poems that are published are beautiful
Every one who writes a poem is proud
Some people give there poems to their girls

Valery Marszalek

Bedside Promises

Bedside promises she always made,
To stop your tears,
She kept you brave.

She made you promises,
And you swore not shed a tear,
But sometimes promises are hard to keep,
Especially not to cry,
So when her whispers left,
ten oceans you must have filled.

You were always told she couldn't stay,
Alas her spirit went away.
Sitting on her window sill,
A bird can be seen,
He seems to gaze at you and then fly off into the sunset.
Was it her? You'll never know,
But then you catch her scent in the breeze,
And hear a gentle laugh.

Bonny Rose Williamson

The Shadows of the Cross

I wonder, they say, what happened that day,
to the man they so freely did kill?

Was it ignorance of life, or the torment inside,
that lead all of them up to that hill.

Our lives were all but gone... it was the only way now,
He knew that we could be saved.

Oh Lord, you have given us hope!
that today we can walk the path that you've paved.

I looked up at the cross as I sat there that day
and wondered what it must have been like?

To be a disciple......and watch our dear loved One...
pierced by the slam of that spike!

I feel pain in my heart, and a tear comes to surface.
and I cry for Him.....for us....and for me.

Oh Lord, I thank you for the gift of life, of hope
and of Your dream that we see!

Cynthia J. Hann

Hush

Listen to jagged mountain peaks piercing the sky
To the song of the clouds that soften their slopes
To the music of oceans pounding rocky shores
Listen to the glow of the moon
The mystery of the stars
Listen to the silence of the Universe
To the stillness that is you

Listen to the glare of the midday sun
Burnishing desert sands
To the loneliness of the owl
The longing of the coyote
And lose yourself in the anonymity of the night
In the silence of the Universe
In the stillness that is you

Listen to the echo of worlds that have vanished
To their voices of anguish that have cried out in vain
To the memories that linger
That will haunt us forever
And listen, listen to the silence of the Universe
Listen to the stillness that is you

Elaine Holtz

The Immortal

From the bottomless depths
To the vast regions of endless space
He goes on forever - without end.
He exists —
Ever consuming life and lifeless
Ever present in all things,
Never resting,
Never giving into the whims of man —
always constant,
Never slowing on his endless voyage —
Controlled by no man, earthborn or otherwise,
Without feelings or desires he touches all.
And yet — He is without form — feared by all.
His never ending journey continues.
And yet — When the universe falls in on itself —
He will still exist —
Alone — friendless,
Immortal — Time.

George Kokali

Dare To Be Bold

To those that love,
To those that dare.
To take a new pathway in life,
There will always be a reason to strive.
To achieve a better goal,
For the ever searching soul.
To find the reason for progress,
In the ever changing world.
To help others find success,
And a reason to be bold.
So just take one day,
And live it as if it were just for joy.
You might be surprised how good a day you had,
And made for a new, or old dear friend.

Donna Beamesderfer

A Shadow

The wind is wailing in the darkest hour
To warm myself I start to walk, then run
My face beholds a mystic, evil pow'r
I turn, another awful chase begun

I know I feel a thick'ning in the air—
The shadow's breath—no worse fume have I known
It chases me and traps me in its lair
Profoundest fear o'ertakes me, makes me moan

Through dusky halls and murky pools I wade
Behind me I hear something steel unsheathe
In desperation, "it" I must evade
In fright it gets so hard—so hard to breathe

I'm cornered; I anticipate the end
"Well now," it says, "I hoped you'd be my friend."

David Siren

To Whom It May Concern

To you, whom it may concern.
To you, the one who turns.
To you, the love is in the air.
To you, the one who is to care.
To you, my one and only love.
To you, the one who's beauty is like a dove.
To you, the one who's love is like air.
To you, the only one that fairs.
You the only one I care.

David Sutton

"Our Love Till The End"

My best friend says we'll be together
Today, tomorrow, now, and forever
Our love together will become as one
We'll have a family daughter or son
They'll grow up and be just like us
Giving us loyalty and all of their trust
We'll grow old together, but our love will still be strong
Our love never died, and it never went wrong
When one of us parts we'll be all alone
There'll be some crying and a lot of moans
But then I'll know you or I'll be safe
Up in heaven with glory and grace.

Diana Bowen

A Lost Child

Too young to fully understand
Too old not to know
Not sure where to find an outstretched
hand
Not sure where to go
Wondering what all the fighting is for
Wondering where all the love has gone
Not wanting to hurt anymore
Not wanting to go on
Praying to God every single day
Praying for all the pain to go away
Hoping that help is on the way
Hoping that everything will be okey

JeNina Nicole Rojo

Trails West

Pinking prongers distance twixt horizons
Tracing the celestial sphere in brazen stride
Their billow borders wraith filigrees of wispment
Splaying glory trails East to West

Hordes have heeded the Horace Exhortation
Pulsing our land from Chisolm to Lindy
Today pronging pinkers mile from Sea to Sea
Hunting the sun's demise

Upon leaving Market Basket and viewing jet contrails in late afternoon

Don Tynan

My Two Worlds

Dreams and stars fade from an ink velvet sky and my day world
transition begins.
Sing with the birds, fly from treetop to tree, I can,
you know, if I choose.
For I have two worlds I live in each day,
I'm here to gain in this life, not to lose.
My day world's a play that is constantly changing,
and I create each role from me.
Sometimes I'm strong or mild, even meek; I laugh, I cry,
I rant and I weep.
I try to bring gladness, to give joy and new hope;
keep promises I gave, sometimes I try just to cope.
As my day world slips slowly to bring twilight then sleep,
my dreams are my night world, my temple of peace.
I listen to my dreams, they are the key to the soul; I hear when
they whisper, I take heed when they scold.
Softly, then deeply, I drift through this world; sometimes dancing,
or falling, sometimes unsure where I go.
Then fairies and rainbows weave their magic through haze,
and I drift deeply then softly to a new dawning day.

Jane Avery Holland

Life Just Happens

A leaf goes drifting through the air,
To lay, where it should lay,
A cloud goes drifting through the sky,
To stop where it should stop,
My heart goes drifting through the world,
To love who it should love.

Jocelyn Ryan

Guenivere

Guenivere had green eyes, like yours
Tresses that show as brightest copper
Flashing eyes wreathed by a countenance gentle and fair
A face effused with love most intense.

Possessed of a body whose limbs
are carried with the grace of the gentlest willow,
well-shaped with curves that
hint at joys and most secret.

I would fold myself into those limbs,
to be caressed by that fair foliage
and to trace those curves to the
inevitable beauty, soft and warm,
inviting exploration, with the
promise of discoveries most wonderful.

With an act so simple as the
clasping of hands, a voyage on a
sea of love can begin.
Nothing is more precious,
more exotic than the soft touch
of your love, my Guenivere.

Christopher M. Lynch

Evening Step

It's evening and I look toward the land of sun.
Trying to speak, the music of words evades me.
I can't clap my hands
on time.
But I can stamp my feet,
dance in the circle and cry,
"Yo! Yep! Ya ya."
It must be rain somewhere.
A cool and damp breeze passed by.
Again I turn and picture the dance
crossing eyes in that jaded face—that old Indian,
cold as the gem.
I hammer my feet
three more times
and this dance is done.

Gregory Lendvay

"To Hold You In My Dreams..."

Always in the summer, always in the fall
Twenty-four hours a day my love
I'll hold you in my dreams...
Once a minute is not enough
Nor is a thousand times a day my love
But each and every moment will suffice
To hold you in my dreams...
When seconds seem long, and priorities questioned
And fatigue is my companion
I'll push it past it's limits, love
And I will be your friend
I'll take and hold you in my dreams...
Though some may smile while others curse
Most will never know
The love I have, the desire that's here
To hold you in my dreams...

Dan Gribovicz

New Life

The beginning of new life,
Two loves prepare as to make one, Romance,
Love, excitement and Fun
Fainting, emptying one's stomach, also soreness of breast
Happiness with tears after the test
Nine months pass by, carrying life inside, eating,
swelling and enlarging one's body.
The day finally is here!
Natural or C—Section, one is in fear. But after all,
A New Life has appeared.
Pain and excitement along with ones cry.
We'll plan again as time goes by.

Cozett Smith

Echoes of the Woods

Quietly and peacefully I blossomed,
Uncultivated, Unadulterated,
In oneness with Nature
And the beauty of the Creator.
The waters ran peacefully below,
And the birds with joy flew above.
The creatures within me in harmony,
Sang of the beauty of the Creator.
And then came that day; the day of doom,
The tool of destruction, man's civilization
Invaded my bowels for expansion
Plundered and polluted the waters,
And shrouded the beauty of the Creator:
The path of man to self destruction, it is.

—Debo Richards Obawole

One Last Kiss

Did you ever find what you were looking for
Under electric skies. Across silver shores.
Searching for the truth as in a little girl
Who finds beauty in this decrepit world

There must be more to life than this
So hold me gently for one last kiss

Ten thousand nights killed by the morning sun
Waiting for the truth to come the
Truth of passion behind closed doors
In your arms I search for more.

There must be more to life than this
So hold me gently for one last kiss

Jennifer Price

Love Song for a Dream

I once wandered far away
Under your Angel's wings I played
My senses seem to soothe me
And I was charmed that day.

You whispered things to me
Of the love between the moon and sea
And with you I will always stay
If you sing these words to me:

Be at peace my love
There is much yet to be done
Believe in dreams and they'll come true
Believe in me and my love for you.

And as you said these words to me
There was something there that I could see
The beauty of a soul I could find
My heart was lost within your Emerald green eyes.

Christopher Rowan

The Orchard

Cotton tufts silently sailing through the sea breeze;
Unknowingly defying numerous gravities.
Apple blossom trees aligned in military fashion;
Their white petals floating with a summer snow-like passion.
Lilac bushes like blots of ink here and there;
Their lavender fragrance perfumes the salty sea air.
A forest of strong determined grass grows ankle-high,
Nursing persistent dandelions under the sun-tinted sky.
Birds find a haven in the bushes' damp velvet leaves,
Providing a soothing symphony that only the earth sees.
During the day young lovers dream and innocent children play.
At night the earth grows and renews itself for the coming day.
Mother Nature made her offices and chambers in the world all around,
But created the orchard for her playground!

Amanda J. E. Gagel

God's Ecology

Beauteous winter whiteness,
Unrelenting loveliness;
A cashmere landscape, broken only
  by an echoing stream.
A crystal wonderland, wherein a
  horse walking aimlessly,
Surveys his pasture.
Spun sugar-boughs overlap-cotton-topped
  posts, and in the distance
The sun is a silvery-gold bauble
Suspended in the air.

Elizabeth Swaim Lawson

Until Freedom Is Won

Stand up for your right, you can't the fight,
until freedom is won.
If you can't work there, don't shop there, where there is no
Freedom to hire can be no freedom to buy.
Stand up for your rights, don't shut-up if you have a
doubt, that is the only way to fight until freedom is won.
Love your fellow man. God made us all. Jesus was
persecuted, jailed and died on the cross, for all mankind.
Man knows what's wrong and man knows what's right,
but if it's a fight for right, continue to fight
until freedom is won.
Don't be ashamed if you have to speak up,
stand up if it's to make things right.
That is the only way to fight until
Freedom is won.

Autrilla Watkins Scott

Mother Constrictor

Welling tears drag me down
Upon my face there is a frown

A lone drop of blood falls from the sky
And causes disaster with no reason why

A snake slithers through my motionless mind
One little thought, and there's nowhere to hide

From my head down to my heart
Ready to constrict and break it apart

Cautiously awaiting a moment to escape
Bend down on my knees and silently wait

Amanda Alban

Untitled

Beyond the wall of mirrors,
Vaguely seen reality glimmers;
In every man, in every place,
but I see only me reflected
In every dream, in you

Committed to myself, I seek Self's goals:

Pleasure, — chameleon-like,
Receding from my ever grasping hand,

Approval, — "See me! Love me!"
Let me see my love of me in you,"

Love, — given briefly, taken,
Until my lover feels the mirror's trap and goes.

Reality distracts me from the cage's mirror image,
Intrudes, distorts my image, in my trance-like dance of Self.
Escape into tonight! Forget tomorrow.
But tomorrow lurks behind the two-way mirrored walls.

Hell is made of mirrors.
The fire that burns the soul reflects the god of Self
And traps me in a shrinking world not big enough for life.

Alex Miller

For Someone Special in My Life

It is for the person I really care about. He is
Very tough, though very sensitive at times.
A warm-hearted person who
Never gives up, and can achieve anything in life.

More than anybody else I've met, he's
A very outspoken person and says what he
Thinks and hardly ever regrets it.
On the other hand he can be very snobby and
Stubborn, but sooner or later he gets over it.

Ana E. Santiago Perez

Terrorist Factions (Nowhere to Run, Nowhere to Hide)

Terrorist factions strike out against the land
Violent action towards the brotherhood of man
Beautiful landscapes reduced to bits of rubble
In the air, the smell of trouble
Endless tears flow into a rising river
Makes your mind boil, it makes your body quiver
There is nowhere to run, there is nowhere to hide
There is no road to walk, there is no ship to ride
Religion is at question, to which belief is right
People disagree, they take up arms and fight
Hostages taken, demands of action made
Political prisoners, make up the balance weighed
There is nowhere to run, there is nowhere to hide
There is no road to walk, there is no ship to ride
Children are left homeless, their families torn apart
Everybody ends up with a ravaged broken heart
This world is catching fire, fueled by hate and greed
We've got to stamp it out, we've got to sow love's seed
There is nowhere to run there is nowhere to hide
There is no road to walk, there is no ship to ride

Charles F. Sierra

The Dove

The dove is the symbol of
things that are free, things that
are good, things that are right.
As she flies, high in the sky, bearing
her emblem of peace, she spreads
her pure white wings as a security
blanket for the whole world.

Marlisa Carrillo

Nostalgia

I roamed over a valley, today,
Visiting the places where I used to play.
The faces of the people have changed
The old neighbors have all gone away.

The Church is gone from the hill, now,
Where as a child I learned about God.
The Cemetery is there and I visited
The graves of my friends who sleep 'neath the sod.

The old school house still stands
With a worn and a stern look.
In my mind's eye I can see myself
Climbing the steps, with my books.

The Black Oak still stands
in the corner of the school yard
a grape-vine still hangs from its boughs,
but no child swings from it, now.

The school friends are gone from the valley
but their mischief still makes me smile,
and the hills around that valley are as beautiful
as when I played there, as a child.

—Helen Neely

Untitled

There she stands across the river alone, dirty, and wet.
Waiting for someone to capture her.
As the wind rushes threw her hair she
Sheds a tear which drops to the earth and
Surrounds the dust below. She finds herself
Falling deeper and deeper. As she falls she
gets bruised and scared her heart is shattering
into a thousand pieces. She tries to walk but
She cannot her face is dirty and her cloths are worn.
She keeps trying to survive in this jungle of pain.
Yet something holds her back what is it?
Is it the pain she's going through or the sunshine
Which makes he weak. As she screams out for
help her heart fills her with tears. No one can
hear her she is slowly withering into nothing.
There is only one thing that can help her which
is love, but she can not find it. She is alone
and surrounded only by her breath.
Her body slowly fading away into oblivion.
She is at Peace.

Dina Mouldovan

Nightwatch

Standing, quietly, patiently
waiting for the arrival of the darkness
projecting itself
up, into the skyline
surveying the scene of open waters.
when night falls its large eye opens
its large shining eye
watching, guiding
keeping the ship away.

Away from the danger
away from certain destruction
among the jagged rocks that line the shore
able to split the ship's hull
like a knife slices through buttermilk.
the ship needs careful watching
not unlike a baby needs a mother
to keep it from danger
to care and to protect it
keeping its watchful eye open
Keeping the ship away.

Aaron S. Anderson

What Will People Think?

I was a child to be protected, to be loved and believed
Wanting to be normal, wanting to laugh and be free
Didn't worry about — what will people think?
No, no one will admit to molesting a child
After all — what will people think?
So you say a child lies, a child makes it up
A child, to be protected, with nowhere to turn
A child learns to keep quiet, not to tell
A child learns — what will people think?
The list, you see is more than two or three
But now the list is between God and me
No more will I my heart and soul bear
No more will I say what no one else dares
No more a child, but a woman with a child's fears
A woman with scars and pains too deep to reveal
No, I can't reach out to family
A family who says — what will people think?
Yes, you said, — What will people think?
Should I tell? I tried. Now, I can't do that
Cry myself to sleep, wondering — what will people think?

Joanne M. Bowman

Jam Session

I was in a jam session,
Wanting to enter the basketball profession.
It was my turn,
And my stomach started to churn.
I went up for the slam,
And made the jam.
I ripped down the goal,
And broke the pole.
I had to pay a lot of money,
But I got it from my honey.
The judges rated my dunk as a ten,
They were all men.
I won the jam session with a perfect score,
Everybody else's score was poor.

Ben Cosman

Silence + Shadow

Muffled crunch of scuffled feet on dead leaves
warns me of the imminent approach of you there
and he there and she there all here
rasping rasping cheese-grater breath
nut-grinder thoughts slam send shards
shrapnel slice my face I weep blood
room for shadow crowded out by hungry
famished souls searching for light
tell me tell me tell me
I wish for return of torturing silence

Curtains drawn over locked door
tell me tell me tell me I scream
strapped sitting soundproofed no one hears
pitter pitter pitter patter
windowpane rain hallway footsteps
blown apart reach teach search
all to find but naught a one
all is done all is undone

Joshua J. Scanlon

A Plain Little Flower

A plain little flower I picked one day I always
thought the flower was magic. Everyone said my
flower was stupid but I didn't listen I just walked
along. As I grew up I still had that flower and now
I am an old woman and I still have my flower.
In my heart I think that flower is magic.

Carmen Mahoney

The Left Turn Dilemma

"No left turn" the crossings show
Round the world we'd have to go.
Left turn friends we'll never know,
You can't go there, the sign says "No".

Ralph E. Williams

Dare To Dream

I have a dream, said Martin Luther King
Was his dream a dream,
That is all it may seem.
To some his dream was a dream,
To others his dream was more.
More I say because they took the dream to heart.
They took the dream and made it a reality.
Although it may never be a reality to all,
I cannot help to feel that,
that will be their biggest downfall.
The dream that black and white,
Can live together with out all the B.S. fights.
That dream will be reality,
When all eyes see each other as though it were dark as night.

Christopher G. Pearson

...And Tomorrow Never Came

Someone made me angry today-

Was it something I said?
Was it something I did?

They should call and apologize
after all it wasn't all my fault -

I miss this person that made me angry today -

Was it something we both said?
Was it something we both did?

We should both call and apologize
after all it was both our faults-
after all we are still family -

Maybe I'll wait for them to call me first-
Maybe I'll call them tomorrow-

...and tomorrow never came.

James Francis Saupan

A Dream of Beauty

As I sit here on my porch
Watching the thunderstorm with all its passion
I am reminded of how beautiful nature is
And my thoughts turn to you

The lightning fills the sky like my love for you fills my heart
The rain washes away the shadows
Like you have washed away my fears of the past

Your smile brightens my day
Much like that of the sun rising in the horizon
And the rainbow at the end of the storm
Is only a shadow of beauty compared to you

As I look at the trees I see the green of my eyes in the leaves
And the brown of yours below come together
To form a bond of Strength Love Passion and Beauty

The rainbow my fade
The storm may pass
And the sun my set
But my love for you never will

For you are my dream of beauty.

Alicia M. Scott

"Suicide or Death?"

As I'm standing in the moonlight
watching the tide crash upon the cliff upon which I stand
I can feel death coming closer to me
closer than I've ever felt before
It's bony fingers are on any back
pushing me into the sea
The water below reaches out
trying to welcome my fall
I'm falling, falling into the darkness below,
falling into the sea
The full moon acts like a light
that burns bright lighting up the dark night
As I hit the rocks below I can hear
death laughing, laughing for he has taken
another life.

Deze Kjersem

The Old Derelict

He said, "Lady, I've been watching you...
...watching you...as you knit.
Reminds me of my mother...could I buy you some coffee."
Asked...the old derelict.

He pulled up a chair...and commenced to talk
...of the twelve or fifteen spreads his mother had made.
...and with due respect...I listened...
Then I said..."my times up...I'm afraid."

As I took leave of the...coffee shop
...others took notice, I know
...and the gossip flew fast...and furious
...of how I had collected a beau.

I wonder if they stopped to consider
...the old man was lonely and sad
...But most of all...did they consider
The old man...could have been their dad!!

Never condemn a man...by the clothes he wears
...don't listen to him if you choose...
But keep your gossip...of the old derelict to yourself
...'til you have walked...a mile in his shoes.

Evelyn Jean Pearson

The Weakness

They are always there,
watching your every move.
You put on a mask to hide yourself,
but they believe it is the real you.
You are two separate people at one time.
You fail to ever reveal your true self to them.
Your peers help you in your time of need,
but they shun you away.
You hide behind your mask to hide your fear and pain.
They think there is nothing more to you than the mask.
"Never show them," you slowly repeat to yourself.
Don't let them see that you are afraid.
Be strong, fight them away.
Don't let them see.
Don't let them know.

Jennifer R. Derwey

The Girl

There she is
Walking around like she's something special
Flirting with every guy she sees
Waiting for them to flirt back
But they won't
They think she's a bitch
So do I

Angela Followell

"Clarity"

We walk in the midnight rain.
Water showers us in soft curtains-beading in our hair;
resting on our shoulders; caressing us from head to toe.
Soft light from a nearby lamp mingles with the rain
adding a pastel quality to this moment.
Colors streak into each other and the whole world glows with
radiance.
And in the center of it all is you, smiling;
whispering warm droplets of laughter;
basking in the illuminated downpour.
Holding your shoes in one hand
and fanning your dress with the other,
you dance between raindrops, splashing and singing.
You toss your head in joy and a stream of diamonds
follows in your wake as tiny beads of water catch the light.
And then there's that playful smile;
the one that leaves me breathless and filled with warmth;
that coy, half smile twisting slightly at the corners,
always innocent enough to hide darker thoughts and wilder actions.
And then I close my eyes, and the rain isn't the only thing falling...

Cory G. Gray

Dawning of a New Day

You are leaving us today, we all will remember this date.
We all are sad, but you must keep the faith.
For around the bend, hidden like a needle in the hay,
Could be something most wonderful, like the dawning of a new
day.

So dry your eyes and wipe your tears away.
Look on the bright side like the dawning of a new day.
We'll miss you everyday and you'll miss us, too, for a while,
But don't dwell on things of yesterday, just remember with a smile.

We know you will do well. Trust in the Lord and pray.
The world will open up for you, like the dawning of a new day.

Geraldine R. Morris

Every Mother

At the mercy of mother nature,
we are.
The lessons of her test -
Not to abide,
Yet, respect and honor.
To ride each gift of day as
the last.
To embrace each peace of night
the same.
For at the heart of her infinite power breathes
Purpose,
Wisdom,
Freedom.
The dream for her children,
we are.

Gina Marie Graham

The Fight

In the shadows of life lurks the face of death.
We are born to die but yet die to live.
When I find myself dwelling upon my mindless desires.
Oh, how I wish I were dead!
Shall I seek the things of the mind,
Only to see that I am blind?
Look to my heart old mind of mine.
There you shall find the death of hatred and the birth of love.
Seek the soul and fill the whole,
With the peace that's true but never meant to hold.
Fade not away from day to day!
For I fear the devil is near and on the way!

Brian Patrick Collier

To My Wife On Mothers Day

Every year in the month of May,
We celebrate a thing called Mothers Day.
We give them flowers and diamond rings,
Cards and clothes and many things.
We tell them "Mom, you are the best!"
Way out in front of all the rest.
Now all of these things are really great,
But why is it that Moms should have to wait?
To be told how much we hold them dear,
Why this should be done through out the year.
A Mother should never be taken for granted,
Cause seeds of doubt could soon be planted.
Then they wonder "Does anyone care?"
"And if they don't, then why am I here?"
And me I'm guilty as any other,
Of doing this to my wife, our child's mother.
So now my dear wife I beg of you,
Forgive me for these things I do.
And believe me now when I stop and say,
My loves forever, not just Mothers Day!

Carl Cress

Untitled

Wonder when all of us people will wake up?
We complain about our air, land, water, and
Most of all, each other!

Complaining and crying about all this is
Not doing any good!
We must stop complaining. Join together
and do something to put an end to all this!
If everyone just believed a little bit,
maybe we could build on that.
The question is; do we the people
believe enough to make a difference?

Carrie Lela Winters

Basic Blue

Common needs, common drives.
We could pull together
And make good things happen.

There is no brown, black, yellow or white.
There are just different shades of blue.
We each are proud of our cultures,
But remember the basic blue.

Common needs, common drives.
We could pull together
And make good things happen.

Let's not waste precious time and effort
Pond'ring reasons problems can't be solved.
Let's level the ground that we all walk.
And win the battle for basic blue.

Common needs, common drives.
We could pull together
And make good things happen.

Dax McCracken

To Good To Be True

This is too good to be true
why do you say I love you
Do you mean it, or do you say it because I do?
these words are sincere to me
they ant given out free
It take's a special person and one that
I fall in love with before I ever say
I love you.

Heather Fall

Happiness?

Can there really be happiness when life is such a chore,
we need love and sharing, but I really do need more.

The gift I need is close at hand, someone who really cares,
who holds me close, wipes my tears and strokes my long black hair.

I need someone to share my dreams and not be so unkind,
to make me feel so good inside that I just want to smile.

Life is hard living each day, I know its not so easy to do,
yet someone standing next to you with love that is so true.

Can help you with the painful times that life can really deal.
Someone to give me all his love is what I need to feel.

Dolly Finkle

Seasons

When it starts to snow one day,
We put all of our Summer things away,
Like shorts, T-shirts, baseballs, and bats,
And get out our mittens, scarves, and hats.
Day by day the snow comes down,
Christmas is near, there's excitement in every town.
Then Christmas is over and snow starts to melt
But everyone remembers the excitement they felt.
Spring is here now it's a nice sunny morn,
And all the baby animals are being born.
Easter is here now and it's Easter Sunday,
Nobody wants this day to pass but soon it will be Monday.
Summer is here now with a breeze so cool,
And all the children are out of school.
It's the fourth of July and there's guests in every room,
Then suddenly there's a loud noise that goes Boom! Boom! Boom!
One day when nature changes and Mother Nature calls,
She says to us as we listen now it is Fall.
Now it's Halloween time with children all dressed up,
It's starting to get cold again as we drink hot coco from our cups.
Again one day it starts to snow,
And then we realize how fast the year goes.

Betsy Olson

"Put Your Hand In Mine"

We listen to newscasts that come daily to our ears
We read headlines that intensify our fears.
But instead of reading headlines that disturb our peace
of mind
Put a smile on your face and put your hand in mine
Everyone is troubled and their skies are overcast
as you try to face the future while dwelling
in the past
If the road seems long and winding and the
end is not in view
There are things we cannot measure, but one
thing I know is true, there is no way to
measure the love I have for you.
I will always be there for you, and will
help you all I can.
Remember one thing now put a smile on
your face and put your hand in mine

Jane Linhard

The Silence Within

Anger and Pain are life's true beasts
who thrash out upon themselves, clashing violently,
spewing frustration's blood upon the inner self
until one screams out it's bitterness and the other lies motionless -
blood flowing from it's gaping wounds, barely alive
until it gains it's strength for the next battle.

Andrew S. Harper

My Brother And Me

We grew up free, my brother and me.
We roamed the hills, had our own wills, my brother and me
We raided watermelon patches and neighborhood trees,
Where all the fruit and vegetables were free!
My brother and me.
He's gone on to higher ground...to roam those hills... without me.
My brother is free!
No earthly bounds to tie him down
My brother can see!
We'll meet on that other shore
Where we could never want for more!
My brother and me
I won't say good bye... brother of mine
just let me know when you find
That watermelon patch in the sky
Where we won't even have to buy!
Where the living is free and easy,
and all our dreams come true!
Where once again there'll be...me and you
My brother and me

Barbara Miller

In the Youth of Our Youth

In the youth of our youth we used to run to the playground
We shouted, we screamed, and we laughed with the crowd.
We'd spin the soda bottle and sit in the grass
wasting time as it so quickly passed.
We'd cross the street and pretend to be bad
But when we returned we knew that we had.

In the youth of our youth we used to run to the playground
We shouted, we screamed, and we laughed with the crowd.
We used to run down the halls with our stupid little grins
Singing long songs and making sins.
We'd shout in the halls
and write on the walls
creating endless crimes
and jokes with nonsense punchlines.
Then it all ended and we had to move on
with our schools and our friends that were soon to be gone.

In the youth of our youth we said our good-byes
with our comforting words, but teary eyes.
So the running to the playground will happen no more
But, the laughter that started will forever soar...

Ashley Neece

"Baby Skates"

When I was a little girl
we used to be together
whatever the referral or weather
he always took time for "Baby Skates"
to be tucked in, with all my prays
read a story in the den
or in his arms I curled.
I was always "Daddy's Little Girl."
Now a success and been 'round the world,
with the tilt of the axis
talking was a twenty-four hour mess.
Though every night I tried not to cry
'cause he was never here to say "Good night."
My only thoughts were
"Please God don't let him die"
and a picture of him wouldn't be my remembering sight
Now traveling most in the states
and trying not to cry while he's gone,
I still want to forever be
"Daddy's Little Girl," and "Baby Skates"

Brooke Bode

The Subway

Faces do not move
We vibrate
To the clamor
Of wobbling steel containers
Scraping rails,
I smell Germany before my birth.

From the ceiling,
Hand hooks gravitate downward
To defective sounds and mechanical swaying.
The boxed horde veers around subterranean city corners,
Catching rat packs in migration toward food,
Chasing this unknown murdering in sewer caverns.
The seated,
With backs to shiny acrylic, wait, watching feet.
Those standing clench fingertips,
Gazing at other fingers and other faces.
Lava man slumps in numb death,
Badly dreaming of being hanged before
His fellow coach-riders.

Bruce Brownstein

Godly Nation?

With tears I view the masses
Wearing their rose-colored glasses.
Plots they're ever stewing;
Vain illusions, they're pursuing.
Some stumble blindly down corporate halls,
Some hide from life in shopping malls.
Some kill their pain with the drugs they brew,
Killing the truth that they once knew
Who is left to proclaim with elation
And honor the King of all creation
In this, so called, "Godly" Nation?

Elizabeth Marino

Farewell

We bid you fond adieu!
We'll miss the greetings at the post office,
the waves as we pass you on that special road.

Yes, we'll miss you!

That road where the deer could be seen
grazing in the field, sharing the green grass
with a sociable fox, a neighbor's sheep, and the friendliest cow!

Looks like a block party, wow!!

Those traffic jams in the morning, not to worry,
it's just the local tortoise, don't be in such a hurry!

Beavers in the pond, flapping tails,
what have they got to say?

I know, "Come on in, let's play!"

Look up...the hawks and ducks, even an eagle.
Yes, the golden eagle whose mighty wings reflect
to guide your car down the winding road.

What sights to behold!
So it is, the air, the water, the land are fine.
How long? How long? For our kind?
The city calls, the city calls. (Cough—cough)

Carol Fyfe

Untitled

As I lay awake in the cold darkness of the night I feel as if I
Were about to dose off
The glinting and glimmering stars seem to slowly fade away one by one until it is pitch black
The only thing that I can see is the white coat of the tall and beautiful unicorn
Now the darkness seems to be in the background as the unicorn gracefully steps forward
It all seems so clear to me now
Its dazzling golden horn is spectacular
Its as if I touched it I
could feel the strength that this unicorn holds
As it stands proudly on its four legs I can feel the strength of 1,000 men as he kicks his hooves and gallops off into the darkness
As I lay in awe over the unicorn I had just seen the stars began to reappear and what had seemed to be dark now was bright and alive as the stars danced in the sky it reminded me of the unicorn that had came so unexpectedly and had left no trace as it Galloped off into the darkness.

Heather Lyon

Graduation

Some of us grew up, some grew apart.
We're making our way, making a new start.
Some of us laugh, some of us cry.
Some of us hope to just make it by.

We finally made it, all the way.
Not that much time, so much more to say.
Starting out not knowing, ending his friends.
We made memories, we made amends.
Each of us with careers in mind,
Walk down the aisle to put high school behind.

Now the time has come, face to face we stand.
Regretting the present because goodbyes are at hand.
We leave not knowing where we're being led.
Only knowing that the paths to our future lie ahead.

Carrie Larrick

God's Tiny Creations

As I looked out my breakfast room window
What a beautiful sight I did see,
Two lovely little humming birds
Looking at me.

I always put out their feeders
All filled with nectar so sweet,
Its soothing to watch them feeding
How vigorously they do compete.

In awe I watch God's Creation
How happy it makes me be,
I wonder what they're thinking
As they look in at me.

Jean Carter

Untitled

A pretty little butterfly
With wings so gracefully lined
Flutters about the garden free
And makes you wonder why

It does no harm to anyone
As it seeks its inner joy
To land upon a rose bud
And grant a wish to a little girl or boy

Hal Larsen

Moon

You are as soft and gentle as petals on a rose,
your beauty is such that a sunset can not match,
you are a jewel from the Orient fit for a king's crown,
you are a man's dream.
And when you smile, the glow that you give off,
brightens up the darkest of the places.
For you are the "Queen of Nights"... you are the Moon.

Al Lopez

He Shed His Blood

He shed His blood that we might live,
What a costly gift for one to give.
With love in His heart, he paid the cost,
Not for the righteous, but for the lost.
He shed His blood for Jew and Gentile,
His heart forgiving all the while.
He bore our shame, He bore our scorn,
So that we might ask to be reborn.
He shed His blood to set us free,
His only request was, "Believe in Me."
He was mocked, He was denied,
So that we might all be sanctified.
He shed His blood for our sin,
"On the third day," He said, "I shall rise again."
The only Son of God above,
The God of mercy, hope, and love.

Catherine M. Fouche

Awareness

As a child my greatest fear, my mother said, was death.
What did she know, how could she know, she was a child herself?
When we could chat I'd ask of her time and time again,
"could you die? But could you die?"
Her answer casual, because;

...as a teen my greatest fear, my mother said, was death.
What did she know, how could she know, she was young herself?
Still searching and still questioning to soothe the obvious pain,
"could you die? But could you die?"
She'd prattle on and on.
Her answer was unnerving, deferring once again, because;

...with age came revelation. Death was an unknown.
Insecurity is what it was, my identity was lost.
Seconds turned into eternity when my innocence was robbed.
For when I questioned "could you die?" metaphorically I asked,
"will I survive?"

Barbara J. Hunt

"Please Look My Way"

Sweet child, when you look through the window,
What do you see? A reflection of yourself?
Can you see nature past man made factories
pouring smoke into our atmosphere, upsetting
our delicate balance?
Poor child, are you that alone that a flower
is seen individually and not as part of a meadow?
Do you see stars as a cluster, or are you so finely
focused to observe and follow just one?
Barefoot child, walk through the meadow and
feel the grass beneath your feet.
Does a single thorn ruin your journey?
Nature's child, whose myopic vision sees the pedal
with buds and stems, who feels no winters cold,
And hears the laughter of children in spring.
Life is not eternal, but a lifetime lasts forever.
My child, look out beyond the window,
for I am as you see
find safety in the window's edge.
for the window - it is me.....

Jim Grudzinski

The World Will Say, "What Mystic?"

The world will say, "What mystic love is this?
What ghostly mistress? What angelic friend?
Read, masters, your own passion to the end,
And tell me then if I have writ amiss.
When all love die that hang upon a kiss,
And with cavil and with chance contend,
Their risen selves with the eternal blend
Where perfect dying is their perfect bliss.
And might I kiss her once, asleep or dead,
Upon the forehead or the globed eyes,
Or where the gold is parted on her head,
That kiss would help me on to paradise
As if I kissed the consecrated bread
In which the buried soul of Alta lies.

George John Guerin

Body Of Water

Sorrowfully sweeping sand castles ashore
what is it you wait not for?
Seven seas surrounding sand
At what horizon does foam tease land?

Starry-eyed Sirens promising Zen
though their beckoning song yields not men
Sinister sea nymphs and Cyclops don't lack
Sending out serpents in a pack.

Sacred sanctuary swallowing whole
all parts edible, disengaging the soul.
Sorrowfully sweeping sand castles ashore
what is it you wait not for?

Carrie Gauthier

Questions

Do you ever wonder...
What is really out there?
Do you ever think...
There has got to be more?
Have I missed something that may be just beyond the horizon
Not far from the shore?

Do you ever want to fly?
Escape from your steel, gray box.
Fly to a new horizon, a better life,
Not far from the shore.

We all must wonder if there is something better,
If we could be more, so much more than we are.
And if this is true, where is that more?
Just beyond the horizon?
Not far from the shore?

There is only so much we can hope for, cry for,
And want.
We must be brave enough to go, seek, and carry out our dreams
To learn if there really is something better just beyond the horizon
Not far from the shore.

Gwen Sharp

Siblings

Across the country from Oregon to Maine,
Younger siblings are all extremely big pains.
Screaming and yelling and drawing on walls,
It is a true wonder anyone likes them at all.
Some like to bite, and others destroy,
All their sisters' and brothers' possessions and toys.
And there are yet others who do things much worse,
Such as making a craft out of big Sis's purse.
Yet there is one time when siblings don't make a peep,
That is, of course, when they are asleep.

Jessica Davis

Time

Time
What is time?
Time is nothing.
Time is just numbers on a clock.
Time, just an excuse for things left undone.
Time is pressure.
Time says, "Hurry! You better hurry!"
Time can be a friend or foe.
Time is unyielding.
Yet without it, we would be lost.
Time is forever.
Yet we are mortal.
What is time?
Time is eternity.

Joshua M. Kingsbury

The Lonely Man

It seems the burden of the world get heaver.
What should I do,
I am like a mother trying to wean her young.
I am only one, I am only me.
When they knock at my door, I know I must answer.
I know I must answer because I am expected to.
In the eyes of the world, I would not be worthy if I didn't.
Whom do I turn to for guidance.
I must help the people of our planet for we are all brothers.
Without each other we can not exist.
So I must try no matter what or if not I must step aside
for another to succeed.

A President

Harroll Armstrong

Untitled

Confusion depletes
what time that is ours.

I curse the anger inside of me,
inside of you,
inside the little children that cry out.
God - how I hate it
when my arms ache
from the hurt I see in their little eyes.

Did we give them life - or
did we take it away?

Pretty little baby face
Angel in disguise
the depth of your tears
pierces my heart when you cry.
So if I could - I'd take you away from all this pain -
far away to sustain.

Pretty little baby face
Angel in disguise.
Pretty little baby face
I hate it when you cry.

Angela Morton-Gould

Bravery

Bravery. What is bravery? Is bravery when a boy or girl, man or
woman makes a stand for what they think is right or wrong? Is
bravery when a man or woman asks his or her boss for a
difficult assignment? Is bravery when a person gets on stage for
the first time? Is bravery when a child asks a grown up for
help with his or her homework? Is bravery when a person has
open heart surgery and tells others, "I'll be fine"? Is bravery when
a child fights a bully or finds a different way to solve his or
Her problems without violence?

Garrett Tomblin

"It's Just a Rumor... Who Cares?"

Word of mouth, written word...
Whatever, who cares?
Only those whose lives it ruins.
Nobody else cares.
It's just a laugh to them.
Who cares who it hurts.
As long as they aren't in the same circle.
Sometimes it doesn't matter then, either.
Giggles, nudges as you walk past.
You wonder why
And no one will tell you.
Everyone finds out but you
And the other involved.
You soon find out... a little too late.
By then everything is ruined.
"It's just a rumor... what is the harm?"
But nobody understands
The trouble you're going through.

Jasmin Gross

Glimpses Of God

I saw a glimpse of God today
When a new flower broke the earth.
The sun rose over the horizon'
To a new day giving birth.

I saw a Glimpse of God today,
When a blind man was made to see;
A child was made to walk
When crippled they said he'd be.

I saw a Glimpse of God today,
When I saw a smile
Brighten a room with sunshine
From the face of a dying child.

I saw a Glimpse of God today,
a man handicapped, useless they said he'd be;
Brightened and Encourage others around him
As he worked his job with such glee.

I saw a Glimpse of God Today;
It brightened my life so much,
I knew I must do my part to help
Show Glimpses of God thru my touch.

Donald Rush

In The Morning Light

God, with joy you fill my heart,
When at dawn I make my start.

Years go by too long for me,
My far off friend sends my spirit free.

The love I feel in many ways,
Makes me wait too many days.

Each morn I pray by flowing stream,
Only to wake to find a dream.

That you were here to my surprise,
The vision gone before my eyes.

Now you are here to hug and hold,
To walk and talk for memories of gold.

Your face to me a wondrous sight,
When I see In the Morning Light.

Frank P. Barrera

Loneliness

I seem to dream at night,
When dusk creeps in like waves upon a barren shore,
That I am once again with you,
And we love the way we did before...

I seem to dream at night,
Of things gone by, and reminisce the days we've been apart.
And a tear falls in my hand,
A tear not from my eyes, but from my heart...

I seem to dream at night,
That you are by my side, although I know this dream can never be,
It's not my lonely, anguish mind that dreams,
It's just the love I have for you in me.......GAL

George A. Lawton

The Way Things Are

When people seem to treat you bad,
When everyone is really mad,
When friends and family turn on you, it really makes you sad.

But, what can you do?
It all seems strictly up to you.

When hard problems come your way,
It's not easy, the things today.

Oh no, It's just not right,
When friends and family have to fight.

Oh why, oh why does it have to be that way?
It's just the way things are today.

Crystal McLaughlin

My Mother's Spirit

One day I sat alone in a dimly sun lit room.
When I saw upon the wall a shadow come to bloom.
As the shadow started to grow, the image became much clearer.
Into the image of a woman that kept slowly moving nearer.
Once she stood before me, she spoke in a voice so plain.
I trembled when I heard this shadow calling out my name.
The shadow woman had no face, but the voice I heard I knew.
Again she spoke, "I hope you don't mind my dropping in on you."
I froze in shock and disbelief as I thought, this couldn't be.
After all of this time that she has been gone, she had come to visit me.
I was amazed to be able to clearly hear the words that she spoke.
All the while I wanted to speak, but there was a lump caught in my throat.
She told me that she missed me and of things I needed to know,
"And now," she said, "my time has come that I again must go."
And missing her the way I did, I suddenly began to cry.
Then this shadow with it's spirit, touched my soul and said good-bye.
I heard her tell me not to worry, that she'd come another day.
Then I lifted my head to only see her shadow fade away.

Cheryl L. Rosemond

My Door

If only you had taken the time to come to my door
You would have found what you were looking for
Trust in me I am your guiding light
I have come to lead you through the darkness of the night
When you knock on my door you will find what you are looking for
So take heed you sinner - for when you pass through my door
You enter my garden - and there you will see -
that there is always room for one more
If only you had taken the time to come to my door -
says the Lord

James V. Gabriela

Untitled

When there was a way, you found the will
When I was down, you helped there me up the hill
When I was low, you were there to make me high
And when I cried, you just let out an understanding sigh
When my candle was burning low, you were there to keep it lit
And most importantly, you were there, not to tell me
But show me, how not to quit.

When I couldn't keep up with life's little turns
You made me understand that in life every one learns
You talked to me, even when there was nothing to talk about
You listened and never, ever, shut me out
You sat and watched with me, as the sun set slow
You stood with me and listened to the wind gently blow

You told me never to rule anything out
To always stand tall and never have a doubt
And now when I wonder where you are
I look up and see your face shining in the star
And quietly say, it's my turn to keep your candle lit
And for you, I will never ever quit!!

Dina Mahshi

Letting Go...Not!

When life seems to let you down; turn around
When love seems to disappear; make it re-appear,
Keep the faith; keep the love; keep the feelings
that are so real.

Soul's that keep holding on when you must let go.
The love holds still tight, for someday it will
Be in the sky to fly away some starry moon lite night.

Just you and me and family of thee;
For hearts that paid the cost; which
Love was never lost. Hold tight with all
your might. Destiny is ours to share, no one
to steal.

For Great Cosmos knows and will
Forever endure, for Universe is forever
Ours to share. Cosmos which is way up in the sky.
Heart follows, stars forever.

Stay young, happiness is ours to share
Burn the bridges, troubles no more
Victory will be us, forever together.
For Ultra Cosmos knows so.

Dody Augustein Randolph

Another Lost Night

Soon that precious hour will be upon us
when the land grows dark;
the only light we will see is reflections of our thoughts
oh so lost; yet so calm
taking hold of our meek gentle hearts
only to restore our lost hopes,
that fade in the deep cold darkness of the night

That deep cold darkness cover us all
with its limitless domain, stretching endlessly into the unknown
caressing all of our hopes for that new dawn
that mysterious night with it empty void
keep us waiting patiently for our dreams
planning rainbows for us all

In its magical wonders of it all
it bring hope to us all
known that relief will soon be there,
providing peace in its feast
that hope will soon arrive
with each passing day.

Just another lost night

Bert. Mosenthine

The Gift

Helen and Henry were left all alone,
When the last of four packed up and left home.
They bought a trailer and traveled awhile.
Country roads, city roads. Mile after mile.
When the joys of traveling left them cold.
They resigned themselves to just growing old.

A plaintive sound mewed outside their front door.
A rain drenched kitten changed their lives once more.
Their front door opened to a wee Calico,
Who, somehow, got caught with no place to go.
Helen and Henry let pity hold sway.
They decided they must let that cat stay.

Windy, seemed appropriate for her name.
For a long while, destruction seemed her game.
Protruding from the end of furry paws,
Nothing escaped the onslaught of sharp claws.
Suddenly, when things seemed at an impasse,
Windy turned into a sweet loving lass.

A gift from that kind gentleman above,
Gave Helen and Henry a brand new love.

Esther M. Slater

Peace

There's a light that dawns at daybreak
When the sun peeks over the hills;
There's a song that fills the air the moment
A meadow lark trills;
There's pleasure that comes at sunset
When clouds are streaked with gold;
And there's delight in summer
When roses first unfold.

There's rest that comes in moonglow
When silver stars are bright;
And rapture when a symphony
Lifts the soul in flight;
There's joy that comes in sowing
A tiny fertile seed;
And there's peace in giving solace
To someone in great need.

Evelyn M. Blanchard

Final Love

The day was dreary and cold
When time was but a chore.
My life was there before me
As I stood on the sunkissed shore.

The light of love lost twinkled
The pain my existence bore.
Hope had all but left me
As I walked that endless shore.

I wondered as the sun boiled into the sea
Was there a mastered plan?
Was I to pass unnoticed
a humbled broken man.

I paused before my final breath
to reflect on what been.
If only I could have loved her,
then....

Daniel F. Kesack

What Is A Mother

She is my warmth when the world is cold
When times are cruel and ever so bold.
She is my sunshine on a rainy day
Which makes the clouds fade away.
She is my enormous burst of pride
I often feel deep inside.
She is my sight when I cannot see
Which helps me get where I want to be.
She is my receiver when I cannot hear
Which helps me understand what is not clear.
She is my guidance when I fall off track
Which helps me find my way back.
She is my strength when I am not strong
When times are hard and days go wrong.
She is my hope when all else fails
Which lets me know I will prevail.
She is my reason I want so to live
To enjoy all the love she has to give.
She is my memories I will always save
To carry on my path she has paved.

Delores Moore

Mom You're the Only One

Mom I'm so proud of you for being my guild
when times were bad
You were the shining star that glittered
in my eyes when I were sad

Mom I'm so filled with joy how you've
always been responsible for everything I do
Because there's no one else to take your
place when my grey skies turn to blue

I guess that's why we should always be
thankful for each moment we spend together
Because we know that even the best
things in life don't last forever

So I'm sending this message to tell you
that mom you're the greatest and you will
always last forever to me, and a day

And that you will always be thought of
forever for life as we go our separate ways

Mom I'll place no one above you, for truly
you're number one, and I will always love you.

Gwen D. Brock

Untitled

I'd like the rain to come for me
when unhappy and away from thee
It comes to cover up my tears
it drowns my sorrows and my fears
It dances on the walk with bliss
makes me laugh and deludes my consciousness
For the moment under skies of gray
I'm hidden from the sunny day
Till once again I see your smile
I want the rain to stay awhile
And when you come to me at last
the rain will stop quick and fast
But if again comes the storm
this time there'll be you to keep me warm.

David Russ

Steel And Flint

You and I are like steel and flint.
When we first met, sparks flew.
Then again it happened, until finally,
A flame burst into life.
Small and flickering it was, but it was alive.
Then we fed it.
With time spent together, secrets shared,
Weakness laid open, and strengths made obvious,
This tiny light grew into a bonfire.
One that burns with incredible intensity and
amazing light.
I pray that it never dims.
I feel so much for you,
That every thought is like fuel
That causes it to burn brighter and hotter.
Yes, we still spark and dim in the wind,
But our fire will never fade.
You and I are like steel and flint,
Without one, what good is the other,
But cold and alone?

Bradley D. Bowditch

My Friend

I've often thought of long ago,
When we were young, but even tho'
Our lives have changed, and so have we,
My dearest friend, you'll always be.

How could we know, what paths we'd take,
As we learned of love, and made mistakes,
And even tho' we're miles apart
You'll always be first in my heart.

As we roamed the hills, and valley's low,
My...that seems so long ago,
But fun we had, back then, my friend,
Oh...but to go back again....

The simpler things of life we sought,
Like fireflies in a jar we caught,
Wildflowers picked, pressed in a book,
What tender care we often took.

I know these days are all but gone,
But precious memories linger on,
The love, the joy, remains within,
I dedicate this, to you, my friend.

Deborah E. Richard

Heartbreak

It is heartbreaking to see
when women and children are in pain.
Men and young boys out in the fields,
mothers and wives trying to heal.

It is heartbreaking to see
children grieving for food,
everyone being so very destitute.
It is very hard to wish for a panacea.

It is heartbreaking to see
Men and women dying from war.
Nobody taking the time to care.
It is so very hard for people to share,
whether its love or help.

It is heartbreaking to see
when I look at their faces filled with tears,
I never thought I'd reminisce,
to see their eyes all filled with lament.

It is heartbreaking to see
My country fall apart, everyday; hour by hour,
and everyone grieve for their country to be.

Heela Popal

I QUIVER

I don't know what it is that makes me quiver the way I do when you are near, and makes me take a deep breathe when your voice I hear.

I can't explain the power you have that beckons me when I see the smile on your face, as I secretly follow you with my mind leaving no trace.

I wish I could grab and hold you close to me while gazing deep within in your eyes; how you make me feel, you'd never realize.

I feel your presence and your touch as I dream and my imagination runs free; and I cringe with desire as if you were right here with me.

I crave constantly of your closeness, as the pain of wanting you I know shows the desperation of increasing passion that continuously grows.

I just don't know what it is that makes me tingle inside the way I do; but, I'll just fantasize me wrapping my feelings and arms around you. For as I dream, I QUIVER.

Avis D. Anderson

Poem for Nora

Since I've met you I've never felt this before
when you entered my life, my heart opened it's door
When you enter the room, my heart surely does pound
for I am certain there's no other love to be found
when you are away, my heart yens for you
Because no one can make me feel the way that you do
You are so gentle, so sweet, so loving, so kind
and when we're apart, your all that's on my mind
My love for you goes ever so deep
and when we're apart, your memories I keep
So deeply I love you, with you is my place
I long for the moment of total embrace
I love you, I need you, you are certainly my life
and I pray ever so hard for the day your my wife
When our eyes meet my heart throbs for you
Because never before have I loved someone as you
I feel as if you are a part of me
and my life along side you is filled with glee
So sweet Nora believe me when I say this is true
My life is unfulfilled unless it is spent with you

Joe Potts

Love Hurts

The hurt inside is beyond despair,
When you feel the one you love does not care;

You wonder why your heart beats so strong,
And how the feeling could be so wrong;

One day you feel he cares and the next day
you feel no one is there,
Your life is on a roller coaster ride with
ups and downs beyond compare;

You love within all the boundaries that God
has allowed,
And you and he will always be above the crowd;

Hold on to your feeling and never let go,
For there is more to your feeling than you will ever know!

Alice E. Moeser

Untitled

When you smile, I smile too
When you laugh, I am laughing along with you

When you cry, I cry too
When you sing, with all my heart, I sing with you

When you dance, I dance with you
When you write, I write too

And if there should be something you can't do
I will smile and gladly do it for you

We may be miles and miles apart
Or so close, we stand heart to heart
But you should know no matter where you are.
I will always be with you, near to far.

Anne Forrest

Frank

This all started one day,
when you were standing in my way.

When I looked up, your eyes met mine,
it was then I saw your face for the first time.

I knew I had never seen you before,
because you had this look that just made my heart fall to the floor.

I remember one thing that took me by surprise,
it was your gorgeous blue-green eyes.

Even though I started to like you three months ago, you'll never know,
how my feelings for you still grow.

You're probably wondering why I never said hi,
well it's because I can sometimes get really shy.

Even though the year is coming to an end,
I truly wish I could have been at least your friend.

Although I'm a person you're probably gonna forget,
I had to tell you all this, because if I didn't, I knew it was
something I'd always regret.

I knew you weren't always going to be here
which only brings one thing to my eyes, a tear.

Anna Russo

"Parting Parts"

As we get old, and bent, and gray
when young, we thought our parts would stay,
for ever, and never go away.
Our hair falls out, our teeth decay, our eyes
blinkout, our bodies sway.
we wrinkle up, like dry creek beds
and some get noses big and red,
Nails get hard as concrete and rocks
we cant bend over to put on socks
Finger joints get big and sore,
Heavenly days! Can there be more?
Waist lines disappear, some get a big rear.
We droop, and hang, and sag, and creek
look in the mirror, and see a freak.
women sprout whiskers, and moles, and spots
we feel all around, and find big knots.
and varicose veins, we have lots.
we sit and nod, and fall asleep never have to count the sheep.
When we were young and big and stout, slim and trim, we had no
doubt.
But as we age, we fade away, and find out parts, just will not stay.

Bonniebell Turcotte Miller

How

How do you start living again
When your world has been torn apart
How do you start loving again
When there's only pieces left of your heart

How do you have hopes for tomorrow
When you can hardly get through today
How do you keep building castles
When all the sand has been washed away

How do you begin to start a new life
When you're afraid you'll fail if you try
How do you face the world and smile
When you're afraid you'll break down and cry

How do you learn to trust again
When that pain won't let you care
How do you learn to give again
When your fears won't let you share

I want so badly to reach out to you
Take my hand and hold on tight
For although it was love that made things so wrong
Only love will again make them right

Eilene L. Cross

Victories

Victories make you feel good inside,
When you're down in the dumps, your frowns will reside.
As you get back that really hard test,
You pray and pray you did your best.
Then you glance at the "A" in red ink,
You feel so good you can hardly think!
It's a victory!
As you kneel on your knees to pray,
"Jesus, come into my heart," you say.
Then you stand up with a smile,
You think," It's all worthwhile."
It's a victory!
There are 10 seconds left in the quarter,
And who's on the bench? The best scorer!
So you block and you steal,
You make three points, what a thrill!
It's a victory!
Victories make you feel good inside,
When you're down in the dumps,
Your frowns will reside.

Deanna Gardenhire

"My Love"

I love the light that shines in your eyes
whenever you look at me,
I love the glow that flushes your cheeks
for everyone to see,
I love your soft and tender touch when you
tell me of my charms,
I love the endearing phrases when you hold
me in your arms.
I love everything about you from your hair
down to your toes,
I know this love shines out from me
so everybody knows
I love to talk and laugh with you because
life now seems so sunny,
What I'm trying to say in my feeble way
is "I truly love you honey!!"

Ethel R. Galeskas

Nostalgia

My mind is the heart
Which revolves the way the earth does
But it has neither darkness nor light.
Even it contains neither rain nor sunshine.
It has only love,
And four seasons to miss you silently.

Viet Quoc Tran

Dinosaurs

Dinosaurs Dinosaurs
Where did they live?
On the earth eating meat
And leaves from the trees.

Dinosaurs Dinosaurs
How did they live?
Fighting and clawing all the live long day.
Past the summers and past the day.

Dinosaurs Dinosaurs
How did they die?
A big explosion
And dirt covered the sky.

Dinosaurs Dinosaurs
How did we find them?
We digged and looked and hiked
Till their bones were gone.

Dinosaurs Dinosaurs
Where do we see them?
At the museums
Where they've always been!

Erica Navage

Of Red and Green

A frosty cool evening ends another day,
where each blessed child, young and old brace
themselves for a new window display.
Boxes veiled with bows affix,
Beneath the Douglas that is facade.
How did they appear, with a new trick?
"An old man appearing elf-like,
came from the north brought them,"
I thought what a grand delight.
Dressed in scarlet bordered with white,
with him a large red pack to convey,
would provide me shelter for a night.
Yes, I remember that wonderful tale,
warmth, and love my parents would display,
warming my heart but to no avail.
A haven admired but scarcely seen,
above me lights of red and green.

James R. Blake

Peace, Love, Happiness

Once there was this peaceful little town
Where everyone was so pleasant and mild
Every little shop sold the perfect gown.
One day there was a scream from the wild.
An army had come and started a war.
This war demolished this peaceful place.
For there was nothing left but an old door.
Someone just sitting there drinking a case.
This town wasn't so peaceful after that.
People hated others for no reason.
Some people noticed this hate but just sat
Wondering if they'll see the next season
Hoping they will afford their next bill
To frightened to say they might be killed

Elizabeth Newell

Winter's Forest Floor

May there always be the forest floor!
Where hidden treasures wait for coming Spring.
Where sounds and smells lie still along the shore of
some small stream where blue birds wait to sing.
The cold, damp hardness there, which will make way
for warmth and life and color, come that hour
when Spring arrives all dancing on a day.
When each small stem presents the air its flower!

The forest floor! That wondrous treasure chest,
Of fiddle heads, and needles, moss and mold;
The forest floor! Enduring winter's test...
Will sing again... its silent song unfold!

Bertha Roosa

My World

Writing is where I run, is where I hide, is where I breathe.
For realities air is too thin and my world is anything my words make it to be.
For words can create lands and seas untold, and places unknown.
Silence can create mountainous barriers, and stone walls, and never-breaking chains.
Words are the keys to so many things, all you have to do is create them.

Debbie Lipscomb

Death of a Country

Alas! The mighty eagle shall falter, and fall to the earth
where she shall lie dying.
A mournful sound shall forever be heard...
the sound of her children crying.

And hence, many small nations shall grow within the body.
Like cancer, they shall spread
until a nation, once so bravely fought for...
soon after, shall be dead.

Around the spot, where the eagle lay, blood stained stones
lay stilled.
And shall loudly speak the names of those...
by whom it's blood was spilled.

Destroyed by but a few greedy men hungering for sole power.
Begun by a single minute seed, which shall grow quickly...
to poison both country and creed.

The mighty eagle shall soar no more, but lie rotting upon
the barren ground
which once was held by the proud and the brave...
For the children will have divided into many nations...
and with this the mighty eagle, shall not be saved.

Colleen Ringgenberg

September

The Children are going back to school
Where they will hear the Golden Rule
So it will be back to blackboard and chalk
And teacher's gentle, happy talk.

Some boys and girls are happy
And some are sad
But I'm sure the parents are really glad
It gets kind of hectic in a way
When children are around all day
They say they are bored-with nothing to do
And it makes parents weary hearing this too.

Edith Trank

My Marching Memory Band

There was a procession in my heart
where tin soldiers marched in cadence
in lock step to the beat of the never ceasing drum
I watched them go through their paces
never out of sync always in time
perfect precision—a perfect line
It was a marching band where no music was heard—
Just the soldiers marching in cadence in lock step without a word.

I watched them and tried to join in, but they never saw me
never knew I was there, I was too small for them to care.
But I didn't go away—I continued to watch
as they stepped so high when they marched on by
until the rhythm finally caught up with me
and I was ready to take my place—and without breaking the line
I waited for the right time to march in cadence with the rest
but where was I—can you guess? I was the leader of the band
leading the procession of a million memories marching through
my heart—they were in their proper order—like little toy soldiers
all in a line—but now with one big difference—
I'm not theirs—they are mine.

Celestine J. Patterson

Ain't I Enough

as i look back i wonder daddy
where you buried the memory of those
hugs-and-i-love-youS-and-don't-worry-daddy's-hereS
i don't understand mommy
how you erased that nobody-shall-hurt-you-baby

i receive a greeting card and mommy nothing
i get a kiss strangers get a kiss and daddy a wave
i don't understand

on those rocks i stumble
when other kids' reports bear two signatures
when monday morning i report about
my stepmother and mommy's boyfriend

mommy a tissue can't reach my heart
every time your car takes off and i see my friend
down the alley hand in hand with her daddy
daddy that i-love-you on the phone and greeting cards
doesn't fill my heart when your voice
can't make mommy's eyes gleam

daddy mommy I say nothing but
ain't i enough to patch up differences and heal frustrations

Alimasi Ntal-I'Mbirwa

Being Lost

I was so awestruck by that lake,
where's the boat landing for God's sake?
We went through each and every cove,
for hours and hours we drove.
It made me feel suspended in time.
Even though I felt fear,
that moment in my heart became dear.
For I became alive and free,
feeling the loving hand of thee,
realizing perhaps I was a little afraid of me.
With that confidence we found where we might be,
it was then the boat landing we did see!

Joyce Peterson

Teenagers with Guns

As I sit here wondering day by day,
Which bullet will take my next homey away?
They're starting to call us the generation under the gun.
A friend of my mother's just lost her son.
Every day people are losing their friends,
My question to you is when does it end?
The saying on the streets is shoot or be shot.
Just where-o-where are these guns being bought?
Don't people understand that children are dying.
Friends, families, and lovers are crying?
Kids used to be scared of lightening and thunder.
Now they're afraid of going six feet under.
Metal detectors are entering schools.
Is having a gun really that cool?
Gangs are being formed minute by minute,
Are your friends and relatives gonna end up in it?
We are the lost generation and we don't understand,
That the selling of guns should really be banned.
Some people say. "If you only knew,"
Here comes a bullet, is it headed for you?

Angella Elam

"Seasons Of Life"

Life is much like the seasons
Which quickly come and go
What we accomplish within each one
The end result will show

We spring into life at birth
Summer is the time we grow
Fall is the age of maturing
The other seasons teaching - winter will show

Study the Bible, God's holy word
Read and live by it day to day
And no matter your season of life
He will guide and show you the way

We are all results of his creation
And when faced with earthly toil and strife
Should always be mindful of the fact
The greatest gift comes from him.
"The Gift of life"

Doris Aline Coffey

Tales Of Two Cities

One sees the gleaming lights of Broadway,
While one sees the deadly lights of gunfire on the walk ways.

One sees the city with all the glamour, fame, and riches,
While one sees the city from cold, dark ditches.

One sees the city as the Big Apple,
While one sees nothing but the rotten core of that apple.

One sees, in that city, so many hopes and dreams,
While one can't even see himself hope to dream.

Deborah Holman

Flights

Fright of flight o'er railroad tracks
while signal hails of coming train -
Ecstasy of hot blood rushing
into long-forgotten veins.

Orange spray-painted boundaries mark
arena of debris and body parts lain.
What horror they must have felt descending
6000 feet in a nose-diving plane.

Timothy D. Deming

The Parting

The heaving and sighing of the autumn days,
whispering goodbye to summer along the way
The lands are ablaze, a Van Gogh's palette.

Leaves, gracefully departing from trees
swishing, swaying around our feet as we walk
through the park
Scampering chipmunks, a lone red fox darts out
Birds that stay home of various colors flying about.

As sunlight comes creeping through,
I pluck a crimson leaf as I go
and a shower breaks anew.

Near the path a white birch grows,
a silent drop of rain trickles down its' trunk
like a tear
Perhaps for the parting, the summer truce.

Diana Dolhancyk

F. E.

There once was a guy Fast Eddie
who always thought he was ready
But then one day he ran away
Only to return one dark rainy day
He lived it up on Brandy and run
With his son he fished for the fun,
He won the lottery that's really true
Only to throw it away on a horse named blue
His drink is now famous
If that's a clue
It's the same as his name
And it's not a brew
He loves a fine women
Who uses a spool
This story can't end
He's no fool

Edward Widmar

"Celebrate Challenge"

"O praise our creator redeemer, and friend"
Who called us as shepherds God's children to tend.
and given us talent, lives laden with gifts
Our darkening clouds to new bright skies God lifts.

"Though sound and mobility, sight are not ours"
Yet lives rich with blessing our God on us showers
We hear that voice calling, I need you to go
For my ways, my truths, and my glories to show.

"We celebrate challenge and grateful we feel"
That was wounded healers the once lost we heal
Yes, touching and healing are part of God is work
We pray that our calling we never will shirk.

"Our eyes now are clouded, and lacking in sight"
Yet still looking east to the clear radiant light
'Oh take now our full lives and gather our hearts
That each to a world lost in pain love imparts.

"With Christ leading we focus not on our loss,
But eagerly carry our share of the cross
The spirit infuses with grace from above
Empowers and quicken all work done in love.

Bobby McIntyre

Untitled

Who are you? I need to know.
Who do you call mom? Where did you go?
Are you near me or far away?
If you met me what would you say?
Do you feel hatred for me?
Or do you understand it had to be?
I gave you up against my will.
I gave you up, but I wanted you still.
I didn't do it for me. I did it for you.
I wasn't ready. It was all new.
I was too young to care for a child.
I was too young; too carefree and wild.
Now I am older and wish you knew:
You don't know me, but I love you!

Dionne Wilson

A Wonderful Lady

There is a wonderful lady
Who is always good to me.
And when I'm bad, she corrects me
For she's my Mom you see.
This wonderful lady teaches me
To be good and to be kind.
Most of all, she teaches me
To love God with my whole heart and mind.
And when I go to bed at night,
This wonderful lady is at my side.
For she wants to hear me tell
Little Jesus, for Him today I tried.
My little tongue cannot tell her
How much I love her so
But when I die dear Jesus
You'll be the only one to know.
This wonderful Lady, I ask you Jesus
To watch her carefully each day
So that when the Pope canonizes her
"That's my Mom," I'll proudly say.

Doris Harvey

My Daddy

I know a man who is tough and strong
who is usually right and seldom wrong
this man is very special to me
why - because he's my daddy

We laugh and argue over nothing at all
And when there's a football game it's me he calls
I love him so much it's hard to explain
It would probably be easier to stop a train

He's one of a kind - the best dad in the world
Even though he's had it tough - he still has the time for his little girl
Yes, my daddy is very special to me
I love him more than anything

He has taught me well - showed me how to do things right
So I could succeed in all areas of daily life
My daddy is more than a parent - he's a valued friend
With him around I will always win

For him I could truthfully give my life
That may sound corny, but not to me
Because you see - he's my DADDY!

Joanna M. Burgan

My Special Friend

I have this special friend
  who is very close to me
She is caring, loving, and patient
  everything I need a friend to be.
She is always there to listen
  and freely gives advice
I hope she knows she can always count on me,
  She never has to think twice.
I have this special friend
  She really is a gift
She comes from God above
  and gives everyone's heart a lift!
She is like my guardian angel
  I'd die to save her life
As long as she's around,
  I know my life is without strife.
I have this special friend
  You see, she really is special to me
Because this friend is my sister
  the best friend a friend could be!

Beth Loftus

Dedicated To My Six Daughters

There once was a lady who had six daughters,
who were as pretty as could be.
But alas poor lass she lost one beauty and then five were left
And nothing was ever the same.

And now all her daughters have grown up and left.
One got married and left her home,
two decided to get out and roam,
the other two stayed home and moaned and groaned,
and nothing was ever the same.

And now the years have come and gone,
and they're getting old and gray.
Four are still married with kids of their own,
but where is my fifth one nobody knows.
For she has no place of her own
but I hope and pray she will always know
there is a place in my heart
that she can call her own.

Henrietta Casselberry

Shannon

What are ya going to do, when you're forty and alone.
Who ya going to talk to, when theirs no one on the phone.
Who's gonna love ya, when you push'em all away.
Who's gonna be there, when you won't let no one stay.
I don't want to see you, sad and all alone.
You can't always be a gypsy, one day you must come home.
But when that day comes, what do you think is there.
But an empty house full of memories, of those that used to care.
So many times you hurt love, by hitting it in the face.
Although love goes on forever, the body just won't wait.
So go on being a joker, and play your dangerous game.
But when reality deals the cards,
you'll find...... you threw the winning game.

JoAnn Snow

Always

The best thing in the world for me,
with you "my love" to always be,
With peace and harmony so right,
You make my world shine always bright.
Not silver, not diamonds, not shiny gold,
But you and your beauty I will always hold.
If someday we should ever part,
I'll keep you always in my heart.

Joseph James King

An Expression of Love

Your love lies deep within my heart,
When we're together or when we're apart.
It doesn't matter where you are,
It doesn't matter who you are.
All that matters is you and me,
United together we shall always be.

Patrick Harrison

For Father's Day 1985

This is a poem for my father
  whom I have loved for 55 years
Whose graceful, smooth, beautiful hands
  bear witness to God's artistry
  whether Lou is creating art in the
  barbershop or fashioning miniatures.
Round-shouldered, tall and handsome.
I thought you a black Clark Gable,
Especially in the photo where you're
  wearing a homburg.
A ready, wide smile - but sometimes a
  furrowed brow. Easy-going.
Extending a helping hand, almost to a fault.
A youthful spirit, a teller of tales,
A self-made man. True-blue; that's you, Lou.
So I write this for life, for love,
  so you'll know the score.
For you, my compassionate, loving father,
  age 74.

Eleanor Speer

Untitled

I've lost my high school sweetheart
whom which we vowed not to be apart.
I never thought this would happen,
for I have found my heart so sadden.
Our marriage words say "Till Death Do Us Part"
but dear Lord, where should I start.
He's left his loved one so shaken,
wondering if they've awakened.
A beautiful family he has,
of blood and brotherhood.
Two sons we beared, loving every moment we shared.
My love for him will never die as I hold my head up high.
My prayers for him are filled with love
as we treasure the vision of white doves.
Please God, no matter the length,
give me the strength to carry on
our memorable bond that we are so very fond.
His spirit fills my soul
and I shall continue to carry on our goal.
To love, honor, respect, and especially never to forget.

Delia V. Hernandez

Reticent

There was once raised a humble child
Whose ambience became the open wild.
He searched and found a magic kingdom
And from there he learned true love and wisdom.

While mortal man was flying high
He revered and scrutinized the butterfly.
From them he learned and lived on dew
And kept from all the esoteric secret that he knew.

His erudition from this kingdom he still treasures
And digresses to this kingdom for life's pleasures,
But to tell this world his secret is inane,
Since the human race has proved itself so bane.

Humberto Cappas

Metamorphosis

I was the young monarch of all those great solitudes
whose kingdom was trees, sand, sea and wind.
I had no dreams but to reign over space, the chaste kiss of salt,
the fragrance of the forest living and decaying,
and to give obeisance only to the howling buffets of the biting wind.

What overpowering malignancy transmogrified my realm?
Why am I exiled to a hostile clime of cemented sand
where the sea surges into gigantic waves of glass,
the frozen trees enmesh in a cooper web,
and the pliant wind ducts through fiery cylinders?

From this cruel banishment
ultimately I am freed to obedient slavery
in that pure realm of charred memories
where transparent waves forever rise and dissipate
in their eternal battle with the drifting sand.

James Kohfeld

Untitled

I see pain in your eyes
Why are you crying
Come with me
Tell me everything
I want your pain to go away
I would take it
If it would make you happy again
You're my friend
As you begin to tell me
You cry
Don't cry
I'll take your tears and put them in my eyes
If it would make you happy again
You're my friend

Angela Brixie

A Letter from Betty

July 1994
Why did you have to break my heart?
Why did you tear my world apart?
Can you see me - can you hear me?
Did you ever even care?
A life so short - so unfair.
Elizabeth has your eyes - so vivid blue.
So strange it hurts each day anew.
Did I treat you unfairly - can your heart forgive?
If the answer is "No," I don't want to live.
I want you back - I need you in my life.
Knowing that's not possible cuts like a knife.
I'm not getting better - I die a little more each day.
Please, Felicia help me - I need to find the way.

Betty Poteet

Yin And Yang

We live a lifetime learning to know
When to control, when to let go,
When to relax, when to give in,
When to fight in order to win.

To live is a balance of might and reserve.
Equilibrium gained, we're then thrown a curve.
Discovering that force won't insure living longer,
We learn that our weakness is sometimes the stronger.

Gloria Bush

Conversations with God

There are many who would describe our conversations as strange.
"Why do you converse in questions?" they would ask.
Remember early in our relationship, My Lord, when I was freshly
born anew, I inquired of you your color—
"Are you black or white or what, My Lord?"
Your reply—Does it matter?
I thought and thought. No, actually it doesn't, not at all.
Many many times I came to you in prayer, begging for your counsel,
At times shouting for your help—-
"Why aren't you there? Why don't you hear me?"
Your reply—Do you not remember?
I thought and thought back over all the years and all the answers.
You were always there. You always answered.
Yes, I do remember.
And still again— "Why didn't you do this, and why did you do that?"
Your reply—Have I ever given you a stone when you asked for a fish?
I thought and thought. No, you never made substitutions.
My final question—-
"Why do you answer all my questions with questions?"
Your reply—Don't you know?

JoAnn P. Mills

Weeping Willow

Weeping willow
Why do you cry?
It is because he's way up high.
Is it because he left you alone?
Is it because he can't be reached by phone?

Weeping willow
Why do you weep?
Is it because he's fast asleep?
Is it because you lost his love?
But he still loves you from up above

Weeping willow
cry no more
his love is now brighten than before
He still dreams of your long days together
He will cherish the memories forever.

Dayna Marie Occhiognosso

Never an End

Oh Life, Oh Death,
Why do you puzzle me so?
Is it because of truth,
Which lies in pain?
Or a simple revelation,
That comes from gain.

My, how we ponder these questions,
As time seems to slip us by.
We never gain any ground in our quest,
To open the doors of our minds best
But stumble through life with a sigh.

So, what of Life? What of Death?
Is it more, is it less?
Is the Beginning-Life, and the End-Death?
Or, is the end, the true beginning of Life?
And the finishing of all our strife.

Janice N. Williams

Mother and Child

Tell me my child
Why have you no quest
Come, lay your head in my lap
Stay a while and rest
Why is it Mother So Dear
My heart is overwhelmed with much fear
Why is there no longer a Golden Rule
Is it because of a certain young fool
The one with the gun, the one with a knife
The one who values no life
And why is it we cannot drink from the same cup
Or even invite someone to sup
These things you speak of certainly all true
The ones of the lost, the ones of the fool
They will all change someday you will see
If mankind surpasses hatred, bitterness,
and loves one another as I love thee
Do all that I've taught you,
Do your very best and fear not my child
and proceed with your quest

Eve M. Gomez

The Shadow of Night

Why must I live in this shadow of night?
Why must I hide from the darkness to fight?
Why must this world be filled with death and despair?
Why can't we live together - to share and to care?
Why is there fighting, fatigue and weakness?
How can anyone live in this bleakness?
Is there a way to escape this dark trap?
If I can find it, I'll give others the map.
Until that time, I'll keep up the fight;
To try to continue in the shadow of night.

Cameron M. Hall

"Tell Me Angel"

Tell me Angel
Why you hide your face?
Was it you that said goodbye
On a coldest, winter day?
Tell me Angel
Do you know it's me?
All those years just flew on by
Leaving only memories
  Oh, white angel
  Tell me, can't you see?
  All those broken hearts you've left,
  Don't just let them be.
  In your shadow
  We can hide our tears
  Keep us warm for as long as it takes
  Under your protective wings.
Tell me Angel
When we meet again
Will you be my guiding light
Will you take me to the gate?

Beata Andrzejewska

Leaves Of Mint

As autumn approaches and leaves turn to gold, my heart is a flutter
With memories of old, the echoes of school bells ring loud in my
ear, announcing another semester is here. Children in cities and
country alike, who basked in the glory of summer's delight, will
now make their journey to bastions of learning.
Professors and teachers as learned beseechers, will seek to
anoint you with wisdom and knowledge, and guide you through
grammar
and high school and college.

Joseph Coyle

Heights of Redemption

(Piero Moreschi, implorable broken heart of love through his open window to the sky of Brianza home is beseeching aloud Matilde of the beautiful white castle beyond lake of Como.)

Brightest of distant lights, joining the planes
of sky and earth from a luminous wave of the sun,
she is coming....Matilde!...my sweet Matilde.
Come and stay beside me, my angel, my vision of love!
Let me hear your voice, I cannot live or die
Without your soul. Please, Matilde, don't make me suffer
Come to wipe my tears. Take my hand and lead me
Where you will. I'll do all you ask.
Oh, greatest envoy of the king!
Forgive me. My faith is free again
My promise I will keep.
Beyond the power of the mountain's rising
In higher art's own symphonies inspired
In skies where bluest clarions are sounding
And speaking many things within our blending spirits,
In unison we shall find
Those gleaming spun-streams of truest immortality!

Franco Buono

Deep Within

So many times I've thought of him
Wishing he knew my feelings deep within
Wanting him and wanting him by my side
Wondering and wondering why he lied
Remembering the times we had
All the times I loved the good and the bad
Thinking if what he said was true
Wondering why I feel so blue
Feeling the sadness deep within
Asking myself if my love for him is a sin
Knowing the next time I see him I'll
be wanting to know what he's thinking
As my heart slowly begins sinking
As I look deep into his eyes
Wondering if all that he speak is lies
Does he want me or do I only want him
I wish I knew his feelings deep within.

Andria Crosby

Untitled

I lay in bed late at night
Wishing you were here to hold me tight
I'm sure you've found somebody new
but yet my heart still aches for you
The way I felt when we were together
is the way I want to feel forever
As I sit and shed my lonely tears
for the love I haven't felt in years
I faintly imagine your presence and grace
and in my mind I see your face
I remember us hand and hand
and remind myself I was like a one night stand
For I know you never loved me
and so you chose to let me be
Us together will be a never
but my love for you will last forever!

Brandy Caine

Keri

There was a young girl I wish you had known
With a light in her soul, my, how it shown
Her quietness was soft, like a warm summer's breeze
Her life was kept simple, with the greatest of ease.

Her soul was as clear as a diamond you see
Her virtue was kindness, her desire to please
You sensed her presence when she was around
More often than not, she would speak not a sound.

A chuckle might come and crinkle her eye
Or she might shake her head, then lean back and sigh
Love and trust was all that she knew
She was a breath of fresh air, she was the morning dew.

What a shock it was, to see the world hard
She crumpled, she fell, she lost her guard
Life broke her heart, and she went away
To that heavenly place where only angels stay.

I shall always remember, it was herself that she gave
What a wonderful memory to cherish and save
But I am so rich along with a few
To have known this young girl as fresh as the dew.

Becky Hansen

My Best Friend: Till Death Do Us Part

I never knew there was such a friend, until the day I was blessed
with being united with the only friend that touched my inner being.
I realized then, I found my best friend,
whom filled the emptiness inside me.
My best friend, respects, loves and nourishes me for whom I am
with no exceptions or expectations. Believes in me and my dreams.
Gives me unconditional love, support and great ambition in my life.
She is there for me when I need advise,
guidance and a loving shoulder to lean on.
Always there to open my eyes to fault with such grace and dignity.
She is reliable and comforting in good times and bad.
She is more special to me than life itself.
There are no meaningful words to describe the feeling
I have deep inside, for I was blessed with my best friend.
The love and trust I share with her is more faithful,
and true, then my fairy tale marriage.
That is why I can say, To my best Friend:
Till Death Do Us Part.

Julia Annette Greco-Weisgerber

Freedom's Call

Scattered leaves upon the ground
With blades of grass woven 'round:
Once on branches held high above
Protected by the great tree's love.
All their lives held by the hand
But longing to soar above the land.
These have leapt off of the branches
Not once considering the chances
Of returning if they could not fly;
Each tiny leaf thought only to try.
With a burst of defiance they suddenly leap
While their tree prepares to sleep.
She calls out to them, but to no avail
As they slowly drift along a separate trail.
The moment they've awaited has finally come
And they quietly dance to a silent hum.
The faraway ground soon becomes near
Though each knows it has nothing to fear.
Their journey is over but they do not care
For they have succeeded by taking the dare.

Cindy Griffiths

Rust to Gold

Life is a cluttered path.
With blinding branches to hinder one's view,
And frightening darkness that blackens one's heart.
Tall swaying grasses with a rhythmic pattern,
That embraces the sorrow of my soul.

Yet, Mother Nature has no knowledge of how dreary a place could be.
The sharp needles falling beneath the hovering trees,
Punctures and reveals my hidden past.

But, when the sound of chirping birds fill the heavens above,
It engulfs within me, my dreadful fears.
Sun shining and flowers blossoming,
Possess this cluttered path,
And expose my shining destiny.

A fellow dreamer never dreams alone,
It is bounded by our destiny to enrapture one's soul.
To understand the unspoken word,
Which hides in the soul of all mankind.
That changes light to day,
Sad to unbearable astonishment.
Turning Rust to Gold.

Jessica Albertini

"Angel Sugar"

Were you ever kissed by an Angel?
With blue eyes and curly blonde hair
Well I was several times daily
If you doubt it you should have been there

Yes you guessed it He is my grandson
And grand he surely is to me
Although he isn't yet quite talking
He knows that I am Grand Mother Bea

We go daily for strolls in the neighborhood
Getting outside is what he likes best
But you never can tell about that boy
He sure enough puts me to the test

I do everything I can just to please him
He will be a baby for such a short while
For me it is indeed very rewarding
Just once again to see my angel smile

When I go home I sure will miss him
And we will be somewhat far apart
Yet we will be close to each other
Because love lives forever in our heart

Beatrice S. Noble

A Planet Of Love

A planet of love on which we once lived,
with eternal goodness for us to enjoy
the blue ocean water, the men ahoy,
a toy wouldn't bring a child more joy

A planet of love on which we wish to live,
will bring a child happiness
in the eyes of sin,
we wish with such might,
to bring love into sight
oh, why does everyone have to fuss such and fight?

A planet of love,
on which we'll endure
only hope will be the way,
to be quite sure

Christina Eulo

My Mama's Hands

My Mama's hands were long and slender
With callouses inside, my fevered brow they stroked so tender;
Wiped away my teardrops when I cried.

My Mama's hands raised eleven girls
Bathed and fed them all with love.

My Mama's hands made biscuits, they kneaded the dough,
cooked the meals, then the cleaning they did do.
They built the fire in the old wood stove for warmth all to have.

My Mama's hands did all the baking and canning from fruit trees we
grew. Her hands were calloused when she was done -
But no complaining was ever sung.

My Mama's hands kept us a'living
Now they lie so cold and still.
They wove a tapestry of giving,
Other lives with love to fill.

Now my Mama, she's in heaven, before the throne she quietly stands.
I see my Mama there with Jesus,
and he's a'holding my Mama's hands,
and he's a'holding my Mama's hands.

Catrinikia Ann Bailey-Taylor

The Black Woman

Oh how beautiful you black queen,
With colored skin of hues supreme.

From africa's heart you were taken,
But your african beauty was not forsaken.

From this night-mare journey you did survive,
To this unknown world they knew you had arrived.

Many years of caring, and of giving your best,
Never did you know you would pass all the test.

Forever in your heart a love misunderstood,
For you gave love like no others could.

So to you, of africa's past and america's present, I sing.
May your future be as bright as saturn's ring.

Clarence Keen

Dreams of Flying with God

Whenever I'm unreasonable during the day, at night I dream of
flying
with God in the heaven where the sky is so blue, and the clouds I
touch rejuvenate my life.

When I'm flying with God. He tells me "you're at peace once
again,
if you believe."

When I'm dreaming there's fear of the unknown and I fly with God
over the oceans, that's sea blue which give me serenity once more.

I dream of fear, truth, trust, and faith in you God,
but you give me the ability to fly once more.

When you fly with me you do believe in me and you trust me and
you
love me. Thank you God for being with me in surgery, helping me
make a decision on my career changes, and life on it's own terms.

When I dream of flying I feel free as a bird. You have given me
new freedom of self. Once again I thank you for life. I need you
and all types of people in my life. I will ask you and them for
help. Today I know I'm never alone.

So I fly with you in peace, love and faith to all mankind. Please
help me, God, to accept what I do not understand, and to believe
that which I cannot see, and to trust that which is beyond my
comprehension.

Jennette Spencer

Don't Put Off Your Dreams

Don't put off your dreams 'til tomorrow,
with Gods help, live them today,
Don't wait until the day brings sorrow
or other problems that come your way,
catch a snow flake on your finger,
Watch a cloud as it slowly drifts by-
Listen to a Bluebird sing - let the melody linger -
Even though soon, away he will fly! -
See the rainbow in its splendor
As the rain drops gently fall
The pinks, and greens, and blue's that blend are
Gods most beautiful creation of all.
Tell someone how much you care
Hoping that they care too
Maybe they would love to share
Some of their dreams with you
These things are all around us everyday, tho' we may not see
we walk with our eyes cast down, hearts filled with misery
So - Don't off your dreams - my dear ask God in His own way
To help you lose all of your fears
And find fulfillment of your dreams today!

Ava Lois Halstead

Love of Our Postmaster

To Nell our postmaster who we all know and love
with her quite voice, like the coo of the morning dove
and everyone knows as they travel down that long trail
that upon arrival she will always have up their mail
she takes time out to talk with you with her sweet charm
and is very caring, compassionate, and never cause you harm
she is on her feet most of the day, and never seems tired
that is why she is very much thought of and so admired
when she does retire, the post office will be a lonely place
because we will all miss her, greeting's and smiling face
But we all know she was the very, very best
and deserves her retirement and long earned rest

Alvyn F. Haley

Eagle

High is the eagle drifting. Eyes blazing
with keen vision before the river crawling.

The spirit guiding the lone brave neath
the oak, beside the stream.

Oak's his father. Strong and stable.
Blessing he must abide.

Scream, the eagle flashed - a thunderbolt
to earth descending.

Showing, swiftly the mark, the prize is
now. Worthy is the sacred vestment of his Chief.

A smile warms the soul.

Clayton H. Stone

On Wings of Thought

On wings of thought you come,
With pockets of air that gives freshness to my being.
And with it new roots are planted for growth.
Through it all I experience a COSMIC fire that immerses
me in creative overflow.
The water of life is present, a water that does not put out
the cosmic fire and a fire that does not overheat the water
of renewed life.
So we have the air of life, the fire of being, the roots
in the earth and the water of total being.
Renewal, Purification And Expansion Of Mind And Spirit...
all in one single communion of two souls.

Bernice Prill Grebner

The Encounter

Two traveling each a different path; one through forest deep
With obstacles along the way, a perilous path to keep
Walking with a careful step; pausing now and then,
To contemplate the splendor of God's magnificent plan.

Two traveling each a different path; one on sandy strand,
Unmindful of the greedy waves steeling o'er the land
His progress slow and cautious as he wanders on his way.
Meditating all God's gifts so lavishly displayed.

Two traveling each a different path, direction yet unknown.
Proceed on their precarious way content to be alone.
Will meet in quit wilderness as separate trails converge;
Oblivious to each other,yet in Gods great plan will merge.

These travelers now encounter and share the gifts so vast.
Exchanging recollections of the wonders each had passed.
Painting vivid images with pallets of heavenly hues,
Contemplating days to come and the paths that God would choose.

Two traveling each a different path; for again their paths depart
But each is now attended by the gifts of the other's heart
They've shared in God's endowment - the wonders of His land.
Two traveling each a different path - their spirits hand in hand.

Barbara K. Schultz

Untitled

Looking skyward you can see clouds
with outstretched fingers
reaching for what no one really knows
to be an onlooker, you'd think
they were reaching for nothing,
to be involved you can see them
stretching for an eternity only they can reach.

As the outstretched fingers
curl towards an imaginary palm,
they seem to be saying,
"Come with me and explore the universe"
If you deny yourself this opportunity
you may lose your only chance to be inspired
to explore yourself through exploring nature.

Cheryl Ann Vaughn

The Hill Walker

There is a walker on our hill,
With stick in hand and sprightly step he roams.

A jaunty wave. A smile.
I wave ... and go on.

Through countless years,
In all the seasons,
The walker keeps his steady pace.

My love moves through the desert of despair,
To final, blissful death.

AND ... the walker walks.
I wave ... and go on.

Ann B. Streeter

Wintery Dreaming

Oh cotton clouds of the wintery winds,
your flurries of flakes enlighten my eyes.

I widen my world, perceiving their pleasure.
of tingling my tongue with a sparkling sensation.

Cascading down upon our edgy Earth,
Gracefully encompassing this Northern night,

I'm part of a miracle, observing their splendor,
of silently soothing our ways of the world.

Craig Rigler

It Is Spring Time

Almost everywhere around the world, It is spring time,
with the grass giving out that fresh scent of lime,
From the deepest valley to the highest plateau,
From the sky above to the ground below,
It is spring time! It is spring time!

The sun shines bright to awaken you,
While drying the grass that is wet with dew,
If that's not a reminder, that it's spring,
Just lie there and listen to the birds sing.

And when you have nothing to do on a boring day.
Just take a drive along any highway,
And watch the beautiful trails of scenery,
The dainty little flowers, to the picturesque greenery,
That wasn't all put there by man,
That's what I call springtime in any land.

I think everyone enjoys this season,
For whatever, everyone has their reason,
The young, old, rich and poor a like,
If it's just to get out or take a hike,
It is springtime! It is springtime!

Aneise Brown-Mayo

Elegy for an Infant

The day rose dark and cold
with the ringing of a bell.
The bell told a solemn tale
that no one wished to tell.
The house arose with a hasty
scurry.
To meet the coldest flurry.

It continued on to become a day of death and sorrow.
The only thing that kept them going were the dreams of tomorrow.
For without those dreams, the babe that would die.
Would never have seen its dearest ones cry.

The memories are still in the heart
Of those who fell apart.
When the news touched everyone who cared.
They started to remember the moments that were shared.
That memory would never be forgotten by those who were there.
When that tiny body became as still as the air.
As the days kept going on without that dear child.
Everyone always saw the tiny face that always smiled.

Erica E. Carroll

"The Seasons"

The beauty of the Autumn leaves
with their colors of oranges, red and greens.
Gives me pause to reflect on my
idle dreams.
With the harshness of winter
soon to approach,
The cold, the snow, and
sometimes the rain.
Then I can look forward to the
glory spring.
With it's lovely scents of the
blooming trees, and also
it's soft gentle breeze.
The skies will be blue, and
have puffy white clouds.
My love of these sights have
no abounds.

Dorothy Ayres

Why?

(Dedicated to a wonderful person — Jimmy Creutzberg)

My uncle discovered he has AIDS,
With this disease your world just fades.

Someone like him doesn't deserve to die,
Oh God, please tell me why.

It really made me sad, you see,
When I first heard of this tragedy.

I cried and cried and cried and cried!
I couldn't hold it back, though I tried.

It made me think of the good times we had,
Those thoughts make me feel really glad.
One time we went skiing,
Through him, the world I was seeing.

Society doesn't know how it is...
Not knowing how it feels to have a life like his.

People with AIDS are rejected,
Just because they are injected.

People are scared and say they don't fit,
They don't understand the seriousness of it.

I realize now, everyone must die,
But not from "this disease," Oh God, tell me why.

Debbie Gamet

Sleep My Child

Sleep my child in your wee little bed
With your Teddy beside you, after you have been fed,
A smile is showing in your little round face
You're sleeping with Teddy, so tightly embraced.

Went straight into dreamland, my Teddy and me
I was as happy as a lark on top of a tree,
My sleeping hours lasted throughout the night
When I awoke, the sun was real bright.

Each day was fulfilled and it quickly flew
My Teddy got older and I noticed I grew,
I found myself growing, but my Teddy stayed small
But that wasn't all about my Teddy, I recall.

Dear Teddy has been a great part of my life
We've shared together many a loving night,
The time is coming when I will leave Teddy behind
I'm growing up now, have other thoughts in mind.

I will always remember the life with my Teddy
He gave me the start, I feel now I am ready,
The memories of Teddy come back in many ways
He will always be a part of my childhood days.

Antoinette I. Roccio

So

So much to control so many smiles to hold back when I was
young with rage I used to run to you like a seeking eye am
but a blur like this field after rain I find my self a
softened blaze just looking back when I get old "yes" I
said yes in the past is the future lied to me it's a fault
of course she's yours it's not your fault it's not a fault
and now she sits in front of me braiding our lives together
knowing there's no perfect circle no perfect lie braid it
well keep it tight I've lost all mine but you have such a
nest full of hair so much to control so many smiles

Aylin An

Why Did It Happen?

The shouting, the angry words!
Words that hurt, words that can destroy
a person little by little.
Why they shout, why they scream!?
Why did it happen?

As I sit on my bed listening.
crying because I thought it was
my fault for them shouting at each other
Afraid as I was when I was a child
What goes through my mind now.
Why did it happen?

Why does it happen?
Is it because no love is there anymore
no caring, no friendship.
Why does it happen? No one knows

Sometimes at night I still cry of
the shouts and the angry words that
were said. But I knew somebody
was there that I could hold for protection.

Jessica Guglielmo

All Wound Be Still

If I should die before my time, let it not be in vain. For the sorrow
would of ended, the emptiness would be gone. And there would no
longer be pain. There would no longer be life no more hatred for me
to feel, No more anger to be displayed, no more lies, denials sins, or
secrets All would be so still! So if I should die so quickly that I
am unable to say my goodbyes My goodbyes I say to you now. I
ask only
that you not feel sorry, do not be sad, and to some of you I ask not
to be glad.. For all would be still.
I will no longer be seen by your eyes, but I will always be there in
spirit. In spring when the flowers begin to display there beauty I'll
be there. And when your camping out under the stars and you hear the
river rushing in the distance I'll be there.. and even in a smoke
filled room a billiard amongst ice you hear the clanking of the balls
I'll be there and all will be still.. I'll miss the smiling faces of
family and friends your hugs and kisses I'll no longer have the
beauty of the earth I will no longer be able to enjoy, but the love
I felt throughout my life, the happy times and the joyous memories,
these things I will not miss.. for these things I could never forget,
These been embedded in my soul for me to take whenever and
wherever
I go. And there all would be still...

Cynthia Morales

A Seasonal Flower

In rain forests the gorgeous epiphytes
Wrap their roots round treetops to steal the heights,
But no self respecting tree would complain
At such flattering company in the rain.

In the tropics, the ice capped volcanoes
Bubble with lava inside, melting the snows,
As my Caribbean love's icy shell,
Thaws quickly when her passions swell.

Through the coldest winter she stayed warm
A tropical bloom defying the storm
But like an early rosebud nipped by frost,
Her flowering came too soon, was lost.

Windward blossoms, hardier than they seem,
In the cruellest of seasons they still dream
In the summer's heat, they'll bear fruit once more
Embracing tall trees as the warm rains pour.

Ian Collymore

The Children

I dream, believing in compassion, love, forgiveness,
Yearn for a sweeter gentler, less hostile world,
It will come, it will come. I hope it comes for the children.

I care, about my past and my future family,
The sweet and bitter fruits of a strong, not so perfect heritage,
It has changed, it will change. I hope it changes for the children.

I weep, because; life is good; we are a hurting breed; everywhere,
The world calls my name, I hear their voices;
I weep for everyone, I weep for their children.

I laugh, for all the people who think they cannot,
The fearful young, wayward, lonely, confused, elderly,
I laugh for the children.

I hope, that people everywhere will dream,
And care, and weep, and laugh,
For the children.

Beverly A. Babin Woods

Tenderfoot Tramp

The ol' man spits tobaccy juice through the space in his stained
yella teeth
It hisses in the flames
Lands with a ping 'gainst a soot-black kettle in the middle of
the campfire
He bids me set and warm a spell
Says the beans are cold but the java's hot
Half froze and near starved I hunker by the fire
I ain't never tasted nothin' so good in all my sixteen years
Howlin' wind blasts my backside
I cuss myself for runnin' from home
He stokes the fire and sizes me up
Wants to know how long I been on the rails
Nigh on two winters, I lie, pullin' my dirty hat low cross my face
so he cain't read me, but he does
He pours me another cup, narrows his sharp black eyes
Says he travels alone, likes it that way
That a freight switches back in this yard at midnight
Reckons I best be on it, so my Ma don't fret

—Colleen Phillips

The Game

The game of life is an ordinary game,
yet different at the same time.
There are the backs and forths,
ups and downs,
times where you move forward,
fall backward.
There is the constant questions;
will you win the challenge,
will you lose the race?
You learn from the little details of this game,
you develop a knowledge from you experiences.
But unlike any other game,
this game is not dependent on the roll of a die,
the spin of a wheel.
It is instead your choices,
which provide the outcome of this game.
If you win or lose,
If you are successful or unsuccessful,
the choice is yours.

Alison Pedalino

We're On Our Way!

Our world, our planet, is our debt to existence,
Yet it saddens my heart, that which I sense.
From nature, and with nature, we live with unthinkable persistence
To consume and alter nature's delicate mence.

We've failed to control population explosion
Well knowing our land mass cannot grow.
From nature, and with nature, we discovered atomic implosion
For weapons, energy, and radiation's death blow.

We've failed to subordinate our differences among nations
Without the presence of mind that we have but one earth.
From nature, and with nature, we live mindless of rations
With vengeance and lust for material worth.

We've failed to realize that there is no place else to go
And I fear we've reacted too little, too late.
From nature, and with nature, we've created an irreversible flow
Which will inevitably stamp the seal of man's fate.

Albert Guth

In the Driver's Seat

Strapped, seated in this well-equipped body
You are Lord.
So secure I am Lord of this God-given temple.
You dwell in me and I in you.
Help me never forget that you're the driver
And I the passenger.
Teach me to be a driver like you
Let me know the way to go
Help me along the highways and byways
Defend me like you do the other drivers.
Slow me down when I'm anxious and in a hurry
Let me look around
And see how safe I am in your care.
Steer me in the right direction, Lord.
When I'm lost, help me not to panic
But make a right turn and find my true-way.
Even when I'm parked,
make me to know you are still in the driver's seat, Lord.
Thank you, Father.

Beulah M. Nedd

Shadow Seekers

Why do you wish to change me so?
You are not me. I am not you.
I have not a child's mind.
I have a child's heart.
My heart can be broken,
My mind is too strong.
My mind confuses my heart,
My heart confuses you.
You will never understand me,
But I understand you.
I know who you are.
I know what you want.
I can feel your eyes searching me for answers.
I laugh at you and let you marvel.
Never will I tell my secrets,
Never will I shed light on my darkness.
You will never change me,
So why do you try so?
I am not hateful or uncaring. I am not a child.
I child can be hurt, I cannot.

Dina A. Atkin

"Fear Not My Friend"

Fear not my friend,
You are part of the Universe,
From stardust toward eternity,
It is a destination beyond imagination.

Forever you'll remain the one your mind and heart dared to be
In thoughts and deeds,
And if you chose to be bold and wise,
Then fear not my friend because your destination will be far,
Far beyond your imagination.

For what you chose to be in mind and heart on earth,
Is what you'll be for eternity,
So fear not my friend,
Stay bold and wise.

Art La Chiusa, Sr.

Untitled

Like the sunshine that wipes away the rain
You are the brightness that eases my pain.
I love you more and more each day,
But I have feelings that are more than words can say.
When you put your arms around me,
I feel some kind of warmth surround me.
You are the happiness that makes flowers bloom;
Your smiles simply wipe away the gloom.
I wish I could see you everyday,
But those are words I simply cannot say.
So stay with me now, so I can remember
The hours we have shared together.
So hold me close, and don't let go.

Dana Truszkowski

"Your Way Home"

When it came time for you to leave,
you brought great grief.
You brightened our life's, but not for long.
Cause you where finding your way back home,
all on your own.
We would of loaned our lives to you
but who knows what was to become of yours.
But now you are gone,
back to your rightful home.
Where you belong brighten life's all over again,
and living in no harm.

Amanda Ellis

You Can Talk to Dogs

You can talk to dogs,
You can say anything,
And they'll just sit there and listen,
While you tell then your pain,
They won't put you down in any way,
Or tell you, you are the one that's wrong,
They'll just sit there and listen,
While you tell them your song,
They won't say your selfish,
Or even that your conceited,
They'll just sit there and listen,
While you tell them your not needed
They won't say your crazy,
Or even walk away,
They'll just sit there and listen,
To anything, you say.

Christy Simmons

"To Lisa"

Thank you for the St. Patrick's day meal
You don't know, how Irish, it makes me feel
Coming over this morning, must have been fate
Even though, the "serving", was a day late
St. Patrick, St. Patrick, my green hats off to you
All the Irish are happy, you were born a Jew
The Jews in Israel, on the dawn, of St. Patrick's day
Eat kosher corned beef and cabbage, and for you, a prayer they say
All the Irish are happy, that Irish whisky is brewed
In Israel where it is brewed strong, and you can get stewed
So that's the story, for under the skin
The Irish and Jewish, are next to kin
It has been known in history, a long, long time back
A corner of Ireland, had a huge crack
That corner fell off, believe me that's real
And the Irish called, it, the land of Israel.

Harry B. Sherr

Love

Love, an illusion, a game.
You dream about it all the time,
But it's never quite the same.

You search your life for someone to cherish,
Someone to care for.
But in the end you just wind up
Getting hurt more and more.

Love is there one minute,
And gone the next.
It can be very hard to handle,
And even more complex.

It's hard to hold on to,
No matter how hard you try.
But no matter how hard that is,
You always have to say goodbye.

To the one who could make you feel special,
Yet break your heart.
Maybe it was meant for the two of you,
To forever be apart.

Barbara Nick

Untitled

When you're on it
You feel very free and light
Like you're floating
Look up at the stars deep enough
And all of a sudden you're there
Up there is very peaceful
Nobody to control you
You're your own person
Nobody's opinion matters
You're free!
Then close your eyes and escape to the field of flowers
Wonderful, colorful flowers
Purple, Red, Blue, Yellow, Pink
And colors you wouldn't even think existed
It's so beautiful, so free, colorful, so me
sometimes when I'm not on it
I can fall deep within myself, and I'm there again
At the field, in the sky so peaceful

Elizabeth Martinez

You Are the Lily of My Heart

You are the lily of my heart,
you gave me a reason to make a new start.
You picked me up when I could not stand,
and gently gave me a helping hand.
On a rainy day you'd walk a mile,
Only to render that loving smile.
When I look at you, I see love
It glows in the night like a snow white dove.
You are like sunshine on a cloudy day,
You are the lily that paved the way.
You give me wisdom beyond compare,
To turn it away, I would never dare.
You build me up when I am down,
And make me feel like wearing a crown.
Lily of my heart I want you to know,
You are the lily that tied my bow.

Christine Avery

Eternal Arrow of Filial Love

(To Christian)

Immutable young Osiris,
you had fly away finally
and slowly
by the milky way of St. James
replete of diamantine starts.

That fugacions shinning in which you raised,
similar to the lighting
was seen by two pure virgins of this life
to be witnesses
that the eternal tent of the lamp-lighter
of the existence
start in a tunnel of light.

Your lute singing
drives you to latitude 450
of north equatorial line ascendant;
ironed soul was yours,
protected
on telluric - collectives ideas
of million of years.

(A fragment of the poetry book, "Eternal Arrow of Eros.")

Beatriz Mayte Santiago-Ibarra

Letting Go

"You" hung over me for so long
"You" hid the warmth of the sun
And blocked all beauty from my eyes.
There was no pleasure in my life -
Only more days like the ones before.
I reached out and pulled you closer
"You" became my protection from hurts in life
I went through the motions of living
with you by my side.
Then came the time I had to let you go
"You" left me slowly
Again I could feel the warmth of the sun
I could see beauty and enjoy laughter
You faded into the past - to only
come back occasionally
No longer do you cloud my every moment
What was this "You" that almost destroyed me?
"You" are grief. I finally set you free.
In turn - I freed myself.

Bonnie Ledger

Daddy's Little Girl

Just call me daddy's little girl,
You know, it's been a long time.
When things were so simple,
And I had peace of mind.

I was daddy's pride and joy,
The apple of his eye.
I was raised like his boy
and one day, he just died.

Oh, how I miss him,
and the things we used to do.
He was always there to save me,
But there were times when he scolded me too.

He taught me a lot in ten short years,
How to be strong, no need for tears.
He was a big man, about 6 foot 4,-
He'd ride me on his shoulders,
We'd have to duck through the doors

My dad would be proud, now that I am grown
I have a good man who loves me
and I have sons of my own....

Christine Gipson

The Moon

Oh moon...Balsam of inspiration.
You look like a pregnant woman.
You give birth every month.
You make all feel in love...
With the love of the fetus
there in the face of the sky.

You have the lyric of inspiration
for love and lovers,
because our eyes look at you
with a prayer from the heart, soul and God.
From the sadness, from the happiness.

You are the inspiration of the poets,
of the writers and singers,
of the rivers and lakes,
of the birds and valleys.
And there you look like a virgin in paradise,
hanging in the infinity of the sky.

Fresia Csoke

Homeless

Even tho you're homeless
You must not walk in fear
Our Heavenly God and Father
Is presently with you - right here

Gods holy spirit dwells among you
To reach the deepest part of your heart
To bring you the joy of knowing Jesus
And never again to part

Trust God to protect you
To give you inner peace
Be willing to accept Jesus
Your burdens and sadness will be released

I have come to forgive you all your sins
And to heal you broken heart
You are so very special - so trust me
I promised this right from the start

Praise me, thank me, give me all the glory
I'm preparing your heart right now, to feel
My peace, my joy and my forgiveness
And to tell a whole new story

Geraldine Nowicki

Letting Go

Anticipation marks each day.
You plan, you dream, you hope, you pray.
You feel each move, each kick, each breath,
You long to hold this child, and yet....
Sometimes love is letting go.

He laughs, he cries, he sings, he talks;
He rolls, he crawls, he falls, he walks.
Now to read, and write, and rule,
He squares his chin and starts to school.
Sometimes love is letting go.

Then it's graduation and degree.
He lives in 'now' and 'yet to be'.
Ahead lie marriage, children, home.
Now he walks and stands alone.
Sometimes love is letting go.

When the time for me is due,
The time when all seems clear and true.
I'll leave these words as legacy,
Grow on and never grieve for me.
Sometimes love is letting go.

Elizabeth A. Reynolds

To My Easter Bunny

What's up Dockett?
  You really light up my socket!
My eyeballs almost pop out when I see you!
  You're a real knockout!
  No wonder I love you like I do!
I'm hunting my special Easter Bunny!
  I'll be yours if you'll be mine, Honey!
At times I'm so lonely I don't know what to do.
  Honey Bunny, I know you must be lonely too.
It makes my life a little more fun!
  Special times, I share love with you, Hon!
Life is filled with fads and bugs.
  I receive healing from your hugs.
It doesn't matter that life is annoying.
  It's your friendship that I'm enjoying.
B de a! B de a! B de a! Dat's all!
  Please write to me or give me a call!

Al Thomas

Ode to Mount Wilson, CA Soul

You asked for relief from the thoughts on your mind
  You said you were weary of this endless grind
You came to this haven of peace for the soul
  You wondered if this was your ultimate goal

You were not alone on this high mountain peak
  There were birds at your head and squirrels at
your feet

They sang and they chattered in endless confusion
  and the deer at your side were not on illusion

Suddenly it was evening — the sun went to bed
  and the silvery moon now ruled in it's stead
Wrapped in it's veil wearing diamonds past number
  The wind through the pines gently lulled you
to slumber

Awaken, my friend, and start out anew
  erased are the thoughts that troubled you
Return to the grind with this word of advice
  You, poor fool, were in paradise!

Dorothea Montgomery

Agoraphobia

Panic sets in....It takes control of your body
You shake inside..... then your mind loses control.

The Door.....Don't close the Door!
I'll die....the air will be gone,
I can't breathe.......I Have to get home!

I'm inside......This is my home!
Don't make me leave
The "Door" protects me,
Hurt can't get to me here!
Fear surrounds me....Terror overwhelms my mind
I'm not in control
If I "Have" to go "Through That Door!"

The door is my friend.....my protector!
It keeps out the hurt......no strangers in here!
No one can hurt me
They can't tell me things "I just can't understand!"
"Keep The Door Closed!"
"I Need The Protection!"

Char M. Reese

Dear Mother

Dear mother, on this day to bless mothers,
You stand above all the rest in my heart.
If I could choose my mother, no other
Could ever take your place or play your part

In my play of life that's not yet written,
Though the scene is set and the actors grace
And folly the stage, some with selves smitten.
And the playwright sits in the sky defaced.

May there be a very happy ending.
A happy first act, too, to our wee play.
The play that starts with my mother spending
Her time to raise her children day to day.

I thank you, Mother, for your time and care.
You've taught me how to love and live and dare.

Brian N. Bailey

Addiction

You lost all you had, now you want more;
You think your bad, and maybe you'll score.

You've done so much dope, your afraid it's all over;
You've given up hope, your flesh getting colder.

You hang on a rope, we thought you were bolder;
You grabbed the rock, instead of my shoulder.

You lost all you had, you wanted more;
You thought you were bad, but you didn't score.

Now your dead, you're casket was carried;
Your spirit has fled, your bones are all barred.

Your loved ones mourned, from dusk till dawn;
They were all warned, that you would be gone.

No one cared, or so you thought;
But you were wrong, yes, you forgot.

I've seen so many nightmares, from this dirty dope;
So many fears, and friends that can't cope.

I ask you one favor, don't do coke;
It's you life I savor, and I won't give up hope...

Belinda Cox

Unforgiven

Driving home
You try not to roam.
You take a left on memory lane,
And try your best to hold in the pain.

You see the flowers
And it brings on that painful shower.
You think of the kid with the gun,
Who swears it was an accident in fun.

You hear the sound of the fatal crack!
The same kid is down the street
But this time, he falls to his feet.
It's his face you see under the white sheet.

You wonder why it comes to this?
In your mind, you still miss.
You paint the bloody picture in your mind.
You wish to rewind and go back in time.

You wonder how you can win?
It's already been done, on paper that's thin!
The ones who commit the sin,
Are the ones that are the "Unforgiven"!!!

Donna Church

Someone Must Tell It...Yes, Jesus Saves

You need shelter from the rain?
You want to cover up the pain?
You feel all alone, you call misery your own?
"There is hope, you can cope, you can find Jesus...there is hope

Someone must tell it...yes, Jesus saves

There is salvation from crack,
Salvation from your mind
When you are down on your back
He'll still take the time
There is relief from the pain
When that's on your brain
You have hope, you can cope, you can find Jesus
In your heart find Jesus the Christ
There is hope...you can cope

YES, JESUS SAVES

Jimmy Vincent

"Dad"

Ever since I can remember
You were all ways there for me.
When no one else would remember me
You were the only one that did.
I can't phantom someone else taking your place
You're my father and my friend
Some people don't have neither one,
I'll all ways recapture the memories
When you would all ways made me laugh,
Helped me understand life's little mysteries,
And when you would yell at me,
When I even knew, that I needed to be.
Don't ever doubt that I don't appreciate.
All the things that you're done for me.
I can't express the love I have for you
The words that I want to use
They don't compare
Your love is greater than words can express.
I'll all ways think of you where ever
I may be.

Angelita Benavides

Heaven Sent

Of all the guys I've ever met, you're the one I can't forget.
Your love is like a pot of gold, hard to get and hard to hold.
But did you know the Lord above, created you for me to love.
I had a heart and it was true, but now it's gone from me to you
Take care of it as I have done, for now you have two and I have none.

Dig my grave and dig it deep, with marble stone from head to feet,
And place upon it a poor white dove to show the world I died for love.

If I get to heaven and you've not there, I'll paint your name on the golden stair.
And if you're not there by judgement day, I'll know you went the other way.
Just to prove my love is true, I'll go to Hell to be with you.

Jaccie Christian

"Mom" One Worth The World

Putting your faith in others, sometimes never succeed -
Your picture of life sometimes - scattered like beads
Force to take a road, that wasn't planned by you -
Many of your "dreams" - you had no means to make true
You have shed many of tears -
You have become strong in your fears
Your tasks always go beyond dawn -
But with faith and strength, its always done
You always gave to others, but not to yourself -
Many times for you, there was nothing left
You are never to busy to lend a hand
If you can do it, you help your fellow man
The children you've raised, disappointment you see -
Their lives haven't been what you wanted it to be
We too have taken a road we didn't prepare -
Though we fall - you're always there
To teach us rules that were learned by you -
"Always do your best - with what tools you choose."
To show your effort was not in vein -
We are teaching our children and mention your name

Dee Rivers

I Speak of Time and Dreams

does a secret lie in a dream?
your worst fears lie between legends of the mind.
i would like eternal life with you
small moments with you, walk with you,
watch you sleep give you love - DREAM.

TIME - is all we have.
like the splendid, solemn, heroic, shining, burning
great magnitude of oblivion.
able to learn wisdom and sorrow
protect you carefully

then tragic events, unnoticed may not happen.
my heart clanged, squeaked, trembled, banged.
fingers closed the air.
the long month that words stopped.
silent love SPEAK! and never stop.
my very soul afraid.
i dread losing you. - it hurt.
for now, I would like sleep.

Deanna Conner

Sound Of Battle

To hear the sound of battle will chill you to the bone,
You're in a distant country and oh so far from home.

Too well you still remember the ones you had to leave,
The tear's you tried so hard to hide, the ones they didn't see.

A kiss good-by a gentle touch will somehow have to do,
Until the fighting's over and I come home to you.

At night I lay here in my bunk, thought's run through my mind,
Of how I miss my family, the ones I left behind.

Somewhere in the distance you hear the awful sound,
Of mortar's going over, exploding on the ground.

The night sky's seem to light up, from the tracers overhead,
Not caring for the ones they'll hit, the ones that they'll
Leave dead.

The sight of death is all around a pain you know so well,
The morning sun will soon be up, but tonight's a living hell.

The dead will all be counted, for them the war is through,
They gave as much as they could give, they died for me and you.

I hope to someday leave this land, the days I'm counting down,
I've seen the sight of battle, I've heard the Battle sound.

Gene M. Koonce

Destiny

You've searched for wisdom and sought the truth.
You've pushed the limits to scale the wall.

Success is achieved; the pinnacle's reached.
Conceit bears fruit - the snare's soon set.

So you turn away, forsake the law,
and reach for vices to slow the fall.

No echo sounds from the words you spoke.
Darkness devours - your destiny's met.

Sheol awaits with open arms.
Warm compassion; she starts to call.

You hear her voice; sweet words enchant.
Your finest hour - she casts her net.

Dwayne Candler

Love Them While They Are Here

They say one dies and a new life comes in
Yes, life is beautiful when you hold someone dear
A world without it would just be a sin
So please, love them while they are here

Life is too short for fussing and fighting
And it can hurt someone enough to shed a tear
Being there for someone can be enlightening
So please, love them while they are here

Don't put off loving someone until tomorrow
Let them know by holding them near
Especially when their heart is full of sorrow
Just please, love them while they are here

Christina A. Jones

My Perspective from Africa to Black America

Abandon your way, my way is better, not deep, dark and mysterious as yours. I learned what I learned from the hands of a hard task master.

Farewell to your language, customs, traditions, and tribesmen. There is no stopping change now. Taken from the school of my mother's lap I learned a new way against my will.

Recapitulate, to me and be what I want you to be, away with you, my way is better. I learned to give you my mind and my soul and to forget from whence I came.

Illusioned by my entrapment, NO! But helplessly I followed. I learned to be what my master wanted me to be.

Cleaving to what's left of me and my past is not easy to do. Once my storytellers were scattered I learned from the people that I loved until that was too good for me. No longer do I know my sisters, brothers, can vaguely remember mama. And dad, who can ever know?

Not all primitive, rings in their noses, undressed and full of wizardry, as some may think.

Punish me no more for who I was or who I am. Come to know and respect me as you do your own. You'll come to find that I'm not so mysterious after all. Come face to face with me and see how much I look, love, think and have the same feelings as you do.

Ella Williams

Nature

One lesson, nature, let me learn from thee:
With no education, no training and no books to read
How does thou paint the world a vibrant and eloquent green?
It's the first of April, the birds sing joyously and flutter;
The branches are bare, swaying by the breeze to capture life.
Within two weeks, the scientist in thee makes the pigment chlorophyll
And splashes it across the rivers, the mountains and the meadows.
How doest thou make it at normal temperature, and with no fancy equipment?
You baffle me nature, because it takes ages for humans to make chlorophyll
Also the yield is poor, with many byproducts to plague the scientist.
As an artist, thou art the teacher of teachers, the delight of students.
Let me learn, nature, let me learn from the artist and the scientist
in thee.

Bail L. Rao

The Path

One day as I was walking down a path I was thinking of my worries and my past. As I continued I realized that the path was was getting darker and I soon began to fear the darkness the emptiness all around me. I began to walk very slowly and my fear was growing stronger; I soon fell to my knees and cried. I heard a whisper in my ear and it softly said do not be afraid for I am near just reach out and grasped my hand and I will lead you to the lighted land.

John Plunkett

All Because You Cared

I was like a leaf blown around and around in the air.
No one seemed to give a care.
Sometimes I fell to the ground were few would bother to look down.
There I would lay day after day, after day waiting for death to take me away.
Then you came and picked me up and told me I was loved.
Now I know people care and all because of you.
You made me into a blossoming flower and all because you cared.

Kristen O'Shaughnessy

"Angels"

A glowing star shines down at night,
Looking in homes even without windows,
Guiding all through wrong and right.

Watching over worlds with powerful might,
In summer sun and winter snows,
A glowing star shines down at night.

With all of our sadness and every plight,
A presence is there to watch us grow,
Guiding all through wrong and right.

When aspirations reach new heights,
And we need a push to help us go,
A glowing star shines down at night.

Persistence keeps us in constant sight,
And it shares with us all it knows,
Guiding all through wrong and right.

Wisdom knows no black or white,
It only sees a person's soul.
A glowing star shines down at night,
Guiding all through wrong and right.

Nadia Nakonecznyj

Why God Why

God called and took the son we
loved one cold and snowy day, then
led him to a wondrous place that's
not that far away.

He had to leave to early and it
didn't seem quite fair, but, God has
promised many times there's no pain
or sorrow there.

Someday we'll see him once again
and then I'm sure we'll know, the
reason that God took him not that long ago.

On the faces of his children his
loving, smile we can see and in
our hearts we'll always know our
son he'll always be.

Margie Flann

Love Is

Love is a river that flows to the sea,
Love is like a tall oak tree.
Love me tenderly and be kind,
Because you might find some lovin' in me.
Love is an ocean that covers the land,
Love is a mountain formed out of sand.
Look for my love deep in the sea,
Find it is my love in the leaves of a tree.

She stole my heart and left it at bay;
She stole my love and then lost her way.
She took my love in the palm of her hand,
She looked for words written in sand.
She took my love and on bended knee,
She took my love down to the sea.
Love like the river flows to the sea.
Love is like a tall oak tree.

Whispers my love are the sweetest words;
They fly away on the wings of birds.
She stole my love and on bended knee,
All of my love was washed to the sea.

Norma Byerly

"The Change"

The animals and the Indians, friends, hand in hand.
Living as a family, being one with the land.
They got along so good, they were all so free.
Until something changed, making them have to flee.
That change couldn't lose, it does all that it can.
It destroys the people, it is the white man.
They came in groups, taking over the land.
Causing Indians to leave, not daring to take a stand
The white men started building, those places they call towns.
They called it civilization, moving Indians from their grounds.
The change still came, just like a brand new day.
The Indians tried for peace, but there just wasn't a way.
The white men put them away, put the Indians on fenced land.
They weren't used to being held, not beaten, not broken, not banned.
They had to work so hard, for a child, a nephew, a niece.
Ending with less than nothing, and all in the name of:
"Peace."

Suzanne L. Jones

Brighteners

When you get up in the morning,
Look around!
And see all things in nature
That God has made abound.
See the squirrels and chipmunks,
The cats and doggies, too,
The cow out in the meadow
Who gives a gentle moo
(and milk, too).
The trees and grass and birds and flowers
can brighten even the darkest hours.
We can enjoy them our whole lives long,
And keep our hearts in constant song.

Margaret E. Traband

"Look To God On High!"

Lift thine eyes to the Lord-
look to him on high,
seek his strength, read his word-
unto him draw nigh!

Look to him for your answer-
he alone can fill each need,
you will always find him there-
to nature your spiritual seed!

And he too, can take care of earthly strife,
for he was sent unto this world, to bring abundant life.
so trust as a person, to walk as a child of God-
he is everlasting, let him come in, wherever in life you trod!

Jody Raelene Hodge

The Earth

The birds are in the tree,
Looking down at me,
Bees are making honey.
Fish are swimming in the sea.
Flowers are budding faster than lighting in the sky.
Then a beautiful butterfly flew
right past my eye.
Then I heard an eagle call.
After the sun grew dim,
All I heard were crickets cry
within the deep dark sky.

Kandice Shirley

Society Problems

Sitting on my bed
looking out my window
I lose myself in thought
Thinking about all the problems in our society today
Babies crying for cocaine and dying from the lack of it
Kids picking on kids and being rude and rotten to each other
Teenagers killing teenager over a stupid little dispute
(an accidental push)
Adults being disloyal and deceiving; only out for themselves
What is wrong with our society?!
Everyone complains about the problems in our society
They want peace
They want everyone to get along and love each other.
But they never do their part
They're always waiting for everyone else to do something
But yet they complain and want peace
What is wrong with our society?!

Nadine Di Spirito

Love Is

Love is a tender feeling of affection.
Love is a special connection.

Love is mutual devotion,
Love is emotion,
Love is progressing together in forward motion.

Love is a great fondness for one another,
Love is a sensation that makes the stomach flutter.

Love is passion in a particular fashion.

Love is attachment,
Love is enchantment,
Love is sentiment,
Love is enjoyment.

Love is an intimate kiss,
Love is bliss.

Love is yearning,
Love is together learning.

Love is sexual, emotional, physical, and mental attraction,
Love is a warm, caring interaction.

Love is glee,
And most of all, love is you and me.

S. Kunkle

Love Is

Love is like the ocean, deep and blue,
Love is like a smile, warm and true.

Love is like a rose, soft and gentle,
Love is like a lion, fierce and temperamental.

Love is a heart of mixed emotions,
Love is a mind full of strange notions.

Love is like heaven with halo's and glitter.
Love is like hell, all cold and bitter.

Love is like nature, perfect in formation,
Love is beautiful, like all God's creations.

Patrice Lanneaux

The Time Is Now

If you are ever going to love me,
Love me now, while I still can know.
The sweet and tender feelings.
Which from true affections flow.

Love me now, while I am living,
Do not wait until I'm gone
And than have it chiseled in marble,
Sweet words on ice-cold stone.

If you have tender thoughts of me,
Please tell me now.
If you wait until I am sleeping
Never to awaken
There will be death between us, can't you see
And I won't hear you then.

So if you love me, even a little bit,
Let me know it while I am living
So I can know and treasure it forever and ever.

Amen

Patricia Grimwood

A Kiss and a Song

As I lay here searching death's face, I feel, yet did not feel, my loved one's embrace. As this macabre countenance hovers over me, I look at things I see, yet did not see. I picture houses, yards, and faces in my waning mind, and many others things I'll leave behind. In the vanquished condition I am in, I realize I will never see them again.

In this condition, about myself I do not worry, for life goes from me in a flurry of memory and wishes, of leaving my loved ones in material riches.

I am finished with this imperfect world, and my past life is now a legacy unfurled. Though over me they may call and cry, they shall forget and their tears will dry. I am the star now, they the audience, but each of these will go in accordance.

Yes, this silent face before me knows that all are equal, and that all for this are eligible. This is the last requisite for this human life, to give it up, whether in happiness or strife.

Alas, mourners, do not be sad for long. Finish your life with a kiss and a song. For with a kiss you show love, and with a song happiness prevails. With these visions and the wisdom of God above, you will be swept to Him in haste, as a small vessel in a gale.

James A. White

Reversals

The repressed, eternally anxious, grey underbelly of bisexuality
Lunged ambivalently from yet another closet
Wreaking more damage than you anticipated,
Threatening your first self-therapy session already in the works:
A rebound diversion fearfully thought out,
Desperately needed and touchy as a raw nerve.
How resolutely you then changed, without pause
From partner to enemy, a fait accompli, without grace.
Cold heartedly you burned your past, at times in derision,
Quivering with arrogance from your fragile new base,
Yet secretive and evasive as a coward in appeasement.
Tired, pudgy faced, pouting and hostile,
A volatile mixture of aggression and insecurity,
You freak suddenly when asked Why?
Like deer caught in the headlights,
Confused about which side of the road it came,
You bolt into the shadows of your duplicity,
Spewing evasions, stabbing at your past to kill,
Hanging on to a thin, fragile, wafting bubble of masculinity.

Steve Harper

"Futility"

Is life mere Eden, face to face,
Made to choose of hell or grace?
Or where is choice if fate hath led
The mockery of life to dread?
Or is but joy a bitter curse,
To breach one to despair, or worse?
Is memory but a conscious will
To blot the pain? Or better still,
Is hope a cushion made to rest
A soul, until the final test?
Is faith narcotic to the awe of hopelessness, or not?
Is taunting rue but the just price
Of one's own choice begot?
To ride the waves of life and still
Accept as fate the final toll,
Are you the master of what waits?
Or he the master of your soul?
'Ashes to ashes', the final fact,
But where is the choice the moral lacked?
Yesterday passed and tomorrow is due
So bide the time, and tomorrow, too.

Patricia L. O'Donnell

To Be A Human Being

Born and conceived by what is love
Made to feel that what above
Is something to deep to understand
They say - keep it low and don't make demands,
Be good, obey, conform to what is true
But what is truth? Truth for me or truth for you?

Break through the fear and insecurities
Find your love, your truth, your reality
Don't believe that what they say cannot be
Turn your spirit into an entity.

Positive energy is what we need
Believe in that power and feed!
Feed your hunger as your appetite grows
Yearning for knowledge...but again who knows?

Feel the love grow within your soul
Let it take flight and go beyond the threshold
Fly on, fly on, spreading peace from within
Take a breath and feel what it means
To love thyself and to be a human being.

Troy Packwood

Nature Of Love

Mountains in the distance, Eagles in the sky
Makes me dream that I can fly.
Soaring through the tree tops, With rivers below
Echoing the sounds of a long time ago.
Beauty in the leaves, Beauty in the grove
Makes me feel like a long-stemmed rose.
With the glimmering sunshine, Through the morning dew
Makes me feel all my love for you.
With the singing from the birds, and the rain from the sky
Makes me wonder why you should cry.
So fly away, fly to the trees,
Nothing will change my love for thee.

Kendall S. Anspach

Reflections

Our minds are full of wheels that turn
Making us to think of things
That are sometimes better left to die
Some songs we shouldn't sing

Leave them buried in the past
That's where they all belong
Don't bring them up or think of them
Remembering would be wrong

We punish ourselves for things we've done
Just never letting go
Don't speak of it to anyone
No one else should ever know

Wake up every passing day
It's always on your mind
Go back to sleep forget for now
Just pass a little time

Never will you forget this thought
This memory you locked away
Just do the best you can somehow
And deal with it day by day

Sherry Grady

The Prize

I'm climbing, struggling up the slippery metal steps.
Mama's there to steady my fears.
"You can do it. The slide down will be your prize."
Daddy cheers me on. Another cautious step up.
But then he's not there to watch.
I continue the climb, stronger now, but it's not as fun.

Mama is farther away now, but still there, smiling up at me.
"You can do it. The slide down will be your prize."
So hard, so long, this struggle to climb the slide.
I have to stop at times to catch my breath
But I keep the prize always in mind.
Others join me in the climb, to help or hinder.

When did I reach the top?

I don't know but this is too fast and too rough I don't like
this slide downhill too fast and too rough I've scraped my
leg and hurt my arm get me off.

A wrinkled hand stretches out to steady me, to slow me up.
The jolt hurts her brittle bones, but she smiles.
This slide down is not my prize.
She is.

Polly Adkins

"The Dance of a Maple Tree"

Hello Maple Tree!
Maple says, "Come closer, unite and do a wind dance with me.
Gently touch my branches, let my leaves caress your fingers.
Close your eyes, lean your body close and feel my energy.
Now, let's dance!"

Maple Tree, there is freedom in your supple branches.
With sweeping flow, you rock me high and low,
propelling me in your arms.
Your leaves laugh as they urge me to keep up with the song.

I leap and soar in a wind choreographed ballet,
that is as timeless as the earth itself.
Before, I only saw you rooted to the ground,
or playing soft music with your leaves.

Ahh, but my how you dance!

Terry Wood Galbreath

The Gifts We Gave Each Other

Long ago, as we remember, we gave our love so warm and tender.
Many days of joyous sunshine, silly things that make fun shine.
Days of happiness and laughter, deeper love forever after.

These are the gifts we gave each other.

The years went by, both good and bad, somehow we made each other glad,
Glad we had each other to share the problems that we had to bear.
A sorrow divided is half the load and easier to travel the stormy road.

These are the gifts we gave each other.

Sometimes, when I felt depressed, I'd look at him knowing I was blessed.
He made me feel that he cared, he let me know my grief was shared
If sometimes I had to cry he understood the reasons why.

These are the gifts we gave each other.

The years go by so very fast, what now is present soon is past,
But two in love can stand a lot because of strength within the knot
The binds them each to one another, a tie that's stronger than any other.

These are the gifts God gave to us.

Marie F. Endicott

One for the Book

Muse a pressed rose embossed upon the fern it entwines
many passionate wonders undiscerned as to why
this subtle one was left alone to wither and die
another page to be turned and pondered, nevermore
a symbol of the beauty it spurns eternal bliss
with no attention in words a reply to ignore
extinguished colors burned deeper than a flame's first kiss
explores just to learn where everlasting love will lie
a brief infatuation drifts separate of all tie,
dead in winter white pages, expressed with a sigh.

Will Cline

Invalid Poetry

He moves in mysterious ways
Me, I move in jerky motion
We could be on Broadway!
If we ever got our acts together...

Some like it hot
Some like it cold
But no one likes it luke warm, except my brain.
"I will spew you out of my mouth"
Oh, so that's where I've been all this while
And I thought I was being slowly digested in huge barrels of HC1
Industrial strength. The new, improved formula.

In sickness and in health
In poverty and in wealth
In everything always
Bless the Lord Jesus, O my soul
Preferably in health and in wealth,
but hey, who's complaining?
Just my poor, sick soul

Limin Lee

Untitled

My life has gone by so very fast.
Now that I'm older I remember the past.
It seemed a lifetime to get to sixteen.
And then twenty-one and fulfill all my dreams.
But now its much later and life slips on by,
Ever so fast and I don't know why.
If time could slow down just a little each day,
I'd take time to enjoy it in every way.

Laura L. Riley

Untitled

The summer breeze moves through
me; it strikes quickly to lighten my head
faster than any drug.

Across the yard carpeted in green
stands a life, with a pink and gold back drop
the tree dances.

My eyes marvel in the vision of
what my ears can not hear.

A rhythm in the breeze that makes
the menacing oak glide like a swallow in
flight.
Singing madly with every russell
and arabesque's towards the threads of gold that flow to the earth;
when the lady of the sun lets down her hair for the evening.

M. Henry

Thoughts

As I sit before the window on a cold and rainy day
Memories of long ago came tumbling in my head
a warm and cozy kitchen where mother baked our bread
of a little boy who sat upon my knee, for all the world to see.
As I sit before the window on this cold and rainy day
the memories of life keep tumbling in my head, little girls
with dark brown curls, a dog a cat who use to spat.
As I sit before the window on this cold and rainy day it
brings a little sadness of all the bygone days of a father
who worked so hard with toiled hands who loves the music
of the great bands.
As I sit before the window on this cold and rainy day
I see a little sun to brighten up the day.

Nancy J. Faust

"Battleship Arizona"

Way out there on sea watch BATTLESHIP ARIZONA
Memory still holds flyin' Japs responsible
For the once proud ship now a submerged rustin' hulk
But ninth sailor's returned to man battle station.

Way down there cold streams wash BATTLESHIP ARIZONA
Mis'ry makes ninth want blood of those responsible
And now once more he's ready to fight risin' suns
With twelve hundred who stayed at their battle stations.......

Sunday rerun those suns on zeroes come in low
From those ship turrets gun fires glow
Sailors hope a diff'rent outcome goes up in smoke
Does most smoke float from aircraft or boat?

They fight there to save their BATTLESHIP ARIZONA
Their adren'lin flows fightin' odds surmountable
So you think this is impossible and can't fathom
No way can you see that this time sailors have won
Blind faith won't let you see divine thing that has come.

Sam J. Alcorn

Knowing Sadness

Have you ever heard a tear drop?
Or a heart break?
I've seen the remains of shattered dreams,
And passed the graves of dead hopes.
I hear the echoes of forgotten memories,
And I know where to find lost love.
I hold on to fallen stars,
And know sadness all too well.

Kristen L. Putnam

Forever Spring

We walked leisurely through the flowers
Midst twilight's fading glow
And gazed enchanted there for hours
Upon God's beauty there below
With a heavenly fragrance in the air
And trees dripping with evening dew
Our hearts seemed to lose their earthly cares
Life was filled with meaning anew
We felt so calm, so free and happy
As we strolled on arm in arm
Although we then felt quite sadly
That not all the world possessed this charm
As we stopped to rest before a country lane
Where fences mingled with springtime blossoms
We craved to walk barefoot again
Through soft moss and dreams not forgotten
We looked deep within our hearts
And thought—More than anything
Love could bring happiness
And make Forever Spring.

Lisle G. Russell

Who Are You?

Once present upon all the land, roaming as nomads,
migrating like buffalo to fruitfulness of land and element.
Who are you? Living with nature in harmony as one, taking only for
survival, not as villains on the run. Who are you?
Life full of spirit, culture, heritage, all blended in splendor
on its own. Knowledge of all seasons, their reaps and rewards
Who are you?
Through invasions standing tall, although conquered did not fall.
Who are you?
Stripped of culture, heritage, land, numbers dwindling like grains of
sand. Who are you?
Kneeling in silence, head bowed, saying nothing, very humble, never
rebelling, never questioning. Who are you?
Culture fading, heritage, language all but gone, lost and forgotten
in time and era. Who are you?
In Statistics and surveys not counted, not even a hint of existence.
Who are you?
I know! I know who you are, as extinct as the buffalo. You are
native American or are you?

Sherry A. Smoker

A Great Big Part Of Me

Not all grandmas are alike, specially
mine I'd say, for she was so very special
in every single way. From the way she
combed her hair, to the way she wore her
clothes, even when she'd twinkle around her
little toes. Not all grandma's are alike,
specially mine I'd say, she scared away my
fears, and chased them all away. She was
kind to everyone, and all she brought was
joy, even with the littlest trinket or toy.
She always made me happy, she always
made me smile, but now she'll pass on
for just a short while.
I know I'll see her again. I know I
will someday, but for right know, in
heaven she will stay. She is a great big
part of me and that she'll always stay.
For I love my grandma in every single way.

Maria Kostrach

Untitled

Seconds turn to minutes as time goes speeding by.
Minutes turn to hours and my soul still waits to fly.
Hours turn to days, and days again to years.
And still I wait and watch time pass as I hide behind my fears.

No longer can I stand idly by and hope that life will flare.
It's time to take the whole world on - live out my dreams and dares.
There are no things to stop me - only some that want to try,
But I'll brush them off for life awaits to show my soul the skies.

I'll touch the stars, I'll ride the wind, I'll climb a mountain peak.
I'll do all that my heart cries for, I'll find all that I seek.
And when I've had my victories and I've let my spirits soar
I'll stop and reflect for a moment or two. . . . .and then go
back for more!

Michael Barlow

Heed The Wind

Seeing beauty, hope, and expectation,
Mirrored in the eyes of the new.

Time flies away, cradled by the Wind.

Smelling of sweetness, hope, and expectation,
The new blossom into the young.

Take wisdom from the wise, young blossom.
Heed the Wind.

Tasting bitterness, hope, and expectation,
The young emerges as mature.

Time rushes away, running with the Wind.

Feeling content, hope and expectation,
The mature evolves into the wise.

Take youth from the young blossom.
Heed the Wind.

Seeing, smelling, tasting, feeling,
All that we are and can be is the duty of,
The new, the young,
The mature, the wise.

Time slips away.

Head the Wind.

R. A. Yale Morante

Baby Don't Cry

Baby don't cry, baby don't cry
Mommy will never say goodbye
Baby don't fret, baby don't fret
All that you need, I'll be sure that you get
Son don't grow, son don't grow
Mommy knows one day you'll have to go
Son don't leave, son don't leave
Without you here my heart will grieve
Mom don't cry, mom don't cry
I will never say goodbye
Mom don't fret, mom don't fret.
All that you need, I'll be sure that you get.
Mommy don't die, mommy don't die
You told me you would never say goodbye

Keith Reeves

Regrets

There are things in life we want to forget
Most of them are things we'd always regret
The pain that stings to our innermost souls
We hope to keep secret so nobody knows
It's no fun to remember the pain
Only our sanity hoping to gain
So make the best of today and leave yesterday behind
For there is nothing we can do
But look tomorrow in the eye

Valerie D. Jackson

In Praise Of Book Reviews

There's so many books that I want to read,
Mostly in science, and math indeed!
Yet I am lazy, browse and read part,
Most that I relish, I don't even start.
The best-seller list, is bristling with gems,
Its from the titles my eagerness stems.
So then in despair, I give up all hope
Of joyously reading the book in full scope.
But wait! There's salvation; I often do find
In some magazine the balm for my mind:
The book is reviewed, by critic of style,
And all its great contents are summed with a smile.
So I end up real happy with gist of the book,
And if its appealing, I'll really go look.

Maurice Machover

Diaspora

Ruth,
mother of Obed who begat
Jesse father of David
King of Judah and Israel,
gleaned among the sheaves,
an alien beholden to her host,
gleaned without reproach in Bethlehem.

Compassion, tenderness and pity —
without which I'd be ruthless, but I'm Ruth
who bore Adam and Michael and nurtured
various cats and dogs,
one bird and a hamster.
Ruth drives on, a transient
mired by the smog of minutae,
too often neglecting
ruth.

Ruth W. Ereli

Untitled

I am a desert,
my emotions whirl in the wind.
I am the color yellow,
my happiness shines like the sun.

I am a coyote,
my playfulness runs with the sand.
I howl at night pleading to say up longer.

I am a cactus bloom,
I open up in the morning to start the new day.
I droop in the afternoon as the heat darts after me.

I am a rock,
the lizard scales of freedom race across me;
the sunlight glares as it sets behind the mountains.
My adventuring falls with the night,
I cast my shadows as my sleepiness grows...

I am asleep

Zoe Randall

Fire and Spirit

I came to life as you went to death,
My eager, reckless Papa.

It has taken me fifty years to find you
after you were blown to bits in the war.

I found you in a tiny French village
in a room at the top of the stairs.

I found you in your camp on the coast of France
sharing your whiskey with your men.

I found you in Aachen
as I entered the valley of the shadow of your death.

I found the "wooded section."
I found the crater made by the bomb that ripped open the earth and you.

The earth is still carved out,
but it's covered now with ferns that ripple in the wind.

Barbed wire that marked the spot fifty years ago
enters at the centers of the trees.

I sat down on that holy ground
and I talked to you there.

You would be seventy-five years old today.
I raise my glass to you, dear Papa, fire and spirit!

Susan J. Johnson

My Window

I look through my window, only to be stricken by the sun
My eyes close tightly, my face becomes undone
I sense a feeling of dimness surround me in my room
Only to notice what had struck me is now a shaded gloom...

I open my eyes so gently, creeping a little light in
What I thought once was so bright has now grown so dim.

A breath of loneliness is upon me and so I wonder why,
When such a short time ago, I woke up by the sunlit sky...

When next I look through my window and the sun strikes me
face on. I will hold on to that feeling of brightness,
because now the gloom is gone...

Yvette Azor

Dream Again

I lie here awake
My eyes closed hoping to dream again
I can see the dark emptiness of my thoughts
I gaze over at the clock next to my bed periodically
I wonder if I will sleep tonight
Or ever again

Past, present and future
Are all parts of my conscious thoughts
Dark and empty like a midnight sky
I gaze over my limp old pillow
To see what the clock has to report to me
A minute has passed since the last time I looked

I lie here awake
I wonder if I will ever get to dream again
Another minute has passed

This night is all so dreadfully long
I really hope to dream again
What am I going to do
Yet all I want is to dream again

G. W. Pepin

In His Eyes

He makes my foot falter
My eyes don't want to stray
From ever shining, deeply blinding
glory of the day;
Reflected in such away.
With him he begs me please to stay.
In his arms he pleads for me to lay.

He loves me is what I hear say.
He loves me in the most divine way.

I watch as his hand along my skin does play.
The words, if I could find them, my mind to numb to say.
My body turns to clay.
In his arms the outside world is held at bay.

My heart in pain does delay,
For he speaks and takes my breath away.

Words too inadequate to say
In his eyes his love's displayed.

In my heart a calm despair.
With you this story I do share.
From such love do beware.

Melissa K. Puckett

Free

"Nothing in this life is free",
My father always said to me.
"You must work hard for what you get".
How true his words, I'd found, and yet
As I walk by the sea so blue,
All he said was not quite true,
For here is calm, and beauty too,
Put here by God, for me (and you).
The birds that fly, the trees that grow,
The sun that shines, white fields of snow
So look around and you will see
There's quite a lot in life that's free.

JoAnne Minar

Thank You, My Friend

(To Barb, a very special lady.)
My friend
I met you while I was in the midst of trouble and strife.
You touched my life.

My friend

Your smile brightened many days for me, you were kind and
caring from the start.
You touched my heart.

My friend

Through good and bad times, our friendship continued to grow.
You touched my soul

Thank You, My friend

Penny Taylor

Dreams Can Come True

No matter how big
or small it may seem,
everybody has a dream.
And every dream can come true
if you really want it to.
But the key is to never give up,
for the dream that seems the farthest away
might come true for you one day.

Lisa McAloon

My Love, My Life!

I'm cracking!
My head is going to explode.
My heart is breaking into millions of piece!
I feel like I'm breaking down, my insides corrode.
My life is close to the end, me it pleases.
I don't want to live anymore
Why should I live if my life isn't worth living.
There is nothing to do I am such a bore...
I can't offer anything, I'm not getting.
My love is not worth having, why should I give it!
No one wants me, I might as well leave.
I can handle the strain of my world.
I should just crawl in a hole and die!
Gave my love so freely, I shouldn't kept it inside
My first instincts were to love, or second thought.
I could have built a wall, should have.
Maybe if there's a next times, I will!
Maybe not! No next time!

Jodi Lee Vance

Untitled

Somewhere deep within it's hiding from the truth
My heart will not continue to grow for others.
Lost in the confusion of pain it does not exist
Becoming such a beautiful person and sometimes caring too much
That lies within the hiding
Easing my troubles by taking away my sadness
Thinking of those last moments?
Remembering with family and friends to find the answers
What is hiding shall never surface.
And if it shall, it will be the time.
Moments of loneliness
Times of tears
Cries for someone to listen
If you only knew I was there.
My guardian angel, I still am.
I too am hurting.
Losing a love, a friend, a companion.
Decisions that shouldn't have been thought,
That didn't need to exist in blind fate
Growing stronger for you, growing farther for others!

Shannon Elizabeth Rogers

Untitled

My heart is full of emptiness,
My mind is full of despair
My arms are reaching out,
But no one is ever there.

During the time of need
The world comes crashing down.
Still no one is there
To pick me up off the ground.

My heart wants to be full of love
My mind wants to be full of happy feelings.
My arms want to hold someone tight
Then and only then, will life have some meaning.

Twila Krauser

Unsung Hero

Walking through the black forest.
Lost in a world unknown to man.
Struggling to see beyond the darkness.
Doing everything that you can.
To see the light of a new tomorrow.
And hold the hand that is reaching out.
From a distant place that knows no fear.
And will guide you through your every doubt.

Nicole Mason

Dreams

Our true existence is based solely
on our hopes and dreams. Life is only
a shadow if we do not attempt to
make our dreams come true. When you
dream and believe in yourself and your dreams,
your dreams will come true. For if we fail
to dream we fail to exist.

Lori Bakken

The Playground

I'm safe in this place.
My mommy-daddy red box that's always sunny.

In the sandpit where we play
We make castles and kingdoms that shine in the sun.

And there's a tune I hum,
With words in my head and my heart that I don't quite know.

And there's a stone she can hold,
Smooth and cold. Fly like a plane if she'd just let go.

And the words of the song are wrong as I sing,
But words, not like stones, fly soft and slow,
land with a sigh and fade.

With the speed of a jet the stone stings,
The sun stuns, bounces round my box, my safe box, like a blade.

My eyes cry, my mouth screams,
But the blade cuts the sound and my heart still sings.

Nina Hollier

Help Me I'm Drowning!

As emotions fill my cranium and the water fills my eyes
My muscles get tense and my fist clenches tight.
I'm fitted in a rage of anger,
like a madman in a straight jacket.
For I am drowning in feelings that have no meaning.
Yet these same feelings I feel can take life,
or will they bring life?
How shall I know if I am suffocated by life,
and their everyday realities?
Grab my hand and save my life,
for my lungs are filled with the world's hardships and I
don't wish to die.
Just yet!!!!

James Neumann

Behind The Door

The door is closed.
My sister and I sit immediately behind it.
We are silent afraid to breathe.
Listening yet not wanting to hear.
Wanting to know yet afraid
that our hopeful security
had again been shattered.
Our tears fall for the cruel words
they speak to each other,
but our sobs are silent.
We don't want them to hear us cry;
it might make it worse.
No sides are taken as the story unfolds
day after day, year after year.
We bond together as the blanket unravels.
We share the pain, the fear
the scary feeling
that tomorrow may bring us
together again for silent sobs
behind the door.

Karen Brofft

Jordan Awaits Me

At the crossing of the Jordan
My truest friend awaits
To join his hand in mine
And lead me through the gates.

My heart is filled with gladness
My eyes are filled with tears
To think I have walked with Jesus
These many many years.

Each year it gets sweeter
As down life's road we go
Drawing closer to the master
As his precious word we sow.

I see the lights of glory
They are shining so beautiful and bright
All its splendor and its beauty
We've never seen such a sight.

Sue Madden

Nation Against Nation

Without love there will be nothing but hate
Nation against Nation, State against State

We need to take the time to accept appreciation
No country has the right to destroy GOD'S Creation

We should not be fighting because of our religion
Whether we're Baptist, Jews or Islams

For it is so written that thou shall not kill
Nations put down your weapons we all wish to live

Lets share in our wealth as well as our loss
Stop putting the blame on each other we all are at fault

Why must we be selfish, eager to out do each other
for it is written in GOD'S WORDS, we are all sisters and brothers

Without love we are a world filled with hate
Nation against Nation, State against State

One country has gold, one land, one oil
We are all rich, what are we fighting for

If we share we all can finally communicate
We will be nation of love instead of hate

So all my relative, neighbors and friends
Fighting stops .... when love begins

Katrina Denise Hunter

Out the Open Window

Out the open window I can see
Nature progressing with life.
The birds singing to each other while
The trees dance in the breeze.
As the birds and the trees and the breeze
Sing together it is like hearing "Nature's
Orchestra." Whenever you are bored,
Look out and see if you can see
What I see through the "Open
Window".

Molly Nesbitt

Untitled

Always and forever I will love you,
Need you by my side both day and night.
Never forgetting promises we made each other.
In sickness and in health and in God's sight.
Very few have what we have together.
Even when we sometimes disagree.
Richly we've been blessed with all that matters,
Special friends and a loving family.
After all these years I still love you,
Reaching out and knowing you'll be there.
You will love me always and forever, this is my silent daily prayer.

Lona M. Lawson

The Last Time

I swore that the first time would be the last time
Never again would he hurt me.
I wouldn't cry anymore
because it was the last time.
I wouldn't wake up crying missing him so
Because it was the last time.
I wouldn't start trembling at the mere thought of him
Because it was the last time.
But little did I know that the last time was only the first time
And he came back for a second time.
For a little while
I smiled, because I awoke with him in the mornings.
I trembled, only because of the life that was running through me.
I cried, only because of the love that filled my heart.
But this was only for a little while, because he left.
He left just like the first time.
The only thing different was that this was the second time
And the hurt and pain had doubled in intensity.
I have to wonder if I've really learned this time
Will there be a third time or would it be the last time?

Kristen Zerbst

River Of Life

The river of life flows freely at will,
Never ending, never still.............

In the beginning the journey of the river
Is detached from its one Source, free to travel its own course.

Hidden obstacles are barriers in the way,
Bidding us to continue or prolong our stay.
Time teaches the relentless river to flow on,
Not to be trapped in a swirling whirlpool for long.
Why be detained with envy, jealousy or strive?
You only contaminate your river of life!

My river wound through mountains and valleys of time.
Forgive and forget is a lesson learned of mine!
I have gone with the flow of the good and the bad.
Live life now, enjoy today, know love, and be glad!
For the past is only water under the bridge,
Allow your river freedom to find the next ridge.

In the end the peaceful journey of the river
Merges with the endless sea, flowing through eternity.

The river of life flows freely at will,
Never ending, never still.............

Marcella Cokkinis

Prisoner of Love

Hold me close, hold me tight
Never leave from my sight.
I was slow to say these words
For now we are separate and hurt.
Cells so plain and bars of steel.
Tears roll from my eyes for pain they feel.
I try to reach for you but my hand is blocked
By glass, reality, and clocks that don't stop.
All I can do is wait for the time to come
When we are reunited again and become one.
So many things yet to be discovered.
So much pain we have to recover.
I have faith in all we do.
For I now know there's nothing we can't get through.
Love is now putting us to the test.
I just ask you, keep holding on to me and
Love me, for God will do the rest.

Jazman Lopez

Ode To Great Men

Men, who aspire to become great,
Never, never, do they abate;
They do their best their whole life through,
While they pursue the great anew;
Great men make this, a better world,
As their unique lives are unfurled;
They leave legacies, rich as gold;
They are legends time does enfold;
They do deeds that prove they walk all,
Deeds that sound down time's timeless hall;
They live lives that are so sublime,
They light the corridors of time;
Great men, then, need to give their nod
To the glory-grandeur of God.

Virgil E. Graber

Birthday Thoughts

First the proud announcement "It's a boy! on May 3rd 1973."
Next, the ups and downs of early childhood that were meant to be.
A negative prognosis from the doctor with much sympathy
"five years to live," is what he said of me.
Yet, life goes on.

"When it rains it pours" they say.
Vows taken on their wedding day, ending in divorce!
My parents added to my fears, quite naturally.
And life goes on.

God in his mercy heard my childish prayers?
He sent an angel in disguise to rescue me,
With added faith and prayers to heal my scars.
My "Nana" shared my cares; I did not die!
And life goes on.

That "baby boy" of whom I speak is me,
Right up the ladder of my destiny.
I count my blessings, great and small, that come to mind.
My childhood cares and fears now left behind.
Today at twenty-one, I am an man! praise God!
And, life goes on.

Wayne F. Jackson

Soul Of The Seasons

Sun exploding into heat;
No breezes to lessen the heartbeat.
Together they are summer burned
and everything is learned.

Leaves on a tree know not care,
as they swirl and float down from the air.
Reflections of love, fearing as they fall,
but fall they must-vulnerable to all.

The impressions of his love
drift indelibly upon her heart.
As the first snow of winter covers softly,
like the strumming from a harp.

Renewal of the spirit comes like April rain.
For the misting of a soul is fame
and eliminates all past shame.
The soul of the seasons can never be the same.

Mary Harris

No School Today

Daddy, can I go to school today?
No child, you have no time for school or play.
I need you to help me pick this cotton.
History, Math, Reading, I have long forgotten.

Daddy, can I go to school today?
No child, you got no time for school or play.
At age seven, I worked. I didn't complain,
I too, wanted sunshine. God sent rain.

You know child, I didn't asked to be a part of this earth,
Certain things were given me at birth.
My mother died when I was three,
I didn't know my father, you see.

So at age seven child, I became a man.
I worked hard everyday, with my hands.
This is all I know, all I have to give,
So be honest, be peaceful, love others, you'll live.

Daddy can you tell my heritage to me? It is such a delight.
I need strength, I need hope, I need courage to fight.
This unending battle given me at birth,
I want to be a STRONG WOMAN while on earth.

Lovely A. Thornton

Silhouette

I wander alone through field painted lights,
No foreseen path will guide this dark night
Unfamiliar surroundings
Absorbing my eyes,
I'm searching for you
To unveil my disguise

Unknowing questions will never be heard
the lights guide my sight
and my words to be heard

I'll sway from the darkness,
Not wanting its touch
I'll stay with the light,
For it guards each tonight
Afraid of my darkness
and my heart to stay shut
I'll walk with the moon
For it leads to your touch

Sommer Molnar

Goodbye

It's done;
No more running around behind our lovers' backs.
Neither emptiness at night nor passion during the day,
It's over.
Yes, I love you and you love me,
But does love always have to include a torrid affair?
The end.
Maybe we can love as our love was meant to be,
Ethereal, yet earthy enough to be real.
Friends.
Can we do it; can we return to the point where we began?
No use.
It's time to move on; yet, I feel a sadness in my heart.
Goodbye.
Sometimes the easiest part is knowing when to leave,
Sometimes the hardest part is simply walking away.

Rory Bircz

A Mistake

I am very ashamed.
No one but me to blame.
I made a mistake;
Yet, please don't forsake.

I knew it was wrong,
All along
I have no explanation of why,
However, don't cry!
You have taught me well,
Though, somehow I fell.

Curiosities may be;
Why this has happen to me.
I've been more painful than any sore.
How could I have done something so deplore.
Do not devaluate.
And please don't hate.

You may not believe,
Still, I will try not to deceive;
Praying you and the one above,
Will soon forgive and love.

Mandy Harrelson

Love

Love is a word which is used by so many but completely understood by
no one. One meaning of love is a relationship between two people which is created over time. Which at times is like a storm that makes your heart ache with the fury of it all. For in this storm are all the passions of life itself which are sorrow, happiness, sharing and pain. When the fury subsides sometimes we lose and sometimes we gain. Another meaning of love can be animals or other
things. That's why each person's interpretation of love is not the same. Love can be expressed by animals as they protect their young. Another expression of love can be of a person stroking a pet as it lays at their feet. At times love can leave you calm and completely at ease with the world. Forgetting when the ships of despair, anger and hurt had your life in a whirl. At times we love blindly, listening not to common sense and full of faith. Finally we day we come to the realization we loved with blind obedience to our emotions and acted in haste. For each of us sometimes love works and sometimes
not. But until each of us experience the passion, fury storm called love of love we know not.

Willie C. Williams

Flying Free

Let me go, let me go, they've all let me go
No pain to feel, no love to show
Free in the air, fly away from the pain
Never return if I want to stay sane
See beauty in nature, find in my soul, peace
Never again will I be the love beast
Crying in anger, hurt in my tears
Falling is one of my very worst fears
Life in the air, death in the sand
I'll live in the clouds if I'm not on the land
Free of the lies, I'm no longer the fool
Love, just like death, is torture and cruel
Forever alone, I fly to the air
Away from the love and all of the care
I believed in love once, but the fact came and went
So I take to the sky where the pain had me sent
I see all the hurt as I look from above
And know I'd still be there if just once I'd been loved.

Rebecca Machala

Peace, Love, Empathy, Kurt Cobain

The words aren't there
No screeching, tearing, scathing words
Spewed forth from the pit of your burning nauseous stomach
I know the words aren't there
But I can't say good-bye

Didn't anyone ever tell you
You would catch your death out there?
All the fuzzy lime green sweaters in the world
Couldn't keep out the cold

You caught your death alright
Out there In here
It waited wickedly in a sporting goods store
Until you were ready to take it home with you
(And you weren't even wearing your sweater that day)

It's the beginning of the end now isn't it?
And the end of the beginning all at once
Life kept coming closer
When all you wanted to do was die

Kurt, I hope you got your Leonard Cohen afterworld
I hope you sigh eternally

Siobhan Eadie

Brown Eyes

They speak of things that are sacred.
No secrets do they keep.
Reflecting all that's kind and good.
And love they hold so deep.

They're dimmed sometimes with tears of pain.
of worry, strife and woe.
Some act I've done or word I've said,
And some I do not know,

But when they're clear and bright with joy.
It brings gladness to my soul.
And tell's me things for which I seek,
And pleasure yet unfold.

If they could see what's in my heart,
They would never mere despair.
For the love that keeps them shining,
I am sure she'll find it there.

Martha B. Spears

Endless

In the dark of the evening the anger rages
no way out - the cloud hangs so low its
suffocating, I scream, but all I hear is
my heart beat louder, over and over I try
to escape the pain, but there's no way out -
I look hard to see a window, but it's so
far away, the room seems smaller with
every passing day, I know there's a door,
but I can't seem to find the key
there's no way out - I'll stay till the end
maybe then I'll find my way out.

Sabrina R. Garrett

Nobody, But Yourself

Who's to blame for all the pain your feeling inside?
Nobody, but yourself.
When you can feel death beside you.
Who do you call on? Who do you talk to?
Nobody, but yourself.
'Cause Nobody else cares or tries do see from your point of view.
They just don't understand you.
When you're down in the dumps and don't give a crap.
Who's there to comfort and hold you?
Nobody, but yourself.
'Cause your good for nothing so, you're all alone.
When you need a friend, who's there to be one?
Nobody, but yourself.
Everyone else is too busy or hates you
Seems to me you're Nobody.
That's what everyone says and that's what you feel.
Looks to me like Nobody,
but yourself, is your best and only friend.
But please, don't commit suicide! I'll be your friend!!

Martha Martin

Despair

Nobody loves me; nobody seems to care.
Nobody wants me no matter where!

I feel lonely - all alone.
It really hurts right to the bone!

No one calls; they don't care.
Oh to hide I know not where!

Despair

Dependent Exist - Sulk - Pain - Anger - Imperfect - Reluctant
No! No! I can, I must, I will!

Despair

Desire - Energetic - Satisfaction - Peace - Allow - Interest - Relax
Yes!

Marilyn M. Basher

Untitled

We were just friends from the start
not knowing love was deep in our hearts.
It seems we only had a few months together;
but the laughter and memories are forever.
One little kiss changed so much,
I know I will miss that very touch.
All the walks we've taken and talks we've shared,
I want you to know I will always care.
I love you more everyday that's way
it's hard knowing you can't stay.
But the distance between us can't keep us apart
as long as there is love deep in our hearts.

Stacey Prescott

Untitled

It isn't you I want,
Nor all the things we had together,
For you are gone and I am glad
That everything is over.

Even at the peak of my devotion, I always knew
That some day we two should walk out of Paradise
Never to return.

I was wise enough, even then, to count the cost,
If such cost can really be counted,
For months and years of loving you.

I was aware of the price that might be exacted
For lovely secret hours spent in an enchanted wood
Or on a hilltop where the stars were so near
I could almost brush them from your hair.

I knew, I knew at the height of my joy and laughter,
As we lolled in the sand by the River,
That we were living and loving in a state of impermancy.

Opal B. Koehl

Forever Free

I hear the geese as they sing their way
north.
I see a fawn take its first steps forth.

I shiver inside when a distant wolf
sings,
and smile at an eagle with its outspread
wings.

The birds of this world fly where they
will.
The animals wander from valley to hill.

They have no taxes, no laws to enforce.
They don't go to stores; the land is
their source.

It fills me with envy; I wish I could be
as one with the wind and live forever
free.

Sherry Preston

Glimpses Of The Past

A father's loving touch that wipes away a tear
not a tear of joy, but a tear of fear.
It's in the father's eyes that others can see his love
it's a tender character that's sent from up above.
A loving memory that's in the child's mind.
only a father can bring a memory of this kind.
A memory of you and me sitting on a swing,
wishing that time had no wings.
Time that went by so fast-
now all it is, is glimpses of the past.
I see you now and all my world has changed,
my whole life has now been rearranged.
The times we had are lost forever;
now I know that we will never
find a love that was so dear
in that first falling tear.

Jill Kauffman

Sea Horses

No one person looks exactly like another.
Not everyone belongs to the same ethnic group or religious group.
Not everyone is the same race nor does everyone have the same cultural beliefs.
No matter what our differences,
We all have a beautiful soul deep within us that God created for everyone to love.
Sea horses can teach people a lot.
A rigid and not so pretty appearance is what we see.
So why are we attracted?
Their actions are what attract us.
If everyone understood this,
There would be no hatred.
It doesn't matter what's outside,
But what's inside.
Even still, people insist on racism and prejudism.
Can anyone answer one question?
Why?

Sherry Rose

Little Michael Sleeping

Little Michael sleeping at my feet,
Not wanting to leave my side, not able to stay awake.
So peaceful in his rest. So rowdy in his play.

I must not forget his playful ways for all to soon they will
Be gone.
gone to a grown up boy, and then again to a full grown man.
I must not give these precious hours away to "be quiet," "go play" or "not now I am busy."
These words will rob me of hours of his love and years of memories of times we spent together.

Little Michael sleeping, his little face dirty with cookies and milk
Little Michael, holding the kitten, Gracie upside down,
Taking off all the knobs off Papa's radios, running off
without anything on. So when I'm at my wits end, I just
Remember how much I enjoy watching little Michael sleeping at my feet.

There was a time not so long ago I watched his mother
sleeping at my feet.
Time has a way of waking little sleeping children into
grown-up people
So while I have the time today, I'm going to play with Michael.

D. C. Parker

Destiny

They were born apart but joined together by a bond they knew nothing about. And carried their lives without purpose of who they were or where they would go.
She had her parents love, more so then she could ever know,
and grew in the shape of beauty that few boys could deny.
But none she gave into or minded and did not think to wonder why.
He far away was much the same leading his life with an unforeseen purpose. Not being able to think ahead in years
for years as a child are nothing more than days.
So life goes on as it does the only way it can, forward in years but close in mind they journey side by side down two different roads.
Apart in body but close at heart till one day they are thrown together by life, their purpose clear and lives joined inextricably together till death.
And this miracle they call destiny.

Robert Huitt

Autumn's Magic

There was fog on the river this morning
Now and then there's a chill in the air,
We know the season is changing
There's subtle signs everywhere.

As the autumn season approaches
I watch pheasant and quail dodge from sight.
The deer are more restless than usual-
The birds start gathering for flight.

The bob-white doesn't call from the meadow,
The tiny wren has vacated her perch-
The robin nests are all empty-
The squirrels scurry along the white birch.

The harvest moon enhances the season
With it's golden glow of light-
Assisting the field workers with harvest
As they labor from morn until night.

While the trout in the river lies sleeping
Undisturbed by the myriad sounds
My sleeping senses awaken
As autumn's magic and glories abound.

Mildred H. Cannon

Need a Shave

One day a woman said to her knave
"Now dear, you need a shave."
He went to the barber,
While she waited at the harbor.
He came out a different man
so she said,
"Is that you, Sam?"
With a giggle and a laugh
he said,
"No, I'm sorry, but
my name is Charlie!"
As he walked on
She sat in the sun
She waited later and later
till one year greater
she said with a laugh
"Why, I don't think he's coming back."

Suzanne Haessig

Notes From An Alien

This world is such a scary place,
now here they all have to live in the human race.
Look behind every corner and tree they say it all so well,
they tell this to their children and expect them not to fail.

Danger is lurking in every step they take,
can anything be done to stop this monster's wake.
Drugs and violence are down their streets walking hand and hand,
in place of yesterday's lovers I just don't understand.

I really wish the sky would just harshly erupt,
and perhaps the voice of God be heard to tell all to straighten up.
Do they need such a drastic message to tell all to be kind and good,
for this might be best for their fates yes I believe it would.

I'm flying back home now and I'm glad you see,
where peace and love prevail along with faith and honesty.
I don't think I'll be back this way ever with my ship,
to me it's not worth my fuel or the long trip.

It's so very hard to look as we were once this way,
until we had a catastrophe that's all that I can say.
Earthlings I'm leaving these notes with your heads of state,
so in hopes you all will change before it's much to late!

Rebecca Blodgett

Untitled

How can a voice who spoke of love,
Now scream with discontent?

An innocent illusion lived,
came swiftly, cried and went.

Wrong meaning in my interpretation
Your lexicon holds meanings all your own,

Unconventional for the amateur reader
Who reads her dictionary

Quietly,
  Devotedly,
    Alone.

Lydia M. Correa

A Child's Cry

Years ago children played outside
Now they must hide
To play with the ball not today
We must stay stashed away

Violence today is tearing us apart
We just want to play in the yard
Why can't we be children again
Why can't everyone be friends

There's so much to do in the world today
But we just want to do a little thing... play
I don't see a play day and the days are going bye
Could you just tell me why

This is a child's cry all across the nation
Why can't people take this into consideration
Try to help the children play
For this maybe the last day.

Mellisa Strickland

Friendly Advice

Stop and take a look at yourself
now try to look at everyone else
what you're finding that difficult to do
don't feel alone, everyone has difficulties to
all anyone seems to see is race, color, and religion
instead of seeing what could be a friend
We've got no choice, we have to live with each other
learn to deal with race, religion and forget the color
please put down your fist and deadly weapons
change your attitudes and try to be friends
will you take my advice
Stop the anger, racism and especially the fights
let's pray we'll join together and stop the hate
before it's too late
Everyone has to pull together and honestly try
think about our futures then decide what is right,
good luck and for now my friends, good-bye.

Tabitha J. Cowen

The Sea

Upon it, ships have sailed and sunk beneath the waters green
On the bottom lies the briny sand, discolored and unclean
From the hulls of many sunken ships the treasures lie around
But the depths of greenish water keep the treasures safe and sound
True, these jewels were meant for someone,
Maybe you, or even me, but they'll never be recovered
From the bottom of the sea

Wanda Kennard

Class of 1967

It's been twenty five years since we went different ways
Now we get together to remember those days.
Listening to music we know so well
Gathering to hear what we have to tell.
Seeing whose changed; and whose looking hot
Wondering who are working; and who are not.
Guessing who are married or who are single
Finding all this out why we mingle.
There's Randy calling the meeting to order
While Carol and Linda has chances for a quarter.
Shirley so quiet; has not much to say
While Bobby is our class clown for the day.
Henry writes tickets; and boy, don't he know how!
And Charlie runs his family business now.
The twins attended the reunion this time
One of them known for writing this rhyme.
Well, this night soon will end; let's have no tears
Cause we'll see you all back in another five years.

Susan Colbert-Reese

"Goodbye"

One last time to say goodbye,
Now you are in a beautiful place in the sky

Wondering if you look down on me,
Wondering is my love for you what you see?

I remember you is what I say,
Every night as I pray

Can you hear me I love you so,
Can you hear me I want to know

Every day I see your face,
It always seems to be in that place

Time will heal the pain,
Eventually all it will leave is a stain

I remember you from the end and to the start,
Now your always in my heart

Kathryn Chaklos

The Nudge of Strength

As she walks her inertia (strength)
Nudges those who pass.

Playfully stopped they speak to her
Not knowing why they do.

With a beckoning wink she walks on
Knowing that they are near.

Her voice spins out like tangled puppet strings
Enveloping them
Picking them up
And depositing them in her trail.

Many pass
A few are caught
Only one untangles the strings.

Like a dust particle caught in a beam of light
This one
Will
Drift.

Clarice

"Alisa"

Yesterday, I saw an angel walk through my door.

The light of day shown off your face and I was
numbed for a moment by your beauty.

Yesterday, a young woman strolled by where
once a babe with freckles galore smiled up to me.

The same little girl who's picture I still carry
so close to my mind and heart.

Yesterday, an angel came through my door
and I longed to tell you of this vision.

But, I know you would be so embarrassed if
I told you what I felt.

So, I smiled and said "hello my dear" and you
replied, "Hi Dad" as you hurried by, yesterday.

F. C. Grubb

To a 'Woods' Golden Jubilarian

Something of the glory of these Woods is yours,
Nurtured, deepened, mellowed with the years
trees stand strong against the sky
firm yet supple through a dozen storms
drawing nourishment from rains
to lift full-laden boughs anew to sun.
So too your life down through the years.
What matter rains and storms?
You stood the test—
And now serenely tall and graced
you lift a golden offering to the Son.

Sister Catherine Joseph Wilcox, SP

The Wonder of a Dream

Close your eyes and dream
Of a flowing mountain stream.
Can you now hear
A melody of sounds-loud and clear?

You dream of summer nights,
Bathed by the moon.
Life's reflections on the water-
Dance to Nature's tune,

And a strange, enchanting music
Beckons you to sleep-
To travel through a valley
Running low and deep.

When the rays of sunrise mix with morning dew-
And shines beneath your feet,
You open your eyes and awake.
Oh, the wonder of a dream.

Kathleen A. McGee

Untitled

I think as through life I trod,
of a home where each one walks with God.
A grace each day, at the table we hear,
and Our father, each night, are words so dear.
He may be lowly, who 'till the sod,
But what is greater if he walks with God?
A home where love is the key to success;
A place where at night a soul finds rest.
Where peace is found, and all is well
That is the home, where God does dwell.
If these are the things, you seek each day
you will only find them, in this way.

Ruth Crabtree

The Shore at Midnight

Contrast the tranquility and freedoms
of a midnight shore
to the uncertainty and confusion of life.

The shore's tempting desire to be one with the earth,
to be one with the night.

How unceasing the peace pervades
Through the heavy black waters.

Oh, how I wish to see, touch, and live
the freedoms, unconfinements and
strengths of life.

Allow me to visit the solemn depths
of my heart and soul.

Let me see for myself.
Set me free.
Free me from the depths and chains
of these binding waters.

Mona Tse

Phantasmagoria

Is it too much to ask,
Of a restless soul?
Some solitude and contentment.
Should we stand on norms and mores
To define what is?
Even if we lose ourselves in the process.
Who stands to gain?

I will fly like an eagle
I will run like a river
Boundless as time and space
My soul will I bare to the elements.
My end will come.
But it will be in pouring rain
And scorching heat.
Then will I be spent
Like vapor from a geyser.

But a phantom is all you see
Cause I will be one with the elements.
I am the morning dew on the grass.
The dawn of a new day.

William Hagan

Radiant Empowerment

As I began, I stood in the shadow
Of a strength I'd yet to know
Always waiting, impatient to mature
Idly mapping all the worlds I would conquer

And slowly the future became the present
Yet the trials of time made me shy and reticent
I hid the light of strength, that soon would be,
In another soul so unlike me

Then my luminescence faded with age
I realized my loss and I fell in rage
'Til I left the dimness to the other soul
And watched my brilliant being unfold

Knowledge of long ago became part of me
And I learned from each adversity
To relish the present and learn from the past
And that the fate of my future had not yet been cast

As a strange incarnation, I begin
Where with each year I learn to shed my skin
And I stand each time on feet newly strong
And draw on a power I'd possessed all along

Stephanie Schwartz

Col John Davis Bradburn

Born in the echo, of the American revolution,
Of an frontier adventurer's spirit, or mold,
A man who'd in his life time, twice face marriage!
Western the man, wise, stern, manner bold!
Eleven, twelve, children, of his beloved 1st wife,
Later into civil war, torn Mexico, old fierce,
There gained favor, routing, the Spanish, in that's strife;
To gain land into Texas, did he come pierce!
A time of grumbling, between Mexican, Texan,
Slavery was not allowed, yet slaves were brought,
The whole cause of his troubles came then;
Why some men, with him, did contest, fought!
He would live to see Texas, from Mexico, free,
Living yet on the age old Rio Grand,
He died suddenly, in the spring of 1843;
A bold, tough man, for a then, wild, brave land!

Raymond Bradburn

"Dismay"

Why oh! Why should one be deprived
of courage because of fears.
Inner - strength weakens frustration increases
hindering progress in our everyday existence.
Only causing inner cries for help.

Why oh! Why should fears over whelm
sometimes causing inner - destruction
The inner cries increase but the battle not
totally lost - the question arises - what shall
I do? Only awaiting for a helping hand.

Why oh! Why should one be deprived of
feeling gallant, confident, bold, and
most of all fearless.

Why oh! Why does it feel like an entity
instead of one's identity.

Lydia E. Rodriguez

On My Lonely Bank

I sit on my lonely bank, seeing a sea of faces,
Of once special people, now beloved angels.

Their lives on this earth, will never be forgotten,
For our heart forever touched, by their wonderful love.

I sit and wonder about their banks, is it lonely and grieve stricken,
Or is it full of wonderful laughter, and everlasting happiness?

The more I wonder, the more I see the truth,
They grieve nor sit upon lonely banks,
but sit on beautiful sunny shorelines.

My heart yearns to be with them,
To sit on the shoreline and share laughter,
To listen to their angelic voices, to just be near my lost loves.

My heart bleeds just to see their faces, light up in the sunshine,
Their smiles glow a thousand lights, to hear the voice once more.

My time on this earth is not up, until it is and can only remember,
And dream of the times of come, as I sit on my lonely bank.

Peggy Bentley

Dream

As I walk along the rows
of roses lined up along the fence,
I think of the ocean and
The sprays of salt on my body.
The sweet smell of dew on
these luscious flowers reminds me
of a scent given off by a love
So dear that it can only be
thought about in a dream.
Maybe it is a dream.
But oh, to dream this dream;
to see, hear and smell the sea,
and feel the warmth of the sand beneath.
As I walk along the
rows of roses lined up along
the fence, I think of the
ocean and the dream I left behind.

Kathleen Hill

A Late Century Love Poem

A friend of love is the fear
of shedding the heartbroken tear.
The tenderest caressing touch,
felt once then painfully lost,
will rend the heart to shreds and
cause that dread tear to be shed.

Might it be that I could love you?
And that you could feel for me, too?
But alas, our tongues are kept still,
as for the love risk, fear has killed this.

So often love will be missed,
the chance lost before the kiss.
Loneliness is the lover we hold,
for none of us would be so bold
as to touch those we would love,
so we remain within fear's lonely glove.

And so never shall I touch you
with a heart meant to love you.
The way of our hearts shall remain unspoken
for fear of that frail thing being broken.

William Plourde

The Time Of Flowers

Spring is the time of loving hours,
of singing birds and small wild flowers.

Nature's brim full in the month of June,
Never is she more fully in tune.

Lilies crown the month of July,
Proud and graceful, never shy.

The rose, queen of all the flowers,
Fills with beauty the summer hours.

Mums tell of autumn's crisp like hours,
A lovely goodbye to the time of flowers.

Rhea Sheridan

My Man

My man the one and only man for me
Not muscular in any way
Just sweet and meek
Not a girl alive could take my man
Not even an angel that came from the heavens
Cause me and my man have one thing in common
True love

Tamara Banks

Our Life Together

Its been fifty years
of smiles and tears!
I can still remember as if it were yesterday,
all the times we have shared.

The wedding dress of creamy gold,
saved for all the memories it holds.
The tantrums, screams and crying of a child,
now in memories grow mild.

Your grandchildren's children you have seen,
is this better than you could have dreamed?
You think your getting old,
there are many stories you dearly hold.

The house you now reside,
you have lived in most your lives.
It holds many stories of the past,
you have made all the memories in our minds last.

Fifty years are here so fast,
our memories will last and last.
The children with you have formed a bond,
the love you share has been carried on.

Susan Krogman

Untitled

Such a state of mind! Such a state of heart of soul...
Of thoughts running together and feelings running apart...
Not whole—
but scattered into time - unable to impart
the wisdom of listening
to the voice within our heart

How shall we answer? What is our reply?
To knowledge of the truth — the one we can't deny
Do our minds know the questions? Should we even try
to acknowledge the presence of
what can make us cry

To know what to think and to know how to feel
about who we are and about what is real
can sometimes interfere with the way we do reveal
ourselves. In standards too ideal.

Sheryl Clark

The Web

I'm caught, you see, between the web,
of what is real and what is said.

In the maze of words, you can loose your way,
Never hearing the truth, in what people say.

For actions speak louder, than words, you know.
and words confuse me on where to go.

To listen to words, so shallow in thought,
leaves me empty of feeling, of what life is about.

It's a curse done by giving, false words and praise,
with skill and charm, to win others to your ways.

Forgive me for fleeing, to escape the bore,
but I need to find meaning, of what life is for.

To see beyond words, hear thoughts not said,
becomes the challenge, to clear my head.

For to find the motive, will often show,
a lot more truth, than you bargained for.

Roxi Huff

Thoughts Of You

I'm lying here thinking thoughts of you
of what to say, of what to do

I look outside to see what's going on
but I can't see a thing for these tears that fill my eyes

Because of my thoughts and my fears,
all I can see and feel is this pain that I feel inside

I don't know what time it is, I can't see the clock
All I want to do is get up and walk
I have no one to turn to, no one which to talk
I keep thinking of you so strong and true and
I still don't know what to do

Who am I kidding, there's nothing I can do
It's over and done with except for this pain
that runs through.

I will never forget the look on your face,
what you said the time or the place

This is love you will leave me, on this sad note
as I swallow my pride and try not to choke

You have touched me in a way that I will never
be the same, a little different, a little insane.

Kevin Chubb

My Heart

My heart has many windows —-
of which you've been all through,
Each one is cracked and broken —-
all with thoughts of you.
They're letting all your memories in —-
they're there both day and night,
I close the shades, I see your face —-
A smile that made things right.
Yes, my heart is full of thoughts of you —-
of times we spent together,
Things we shared, just you and I —-
what happened to forever??
I try to say, what's done is done —-
but tell it to my heart,
Through broken dreams of yesterdays —-
flows a world you're still a part.
We went from friends to lovers — we came to be just one,
We laughed, we cried, and made love from sun to sun.
Mr. Blues looked in on me today, Ms. Memory asked about you,
Then Brother Tears dropped in to say, your heart has windows too.

Sandra Hollaway

Anatomy Of Thoughts Descending.......

I dream about what's gone before
Of years gone by, to return no more
Into this lifetime of stress and strain
Grieve no more, feel no pain

We have become heartless, discontent
This was not to be, this was not meant
Stop, and think wherein we fail
To recognize the children's wail

We are responsible to their cries, and pleas
stop the anger, the killing,
Get on your knees
And thank the Lord, that we have the might
To end the suffering, but do we have the right?

When did we lose our sense of humor
Was freedom, happiness here.......... only a rumor
Heaven and hell are banging on our door
Which do we choose, before we are no more......

E. R. Troncone

Traveler Small

Ah! Little girl, where are you going?
Off to some far distant shore?
Or have you been and are now returning?
Your luggage tells me you have travelled far.
How many hearts did you leave bursting?
How many eyes were filled with tears?
Your flower tells me you are a child of love.
How may suitors pursue you?
God speed little girl, wherever you go,
to distant shore or mountain top.
The sun and stars will watch over you and
the morning dew will bless you.
Unpack your bag at journeys end.
Lock your gate and try to mend,
the broken hearts you left behind.

Larry Miller

Love

Love is good, Love is bad,
Oftentimes love makes you sad.
You love him he doesn't notice you,
That feeling really makes people blue.
Then the day comes, you tell him how you feel,
He hugs you and laughs, then you know your feelings are real.
His eyes always sparkle his face is so sweet,
He's perfect right down from his head to his feet.
You know you're in love the next day he asks you out,
You face lights up and you begin to shout.
You tell all your friends and you smile a great smile,
You know you will be with him for a very long while.
You are setting at home on that very same night,
And look in the mirror and say to yourself
that everything is going right.

Monica Mitzenmacher

The Bells of Bill Clinton

The bells of Bill Clinton, the bells of Bill Clinton
Oh! hear they are calling
The young man, the true man
Who God's calling from Arkansas
He's traveling to the White House
To become our President, of these United States of America,
Bill Clinton, Bill Clinton our next President.
The people are listening, watching and waiting, speaking and working,
planning and voting for Bill Clinton.
We are proud, we are proud, God's victory is ours
Ring the bells for Bill Clinton
Liberty for all, we are proud, we are proud,
Ring the bells for Bill Clinton, our president.
God loves America

Ola Mae Evans Broadie

Star Owners

Returning from Sanford, Maine
On dark country road devoid of cars -
Our headlights guiding us on the lane
And the heaven above packed tight with stars-
We felt alone there on this planet -
And driving into our State of Granite
And through our woods so black and still -
Saw the lake at last - just down our hill.

And there - under majesty of velvet dome
We stood silently outside our home -
Heads back - gazing into God's vast spaces -
While millions of stars shone on our faces.

It seemed we owned the world and night -
We two together in starlight.

Janice Gray Kolb

Christine

Oh the pain ... Of hearing the news today
Oh the pain ... Not believing what they say

Oh the pain ... It couldn't happen; not to her
Oh the pain ... The hospital was a blur

Oh the pain ... Of putting her to rest
Oh the pain ... Deciding who knows best

Oh the pain ... Not knowing what to do
Oh the pain ... Her life is really through

Oh the pain ... To hear the final prayer
Oh the pain ... In the dress she loved to wear

Oh the pain ... Watching it lower in the ground
Oh the pain ... No one made a single sound

Oh the pain ... It's hard to fight the guilt
Oh the pain ... To see a young life wilt

Oh the pain ... To wish she were just asleep
Oh the pain ... I feel I myself weep

Oh the pain ... Why can't it be a lie
Oh the pain ... My soul begins to cry

Oh the pain ... To watch your daughter die
Oh the pain ... It's time to say goodbye.

Samantha Schafer

"A Mother"

To look upon her face
oh, what a beautiful sight.
And when she speaks
She knows she will always be right.

God gives our mothers knowledge and wisdom
and his very best
We give our mothers heartaches, headaches
and a whole lot of stress.

Her love is unconditional
like a well that never runs dry.
You will push her to and over the edge
and then ask yourself just why?

She's earned your respect
and deserves all life's treasures.
But to give back what you got from her
you will never quite meet that measure.

So ask yourself one day,
what would I do without my mother?
But in your heart you know
there'll never ever be another.

Pamela Cox Slappy

Death Row

If chocolate, is king...hemlock; is an
ombudsman's hostess...caloric!D!D!...
Gag...rules abound...in McArthy-Army rows'...again..
Trap...rats...in any...season...fall field mice...become
winter...food..for bird...cheese-nip...of hep-cat...spatz and
pure...protests..of..all that is biblioethique..and true.
You must first win..to write...history of his weird
world...let alone

Screw up...something more than ye...already have...ere...
Death-benefits...pay better...than bribed...head of
John...the baptist...anonymously grafted...to a
pine..cone..smudged-pot..in ...swamp—country...long ago...

Richard C. Miller

The Rose

Outside stands a rose
on a warm, sunny day.
After being fed and watered
She feels so bright and gay.

Although she's always been a friend
to all the other flowers,
She sometimes doesn't speak to them
for hours upon hours.

The reason is, I say, my friend
is just because and that
the girl, the flower, is only thinking
She isn't where she's at.

She feels she's in a far off place
where she is not to be.
The reason why? She does not know.
It's too hard for her to see.

So, if you see a rose
that likes to think and dream,
the reason the rose is towards the sun
is not always what it seems.

Krista Marie Lemke

A Mother's Wish

As the moon shines down
on a wondrous little town

May evil stop its endless stalking
and goods wonderful chimes ring on

While the sun sinks down over the horizon
and the night sets another paragraph
in the long chapter of time

May a mother hold her child tight
as the helpless child she holds
gets over the overpowering fright

Fright brought on by evil
evil so strong, so strong it can steal
the happiness away from the child
away from her child,
for one unending second
which is one second too long.

Nicholas Joseph

Captain Love

Captain Love set sail,
On the ship Forever Yours,
With two mates on the sea,
The sea of Eternity.

The clouds of hope, filled the skies,
Above the mates, you and I,
Making castles in puffy scenes,
Helping fill our wildest dreams.

At night the stars came into view,
And the winds of yesterday gently blew,
The captain Love, maintained the course,
As we sailed the ship, Forever Yours.

Neal McElhaney

Ocean

The rose colored sunset reflected
on the smooth water,
I stood hypnotized by the colors of the ocean,
The sea breeze swimming through my hair,
I hear light airy voices calling to me,
from beneath the ocean's surface,
melodic voices telling me to forget my troubles,
to come and play,
I imagined myself soaring through the water,
beneath the cool waves,
the cold and icy waves,
the rapid and uncontrolled waves,
ripping at my skin,
then I imagined myself cold and blue,
motionless and silent,
gently swaying with the currents,
the thought made my body shudder,
standing there on a boat
in the middle of the ocean,
cold and afraid.

Trudy Carlson

An Autobiography

Sharing a dramatic and loud entry, with a million others -
On the stage of this huge theatre called world
I was expectant, even jubilant, but all at once I saw -
The lights going out and the audience leaving
And other characters going through -
A tragic, terrible, terrifying act when I found myself -
Being strangulated, drowned or crushed -
To death, at best they dumped me on a garbage-heap
I cried shedding a billion tears and then learnt not to
I toiled to please dear ones around me
I spent my days cleaning, scrubbing, washing -
Almost as soon as I learn to walk
But all my rewards were in the form of -
Beatings and bashings, curses and contempt, I was
Burnt alive or I committed suicide, seeing -
The despair in my mother's eyes
Nay, I was killed in womb-
Curetted out, gouged out, thanks to the great -
Break-through in science, the Ultra-sound.
You see, I am a woman from the third world!

S. Awasthi

The Maze

My life is the paper
on which my life will create.
The paint of confusion I stir
as the blank paper does state.
what shall be produced
on this paper so willing?
This sheet so easily seduced
is memories spilling.
Look beyond the surface white,
Its fibers tell a story.
A tale of one's treacherous plight
in an endless maze of worry.
I must go that way or this,
or I must not move an inch.
I go here but that path I miss,
and stopping to ponder, my teeth I do clench.
Outside the white edges
longing for strokes of thought,
Is a world of many ledges,
What was it that I sought?

Melisa Hayes

Wolf

The brown foliage of trees
Once again I see
When the river banks freeze.

From my burrow
I weep with sorrow
For I don't know
If my mother will live tomorrow.

Her fur was all they wanted,
So down she was hunted;
And death she affronted,
Almost exhausted.

She strived to survive
Though bleeding she came
While we, her babies, still try
To keep up the flame
Of our hearts alive.

We are a severed pack, our mother has died...
We are young and alone to face the world
Which is now covered
With white sparkling snow.
I am the Wolf.

Victoria Ragsdale

"Kimberly"

Ah, the light of heaven like grace,
once before me lied.
The love of fair upon her face, and the moon became her eyes.
My Kingdom of grey, her flesh all pale,
together escaping the world too blue.
Dining on steak, and sipping rich ale...
Alone at last for all wrong's to undo.
Bare on the carpet our torso's entwined...
We acknowledged the essence of love.
All the shadows' of the catacomb then combined,
and her tongue was the flavor of blood.
Oh, the blackness of hellish depths,
enough to pledge insane.
To feel this drowning sensation of darkness,
to open eye's flooded by pain.
My Kingdom of black - her flesh all away...
Those moon eyes have turned to stone.
Dream her at night, think her by day...
Our past becomes my throne.

Kris Triana

Be Smarter Than Drugs!!!

How cruel the cold snow, insane for the desire,
Once you melt the snow, you can't stop the fire;

The wind blows lightly as the smoke clears,
Your emotions explode while the hoodlum cheers;

Satisfied with the fact that you'll be back,
Instead of feeding your family, you're making strangers fat;

Return to earth jerk, before you end up hurt,
That's not the worse, fool-you could be covered with dirt;

Be what you were born to be, not what you become,
Any kid can tell you: Doing drugs is stupid, as well
as dumb!!!

Willie Carter

My Two Sons

I have two sons, who are very dear:
One lives far away,
while the other one's near:
One's name is Richard,
the other one's Brian:
Sometimes I miss him, and
want to start crying:
I know they both love me,
without being told:
I wouldn't trade them, for
silver or gold:
I tried to raise them,
and bring them up right:
I tried to teach them, to stay out of fights:
Richard has two kids,
Brian has five,
I pray to the "Lord" to keep
them alive:
I pray to the "Lord" every night:
To watch and keep them, safe and alright:

Mary Lou Parsons

If the Humans Can

Two little flowers growing all alone
One turned and with a mournful moan
Said to the other. Do you remember
When we slept through September?

Yes, we awoke came the spring,
We knew because the birds did sing
But now they are all quite silent
It's all because the world turned violent

The humans destroyed the world you know
They reaped what they did sow
Grief and destruction covered the earth
Nothing was left of any worth

Standing here we saw it all
Each winter, summer, spring and fall
We are the last to leave,
And not a soul is there to grieve

Wait said the flower it was only a dream
But so real it did seem
It's still not too late
If the humans can overcome the hate

Mary Jasilionis

I, Desire

I, Desire a man who will fulfill all my needs.
One who will have me over-flowing with joy at all his good deeds
Delight me with his Manliness and lust.
One I can have to hold, cherish and trust.
For my soul he can have, hold and control.
Because my deepest emotions and feelings he has stole.
Who I will always treasure.
Who will stimulate me with his intimate pleasures.
One who will devastate me with his very presence.
Have me sensing his every essence.
He who is gifted and talented, and molded to perfection.
For he is the only one I will give all my love and affection.
Not by death do we part.
But from the start and forever, You knew you were always in
my heart.

Shirley D. Harris

Stop The Hate

If I could change one thing in this land,
One would not be injured by another's hand.
Violence has no respect for any common law,
Sooner or later a gun will be in every youngster's paw.
Gangs are tearing apart every neighborhood,
Police are working hard doing whatever they could.
Slowly gangs are becoming superior,
While the cops are getting wearier and wearier.
Senseless shootings are killing one another,
What ever happened to "Love Thy Brother?"
News is slowly becoming an obituary column,
This major problem turns everyone very solemn.
Without violence we will all be here awhile,
So let's not shoot and kill, just smile.

Joshua Rhett Miller

The Scent of Roses

Oh! What is the sweet odor that calls to the bee?
Opiate in composition, its life's greatest addiction.
The rose, the rose oh! How it calls to me
Promises of love pulse from stem, to petal, to leaf
Cut from the root and trimmed of the thorn
Fear of pain and dissection is gone
Ironic but fitting, it's dying breath gives
Lovers memories of feelings no storm could ever weather
And for that moment, the scent of the rose is....,
Forever....,

Louis A. Williams

Getting Ahead

Life has its ups and downs you know
Opportunities will come and go
When things seem to look really bad
Write down your problems on a pad
Only you are responsible for your direction
Figure out a strategy for needed correction

Life is tough and gets tougher each day
If you're not getting ahead - why do you stay
Check your options and take a chance
Take a look at yourself - what can you enhance
It's up to you to make the decision
Put yourself in the right position

Life is what you can make of it
Take a chance - you'll be a hit
Remember - don't cop attitudes
Keep in control of all your moods
Get up your confidence and make your move up the ladder
Because your career is a very important matter

Joanna Huestis

Touchstone for Liberated Daughters

Bed with anyone you choose, but never bed with anyone, by choice
Or chance, unless (all other things being equal) given the chance
To bear his child, you would, and would rejoice. It is a
two-way test:
If he might father on you, he may husband all you have. (Best
To make few babies, over all. All other things are somehow
seldom equal.)
Make free, take loving gifts, aware: having is giving's sequel.
So you may choose with anyone you bed, so you may give,
and so you may be wed.

Virginia Kidd

Missing Jera

I wish there were a story I could write,
Or a little prayer I could say each night.
But all I have left is a smile on my face,
And in my heart, a very special place.
Where I keep all of the memories along with the laughs,
That we had made throughout the past.
Also, though, there is a terrible pain,
Knowing that I'll never see you again.
For you have left the world we all know,
So you can watch us as "the ones below".
By saying this I mean that I know you're in Heaven,
And that you were just another of God's little blessings.
But try as I may I just can't understand,
Why it had to be you that answered His demand.
Because no matter how badly He wanted you up above,
You could've stayed here, surrounded by our love.

"I love you and miss you."

Kelly Myers

For Nana and Papa

When I saw an evening sunset
or felt the gentle rain,
it broke my heart to think
I'd never see your face again.

Reality stepped in,
death was so cold and black,
it seemed a part of me was gone
and I could never get it back.

But in Gods word it told me
if I sought him I would find,
that my loved ones were not lost at all,
they had not left me behind.

They are merely in another place,
a land where they are free,
awaiting till that special time
we are joined as a family.

Now I see your face in every thing,
and I feel you in the rain,
I'll hold you close in memory,
until we meet again!

Kelly McGowen Boone

Save The Earth

Don't pollute our rivers,
or it will give our fish the shivers.

Don't pollute our air,
we'll not be able to breath, which is very unfair,

Don't cut down our trees,
or you'll take away our pretty leaves.

Don't litter our parks,
or they could go up in sparks.

Recycle your cans,
and you'll gain many fans.

Saving the Earth is a big job,
so please do your part,

Don't Be A Slob!

Jeffrey Franke

Justice

We know that there is something wrong
Or there is something that doesn't belong.
All I can say is that we must
All work hard to find what's just.

Kids are killed for their clothes,
And we stand there as that gang throws
Bricks at the glass, at that man,
And listen to music that people want to ban.

People are thrown against a wall,
Searched for powder, rock and small,
But it is already much too late,
Because the last buyer's signed his fate.

The world may not always be right.
But it doesn't mean we have to fight
With each or our minds.
We must look for the peace we just can't find.

This is the answer to our puzzle.
On the mouth of hate we'll put a muzzle.
To stop our pain we must
Break the natural rhythm.

Jason Poe

Take a Moment

Arise to another beautiful day, whether the sun is shining
or these is snow on the way, take a moment.
Venture into the outside world, and this day make a difference
when you meet a boy or a girl, take a moment.
With the hustle and bustle from day to day, its no wonder the young
and old stray, take a moment.
Take a moment to relax and enjoy each day, then you can better
plan your way.
Take a moment for others, we are never alone, because a bench in
the park can one day be your home.
Take a moment to share, maybe a kind word or a deed, today's
world
is full of all kinds of needs, just take a moment.

Nellie H. Murray

Jason

He doesn't know why the world goes 'round,
or why there's 16 to the pound.
Why moon and stars are up in heaven;
his name is Jason, he's only seven.

He is smart for his seven years,
and there is nothing that he fears.
His heart is always full of love
he came to us from up above.

I don't feel that I should boast,
but Xmas time he loves the most.
He's not like any other boy
when he opens up his little toy.

He brings in the paper and the mail,
and then he wags his little tail.
If you haven't guess and in a fog
Jason is my little dog.

John M. Antonucci

Incredible Illusion

After a summer
Thunderstorm, a gigantic
Multicolored arc
Permeates the eastern sky.
It is a vivid rainbow.

Virginia Hovdestad

Faith

When nothing seems, to be going your way
or you're having the worst, possible day.
When hope is gone, and quitting is near
or a day feels like, an entire year.
When you think to yourself, you are down and out
Have faith in God, instead of doubt.
He who doubts, his love and care
Should honestly try, meditation and prayer.
He will listen, to every word you say
And help you out, in any way.
He'll answer your prayers, and give you strength
To complete each day, no matter its length.
When in the hands, of our father above
You can always have faith, in unconditional love.
So when times get tough, you know nothing to do
Have faith in our savior, and he will help you.

Shawn Moon

Summer's Repast

Sometimes a trifling of angst, stirring from unknown
origins serenades to me on sultry summer nights and
bids me to offer up mine eyes, arms, legs and ears
as if in propitiation for some peculiar lassitude:
A too willing nature, pining for languorous existence.

For then I minded less and less the urban fluidity
escaping from an early summer's eve sirocco blast
than the encountering of more or less an urbane populace
with their diminutive caring and companionship concerns,
residing within a cacophony of all metal disturbance.

Our exact relationship to these feckless neon gods are
as uncertain as they are personally anodyne, while
a ghost-riding populace mood macerates on their own
self awareness in lamb-like silence. No bo-peep
substitutions are expiation enough for anyone's poltroonery

Of a wan spirit. No confrontation can be exacted
beyond the acceptable unwritten guidelines
as if this illusive God connective were lost
in a summers' wind and approachable only by imagined beings
who already imitate wandering troglodytes.

Robert Michael O'Hearn

My Swans

Already falling, I'm half way down,
others greet me as I hit the ground,
rain trinkles down, every drop hits my face,
I clinch the ground, oh, just in case.
the trees, all above me, sway in the wind,
the group that is standing, yes, they are my friends,
and they pull me up, help me to stand,
yet I fall back down, fall on my hands...

And the swans see it happen, they're watching me still
the only ones who know exactly what I feel,
as I'm getting weaker, the swans fade away,
we are no better than we were yesterday,
and the stars are all laughing, though nothing was said,
as I'm giving up, the swans fall down dead.

Pamela Palacios

"Bowling"

Motionless, focused on the task ahead, begging the
Lords for assistance. The heels slid as the flanges open up
And released to allow the sound of thunder, as the head
Rolled down the corridor. The windows of your soul
Witnessed the mauling of the ivory red necked soldiers,
Then the eruption pierced the drums of my lobes.
The aftermath, a barren field of maple planks.

Larry Maleson

Untitled

We are his stars, we are his sun, our smiles are his sunshine,
Our laughter is his music.
When we don't smile, when we don't laugh, the sky gets grey,
The clouds get dark, the thunder rolls, the lightning strikes.
And he cries.
I feel the cold mist spill from the sky and I look through the
Clouds and I wonder
Why does he cry?
Does he cry for the sick and for those whose spirits are low?
I can see his clouded eyes in my dreams and the tears pouring
Out of them,
Covering the heavens and the earth in a sheath of sadness.
I feel the pounding of the rain,
And I feel his pain.
We blame the rain on nature's course,
But his bleeding heart is the true source.
And the thunder rolls and the lightning strikes, and the
Sky turns grey and the clouds are dark,
And he cries, and he cries, and he cries.

Misty Harper

What Is To Be

Whispering river on your way to the sea
Over mountains, meadows and a forest of trees
Tell me your story, what do you see?
What is to be?

Lovers in the moon-light holding hands
Dreams of tomorrow in their plans
The glow of a camp fire like fire-flies in flight
Shy forest creatures keep watch in the night.

Whispering river on your way to the sea
Flowing gently, calmly in a soft summer breeze
Tell me your story, what do you see?
What is to be?

Violets sleeping beneath the leaves
Fishermen trolling and lines in trees
Cool rain drops falling in darkness of night
Tall lonesome pines sway in the twilight.

Whispering river on your way to the sea
Ever winding, weaving, cascading in glee
Tell me your story, what do you see?
What is to be?

Lucille Tschaen

Untitled

I sit in silence like the night,
Overcome with a sudden sense of fright,
It is like a chill running up your spine
It grows like the grapes on a leafy vine,
Knowing no boundaries
Knowing no end
It is like the return of a long lost friend,
One that you have tried so desperately to avoid,
Bringing the fears you have tried to hide,
But not all fears
And not all grief
Good moments that seem all too brief,
They seem to go by so fast,
That must be the reason why they last.

Lori Vanella

Silence and Sound

I venture through a world with both pleasure and pain, where the pain seems to double and only pleasure keeps me sane. I've opened the door but I cant get out, I'm stuck in the corner of doubt. I am in this world all alone, but in the distance I hear a tone. The tone being my only pleasure, It's music I'll forever treasure. I can feel the chill run up my spine as I watch sound and silence entwine. Abruptly silence gives in and the wonderful sounds of music begin. The closer the sound the stronger I feel, slowly this world doesn't seem so real. As I watch the colors dance about I begin to leave the corner of doubt. I reach for the door, while I listen for more. But wait! A thick arises and the door disappears, my mind is full of fears. Fears of pain and suicide, I turn and run so I can hide. But the fears dig deeper while I grow weaker, the colors are gone, where did I go wrong? Inside I feel the need to scream, "Was the music just a dream?" I've convinced myself I'm ready now, so I put the gun against my head knowing my only escape is this piece of lead. The tears flow freely down my face, I just want to leave this place. Then there's a sudden blast..... I'm finally free at last! Although silence wouldn't let me be, sound managed to set me free.

Stephanie Andrews

depression

our youths never met
parallel lines
converging years after your true need
now your bruises, cuts, burns
are diminutive
scars along a healing plane

could i have only curved around the hourglass
to whisper words from this future
where your strangled shadow is falling away
i would have told you fear is the archenemy of faith
become a modern Diana, uncurl and spring from Poseidon's ocean

as it was you spent years in that sea
cold rotting and shrinking from the salt
drowned by the glass of water which was not half full but shattered

these long moments later you are no longer
that wet broken emptiness
we chased away your shadow self
hanging alone in a noose

still there is the persistence of memory

Laura M. King

Sunset

When I am old and left alone,
people will say, "Look at the old crone";

Little will they know, or will they care,
I've loved, and had my share;

Each day will be like a new beginning,
some losing and some wining;

But the thought of you, will quicken my step,
it will give me vigor, energy, and pep!;

In remembering how it used to be,
that old sweet song of you and me;

And when my sun begins to set,
I'll know I have loved you, without regret!

Richard A. Miller

Imaginary Places

Far away shine crystal roads to imaginary places. Where the air is pearl with windy blue ice skies. And cascading diamonds are tossed from a calm and blackened sea. I long for wings, for fairy flight, for perfumed breezes on which to rise.

The mountains stand in craggy, smoke-gray silence. Aqua pools form mirror-smooth glassy tombs. Through liquid velvet one may glide, or soar,
or fly And go and visit the bright side of all the stars and moons.

Rainbows shimmer shades of neon pink and orange. Shooting starflowers
streak glittering sparks across the clear-white space. Topaz suns blaze halos of violet fire across the sea at noon. Darkly transparent tree-shadows filter sun like emerald snowflake lace.

Elder Beings come and look, like great and splendid ancient trees
I sweep by, the stark white towers gleaming in slanting moon-lit rays
Cities of alien folk dot the undulating landscape here and there
Twelve blue moons flatly gleam in the lavender haze of day.

I dreamily float through feathery blooms of exquisite-hued sweet flowers. I pass unseen through places guarded by gold-winged creatures at columned gates. I wander far away in time, and in my heart I search for things unknown. And all the while, the things I yearn to reach, already lay in wait.

Rebecca Downie

Catastrophic Justice

Here I am the forgotten victim, jailed.
People lying the court unfair.
Legal rights abused California Justice doomed.
Rejects controversy police brutality cruel.
Deprived freedom, condemned, restricted, cheated,
troubled life entombment disappointment.
The struggle release believing pressure
arraigned bailout.
Confrontation arrest prisoner guilty.
Why anger, pain, fear, shame, confusion,
suffering; frustration, and intimidation?
Protest fair deal; startled failure.
Lonesome, scared, afraid, homesick.
Convicted killer's disrespect
morality disgraceful.
World stress dishonesty
conflicts, cold violent turmoil.
Drug abuse, Drunkenness;
Paranoia slump hurt.
Silence strength threatened CATASTROPHIC JUSTICE!!!!!

Willie Whiting Jr.

Judging

I judge people dishonestly.
People who I believe are less fortunate than I,
people who I dislike for no reason.
I surmise I do this injustice intentionally,
just to make my peers like me.
But the more I do it, the more inferior I feel.
It not only destroys the heart of my victims,
But destroys what might have been a tremendous friend.
A friend who would respect me someday for who I am.
And the tragedy of losing something as special as that is too much.
And I know that the people I judge are eager,
Trying to feel important to me, but I turn away, making their lives inferior, and having them to have to face tomorrow,
Uncertain to what the world is going to say.
I now recognize that popularity is for fools.
Especially if I have to destroy ones soul.
I know I possess the power to endure my true character,
A goal I intend to keep for eternity,
Because there is no remuneration in such vulgarity.
Aren't my victims no better than I?

Nicholas L. Cooper

Meditation Can Be Hazardous To Your (Mental) Health!

Some say that meditation calms one down and relieves frustration.
Perhaps for a few, I guess, it relaxes to take a break from phones and faxes, busy bosses and clientele (so that we can serve them well).
It appears that meditation, spurred on by my imagination,
Is the roof of all my ills (not to mention hospitals bills).
The 'forest' I entered was shady and cool; and in the distance was a pool, a misty waterfall and a brook (with fishies everywhere you'd look).
I cannot scratch ungodly itches due to all the doctors' stitches
Used to close a real deep gash (caused by an unkind grizzly's scratch)
Imaginary deer have made me sick (because I got bit by a tick)...
Lyme disease with funny spots, obligatory rabies shots,
Combined with weird hallucinations from the mix and medications
Given for relief from stress, only adds to my duress!
An easy victim of power of suggestion, I now can't breathe from chest congestion!
It appears that meditation, spurred on by my imagination.
Is the root of all my ills (not to mention hospitals bills).
You can find you're stressed out more than you were an hour before!
Remember that, despite all one's wealth: Meditation can be hazardous to Mental Health!

Susan M. Kennedy

Diamonds

Hello? There was a silence on the phone, then I began to speak. "Perhaps you can help me. I am looking for an old lover. Only he was not filled with love. He was filled with hate and cruelty and despair." Silence. "Surely you know him. Years ago he lived where you live. His habits were the same as yours. He met a beautiful young girl. She was filled with laughter and love. He took all of her love. He swallowed up her laughter in his cold black heart. She loved him more than one had never loved another. She would have given him anything and she did. She gave him gifts, glorious gifts. Gifts. of golden sunshine, ruby smiles, diamond tears. The diamonds
were his favorite. He asked for more and she gave. She gave until her soul was dry and when he asked for more, she gave her soul. She would have died for him and she did. But her body chose to live on. There was no soul there anymore. It was trapped in his black heart. That is why I am calling, I need to have that soul returned. If you see him, would you ask him to lighten that heavy heart? Can he free that soul? Hello?... Hello?...

Jill A. Amendola

Sunset: (The Dying Of Dawn)

The setting sun colors the sky,
Pinkish hues and purple tones.
Bleeding together in a tearful blur,
She sits and looks; Seeing not.

Alone in the world; Just learning to survive,
Pain seeping through her bones.
Dwelling on memories of the way things were,
She sits and looks; Wanting not.

But how will she learn to live with the pain?
Why does she have to anyway?
Never asking for much, just searching for love,
She takes her life into her hands and wrings it out to dry.

Now she lays under the moonlit sky,
A single star shining above her.
But she doesn't look,
She only sits and stares... Living not.

Velia D'Aloia

Take Me Dreaming

Take me dreaming where I lie.
Place your hand upon my thigh.
I'll be your alibi.

Take me dreaming where I lie.
Together we'll build a bridge of sighs
Heaven high.

Take me dreaming where I lie.
Around our hearts, a ribbon tie.
Of this ecstasy, we'll not seek the answer, "why"?

J. Pierritz

Soul Destiny

Tears, passion and pain ... under cover ... in secret
places ... you talk to me. You are my lover ... my soul destiny.
Dare you ask me ... how I found you ... you knew inside
you ... that it was me. I've come back for ... my one soul destiny.
The night was bewitched with cosmic joy ... as hearts
reunited ... you drew near to me.
You remember the flames that burned ... consuming our
flesh as it melted the empty pit of longing for ... our
oneness. I search no more in this retched world of aloneness
... emptiness. I've found my completeness.
Love waits alone ... watching your captive flesh...
as a beast masquerades as an angel of love ... keeping you
from me.
When the room has been emptied ... and emotions are freed
... what will be left then ... you and me.
The time is near ... love is waiting. I knew someday
... you'd come back to me...
No chains to bind us ... no burden here ... just you and me...
... in one soul destiny.

Laura Reno

The Travelers

Across the mountain ridges, and across the desert
plains—through the jungles dense
with swamp, through the filth and rain—traveled nine brave men...
Weary, hot, wide-open spaces banked with droughts of mud—came
the nine hard staunch
faces, and the smell of blood.
Drought, drought, drought, and the heavy march of feet; Swish,
swish, swish, and no sun did beat.
Oh! now the moon lit up the valley, the stars were in the sky,
but the nine brave travelers had not time to die.
So night came, and night came, and the weeks fled bye.
And the men they kept on traveling, to rest was to die.
These men they fled from prison—they said that bars would keep.
They broke away from prison and the bars they said would keep.
Ah! nine brave travelers, onward through the night.
Plod, plod, plod, and the endless-endless night.
Somewhere into nothing so the theme should go—on the
ground, then in it, these men they did go.
For when the sun rose in the morning; they were shot and placed
there so. . .
Etched in the moonlight, and they never saw the day,
but sometimes I wonder if they really didn't get away.
Nine brave travelers hit the dusty grave—Nine brave travelers,
did they get away?

Si Simons

Stop

You can try but you will not stop me,
my powers are to great you stand
not a chance fighting me, so go,
go back where you come from,
your presence is no longer wanted here,
for your sin has not been forgotten
Your soul shall be and will always be doomed!

Trevon Hollingsworth

Little Girl

Little girl, don't look at me.
Please do not wave; do not smile
Because I will scowl in return
And it will surely break my heart.

This old man with his numbered days
Knows that danger and evil are everywhere
And he instructs you, little girl:
Trust not him or anyone.

But, oh, little girl, you instruct him, too.
Your innocent trust is surely heaven based
And is his sweet reassurance:
Heaven must be! Heaven must be!

Ross Byers

"Please Don't Forget"

Please don't forget, I am not the world.
Please don't forget, I am just a girl.
Please don't forget, I can't change fate.
Please don't forget, big isn't always great.
Please don't forget, I am small.
Please don't forget, that is not all.
Please don't forget, my heart is sore.
Please don't forget, there is more.
Please don't forget, at night I don't sleep.
Please don't forget, all night I weep.
Please don't forget, I like to paint.
Please don't forget, I am not a saint.
Please don't forget, I know you're proud.
Please don't forget, I wish you would say it aloud.
Please don't forget, I have a mind.
Please don't forget, I am a kind
Please don't forget, I love you.
Do you love me too?
Please, don't forget.

Lexie Murphy

Hear My Soul

Smoke fire burns emotions damage soul
Please no special treatment
In a chair of judgment you look down on me
Fear is not the reason that brought me here
Prayed when I was wishful a child with a dream
Prayed when I was fearful of the beating of my peers
Prayed when no one listened I thought you would hear
But you never heard me
Never treated me like a friend
Instead you thought me like a leper
Someone very dead
Although you claim to give yourself to very special friends
Never once came to my house
Maybe shame to enter
Into a house of taboos and rotten pain
No longer visit temples never take your grace
Only pray to you
So you understand and my pain

Terance Miguel Beason

Insane Forest

The moon dimmed in the cold night
Owls screamed at standing trees
While far above the deer sang "Hallelujah"
Laughter and moans were heard
Through the night
Walking birds laughed at talking fishes
Insane forest was a very
weird sight

Vanessa Holder

Life Then - And Now

It's 10 p.m. and I'm in bed
poetic thoughts racing thru my head.
I'm one of six sisters and three brothers.
Lived together spring, fall, winter and summer.
Got up early and got a good start
Currying horses and milking cows
Better than 'slopping' all them sows,
Hurried to school and we did walk.
Back then there wasn't a 'bus stop'
We learned, reading, writing and Rithmetic
Teacher kept order by "black stick"
We learned to write in 100 days,
Read the Bible and we did pray.
What's wrong with school today?
Trouble is they no longer pray.
Left God and Prayer out of school
Are we producing educated fools?

Patricia A. Glodek

Romance

I carve Egyptian cats into
polished jade bedroom walls;
hoops dangle from shark-tooth ears
like broken wrists in your handcuffs.
Beneath your breathing window,
turquoise ferns quiver and squirm
like you used to
when my finger was a worm. Zeus,
a swan, between my legs,
or is He a goose we seduced
from unswept pond with the dregs
of breadbags? Pot-bellied tyger,
ghost-white with black bands,
swears nothing but rigor,
slips his paw in your hand.
Candlewax cataracts crust milky eyes
and our sheets, dyed blood-red, hang out to drip dry
and saltwater stains are all that remain
of the pointless existence that trickled away
through carvings we made in jugular veins.

Nyx

"Lonely Rider"

Speeding faster with his feet lightly strained,
pressing downward with all his strength.

Riding through the darkness his hands red with grip.
Thoughts in his brain scattered no longer caring
to be battered.

It is the end slowly showing he does not care, for
his thoughts are flowing.

Quickly it approaches to his surprise, then darkness
falls over his frightful eyes.

The lights surround him, flashing red, flashing blue
each one brightened through and through.

He does not hear their cries, or see their lights,
he does not even feel their tears, which fall from the
eyes of his loved ones goodbyes.

There in the darkness he ends it all, for he did not
fall, he simply drove to forget it all.

Michelle Dahman

Untitled

Pretend like it's nothing when you see he doesn't care,
Pretend like it's nothing when you see it there,
Go on and pretend like it's not meant for you,
Even if deep down you know that it's true,
Pretend you don't care what he has to say,
Pretend, cause it may be the safest way,
To mask the feelings burning deep down inside,
And pretend that you have no emotions to hide,
But then one day you'll see and notice the light,
You'll quit pretending and begin to fight,
And one day you'll find that something is there,
Because, just like you he's begun to care.

Linda Franklin

Pledge Of Allegiance

We are the soldier's in uniform,
Proudly, we salute and say
We love both God and Freedom,
And our sacred U.S.A.

Our duties for Liberty are many
To keep "Old Glory" flying high;
To guard and to guard well
Our security, lest we die.

Thank God we live in America,
The greatest Nation on earth;
The land of "Pilgrim's Progress",
The land of Freedom's birth.

We hold high the "Torch of Freedom",
May the light forever shine in the sky;
Liberty, Justice, the Pursuit of Happiness
Depends upon you and me.

We are the defenders of America;
We pledge allegiance to our land;
In God we trust in peace and war;
For Freedom, united we stand.

Roland A. Johnston

Where Do We Go?

Crazy lines of white manipulation
Pull the strings of the sublime.
wasted time of a martyr
on a population of crime.
When do lines of distinction Arise!
and awaken our souls When do we
as a nation decide to gather and revolt?
Silly Girl, you think you can
change the world with a Bat
of your eye and the muscularity of your mind, Wrong
depravity will cause the eruption of your mind to
swallow your faith. Do not bear the cross or
milk the moon, it causes backache and blindness
Rather, wander, shop and reap what you sow for
a Man will not be the Answer!

Traci Tompkins

Weeping Willow

The weeping willow
sheds its tears in a variety of hues.
green, yellow, purple, orange and more
weeping weeping while its leaves it does loose
nothing can stop its tears
though we do not know why it is weeping
it will keep on weeping through the years.

Melissa Lindbloom

Precious Slut

Paint your pretty face
Put on your garish plumage
Dance! Show your teeth, your taut ass
to your adoring public.

You have need of no more
than their adoration
(they see you as a freak if you
really care to know,
my strutting little whore!)
And your TV cartoons.

For you I'll no longer slit
my minor-league heart.
You stuff it every time with ice -
with barbed wire.

(I'll be waiting for you at closing time,
my sweetest)

R. A. Hoge

Happiness: Faux Pas

Smoke tangos in the Bop Shop. Late night spent drowning in the haze.
"Put some english on it," Her jaw teeters.
Luck smacks the win or lose one in.
A series of colors burrow away from the caucasian left
on the green fair ground. The end has occurred.
The victorious return their weapons to the wall.
Seated with her, our elation rests in the cold bottles.
The dank room is filled with content.
Whole notes ricochet against my ear drum.
We sit staring at nothing intensely.
Blinking, she pauses as if to warn me to listen.
Stagnant air remains, because she says nothing.
The cigarette machine reflects neon, On her vacant expression.
My profile is heated by her searching gaze.
We walk out into virgin wind. Shuttering follows,
as the repetitious breathes are ushered out. A plastic
embrace ushers you home and away from her.
Twelve noon knocks it's welcome on your foggy brain.
Reminding you last night was simply happiness faux pas.

Ozana Horel

What Is The Point?

I'm running, I'm searching, I'm hoping to find, the answers to my questions before I must die. What is the point? I just don't understand. Why do we live like this, in a hell-like land?

Disease, hunger, and all types of abuse, it is obviously not our choice, or else why would we choose such a horrible life, to live out each day? If you knew there was something better, why would you stay?

Maybe we have no choice, and this is all there is, but we'll never find out unless we try to live the life we want. We can't just say the words. We have to mean it and not think it is absurd.

We have to find some hope, a little is all it will take to get you through the pain, and somehow make our lives much better. We can't give in and pretend that this is all there is. We can win. We can have peace with ourselves, if not with each other. We must change our surroundings before they cause us to smother, and choke to death in despair.

If you are in a bad situation, you must get out of it, or hold on, if you have the strength and wit, to get yourself through. Find the hope within yourself, if you think you can, and never be afraid, to ask for help.

Victoria S. V. Collins

The Angler

Patient is he.
Quiet as the grass
on a warm summer's day.
Watching the pool of swirling water,
reading it, as a map.

He finds the spot.
Light Cahill should work.
With ageless knowledge he casts the fly on the calm, still water.
Quick! A flash a silver!
Nimble fingers set the hook, firmly.
The tenseness disappears as the angler relaxes with joy.
The afternoon stillness is broken as the fish leaps and falls
fat, gleaming body thrust high in the air.

Yet, he is tiring.
The net is drawn from the angler's strong back.
Its handle worn from years of triumph.
As the fish slides into the aged net,
A slight grin appears on the angler's face
He casts again
All is well.

Pilar A. Patterson

Good-Bye

There he lies
quietly
on his side; silky stubby velvet paws clutching
his daily carrot.
My lovely little lop-ear.

I stroke his ears.
Incredible
the soft and silver fur I'm touching.
Still springy.
My gentle little lop-ear.

There he lies
as if asleep
on woodland ferns. He spurns
our world forever.
God's peaceful little lop-ear.

Sigrid Lohss

The Way I See It

The way I see it, most people can't look beyond the race, or the color of someone's face. They look at a person's skin, they can't look beyond - at what's within.

No matter what the color be - everyone's a person - same as you and me. Because - God didn't create war and fight. God created peace and right. God didn't create lies and hate. God created love and fate.

If we'd look closer, we would see - children Are role models for you and me. Children aren't racist, hateful or nasty - children are loving, caring, and happy.

If we'd just look closer, we Would see - that life could be better for you and me. And if we'll look deeper we will find - life Is much better when we become color blind.

Stop the fighting, stop the hate. Life could be wonderful, life could be great. We need to learn to live and let live, we need to learn to love, and give.

Children are wonderful, if we'd follow their examples life wouldn't be such a pit. Young kids know what their doing - and that's the way I see it.

Mandie Fitch

A Picture of Majesty

The deer frolicked in the pasture. The children ran through the high grass flying their kites in the soft breezes. In the distance one could see the tall trees with their leaves beginning to turn to rainbow colors. The sounds of the birds chirping and singing to each other while flitting from tree to tree. Varied colors of wild flowers made a pattern that only mother nature knows how to design. Looking past the meadows, siting of mountainous hills graced the valley with their straight and majestic trees.

A waterfall in the midst of the hills, rippled down, spreading streams in different directions through the valley. Ponds decorated the land with colorful and picturesque water lilies. God has graced the land with his majesty. Oh what a picture! A picture of sovereignty. A picture of tranquil and serene majesty.

Mary C. Ragland

Alberta

A wildflower from the south
Re-acclimated to New York asphalt
And the kitchens of the wealthy.
Always your hands were busy,
Your spirit turned to the light.
With me, a woman of few words;
What did you think of what you received from life?
The rattling of pots and pans
An underlying rhythm
For the lives of your children
Offset by the beat of clothes against a washboard;
Housewife jazz.
In later years, you were
Transformed into a gypsy song,
Traveling music.
When you did come to rest
It was in an empty house
With the heart of summer heat around you.
Silence and the heat of yourself
Were all you left behind.

Sheryl Singleton Lynch

Death

Death is at the top of the staircase of life,
reaching up at extraordinary height.
It is when death beckons for you to reach the top,
And when you are up so high it is impossible stop.
There you are in heaven as happy as a fawn,
you are cured from all the pains and sorrows after the dawn.
You are now in the eye of the Lord,
King of peace and love.
And now you're an angle with wings of a dove,
You have a bright gold ring high above your head,
While your family is grieving because you are dead.
They all know you're cured from all of your pains,
But their mixed emotions are driving them insane.
They all know they'll see you again in the sky so high,
So for now all they can do is say Good-Bye.

John Thomas

Making Your Day

Will you bring sunshine someone's way?
Or will it be rain and clouds for the day?
Will you hear thunder or make that loud sound?
Or will you strike out as lightening and cause pain.
To the closest ones around?
You can make your day, the brightest of all.
By thinking the weather and not letting it fall.

Sharon K. Peyton

In the Crowd

Judged by how I look
Read by what I say
Pushed into the common way
Not being the same is considered strange

I live in a town where people stare
I can't hide, all I can do is ignore the glare
I can't be myself without being called a name
Just because I'm not the same

People look at me in question
They wonder why I am the way I am
When I try to answer, they still don't
understand,
Can't get away from this worldly hate
Stuck in glue, I try to make it through

All I can say is I'm happy being this way
My thoughts of sanity are no longer the same
Shuffling down unfamiliar streets
Ignorant of who I might meet
Here I am in a crowd standing alone
Can you pick out which one is me.

Karie Hambrick

A Message For You

Dreams come from the heart
Reasons come from the head
Maybe all the hate in this world,
We can turn into love instead.

Drugs, sex, and violence
Need to be a thing of the past
And love, happiness, and kindness
Shall show itself at last

Of all this love in the world,
There's not enough
But don't give up hope
Even though it's going to be tough.

Today's teens have brought back the sixty's
A time of carefree and peace
But why has that changed
And that prospect dared to decease.

Show today's people a little love
And the kindness they share,
Because even if everyone else gives up,
I'll always care.

Stacie Orsburn

"Every time" I See You

"Every time", I see you, my heart brings me to "remember"....
Reminding me of a "love", "we had once shared together"...
The reflection of those "old memories", that had once
"flooded the depth's of my soul"...
And "how painful" it was to let it go....
And "every time", I see you, "I say to myself", "life goes on"...
What we once had, it's over and gone!....
Although, I wished it hadn't went wrong...
"Now", "I must" put it all behind me, and "move on"....
"Time", will heal my wounded pain!....
"I will be alright again"....
Although it may seem, "like the end"....
In my heart, "I know", we will be "friends"
"In my heart!" I know, we will be
"distant friends"....

Margaret Barrera

He Lied

I cried, again, as hope lay scattered at my feet
Recognized, once more, the unfamiliar slam of failed defeat
Joy unspeakable gone, no more the child-like trust
Crushed and ground, without a look, beneath his heel to dust.

One involuntary act caused my heart to thus react
The damage quickly done, again the bottle won
I lost, again I've lost, and who can count the worthless cost?

Why did he think it wouldn't hurt
To stomp upon my heart, throw it in the dirt
And dust of life's decay... It could have gone the other way.

I loved him and believed him
"I'll never hurt you..." he pledged his word
Now the shot-down dreams of future hope
Have died, a waste; lesson still unlearned.

Because to me he visibly thought, then chose to lie
In that brief moment, something in me died
And I mourn the innocence now gone, now lost... again it's lost.

Sometimes things remain the same, forever losing insidious game
It's done, it's through, the battle's won
And I am nought, my hopeless mission done.

Patricia Lowrey

Burdens of the Father

Images of crystals, sparkles of light,
reflections from the tears, that streamed
against her ebony face that night.

Somewhere in the darkness, a clicking
sound, as the crowd moved in to witness
the dead man lying on the ground.

The gun now empty, gripped firmly
in her hand, still squeezing the
trigger at that violent man.

Ashen clouds amassed, hovered overhead.
The deaf ear of justice once again turned its head.

She closed her eyes, tried to remove
the vision of his face, only to discover
his burden was now her disgrace.
She would not forget, no matter how hard
she tried, the first time he raped
her, the night her virginity died.

No one heard her silent screams,
no one calmed her fears, as the
empty clouds shed the last of the innocent tears.

Patri

Theory

As we live our lives,
Remember yesterday,
When you were someone else,
In a different time and place.
Could it be we live our lives again?
To see the results of our mistakes.
Reborn in a different time and place.
May it be we're given a chance,
By living our lives again,
To prove ourselves worthy,
To be chosen for the land.
Will we finally do our share,
To care more for the world and other people
Then will we go to rest?
Or will we live again?

Rohnda Millinger

Two American Beauties

Against the odds: Poverty,
Rejection, discrimination
After the civil war, along the South
They survived pains

Like flowers sprouting in Spring
After the winter snows, cold winds, rains
Symbols of inspiration Admiration

Two lives to be emulated
Unselfishness, perseverance Love

Portraits of a past family that exists no more
A life many today cry for
When mom, dad, sisters,
Brothers were a real family
With hearts full of hope, faith Charity

Two sisters: Sadie and Bessie
Ages over a hundred years today
Patriotic until this day
When they proudly like to say
"Lord ain't it great to be an American"
Truly, two American beauties

Veola Victoria Barnes

Aspiring To Sacrifice

Take my eyes so I can see
remove my tongue so I can speak
refuse to abuse the capacity to use
my ear to hear the wisdom clear one is in need
I live by this creed it takes all of my soul
to plant one tiny seed
to raise up a tree so it can be said
that many are happy
when their mouths are fed
servant to all and master of none
pick up a pound when bearing a ton
fellow traveler
as on trail you tread
when longing for rest
you may sleep in my bed
if your clothes have been taken
receive all of mine
I bury my flesh to seek the divine
and nothing of worth will ever suffice
to be a replacement for sacrifice

Nicholas Malewski

Untitled

The peachy orange sky of the retiring sun.
Replaced by and awakened moon.

Birds in formation;
Swooping and diving from tree to tree.

Leaves shedding their green color,
and drifting off freely.
A squirrel sipping gently from a puddle,
just after a cleansing rain.

Water gliding softly over the ridged
sculptures in the creek.

A newborn baby just opening his eyes
to his brand new world.

A grandfather sharing his wisdom
before his time comes to rest.
ONE special bond.

Kimberly Walker

"Tell Me You Love Me"

A chilling voice echoes - echoes
Resonating through the chambers of my reason
Sensations of desire take form
As the vibrations move through my body
The voice cradles my heart and stirs my soul

Awake - am I awake?
In a dream - it feels like a dream
Your hand slides down my back
My body quivers - oh, but the feel of your touch
I slowly open my eyes - you are so beautiful
Just to lose them in yours
"I love you" - how I do love you

Lisa R. Rowley

Our World Is Falling Apart!

Our world is falling apart
Right before our eyes.
With a druggie's desperate lies.

The pieces of the puzzle
Are coming apart.
With a ten year old stealin'
Just breakin' his poor mama's heart.

Our country's dyin'
From mystery men in suits.
Gangs walkin' the streets,
Just lookin' for new recruits.

The struggle between life and death
NOW! Began.
It's gettin' harder as the years past us by.
But over all the battle between life and death
Will be won.

Sherine Ramnath

Fantasy World

Waves moving across the sea unbalanced by reflection.
Rising up and the sun overlooking a perfect picture.
Images of life reflecting uncertainly.
Not knowing if the sea will connect with the sun.
Time still moving, yet caught up into two perpendicular axis.
Where, where, where.......
Self image reflects reality, innerself and insanity.
As the moon rises, the sun shines.
The more emotion the less energy.
Emotion, shining high, yet physically draining.
Do we stand in the middle of forces that are uncontrollable,
or exist in a Fantasy world.

Pamela J. Stevenson

Good-Bye

As you get in the car, tears
roll down my face, knowing I'll never see
you again breaks my heart.
The memories we shared
will be with me forever.
I was afraid to let someone
In my life, afraid of love, but with you
it was different, you made me feel wanted,
cared for, for that I thank you.
Well now it's time we must part,
I'll miss you so much words can't explain.
As you drive away, I wave goodbye
with a lump stuck in my throat, and those
words I never said, I say those words now
Goodbye; I love you.

Tammy Cook

Impossible Possibilities

Possible things come in every color
Save a certain shade of blue.
We put out a house for bluebirds
And a few days later
The family was all moved in.
Don't tell me they
Sensed that tiny hole.
The world is much too big
For this kind of radar.
Impossible things come in the color blue
But only the blue of bluebirds.

A. Roy Eckardt

To Your Door

I wake and toil in the sweaty sun because of me being poor.
Saving every penny to buy you gifts galore.
We go to a movie and dinner, wishing I could give you more.
The meal eaten to the core, the silver-screen simple lore.
On the ridge you see the lights of the city.
All day in the fields, I am tired and sore.
I ask you how long have we been together?
Has it already been a year times four?
I tell you, tomorrow I have to go off to the war.
Don't cry, not one single despaired roar.
Given to you, a poor man's promise ring.
Inside of me, I feel from limb to limb being torn.
You say will wait for me, and will keep a light on for me.
You are mine and I am yours.
If I don't come back, know that I love you forevermore.
I ask you, just one last request before I see you no more.
May I walk and escort you, to your door?

Jacob G. Johnson

Pantophobia: The Fear of Everything

The psychopathic man sits shivering,
Scared of everything, alone and quivering.
In the corner where he sits it is dark.
He shrieks at the distant sound of a dog's bark.
The man is bald because he's afraid of hair.
Why not shoot himself? No one would care.
A man walks by and drops him a dollar.
As he throws it aside he bellows a great holler.
Money, like everything else, is one of his fears.
He looks at the gun and thinks, as the end nears.
He lifts the gun to his head ever so slightly.
Then cocks, and pulls the trigger ever so tightly.

Patrick G. Williams

A Child's Point Of View

Ten toes wandering aimlessly amid the morning's dew,
Searching for a robin's nest, a butterfly or two,

Whispering secrets to a pup or favorite teddy bear,
Saying hi, being shy, taking time to care.

Fueled on hugs and kisses, a sandwich and a nap,
Two good stories, maybe three, on top of Grandpa's lap.

Color doesn't matter, friends all seem the same;
Only difference is perhaps, the sound of each one's name.

Not concerned with time you know, the way we seem to be,
Life's a magic circle they dance around with glee.

You say you can't find answers - and peace won't come to you?
Then look at life quite simply from a child's point of view.

Pamela Hoffman

Searching — Searching

Searching for something,
Searching through the day.
A better tomorrow,
A better way.

Searching can be such a strain,
Searching life, searching in vain.
What is it that takes us astray?
What is it we seek each day?

The answer my friend, is hard to say.
We search at work, we search at play.
Someday into the tomorrow,
We who search, seek not sorrow.

We as humans, do strange things.
We as humans, have no wings.
Searching searching life each day,
For peace of mind and freedom to say.

Each of us seek the same.
May we all be free of pain.
Being human and searching on,
Can only take us to the great beyond.

Lyell Thomas

The Secret Of Success

The secret of success,
Seems to be easy I guess,
Only the strong survive.
It takes patience, honesty
and the gratefulness to be alive.
It's one day up, one day down
and that's just a start.
The secret being,
it's what's in your heart.
Love yourself first, but keep in mind
The planet has plans you can't control.
So do everyone a favor and go with the flow.
Make things happen, you have the choice.
When anger appears silence your voice
Life is short, so count every minute.
You only get out of life what you put in it.

Sharon Gambatese

Your Loving Touch

Your loving touch of sweet embraces,
sends my heart into racing.
Without even knowing the true meaning;
those gentle caresses sends shivers of,
excitement throughout my being.

Your tender eyes reaches out with a
loving touch;
That caresses the very depths of me,
leaving feeling of your nearness so much.

Should the night arise with you lying
by my side;
Your loving touch of sweet embraces,
and gentle caresses;
Could make the moments slip into
hours with hearts a racing.
And if hours should decide to slip
into the dawn,
Then it would be alright as long as
I'm with you lying by my side
in your arms.

Rubie Cox

The Great I Am

The One who is and was
shall always be
Who directs us home
by means of His shed blood on Calvary

With outstretched arms
peace and grace
He leads us on
to our chosen place

His will for my life
I leave in His hands
what greater place can there be
understanding His love and prompting commands

Dear Father in Heaven
almighty in power
please grant to me the strength
I need for this hour

I am in the place of care
You have chosen for me
I am in need of Thy Spirit
Your word please allow me to see

Lawrence D. Lindberg

Tears of a Father

I once knew a child,
She belonged to me.
She was the cutest baby,
That I would ever see.

But one day,
I gave her away.
And now it seems for that mistake,
I will always pay.

To her I am a stranger,
A person she doesn't know.
I'll never see her smile,
Or see how big she's grown.

Over the years I wish I could see,
What this child has grown up to be.
To see the relationship we could have had,
In my mind I will always be her dad.

Thomas E. Buckmaster

The Cross

My only concern was over the death of a young life, a child
She had not yet begun to live, and so-died
Nothing can grip the purple taste of death as one so young
In your arms, unafraid; totally unafraid

Children fear what they do not know, they are conditioned
Adults tell them that the unknown is a thing to be feared
And she lay in my arms, all 3 and a half feet, 57 pounds
of her, and she smiled before she died, poor child

I wept aloud, uncontrollably for two hours. I could not talk
The smile still on her face after she was gone, a mute
reminder of what she was, had been, was becoming
And I lay awake all that night thinking of the girl

I had not known her, had only seen her from a distance
A couple of times before at the same crosswalk
I drove home that way every day, and she smiled at the
familiarity.

The brakes just gave way and I hit her, hard enough to knock
the very last breath out of her, and she died in my arms.
And I could not bring myself to forgiveness. And her parents
did. And in some strange, smiling way-she did, too.

Mark Storer

A Mother's Love

A mother's love is something special.
She holds her baby, tenderly.
Reminds me of the special way
Jesus cares for me.
Reminds me of the special love
Jesus bears for me.

And as he grows, a mother knows
that soon her love must set him free.
Reminds me of how Jesus' love
sets free you and me.
Reminds me of the special love
Jesus bears for me.

Then soon he's grown and on his own.
He forgets his mother's name.

He uses her abuses her;
But she loves him just the same.

Too soon she's old. Her body's cold.
And her son cries for his loss.
Reminds me too, how me and you put Jesus on the cross.
Reminds me of his special love that nailed Him to the cross.

Lorraine Standish

Cocoon

She comes forth from her sleep at break of day.
She opens up her eyes and with a groan,
She pleads again in that remorseful tone,
And pleads for one more minute she might stay.

Her eyes will open, this time all the way.
She says, "Good morning" with that morning groan,
And with that lazy manner all her own,
Rises up to great a brand new day.

Why is it such a task for her to wake?
Is not the morning beautiful and bright?

And as she rises and her bed forsakes
She seems to blossom in the morning light.

I don't know why it is this way
But that's what happens every day.

Patrick L. Whittle

Best Friends

The island is my serenity, she and I are one.
She quietly calls as I draw near, through waves, wind and sun.
The eyes are the true key to the soul, look down, deep inside.
You will find honesty lives within, this we cannot hide.
There is not a secret between us, the truth must be told.
Long lost loves and fantasies fulfilled, daring to be bold.
She knows of the passion in my soul, the fire in my heart.
The sexual power held within, tearing us apart.
Dangerous liaisons come our way, memories to hold.
All caution thrown to the winds above, destinies unfold.
Adventure will always entice us, master of the night.
Sensual desires take wing and fly, breaking dawns first light.
The fantasy is overwhelming, a hunger inside.
No man will conquer the spirit here, though many, have tried.
The spirit we share that is our soul, never calm or tame.
You cannot claim what you never had, freedom, is our name.
The meaning of life is not withheld, in her heart or mine.
The simplicity of what we share, mighty oaks and wine.
Forever a part of the island, she and I are one.
Cosmic energy body and soul, until, life is done.

Terri J. Schwalbe

I Wonder

I wonder if the rain that falls from the sky, the gentle tear we
shed from our eye; or just another lonely heart saying goodbye?
or the sun that shines so bright in the sky,
is it letting us know why we should try?
or the grass that's green,
is it showing us there's a place we've never seen?
or the flowers that bloom on a bright summer day,
are they showing us, there is a better way?
The winds that blow, are they showing us the right direction to go
or just a whisper saying "I told you so"
The tides in the sea are they telling us there's a better place to be?
or is it just something pretty to see?
The suffering and the pain, what do we gain?
I guess we'll never know till we ride on that train.

I wonder...I wonder...
and now I know there is a better place to go!
I wonder do you?

Tonya F. White

She's Rich

She's perfectly polished from her head to her toes,
She's got money to burn and it certainly shows.
She's manicured, coiffed, and her eyebrows are tweezed,
She looks in the mirror and she's nothing but pleased.
The jewelry she wears is the real stuff, not junk,
She's always got dates, and it's usually a hunk.
Her car is expensive; a foreign-made ride,
The fur that she wears is a genuine hide.
She owns forty horses and sometimes she'll ride,
Or walk through her acreage, her dog by her side.
She works on her tan while she sits by the pool,
She sips margaritas to keep herself cool.
She's climbed in the Rockies, she's sailed on the seas,
She's gambled in Vegas, she's shopped in Paris.
She eats fine cuisine that her chef has prepared,
Caviar is a staple on her bill of fare.
She gives to the needy, she helps feed the poor,
She'd give all she could if she only had more.
She's got lots of money; she hasn't a care,
But what makes her the richest?—She knows how to share.

Michelle Glad

Nobody's Perfect

Overweight; bad breath; oily hair;
short in height, nobody's perfect right?

Punish a child; get into an argument;
convicted of murder; quit a job;
tell lies, nobody's perfect right?

Skip school; be cool; do all the bad
things people do, nobody's perfect right?

Good grades; a great paying job;
love and affection; that's no loss.
But wait, nobody's perfect right?

Alcoholism; homosexual; drug overdose;
suicide, nobody's perfect right?

You can laugh;
You can cry;
You can make fun of people,
but you should realize,
Nobody's Perfect. Right?

Kristy Gorrell

The Lonely Nights

The nights I sit up in bed, when I
should be sleeping. I think of you instead.
I think of all the good times we had
together and how happy we both were.
When you held me in your arms, I felt
secure. But when you let me go, I
lost the security, but still in my heart
I still felt secure. And no one will
ever tear us apart. No matter what,
you will always posses my heart. And
if any one takes my heart away, you
will always be there when I need you
the most. No matter what you will
always be by best friend.

Melissa Garrett

True Hate

When thinking of the things I hate, of people, qualities and fate
Should I attempt their sum to keep would leave me little time to sleep

The foremost rule of all I see is "Hate all those who now hate thee".
If fact does not this hatred prove, suspicion should all doubt remove.

Another set 'tis safe to hate are those I have not met to date.
Is it too far fetched to assume these meetings to be filled with doom?

I hate with pleasure all of these, those strong or weak or with disease.
Those red or brown or black or white in every group are those I spite.

I hate those who depend on me, I hate those yearning to be free.
I hate the rich, I hate the poor, I hate when two and two make four.

I hate to have, I hate to need, I hate to hunger and I hate to feed.
I hate the wet, I hate the dry, I hate the earth and I hate the sky.

I hate those who with me agree never from hatred to be free.
I even hate that part of me that makes me hate all that I see.

R. C. Cordoze

If Only

If only there was peace!
Silence in the air, no fighting anywhere.
Weapons put away, nothing bad to say.
Prisoners of war released, mourning for deceased.
America, such a sigh, no violence, not a fight.
People shaking hands, as their friendship expands.
No racism anywhere around, everyone safe and sound.
People getting along, and not treating others wrong.
By others, meaning colors.
Whether Black, Hispanic, Oriental or White,
We're all equal in God's sight.
Treating others with respect, getting back a positive effect.
Judgment isn't right, that's one reason why there's fights.
Respect for the flag, because it represents the
freedom and peace we should have.
If only these things came true,
maybe there could be more peace for me and you.

Liana Behrens

How Long?

How long has it been
Since you picked up a pen
And wrote to a friend far away?
How long has it been
Since you managed to grin
And cheer a poor comrade at bay?

How long has it been
Since you forgave deadly sin,
Enfolded transgressor to breast?
How long has it been since you spoke to a kin
And laid all past troubles to rest?

How long has it been since you picked up a pin
And though of some soul who would like it?
How long has it been
Since a rumor you heard
And right at the start did spike it?

In spite of your "love, if for each the above,"
Your answer is long, very long,
It's your slip that is showing, believe it,
And the time is right now to retrieve it!

Thomas D. Gillis

Twenty Years

It's been twenty years
Since you've gone away
I never said goodbye
I had nothing to say

You left me quickly, and without a word
But I felt your pain, and your cries I heard
When I heard the news, I cried and I cried
Then I looked to the heavens, and asked the Lord why

It's been twenty years
Since you've gone away
And I never said I loved you
Until this day

My heart was filled, with sorrow and pain
But I knew it wouldn't last, because I'll see you again
You blessed me with children, that are precious and two
And my heart is filled with joy, when they asked about you

It's been twenty years
And I never said goodbye
Because I know in my heart
That you never died

Richard D. Sterling

A Dream of Heaven

Outside lies a world far from our reach where small birds sing and children play. In this world only goodness exist and evil is something that belongs to the past.

Little creatures smell their way through the gardens of fruit that never grow old while insects climb up the plants that forever stay green.

Clouds of billowy white and gray move slowly across the sky bringing showers that keep me dry. The smell of hot fresh bread passes under my nose filling my stomach and suddenly I become satisfied.

Walking every inch of land trying to spot the face of our creator, my legs only feel to walk longer and farther. I ask myself, where is this Supreme Being that created all of this beauty? My eyes slowly gaze above the rumbling mountains to feel the presence of are one and only God.

Rosemarie S. Behzadpour

The Artist

The artist starts with sheet of white,
Slowly paints the background bright;
With paint brush held within his hand
starts to paint the landscape grand

First a purple mountain crest
A tall green pine with birds at nest
A river clear and flowing blue,
Banks of flowers in vivid hue

A dirt brown road winding down,
To the rooftops of an old quaint town,
The artist signs his name with pleasure
Hoping someone will buy his treasure

Wanda L. Young

Life

We all start out as children.
Small, helpless, children.
As we grow we make new friends
Some come, some go
People play an important role in the environment.
Beautiful flowers clutter the ground.
Animals roam our lands.
Carnivores and Herbivores exceed many
The earth contains strange species.
Many not discovered yet.
God created all things in his thoughts.
And all was created with Pure Love!

Rachel Riley

"Beware"

Beware of handsome men with gorgeous
smiles, for their looks can be deceiving.

Beware of their blue eyes which sparkle
so bright, for eyes cannot lie.

Beware of their promises and whispers in
the night, for they are unkept and
usually meaningless.

Beware of tokens of love and appreciation,
for love cannot be bought.

Beware of their fast talk and swift action,
for they cannot understand the
meaning of sensuality.

And most of all beware of the love
that you give willingly and freely
for once it is gone, it shall never
return.

Sabrina Ferrara

Softly Falling Snow

Softly, gently, all around,
Snowflakes fall quietly to the ground.
They flutter silently as if on air,
On and on they dance, without a care.
They swirl and swoop, flying with wings,
They weave a melody no bird sings.
Down, and down and down they cascade,
Going on and on with their graceful serenade.
They wisp and twirl floating here and there,
And one cannot help, but sit and stare.

Rachel Dunsmoor

Friendship

I had a need for some little things,
So bought then for myself.
Brought them directly home,
And put them on a shelf.

In the homes where we all live,
There are many master keys,
A man entered-I was away
My things disappeared like a freeze.

In time he must have realized,
A big mistake he had made,
Given a chance to make things right,
Put them back where once they laid.

Given a chance in this land of ours,
He may become a man of fame.
To ruin his name at an early age,
Would put us all in shame.

Don't mention to me, his name
I know he's on the mend.
Don't make me hate the guy,
He could be my best friend.

Leo F. Hodgson

Memories

I hold tight the memories we shared
So few, yet so many.
If only we could have shared more.
I would have liked that,
and I know you would have too.
But, you had to leave.
I understand, I think.
You had to go to a new place
A place where I will meet you someday.
It will be there that we will meet again
to share more memories.
I will like that, and I know
you will too.

Kathleen Carroll

Raindrops and Rainbows

God sends "Raindrops" to make flowers grow;
So from the sky, they fall real slow;
Before long they hit the ground:
Yet; so small they make no sound;
I even go to see where they fell;
But when I get there I cannot tell;

Yet; these "Raindrops" hang on rose petal like dew;
They send out a fragrance that smell so new;
This is how God shows his beauty to me:
When life is troubled and hard to see:
He did promise when trials come my way:
He'd give me "Grace" for that day:

I love to see a colorful "Rainbow" bright:
After the "Rain" what a beautiful sight:
As I see the colors in full glow,"
I want to stand at the end of my "Rainbow,"
Yet I know this beauty's out of reach
Just as there's lessons yet, for God to teach!

Lou Leann Tucker

"Mama.....Are You Mad At Me?"

At thirty-two she spoke like a child,
So haunting, so scared, so terrified.
Listening I found myself appalled at what I heard....
A pleading....I'll never forget.

"Mama...are you mad at me?" She said.
"You know I don't like you to wear your hair down,
it's prettier up".
"But Mama, I like to wear it down" she softly said.
"You should wear it like your Mama wants it sometimes",
her mother said.

They looked at each other with tears in their eyes
Each waiting for the other to approve or give in....
It was not to be... as the silence continued
I heard a weak sigh....
"Mama....Are you mad at me?"

There were no more words the rest of the way,
The two women, the child within... and me.
The echoes surround me still as I feel
intensely inside for this child...
"Mama....Are you mad at me?"

Maureen Barraford-Soobitsky

A Clue

Just give me one little clue
So I can do,
What I have always wanted to,
That is to find YOU.

Who are YOU?
What is your name?
Your claim to fame?
An identity
That connects YOU and ME.

A secret so carefully kept,
For years the tears that I have wept.
All of the thousands of scenarios I have thought,
All of the books on adoption I have bought.

I respect the privacy of my mom.
Where did it all go wrong?
Why do I yearn to know the truth?
It started way before my youth.

Oh Dear God please help me to know,
Which way I must go
To allow my life a balanced flow.

Mary S. Butler

Life

As the morning sunrises upon the earth.
So is life on our day of birth,
It's path is scheduled throughout the day,
Ours is not, along our way, clouds appear to hide it's rays,
As troubles may among our days.
By noon the sun is overhead, half it's journey now the past,
We taken this time to plan ahead,
Then our aims in life are cast.
As the sun continues on it's way,
It's warmth and light come into play,
We use this time allotted us,
For good, not evil, which is a plus.
As twilight nears and time runs out,
Was our time well spent, without a doubt?
The sun will rise again tomorrow,
Without us, to some a day of sorrow,
Our memory to them we leave behind,
So make it worthwhile, the very best kind.
The sun will have a smile upon its face,
Bringing new life to take our place.

Jack D. Green

A Mother's Prayer

As thou didst walk in Galilee
So loving Saviour walk with him for me.
For since the years have passed and he is grown
I cannot follow, he must walk alone.
Be thou my feet, that I have had to stay
For thou canst comrade him on every way.
Be thou my voice, when sinful things allure,
Pleading with him to choose those that endure.
Be Thou my hand, that would keep his in mine
All, all things else a mother must resign.
When he was little I could walk with him and guide
But now I pray Thee, Thou be at his side.
And as Thy blessed Mother folded Thee
So kind and Loving Saviour guard my son for me.

John Garrod

Rwanda

Rwanda
So many ways to die.
What's singular, the spiral downward.
Holocaust revisited.

Monstrous menace man,
Any balance, upset by conquest, Imperial Lust,
And human nature? Us and them a must?

Hutu and Tutsi, we are you.
No relation, you say,
'Tween Kigali and LA?
Then listen to the words
Rodney and Luther King did say.

Morally right is prevention, tyranny detention,
Pay no attention, allow ascension to the royal seat,
See Rwanda repeat.

New nation-states, miracle machines,
Epics of this century,
All pale to compare,
To the genocidal flair,
We bequeath our progeny.

Richard M. Gross

Pink Lemonade Kisses

Pink lemonade kisses
So sweet and so sour
The kisses to bloom
The love is to flower

So good I can't stand it
Let it open so wide
Kisses to your soul
Please let me inside

Those pink lemonade kisses — you don't even know
That flower that I spoke of, let it grow, let it grow
That gentle sweet flower, that pink lemonade kiss
It's for you that I long and it's you that I miss

And it won't be long,
Each day that I wait
Those pink lemonade kisses
Make me tremble and shake

Those pink lemonade kisses,
You don't even know
That flower I spoke of
Is my love, does it show?

Lucy MacDonald

Mother Dear

Most purely devoted mother
So thoughtful and granting
Where in dire needs and help
Where no one could ever accomplish the dreams
That she tainted for her child.

Irresistible dear mother
Who is so fame and worthy
Of all the gifts that God
had given her child the chance
To see the light of nature.

Amidst the midnight through
Caring her child for shelter
Keeping warm and gentle
Sharing all the comfort
That no one can give the best of everything.

The Universe is full of wonderful things
But not all that glitters are gold
The sacrifices and teaches she rendered
Never someone could repay
Beloved mother is the greatest of them all.

Jonalyn Bautista

Once...

Memories fall like gentle snow,
Soft and pure and cool to the touch.
The explosion of light from a fireworks show.
The crackle and crispness of a paper bag lunch.
The sap on you hands from climbing a tree,
A time when bikes became airplanes in flight.
When you stayed up late before Christmas wondering who you would see,
When shadows became goblins in the darkness of night,
And the bogeyman hid under your bed.
When bushes became jungles and berries became bombs,
When dreams of fairies and unicorns remained in your head.
When the clap of thunder made you run for your mom,
A time of innocence and happiness that drifts through your mind,
As you realize it's gone,
Trapped in another time.

Killeen Tracy

Untitled

When I watch the news at night,
Some of the stories give me a fright.
I sometimes wonder what will happen to me,
Will I be who and what I want to be?
This world is tragic all over the place,
Guns, Drugs and violence take up much space.
We can help it if we try,
We don't need these people to die.
Innocent victims being killed or slaved,
We can give people homes, get them bathed.
We can dry the tears of kids who see,
Sad things in life thinking "it could've been me."
Just remember whatever you do.
Things can happen especially to you!

Lisa Philbrick

Puzzle Pieces of Our Earth

Once the Earth was clean, beautiful land perfect.
Now the Earth is clean, but dirty the puzzle is missing a piece.
Later the Earth is dirty and the puzzle will lose all its pieces.
Now we can help from losing more pieces to our Earth.

Melissa Zirbes

Wild Thing

I'm a wild thing,
The name has a ring,
Every time I say it I hear Ping,
Cause, I'm a wild thing!

Nicole Cannon

Goodbye

The days are quickly passing,
Some too swift for me.
While the sun shines brightly
And the sky is blue and warm,
We will gather every minute
As a treasure for to store.
Time is the master of all things,
A gift to all mankind,
But the most valuable prize of all,
The moments we have together.
The weeks go by and days do fly
Until the happy, dreaded day is here.
Then, my friend, so special that you are
Sit back as you sail away and recall,
The moments of the past gloriously filled by we.

Rheda J. Pell

Just a Woman

I'm just a woman.
Someone who has feelings just as you do.
Someone who loves with all her heart and hates with all her soul,
Someone who believes sex does mean love or even like.
I'm just a woman.
Someone who has the gift to care for others just as you do.
Someone who rescues her friends from loneliness, despair,
able to listen to problems and help them out of hopelessness.
I'm just a woman.
Someone who possesses the gift of life just as you do.
Able to feel life growing inside of us, moving, breathing,
Able to innately know that this is the true essence of love.
And I'm just a woman.
A woman that has all these characteristics and more.
The intelligence, the beauty, the innocence of angels,
And the knowledge that women are a gift from God to all.

Kim Anderson

Farewell My Furry Friend

It's hard to say farewell to someone so close,
someone who's been around for so long.
For seventeen years he brought us such joy
and then, in a moment, he was gone.

"Ming" was a very handsome Siamese cat.
His personality was so "laid back".
It didn't take long to get hopelessly hooked
on this "kitty", who was tan and black.

And then during the summer of '93
he started looking frail and thin.
Off to the Vet to discover the cause.
We did this, again and again.

The news from the Vet was not very good,
Ming's liver and kidneys could not sustain.
We brought him home, to return the next day,
to put him to sleep - OH, THE PAIN!

My husband wept as a coffin he built,
the next day we laid Ming to rest.
Through all the memories and even the pain,
we'll always know we had the best.

Shirley M. Payne

Untitled

Can you help me?
Something hurts
A persistent pain
Dull, but extreme.
I close my eyes only for a moment
And that moment is gone.
All my dreams pass before my eyes
I can't reach them
Can only see a blur.
Something hurts.
Can you find it?
Take my pain away
It keeps pulling me further and further down.
I can't pick myself up
I can't let go
Though I know nothing lasts forever
I'm too numb to cry
Too confused to try
Try to think of why
Something hurts.

Jenny Snell

Let Me Be Me

When was the last time you took some blame...
Sometimes I wonder if you even remember my name...
Tell me dear, what is your game...
You leave me crying and feeling lame...

You take my feelings and toss them aside.
You rip my heart and I begin to cry.
You lie and say you understand, how can you when
you had a loving mother's hand...

When my heart needs you, you always leave.
Tell me dear, what do you really need.
You give everything to me.
Everything but what my soul really needs...
Maybe someday I'll be as free as a flying bee.
Until that day babe, it's you and me.
Just let me be happy, free and me...

Tina L. Gerjets

Sometimes, I Wonder

As a mother you gave me life.
Sometimes, I wonder why!
If you love me, why do you leave me,
when times are filled with strife?
I know for a fact, you don't have to go.
Sometimes, I wonder, "Do you really want to show?"
You say you do but you just can't.
Sometimes, I wonder, "Is that a useless rant?"
Once or twice that wouldn't matter but
you've done it enough to make my heart shatter.
Of course I'm angry and even hurt
but someone has to feel like dirt.
I have to love you because your my mother
but you should put me above your significant lover.
I'm not saying walk away
from a love that seems so true.
I'm just asking for you to show your love
like other mothers do.

Rachel O'Dell

Goodbye

Pictures spread across the wall
sometimes I'd like to forget them all
It still hurts after all these years
a love that still brings those tears
I kept every letter underneath my bed
every word every little thing you said
Living with your memory, it pains me so
not because your gone, because I can't let go
Last time I saw you, you looked so handsome lying there
without a worry, without a care
We were to be married in a month or two
and the last words you said to me were "I love you"
I placed my engagement ring in your pocket
also a picture of us I kept in my locket
I gave you one last kiss and prayed you saw the light
and as they closed the lid I said my last good night
But for all the tears I still cry
the time has come to say goodbye

Veronica York

Piece By Piece

Piece by piece the puzzle fits together.
Sometimes it seems to take forever to figure where just one piece goes
But eventually you find the right place.
Sometimes you think a piece goes somewhere that it really doesn't belong,
But after you look at it from a different angle,
you realize it was wrong.
Sometimes you may want to give up putting the puzzle together,
But you cannot give up.
You have almost solved it.

When all the pieces are in their place, the puzzle sure looks great.
But, sometimes, unfortunately, your puzzle may fall and crumble...
But that is O. K.
Because you know now where the pieces go.
You can pick them up and go on.
Piece by piece life also fits together.

Paula M. Lee

Dad

Dad, I love you with all of my heart
Sometimes you build me up to feel smart.
It's hard to tell you what is on my mind,
Because I don't know which dad I'll find.

One is the greatest I'll ever know
The other I wish would pack up and go.
To live with two dads is not very easy
I find the bad one makes me queasy.

I get my hopes up, my dads going fishing
The other dad comes and my dreams turn to wishing
Make that other dad please go away
Bring back the good dad I love everyday.

No one knows what alcohol can do
Until you live with one dad, that's two.
You try to separate you feelings somehow
Please give my dad the strength to stop drinking
God "Now"

Virgene Kobbe

Going Home

I dream of a land far away nestled in the pines and bathed in the light
of God's love.
Where rivers flow swiftly and long and rainbows hover above.

The cottage with the old thatched roof
stands shrouded in a morning mist watching the deer with their
babes—alone and aloof.

Where wood crackling in the fireplace dispels the cool dampness with a
slow deliberate pace and the mad dash of corporate politics was
eliminated early in the race... in favor of calm solitude and peace.

In my dream I see the roses climbing the trellis on the white washed
porch and corn stalks glistening with the morning dew.
Where life is good and troubles are few.

I have dreamed of this place for many a night and I know it must be.
My goal now is to find it, to gaze upon its beauty, my own eyes to see.

My search now begins to seek out this place where I was meant to stay,
no matter it may be a far journey.
I don't mind that it's so far away.
I'm going home.

Phyllis R. Gentile

Sudden Farewell

I heard a sad song today. The melody was sweet, the words were sad. Singing of things they would have done, if only they had known. The verses brought up the memories, feelings I had bottled up, all of this anger and sorrow inside me, making me wonder:
What would I have said to you if I had known that one person would have done such terrible things to you?
What would I have said to you if I had known you would be gone in a blink of an eye? What would I have said to you if I had known that I could never confide in you again? What would I have said to you if I had known there would be no more laughs, only tears? What would I have said to you if I had known the magic would end for you? What would I have said to you if I had known there would be no more shared birthdays?

I wish I had said thanks for being there when I needed someone to listen to me and thanks for being a friend. But mostly I wish I had said I love you like a Mom, even though you're someone else's.

I'm mad I'll never know why he killed you? Now all I can say is:
I miss you! And Good Bye!

Risa D. Carter

GA

Neighborhood-you ain't changin', truth is you was born that way.
Pretty girl told me so, under the mouth of the C Train—the breath
was bad but the buns was good.
Who was I to complain, stroking the blade in my jacket pocket
As I stroked the blade in my jacket
pocket

"False hop[e] and the prophesy sayeth"—typical of me falling
asleep when the Rev. Farakhan was speakin'. What is this brother your
my brother jive-TONIGHT ONLY- BLACK MEN

Outside I lit a salem and looked up and saw his black
wings unfolding over the city—I swear it wasn't no superhero
There are no superheroes when I am awake.

Ghetto Angel I got a plan you will be pleased - every door, window,
car, liquor store is covered

Here's the deal - stop torturing the neighborhood so slow
Speed it up man, speed it up

Take us now all of us take no prisoners
Start over Ghetto Angel and would you throw in more flowers for me.

S. M. Garfield

Lonely

The sky is gray
Like the scene in my heart today,
Never seeing nothing but my solemn self,

I stand upon my pedestal
Looking forward for want of more,
Wanting only to please my greedy self.

All of those who know me well
Can only say that they knew me well,
Standing here on my empty ground, forced
To stand by myself, all by myself.

All by myself.

There was once a humble voice in me
Speaking only the choice in me,
A warm voice of sweet romances,
A kind voice that spoke of better chances,
A fine voice of bitter happy days;
And better ways.

Harvey

Needy Child

When I looked at her I saw a
little child with string hair and torn
clothes. She was a needy child.
I saw fear in her eyes and tears
stained her face.
I knew in a glance she didn't trust me.
As I looked into her eyes I saw
years of abuse and pain.
Oh how would she trust me?
I spoke softly to her.
I told her I knew of someone who
could take the hurt and pain away.
She looked at me with tears in her eyes.
And hope in her face
She spoke softly who!
Only Jesus I said.
Only Jesus!

Tammy Ruse

Kanna

I watch you from a distance
Like the snow on the tree's you glisten
many years of knowledge you have retained
Remember running through the Fjords in the
arctic rain.

A family you helped to create all special
to you in your own way
When they were wrong you seemed
to find sunlight to brighten their day.

As time goes by you're still keeper
of the flame.

When one falls you still help
them when they cry out your name
you find goodness in all of them
When others seem to turn away
I guess a mothers love is stronger
than steel in this modern day
Kanna's your name, but not by birth.

It was given to you by a grandson
your first.

Travis von Bischoffshausen

Caribbean Dream

Crossing the threshold
I am captured by Sweet Mother's tropical cornucopia.

Sun, crowned with gleaming amber,
Casts burning streaks across the sky.

Flaming blossoms dazzle and delight.
Licked by scented breezes.
Hypnotic, exotic - ginger, jasmine, gardenia.

Joyful butterflies careen from red to yellow
Dripping sweet nectar.

Sparkling sea kisses and caresses.
I peer through liquid glass at sunlit slopes.
Secrets are revealed, one by one;
Coral forests whisper,
Purple sea fans beckon,
Neon fish flaunt crimson, yellow, electric blue.

Awestruck, I melt in Earth's ripe womb,
Dissolving, merging, until I realize at last

I Am all this and more. . .

Roberta Hill

An Illusion

I exist only in your mind
I am just a thought that you have carried thru time
I appear when you want to be near me
And speak of love when you need to hear me
I am only what you make of me
A reflection of your own naked beauty
And although at times you may think I am real
I am simply a part of the way that you feel
The joy and happiness of being alive
In a time and space where lovers thrive
I am the color of passion in your rainbow eyes
That cannot disappear with simple good-byes
Nor leave you in darkness while the moon cries
For I am an illusion -
That never dies

C. P. Olive, Jr.

Why?

As I sit here crocheting and meditating
I ask a question of myself.
Why does God keep me here on Earth?
Why am I not "put on the shelf?"
It's over ninety-two years since my birth.
What do I have to offer? Who really needs me here?
What Treasures can I proffer? Well, yes, a word
of cheer to someone who is lonely, to someone who
is sad. It may bring a ray of sunshine - might
even make them glad. So, maybe there's reason
My Lord wants me to stay at least another Season
before he carries me away. I thank him for my
friends and my beloved family. They are so
dear to me. And pray that He watch over us
And keep us safely.
Yes, Lord, I put my trust in Thee.

Maryan Norberg

To My Darling Wife

A rose is so fragile its purity is true
Its innocent touch reminds me of you.
Its beauty breathtaking in the dimmest of light
Inspiring lovers and poets just by its sight.
It has Thorns to protect it from things that appose
So let me be your Thorn and you my rose!

Steve Vanslyke

Walk With Me

Walk with me, walk with me,
I asked ,will you be my friend?
Will you walk with me till the end?

Will you be there in time of sorrow and joy?
Or will you reject me like a broken toy?

Will you stay with me when I need you most?
Or will you turn away?

Will you walk with me
Will you be the things I ask
Will you be my friend?

Lori A. Clark

What A Day!

In 1992
I bought a pair new blue shoes
Hoping to see Bob Barker and his crew

So I went to make the days plans
Finding out I'm traveling in a van

When the day came
It was a shame
Knowing Mr. Barker
Had to wait for his carpenter.

I'm sorry to say that didn't make my day
But figured it seemed to true
So I went inside and listened to some blues

The following day I went to the park
Listening to the dogs bark

The happier Mr. Barker seemed
The more his face gleamed

Maybe if I pray
I'll be able to say
Goodbye everybody and have a nice day.

Rodney Chevremont

Reality

In the strains of life
I breathe through you.
In the fate of time I see
through your life's illusions growing to uncertainty
Soon reality becomes the illusion we once knew.
In reality is where the past haunts us.
In the state of unconsciousness
is when we are what we want to be.
Time can heal the pain and
also drown the scars.
Time is the present, the future
and soon to be the past, but our dreams
are our fulfillment, the life we never had.
With loves and laughs comes
hatred and tears it's what all of us fear.

Rochelle Shamaley

Freedom

Words like Freedom are good to know
Make it your life wherever you go
North, South, everywhere the world turns
This thing called Freedom each place yearns.
In torn, ravaged lands of injustice
The struggle and fight seems hopeless
But the beacon for which they fall
Is a Golden Horizon for all.
I say words like Freedom are good to know
Make it your life wherever you go.

R. Ess Brown

The Sandman

Sandman, sandman flying through the air.
I can't see you anyplace, but I still know
you're there.
Checking heads that lie in beds in
pillows sunk so deep, making sure those
eyes are closed, then send them fast asleep
So sandman, sandman come and visit
me. Sprinkle some sand in my eyes so
I can fall asleep. So I can dream of
toy's and candy I can eat
Sandman, sandman come and visit me.

William Seaman

Salesmanship

The owner said he'd sell the car and give me a fair price.
I checked the paint and found no rust, the upholstery was nice.
The dipstick showed the oil was full, the belts were fitted snug.
The exhaust pipe was not burnt, to the tires I gave a tug.
The mileage low, the radio worked, the clock, it even kept time.
It was a great second-hand car, the best I'd ever find.
I bought the car, I paid cash, for the owner was in need.
I drove it to the corner, but the brakes, they would not heed.
It came to rest on the railroad tracks, a train was coming fast.
Terror filled me and I jumped out, I was safe at last.
My poor car was a tangled mess, just a metal hunk.
So, I sold my car for scrap and I got more for junk.

Mary R. Stanley

Life

I was thinking about something earlier today.
I do absolutely nothing, but waste my life away.
I just sit around, and don,t do anything at all,
While other kid's run, swim, and play ball;
Yes, I was thinking about it
And I can't figure it out;
What's the purpose? What's "life" all about?
When God put me on earth, I had my first glance,
He gave me a "choice", and he gave me a "chance",
Now I've taken the "chance", and I'm wasting it away:
That's what I was thinking about earlier today.

Lana Badart

You Changed My Life

You changed my life so many ways, there are so many,
I don't know which ones to say. I was a child before I knew you,
but I grew up more than you thought I would. You made me a woman
that only night, when you took me in your arms and held me tight.

I believed everything you told me and I trusted you, when I opened
my eyes I realized the truth. You made love to me and left me laying
in bed, I still remember the cruel words you said. You hurt me, and
you hurt me deep inside, you left me with nothing but tears in my eyes.

I loved you and I loved you very much,
I loved your kiss and your warm touch.
You changed me and you left me alone and sad,
You stepped all over the dreams and wishes I had.
I loved you but you are now the past,
Although I will never be able to recover
from you so fast.

Ledy De Jesus

"Scrawling Back; An Ode To Alcohol"

Scrawling Back; an ode to alcohol
I drew a picture of my soul and set it on a shelf,
The dust collected on my soul and I forgot myself,
Each feeling yellowed form neglect and yearned to have a say,
But I enslaved my thoughts to him and failed to frame them for display,
I taunted his arresting taste and dared to try and run,
He simply smeared my soul with actor's black and reveled in his fun,
The paper thin image lie quiet and trembled with each stroke,
I prayed for lightning rescue and the fragile lines were broke,
Impatient drops of water fell and smudged the paint away,
My soul sucked a breath of peace and feelings asked to play,
So I tucked my soul inside and cradled each emotion,
While welcome pangs of sorrow lingered and tempted my devotion.

Winona Ann Petersen

Bridge Of Love

As I occasionally muse back through the corridors of my mind,
I encounter a bridge of love transcending the river of time.
The evening grows dark for the hour is late
When two lovers meet to test the winds of fate.
Their love is enshrined by the canopy above,
As they cherish this moment on the bridge of love.

The river of time flows relentlessly along
Murmuring a tune from loves old sweet song.
Will this love, the ravages of time, endure?
The answer to this question can never be sure.
No matter the course, loves memory will stay behind
For the bridge of love transcends the river of time.

William A. Cooney

Untitled

As I enter
I feel cold and lost
I light a candle and feel as though it will
be my guiding light
We all need a guiding light to help us in
the future
To give us a shining light for that
cold, dark room you enter.

Pete Gabarro

Something There

There's something there,
I feel it in my soul,
It's not lust,
It's not despair,
It may not be love,
I just know that I care for you and always will.
There's something there,
So come and see,
The soul that cries,
The heart which aches,
The feeling of emptiness,
Only one can enter and be keeper.
Keeper of the something in my heart which
will always be.
So find the key and look inside,
And you'll find the something there,
Inside, waiting.

Kathryn Elgin

Confused World

Spinning, the world is spinning around me; dizziness is all I feel. Why, why the spinning around me?
I cry out, "Help me understand!" No one answers; why does no one answer?
I get dizzier as the world spins around me. Then I, too, start spinning with this confused world.
Confusion and chaos is all around me. But why, why does my world have to be this way?!
I cry out again, "Does everyone feel this way? Is everyone's world this way?!"
As I say this, the spinning is too much for me to handle. I blackout of my confused, chaotic world.
Forever. Never to come back again.
Calm, I am calm now, calm and peaceful. I have no world to live with anymore.

Melissa McMullin

"And I Began"

I felt the flash and I began to see,
I felt the wind and I began to breathe,
I saw the flower and I began to smell,
I saw the music and I began to hear,
I saw the tree and I began to climb,
I saw the water and I began to swim,
I saw her skin and I began to touch,
I saw the hurt and I began to feel,
I saw the pain and I began to cry,
I saw Him and I began to hope,
I looked at all these things and saw life,
... and I began to live.

Rob Gallavan

Distant Love

Once in my life
I find what I'm looking for
Now he's leaving
Nothing to do, nothing to say
Have to take it
Day by day
I watched him work his way into my heart
Now it's over and it didn't even start
I'm losing him like minute grains of sand
slipping through my fingers
Trying to hold on, but my fingers are frozen in place
Only to sit here and watch
He's gone without a trace
Watching the best thing that ever walked into my life
Walk away

Lorraine J. Ludolph

Despair Not!

Up the mountain as if by magic
I found myself, mood dark and tragic
I cried; with life's downs, pray, how may I cope?
And back came the mountain echo; HOPE!
From despair and pain I can't take leave
Back came the mountain echo; BELIEVE!
Heavy's my cross, help, heaven above!
And back came the mountain echo; LOVE!
So I now BELIEVE and LOVE and HOPE
And with life's ups and downs I can cope.

Michael John Constantinides

Remembrance

In the early morning hours
I gaze upon the sun
I remember when I was just a child
And always having fun.

I ran and jumped and played,
All day I would do this
Until 'twas time to sleep
And I would put my P. J's on and give my parents a kiss.

And now as I grow old
And I am sitting here
I remember my childhood
Was also filled with fear.

Fear of dark
And fear of height
Fear of wolves
And things that go bump in the night.

But in the morn when I awoke
These things were forgot
And I would go and run and play
For I was just a tot.

Steven Petrie

My Gift to You

My love, my sweet, herein is my gift to you
I give you my very life
Since it's the legacy
That I have set aside for you

This gift of life comes
In three fashions: My body, my soul, my spirit
Each one of these are three steps to pleasure
Sexual pleasure, or is it,
Emotional pleasure, might it be
Social pleasure

This gift is all sufficient
It shall make you a satisfied,
Enriched and rejuvenated person
You will sigh with pleasure
As you feel me entering your life
I love the way, you receive me

I am the gift to you, wrapped with tears
Tears of longing
Longing for the comport of your bosom

Ruth Derrell

"With the Drop of a Dime"

(Dedicated to Benjamin Michael Cool)

Who would have thought it would end so soon,
I got the call shortly after noon;

You had so many plans, so much time,
but it all went away with the drop of a dime;

I wish I could have hugged you and said goodbye,
but now you're gone and I'm left to cry;

I'll never see your soft smile or warms eyes again,
at least not until we meet in Heaven;

You're in God's hands, you're in his care,
Your memory is alive everywhere;

I'll never forget you, you'll always be loved,
I'll see your image in the skies up above;

If I ever feel lonely or need a friend;
I'll think of our memories and the loneliness will end;

You will be missed for quite some time;
but we'll all meet again with the drop of a dime;

Samantha L. Cridler

Poor Boy Blues

Forgive for not smiling
I got this poor boy blues
I got this little problem, a señorita
Day after night
I get the courage to ask
She always had an alibi
A heartbreaker I gave it a shot
Now, I'm dragging my heels
Throwing myself at her feet
Is it a crime or is it a sin?
I pray to the Lord above to make things right
Now, I'm drowning myself on paper
Thinking of love songs to write
Fingers getting numb
Pushing my mind to the edge
Emotions slipping away
No matter how hard I try
these feeling won't end
No one can stop me from
singing my poor boy blues.

Ramil C. Laudico

"Q & A"

as i was a-wandering on this fair earth,
i got to a-pondering what life was worth.

others say it is money that makes the world spin,
and every day is sunny if the game you win.

still others desired fame: awe-struck faces amazed,
for the prize in this game: adoring eyes upraised.

this is where humanity made its mistake,
thinking its own vanity is all it takes.

when will they "all" learn that love and care were it;
sorrow no more burns with acceptance of it.

"then why doom, destruction and death?" the ones with hurt cry out,
"why agony in every breath to those faithfully devout?"

you and me dared ask, "Why?" and what the meaning of all was.
the goddess smiled wry and answered with a tear, "Because."

Stacy Wong

Falcons and Sparrows

Come on little one come sit on my knee
I have a story for you it might be scary
A story about birds one great and one small
A story about us and how to stand tall

When God made the birds he made many kinds
Sparrows and falcons the latter one fine
Sparrows are small and they hide under trees
They run away from everything they must not be pleased

Falcons, on the other hand are great and so fine
They are graceful and confident and live in sunshine
They're afraid of no one and they take on all comers
The falcon has power and he flies with no others

Falcons are boys and some falcons are girls
Some are quite dark and some look like pearls
You see it doesn't matter a falcon makes his own flight
He flies with the sun and uses all of his might

Now as you grow older you will have choices to make
Remember the falcon and life's yours to take
Fly high with the sun and never look down
Don't follow the others...the sparrows on ground

Roger Beery II

Eighty - "80"!!!!

Life begins at 80, so come to the FRIENDSHIP CENTER.
I have GOOD NEWS for YOU....... The second 80 are
A succession of birthday parties.

Once you reach 80, everyone wants to carry your
baggage and help you up the steps.

If you forget your name or anyone else's, and appointment
even your own telephone number, a promise to be three
different places at the same time, or how many grandchildren
you have, you only to explain that YOU ARE 80.

Being 70 is no fun at all, at that age they expect you to
retire to a house in FLORIDA and complain about your
arthritis (they used to call it LUMBAGO) and you ask everybody
to stop mumbling because you can't understand them.

When you reach 80, everybody is surprised you are still
alive. They treat you with respect, and seem surprised
that you can walk and talk sensibly.

So try to make it 80, or enjoy it after 80. It's the
best part of life. People forgive you for almost anything,
except if you QUIT ATTENDING OUR MEETINGS in the
FRIENDSHIP.
CENTER. LIFE BEGINS AT 80!!!!

Russell Sisco

Moon Sweeper

Tiptoeing through the moonlight and staring up at the stars,
I have got my sweep over my shoulder and my bag full of jars.
No time is there to play, my job has to be done.
The moon must be dusted before the rising of the sun.

Jumping from star to star, I am careful not to fall.
Climbing up to the moon can be one long haul.
Once I have dusted the moon my job will only be half done.
After having collected all the moon dust, to the fairies I must run.

On the nights I am lucky I will see the man in the moon.
He helps me pack my jars with all the moon dust that was strewn.
Pardon my sudden departure. For I am running out of time;
The skies are getting lighter and the bells of morning are about to chime.

Marianne Ware

A Personal Lament...

O' woe is me when all hope is gone
I have no reason to carry on.
The silver linings from my clouds are done,
O' woe is me when all hope is gone.
Sunk in the pit of despair—I see no hope for me,
There isn't a place for me anywhere.
The moon and stars are gone from my skies—
In daylight there is no sun.
O' woe is me when all hope is gone.
But wait — is that a star after all,
To light my way and lead me?
No — not a star — but my tear drop glistening.
O' woe is me when all hope is gone.

Linda Pittinger

Tears Of A Clown

I went to the circus and to my surprise,
I found a weeping clown drying his eyes.
I decided to try and cheer him up,
by juggling four balls and a polka-dot pup.
He flashed me a smile and thanked me kindly,
because he realized that I now know finally.
A clown appears to always be smiling,
but you never know if inside he's crying.

Samantha Scotto

The Memory of You

There's no way I can explain the feelings I feel inside,
I have them all locked up and I'm trying to run and hide.
Feelings of anger, guilt, and desire,
Like I need a love to light my fire.
Crying over every little thing I hear,
Wanting a love to hold me near.
The only thing that can fulfill my needs,
I've been searching for among many weeds.
You were the only thing that mattered to me,
You were the miracle that made my life complete.
We had a love that couldn't be torn apart,
Then you left me without a love in my heart.
Now the only way I can get through life's cyclone,
Is to leave the memory of you in my heart alone.

Stephani Sinyard

Thank You

I been givin' so much/but to date
I haven't been able to match u're gift/takin' it all away
You see/somethin' inside died
when you drained blood outta my rosebuds
just as they were beginnin' to open up
for a long time afterward/I experienced pain
in all the colours of the spectrum
I lost Perspective
forcin' deals with Black and White
LIFE
is a cycle within a cycle within a cycle
winter precedes spring precedes summer precedes fall precedes winter
and while I got the browns today
in MY season
I will flourish
I will once again seek solace in every hue of the rainbow
this is just a note/to thank you
for providing me with the opportunity to feel
even if my feelin'/has to be bad/right now

L. Barcliff

The Unheard Voice

I was brought here, but not at my choice.
I hear a lady's voice.
She may not keep me.
Does she not want to pay the fee?
Or have to make care of me?

Was I something that was unplanned?
Please explain 'cause I don't understand.
Will I never play with toys?
Or live long enough to feel the joy
Will I never shed tears?
Or live to conquer my fears?

If you let me live I'll try not to be a bother,
This is a promise from me to you my mother.
I don't think it is too much to ask for.
All I ask for is to live and I won't ask for much more.
I'll ask you again,
Please give me a chance to begin.

Rachel T. Nguyen

"Azure Apparition"

Night lowers her arms, and an indigo velvet dress descends.
Its folds are turquoise and teal, deep and rich.
The stars at the garment's bosom are not pale yellow dots,
but glistening aquamarines.
At Dawn, Night will change her gown from royal to sky/ice blue
or maybe to slate grey,
depending on the day.

Victoria Adonnino

Love's Song

Doves circle the pure, good and righteous.
I hold my lovers hand in mine.
The winds change to a soft whisper,
calling out our names.
We become distant, the whisper is now louder.
You recognize her voice, beauty is her tone.
Love, is slowly bring us together.
Your eyes are big, and filled with mine.
Your caress, soft as a doves wing on my cheek.
Loves beauteous tone with grace, has no race.
Her powers great. I can not fight you.
My lovers hand will not bring us apart.
As if we are flying high above the clouds.
Love songs her song. We find ourselves
oblivious now. Love sings on.

Tina Schroeder

Thank You Mama

I'd like to say thank you, mama tonight
I just want to thank you, for raising me right.
I'd like to say I'm sorry
for all sleepless nights,
And ask you to forgive me for what I did that wasn't right.

I'd like to say thank you, just for loving me
For telling me of Jesus, while I grew beside your knee.
You told me of your saviors love, and how he died for me
How he hung upon a cruel cross, made from a rugged tree.
How he shed his precious blood to set the sinner free.

I'd like to say thank you, for the things you've done for me
You've helped me through stormy weather, and many turbulent seas.
Your strength is like an oak tree standing in the breeze
Sometime swaying, yet never breaking, always praying with heart aching
forever giving and never taking.

I'd like to say I love you
one more time before I go,
I'd like to say thank you
More than you will ever know,
For all the things you've done for me - Mama I love you so.

Louise Hollis

The Vigil

I did not want to return this night to my home.
I knew you'd need me, instead,
to guide you through the end
Was glad to be with you to meet this
long awaited death
Not with pleasure did we greet this death of yours
but we knew that this life held no value
for you as you are.
No voices did you hear.
Nor words could you speak.
Your vision was fading away as well.
You were a prisoner in a body so long gone wrong
with stroke upon many strokes
Your life eroded away.
But we bravely met your timely death
and shared the moments of gasping breath
to find a peace within us both.

Linda Decker

Honestly

I tell you I love you
I know it's the same toward me
But there's something I have to tell you
That's bothering me.
I gave you my trust
Which that you have earned
But then you turned your back
And I was the one burned.
If I was to deserve
I like to know why
Cause deep down inside
I let out a cry.
I'm not mad no longer
It was stupid of me
I was foolish like a loser
And too dumb to see
That you care for me a lot.
and honesty is the best policy
especially when it comes to me.

Shannon Kauffman

Forever and a Day

I see you in the halls, but you don't see me.
I know when you look down you do it purposely.
I don't know how to show the feelings that I feel.
When I see you it's like a dream, but I want it to be real.

I know there is no chance for you and I to be,
But when I see you in the hall it makes me so happy.
When you smile at your friends, I feel like I will die.
And knowing there's no us makes me want to cry.

I'm so happy you are here but I know you'll soon be gone.
Knowing the pain I will feel I want it to be done.
But when you leave, I know the pain won't end.
Why did I see you? Why did it all begin?

The truth is you have to go but I need for you to stay.
When it's time for you to go, I won't have a thing to say.
For how can I ever say to you goodbye?
A pain in my heart forever now shall lie.

Once you leave I'll keep on crying silently.
But you'll go on with your life, with no memory of me.
With years to come will I remember the boy that went away,
And will the pain that's buried deep last forever and a day?

Tricia Anne Parmarter

"Mother's Shoes"

Life is a breeze. I thought with a smile
I learned later - children really think
Only once in a while!
I watched mother as she worked each day
I stood by her side as she bowed to pray.
"Why", I would ask, many hours a day
No wonder Mother gets lines and her hair gets gray
Oh, it's fun to wash and clean
And bake those cakes and pies
Why Mother got so tired, I couldn't realize
Babies grow up by themselves, I thought
As Mother held them on her knee
But those thoughts I had when I was only three!
I wish I had listened to Mother so wise
Experience had taught her
Problems are real - no disguise
As I have grown older, I have changed my views
Because I am standing now in Mother's Shoes!

Vi Marshall

NH Talking Trees

As I go walking through the woods,
I like to listen to the trees,
And though they never speak a word...
I listen to them calmly.

As they whisper and they whistle,
And friend wind howls back,
I seem to wonder why they keep on talking.

In winters brittle light,
Or in summers scorching sun,
Or even in the rainy season;
When the floods run.

Or when autumn winds make them bare
Why they keep on talking is a puzzle to me...
But maybe I should let them talk,
And wonder why they keep on talking.

Melissa Wyman

Untitled

As I sit here and think and wonder why
I look at his picture and begin to cry
It seems he's sitting right here beside me
Then I realize it's only a memory
I remember how he said he loved me and would never leave
I knew the truth but I just had to believe
I'll remember our walks through the fields and trees
And everything he ever did, he did for me
I'll remember his laugh and the bounce in his walk
And always his willingness to talk
I look in the mirror and see his face
I know its there but it seems to out of place.
I want him here beside me to look into his beautiful eyes
I want him to tell me he'll come see me soon
To walk with him again underneath the moon
As I stand here looking at him with tears in my eyes
I lean down beside him and whisper good-bye.

Megan Holthouse

"Black"

I look up, and see black.
I look down...
More black.
I look everywhere around me,
Yet my world is still the same black hole it's always been.
I keep trying to climb out,
But I think I've lost hope.
I'm distressed that there's no lended hand
Or understanding ear.
There is no escape to this life.
I fall to the floor and try to cry myself to sleep,
But my sleep doesn't come.
One day I'll close my eyes
And forever, I shall see black.

Toni Palazzolo

Ron and Christi:

God works in mysterious ways,
Sometimes he giveth and sometimes he taketh away.

I don't know his reason nor his rhyme,
It must not have been just the right time.

On the saddest of days I promise to thee,
God will allow you to extend your family.

A flower of hope I will place at the Virgin Mary's feet,
For blessings that what you next sow you shall reap.

Robin L. Engberg-Maluvac

"My Darling"

How do I know you love?
I look in you're eye's, and see nothing:

You're mouth is firm, and show's no sign of a smile;
I say, I love you, but you look away:

I turn you're face, so I may look into
you're eye's, and I see a tear;
Suddenly, you put you're arms around me,
so I may feel secure:

You put a smile on you're face, and gave me a kiss;
I wiped the tear from your cheek, you hugged me:

Then you looked me in the eye's and said;
Never fear my darling, I will love you always and forever:

Lisa Elsing

Untitled

He sat there across from me and spoke the words:
"I love her and I can't live without her."
My heart pressed against my chest and tried to beat its way out.
The door slowly closed as he left.
I sat in the hollow hall of despair and the silence crept through
my skin into my soul.
I wept.
Tears zig zagged across my face while the quiet turned into a
thunderstorm as they hit my blouse catching my hearts explosion.
My body tremble with the agony.
Suddenly it was quiet.
I raised myself — walked into the kitchen —
and washed the dishes.

Linda Canepa Butler

Tree

I'm a tree so tall and strong,
I love my home cause that's where I belong.
No one can hurt me,
Cause I'm friends with a bee.
If someone tries to cut me down.
I'll have to leave all my friends with a frown.
One day someone came out of the blue,
'Cause suddenly all my birds flew.
After that first blow come around,
I knew I'd soon be fallin' down.
After I was gone that day,
there could be no more than I could do or say.

Kristen Elizabeth Keels

Sounds of Evening

The forest
I love the sounds of evening as they whisper through the hush
That gently paints the forest land with Night's unhurried brush.
It always seems to me that then the earth is like a church,
And murmuring in lofty prayer are pine and oak and birch.
The breezes come with fragrant breath across the wooded miles
And wend their way a-sighing through the purple forest aisles.
The birds in choir softly hymn and sermonize in song
While shadows stretch their fingers out and pull themselves along.
From countless secret corners of the congregation met —
From furtive little runway to the highest parapet —-
There comes the muted chorus of a last devotional
To mark the parting day before the soon dark interval.
In many voices speaking come the eventide's array;
No language set in books of man can tell the things they say.
I love the sounds of evening as they whisper through the hush
That peacefully the forest clothes ere Night's descending crush.

William N. Anthony

I Love The World

I love the world when pine branches dance around in the wind.
I love the world when clouds swirl in soft colors.
I love the world when the sky is of fire with reds, yellows and
pinks.
I love the world when grass is almost glowing green.
I love the world when snow falls softly and shines like diamonds.
I love the world when crickets play their song of peace.
I love the world.

Laura Shapiro

I Just Lived

I never fully understood why I came to be — I Just Lived
I never fully realized my purpose in life — I Just Lived
I opened the door everyday to move forward in my journey
my head held high
I stepped a fierce step — Just to Live
And I didn't expect the anger — the rage
to overtake my living
'cause "oh no" it could never happen to me
but the role played out and I open the door
to move forward once more, but I don't make it
I propel back and down
and I lay in the fluid warmth reflecting on
the doors I opened
the songs I sang
the party's I played
the people I loved — the Life I Lived
Who would have figured
How could it be me
I never hurt anyone
I just opened the door to Live.

Wanda C. Outlaw

"The Indian Woman"

There was once a woman that
I never knew but, how I grew fond of her
Because, her love was pure and true.

They say this woman was
Indian but I will never know but,
She was my Grandma and I loved her so.

Here she stands alone,
Wrapped in her blanket with moccasins on her feet
and long dark shiny hair braided so neat.

When she speaks everyone
comes to hear, because the language,
and the words she spoke, were so clear.

She went to heaven when
I was only two or three, this woman,
I will never, get to see.

Now the Indian woman
Is gone and I do regret, but
She was a fine woman, that I
will never forget.

Mary Winham

Mother

They say diamonds are a girl's best friend
I know that isn't true
A mother is a girl's best friend
There's nothing she won't do
To make sure that her "little" girl
Is happy as she can be
I know my mother is my best friend
She's always there for me

Kathie Scott

Seven Dolphins

Seven dolphins struck the sky
I never saw them jump so high
The waves hung beneath their fins
Their bodies appeared to ride the winds
Early mid morning yesterday
In a cold January's winter sway
An eagle rose from its frozen perch
Heading skyward with a sudden lurch
How the eagles do soar up there
Flying high as we stand below unaware
The wind blows cold, wild with gust
The eagle's wings pushing upward with thrust
Suddenly, it left the sky
Was it wounded or did it die?
I saw it no more, but it still remains in my mind
Can't drive it out, no, not this time
But seven dolphins touch the sky
And to this day I don't know why.

Morris B. Taylor

A Child's Cry

Please Momma, take a second glance,
I plead and beg for just a chance.
Even though by you I'm not wanted,
A great child would I be, for I'm anointed!
Someone's life I would enhance.

Somewhere a couple weeps for me,
They want a child desperately.
Please someone hear my cry,
I am alive, I don't want to die!
That couple's child I want to be.

To save lives my killer is taught,
Yet my death my mother has bought.
Will the killer go to jail,
Or be commend for a job done well?
Which will happen if he's caught?

They believe in God they say,
Yet my life they take away.
I ask what type of world is this,
That greets my life with death's kiss?
Don't they fear judgement day?

Shelly DesOrmeaux

Remember Me

When I close my eyes
I pray I will never have to open them again,
That my very soul shall cease to exist
And hurt those so dear to me.

I look back on my younger days;
Always smiling, searching for a rainbow,
Never pondering on what tomorrow may bring
Nor the pain that lay ahead in the near future.

I never meant to hurt you,
For I love you more than I can ever say -
And I always will...
But not even love can save me now.

I have failed.
Now I can only move forward to a hell of my own creating.
My woeful cries of anguish
Shall echo forever along the walls of time.

Remember me.
Remember our ephemeral time of happiness.
Remember me as the person who lived through your dreams....
Not as the person I have become.

Marie Ellene Belton

I Meant To Do My Work Today...

I meant to do my work today,
I really did, you know.
But my puppy tugged at my shoes,
As if to say "Let's go!"

I meant to do my work today.
I really intended so,
but the blue birds and the robins called,
as if I didn't know!

I meant to do my work today,
I really tried, you see.
But how could I stay and work
when mother nature called to me?

So, this is an apology,
or something of the sort.
I meant to do my work today,
but I came up a little short.

Patsy Estep

This Small...

As I sit here quietly watching them sleep,
I reflect upon their day
And I find myself beginning to weep
For, this small, they won't always stay.

They look so peaceful, all snuggled and warm
(Tuckered out from a long day of play...)
Never wanting for love or security,
I'm keeping their heartaches at bay.

They need me now, to calm their fears,
To ease their pain and dry their tears.
I wish that I could freeze these years,
But the future is on its way...

I suppose I should go back to bed now,
Reassured that all is "ok",
But I'll sit here a little while longer,
For, this small, they won't always stay...

Yvonne Flynn

You Knew What It Would Do To You

They said that it wouldn't hurt to try it.
I said no, knowing what it would do.
I know that you knew to.
But you're so easy to persuade.
So you tried it.
Did you like it?
You told me that you did at first but you
said that you needed it.
What for, I wondered why.
You started to skip school.
You never did that before.
I asked you to please stop.
But you told me that I was out of line,
just like the time I told you not to take it.
When the cops told me that you O.D.'d
I was angry at myself for not forcing you to stop.
But how could I?
You made your choice.

Windy Davis

Lost and Found

I looked for love...but I could not see
I searched for peace...but I could not find the key
I reached for life...but I could not be free
I sought my Lord, and found all three.

Michael D. Romolini, Sr.

Keeping Busy

When I found out; I had to have surgery,
I said, "Oh No!" and felt sorry for me.

Then all of a sudden, a thought came from above,
Saying, "Do something for someone you love."

So off I rushed, to the Fabric Store,
Searching through transfers and thread galore.

My eyes were drawn to these precious bears,
That's the ones I'll sew; to diminish my cares.

So, My Darling Daughter, believe me, when I say,
"This project kept me busy for many hours each day."

The time passed quickly, whether dark or light,
It helped to bring joy, to my day and night.

Yes, Oodles of love, and lots of wonderful wishes,
Went into making these towels; to wipe your dishes.

Sue A. Sayles

Animals Are Teachers Too

At the Zoo,
I saw a monkey share his food with a giraffe.
In the tree,
A squirrel helped bird build his nest.
On the ground,
I saw a mouse protecting butterfly's cocoon.
In the sky,
Both hawk and eagle flying west.
On T. V.,
I saw a mouse mending lion's splintered paw.
In the yard,
I saw a cat and dog at play.
Animals are teachers too.
Just reread this poem.
Then perhaps.....
We can learn to live their way.

Vanessa Epps

Eagle Flying

One day while I was looking out my window
I saw an eagle flying
Oh what a beautiful sight
That made me think of our saviour Jesus
And how he is so beautiful
Loving me the way he does
I sat and watched that eagle
For a long time that day
Just watching him flying
So high up in the sky
He would fly low
He would fly high
Just spreading his wings
As wide as they would go
Just like our saviour Jesus Christ
When He spread his arms
And said this is how much
I LOVE YOU

Linda Beech

When She Died

Rain, it filled the sky
It splashed like tears of sorrow.
Clouds filled the sky. Her aunt,
numbed and dying slowly.
The sky cried for her Aunt and her numbness,
But it stopped the sky was blue again.
The sky stopped crying, for her aunt found peace.

Kate Uyeno

Ceiling and Visibility Unlimited

Upstairs ten thousand, more or less,
I saw the air, sheer nothingness,
Become in one celestial sweep
A lake eight hundred fathoms deep;

From crest to floor a liquid shimmer,
Not crystal clear but somewhat dimmer;
I almost thought to see a trout
Break the surface and splash about

And ruffle up the tranquil clouds
That flecked the pool like snow-white suds,
As if Hyperion had been there
Shampooing of his golden hair.

Robert I. Thiel

"I Hate Myself and I Want to Die"

(In memory of Kurdt Kobain 1967-1994)

When I look at life through obscured eyes
I see naive and immature people
They try to understand my teenage angst
But they can't grasp why I stand alone
Is life meant to be self-destroyed
Or do you wait for the course of nature?
Should God have his way with you
Or is suicide a true scapegoat?
They try to analyze his lyrics
But he may not have understood them
They are stomping on a dead man's grave
And tearing apart his past to find the answers
The press shredded him to pieces
And he could no longer handle them
Ironically enough they aimed to be unpopular
And soon enough he was "The Voice Of A Generation"
They say his screams were for "Generation X"
But they were for no one but himself
He had an ongoing feud with life
But unfortunately on his final day he was not a coward

Nathan Tibbetts

A Snow Enhanced Memory

With the wind the snow it came
I see silver mountain ranges
Trees with partly green branches
From winds designing changes
The snow dances painting white all
The picket fences falling top on top
Covering the fields with a snow white crop
Dimmer is the light that moves slow in to the
Night a lost tern rest's on a bush
That looks like a sea-urchin hush it flies
Away and I am drunk from dreaming about
Places my heart and soul flashes me the places
Where children young and old sledding down
The hill the joy and laughter I can hear it still
I travel where I go there are no footprints
In the snow.

Ruth Culver

Outside

From the outside...looking in
I see that you are trying to hide
I'm not trying to analyze...pass judgement,
I'm not trying to pry...
From the outside...looking in
Behind your smile...behind your eye's
It's not the same...it's pain
It's not a trivial thing,
Self destruction...is a major production
From the outside...looking in
I see that you are trying to hide
One day...if you try
You'll find peace of mind
From the outside...looking in
You need a friend.

Ruth Yates

To Be Free

As I sit looking out to sea
I see the waves as they bounce Free
How I wish I were Free
As I watch the leaves fall from a tree
I think to my self how Free they must be
Oh how I wish to be Free
As I look to the sky I see snow fall
The flakes so Free don't hear my call
Oh how I'd give anything to be Free
As I see the river flow so smooth
The Free looking waves they soothe
Don't think you're not Free
You really are as Free as can be
Our souls are confined for only a time
Then our souls wander oh so Free

Mary B. Everett

The Special Window

As I sit and stare out the back of my window
I see the world in a different way.
It's so much quieter and yet so still.
The animals run free, the land and water look clean and dear.
But it's different when we step out our door into the real world.
The air is dirty, and as you walk down the street
there are people walking around with no where to live.
The ground is dirty and there's violence.
Sometimes I think to myself that I wish
I lived in what I see out the back of my window.
When I'm home I'm glad to be safe looking out that special
window.

Stacy LaVorgna

Unsaid

How often has Father Time, in years gone by
Seen useless quarrels or watched a young love fade and die
To be replaced by something less
Disappointment.
Sorrow.
Loneliness.
How could this world of ours have been changed
If thoughts behind the words were read?
How many lives would have been rearranged
If one had known what lay within the other's heart
Unsaid.

Sandy Eckhardt

The Encounter

On a warm sunny afternoon, quite a beautiful day
I set out for a stroll along a beaten pathway.
I was walking and thinking, not paying much mind
when I heard someone call to me from behind
I turned and saw a timely old gentleman standing there
in tattered clothes and graying hair.
"Pardon me Miss but I seem to have a problem" he said,
"Can you see from where my foot has bled?"
I bent down and placed his fragile foot in my hand
And my heart went out to that kind old man.
I gently wiped away the blood and was surprised to see
There wasn't anything there to cause it to bleed!
I looked up and saw a smile come across his face, a smile that my
memory will never erase and then he said "brothers or sisters I
have none for I am the only begotten son."
"Your act of kindness will someday be repaid,
along with all the promises I have made"
At the moment I did not know what that man meant,
But I know the time we shared was very well spent for I didn't know
then but I knew after, that timely old gentleman was our Master!

Teresa L. Barnette

Glass

Reminded every day,
I sit alone, emptiness inside
that is wanting to break free.
To dwell on the fictitious fact of life,
yet so scared of the outer core.
Always enchanted by fascination,
the crucifixion, never once scared,
but somehow seen dearly
through the eye.
I'm left to let go of the swinging rope,
and fall dumsily to the ground,
letting go I drift off into
the world I call my own,
which seems to be filled with many.
Only to enter with an injection of thrill.

Shannon Littlefield

An Emotional Feast

Once in a while in a brown room
I sit down to dinner with my emotions
They fill all of the chairs
at the long dining table
There is conversation among them
I sometimes find myself listening
but as words drown others out
I slip into a white room
with no furniture, windows or doors
How do I get out? (How did I get in?)
I can't!
I stay and wait, my visit here is long
Finally, I hear the conversation again
but I realize that it was just a distraction
I now see through the top layer
and I AM DINNER
My emotions attack me: they cut, tear, rip
bite, chew, and swallow
Now I am just tiny bits inside each one of them-
There is nothing left of me....I am no longer whole

J. Gibbs

Kol Nidre

On this day
I sit
under the
all knowing tree

I am to atone

The shadow
from the tree
covers me
like a cupped hand
over a candle's flame

To whom

A cool breeze brushes
against my back

Make an oath

I look up to
the absolving sky
patches of blue
through the red orange
and brown lattice work

Release me

My hands feel the firm
annulling earth
cold black underneath green

I am bound

I am here now

Repent I am alone

Jerry Spivack

My Imagination

On wings of imagination, across love's sweeping sky,
I soar again with you, up to the moon on high.
I feel the tenderness, that throbbing sweet sensation,
And love is born again...in my imagination.

In my imagination, our love still resides.
There it does withstand reality's crushing tides.
Though we were torn apart by deceit and suspicion.
Our love lives once more...in my imagination.

The wings of imagination carry me away,
To another time, our love filled yesterday.
They let me know again the joyous elation
That I can only feel...in my imagination.

In my imagination I hear love's sweet refrain.
You are still close to me, in my arms again.
There our love can survive, outlasting fate's decision.
Happiness is ever mine...in my imagination.

Jess Kelly

Untitled

Hello stranger - it's me again.
I stopped to say hello today. —
Talk about our changing lives.
Of course, once again you listened,
You gave me advice and showed that
you cared.
It's been difficult since you opened
your heart to me and I shut you out.
I miss you not being there to lean on -
To act as my best friend.
Things may change in our lives
But you'll always be very special to me.
There's no one like you in the world.
Hello my friend - it's me again.
This time I promise I won't leave.

Melissa L. Pedri

"A Letter To God"

I look out upon this world and smile
I thank you for all you've given me Lord
In my darkness you give me light
My sorrow disappears

I ask your forgiveness of my sins
I ask that you watch over me in all I do
I can only give you my love
And serve you eternally

Dear Lord when lost and alone
You are there to comfort and guide me
When I slide somewhat backwards
You forgive and still love me

My heart be full and strong
My life be yours to command
My faith shall never falter
Your grace stays close at hand

Lee Devore

"Discipline Problems"

I walk, I run, I race, vroom...out of my room.
I think, I ponder, I wonder...did I blunder?
I miss, I mourn, I lament...times I was heel bent.
I wonder, I worry, I dread...the days ahead.
I didn't, I won't, I can't...rave and rant.
I delay, I stay, I pray...that I'll find a way.
I attempt, I muster, I try...not to cry.
I moan, I groan, I grieve...it's hard to believe.
I recognize, I realize, I know...I have seeds to sow.
I figure, I determine, I surmise...I have to rise.
I shall, I can, I will...get over this hill.
I beg, I plead, I cajole...I play the role.
I must, I insist, I demand...I take a stand.
I endure, I resist, I survive..."learning" stays alive.
I fix, I remedy, I discipline...while I grin.

Kathleen Doran Wood

As I Slept I Dreamt of Sorrow

Sometimes it's really hard, I try but just can't sleep
I think of life without him, and then I start to weep.

I thought he would be near me, when we became close friends
But now I'm finding that the road to him never ends.

I never thought the day would come, when we would say goodbye
Yet now it is so fatal, for my love is soon to die.

I loved the times we spent, by one another's side
I won't forget the times he spoke, "It's alright, please don't cry."

I can't help but wonder now, what we did so wrong
For God wants him in heaven soon, but won't let me come along.

I don't know what I'll do, when I lose my precious love
He tells me not to worry, he'll be watching from above.

The last time that I saw him, he washed away my fears
He said he would be leaving soon, and wiped at his own tears.

He asked that I not forget him, all the happiness we had shared
He picked a red, luscious rose, to show how much he cared.

We left each other at the gate, leading to my door
And as he walked away from me, I whispered love once more.

That night I cried myself to sleep, and shivered in my bed
And as I slept, I dreamt of sorrow, for when I woke, my love was dead.

Rebecca Nucci

If I Could Give the World a Gift

If I could give the world a gift,
I think that it would be
An unpolluted environment just for you and me,
A world full of green trees, clean lakes and litter free.

If I could give the world a gift,
I'm sure that it would be.
A world full of joyfulness, love and harmony,
A world full of peace near and afar,
A drug free world wherever you are.

If I could give the world a gift,
I'm sure that you would see.
A world that is sickness and poverty free.
A world that leaves no one homeless or starving in the street.

If I could give the world a gift,
I pray that it would be.
All the things I've said above for all eternity.

Sarah Jean Coffman

He'll Never Know

It was many many and a year ago
I thought he would never know
Though he was loved by another
Which he did not know that she loved another
I knew he was to good for her
But when I thought he saw me it was just a blur
But I was so obsessed with him
I thought I would be out on a limb
My life was incomplete
Then I knew I would have to complete
When he finally met me
She was there to get rid of me
Then we bumped into each other
Then he told me that he found out about her
But he did not know that I set her up
She then found out and wanted to beat me up
He then found some one else
But else was not me
Then I knew he would not love me
then I knew I would ever nor never love he

Melissa Ross

Untitled

I told you I was going to give you my heart
I told you that you didn't have to give me yours in return
I loved you from the start
If you knew you were going to hurt me, why didn't you stop?

You took my heart anyway
You accepted my love and gave me yours
I made myself think that you would stay
You told me that our love was pure

Instead you threw it back at me
and you ripped it into pieces
Are you blind? Couldn't you see?
Now I have no peace

I wonder around searching
Searching for something to fill the emptiness
Searching for something to satisfy this empty vessel of a
  human shell
I'm lost searching for something I know
  I can never find or have

Tammy Elaine Miles

Darling, I'll Go With You

Darling, I tried my best, to make a home for you.
I tried to raise our children right, and tried to get us
through. I know our house, it ain't so grand, and our
clothes are rather plain, and I know I ain't no movie star,
but I love you just the same.
We've always stuck together, when the money wasn't there.
And I'd work a little harder, because I know you cared.
Now they say you're gonna pass, onto heaven, that I'm sure.
And all I can do is hold you, and feel your heart so pure.
But there's something you must know, now don't go looking
blue; when the angels come to take you home, darling,
I'll go with you.
I'll go with you to the highest star, to our eternal home.
We'll never lack for nothing, we'll never be alone.
We'll spin and dance and laugh and kiss, like lover's always do.
When the angels come to take you home, darling, I'll go with you.

Mark Czaja

Trying to Change

My only income is ADC,
I try to change that but they wont let me,
studied hard in school, made it across that stage,
went out, found a job, making minimum wage,
on my job, I worked harder than two champs,
then to my surprise they cut my check and food stamps,
 minimum wage can't fulfill all my needs,
I have a house full of bills and children to feed,
called the system to see what was up,
they said now that you're working, we'll have to deduct,
so now I feel nothing but confusion,
and feel that I have to reach some conclusion,
First I got really scared, and felt I had no win,
So I decided to give the system a try again,
Then as I stood there puzzled, hurt and feeling shame,
I decided never ever, stop trying to change.

Sherry Elaine Paymon

A Letter to a Veteran

Although I did not fight it,
I try to comprehend,
the way it eats inside of you,
and the messages that you send.
  I can't learn it from the books,
  the system has it all wrong.
  I can't judge it by it's looks,
  because the picture isn't that strong.
The way you fought for our country,
and the welcome you didn't get.
Your brothers and sisters that aren't free,
is like the family you never met.
  Those years they made you suffer,
  those dead you'll never forget.
  those missing that are still in pain,
  for a war we'll always regret.
I send to you my sorrow,
for those of you that died.
Not for the parts that live tomorrow,
but for the soul you lost inside.

Kerryann Miller

Untitled

In the quiet whisper of hushed and penciled pines
'Neath the spell-bound silence of the silvered heavens
My soul stretches.
In the warring madness of the penciled pines
'Neath the thundering voices of the silvered heavens
My soul stretches.
By what instrument, o man,
Will you measure the greater distance?

Lorraine Wiley Young

Love, Then Go

Teach me how
I want to know
how you learned to love, then go
With your love I felt I was needed
but in one breath my heart
was defeated
Needing your comfort, take away
my pain, breaking my heart
with the slightest touch
I didn't know I could
love someone so much; Standing the sorrow
fighting the pain
wanting to learn how to love once again
I finally figured how,
now I think I know just how you learned to love, then go.

Kristy Lane Newman

Untitled

Before I prove my insanity
I want you to know I'll always be.
I'll be in your mind, but not in your heart,
so you can get off to a brand new start.
I can't use magic and make everything okay.
I ponder on this all through the day
while I sit in my room and start to cry.
I really wish we hadn't said "goodbye."
A loser is what you classify me as.
If you don't, why not? Society has.
I am the monster you left behind
for someone else to look for and find.
Now I am trapped and can't come back,
but in your eyes this isn't a fact.
Maybe I'll be old enough to say,
"You were right that awful day."
but until that happens I'll tell you the truth,
yes, I am a troubled youth.
Since in the end we're not the same
then I have just proven I'm not insane.

Sahra Firestone

Chance at Love

I was serious, you laughed.
I was hurt, you were glad.
I am alone, you still have friends.
I feel pain, now you have love.
I cry tears, while you sit and smile.
I gave you everything,
You took it all, never wanting to share.
I needed you, but...
You walked away.

Now I am left here, and she is with you.
I hold your picture, she holds your hand.
I have your memory, she has you there.
I feel your pain, she feels your touch.
I cry your tears, she keeps you holding on.
You gave her everything,
She took it all, just as you did me.
She left you, but...
I am still here.

Mandi Lee Tromm

"A Way to Keep Out of Hell"

It was a really hot day in the middle of January
I was resting on the steps feeling tired and weary
All of sudden, from the corner of the house
Came a little dog no bigger than a mouse

He asked me if I had seen the farmer in the dell
You know, he said, he's forever ringing that church bell
I told him that he was down there by the well
He's telling people a way to keep out of hell

Believe in the Lord, turn from your wicked ways
Repent, repent, he said, Jesus will love you always
He has a place in Heaven that he has prepared just for you
It's really very simple, not much for you to do

Just ask Jesus to come into your heart
That's the beginning, that's where you start
Pray and ask God to be merciful to you, a sinner
He will forgive you, you'll be a winner

Take Jesus as your Savior today
Please, please don't turn him away
Put your faith and trust in him without delay
He will give you eternal life, debt free, you won't have to pay

Myra Staudt

Banished Memories

Standing in the rain listening to the rhythm of my tears.
I watch the moon over my head vanish in the clouds.
I scream so my soul can call his.
His soul does not answer.
I now cry through tears of blood.
I remember the flowers I placed on my destiny,
fate, and joyful love.
I stand in a field where people lie under me.
They are cold, damp, and lonely.
Suddenly I feel his presence he embraces
me and touches my heart one last time 'till the end.
My body does not want to let go, but my soul
knows we will be one again.
So I drift from his eternal touch to
return to his world.

Meriam Kelada

An Answered Prayer

In 1988 the Lord said wait
I will send a pastor before it gets late
So we waited and there he was
a small man with lots of love
And now we know what God meant
because we know for sure John was sent
You have a great big heart and
You show love and care,and we thank god
you are here
You have a lovely wife whom we love
and she shares in your work that's sent
from above
So you see Brother and Sister we
love you very much
and we thank god for the lives you have
touched
May god keep you both in His care
and always remember we love you here.

Wanda Krall

"Making Love To My Father"

"I'm glad it's over," she said to herself,
I wish my father would give me rest.
Anytime he feels horny, he calls my name,
but who the hell can I blame?

I've been doing it for so long, hurting so bad,
the reward I get is driving me mad,
I hear strange sounds when I sleep at night,
what I'm doing must not be right!

I've pleaded many times to stop this doings,
my mind is ruined from so much abusing!
Many times my tears turn into hollers,
when I think about making love to my father!

Saleem Abdur Rahiam

I Wonder

The sun comes up from another mountain top,
I wonder, as a wakingness, will it ever stop?
The pain on another face I see,
I wonder, will that pain in turn hurt me
The sky turns from blue to rusted black,
I wonder if its happiness will ever come back
The moon shows light of an ended day,
I wonder, will it always end this way?
In time should I learn?
Maybe in time they will yearn.

Valerie Jones

Midlife Smile

As I sit by the warmth of the vibrant fire
I wonder what life's treasures have passed me by
Soon I will reach what is known as the midlife mile
I can't help but wonder how different my life would be
If I had made other choices and decisions concurrently
Would I now be sitting by a different fire in another dream?
Could I have known a fascinating world filled with exotic memories?
Or would I have known a life of mundane and endless doubts?
I am satisfied but full of wonder of what might could have been
I suppose I am now facing what is known as the midlife crisis
I thought it would never happen to me
I have always known who I am and what I wanted to be
But here I sit by the open flame
Dreaming about what life would have been
Had I made choices and decisions differently
I smile to think I could have been as important as President
Or perhaps even a missionary or world visionary
But, here I sit with my mug of tea
Smiling and happy only to have become me

Sandra L. Broadway

Untitled

As you sat in the big old chair
I wondered what to say,
I never really knew you well
For we spoke in a different way.

We always shared our foreign words
In the most unspoken way,
With this I learned a Grandfather's love
Is never too hard to say.

I may cry and wish so hard
That you were here with me,
Always fishing in the yard
Is what I'll always see.

I know that you are happy now
And at peace is how you'll be,
Remembering you always
Is not to hard for me.

Lisa Beth Iwaszkiewicz

The Love I Have For You

A cool breeze across my face or my feet on soft sand,
I would gladly pass these by for one touch from your hand.
The bright flash of lightning or a flickering flame,
The sparkle in your eyes puts these to shame.
The bold colored rainbows or the starry nights,
Comparing them to you, these are bland sights.
A small butterfly or a delicate rose,
Just like they will, my love for you grows.

Melissa Shartle

Valentine

If I had a chance to bring the world to a still
I would tell you that I'm sorry, that my heart has left my will

I would tell you that I miss you and that I am so very sad
and I would tell you that without you, my life so meaningless and mad.

Where is my precious moment and where my precious heart?
Where is my hope for loving you now that we're worlds apart?

Yet, through words and some confusion, it all seems so unfair
I miss you very deeply, your eyes, your smile your hair.

I am so very sorry, forgive my foolish way
Remember just the moment when you asked me to stay.

...and if my lips could tell you don't go my love divine
Obsession of my dreams my sweet sweet Valentine

Sheikha Susie Hobeiche

Untitled

As I sit at home in my lonely room,
I write this poem for only you,

Oh how much I miss you,
And wish you were here to guide me through

Even though I know it had to happen,
I can't help think why it had to be you,

But, I know one of these days,
We will meet and then you'll stay,

Somewhere, in the stillness of might,
My heart will become numb,

Then, I will finally meet you,
There, at the golden gates,

As precious as life may be,
I'm awaiting you Lord to come free me!

Nora Pomerleau

How Can I Forget You

How can I forget you, it is not possible
if I carry you so deep.
How can I forget so many memories
your caress and your kisses.

How can I forget your smile
the softness of your hair.
How can I forget your concern
in my sleepless nights.

How can I forget you my love
after we lived so much time
the passion of a single kiss.

I need not ask the heavens,
to help me to remember you
because I can not forget you

Rudesindo Montoya

Memories

When day was done and night was nigh,
I'd hear a murmur and a sigh
As in your loving arms I'd lie
Until the dawning of the sky
And day begun.

When day was done and night was nigh,
I'd croon a wee one's lullaby.
A son so small, so dear and sweet,
Who for our love did now compete
When day was done.

And so the years sped quickly by.
The numbers, now eight, have heard a lullaby
When day was done.

Now day is done and night almost o'er.
And you, long years on a happier shore.
Without you I am sad and a feel so alone.
But memories fond and always clear,
Bring back your words, "I love you dear".
Now night is done and morn is here.

Ward Glenn

Today's World

Were I to enter the world today
I'd shudder to think at what I'd say
Would I be happy and have a long life filled with cheer
Or have a short one filled with fear?
Nothing to gain, nothing to lose
Is this the kind of life I have to choose?
Thing's must get better for all of our sake's
No more brutality, no more rapes
What sadden's me the most I have to say,
Is, will I make it to my Wedding day?
Does this make me a pessimist, I muse
Or does this all come from watching the New's?

Sidney S. Kampf

Children Our Heritage

Have you ever given any thought to how dreary life would be
If all the children in the world suddenly ceased to be?
There'd be no childish laughter, no pretty curls to comb,
No rowdy boys with puppy dogs to clutter up the home.
The house would be real tidy, the rooms all clean and neat,
But oh, the change that could be wrought with the patter of tiny feet!
The very walls would come alive with the pleasure they could bring
And, speaking from experience, they cause the heart to sing!
Some folks think they have the right to say this life must end,
But they will drink the bitter dregs for they are wrong, my friend!
So stop and think before you act, 'twill only cause more strife
And know for sure the very deed will haunt you all your life!
For a house can't truly be a home until it's known the joy
Of sharing all the sights and sounds of a little girl or boy.

Maxine K. Sorge

Missing Grandpa

I sit here wondering how things would be,
If God didn't take you away from me.
A thought of you always pops in my head,
A song, a memory, or something said
Which gets me teary eyed and blue,
As I try to remember you.
But it gets harder and harder each day,
As my memory seems to fade away.
Someday I know I'll be with you again,
Even though I'm not yet sure when.
Just know that I love you and I'll have no fear,
Because I know you'll always be near.

Kim Klish

existence

An existence without you is lonely;
if I wasn't so cruel, if only...
I could keep you tonight, by my side,
if I wasn't a fool... who had lied.
A fool without repentance.
A fool... to live alone... existence.

Beyond my window, steady rain
rolls down the glass like our tears...
without shame.
I hear the echoes of laughter— somehow gone sour.
A memory of love... that once grew like a flower,
and wilted, just the same... devoured.

And existence without you is lonely.
If I wasn't so cruel, if only...
I could keep you tonight, by my side;
if I wasn't the fool... the one who lied.
A jester in a game too intense...
if only I'd known I'd be alone...
ever since...
existence.

Miko Starr

Reflections On A Sudden Death

Churning Thoughts - Why didn't I - ?
  If only I had -
  What If I had - ?
  What didn't he - ?
  Why didn't he - ?
  If only he had -

Negatives - How could he leave me with all this - ?
  How will I manage - ?
  What do I do first - ?
  There are all the Taxes -

Positives - At least he did not suffer -
  Its good he retired early -
  I'm glad we took the trips -
  Over all he had a good life -
  He is taken away from the evil to come -
  All the changes in the world
  Will no longer trouble him.

Conclusion - God is merciful.
  With his help I will manage.
  Take only one day at a time.

Mary Firehammer

Reality

Kids these days are trying and using drugs
If they keep on
Later on in their lives
They will become thugs!

Walking up and down
Up and down the streets
Looking homely without enough to eat!

Instead of fighting the battle
They let another day pass.

Then they begin to weaken
And slowly start to die.

And so you see my friend drugs
Doesn't pay!
It only causes heartaches
But it happens everyday!

Lanetta Kennedy

Baby Steps

We all must practice steps to get the process started.
If we fall down or slide a bit, we won't be brokenhearted.
The little lessons that we learn by doing every day
Will make us strong and re-enforce our skills along the way.

We have to try and try again before we will succeed
To make some progress on the road to get the things we need.
Perhaps today we have to risk to find a brand new friend
Or maybe now's the time to say, "I'll let this friendship end."

I think today may be the day to do something for me.
I'll try to take a bubblebath or make a cup of tea.
I'll use the phone to call a friend; that is a special treat.
Or take a walk around the park and find a shaded seat.

There are so many choices that I can make each day
And many healthy things to do to speed me on my way.
But first I must remember before I try to run
That even with the help of friends, I am the only one

To take My baby steps———

Marion Kamerling Kleiner

Seasons

I love the sights and sounds of spring; it is my favorite season
I'll hereby make a list for you of some of my best reasons.
Thunder crashing, colts dashing
Grass greening, peacocks preening
Rain falling, birds calling
Tulips blooming, cats grooming
Lambs bleating, chicks eating
Air warming, bees swarming
Trees budding, windmills thudding
A lovely time for cleaning along with a bit of dreaming.

I love the sights and sounds of fall; it is my favorite season
I'll hereby make a list for you of some of my best reasons.
Leaves turning, wood burning
Skies paling, winds wailing
Buses clattering, children chattering
Grass browning, scarecrows frowning
Pumpkins yellowing, apples mellowing
Squirrels debating, geese migrating
Air crispy, clouds wispy
A lovely time for a walk and a friend with whom to talk.

Mary Sue Harrold

I'm Fine — How Are You?

There's nothing whatever the matter with me.
I'm just as healthy as I can be.
I have arthritis in both my knees,
And when I talk, I talk with a wheeze.

My pulse is weak and my blood is thin,
But I'm awfully well for the shape I'm in.
I think my liver is out of whack,
And a terrible pain is my back.

My hearing is poor, my sight is dim,
Most everything seems out of trim,
But I'm awfully well for the sharp I'm in.
I have arch supports for both my feet,
Or I wouldn't be able to go on the street.

The moral is, as this tale we unfold,
That for you and me who are growing old,
It's better to say, "I'm fine" with a grin
Than to let them know the shape we're in.

Shirley Linville

What Is Your Name?

Fear is my name, what is yours?
I'm known in dark places and behind locked doors.
I am known today, as I was known long ago
I am known in high places and to the depths of ones soul
I live in mirrors and shadows
And on distant shores
Fear is my name, what is yours?

I live in books and around strange corners in strange places
In many disguises and have many faces.
I live in the heart as well as the mind
I live in the true and the untrue, both are of one kind.
I live in your springtime as well as your fall
But I grow in your winter most of all.
My name is fear, what is yours?

I live in the trees and the things that fly
I live in the years that flow swiftly by.
I live in the beasts on two legs, or that crawl on all fours
My name is fear, what is yours?

I've guessed your name, I knew it all the time
It rhymes with mine.

Michael Lee

The Way I Will Perish

Death surrounds me
I'm not afraid
Death taunts me with its claws
I'm not afraid
Why should I be?
Come and take me away, death
My fear is your weapon
You have no weapon with me
Take me in your arms, death
And you'll take me with a smile on my face
Can't you see?
You are the last at best
For I'll see my companions in life again
You'll see

Miki Kajiya

Floating To Freedom — Version Two

I'm floating to freedom
I'm riding the tide of pride
The black knight has guided peace on earth, and I can see the light.
The light gives me the power to fight the sharks of slavery
and the black knight gives me the faith to dream forever,
and the blue moon carries my tune out of the cruel cold of
winter and into the new month of June.

My band finally reaches the island of freedom.
I don't need my coat anymore because the sun is going to save me.
If love is a rose, as a song once told me, then
freedom is a flower as transparent as gravity
Freedom is a tree leaf as transparent as the rain that flows
from the clouds and inspires my life on earth to grow.

Walker Hayes

The Special One

I write this poem to tell what's in my heart.
So here comes the hard part.
I'm talking about those beautiful brown eyes.
The ones I hope I never see cry.
For the way you smile at me I have no words.
It's the perfect way to end the day.
I think of you in wake and in sleep.
If I lose you I just might weep.
And for days to come in my heart there'll be no peace.

Jack E. Williams Jr.

Thoughts...

Everything is so confusing,
I'm trying to fit the pieces together,
But it's so depressing,
I don't even know why I bother.

At times things seem so smooth,
and others, I'm afraid to know what's ahead.
with you, I must assume.
my path was misled.

Why? I ask myself, time and time again,
I've only confused myself
I just need a close friend,

Love is hard to find, it's only when its right,
you have to find the "one of a kind",
it could be love at first sight,

We were only friends somehow it lead to more,
The friendship doesn't need to end,
'cause I need no less, and no more
Thank's for being there, friend,
I guess I should say no more, don't let our friendship end,
Because that's what friends are for

Sara Pike

Imagine That

Imagine a world with none of the crime
Imagine a world with none of the war
Imagine a world with none of the grime
Imagine a world where no one is poor.

Imagine a world with no pollution
Imagine a world where no one is mean
We must come up with some sort of solution
What we're doing now is truly obscene.

If we can clean up this huge world of ours
If we can stop people from being shot
If we could have those tremendous powers
If we could stop oil spills on the spot.

Our children could have eternal peace.
If pollution and crime would only cease.

Kimberly Nicole Newman

Broken

Fractured, sharp
Irregular edges,
scattered haphazardly, gleaming,
now screaming "danger" in glistening heaps,
I'm broken, fragile as ice not fully frozen,
skated on by pointed blades.

There were no visible signs of thaw
to signal you to stop...to tell you "beware"

I presented my secure front,
smooth, unbroken illusions,
and watch as you lace the skates,
supporting your tremulous steps as you begin to glide
fearlessly flying toward the middle, unknowingly
causing small cracks, each leading to the spot
marked faintly with "x", I crumbled, I'm broken

Renee S. Moore

Children of the Light

Far far away, in a meadow by a stream...
In a place accessible only by dream.

Shines a light for those who've fallen asleep...
Asleep to all darkness while loved ones weep.

Becoming like children as they enter the light...
Wearing stars as crowns while doves take flight.

Awakened by sleep, the nightmare is done...
The children are home with the light—-
They are one.

Thomas Fulton Navarra

I, Myself, and Why

I grew up where I used to live
In a strange but happy way
But still I can't understand what
happened to me one day.

I was on my way to school and
someone said "Hi"

I kept on walking but soon he was
at my side.

He asked me for directions and I did reply.

But that wasn't what he wanted and a knife
was at my thigh

And even though I got away
The pain and hurt still stays

Perhaps I will forget one of these good
ole days.

And even if I don't, it helps me just to say
Keep walking, keep watching, it could
be you some day.

Sonia Green

Ask, Tell

Ask yourself if there is justice,
in a world obsessed with hate.
Ask yourself the meaning of the word love,
cause this world doesn't know it.
Tell me the meaning of the word peace,
as I have no experience.
Give me the word hate,
and I'll give you a thousand examples.

Rebecca Richards

Invictus

Far from Erin' green and lapped shore
In darkness waits for sweet Aurora's smile,
A lonely barque which no deserted, bore
A once and precious cargo to beguile
Such Gaelic charms as ne'er were put to trial.
From love' tribunal sweeter penance drew,
And Ero's bow pierced deep the precious while.
And lips that could not stay the bitter yew
Which stung the heart that felt no more as thru
The anodyne of tears, my bootless cries
Thru heaven's vault arise, Alas, perdu!
The lie has found the truth that love denies.
So sleep my love upon they verdant bed,
While fair Adonis palms thy fustian head.

James W. Hutchison

What Will The Children Know

When they are grown, what will the children know?
In Ireland a car explodes and the people on the
street weep in anguish over the familiarity as
much as they do for the tragedy.

In South Africa where people who hold strong to their tribal
loyalty kill one another with sticks and bricks-disunity
as the white seats watch without seeing.
When they are grown, what will the children know?

In the streets of Beirut and many forgotten Baltic
states people die for land and purity of lineage and
heritage and old and new regimes.

In streets of so many Americans cities; from sea to
shining sea; people gone now because of the colors
they wore or the power behind the American drug dollar.
Those who's heart never even beat outside the womb
that became their tomb.
When they are grown, what will the children know?

Steven R. Lebre

Faith in a Hope that Strengthens

"Dear Lord, please give me Faith to do thy will
in life. Please help me to accept a trial as JOY
not bitter strife.
Help me to LOVE my neighbor and give HOPE to the
distressed. Give my heart an abundance of STRENGTH
to faithfully pass the test.
Let me have HOPE that one day I will see your face,
that I will live with you forever, showered by
your GRACE.
Dear Lord, help me to FORGIVE my enemies and
PRAY for them always. Help me to BLESS and not
curse them for the rest of my days.
Help me to be more like Jesus and follow where
His steps lead. Let me be more worthy of the case,
for my sake He will plead.
And, dear Lord, if I have left anything out of
this HUMBLE prayer I give, please provide me FAITH
IN A HOPE THAT STRENGTHENS to brighten the life
I live —
AMEN.

Sophia V. Owens

In My Dreams

In my dreams, only strange things would happen.
In my dreams, I'm either in a fantasy deep deep in my mind,
or thinking of a palm tree that I'd like to climb.
Funny things happen, that may not
have any meaning, and is worth not the believing.
But it still happens in my dreams.
In my dreams I like to fly and observe
the world from above, in my dreams I'd
like to be floating in the sky when the winds blow.
It would seem strange to you, but if
you dreamt my dreams you would of known.
What it seem like is a figment of my
imagination, or just a plain deep exaggeration.
Some say dreams are repressed desires
of things we would like to have happen.
My dreams are weird as good as it may
seem, but even so it still is in my dreams.

Sherry-Ann Jules

The Birth Of Winter

Times seen and unforgiving
In my past, I am living
People rejoiced and reconciled
The season a cold winter mild—

The colors illuminate in black and white
A scene of pure, solemn delight
To nature the life has been lost
Come forth now the snow and the frost—

The winding stream gently slows its run
Set apart from the distant sun
Depression spreads across my face
As a majestic sky outlines all beauty and grace

The crystals begin to dance in the sky
Do not let these moments pass you by
New footprints break the virgin snow
A feeling of love, seeming to grow

Winter matures now to its final extreme
Just like a child's vivid little dream
So when its memory fades for yet another year
Always remember that winter once lived here.

Shane Darren Retter

Lonely

Lonely is the heart that waits
in quite desperation.
Lonely is the mind that wanders
and never finds.
Lonely is the one who seeks acceptance,
only to find rejection.
Lonely is the love that is given and
is never to be returned.
Lonely are the people who live life
within themselves.
Lonely am I without you.
Lonely is one.

Steven Roberts

Untitled

Oh though who holdeth the stars
in space, look down and fill my
heart with thy grace. Purify and
make me thine. Help me Lord the
hill to climb. To the land of
sun shine and joy, where nothing
can our peace destroy. In the
heavenly plain so fair. Fit
me for a dweller there
Make me Lord a labour here
Faithful to work with in my
sphere. Telling others of thy love
until there shall call me home above
Oh thou who holdeth the stars
in space. Keep for me in thy
kingdom a place.
I was 90 years old
August 7. But I wrote it long time ago

Lesley Bebbir

Within Sight

As I sit and stare
through the window
of my soul,
It's sad to realize
that windows
have no doors.

Jayme Gruden

To SKN — With All My Love for This Lifetime

It's the feeling that comes with the setting of the sun
In that moment I realize one more day is done

It's just when I believe that I have done my best
It's the time that I ache for one moment of rest

When I sit and reflect and remember who you are
When I wish and I hope upon that shooting star

It's the time when I feel you envelope my soul
When you are too far away and the world is so cold

When I am tested for strength time and again
It is then I'm reassured you are my dearest sweet friend

There is no other voice that I hear through the crowd
There is no other being that my heart will allow

You come to the place that I hide from the world
You tread ever so gently on this scared little girl

You know just how to sooth me, you know precisely what to say
You come on that journey that takes this world away

You have always been the keeper, I have known it from the start
God sent you as the shepherd who tends to my heart

Nancy Jo Meehan

Shadows in the Darkness

There is no difference in all of us in total darkness.
In the dark, the naked eye won't see any intelligence.
Nor will it witness any type of ignorance.
When the light shines, we all must open our closed eyes.
In that way, we can all realize...
That racism, as well as any type of discriminating doesn't have to be a part of reality.
Not if we all take time out to correct our mentality.
Night after night and day by day...
We must all remember not to let our correct mentality astray.
Equality is what the ignorant ones must learn and know.
Once the ignorant ones identify this we all can grow.
To have a perfect, peaceful and harmonious community.
Just like I imagined it to be.
We must all come to realize that there is only one race, the human race
Fighting among ourselves will only result in loss of our place.
On this here planet that we all call earth.
So please practice equality from birth.
If not, you will show nothing but ignorance.
And yourself chasing shadows in the darkness.

Mark N. Lewis

Untitled

In the beginning we were whole,
In the end we pay our toll.
The sacrifice of me and you,
Create a life, and start with new.

Go towards the light, believers tell,
To cleanse your soul-of sin you dwell.
The light of life, the dark of dead,
You live in sin of death you dread.

The thought of everlasting sleep,
For someone else to live and weep.
It's not for me to say who goes,
We give our lives so others grow.

This game we play is dealt with care,
The hand you get is your's to bare.
If you lose it is time to fold,
Because death's hand is what you hold.

Let others come and learn to play,
Your time is up you're on your way.
To the place you have practiced well,
Light of Heaven, or dark of Hell?

Lisa Mulligan

I Saw God

I saw God in the sky today
In the gothic clouds and the sun's bright ray
All pink and black with a yellow hue
Forcing its way through the skies of blue
The quiet farmland an awesome contrast
To the powerful clouds and the sun's bright blast
No artist could paint a more beautiful scene
The close of day in an early spring
With the trees all bent and swaying
To the wind's restless music-making
A quiet time, a tender kiss,
A moment shared in marital bliss
A gift from God's bountiful storehouse above
A promise fulfilled by His Unending Love.

Norma Jean Trice

In Absentia

Along the shore
in the gray-blue of daybreak,
The sand,
washed clean by the fingers of the sea,
Stretches for miles in its new virginity.

The waves
lazily lap the shore
in short sleepy kisses,
Echoing a rhapsody of calm.

The sun
peeks its drowsy head
over the horizon
And gazes at its golden image
in the waves of the sea.
All is peaceful.
All is serene.
Man has not yet awakened.

Shari Lee Whipple

Legacy

My grief selects a glistening, white horse
in the outer row on the what-goes-around-
comes-around carrousel.

A continually lonely little girl, mute and neglected
copper-hued braids dipping in the black-as-a-deep-
well-at-night inkwell existence.
Orphaned — she and I danced to the tune of Melancholy
from early on.

Mother's loving legacy
an obitchyouare obituary
and an ancient dear John
blasting my shortcomings.

She who laughs last —
your physical remains finally stripped
of their caustic bitterness
now floating out to sea
Laughs Best!

Nicola M. Shugars

Twilight

Time between night and day...
Where lovers meet...
Under the stars...
Hand entwine...
Lips join...
Tongues touch...
All at twilight.

Jennifer Sternal

Room Of Rain

Wet your lips
In the room of rain;
Where sugar is wet and the rain is
Sweet suckle that runs down my nose and
Touches my lips as my tongue brushes by to meet
Wet bodies pressed together
Dipping their wings
Into shapely things,
Making a song only they two can hear.
But can you hear me?
I have secrets to tell.
Touch you lips to mine,
Can you hear them?
Then let us do a turn to make our bodies yearn
For one more night
In the room of rain.

Shannon Dixon

Human Season Change

The hardships of home change like seasons.
In the summer you were warm to me. Accepting what I did.
In the fall you discourage me from things I want to do, as though
warning me of the winter coming up inside of you.
But I already felt it. You waited to long. And now I just
wait for that first day, when everything will start going wrong

I see the snow start to form in your eyes as
you glare so still. Every move I make I am cautious not
to let it snow to soon. But if I get through that time of
trouble I will be happy to invite the spring in. Where
everything starts to thaw and bring new life, but still
dread the human season change to come again.

Jesseca Stein

Golden Rule

You seem to all be looking for the right thing
in the wrong place

To make so awfully difficult
Something simple within your face

Trying all religious
Reading all the books
Just searching for the answer
In every corners nook

Life's answer was always with us
It's the Golden Rule you see
But none of you'll accept that-
"It's too easy that can't be!"

But if you'd only try it
A chance to it you'd give-
The fullest, richest, love-filled life
Would be the one you'd live!

Sharon K. Douglas

Goodbyes

All your life you dread
saying goodbye's until
the time comes you must.

You feel as if you can't go on
But as the days pass the pain
grows smaller, but the love grows stronger.

It seems as if you have lost them
forever, but even if they're not there
in person, they'll always be in your heart.

Jordyn Wells

Puppy in the Alley

On one cold winter's morning
in the year of Seventy Five,
I looked through the window
And their to my surprise
was a little baby puppy in the alley down below
As I ran down the stairs and opened the gate,
to pick up my puppy who was the gift of Faith,
I went to the house and drew a warm bath,
to wash my little puppy who was no bigger than a rat,
As I dried my little puppy and looked into his eyes,
I told him that I loved him, and he would be mine.
As the weeks and years went by,
my little prancing puppy, brought lots
of joy and love to me, until the
year of ninety two, when he said
Good-bye to go to heaven up above
I Love my Little Baby Puppy

Kathleen Laurich

Their Feelings

Sometimes people do things they regret.
In this case they regret something they didn't do.
The thing they are worst as it expressing their feelings.
Hiding love and feeling frustration and pain.
Keeping anger bottled up and also feeling frustration, but the anger
Also grows more intense.
How can they show their feelings without hurting others,
or hurting themselves? Its easy for most people,
people who have confidence.
These people haven't gained confidence yet.
Their feeling's kept inside, building up within them.
One day along the road, the emotion will burst out of them,
And hurt everyone they need them from yet in the end hurting
themselves the most.

Lisa Bosworth

The Love Of A Child

There are many things that come our way
In this walk of life we take,
The end results will all depend
Upon the choices that we make.

Of all emotions we'll encounter
As we walk upon this land
There's not a feeling can compare
To when you hold a child's hand.

From the day you have been blessed with them
The love, you can't explain
when you look to their soul, through their loving eyes
You know there is so much to gain.

The bond in which you create with them
will be so much worth your while,
When your love is then returned to you
Through their hugs and unique smile.

Their touch is very gentle
So tender and so mild,
Please cherish them with a lot of love
For there's nothing like the love of a child.

Penny Smith

Nirvana

Nirvana, never mind, no way back, loss of time
In too deep, too high to sleep
Real to the night, yet it turned to fright
Variations of my songs, show me doors, right from wrong
Allegations, transfusions, abusions, simply accusions
Never let Courtney cry, never let Francis get high
All in all is all we are.

Tiffany Harris

A Mother

A mother knows how sad you feel by looking
in your eye,
A mother knows how hurt you are before
you start to cry.
A mother knows and understands everything
you do,
A mother knows you better than you will
ever know you.
A mother knows just what you'll do before
you ever do it,
And if you have an ache or pain, a mother
knows how to soothe it.
A mother knows not how much she is needed,
For if God had made no mothers, the world
would have been cheated.

Susan Younger

To Comfort You In Your Loss....

Our Father in Heaven will comfort you
In your trials and disbelief
In your tears and in your sadness
In your pain and in your grief.
Our Father He will always lend
Forever a helping hand
He'll leave you strong in your sorrow
And help your feet forever stand.
Our Father He has taught us
That this will not last forever
The best of all the rainbows come,
After the worst of bitter weather.
So when days are long and lonely
As you are dealing with your loss
Just remember our Father was grieving too,
When his Son died on the cross.
Our Father He's our comforter
When trials come and hardships too
He's looking down from Heaven
His love's shining down on you!

Kirsten Megill

An American

You don't have to be gay to understand
Indifference?
You don't have to be black to understand
Prejudice?
You don't have to be a women to understand
Loneliness?
You don't have to be a minority to understand
Minimum wage?
You don't have to be a child to understand
Abuse?
You just have to be
An American!!!

Pat Ruzicka

The Seed

Although I'm no bigger than a pin I'm alive
Inside here I know no sin I'm alive
Can't hear, see or even speak I'm alive
Keep that wire hanger away from me I'm alive.

Let me grow and develop just like you
Let me smell flowers hear birds see it all
Let me nurse my mother
Let me grow tall

Love is what I want
Love is what I need
Love is why I'm here
Love me protect me I'm your seed.

Williams Davies

January's End

The gusty wind roars harshly enough to etch the cliffs of tomorrow.
Inside the comforting tick of the ancient clock permeates the warmth
with a feeling of tranquility.

Mixed emotions of smugness and remorse play tug of war as the relentless wind blows over the jobless streets of hunger and foraging.

Suddenly the arctic gods are appeased and saffron sunbeams glimmer and
leap off precious keepsakes.

Like the wind, feeling of guilt and regret are tucked away...only to be withdrawn on another windy day.

Patricia Ann Halek

The Grand

Rich and majestic is her cat eyes glow
Instruments in tune make energy flow
The grip of her wheel and touch of her keys
Renders forth a thrill to tingle and please
A sight to behold, a sound of delight
She transmits pleasure like opera at night
A turning response brings notes sharp and quick
A cherished possession, she's what I'd pick
A partner in travel, a mate on stage
A match like this one is heavenly made
To tell of the love developed for both
Demands expert mechanical notes
She's awesome, she's Grand, how lucky I am
To sit at the helm conducting the Grand

Kay Maddox

Tapestry

Rich heavenly hues
Intense pattern nestled within the fibers
Rough to the touch, yet somehow soft and inviting.
Crests and crevices throughout the design
Vested in tradition, a valued inheritance.
Artisans since time immemorial have treasured their creations

How very like human spirit!
Tapestry; tangible parallel to the soul.
Purple, mauve, jade, ivory, lapis, silver, gold all elude to vacillating emotion.
Solid lines, furrows, curves, cables, paisleys are as life's adornments enriching a soul.
Greed and humanism yielding to a merciful Savior.
Blessed by Grace—Forged by the fire of trials, tribulations.
Morality, idealism pass to tomorrow's generation.
The Lord, God is the soul's artisan; Yea, since time immemorial.
Unto today He treasures His creations.

Karen A. Peterson

"A Child Is Born"

A child is born
Into this world
Of waste and haste
Where the city has no pity
Where people are always
Pushing and rushing where nothing is free
For everything has a fee
Where the streets aren't
Covered in gold but there only old
Where there is a lot of crime
But never enough time
Where the smog is thick as fog
Where the prices are high
And there never low
Where everything is slow
And nothing is slow
Even our towns are going down
For a child is born into this world
God help this child for it's a wild world
We live in!

Thomas Erickson

Imagine That

Imagine that there is world Peace.
Imagine that there weren't any riots.
Imagine that there weren't people
beating people of different races.
Imagine that there weren't people
killing other people.
Imagine that there weren't starving
homeless people on the streets.
Imagine that we weren't feeding
starving people in different countries,
but feeding our own people.
Imagine that there are no more wars.
Imagine that all the people in the
world weren't starving to death, and getting
along with each other, but all I can say is
Keep Imagining!

Shannon Anderson

To Love

To be able to love someone,
Is a feeling of joy,
That's like no other.
Can we honestly appreciate love?
Give love without condition?
We tend to say, I love you,
And that's good,
Only if we act on that love.
Why do we utter words of love,
When we cannot show that love.
Is it because we are afraid to lose control?
Is it because loving someone is not easy?
Maybe we simply do not know, how to love
If we are to know, truly, the joy of loving,
We must start by truly loving and accepting ourselves.
So when we say, I love you,
We truly understand, what it is to love.

D. Sainten

Those That Listen

Where ocean meets the sky,
Is a place to ponder why,
Some of heaven, some of earth,
rise and fall to decay and birth,
Light and shadow side by side,
Common thoughts do abide,
To earth some eternally bound,
As heavenly chorus resound,
Of the courage, of the strife,
Moments of faith appear in life,
Pilgrims journey do sometimes embark,
In the shadows where light almost touches dark,
Rivers will rage, stars will glisten,
Answers come to those that listen.

Victor T. Greene

Friends

A person who is kind and loving,
is considered a friend.
A friend is always there with you.
Until the very end.

A friend is there to stick up for you.
When your self-esteem is down.
They help you feel happy,
and to wash away your frown.

You should take friendship seriously.
Now as we speak.
You should guard them with your life.
Because they are so special and unique.

When we become older,
our paths will start to part.
But friends will always have a special place,
forever deep down in our hearts.

Laura Wiercioch

Life to Death

Why must we live just to die?
Is happiness just an ugly lie?
One day just seems to run into the next.
Are there answers-someone please write the text.
Give us directions to a happy life.
Why the suffering, madness and strife?
A beautiful child's hopes and dreams
Abused by the world, filled with screams
Adults tortured and full of fear
Mindlessly living another year.
For what goal or what price
To be as lonely and cold as ice?
Put beneath the ground under a stone
Cold, wet and all alone.

Michael J. Osborne

Ode To A Passive Aggressive Man

Why do you keep doing this to us?
Is it a pattern, a pattern that
speaks of a child's pain on
seeing his mother belittled and abused?

Is it the pain of a man unable and
unwilling to express his anger to his
woman, whose only recourse is to find a
new woman - start the pattern all over again?

Meanwhile, those of us who continue
to love you and have been discarded, ask,
"Why do you keep doing this to us?"

Valerie C. Dhanens

Death

What is death?
Is it going through the tunnel into the light.
Is it passing into another life.
Is it the sweet sorrow song by a bird.
Is it wind blowing through a pussy willow.
What is death?
Is it the weeping widow
Is it flowers
Is it the tissues that wipes away the tears.
Is it the empty feeling
Is it the tears running down your face.
What is death?
It is a part of life, so don't cry.
Just remember the good memories that you have.

Patricia Paruolo

Daddy's Girl

Why do Daddies love little girls?
Is it the smile or the pretty curls?
Or is it a very special love
That's only sent from heaven above?

A little girl has a very special place
Only she can fill with such tenderness and grace
I guess that's why Daddies worry so
When little girls grow up and go
On their own, away from home all alone

A Daddy will always feel
That she is still a little girl and it hurts him so
When he knows he must let go but, let the little eagle fly
Try out her wings against the sky
Because no one can ever be
Complete, fulfilled unless they're free
And it takes a special love to give the eaglet the final shove

And so a Daddy's love must be
Tender, kind, yet oh! so free
But Daughter remember this for sure
Your Daddy's love will long endure.

Richard G. Vollmer

Spellbound

(Dedicated to Charles Munch)

He who spun this thread of gold,
Is lost in rapturous ecstasy,
When from the very depths of his soul
Arose this flame of mystery,
And with those graceful eager hands
He molds precious tones into glittering gold,
Blending its colors ever so bright
Into rainbows of jewels that shine like a light.
So enchanted am I by all this beauty,
That this spell you wove so exquisitely,
None shall break till eternity.

Victoria Onanian

Love

The day is long, the night is cold
My heart is empty and so is my soul

I've longed for His love day by day
And never understood why he stayed away

I thought I found true love one fine day
But now this love has run away

Now I found love at my best Friend's hand
And I wonder why I looked to another man

Katherine Pennington

Things Unseen

This very first thing you can't really see
Is something when blown can move the tree.
It's here, it's there, it's everywhere.
Have you guessed what it is?
It's something called AIR.

This second thing is invisible, too.
It's everywhere, including in you.
It's all through the dirt.
And all over worms.
Have you guessed what it is?
It's something called GERMS.

Number three is oh so wonderful.
It's been here since the beginning.
It's all things bright and beautiful.
It knows all we think, and all that we do.
It helps us believe.
It's all pure and true.
It's chock full of splendor and worlds it has awed.
Have you guessed what it is?
It's something called GOD.

Kristina Zanotti

Legacies

I raise my tiny head seeking life, warmth and freedom. Long is the time I came into being.
Luxuriously I stretch and begin to unfold. Reaching, ever reaching. Layer by layer I reveal my softness. The beauty of my creation.
In full flower I am embraced by the Son. Behold! I have arrived. Reach out for me and feel the vibrancy of existence.
Without warning I destroy the delicate softness of your soul. As a rose, I have thorns. My imperfection comes full focus. Those who have created me caused the poison that foretells my destruction.
Inch by creeping inch I fold upon myself. A swarming mass burns away my form. I wither and melt away. Loosing the whole in ever increasing stages.
A beginning and ending upon that same first breath. My creators of life, Your legacies gift.
AIDS !!!!!

Karla Kovscek

Death

Where is it that we go when we die?
Is there really place where we can fly,
Way, way up in the sky?

Is there really a place,
where everyone knows you,
for you not your face?

Where the pain goes away,
and you're filled with happiness, joy, and love,
is there such a place way up above?

Where you can go,
where your memories will never fade,
where you can look at all your accomplishments,
and all you've made.

Remember to love now,
and never forget,
for you'll then remember by, and by,
even if there is no such thing as heaven,
you still got to fly!!!

Merri-Jo Campbell

The Wondering Wolf

The matter of which I'd like to know
Is whether the wolf is friend or foe
To watch him preying on a herd of deer
I watch in awe, I feel such fear
He senses the presence of someone else
He looks around and finally sees
I'm looking at him, now he's looking at me
His frightened eyes are meeting mine
But I feel a bond, like we're intertwined
He now seems calm like he feels the same
He's approaching me as if he were tame
He perches himself next to me on the
hilltop
The wolf glances at me, then at the moon
He points his muzzle up to the sky
And lets out his beautiful howling cry

Laura Gomez

The Kiss

Intimate sharing, most precious, passionate, all encompassing.
It begins with a single kiss. How can it be taken lightly?
The most personal gift. It often ends shared pleasure,
sometimes, shared pain. Or is it really the
point of continuum; the act that says, "we shall go on"?
All important in this life, it is a symbol of love, caring, warmth,
emotion, and humanity. Great power. A kiss betrayed Christ.
How can it be taken lightly?
Over lips travel words of love, or fear, pleasant honesty, images of
the way men wish to be perceived.
Over lips travels nourishment to the body, music of the soul, smiles
that light the darkest hours, the sigh of whispered prayer, the breath
of life. How can it be taken lightly?
Eyes cannot lie in this personal space.
Feelings flow unchecked and exchange, running over freed in truth.
This touch, this shared breath,
in a moment, says, "I choose you, share with me, know me,
love me, I am your friend, I am human,
share beautiful soft lips, kiss with me.
How can it be taken lightly?

Valerie Polacek

Rainbow...

When a rainbow fills the mountain side
It brings happiness to my eyes, my heart, my soul
A sense of closeness with thee
To appreciate things around me
Hope instills my ever living
To see nature always giving
Distant as it may seem
Never losing sight of it's gleam
It's colors tell me that I live
To be free, so I can see
A rainbow just for me.

Mapuana Kahanu

Fog

Fog rolls 'cross the Bay at a menacing pace,
It dampens my hair and cleanses my face,
It sends a cold chill right through to my bones
And silently tells me to hurry on home.
I shiver and shake; I quicken my step;
There's fog to my right and fog to my left;
I'm startled that buildings ordinarily tall
Have lights that are blurred and no tops at all.
The fog turns the scene into very fine lace
That covers my hair and encircles my face,
But with the cold chill seeping into my bones
I hasten my step and hurry on home.

Myrtle Gartman

Unknown Presence

What is this strange presence that overpowers all?
It brings trouble and toil;
Fear and fate, and unwant.
But, why do people search for its presence?

What is this thing that joins two people together
That at the same time could tear them apart?
The thing that makes a union struggle with themselves?
What is this, and why do people search for its warmth?

This monster of destruction also creates.
It brings happiness and comfort,
And all of the golden things in life.
But why, why do we long for this stranger of creation
and destruction?

Ah, maybe it is the essence and glow it brings us.
Or the sorrow that mangles and leaves us.
It is shared by many, forgotten by some, and longed
by few.
So why is it that we search for this presence and yet
have trouble with it?

Michael G. Murphy

Place In Life?

I've lost my place in life and I can't find my way out.
It caught me at all the wrong places
and all the wrong times,
I've lost my place in life and I can't find my way out.
I have even lost my mind,
I can't remember the last time I look a shower
or the last time I was even funny,
I've lost my place in life and I can't find my way out.
Hell, if that's how life is I reckon
everything can't be roses,
I can't see anymore and I can't hear anymore
so why does this all happen at once.
I've even lost the beat to a different drummer
and I can't find it anymore.
I've lost my place in life and I never found my way out.

Sean W. Pritchard

Memories

There is that about a back house which attracts my baser mind
It could be the seats, hewn circles, tailor made for my behind

It was there I did my reading in an atmosphere quite ripe
In that time of blissful being; aft the call but ere the wipe.

I have dreamed so many daydreams but the best that I have known
Have been conjured up while sitting on that any weather throne.

Now we have a fine new bathroom and we've thrown away our pot.
Gone now is the aged back house, weeds now flourish over the spot.

They tore it down and burnt it, it was only in the road.
Now my backside makes acquaintance with an up-to date commode

What an awful lonesome feeling when I get the days warm heat.
I remember how the sun rays used to warm the out house seat.

But it's gone and I'm aware now that here's the gist of it
Where it used to be a pleasure, now it's business when I sit.

Roberta B. Beatty

Gone?

You think I'm gone, but that's not true,
I'm in all you say and do.
I'm in the sun, the sea, the sky,
I'm in each breeze that passes by,
I'm with you now, and shall be,
until you can't remember me.

Frances T. Bowen

I Hear the Silence (On My Last Day of Teaching)

Suddenly I hear the silence I sometimes demanded.
It does not smile or look at me from innocent eyes
That say, "it wasn't me."
Why do I miss that movement all around me?
Is it only that I formed a habit looking at those eyes
And hearing those voices?
Why do I wish it was noisy when I have many times craved
To hear "a pin drop."
Because this silence means they are no longer part of my life
They have gone to others who will continue smoothing the edges
Building skills, attitudes and honesty, and character that will
Forever be a part of them.
Dear God, How dare I to teach, to mold, to build on these images of
You. I pray that I, for a while, served as the "splinter"
That held the twig so the tree would grow straight and tall and
truthful and honest and loving.
Then silence, I can laugh at you because you cannot erase those
smiles and those innocent eyes from my mind because they will
always be a part of me as I will be a part of them!

Mercedes Conner

For You

Every drop of rain that falls from my face,
it falls for you.
Every step I take,
I get closer to you.
Every sound to make,
I make to speak to you.
Every chance to take,
I take it just for you.
Every day I live,
I live to be with you.
Every time I love,
I love only you.

Shawna Brewer

Fall

That night the moon shone in the sky like a big silver marble.
It filled the sky with a silverish light.
It was as if I were on a planet of ice.
The water moved quietly and cautiously over the rough rocks.
The only sounds were the crickets making their music.
Listening, hushed I fell asleep to the gentle sound.
The next morning was beautiful; there weren't any clouds
in the sky.
There was a light, cool breeze; the sun was shining.
As I ran through the different colored leaves, I knew it was fall.

Sara Sullivan

Touched

Touched by a feeling full of light
It fills my soul with power and might
I can conquer the world if I try
I can heal the people's desperate cry
Screams fill my head day and night
I read about a life destroyed without right
The right I'm told is by the mother
Does that mean I can kill my brother
This crime happens everyday
But we just read about it and go on our way
No one gave that life a chance
It missed the world this big "dance"
"One nation under God" is that what we say
I think we left that foundation back a ways
You hear the people preach about the rights of mice
Then go to the Doctor and destroy a life
Maybe I'm wrong in what I say
But I would rather have a brother than a mouse any day.

Mandy Ray

You Are The Dream That Lives In My Heart

The dream of my childhood
it has been from the start
to change me into motherhood
the dream of my heart

My dream lives but not in my heart
as she cries and plays
as she sleeps and eats
She is the dream of my heart

My dream lives but not in my heart
as she teeters on the brink of walking
as she becomes a chatter box from all her talking
She is the dream of my heart

My dream lives but not in my heart
as she grows from a tot to a sweet little girl
as she goes from home to school
she is the dream of my heart

My dream lives in my heart
as she is dressed in white
as she journeys towards the light
once again you are the dream that lives in my heart.

Mary E. Andreko

"A Wonderful Man Is Leaving Us"

A wonderful man is leaving us
It hurts me so to say
That this man who has worked so hard
May not live another day

A wonderful man is leaving us
And soon will join his beloved wife
And receive his rewards in heaven
For taking such good care of her throughout much of her life

A wonderful man is leaving us
But the good life he led will not be in vain
For every time someone thinks back on his memory
They will be reminded of his virtue again and again

A wonderful man is leaving us
And it is hard for his friends and family
Because without his smiling face
Our lives will be a bit empty, you see

A wonderful man is leaving us
But the kindness and friendship he bestowed will be with us forever
And one day we hope to join him in heaven
Where we will all live happily together

Melody L. Hanscom

My Love

It is something I can share with you.
It is all I have to give. It may not be
much but I want you to always take it in your
hands. I trust you with it and would hope you feel the
same. I am so happy I have found you, someone I
can trust and who respects me. With the time we spend
together I feel that you will not harm me in any way and I
hope I can keep that feeling in my heart. There is nobody who
could ever match up to you. I need the security and hope that
you will give it to me. You have shown me the meaning of
happiness and you have given me the love I have long waited for.
I have a friendship with you, I have never seen before. I know
that when I say I love you it may not seem that I mean it
but I really do. You say that you love me and are so lucky to
have me but it doesn't sound like you are lucky. Who could be
so lucky as to have me in their arms? I don't think it is
luck, I just think you come at the right time in my life!

Michelle Ann Grote

The Power Within Me

There is a power which is deep within me
It is deeper than the eye can see.
It helps me through the daily fight;
It gives me strength; it gives me might.
I don't know what I'd do without it;
It keeps me light inside me lit—
It gives me humor and also laughter—
It relieves my stress, bit by bit.
It helps me mentally stay awake
For all my surroundings' and peoples' sake.
It helps me make it through the day,
So that at night I can wander "away"
It helps me act and be polite;
It helps me reach unheard of height.
It tells me what is wrong or right;
So I can find joy in a beautiful sight.
It helps me reach my goals and dreams
To learn what life is and what it means.
So every day as I walk along,
I think of my very sacred song.

Paul Martini

Life

Life is all a big game, sometimes you win, sometimes you are blamed.
It is no wonder the fortune and shame, but somebody always
Has to play the game.
Sometimes you win sometimes you loose, but you never know
Which one they will choose.
Life is nothing but a big game, so why don't someone just
Take the blame.

Tina Pittock

Bowling

Bowling is a great sport,
it is played by millions.
Instead of an outdoor court,
it is played indoors in any season.

Anyone can play this game
no matter what kind of shape you're in.
If you're disabled or not, it's all the same
as you can have fun and still win!

You can be short, you can be tall,
you can be fat, you can be thin.
As long as you can pick up a ball
and knock down lots of pins!

There are many leagues and tourneys to choose,
just pick one and sign up!
Maybe you'll win or maybe you'll lose,
as long as you don't give up!

What's the matter, can't decide
whether to give bowling a shot?
Well, you can open bowl, just give it a try
and see if you don't like it a lot!

Steve Tardif

The Path

As she walks along the narrow path,
It is raining but not to worry,
The berries are bright, the leaves are green,
And the little white flowers smile as she passes by,
This is what warms her heart inside.

And now that she is older,
She still walks that narrow path,
The path that we must all face,
The path of Life,
The path of Faith.

Lara Lynd

Light Steps

Don't look backward over the road travelled -
It is the distant past.
Go forward in love and wisdom
These are the things that will last.

Life has its way of molding us of bending us, and sending us
Into experiences of cleansing us to purify and clarify -
That which is not real accept the challenge of the path
Leaning on those who have gone before
They have travelled this way you took
And they stand ready to open the door
To newer joys, the same love that carried you through
They rejoice with you at this moment knowing the cycle is finished
You are through

You did your best in the consciousness
You were experiencing at the time
Now move on to higher mountains
Give up appearance - give up time
Live in the endless flow of eternity
A new start, play the part my
Silent mine

D. Jumel

Dancing Stars

A moonbeam came through my window last night
It kissed me on the cheek
It's coolness had a power that brought me to my feet
It came with an invitation to the greatest laser show by far
Put on by the dancing angels
Everyone of them a star
I watched as they danced the greatest ballet
Each one in its place
They surely are Gods angels
Dancing there in space
Then dawn arrived with an encore
Of color oh so bright
That left me with a promise
Of another dance tonight

Jean McNutt

"Camp Light"

There is a certain light I like
It makes me feel so good at night.
It moves by something felt not seen
It's brilliance is more than just one beam.
It's warmth is measured only by me
Just by adding parts of a tree.
As I lay and stare
Not too close do I dare.
It takes me far, far away
Even farther than the next day.
But sadly there comes a death
To my life-giving breath.
As a distant great light appears
Mine lies in it's own tears.

Jay K. Potter

The Coming Rain

Rain falling gently, softly, hard, loud,
lightning flashing, thunder roaring damp
and cool, a tender breeze is blowing
that rainy scent seems to float. Your
blood flowing you can touch it, play
in it, hold it let it run through
your fingers feel it on your finger tips.
Watch the flowers grow and the tree's
leaves bow down to its every touch as
it brings with it life.

Jamine Williams

"Prudential"

She stands upon the prudential, teary-eyed but proud.
It must have been essential or it would not be allowed.
He went with such bravery, fighting for his life.
It was not a bit of slavery at all throughout his strife.

He always was the best they told her.
Would've carried them on his shoulder.
She always knew there was a chance, but hope had filled her mind.
Love had put her in a trance, made her totally blind.

Then the telegram when the doorbell rang.
"Excuse me ma'am," the postman banged.
Her hand too weak to turn the knob.
A pain so bleak she couldn't sob.

Now she wept and fell slowly down.
As her husband had crept and been shot to the ground.
As she stands on this great cliff, her hair long and wavy.
The wind blows, her hair lifts, and she slowly salutes the Navy.

Lisa Remillet

Waiting Here

Although we're in a room filled with people
It seems as if it's only us
Only us again
Like all those times alone
But those were good times
Not like now

You refuse to meet my eyes
My eyes that still hold the red from the tears
Would I be able to meet them even if you did
I still love you
You know that
And I'll still be here loving you
Waiting

Tanyia Shaw

Darklight

Darklight
It shrouds the stark reality of day with a veil of illusion
Beware of Maya
The woman I am... is the child I am
Free... to be
To dream the child dream ... Sleeping Beauty
The babes are sleeping ... and I am free ... to be
Moonlight casts fairy dust in my hair
My spirit lifts and shines it own light
My dreams take flight ... I fly the great Pegasus
The Fairy Prince unbraiding my hair in the starlight
The gossamer strands drifting back to caress his nakedness
Gold and raven tresses weaving a tapestry of their own
A gift to gentle Zephyrus
And I am the light
I feel his lips brush my shoulder
And he raises me up to the top of the World
I am free ... I soar the heights of ecstasy
Then Daylight charges in on his shadowed steed
Dreams are shattered ... I am only me.

Susan K. Baritell

Random

On a table the light lies
It spreads its hope throughout the ancient room
Age old logs will be my warmth
shall protect me from nothing
In the corner is a generous skunk
Damn! Too generous and it scurries off
I ungratefully burn its gift
Now I try to nod off wondering;
Will soft serve ice cream ever come in more than four flavors?

I awaken, a new day, a new journey and freezing cold. I exit.
Hungary not knowing for what, I eat wild berries
They quench my hunger; What would it be like to have three hundred
and sixty degree vision?

My generous friend is back I don't want more gifts,
run, panting, sweating, How did jelly bracelets become so popular?

Finally, I reach the road leading to my house
The smell of fresh cut grass enters my nostrils.
I reach the door, unlock, and enter.
Closing the door behind me I realize something —
Jumping up and down and saying bouncy is fun.

Peter Santos

If I Could Give The World A Gift

If I could give the world a gift-
It would be a stop button and a rewind.
I'd press rewind to run backwards
away from the fake smiles
used to cover the war's death toll,
I'd press stop to end
the long death of the farmer
who watches his field burn.
I'd press stop
to end the foolishness of this world,
to kick it in its side, to open its eyes,
force it to see our ruined earth.
Let it see the pollution, war, and mess.
Let it see the poverty, hunger, and pain.
Let it see our perfect little world -
Let it see, let it die;
why force the Earth through all of the pain?
Press rewind to see where we went wrong.
Press stop to end it all.

Trescha Miller

If I Could Write A Poem About Sister Nancy

If I could write a poem of what I feel and what I would say,
it would read like a book about my Sister Nancy, who I think of every day.

There would be beginning, a story within, telling all the wonderful things Nancy had been.

It wouldn't be a short story, but one with out end, one that would continue, day out and day in.

A continuous story, with cliff hangers and all, a story of my Sister Nancy, who God caught each time she stumbled, each time she might fall.

God extended his hand during her times of despair, reminding her each time that he would always be there.

Also reminding her of the rough road he had told us we would travel, a road with many turns, and one with many battles.

Nancy is no longer with us, she has gone to her reward, to be with our God, where another lifetime is stored.

Yes, if I could write a poem about my Sister Nancy, you would know at its end, you'll find another verse of "MY Sister Nancy", written with Gods holly pen.

James Howard

Black Wind

The sun should be out
it's a good day, after all
but black evil holds my heart
and keeps me from moving on
the clouds are out, dropping rain
on our faithful minds
the clear words now unseen
the clear ideals now forsaken
because I missed my chance
go back as in a dream
romantic figure stands, hooded in a black
devils cloak, demons cloak
hair dancing in the wind, everything caught
too late, figure it out, to be real
vibrations of music catch me for forgiveness
from the guilt that binds
rather than love
because what I want most
by my own fault is gone
except in the darkness and rain and wind.

Lenore Palladino

The Puddle

Staring into the puddle,
it's another world I see:
that of unreality.
Images are so subtle
of glimmering reflections.
My mind is filled with deflections.
Vaguely, I remember it; the truth concealed within me.
I wonder my destiny.
Seems as though my heart has split.
I can not set the hurt free.
It still haunts my memory.
The puddle reflects a dream.
Illusions are what I see.
They are not reality.
The puddle dries; tears still stream.
I watch it disappear just like those I thought did care.
The puddle's dry; it is no longer.
My eyes still cry, but so much stronger.
I stare at that spot through my blurred eyes
As trust and love within me dies.

Lisa S. Hilliker

China's House

The flowered portrait stared at me through
It's blanketed shadow and the wall made
Sure I would not walk away

Excuse me, but could you spare a friend
And exchange my seltzer for a cup of tears?

Why does my staircase go straight, instead
Of down and up and why is life temporarily
In a shoe box?

Will you drown in my puddle, cause if so, I
Won't cry and when my eyes hear what my ears
Won't, will you run away?

I lost your name tag, so tell me who I am
And when it begins to rain, don't forget your
Sponge

The wind will carry away high temperature
And the butterflies will come back home to
Find their Greco-Roman nest clean and their
Mother dressed for Sunday mass.

Steven Postiglione

Autumn's Treasure

You dislike the thought and site of autumn
It's colder temperature chills your bones
and turns your flesh to stone.
I've never spent an autumn with you,
though if I could, I would tear this fear
from the pages of your calendar.
Before the first kiss of virgin snow
which buries the roughage of summer's glow.
I see the sky meeting a burnt red sun.
The heat of summer passing.
As a lovers passion send droplets of sweat
Between the snow white breasts of his love.
As I gaze into all the colors of autumn
which are your eyes,
I feel the warmth of smoke from burning leaves,
As though the warmth of your embrace.
The wisps of smoke thrown around by the breeze
Give way to the scene of golds, reds and browns
Mixed as if they didn't care and mingled with freshness
as your autumn hair!

Thomas J. Vana

The Right Game

I want to say I love you, and I need you every day.
It's kind of hard to come up with words that tell you in every way.
It's impossible to live without you.
Without being in your arms; and when
I think about your sweetness and all your romantic charms.
It makes me wonder if I've met you in my dreams,
or if I've loved you in another life,
because it's just the way it seems.

The tenderness in your words that melt
my heart in a snap, comes rushing back
when I sleep or try to take a nap.
I just can't stop thinking how your soul just seems to shine.
I think I'm the luckiest girl, and proud to say you're mine.
If I have you forever and if you feel the same,
our life will be so perfect, loving in the Right Game.

Nicole Link

Forever Together

You have my love as long as forever.
It's my fondest wish that we're together.
I'll always love you with all my heart,
The moment we met I could not part
From your gentle heart, your special ways,
You always do something to brighten my days.
It maybe just your cute little smile,
Or we may sit down and talk a while.
No matter the choice it is you choose,
I won't be able to stop caring for you.
Sometimes today may seem like never,
But we both know someday
We could be spending forever together.

Kathy Rombach

Love Will Follow You:

Sitting here thinking of you
Knowing this love is so true
Wishing that people feel all the same
Wishing to give up this hating game
Willing to learn what this is about
Willing to scream out loud
Trying to work for peace really heard
Finding that this would be a great start
Hoping you feel like I do
Than love will always follow you!

Susanne Smoak

I Don't Believe In Falling In Love

I don't believe in falling in love;
It's not a descent from somewhere above.

Love is more like a road that is always ascending.
And not like a pit; into descending.

The type of love that lasts for a lifetime,
starts with one step then continues to incline.

A fall suggests an event that is tragic.
But, real love rises, and is truly romantic.

So beware of the fall for the bottom is deadly,
but rather seek for climb that is never ending.

S. A. Yates

Priceless

Don't tell me that I'm worth nothing, because I know I'm priceless!
It's not conceit, and I'm not stuck-up.
I'm just tired of not being appreciated, for the struggles I've been
through.
Tears shed, women dead. It's time to unite as one.
We can't subject ourselves to this abuse forever.
Whether it's a punch, or a slap, or verbal slurs,
If I left you, I'm sure you'd be crying!
You'd swear you'll change, and never leave,
and that you're love I'll always receive.
But why should I believe you?
Don't tell me that I'm worth nothing, because I know I'm priceless!
My mother always told me to look for the "good in people"?
You tell me, what's so good about you?
I guess you never cared enough to show me that side of you.
And tell me, what have you done for me lately?
Why do I get the impression that I'm doing all the giving,
and you're right there with your hand in my face, for the taking.
Well not anymore! You don't get another chance, because my
future
I plan to enhance.
So don't tell me I'm worth nothing, because I know I'm priceless!

Nicole A. Ashton

"Story Time"

I'm about to tell you a story about me,
its of my dream of death as it overcomes me.
Someday you'll find me, but don't be scared.
You see this time, I went further than ever dared.
While my body lie limp, and a bullet in my head,
don't try to revive me, hopefully I'll be dead.
Blood will appear, and won't that be a sight.
If my heart stops beating, I know I've done it right.
My body will lie there and slowly not away.
My color and life is gone, but my smile still stays.
The blood that was shed will leave the reddest of stains,
the bullet is not to be found, for it is still in my brain.
By now I should be decomposing, and spoiling away,
my flesh will be gone, but my spirit will forever stay.
My story may be over, but I'll push my self into your dreams,
I'll make them bloody and fearful,
waking you with the loudest of screams.

Sara Marie Everson

In Memory Of My First Love

I cannot believe that I've loved you this long!
It's ridiculous really, I know, yet how
strange that your memory still calls out
to mine with such power it never lets go.
I cannot believe 50 long years passed by
and this tender, sweet feeling remains,
Lord, I am so grateful that You did not
jest and kept our precious loving unchanged.

Patricia Parhad

Lobo Lake

In Levelland a lake I saw, its deep green waters were setting still
Its surrounded by its city streets and rather high man-made hill

Small children come and go...to gladly feed the ducks below
I watched silently and in awe...
my eyes marvelled at the beauty that I saw
I sadly sigh from the bottom of my soul for soon I'll leave this
pretty nature's scene
and other places that I've been

A part of me will stay behind with two precious ones that stole my
heart
My two grand children
whom I dearly love and cherished always from the start

My mind fondly reminisces the moments I spent here, when with
utterly delight
My grandchildren happy I watched; roaming, laughing and
carefree,
their gentle hands the ducks were feeding
I watched with love this moment fleeting

I tried to capture it with my mind
for soon all this I'll leave behind
A sweet memory it will become!

Maria Perkins

Sisters

It must be wonderful to have a sister.
I've always wished I did.
To have someone share life's ups and downs.
Forever, since a kid.
I'll never have a sister. This can never be.
But it makes me very happy and I pray will ever be
That my daughters have each other.
How wonderful that must be!
Thank you Lord.

H. Vivian Beck

The River

I've seen the man
I've seen him play the game
he gets a fire in his eye
and everyone knows his name

He gets carried on the shoulder
of a team that won the prize
He's a hero now
look at the sparkle in the young boys' eyes

We worship the gift
but we do not see the giver
He's at our fingertips
but we wash him away
In the river

Scott Harpt

"Heart Burn"

Her love reached in and pulled out my heart,
Like the quickness of lightning bolts.
Our hearts had danced among the stars,
With the energy of newborn colts.
Thoughts and feelings have come together,
To bond us like no others.
Time will test the strengths,
Of true love to it's lengths.
As one in time may loose their love,
Never close your heart of showing love.
When the hurt and pain continues to bout,
Never let that fire go out.

Kelly M. Garrison

Marital Romance

Goodwife rents three videos
Julia Roberts, Michelle Pfeiffer, Sharon Stone,
as protection against his mood.

She buys Chivas Regal
to ameliorate hers
and a six-pack of Coors
to keep his stable, less or more.

Inspired by the moment,
she grabs a copy of Penthouse
and fully armed by Victoria's Secret
returns to her now childless
condominium by the sea.

On their anniversary,
she drinks beside
the husband she still loves,
hoping something would remind him
why he picked her up
on the dance floor of a discotheque
twenty years before.

Kent Braithwaite

Just Be My Lady...

Just be my lady, for a moment - after awhile
Just be my lady, for whatever time allows
Just be my lady, for I ask you so
If you were my lady, this is how the story goes

My lady would wear a diamond ring
  she would lack nothing and have everything
She would carry a name of great ponder and cheer
  have an accurate knowledge to continue her career
My lady would bare a child of our own
  a home, garden and private listing by telephone
She would only call on the good, overlooking the bad
  prove her happiness exist, outweighing the sad
My lady would love only what's right
  loving me by day and all through the night
She would give her prayers to God in heart
  growing old together, till death do us part.
My lady would live in memory of this poem
  she accomplished life's successes
    of the sweetest love song
Just be my lady, for a moment - after awhile...

Tequan Sabre Graham

"Lessons"

I remember our talks as we sat in the swing,
just enjoying being together and listening to life sing!

Your hands were so calloused from living a hard life,
but your heart was so tender through good times or strife!

You taught me of life, to be honest and true,
to stand up for what I believed no matter what
I had to go thru!

You gave me your pride, your reasons for caring,
you showed me your love and taught me of sharing!

For life you prepared me, but there's one lesson left,
Dad, you never taught me how to deal with your death!

How to keep on going without seeing your smile,
or just sit in the swing and talk for awhile!

The hardest lesson I've never gone thru
is learning to live and not having you!

Leanne Zachary

My Special Valentine

This Valentine poem was written to let you see.
Just how much you mean to me.
From the smile you wear to the little things you do.
I could never do enough to prove my love for you.
This day takes on a whole new meaning since you became my wife.
It is so great knowing that you are my Valentine for life.
I just tried to jot down a few lines to let you know.
That no matter how far or wherever you may go.
There will be one thing I hope you will always know.
There will be no storms our love cannot weather.
Because you are more than my Valentine, you're my best friend.
One who'll stick with me till the very end.
I wanted to tell you these and many others things.
So I searched and searched and this poem became the means.
To let you know I want you to be mine.
Not just today or tomorrow, but until the end of time.
I hope you get the massage I'm trying to convey.
Because for me on this Valentines' Day
There is only one and that one alone will do.
I love you so very much sweetheart, and my Valentine is you.

Marshall Jones

Wisdom

Where did the time go?
Just yesterday I was young
Today I feel so old.
All my dreams have gathered dust
Some dreams I tried, some dreams I forgot.

The fine lines are starting to show
Hot flashes come and go.
The wisdom of age has started.
What does wisdom do?

When you get the wisdom you need.
It seems too late to use all,
The wisdom you have gathered thru the years.

Now, I'm alone with my dusty dreams
and all my wisdom I needed years ago.
When my dreams were not dusty.
I have energy to fulfill them.
When I taking a chance.
Was worth chasing my dreams

Now I feel old and empty and wise
Just waiting, waiting, for the unknown.

Sara Cook

The Crow

Circling high above the graves of long dead kings
Keeping a vigilant watch over the mound that rings
Ringing with the echo of glorious battles past
Honor, glory and valor lie here at long, long last
Blood as red as the setting eventide sky
Fertilizes this barren land as the crow hovers ever near by

Souls that have lain here for ages and will lie
Yet all have tales to tell of a thousand and one ways to die
"Thy fate is in thine own hands, my son," you can hear
the dead faintly say
For who but the crow and the dead knows what
toll to the fates we must pay?

Todd E. Shawell

Shyness

Shyness is a kind of humiliating feeling,
kind of like your face is peeling.

People may say you are prude,
but you're just trying not to be rude.

I know I am shy,
and I wish I could die.

But I know I can't,
because I hear God's chant.

I wish I had the guts to kiss,
but when I want to, my nerves melt into
nothingness.

Roses are red,
Violets are blue,
My nerves are gone,
But I still love you.

Joe Dunn

Mother and Son Eighteen Years Today

God, I never really did
know just how to raise a kid
I mean, I thought I should
and hoped that I could and, of course,
I knew I would
Fourteen years old and so alone
My mother tried to build a home
With little to go on, alone she fought
to give us kids all that we got
Searching for love, the faces were many
Searching in vain, I found not any
Quite early in life came this bundle of joy
My very own, my baby boy
Here was the love I desperately sought
For hundreds, for millions, it can't be bought
He would love me and know me
like no one you see, and like no one
accept me unconditionally
Unfaltering he's loved me from that day on
and from that day on I love You My Son

Tena M. Wagner

He's Irish, He's American, He's Hank Locklin

A twinkle in his eyes,
Known from Dallas to Dublin for there's no doubt;
Especially in the land of his ancestors, could Ireland where he is popular as the shamrock.
To give you a better insight this country music artist was born in Northwest Florida.
As his popularity grew in the Fifties, he signed an exclusive recording contract with RCA Victor, with Chet Atkins Producer.
I see it only fit to mention that he was country music's performer of the year in 1960, the same year he joined the world famous "Grand Ole Opry."
Singing a tribute to country greats, with his rendition of the "Country Hall of Fame" just one of his many hits.
As his beautiful Irish tenor voice became his trademark far and wide,
I feel certain the next time you hear the classic standards, "Send Me the Pillow You Dream on", or "Please Help Me I'm Falling"
You will be inclined to say that's the Mayor of McLellan, Hank Locklin.
For he's "Flying South" to Dixie, & what a "Happy Journey" it has been

Stuart Pooley

Without You

The days have no ending,
Lasting into an eternity without you.
The thread that binds my heart to you
Has stretched taut- and soon will snap,
Leaving an aching wound that once was my heart.
The sun burns blindly;
Once I thought it so gay and bright.
Now, I long for the shelter of night
To cloak my heart in its comforting mask of darkness,
Away from the sun's mocking rays.
You're gone. My mind tells me,
But my arms reach out to bring you close;
My fingers, grasping for the warmth of your hand,
Encounter only the cold emptiness of air;
And my heart cries out to you
- Silence is the only answer.

Nancy Foord

A Meaning of Friendship

How can words ever explain our friendship? Our every cry, our every laugh, and our every whisper? We've been through all the good and all the bad times, and yet, we're still here.
How can words explain everything we've ever shared? Our every word,
our every thought, and every feeling? Fate brought us together and time brought us closer, and yet, we talk about tomorrow.
Friendship, not a word to explain, but a word that is felt.
A word sometimes misunderstood, or taken for granted,
but yet, there are those who manage to keep it straight.
If anything else was included, wouldn't it be called Love?
It's a love of two friends as good as you and me, and nothing can ever make it change.
A feeling which is never forgotten, because those who touch and enter you heart, never leave. I'm glad you were one to stop and learn, to stop and understand, to stop and care; because
all I can say is that I love you.
Just always remember and never forget, because your best friend never will.

Lizbeth Duncan

Once I Loved

My boundless love for thee -
Leaves me in breathless wonder.
Its vastness liken unto the sea;
Its mystery as intriguing as the darken paths of yonder.
Warm, like a hot summer wind;
Caressing my soul and filling my heart with a burning glow.

I stand captive by this love until the end.
A sweet surrender,
Worked by your magic, gentle and slow.
Whence remembered in my golden years,
Whether or not thou be with me in your physical being,
Shall, I am sure, never fail to bring a tear;
And, fill my heart with inner singing.

Jann B. Nelson

To my Husband

Happy anniversary to you my dear,
Just think, we have reached our fiftieth year.
Remember the day when we were spliced,
The weather was freezing and everywhere iced.
When I arrived at the church and they opened the door
All I could see were soldiers galore.
When I walked down the aisle and saw my Frank,
I knew he was my one and only yank.
Once again love best wishes from me,
Wishing this was just our first anniversary

Kathleen Bassillo

Yonder Calls

Heaven is calling and he'll soon go.
Leaving behind loved ones below.
But he'll be happier in that far off place.
In that distant horizon beyond our space.
He will rejoin his family that have gone before.
Where he'll catch up on the news and be given a tour.
Here he will be free from worry and stress.
And be able to receive a much needed rest.
Although in distance he will be far.
Just look in the sky for the brightest star.
That will be him, shinning his light.
To guide those that follow in the dark of night.
He will go willingly as he mounts the stairs.
For he knows God has his reasons for calling him there.

Shelby Jean Aldridge

Grandmother

Soft bare feet walking to work on the abandoned tracks.
Leaving early to pick wild berries on the way,
Moving slowly past dirty, old factories that
promised jobs and left behind lives and smoke stacks.
She whispers "In its day."
This lonely lady of wisdom, grey hair, and love
For others, wonders like an ancient priest past
shanties and shacks.
In the cool morning, when the stars still shine,
she tells good stories full of sweet sadness,
and serious things. She quietly had a lot to say.
was I listening?
Sitting in the shade of the monument trees,
This single rose cannot convey the love of
80 years. I drop to my knees and merge
with living memories of this silver haired
lover of dogs, gardens, children and of me.

Rick Payne

The Journey

Come and go this sailing ship with me
let the winds carry the sails on high
the breeze will blow and set us free
to chase the sun across the sky

Capture the moonbeams in your smile
and hold them for all of time
and answer from the heart all the while
to follow life in life's rhyme

the time is near for our depart
we must ready the ship for rugged seas
and sail on with moon-lit heart
on this sailing ship of you and me

For life is a journey of ups and downs
like the waves of the seas we sail
so listen close for the warning sounds
of the sirens beckoning wail

Let the winds take sails and golden hair
and lift them from bow and brow
to find a life that's free from care
and make tomorrow now...

Rodney T. Bruce

Untitled

A precious little angel
  lies sleeping in my arms.
Her tiny hands and tiny feet,
  her tiny smile that charms
remind me of another child
  not very long ago
who rested in my arms this way.
  Why do they have to grow?
Time seems to have slipped by unnoticed
  while he grew so very tall
and the baby I once held this way
  is not a baby at all.
What I would give to keep them young,
  to hold them close to me,
would seem so little in compare
  to what my joy would be.
So sleep now, little angel,
  and dream your baby dreams
for soon you'll grow and then you'll go
  to dream of bigger things.

Karen A. Golden

I Should Have Surely Died

Why did I live to meet you, only that I may cry every day of my life?
You took my heart and then you had to part, Oh why did I not die
without you?
I am empty I want to tell you simply, why I could not admit it
until you said good-bye.
I will always care and always be there, just think of me and I
will start to cry, because you are a part of me and will not let me die.
I care so deeply I don't wonder why I would run away to meet you in
the night, help me make the journey say you'll meet me when I reach
you and tell me that you care.
Oh, for another day to come maybe if you come to we can love so
divinely until the end of time.
I care my dear no matter what people say I'll think of you every
single day.
so now I will say till we part at our graves, my love I pray is not
in vain. So truly hear me say I do divinely want you to be mine
until the end of time.

Lee Ann Coody

Retirement

"It's a great life if you don't weaken."
"Life is for the hale and hearty."

Retirement...
It's a blast if you have the dough!

In order to have the dough,
you have had to go and go (before...Retirement!)

Retirement's great if you're hale and hearty.
How many of us are?

Our minds begin to go-
our bodies too!

Retirement! - It's a great life
If you don't weaken - Somehow!

Mind or body, it doesn't matter much where!
You can begin to go in either direction, but...

If you don't...
It's a great life!

Retirement!!

Nancy Karns

"I Had A Dream"

Almost everyone has their dreams, going through life, searching it seems, to achieve them.

I too had my dreams, always trying to make them, come true, sometimes thinking, do I have what it takes?

Where would I turn, how could I do it, alone?

Could I write a poem, for each of those I love, send it to a contest, and have it chosen and be published? Some dream

So I pulled myself up by the boot straps, sent in my first poem. It was chosen, by the editor, for an award, also to be published. This happened five times, what a feeling! Of happiness, and pride. For me success! For friends a pride, in a friend, for family a pride in mom.

We can all reach our dreams, no matter what they are don't give up on them. Keep reaching and you'll succeed.
A goal for yourself, and a reason to go on, living, making your mark in this world, and leaving a memory for those left behind, maybe giving them a desire to reach their dream.
As I have reached mine.

Margaret A. Brewster

Girl Friend

Time's are hard and it's difficult to see
life will get better if you just proceed.
Feeling alone like no one cares you'll
say to yourself this isn't fair.
A momma of three, yes we see
you are alone raising his seed.
Tears flowing from your eye's feeling
like you can't provide, girl friend!
Give yourself time.
Look up in the sky open you heart and mine pray
to our heavenly father, he'll show you sign's.
He's the only one greater then men in the world,
when feeling like you just can't go any longer
get down on your knees and give him yourself.
Burden's will be lifted just you wait and see
cause our heavenly father doesn't live selfishly.

Marilyn Suratt

The Storm's End

As the storm comes to its end,
light begins to comfort all
That has been scared and threatened.
The fierce black rumbling clouds
Give away to hope filled , piercing rays of tomorrow.
For at the end of the storm,
There is a new day, a new beginning.

This new day holds wonders and joys.
For life is the wonder of all.
The wonder of love and laughter,
The joy of romance and togetherness.

But, in each new day
Life begins again. And this, is specially true
At the storm's end

So, after today my love,
Our storm will see its end
And our life together
Will embark again.

This will be especially true
After this storm's final End.

Wes Sprinkel

A Perfect World...

We strip ourselves of our body and skeleton
Lightning bolts flare from our heads
Floating upon cotton clouds we come
together, we are one.
With violet flames roaring we fly
around the world
Bringing joy, happiness, love, and positive
energy to all who are awake
Knocking on unconscious minds we
alert those yearning to be free
Our triangle of light brightens and
opens up to new fireflies
experimenting with their true inner self
One day the Earth will be no more
and spirits will peacefully roam
throughout the wide open universe
Leaping over planets and dancing
with stars, this place is ours to experience
We must live life to it's fullest and
realize what we hold within.

Nicole Smith

Evil

Evil strikes its victims
Like a blow in the head
Leaving me hurt and agonizing
On a raging cold floor.

The pain, the sorrow of evil,
As it lurks my sole
Turning me on to insanity
and I patiently wait for it to disappear.

It turns into eternity
A burning sensation,
Anger, that won't fade away
Anger, that grows stronger each second

I wait, but it won't leave
I fight, but it's too strong
I scream, but it's deaf

It isn't alone.
It's now around me,
Around what I one loved.

No one seems to notice,
No one seems to care, No one but me.

Mariana Negron

Death

Many times, death strikes fast,
like a boat opening its mast.
I too am one of the dead.
Here, my rotting carcass sits,
waiting, hoping, for someone to dig,
hit a box and open it.
They would probably find my body
Full of insects and dirt fighting to get out.
Death separates families
It gives no warning, but comes like
the grim reaper in the dead of night, and
leaves the silence of sadness upon loved ones.
Death robs us blind, sometimes it's
all in our mind.
Death strikes us all, but
some of us don't grasp and usually fall.
My accomplishments would become a
disaster if death struck me.

Ugochi L. Anaebere

"Ice"

The favored pen glides
like a skate on blue ice
making perfect figure eights
with blades dipped in the ink of vice
'til the marks became marred
in droplets of frozen blood
Smeared by poor judgement
blotched by bad timing
the once clean page
becomes a patchwork of flat destiny
the once pristine ice
a jigsaw of diminished reason
the once well place thought traced and sought
Lost in the endless turns
of the pen, the blade
and as always...
no returns are made.

Nola Chapman

Invitation

Crawling across the summer night
Like a soldier low and sneaky on
His marshy field of battle,
The falling rays of dusky sky
Kiss my forehead and
Lift me
Out of time.
Home at last, I see myself
Differently
Brighter
Alone.
But it is the sweetness of the blue grass
Bowing to the stars,
And the kiss of yesterday's zephyr
On my tear-stained cheek
That squeeze my innocent, misplaced heart and
Force the emission of a lone
Melodious
Contended
Sigh.

Lorelei Bonet

Where Did It Go

Where did it go it started when I was young
Like a song of nature it faded soon after it begun
It seemed so short though can be proved to be long
I don't understand it do I really belong
I saw it grow longer as each day waved goodbye
How long will it last I don't know...but why
It soon reached a climax of a well known hill
Hoping to remain there hoping to stay still
But it had to move on no way to stop
Able to look back and over the top
But it had to progress until it reached this very spot
Where will it lead me where will it stop?
I don't know when it'll stop I know it's gotten slow
But these questions are what make it great,
Where did it Go?

S. Laframboise

Untitled

My life fell apart
like a well-weathered rose
Lost its color steadily
as it's roots were ripped from the
unstable grounds
Then each petal was carried a separate direction
by the ruthless hands of the wind
I tried to grasp what was left of the
mutilated rose
and now my hands bleed
from the eager thorns of destruction

This is why I hesitate
to save what is now remaining
For I fear I will hurt again...

Cristin N. Jones

Dreamy Masterpiece

Cool water glistens on mossy rocks
like diamonds sparkling on green velvet.
Fish swim lazily past my dangling toes
as they did the wriggling worms on yesterdays hook.
The buttercup yellow sun warms me
while I sit...and dream.
I smile to myself
and imagine God painting.
His sunbeam brush dances lightly
across the canvas universe.
I lean back absorbing the finished masterpiece.
Its pastels and vivid colors come alive
where I lie, dreaming and enjoying.

Valorie Thies

Untitled

-Behold, our king on his throne!
Like pillars of fire
are his eyes. Nostrils flared,
His white steed stands: Alert, abreast, ready!
The enemy surrounds the beloved city!
Yes, the jewel of the crown.
Arise, mighty one, with
The sound of a trumpet blast!
-Behold, our king upon his white stallion,
Fast, cloaked with
The armies of his vengeance!
And he himself treads the fierceness
Of his wrath through the valley of decision.
-Behold the glory of our City,
And taste the yoke of peace!
-Behold our kingship and head!
Daylight has spilled over darkness
and freedom has subjugated bondage
Forever more!

Thomas Lee Miller

A Mother's Love

A mother's love is rare you see
like a precious jewel or a pearl sea deep.
A kind of love that's one of a kind so pure,
so sweet and so divine.
A mom's a gift from GOD!! above.
As I grew older I learned to respect her love.
My mom means the world to me.
I'm apart of her and she's a part of me.
My mom's a gift I'll never exchange for wealth
nor for money nor for fortune, nor fame.
But even if we are to part (by death)
She'll always forever!!! be in my heart.

Vickie Dennis

Derrida In Winter

Signifiers significands disconnecting
like promiscuous partners slipping away
coupling uncoupling finding stray beds.

A revolution in language theory has taken
hostage the thing.

Life without things? To what will we refer?
Can speech ever be of things, like it used to be?
About that crack in the pane of the
bedroom window that so annoys you
and that I still have not tried to fix
and from where we watch
the blue icicles gargoyle-shaped
shimmer in the morning sun.
No.
All we speak of, can ever speak of is language.

But in speaking of language we are evicted, thrown out
into the shattering and silent evaporating world of things.

Joseph H. Holt

The Blue And The Gray

At dawn by the sea, gray meets blue.
Like the uniforms of soldiers, fallen, along with enemies.
The wind carries, the sound of wailing gulls.
They circle, white wings beating the air over the slain.
Crying of the battle, by the sea.

The world of reality.
Or is it a dream?
Our dreams are of mermaids, and crystal palaces.
Nonsense words, with no other place.

Gray and hazy is our future.
A dreary road, stretching to the skyline.
So the white gulls shriek, with rejoicing or with fear?

A gray haired woman, sits in a rocker,
Gazing out a window at a gray sky.
She bares the weight, of many seasons upon her frail shoulders.
Her man never came home.
War was a curse.
Many tears have fallen from her blue eyes,
But no more can come.
Life is gray.

Kristin Seim

Metamorphosis

Love came into my life, my lonely life,
like quicksilver in my veins.
And illumined my life, my lonely life,
like lightning on the plains!

Like the moon draws the tide away from the shore,
God's love attracted my soul.
Upward and outward his heavenly love
drew me toward my goal.

It was this I was made for, this that I prayed for,
the spark that made me immortal.
Love was the catalyst, love the propellant
that lifted me through the portal

Into the light, the lovely light
of the Author of all that is known,
To dwell in His love forever above
in my infinite heavenly home!

Marian Umscheid

Father

As I look at the picture's we once
Knew, I think of the past we once
Shared. Days that were spent on
Birthdays and Holidays. We all loved
Each other, why did you have to leave?
We all loved you not only as a father,
But as a friend. We shared days and
Years with each other, but now that
Your not here with us, we feel not wanted
Since you left we all had fallen apart.
Were not close like we were when you
Were here. If there was a wish
That I can ask, is for you to come
Back and not ever leave

Maria T. Guzman

Beaten Down (Survivors)

We smile, and grin, and try to be polite.
In their eyes we are always wrong, we are never right.
They divided us to conquer, and stole our native tongue.
They fill our neighborhoods with dope, and automatic guns.
And we are beaten down, we are beaten down.

They try to steal away our dreams, as we sleep at night.
So be prepared to catch all hell unless you're lily-white.
But now the time has come, when we must take a stand.
And show those hooded sheets who is the better man.
And we are beaten down, we are beaten down.

You brought us here to pick your cotton, and wipe your children's nose.
We are kings and queens from the dark continent, who sat on mighty thrones.
You have robbed us of our diamonds, raped our women, committed genocide.
You strung us up from trees, and tried to strip away our pride.
And we are beaten down, we are beaten down.

We are strong black people, who are a mystery to you.
Because you sit in awe, and think what else could we possibly do.
But you can't break our spirit, even, when you made us bow.
Because when Gabriel sound his mighty trumpet, you will feel God's
wrath come down.

Trayce Turner

Velcro War

Standing still against the pain
I start pushing towards this thing
Looking for something to keep it right
Armies dying it's a winless fight

Balance of power losing ground
Scales tipping, spiralling down
Cold hearted leaders with recipes for hate
We watch with anger as they choose our fate

Freedom now nothing more than a joke
Liberty and justice being choked
Where have all our hero's gone?
They have been stomped out or stepped on

Kennedy, Mandela, and King
Men who tried everything
But when faced with harsh reality
Forced to accept death or brutality

So always remember to push further
Because they can't kill every soldier

William Bumgarner

Life

Life can sometimes be like the weather; calm and beautiful, with love, joy and happiness; sometimes cold and stormy, with worries, problems and lost love.
As a child one lives at home with no worries and no cares. Everything is like a sunshiny spring day, warm, calm, not a cloud in the sky.
As you get older and eventually find yourself alone, the weather seems to get worse. Loneliness, financial difficulties and personal problems seem to be the beginning of a large storm, dark, cloudy and depressing.
If you are lucky, you may find love and suddenly everything seems to clear up again. The sun is back, the clouds are gone and you are alone no more.
However, this could only be the eye of the hurricane, the calm before the worse part of the storm. Then it hits, like a bolt of lightning! The one you love is gone and you are alone once again.
Eventually it will pass, but it will take time before the sun shines again. Others will tell you, "that is life, and it is rough sometimes" and that is true. I can understand the good times and the bad. But I can't understand why the storm has to last so long and hurt so much?

William Mueller, Jr.

To You Mom

Yes, I know we've had many fights, you've taken away some of my rights.
I always get mad at you, I'm a teen what else am I supposed to do?
At times I've been really scared,
but you were the one who was there that cared.
Yes, there are people who had
worst times than us, but we had to really fuss.
You have to play two separate parts,
you have to care for two different hearts.
You've tried to teach me wrong from right,
you tried to show me the brightest light.
but knowing me I didn't listen,
I walked right away from the glisten.
You told me all the things you've done,
so I wouldn't try them and have no fun. It's hard in this world at this age, you should just lock me up in a cage.
You've held me in your arms, just so one did no harm.
You've sat there and said "you're making your own bed."
I said "Yea, whatever" the truth is you were so clever.
I know having me is a pain, I know I sometimes make you insane.
We've been through a lot together Mom, thanks. I love you Mom.

Shalene Brown

A Love That Will Never Be

Every time I talk with you, I learn more and more,
I am longing for the day when there will be more in store.
You seem to look at the bright side of things,
Instead of dwelling on the negative, that a divorce can bring.
I believe you will become a special friend and maybe a friend is all.
Primarily because you are a married man and for that I can not fall.
Although your divorce is pending and you say the divorce will be,
Given all the years you spent with her it may be harder for you to see
That your love is everlasting but I hope that you will remember me.
Every time you look around, I hope you think of me,
I am longing for the day, when you will be free.
Look to God for all your answers and your choices will be clear.
With God as your source of understanding, there will be no need for fear.
I will pray that your life, will be full of love, instead of lots of pain.
As long as you have God on your side, you have something special to gain.
I will like to get to know you better, primarily because you are so nice.
Although, you have made it quite clear, that you would like a lady in
The church of Christ for a wife.
Given all that information, I pray that she will be,
All that you really hope for and an everlasting life you two will see.

Linda Ann Jarvis Davillier

Recognize Me

So late at night
I get long phone calls
By some great guys
Guys who would never
hurt their women
And to me I think
They are the best guys in the world
for that.
They deserve the best.
I just wish they would recognize me.

I'm here -
Holding out my hands to you
You guys who are so sweet
And sensitive
So sensitive that
I can't even believe it.
They are just the kind of guys
The kind I have always been waiting for.

All they have to do next is
Recognize me.

Carrie Graham

When I Was Born

When I was born,
I had lots of hair.
Then it all fell out,
Gee that wasn't fair!

When I was one,
At the beach I found a feather.
My Mom thought it was cute,
Because my name is Heather!

I had a Care Bear Cake,
When I turned three.
That was real neat,
Happy Birthday to me!

My Mom had Andrea,
When I was eleven.
The minute I saw her,
I knew she was from Heaven!

Heather Grudis

Save Some Time For Me

I have no time to read
I have no time to write
I have no time to be

Up at eight
Now don't be late
There is no time for me

I have no time to clean
I have no time to sew

Home at five
Barely alive
I have no time for me

Once more
Back to the store
There is not time for me

The kids are grown
No ringing phone

I need some priority
Maybe write poetry

Save some time for me
Special time to be.

Cathy G. Schultz

I Found A Friend

I think I found a friend-she seems so very kind.
Is this only a passing trend? Until she learns of my true mind?

She has such a pretty smile-she seems to like me.
At least for a little while-until at last she will see.

What if I said what I really thought? Opened my heart like a book to be read.
This friendship I so desire would be nought-I so want to share but can't help the dread.

My whole life fell apart when I was nine-what will she say? How will she react?
The decision to have sex was no longer mine-the look of compassion her face did not lack.

My words were out, no longer hidden-oh, the joy to feel the release in my heart!
Like a wild horse having been ridden-can this hope of friendship really start?

She didn't just seem to understand-her own personal story was so familiar to me.
After feeling as an alien from another land-no longer just I, now I could say "We".

She told me of her abusive life-how lowly she felt for not taking her stand.
We both shared our stories of mutual strife-how comforting, that
together our lives could land.

I know now I've found a friend-she truly is so very kind.
This is no mere passing trend-she knows and understands my true mind.

Linda Euless

Reality

The evening breeze was wistfully gracing our bodies as we were lying
in a field,
The grass felt as that of a soft bed,
Lying there — just the two of us, feeling completely as one, with our
hands interlocked together.
The clouds appeared as though they were mirages of cotton filtering
out the last rays of sun for the evening,
Looking up toward the light blue sky—just resting there - alone,
Knowing each other, thinking as one, and feeling the same with one
another.
All at once a cloud burst!
Rain was falling heavily upon us.
As I reached up to wipe away the water, I found that the water
was tears on my face,
It was only a beautiful dream.

Valana L. Friedrich

I Wonder....

I wonder if you think of me when it's quiet and you're all alone.
I wonder if you remember my phone number, when you look at the phone.
I wonder when you're phone rings, do you anticipate it being me on the
other end.
I wonder if you remember the smile's I gave so freely.
Or all our little talks when the light's were turned down dim.
I wonder if you stop to think of me every now and then, and wonder how
I'm doing or how I've been.

I wonder if you hurt inside when you hear our love song.
I wonder if you yearn for me when you see other couples strolling by.
I often wonder if the memories keep you awake at night, and sometimes
if you wish we never met that night.
I wonder, and I wonder till my mind goes numb.
But most of all, I wonder if you wonder, what I wonder about.

Olga Ilievski

An Ode to Friendship

Friendship Cemetery is a giant obituary of time that used to be.
Overlooking the Tombigbee she's a quaint commentary of what's destine for you and me.

Three links by design, she's one of a kind, sharing Friendship, Faith, and Love.
Given birth by Odd Fellows her history but bellows of time fleeting fast as a dove.

Four ladies they say, came together one day to remember the Blue and the Gray.
From this humble beginning one nation began mending its heart on Memorial Day.

To the great and the small Friendship says to all "here lies your final resting place."
So friend it won't matter what records you shatter, what counts is God's saving grace.

Sherrill Bennett

Many Loves

I shall learn someday
I have not searched in vain.
Love comes to me but once, I feel -
But who am I to say?
These mountain roads I love to see-
A touch of flaming red - a tree -
And all around wild flowers - blue -
My heart they surely hold 'tis true
Many loves in many places
I search for peace to be
Within my heart - contentment - yes
A tree, a flower, or thee?

Bonnie Fester

The Catering Truck
Is At The West Door

Hark!
I hear the pattering
of the catering
Wagon
Dragin'
To a haltering
On the asphaltering
Immediately to the west
Of all the rest - - - of us.

Donald Buffenbarger

Whispers

At night when I lay in bed
I hear them, gently lulling me off
to sleep, sounds coming from
nowhere, but somewhere.
In my head, they dwell,
until my cat heard them, too.
Listening, hearing, yet not knowing
who, or what they're saying, but
understanding, pitying.
Trapped! The whispers are trapped
in my mind and house forever,
Never leaving never knowing
What happened and why they're
here, just content that I alone
can hear, who can find the whispers,
and hear what they say...

Amanda Boyes

My Window

When I look out my window
I imagine a world with gladness.
But when I open wide my window
In reality I find sadness.

When I venture out of doors
Into a land filled with sun
I see that truly, the rain still pours;
The damage has been done.

When our souls confess gratefulness,
When our hearts are bright,
Can we reverse this darkness?
If we concentrate on the light.

Erika Marie Leolyn Dahlin

Untitled

Someday,
I know,
I will find a place.
A place full of truth,
happiness,
and
love.
Where everyone is accepted
And no one rejected.
United
Everything will be real.
This is my dream place,
for now I am lost,
a lonely soul
in the "real" world.
Lost in my emptiness
without truth,
where no one can be trusted.
Alone

Cynthia Law

Marijke

Marijke.
I long to be with you
As the morning dew cascades
Over each budding blossom.

You and I in a union
Everlasting.

Marijke.
The hazy summer days
Cast us into a dreamlike state
From which we wish never to awaken.

You and I
In perfect harmony
For an eternity.

Marijke.
Time passes us by
Yet we stand still in time.
Your figure silhouetted in a red, fiery sunset.
Warm. Glowing. Vibrant.

You And I
Together forever.

Byron C. Mason

Ocean and Beaches

I love my bare feet in the sand.
I love the salty taste of the air.
I love sunrises on the ocean.
I love sunsets on the beach.
I love the waves again my feet.
I love the sound of the,
Waves crashing and sea gulls singing.
I love to look out to the sea,
And see it was never ending.
Ocean and Beaches is good for,
The soul and peace of mind.

Belinda A. Linkous

Tall Man

How are you today
I must say
If it would rain
You'd know first
If you got taller you would burst
You should be at the circus
You should be at the fair
You could be a tree.
Or even a bear
Your are so tall
I must say!
See you tomorrow, O.K
Hey...
Where did you go?
I was talking to you!

Heather Bergfeld

We Will Never Part

We will never part
I promise you that.
You will always be with me.
My laughter will be your laughter
My joy will be your joy
My journey will be your journey
We will stand together forever.

Though you are gone
You will live within me,
See through me
Feel through me
Touch through me.
My soul is your soul.

Death will never part us.
My heart is your heart
My brain is your brain
My being is your being.
So long as I am alive
You too will live.
We will never, never part ...

Cecile H. Pichel

Darkness

As I look into the rain,
I remember all the pain.
As the gun powder blows,
I shudder softly at my window.
As I sit in my wheelchair,
I can still hear the bullet
whizzing through the air.
I always get a chill, when I hear
people gang bang for a
thrill.
I can see the play of kids,
And I hear parents shout "Shut your
lids."
To think of all this hate,
No wonder children have bad fate.
If everyone would look at me,
Then maybe they would see.
Out of the darkness we must fly,
And into the clear blue sky.

Dawn O'Neil

Graduation

My dear, it is graduation.
I sent you my congratulations.

To you I have no gift to send,
So I'll be your lasting friend.

Won't you let me help you, too?
I'm a friend both tried and true.

We have a Friend who is above.
One we both cherish and love.

If to Him we provide sincere,
We never need to worry or fear.

Let our friendship ever be,
True, sincere and ever happy.

The separation may be out lot,
My dearest friend, forget-me-not.

Dorothy Garrity

Reflection Of Love

I love you as I watch the stars,
I love you while the sun does shine,
I love you as the earth turns around,
I shall love you always and forever,
I will never again love like this,
You alone have given me all I need,
We will share our love for one another,
We shall keep the love fires burning,
For you and I shall share eternity,
Together with each other because of love.

Gloria A. McDonald

Memories of Yesteryear

One dark and dreary evening
I was sitting home alone
There was nothing on the TV set
And no one on the phone.

So I curled up in my easy chair
And thought I'd take a nap.
With a shawl around my shoulders
And the good book in my lap.

I dreamed about the good old days
At home with mom and Dad
My brother and my sisters
And the good times we all had.

My Dad played the organ.
We all gathered 'round to sing
All the good old gospel songs
Oh! What joy that did bring.

One by one we left our nest
And entered the world to do our best.

Bee Paden

Passion

When I come in
I smell
your tirade
before I hear
your burlap-wrapped tongue
Lash Out
at me
the kids
the neighbors
your boss
your friends
my friends
the IRS
IRAN
then...
your tongue swathed in satin
slithers to my ear
and hisses...
I want you

Bev Lear

Alone in the Night

In the middle of the night,
I think of what you said,
You didn't love me,
Now I'm alone in my bed.

You left me for another,
Said I couldn't provide,
You didn't understand,
Now I'm dying inside.

You could have heard,
All I had to say,
You didn't listen,
Now you've gone away.

I really loved you,
You wouldn't believe,
I wanted you to stay,
You had to leave.

Now you're with him,
You've forgotten me,
I must go on,
To learn to be free.

John R. DeFina

Love N' Time

Time was fleeting with love.
I took time out to care,
with love to share.
I touched time with soft
words. I caressed time with
beautiful thoughts. Time was
still....Holding those lovely
moments.

A. Eugene Massagee

Untitled

We cannot possibly
appreciate what we hold
dear until we can no
longer hold it...
And not until then
car we fathom the pain
and grief of
having to let it go.

Kara L. Ellis

The Truth Is In Our Eyes

Alone at night
I walk the empty streets
The strangers
They ignore me.
Am I inhuman?
Is my soiled skin contagious?
No.
No pity or sympathy
Freedom
From this hell we live in!
Come close
Pay Attention
The truth is in our eyes.

Inge-Lisa Harris

Steeped in Senescence

My love, I barely see your form
I want to kiss your thigh,
To touch you where I know it's warm,
and then I wonder why...

Remember dear, when you could hear
it wasn't long ago,
I used to whisper in your ear
and feel your passion grow..

My senses are fading
but I'm still charading,
There is this urgent warning...

Your lips don't taste the same
yet we can "play the game"
It's like a new day dawning...

But if by chance I fall asleep
will you love me in the morning?

Bernard Criscuolo

You'll Always Be First In My Heart

Wherever you go
I want you to know
You'll always be first in my heart

Tho somebody new
May be loving too
You'll always be first in my heart

Tho I choose someone else
To help me forget
You'll always be first in my heart

Even though I said goodbye
For until I shall die
You'll always be first in my heart

Bonnie Ann Espsoito

May

There I was in the month of May,
I was on the bay,
I felt so gay,
I felt like the bay was
the right way,
I couldn't believe I felt
So gay all in one day.
There I was on the bay on one day
in the month of May.

Alexa Wolford

Between You and I

Between you and I there is nothing
I wish love is there but is not
I look in your eyes, lust your warmth
I wish to have what I have not

I see your expression and wish
Your eyes will lock mine and you'll see
That I am the one that you want
And all that you'll look for is me

Still in fear to admit you're my heart
That the hurt will seduce me to cry
Many times I have been there before
And there will not be you and I

Dawn Pagliaro

I've Got Jitters

I've got jitters and I'm all alone.
I woke up trembling and heard my groan.
My skin is damp. I'm cold to the bone.

Friends all laugh but they do not care,
It's only a mask to hide their fear.
Most of us laugh when others are near.

Oh! dear God, have you forgotten me?
I've got the jitters - can't you see?
Without you, where will I be?

I'm depressed. I feel low.
I can't take another blow.
Oh Lord, where did you go?

I've got jitters. Is there hope for me?
Some say with faith a light I'll see.
There is a flicker. Is that the key?

Irene Volkman

Country Living

Wouldn't it be nice,
If each city kid —
Could spend a week in the country,
To enjoy what we did?

To see nature at work,
The leaves sprouting from trees —
And maybe help,
With planting the peas.

Watch the corn grow,
And the hay fields, too —
And perhaps they will hear,
The cows when they moo.

Sure would be better,
Than some city streets —
When gun shots ring out,
Must give 'em the creeps.

Keep them all safe,
Stop the gang wars —
Take away all the pain,
Won't even need to lock doors.

Joyce P. Keeler

Would You Trade Your Heart for Mine

Would you trade your heart for mine
If I gave a lifetimes guarantee,
To take care of its every desire
And keep it close to me.
Would you trade your heart for mine
If I promise to protect it with my soul,
promising to keep the fire burning
and for it to never run out of coals.
Would you trade you heart for mine
If I promised you eternal love,
to give you all that I can give
even if it's not enough.
Would you trade your heart for mine
understanding the way I do.
Promising me your eternal love
the way I promised you.
Would you trade your heart for mine
If I said I would die for you,
if I promise to cherish, and promise to hold
....Can't you see my love is true?

Chad Sangster

Don't . . . If

Don't tell me that you love me
If it will only be a lie.
Don't tell me hello
If it just leads to good-bye.
Don't make me promises
If you don't want them to keep.
Don't say it's forever
If you'll be gone next week.
Don't tell me you'll be there
If you won't show up.
Don't kiss me more than once
If you want me to forget.
Don't take my heart
If it's not what you want.
Don't leave me alone
If you want me to stay.
Don't misunderstand what I'm trying to say
If you truly love me, you won't go away.

Andria Houston

Prayers

Do prayers always reach you,
if you are away,
do I have to talk real loud,
or kneel on my knees and pray,
can I seal it in a cloud,
and send it up to say,
what I have on my mind,
or should I send it another way,
can I ship it by boat,
sailing on the sea,
giving you a message,
especially from me,
Possibly by plane,
maybe car, truck, or train,
any way to send my message,
to release my pain,
may I send you it by rocket, if it is OK
I hope you'll keep it,
close to you,
in your heart to stay.

Amanda Wood

Positron

Hunt for me in the particle accelerator
I'll be with the other electrons
Whirling about the magnets
And thinking of you

Stalk my sighs in the cloud chamber
I'll be waiting at the speed of light
For you to howl my name
Until the moon crumbles like a mummy

Take me when I'm sleeping
On a gamma ray
And dreaming of you
Dearest Positron

Collide with me
Kiss me
Annihilate me

John Abraytis

Imagination

Let's pretend I am a bird
I'll fly and fly so high;
To places I have never seen
And see God's beauty from the sky;
I'll spread my wings and soar away.
Although I am a creature small
I know God loves me best of all;
I say to all mankind,
Just for today be kind
Give thanks for all His blessings
How fortunate you are,
Give thanks I say.

Becky Chee

Invasions

Sometimes I'll see you
I'll glance at you then turn away
The reasons you see
Are basically the same
I guess because the past
Seems to invade my thoughts
Actions take control
I turn around to talk to you
As if to say "Lets talk"
Yet the words are never spoken
The memories never told of
The separation continues
We pass each other
We say nothing.

Joyann Dunkelberger

Untitled

You are miles away from me now,
I'm here and you are there.
Even though I don't know how,
I just know that you really care.
You give an answer for every letter,
Make me feel that I am above,
And there is no feeling better,
Than the one, that I have your love
With your love I'm never scared,
And you have always made me smile,
And every thought that we've shared
Brought us closer one more mile.

Galina Velikovich

The Real Me

No one knows the real me,
I'm just a person they can see.
Every one thinks they know the real me,
But no one can see the real me.
Every-one is so vain,
Can't you hear me crying in pain!
Please someone rescue me!
Some-one come and find the real me!
As tears stream freely down my face,
I start to panic, I can't keep up pace.
Someone crack my shiny veneer,
And take away this great fear.
someone please help me,
Help me find the real me.

Jennifer Kraus

Hurt

I hurt for someone so.
I'm willing for love.
I have lots of foes, but no love.
Some guys come and some guys
go, but no guy stays
for he is far away
and can not see me.
I hurt for someone so.
I have many foes, but no one for love.

Hiedi Dent

Pain

The pain
Immense
entangling
writhing
suffocating
smothering
The pain
Will it last?
Is there an end?
It is so close —
Cutting through the realms of my heart.
This anger, bitterness toward God
Oh why did he take him away?
Why? Oh why?
The pain
gnawing at me like a bear
Slowing down my every move.
Controlling my mind —
like a machine.

Carrie Garner

Secrets of Mistake

Hides behind a blanket of shame
In a dark shadow she dwells
Beckoned back into reality
But she does not leave her shelter
Fearing the humiliation
And frustration
Her screams of anguish
Are not heard
For she buries it deep inside
Mistake made once to often.

Brandi Long

The Rainbow

The rainbow was glowing,
The sky was showing
The river was flowing
As my love was growing.

Teresa Ciarlo

Too Bad

There he was, beer in hand,
In front of the all nite store.
There he was, like he was,
So many, many times before.

Guess because it was Christmas nite,
He captured my attention.
Alone in the snow, with no place to go,
Too bad this is true, not fiction.

No ordinary bum was he, you see,
He had a degree from Yale.
Once his future was big and bright,
But slowly it started to pale.

He really could've made a difference,
Instead, he had another beer.
What a waste, what a pity.
Life is precious. Do you hear?

Barbara Lengel

In Love with You

I've often been
in love with love
And when I did
soared like a dove
But now I know
in fact I'm sure
That not with love
am I in love
But with just you
forever more.

'Tis really true
I'm sure you know
I am in love
with none but you
But if you doubt
my feelings, dear
Do not forget
our days of cheer
I truly love
just only you.

Daisy I. Infante

"My Special Place to Play"

On a mountain top, far far away
In ole Kentucky.
Where I use to play.

Wild flowers blooming everywhere
I picked some daisies for my hair

A special place by a little pine tree
There's a place I longed to be

Where I lay my head to rest
That's a place I loved best

Look up at the blue sky above
Thank God for giving me all
these things to love

Carrie Payton Crump

Many An Hour

You can spend many an hour
In the garden with the flowers

Sitting in the shade of the tree
Caressed by the gentle breeze

Watching the fluffy clouds go by
And the birds flying in the sky

Oh what pleasant place to be
Oh so much there is to see

The wonder that from small seeds
Comes the flowers and the trees

With love the gardener does sow
Weeding and watering for it to grow

Now is the time to enjoy
for the patience now comes joy

Contemplating the magnificent power
You can spend many an hour.

Barbara G. Schinler

Untitled

A slash
in the picture
bright blades ripping
rocks and roofs
and sea and sky
torn asunder
shining silverpoint
whistling in sharply
and like thunder comes
in the Light.

Helen M. Waters

Tongue of Rage

Everybody has a right to do anything in this world of hate.
Every step you make in your journey of life, the closer you get.
Every corner you turn seems like a different world.
Drugs, poverty, violence, prejudice.
The smell of Death.
Broken dreams, fantasies that will never come true.
Faces littered with shattered hopes.
Someone is always worse off than you, spiritually, financially.
People sense emotion.
Even though you can't save the world.
Smile.

Jennifer Karstetter

Wee Wee Little Lady

I'm a wee wee little lady
In a wee wee little house
And I know that I am living
Like a wee wee little mouse

But when these trials are over
And the wars have all been won
I have a home in heaven because
I Love God's Son!!!

Estelene McDermitt

"The Gift"

There's a gift for you and me,
In which the taking is quite free.
If you'd ask what this gift might be,
It's a gift you need not see.
But instead, a gift in which you feel,
Deep inside, and oh so real.
This gift is one that can be shared,
One that need not be prepared.
No wrapping paper is required,
The uniqueness is spiritually inspired.
Will certainly never wear out,
Cannot be bought without a doubt.
Without anymore delay,
It's time to bow our heads and pray,
To receive the gift of eternal life,
Only found through Jesus Christ.
If you have just received this gift,
You're guaranteed to feel a lift.
Share this gift with everyone,
The will of God shall then be done.

Janet L. Hollenbaugh

Christmas Nostalgia

No more we search for Christmas trees
In woods at the old homestead
No more we gather holly leaves
With berries bright and red

We miss the sound of the rushing creek
The crunch of fallen leaves
And the scents of pine and cedar
The cool damp winter breeze

We miss the joy of exploring the woods
As we hunted that "perfect" tree
But you know, God had provided
And shared those woods with me

It was there that I first met Him
And felt His protective care
And this beauty He had created
Became mine to have and share

Although those years have long been gone
And I am no more a child
Yet God's love remains within my heart
And His presence is alive!

Ibera Garner

Natural Beauty

I took a walk alone today
In woods not very far away
And there before my very eyes
Beneath the almost cloudless skies
I saw the trees as never before
Green and swaying as in days of yore
When I was just a child so small
Never understanding it at all
What natural beauty we all share
But never seem to know its there
Like wild flowers, birds and bees
We never seem to notice these
So untouched by today's fast pace
Yet always there to take their place
Until one day we know their worth
The reason why they are on this earth
It's God's great gift to all mankind
To have and enjoy until the end of time!

Helen H. Carswell

Centipede

Creeping, crawling centipede,
Inching up the wall,
Do your many feet get tangled,
Ever causing you to fall?

A hundred feet are great for you,
But two for me are fine—
Tying shoes would take all day
If all those feet were mine!

Dianne K. Roark

Drowning

Huge gasping breaths
Inhalation smothered
Cold wet gushing
Streaming pouring
Filling my insides
Eyes round large
Horrified staring
Confusion solitary
Jaw straining
Ears pinching aching
Suffocation
Filling my insides

Dawn Piontek

Untitled

The whisper of all blowing trees
is all I hear.
The darkness of a summer storm
is no where near.

I'm all alone.
Or am I?

The gentle rustle of the leaves
is a close dear friend.
How quickly these autumn days
are coming to an end.

I'm not alone,
just peaceful.

Diane Snow

Summer Moon

The full moon at night
is chandler of lights
stars fill the skies
like flickering candlelight
the warm summer breezes
on those special romantic nights

She wearing her sheer dress
the chandler is behind her
her woman hood confess
the candlelight dart
dancing all around her
the goddess of the heart

The whispers of there voice
murmuring sweet romantic things
that makes her warm and moist
it makes his life feel right
to take her home and love her
on that very romantic night

James A. Rumbold

Water

Water! What is water?
Is it some thing that can destroy,
harm or even kill a living organism,
or is it something that is quiet,
peaceful, and keeps us alive.
I've thought long and hard about it
and I've come up with a conclusion.

"Water is what ever it wants to be"

Aileen Arens

"Left Alone"

I'm feeling an ache, and sorrow
is showing within my heart.
Until he left me alone in this world
I never thought we'd part.
We got the call of worry on a bright
and shiny day.
If I look he won't be there, but in
my soul he'll stay.
He watched me from his open world
I never really knew why.
now he's gone and I'm still here,
but he watches from the sky.
I was strong but now I'm weak.
My older cousin is what I now seek.
He's the best cousin there ever will be
He's up in the sky, he's an angel you see.

Haley Pool

A Mother

A mother is something to cherish
is someone to honor and never
forget

She is strong, pure, loving and
deserves all attention and respect.
A mother is best a friend, a
helping hand when in need a
person who encourages you and
helps you to succeed

A mother is a person who listens
when nobody else hears

She is a discipliner who also
holds you close and drives
away your fears.

She is a blessing that helps
you when sick and dries
all your tears.

Ajeenah Seifullah

My Locket Of Empty Dreams

My locket without your picture,
is the locket of empty dreams.
For inside my locket are memories
of a life that is not what is seems.
I think of you each day, my love,
as I pray to heaven above.
The beat of the sun continues its beams
on me and my locket of empty dreams.

Annette Albin

Where Does The Sky End?

Where does the sky end?
It ends in his eyes.
It started as friends.
And ended in lies.

Where does the sky end?
In the warmth of his hand
Oh, the warmth he did send.
As we played in the sand.

Where does the sky end?
In his gentle caress.
My heart cannot mend
He could only have guessed.

Where does the sky end?
In his heart made of gold.
His heart she did steal
As in stories of old.

Where does the sky end?
At the end of a rope
The same way that life ends...
Without a glimmer of hope.

Brandi Linne

"Memories"

There's a strange feeling inside me;
It feels like happiness
or fascination.
It reminds me of you
and of the times we shared together.
Sometimes I wonder if it will ever
disappear
and never return to me.
There's a strange feeling inside me
tearing up my soul.

Jana Bryan

Untitled

Look at the world around us,
It getting worse each day,
There's pollution, fighting and homeless,
And soon we'll all have to pay!

When the worlds to polluted to live in,
When nobody gets along,
That's when we'll end up paying,
Cause we have all done something wrong!

We have polluted ocean and seas,
We have polluted the air and the trees!

We have stuck people on the street,
With not a bite to eat!

We hear about new wars everyday,
And no matter what we think they're
not just going to go away!

These are all problems were facing,
In this awful world today,
And were all going to end up paying
If we don't do something right away!

Gimmi Fontenot

Untitled

The muck drips from my head
Into the pool of thought
Causing ripples on the surface
Disturbing the reflections
And the pool gets deeper

Eric W. Carroll

Life Is What?

My life is like a basket case,
It is always to closed,
Through teenage angst and saving grace,
It is tied up by a lace.
In it is one black rose,
Morbidity is which it stands,
I finally could see,
Through all this dying of agony,
I am free.

Cheryl A. Valdez

Untitled

Melquiades - my man.
It is carnival time
displacements
transmutations
permutations,
explorations-
inventions
disguises
illusions bells
pipes and kettledrums-
that lend credibility
to the idea
that carnivals are about
delusions-
when carnival time is a fun
time about
the real- real
as the earth
prepares for a visitation
from heaven and love.

Betty Geyer

Abortion Murders

Hello Mommy
it is dark in here,
but when I hear you laugh
I have no fear.
I hope all the world
is just like you,
gentle and loving
and tender too.
I can not wait
to touch your face,
for you to hold me
and keep me safe.
Mommy help me
what is going on,
why did they do this
are you now all alone?
Though it is done
I still feel the pain,
all I did was love her
and Mommy had me slain.

Audrey Hullette

Advent Wreath

Light one candle on Advent Eve,
Illumination for those who believe.
Light two candles, instead of one,
In loving honor of our Lord's son.
Light three candles, and then begin,
To pray for peace among all men.
As the fourth candle begins to glow,
So shines God's love, on the world below.

Gloria Rees-Hansen

It Torments Us

Death,
It is too real
Confusing us
With it's coming and goings
Leaving us frightened
And bereft of all courage.
It knows our fears
And touches us there,
Deeply
Sending us into a
Frenzy to hide
Within ourselves.
It torments us
With it's knowledge
And pierces through
Our skin slowly,
Entrancingly.

Adria Reinhart

My Inspiration

God is my Inspiration
It is unbelievable what He can do.
But when you are tired and weary
He is always there for you.

He furnishes all the wisdom
When decisions I have to make
He gives me the strength to walk
And I thank Him for each step I take.

Any talent that I might have
He gives to me for free
And when it comes to reading
He made my eyes to see.

He made my voice for speaking
or sing, if I choose to do
If I have any obstacles in the way
He is there to carry me through.

My body is the temple of God
and it is cleansed, without hesitation
But all the praise and glory goes to God
Because He is my Inspiration.

Estella Vineyard

Love

What a strange thing.
It makes you happy
in a painful way.
It gives you
all the joys you want,
yet,
it tears you apart
like nothing else can.
It is an energy
that we need
to survive and die!

Andrea Schilling

Winter

Gray twilight seeps
Through my eyes.
Days and nights are
Intertwined
And I desperately
Try to remember
When we made
Angels with our hands.

Katie Cook

"You'll Never See Night"

Yesterday a door opened.
It opened very wide.

The door called to me,
and told me to step
inside.

When I took a step
towards the door, it
closed tight.

In fact, it closed so
tight that it locked in
the night.

If this is true, will I
ever see night?

No night? That means
the sun will have the job
of always shining bright.

Colleen Magee

Deception Of The Heart

Deception is the devil's toy
It wraps our minds with lustfully joy
Selfish hearts are all the same
Stalking the desires
It wishes to tame
The hand says
It wishes to please
while ripping the heart
off its lover's sleeve
over and over
again and again
pure hearts
are filled with sin
Day after day
Time after time
The body loses control
to the twisted mind

Anna Standifer

My Life

Operations here and operations there,
It's a pretty good scare,
And no one can compare
It's just not fair,
Sometimes I think I just don't care,
But who, who am I kidding,
For it will always be unfair,
My goal is to model,
But what a laugh,
I know it wont come true,
But I won't know until I do,
I'm only fifteen years old,
And my legs are a fright,
Because their not a beautiful sight,
It's just not right,
I guess it could be worse,
For this is not the first,
This October I will be in a cast,
But I guess it will pass,
I just have to focus on the good and not the
bad.

Denise Marie Acosta

The Game

Love is nothing
it's all a big game;
The way we degrade it
is such a shame.

In and out
heated and fast;
Is this what it takes
to make love last?

It seems we've forgotten
all about dignity,
all we're concerned with
is loosing our virginity.

I feel sorry for
the player who plays,
because there's a new game now
and that game is AIDS

Amy Wasz

The River

The river is cold and wet,
it's dark and mysterious.
The river holds life, and to
a certain degree death.
The river can be calm but
it can also be rough, like life.
The river holds secrets to
many things and yet tells all.
I wish I were a river, free flowing
and care-free.
If only life were like a river, always
moving ahead never looking back.

Jennifer Lowe

Love

Some say love is blind,
It's not, it's just hard to find.
Many suffer from a broken heart,
You'll pick up the pieces, if you're smart
Love is great, don't get me wrong,
Although, not all love is like a song.
When you find the right one,
Don't lose that special someone.

Dannie Thudium

Wings

We've all seen the White House,
It's the symbol of our nation,
And, the reason it's still standing,
It was built on firm foundation.

A tree grows straight and tall,
As we enjoy it's fruits.
But, when the winter comes,
All that's left is trunk and roots.

We cross bridges when we get there,
And trust them without question,
Because they've never let us down,
They're rarely even mentioned.

A ship must have an anchor,
To keep it off the sand,
And you are living proof,
God needs a helping hand.

There is nothing quite as heavy,
As the burden love can bring.
But, if it's any consolation,
You've already earned your wings.

Jim Gorman

"My Beautiful Daughter"

At evening when the shadows fall
It's then I hear my darling call.
With words so soft, so sweet and light
Goodnight I love you goodnight
When the night is dark and still
Sweet memories bring my heart its thrill
Of days gone by when things were right
Goodnight I love you goodnight.
My work on earth is almost done
My face is toward my setting sun
Before my soul and body part
Goodnight, goodnight dear heart.
The last sweet sound I want to hear
The sweet, sweet voice upon my ear
As my spirit takes its flight
Goodnight, goodnight, goodnight.

Dorcie Warren

We Can

The fall air provides
just enough chill
To make warm arms
softly caressing you
Welcome comfort

The casual breeze
brushes the tips of your hair
As hands clasp and together
you stroll
Through the colorful leaves
quietly floating down
Becoming a beautiful blanket
for the naked earth

The blue sky with
fluffy whipped-cream clouds
Is the hope,
the freedom of growth
Endless, for each - alone
endless, for both - together

Joan McCaw Lincoln

A Brand New Start

I found a baby kitten,
Just the other day;
While sitting on the doorstep
passing time away.

It cried in sounds of hunger
I couldn't help but sigh;
With bones so sightly showing,
I couldn't help but cry.

I brought it in my kitchen-
prepared it milk and bread;
It purred and purred so mercifully,
while waiting to be fed.

No longer had a minute passed,
the little dish was dry;
It's tummy full of happiness-
meowing in reply.

I picked it up, and held it close,
much love had filled my heart;
To know that I had given such life-
a home, and "A Brand New Start"

Brenda Lichman

"Lonely"

All I want is time
just time with you
with no one to bother us
no one to tell us what to do
what ever it maybe
holding you.
just you and me
knowing your there
knowing your in my arms
and knowing you care
that dream will never die
for now I hold back
before I cry.

Glenn R. Texeira

Master of the House

His sure aim yesterday
killed the game birds
he watched fall to the ground
making him feel masterful,
in control.

Now, the master of his house,
he aims at the spirit
of an easy target
so close at hand.
She was trained from childhood
to take the assault.

He watches her spirit fall
like wounded prey
shot in the field.
Her smile will mask the familiar pain.

His calm returns
He's in control
feeling masterful.
For a while.

Joann Boote

Dear Ms. Or Mr.

Love
Kindness
Friendship
Care

For me it's hard to say.
But open this gift with no delay.
And you will see my love
Describes all of the above.

Ashley Christen

Forever My Love

Inside my heart of hearts,
knowing where friendship stops
and love starts.
Forever my love; that's
what you'll always be.
You can't begin to imagine,
how very much you mean to me.

Forever in our hearts, that's
where our secret must lie.
To always believe, that
this everlasting love,
will never,
ever die.

Amanda L. Ryba

There Is Always Tomorrow

If you store in your brain,
knowledge from strife:
Fire or flood,
can not change your life.
For from deep within,
all that you have gained:
Can be rebuilt,
when sorrow hast rained.
Waiting and wishing,
just slows one down:
Till there is no spirit,
in any sound.
Bent from life's burdens,
one must not stay.
Remember,
Tomorrow Is Another Day.

Doris Kasper Lobner

Untitled

In sackcloth gird yourselves
Lamentation, the nations blue
as a spring gushing forth
from a mountain crystal clear
Unto a waterfall, her eyes
Airy and light she cries happy tears
Awaken peoples, tongues, nations
with the armor of kings
Mount up unto the Son
Ask and you shall receive
Seek and you shall find
Bind on earth bound in heaven
Loosed on earth loosed in heaven
None shall bind as he binds
All I will, see as he sees
At the crossroads which way to go
One knows the way the truth the life
The first the last the beginning the end

Dale K. Wright

"Recycled"

Almighty God, You
lashed my soul,
like the rolling
thunderous sea.

I am helpless,
like mere 'driftwood',
tossed ashore for
all to see.

Sun beats down
upon my being—
hid among
sharp shells, 'debris'.
You have cleansed,
reclaimed, accepted
all I am...
or hope to be.

Ethel Brice

Dear Myself

Why do I keep
this secret to me
hidden so deep
under the tree
I sit there a lot
in the same spot
under the tree
to see my destiny

Megan Teminsky

I Want To Be Free

I want to be a flower child
Lay among the fields awhile
I want to feel peace everywhere,
I want to be free to dance.
I want to be an angel girl
Look down upon this messed up world
I want to fly against the wind,
I want to be free to soar.
I want to be a beautiful sunset
Something people just can't forget
I want to shine and glow sometimes,
but I want to be free to fade.
I want to be a dreamer's dream
flow across the sparkling sea
I want to be wonderful and true,
I want to be free to live.
I want to be a courageous heart
Keep some life from falling apart
I want to see things special and clear,
I want to be free to love.

Jessica Collins

"Going for the Goal"

In this life you should
Learn all you can,
You should endeavor to be
A success whether you're woman or man.

Never quit or pull out, because
You will have rough days,
Keep on climbing for your goal
As you journey through life's phase.

You must have courage to obtain
Your ambition,
And don't surrender until you've
Reached your mission.

Remember, your objective is not
Achieve unless you work hard,
And many pleasures of life
You must dis-regard.

When you've reached your goal
You'll feel blithe inside,
And the accomplishment you've
Earn will feel your heart with pride.

Earl Nash

Intermission

Wake up, sleepy - slumbering Earth.
Let me hear sounds of life returning,
Let me see signs of new arrivals.
Fill my heart with shameless yearning
To be life's blooming survival.

Wake up, sleepy slumbering Earth.
Calm the cutting winds that chill
and cause the infant boughs to break.
Let naked trees once more be filled
with robbins seeking a home to make.

Wake up, sleepy slumbering Earth;
For I long once more to see
the verdant splendor of God's Creation,
unfolding so majestically
His masterful plan in transformation.

Wake up, sleepy, slumbering Earth;
Let warm breezes of a welcome Spring
blow gently, bearing messages of love,
for without love, we have not anything.
Yet, we have everything from Him, above.

Eleanor Busby

Untitled

Give me a Tall ship
Let's hoist the main sail.
Pull up the anchor.
Slice through the waves.
Smell salty sea air.
Feel the windy breeze.
Hear Gulls on high.
See the billowy clouds.
Give me a Tall ship
With Hearty crew.
Working from down
too dusk.
Picking up the cargo,
at the other end of
the line.
Give me a Tall ship.
Where the journey never
ends.

Annette M. Reville

Let It Be

Now it's over
let's start again
No, no not again
Let it be

It's been a blast
don't look at the past
Now the time is new
let us renew
Let it be

Oh John how long has it been
remember the times
No, no not again
Let it be

How Paul, George, and Ringo wish
that they hadn't drank like fish
remember the times
No, no not again
Let it be

Clint Durham

"Dream Boutique"

A gypsy's votive candles
Light her scattered saints
Little plaster statues
Their skin are chips of paint

A shabby curtained window
Beckons forth ... a palm
Come and see the future
Within the sea is calm

A book of yellow pages
Her Bible old and fray
Sits upon an alter
With a chalice made of clay

Inside the incense simmers
Pungent with mystique
It's here we shop...God won't be mocked
Within the dream boutique

Anthony J. Cassarino

Miles Away

The wheels turn, horns blow,
Lights blare their neon noise.
Voices sing, children cry awake,
Radios blare, cans pop, paper rattles,
The miles away.

The endless roll of the road
Sweeps beneath the iron beast.
Sun's rays beat, winds howl,
Restless people squirm and bleat
The miles away.

Within this, my body moves,
As trees and mountains pass.
Valleys green and unknown towns
Unseeing and uncaring let us pass
The miles away.

Yet my heart has never moved
From you, or felt so full,
For inside my own I feel
Yours beat, and move, and love
The miles away.

Henry Benjamin Askey

Life

You grow from inside
like a flowers every glow,
and take what you can get
as the Earth's first snow.
In the middle you lean
like a tree often does,
and think your half done
when you've only just begun.
Now do what you want
and what when you can,
cause life's it-
that's all we have.

Angela Mattice

Old Age

All of us are on its "Hit List"
Like a wild animal stalking its prey;
Old age is creeping up on us,
Stealthily, day by day.

A wrinkle here....a gray hair there,
We are gradually losing our youth;
Sometimes, in spite of all we can do,
We may lose another tooth.

Someday, before we realize it,
We may be hobbling around with a cane
Trying to cope with being feeble,
In a body that is racked with pain.

So before old age catches up to us,
I think what we should do
Is enjoy life while we're able,
And share it with other folks, too.

'Cause when old age says, "Gotcha,"
You will discover it's too late then
To do lots of things you planned to do,
But couldn't decide just when.

Dorothy Slaughter

Snowsteps

Snow on the hillside
like dancing ghosts,
windy footprints.

The sun a cloud-covered
man, shifting through
with bent and burning rays.

But the snow doesn't know
enough to go away,
so all stays quiet, faint,

Bleeding through
a trickle of mountain water,
like dancing ghosts,
or my windy,
vanishing steps.

Gregory Ball

Ocean Song

Strive
like the Tide;
Always reaching,
Never ceasing,
Constantly pulled Back.
Reaching yet again,
So much farther than before,
Only to yield once more.
Never to defeat.
Though time may deride,
Still she must repeat - strive
like the Tide.

Angel Swartz

Our Leader Builds

Common people
Like you and me
Are builders for eternity
Each is given a bag of tools
Each is given a book of rules
No stumbling block
This Jesus Our Rock
You toil you pray
You're '94 today

You dream
You plan
You stretch forth your hands
Open doors with a will
So the weary may come
And with you go on home
For the mansion God planned
It's not built with our hand

Bessie S. Burkett

Listen to the Desert

What a peaceful place.
Listen to the wind
howling through the desert.
The animals coming out
to play on the sand.
The sand smoothing the rock.
At night see the shadows
dancing around in the sand.
Listen to howls of the coyotes
The crickets humming a merry tune.
Watch night turn into day.
What a peaceful place.

Dylan Barry

You

All alone in my room,
Listening to a saddened tune,
Knowing something's not right,

Knowing inside what should be said,
Thoughts of love dance in my head,
I wake up in the night,

As the tune comes to an end,
I stop and think what might have been,
But I don't know what to do,

Not feeling too sure about myself,
I see a picture on the shelf,
I stop and think of you.

Jonathan DiVito-Naas

A Friend

A friend is one who
Listens with her heart
As well as her ears
Has loyalty and love
Through all the years
Shares good and bad times
In sunshine and rain
Can join you in laughter
Shed tears for your pain
Has many precious memories
For all the past
Is secure in the knowledge
That friendship will last
It's a priceless gift
To receive or give
Between two people
For as long as they live.

Betty Pinson

Sunny Shores

Across the seas, over the water
Lives a Czar's beautiful daughter
Far beyond the horizons blue
She stands so pure and innocent too

Her face is hidden by a home remote
Only reached by way of boat
Surrounded by water, are sunny shores
She's all secluded by drugger's wars

To break away is her only hope
Gaining freedom from a prison of dope
At night she sits to cry and weep
Yearning for love as she falls asleep

The guns and crime all around her
Have set up the walls that surround her
Locked within the gates of hell
A perfect place for loneliness to dwell

Of all her wishes her father ignores
Is the desire to leave the sunny shores
Knowing her dreams could never be
She'll relinquish hope of ever being free

Delton Jessee

Love Sees No Color

Stabbing at your heart
Love is here it's there
Running away like a thief in the night
Knocking on everyone's door
Not knowing if your ready or not
Love is like a cloud covering all the hurt

Jamela Yacubu

I, Myself, And Me

I am only one person
Living as three
Loving, caring, and sharing
As I, myself and me.

Going about my daily duties
As time goes fleeting by
Though I have a loving family
It's just me, myself, and I.

Myself, that's who I am
And lets forget it not
For when this life is over
What else have I got?

So, me, myself, and I
Must be one in three.
As I said at the beginning
Its just I, myself, and me!

Corinne B. Hein

Hell for Hellen

Hellen.
Living Hellen.
Living Hellen the hard way.
Living Hellen.
Hellen. Hellen.
Living Hellen the hard way.

Hellen
I can make you see Hellen
Open up to me Hellen
Don't you know you're wrong
Hellen
Only good is strong

Hellen
Shut these voices
Out of your red, screaming mind
And you'll find,
Hellen, Hellen.
And then Hellen, you will find -
yourself. You'll.

Find. Hellen.

Byrd

Untitled

In peace loving times.
Man and Nature
communicated in harmony
with an exchange
of honor and respect,
neither one taking nor
borrowing without being
granted permission first.
Now man has ceased to
communicate or listen
not only with nature
but with his own kind as well,
thereby becoming void of
honor, respect and reason
and this ever so sadly
has all come to be,
because man has attempted
to uplift his own importance
above the Ultimate Unity of the Universe!

Brenda Kimball

My Love

It has never entered in my mind,
losing you is not a fear.

You have always been the love
of my life, my dear.

Your touch, smile and laughter
has grown in my heart.

From the day I met you,
till the day we married, I got smart.

We have been together for more than
seventeen long wonderful years.

Through thick and thin and lot's of
happiness, joy, sorrow and some tears.

Our life is special, with our 4 children,
and you always by my side.

Even when at 2 o'clock in the morning,
changing diapers or clothes washing with
tide.

We have a lot of memories of family
and friends through the years.

God willing I pray we have many more
memories
to make with our families and friends and
little dears.

Diane L. Provost

Untitled

How soon the flame of
love can die. How
soon "goodnight"
becomes "goodbye".
You're gone now and
life goes on but "all
the fun is gone".
Time can bring a
change of heart and
love can make another
start. Someday, you
may come back to me
but who can say "how
soon, how soon".

James H. Hanks

Departing Sorrow

To the war my friend must go,
loyalty to his country he will show.
He acted brave with head held high,
he never let us see him cry.
I know he's scared it's in his eyes,
to see those bombs up in the skies.
He tries to laugh without a care,
the thought of war he tries to bare.
The day had come for him to go,
departing sorrow we dare not show.
He stood so proud with bags in hand,
as his ship pulled from the land.
We raised our hand to say farewell,
to our friend who's scared as hell.
We'll think of him and all who's there,
and every night they'll hear our prayers.

Chrissandra Buchko

Untitled

Sing songs of wonder and
lust after meaning in the faces of J
deep inside the chilly steel cerebral
closet bursting with brass feeling.

The base nova super that was mom
dances in Jack London Square while
father Red's three jobs memorize the
slavic rhythms of her
holy spirits stolen by
noisy unknown earth matter.

Gregory R. Neidle

Fantasy Ride

Somewhere in the world, there is a
magic land,
Where everyone is close at heart, side
by side and hand in hand.
If you want to go there, wish with
all your might,
Just jump aboard the Fantasy ride
for a magical flight.
Everything you will see is a magic
sight,
Everything is perfect, morning, noon
and night.
You will get a wonderful feeling,
and won't ever want to leave,
But then you will awaken and realize
it was just a dream.

Chrisy Russell

Untitled

Hush little baby, go to sleep.
Mamma doesn't want to here a peep!
Worked all day and worked all night
Don't mean to give you such a fright.

Hush little baby, Daddy's here
Sleep my little darling, don't you fear.
The angels are watching all night long
And getting ready to sing their song.

In the morning we'll play all day
You can have it all your way
But for now little baby, go to sleep
Mamma wants to see you fast asleep.

Carmella Donato

The Enemy's Eye

Dream warrior acknowledge
me to be his serpent. Though he
did not speak of whim, but
rather I ignored the consequent
and the devastating loss.
Hush! said, the Grasshopper
Hush! said, the mosquito
though I was lost in so-called
dignity, that I was blinded
By my own luster.
The way he flew
The way he moved, was
essential to thy need.
though I became a victim of an
Ultimate ritual that abandon me.
Yet!!
inspired by my own dignity.

Inam-Ur Rehman

Hope

We hear the pain across the ages
Men and women in their cages
Children with their pitiful cries
Tears of hunger in their troubled eyes.

We know we are the cause of it all
Surround our hearts, a thick stone wall
Around the world this agony we share
War is killing, no one cares.

Another generation grows
Fear and hate are all it knows
Life to them is not a gift
Through the rubble they must sift.

We hope to see in our lifetime
No more hate, no more crime
Poverty and hunger will be at an end
The silver lining around the bend

Together if we work and pray
Maybe that joy will come one day
The day that suffering will cease
The day the world will be at peace!

Elena Kozlowski

"Love"

The thought you have of touching me
misses me entirely.
Inwardly I sigh and pretend
that nothing's wrong.

Nothing wrong with me,
nothing wrong with you, or us, or ...
Nothing wrong with ignoring lies
and turning away in pain.
Nothing wrong with furtive boredom
and glancing at your watch.

I try to be what you want,
and that's wrong - but - you
would never see that.
if only I could say to you:
"You don't love me because you can't."
and:
"I can't love you because you don't let me."

But we both prefer to lie;
there's nothing wrong with that.

Amy S. Whitaker

District Byzantine

Nicaea D.C.
mon amour!
Sunshine n'water,
music,
enigma waves,
in medieval chaos!
Sous l'arbre
Manuel Rontriquez,
Jeremiah Smith, Jr.,
et quelques autres;
scenic reality,
eternal aspects,
Byzantine mix!

Constantine A. Stratakis

Forever Longing

That this sorrow might depart,
My fingers grasp a loving heart,
Forgiveness be a comfortable
Old slipper.
Intimacy less appalling,
Idols refrain from falling,
Misfortune be as barren
As a desert.
Trust never forsaken,
Innocence awakened,
Consent become a choice
Not a given.
Bleak opposes future,
No wound in need of suture,
Obedience doesn't come
With a debt.

Felicia K. Napier

"The Eve of Tomorrow"

On the eve of tomorrow,
my life may be at end.
But I have seen life's purpose,
In the essence of thy hand.
If I were to borrow,
Another eve of tomorrow
I would hope my life to be
More in the harmony with thee!

Judy M. Walker

Breakfast

Dormant
My mind craves.
Solidness
To strengthen this slave.
Famished
I need some bread.
Destitute
For I have not read.
Meat
Not of this world.
Growth
Digesting Truths unfurled.

Christopher M. Hilliard

Tender Rose

Please don't touch me please,
My peddles will start to wilt,
Falling toward God's green earth,
There won't be anything left,
For if you leave me all alone,
I'll live forever never to be torn,
Just touch me once is all it takes
To end the love God had create.

Joy Madison

"Vision"

Who pierced the camels of our sun
left dromedary humps to wane,
weakened wanderers with mirages rampant
in the thirsting travelers brain;
Can hoof or nose or spitting mouth
tear the tearful rays from sky,
which warm the cane whips of the riders
who guide the camels of our eyes.

James M. Tracy

Riding

Rippling muscle under chestnut velvet.
Pounding hooves in sync
with my heartbeat.
Upon a half-ton of boundless strength
I soar
With stirrups for wings.

Beverly J. Justice

Older Eyes

Years that pass my heart confirms,
My points of view revise.
Things once held so important,
I view with older eyes:

How constancy is precious —
Eternal, better said.
How what just a preface
Grows better fully read.

How vision growing fainter
Is only outer sight.
How truth unfolds in what we see
By the surer, inner light.

Where what we love counts not at all,
Nor how it comes to be.
But who we love is all in all;
It's all in who we see.

To you I raise my honor,
And with such vision rise,
Eternally to read you,
And kiss you with my eyes.

Bruce W. Cummings

Mrs. Stout

To the nice old lady's house we go,
my sister and I.
The fairy tales she reads to us
sit on top a little organ.
We slowly swing,
back and forth while she reads.
She's getting older and older,
as the years pass by.
I need to visit her more,
she'll soon be gone,
I have no time,
no time at all.
In the night I watch them
as they drive her away,
away to the hospital.
Soon she died,
put deep into the ground.
She's gone, I'll never see her again.
Just one more time?
PLEASE!

Emily Caroline Havens

Ol' Jay

There once was a man
name Jay, who came
to town and couldn't stay.
He had to keep movin', up and down,
hoppin', skippin', runnin'
round, but he just couldn't get it down.

I guess Old Jay
will just keep on movin' till this very
day, chasing after his kite that had once
led him astray.

Ashley Hill

Untitled

Never spoken of
Never expressed
The only real love
Ever possessed
It started one day
The day of our birth
Not knowing if
Their trouble was worth
My mother the beautiful
Blessed and strong
My father the gorgeous
Too good to do wrong
Blended together
And divided in half
Gave life to twins
To love and to laugh
They never stopped giving
Since the day we were born
They are the rose
I am the thorn

Amy L. Manfred

Strive To Be Free

Strive to be free
Never quit, 'cause you're different
Never turn back, 'cause
Peoples words brings you down
Reach for the sky
The Lord knows your trying
He'll make you free
Just believe in Him
And you won't have
To strive to be free

Gabriel Cardenas

Home Is Where My Heart Is

Home is where my heart is;
Never to leave through the door.
I like to think of the joys
that may never come no more.
As I grow older,
I try to share what I have;
but I think of the tears
that stay outside my door.
The trouble and the disappointment
that may come my way.
If there was away
to change this world,
I guess I would have to say,
May I have the struggles
and the memories
To keep me warm at night.
For home is where my heart is,
And my days are not that long.

Eliott C. Ponte

Untitled

I walk through the tunnels of darkness
never to see the light
I fall through the pits of sorrow
to be consumed in my agony
I lie on the bed of nails
I feel no pain
I swim through the turbulent waters
never to reach my destination
I fly through the morbid skies
secluded from the world I once knew
I walk through this hell...
absent from my bodily misery.

Erica Witte

Untitled

I live my life
next to the flowers
of a still life
fading, oil lamp shadows
at noon from my
window overlooking the prairie.
Someday you might see me
peeking from the roses
or eating bread crumbs
watching your mouth water.
Here, I, nothing
but borrowed and
rearranged memories, sit and
search for lonely artists
defining a new Eden
out of the infinite
shuffling the signature
of a masterpiece.

Andrew T. Kemp

The Eternal Question

The eagle soars through limitless sky
No fence to restrict his lone flight
He is master of his spacious domain
The fabled eye focuses on the rooster
Who struts about in his fenced pen
Surrounded by his mistresses and kin
He senses the eagle's shadow
And cocks his eye skyward
Each is aware of the other
But who is the envied one
The rooster who is king
In his own little place
Or the eagle as he soars
Through limitless space

David Keck

Explanation of Death

If you fear death
no man is free

To walk the path of
freedom and harmony

Everyone's time will come
some young, some old

Just stand strong
firm and bold

Nothing can be done
to change the Lord's mind

When he calls your name
It must be your time

So when all is done
don't cry or fight

It's just temporary darkness
and a new sun for light

One day we'll meet, once again
It's a new beginning, not the end.

Duane Phillips

Depression

Is my life nothing but a dream?
No more than wasted time?
And why do all the people seem
To think my love's a crime.

Sometimes I cannot help but feel,
Like I have lost myself.
My heart is like a weight of steel,
Without a friendly wealth.

Good things I see without my eyes
But with a hate so strong.
It's like I loathe all passers-bye,
And those who stay too long.

I can't be pleased or satisfied,
I always hunger more.
There are so many I've denied,
To leave them sad or sore.

As I grow old I start to see,
What I've done is so wrong.
And now hell is my destiny,
My soul is almost gone.

Cheryl Christie

Ghost Ship

Ghost ship tossed upon cloudy seas,
No movement save a sharp, brisk breeze.
Lapping waters against the bark
Whisper curses to the falling dark.

Once bold men lay about its deck,
Jutting rocks look toward its wreck.
Towering masts against the sky,
No sound save the sea gull's cry.

Blood-stained wood boasts of battle.
The rotting boards begin to rattle.
Footsteps sound on hollow floor.
Flickering light at the captain's door.

Shadows cast on broken beams...
Sudden moans and chilling screams.
Cloak of darkness shrouds the prow.
Lifeboat can save no one now.

Starlight streaks off scattered gold —
None left to tell this tale of old.
Lone avarice the victor here,
Left to claim a prize too dear.

Gloria S. Yatsko

The Most Fun Wins!

Now if you play a game
not for fortune or fame,
And you play it for fun,
then you've already won!
Just try to learn each day
from the games that you play.
You'll be your own best fan,
think and say yes I can!
And before games begin,
know that the most fun wins.

Don Fogle

Simply

Stand beside me,
not in front,
not behind,
Simply beside me.

Be my friend,
not my ruler,
not my servant,
Simply my friend.

Be my comforter,
not my critic,
not my excuser,
Simply my comforter.

Be my lover,
not my abuser,
not my worshiper,
Simply my lover.

Simply beside me,
Simply my friend - simply my comforter
Simply my lover,
Simply my man!

Amber Lolita Price

Why Can't You See Me (Who I Am)

Why can't you see me for who I am!
Not what I am?

Should it really matter that my
skin is not white? To attack
or hate me? That gives you no right.

Why do you keep me from the things
that I deserve? Try to oppress me,
get in every single nerve.

Should it be a problem that my
skin is black? Only on the surface
as a matter of fact.

I am a person created in God's own
image, and because of this I'm entitled
to every privilege

What I am saying, is I'm running a
race, trying to stay on tract, and
that gives me the right first to be
human, and then black.

Des'Rae L. Strome

Sex After Sixty

The pace is slower
now
The frequency is lower
now
The force is not as
strong
The time is not as
long
The urgency is less
than it was
The action though still
gives me a buzz

George Stroud

Ink Spots

Words rolling over paper,
Oceans of words without end,
No end,

No end...does a sea of ink deliver.
Mind and pen being understood,
only by it's maker.

Days on end, time wasted,
Rivers of white, stacked...
With indigo highlight.

Screams for explanation written,
None to know or care,
Until sent on it's way.
Never reaching intended.

Eternity, time wasted,
Once a goal to meet,
Words returned to not.

Riddles, all this be,
misjudged, the thought.
I play the waiters game,
Awhile...then, then... naught.

Carol O. Melquist

The Burning Field

We were walking tall and proudly
O'er the rich and fertile ground
Mama peacock and the family
As they followed me around

Every color in the rainbow
Was displayed upon our frame
But to this color-blinded peacock
All the pigments are the same

Tell me why our field is burning
Tell me why the land is bare
Why the sun's no longer shining
For the smoke has filled the air

Did a passerby get careless
As he fumbled for a light?
Was it just a bolt of lightning
In the middle of the night?

Could it be the flame of hatred
That has set our field aglow?
Friend, my little ones are asking
And, the answer, I don't know

John L. Mullins

This Red Hat

A dragon fly
on this red hat.
See that she is wanting.
Quick as fragile wings do flutter,
she needs a tender landing,
hopes for understanding.
Often she catches the wind
and takes flight for freedom,
but this seemingly busy release
is a moment only for peace.
As always she comes again,
searching warmth.
Crying soundlessly for company
to share her gently nature.
She stills a moment
on this red hat.
The dragon fly
then flies again.

Hannah Moon Hood

Earth Child

On the dark side
of a faceless moon
A seed fell down
To fill the Earth's womb

There I was born
And here I stay
Feeding on life
In every way

And in the abyss
That is my head
I dream of things
Long been dead

I see my brothers
Rise so tall
Their seasons change
As their leaves fall

I am the child
of the Earth and Moon
Brother to the trees
Who heal my wounds

Brandon Erwin

Bouquet Of Life

Life is really a mixed bouquet
of scattered joys along the way
a fragrant rose, a friendly smile
a love that makes it all worthwhile.

A friend who's tested, tried and true
some work we love, a joy to do.
A child's quick hug, a loving kiss
Life has no better joys than this.

And at life's end, we closely bind
the joys of life of every kind
and savor them in every way
This life of ours and its bouquet.

Evelyn M. Strom

Invisible

I sit buried in the fangs
of your smile
while you pretend to exist
in the present tense.

You sit surrounded
by unopened boxes,
empty walls
peeling in the twilight,
unseeing,
frozen in another time.

You stare with piercing
blankness
as the angles of my face
disappear.
in the silence.

John Kaufman

Disappearing Sun

As I sit and watch the
Sun slowly go into the River.
The clouds change form and Color.
The river sings of a lovely song,
The orange, red and blue
colors call out and say,
would you like to follow me today?

Doris Martin

Untitled

When one is old
One becomes bold.
The truth is told
As it is viewed.
If not told when old—-
One will fold, fold, fold.

Gertrude G. Ronk

Rebirth

Open up for me
Oh sweet dark sky
Fill me up
Give me life
Breathe into me
As you do
All things around me
Fresh and new
Wash away the pain
Of winter's past
Beat down on me
Hard and fast
Then move aside
Sweet dark sky
Make room for the sun
And all her pride
Allow her to drench me
In her warm soft glow
So that I may have
The strength to grow

Carolyn Leake

Untitled

Gone like the wind
on a flower blossom

Away blows the pollen,
away blow the petals,
and soon
only the base is left
there to die.

Quite like life
Are the wind and the flower
They go with the flow
awaiting another tomorrow.

Cynthia Geronsin

Away From Others

Alone tree stands,
On a long stretch of grass,
Away from her companions,
Swishing her splendid crown of leaves,
In a magnificent rainbow of colors,
Against the wind and the sun,
Who admired her longingly,
While she swayed gently,
To and fro,
In her world of her own,
In an aura of glow,
Singing a song of crinkling leaves
Held by her many branches,
Supported by her powerful trunk,
Of curving grace,
Flowing beauty and vitality,
From her graceful figure,
Dancing in her infinite world of pleasure,
And of joy,
Away from others.....

Carla Acuna-Neely

"Doll Upon Your Shelf"

Bitter tears I can not hide
on my cheeks have dried,
Sitting here all by myself
Just a doll upon your shelf.

Collecting dust forgotten now
imprisoned love I feel some how,
through it all can't help myself
Just a doll upon your shelf.

Alice Johnson Williamson

"Hatchling"

The courageous hatchling wavers,
On the nest's narrow edge,
Uncertain which side he should jump to.
"Take a chance.
It's your first time.
Nothing'll happen,"
Assures his withered brother.
He's convinced,
Despite his fearful instincts,
And plummets.
Pedestrians carefully step
Around the hatchling's lethal choice,
Splattered on the pavement.
None stop to scrape up his mistake,
No one stretched out their soft hands
To catch him either,
On the hatchling's first time.

Bev Nordahl

On Moon

Break the bloated marble moon
on the sharp of a star
Silver cleave her graceful lies
Slay silent her liquid,
tuneful lips
For come gulling dreams
forth this casket of skies
And these
the tall grass
that well hides our path
to the stars.

Craig Braginsky

C'est La Vie

I will remember you.
Once when my skies were gray.
You came with magic and my cares
Took wing and flew away!

You called me "Tuter-Puter"
With a soft and whispered sigh,
And I called you "My Butnus"-
I really don't know why.

You were my shining knight
On a white steed-riding,
Destined to blend your pheramones
With mine- and nothing hiding!

On a starlit summer night
I turned to find you gone!
No time to grieve — there was Steve,
Who claimed me for his own!

I stumbled on you in my dream;
Now I know where you are,
Conning some pilgrim and smiling
And lost on a distant star!

Elizabeth Gamble Kopp

Time

Time flies by so fast, so cold
One day your young, next day your old
You look back through Time to see
One point in life, you were free
You were free in Times great sky
You were there without a lie

But now you're here
It's all caught up to you
That is why you feel so blue
So please don't cry
As Time flies by
'Cause Time was here without a lie

Amy B. Cheeseman

Angelic Encounter

I met a girl
One June night
'Twas at a fair
The mood was right

I had to turn
At first sight
For there I saw
A splendid light

My breath she stole
She wore white
The hue of clouds
My thoughts took flight

I soared into
A new height
I wish these thoughts
To become finite

I someday hope
That we might
Together read
These words I write

David D. Vanderveer

Grandson

For three months he was ours.
One night, the angels woke him up
And took him home...
The death of a child
Defies description.
This much I know...
During their short earth time
Their Moms had a glimpse of heaven.
And, when it is the mother's time,
Her journey - to eternity
Will be a straight line.

Ann Milliron

I'm Lost

Now that you're gone
Life must go on, without you dear
I'm lost.
Days are so dreary nights are so
weary. Lonesome and blue
I'm lost.
You were my dream, you were my love
Now you're in heaven above.
I'm lost.

Isabell Williams

Life

There is one thing that never stops,
One thing you can never rewind or erase,
Life.
You think that you'll die,
But you won't.
It has good and bad times,
Frustrating and happy times,
Confusion stress, and anger.
But behold,
Bad is followed by good,
And misery will always end.
Life is always changing and moving.
It will never stay the same,
Never perfect,
Never full of horror.
That's the way it will always be,
And has always been.

Donna J. Olson

Street Corner Flies

To triumph in the mind
One thinks, not speaks
This is carefully missed
By the speakers of man

An observation in eloquence
On any street corner
Is, at best
A hurried demise

For thinkers are not found
In the dregs of town
As in churches, or state
No participating clowns

But on my window sill
Sits a fly thinking
Of last nights rain
The residue, its drinking

On the street corner
Broken lift the bottle
How, like a fly
Its residue their drinking

Andrew S. Gill

Untitled

If words could be like butterflies
Only beautiful to see and hear
Instead of like the bumble bee
To hurt and bring a tear
If people could give out more love
And run out of hate and fear
If everyone could listen
With an open heart and hear

I wish I could reach inside myself
And pull out all my feelings
I know the words are in there
If I could only say them right
When I try to talk it comes out wrong
Maybe the right feeling is wrong

Arlyce Anderson

"Meta"

From dust, an infant cry:
One of lifetimes pondering why
Ere dust chokes the final cry
Into the folds of timeless time
Wondrous dreams, subtle games and
Hope ever sublime...

Gordon L. Cathey

Addiction

Do you know where you are?
or even where you're going?
You are hiding something,
It is slightly showing.

What a savage man,
to steal such a wonder.
I don't understand,
why it makes you go under.

Did you ever possess a lucid thought,
or even a straight mind?
It's always there to be bought,
And it's robbing you blind.

So try and fight back,
and reach me your hand.
You're slipping through a crack,
You've entered a new land.

Andria J. Holstine

Son

I can not teach you life's desires
Or hold your hand to journey's end
Nor sup with you at passions fires
For in our ways our paths will bend

I could wish that we were one
Then in our mind together see
Of which fulfills and then is done
Or better yet to let it be

For it would be a wearisome mind
To drink the cup we never fill
Not glory in our separate find
Not know desires of our own will

Then what is left to offer
To aid you on your way
Not gold as from a coffer
For this in life is clay

The life that we must travel
Will fly as though a dove
Then ere we sound the gavel
Look home for lasting love

George H. Eckert, Jr.

Untitled

Marriage is not a piece of paper
Or the saying of "I do"
But marriage is a special love
Often shared by two
Marriage is not just a honeymoon
Or a dinner by candlelight
But marriage is getting over
That silly little fight
Marriage is not a game to play
But marriage is an art
Marriage is being able to see
Not by your eyes but with your heart
Marriage is not only the pros in life
But the cons that you will see
And when those cons are seen together
Your marriage was meant to be.

Cheryl Roberts

This Day

So on this day we mourn our dead,
Our family and friends we've lost.
To drugs and booze, disease and war's,
"Oh Lord, we know the cost."

We've cried the tears and song the songs
And suffered with much pain.
With broken hearts and loneliness
We ask "Lord, what's to gain?"

For life my friend is short at best,
Only a small parade.
Live it right and do Gods will,
Don't live in a charade.

And when you get so weak at heart
And have to have that drink:
You think that you are desperate,
At least that's what, you think.

Reach for that phone-give me a call,
I'll set your sobriety straight.
Don't waste your life as others have
Remember, we all, have our date.

Harold Raymond

Epitaph

"Work is liberty..."
Our fragile bones say.
My trapped years beginning.
I could die today or maybe tomorrow.
I want to escape this pain.

Cold afternoon—
Don't you recognize me?
I'm kept within an open tomb.
Your honor has become so vulgar—
Slowly as we approach our last day.

My time has come now.
I must face Hell or Death.
You now wish to say many things.
One moment short—
Concealed within darkness.
You never read our epitaph.

Heather Erickson

Our Mother

Our mother is pleasant
Our mother is love,
Our mother's an angel
Sent from above.

She nursed us, she fed us
She wore herself out, when your a mother
That's what love's all about.

Our mother is old
She's fragile and frail,
We know it's our turn to carry the pail.

She ails and she suffers
And you wonder why?
But never forgets to kiss good-bye.

you wish in you heart
You could turn back years,
And oh! how you fight
To hold back the tears.

You know God in Heaven will call her
away,
But forever in our hearts
She will always stay.

Judith Stacey

Gift

Butterflies
Spider webs
Queen Anne's lace
Intricate beauty
Infinite grace.

Margaret H. Moore

Sweet Baby Jesus

'Twas within a makeshift cradle
Our sweet baby Jesus lay,
More beautiful than a porcelain doll,
On a mattress made of soft hay.

His mother kept close by Him.
His father watched from on high.
In the stable the light was dim -
Where the cattle lowed a lullaby.

A halo glowed around His head;
He was special from the start.
His mother took Him from His bed
Then held Him close to her heart.

He came to save the world from sin
And take on Himself all the pain.
His love will give a peace within
And give sunshine through the rain.

This sweet little baby Jesus Boy
Was born our Savior and King.
This Christmas, bask in all His joy;
Let the anthems of His praises ring.

Carol Gideon

Do You Want To Dance?

With my heart I step forward
Out of fear you step back,
Your rejection spins me around
Your neediness grabs my hand
And pulls me close.
With my heart I again step forward
Out of fear you step back
Do you want to dance?
or would you not rather
Walk hand and heart
And the music we hear,
Will be the sound of our feet
Walking in rhythm
To friendship, trust, and love
Or would you rather
Dance the next dance?

Glenda Hatley

Creations

The setting sun
over distant seas
the stars at night
a warm summer's breeze
snowcapped mountain ranges
the trees' autumn changes
children's laughter at play
the dawn of a new day
The beauty of God's creations
is a wondrous sight to behold
but of all of God's creations
His most beautiful creation
is you

George T. Peacock

Beautiful Christmas Eve

As the snow touches ground
Painting white our town
You can see it's Christmas Eve.

As all bells ring in song
All the night long
You can hear and can believe...

Christmas Day is almost here,
Peace on earth to men everywhere.
A day of giving
That makes life worth living,
Beautiful Christmas Eve.

If I had my way
Then, every single day
All would help to conceive
The spirit of giving
That makes life worth living
The spirit of Christmas Eve.

Carolee Gavigan

"My Destination"

My destination is a place of
peace and harmony,
A place of happiness where I am
free.
A place where I can shout and
run,
A place where I can be alone
but still have fun.
A place where none could bother
me,
If I could be anywhere this is
where I would want to be.

Christina McIlhenney

Tears

People show tears when they cry
People show tears when they are high
Tears of Joy are seen in marriage
Especially when you look in the
baby carriage
People have tears of fear
Even when you have a nightmare
I love tear of joy
Comes also with a baby boy
or even a girl
One of the sweetest things in
the world
I have one special tear
in my heart
Because you share a very big part..

April Ray

Time-N-Friendship

Time goes so fast
Life asks so much
No wonder friends
get out of touch
But in our hearts
deep, true, unseen
friendship stays forever green
with love

George R. Stumpf

Love Joy

Love joy
Please don't you go
Love joy
I need you so
No baby don't you leave
Stay my baby, stay with me
And give to me what I need
Your love baby and harmony
I love you baby cant you see
I need you baby here with me
To set my soul and my spirit free
From all my pains and agony
Do you believe in loving me
Come on baby stay with me
Please my baby don't you leave
Without you baby I cant be free
From all my pains and agony
Do you believe you set me free
From all the pain's of misery
Stay my baby, stay with me.

Greg E. Williams

The Beauty of Fall

The scarlet oak looks
proud and tall, it keeps
its leaves longer than
all. It drops its acorns
in the fall. To feed
the squirrels who gather
the nuts in their fat
cheeks and run for their
trees near the running
creek.
Holding the mystery of
the night.
In their trees as
they cuddle all night.

Jane S. Fabrizi

On Parents

I bring home my test,
proud of my B.
"You could do better,"
is what they say to me.
I jump and run,
Let out a screech,
They say "act your age,"
along with a speech.
After my game,
I sit down and rest,
All they could say was,
"You didn't try your best,"
They expect of me,
what I cannot give,
and are constantly telling me,
How to live.
Now living with them,
is kind of tough,
Especially when nothing,
is ever good enough!

Daniel L. Voelkel

Sleep

Sleep soft star in yonder sky
quiet is nights beckoning
calling deeper and deeper
into sub-dark dream paradise.
Sleep
Our journey placidly continues.
Snore louder!
Ball-up into a fetus knot.
Stretch
And day is upon you.

Dwight Hayes

Friendship

The waves ripple gently,
Reaching out to the sand,
They try to touch it,
Just like the human hand.

They try to cure its problems,
In such a way,
Even though they fail,
They try every day.

They never will stop,
It's the friendship that's true,
You know they love each other,
It's what friends should do.

Chrissy Wise

Untitled

I am a flower
Ready to bloom
Something is killing me
Wilting me before my birth
Silently I die

I should have fought to survive
Without water
Without soil
Instead, I died
Before I bloomed

Christina Lang

"Suicide"

Did you ever slip on
red blood?

Warm and thick, it runs,
in tiny rivulets of its own design.

Across cold white tile
uncaring and unyielding
to red blood.

Splashing pin sized droplets
and curling in a corner
with nowhere left to go.

Pure and hard, the tile
does not accept,
the faintly sweet smell of red blood.

This pristine room
remains indifferent
to red blood.

Amy S. Whitaker

Mortal Art

Reticent contemplation
Retrospective of this work
Aesthetic line
Pulsating red water colors
Joined by gurgling bubbles
Symphony of passage

Death, the eternal blink
Solitude, my companion
Spiraling emotions into nothingness
Blackness, cold and eternal

Albert Valenciano Desonia

Untitled

A strange rain approaches and thunder
Rolls from within my head
The mirage is shattered by the
Words I've said.
Is this storm real?
My chin in my hands I sit and wonder.
If the sun before it, that shone
So bright
Was only a reflection of your mind.
I find myself in the dark
Without so much as a speck
of light.
I could have swore I was right.
But no one cares.
In the middle of the night.

David Reynolds

Explanation

Shelves are filled with proper toys—
Rows and rows.
With golden cords and ribbons and bows
From a package world,
Each comes labelled and guaranteed—
In boxes and bags
With instruction sheets.

But love, my love, is an old tin can—
Bouncing along and up and down,
Hit with a stick,
Or pulled on a string,
Making up rules as you go along.
Love, my love, is an alley thing.

Joe English

I've Been to Jekyll

I've been to Jekyll, the golden isle
Saw homes of wealth with gracious style
Along its shore, watched dolphins play
Saw sun come up at break of day.

I've been to Jekyll, the golden isle
Walked the beach, my heart did smile
Felt sun so hot, the body warm
Saw evening sky alight with storm.

I've been to Jekyll, the golden isle
And though I only stayed awhile
Saw oaks so tall and spanish moss
I've been to Jekyll; my soul is lost.

Joyce A. Przelenski

With You

Written in blood; and
sealed with a kiss.
If you love me; then
you deserve this.
Babe I love you, so
please be true.
Can't you see that
by the things I do?!
And when I go to
heaven and your not there,
I'll write your name
on the golden stair.
But If your not
there by, judgement day,
I'll know you went
the other way. Then I'd give the
angel back their golden wings.
You knows what else
I would do? I would go to
Hell to be with you?

Adrianna LeRoux

Love Unending

Look for an answer,
Search for a sign.

In all God's wisdom
And earthly design.

You'll know when it happens,
He'll show you the way

All you have to do
Is learn how to pray.

The answer is simple,
Don't waste a day.

Accept the blessings
That come from above.

Take all God's bounty
And share his love.

It comes from the heart
As all things do.

Love is the greatest
For me and you.

Dorothy Slack

Untitled

Silence settles in again...
seeking its level.
The storm has passed;
It's effects permanent in the cosmos...
infinite, never to end...
Everywhere and all in one place,
even as we spoke or felt them.
Thoughts. Emotions.
Loneliness rides the silence;
a familiar figure from the past.
I cannot more forward nor go back.
Memories flood this my empty world.
Home again. I wait...
for the Light.

David Stephen Isaacs

Untitled

Unspoken words....
SHADOWS come.
Spoken words....
Death calls.
Together make a darkness fall.

One lie makes a web of spoken words
That casts a net of thoughts that could
Of love of life and words said,
It die's of what unsaid!

Thought and deed in mind is set,
Of word and touch... Oh regret.
Of word and pain like a knife edge,
The cut is clean.

Bill Zimmerman

Birth

What she told herself was a lie
She asked herself why?
What could she do
Who would of knew
That it would happen to her
Her mind was in a blur
She thought she would be o.k.
The man told her he would stay
But he ran far away
Now she is left a stray
Who would take care of her
And the miracle inside her
That she was going to give birth to
The one she would bring to earth

Amy Coey

The Mirror

I know a girl who's really sweet.
She keeps her room nice and neat.
But, there is something mysterious
about her she never goes out nor
Do I for we have lost someone
deep in our lives I don't know
Who she is or what she
is I just know she's there.

Crystal Estes

Missed Expectations

She didn't say she loved me
She never said she didn't
She never said she cared
Nor did she say she was unaware
She didn't promise to write
Never did she say she wouldn't
She might have said she'd call
But then again she didn't
I will send her flowers
Perhaps candy would be best
I can't seem to please her
What can I do to appease her
I hope soon that I can forget her
But then again I haven't met her.

James A. Grimes

"She Sleeps Alone"

Reminiscent of an ageless glamour queen,
She sashays through her world.
With sophisticated vibrance,
Her elegance proudly unfurled.

Her quest is for fulfillment,
Both inward and outwardly.
Surely a happy home; a passionate love,
Would set her spirit free.

But Fate has not been kind,
To one so meek and fair.
Her mind is burdened with anguish,
From burned bridges beyond repair.

Confusion is her daily comrade,
Whose kinship breeds despair.
But her wisdom lives in knowing,
That she will find her peace somewhere.

I hope she finds her special place,
She's deserving in her undying goal.
But who's to say: "It hasn't all been in vain?"
Because even still—She sleeps alone!

Joe C. Weidner

Inside Cage

They say the child in me
Shields the woman from the pain.
The pain has a life of its own,

Uncontrollable, unrecognizable,
all consuming.

Must the woman feel the pain,
To kill its life?
The pain is Victor, it is obsessive,
The woman is the child.

Denise A. Bell

Hope

It's been a long time LORD
Since I've felt your presence near,
Or felt YOU cared about me
My cries for help YOU'D hear.

It's been a long time LORD
Since I've been on bended knee,
Or bowed my head to seek YOUR help
Your will for me to see.

It's been a long time LORD
I've lived it all in shame,
In fact, it's been forever
Since I've even called YOUR name.

It's been a long time LORD
Far too long I know,
And now I'm fighting for my life
I've no place else to go!

It's been a long time LORD
I hope YOU still are there,
I'm counting on the promise
OF YOUR abiding care.

John W. North

I Am Your Friend

Today, I heard a water bird
Singing to her friend
She sang to her a song of love
That I hoped would never end

Will you be my friend, she sang,
And love me 'till I die?
Will you be my wings, my friend,
When I am weak and can not fly?

Will you be my eyes for me
When I am blind and can not see?
Her friend just nodded lovingly
And accepted unconditionally

Of course, I will be your friend
Through the good times and the bad
I will even wipe the tears away
When your heart is soft and sad

But I am already your friend
So you need not have to ask
I will always fly by your side
Whatever might be the task

Corky Carpenter

"The Farmer"

The wind through the old straw hat
sings its rehearsed melody,
as the sweat slowly flows down those
old familiar valleys of his
wrinkled, leather face.

His hands, chapped and strong, move
as if hard labor were all they
had ever known.

The galluses of his faded overalls
echo his torn, but steadfast,
existence.

His steps, sure and forward, lend
not to regret and unfulfillment,
but to the hope of harvest and the
art of creating and sustaining life.

Cortnie McDougal

Night Sounds

High upon my rooftop
sitting quietly,

I hear the sounds of nighttime
echo softly through the trees.

Crickets play in unison a haunting
melody,

Din and patter of the traffic
plays night rhapsody.

In the distance, I can hear a
haunting whistle blow

And overhead yet far away an
airplane lulls my soul.

I cannot help but feel that
all these sounds combined

Join the sound of heartbeats
to play night symphony entwined.

Barbara A. Opyt

Alone

In the bayou,
Slowly guiding my perique.
I am alone.

The overhead cry of a hawk,
startles my thoughts.
I am alone.

Honeybees in an ageless cypress,
humming their own tune.
I am alone.

A breeze stirs the spanish moss,
it makes no sound.
I am alone.

A gator wakes from his nap
to watch me pass...

In the bayou,
Slowly guiding my perique.
I am alone.

Anita Horn

Touch

Let me touch you,
Slowly strip you,
Caress your smooth soft skin.

Let me kiss you,
Gently excite you,
Explore your flawless body.

Let me entice you,
Seduce and arouse you,
Kiss your soft moist lips.

Let me take you to the heights,
Of sweet ecstasy, all through the night.
With a burning passion we will kiss,
How much can you take of this?

Demetrius Sarigiannis

Metamorphosis

The black curtain falls
slowly, unfolding before
the eyes of its victim
one pupil at a time.

Total darkness approaches
As rabid dogs
Close on the brain
devouring thoughts and memories.

This world has left
me behind, closing the
mind to all known
But beginning a new life.

James Gooch

No Name Cafe

Angela used to go to the roadside cafe
She used to sit in the booth,
Always the same booth with her friends
All her memories and dreams lived there
And now even though its closed down
She sometimes goes and stands outside,
eating a tangerine,
Remembering everything that still lives
Hidden behind its broken windows.

Jaylene Day

Untitled

Be happy, my golden one
Smile your beautiful smile
Laugh your merry laugh

Think of all that is good
The earth, the sun, the rain
Smile at the sight of a rainbow

Dream your childhood dreams
Know they can come true
If you want to be loved by others
Love yourself

Let your heart be free of anger
Free of hatred, free of death
For you are alive!

You alone can live the life you are given
Cherish it
Regard it with the wonder that it is
Let every moment that you live be
Your past - Your present - Your future

Be happy
My golden one.

Cynthia L. Lyons

An Archer's Day

So soft the air in mid morning flow
  Smooth and silent as an archer's bow
Waiting to find a majestic display
  Of a white tail buck coming this way

Still time is heavy and pressure mounts
  Starting to think of watery founts
Believing it's time that only counts
  Till a lurking buck begins to pounce

But oft and oft to try again
  To view a wild grouse hen
A squirrel is clamoring over head
  Crows pulled the last thread

Tension mounts to explode
  An archer knows his mighty woes
He looks as though he has no foe
  As he packs his bag and starts to go

Charles E. Oxenford, Jr.

I Do Not Understand

I do not understand why there is
  so much fighting.
I do not understand why people have to
  live in the streets.
I do not understand why
  there is a devil.
But most of all, I do not understand why
  we can't have peace and
  why we can't stop pollution.
I do understand that God loves me and
  will protect me during the bad times.

Jennifer Denise Carter

One

Two bodies
Two minds
Two souls
Two lives
Two hearts
One purpose

E. M. Thibodeaux

Missing Children

I am missing, from my home
No, one seems, to know where,
I am, gone, my mother and,
Father, are very sad, they,
Will be, glad, when I return,
I hope, it want, be very long,
Before, I come home, that where
My heart is, and that where,
I belong

Annie J. Monk

Memories

Empty room full of thoughts.
So much garbage,
I can barely walk.
The bed is full
of all the times we made love.
The empty closet is stuffed
with the memories of your clothes.
The floor is overflowing
with your foot prints.
In the mirror your shadow still remains.
And in my heart there is still pain.

Judith Tamayo

Dead Inside

She hid beneath the limelight
So no one could see her pain
her meaning had been long forgotten
now she's just a name

She was tired of being used
she was tired of all the lies
no longer was she taken seriously
the pride she held had died

She began to grow mischievous
with the intention to rebel
when there's no one left to trust
your life becomes a Hell

When everyone betrayed her
used her for a name
it left her feeling helpless
she began to take the blame

They said the jump had killed her
as they pulled her from the pit
but she was dead inside
long before she hit

Julie Wilkie

Children

Children are so special,
so small, so sweet.
They bring love, laughter,
they are such a treat.
Without children where
would we be.
In a world full of
hate, crime, and misery.
Each child has a mind
of its own.
And each one deserves
a loving home.
Whenever you see a
child give them a hug.
Because each child
needs to be loved.

Cathy Kilpatrick

Yours of a Woman, Mine of a Man

Let us clear up things between us
so that we can clearly understand
that the feeling we have between us
is yours of a woman
and mine of a man

Sometimes our feelings cause us anguish
Because love and pain go hand in hand
But the love that is between us
is yours of a woman
and mine of a man

We will always love each other
and want to be together all we can
for we both know the reasons
are yours of a woman
and mine of a man

To go through life together
is what both our feelings demand
the plans we have for each other
are your of a woman
and mine of a man

Duane E. Bible

Marium Swenson

She's wobbling her head
so very young at heart
painting her projects
from the glazes off the carts.
Is there not a care
within that woman
with the snowy hair?
I hope never to see
a deepening clear tear
from that elder woman
with all of her hidden fears.

The jar full of fears
were abruptly broken
Streaming of tears
but nothing to be spoken.
Emotions soared above
all else that meant much.
As did this dove
now buried in the dust.

Amanda Ostrander

The Journey

Marching, marching, marching
Soldiers of fortune
Across the sands of time

Marching, marching
Minutes
Into hours
Into days
Into years

Marching, ever marching
Into the last twilight
As the winds of eternity
Sweep away every trace
Of their entrance
Into
Oblivion.....

Joan Morgan

What Can We Do

Some can help it
Some can't
But I'm sure if we tried.
We could stop it
If there were more jobs
if everyone was kind
There would be no more homeless
Everyone would be fine

Bambi Giles

Untitled

A window to a world
Someone looks out at me
Do I know her?
Is she real?

A window to my world
She looks at me with wondering eyes
Am I real?
Or am I just her reflection?

Becky Tulloch

The Search

Searching, for a companion
Someone, who understands
The alikeness and differences
Inside of every man.

Having a sense of purpose
In living every day
Taking note of the changes
Happening along the way.

In using the information
We worked so hard to attain
We're learning all the answers
And relearning them again.

Finding some so temporary
Others seem to last
You've got to keep changing
To void living in the past

Reaching the very top
Without standing in line
But most important, obtaining it
With a peaceful state of mind.

Donna A. Langdon

Special Friend

A special friend is hard to find,
Someone who's caring, honest, kind.
Someone to tell your troubles to
And cheer you up when you are blue.
Someone to listen as well as talk,
Someone with common ground you walk.

Friendship is a two-way street
Where two hearts and minds together meet,
To share each other's common goal
Which comes from deep within the soul.
And if you're lucky to possess
A friendship sharing this closeness
And strong bonds that cannot be severed,
Then you have found a friend forever.

Janice Esposito

Little One

Oh precious one, little one
sometimes feeling forgotten,
don't you know how much I love you?

Oh precious one, little one
making effort to do my Will,
I appreciate all you do
though you don't hear me
speak to you.

Oh precious one, oh little one,
be comforted by my love.
Please know that there's
so much blessing for you
coming from above.

Gerianne Meyer

"40 Years with Wife and Ware"

Forty years with cooper bottoms,
Sometimes I wish I hadn't got 'em.
They were a gift to you,
But you made them mine,
Best I give them another shine.
Now all your pans have shiny bottoms
They look so good, I'm glad I got 'em.
After forty years, dear
You're both top rated.
I'm glad your bottom
Wasn't copper plated.

Irving A. Russell

Untitled

Feelings can be so weird.
Sometimes it's like
their unknown or not there.
Like a person without
a name or personality.
But in some way it could be good.
Personally I wouldn't like not having
a personality because then
life would be so dull.
Also I don't like having
unknown feelings.
So I guess I need to grab
a hold of my feelings and
act like myself, so that
means I'll have to show
my personality.

Gail Patterson

My Lisa

Warm is the glow she radiates...
sparkling are her sky-blue eyes
as she reaches out smilingly
to hold...to hug...to love...to try.

My Lisa, daughter beloved...
full of God's charm and grace,
dreams dreams that will come true...
in time...someplace.

She is always "there"...
always ready to care...to guide,
She is blessed...a child of God.
I am blessed and full of pride
because, you see, she is mine!

Jean Schubert

Internal Excursion

The other side of the mirror
Speaks to me with repulsion.
Darker than an emotion of life,
The truth becomes my affliction.

Looking deep inside my head,
Violently searching for sanity,
I close my eyes to escape
The shadows formed from misery.

Reaching for a change within,
I drown in seas of fire.
Seeping through a tight embrace,
Feeling the burning desire.

Damn the presence of mystery,
I stand alone, morose.
Reality has brought destruction,
Blood descends from my ghost.

Jennifer Kousek

Seasons

As summer emerges into our grasp,
Spring becomes a part of our past,
Bringing hot weather along,
Summer sings a sunny song.

Soon summer is gone,
Then autumn dawns,
Bringing colorful sights,
Falling leaves dance like kites.

Autumn fades away,
Bringing winters chilly days,
Snowflakes falling down,
People buzzing 'round and 'round.

Suddenly springs back in view,
Bringing things to anew,
Budding flowers everywhere,
Spring is in the air.

Amanda Thornton

Surf Fishing

Translucent green straight ahead
Squeaky tan at my feet
Azure blue overhead
On the beach where all three meet

Looking down the interface
Where distant objects disappear
I think myself in time and space
Must also be as nothing near

I cast my lure just past the spray
And jerk it back with animation
A hook up may give eve's entree
If only fish will take a notion

Many times I perform this ritual
Resharpening hooks retrying knots
Counting 'one hundred' becomes habitual
Till the sun grows dim and drops

Now it's time to pack it in
Feed the crabs and sea birds scraps
And thank the creator once again
For life and thought, and all that's that

John W. Knight

The Cloth

I offer up my Baptismal Cloth,
stained by my sins,
blood red
like Christ's Shroud.

This discolored cloth,
shows to Him
my faults,
my failures,
my disappointments.

This cloth I offer up,
again and again,
rejected in my self pity, yet;
He returns it to me
clean like a sunrise!

I lift my eyes
out of my tears of joy
and see His love for me unceasing,

as

I offer up my Baptismal Cloth,
stained by my sins,...

Bart Stafford

Best Friends

Friends forever
Stand our guard
Through the right and the wrong

Closer then ever
Never apart
Always together
Heart to heart

Then one day we're separated
You were shot, your life invaded
Torment and tragedy fill my eyes
I cry awhile
Then ask God why

You didn't have to go
I wanted you to stay
We were best friends
Until that day

Jamie Zakian

Love Dies

On a glorious golden day.
Standing on the rocks by the sea.
Where is my love I say?
But no answer came to me.
A dove! A beautiful white dove
flying above in the sky.
Take this message to my love,
So my heart won't have to ask why
Why I feel this pain so great
I could die
From the dove I wait for a reply
please, please hurry back I did cry.
On a stormy thundering midnight
Standing on the rocks by the sea,
My beautiful white dove comes in flight
with tears in its eyes it looks at me
and falls dead by the sea

Geneva Mata

Abandoned House

An abandoned house
Stands empty and alone
Inside
Are echoes of past life
Shadows of people
Dance on the walls
Faded colors
Gray, black, white
Spirits fill the house
Of what once was
A life
Now gone.

Amanda Sedlak

Ars Poetica

Adventure in a word
stepping out upon a phrase
discovering a turn
moving on beyond one's expectations
surprising landscapes
sudden forms—
poetry.

Jeffrey H. Kaimowitz

Untitled

Reflections of your youth,
still linger at your door.
Because of love and
happiness you feel
it so much more.

It holds your hand
and strengthens your soul,
but the memories break
your heart.
They seem to know how much
you really cared
and how hard it was to part.

Although the intentions
were good,
the love that was shared
will never be understood.
for life is not
a simple thought, but
a secret cavern with much
more to be sought.

Jenny Kish

In My Eyes

In my eyes you will find
Strength to overcome your weaknesses
Courage for all your fears
Sympathy in your every pain
Grace for all your trials
Joy for all your sorrows

In my eyes you will find
Hope for all your dreams
Faith in all you say and do
Trust in your soul
Desire in your love
Belief in you
Friendship full of trust
Happiness when all your dreams come true

And in my eyes
You will see my heart
Where there's that special place only for you
And you will know how much I love you

Allison Sova

Ray Of Sunshine

Walking on sunshine,
Strolling in the air.
Everything seems fine,
But the feeling is too rare.
Don't follow the ray on its decline,
Nothing is there.

Cheryl L. Wills

Behind The Wall

Lifeless and lonely wall
Strong as a heart
Between nature and civilization
It rests
It protects us like a father
So we will be free from rain.
But it is sad
For we decorate it
without its permission.
It bleeds by the puncture
Of nails and pins.

Carrie Wang

"Compliments Only Of Wolf Lake"

The lake, the trees, so serene,
sun, fresh air, the perfect scene.
Cleanse my soul of yesterday,
the path I choose will go one way.

On the edge you stop and stare,
calm and quiet everywhere.
Feel the breeze swirl in stone,
Let it loose, you're now alone.

For the moment you are free,
escape the harsh reality.
The hurt you feel will all subside,
absorb the peace, enjoy the ride.

Take it in because you know.
The dream is over when you go.
Can't take it with you, it's not real
but, this is all you want to feel.

You went to leave it all behind,
and now you have it, peace of mind.
Let go of feelings you can't fake,
"Compliments only of Wolf Lake".

Cheryl Brasso Holzberg

A New Day's Dawning

A new day's just beginning
Sunlight drifting through
the trees
Here and there Mother Nature
Is waking up her children
The peep of new birds calling
Hungry mouths open for feeding
Squirrels are running to find
food
For their families are waiting
All to greet this new day's dawning
In the forest on the hill

Albertina C. Serpa

Fragile

Gale, mighty wreathe;
switching exertion-
disarray
Breathe-your membranous
branches inflamed
naked and asway

Pale and closely-grained
quiver-trembling
by rage-infer
Sap/withstanding
hearth a-frail

Patience in passing
revival,
zeal,
spring time-birchen,
glorious.
Will prevail.

Greg Hamel

Lonely Tears

Alone I sit crying my lonely
tears.
Remembering when we were still
together.
All the good and bad times
we shared.
Didn't he know he didn't
have to lie.
That I cared enough to
understand the truth.
I guess he didn't know how
much I cared.
Cause, alone I sit crying
my lonely tears.

Angela Pope

"Alicia"

Oh Alicia, sweet Alicia, our Alicia
Tears of joy filled both our eyes
Hearing your first cry

Oh Alicia, sweet Alicia, our Alicia
You are beautiful even when you sigh

Oh Alicia, sweet Alicia, our Alicia
You were made with two hearts
both in loving harmony

And we know with love so pure
You'll return this love we're sure
My God be with you through eternity.

Gary D. Miller

Today

Today is fullness
like a fruit...
when it is ripe,

Like a benevolent rose
...fully opened
to the sun
to the rain
giving of itself entirely.

Anita Wood

"Grandawl"

Tell me bout the good old days.
Tell me bout the clothes ya'll wore.
Tell me bout the song and praise
Grandpa offered to his Lord.
Tell me bout God's holy hand.
Tell me bout the promised land.
Grandmaw, tell me bout the good old days,
Tell me of furrows across the land.
Tell me bout the cross you bore.
Grandmaw, make me understand;
Tell me bout forever more.
Tell me bout an old milk cow.
Tell me of the sun's hot rays.
Tell me bout the dirt and plow.
Tell me bout old family ways.
Tell me bout the holy vows
Tell me faithful marriage pays.
Oh please grandmaw,
Tell us bout the good old days.

Howie Patterson AKA Lot

Santa Claus

Daddy! Daddy! Daddy!
Tell me it's not true!
He said there's not a Santa Claus;
He laughed and said that Santa Claus
Was only Mom and you.

"My son" (with lump in throat) I said,
"Your Santa is not dead.
He never was a real, live man,
But lives inside of every man.
He's that which makes the act of giving
First among the acts of living."
"No! No! My son!" I quickly said,
"Your Santa is not dead;
He still is living, sound and whole.
And now that you have met him
I pray you won't forget him,
For he'll light the spark
Which fills the dark
With sunshine in your soul."

Austin J. Simpson

Forever Love

I love you so much, more
than words can say, to be
with you each night and
each and every day. Your
the one I love, yes, the
one and only. Your the one
I want, when I am feeling
lonely. Today is your
birthday, and may your
wish come true ... In
everything you say or think...
In everything you do.
Even though our love is
young, we're growing older
fast... And I want our
love for each other...

To always and forever last!!
I love you!

Jennifer Marie Dunlap

Dream World

I have a world
That belongs to me,
A world that no one
Will ever see.

It's a world made of
Dreams and wishes,
With lots of love
And hugs and kisses.

It's a world that has
No murder or crime,
And when people ask how are you
You can mean it when you say your fine.

Now you understand
When I say this world belongs to me,
Because a world like this
Will never be seen.

Jackie O'Melia

Trains

There is a train whistle,
that blows in the air
Bringing back memories
of when I was there
The clanking of wheels going
round and round
Echoing along the rails
with a magic sound
Today they still whistle, the
wheels they still hum
But now they're turned into
a "Dinner Drum"
As dining you go upon the rails
Forgetting historic events
they entailed
Even today we can all agree
without the rail system
Where would we be?
We have gone forward, but still can look
back
As the wheels on the train go clickety-clack.

Gladys Perttunen

What Is A Great Grandchild?

A great grandchild is a treasure
That brings much pleasure
Something money cannot buy —
It makes you laugh instead of cry
It stretches your joys of life —
and makes your years bright.
It recalls happy days of your
childhood ways —
Also your child's ways —
How happy were those days!
The grandchild appears —
Then the great grandchild appears
Where are all those years?
How blessed is a great grandchild!
Wonderful!!

Buena A. Crume

Untitled

Love,
is a cat,
moving gracefully,
walking quietly through a
field of flowers and thorns.
Often eluding those who seek it.

Aimee Zollinger

Why?

Love is poison
That burns your soul
Shrieks of fear
Tears no more
Cries of pain
Taste of hate
Drink the blood
Life's a waste
Running for life
The paths are gone
Turn around
your life is done

Deborah Smith

Creativity

When we write
it is surprising
how much we know,
stored,
waiting,
trance-like,
poised for release,
expression denied only
by self-inflicted reticence.

Pain and joy intermingling
should rise or fall,
in accent sweet,
or low,
but never restrained
by lack of surety
of what the world might say,
or know.

—Carol Poppenger

Something Else Beautiful

There is always something else
beautiful about
MOTHER,
She's your comfort and she's
your guide;
And when you call her she is always
there to answer too,
You can always in her confide.

She acts; to open doors for you,
She prays; that God will see you through,
Though many sleepless nights from you
she may hide;

You see, there is always something else
beautiful about
MOTHER
She's God's gift to you:
His joy and His pride!!

Gloria W. Roper

Silent Watcher

A Silent watcher,
Over the rough ocean.
A guide away from danger,
A welcome sight to any sailor.

The taste of salt in the air,
The warning of a storm.
The lighting of the wick,
And the cleaning of the glass.

A symbol of safety,
And a maker of times past.

Chrystal L. Jones

Rain

Rain,
A calming sound
Trickling down from the sky.
Every drop each an individual soul,
Merging into one another,
To form a sea of life.
It comes down from darkened skies
Hoping to keep its process a secret
Yet, like tears
Its source is its expression.
Never ending,
Ever flowing,
An expression of love, beauty and pain.
It comes from within,
A release of the impurities of the soul.

Gail R. Fox

Moving

Another key
a change of place
yet...we begin again

A larger place?
A smaller place?
Away from grass and trees

The roots are torn
the spirit gone
another key of tin...

Helene Peckar Cartwright

A Child's Bond

A parent is so proud when
a child is born.
As they watch the child grow,
and the flowers bloom.
They think of the child as the
most beautiful, perfect creation
in the world.
Parents never expect the child to
get sick.
They cry together, and mourn
together.
Parents always feel their
child's pain.

Elizabeth Dzichko

Mama's Hungry Babe

A babe in arms cries out in pain
a cry with so little to gain.
Mama holds him close
giving love in a strong dose.

He cries with great strain
his tiny stomach hurts with pain.
A tender touch of mama's hand
still it's hard for babe to understand.

A cry of pain pierces her heart
that just tears mama apart.
She sings those special lullabies
hoping babe will soon lose his eyes.

A babe in arms cries out in pain
still with nothing to gain.
Mama holds him close
and still only giving love in a strong dose.

Denise M. Gotimer

The Red Flag

He lied and then he gave the man
a drink and the man swallowed it as
he swallowed the truth and coughed
he coughed the juices of strong
sensation neither vodka nor betrayal
he simply coughed up bitterness but
he no longer had the strength to
regurgitate what was harshly thrown
at him and when youth allotted him
this power he did not recognize its
necessity and so then he covered his
eyes with his hand and he never saw
the lying man next to him covering his
eyes for shame of his tears.

Gabrielle Tito

Love!

Love is something special
a feeling in which we share.
and no matter how hard we look
there's no other that can compare.

It fills our hearts with joy
and often causes us pain
But after the hurt is gone
the love will still remain

So keep these words I've written
deep with in your heart.
always hold them close
don't ever let them part.

You've read this poem alive written
and now you wonder why
It's because this poem I've written
is with out one single lie!

Dennis Brock

My Mother

A tear for my Mother
a flood of tears
yet it still hurts
now and then
a memory here and there
She woke us with a kiss each day
She was imposing, but never imposed
The frail, little bird has flown away
left us behind
Tears of happiness for her
and tears of loss for me

Juanita M. Villalobos-Bell

Today and Tomorrow

Here's hoping that you have
A happy Christmas holiday
Here's hoping that the new year
will bring happiness your way.
Here's hoping that the future
Will bring good luck to you
In every thing you want
And everything you do
Wherever you may travel
Or wherever you might be
Whether it is on this land
Or traveling o'er the sea.
Be thankful with the thought
How blessed for you and me
To live in this America
The wonderful land of the free.

Jeanne Eberle Selman

"The Poison Kiss"

He was the love of my life,
a gift from God,
his kiss was the knife,
that killed in cold blood.

I always had hoped,
to find one like him,
but he had the rope,
to hang my heart in.

Like poison in vain,
his kiss was so good,
I knew I'd always remain,
in his arms.

When the poison ran out,
and the rope was cut up,
I wanted to shout,
as the knife grew dull.

The love of my life,
who always had thrilled me,
left me with strife,
for he had now killed me.

Candice Higdon

Remembrances

Do you recall a starry night
A long, long time ago?
When fiery passion burning bright
Set out souls aglow.

Do you recall that starlit eve
We strolled hand in hand
And barefoot, danced among the waves
And kicked the glistening sand?

We watched the pipers run with glee
Along the water way,
We watched the sun set fire to the sea
At the end of a perfect day.

Since that wondrous time with you
A thousand suns have set,
A thousand wishes all came true
A thousand joys ... and yet,

Memories linger, ever bright
And thoughts that will not quell.
Do you remember that starry night?
I recall it well.

Jim Jackson

Grandpa

He is not an actor,
a millionaire, or
a CEO of a company.

He does not wear designer clothes,
drive an expensive car, or
own a mansion.

He is just my Grandpa,
The greatest man I know.

Cressida J. Mark

Walk To The City

This small place is where I'm from
A place where I know everyone
Me and my things together as one

Step out the door and I see; familiar
Take a few strides I see; safe
Today is the day I leave this place

I keep walking at a slow pace
Now I am leaving this small place
Tears are running down my face
I think to myself, goodbye familiar
goodbye safe
goodbye small place

Christine M. Farrah

A Kiss

A peach is a peach
A plum is a plum
What is a kiss without a tongue?
So open your mouth
And close your eyes
And give your tongue some exercise

Jaime M. Crakaal

"God's Gift to Me"

Not long ago, I learned of you,
a precious gift I treasure.
A gift so freely given,
with a love beyond all measure.
My heart is filled with so much joy,
overflowing with grace,
anticipating that special day,
I meet you face to face.
It won't be long, my beloved child,
before all the world will see,
just how much that you are loved,
and what you mean to me.

Felicia Plunkett

The Angels Cry

Tonight the angels cried

The violence creates
A sad lullaby

Through deafening silence
An innocent child died

The mist of their tears
Fall softly upon the night

They weep for those
Who could not cry

They cry for children
Who should not die

If you listen closely,
You can hear an angels cry

Angela Andrews Pifer

Untitled

"Now is the time,
For giving thanks
To our belov'd overseer
For it's the beginning,
Of the end
Of this,
Another year."

Hughie Dale

Untitled

A sheltered love
A shattered heart
A happy family
Torn apart
A window glass
A reflecting mirror
What is pain
Is it in a tear
Can you go through life
Without ever living
Can you love a person
Without ever giving
What is a home
Is it only a space
What is a parent
Is it only a face
I don't understand
Why there is so much pain
Can souls be renewed
By a fresh, living rain?

Jennifer Jean Luce

Where Eagles Fly

It was way out in the distance
A silver slash
Flickering magic in the air,
Vanishing through the mist of the clouds
my eyes playing tricks on me a U.F.O.
A flying saucer
Then towering straight up
through the crashing winds
gracefully appeared a beautiful
Span of wings
Rolling, curving
freely in a pool of air
A glistening white tale
Sparkling off the mighty sun
Soaring ever
And furthermore

Dean Knapp

Snow Man

A child places the face of
A smiling snow man in the window
And hides behind it;

He waits and then in deep anticipation,
He peeks expectantly from behind
His secret hiding place;

Passers-by do not see the smiling
Face;
They do not see the cherub's head,
The face of innocence behind it;

And now this innocent face;
This vibrant smiling child's face,
Turns from the sun,
Turns from the brightness of the
Day,
And looks away;

His first furrowed brow appears:
And from his eyes, now filled with
Dew
Flow tears.

Burton H. Boroff

The Beach

The wave's roars.
A sound of anger
or
A welcoming?
The sea gulls.
A beckoning
or
A sound of peace?
The sand.
Captures memories
or
Drifts away like
Time.

Amy J. Coleman

Appreciating

I touch you gently as can be
A sweet soft dove who'd fly from me
So shy and fragile is the dove
So sweet and gentle is my love
Your eyes as lovely as can be
Your breasts so soft, so heavenly
Oh, how I love to touch you dear
How wonderful to hold you near
It's my love that I'm relating
With hands and eyes appreciating

Bob Strauss

Tell Me My Heart, If This Be Love

When Steven on the plain appears
A wed by a thousand tender fears
I would approach, but dare not move:
Tell me, my heart, if this be love.

Whenever he speaks, my ravished ear
No other voice than his I can hear
No other with but his approve:
Tell me, my heart, if this be love.

When he is absent, I no more
Delight in all that pleased before
The clearest spring, the shadiest grove;
Tell me, my heart, if this be love
One day he turned to me and said
That this is true and real:
So, lets make us a deal,
My heart said yes, that it is love.

Debby Kush

Untitled

The roseate clouds drifting
across the reflective sky
slowly part to reveal
the first crystal star of evening.

Dark darker darkest
black turn the green-leaved trees
as light also slowly drifts
away from the visible sky.

Wisps of now colorless clouds
float through the dusky mists
a flash of star then veiled
it is night.

Beverly Mulconry

"Unfortunate Find"

As I travel the sea of gypsies
Across the sands of time
My future is of sadness
Searching for a different sign

I see a hollowed darkness
Above the darkened sky
Across the land of gypsies
For which the humans die

It is a sacred journey
For the wise and old
They hope to find sanctuary
Beneath the sands they hold

For the cause they've come for
Across the sands of time
To perish in the gardens
For which they could not find

Jerald Nicolaides

Connections

The moon creates an eerie light
Against the sky's gray hue
A sense of danger in the air
There's trouble there for you

So please beware of what's out there
Of warnings you can't see
And heed the call that you can't hear
Within you there is me

Jan Preston

A Reflection Of The Motion Of The Mass

Crimson sap tears congregate at my navel.
Against the whiteness they look festive
For the holidays.
Considering,
It's not a holiday
Or anything.

Then, a single droplet separates
And rolls down my thigh,
Picking up speed on the Journey
Over my knee
And past the bruise on my shin
To drip off the end
Of my big toe.

More follow.
Until they gather at my feet
To form a puddle.
Curiously, I look down
To look up
At myself.

Emily M. Christiansen

None

Life with you is all or none,
I gave my all, you gave none.
Through your derision
I made my decision.
By opting for none
my life has begun,
proceed with the fun.
To hell with you
O arrogant one.

Daniel A. Cunningham

From My Heart

Oh how I love you my turtle dove
Against time I panted after your love
What many tears were shed at night
How I longed in your arms to delight

Thanks be to God who knows how to bless
You are now bones of my bones
And flesh of my flesh
May be continue in our love nest

Love never cease
It will go through the years
Even though in love
I seal these lines with tears

Anthony G. Atkinson

Gloria

It's been fifty years
ago today
Since He took you
by the hand
And led you away.

He took you to a far off
and beautiful place
Where forever you'll dwell
in beauty and grace.
My heart bled when
He took you away;
A part of me died on
that very day.
Your place in my heart
can be filled by no other;
So great is the love
God plants in a mother.

Johnsie P. Amerson

"Ghost Town"

Boomtown buildings-
All askew;
With windows set in —
Two by two.

Empty eyes that stare
and yearn—
For days gone by-
But can't return.
False faces turned
up to the sun.-
To dry and warp;
and colors run.
Your boards curl up
and splinter, — rot —
You tell of times -
when people thought
That they were lucky-
(But were not!)

Dege McCoy

"Untitled"

Love is a feeling,
found in your heart.
Love keeps two people together,
never apart.
When two people meet each other,
and love is found.
They stay together forever.
Their hearts are bound.

Josie Collorafi

Untitled

You are all I dream of
All I think of

When I clear my mind
And dig deep into my soul
to find what I am missing
what I am wanting and
what I am needing

I find you reaching to me
with empty open arms
Calling to me to fill them
and never leave them

I do

I hope this is not just a
dream but an insight
to one reality of our future

Jennifer Mone'

Simple

All I want is a smile in the morning.
All I want is a hand to hold.
All I want is a little extra sunshine
For when my day gets extra cold.

All I want is peace of mind.
All I want is another song.
All I want is to live forever
And bring my loved ones all along.

All I want is one less worry.
All I want is one more day.
All I want is for the world to listen
Even when I have nothing to say.

All I want is one fair chance.
All I want is one good shot.
All I want is to break even,
I'm not asking for a lot.

All I want is to say "I made it."
All I want is to meet you there.
All I want is to stop for a moment.
And then continue on without a care.

Jeff Terry

White Crosses

They stand in far off places
All neat in a row.
Those terrible white crosses
That once were smiling faces.

Rows of white crosses say it all
Marking the final resting place
For those who stood tall
Many unknown, many only a trace.

Sacrificed for freedom, country true
On beaches, in jungles, oceans too.
They got white crosses
Families got red, white, and blue.

Brave men and women of all races
Who fought and died without fear
We write song and graces
About the souls who lie here.

The veterans of war try
With monuments, statues, a wall
To honor and remember you all
White crosses forever make us cry.

Jerry A. Walsh Sr.

My Eyes

Look inside my eyes and see,
All there is to know of me.
My eyes are the windows of my mind,
Look and see what you can find.
My eyes speak without a word,
For my thoughts to be heard.
I sit behind them and watch the world,
As my life is unfurled.
There is so much to see,
Won't you come and watch with me.

Brenda Lee Bickta

The Mask

I saw the man behind the mask,
although he tried to hide.

I broke the barriers he had build,
though they were strong
and packed with the pride.

And little by little his love
leaked through
and the bricks began to fall.

Slowly but surely I got to know
the man I love most of all.

Heather Riney

Am I Doing My Part

Do I measure up to the Father?
Am I doing His will?
Do I try to Understand Mother?
Or am I hard-headed still?
Am I sincerely helping others
Because it's from my heart?
Or is it just my duty
To do my meager part?
My Bible says to give my all
To others every day.
I try to do the best I can,
But sometimes short I fall.
I know no person can be
As perfect as He,
But if we strive for perfection
His Glory we will see!

Janet Wible

The Grave

He lifts his face to the sun,
An attempt to dry his tears,
But they just keep falling,
About one for every year,
How can the sun shine?
On such a dreary day,
His true love for years is gone,
She has passed away,
No longer does her gentle presence,
Fill the darkened night,
No longer does he have,
The strength to fight,
He will die of mourning,
Like so many spouses do,
When their true loves have died,
Their lives might as well be through,
So as he places a rose on her grave,
As they will do to his soon,
The tears gush like falling rain,
But will not heal his wound.

Echoe Markland

Myself

If I could leave this life I live,
and be just one thing else
I think a dolphin free at sea,
would really suit myself

Or maybe a parrot high in a tree,
looking upon the land.
Flying across the jungle air,
my colors so bright and grand.

I could be a chameleon, that would be fun,
changing colors wherever I go.
I could disappear without a word,
and no one would ever know.

A manatee big and strong,
swimming gracefully in the waves.
To bad there aren't too many left,
and could be gone someday.

If I could leave this life I live,
and be just one thing else.
I think of all the things in the world,
I would like to be myself.

Adam Johnson

In Splendor of the Day

The soft morning sun kissed the early dawn
And brought a blush to the rose.
Dew sparkled upon a field of green
As the new born day arose.

All nature's creatures sang to the dawn
In sparkling crystal tones.
The music of their song
Pierced me to the bones.

I heard the robin and the whippoorwill
Calling to the jay,
The birds were all rejoicing
In the splendor of the day.

I stretched and sighed so softly
Their music was so gay,
I rose to see the sunrise
On another beauteous day.

I'm glad to be alive, Lord.
To see the world you made.
A chance to live beyond the past
As memories slowly fade.

Jacquelyn A. Frederick

My Meaning of Love.......

If the rain slithers down,
and dives to the street,
my love for you can not be raptured.
Like the birds dote their songs,
or the plants cherish the sun,
my love for you is much greater.
The love we divulge,
just you and me,
is crystal clear,
like the sea.
Hold me tight,
in your arms.
Caress my delicate back,
and tell me you love me.
As days go by,
one by one,
our love stays strong.
Like a flower in the rain,
we all have our own song.

Arianne Saenz

Nirvana

It was as if a sparkle fainted
and extreme blackness came
In instantaneous burst
of multiplied bareness of colors
we are tempted by time and space
For one cosmic second
we are in the midst
of God's breath
We experience the brilliance
of matter explosion

Elizabeth Lewicka

Thanks to God

Thank you God for trees so green,
and for the air so fresh and clean.

Thank you God for skies so blue,
And for the clouds I thank you too.

For flowers, grass, sun and rain,
for mountains great and open plain.

Thank you God for light of day,
and for the music the wind doth play.

Thank you God for snow so white,
thank you too for dark of night.

All these things you give are free,
I thank you God for loving me.

Dolores M. Trapp

At First We Were Just Friends

At first we were just friends,
and friends was what we were going to be.
But then we grew closer,
walking hand in hand by the sea.
When you came along,
I didn't know what to do.
But now I realize,
that I've fallen in love with you!
At times you seem so close,
but yet you are so far,
I've always wondered if we've wished,
on the same bright star.

Clelia Angela Scaccia

When I Pray

When I kneel beside my bed
and go to God in prayer,
I thank Him for another day
and for His love and care,
I thank Him for the home I have,
for family and for friends,
for the food and cloths He gave,
But most of all for Him.
I ask Him then to heal the sick
If it is His will,
for the ones who don't know Him
And for the ones who just don't care.
Then, I thank Him for letting me
come to Him, this way,
Whatever problems I might have
I'll leave with Him today.
Someday soon, I'm going home
My Jesus I will see,
for these prayers are not in vain
I know my Lord was there with me...

Frances Tilley

Without You!

'Tis spring again
And I am pushed to remembrance
Of happy days long away
When dreams were new
And come what may
Were acted upon and loved.

'Tis spring again
And longing fills my soul
To know again the joy of love
Once freely given
And quickly garnered
to be protected and savored

Tis spring again
And sadness haunts these moments
When "might have been" sounds hollow
And wishing clouds my way
And I must live another day
Without you!

Jennie F. Beasom

Young Love

You whispered my name
And I felt all aflame
For the word you had hesitated to claim.
You whispered you wanted me
And I felt the same.
We spoke of our love
That nothing can change.
But the words that you uttered
That made my heart shutter
Were "I need you, more than anything."

Dedra Hubbs

"God's World"

The time has come to leave this earth,
And I have No regrets
I did my best for what 'twas worth
And justly paid my debts.

I cried at sorrow, laughed at jokes,
And more than did my share
I was so good to all the folks
And let them know I cared.

If any place I missed the way,
And if I hurt someone
I wouldn't miss a single day
To bring some sun and fun.

And so before I leave this life,
And leave my flag unfurled
It hasn't been all pain and strife
God's made a wonderful world.

Dorothy C. Black

Liquid Sunshine

Silently,
falling,
Unheard drops of emotion.
Only I can hear
What they always tell me.
My emotions are
Liquid sunshine.

Artrece Sanders

"Never Grow Cold"

I hear a train whistle blowing
And I know where it's going
It's destined farther south
Where it never grows cold

I see the people at the station
And I know why they're waitin'
They want to chase their dreams
Before they all get froze

Up ahead in the distance
The train moves with persistence
I can't believe I'm leaving
My childhood home

As I stare at the masses
They call for boarding passes
We're going to ride the rails
Where it never grows cold.

Clint Elwood Lacy

If

If I let you in
And if I did hold you
It wasn't for keeps
I think I might've told you

If I tried to see things
I tried through your eyes
If I tried for closeness
I told you no lies

If I gave you strength
Take it, use it and fly
If I gave you peace
We'll share it, by and by

If I say I love you
Please don't take it wrong
It's love of friendship, of life
It's why I wrote you this song

Lazarus Tarmac

Holy Traveler

I will travel through this way,
And if only for awhile,
I want to live like Jesus,
And reflect Him in my smile.

Lead the way dear Jesus,
And let my heart be always true,
Let me be a holy traveler,
And walk each step with you.

Betty Muschar

Feeling Blue

I laugh
and joke.

At my belly
I poke.

I won't flick butts
'Cause,
I don't smoke.

I'm sitting and thinking,
of something to do.

To, chase away,
that feeling of blue.

Greg Major

"An Old Arabian Proverb"

He that knoweth not,
And knoweth not that he knoweth not,
is a fool — shun him.
He that knoweth not,
And knoweth that he knoweth not,
is a child — teach him.
He that knoweth,
And knoweth, and knoweth not
that he knoweth,
is asleep — wake him.
He that knoweth,
And knoweth that he knoweth,
is wise — follow him.

Edith Wright

Build Me a Castle in Your Heart

Build me a castle in your heart
And let me live there with you
Let's sit by the fireplace
Our arms in warm embrace
Fill my heart with love
Your everlasting love
Walk by the radiant stream
Stroll by the unresting sea
In the castle in your heart
Serenade me with your song
Inspire me to be strong
Because you are my everything
Climb a mountain in the sky
And watch the swallows fly
For our quest is true love
Our everlasting love
Walk in the lanes of home
Be with our heavenly host
In the castle in your heart
Where love will not thirst nor hurt anymore.

Candido M. Manal

The Stallion Full of Hate

He is black as night
And likes to fight.
He is big
And likes to do a fancy jig.
He has a diamond on his forehead.
That makes him look like a king.

His teeth are bared;
His eyes are red.
These are sinister eyes.

He is full of hate,
Life and viciousness,
Which makes people shiver.

His name is Satan,
Black's son,
Who rears, bites and kicks.

He would try to kill anything
In his way.
His nickname is KILLER.

Julie Laing

Untitled

I have depression, I believe,
And my case is not severe,
But it lingers and will not leave,
And hides behind trees, always near.
To cemeteries sometimes I go,
Where the deceased lie inert;
The kind of world that they know
Has no goals, no anger, no hurt.
Each day brings new difficulties
To take the place of pleasure.
Suicide? No, my judgment sees
It is too drastic a measure.
I live on, challenges taken,
Enormous tasks not forsaken.

Evan Werner

Whenever

Whenever your lonely
And need a friend
Call on me
I will never leave your side
Whenever your scared
I will be right there
No matter what
You can reach me
Whenever you want me
I will want you always
Never doubt it
I will always care
Whenever your lonely

Angela Schwingel

On Being Sixteen

How wonderful to be sixteen
And not be afraid to say
The thoughts and words that come to mind
On this your own birthday.

To love the world as you do
Is great, don't let it fade,
Animals love back when they are loved
The world, too, like this is made.

Your outgoing spirit shuns no one
And yet you seem to get your way,
Continue so with man and God
So each one, will be a happy day.

Alice Rogers

Given a Chance

I can do that
and not... "If I try"
I can do that
I will show you why
Give me an eye
You will see
Your heart can be opened
but you hold and hide the key
Warmth can flow hither to there
Love can whither unless you share
give me your heart
I will take that chance
for our souls to entangle
for our souls to dance
for I can do that
If your heart will say
for we can do that
If only you may

Daniel R. Simons

Made of Honor

To be so near your
And not to touch you.
To hear your voice
And not speak.
The scent of you
So sweet.
Your voice a melodic whisper
"I Do"

Your tender heart,
Your loving ways,
Perfected in her eyes
And echoed in my heart.

Alice Bussell Burkee

I Was Blue

I was once blue.
And only my father knew.
And no one else had a clue.
That my heart couldn't be glued.

Then he sent me my destiny.
Which I didn't know.
To makes my heart a new.
So I wouldn't be blue.

So now my heart skips a beat, one, two.
For it is as good as new.
Thanks to you.
And I am no longer blue.

Betty J. Bible

The Light of Hope

I look to the sky at night
And see a bright light.
A light of mystic and wonder,
I see the light every night.
It gives me hope to go on,
Like the shining light at night.
This light I see,
Is the moon at night.

Albert Gonzalez

The History Tree

How many see a tree
and see history?
Eras gone by, captured
in each ring;
wild flowers encamped below
where once soldiers lie
shivering in the snow.
Suddenly, minds clearing
they whisper a last goodbye.

See the mighty oak
cornered in a farmer's field;
his mule plowing, wheat it's yield;
weathered skin, a straw hat, his cloak.

If fear of doom be a concern,
let one lesson man learn.
Hope is beneath the debris.
It is the seed of a tree,
man's future to be,
the tree of history.

Carol S. Kannan

Science

Planets unite!
And see what I see
The universe is
Such a vast grain of sand

Sand
What do you mean sand?
How do we know
To others, our universe is
Not just a grain of sand

Science proves it
Science says the universe is
The limit of all things!
Science is a bunch
Of psychotics roaming
Around in white coats

Andrew Wright Milam

Despair

Creeps into my being
and smothers my soul
with its blackness.

Slowly
swirls and squeezes
pukes and chokes
until I am a solid stream of waste.

Oozing rage
that rumbles in my belly
heaving hot breath
That rushes and roars
out of my mouth.

Not me!
Then who?
No more!
Then what?
O God!
Help me?

Jacqueline Hinton

Gifts

Rainbows and sunsets
And soft breezes at twilight.

White clouds and angels
And the Heavens in starlight.

Lilacs and lilies
And springtime's warm sunlight,

Music and laughter
And the ocean in moonlight.

Bluebirds and robins,
And the gray mourning done
But mostly I'm grateful
For God's gift of love.

Doris Hall

Fuji's Poem

The sky is blue
and sometimes black
reminds you, huh
of the next life
so then its back
to what it was
just simply,
Black and White.

John "Fuji" Santiago

Thank You, Dear Lord

I never ask for much, Lord
And still I can't believe
All the many blessings
From You I do receive.

When I sit in total darkness
You always send me light
A guide for me to do things
That are pleasing in your sight.

The greatest gift you've given
For my life and soul to win
Is the Precious Blood of Jesus
To wash away all sin.

The Songs and Poems you give me
The beauty of each day
I ask of you so little
You send so much my way.

For all these things I thank you, Lord!
That come from up above
They make me feel your presence
And tell me of your love!

Eugene W. Miller

Go Rose

Go rose
And tell me why
The relationship everybody knows
Must die

Be the symbol
of my love
with simple beauty
like a dove

Our love will burst forth
As if a new bud

But our love will not fade
And die a simple bloom

it will grow strong
And deceive a certain doom

Boyd Railton

Existentializing

Let the silver cord be broken
and the dream deferred.
Let the cradle be robbed
of its trusting prodigy.

For I have been to the mountain top
and have been denied.
I have sought the meaning
and have been perplexed.

So let the sun rage on
and Mersault put to sleep.
Let the surveyor lose his way
and the whiskey priest his soul.

"For I have touched the sky"
and found the earth hollow.
I have looked beyond.
and found the nothing.

Don E. Peavy Sr.

The Still Of The Night

I look out my window
and the night is still

Unlike my incessant love
that I wish I can kill

If only it were so easy as
to just take a pill

But I fear that instead
I would just become ill

The trees are so green
but just won't move

But it is my love for you
If only I could prove

It is the still of the night
that drains my might

To forget about you
and give up the fight

But fear not
because I have surrendered the plot

And honor your will
As the night remains still

Frank A. Melfa

The Unknown

Show me the way to the tides
and the sea

I'll show you the way to the
unknown me

How I feel inside I always
will be
Afraid and alone is what you
can't see

But I keep smiling but really
I'm dying
Of what I can't be and dream

Crystal H. Verver

Siesta Key

As the waves come crashing in,
And the sun begins to slowly sink,
I sit on the terrace looking down below
With nothing to do but think,

I get caught up in dreaming
As the pelicans fly by
And await the coming of evening
With it's wonderful starry sky.

Its a place to sit back and escape
from the hurt and pain we often feel,
A little world within itself
Too magical to be real.

Let the feeling of this heaven absorb
Into your body and your soul
To fill the empty space inside
And once again feel whole.

It's a place to just put everything behind you
And let your mind wander free,
For that is all part of the magic of
beautiful Siesta Key.

Amy Caccamo

"Love Hurts"

He took my love
And then he left
He made me feel so wanted
He told me that he loved me
Then never came again
What's wrong with me, that he
doesn't like.
Or was it just lust for him
Even if I never see him again
My heart still holds him dear
I see his smile
I feel his kiss
His arms so warm and sweet
Just one more night of heavenly bliss
That's all I need from him.

Edna M. Garris

Nostalgia

Did you ever sit by a fireside
And watch the embers glow
Thinking of happy days gone by
And friends you used to know,
Recalling the past, when you were a kid,
That wonderful, carefree time,
And thinking of crazy things you did
And what you could buy with a dime?
Remembering the fun you had in school
Remembering green apples you ate
Remembering the times you broke a rule
Or swung on a neighbors' gate?
Did you ever sit by a fireside
Watching the embers die
And turn away to go to bed,
Then stop...and smile...and sigh?

Eleanor J. Hollahan

Love Me

Did you ever love someone,
and wish they loved you?
Did you ever feel like crying
but what good would it do?
Did you ever look into his eyes
and say a little prayer?
Did you ever say "God I Love him."
but I bet he doesn't care!
Did you ever stay up at night and
dream of how it could be?
Did you ever wonder how he could
overlook a love so easy to see?
Don't ever fall in love my friend
the price you pay is high, if I had to
choose between love and death I'm sure
I'd rather die!
Don't ever fall in love you'll hurt
before you're through, you see my
friend I ought to know, I fell in
love with you!!

Christina D. Grande

Forever

Forever is the dirt on the ground.
Forever is the stars in the sky.
Forever is how long your suppose
to love your spouse.
Forever is an eternity, it never
ends, good thing this poem isn't
Forever.

Jennifer Williams

Untitled

My age, Experience
And wisdom
Has not enabled me
To understand,
Or attempt to equalize,
The imbalance
Of forces
For which I'm attracted.
That allows some
To give so little
And yet so much,
While others
Give so much
And yet so little.

Eva Barksdale

Black Or White

I am white,
And you are black.
Our races usually fight,
But not tonight.
Tonight is the night of Jesus' birth,
A day when all men were created
Equal on earth.
We now play together
Like birds of a feather,
Though some still fight
All day and all night.
It is very sad,
That some are still mad.
But now can't we be friends?
Because our colors can blend,
And we can still be the best of friends.

Darlene Marie Loede

Exchange

One day I want to be like you,
And you could be like me.
We would have different hobbies
different tastes, we would see a
different face.
We would have different religions,
different brothers and sisters,
and different friends nearby.
Different rooms, different laughs,
we would hear a different sigh.
So, what do you say?
One day I could be like you,
And you could be like me.

Jamie Durham

I Don't Know How

The waves are breaking,
and the sun has set.
So I'm standing here thinking
that I don't want to leave just yet.

I don't know how to say good-bye,
and it seems so sad.
I want to cry-
for my heart is breaking.

The trees are swaying,
and I can feel the wind on my face.
I can still hear you saying
good-bye as I leave this beautiful place.

Elizabeth A. Smith

Untitled

May your life be filled with laughter
And your heart be filled with love
May happiness embrace you
Like the sunshine from above.

May your mornings wake you gently
Your days be what you please
And when the nite befalls you
May you always be at ease.

Should your eves be lonely
I wish for just one star
To twinkle thru the darkness
Glowing from afar.

Wishing you all you wish for
What you dream and then desire
From today until the next year
May all of these transpire.

Dottie Race

Quite Night

As I lay here in the Dark
another day done.
Crickets and whippoorwills
Sings me a song of summer,
They are happy to be here
They ask me If I am?
"Sometimes".

A soft warm breeze blows in
The window and brushes my face
The scent of Cedar all around.

"I miss you" I say softly
to myself-
Another night lonely.
Can't anyone ease this pain inside
I close my eyes to restless sleep
In the quite of night.

Diane Rice

Finally Happy

Three friends sitting on a bridge,
Another on a rock,
The current carrying ducklings by,
The sun shinning,
The lake glittering,
And us,
Smiling,
Laughing,
Talking about boys,
Our reflections on the water.
A reflection of our lives.

Jenny L. Roizen

Sweet Words Of Love

Sweet words of love,
Are all that I hear,
Where ever I shall go,
They're always someplace near.

They stand and hover over me,
Like an umbrella in the rain,
They protect and cover me,
From all the worldly pain.

They'll stay with me forever,
Something I'll always think of,
I'll forever remember them,
Those sweet words of love.

Jennifer Jimenez

A Passerby

She wore her bandanna like a crown
Expression on her mahogany countenance
like an intriguing saga
A pair of bleached jeans,
draped about her voluptuous body,
like a tribute to mankind.

Dorothy E. McClinton

Intricate Feelings

You
are on my mind
not some of the time
but all of the time.
What is this?
I can't sleep for dreaming
I can't think for you being on my mind.
What am I to do?
This I know not.
Feelings diffuse into my heart
some good, some bad.
My heart is saddened
by you knowing not, these feelings.
When I am blessed with your sight
the sun shines with pride
troubles are forgotten.
Respect is the word.
Without you, my heart is empty.

Jonathan Caudill Jr.

Imaginary World

Only in an imaginary world
Are raging waters calm
Only here can you hold your dreams
Securely in your palm

Only in an imaginary world
The winds are peaceful above.
Only here can you count on finding
True happiness and love.

Only in an imaginary world
Can you tame the mountainous land
Only here can you find your strength,
With a gentle, yet guiding hand.

Only in an imaginary world
Can your thoughts and spirit run free
Only here can that happen
In this world, so imaginary.

April Mankin

The Oak

Once, I was thought of
as a strong old Oak,
Never was it thought ever,
my limbs would be broke,
Standing firm in the ground,
strong as can be.
Thinking nothing could ever
penetrate me.
Now a branch has broke from
this strong tree.
And yes, most truly it
has devastated me.
I'll remain standing, firm
and strong,
Until the next Lumberjack,
comes along.

Daniel Thomas Dennis

At the River

The river slowly winds and bends
as along its way it wends
round little islands
sitting in the sun.

The wind makes ripples on its top
and little wavelets never stop
tickling sandy beaches
as in and out they run.

The children come to splash and play.
They love to walk around all day
through sand and water
having so much fun.

Some porpoises put on a show
as little fish dart to and fro.
It seems as if no
end will ever come.

The boats glide by with sails so bright
but all too soon day turns to night.
So home they go
a happy day is done.

Dorothy Keyser

I Wish I Could Sing You a Song

I wish I could sing you a song,
As beautiful as you are,
but songs don't come like that,
not at the least by far.
If they did I'd let you know,
that you mean everything to me,
And if I could spend time with you,
I'd start from now through eternity.

Colleen Ann Jaros

"The Way We Live"

Life is like a story,
As day by day it unfolds.
We can't change the past,
And we can't see what the future holds.
But if we could view our life,
As a play on a stage.
There would be things we'd change
As we turn back a page.

When we're young and foolish,
We think life has no end.
We live for the moment,
Never wondering what's around the bend.
But as time slips us by,
And our hair turns a little gray,
we have to stop and wonder
why we lived our lives that way.

Judy C. Wishon

Night Time Nirvana

Sometime late at night,
as I lye awake in bed,
All sorts of thoughts keep running
through my head.
Some are bad, some are good,
some of them just aren't understood.
When I think of life and love,
I look to God above,
even though he doesn't answer me,
I know it's my love that holds the
key, and I'll always be free,
I'm sure.

Dawn Marie Wright

Scorn

The memory lingers
As stilled images lie
Cast by forces unknown
Laughing with tears

Shadowed by illusion
Weeping with fear
The pagan ritual began
Dancing with the devil

Escape of imagination
Freedom from gravity
Society smiled while
Taking the swollen fruit

The feathers now fly
Driven by need
Of sanity not tainted
I pillage with intimacy

Through hidden desires
Of young thoughts
Innocent becomes deviant
I am reborn

Christine Vitale

Change

Things have changed
As tears run down my eyes.
You may not love me with all your heart,
But I feel you still care
Why you treated me so bad
I will never know why.....
someday when you're alone,
You will remember me
And you will feel the loss
This is my final goodbye.
With a sad good-bye,
I say to you "Good luck and farewell,
My love...."

Jennifer Joy Ginther

Sounds of Enchantment

The rustling of leaves chime
As the wind gently blows east
It's almost as if they are quivering
For it's the sun's turn to rest.

Sounds of rain
There is running water nearby
Making its way to the sea
Creeping in every tiny crevasse
Only to join again as one.

Sounds of enchantment
That's what this is
Sounds of enchantment
That's what this is
The wind has no limits
And the water as one
Sounds of enchantment
That's what this is.

Heather Shaffer

Contentment

A wisp of hair
A flippant smile

The look of love in
the eyes of a child

Tom Owens

The Beach

Waves lap quietly;
as they rush to the sand.

Wind in the trees;
gently blowing across the land.

Carefree gulls hover...
floating along

The morning sun rising;
spreading rays like a song.

Quiet time spent;
all alone on the beach.

Collecting rare treasures;
or relaxing by the sea.

Time that is spent;
by the waters edge.

Are but memories for later;
which may be revisited again!

Debra Kelleher

'Trust'

If things go wrong
As they sometimes do
I ask the Lord
To see me thru.

One day at a time
Is all I ask
Took God seven days
To finish his task.

If we follow his road
No curves or bends
He will see us through
To the final ends

My eighty years
Will soon come to an end
But I'll always rely
On my trusting friend.

When I awake in the morn
And see the sun
I say Dear Lord
Bless everyone.

Eona Prellwitz

Thoughts Of The Mighty Oak

To live in a forest,
As time never ends,
One might think I'm lonely,
But I have many friends.

The squirrels dance about,
Seeming so gay,
Leaping through my branches,
Day after day.

Sunlight and wind,
The still and the rain,
All of my friends,
I know of no pain.

The seasons change,
My trunk adds a ring,
Standing tall and strong,
I am sure of one thing.

If given a chance,
For fortune or fame,
I would not trade a thing,
I'd stay just the same.

David A. Stoltz

Tonight My Love Tonight

Our blanket blew gangly in the wind
as we stood beneath the levee
arm's grasp the midnight air
was chillin' the moon shown down
with heavenly glare.

Then you kissed me there
I was adorned by high spirits
Captured in your love and for a
moment heaven and earth grew close.

Owls hooted in the far off distance
the stars sent glittery shadows
across the water your eyes sparkled
like diamonds as we stood in the
chillin midnight air.

Your kisses warmed me yet your
charm captured my heart and soul
then you whispered
tonight my love tonight

Dorothy C. Taylor

Special Moment

It was a nice spring night,
As you were such a beautiful sight.
Hearing you cry
seeing your smile,
Certainly was a wonderful delight.
I have the Lord to thank for such a
precious gift,
sent from above,
and from that special moment,
Its you I shall forever love.

Elsie Kleinz

The Rustic Little Church

There's a rustic little church
At the foot of a hill,
Where we go to worship
'Cause we know it's God's will.

There's a sense of elation
And emotions that are strong,
When we listen to the music
Of an old gospel song.

There's feeling of reverence
As we bow our heads in prayer
And know we're in his presence
Because Jesus is there.

We listen to the message
Of God's holy word
And many many truths
From the Bible are heard.

So, come worship with us.
We sure hope that you will
In the rustic little church
At the foot of a hill

Byron C. Casey

Untitled

The moon in the sky,
Brightly shining on the town.
How pretty it looks.
The stars help it shine.
It looks like it came to life
By simply being in the sky's darkness.

Amanda Kenney

Reflections

I stand alone just looking
at the image of a man
hanging there upon the wall
lost in wonderland.
Who is this man I see,
I feel I know him well.
He appears quite familiar
yet I cannot really tell.
I stare into his eyes
trying hard to read his mind,
I search his face for answers
but only questions do I find.
He looks so lost and lonely
as if he doesn't know
the meaning of his life
or which direction he should go.
Who is this man I wonder
as I turn and walk away;
the picture becomes empty
and awaits another face.

Justin Low

My Wish

By the wishing well I stand,
Barely reaching out my hand;
Waiting by the stepping stone,
Where a gentle wind has blown;
Remembering from within my heart
Why it is we had to part;
Thinking of your tender smile
And why I couldn't stay awhile;
Recalling the times I smiled the most,
And the gentle way you held me close;
This I remember and wish for today,
I extend out my arm, then I pray.
My fingers slowly open and the
Coin begins to fall,
My wish is for you - it's your name
I call.

Elizabeth M. Bihm

Untitled

The unicorn lore
Be at your side
To protect and guide
So love never dies.

The strength of a man
His power and pride
Adds wisdom and beauty
To his child bride

Her grace is magnificent
As she walks in glory
By the spirits of
Earth, wind and fire

An unspoken love
Of the element's around
Graces the land
And knows no bound

The treaties of old
Behold thy daughter
Maiden of virtue
Virgin so pure

Elaine Yovonne Fugate

Untitled

Should our hunger for each other
Be so very strong
No matter how hard we try
To be with one another we long

Night and day we'd be together
If we could have our way
Consumed by each other
Is exactly how we'd stay

One heartbeat is all you'll hear
Our bodies melted together
Unable to separate us
We'd live off the love we feel forever

The feelings grow more intense
As the days come and go
Yet we keep them hidden
So only you and I really know

The depth of our emotions
And the fervor of our love
This bond between us
Must have come from above

Edith-Marie Innocenti

I Often Wonder

I often wonder what life would
be without the spring breeze,
the bright sun on a hot summer day,
or the beautiful white snowflakes on
a cold winter night.... I often
wonder.....

I often wonder what life would
be without love and happiness...
Sadness or loneliness... I often
wonder.....

I often wonder what a falling
tear means, or a great big smile.
Behind it all there's always a
hug or the sound of laughter... I often
wonder.....

I often wonder what it all really
means.....

Amanda Wood

Moonbeams

I see moonbeams
Beautiful moonbeam
Flowing down from the sky above
Flowing down in a sea of love

Their beauty lights up
Our wonderful sky
The moonbeams dance
The moonbeams fly

And as they fall
They touch us all
Like little darts
They light up our hearts

Beautiful moonbeams
Loving moonbeams
From out of the midnight blue
So lovely - they remind me of you

Bill Keller

Forever More....

Moments have come
  Between you and I...
Beloved thy name
  That will be thy be ours

Love to thee
  is for you....
To hold
  and be held
  through your arms
  with warmth
    and comfort...
That I have for you...

Nor perhaps
  I shall be blind
    to let you go;

Because forever more
  I am love to thee
    in love with you...

Agnes Zabale Reyes

Tired and Worn Out

Saggy breasts and baggy chin,
Blotches over wrinkled skin,—
Is this the way we must grow old?
That's half the story, I am told.

Go find a chair in which to sit,
Tired now, have to rest a bit.
Find my glasses and a book,
Sit again and take a look.

Bed is better than a chair.
Think I'll totter over there,
Pull up cover, close my eyes,
Just do nothing while time flies.

Clara Lacy Fentress

Sound Out, Mighty Bugles!

Sound out, mighty bugles!
Blow with strength to end battles!
Piece the smoke-heavy air
With your strains of noble commands!

Calls for the weary,
Calls for the wounded.
Sound out to guide,
Sound out to fortify.

Warm the soldier's heart,
Ease the officer's burden.
Sound out, gentle bugle,
Sound out to end.......this War!

Jerry K. Pollard

Untitled

I watch a flower petal
drop to the ground.
It slopes and staggers
'til it lands softly down.
You never see them pounce
to the ground.
There so gentle and relaxed
'Til another one falls right down.

Jamie Fieger

Fate

We're two wounded hearts,
both victims of love,
Painfully burnt by the flames.
Stripped of our souls,
unable to trust,
Stranded with nothing but shame.
Travelling alone, the journey of life,
Striving to forget of the past.
Hoping someday that if patience
persists,
We'll discover a love that will last.
Then oddly one day,
our paths had crossed.
It was a sign that was sent from
above.
Telling us both,
we finally had found,
The one we can trust with our
love.

Jodi Sostarich

Eternity

We stand on the edge of eternity
Bravely holding on
To the space that lies between
The heaven and the dawn

And in that place there's much to see
Whatever's going on
The atom fused and Newton
The jenny spinning yarn

The sun comes up to warm the day
As wildflowers bloom
Lovers walk to the sea
Underneath the Moon

Mountain strong, against the sky
Rives flow away
Stars shine bright in the night
Along the Milky Way

But all the army and marching band
That's very plain to see
Slip over the edge, their turn will come
To meet eternity

Gene Evers

The New Life!

It is a big deal to
bring up a new life
into this awful world.
It doesn't even matter,
whether it's a boy or a girl!
It should take every
strength you've got,
to raise your child.
You wouldn't want him
or her to grow up, wild!
To be a good parent
takes hard work and
has its ups and downs.
But the biggest reward is
worth having them around.
I can't wait to give all
my love to the child
or children, I may bare.
For he or she will always
know that I'm there, to care!

Colleen Kirby Rosario

"Glass Garden"

Moons glowing orb
brings midnight sun
crickets of late
trilling words sung
Safe and alone
rest variant room
faint stifled snore
of seven year groom
One loyal consort
sleeps underfoot
dreaming of game
bones at the root
Atrium hall
surrounded by green
add comfort and warmth
to hallowed moon beam
Lighting abode
as if it were day
she quietly sits
till orb goes away.

Constance E. Radin

Supplication

In castle walls I dwell secure,
Built ever to protect, endure;
Who dares to knock upon my door,
With skillful hand, who does implore?
The oaken door with iron bands,
Withstand the shaking of your hands.

Another stood where you now stand,
Surveyed this field, claimed this land;
The gate was then but crimson gauze,
I opened gladly to her cause;
I felt the pain, I heard with dread,
I dug this moat with words she said;
She filled it full with shame and hate,
Her laughter built the wall, the gate,
That hold me prisoner.

But if by chance you find a key,
Unlock the gate and set me free;
I'll drain the moat, breach mine own wall,
Unarmed before the conqueror fall;
I want to be your prisoner.

Denis H. Dieker

Victims

They are selfish
But,
I cry for them...
These children
The victims
of our society.
They have so much...
to offer,
But are convinced
have so little...
to gain.
Intelligent,
Creative, manipulative
Geniuses
Twisted inside out
Confused, apathetic,
Powerless, victims...
A product of our society
Dammed this society
We are selfish.

Donna McCann

"Hard to Say"

It's hard to say "I love you"
But how you gonna say it
It's not only you saying it
But you must feel it in your heart

Some times you say "Love"
But there's another word more
Some people say "I love you"
But they don't realize
What they saying

You must feel it
The way you say it
And you will realize
That "I love you" means a lot
For many people like me.

Gabriela Albano

Something Wrong

I'm so sleepy,
but I can't rest;
So I'm dopey,
without a test.

I have a stomach ache,
and my arm is numb;
But there is no medicine to take,
and it makes me feel so dumb.

I'm having chest pains,
it's a heart attack;
So if I say this, I'm not insane,
you might as well put me in a body-sack.

My head is in tremendous pain,
only more than that;
Don't tell me it's my big brain,
because it feels like I got hit with a baseball
bat.

Don't tell me they are all fibs,
I'm not being sore;
It's all part of being a kid,
I'm Just Bored!!!

Corey Cashen

"You Where Not There For Me"

You say you love me,
but I think you don't.
If you want me home,
then why don't you do what I ask?
I want to be home please let me!
I pray to God everyday to make him dead.
but me and you know God don't like me
God put me hear to go through hell
I am going through hell by myself.
No one is here for me,
No one is ever around for me.
Not you.
You are just there for him.
You have other children,
why not spend time with them?
I loved to come home,
but I will fell so alone.
I know because you where never there for me!
I was there for me and me only.

DeAnna Jo Klebs

Fait

White hands of snow embrace me
but my body burns with cold.
A thousand sands of time erase me
but my stories will be told.

Please hold me close and comfort me
make sure my life be fair.
Hold me tight to be one with me
make sure that joy comes here.

Instead my need are never meet
my life so ragged and rough.
All my life I was raised upset
my roads where pathed so tough.

I arise through fire and burning smoke
I succeed through all your hate.
To me all your trouble's a joke
because my destined life be fait.

David Paschall

Less Everyones, More No Ones

Everyone wants to be born,
but no one wants to live.

Everyone wants peace,
but no one wants to stop fighting.

Everyone wants to jude,
but no one wants to walk a mile in
that persons shoes.

Everyone wants to receive love,
but no one wants to give it.

Everyone wants to watch,
but no one wants to see.

Everyone wants to listen,
but no one wants to hear.

If you're an everyone step back
and take a good look, because
if you look hard enough you'll
see our world needs more
no ones.

Christina Morgan

Dreams

I once dreamed of a Genie,
But she did not stay,
I once dreamed of money,
But uncle sam took that away,
I once dreamed of freedom,
But then I committed a crime,
I once dreamed of a hobby,
But figured it would take too much time,
I once dreamed of love,
But no one really cared,
I once dreamed of a friend,
And you were always there.

Eric M. Swat

Love

I love you so
I see you know
But now it's time
To let you go
But which I can't
See you cry
I guess it's time to say
Good - bye

Misty Daniels

"Whisper She Does To Me"

Her life span is unknown,
but she is very old.
Her knowledge undiscovered,
yet she is very bold.

Large in size,
Yet small on scale,
She spins in a circle,
with no reason to tell.

For life she does support.
A mother to all is she.
Teachings have been shown,
in a history left to be.
And at night as I lay upon her,
whisper she does to me,
all the great wonders,
that are still to come for me.

Brian Beisigl

Arising In Me

I was born of seekers
but they are too scared to seek.
I know they yearn for truth,
but settle to keep things smooth,
they desire to love,
but the fear of appearing foolish
keeps them for a time
in bondage.

I have tried to live that life,
but something inside me cries out
This can't be
the time is short
you must cross that line -
that illusion
Appear the fool for in your heart will
sing a song so deep that you will die
to what you thought was real
and be reborn to what you know is true

Deborah Palmieri

The Toast Of Death

You, I have gained,
But yet I have lost.
My life is deeply pained.
A high price my life did cost.

Deeply saddened and troubled,
My time simply had no meaning.
My heart hast not doubled,
Sheerest of silk is the screening.

With a wound I did covet,
The silken red sheet covered me.
Red and crushed is the velvet,
My heart and soul would not set me free.

The red stained and gathered,
I drink to the death of thou.
Now, down I go withered,
My future I will not endow.

Thou hast coveted it,
To the host.
I go deep into the pit,
To the death of thou I shall toast.

Amy Christine Lynn

The Forest Sings to Me

The forest sings to me at night,
But yet it sheds little light,
on the fact that I am alone.

Sometimes it is sad to hear them sing,
a song of happiness and joyful thing,
because I am alone.

I hurt sometimes when I hear them sing,
It is sad to hear the soft ring,
because I am alone.

The forest sings no more to me,
Now I wish it would sing, can't you see,
because I am alone.

Christine McQueary

You

I see you in my dreams
But you have no face
I look in your eyes
But you have no face
I hold your hand
But you have no face
I kiss your lips
But you have no face
When I meet you out of my dreams
I hope I recognize you.

Deanna Holley

You Touch the Future

Live for today
but you must build for tomorrow.
Give your time, give your strength,
and it will give you life.
You have come to understand
that there are choices to be made
so embrace the past and
pursue the future and its challenges.
Take your stand and
make your commitments
for the future is yours.
Remember this time and
teach others what you have learned.

Helen Guckenheimer

A Thankful Heart

The sound of wind chimes captured
by a splendid summer breeze,
The tree tops swaying, hearing the
sound of rustling leaves;
The bright sun glowing with a hint
of expectancy in the air,
Being a part of God's Universe
so rich, so vast, so fair!

What a joy to experience each
thrilling new day,
Beauty unfolding in its' multitude
of worth;
A day filled with happiness and a
remembrance to pray,
A thankful heart, a loving spirit, and
a miraculous re-birth!

Anna Rose Whitlock

"Life's Entity Of Beauty And Love"

Awakened one morn at the age of 4
by Mama saying; "Hurry Lil' Ada
before the girls my 2 other sisters
come running through the door.
To eat all of the pastries that
was left in the oven and Papa
started the coal and kindling fire
and burned most of the pastries;
left for Santa Claus, and forgot
to take them out of the oven first.

We all had a tummy ache
afterwards but how sweet it was.
10 years later after years of Santa
coming down the chimney. Many
Christmases afterwards and many
offsprings later repeatedly and
much more exciting and going
to bed to give Santa his space
to make every one as happy
as was designed to be. Merry Christmas

Ada Kimbro

Alone

Alone...
Caged in a jail
Wall within wall
Can't see outside
Trapped in this hell
No escape, no light
No air
Suffocation
Mind is dead
Body will follow
World without comfort
Mind without thoughts
No life
Babies need a mother
Teens need compassion
Adults need love
Unconditional companionship
I have died
...still alone.

Elizabeth Reuter

This Love

Cannot live
Cannot smile
This sadness inside
Is staying a while

Cannot breathe
Cannot eat
In my heart
I feel a defeat.

I feel the hurt
I feel the pain
I feel this love
Driving me insane.

My world is only darkness
These days are never bright
I hope that one day soon,
I will finally see the light.

Amanda Cortes

"The Joy Of Jesus"

Oh the joy of "Jesus",
centered deep within my heart.
When troubling times do come,
I know "He" will never depart.

Oh the joy of "Jesus"
A continuing source of strength.
Despite of myself and weaknesses.
It's "He" I can depend.

Oh the joy of "Jesus"
in these days of happenings.
It's good to have "Him" with us,
for truth and comforting.

Oh the joy of "Jesus"
Every heart should know the feeling
Oh the joy of "Jesus"
the event is just so thrilling.

Fred A. Lindsey

Circus

Circus ceiling
cirrus discuss
Crescent cascade
aural chorus
Ethereal aesthetic
cerulean centaur
Aerial chariot
escalating gate
Equality transcends
enchanting dance
Chemical romance
emancipate chance
Circumstance coincides
anticipate consequence
Cosmic consciousness
concentric circles
Electric circuit
chiropractic canticles
Sincere sacrifice
celebrate Caesar

Brian Farrell

Untitled

Fly where the eagle glory
Clean fresh fair air
Hark hear the God story
A tear is warm
As a bee in a swarm
Swoop low my regal
Raise all as a bow
Oh arrow fly as the eye
Go life grow
And let me know

Helen Sherwin

Friends

Friends.
Friends.
Friends laugh,
Friends cry.
Friends hit
But friends never lie
Friends
Friends.

Sara McVicker

Untitled

We don't get along in the garden
Argue where to plant cabbage and beans
You refuse to wear a sun hat
I don't care a fig for your jeans

So we'll raise beefsteak tomatoes
And a kind of lettuce called Bibb
I'll comfort you with apples
And never crawl back in your rib.

Dorothea De Woody

Sleeping Hope

I am the essence of the midnight
cocooned between time past and
time futured.
I am the void of all voids
within the silence
of the universe -
my nothingness gathers momentum
growing...expanding...until
in blinking shock
this nothingness jolts
against the broken edges of
lost midnight thoughts
catching
burning
exploding
on contact.

Quiet settles upon quiet
and in the muffled deep
the infant phoenix stirs
in surprise.

Erina O. Goff

First Snow

The winter wind howls up its
cold breath and shivers across
the land,
the trees seem to groan against
it's current, bending to the point
of eruption, and then swaying
back in the pause.
White frozen rain beats repeatedly
into the ground, forming a shroud
of quiet despair
all things are slow motion
for winter is now upon us
and we will endure.

Hugh R. Schumacher

Mirrors

Grey, as the sky on a
cold winters day;
but with a softness
and warmth as elder down.

Sandy brown, like the
leaves of autumn;
but with a hint
of sunshine.

Tall, strong and foreboding,
like a mighty oak tree;
but with the soft touch of a women's
caress, you yield
with a gentleness
called love.

All this I see in you, dear,
in the mirrors of my mind.

Jan Francis

Oh Sunshine!

Shine down on me, oh sunshine
Come walk with me a while
Let me feel your warmth
Come, walk another mile

Shine down on me, oh sunshine
Cast your shadows through the pines
Don't let the darkness find me
In this lonely world of mine

Smile down on me, oh sunshine
I sure could use a friend
On this lonely road I walk
Which seems to have no end

Shine down on me, oh sunshine
Keep me warm with your light
Give me strength to make it
Through another cold, dark night.

Ann Hughes

945 Coast

Sunlit mornings
covered in your dew
warm with passions fill
tranquil echoes of musical sounds

Entirety seems askew
through loves concave window
reflecting a hero
masked in ordinary hues

Complete
and whole
as the infinite lines of time
intersect

Jana Fox

A Galapagos Tortoise

A Galapagos Tortoise
Crawls alone
Through Equadorian-nights
Weighing a hundred pounds.

Seek it out—-
Through search light procession
There I am hiding in a tree-top
So to wonder why?

Prehistoric fauna
Live on
In the dream
Of a torrid zone —
Night!

Eugene Zaia

The World Is Your Mirror

Laugh, and laughter ripples back,
Cry, and tears will surround you;
Smile, and the world will smile;
Frown - and you'll find frowns too.

The cheerful "Hello" will echo back,
An unkind word brings only gloom.
A happy face warms the atmosphere,
But, a cold shoulder chills a room.

Decide what it is you'd like from life,
For, as you live, so the world appears
Live and act the part your self:
The world reflects your smiles and tears.

Daysha Shunn

A Mother's Lament

Narrow slits, hooded thoughts, cold
dagger stares;
Lips pursed in simmering rage.
Stony walls - no warmth or light.
Struggle of ages, daughter of mine.

Love and hate,
Need . . . revulsion. . .
Warring parties of your
Child - woman heart.
Struggle of ages, daughter of mine.

I stand before you unswerving...
As my mother before me, no compromise.
Embrace the pain, swallow the fear -
no tears.
Struggle of ages, daughter of mine.

One day . . . no more.
My only hope is tomorrow.
Open arms tremble, waiting for
your return.
Our struggle of ages, daughter of mine.

Hanne E. Moon

Days Creation

At twilight, I stared, as the
day broke into a spectacular
time of wonder
It was a chance to toss all
my sorrows together and ponder
that a my future must continue
into different way
There would be joy tomorrow
because of the beauty of today.
If we but look into the
stillness of the quiet morning -
there lies a gift to all who care
to see and feel
The treasures are real.

Eva Poynter

Transformation

Dormant
Dead
Empty
No memories
Without love

Colorless
Beauty
Hidden
No light
Consumed by darkness

Seasons
Years
Months
Leaves green
Form, awesome, life

Voices
Emotions
Touching, sharing
Enclosing, unfolding
The rose

Juanita Marie Donahue

Since I Found You

I never knew such joy and peace,
Dear God, till I found you,
And now I have my whole life through,
As long as I'm in touch with you
Throughout each passing day,
If I become confused or lost,
You help me find my way.
And when sadness fills my heart,
As happens now and then you're
Always there to lean on,
And renew my faith again.
I wish everyone could have
The peace of mind I do,
And the joy and love, dear God.
I've had since I found you.

Eva M. Carson

Hatchets

Water silk, Mystic rage
Deeper clouds, Thunder gage

Sulken spot, Burrowed words
Caterpillar creep, Nothing heard

Sooner sleep, Left behind
Giving in, Fill my mind

Rising tides, Coming soon
Faster now, Harvest moon

Left alone, Death becomes
Light approaches, Darkness runs
Gust of wind, Surge of power
Nothing there, A pouring shower

Start all over, Find new hope
Like climbing mountains, Without a rope

Into the sky, Up and away
New happiness comes, With each new day

Cara Weimer

The Rape of My Soul

You walked into the room,
determination on your mind.

You'd been drinking heavily
and knew what you wanted.

Nothing I thought or felt
made a difference to you.

You trapped me in a corner
your sweaty, manly arms about me.

My smile was the reason
you gave for your actions.

Since when is a smile
a license for rape?

You gave me no choice to make,
but then I gave you one.

You had to make a choice -
leaving my body alone or acid down your
pants.

You may not have taken my body,
but the torment raped my soul!

Holly Lee Hann

Confidence

Confidence is what you have,
Do not let it go,
Keep it when you're feeling high,
And when you're feeling low.
When everything seems hopeless,
And you are feeling sad,
Just keep up your confidence,
And you won't feel so bad.
Keep it when you're having fun,
Running, jumping, screaming,
Keep it when you are asleep,
Even when you're dreaming.
Keep it when you're sorry,
Crying out of pity,
Making something ugly seem,
Extremely pretty.
Just remember to hold on,
Keep that grasp so tight,
Then you'll win every battle,
Victory day and night.

Alvin Krinsky

"Homeless"

Who are the homeless?
Do we really want to know.
They roam the streets
With no place to go.

They look poorly and sickly
With no thoughts of tomorrow.
To end up this way
Is such great sorrow.

What should we do about
this situation?
Look the other way or give
it attention.

The answer is within us;
Let conscience be our guide.
But whatever we will,
"Let it be with pride."

Evelyn Goldberg

The Promise

Watchman, how goes the night?
Do you yet see our Lord?
The wait is long, yet still it's right;
Watch for His holy Light.

Faithful, we wait for you,
The promise yet to come;
Though made of old, still it is new,
You've shown Your Word is true.

Hope strengthens every heart.
It makes it very clear,
As we believe in all you art
So does Your Kingdom start.

Let us sing joyfully.
Let us Hosannas sing.
The Babe, the King, with us will be;
His love will set us free.

Watching, we see our Lord;
The Promise 'filled anew.
Hope makes it clear Your kingdom's here.
Let us sing joyfully. Amen

Ann Marie Evans

Just Because

Just because you can't see me
Does not mean I am not here

Just because you can't feel me
Does not mean I am not near

Just because you can't hear me
Does not mean I do not speak

Just because you can't touch me
Does not mean I am out of reach

Just because you can't hug me
Does not mean I am gone

Just because I had to die
Does not mean our "LOVE" cannot live on

Janeen Kerrigan

"A Smile A Day"

Smile in your time of trouble
don't fall into the rabble.

A smile can bring joy
to every man, woman, girl and boy.

A smile will brighten up your day
and help you along life's way.

When you smile, others will smile
joy and sunshine will spread a mile.

O how happy our hearts could be
if we practice smiling and wait and see.

Edna Warren

Don't Push the River

Flow with it,
Don't push it,
Accept what life brings.
Weep for it,
Laugh for it,
Hear what it sings.
Love when you can,
Learn when you fail.
Flow with the river,
Let peace be your sail.

Edna Price

Our Commonness

Stop, Brother! Stop, Sister!
Don't walk away from me!
We have something to talk about —
that common thread
running through our ancestry.
We may be red or white,
black, brown, or in between,
but that's no reason,
Brothers and Sisters,
for us to overlook our commonness
in many things unseen:
our capacity for love,
compassion, and sympathy.
Let's treasure these,
not hate and jealousy.
For, if we take stick and stone
to break a bone for justice and equality,
we inflict on others
our own brand of misery.

Ben F. Bufford

Tears

Raindrops of pain
Droplets of sorrow
Falling in vain
Today and tomorrow
The tears don't stop
They keep falling
More than a drop
I'll keep bawling
I can't make it
You will see
Then you will
Come back to me.

Angie Prax

Rainbow of My Being

Colors connect me to my soul,
Each one special in its toll.

Red to Passion! Fire! Sun!
Anger! Violence! Battles won.

Green to healing, love and calm,
Nature's wondrous, soothing balm.

Colors connect me to my soul,
Each one vital in its role.

Blue to spiritual, ethereal lore,
Endless thirsting for much more.

Yellow to knowledge, endless yearning,
Joyful pursuit of ancient learning.

Colors connect me to my soul,
Make my life complete and whole.

Orange to joy, to fruit of life,
Strength and courage amidst all strife.

Violet to wisdom, majesty, grace,
Desire to find my sacred place.

Colors connect me to my soul,
Focus me on my life's goal.

Ellen M. Curtin-Contabile

poison eaters' society
electric visions
of hope
or death.
i saw Nirvana
and could taste it.
She slept
and felt her life slip away.
Phobia.
i still feel their finger
penetrating
My neck at chosen points.
he made me see myself.
laughter.
Uncontrollable laughter.

eric irving

Untitled

You take me from my self - imposed
cage and help me soar

And when I tire of flight, you
return me to my refuge - contented

Leaving me hoping that you'll
find your way to me once more
and help me spread my wings again.

Alice Vedral Rivera

Names

Tom, Dick and Harry, Jack and Jill,
Elizabeth, Kate and Mary,
These eight or many other names,
Are synonymous with the people.
Simple words that stand
Sturdy as English yeoman,
Redolent of the soil;
Words hackneyed and harmonious,
Essence of our history,
Ancient as our tongue,
Invested with tenderness
Bestowed by time's association

Genevieve F. Miner

Winds of May

Winds, winds, winds of May
Embraced by swaying trees
Your winged feet escape their arms
And onward flows the breeze

Winds, winds, winds of May
That heralds summer heat
Your scurrying fingers comb the grass
With steady rhythmic beat

Winds, winds, winds of May
Where do you wish to fly?
I feel an answer whisper down
An echo says, "The sky"

Deisel A. Tykeson

The Silent Telephone

There's a phone upon my wall,
Ever present for a call that
never comes.
Who cares you ask?
As you proceed with a task that
must be done.
I often call a friend,
With a bright and cheerful end,
Leaving me alone, once again,
So I'll wait for time to come,
When I'll go to Heaven's home,
Where there will never be a
silent telephone.

Fayetta P. Landers

Empty High School

Look good.
Feel Good.
Wonderful f___ing years.
Whoever said that
High school is the best
Time of your life, lied...
Look Good, I don't.
Feel Good,
I definitely don't.
F___!
Anger with tears.
A pain in my gut.
Don't give up.
Help me!
I'm sinking,
Drowning,
In a sea of people.
Help.
I'm gone.
Nobody noticed.

Jana Amberg

God's Trees

God's trees are everywhere.
Every kind you could guess.
Some trees are evergreen,
You choose what is best.

Some trees give us delicious fruit.
Some give us shade to rest.
Maple trees give us syrup,
Trees for birds to build their nests.

We have trees to build houses,
And buildings built so high.
We have wooden chairs to sit on,
When we eat apple pie.

There are trees big and small
That dot the whole earth.
Leaves of many colors,
They all have great worth.

As we travel along —-
God gives us a song.
His creation is so perfect,
Praise the Lord all day long.

Clara I. Nelson

Woman's Loving Touch

Her hands are silky soft,
every time one feels them;
her breast fully firm,
upon one's gentle caress;
her eyes sparkle with desire,
and her heart burns with passion;
her embrace is intoxicating,
with all the force of nature;
her body glistens with sweat,
but smells as sweet as a rose;
her arms shelter the fear,
and one can only love her;
her legs welcome for desire,
that she shares with her lover;
her touch is loving,
filled with natural warmth,
as only a woman's touch is....

James Earl Cook

"Eternal Road"

Curving eternal winding road
Excessive intersections to fly by
Sentinel waste obscures the mind
Beastly squalors by your side

Constant temptation to unwind
Negative donors go to die
Friends decay in disjunction
Absolute depression in function

Immorality invites deception
Purity seen at a distance
Gulosity invades your mind
Obligation has no time

Lively fast lanes only tell
You are living in living hell
Then your life can be showed
On the eternal winding road

Jeffery Amsden

Snowflakes

Snowflakes snowflakes
Falling on the ground.
Snowflakes snowflakes
Falling all around.
Snowflakes snowflakes
Falling on the trees.
Snowflakes snowflakes
Swaying in the breeze.
Snowflakes snowflakes
Dancing in the air.
Snowflakes snowflakes
Dropping everywhere.
I here mothers calling
Carried in the wind.
Come in now frost is in the wind.

Adrienne Kraft

Take Me Away

Take me away,
Far, far away,
Where you can't hear the gunshots
Or the screams of the helpless.
Take me away
To a beautiful day when silence and
Dark are non-existing,
But the laughter of the young and
The wisdom of the old are filling
The earth
From the high mountains to the
Deepest ocean—
Take me away.

Anisa Al-Turki

Silent But Screaming

Lost in the crowd
Feel so unproud
Do you know the name of pain?
Have I gone insane?
What's wrong with my brain?
I can't break these chains
Silent but screaming
Dead but dreaming
Backsliding again
Don't ignore my affections
Don't refuse with objections
To you this love I send
I'll get you in the end
Surrounded by idiots
And the women who love them
I am so hostile
Love me!
F___ me!
Damn you!

Gerardo Munoz

What's Wrong

Walking through the night it rained,
Feeling lonely, so much in pain.
Thinking about what you did wrong,
Tonight just feels so really long.
Teardrops falling from your eyes,
Nothing to do, but just to cry.
There are so many broken hearts,
You've never thought you'd be apart.
Well.... just believe it, it is true,.
'Cause it's called love, it's happening
to you.

Amy Ha

"Dark Tides"

Waves pulling me in
Feels like the unknown
Angels and demons pull out their swords
Two forces are pulling on this poor soul

Dark tides surround me
Waves getting so high
I'm alone at sea
Alone to the naked eye

No one can save me
Not in this night
The storm's getting closer
But I won't give..
No, I won't fall in..
No, Not without a fight...!!

Emilio Rodz

First Day

Gold first light
Filigrees across the sky
A prelude to each moment
The moment which holds
Anticipation, experience, wisdom
The moment which grows into each hour
The hour which moves through the day
To see the first star
In the clarity of the night
A first night which surrounds the way
To the next first day

Barbara A. Flaherty

Moments

Moments, moments - oh, so sweet
Fill my heart with gladness.
Guide me, help me to retreat
And banish all my sadness.

The earth can tumble into space
While sunbeams cast their light.
An ocean's roll can soon erase
The sand marks from our sight.

Moments, moments - oh, so troubled
Feed my hungry soul with rapture.
That I may lose a burden doubled
Leaving joy for me to capture.

Humbly seeking quiet refuge
Amid encounters of the day.
Sway my thoughts - do not refuse
The promise of time to pray.

Moments, moments - oh, so still
Cast your shadows like a balm.
Build my strength and so fulfill
Moments, moments - oh, so calm.

Frances Y. Dunn

Untitled

When you first set
fire into my heart
I was uneasy
but now in the burning
embers of my soul
My heart is crackling
on this painful day
As the flame of my
life slowly burns away.

Dawn Runstrom

Fall

Brilliant leaves - rustling leaves
Flamboyant range of colors
Autumn of the year is here
Yet not the bane of mothers
Children running off to school
A few who lag behind
Bring memories of my little ones
who've grown in size and mind
This time of year - the harvest
Corn and pumpkins in the field
A scarecrow - now his duty done
Is just about to yield
Ghost of another season
He too - lays down to rest
The earth preparing for a nap
Has passed this summer test
Rest well - old earth - as nestled
in your folds of deepest brown
The seeds of next year's harvest
Sleeping quietly are found

Carrie E. Autry

Love

Your love is like a boat
floating in the sea;
Your love is like fire
burning brightly in me;

Your love is powerful
so shocking, so new;
Your love can't be found in no other
because there are very few;

Your love is determined
to seek us through;
Your love makes me so happy
I'm glad that it's me and you;

Your love is so precious
to me, you see;
and I thank God always
that you've chosen me.

Jennifer M. James

Night Sea

The soft, warm night
flowed over me, in a gentle touch
caressing my body, in its embrace.
I looked with wonder
at sparkling stars
dancing in a moon flecked sky
that reached down
to paint the sea
in silvery beams
dancing in the breeze.

The gentle lap of waves
against the hull
of Taru, rocked her to and fro,
her main and jib were folded so
to spring to life at dawn's first glow.

Were I a painter or a poet of fame,
could I express with brush or rhyme
that exquisite magic which was mine
in that moment, on the sea
when heaven reached down and kissed me?

Dorothy Irene Hjelle Sjogren

Life, What A Beautiful Choice

Life, what a beautiful choice.
For a baby whom yet has no voice.
To say what's right,
Or even try to fight.
It's up to us,
To make a fuss.
Don't do what's wrong,
Let a baby live long.
For a baby whom yet has no choice.
Decide that life is a beautiful choice.

Cristina Aya

Life's Too Short

Life's too short-
for a family feud
Life's too short-
let's not be rude
Life's too short-
for jealousy and hate
Life's too short-
no time to wait
Life's too short-
stop - and smell the rose
Life's too short-
for a picture let's pose
Life's too short-
to not forgive and forget
Life's too short-
our Maker soon will be met
Life's too short-
the storm clouds will gather
Life's too short-
let's put the pieces back together

Betty Rinerson Paulson

"Do We Thank Him"

Do we ever thank Him,
for all that he has done.
Do we ever look back,
and see where he brought us from.
De we ever thank Him,
for good times he's sent our way.
And do we ever thank Him,
for keeping us safe day by day.
Do we ever thank Him,
for the little things and the big.
And do we ever thank Him,
for meeting our daily needs.

Billy Jackson

Hopes and Dreams

I have a piece of hope
Deep inside my heart
It's so very special
I won't let it part
It carries me so very far
And lets me live each day
It gives me strength
To take each day in a new sort of way
Life is not a bore
It's not a silly game
Hopes and dreams give me courage
To take each step and never be the same.

Allison Green

"The One I Love So Much"

My heart is full of fear,
for all the answers are clear,
The one I love so much,
I cannot longer touch,
We promise to each other,
that never shall we part,
But now you are gone with another,
Leaving me a broken heart,
your smile keep on haunting me,
morning noon and nite,
My peace and joy you rob of me,
Oh God it's this right,
Time has pass and my heart is heal,
But the wound you give me yet I feel,
your face I am longing just to hold,
Sure my story will be told,
Now my knees are shaking my back is bend,
yet you will remain my very best friend,
I cannot love another so,
for you my love will always grow.

Bissoondat Ram

Do Not Be Sad

Do not be sad when I depart
For I shall come again-
I shall return some spring
In the softness of the wind.

I shall be as a drop of dew
On the petal of a rose.
I shall be as a rainbow
Colorful in repose.

I shall whisper in the willow trees-
I shall whistle in the glen-
I'll touch you as spring rain
And brush your hair as the wind.

The warmth from the winter fires
And the snow so soft and cold
Are feelings I'll project to you
From every little knoll.

Bobbye Tubbs

Give You My World

I would give you my world
For just one more chance
To see your face
To look into your eyes
For just one more minute
To hear your words
To drown out my cries
I would give you my world
Give it all up, every last drop
Just to be together with you
That's what I would do
Give you my world

Brenda Holmes

Bam Pam Ram

I bam
I Pam
At ram

Shane Paul Allgeier

Untitled

My mind is too free
For my body tied to this tree.
This brick and bar can't hold me here.
Captivity is all I fear.
Chained and locked for so long.
Satan keeps my life prolonged.
Jesus is on my mind.
But I can't find the time.
I die to try to pray out of my cage
I feel my anger and a satanic rage.
My life will never begin.
Unless I'm free of this worldly pin.

Eric Wright

"One Last Rose"

A dozen American Beauties!
For my love to show!
To somehow assign
The inner me
As one on one, only!

Roses on Valentine's day!
With the bubbly!
To etch my feelings,
Growing grandly!!
With love felt deeply!
As one on one, only!

Roses, for my love to show!
Until it wasn't wanted
Any more; so, my gift,
Of "One Last Rose", a book with
Petals of love pressed between the pages!
As one rose, on one last rose, only!

Hugh Phillips, Jr.

The Best Gift

How do I say thanks
for something like this?
Do you give them a hug
or a great big kiss?

This gift is so big
and so hard to describe
How long will it take?
as long as I'm alive?

Its hard to understand
this wonderful gift
It takes love patience
And a great big lift

Its the best gift
A person can give
As long as they try
As long as they live

This gift is a miracle
It needs a loving husband and wife
This gift you want to hear about
is everyday life.

Angela Gertsema

"A Father To Be"

Come November we'll be able to cheer
for the laughter of our baby
that we shall hear.
I know in my heart
A great daddy you will be.
And I will see the love in your eyes
for the first time
when you hold our baby
And bond your ties.

Aleicia McDonald

Thank You, Lord

Did I say "Thank You" today, Lord,
for the many things you've done?
Did I express my gratitude
for the battles I have won?

Did I stop for just one moment
and say "Thank You" for your care?
For setting me on my journey,
and safety getting me there.

When darkness was all around me,
and nothing seemed quite right,
did I thank you for your mercy
as you lead me to the light?

Could it be that I've forgotten
how you get me through each day?
Am I grateful for the blessings
I've received along the way?

If I forget, Lord, please remind me.
You see, I depend so much on you.
Thank you, dear Lord, thank you,
for all you've done, and continue to do.

Jacquelyn C. King

Day By Day

A child's tears I can not stand,
For they are the saddest
Of all the land.

A two-year old stands here crying,
For he is so young to be dying.

Dying, a cancerous death.
For any day now,
He may draw his last breath.

A sad tear rolls down his cheek,
Rolls off his face and to his feet.

Please, child,
Please, don't worry.
For God will save you in a hurry.

God will take your pain away,
And you will live
Day by day.

Doris Evelyn Bowen

Hope

I know I can cope with this,
At least I hope.
I know you will see the same as me,
At least I hope.
I know I will always be with you,
At least I hope.

James Stone

Through All Things

Best friends are together
forever, from across the country,
to across the world, and into
the endless skies. Through fights
and quarrels, and your first love,
And when you fight, you can't
bear it.
When all goes wrong
and it seems no one is there
for you, your best friend gives
you courage to do anything.
Like being a friend through all things.

Jennifer Brown

Bruthas, Drop Your Guns

Genocide
Fratricide
Bodies
Float out with the tide
And why?
They're on the other side?
A different tribe?
For ethnic pride?
Our skin is all black
Our noses all wide
And we all cried
Hearing how many have died
Tutsi and Hutu
Haitians, Somalians
Crips and Bloods
Brothers gotta work it out
Let these tears be dried
Stop this suicide

Ernest Morrell

Falling Leaves

Having fallen turn
From green to gold

Tear shaped raindrops
Pulled to perfect round
Splash into crowns
Upon the ground

The great pattern
Is a straight line
Within a glorious circle

Eric Stanley

Mother

I was sent to you
from heaven above;
You gave me life
you gave me love.
No sweeter person
could there be —
God's special gift
was you for me.
I owe you much,
I can't repay;
I love you more
each and everyday.
When God made you,
He made the best;
To find more beauty
is an impossible quest.
He made you perfect,
He made you so fine;
But I thank Him most
for making you mine.

Jeffery Rosemann

Grandpa

G - Is for the goodness that comes
from the heart,
R - Is for remembering things
from the start,
A - Is for ability the strength we
always find,
N - Is for navigator to help us
when were blind,
D - Is for dear the people we
keep in mind,
P - Is for positive no matter how
hard things are,
A - Is for always if were close
or very far.

Darla O'Leary

Always Together

Your ashes sift through my fingers.
Floating on the breeze, they scatter
over the garden.
Sunshine and rain melt you into
fragrant blossoms.
Smelling and caressing the flowers,
I cling to the ashes of my love.
Knowing: Tomorrow we will grow
.... again together.

Jana Yeates

"E.T.P."

Tho there are many miles
from the old, to your new home
We'll always remember the smiles
we shared before your roam
And tho we may shed a tear
Remember you must "Endeavor to Persevere"

For it is with a great pride
and a greater love in our heart
That we are on your side
No matter the distance we are apart
So go forth my son without fear
For we must "Endeavor to Persevere"

Abel J. Flores (Poppers)

The Dog

Oh! Fred Boy you came
from the street.
Right away you melted
our hearts.
What joy you brought
And we were caught
In your spell
You were so sweet.
Tho' you've been gone
many a year.
We loved you so
When you were here.
We think of you often
with a tear.

Ethel Irene Duran

The Love I Still Feel For You

Even though my heart is crushed,
from the tragedy you made for
the two of us.
I still love you and will never
stop, because in my heart your
at the very top.
Even though we didn't made love
that doesn't mean you have to
hate my guts,
I think of you day and night,
when the sun is not shinning
as bright, like your face in my
eyesight.
I love you dearly, so don't forget
me, cause I haven't done
anything to loose you my honey,
and please remember you'll always
be my one true lover.

Aleta E. Flores

To Mom with Love

I thank the Lord
from up above

For giving me to you
to love

You made me grow
all through the years

There was laughter,
there was tears

I miss the times
we used to share

But yet I know
you will always care.

Now I carry
all the joy you gave

Within my heart
for me to save

To someday share all I have
learned from you

With a child of mine
someday too.

Bonnie Johnson

Husband

To look into your eyes is to
gaze into a pool in which I can
drown with no pain.

To kiss your awaiting lips is
to feel the purest of silk against
my mouth.

To be in your strong arms
is to have protection like a home
that is always open.

To be with you is to be
with the kindest of men with the
warmest of hearts.

To love you is to feel joy
like this women has never felt before.

Jennifer Miller Gill

First Love

Like the sunshine of early spring,
Gentle, brisk,
Your kisses and embraces.

Like the new moon hidden in cirrus,
Coquettish, shy,
Your glances and poises.

Like the snow covered peaks,
Pure,majestic,
Your promises and sentiments.

Like the fresh morning air,
Freely given and taken,
Your care and solicitude.

Like the dawning aurora,
Emitting all the hopes,
Every time you smiled a smile.

Alas, let me rid of all the sorrows,
And love you as I drank the elixir of wines;
Let this moment be filled with ecstasy!

Bai fuh

Untitled

Over coffee
gently how we seem to
forget the presence of ordinary others,
This myriad of bland,
Of personalities so foreign
to us -
Who may not want
to know
how two minds can
be fused
Like kindred dialects
of a language
when stimulated by
love and tenderness and
the illumination,
the presence,
and the passage of long, long years.

Allyson M. Carneal

"Winter Picture"

From my window I can see
Gifts of nature and all are free.
A tiny titmouse on my sill
Nibbling at seeds, his thanks a trill.
Naked trees with arms outstretched,
Against the leaden sky are etched.
The lacy birch, standing so tall...
Lovely in every season,
Winter, Spring, Summer and Fall.
Mounds of snow like paper-mache
Makes perfect the picture
On this winter's day.

Helene B. Dillon

Work

The carpenter cuts and hammers
driving his nails deep
into the wood of a new house.

The tailor leans into his table
stitching the ripped hem
of a rich women's dress.

The poet sits and scribbles
seeking to sift something lovely
from the ashes of his life.

Bea Scribner

Nostalgia 101

Many years ago when I was just a boy,
Growing up in fancy farm with friends
like Harold, Rudy, JW and Mr. Roy,
Times were tough and very lean,
And people worried more,
Most confessed to unpaid bills,
At Hobbs and Cashes general store,
We all remember the red brick school
Named after the great Saint Jerome.
And the Nuns that thought us
the value of family friends and home.

Carneal Thompson

Two Hearts of Gold

My husband George
had a heart of gold
and in loving him
he gave me a heart of gold.
How two people meet and
love and say good-bye is old; for
we had hearts of gold.
as I sit here on the
beach, with him out of reach,
My heart of gold is cold,
for only with him did it beat;
my heart of gold.
Two lovers where we,
with hearts of Gold....
By his wife of 28 years.

Joyce Orphanoudakis

My Love Will Never End

Why do things like this
happen, I say, Dear Lord
tell me as I pray.
His body so sick and full of
pain, never did we hear him complain.
He came to us like the
warm sun, tried to make each day fun.
I can still hear him, but know
he is gone, he has lost life's song.
You will never wipe away my
tears, no comforting arm to
take away my fears.
His love gave life to me,
I will always remember
the way we use to be.
I see your eyes in the stars,
your presence surrounds me near and far.
I will hear your voice in the
wind, my love for you will
never end.

Carolyn Thorsen

Wicked Eyes

Piercing my soul
Her wicked eyes watched me
An enchantment she has cast upon me
Captivating me in her gaze
In those dark lovely eyes
Do I dare break the stare
Or lose myself within it
Oh how her gaze frightens me
Yet there is comfort in it
Like beacons her eyes shine so bright
I like a deer am frozen in their light
Should I take the coward's flight
No I shall linger another moment

James W. Harlan, Jr.

Evening

Evening in her gentle way
Has gathered up the fringe of day
And tucked each little thread of light
Beneath the blanket of the night

She drew a shade across the sky
And as the shadows hurried by
She gathered each in warm embrace
And laid it in it's resting place

Every creature, bush and tree
Settled down contentedly
As she spread her gentle hand
Across the bosom of the land

And when the final hour had come
And she had parted with the sun
A quiet contentment filled the air
As evening raised her face in prayer

Forever it will always be
These lovely things we hear and see
Stay with when, with sleepy nod.
We whisper our good night to God

Jerry Caldwell

Untitled

High in a pale blue sky
he began to wonder why
but it brought him naught
without worry and taught
him enough to make his
head spin and spread
everything out real thin
between the hawk's angry eye
and a fair maiden's deep,
summernight's sigh.

Joseph A. Belanger

Creations

When God created cousins,
He made close friends to share.
Our secret hopes and dreams
And the burdens that we bear.
When God created cousins,
He made warm hearts to care,
With gentle understanding.
And an insight that is rare.
When God created cousins
He has answered every prayer
That has asked for a someone special
Whose love is always - always there.

Jessica Rice

My Answered Prayer

I asked for power that I might achieve
He made me weak so I would receive
I asked for strength to make me strong
He gave me deliverance from all wrong.

I ask for riches I had much greed
He gave his word for me to read
I asked for a big and beautiful place
Instead he gave me sufficient grace.

I asked for knowledge to make me wise
He gave me favor in his eyes
My prayer was answered in God's own way
So I'll be with him in Heaven one day.

Delta McLauchlin

My Heart's Prayer

Lord father in the heavens
I come to you today
In hopes that you will read my heart
And hear this prayer I pray

I thank you for the life you gave me
And for this world in which we live in
For all my friends and family
And for the sister's I've been given
Throughout our years of growing up
And through the loss of mother and Dad
You taught us love and gave us strength
And showed us good in bad
No words could ever express
The love that we all share
A bond between three sisters
That will always be right there
And though our future lies before us
We know this world will come to end
I thank you Lord for making us sisters
And for the love that made us friends.

Carol A. Diegel

Secret of the Heart

I find my life confusing,
I don't know which way to turn.
No matter what I decide, some
one will get burn.
I try not to think about him,
but no matter how hard I try
I remember the first touch,
the kiss that left me shaking inside.
Then I realize it can never be,
and I try to make my heart see.
Our love is special,
but one that will never be.
I know our love is forbidden,
for neither of us if free.
But we started out as friends
and friends I know we will always be.

Arleen L. Tatum

Me

I don't want to try to be pretty
I don't want to try to be beautiful
I just want to be me.
I don't want to try to get attention
I don't want to try to be the center
I just want to be me...
That's all I can be.
I would like to be respected
I would like to be loved
But I need to be me...
That's all I can be.
Any beauty I may possess,
I hope you can see it.
Any attention I may receive,
I hope comes from you
But your love and respect
I hope I receive
Only because I am me...
And that's all I can ever be.

Felicia Thomas Williams

Touch Me Now

As I dream... I dream only of you
I dream of all the things that we
have been through. As my mind
wonders off into the night, I can feel
your touch as you hold me tight, so...

Touch me now, let's run away
let's whisper our love in each others
ears, 'cause we have the love that will
last for years.
Fast asleep I fall, in my dreams
I see myself crawl to you... to be
by your side, I feel so safe in
your embrace and with you there
is no problem that I can't face, You
touch me lover and for me there
is no other, so...

Touch me now and
let's run away, let's whisper our
love in each others ears. 'Cause we
have the love that will last for years.

Donna Wright

The Earth Beneath My Wings

Like a bird,
I drift off into the sky
Looking down below,
To the earth where I sleep
With the wilderness of peace
That I seek shelter.
The beauty of my wings
Let me go where no bird
Has gone in life.
I adventure many places
Along the sparkling river
Where in a old, oak tree
Holds the life I given to
My yearlings
Soon there wings will be
My heart
Then they will be looking
Down below,
Where I lay, with my soul

Christina Witucki

"My World"

When I look in your eyes,
I enter your world.
For you just entered mine.
You, so innocent,
Though you do not really know what kind
of a world you're in,
One of violence and hatred,
And yet you have no fears.
I can't protect you from this world I
brought you into.
I wish I could!
It hurt me to know it's my fault you're
here in my world.
I love you and want you to be safe
from harm.
So, I'll try my best for you to be safe,
Until you understand my world!

April Cole

Betrayal

Should I live or die
I find myself asking why
As I sit all alone
Weary to the bone
Of the life I am living
That turned very unforgiving.

It started out bright
Then eclipsed into the darkest night
As the innocence of my trust
Fragmented into dust.
My soul cried out
"What is to come about?"

That decision I fear
May cost me dear
If I can't find
Some peace of mind
Before I decide
That I will have to unreside.

Anthony S. James

For Tina

I loved you more than any other
I gave those things I thought
I would give no other.

Blinded, I believed your lies,
Ignored your treachery
And laid bare my soul.

You took my soul and crushed it.
Stomped upon my heart
And laughed as I lay dying.

All my love is turned to hate
Venom has replaced what once was sweet.
That is your gift to me..

John Ditchman

My Black Widow Poem

I am not worth the time you spare
I am a creature of the night
Beware!
A black widow waiting for her prey
I lure you into my arms at night
and belittle you till the morning light
I'm as soft as morning sunshine
Eyes more innocent than a doe
And if you think that I love you
How little can you know?

Bobbie Jo Beeman

Thank You Lord!

Thank you Lord for all you've done
for me!
Thank you Lord - for helping
me to see!
Thank you Lord - for each and
everyday!
Thank you Lord for showing
me the way!
Thank you Lord for birds
that sing!
Thank you Lord for
everything!

Edith Macko

Untitled

The Lord is weeping for all His children sleeping
Somewhere in the night there stands a lone light
Somewhere in the world there stands a lonely girl
Who prays to the Lord to stop the destruction
and bring on construction, she says
Cry for your nation
Bring back God's creation
He believes in you, believe in Him too
Give Him your heart and let's make a fresh start
We must stop the fighting and crime
Cause we're wasting precious time
Let's stop the hate and start a new trait
We need to change this place for the whole human race
We must change our ways so we can all stay
We must stand up tall before the big fall
Cry for your nation
Bring back God's creation
He believes in you, believe in Him too
Give him your heart and let's make a fresh start
Cry for your nation.

Tammy Post

The Cradle

Cradling me in your arms.
Soothing words.
Soft fingertips moving gently through my hair.
His kiss is warm and luscious.
I close my eyes, my pain leaving my body
I feel safe and cared for,
My tears diminish and I wait for you
to take me away from misery.
The rain hardens and thunder breaks.
The water cascades down the glass...
The memories return
and the tears fall once again.

Julieta Banan

Love Never Dies

Early A.M. rolls and still awake
Sounds of clock ticking reminds my heart to ache

Memories so beautiful; yet so devastating
You went away; my heart breaking

Togetherness was forever or so we thought
Life is short; difficult to hang on to what we've got

Your spirit, often so close, still lingers
Always touching my soul with delicate fingers

Death is rude, it doesn't care
Many lives it has yet to tear

Although our time was short
Our love, shall be, forever more

Lisa D. Hofmann

Adoption

A modern - day Moses,
Spared from destruction,
yet sent on my way
To navigate the river of life.
Saved out of water,
yet how did you know,
I would find the Pharaoh's daughter?
That the tide would turn.
The beating waves would subside.
And I would no longer have to hide
Behind a sense of betrayal and rejection.

Louise Bonnett

Momma Said, "I Can"

I'm a future star, so brightly do I shine
Sparkling with life and a brilliant and capable mind
I can be a teacher, an instrument for learning
Or an environmentalist and help stop the ozone from burning
I can be a scientist and cure a dreadful disease
Or a humanitarian, to comfort those in need
I can be an attorney and vindicate someone's rights
Or an accountant, balancing books, both day and night
I can be a surgeon and repair a broken part
Or a cardiologist and heal an ailing heart
I can be an engineer creating marvelous sites
Or a chef, preparing pleasures for the appetite
Yes, If I work diligently, I can be what I desire
Momma said I can, and momma is no liar

Patricia A. Wooten

Assurance

Wispy threads of doubt dance through my mind,
Spinning webs of fear and of dismay;
My thoughts become entangled therein
And prophesy my failure today.
Lying words form as if from nowhere;
Ever so beguilingly they scheme;
Telling me that I am worth nothing;
They assail all of my lifelong dreams.
Peers speak and I am torn asunder;
Even friends align themselves as foes;
Misguided reproofs cut me like knives;
adding strength to my ever growing throes.
Just at the point when life seems worthless,
And I'm almost convinced of my lost estate,
God's voice speaks from unexpected sources,
assuring me that my future looks great.
"Listen to me my child", he urges,
"Those other voices don't mean a thing.
I am the one who gives assurance
That you are a child of the King".

Thomas Straitwell

A Special Miracle For All

As I walk out the door I breathe in that smell of the glorious spring thaw.

It is the first sign of spring and to me it is a miracle of life.

Slowly but miraculously the flowers start to pop up from the ground.

The bud of leaves on the trees start to bloom like a trumpet of hope being blown at all might.

The sun swings around to greet me with another season of new life for me to cherish all winter long.

At last spring is here for all to find and greet hope, joy and love.

Mari S. Wilpiszewski

My Friend the Dolphin

From the roll of the harbor wake to
the taste of spray he takes.
On a promise to be free. In colonies
of mermaids among gilded galleons
Spilled across the sea floor, listening
to the songs that the rigging makes
as the currants go to and forth.
Seeking no treasure only the promise
to be free dolphins playing in the sea.

W. C. Ramsey

Coastal Storm

Wind tears at solitary scrub pines
Standing as sentries by the shore,
Bowing and scraping,
First rhythmically and humbly,
Then in wild frenzy
At harder bites of the blustering North-Easter.

Agitated stone and shell bits,
Long ago pounded and pummeled,
Powdered infinitesimally small,
Leap from dunes' bosoms
And fly inland on wisps of tawny cloud.

Whipped by the wind, the waters flinch,
Draw up mightily, then collapse.
Pushed and shoved toward the shore,
Legion upon legion, the waves advance,
The waves advance,
Then tremble, fall and expire,
Emitting thunderous roars
In their last agonized convulsions
That presage final extinction.

William John Giacofci

James

The years have gone by and the memory of you
stays, I think of you quite often, especially
these days.
To think of what might have been, of your
life growing up, to hear your little laughter
and see you drink from a cup.
Missing you although I knew you not long,
I'm wanting to hold you and sing you a song
To see your little smile and hear the pitter
patter of your feet. Thinking of these
thoughts makes my life somewhat complete.
The sorrow and the grief that I felt that
long, long day. With strength and time was soon
to be swept so far away.
I loved you as if you had been my own, I'm
sure together we could've had fun.
Little brother James I assure to you, I'll
be there when my time has come

Kristie Deford

Stretch Out Your Hand, Friend

In life's darkness and lonely times it's hard to find good friends.
Stretch out your hand to me, let me hold it once again.
Let me comfort you and make your problems melt quickly away.
I shall guide you in the stormy seas, by your side I'll always stay.

If it's counsel that you seek, you only have to ask.
I've always and will always be there, it's a humble task.
For your pains and your joys is something we can share.
Grab your troubles by the reins and let's ride that wild mare.

Life's obstacles help to form who we really are.
Vanquishing dilemmas make us strong and go far.
There's a knowledge you acquire when all is said and done.
Though that ride was rather rocky with little time for fun,
You'll emerge victorious now that the battle's won.

I'll bid you farewell and walk tiredly from the wear.
Pause a moment lift my eyes and towards heaven I shall stare.
Thank God for the endurance and the right for me to care.
When my friend needed help from me during those tough and trying
times,
God gave me strength to help....so quietly it was as if almost mime.

We can now go forth in life for better things to come.
For that battle that was fought...my friend and I have won.

Yolanda McCool

Sea Wisdom

(For Raquel — My lovely daughter who inspired these line as we strolled the Florida Panhandle Gulf Beaches — eyes seaward— to catch a glimpse of these graceful creatures.)

Can you fathom the wisdom of these ancient seas
As they roll their waves over these shifting sands?
Can you read the scrolls unravelling there
Which bring us words from those distant times
When man was not and time was young,
While in the seas the code was forming
With which to write the age of man.

That may be the song the dolphins sing,
If we could only read their tune.
For they may read the code that's written
And the wisdom that is harbored there
Within the flowing silent deep,
And reveal to us our heritage
And the future scenes of man.

Richard H. Steele

Untitled

I am me;
strong as I need be:
Strong of body, mind and spirit;
making me complete, embracing a sense
of perfection within my world and I don't
fear it.
Knowing my faults, working to correct not
conceal them from my sisters and brothers;
being honest with myself, learning to
love and find contentment within me
in order to find it in others:
I am he who controls his own destiny,
as you are with your own;
I am the answer to my problem as you're
with yours, this is known:
If my deeds reflect my prosperity of demise;
Then tell me, what course in life
would be wise?

Shonn L. Banks-Bey, Sr.

The Man with the Cane

The man with the cane
Struck a note of fear
In many a child when he came near.

He walked with a limp,
He didn't stand tall
His body was bent his head was bald.

But he was a man
Of beauty within, of strength and courage
Found in few men.

When the great storm came,
He gave the word,
"Get under your desks!"
Their prayers were heard.

You may not agree
With the way that he ran
The old school with his iron hand,
But our lives are all fuller
With knowledge we gained
From knowing this great man,
The man with the cane.

Mildred Hardy

The Preacher

He walks proudly in his every stride
Suggestive of the great spirit inside
To emulate one must pay great dues
Or even venture to walk in his shoes.

He ministers with very strong faith.
And he teaches as he deliberates
A man with renown character is he,
Make him worthy to be the honor-ee.

He who is filled with heavens fire
Fueled with power that comes from on high
He tells the story with joy and pride
Of Jesus who lives although he died.

He has many expressions that we enjoy
But his message from heaven we mostly employ
He talks of the man who was pierced in his side
It was Jesus who "lives" although he died.

Penick H. Wagstaff

Winds of Time

The winds of time have changed my life

As I walk through a rocky road I realize the
sun will rise on a new horizon, and so will I

Looking for the truth as obstacles become
harder to climb, I become confused

Rivers flowing, cleansing the earth for the
new seasons to come

As the moon rises the sun sets, I become
calm and I acknowledge my most inner-soul

Today is new.

Mary A. Waddell

Alone with Myself

My heart is heavy
Sunken deep within me like the lost treasure it has become
Cracked in more places than one
Waiting desperately to be discovered and brought to surface light
While threatening at any moment to shatter ... completely.

Surely there must be more than this?
Pain is my constant companion. Loneliness rules my day
And since misery loves company
Sorrow and sadness have also come to play
Squatters all, refusing to vacate the premises

What is the matter? What can it be?
Am I unlovable or misunderstood? No.
Just broken from within with no fix in sight
I long to laugh again just for the fun of it
Live life and explore it

Instead I am alone with myself
In a forgotten place that seems strangely familiar
Swirling in a vacuum no one sees
Treading on the edge
Where I hang by a thread ... to reality.

Yvette Anglero

Untitled

Bright blue eyes filled with tears
Reaching out for that special someone
Yearning for the love
Always given to another
Never understanding why!

Amy Wolota

Miracle

It was quiet outside, "night had appeared, the moon,s
sunlight shines on her tears." Why is she crying, this statue
of mine - She,s the Virgin Mary, Mother Of Our Divine.

Rose petals, are falling! "What is going on?" There around the
Holly Mother, out on my lawn.

The aroma of roses fills the air, "I stop and glance at mary
who,s standing there." She says blessed are these petals
That fell around my feet, gather them and pass them out to
the sick, homeless, and meek.
Miracles will happen, to those who believe, "that my son
Jesus was the one I conceived.
he died on the cross for all mankind, "he died for our sins
your,s and mine.

He who shall ever believe" :Shall have ever lasting life.
"and the aroma of the roses," still remains alive.

Nancy M. Jackson

Untitled

He sits alone with his thoughts and ideas, his unspoken feelings.
Surrounded by gloom as thick as London fog.

He can still hear the others around him,
but has grown weary of reaching out to find nobody near.
I can see him sitting and wonder, "why is he there?"
Can he not see the light I shine before him?

He looks up and vaguely smiles,
his eyes fill with forgotten memories.
Puzzled, I wonder, does he think me to be an apparition?

Alone he has been for an untold time,
Too long has he sat there, now only sadness fills his mind.

I call out to him but still he does not stir.

He sits alone, all he sees is bleak.
Has he forgotten the children's laughter.
the warmth of the sun,
the touch of a lover?

Can he not see
this flicker of light shone before him?
He sits alone with his unspoken thoughts
unaware of the angels beside him.

Naomi Vasquez

You, My Father

You, my father, held me when I was no larger than your hands,
surrounded me in your grasp, and so secure I was,
yet knew not the love that encompassed me.
I grew, but you were always larger, it seemed I would
never catch up, even when taller I became,
I still was not as tall as you, larger than life.
We travelled, and I saw, saw things through my
eyes and your eyes, I viewed the experience
and the scars that your body bore, frightened me.
You have been there for me when I needed you, you have
held me when I needed to be held, perhaps you
will let me give to you, as you have given to me.
My love does not abate, but grows stronger day to day,
with memories etched on my child mind,
of being held aloft on the shoulders of a colossus.

Stephen W. Sanders

Pulse

Fragrance overwhelms me as I sit;
Sweet florist's gift beside me;
Plumes of green encompass;
Garnish of moss springs curly grey;

Ruby hearts glisten in the evening shade;
Pistles reach Proudly
  Pleasing to guests;
Palms extend;
Veins shoot, nourishing cells;

Tightly spun petals laugh;
Twirling branches dance;
Spotted tongues and whiskers-six
  Tigers roars
    spilling their essence into the air.

Scott Douglas Spencer

Little Girl Lost

Each and every day you are in my thoughts
Sweet precious Holly, little girl lost

A holiday blessing, so wondrous and new
Unknowing what life had in store for you

A brand new being, a delicate little creature
I close my eyes, and recall every feature

My arms never held you, through a window I could see
The beautiful child, that would never belong to me

A child myself, confused, uncertain what to do
Somewhere a loving couple had been praying for you

In God's wisdom we are taught we must believe
Through me a child given, their blessing to receive

To give you all, at a time when I could not
A stable secure future I prayed was your lot

The years have gone by, now you have grown
Married perhaps with children of your own

I pray from my heart that you may one day see
The choice I made was most painful for me

We may never be together, my punishment to bear
Forgive me my child, know that I care

Susan Nabb

Communion

Again, I offer my Body to you, like the Host upon a sacrificial altar
Taste of me, consume me, and know that the Anointing lies within
Inside you, my world has sought completion and found Heaven's gate
Fly with me and touch me and seek the Hawk's wings

I soar ever onward and up to the heights glancing in your eyes
Could it be that the Lady has betrothed us one to another
Priest and Priestess to bring in her power
And to love

Still I miss your breath upon me and I cry for you
The Time, the Space, have become enemies of a sort
And I banish them away from me, seeking the limitless
Only to see your eyes before me and remembering Communion

Thomas Downing

Says Who? Says Me!!

It's been said for years and years that baby dolls don't cry real tears, but Thumbalina wets and cries cause I'm the one who dries her eyes-and diapers...

It's been said for years and years that kids don't like to wash their ears.
That's not so, I'll tell you why! Washing your ears means going bye-bye-and hamburgers...

It's been said for years and years that kids are filled with silly fears.
Don't you believe that kind of talk, you'll be afraid to go for walks - and ride your skateboard...

It's been said for years and years that when asleep, kids are dears.
That's kinda true, as you can see, cause I'm as mean as I can be - cept jest fore Christmas...

So kids don't believe what's been said for years. Toss away them silly fears.
Wash your ears and go bye-bye and try your bestest not to cry.
Ride your skateboard everyday and don't be naughty when you play.
Be the best that you can be, jest maybe you'll grow up like me.
Cute and smart in everyway! Ask me anytime, I'll say.
Says who! Says Me!!

Patsy Fields Ritchey

The Shadow

Tears of grief.
Tears of pain.
Tears rolling down a mother's face.
Tears keep falling until there's no more left to fall.
Then comes the sweat pouring down your face.
Nightmares of death and blood.
Nightmares of killing another, and waking in a cold sweat.
Nightmares that repeat themselves over and over.
Then the tears start to fall again.
Though this time it is you that is crying.
Tears that fall 20 years after it happened.
Tears that are still falling over a lost war.
Tears that are falling over a war that never should have happened.
Then shadow will be over us,
  FOREVER!!

Yvonne Zeitler

Before I'm Gone...

Only once will I pass this way.
Tell me, do you need a friend this day?
For the span that I am here.
I'm more than willing to lend an ear.
And if you need a shoulder to cry on,
Let me know before I'm gone.
Time is precious to me indeed.
Tell me now, if you're in need.
For each friend I don't neglect,
Will be taken in account in retrospect.
I want to share all the love I can spread,
Before the last time I rest my head.
Therefore, any good that I can do,
Let me not defer from you.
Even though I shan't pass this way again,
Know in your heart,
  everlasting,
    you had at least
      one friend.

Mary K. Mucker

Ocean Dawn

Anticipation. A quiet stillness.
Tended by the Goddess of Love.
A closeness to the power of the Creator.
In the deep recesses of your mind,
Recognition of a time before time.
Slowly, the sky streaks with gold.
A finger painting by the hands of God.
The glowing orb emerges from the sea.
As a babe springs from its mother's water,
Breathing the sweet air of new life,
So is born a new day.

And just beyond the horizon,
With the same majesty,
An old one dies.

Tom Wyche

Date Rape "15 Minutes"

Something that starts out innocent, and sweet. Could end up horrible,
terrifying and beat. I say no, he says yes. All of a sudden he's unbuttoning my dress. I still say no, but yet he still ignores. He must be mistaken me for one of his whores. He tries to trick me says "He'll be there" But deep down inside he really doesn't care. He says that we will be, together forever, and this shall be something that I will forever treasure. So I gave in, how stupid can I be? To let someone like him be able to hurt me. The way it happened its not the way I planned, we started out innocent and it got out of hand. Fifteen minutes that's all it took, a smile on his face but he misread me like a book. A special moment in my life, that ended up cutting my heart like a knife. For a day or two things we fine, until our
our relationship got in a little bird. Then one day, he says goodbye, I just stand there trying not to cry. I thought he cared and loved me too, I must of be mistaken cause after it was Natalie who.

Natalie Markh

Mr. Postman:

"Neither rain, snow, sleet nor hail,"
Thank you, Mr. Postman, for delivering my mail.
But I wonder if in days of 'yore'
They had in mind you having to climb
Over ditches and road construction
To reach my door.

If a bulldozer you should meet
In the middle of my street
And if you find your little cart won't go around
One of those great, big dirt mounds,
And if all you see before you
Are insurmountable hills,
Then, please, Mr. Postman...
Just keep my bills.

Patricia Braddock

Life's Spectacular Wonders

Spectacular fireworks in the sky,
sweet smelling flowers on the ground,
people sitting bee's flying all around;
the way you see it is the way it is.
Life is an on going display of fireworks,
people sitting motionless starring
and gazing at a new display of
man made beauty.
Everyday you see new things-
smell new sweet smells, and
take in what natures beauty
has to offer

Vanessa Horne

Roses

A family is like a bouquet of roses
That begins as a bouquet of two
Then Jesus added seven more to our bouquet
Six pink ones and one a bright blue.

He saw one that stood out above all the others
And that Rose — Bud was you.
Now our bouquet has changed since your parting
For there are eight lonely roses so blue.

Our family was a bouquet of roses
Till He saw the one He would pick,
For He knew how much you would suffer
And He couldn't bear to see you so sick.

He has promised we can come to join you
Where our roses will not be discrete.
We look forward to that great awakening
Where our bouquet will again be complete.

Marjorie P. Miller

Losing Weight

I've inherited from my parents a certain shape
That causes me much anguish to this date
For every time I pass near food I realize
I tend to expand to the very next size
Food seems to add to my butt, stomach and side
All the fat that can't be burnt in one bike ride
Even when I watch what I eat
My stomach prevents me from seeing my feet
I walk two miles a day as often as I can
Because of my age I walk where I once ran
Hoping to make the inches shrink or fall
From my chest, stomach, butt, legs and all
But it seems at times a losing battle
No matter how many hurdles I straddle
Trying to have my weight go down
I'd have to walk all over this town
And then not eat a single thing all day
Hoping to have the pounds start falling away
I've always had this problem with weight
Which in our family seems to be our fate

Walt Schmidt

Seventeen

I am seventeen year old, that smokes too much...
That cries a lot, and losing touch...

With the things in my life, that I hold close...
My Father died two years ago, I can still see his ghost

Did I forget to mention, that I am gay...
And have to listen to the slurs, my peers tend to say

I go blank sometimes, and forget who I am...
But I can count on my peers to remind me I'm supposed to be fem

It feels as though I'm drifting, a hopeless castaway...
In the land with "Freedom of Speech", yet still we monitor what we say

I can't go on feeling like this, But I know that I can't leave..
I still have the whole world to conquer, after all, I'm only seventeen

Stanley Fitcheard

Genesis

In Genesis it is written
that God created man
and He liked what He saw.
Since then we have cursed Him, damned Him
used His name in vain
blaming Him everything
fire, wind and storm.
Perhaps we should question just who created whom
did we create this image
to blame and to curse
to take away the guilt for things
that we ourselves brought forth.
It's a question that needs an answer
you decision must be now!
for what God has created
He surely can recall.....

Richard E. Wise

Again

It happened to me once before,
that I care for someone so devotedly
I don't know why it happens to me once again, having the same feeling as what I felt before, but it is even stronger now 'cause I can't stop thinking about you for a minute or even just for a second.
I think I've lost my mind for falling for you.
So scared that there will be no future for our relationship,
no hope, no support, nothing at all.
I'm not even sure if there is something going on between us 'cause I'm living my dream with every good fantasy that I created, especially about you.
And all these have to end eventually,
so let me start by saying good bye.

Joyce Aryani Gunawan

Venus

I had a dream
that I was walking on the moon
and the secret to love
was right in my hands,
but no one really cared.
I flew down to the earth below.
and looked up at the moons lonely face.
The stars shone like diamonds
and Venus was a glowing blue.
Alone I sat
in my dark room
And put my head to sleep.
With close eyes.
I saw stars and planets
and hearts
and thought of you.

Leyla Mahdaviani

Scents Of Earth

Joined together by hope, a dominant wish.
Through our eyes we cannot see our future,
only glistening tears.
Man is destroying, bloodshed is no longer
just a vision.
Mother Nature, reaching, crying for mercy.
The eyes of a dear, igniting in fear.
A rose blooms out in the open, the sweet
fragrance of life.
Slowly, adjacent from the world.
Peace on earth, an illusive dream.

Jennie Casterton

Miss You

I miss you! I said, don't miss me, but I guess that is the way things were meant to be.

Times were hard when we said good-bye, but the need to go on and have fun in our lives.

As I go on living day-by-day; I'm still missing one smiling face, which makes me cry and feel so out of place.

It ain't the same looking across this old farm land, but I guess I have to continue doing my job and take it like a man.

As the seasons pass by, Fall, Winter and Spring, or as I see or hear a plane or a train, my heart beats fast just once more, just hoping yours is the next knock on my door.

Ronald Eugene Burke

Wonderment of Life

As a youngster growing up you never think
That life might cause you to want to drink.
You find the right mate, HEAVEN appears
Marriage, children, job security—-
sometimes hell is near.

But love, the smile and antics of children maintain
Courage, hard work and patience sustain
The years fly by, children leave the nest
Your soul mate retires and you think you both can rest.

Omens of fate have another aim in store
They say, you must suffer a little bit more
Illness and pain—three years long
How could anything go so wrong?

But love conquers all, or so they say,
And there you are, well again one day.
Together you've made quite a team
Knowing and growing about what life means.

Polly Nelson

Untitled

The morning's early light will let you see
That past my cold, dark shell there lies a pearl
As radiant as Aurora's rays make thee.
The strongest sails of friendship will unfurl.
Once the dawn of love deep in us shines,
The noontime's Phoebus warms us, guides my eye.
I see you, you see me and we divine
That we are one, one ship on Neptune high.
The seas of life are calm, the sun has set;
Diana's beams illuminate us well.
Our cruise complete we anchor and then we let
The evening come - we know the tide will tell
Of you and me. I saw you truly then,
One day when Cupid's arrow was my pen.

Sammy Sohi

"Our Will Or His"

Some of us must work harder than others,
to fulfill the dreams of our fathers and mothers.
But the Lord sets aside good things you see,
the benefits for those with like minds as he.
For through God I can find such sweet
contentment, there many may find only gross
resentment. No man can understand God's
will, but the righteous know him by
being still; still to God's will, free
from his own, soon I will arrive,
home sweet home.

Sunzie R. Nix

A Friend

You need a friend in your present,
that stays with you, even if you become the past.
You need a friend that sticks with you,
a friendship that lasts.
A friend that you can call anytime,
and say what's on your mind.
A friend that listens and answers,
in a voice that's kind.
A friend who believes in you,
and understands your feelings and fears.
A friend who calms you down,
and will dry your tears.
A friend who can listen,
and will always understand your pain.
A friend is someone you believe in,
and they have nothing to gain.

L. Fern Barlow

Manitou

Bluish is the light that
That wants me to be
Neither happy nor sad
It looks so fine in my mind
Back to back insanity dazed forthright loneliness

But now I see the problem
It is not me nor you
It is them
With their attention-hungry fangs
Screaming for more
Whimpering in ecstasy

Every minute spent whistling
Through the holes in the trees
As the dogs laugh run to stone

Turn into the light that feeds me
More is what I want
Not pity for the trees that swing lifelessly
But the heat from my flame
Rage and cringe to my own
I dream of a day full of nothing

Patrick Gunn

Memories Of Youth

Close your eyes, and let's pretend,
That we have found our youth again.
Let's step into yesterland,
Where dreams occur at our command.

Do you see the roses' blush,
Blossoming beside the thrush?
Buttercups and daisies bloom,
To fill the air with sweet perfume.

Clouds of beauty, drifting by,
Painting pictures in the sky,
Sewing threads of memories
Weaving webs of fantasies.

Let's walk the pathway through the woods,
Stand on cliffs, where we once stood,
Let's listen to the whippoorwill,
And swing on vines to test our skill.

Now, let's dance among the trees,
Hearing tunes within the breeze,
To celebrate days long gone by,
Enjoyed by folks like you and I.

Marie Holman O'Neil

A Thought...

There are times when we realize
that we have known someone all of our lives.

Yet we recognize that on a deeper level
we might not know that person at all.

Still because of the lifelong sense of knowing
that person on some level,
the feeling of friendship seems real and strong.

Sometimes we notice that our feelings and perceptions
change toward such lifelong strangers
and we begin to long to get to know them
on a different, more intimate level...

And such thoughts engender fear
and a sense of great anxiety,
because no one wants to risk loosing
a lifelong friend,
for something that may not last.

Lawrencine Smith

If Only But A Dream

If only but a dream,
That which has no truth in reality,
But a mere flicker of hope, awaiting to burst,
Like a shimmering flame of destiny.

If only a dream,
One's search for the true happiness,
One's plea for everlasting peace,
And equality for all races.

It only a dream,
Shall not the light of faith ever waiver,
Shall not the bitter kiss of death
Rob the soul of eternal pleasure.

If only but a dream,
A mortal's hope for immortality-
A precious, golden quest in life,
May it have truth in reality.

If only but a dream,
We shed all miseries with fervor,
And in the richness of the everafter,
We dream our dreams forever.

Marsha J. Davis

Kiss Her

He set upon her lips, the very first kiss
that would alter everything
She knew this was going to be special.
the way he bent over, very cautious,
barely touching his lips to hers.
Very tender, very sweet, very torrid.
Innocently
Not too sure of the response he was to get.
It had made her forget the chill
She didn't be think the numbness of her body.
All that mattered was him.
And the few seconds it took,
seemed like hours, somewhere else, far away.
Yes, he was a fine kisser.

Michele Ziarnowski

Memories

There's a ditch of broken bottles, trash and empty cans.
That's all that's left of all that used to be.
The house that daddy built for us, and mama's garden plot.
These happy times are just a memory.

The well that daddy dug out back, with two hard working hands.
The barn and lots are gone now, it's a shame.
The out house with the broken door, beneath the old oak tree.
An old rope hanging where we used to swing.

There's a creek down in the meadow, beside a mountain trail.
It wind around the boulders, and the bend.
I guess it's all just like it was, I really couldn't say.
Since I left home I ain't been back again.

I'm sure the dust has covered that old ditch, and all that trash.
Texas sometimes has a lot of wind.
The dust storms and the wind storms, can change the face of things.
And like I said I ain't been back again.

It's a crazy world that takes us from the things we love the best.
It takes away the kin folk, and our friends.
And puts us on a crooked road with no way to get back.
A road with only detours, and no end.

Nancy Holaday

Peace

Picking up the pieces of my life and moving on
That's what it is all about, from now on
I've been through the sadness and pain
Now is the time to enjoy life and gain.

All the good things that I deserve
Getting away from doing for others, to serve,
Life is what you make it and now I see
I need to take time for myself and think of me.

I need relaxation and peace
All the fighting has finally ceased.
I need to smell the flowers and take the time
To get myself rejuvenated and everything will be fine.

I need solitude, warm breezes and the sun
Listening to the birds until the day is done.
I need to learn to sit and do nothing
I have to quit always doing something.

Stop feeling guilty about wasting time
Enjoying each moment and make it mine.
Little by little I'll learn to be
That what God intends for me.

Rose Calanni

The Greatest Gift

Away in a manger. No crib for a bed.
That's what the beautiful old Christmas song said.
The wise men, they traveled by day and by night
To bring precious gifts and catch a glimpse of the sight.
To think that a Prince was born in a barn and lay in a manger
To the virgin Mary, yet the story gets stranger.
He grew up, the great Prophet, the Lily, the Rose,
And died on the cross in front of his foes.
On the third day, he arose from the grave where he lay,
And, o' what rejoicing was done on that day.
So, as you gather around the Christmas tree,
Remember the man who died for you and for me.
As you open the presents and eat the big dinner,
Remember the man who gave the greatest gift of all,
The man who died for every sinner.

Traci L. Purvis

To Be Free

Out on the ice isn't everything nice.
The wind in your face the feeling of grace.
With a blade a curve is made.
The toe goes in then jumps begin.
To spend some time in a climb.
Up in the air without a care.
To fly so high in the sky.
To be so free that's what's for me.

Lisa Rassel

Trapped In Twilight

Lonesome trees upon this winter screen
the air is brisk again
Faraway out like a dream
crashing towards and beyond me
are foreigners of fate
ancient Gods of those who determine to hate
Parodies of always
smiles of true days
Wavering, standing there, faces like stone
yelling out, I hear you in some strange way, laughing at me
Oh, it's a strange day when you're trapped in twilight
Traces of this heaven's cold
My feet sink into ice and snow
Your smile, ironically dangerous as you crossed over
this forbidden line
Telling me what has got to be mine
You whisper away a winter's night, holding me gently
in arms so tight
Feeling strangled and wanting to run but your hold on me
so long ago has never gone.

Samantha Friello

Fall On The Flake

Primal mists gently overflow
the arms of sylvan guardians,
and fall with gentle rhythms
to the waiting earth below.
The wind picks up a leafy melody,
and a hammer in the boatyard sings metallic.
Now harmony begins to grow.
It's the music of a land shedding summer.
Putting off her warm and verdant raiment,
for more brilliant Autumn hues, aglow.
She's singing of a time that's quickly passing,
and of another season soon to dawn.
But for now, Fall glory be alive! Don't go!

Sheelah S. Browne

Endless Movement

Reality...
The awakening
from a dream state
In which you have been submerged
for longer than you can remember.

Consciousness...
The unclouded,
understanding
of views and decisions
that you are afraid to make.

Eternity...
Endless
movement
through
Conscious Reality.

Lisa Renee Duran

A Still Life (For Mo)

We gather the apples fresh in morning fog
the basket on the table in the sun

In the orchard you clench your fists
I hide fruit in the tall grass

You open the cupboards one by one
I stand on the porch hands in all directions

The sound the grass makes as it dries
like you talk in your sleep of other places

If we could be the children we see
as we look back and stand still in the orchard

the plants stretch quietly across the sill
one drop of water rolls down a leaf
to the floor

You rearrange things by their sound
I change the air with my hands

The trees were planted before we were born
and again every day after
And now though we are no longer here

Mark Chadwick

"Fall Is In The Air"

Fall is in the air
The beauty of the season one sees everywhere,

Leaves are gently wafting in the breeze,
Gliding, swirling, in a dance of ease;

Increasing momentum with each gust of wind,
No path in mind and to the porch cling;

Children riding horseback, spreading vapor with their conversation,
Manes and tails flying in gallop - falling gently with each hesitation

The gold of the poplars dot the countryside,
With it comes the turning of the autumn tide;

Bright, the gold is like the sunlight
So overwhelming as to blind one's sight,

None must forget the greens and reds,
We saunter, kicking our toes in the 'crackle' of the leafy beds.

The nip of the morning air, fills our lungs and sharpens our minds,
Bodies invigorate, and our hearts are kind;

The mountains glisten as light dances on the snow,
Season such as none e'er knew is spreading elegance in afterglow;

All to soon, we'll feel the winter's blast,
"Where is the glory of autumn? all will ask.

Thelma Reusser

In the Corner

The room was dark and bare
the bed was covered in cobwebs
an inch of dust had settled on
the bureau drawers
the chair in the corner was chipped
and broken
the clock on the wall had stopped
the room was still
In the corner by the window was
an object
it was long and frail
something about it made it visible
it was familiar
shoes, socks, dress ......
a tiny face-not a normal face
disfigured, grooved and dull (a face of death)

Star Ursillo

Leaves

The soft wet rain bathes them
The big oak gives them life
The onlookers admire their color
With the spring they are regenerated
Each life is short though not without impact
The fresh brilliant green of their rebirth
Brings joy to the onlooker
The vivid colors of their death
Brings sentiment of life to the onlooker
With their short life, they teach the onlooker
Of the beauty and swiftness of time
They remind the onlooker
To be aware of what is important
For each one the answer shall be different.

Theresa K. Allgood

The Beach

The rushing of waves onto the sand,
the blue water, always moving, almost never still.
The rustling of the wind all through the land,
speaking a soft voice, telling a little story.

The shrieks of the sea gulls flying over your head,
their song continuing, echoing in your mind.
The shrills of the dolphins, looking to be fed,
their beautiful figures leaping up in the air.

The golden sand in between your toes and all around,
the palm branches swaying as the wind blows,
so green and delicate and carefree.

You walk some, listening to the waves brush up on the beach.
You search for something or someone, but only nature stands
beside you.

Jill Johnson

He Isn't Ready, Child

Jesus, what's the reason for this second chance?
The body so near to slumber, the heart beats, the lungs breathe,
But there is not twinkle in the eyes - only a stare
Why wasn't God ready for him, yet?

Jesus, is this an example of real life?
The throat makes no voice, no warm "hello" no "good morn""
No sweet sound of "I love you with all my heart"
Why wasn't God ready for her, yet?

Jesus, what can we do to help cope?
We want to do our very best.
Lots of cards, bouquets of flowers,
Stuffed bears and dogs, a wide-eyed frown anything at all
Why wasn't God ready for them, yet?

Jesus, can you hear our heart felt prayers?
The struggle to return to us,
Tries our patience breaks our will,
But, if this is all there will be - and nothing more!
Tell God it's time to let them rest!!!

Susan J. Andrews

Untitled

A hug, a word, a gift of love
this comes through you from
God above.
A safety, a haven, a peaceful rest
this is what you give, nothing but your best.
A smile, a prayer, a kind deed
this comes from you in times of need.
Of all the gifts that God has
given, you're the best he had,
sent straight from heaven.

Reni Snellgrose

Tuesday Evening

Watching the sunset - I think of you...
the calming effect night has on day...
as you have on me.

The sounds are soothing...
...reassuring.
Birds chirping to young ones
giving them their final meals of the day.

Crickets saying hello...
...it's their time to speak.
When I hear your voice
- you reassure me...
...you soothe me...
Fireflies begin to light up the sky...
...as if in celebration of night.

When I'm with you - I feel the same way.
I fear the night is too short and
their will not be another sunset
as spectacular as this one...

...Tuesday evening.

Patrick T. Smith

My Picture

I painted a picture in art today.
The clouds are green, the sky is black,
the flowers are dead, and the grass is purple.
The art teacher asked me what it was
called, with those fearful eyes of his
"The Way Things Look To Me" I answer.
I laugh.
He doesn't.
He asks "Are you having any problems?"
When I say no
he says maybe I should see the counsellor.
I notice when he says that his
cheeks turn the color of my grass,
I think about telling him this,
but I decide against it.

Talia Epstein

Timeline of Life

The measure of time never varies scientifically,
the constant flow of events is measured in a standard way—
It's order never fails, like a finely tuned symphony,
as the minutes turn to hours and then into days.

But time is only a relative measure,
controlled by the perceptions of the mind—
What the young ignore, the old do treasure,
as the clock of life slowly unwinds.

As we grow older life seems to slip by ever quicker,
with time only to reflect on daily laments—
Till one day our existence seems only a flicker,
in an infinite sea of obscure events.

Michael A. Deterling

Angel's

There are many different type's of angel's.
They help you, guide you and protect you.
Angel's love you unconditionally,
They save you form disaster and tragedy.
They comfort you in special way's,
Through family, friend's and other way's
Look for your angel's and you will find them there,
Because they are there to help and care.
Listen to them with your heart, soul and mind,
And you will find that they are with you all the time...

Zelma D. Cagle

The Door

Hold on to the past
The cycle, at last, guides me towards you

Know someone's there
Counting the squares, opening the door

Remembering
Times we knew

You don't have to say
Won't tears on my face answer all for you

Thoughts in my mind
Like storms, arise. Closing of the door

Outer darkness

Time we choose

No, don't turn away
From this place I made only to greet you

Time beyond time
When you arrive, please, knock on the door

I will be there
There for you

Nora Devlin

My Special Friend

A night has come.
The day has end
I met and talked with this special friend
He was stranger than any I knew.
Said dear child I love you.

He told me things I didn't know.
Then he turned and said I have to go.
To meet my father on His throne.
When He calls His children home.

When we meet in the promise land.
There we will join with the angels band.
To be together in that Heavenly Home.
At the touch of the Masters hand.

No more sorrow or pain to bear.
For it will be different over there.
We'll walk on the golden shore.
All of His love we will share.

Mary Bunnell

"I Wonder"

The mailbox stands by a lonely lane.
The day is hot and dry.
A farmer searches hopefully,
both the mailbox and the sky.

He slowly walks back to the barn,
With coveralls filled with dust.
Turn eyes toward heaven and murmurs low,
"'tis you O God, in whom I trust."

The shade of the barn in a welcome place,
to rest awhile then pick up pace.

His mind begins to wonder along
As he sits on a wagon scratching dust with a prong.

"Before the flood of Noah's day,
his mind goes back in time.
Who was sitting in this same spot,
before this land was mine?

Did another life live here before,
did their hearts and minds know you?
Were they happy or sad, serene or glad,
was the sky then just as blue?"

Patsy Spaulding

Mothers Divine

Well that day is finally here.
The day you are honored once a year.
It's not much considering all you've done.
You counsel us when we've lost, you're the first to praise us
when we've won.

When we're sick, you answer our every call.
You're there to pick us up when we fall.
And though sometimes we make you sad,
You're still willing to take the risk, and save us from
the wrath of dad.

We're sorry about those walls we cause you to climb.
We praise your love, for it is truly divine.
Mothers are blessed, we all will give a nod,
For it took a mother to give us the son of God.

L. Robert Green

Woman With Gold

Each time she turns her head hits the pole
The doorway she sleeps in sprays her with stench
Her blanket gets caught, caught on the nail
Sticking out of the wall
She is caught, caught in this city of gold
Golden streets and golden shelters
They serve shining yellow corn at the soup kitchen today

She takes the leftover bread, wraps it in the white napkin
Drops it into her bottomless pocket
The pocket that holds the tainted secrets of a once joyous
Now twisted life.

The bread falls
"Come through our Golden Gates"
The doors of institutions
Fly open
Find color on the streets
In a hole
In her eyes
The eyes that doorways cover like lids
With Golden shadows

Megan Bourne

"Something"

Totally inspired by the elements
The earth is moist
Enough blue sky for a thousand lakes
Reflections of the soul are abreast
Turbulent seas, minds awash with artifact
Seasons beginning
Nature in solitude, blooming into perfection
Absolute reincarnation of the soul taking place
Amidst the never ending phases of reality
Confronted in time with memories
Being led as if on a harness with reins
Suffering at times intolerable pain
Within our character we abide in wisdom
Passed on to us from earlier generations
Forever searching, forever reaching out
For that certain something
Our heart rendering goal
For if one does not search
Life is as an ember return into coal...

Mary L. Jansson

The Family Tree

The family tree is both majestic and profound
The epitome of royalty
It stands tall and very proud
For all the world to see

Children bring parents so much happiness and joy
Their hearts are so light and free
They know they've done their best to make more complete
The beautiful family tree

There is not enough money in the entire world
Nor will there ever be
To purchase the love in a parent's heart
For their beautiful family

As the oak tree needs the sun and rain
for nourishment to grow strong and stately
The family tree gets its nourishment
From love, kindness, and integrity

Marvin D. Fielder

Untitled

A parent's fight is hard you see
The fight is for their child
A battle that they will win and yet
The war is the call of the wild.

The children cry so often now
They see violence in the street.
Do they deserve the world we've caused,
The blood spilled at their feet?

They are a frightened generation
So scared and fragile to the touch
And they look to those they love for help
But can they trust them just as much?

The parent's fight is long and hard
They need God's strength, courage, and will
They've seen enough of the sadness strike
They've had all of their fill.

So stand beside your children now
Speak for the innocent who have no voice
For you have their love with you
In return, leave them a world of choice.

Kim Martin

Driftwood

Three men a time ago put out to sea,
The first (a strong, strong man, you see),
Rang up the sail and said, "It's true,
A man is not a man who fears the Great Blue."

Out at sea, in the second man's schooner of small size,
The second turned and looked up—away from his small prize,
And said, "I believe it through and through,
a man is not a man who fears this Great Blue."

The third man, a sailor most his life,
Had kept quiet for a time, just sitting with his pirate's knife,
But finally he stood up and said, "Of this I knew,
A man is not a man who fears our Great Blue."

Halfway 'cross the ocean, they spied a storm on the 'izon,
Said the sailor, "I fears me a 'cane arisin',"
Replied the first, "That's rubbish," and the second. "This too—,
A man is not a man who fears the Great Blue."

So the schooner kept a-blunderin' on
Until they met the hurricane head-on,
And on a piece of driftwood (washed up the next week) was carved:
"It's true—a man is not a man who fears the Great Blue."

Kevin Griffin

Untitled

When I thought of you it began to rain and my memory was clouded
the fog hung low on your smile
and the puddles splashed my face to wake me up
the road was like a mirror and the lights were shocking to my eyes
the rain is frightening but it soothes me
and then the crash and flood of light and you were gone as easily
and quickly as when you came into my life
the rain poured over my head and face
and alone I stood so open to the bitter cold
I did not seek shelter right away
I thought maybe you'd be back to cover me
but you were warm and safe while I stood in the rain
until the clouds broke
and the sun came
again I was warm and dry
on my own without you to protect me from the unpredictable sky

Stephanie Hughes

In My Heart

I look into your eyes and see passion, a desire.
The gentle touch of your lips sets my body on fire.
When your arms wrap around me. It is love that I feel.
I can't explain my emotions. I only know love is real

Two separate lives are somehow bound together.
You have entered my life. You'll be with me forever.
What the future may hold we are not readily aware.
This love can last forever. It's not something to fear.

Our lives intertwine. For a reason? I don't know.
I have opened my heart. I have bared my soul.
It is a beautiful feeling. so tender, yet strong.
What I feel in my heart tells me I cannot be wrong.

With my eyes closed I see you. Your smile brightens your face.
I taste your sweet kisses. My heart quickens its pace.
You are with me forever. the memories are clear.
In my heart I will hold you and you'll always be near.

I will not forget your smile or the color of your eyes.
When our lips come together your kiss tells me no lies.
Special friends last forever. For your happiness I pray.
In my heart we're together. In my heart you will stay.

Linda M. Sinagra-Smith

"Between Us"

The winds of time drift softly by.
The hours pass you start to cry.
So far apart I couldn't even start,
to count the miles between us.
Then the depression of loneliness,
settles its weight upon your chest.
For you my love flies higher than the dove,
but to believe all you have is trust.
Soon the ship will set a sail.
For others I will leave no trail.
Then we will be together and free,
with nothing to count between us.

Kevin Roby

Post Meridian

White walls and plastic fans blowing at my blue sheets
The taste of dried milk still in my mouth
My mothers lonesome breast above me
Staring hungrily at her semipellucid peach nipples
The struggle of my cobalt lips left sour
The quiescence of my body in the post meridian
Wintry flesh discernable against the darkness
The cry of my rattle.

Mardesia Sapien

Make Us One

Let me love you, just a little bit my sweet
There's a need in me, that only this love can fulfill
Make my life begin again, as we tenderly embrace
Let this feeling that I have, make us one.
When I hold you in my arms so tenderly
All the love I have is just for you and you alone
Say that we can be as once, and our lives for ever more
Will be lived in ecstasy-be my love.

Ralph L. Daudet

The Informer

I notice the hour and lay pen aside,
The house is orderly, quiet, and neat.
I close my book, its completion denied,
Then silence is broken by tiny feet.

Her voice is high, telling her story
Of how games were played and friends were fooled,
Of injuries that are always gory,
Of puppy dogs and swimming pools.

I watch her face and hardly hear a word.
Her eyes are wild, her cheeks so red,
To interrupt her would be absurd,
So I just feign interest and nod my head.

Of her story I barely make heads or tails,
Alternating with happiness and sorrow.
But I'd never take the wind from her sails,
Because I'd hate to miss the next story tomorrow.

Michael P. Mahoney

"Remember When"

The years have passed; they finally meet again;
The joy upon their faces is plain and good to see.
Their eyes light up and their faces glow
As they turn back the hands of time from "Long Ago."

They look back on those younger days
And choose to remember the good;
And not the hours of loss, hurt or pain.
Time adds a golden luster to the days that have been
When their hearts return to
"Remember When."

Linda S. Lia

A Youth Through Ages Eyes

He sees tomorrow as an endless time,
The joys of now the only hills to climb.
His yesterday is still a present part
Of purpose without plan and without start.

His thoughts posses his mind, he rules them not.
He hasn't learned to own his reason, bought
By time and failure, love and loss and life;
Control that's found through overcoming strife.

A body that responds without complaint
And goes from strength to stronger without taint
Of weakness born of years. He doesn't feel
And cannot know the vigor age will steal.

I would not trade my years of wisdom earned
Through trial and error - life's great lessons learned.
And though my body ages with each breath,
It is the one I'll carry into death.

He is the future, he's the dreams - the hope;
A bit of immortality. He'll cope
With that which God has for him preordained
While I can know life's victories I've gained.

John B. Westfall

The Keeper of the Breath

The keeper of the breath, that was I.
The keeper of the breath, until he shall die.
It is sad to see a strong and viral man,
Give up and go to never land.
To watch each breath that he took,
Carry him closer to death with a look.
But, his passing was quiet and over he went.
Such a peaceful look and his life was spent.
I could see him drifting up to the sky,
Where he reached out his hand after he would die,
For there on the other side of life,
Was my mother, his love and wife.
And they went off into eternity
Maybe one day we will all meet thee!!!!!!

Mary Koval

Halloween

It was Halloween night.
The kids were about,
But when it struck midnight,
The witches came out.
Cackling, cackling, louder than the sea
There was only one person watching.
That person was me.
They were riding on broomsticks.
Two hundred or so,
But I just sat there alone in the snow
I just sat there struck with fright.
The witches were dancing for half of the night.
Still I sat there suddenly I took a gasp,
A witch a witch flew right past!
Goblins and ghosts ran after me!!
I am so glad it was only a dream.

Sarah Rose Peacock

Halloween Night

Halloween night was here at last
The kids were dressed in a fright
The people in the house were the last
To see the kids dressed just right
As the kids in funny costumes passed
Each one with just a little light
So the drivers could see as they passed
The kids went from the house to house
When the door was opened the kids said trick or treat
At one house the door was opened by a big mouse
The kids ran right into the street
When it was time for the kids to go home
Each one tired and sleepy
The parent ask if the kids wanted an ice cream cone
The children just got ready for bed
The people in the houses were sleepy
The people called it a night

Margaret Bitterman

"Coping"

The industrious beaver builds a dam in the water
The ant builds a city on land
The squirrel saves nuts for the winter ahead
and the camel stores water for a trek over sand
The dog loves it's master till the end of it's days
The bird feels safe in the top of a tree
The bear spends most of it's winter in bed
And fish find their place in the sea
They live their lives the only way they know how
And don't ask the reason why
They let nature chart their course
Why, then, oh why can't I?

M. James

America

To this great land we live in,
The land of the free and the many great men,
We need to show more respect and pride,
To keep it clean and in it's laws abide.
To our fellow man show much care and love,
And work sincerely through God above.
We should always honor the red, white, and blue,
To the flag of America our hearts forever be true.
For this country to us will always be,
The home of the brave and the land of the free.
Our education - the highest from the schools we attend,
The President, a leader, to always commend.
Wake up America before it's too late!
Get rid of the crime, the selfishness, the hate,
Before the Communist rule and you've met your fate,
Show love, respect, and pride in each state.
Just do your best for this great land,
And always be willing to give a hand,
To help make it better in all that you do,
For America, the land of the red, white, and blue.

Virgie Neiman

Visions of Fall

A soft wind blows them here and there,
The leaves float softly through the air.

The summer breeze turns slightly brisk.
Trees turns crimson, gold and crisp.

Fall is a beautiful time of year,
The season I've always held most dear.

Cornstalks and pumpkins will be festive soon,
You'll see halloween witches fly past the moon.

Indian corn will decorate doors,
And trick of treaters will come as before.

The mirage of colors will be gone before long,
And the last of the robins will give us his song.

The trees will look bare, all their leaves on the ground,
They'll be a blanket of colors and a crisp crunchy sound.

Maureen McCoy

A Refraction In Vermont

To her the view was like a painting. The season was Fall.
The leaves on the trees were splashed with gold
As if the gold had been carelessly spilled over the tops of the trees.
Her eyes watched the view nervously while her fingers crept across
the desk and touched the metal letter opener.
In one frantic moment she held the letter opener up-right
And slashed at the painting splitting it into two halves
As if the view had been painted on a sheet of transparent plastic.
She thought she even heard it rip as she slit it open.
She hesitated. Then, putting the letter opener down
She reached up and with her fingers pried the slit apart
Searching for what lay behind the painted picture.
She was astonished to discover
All that lay behind the painting was air. A sort of vacuum.
An empty world with no one in it. No sound whatsoever.
No movement of any kind. So, she retreated.
She had touched the surface of the painting
Sensing that death was not what she was searching for.
(At the moment) Then in an instant the painting became a view again.
The gold was on the trees, the leaves undulated in the autumnal air.

Richard T. Lebherz

Life/Afterlife

The life we see, it is not infinite in meaning.
The life we lived, it is no matter now.
The life that we did dwell in is,
but a moments notice.
We come, we go, and life continues on.
We wish we had the spark on earth
that radiates within us now.
We see beyond those days of yore to what
we could have been.
And yet, we do not weep my friend for in the end,
we did our best as men.
The past is sealed, the future opens up. We blossom
with our wings unfurl'd to do God's work aloft.

Marilyn J. Waugh

Aaron's Pine

With G I shovel gripped in hand
The little boy and grey-haired man,
Knelt together side by side,
Planting the tree with equal pride.
The grandfather viewed this special time
A legacy of love to leave behind.

As the seasons pass and the needles fall,
The tree grows straight and true and tall.
The young lad grows as does the pine,
And the boy recalls another time
When he was young and with "Poppa Don,"
They planted a tree on the verdant lawn.

The years pass——the grandfather old —
Watched the tree through winter's cold,
Through summer's heat and autumn rain,
And longs for April once again.
Roots grow deep beneath the sod,
A man, a boy, a tree and God.

M. E. Spence

Dream World

I scream in darkness.
The loud noise in the already silent room,
bounced along the walls.
An empty voice with no response
So familiar. So real.
I'm waiting for an answer to keep
myself from breaking down.
Leaving reality I begin to dream.
I dream of a fairy tale wonderland.
Criticism are no longer repeated in my head.
In the real world, where I could trust no one,
is now replaced with happiness and joy.
I am no longer alone! I no longer feel betrayed!
I love it here! I shall come here more often.
Fading away from my dream
I slip back into reality.
I slip into a world of despair.

Marea DeMarco

The Cat Will

Quiet as a shadow, strong as a rock,
the Cat will lead.
Free as a cloud while the night floats by,
the Cat will slip away.
Prowls like a whisper, sleeps sound as fog,
the Cat will squeeze through.
Fur soft as cotton, whiskers stiff with pride,
the Cat will fight true.
The Cat will.

Sara Ahern-Sawyer

Missed Treasures

Be careful Dear to recognize your treasures,
the hand prints on your fresh white walls,
muddy foot prints across your halls,
kool-aid spilt down that Sunday dress,
for the spider feels the fly's disruption of its web
and wraps that fly in satin white
to hold it for those long lonely nights,
but breezes pass through the web,
the spider all along unaware.

Viola Gay Davis

Love Has It's Ways

I can't hide from this great, warm feeling in my heart.
The love I feel is like putting on a comfortable bathrobe.
It feels soft and loose, but yet it knows every
curve on my body. It feels like a fireplace
that doesn't stop burning in my heart.
I can't express my love right now. Please,
believe it's going to always be there for you.
I wish that I could talk out my feelings.
But, I'm not ready to do that at this time.
In the months to come, I will open up as I relax.
I can't believe how perfect this feeling,
love, seems to be. I feel as if I can
mess up and always be loved like right now.
I want this perfect love to last forever,
but in time, feelings can change.

Melanie Brown

When Still All Things Are

When still all things are,
The moisture laden Moon descends.
Like heavy dew in the morning hours,
Its life giving beams coat the whole World.

When still all things are,
The Moon, a cool star,
Larger than the Sun,
Quenches all things.

The Hungry, She feeds,
The heavy laden, rest She gives.
The ones that inside find Her,
Blessed are they forever.

Her names — Many,
Her forms — Many,
Her worlds — Many.

But, with one Name, one Form,
And within one World,
The deep She fills.
When still all things are.

Steve Elmer

The Sun, the Moon, and the Stars

The sun watches you all day long.
The moon takes over at night.
While the stars always watch you.

The sun is your guardian of the day.
The moon is your guardian of sleep.
But the stars are always by your side.

If it is stormy and you feel alone,
because there is no sun,
and when you look up to the sky at night
but the moon can't be found, don't worry
they are just on a short vacation.
So the stars will protect you till they return.

Lera Watkins

Open Your Heart

Open your heart to the love life brings
The music from the bird that sings
The deer in the meadow by the fence row
Enjoyment of watching the red rose grow
Mother nature planned things well
To bringing the hard hearted out of his shell
Freedom to walk along a peaceful stream
Or lay in the grass and enjoy a dream
The snow on the mountain beautiful and white
Glare on the water from the moonlight
Flowers growing free in a field of green
So many things of beauty can be seen
If you take the time to enjoy and look
It's so much better than pictures in a book
Relax, enjoy, don't be a fool
No matter what they say...
Nature is cool

Ronald A. Wilson

The One I Need and Want

Your all I need here to hold me tight
The one I want to love me through the night
Your all I need to make my days shine
The one I want to tell me everything will be fine.

You're the one I need to be my light and guide
The one I want who I know will always be by my side
You're the one I want to love and adore
The one I need more than I ever needed anyone else before

Your all I need to comfort me when I cry
The one I want who would never lie
Your all I need to make me feel good
The one I want who I know could

Love me for what I am not what I can try to be
You're the one I want and need because I know you will always
love me for me
You're the one I need so please don't ever change
The one I want who I know will forever remain the same.

Tracy L. Smith

Who Is This Man

Who is this Man that laid down His life for me?
The One who suffered a terrible death upon a cruel tree.
He, who called me to be His very own;
And said I'd never, ever have to walk this way alone.

Who is this Man that sent His Spirit to abide?
Said He'd be there forever, my way He would guide.
Give me abundant life, if His servant I would be;
It seemed the very least I could do after all He'd done for me!

Who is this Man that laid down His life for me?
He is the Christ, the Saviour, my Redeemer don't you see;
The expressed image of Jehovah-God, His only begotten Son,
The Lion of Judah, The Prince of Peace, God's Holy One!

I know He'd have laid down His life if only just for me;
But He didn't, my beloved, He also laid down His life for thee.

Margaret Campbell Riddlebaugh

Sunday

It is a beautiful, an ethereal day.
The foliage of the trees is green; the sky above
Is as evenly blue as a whisper of May...

I can touch a shadow; I can hear a silence;
The beak of a pigeon is biting a sunbeam.
It is a day when one would sing forever more...

Maryse Elot

Asparagus

Asparagus, you baleful stalk
the only veggie at which I balk
a plant of greenish, pallid pallor
to some an edible, phallic power
makes me shake, quake, and quiver
turns my stomach and assaults my liver

What fiendish fellow did discover?
What careless cook did uncover?
this loathsome ruin of vegetation
this reject from the grand creation

It's smell alone makes me nauseous
and Gods in heaven must be cautious
in their holy, celestial kitchen
I alone, can hear them bitchin'
for even they must be disgusted and think their mothers maladjusted
to serve them such a nasty beast saying it's a godly feast

This plant of evil dark design a crucifix of ancient times
It was sent by Satan I can tell to torture souls in a living hell
I hate you! I hate you! What more can I say
so for now I'll bid you a fond good day.

John Thomas

Fuzzy and Warm

Love is like a peach
The outside shell feels slightly mysterious
but enough knowledge about this fruit, makes it easy
to erase the blank slate of unfamiliarity.
As it waits to be torn open with your teeth
you wonder if it will stain your shirt.
How absurd, you are too self-conscious.
As it squishes in your mouth,
the napkin you hold catches the downfall
and you are silently relieved
that the etiology is in your control.

Laurie Christenson

The Other Side

The year is 1942,
The person, a gentile.
He helped a family hide in fright
but alas he's in there, too.
For 13 months they were believed
to have escaped the Nazis.
Until one day, when Aryan's found out
and turned them in to the police.
Three men, two women all led away
Never again to see the light of day.
I visited the men-we spoke through a fence,
Out of the blue, three gunshots rang out,
The boy, my new friend, lay dead on the ground.
He died with honor - proud of what he did,
Even though he was on the other side.

Robyn Smith

Till Death We Do Part

And there she was all withered and white, so warm against
the black night.
She looked as if her heart had broke, oh if only she had spoke.
She walked with the grace of a beautiful white deer, she
seemed to glide across the floor so near.
A stairway appeared I had never seen before and at the top
of the stairs such as beautiful white door.
She went up half the stairs, then turned to look, the picture
I saw was like in a fairy tale book.
She shed a tear but wiped it away, then she turned and went
the rest of the way.
That was the last time I saw her for God has her now.

Penny Strbik

Dreamland

I dream of a beautiful dreamland,
That only I can see,
And when at night I close my eyes, I dream of what it can be.
It can be a world of my desires, a world of fantasy.
I can imagine a world of wonder, because I have the key.
When I wake up in the morning, my dreamland goes away,
But when I go to sleep again, with me, it's here to stay.

Susan Agudo

Twelve

I'm trying my hardest to be
the person that they say they see,
When down deep inside I sometimes
must hide the person that I see in me.

Sometimes there is room in my mind
For me to search through me and find
I'm too young or too old or so
I've been told,
Life's not always fair or too kind.

It's hard being stuck in between
there's still so much more to be seen,
I know there is more, a great
Life in store, can you die from being preteen?

Tracey Faunce

Belfast Blues

A boy rushed in, his voice like mist
The police, the bloody police, they know I was there,
I've made their list

His mother cried, then sighed,
You've got to go, you've got to go
What have you done? What have you done?
The boy stood tall, then sagged
against the wall

I know, I'll go and fight them from afar

The mother, Kathern from Cork
rocked and thought, have I won or have I lost?

My son will be gone, but safe
I'll weep and shout, perhaps in God will doubt

But then I'll hold my head high
I'll pause to pray, to laugh and say
This is what we Irish are all about

Richard M. Caimens

The Prize

My heart has weathered every turn,
The prize it sought was one.
My heart was happy beyond belief.
And then the prize was gone.

Slowly, day by day my heart has died,
Little piece by piece.
And now I found that was so hard to accept
Is leaving me with peace.

In two days my prize is gone.
I barely even get to say goodbye.
And maybe someday the prize my heart once sought
May be found again.
And I can go on every day.
Like it was before it was stolen away.

So, for now I will try to weather the storm.
And every turn that comes along.
And someday my prize will return.
And I know my heart will be alright again.

Joy Smith

Uncelebrated Things

The one that got away
the pulled tooth, and shining new ones
the baby bird I put back in the nest
a bandage, that mama put on my knee when I
fell out that bird nest tree.
The ball I hit out the park
that day I fed my brand new baby brother.
All these things are great to me
though uncelebrated - thou they go
unnoticed, they are very much
celebrated to me.

James A. Wiggins, Jr.

Oasis

There are times, when I feel longing for
the quiet solitude of a mountain forest.
Where soft green mosses blanket the stones
and fallen trees that rest along the clear
sweet waters. As the wind whispers through
the forest, I hear the voice of GOD in all
creation. Soothing my soul bringing peace.
Delight is mine while soft beams of sunlight
filter through the forest like Fairy light.
sweet air purifies the body with its cool
fragrance, such that the senses come alive
with wonder at such pleasures. In a world
so wrought with the realities of humankind —
there is an Oasis. Far away and safe from
the unclean influence of "Progress". Yes
there are times I long for paradise in the
quiet world of green leaves and bright petals
of color, and the breeze carries the promise of peace.

Kevin Kirkpatrick

The Rapids

Swollen with winter's melting remains
The Rapidan, augmented by spring rains
Breaks from its banks
Into myriad streams.

The simple oneness
Unfolds its endless seams
Change born of diversity
Rushes toward plurality.

Yet, when the process is circumscribed in space
The distinctions shared and channeled through the
prepositional case
Cause the many to form anew
the one made rich in complexity.

The Rapidan of summer's end
Falls back upon its banks,
The ghost of the lady-in-wading
Closes shut her multi-spawned fan.

J. R. Dwyer

Untitled

Was it by mistake or purpose
That two stars were left out of the skies
And placed, with their brilliant resplendence,
In the soft beaming green of your eyes?
Did the angels, in a divine mistake,
Create for the Earth this mortal's delight
By giving these stars to you,
And thus depriving the night?

Melanie J. Lockridge

The River

She sits on a rock as the water rushes by.
The rapids are rough today.
Each wave trying to go their own way.
Struggling to be set free from the pain.
Yet holding on to the safety around them.
Some trees are bent, looking down.
As if to say they're better than everyone.
Some branches fell loose and now float on top.
Banging into the edge, wanting to cling on to something.
A tree lies across the water.
Either you walk across or stay where you are.
This is the river.
Everything here has a meaning.
A symbolism of life.
But in the end, they all go down the waterfall.

Lori A. Raymond

Pressures

The pressures of life seem to be weighing down on me,
the responsibilities are getting heavier, you can see.

Sometimes the pressure is intolerable, I think I'm going to crack,
but sooner or later, I'm going to push the pressure back.

At times like this, it seems with me the pressure will always stay,
but, in time, I know that it will all just go away.

Serenity is all I need, this I know too well,
but I don't know when, I guess that only time will tell.

Tension and uneasiness are always building up,
to those people building it I will just say "Shut up".

All these pressures will go away when I die,
forever these pressures will be gone and in peace I'll lie.

Kari Carlson

Reflections at an Abandoned Schoolhouse

Time passes. Things and people change,
  The river wears away the stone.
The old schoolyard looks sad and strange
  With weeds and ivy overgrown.

And we, whose sandals loped the dust
  Of random playgrounds long ago,
Walk only when and where we must,
  And then with painful steps and slow.

Though years erode, and age grows grim,
  A cruel compassion underlies:
For as the fading flowers dim,
  Perception dims in fading eyes.

Oh precious youth, so sweet, so bright,
  And so impatient to be gone,
Leave us one candle for the night
  Before you come again, at dawn!

Virginia Wayland

Rainbow Eyes

I wished on every star I saw,
To see life differently,
That the song carried in a rainbows path,
Would someday come to me,
And when the wish was over,
I turned and looked your way,
To see the rainbows dancing in your eyes,
With a song for every day.

Mark Janelle

The Road Of Life

I sit and watch the years go by
The road is dark and narrow
Each curve sends a jolt
The signs are blank and unmet
The past is a curving one way road
One haunting look back and you're thrust Forward
Reaching out for things you can't have
Upset and depressed life goes on
The future opens new gate ways
The forks in the road make you decide
The uneasiness of what lies ahead grips you
Fear pins you down and you keep moving
The road suddenly comes to an end
You run off into oblivion
No more fears or uneasy paths
The serenity has you at peace
There is no road you chart your own way
The map is your to navigate

Jennifer Peterson

Love

Every night when I crawl to bed
the same prayers and hopes always are said

They are my dreams
of what tomorrow will bring
They are the songs of freedom
We all shall sing

The battle before us will take
Courage and might
We all have to help; we all have to fight

When love sees no color
When we can look past the skin
When the first thing we notice, is the beauty within

When the last man is shot
For the color he wears
When you can walk down the street
and no longer feel the stares

When all of this is accomplished
When we no longer will fall
It means no more colors;
Love conquers all

Robyn Evangel

"On The Prairie"

On the prairie the wind will blow.
The seasons will come, the seasons will go.
On the prairie the grass is brown,
Yet it gives no reason to frown.
On the prairie the grass is brome.
On the prairie is my home.
On the prairie the sky is blue.
At dusk it gives a purple hue.
On the prairie the land stretches out
So far that you can't hear a shout.
On the prairie life is wild and free.
Life is like it used to be.
On the prairie you live the old way.
For survival, you have to pray.
Yet beyond the prairie, I'll never roam.
I'll stay here on the prairie that I call home.

Jamie Dorn

Fields Of Amber

On fields like these, in distant places,
The silent wind carves out traces,
Of each oarsmen and brave grenadier,
That marched, or prayed, or even died here.

For in my hand, your soft hand,
In loves comfort finds its place,
As we lie in grass upon this land,
Where the infantry drummer signaled the pace,

This quiet meadow in sunbathed bliss,
Embraces us, while yet we kiss,
For loves moments more than these,
Every combat soldier feels and sees.

Did robins and skylarks witness smoke and
Blood?

Or gaze upon the dark red mud?

As now they gather and watch
Us play,

Loves whisper upon the wind
This day.

Ronald S. Hoard

My Child Drew a Picture

My child drew a picture, as children will do,
The sky was all red, and the sun, it was blue.
I watched her with pleasure, my heart full of pride,
And when she was finished, I took her aside.
I wonder why you chose those colors, I said,
You made the sun blue, and the sky cherry red.
She looked up at me with those innocent eyes,
Then a smile lit her face as she said, with surprise,
Oh, Daddy, you're silly! I know the sun's red,
But blue is the color I made it instead.
It wasn't exactly the color I planned,
But that was the crayon I had in my hand.

Sherwin A. Kaufman

Rainy Day

It was a beautiful rainy day.
The smell was so refreshing you wish you could breathe it forever.
So surprisingly it speeds up and slows down.
The trees sway like their dancing with joy.
The sea blue sky darkens with grey clouds,
as if it were trying to fool us with a sunset.
The air develops a chill,
as the storm approaches.
The lightning Bolts!
The thunder Crashes!
The rain pounds on the window, like someone you have been
longing
to see, trying to pound their way into your heart again.
The rain stops.
The birds come out as if god were sitting upon their shoulder.
The wind in nippy.
The sky is dark.
Someone loves me to give me such a extravagant day.
Now I can sit with the window open and smell
the sweet smelling afterthought of that glorious spring day.

Tonya Staples

Graffittico

Why is it I always come back to a child's trend?
The smile on their faces' a perpetual blend
A little child hiding in a attic....writing in their diary
All to familiar a dreadful tactic...a child must be dreaming
of a fairy
What's happening to our child's dream?
So sad to think a child's eyes leaving no gleam
I can never write enough of a child's inefficiency
Economic need our child's lack of sufficiency
When it is wrote? Perhaps someday it will be done
So alone seems almost gone
God surely knows their meager existence
A child's exigency creating pestilence
Take a child's life and began at creation
Healthy wombs and healthy diet create a path to better
children's education
I came back to the children to lend a hand
God knows someday it will be their land
Graffittico! A cry out of the dark
The cry of the lark a bit stark.

Robert G. English

A Child's Innocence

I put my boy to bed last night while tears were in his eyes.
The spanking that he had received I felt was justified.
Of course I do not like to scold or punish my own son!
But the duties of a father require at times such things be done.

But now, while I stand watching, he in a blissful slumber lay.
His face beams strong of innocence, the tears have gone away.
Was I wrong to strike this little boy? Had he been so terribly bad?
Or did I vent my own frustrations on this helpless, innocent lad?

I want to pick him up and hug him, to never let him go;
To tell him how much he means to me, and that I love him so.
But my boy lay peacefully sleeping. To disturb him would not do.
So in sadness I turn and leave him, and I hope he loves me too.

A shake, a tug; as I wake what should I see?
A cheerful face on a little boy. "Daddy, will you please play with
me?"

Oh, my little man, there's so much for you to learn.
I will teach you all the things I know, we will take each one in turn.
To throw and catch, to ride a bike, to swim, to read and write.
I will teach you how to understand what is wrong and what is right.
I will teach you all the things I've learned, as all good fathers do.
But please, can you teach me to forgive and love even half as well as
you?

Kevin J. Ward

The Lord of Glory

The Cross stands tall upon the hill.
The stains of blood show forth the kill.
The tomb is quiet and dark with sorrow.
The women are weeping with no tomorrow.
The Man called Jesus, who hung there in agony,
Has gone into the earth to bring forth captivity.
His body, still chained to the shackles of death,
Bursts forth with life in Heavenly breath.
Never to die, He will seek out His wife —
The Church of the reborn, saved out of strife.
Out of the tomb, He showed the disciples His wounds.
He walked through the walls of their upper room.
Bringing words of comfort to all who would hear it:
The promise, all powerful, the sweet Holy Spirit.
The sky unfolded. He was caught up to glory,
But only until we have all heard His story.
Then out of the blue He will ride down in splendor,
His sword dipped in blood to cut evil asunder.
You know in your heart you must surrender,
To the One called Jesus - the Eternal Ember.

Ken Smith

Heavenly Host

I can see God's heavenly promise in
the stars agleam.
Millions of galaxies tell me of
a radiant beam.

The magnitude of God's greatness is
amazing to see.
Vastness of His big universe;
a shooting star spree!

Tells me there is a miraculous
"Lord of Host"
"God of Jacob" I can substantiate
and proudly boast.

I can look upon THE STAR - have no fear,
my sins are as white as snow.
"The bright morning star" - is showing us
a heavenly marvelous show!

J. W. Mahan

Stepping Stones

I carefully step from one stone to the next on
the stone pathway.

Never looking down to see what is waiting for
me and never looking back to see what I
might have missed.

Thoughts of falling into an endless pit race
through my mind as I take each step.
All my concentration is locked on what lies ahead.

I hurry to reach the other side where I will
be safe, but each step I take closer to
the other side takes me to a new beginning.

Regina Clark

Untitled

In the deepest of winter with the ice turning blue
The storyteller warms them with tall tale and true.
He tells of the legends of raven and bear
Of battles with Blackfoot so real you are there.

Tales of the seasons that still come and go
Of creeks, streams and rivers that forever will flow.
All winter they come to his place by the fire
To hear of the great ones, tales of which they don't tire.

When the snow is all gone and starvation no fear
The band moves to the plains to start a new year.
The cycle of life and the roots of the tribe
Are passed down in story and painted on hide.

So remember your past and where you are from
And keep memories stirring in stories and song.

William G. Page

Place of Peace

A place where I can go...
To walk barefoot through the cool, damp grass;
Or maybe just sit and watch.
The mothering, blue sky lays the sun to rest.
Chaos down the street doesn't bother me, but gives a needed
dose of reality.
The air carries in it's stillness, the potpourri formed
when the scent of the flower garden met that of the grass.
It brings me peace.
Even the thought of it provides a feeling of tranquility.
This place...my own humble paradise.

Stephanie Brokstad

Jessie

Courage is beauty and you are beautiful,
The strength you own emanating light of day;
Nourishing those of us who know and love you,
Bright'ning each our lives with ev'ry glist'ning ray.
Jessie sweet young lady, our inspiration,
Swagg'ring defiantly at the storm now met;
Captaining your ship above each mighty wave,
Never falt'ring from the course that you have set.
We the crew helping sail with you our leader,
Sextant aiming at the stars that be your guide;
Their hands holding while you steer through this vast sea,
Vessel cutting like a sword through any tide.
Soon a land will appear on the horizon,
Harbor waiting to envelope you with joy;
Off'ring richness to a seasoned sea captain,
With an ocean of perspective to employ.
Your future stands in front of you, dear Jessie,
These waters traveled as a fading mem'ry;
Those winds so weathered against your unfurled sails,
To make a woman that all would wish to be.

Lawrence Uniglicht

Earth's Four Seasons

Wind rustling through the trees, birds singing melodies
The sun's brilliant glow illuminates new sights and smells
Spring is here - it's all around.

Now the sun's warmth grows in intensity
Until it parches all in its vicinity
Every living thing must bargain for its share
For summer has come, leaving no water to spare.

The leaves begin to turn in color, orange, brown, red and yellow
Falling to the ground as if to implore, come, see me once more
Cool crisp days lead to heavenly nights
Clear skies, countless stars, aboundless heights
Autumn is here to have its way.

Cold, wet, the weather has changed
The sun's shine is short, the moon's glow long
The leaves have all fallen, only the evergreens remain
Winter has taken its toll on the Earth's domain.

Our seasons they come, only one at a time
Each takes its turn in the seasonal line
But oh what a dreadful place our Earth would be
Without the Four Seasons to mesmerize me.

Sally Brannen McDonald

A Soldier After Battle

The battlefield lies silent - dead bodies scattered about.
The suns rays breaking over the horizon. Smoke from the bombs
dispatching into the air.
Alone soldier marcher on. He feels the wastefulness
of was - the hatred. Knowing innocent people
died for the beliefs of rival countries.
Soldiers marching on to die for a cause they
may or may not believe in. The fear of dying, the bravery.
Not knowing when you too will be killed.
Seeing your best friend dying in your arms, covered
with blood, blown apart - the sorrow.
Yet, he finds the courage to go on.
But, in the depths of his mind, the war will
rage on forever. He feels the thrill of coming home-heroes
But the sorrow for the lost comrades killed in battle
Still lie fresh in his mind.
He will carry these memories forever - hauntingly.
Trying to cope with all the blood-death-sorrow.
Yet striving to become one with society once again.

Leonard F. Cavaretta III

Wedding Day

Love is like a flower that grows with
the sunshine and the rain,

Love is a marriage that grows with
the laughter and the pain,

Like a baby's first step everything
will seem so new,

There's a whole new world out there that
has been opened for the both of you

There may be times in your darkest hours
that follow with discontentment and strife,

But may your love for one another overshadow them
all, and may peace and happiness fill your life.

K. Nick Long

Helplessly

A tear for a life that didn't get a chance to live.
The thought of seeing your little heart beat, beating away.
A great feeling of sadness overcame me,
the tears poured from my eyes uncontrollably.
As I thought of how it must feel to be safe one minute
and at the next have it taken away.
Gasping for air, but your little heart just kept beating strong
as you laid there helplessly fighting so hard for life.
All I could do is stand there and stare.
If there was a something I could of done to have saved you
it would've been done. But there was nothing.
Your heart kept beating strong not wanting to give up
but at a loss you couldn't go on you, fought so hard
that you became weak and your heart stopped beating.
I swear after you were gone. I in my mind could still hear
your heart beating strong. Tears fell from my eyes as I saw
all the life drain out of you and as you said goodbye
to a world that only for a mere sad and helpless moments -
you were a part of it.

Yolanda R. Garcia

Maya Sings

You stood upon the platform crest,
The throngs around abound.
Your words rung clear the spirit's test;
Love sewn within each sound.

The throngs abound around your feet,
Not one creature seemed to move.
Love sewn within each sound you preached;
Turmoil it came to soothe.

The throngs abound around your feet,
Words ringing the spirit's test;
"No, not here! there's no hiding place!",
You sung upon that crest.

Robert L. Lewis II

Sharing

Two little boys, who share each others toys.
They also share some thing sad!
Not having their very own DAD!
Their happy and bright and don't seem to mind,
That's something missing, they may someday want to find.
One is five the other four-sweet little
Guys any one would adore! They need
someone to teach them to be tough and strong!
To know the difference between right and wrong!
There's something missing I'm sad to say
They need someone to love them in that "special way"

Pat Maria

Pucci

He lives in me as if he had never left.
The times together, which seem so short are cherished
and will never be forgotten.

The humblest of men with the heart of a thousand.
Always looking for a laugh, a game, or a cup of coffee,
he always bought.

A snooze was his weekend afternoon chore, listening
to the crack of the bat and a cheer from the crowd
next to him, of course him and Duke spent every spring together.

Let's not forget the daily mail drop or the never ending rides
to town. His slow wobble walk and the pace he set, never
fast enough for anyone, but him.

There was a style in everything he did. Opinions that were
questionable at best. If it wasn't "Punch it thru the hole,"
well we each have our favorite saying that keeps his spirit alive.

The times missed are not important but the ones shared
have a place in my heart that cannot be touched or forgotten.

Steve Howell

Flight

I stood, weary, waiting for my bus, alone, the sunset to my left.
Around,
the trees on the horizon made a rasping wheeze.
The sky was clear above, no cloud in sight,
But to the west a sailor's red delight.
I stood—weary, waiting, sighing.

In hearing only first, but then in sight
around me, all around me, they took flight,
a thousand pair of wings and more. They called
to me and one another, words I knew—
if I could just remember. Birds! They flew,
advancing, then retreating, dancing high
above the ground. Their only watcher, I
stared in delight. I longed to dance, to share
the flight. My heart swam gaily in the air.
I could not move, I dared not breathe. Above,
in symmetry and perfect grace, they flew
and turned and soared and slowed and raced anew.

When they settled in the bone-dry autumn trees, the sky was
empty once again. I stood there waiting on the ground,
a man by Newton's chains to earth still bound.

Kevin Vail

Troubled Waters

I envy the sea.
The unchanging nature of the tide.
Its constant repetitive rhythm.
Its permanence.

Set into motion so long ago.
The tides are still rolling.
In the same hypnotic cadence.

If only life were that simple.
Traveling a course immune to change.
Making only slight deviations along the way.

But my life is a sea of conflict.
A cesspool of fears and unanswered questions.
Filled with confusion.
Lacking any meaning or stability.

I keep holding on to the past when life was so simple.
While the sea keeps pushing me further into its depths.
Trying to drown me in its cold darkness.
Sweeping me away, never to return.
But I keep groping for the shore.
Fighting for one more chance.

Lisa A. Lewis

Naked

I walk naked through the sand,
the water and the sky.
Just to have the wind in my hair,
the water to my thighs.
To feel and breeze of innocence,
discover beauty sights.
Have sand travel between my toes,
Here and lovely things.
To see the naked people having graceful fun,
satisfying every need to wish would over come.
I humor this in which I tell,
I say this only once,
I shall walk, naked through the night,
and try to have good luck!

Kara Lillethun

The Ocean

The ocean is a beautiful place,
the waves seem to flow to land.
The sea gulls fly with grace
and the children play in the sand.

The water seems to never end,
you don't even notice the heat of the sun.
Everyone is with a friend
and everyone is having fun.

It's so nice to go at night
and see the waves come to the shore.
With just the stars and pale moonlight,
all you see is the ocean, nothing more.

Sarah Salm

Real Love

The throng of people yell obscenities and laugh.
The weight laden wood cracks and creaks.
The pain is agonizing.
The lips are silent.

Throbbing points of pressure pierce the bowed head.
Trickling blood stings the tear filled eyes.
The pain is consuming.
The lips are silent.

Splinters of wood tear the weathered flesh.
Cold hard steel penetrates the gentle hands.
The pain is numbing.
The lips are silent.

The scoffing crowd dissipates.
The body is limp.
The pain is silent.
The death forever shouts - I love you.

Robin Ferrin

In One's Time

I walk forward undaunted into time
to the point not ahead of me, but now surrounding...
Faced with my significance.
Expansive as I come to this, the splendor of disclosure.

The unobstructed view upon me,
having walked it, now I see...
Action, rewarded with a purpose.

My place in time is a horizon, never ending, yet complete.
I am a fingerprint of time.
Infinitesimal but distinct.

Sandra Lee Messer

A Union Of Earthly Elements

A forceful movement near the ocean erupts.
The west wind blows his breeze.
He beckons the overflowed ocean to corrupt,
the untouched maidenhead of the beach.
Under the rise of a full moon,
two natural forces collide,
in rhythmic and redundant rapture.
The turbulence of a tide,
causes a period of peaks.
A thunderous wave ride,
between water and land creation.
It is a union of earthly elements.
They are engaged into entangled elation.
Water and land creation surrendering,
themselves in the dark night.
A little later, the ocean activity ceases
at the sun's rising light.

Theresa Rose McMiller

My Friend Willie

It was a cold winter nite, under the Willis Avenue Bridge.
The wind biting my face, with a chill to the bone,
Winter was laughing.
I heard a faint cry, and a dirty, black, calico cat,
Comes to me, on wobbly legs
Sick, skinny, afraid, but starving overcomes her fears.
I take her into my arms, and she shares my late snack.
At home she sleeps little, on guard of every move, and sound.
But slowly she regains her strength, and relaxes with
Her new environment.
At first, she is untrusting, ready to bite, and assume
The attack position.
As time passes, her aggression turns to love, and today she
Is a beautiful creature.
Dark, black hair with a hint of orange, her, under carriage
White, slender in built, small lack of growth, but a
Beautiful cat, never the less.
Her name is Willie, after the Willis Avenue Bridge

Lenny Mastro

Promises In The Wind

There are no promises in the wind, they say.
The wind caressed my naked flesh,
Then the wind began to blow the other way.

I gaze up into the gloomy, gray, suffocating sky.
As the rain commences, we let ourselves free,
and together we cry.

I hold myself tight, as I curl into a ball.
I watch the day possess the night and listen
to the hushed voice of the blowing wind
promise that it won't let me fall.

I turn my head away.
for I can't bear to listen anymore.
I had listened to this familiar faint voice
on too many sleepless nights before.

For there are no promises in the wind.
Don't believe what the wind has to say.
It will cast shivers up your spine,
Smiles to your heart and put fire to your soul.
And with a sharp, gusty blow, the wind
will carry it all away.

Melissa B. Rogers

Carrying Love From One To The Other

When a man loves a woman more than life itself
The woman will return his love like an a abundance of wealth
Love is the highest expression of all human emotions
And only works when the two involved share it like a love potion
When they are separated to do their daily chores
Reunited again at home, they will share their love behind closed doors
When all the love and passion has been shared
They know that each has shown great care
It completes a love that only a man and woman could know
For love making is better than watching the late night show
Now that they have carried their love from one to the other
In God's plan they will always be together as life long lovers

Priscilla E. Princler

I Believe

Remembrance of the good times we once shared
The words of love and the things we dared
Through all the triumphs that life presents
The bonds of love prevails to no extent
Reflection of time and thoughts of you this night
Reality of darkness become visions of light

Promises made are sometime broken
The love we give are sometime tokens
Facing decisions in the cross roads of life
Decisions we make alone are not always wise
Words of truth you have given me
The love and commitment so endlessly

I believe by the words you care
I believe by the love we share
I believe in the things you do
I believe in you

Larry Fisher

Friends

Friends will last a life time if they are truly friends, their friendship shall never, never end.
If they are special, tell them today, they need to know before they pass away.
They share your hopes and dreams, they share your sorrow and your pain.
They gain your love forever and for eternity, they want to show their love for you constantly.
In times of sorrow and in times of need a true, loving friend will never, ever leave.
A true friend really cares and they always will. A true friend will last forever and always, until the end of time.

Patricia Marie Kolesar

My Dream

I dreamed that I was in a mist so thick I could not see.
Then I saw this light coming towards me.
As the light come closer I could see.
That it was a man walking toward me.
He held out his hands and I could see.
The scars where he was nailed to the tree.
I could see the scars that was made.
Where the crown of thorns on his head was laid.
His eyes was so loving, I knew that he could see.
Everything that has been, or ever will be.
His robes was a glistening white.
For Jesus was pure light.
His voice was so gentle and kind.
He said, my child, it is not your time.
I have a work for you to do in this land.
You must be a witness for me to man.
Now I know that Jesus is with me day and night.
For He is my saviour, my guiding light.

Mildred O. Kitchens

Distant

Your first spoken words to me made me wonder.
Then I see us now.

Your touch sends chills and your smile I need
no words.

Your eyes are like those of a lost puppy.
Lonely but dark, hidden in an unknown world.

As I take a deeper look I realize that I am
the lost one the unknown one.

How, oh, how can I let one in?
We are so distant, but we are as close as a
leaf tenderly touching a branch.

Your seconds from my heart yet miles away.

Kathryn Rowton

I Remember When

I remember when, we used to be friends.
Then something happened...
What? When?
Things changed then!

I remember when I used to try to get us to do things together.
You used to say, "Go away! Go away!"
It felt as if you had no time for me anymore...
I tried time and time again. You used to say, "No".
That you were doing this or that or had plans that just
could not be changed or somehow rearranged.

A few moments of your times was all that I had asked.
But now, time has passed. I seldom ask.

I grieved and yet made a life of my own.
But now, you seem so all alone. I've grown and left you
somehow behind. If that's unkind, then I'm sorry.
It was not mean as such.
I love you much! And I hope that God will help you not to feel
so all alone.

Sherry Jackson

Destiny

From the depth within my soul
There comes a yearning that only one can control
The one that is so close, but yet so far
And from this soul so alone
That he can conquer with only his own

The years have placed us far apart
Not within our arms could we play
Memories that linger and touch both souls
Live deep and very bold

But what was meant to be will be
And the love of these two souls
Will finally touch and hold
Once together they are finally complete

No yearning, no lonely dreams
Far the now and future the lonely souls are one
Their goals they did reach
To have and to hold each other finally complete

Lynn Bradford

Happy Mothers Day

My dear sweet Mother
There could never be no other

Always giving and sharing
A Mother who's so caring

Everything you've done has been for us
You did it out of Love without a fuss

You've always put us first ahead of you
We were young, if only we knew

You took a lot day after day
I am sure there were times you didn't want to stay

Your a wonderful Mother without a doubt
You show true meaning of what one's all about
I am sorry it took so long to wake up and see
What a truly Great Mother you've turned out to be

I have so much love and respect for you
I don't think you realized or had a clue

I think it's time to give a credit to you
It's one that's been, way overdue

And just one more thing I'd like to say
I LOVE YOU MOTHER, HAPPY MOTHERS DAY!!!

Jamie M. Schroeder

Dressing Up

Up in the attic in the very, very back,
There is an old trunk I'm allowed to unpack.

It's full of the neatest old shoes and clothes,
And I know every piece and where it goes.

There's my dad's old navy uniform,
I can become a see captain in a heavy storm.

My mom's pretty wedding dress,
Turns me into a little princess.

There's rubber galoshes and coats and hats,
And I even found grandpa's snappy spats.

Old jewelry and baubles make a gypsy of me,
Or put in a chest, a pirate at sea.

I have so much fun playing with these old clothes,
My imagination can take me to places untold.

If you have an attic, look way in the back,
And see if there's an old trunk you can unpack.

Patricia M. Rondeau

Divine Intervention

Where dreams and purpose dance,
There met I a friend.
My life He did enhance.

Knowing of Him, yet not knowing Him
One night He came, a vision beckoning.
My dashed hopes to reclaim.

No mention of wrong, nor did He threaten.
Love emanating through every word spoken
His life He laid down, not a token.

"Believe on Me," still echoes through time
His love never changing
Crippled lives, He's into rearranging.

What He'd done screamed through my brain.
No condemnation did He throw,
And in Him now I ever grow.

Katie Figueroa

Rocks in the Forest of Fontainbleau

In the lush greenery of the woods a solitude rock, there, sits alone. It beckons, weary, a traveler to come sit on the rock.

There, that person sits and is surrounded by sound, birds, squirrels, and chipmunks are all around.

By the rock runs a stream, shallow, so crisp; yet clean. The travel looks around and sees such beauty go untouched. He hears a sound, a snap from the nearby brush, he looks up and sees a majestic unicorn. As unreal, but very much there. The unicorn drinks from the stream.

Fontainbleau, home to the magical unicorn, the realm of peace and harmony. For you see in the lush greenery of the woods a weary traveler sits, and learns a lesson of peace, and how man and beast must work together against destruction of such a place. A place of never-ending grace.

In the silence a world of non-violence, a peace known to few; kept secret, wrapped among the green hue.

Kelly Rine

Budded Rose

In a small little garden one of many in these lands
there was a budded rose and you took her in your hands.

You admired her beauty as you touch her with your fingertips
you saw of her worry and granted a kiss from your lips.

You offered her your company and watched over her all the night through
you fell in love with this budded rose and restored her honeydew.

And when the night had ended and light grew in the skies
it was a beautiful morning among the pink sunrise.

You turned to the budded rose and gave out huge sigh
for the rose bloomed to your surprise.

No more worry upon her you see
for you showed her courage and opened that bud free.

Now when you admire your rose you've earned some credit for your care
this little rose grew because you've showed love and were always there.

This single rose you've made her bloom never to take away
instead of one this little rose now a whole bouquet.

Lori A. Gilberto

The Flicker

I was born in the early spring of ninety three,
There were in the nest just a few don't you see.

Feathers grew larger and we spread our wings,
All three of us turned into beautiful things.

After some time all of us took flight,
You never saw such a wonderful sight,

In a short time separate ways we did wander,
It was great fun to fly hither and yonder.

I had beautiful feathers on my tail and wing,
The red patch on my head was an attractive thing.

I had very sharp claws and a strong sharp beak,
To get into trunks and logs for insects I seek.

In October I was preparing for migration to begin,
When on a pole an insect was sighted to win.

I swooped down to get him before he got away,
An electric breaker was my downfall this day.

A boy and his grandfather under the pole I was found,
They buried me with love and dignity under the ground.

In the end my name tells this story of mine,
I was just a flicker in the winds of time.

Robert L. Inskeep

I Lost Another Friend Today

I lost another friend today
There were so many things I had meant to say

How I treasured her friendship all these years
How we shared so much happiness as well as tears

She is one of several recently, I had to say goodbye to
It breaks my heart, for soon there will be only a few

As I grow older, life is rushing by so fast
Nothing stays the same - nothing ever last

I thought I had plenty of time to tell her how much I care
Never thinking that she wouldn't always be there

I must hurry and tell my friends, who are so dear
How much I love them, and so glad they are here

Friends are my most precious possession
Without them, life would be empty, there's no question

I need to answer the phone, its rung for so long
Hello, oh! No! you say he is already gone

I lost another friend today

Maxine Burns

Depression

Darkness fills your life
There's nothing but pain and strife
All around you see despair
But to most they are unaware
Life that once thrived
Has withered and died
Tomorrow is so far away
You fear yesterday is here to stay
Constant troubles disturb your mind
Like vines overgrown all tangled and twined
Weary days and endless nights
Always anxious and hopeless with fright
Empty and numb
You're coming undone
Trapped in a place where you don't want to be
Your life is painful, and you live in agony
Gone are those days of laughter and song
You only think now of all that went wrong
Depression hurts and can even kill
When people give up and lose their will

Kathy Stellato

Hands

These hands used to scold my children.
These hands used to play beautiful music.
These hands used to work as swift as the wind.
But they can't anymore.

These hands used to hold precious things.
These hands used to dance in lather.
These hands used to be soft as silk.
But the silk is gone.

These hands used to hold a beautiful ring.
These hands used to hold icy cold drinks.
These hands are as cold as ice.
Because I am dead.

Tori Botticelli

A Daughter's Tribute

A Parent's love is special and true,
they are always watching over you.
When hurt or harm appears,
we need never fear, because they are always near.
Most times our expressions of thanks are few,
but we really do appreciate you!
Your love overflows from a heart of pure gold,
like a precious gem could never be sold.
The happiness and comfort that you instill,
has settled within us, our lives you have filled.
A heart felt love for you is written in this rhyme,
this infinite bond to share until the end of time.

Teresa Oberholtzer

My Grandmother

Her eyes shine so bright
They are an unimaginable sight

Her hands are soft like pillows
She strengthens even the weakest of willows

Her wisdom is far beyond her years
Accumulated through many moments of laughs and tears

Her smile is so kind
It automatically eases your mind

Her heart is like an open book
No one can take just one look

She will mesmerize you with her charm
Never has she done anyone harm

Is she only a dream?
Or are my words as real as they may seem?

I can never tell you is she is real or hocus-pocus
She passed away before my child-like eyes came into focus

So I am left to draw my own beginning and conclusion
My grandmother is only an illusion

Karen Alexis Adamcik

The Forgotten Children

There are children being born, neglected and abused
they are born into this world, being used

Black or white, which ever color you choose
before they even try, these children will lose

To see the let down look in their eyes, is to me a terrible shame
How can we keep ignoring their cries,
where will we put the blame?

The lives they live are filled with pain
they do not have a choice
Nothing ever seems within their gain
These little human beings have no voice

I watch them on the news at night
I see them and I cry
Because children should be born to live
and not to wither and die

These forgotten children are prisoners of their very being
The proof is in the helpless stories we are seeing

If people don't make an effort to bring them relief
then someday we will all be the prisoners of their grief

Kathy Whirity

Remember the Place that Holds the Memory

They came from among us and brought war with them.
They betrayed their country and called it justice.
They bent the people to their will and called it freedom.
They turned the soil crimson with blood and called it a new life.
They devastated the land and called it peace.

We abandoned our home, but we brought with us pain and remorse.
We survived inhuman misery, but we call that courage.
We suffered tragic hardships, but we call that dignity.
We overcame insurmountable odds, but we call that hope.
We healed the scars of a broken spirit, but we call that fortitude.
We rebuilt the wreckage of our past, but we call that faith.
We will endure, but we call that victory.

I remember a place and a time where
Every image of beauty and serenity,
Every song of love and bereavement,
And every proverb of wisdom and experience once was.
The complete drama of our four-thousand year old heritage
Exists there and then. The memory is the legacy.
Remembering will preserve the place.
The place remains as long as we endure.

Quang X. Nguyen

The Flowers' Opinion

In spring the flowers burst in bloom for joy.
They danced and laughed and sang and put on airs.
The rose denounced, said "With death you toy,
The noise you make will wake the sheep and mares."

The flowers cocked their heads at her and said:
"Dear rose do not denounce and call us done.
We know precisely when Death us will bed,
This is revenge we take on him for fun."

The rose cried out and begged and begged to know
When Death will come to her and bed with them.
The flowers shook their heads and said, "Oh, no!"
You must enjoy yourself before the End."

"And why must I enjoy?" complained the fool.
"Do just as you would wish!" said flowers, cruel.

Kiran Aftab

Only One Mistake

Only one mistake,
they did it too late.
All our men who fought for our country
we're seen and we were proud of
for what they were fighting for.
But, only one mistake.
Our men fought for Vietnam
were not sure of what they were fighting for,
they didn't want to fight for something they didn't believe in.
Only one mistake.
They did it anyhow, for which for some was a mistake.
When they came back and we were not proud
of them for what they were fighting for.
Which the things they have seen with their eyes,
the tears, the pain, the lost.
They went through fighting this war.
Only one mistake
they did it too late.

Melody Hause

Hope

In the fall, the flowers begin to die.
They fade ever so slowly with a pitiful sigh.
Another season has passed as they drift to sleep.
The earth is cold and bare and slumber is deep.

We humans are as the flowers of the earth.
While we are young, we are full of mirth.
As the years pass, we slowly fade.
Then our bodies die and in the ground we are laid.

But the seed remains, which is our soul
When Jesus speaks, we will again unfold,
Into a beautiful flower which will never die.
Thank Him, Believe in Him, for He Cannot Lie

Toni Spivey

"The Perfect Couple"

The perfect couple has become a rare breed
They have become extremely hard to find
Different people will give different reasons,
but most agree it's a state of mind.

The perfect couple must listen to each other
and lend an ear in a time of need
For a person who speaks but doesn't hear,
is a person full of nothing but greed.

The perfect couple must at times laugh together
and realize life isn't all work and sweat
To be able to smile while other people frown
and looking at us, their problems they soon will forget.

The perfect couple must at times cry together
and accept their tears as a part of life
In every relationship there is assured to be sorrow
be it a young dating couple or a husband and wife

The perfect couple has become a rare breed
They had become extremely hard to see
If anyone wants to see one of the few still left,
they can come and look at you and me.....

Michael Neuberger

To Dream

They tell me to dream is frivolous, I say, "it's necessary,"
They look at a plant and say it's weed, I say "I see a strawberry."

They say "isn't she sweet? she's such a happy little girl,"
I see sad eyes and a black-and-blue bruise under her curl.

I dream of a world filled with happiness and love,
Gang members only know how to hate, shoot people and shove.

I dream of a Knight In Shinning Armor carrying me off on a white horse
But in reality, there is no such thing, I know this is my heart of course.

I dream that all the prejudice in the world will soon be gone,
The White Supremacist says, "it will be over when only white people remain, and they will be number one."

I dream of a day when adults become as smart as children and don't notice any difference in each other,
But in reality very few of us ever say, "He's Not Heavy, He's My Brother."

I dream of one day receiving my degree in Psychology and helping as many abused and troubled children as God sees fit,
I'm halfway there, and I am going to finish, the reality of this dream is that it is going to come true, because I will never quit.

Pauline Davalos

Harmony

I watched two fleecy cloudlets in the sky,
They met and kissed each other tenderly,
And then I saw but one cloud drifting by,
The two had merged in perfect harmony.

I watched a brook flow down o'er rocks and rills,
And heard it fill with song a woodland dell,
The flowers that bloomed along its course bent down
To greet the singing brook they loved so well.

I watched a happy lark soar through the air
To make his concert stage upon a tree,
There in the glory of an early dawn,
He filled my garden with his melody.

Oh, God has made this world of ours so fair;
All nature plays a wond'rous symphony,
No deed of mine must mar its beauty rare,
Or be discordant note in harmony.

Rose Marie Camerota

"Old Age"

When you get funny looking you're not the same
They tell me mother nature is to blame
You can try and try as hard as you like
But eventually you will lose the fight

My hair is getting thin and if his turned gray
I have lines on my face, that are here to stay
My teeth are gone, dentures I've got
And let me tell you, they are not so hot

I have pain in my shoulders, it's hard to sit straight
If I sit too much, I put on weight
I've a little pot that's hard to control
So I get down on the floor and rock and roll

I bend a little here and twist a little there
Hoping it all will soon, disappear
But then my knees begin to ache
So I have to stop and give them a break

I crock and creek from head to toe
My steps are getting a little slow
It's hard to remember what I forgot
Cause my thinking cap is pretty shot.

Olive Showalter

Slow Dance

Your shapeless, coppery arms hypnotize me.
They waver slowly at first —
Slow-dancing and seducing me.
Then suddenly they throw me to the floor,
And I crash like a pine tree in a forest fire.
Your flames lick at me, tickling and burning all at once,
And I can't decide whether to giggle or scream.

So I lay motionless, breathing in your second-hand smoke,
expecting to gag on grimy fumes.
Instead, I feel high and I float above you
Until your heat finally overcomes me
And sucks me into your hearth.

I feed you, and you swallow my ashes,
Burning me clean so there is no filthy soot left —
Only a clean, white haze that escapes from your mouth
Like breath crystals on a snowy morning.

Suzanne Czehut

What Is An Angel?

God created the angels before us
They were made to obey and to serve
They are holy and yet something's missing
Perhaps passion, or suffering, or nerve

God gave one of them freedom to choose
and he chose his own selfish way
So the Lord sent him out from the glory
but then He made us like him one day

We can choose God's direction of Satan's
We've a helper to grow either way
We can grow in God's light and his love
or find darkness and anger each day

If we choose God to guide and direct us
we may find that we stumble at times
But we're doing the will of the master
and He's paid for the sum of our crimes

What's the difference 'tween us and the angels?
We've the power to turn from his love
or to the power to reach up and grasp it
when we'll rise o'er the angels above

Victor I. Fredda

Dreams

Dreams are the stars in your eyes,
They will never leave you, nor pass you bye.
Dreams are what keep us going in life,
You could be dreaming about a wife.
If you do not have any dreams,
Your life may be going down a stream.
If you look into the future,
Your life and dreams will be a beautiful picture.
If you dream about your family far away,
Don't you worry it will be true someday.
Sometimes your dreams may be history,
And to some that could be a mystery.
You may be dreaming about a new car,
Don't you worry for it may not be far.
Life is full of hope and dreams,
Even when life's coming apart at the seams.
For when it seams all hope is gone,
Dreams are what keep pushing us on.
For do not give up on your dreams,
For life may not be all that it seems!

Shannon Marie Averitt

"My Thoughts"

My thoughts for you haven't changed
They've actually increased
I thought this feeling for you had finally left my heart
So we could grow apart
Not a day goes by without me thinking about you
I promise I'll be true to you
Patiently I've waited, and somehow I've made it
My days are getting darker and darker
I've tried and I've cried
What other possible thing could I do
Nothing has worked
My minds completely on you
I wish you felt this way too
Sometimes I have high hopes but as soon
As I see you I know the love from you couldn't be true
I just want one more chance
Please believe me, this isn't a lie
You left me and didn't look back
That must mean your thoughts for me have left
Why couldn't I do the same for you...

Yoon Choi

Life's Fulfillment

You're sitting under the tree where
they've been before you,
In the shade, with the breeze lightly
brushing your hair,
imagining the quiet peacefulness before you
you're sitting on the ground, gazing at the
wheat, the wind singing through it,
wondering what the rabbits did to make them so lucky.
You're looking at the flowers, with
the bees buzzing around them,
wondering if the bees have found life's fulfillment.
You're sitting on the chair, on your
deck, the umbrella catching the sun,
the wind breathing softly in your ear,
wondering if you have found life's fulfillment.
You look around and see the
bees, the trees the rabbits hopping madly
and you understand. SAS

Shawn Anne Spencer

Creatures in the Night

Creatures in the night, you'd never
think it so, but listen very carefully
and then you'll know.
The crickets they sing a very lovely
song, the owls they hum it right along.
Creatures in the night, listen very
close, a rustling rabbit you would
think it's a ghost.
Creatures in the night, the bats
they soar, and maybe in the distance
you can hear the wolves roar.
Morning comes and all is quiet,
you would never know, the creatures in the
night were out just hours ago.

Shelly Lynn Duplaga-Gardella

Girl Why Did You Have To Leave Me This Way

Girl why did you have to leave me this way
Think of the love we use to share
And try not to bare
The love we had was special to me
It was not a sparkle in your eye it was a gleam
You leaning on me was hard to think of
You know we were made for each other like hand and glove
Staring at this picture on the wall that was you
Why wasn't your love true
I have been through this plenty of times
I wish I could say that you are mine
I hope you take the time and read this
And soon as you do you will miss

Tony Jones

Intimate Secrets

Intimate secrets my dear friend
This is how our friendship ends.

In your eyes I can always see
I told too much about Lee and me.

You're over there
And I'm over here.

What are you telling them
About me and him?

Now I wish I'd never told you
Because everyday you make me feel so blue.

J. Scarlette Black

Drugs

There you sit under the sky of blue;
Thinking of absolutely nothing to do;
Then there's a thought you never had;
Drugs are the thing! Whether good or bad;
You listen to your friends;
You listen to the news;
DRUGS, hey you got nothing to lose,
One try; one dose is all it takes;
The pain and misery of what it makes;
Crack and marijuana is what you use;
Don't you think your blowing the fuse?
So snap out of it America; and look around;
For its drugs what makes the world stop going 'round;
But some still think drugs is the solution;
But NO! Snap out of that illusion;
For drugs is the leader of crime and assault;
But its the government that gets the fault;
So before you have that thought or spurt;
Realize you'll be six feet under dirt.

Jamie Bratslavsky

In The Light Of Day

I sit and stare into the light of day
thinking of you and the words I can never say.
Try as I might
I shy away with fright.
I fell in love in the first degree
Despite your every beckon plea.
I can write them down, but never say those words today
here in the light of day.

I said goodbye in the light of day
and shed many tears with no reason of why to say.
You ask for friendship as I for forgiveness
But maybe neither can give this.
Should we try again someday?
I await your answer here in the light of day.

As I lie and stare into the fading light of day
thinking of you and these few words left to say.
I realize now the ones that precede me
Have changed your heart from soft to steely.
I no longer hope and pray for your love to sway
Only that you may see me in the new light of day.

Mindy K. Killingsworth

Silent Prayer

Dear God
This is a silent prayer that only you will hear,
Please keep me safe from all hurt, harm and fear.
I know sometimes I don't always do right,
but I always ask for your forgiveness that very same night.
Through all the heartaches and pains I have encountered,
I just ask that you forgive all you've heard.
I now realize that there's no one like you,
the questions you answer no one else
seems to have a clue.
I see now that you are my best
and maybe only true friend,
thank you for hearing my silent prayer

Amen

Monique Perkins

Darren

Goodnight, sweet cousin, and sleep well
This is not goodbye or farewell
But a tender kiss as you fall asleep
And travel thru the land of dreams.

Goodnight, gentle cousin, and God bless.
As you weave your gossamer dreams
We'll feel them in summer's soft breezes
And hear them in the gentle motion of the sea.

Goodnight, Dear cousin, and dream on,
Weave dreams for us full of love and light
We'll see them in the children's gentle smiles
And touch them in the tears that fill our eyes.

Goodnight, sweet cousin, and godspeed
Someday soon our dreams will meet
Until then, take good care
Good night, sweet cousin, and sleep well!

Luciana A. Ceross

The Unbalanced Earth

In days of young when our nation was new,
This land was pure and clean.
Man enjoyed a balanced nature,
And lived off the land and sea.

But then came a time in our land
When fur trapping was on the rise,
And baby animals were liquidated
From their mother's feeding breast.

Caring people came forth to rescue
Animals on land in the seas,
To protect our endangered species,
And to regain our long lost animals.

The days are evitable....with
Harvesters destroying our forests
While metal wastes dregs our water ways,
And chemicals vitiate the air.

As time progresses, time will disclose,
For technology to take its stand,
And man will be stimulated
To regain our long lost resources.

Mafalda Grande Carrasco

A May Baby

In the merry month of May
This little baby came to stay
Right from the very start
She up and stole my heart
She gave it such a twirl
this little baby girl
she's always giggling
and always wiggling
Never does she cry
Unless of course she wasn't dry
She's out of this and into that
Then she crawls upon my lap
oh what a thrill
When she says, grandma I love you still.

Melissa Hart

A Pirate Looks At 60

His hair is graying, but his eyes remain bright blue,
This man of adventure with his own outlook and view.

His years in the sun on a boat or by the sea,
Have tanned his skin like a pirate might be.

His love of the sea and a boat under sail,
Have given him much pleasure, too priceless to sell.

He has no love of money, or things that get in the way,
His loves are quite simple, like the love of a new day.

He's a man of distinction with his own beliefs,
This pirate, my Father, my love he always keeps.

He taught me to sail in a way of his own,
So his seeds of piracy soon were sown.

One child he has, a daughter, that's me,
Adores her pirate as he looks at 60.

Age does not scare him, he has no fear,
He knows he'll still sail for many a year.

His life has been full, rich you might say,
A pirate looks at 60 and smiles at every day.

Kimberly King

Immortality

What is this thing called immortality?
This thing that causes wonder and calamity,
Alas, is it from man all in vanity,
Word, deed, thought or insanity?

Fear of death is what drives every man;
But, is it for us to understand?
Is there really a great plan?
Prove it, some say, if you can!

So, why do many delve and scheme
To arrive at the riddle of the immortal dream,
When nature gives all the answers for you to redeem
As written by the Creator ream upon ream?

Flowers, birds, bees, wind, rain, and sand
Are verses from the Creator's Bible written by His hand.
So, it is up to each of you to understand
The words of the Creator, if you can.

For only in this way will you know immortality
And eliminate the causes of wonder and calamity.
The message of nature shall conquer man's vanity
And eliminate all notion of insanity.

Robert R. Mooney

Take Time for Today

Take time for today - that is all you can do
This twenty four hours - that is so brand new
Take time to notice all the beauty you see
So many things that are totally free!

The beauty of a rose - the ocean so blue -
The smile of a loved one - talking with you
All of these things are there this day
So don't let this twenty four hours - just slip away!

For yesterday is gone a soft memory
And tomorrow is something still yet to be
So take time for today and share it with love
And count your blessings from the good hand above!

Make sure and take time for today!

Nancy Taylor

Guiding Star

The stars are shining, the moon is too,
This wouldn't be true if it weren't for you.
You make the earth go round and round,
But you keep your face turned toward the ground.
You are my friend, my star at night,
You are my once lost guiding light.
You mean so very much to me.
You are the eyes that let me see.
I love you in a special way.
It kills me to see you hurt each day.
The pain is there and it may always be
But please don't stop believing in me
I need you there right by my side,
So please, don't try to run and hide.
So pick your heart up and your head held high,
Don't worry I'll be there for you until I die.

Pam Fetgatter

The Thorns Left Behind ... (The Cuban Exodus)

The land is arid under the greedy hand of the ruler,
thorns grow merrily on abandoned land.
Like wildfire in a hayfield..so the misery spreads,
The old woman's face is scared with weary worry lines.
Her eyes look toward the horizon...traceless of any life,
squinting in thirst for a glimmer of hope,
failing to see any .. she walks on unquenched and parched.
Walking a feeble path amidst the thorns toward the burning sand,
to the shore of her ancestry.. the home of her by-gone dreams.
The scorching sand burns blisters under her soles.
She's oblivious to the pain and the torture.
For agonies of a worst kind... of blood and brutality,
has made her a frail little frame...unfeeling of most emotions,
known intimately to you and me.
Out on the shore...people are boarding anything that will sail the seas.
To disappear beyond the sunset to that far away land free from all misery and disease
The final survival...if attained would be worth the harsh sail,
She trods on to the raft clutching the rope till her knuckles turn blue
looking out toward the swelling sea,
Not turning back once to remember the thorns left behind.

Ramila Liyanage

Love Hurts

Those you don't love are dull
Those you do love are sharp as a knife
And when the loved ones cut you
The wounds are deep, no matter how small
Wounds that can't be healed by words,
But only by actions and time, especially time.
Sometimes wound are visible only to the wounded;
The knife feels nothing - it is cold
And although your warm blood runs upon it when you are cut, the knife can never feel just how deep you are hurt.
After you have been cut so many times
You are left to fall to pieces -
With nobody there to pick them up and put them back together
Yet if somebody was there just to hold you,
The pieces might not fall.
Only when the knife itself becomes warm will it stop cutting - only then
But once there is an edge, there is always an edge
Because those you love are sharp as a knife
And only those you don't love are dull.

Sherry Kaye Pack

The Drummer I March To

The drummer I march to is not of this world;
Though He's a world ruler with a crown that is pearled.
He leads with perfection all goodness is His,
I am His follower — most contented as is.

He leads me to peace, while he shares my load,
He makes right decisions and walks the right road.
He instills me with knowledge of things to come,
He knows all about me and where I am from.

Not of this world is the drummer I follow
The works of this world are callous and hollow.
Now he's been my savior...forgiven my sin
Tested and tried me, I can hold up my chin.

That I may gain entry, make heaven my home,
I passed through the jungle where all devils roam.
But he held my hand when the roads became and blocked.
'Till I could pass over though heckled and mocked.

A road not accomplished without faith and hope
To go it alone, an impossible scope...
As no one could help or provide me relief;
This trial of fire was to test my belief.

Vinetta Bianchi

Who Is He?

There he is with his beautiful smile. I can see it even though it's miles. One day I love him; one day he's gone. Then he can't phone; I just moan. The love between us is the greatest. Then he says, "Oh, you're just the cutest." What's this mean you say, "I'm stuck in between a dream that's locked between the two and wrapped within a bow." He says so. When inside, I'm really about to blow. "I love him more than life," I say, "for him one day, but deep inside it's just a play." Then, it goes day by day, and you say, "Hey who is he," and I say, "It's my sunshine, rainbow, love, laughter, sadness, and boldness — for he's like my mother even though it's my brother...

Olivia Ann Bergeron

Ode To A Pansy

The petals are streaked with blood
though you have no aggression
your gentle eyes grow sad
and the wind caresses your soul
The rain falls silently about you
Causing a sudden droopiness
all the scenes that lie around you
The roses, lilies and lilacs
their beauty shines throughout the day
while yours is ever changing

As the sun rays fill the sky
And the test of nature gets attention
While you sit all alone
Alone in your own dimension
The thunder heads arrive at once
And torrents of rain fall upon you
Immediately your light shines through
Beauty - shining above all others
Beauty - ode to a pansy

Melissa Landon

Untitled

an opal moon
thoughts in her eyes
a clashing of lips in nigh
lilacs thrown in the wind
pain and passion in her kisses
dreams and memories collide
holding, clawing, wanting
nervous exploration
rising, falling not as far, and rising again
curious of the next step
more, wanting more
flesh has never been this good to me
such flavor, such violence when
dreams and memories collide

W. E. Kendra

Rhythms Of Love

Sweet nectar of misery
Thoughts of you forever haunt me
Always in silent memories
Thoughts of you pushes me
Thru empty rhythms of reality
Raking leaves against the breeze
A thought comes to me
if only time could be rewrote
I'd play for you all the proper notes
To bring you back to me
For within my loneliness is a heart felt rhapsody
Lay with me, touch me
Be one with me
For your laugh I often hear
And your smile I often see
Your beauty a sweet serenade
Enchanted by you melody
My heart beats a quiet beat
So that no one will hear
A love song incomplete

Paul J. Simmons

Saquthia

Oh! Saquthia my love, jewel of my heart.
Thoughts of you plague the soul when we're apart.
You, pure, innocent and precious as the dove
And here I stand wretched and unworthy of your love,

Though I thank the lord for the kindness I don't deserve.
Striving for you to be mine to serve.
I don't need the assurance of the world,
'Cause when first we meet my heart did yield.

Loved you since then and forever will.
Forever content with how I feel.
Possibly crazy and mad with this affair,
But never question the sanity of our love (do not dare).

The thought of your desertion I do not fear
For I rest in the belief you will always be near.
No need for your promises or assurance of words.
One kiss and all doubts become absurd.

Beautiful Saquthia. Capturer of my soul.
The future promises our love will only grow.
My whole being is in the control of you
For with it only you know what to do.

Lonnie R. Boe

Untitled

As the darkness of the storm tries to penetrate the room, three lone flames hold it back. Images of you fade in and out of my mind as the Times collide. Scenes of romantic encounters and energetic children are evoked by the dancing light ahead of me. As the flashes of white pass through the glass my mind wanders to another time when people lived and loved by the sacred yellow light. With thunder rumbling through my heart I sit wondering what you are doing and thinking this moment. Like a young girl writing her hero centuries ago I pray that our love endures the time between us. I watched the rain washing away the soil and know our love will not be swept away in that channel.

As the piece strokes midnight, fantasy begins to be overwhelmed by reality. But in that instant I realized the two are not that different. I want to grow old with you, I want us to bring out all of the hidden things in each other, I want our hearts, minds, and spirits to be unified forever.

The storm has passed, but your blanket of love still surrounds. The storm has passed, but the feelings I have for you never shall.

Kelly M. Malloy

The White Sorrow

Who, the genius painter
Threw colour into nature
That the end of fall with red
Yellow and brown in Winter.

It has snowed last night
The forest now whelmed in the whole white.
Who, the genius painter
Threw snow flowers flying above

And dropping on the backs of deer
On the wings of wild birds
On the quiet rivers, the ancient rocks
And on my shoulders...

Who threw colour into nature
Threw sorrow into my heart;
The white sorrow you never got
The immense sorrow spreading before...

Phuc Nguyen

Wings of Love

Just as the birds fly free
Through all the heavens above
Something special has happened to me
I've been touched by the wings of love.

Thinking of you always
The beauty of a mourning dove
I realize now what it can possibly be
I've been touched by the wings of love.

I need you now so very much
As the hand desires a glove
The care-free smile, your soft sweet touch
I've been touched by the wings of love.

With you I could spend eternity
No promise, no push, no shove
Because you mean the world to me
I've been touched by the wings of love.

Come with me now, together we'll fly
Through all the heavens above
Together we'll laugh, together we'll cry
We've been touched by the wings of love.

Randy Mayfield

Rage

It boils, seeping
Through crack and nook
Bubbling, churning
An acidic brook
Linger and burn
To gnaw and to rend
Devour, envelop
A blistering end
Layers, like stone
Splintered and spidered
Know that they fear you
The hate they've inspired
Further it stretches, inch by sick inch
Fermenting alone, you feel the tight pinch
Doubling and tripling, all control lost
Can't take it no more trigger squeeze soft
Orgy and splendor of blood running thick
Screaming and fleeing the pain I inflict
Know now my vengeance feel now my hand
Torment the small boy, but face the grown man.

Thomas Coghlan

Heaven

As I look toward Heaven, what do I see?
Through the clouds, far beyond the trees

The rays of the sun, how they warm my skin
The light of God shining deeper within

What blessings He gives throughout each day
What miracles He performs, if only we pray

For prayer can change things that may be unseen
An angel may guard us far beyond our dreams

I think of these things, as I look above
For I believe in God's power, and trust in His love.

Tracie Lynn Lafferty

Balance

Whispering clouds appear never to stop,
'til they are snagged by a towering mountain top.
Rainbow colors are bright and bold,
'til horizons hide their pots of gold.

Shining stars twinkle and glow,
'til the sun sets it's rays to flow.
Surging oceans roll and roar,
'til they lap the ever present shore.

My love like a river doth pour,
'til is meets your icy shore.
Constantly I give it my all
But, you never return my call.

Larry Brook

Heaven On Earth

I walked in the woods on a February day
Through a frosted, snow crusted world outside
Like a bowl of divinity on Christmas eve
Peaked and piled in frosty mounds
Cut by a shimmering, trickling stream
Beneath a dark branched willow tree
Bearing lacy fingers of white frigid snow.
Whispering winds blowing bridal veils
Causing creaking limbs to crack and fall.
I walked in the woods on a February day,
Where I contemplated if it were feasible
That God's promised Heaven might possibly be
Right here, right now, on earth, to touch.

Mary Morris

The Wedding Promise

Within the circle of our lives we shall be as one,
till all our days have wound away to greet the setting sun.
When you are weak I'll be your staff.
When you speak your mind I'll be your ears.
When you laugh, I'll laugh with you,
and when you cry I'll taste your tears,

Within the circle of our lives, between each dusk and dawn,
God shall hold us close, like two pebbles in His palm.
When I am frightened, comfort me.
when I'm confused please understand.
When I am glad rejoice with me,
and when I feel I can't go on, give me a helping hand.

Within the circle of our lives, together we will find,
our love shall grow, and like a strong oak tree,
withstand the test of time.

Kathleen Jakubowicz

"My Point of View"

Enlarged, lacking any point of focus.
Tilting, rolling, faded, blended

Rocking, spinning, bent, distorted,
glassy, unreal, unprotected from
reality, moving, calm and peaceful,
yet at war with it's imagination.
No back or front.

No sides. No teams, no colors.
Fuzzy, yet supersharp. Concentrated
and deliberated.

Encircling. Liquid, solid, moving,
shaping, mocking.

Staring blankly into an abyss
of loneliness. Unable to comprehend anything
for fear of lacking emotions, creativity
and genius. A statement, not an
apology, taken to mean something
else. Incomprehensible to you or I,
normal to them. Flying inconceivably
lacking any sense of direction.

Rebecca Peters-Golden

To My Beloved

The moon moves silently ore the sky,
Time goes slowly and gracefully by.
Sadness journeys forward, as I cry,
May the distance narrow by and by.

I stood looking, longing in the night.
The moon sailed listlessly big and bright.
Heavenly stars languid, dull and dim
Shown bleakly through a glimmering film.

Stars that lovers wish upon
Hidden in the night forlorn.
Saturnine skies, specked as a fawn
Morosely silent into the morn.

My heart intoxicated by the misty moon
Heard voices of angels, harmonic in the gloom.
My vision then hazy, my mind unsure;
The music soporific in its tour.

The morning bloomed fragrant, pure and white
Scarred only by the remorse of night;
The night before, and the night to be
To be spent alone, and without thee.

Kathryn B. Torme

A 28th Passing: Ode To An Oliphant Sister

Oh Maryanne, a birthday salute,
to a friend of ours of fine repute.
Your demeanor, as always, is great towards all,
is there more to love, ask Wayne and Paul?

We certainly see your birthday grin,
but could that be a double chin?
For when you laugh your throat does wobble,
it's rather like a turkey's gobble.

So to our fraternity of advancing years,
of too many nights and too many beers,
of thinning hair and growing girth,
your many years have shown your worth!

Finally we wish to offer,
a simple thought for your "comfort" coffer.
That we'll be present and ready to cheer,
when you achieve that 30th year!

Paul Maxson

My Love

Come grasp my hand and I'll take you away,
to a world of happiness in each and every way.
We'll never be apart and we'll never be sad,
we will survive on the great love we've had.
My heart is filled with sorrow while you're gone,
but from the support of my family I can move on.
But another one intrigues my mind scaringly enough,
it hasn't been easy it's been rough.
I remain faithful to you as I promised you that day,
that I cried forever as you walked away.
My mind's in a frenzy to leave here soon,
to see you again and our love to resume.
I'll miss the friends I've made here so far,
some distant and yet special like a new star.
Another summer comes to a fortunate end,
and happily I smile because I won't return again.
So take heart my love and know it be true,
I miss you terribly and I Love You.

Leigh Ann Bolon

The Healing Tears

On the sea of life we're often tossed,
To and fro and feeling lost
When storms arise and disappear
In their wake are found the healing tears.

"Why" is tear drop number one
That falls before the flooding comes
When understanding cannot be
Healing tears flow constantly.

When there's no one who seems to care
And no solution anywhere
Consider these a tender friend
The healing tears emotions send.

Forgetting helps when teardrops fall
Forgiving sometimes most of all
Until the heart and mind are clear
We need the ever healing tears.

We have all had tears, I've had mine in every one I've found design
To teach me, lead me, help me know I'm not alone when teardrops flow.

The final tear, I love it best one more trial is laid to rest
Teaching my heart to overcome and say, "Oh, God! Thy will be done."

Lura Maness Myers

Sadness

Sadness is watching someone close so,
to another world were nobody knows.
Sadness is thinking of memories of a loved one.
Waiting for him to get up and say,
"I love you!!"
Sadness is seeing that loved one
for the last time in a coffin, all peaceful,
all alone, waiting to be buried,
in the solid ground on a misty day.
Sadness is coming home, calling out his name,
but nobody answers.
Sadness is going to your loved ones grave,
Knowing he is watching over you like a guardian angel.
Sadness is memories fading away day by day.
Sadness is a part of life.

Maria Bianchi

Lost Soul

A lost and imparted soul cries out for love and comfort,
To be a part of the known and never again be hurt.

This soul indeed, is deprived of all attention,
Of all love and cherish, which is certainly never mentioned.

To be this way in all of you is something you'll never know,
Because of your greed and selfishness, this burden you'll never tow.

This soul hides out under the moon waiting to see,
Something that will never happen, something that will never be

You'll never understand this soul that's lost,
You'll never understand, cause you'll never pay the cost.

You'll never understand this lost soul, you see,
You'll never understand that this soul is in me.

Monica L. Little

What Would the World Come to Be

What would the world come
to be, if it didn't have me?

Would it be happy or would
it be sad, would all the
other children be good or bad?

Would they keep nature, would
there be life. Would every man find a suitable wife.

What would the world come
to be if it didn't have me.

Would my parents have another
child. would people live in the scary wild.

Would they still kill for fun
Could you still get cancer from the burning sun.

Would people die or would
they always live , would those who care still give.

What would the world come
to be if it didn't have me.

Would people still strive to keep the earth together
but no matter because I'm
here and here is where I'll be forever.

Melissa Schneider

To Be A Friend

To be a friend you need to care,
To be there with warm feelings to share.
An open heart and an open mind,
To be a good friend you need to be kind.

You are someone to talk to with listening ears,
To share with them the sorrows and tears.
To share the good times and the bad,
The happy-go-lucky and the sad.

To be a friend you must be caring and giving,
Be able to share the life you are living.
To laugh at the jokes whether good or bad,
To stay with them even when they are mad.

Friends are people who are special and true,
People to talk with and share things too.
If you are true to your friends, they'll be true to you,
And you will stay together all your lives through.

Share the times that you have like there is no other.
Like the love that you give to your sister or brother.
The day just might come when you will be apart,
Then you will cherish the love you had from the start.

Karen E. Bates

Friends And Flowers

Among the blessings that God has sent,
to brighten our lives throughout the years.
Is the gracious love of faithful friends,
who share with us our hopes, our dreams, our fears.

They are like the beauty of a blooming flower
And they are their, with you on your lowest hour.
And when you feel down and on your own
The memory of them brighten your gloom.

As we grow older and wiser, with God in our lives,
We'll always keep the faith and friendship
of one another.
We know with God our friendship and sisterly love;
will stay strong
Like the stem's and the leaves of a flower.

I cherish our friendship as I would
cherish a bright beautiful flower,
on a warm summer's day.

Sharon Appell

To Love A Love

To love a love that has never known
To clinch and grasp at hope's unrest
To yearn for romance where passion's not shown
To marvel at time's powerful test
To dream a dream of intense emotion
To long for love's passionate embrace
To hope for the capture of sensual sensation
To aspire for its eternal face
To believe in your heart's miraculous aspires
To anticipate love's stimulating fantasy
To fulfill all your heart's astonishing desires
To crave for love's zealous ecstasy
And to love a love of the purest heart
Is to love a love that will never part!

Kara Nicole Coussou

The American Dream

Dear Lord, look down on us day by day
To discover and follow the right to pray
Why the world is in turmoil and such despair
And some people suffer and others just don't care.

What can my child expect life to be
With crime running rampant and no morality
From where will they take their own inspiration
To build and hope of the American dream.

Lord, divulge us the wisdom and give us the time
To un-twine the injury done to mankind
By our own mind with no regard
The distress we impose or the glory we discard.

But through our efforts, let it be resolved
That every American will get involved
To make this country the greatest it can be
And restore our people with a strong legacy.

Oh, sons and daughters of this mighty land
Present issues shake the foundation on which we stand
If we struggle for our future then we shall not fear
For the Lord, has equipped us with the American dream.

Paul A. Palma

Across the Miles

When the moon and sun collide the ultimate climax
to ecstasy evolves into uncontrollable passion.

Neither one knows of the other for the miles separate
their beings therefore living in different orbits.

One is cool, dark and desolate filled with creators of
nothingness wanting to feel the warmth of another.

The other is warm, bright and bursts with emotion,
But is still alone to suffer in solitude.

In their dreams they portray themselves as Gods, looking
for their perfect mate to rule along side them.

Slowly they encircle each other using all the
powers they possess to charm the other.

When their adoration for each other is confirmed, their
passion for one another runs wild with fantasy.

Thus leaving all those alone to watch in raging jealousy,
to spite them, and destroy their everlasting love.

Misty Dawn

"The Dance of Life"

In the end, we all want that final dance.
To find the perfect partner to share the dance.
It's not the same, to dance the dance alone.
We search for the perfect partner all our lives.
The partner makes it whole, to fit together,
To know the moves, the timing, the synchronism.
Everyone dances on the edge sometimes.
To some, the dance is fast, flirting with disaster.
To others, the dance is slow and meticulous.
The dance is ever changing; its never the same.
It's nice to find a partner,
To have someone there at every step.
To dance the dance alone, could be hard and lonely.
To dance the dance with a partner,
Means to share in the next step.
To feel the next step, not just decide it.
So find that perfect partner,
And dance the dance of life together.

Karen Ridenour

To Love

To love means to care
To help, secure, and share.
The feelings you have inside
To some one you abide.
To love (pause) to be profound
To say your love one, what a beautiful sound.
To love is to accommodate.
Not to put down of discriminate
Love, a word full of mean and life
A life of wonderful of spice
And basically all that above,
It what I mean by to love.
So if you don't remember anything do remember this,
Even if you don't love me I love you.
I'm sure that's what God would want us to do.

Latasha Smith

Special Breed

It takes a Special Breed of teacher
To help the Special Child!
To know the magic words to calm him when
he starts getting wild.
To anticipate the flare-ups in his world of
mixed up thoughts.
To project a loving atmosphere
Even when you're out of sorts
It takes a special breed of teacher
To help the special child.
You're the mother who is missing,
the father who is gone.
You're the ray of light that guides them
and helps to lead them on.
You're a Special Breed!

Ruth Allweil

Untitled

A long time ago God had a plan,
To introduce a woman and a man.
Intricate details would have to take place,
For these two people to meet face-to-face.
One day in the future, on a particular date,
For them to be united was truly his fate.
Years have passed since these two first met,
They owe one another a gratitude of debt.
For there's a bond no one can explain,
That binds them together through their joy and pain.
Recalling the memories these two have shared,
Is reminiscent of the way they've cared.
The past, present, and future they face,
Brought together by God's loving grace.

Stacey L. Feddern

Cavalier

Wisdom will come, love is her blossoms;
Time will bring us the comfort of her bosom.
Follow her now, reach far above,
Grasp on the stars, reaching His love.

Conceive beyond the realm;
Take charge the helm.
Straight and narrow,
The path you must harrow.
Destiny ours, peace in our hearts;
Sorrow dispenses when we are apart.

With all of my love, I wish you it all
No matter how large; no matter how small,
Each thing that you hold dear,
My love... my sweet... my dear Cavalier.

D. Vitale-Cox

"The Price Of Life"

There is a price that we must pay,
to live our life from day to day,
All sorts of joys from happy times,
and all sorts of sorrows, like murders and crimes.
It's a world of give and take,
the days we share that God does make.
Full of miracles and madness,
of yesterday's laughter and tomorrow's tears of sadness.
Many ups, lots of downs,
life styles of the rich and famous, and the wrong sides of towns.
A baby is born a brand new life,
a man is arrested, he murdered his wife.
It's a very steep and heavy price to pay,
but we're all born to die one day.
Amidst the turmoil, there is found some good,
I'd make everyday worth living if only I could.
But there will always be struggles and strife,
the cost we must pay, "The Price of Life."

Rickie Bentley

From Orphaned Halls

It was time to leave;
To make a passage through sound
Straight into the chest and arms of a waiting stranger.
It was frightening.
I didn't like this first touch.
So I stood there cringing,
Stiffly suffering through the assault of welcome.

Oh God!
After all these years,
My need so dear has solidified
And tempered itself into cold silence.

It was so heavy;
Not a single gesture of affection could move it.
I couldn't make a sound.
But embraces followed,
And the searing pain of freedom shot through me
Until the bronze weight inside cracked.
The bell that had been still all my life was finally struck.

Robin O'Connell

Salt Water Taffy

We couldn't go to Atlantic City
To mess up the affection
Of lovers in a tryst
From a candy confection.

With a diamond bracelet on my wrist
I would reach out to her in my dreams
For shared joys and thankfulness
Yet a brisk stealing wind calls mist's shadows that were.

Salt water taffy,
Under the boardwalk they found love
Sand beneath my toes
With briny tears I look above.

Yet such an important union
Could not resist a spell to admire
Violins for you my dear
For it still was a church with a spire.

And they still sell the taffy by the shore.
Which I saw you eating
In your ghost dance allure
For time's heart was beating.

Susan Reed

Indigo Eyes

I try in vain beyond this pane
To muse the world I spy
It's not a world of black and white
That's seen through my indigo eyes

Oh! Is that a tree that sways so free
And stands so green and bold
Or is that a cat I'd love just to pat
With fur that glistens like gold

If only I'd be a flower you see
With my arms like the petals unfurled
I'd play and I'd run and I'd soak up the sun
And grow with no care in the world

But somehow I know through the time that I grow
This beauty will cause me to cry
I'll bear it a tear so blue and so dear
As it falls from my indigo eyes

Mary Beth Johnston

The Changing

Once, I remember walking into the light
to never emerge.
Now I find that I no longer belong here,
her heart oozes a different sap.
I cannot look upon her new face,
with eyes of cracked glass.
The lover has turned into a stranger,
stranger than most.
She's all gone.
There is turmoil within me,
a sea whose water has become tepid.
Without a host, the future falters,
the stem of my fidelity is gelded.
I am lost amidst a parish
that closes all doors instead of entering inside.
I am crying,
but it serves no purpose.
My mind is a nest of wasps,
and I walk away laughing, almost insanely, into the shadow,
to never emerge.

Thomas Anthony Gass

I Fall To Pieces

Each time I see you again, I fall
to pieces
Knowing I cannot so openly go into
your embrace.
Loving you at times hurts much more
than being alone.
Yet I am patient until it is safe
for us to be together.
At times I wonder how something that
Feels right can be so wrong
Still I trust you and your judgment
just as I need for you to trust me.
Selfish as it is, I cherish the moments
When we are shut away from others
And I have you all to myself.
I am content with thoughts of
you while we are in our separate worlds
But I love the feeling of you
making me whole after
I fall to pieces.

Pamela Hernstine

"Julianne"

Couldn't find a birthday card
to say what we wanted to say
They just didn't have "the feeling"
they portrayed what's said everyday.

Our cute little blond of a few years ago
has captured our hearts, you see
And to send just one of those everyday cards
well - we simply couldn't agree.

You adopted us as your grandparents
which brings many tears to our eyes.
You have made our dreams come true, sweetheart
we feel like we've won the "grand prize".

They say every cloud has a lining
ours was that cute little girl
Who is now 21 and still shining
who captured our hearts with a whirl.

To say happy birthday honey,
is such a small thing to say
But happiness is what we wish you
each and every day.

Thelma Meissner

The Space Shuttle Tragedy

It was the perfect time and the perfect place,
To send the space shuttle into space.
the Astronauts were ready to set their goal,
On their base in Cape Canaveral.
The sky was blue and no clouds were gray,
So at last they sent it on its way.
But even though the takeoff was perfectly grand,
The mission didn't work out the way it was planned.
Suddenly there was a powerful boom!
And before them was a smoky gloom.
Now several different people were going to cry,
Because seven determined astronauts were about to die.
Even though the Challenger failed to fly that day,
The memory of it will never pass away.

Matthew A. Whitted

Untitled

A holy massacre upon the earth
to settle the final end.
The Heavens thundered with the wrath of God,
a message he did send.
For one to have the utmost power,
it is with death that God will make one cower.
For God in Heaven made not the world for
one man's hands.
He made the world for all mankind
to walk across his lands.
Pain and struggle are a natural occurrence
put upon this earth to test our endurance.
God created life as the ultimate test,
for many to pass, many to fail.
It is the most incredible quest,
but only when one steps upon the Lord's trail.

Martha C. Turner

A Discovery Of Love

Two hearts came together one hot summer night.
Two lives changed forever in one candle's light.
Moonlight found us walking spellbound, hand and hand.
Both in whisper talking, making future plans.
Stars looked down on lovers whose time had arrived.
Two who had discovered one sweet love for life.

Rhonda Del Santo

Sagebrush Memories

I smell the sage and get carried away
To the old home ranch and a bygone day.
Clover coming up to the horse's flank,
Cottonwood trees on the river bank,
Fawns hiding in the willow brush,
Cattle grazing in pastures lush,
Horses filing down the rimrock path
To drink from the river and take their bath.

From across the sage you could often hear
A rooster pheasant with his challenge clear.
The binder and thresher and the golden grain,
The hay we stacked to beat the rain.
Whenever I breathe the sagebrush air
These things come back and meet me there.

Roa Davis

To the One I Love

To the one I love with all my heart
To the one I'll promise, "till death do us part"
To the one my heart aches for when I'm lonely and cold
To the one who fills my life with riches untold
To the one who brings me the strength to endure
To the one who loves me so honest and pure
To the one who's been there through happiness and tears
To the one I will love through the timeless years

You, my sweetheart, are the one I am speaking of-
And, to you my sweetheart, I'll pledge my undying love
A love that will carry us through all eternity
A love only shared between you and me
Together we will walk till all days here are done
I love you my sweetheart - you are the one!

Katherine Hermann

"Acceptance"

Peddles of a flower I am blown
to the wind..
Scattered across the fields for within
the deepest corners of my mind.
I am one. With a shadow of darkness
upon my skin.
One to live with. One heart to give Thee.
Heart and soul that is of gold to cherish, and
nurture our lives that we do spend.
In good, bad, happy or sad. Be it angry or mellow — I have
but myself to give.
Please accept me.

Therese A. Garrison

The Witness

How could she love, whom she could not see
To them, the concept, was hard to believe
So, they mocked and teased, and called her weird
Yet, still she loved Jesus with reverent fear

Knowing nothing could pluck her from His hand
With her head held high, she took a stand
She told them of Jesus, and His perfect love
And how he reigned in heaven above

She warned them, in love, of His soon return
Asking, "Will you repent or will you burn?"
But, they wouldn't take heed, to her gentle voice
For they were too proud to make Jesus their choice

And then, one day, as they began to mock
First she was there and then she was not
Looking around, they all became scared
For Jesus had come and they weren't prepared

Niecie L. German

A Wish a Dream a Reality

Beginning with a wish and what we hope for,
To want for the future to open every door.
Next there is a dream that you would hope to see,
To think of or just something you want to be.
If you strive hard enough, you and others will see,
What you dream and wish for will become reality.
No matter how hard life may seem,
There's a time for everything.
Time to worry, time to cry,
Time to live, time to die,
Time to dance, time to sing,
Time to wish, time to dream,
Time to want, time to be,
Time to hear, time to see.
Time for heartache, time for lies,
But there's also time to fall and time to rise.

L. Bernadette Carter

"Risks"

To laugh..is to risk appearing the fool.
To weep..is to risk appearing sentimental.
To reach out for another..is to risk involvement.
To expose feelings..is to risk, exposing your true self.
To place your ideas, your dreams before the crowd..is to
risk their loss.
To hope..is to risk despair.
To try..is to risk failure.
To live..is to risk dying.
To love..is to risk not being loved in return.
But, risks must be taken because the
greatest hazard in life is to risk nothing. The
person who risks nothing does nothing, has nothing
is nothing. He may avoid suffering and sorrow,
but he simply cannot (learn, feel, change, live.
....or grow love...). Chained by his ignorance, he is
a slave: He has forfeited freedom.
Only a person who risks is free!!!

Leilynn Puanani Florence

Winter Is Nigh

Bold gray rocks on a grassy scene
to which tips of trees seem to lean,
and whisper sound in our ears
we all were young, remember those years?

Colors of fire licking the hills,
apples are ripe, their fume over spills.
Then darker grays blanket the sky
announcing the harvest a winter is nigh.

Fallen butternuts, sticky and green,
we run gather all that are seen.
Cakes and fudge, pies and cream
dance in our minds like a bubbly stream.

The new day breaks, a fresh new season.
Labors of past reveals the reason,
corn is cut, stored in silos.
Crackling fires melt frosty windows.

Yesterdays spent while we're able
to catch summer's flavor, set winter's table.

Susan Stowe Phillips

With All My Heart

With all my heart I wish I had the talent to write of things I want to say, and have the words all come together like they should; but they just refuse to leave my heart at times.

My thoughts consist of subjects that we already know, but forget sometimes that the material possessions we see and treasure now, all came from the ground and we must leave them all behind when we are gone.

The way we live and obey God's rules as best we can and do kind thoughtful things for others, are the unseen building materials that are sent along and polished into gems for our new home that is waiting for us far beyond.

So it pays to think twice before we do wrong, and not let that curtain come down before it is time, and end up where we don't want to go.

Remember all the right things we do will long be remembered after we are gone. Also what goes around comes around.

Lucille M. Asa

Through A Child's Eyes

Look outside, can't see the skies
Too much pollution, smoke fills our eyes
Hate, anger, death, and sorrow
We have no future, no hope for tomorrow
Toxic waste, nuclear war
Our friends get shot as they walk out the door
We went to the funeral, all dressed in black
They went to the playground, but never came back
No education, or desire for learning
Booze bottles empty, cigarettes burning
Trying to grow up before they should
They'll be six feet under in a box of wood
A man was stabbed just down the street
You must be wary of each person you meet
Discrimination, segregation
Violence and deprivation
In her room, a little girl cries
At the world, as seen through a child's eyes

Lynsey Strunk

Forgotten Minority

Beautiful but crippled bird held back by father sun;
torn by mother earth...
Lost in a sea of turmoil, waves of thoughts crashing about,
Yet not willing to surface,
Afraid.

Wind gone wild, forcing its way through, reaching for strength
To calm its weary soul stops to catch it breath - finds to strength
And goes on...
Weary.

Eternal cloud weakened by life's moments;
Driven by the purest heart...
Reaching for oneness, torn by lasting pain and unforgiven sorrow only
To find deep sadness - won't let go; becomes one with self.
Alone.

Sea gulls lift the spirit,
Ocean washes by clearing the mind of weakness,
Creating a calmness from within, yet once
The ocean ceases to be free and the waters calm,
Life's ripples stir from within and reality sets.
Confused.

Valeria Michelle Witt

Sun break at the Flags in Tianamen Square

Thousands of figures rolling through the night,
Towards the heart of the city, that beats to the drums,
Calling for the dawn to shed its pale light.
A raising flag and the absence of guns.

Breaking through the mist of the morning hours
A quiet, dry breeze marches in on the square.
The birth of a new day over red and yellow flowers;
A grave of freedom that a billion souls can spare.

A clouded grey sky is mirrored on watered stones
At the feet of the red walls of the forbidden city,
The national anthem reaches dawn to the bones...
Tianamen square at dawn, enormous and pretty.

Nicolas Ducote

For Mama

There is rose everywhere. Softly, sleepy music pervades the tranquility, but the smell is the thing. Roses. A soft quiet, clouds that cushion the soul and roses, always roses, to remind you...

The massiveness of oak and mahogany, the finality of peace... coldness creeps into my heart and the air conditioner lends ice to my heart.
Rose colored cloth, rose colored coffin.

Kenneth C. Mackel

.......To My Unborn Child

Love flows through my being
transcending all fear to touch you,
to surround and nurture your developing spirit.

I love you before I know you
because you are me and I am you.
You are a miracle.
A shift in my perception
is born in your creation.

You give meaning to the
beating of my heart
and the lessons of my soul.

Victoria Gardner

Travel

Yes, Lord, it seems we sometimes travel down the
tree as this little bird,
When we're really trying to go up to higher realms
of life to reach maturity.

Oh, Lord! How we need your wisdom from above,
when we're really trying to live to please you
while we are here!
It seems we stumble and even fall
and out of desperation call, "Help us, LORD!"
We sometimes grow weary in our struggles and say,
"Give me rest and peace, LORD today!"
Refresh me on the morrow and strength from You borrow.
Then we'll struggle on, knowing You care and stand
close by to help us whene'er we sigh.
LORD, you created us and we give you our trust.
For in you is L - i - f - e !
Now and for-ever-more!
Amen!

Virginia Todd

People of Somalia

Baby of the barren land-always destined to be damned
Treeless plain, sand filled dirt-can there be justice on earth

Bloated stomach, filled with pain-Never touch a piece of grain
Sad eyes, loosing sight-Hoping, dreaming for a life

Skeletons, walk around-Ten, Twenty, Thirty Pounds
Child's only true emotion-hunger, fear, no motion

Thousands die, every day-We just let them waste away
Precious life, gone forever-Never reaching their endeavors

Many children roam the land-No parents-No one to lend a hand
If they make it to tomorrow-they will always carry sorrow

Mothers of the barren land-Always destined to be damned
Precious child-Have no milk-Bury child in the dirt

Hear her sorrow, feel her pain-As her efforts die in vain
Searching for a piece of life-Fighting almighty God on earth

Mothers, fathers, children, human beings-destiny, it has no meaning
People of the barren land-Always Always you'll be damned

We watch while thousands die-Mother earth swallowed many lives
I am praying for your souls-Those that passed, those that go

One day, all will see-you deserve to live like me
Life will float upon your plain-Bringing health, no lifeless shame.

Odette Coco

"If We..."

Land.
Trees.
Water.
Air.
That is what our earth is made of.
But if we pollute the water with garbage what do we have?
If we cut down the forest then what do we have?
Without trees the wind will destroy the land.
Without land how can we live?
No land to live on.
No trees to give us shelter.
No water to drink.
No air to breathe, and now we have no more life to live.

Tiffany Cipponeri

The Charm of Poetry

When you are feeling down and out,
try poetry.
Lift up your head and loudly shout:
"I found the key!"
Through poetry I will release
what troubles me and find true peace,
For gloomy thoughts will truly cease,
through poetry.

When looking for a healing art,
try poetry.
And rest assured it'll play its part
to set you free
For poetry can much undo;
refreshing hearts and spirits, too;
Our planet magically renew,
by poetry.

Allow it then to radiate,
so others of it can partake
And deeds of kindness activate
with poetry.

Sister M. Marcy Baldys, CSSF

Driftwood

You freely cast your whispers in the wind
trying to fill tired and tattered sail
now raveling like the dreams you could not mend.
Endlessly you swore that hope would prevail.
In an emerald bottle you bound your dreams—no avail.
Along the shore awaiting—still standing strong,
Far off thunder murmurs—silence assail.
Eyeing the bottle and dreams tumble headlong.
Dark clouds drift in—conquering armada drape the horizon.
Omniscient clouds come rumbling, singing ancient song.
Bring they new hope or another mocking taunt?
Still yet distant—do they come for you or drift on?
Your face now weathered by the salts of time,
Your vision lost—complacency your only crime.

Nathan J. Collins

Number One Friend

When I come out of my mommy's
tummy, I knew that I would never
be clumsy. I was the big surprise
a baby girl, when she held me in her
arms I saw sparkles in her eyes, I
knew at that very moment that I, was
her pride and joy, her best friend and her
daughter and that our love and bonding
would never end, but now that I am
getting older there are changes being made
in my life but our love and bonding will never
change, it will forever stay the same

Tamala Wiggins

I Thought You'd Turn To Me

I thought you'd turn to me.
Turn to me my friend and you will see
How true love is supposed to be.
On my behalf I'd like to thank you for being you
Up real high you make the sky I see more blue
God I'm glad you do the things you do
However I'd like you to see that you're number one in my life
Think for one minute and soon you'll be my wife.
You are the love of my life as well as my true friend.
Only you have given me your heart to mend.
Used to be I thought you were my friend
Down deep inside I have a special feeling for you
Turn to me and ask me to marry you, and I'll say I do;
Up and up and away from us the bad leaves us
Running with you in the night, oh, what a rush.
Now and then you meant the world to me.
True love is what we're in, and our love is meant to be.
On this day of May 6, 1994 all I want to see is the Bride & me.
Exactly where does the honeymoon take place, well, I thought
you'd turn to me.

Steven R. Monetti Jr.

Saturday Morn!

Saturday morn, a time of refreshing content,
Turned into hours, days, weeks of men seeking public sentiment.
What happen to my time to scream and holler,
A group of Billionaires and Millionaires began fighting over a dollar.
Oh sure it's their money and with it they can do as they want,
But empty is life with no umpire to taunt.
Saturday morn, out mowing the grass,
Planting and picking, I hope they solve this thing fast.
Now I realize this game is not a solution to world despair,
But rooting for the home team can temporarily relieve trouble and care
Week day games, they occasionally filled a void,
But Saturday morn, meant Father and Son, a Man and a Boy!

Ricky Williams

Wraith

Ghostly smoke
twisting, whirling, entangling
drifting towards the light
from the memory of a child
and delight in a man
that has lost its shape and splendor
beyond the glass
Smoke frozen sweet in the heart
its foul stench clings to my gloves
its vile potency fills my lungs,
choking me, burning as fire in the words I speak
Smoke hypnotizing, entrancing, nostalgic
rising from the grave of childhood,
fixated in time
loved and hated
in its slitherings
but ghostly dancing
to the eyes.

L. G. Knauer

Precious Moments of Life

On a cold and windy night
Two tear filled hearts were blessed.
They were parents of a little girl,
Who was being laid to rest.

It happened all so quickly
Without a sign or warning,
She took sick on a wintry night
And passed on the next morning.

No more of scattered toys about
The dolls, the paints, the teddy bears,
No more of sneaking out of bed,
Never again an evening prayer.

As the final words were spoken
A light from heaven shone.
God's Holy voice rang within the church,
Come child, you're coming home.

The parent's eyes were lifted
Their hearts though filled with sorrow,
For their little girl they realized,
Would always be a tomorrow.

Sally Ashley

Darkness

Beneath the sea there is total darkness
Under a sheet is exactly the same
Where does it come from, where does it go
From now till forever, we'll never know.

Out from the night as it leaps at us,
We cannot run and we cannot hide
But still we try and try to defeat it
But all we get is everything beneath it.

Total darkness there is nothing worse
Except when riding in a hearse.
For in a hearse you would be dead
And all you'd see is a bed.

And in that bed you see yourself
Looking down all pale and cold.
When did you become the subject of darkness?
When did you lose all life and hopefulness?

Can you prevent the surrounding darkness?
Can you hide in complete terror?
The answers are no, there's no way out
For with darkness you live with terror throughout.

Julie Archer

Phoenix

Emulating Icarus on an excursion toward the sun:
Unmindful of the frigid seas and the turgid surf
that will hurl your hopes against the rocks -
"With nothing ventured there's nothing gained"
(but there's also nothing lost).

So with a palpitating heart and one hand full of trepidation,
the other fist clutching astronomical expectations,
we summon up the courage and expand the tightening chest;
anticipating, for the most part, nothing but the best
(but neglect to pack a parachute).

We then wallow in our lunacy, wishing for a change
issued with a mystical wave from a magical wand
wielded by some wizard from medieval days long gone

Then with outstretched arms to the benevolent heavens
and impassioned pleas to the constellation Orion...
our crying just falls on deaf ears

Through muffled moans ushered from a pillow of despair
we implore the higher powers to fulfill our fruitless prayers
but the gods are bound and gagged and no miracle occurs

Icarus is dead

Stephen A. Beck

Future Blues (The Wastleland... a Slight Return)

Hot winds swirling dust across a dry lake bed
Unseen by water nymphs departed to God knows where
Only when gusts rustle the mule grass does it elicit a moan

The swamp rises but no water flows
Days dawn gray, the sky cries poison tears on barren ground
You gaze into a noonday sun blood red as Mars
A vague atmosphere as still as dreams
Out in the middle of nowhere
People are walking on the highway to oblivion
I fly into the teeth of Time drained by white lips
Junkies are scratching at my door
I spout religion but nobody listens
Even though they're all on their knees
Preyed upon by the dollar squeeze
Takers and talkers form the gauntlet I run
When the line was drawn all stepped across
Save one

Nick Menkee

Elusive Love

Spiritual growth to places untouched and unfelt
Untamed passion
Undone not concurred
Understanding or admiration?
The mind enigmatic
the bodies entangled
the hearts woven
the senses diverted.

Elusive love
there is only strength
the power surges threw the body
the kiss uncontrollable
the touch, desired
the thoughts impudent
the elusive love,
my love for you.

Paige Boilard

Or Grew We Darker?

Can you think of more than trees
Up from where we looked?
Can you think of more than hands
That caught the air screened through the net of green?
Can you think that all the dark dropped down on us
Dropped over others, drowned as we?

Can you think that we grew darker with the dark?
Or showed we clearer, sharper, more like branches
Spread and drawn to cover?
We clung in gladness. But how this gladness
while we grew?
Or grew we darker, darker, became I less of me, you less of you?
Became we one and one with others, dark and lost as we?

Oh, what became we under trees,
Shading, though not stopping darkness sifting
through the net?
Keeping darkness dropping down on us, keeping
darkness pouring in.
We clung and grew darker, knew less of all the dark around us.
We clung, and, in this, are caught.

Pelanie

The Mosquito

The mosquito is an awful beast;
Upon your blood she loves to feast.
And where she thinks resistance low
Upon that spot she's sure to go.

At any gathering great or small
From camping trip to social ball
She is an uninvited guest
Whom all consider as a pest.

And when in bed you there recline
Even then one hears her whine.
Of all the bugs in all the world
She is the very worst;
And if you do not swat her soon,
She then will quench her thirst.

(Note — It is the female mosquito that bites.)

Vincent W. Allin

As the Thunder Rolled

As I sat and listened to the Thunder roll
Visions of flowers, rainbows and Spring
Breezed past the window of my mind
Still cluttered with the refuse of the day—

After the Thunder came the rain,
And although I sat in the
confines of my home,
I could smell winter
melting away—

My heart began to lighten,
My spirit began to soar
And the refuse of the day seemed to be
No more—

I wonder now about the sound,
The Thunder you know,
Could it be God encouraging me
To clear the refuse from my mind
And let the flowers grow?

Lola Longyhore

Going Home

It will not be easy to live with the sea again. Too long I have waited for the tide to be right, too long I have waited for the storms to blow over, "yes too many nights have been fought with the sea and me. But the call of the sea has pecked holes in my coffin on land, and I must leave now. The years of the soul have softened my strength, the broadcast of seeds instead of the broadcast of nets has softened my calloused hands to blisters. But I shall milk brine into my soul and my mind will lose its rust of the memory of fields blowing, and pine coned trees. "So sail and be damned," your voice will reach high pitch— But I shall not feel your switches for the witches of the sea are still married to me.
The brides veil is cresting the foam of my ship, and I must leave now, and sail home.

Ruth M. Sample

Lonely Night

When doth a lonely night
Walk along a moonlit waterway
Weighted tears roll from stars point
As white water engulfs the heedless stones
Laughing trees console a lonely night,
Left to feel exiled
What has the darkness done so wrong
People seem gleeful when she comes out to play,
When music comes to make song and dance
Then the wind came to call,
With a whistle through the leaves
He asked the night why she was so down,
And her story she told
The wind cries "It is you who makes the sun
Seem so warm, the day much brighter, you
Bring peace and quite, the time of dreams!"
Be not a lonely night, you have many friends.

Matthew Griffin

The Beach

The sun glistening at your feet.
Walking hand in hand along the
shore, with all the life there is to
see, the beach is the place to go, and
ripples of waves just missing your toes.
sea gulls, above gliding in
the sky, what a sight to see through
your eyes - a place of peace, a place of solitude;
the beach giving out the auras of
these moods,
Never wanting to return to the
realities of life,
Dreading the moment leaving this
precious sight.

Linda Johnson

Maternal Warmth

I awoke for the first time, she was there
With a look in her eyes that only a mother could have
I fell asleep in a blanket of warmth
That I knew would last a lifetime.

She awoke for the last time, I was there
With tear filled eyes and the loneliest feeling
That I have ever known
She smiled and looked up at me in her loving way
Then she fell asleep forever
Leaving me cold, with a warming feeling
That I knew would last beyond all lifetime.

Ron J. Ritchie

On The Wings Of Angels

She flies on the wings of angels, watching each move they make,
Wanting to fly on her own so bad, knowing the trip she'll take.

They all join hands with the hummingbirds, the butterflies join in too,
Their jobs today are all the same, they know what they must do.

A baby angel was born today in a place so far away,
God picked this angel to take with him and with him she will stay.

They'll teach her what the angels know and what the angels do,
They'll teach her that no tears are here, no feelings here are blue.

They'll comfort her until she grows and learns to use her wings,
And then they all will fly with her, such joy her learnings brings.

And when the end of day is near and her eyes begin to close,
She'll sleep contently in their care because inside she knows,

Angels embrace you from the heart like only a mother would,
And that I'd be there holding her, if somehow, I only could.

Lisa Downer Fulghum

The Little Boy with the Magic Finger

The first time I met this angel of God's
was at a ball game of his sister's, whom he dearly loved.
As I walked near, he raised his tiny little hand
and shot a bullet of love that I could hardly stand.

From that day on he was special to me
with his hat and boots - a cowboy to be.
He even told "Whoppers" like most cowboys do,
and anyone who met Jonathan was captured, too.

His classmates all loved him.
They catered to his needs.
"Come Jonathan," they'd say,
"Let us pull - please, please!"

As a student, he taught us
more than any teacher could teach
about courage and love
and of life's defeats.

There is no way of measuring the strength that he had.
He fought like a true cowboy when things got bad.
His love for his family was beyond compare,
but we know now that he's in God's care.

Winkie Kirby

The Greatest Commandment

The Greatest Commandment Jesus gave to man
Was to love one another, His total plan.
Jesus wanted to see in a congregation of His
There would be wonderful harmony working with.

Jesus wanted to see that Love complete
With his brothers and sisters as they sit in their seat.
Jesus knew what would be in the hearts of man;
They would keep the Ten Commandments as God had planned.

But show the love of Jesus as they sit in their pew
Not singling out their love for just a few.
Jesus wanted His people to have His Love
So the world would know it was from Heaven above.

Jesus said to go out in the world today
Spreading his love along the way.
That his love is shared with all types of men
To bring a lost soul for Jesus to mend.

Lyle Gray

All About Time ("Haste Make Waste")

Time is what our Creator did make,
Waste and haste is what mankind made,
Time is needed to heal a heartbreak,
To increase, enhance, to grow to slow,
Space time, biological or chronicle
Time is there to control lives flow,
Whether we fail, How we can succeed,
Time is an indispensable need,
Time does comes, time does go,
To make use of it, the best we can,
Is what anyone sincerely need to do,
Make the best in life, anyway we can,
A life of fulfillment, one of despair,
Life could be impendingly good or unfair,
Happiness and sorrow, bitter and sweet,
Attempt to be content, having faith and heed,
To the forces that comes from the heart,
While playing fair, thinking smart,...
Life is what Time is made of, beware,
Live it wisely, righteously, it's too precious,
To haste and waste it all senselessly away..

Ludwig Schilling

A Day to Question

Watch the children run and play,
Watch, as their day fades away.
To find themselves content,
with the smallest toy or off-key song,
or, simply, to find a friend or two,
in which to complete their day.

It seems to question,
that I now speak,
that they can find such simplicity,
in which to brighten their day.
Though, then, the Elders can I see,
pale in question, rich in forecast,
Do endeavor in stride, unyielding parallel,
to unravel tomorrow,
before today has begun.....

Thomas A. Mason

Untitled

Love is an illusive shadow covered by a mist
Watching and Waiting
Hoping to find a place — a heart to rest
You can't go looking for love
Love must find you
So you wait
So you hope
Answer when love steps out of the mist and into the light
Catch the illusive dream before it fades
Back into the mist to again leave you waiting

Lois K. Miller

Grandmother

The old woman sits by her window
Watching the snow hit upon the ground
No one comes to see her far from town
The sound of once children playing
Still linger in her mind
She drifts back to those times
A tear falls on the album yellow with age
If only those kids could hear what's going on today
She'll love them always the day is fading night is here
No one to see Grandmother so near
Her life is leaving one breath to take,
But she lived a life time in that one day

Jennie Gaskins

My Tribute To Elvis

I loved you from the very first
Way back there in '55
The way you looked and danced and sang
You really made me feel "alive".
Through the years I kept track of you,
Bought your records, saw your shows
Named the King of Rock and Roll
You were "it and all" as the saying goes.
The best known singer of our time,
Your unequalled fame knew no bounds
And no one loved you any less
Because you put on extra pounds.
When I heard the tragic news,
Oh, what shock! what searing pain,
You couldn't be gone, my heart cried
And my tears streaked down like rain.
You're still a very famous star,
The brightest one in heaven above;
The world still mourns, and though you're gone
We'll always remember you with love.

Joyce Brandenburg

Sisters

My dear sister in the hospital, how can this be,
we are a healthy bunch you see.
We have weathered a lot, growing, loving, fighting, and
crying together.
My love for you is strong, it has been for so long.
You are a part of me, since we sat on daddy's knee.
Since we fought to take off daddy's shoes.
Mom's chili and hot buns on Saturday night.
You and me in the round tub.
The times mom and dad smiled and hugged each other.
Would things have been different if we had a brother?
The five of us so close, God must really love us.
Love, happiness and health, you can't buy them, you can't
steal them.
What we have no one can take.
Mill picnics, sack races, the pig in the snack.
Would I change anything, could I change anything?
What a bunch we are; strong at times, fragile too.
When you hurt, so do I.
I have prayed, I have cried, both have made me feel better.

Mary Rosival

The Single; The One

I am a brother among four.
We are; the Eagle, the Bear, the Cougar and the Owl.
Once young, we soared the skies.

Now, remains only, the one.
Although not alone, I stand, the single the one.

In the whispers of the slowing breeze,
I hear memories; of the four; and of the one.
My heart hears; my brother the Eagle, cry,
and I plead; "Guide my spirit brother as I die."

With the strength of my brother the bear,
I stand to face my destiny. As one, but not, alone.

I pray, to the Owl, "Grant me wisdom,"
The Cougar; courage, the bear; strength,
And the eagle; the spirit, to help me face, "This End."
As the Single the One.

The breeze slows to a stop, but I will sustain.
Only then; will it be
"A good day to die."

Tammy Van Winkle

We Are

We are the weird, the freaky and dark
We are the ones who roam late in the park
We are the sad, lonely but kind,
We are the creatures that crawl in your mind

We are the dragons, fairies and gnomes
We are the ones that hide in your homes
We are the giants, the dwarves and the elves,
We are inside your mysterious selves.

We are the gentle, unknown part of you,
We are the ones, we are the few
We are the people you see everyday,
We are the creatures who taught you to play.

We are the sun, the moon and the stars,
We are the ones that you see up on Mars.
We are the sad, lonely but kind,
We are the creatures that crawl in your mind.

We are you.

Jennifer Larsen

Canoe

Burdened down by loaded packs,
we forge the long portage that leads us to our next
paradise.
Two of us carry canoes, heavy on our shoulders,
In search of untold wonders, we pack the canoes and set out
into the tepid waters of the Quetico.

Stroke, feather, stroke, feather, we glide across the glassy water,
Stroke, feather, - we pause and rest our paddles along the
gunwales of old "Laughing Star."
Droplets of warm water drip from the blades of our paddles
and ripple the surface,
I lean down and let the lake tickle my fingers as I gaze at
the rocky bottom, twenty-five feet below.
I stop - listen,
and only hear
the faint beating of my heart.

Lori A. Augustine

Friends

I had a good friend, but she went away!
We grew up together for a couple of years,
We also shared laughter and also shared tears!
I knew she loved me, for she did not need to say,
I knew she cared for me everyday!
But one day she got angry, and really blew a fuse.
I think it was because of the abuse!
She went to a party and did something bad!
It's not her fault, she knew little of what she had.
She tried driving home because of a fight,
But she did not make it home that night,
She crashed up her car and drove off the road!
What a burden will her parents have to hold!
She died the next day in the hospital bed,
For we all knew that she was dead!
I pray for you all, from this day on
That you don't have to go through, what
I just gone!

Tanya Brown

Remembering Grandma's

From years ago until now, many things have changed
We have all gotten older, and our lives re-arranged
There are many fine memories, from that big old house
The noise of the floorboards, sounded like a mouse
From the big kitchen table, to the soft tic beds
The aroma through the house, of fresh baked breads
Bring about eight, with lots of family around
Easter celebration, with lots of eggs to be found
Walking with Timmy, taking the railroad tracks into town
Our times at Grandma's, I remember no frown
With Amanda in the band, to a cake walk I went
My time in West Virginia, was always well spent
Being a lot older, and having kids of my own
Holding all of these memories, even now that I'm grown
My kids enjoy Grandma's, as I did years ago
Our going to West Virginia, their memories will grow
Quiet sounds of Grandma's, you could sleep from dusk till dawn
We've all built fine memories, to long carry on.

Therese Marie Brunner

Dear Bridget

I took you in.
We need each other, we needed a friend,
It's been quite a few years since you slipped out of my life.
Death came and tore us apart,
But you will always be in my heart.
You didn't walk death's path alone.
I truly believe God sent an Angel from the throng.
You and I were the best of friends.
We stuck together until the end.
I can still hear your bark,
And still see your tail wagging from side to side,
When we would ask you if you wanted to ride.
I know you were jealous, I'm sure you will understand.
He was cold, hungry and homeless, so I took him in.
He won't replace you for that never could be.
Months and months passed, I would still feel for you in bed.
My heart would ache and I would cry
When I would realize you weren't there.
I don't know if we will ever see each other again,
But you will always be my loving friend.

Margaret C. Martin

Freedom's Call

Gathered as one this solemn day,
We remember those in harm's way.
Without their courage and sacrifice
None of us would rest this night.

If we stand before a tyrant's gale
We stay free and not in someone's jail.
What makes a soldier oh so brave—
Would you want to be some taskmaster's slave?

Reflections abound this month of May
Remembering those who showed the way.
If you love freedom's rights
Pray for those who guard the light.

God sits on His perfect throne,
And one day soon He'll claim His own.
But until He calls His people away,
There'll be battles to fight another day.

The USA is free today,
And with God's grace it'll stay that way.
Soldiers and sailors gave their all
Because they heard freedom's call.

(ret. MSGT, USAFR, Vietnam 67-68 + 70-71)

Richard D. Lunsford

A Circle Small

Flowers growing by the house
We see them grow, we think of you
And bend down close like you would do
And love the flowers that you grew

A piece of tin blown from the barn
A silhouette down by the pond
A woman dips her hands to wash
from planting flowers by the house

A table worn and sanded down
We feel the wood, we hear the sound
And watch as hands rub up and down
And feel the grain you must've found

A circle small beneath the dust
We found the ring you thought was lost
After all this time who would've thought
we'd find the ring you thought was lost

The wind blows cold, we shiver here
The wind blows cold somewhere outside
A voice, it sounds so soft and kind
A circle small beneath the dust

Shirley A. Gilley

Grandbabies

Babies, the small miracles of life, are precious to behold.
We take them to our breasts, watch a miracle unfold.
Treasure their growth, as time flutters by-
Quickly and quietly, as if a sigh.
The babies are grown - have children of their own.
Nicknames are given immediately it seems-
'Jewel' has the longest lashes I've seen.
'Pretty Girl' - voiced brings a smile to her face
Blue eyes, blonde hair — a picture I'd trace.

Now I can enjoy all I have missed
As 'Jewel' throws me his first little kiss.
Hugs so tight as fear is shown
Hands drawn back from leaves a blowin'
He makes a path upon the ground-
The flower beds he has found
First words spoken favorite toys-
On and on he brings me joy.
"Pretty Girl"- now adds to my bliss
A part of life I will not miss.

Terese V. Radatz

Something New

We met romantically, not knowing what to think.
We were like children not saying anything about it to another,
We knew just how we felt toward each other.

Then soon I understand, he's nothing, like anyone that I have ever met.
He was the only man my hidden heart that I would let.

And then comes back into my mind, "you never know."
I think of dearest, sweetest, love I start to glow.

I'll see and then I'll find the truth that soon we'll face.
Indeed.
I'll live, but unlike every man I'll race.
In lead.

And after all it changed, meaning my thoughts about
relationships and everything that will surround this fact,
that no one clearly understands although I think I do as
clear as crystal in the light of fire.

Melaina Prusaty

"Love Is Pain"

The beach was the place we met,
we were pulled together as if we were in a net.
It started off like a fairy tale,
and ended up like the deepest pits of hell.
Each minute was spent together,
but then we fell apart like a feather.
It felt right at the time,
but ended up as crime.
Our feelings remained,
but our love was drained.
My heart was a great big knot,
torn into a lot of guilt.
From the start I knew it was my fault,
I knew I should of made a halt.
I never thought it would give me a scare,
now I wish our love was still there.

Tiffany Clark

Super Bitch — The Finite Manager

Blunt with sharp edges; her goal is to control.
Wearing spike heels and short skirts, she moves with purpose,
and in her own direction.
Where her professional interests are at stake,
nothing is sacred.
She prides herself on being a judge of character,
sometimes with little or no knowledge of those she judges.
She prides herself on her ability to make decisions quickly,
sometimes even in a vacuum.
One day, she adamantly opposes a plan; the next, she may see an
advantage, and make you think it was her idea.
She revels in numerical displays, charts, graphs, spreadsheets,
and the art of using statistics in her own meaningful ways.
Approach with caution,
honesty is not one of her finer qualities.
Distrust her benevolence,
for it is only a sham to disguise her motives.
Believe the opposite of what she says about her own modesty and
intentions;
her common sense borders on impropriety, and she has no
conscience.

Marie T. Stephens

The City Band

With tin cans on the heels of our shoes,
we'd do a dance and sing the blues.
We'd hit a picket fence with a piece of wood —
it made a little sound, just like it should.

With an inner tube, cut up, and a can cut down the middle,
we'd make ourselves what sounded like a big bass fiddle;
with a tin washboard and an old rusty nail,
we'd keep the beat, like we heard in the jail.

We'd all make music wherever we went;
we'd play our tunes in the Revival tent.
Were a band that was mighty poor,
but all the folks around would ask for more.

Our "music hall" was the city street —
from all of its sounds, we took our beat.
Now the music's gone, and the boys are men
who will never play like that again.

But if you stop, on some busy street,
and you can hear a special beat,
it will be the music that we made
when we were young and unafraid.

Louis B. Wies

Granddad and Granny's Farm

When Granddad and Granny used to live on the farm,
We'd walk through the fields arm in arm.
All of us kids had so much fun,
And we always played in the summer sun.

We'd ride Polly, the horse, all day long,
And as we'd ride we'd sing a song.
We'd cover every inch of the land,
Which was cared for by their own hands.

I'd go with Granddad to check the cattle.
And ride behind him on the saddle.
We'd count the cows one by one,
To make sure there weren't any gone.

I miss the trees and grassy fields so much,
Knowing it was destroyed by man's touch.
Yes, they sold the farm and moved to town,
And the new owner dozed the trees and plowed the ground.

I miss everything about the farm,
And I wish they could've stayed.
But, we still have the memories in our hearts,
And they'll never go away.

Shelly Searcy

Out Of The Public Treasure

Out of the public treasure comes the private gold
We'll be rich and free and well, no one will grow old
We'll vote ourselves whate'er we need, we'll all be full and bold
Out of the public treasure comes the private gold

Out of the public treasure comes the private gold
We'll be warm and fed and happy, no one will go cold
We'll raise the taxes if we come up short, there's plenty we are told
Out of the public treasure come the private gold

Out of the public treasure comes the private gold
No one will be sick or hungry with the government in control
If someone does appear to lack, we just add them to the role
Out of the public treasure comes the private gold

Out of the public treasure comes the private gold
Look around, see what you want, just trade in your soul
There's no difference anymore, we're cut from the very same mold
Out of the public treasure comes the private gold

Out of the public treasure comes the private gold
Trade in your house, your car and children, for security they've been sold
Now that we're equal there's really no need for you to have your gold
Out of the public treasure comes the private gold

Roy C. Frink

Grains of Sand

Those years together
Were like spending time in a bottle
We were golden
Like characters in a classic novel
So young and unspoiled
With our virgin laughter
Why did the fairy tale end
What happened to our happily ever after
Old photo albums
Is all I have to remember
I feel so cold inside
Like the winds of December
All those tender moments
Sifted through our hands
Like water from the sea
Like so many grains of sand

R. C. Bournea

The Treacherous Heart

The pain that overwhelms me when I look into his eyes, there were many things he gave me one of which was good-byes.

I did love him for many years, and all I gained from it was many tears.

I gave him all I had how could I be that unwise. Oh he was a cruel beast, and his mouth was cursed with lies.

The days I didn't show him love they were very few, at times I wish I could hit him, slap him, maybe even sue.

How could a man take a heart as loving as mine, just to shred and destroy it line for line.

Yes, I believe if forgiveness, in my heart it's known.
But, I can't give it to him he has reaped what he has sown.

I care for many people, maybe even men. If they want my love they'll do what is right forever and ever amen.

Mandy Bomgren

Silent Conspiracy

The songs we heard from Bosnia
Were sad songs of sorrow.
Thousands maimed, thousands slain
And the living cry in vain.
Women defiled and tortured
Joy of motherhood punctured.
Innocent children wade against violence
In a turbulent world devoid of conscience.
Genocide, but the world turns away
And the villains get away.

Same songs of sorrow from Rwanda
The haunting horror of death.
Thousands maimed, thousands slain
And the living cry in vain.
The evil in man rears its head
Motherland swallows the dead
The world turns away
And the villains get away.
But History records man's silent conspiracy
And History reveals man's hypocrisy.

Victoria Edafiogho

"Miles of Silence"

The miles that are between us and... The silence that we grieve,
Were walking along quiet path, as though we were deceived.

So... far away and yet so close, I feel you are so.. near.
I sense your lonely feeling, it brings me silent tears.

The stars is our galaxy, a never ending space,
Love's secret journey to another place.

Like mountain's peaceful secrets and winds that has no sound
or a deserted desert and, the mirage that's not around.

For... time has no ending, like an endless beam of light,
Or the sea's endless waves and the loneliness of the night.

Our time's a distant journey, like... clouds across the sky,
It's a dream that's never ending.... and never knowing why.
The distant miles between us, will never keep us apart.
For love is our essence, as fate is destiny.

It's like an eternal spirit.
That will always forever.
"Be"

Mike Ergen

Were You There?

Were you there to see the fight?
Were you there that night?
Were you there to see who won?

Were you there to see who pulled the gun?
Were you there to see that person fall?
Were you there to see that person take his life?

Were you there when they put him in a bag?
Were you there before he died?
Did you even say good-bye?

This poem is about my father,
Who took his life. I was there
To see him take his life. It
Was a nasty sight, I didn't
Even say good-bye!

Monica Velazquez

Goodbye

We've had our good times
We've had our bad
Times we were happy
Times we were sad
We never quite could stay away from each other
You were mostly my friend
And partially my lover
There were times we fought
And times we embraced
Times I wanted you more than anything
Times I refused to see your face
But finally I had to say goodbye
I still care about you
Saying otherwise would be a lie
I'd still like to re-live all the fun
So I guess it's true and I admit it
Goodbye is easier said than done.

Lara Carcoura

Questions

What can I do with the rest of my life?
What can I do with the years?
What can I do when the days seem so short,
Where is the laughter, when are the tears?
Why is the labor one gave in their prime
So proudly, so freely, now measured in time?
The Moses', the Hemingways, and Pablo too
Showed the way for the elders like me and like you.
So why do I sit in a place for the aged,
Complacent and docile like an animal caged?
Why don't I break out and set my mind free
To write about life and the things that should be.
Like a world free of strife and a world full of love
And a world that believes in a heaven above.
Maybe a world that can nourish its brother,
Maybe a world that respects one another.

Ralph W. Fitzpatrick

Who Am I?

As much as i do around this place,
You'd think someone would notice my face.
But They look right thru me, like i'm not even there
i'm screaming, "i'm over here." and They say, "Where?"
i really don't think They can see me cry,
Cause They just walk away and never ask why.
i talk to myself so i know i'm here.
Will i go crazy? That's what i fear.
No, life goes on and nothing's fair.
i'll worry about it tomorrow, today i don't care.

Wife (Sharon Lucas)

Frame Of Mind

The joys and sorrows of
what could have been,
what should have been
and what might have been.

All lay in waste in comparison
to what is not.

Our thoughts and hopes and dreams,
should focus on what can be done-
to better today, tomorrow, and next year.
Our vision should be an end to
the injustices that man has brought upon man.

Injustices that have men crying out
to God in anger-
-but it is not God we should blame.
It is ourselves.

K. M. Spring

Death To A Child

When some dies,
What do I do? What do I say?
Is death a monster? Can I run away?
Do I tell people how I really feel?
Or do I pretend that this isn't real?
Will they know that I am worried?
Will they know that I am scared?
Will they understand the burden that I bear?

Please don't hide something from me about this.
Talk to me, hold me and give me a kiss.
Be patient with me, o my friend,
When I ask the same questions again and again.
Help me to grieve, allow me to cry
Or just let me sit quietly and give a loud sigh.
I'm just a child, with my own special feelings.
There is no right way
No certain way of dealing.
So... let me say good-bye to my friend
Let my memories heal over and my heart start to mend.

Sarah W. Duvall

Mysterious Love

She is on the trail to a brand new love
What does await her? Will it fit like a glove?

She knows now that she cannot turn back
For if she does her life will lack

The knowledge of what lies ahead
And though the end could just lie dead

She limps along the trail of life
For the stab of love is that of a knife

She knows not, how far the journey be.
I know, for she is also me.

Summer E. Kennedy

United Nation

I dream of a United Nation
where people aren't put down
and religion didn't cause complication
color wouldn't bring you sadness
The girls not having to run from rape
and kids get shot while friends stand agape
Anyone can dream of a United Nation,
but we all have to make a
United Nation.

Lindsay G. Martin

Eden's Shadow

Adam...did you ever wonder or doubt or did you just know
what evolution had evolved in your brain

That you would self-reflect, that you would be in awe
oh so cruel to say that all is illusion and false hope
so cruel to say that it is simply human nature to falsely hope
did you know, did you ever know beyond a shadow of a doubt

What was real, what was true
or was everything just as uncertain, confused, stormed
did you know of these headaches of mine

The loneliness and the dully clanging pain
did you assume all to be meaningless
or did you know love to be true
oh Adam I wish you could hear me and answer me and tell me
but adam I know you are me
and that it is you that is asking the air
oh adam, adam
talk to me
talk to me
(I beg of you...talk to me)

Steven Dow

Ladies' Magazines

The ladies' magazines tell me what to wear
What foods to eat, and how to style my hair.
With the latest procedures, I've found the cure
And my cholesterol goes down each day, I'm sure.

I've tried the new recipes with the greatest of ease
And the children are beginning to really like peas.
Now my husband thinks I'm the perfect spouse
And with the monthly hints, I keep the neatest house.

As I chauffeur them around and travel to and fro
There is just one more thing I need to know.
Why is it,..........I wonder, when I'm busy as can be......
There is yet another new magazine waiting for me!

Katherine J. Hall

Lonely Now

Touching the marble and stone,
What I thought was love is gone,
Dull, firm, blankness, I am alone.
Actions and judgments I could never glean,
Separated by a land, joined by the ocean,
Mixed signals, never indicate what you mean.
My time for love is now, for your it seems later,
Endless cycles, vicious circles, raging water,
Tired compromise, trying to be the abater.
No longer can I be your drone,
But I can't stand being one,
Only the solitary know how to be alone.
Should I be the one to chance,
Leaving my only substance,
You leaving now, it's all circumstance.
Truth is always hard to find,
Invisible, like the wind,
Painful, and never kind.
Someday I'll die in your dreams, you see how,
Waking alone, I wish you were here with me now.

Michael P. Steward

Repair Next Generation's Hearts

Don't do what I do, do what the bible does preach:
What leader's excuses teach, but not Martin Luther;
Practice applying your faith the bible demands:
Example is God's command, Wittenberg found truth here.

Martin Luther imparts, interfering with Rome:
  Stop that "Don't do" manipulation;
And as you ought, do as you say when home:
  For sake of the next generation.

Today it's child abuse to spank for their own wrong doing:
What, hypocrisy not their choosing; but still no change;
Oh, they would rather corrupt their own child:
Than to change for awhile, to expand their opinion range.

Repair their hearts, let your example prove it:
  Stop the word justification;
Restore their thought, apply faith to do it:
  Save the next generation.

Stephen L. Rush

What Is Love?????

Did you ever really wonder
  what love is all about.....
Why it makes you happy
  and why it makes you want to shout......
Why it makes you laugh
  and why it makes you cry......
And why it breaks your heart
  every time you say Good-Bye....
Why it makes you dream
  whenever you're alone...
And why it makes you jump
  every time you hear the phone...
Why it makes you try
  to always look your best...
And why it never gives you
  any sleep or rest...
And why you ask yourself
  will he always and forever love me...
There's never been any answer to these questions
  And there will probably never be.

Kathie Thomas Simpson

"Song of the Rose"

I was there with so many others just like me.
What made you choose me?
I was so young and fresh,
You loved me with so much caress.
You loved me, helped me,
And took very good care of me.
But then you began to neglect me.
You had more important things to get ready.
Pretty soon I began to wither and die,
And so did the love we shared for so long.
Then I was thrown out and just a memory
Replaced by another who was more lovely.

Stephanie N. Morris

Touch of an Angel

What would the touch of an angel feel like?
What magic would you feel and see?
Too much for the mind, body, and soul to possess.
Too much for you and me.
I'm on a journey for that touch.

I seek so far away,
but realize that my answers are so near and close to me.
Because my mother's touch is just,
as well as any angel's touch would ever be.

Michelle K. Meyer

Shattered Youth

It scares me to see
What the future holds
For teenagers like me

The streets are not safe anymore
Not even a knock on the door
A house, a home no more

We see a lot of anger
A lot of hatred——-
A lot of people in hunger
A lot of couple unmarried

The youthful innocence is taken away
The young has been led astray
Where are the leaders to lead our way?
Where are the parents to
  help us day by day?

The color of your skin
  does not matter
Nor does your religious order
To learn to love one another
Is all that really matter

Nichole Tampus

Uncertainty

  We were born not knowing
what we would be or where we were going.
  Through the years
there was happiness and there were tears.
  There were many problems put in our face.
But through life we beat the hard race.
  In our heart and mind
there were ideas of all kind.
  As the years went by our wisdom grew.
Telling the old and hearing the new.
  When our death came the life we had was gone.
But the moon, stars and sun keep burning on...

Rachel Starkey

What Would You Do?

What would you do, if he couldn't live without you?
What would you do, if you couldn't live without him?
Would you die?

What would you do, if he looked at another?
What would you do, if your eyes wondered too?
Would you cry?

What would you do, if he promised you forever?
What would you do, if you had the time?
Would you try?

What would you do, if his time here were through?
What would you do, if yours was too?
Would you say good-bye?

What would you do?
If I said I love you?

Patricia L. Lambert

An Ode to Brenda

Dear little Brenda with your chubby nose
You're just as pretty as a summer rose
With eyes so bright and curly locks so black
You make up for all the riches that I lack.

You're growing so fast though, you'll soon be grown
Then out into the world you must go alone
But remember my child where ever you roam
Take Christ with you and anywhere will be "HOME"!

Sara Claude

Lonely

She is sitting in her rocking chair same as yesterday,
Whatever will she do as time ticks slowly away?
She does the same thing everyday without a change in sight.
She wants to make us happy, so she doesn't put up a fight.
She doesn't want to be here, this fact is well known,
But she doesn't want to be a burden to her children who are grown.
What is she thinking when she's just sitting there?
Watching out the window, brushing her white hair.
Is she thinking of that Christmas so many years ago?
When her children were just babies playing in the snow.
Is she thinking why don't her children come to see her anymore?
They brought her here, against her will, and then they shut the door!
She has so many memories she won't soon forget,
But for these same memories her children will regret.
Because they didn't see her, in her last dying days.
And because they didn't tell her we love you in many ways!

Tammy M. Woomer

"Ignorance"

You crazy niggers
what's wrong with you?
You stupid niggers
yeah I'm black too
You ignorant niggers
but, you can't solve anything with violence
you will find
You poor niggers
that an eye for an eye will leave
everybody blind
You small minded niggers
when you hurt innocent people
because of their color
You foolish niggers
you're no better than they are
My ignorant black brothers.

Sammi Farrar

Kurt Cobain

As a child, you dreamt of the day
When admiring fans would follow your way,

By the time your dream came true
Drugs had completely consumed you.
Despite great success, you were out of control.
Loyal fans & family could not console.
You lived by your lyrics though you died all alone.

Although your inner torture has ceased, and
you've found a new place your memory
will live in our hearts, and in your daughters beautiful face.

Sherri Hughes

Baseball

Baseball comes upon us every year,
When all its fans stand up and cheer.

Baseball brings with it a game of fun,
One that can be enjoyed under a hot summer sun.

Baseball is played by two teams of nine,
One that will lose while the other shall shine.

Baseball this season brought us something to regret,
A terrible strike that will be hard to forget.

Baseball may no longer be played anymore,
The powers that be won't open the door.

Steven Schneider

Knowing One Lives for Eternity

How does one know when it's time to depart,
When all of eternity rests in the heart.
When life seems to ring of each beautiful thing,
When one's spirit takes flight and alights on the wing.
When the time of living has been so precious and free,
Unlocking each door with the mystery key.
Can life's treasures be of the infinite realm,
Not to be left at the moment of death.
But to know in the soul and have in the heart,
A forever place for Forever's part.

Marlo

Autumnal Art

Why do we rake the jeweled leaves
  When Autumn's patchwork quilt she weaves
And proudly scatters them around
  Where summer flowers graced the grounds?

Each showy coverlet would keep
  Our plants alive in cloistered sleep
Until the warblers loudly sing,
  "Awaken all and welcome Spring!"

Could we but keep each festive quilt
  When Autumn flowers fade and wilt,
'Twould gladden eye and quicken heart,
  God's glowing gift, Autumnal Art!

Nell Campbell

God's T.V. - The Sky

The clouds play stories
When God's T.V. is on!
And when the wind blows
Each cloud holds a different theme
  Eagles fly -
  Rabbits run
  Roses sway
Ships of the sea float by -
Look and you will see
Countless stories the wind creates
For your restful hours and your dreams -
"Look up at my T.V.", the Lord said.

Mildred Clearwater Russell

Sleepless Night

Tonight is a sleepless night,
when I close my eyes I think
of you and I see you.
I only hope this will not continue
because a sleepless night is a lonely night
I need the comfort of your touch
I need romance with lots of lust
I want us to be more than a powerful emotion.
I want our souls to burn like fire.
We share more than a sexual desire.
We share thoughts feelings and most of all love.
We are heated with passion our love is deeper than our souls.
This is what I think of us
Tonight my sleepless night.

Nellie Hernandez

My Daughter

You were so precious and so dear,
When I first held you my own love,
How glad I was your cry to hear -
My prayer was answered from above.

I looked at you with pride each day,
And as you grew year after year,
You were the suns own brightest ray,
I clung to you and kept you near.

You symbolized my highest aim -
My hearts desire my dreams untold,
You were to me far more than fame,
Far more than power - far more than gold.

And now you are a woman dear,
A woman good - a woman true,
Be brave and strong and have no fear,
Our GOD will love and care for you.

It matters not how dark the night,
How great the load - how hard the test
HE will be there with guiding light,
To show the way - the way that's best.

Velma A. O'Donnell

My Karma

My heart withdraws from life it seems,
When I forget to pursue my dreams.
To not waiver to not resist,
Forever onward I must persist.
My karma I see is mine to meet,
In time I'll make it very sweet.
For I know the lessons learned,
Can make my life times one less turn.
Up each step of the ladder I go,
The more the God within will show.
Oh spirit guide and God above,
Fill me with abounding love.

Vivian R. Belcore

Sweet Dreams

Lifting my voices I call to the wind.
When I hear no one answer. I call once again.
I look to the sky expecting to see
A sign of a answer to what's troubling me.
I think to myself and then start to cry.
I try hard to yell, but let out a sigh.

Raising my arms I cry harder still,
Trying to silence the pain that I feel.
But all that I've done is awaken the beasts
That prey on the souls of whom hope has released.
I fall to the ground and drift off to sleep.
I dream of my sorrows and smile as I weep.

I am my antagonist.
I reduced myself to this.
My only enemy is my mind.
I live a nightmare all the time.

Ryan Brown

The Ocean and Its Dancers

The Ocean is the place where dolphins dive.
Where the fish swim, and the starfish jive.
The place where the seals do the Mango - Tango.
Where the crabs do the waltz, and the lobsters do the jig.
The blowfish blow up really big.
The clownfish start clowning around some more,
And the clams lay on the ocean floor.

Melissa Passno

I Don't Hear the Thunder Anymore

I was playing around the old oak tree, down by the lane
When I heard the roar of thunder, and I thought it might rain
I looked into the stormy sky, just in time to see.

A mighty bolt of lightning, hurling down at me
Now the rain is softly falling
My mother must be calling
I see her standing in the door
I feel the wind blowing
I guess I best be going
Cause I don't hear the thunder anymore
I saw the lightning flash, as across the yard I dashed
But I never made it to the door
For in the mud I slipped, just as the lightning hit
And I don't hear the thunder anymore
I see an angel coming
It is my mother running
To hold me to her breast forever more.
I see the sun shining
On clouds with silver linings
Now I don't hear the thunder anymore

Melvin G. Cornwell

Going Home

Now I lay me down to sleep,
When I return to me, oh tender spirit being;
To the cradle of my death,
When I return to me, oh tender spirit being;
Beyond the mist of memories, where mankind cannot tread,
When I return to me, oh tender spirit being;
Beyond the Veil of Tyranny, where Fear no longer reigns,
When I return to me, oh tender spirit being;
Weep no more, my little one, our journey's at the end,
When I return to me, oh tender spirit being;
United with my infant Bliss, on gales of joy I ride,
When I return to me, oh tender spirit being.

William M. Simons

Dream Reality

-Do I experience reality when I'm sleep or when I'm awake
-When I sleep I travel around the world experiencing life ...
-When I'm awake I'm bound by the system...

-When I dream I speak seven languages communicating to the masses ....
When I'm awaken I struggle to speak without interruption ....

-When I dream, life has unseen colors and beauty,
When I awaken life is limited to just black and white ....

-When I dream, I am whoever and whatever I can conceive,
When I awaken the chains of society try to bound me to a mere number ....

-When I dream I am no one's property or slave; inferior to no one, master only to my soul ....

When I dream I am free!

—If being awake is reality, I'd rather live the dream and leave reality to those who are "truly" Asleep!

Stephen L. Walker

A New Beginning

I got to know you
when I was beginning to think my life was almost through.
I had tried to be strong
but everything kept going so wrong.
At the moment I was about to give up all hope
you showed me how to cope.
You made me feel good
like I never thought I could.
You taught me how to feel again
when I didn't know where to begin.
I thought my heart had turned to stone
but a way to love again to me you have shown.
If it weren't for you I don't know where I'd be
for it is a new life you've given me.
I wanted to take this time to say
thank you for showing me the way.
And I just want you to know
If I have my way I'll never let you go.

Shanci Brooks

My Life

As I lay here I think about my life
When I was born, when I got my first tooth
When I learned to walk, when I crawled,
I think about all the things in my life
and how if I could go back and
change all the things I did bad
and do good I know now that I could fix
all the bad things I did by doing good now
I learned that if you do a bad deed,
can you fix that later in your life by doing a good deed
I write this for my mother, father, brother sister,
grandma and uncle, I say to them I love you
and I always will remember that I say to them.

Leticia De Leon

The Friend in You!

In time we've grown, laughed and cried—
When I was down, you were by my side...
You picked me up, when I was falling—
Wiped the tears when I came calling...
Gave me joy beyond compare—
I know love, when you are there...
The understanding when things are tough—
That my mere words are not enough...
To let you know, what it means—
To share this friendship, hopes and dreams....
The caring and sharing, our feelings of heart—
Being separate, but not apart...
Knowing exactly the feelings inside—
Never feeling we had to hide...
Being so comfortable to give and take—
A friendship like ours, takes years to make...
Don't ever give up or stop caring—
For there is too much, we've both been sharing...
And I thank God, my feelings are true—
for giving me, "The Friend In You"......

Karrie L. Jackson

Dream A Little Dream

My most treasured moments are at home asleep;
Where I have my own personal thoughts, only I can keep.
The day has come now that I will be wed;
There will be two wandering minds in the same bed.
Two lives will become one, it's time to share:
All personal thoughts and dreams to show I care.
I remember wishing upon that glistening star from above;
My dream has come true - I'm in love...

Tammy Crowell

Dad

Dad, you were the greatest man I ever knew
When I was little, I wanted to be just like you,
You taught me the difference between right and wrong
You always had faith in me to be strong,
You taught me how to love and how to share
And you were always in the background standing there,

Dad, I've made a lot of mistakes along the way
But yet you stood beside me everyday,
You were always ready to lend a helping hand
Even when I thought you wouldn't understand,

Dad, you were always filled with so much life and love
That it fit you like a pair of gloves,
Then came a day - the life was gone from your eyes
I knew this was God's will - it was your final goodbye,
I know now that your in a better place
The memories of you can never be erased,

Dad, you were someone I very much adored
You were the best father, a child could ever ask for.

Linda M. Petterson

"Always With Me"

Should I listen to my heart
when it calls out his name.
Though deep down inside I know
things could never be the same.
How wonderful it would be
to turn back the hands of time.
A chance to redo all the things gone past.
This time for sure, I'd make certain it lasts!
For I would know
all that I need.
To make things right,
and to succeed!
But I know such a thing
could never be!
We must continue
with the life we now lead!
Remembering the lessons learned on the way,
will help us each and every day.
So there's my answer, plain as can be,
in my heart he'll remain...always with me!

Valerie Taitt

That One Cold Night

That one cold night,
When snow and ice were lain.
I shall never be able to fight,
The anguishing pain.
When you went to the party,
You promised to drive safely,
And with that I left you in God's eye.
Later the phone rang,
You had been killed in a wreck;
And I was to say good bye.
I would never get over the hurt of this ordeal.
They say you didn't drink,
Silly of me to think;
Some other careless person has ended your life.
So in heaven to all that have been affected in this way,
I pray.
And to those in prison,
For what they did;
I cry.

Kristen Meysing

"The Awakening"

I knew that someday I would awaken to a world of splendor
When the air was no longer harsh-but pure and tender,

A world that for so long had been dormant-and hidden from view
Would once again replenish itself-with everything new,

Lakes and streams, once still-and laden with ice
Would again run freely, resuming its roles-a catalyst of life,

Trees and flowers that were barren and naked
Proudly flaunt their leaves and blossoms now fully awakened,

Creatures of all kinds, some who'd slept day and night
Would again roam the forests and the fields-to natures delight,

Birds and beasts of all sorts, who'd fled to escape winter's wrath
Could again be seen-in great numbers of past.

Nights that were once cold, unforgiving and frightening
Were now aroused by the clasps of thunder and lightning,

Winds that were once numbing-and carried a biting chill
Were now a memory, replaced by the cry of the whippoorwill,

Yes — it was God's creation and is comparable to none
The stars, the moon — and a life giving sun

Like tomorrow, spring is not promised, nor is a new generation
Just thank God when it comes-bringing joy and jubilation

William Clayborne Jr.

Reflection On Humanity...Self

At times I sit in wonder, wondering about the end of time;
when the judgment of man is handed down, who will be left behind?

Will it be the drunkard with his wine of forgotten time?
Will it be the person carrying on a lie?
Will it be the Holy Man leading the flock astray?
Will it be the murderer who did not know another way?
Will it be the politicians that wage war instead of peace,
Or will it be the soldiers standing at their feet?
Will it be the fornicators who are driven by desire of flesh?
Will it be the people in corporations that ravage the earth for success?

We all have sin in our blood, and a body to carry the acts;
We are imperfect people in an imperfect world and this must come to pass.

So I sit and wonder, wonder about the end of time;
When it comes and His will be done, will I be left behind?

Michael Divittore

Finally

When the brass ring slips from your grip and is lost,
When the nights are so cold you wake covered with frost,
When days pass unnoticed save when years add by one,
When no day seems important and no day seems fun,
When resolve fixes solitude for no family's alive,
When it just doesn't matter even if you survive,
When your mind starts to wander for days at a time,
When you wake in a dark cell not knowing your crime,
When people stare at you and whisper your name,
When the children won't even mistreat you for game,
When your legs start to wobble unable to walk,
When trying to cry out you find you can't talk,
When you lay down convinced that you'll never rise back,
When you know it's all over your breath growing slack,
When the final chill hits you as you fade in disgrace,
When your ticker ticks lastly ... you've a smile on your face.

Tom Mayer

"Supposin'"

When your world is upside down
When the pain seems trouble all around
Just supposin' your life is full of fun
And then some

Supposin' you see the sun as gold
Supposin' you have shelter from the cold
Supposin' you delight in all that's real
And feel - love.

Supposin' you see yourself so tall
Growing in every way
Supposin' you fly a kite so high
The wind takes it away

Think of yourself ("supposin', of course")
As the captain of a stalwart ship
Tough and strong and getting along
And having fun with it

Supposin' the world is made of glass
Supposin' the grass is blue
Supposin' the moon is a silver spoon
And that the Sun is you

Nell J. Griffiths

When the Moon Changes Her Faces

When the night has fallen, and the moon changes faces,
When the smell of darkness spread through
  your head, and you begin to do your dances.
In the wine garden with the roses,
  and their perfume fills the air.
The singing and the music, play on the moonbeams,
With blackness all around.
And shadows creeping in every corner,
  eyes watching; while the moon changes faces.
And my voice was the song,
  my tears were the rain.
My heart was your feeling,
  and I felt all your pain.
I can feel your presence, always here.
Under the black sky, while the moon
changes her faces.

Shannon Minger

I... And The Right To Die

I laugh
when they say
everyone has the right to live.

I cry
when they pray
I haven't the right to die.

When I have a person to love
and bread to eat
and a place to keep me dry
let me live... let me live... let me live.

But when the pain's too great
my mind's too late
and I've earned my fate
let me die... let me die... let me die.

Mort William Fenimore Cooper Elkind

Forever

I dream of a time
When we are together,
Looking into each others' eyes
Wondering what the other's thinking.
We never know what's going on
In the other ones' mind
Maybe we just feel sorry for each other,
And want to make each other happy.
Maybe we're thinking of each other,
Maybe of someone else.
Maybe we don't care how the other one feels,
Or what the other's thinking
Maybe we do care, and let our feelings show.
We hold each other close,
Feel protected, and don't want to let go.
Maybe we're too shy to let the other know
How we feel,
Maybe something will happen, and we'll no longer be together,
In each other's arms - forever.

Nushin Aliabadi

This Is Not The End

The life we live is not the end,
When we leave this world, new things begin,
New wonders are for us to see,
When God does beckon me and thee.

The angels many do abound,
In Gods sweet light is where they're found.
A place for you, a place for me,
Our many loved ones we will see.
So do not worry or be afraid,
when called by him, our soul to raise,
Forever in his place to stay.
Rejoice on that most Holy Day....

William K. Sherman

To My Husband

It was the 10th of February, 1968
When we were on our first date.

You were quiet and kind of shy
You were nervous and so was I.

We hardly spoke the whole night thru
But yet I realized I wanted to spend my life with you.

We made our plans for our future together
And then decided to marry in the cool fall weather.

We finally wed on that October night
Everything was perfect and turned out just right.

We started our life together as husband and wife
You brought so much happiness right into my life.

Somehow we made it helping each other
The next thing we knew we were a father and a mother.

We have two wonderful sons who now are full grown
And here we are with so much time of our own.

With each passing day since we said I do
My love grows stronger as long as I have you.

I love you and I know you love me
And so it will be till e-ter-ni-ty!

Susan Margolis

Kaylee

All my wonderful memories of little Meg have become the past,
When who should step out but little Kaylee at long last!
A delightful little brilliant ray of my very sun,
That shone on me precious love that my time had won.

Whisper through time and bring back this fresh breeze
As this wonderful child will laugh and I will please
Because to live in her presence is the answer to my dream
Together we will form our hearts into life's team.

Watch as her wonder dances through her delicate features.
Look on as her brilliance amazes all her teachers.
Listen as the melody of sunrise plays on her fingertips,
Hear the golden sounds of heaven float through her lips.

When she cries you must hold her tight.
Reassure her in the dark that everything is all right.
Love her in the morning, during the day, and all through the night
Because she is my heart, Kaylee, my very light.

Margaret Mitchell

That's When The Teardrops Will End

When will the teardrops stop?
When will I laugh again?
All my hopes for our tomorrows
Left with my love and my heart will not mend.

When will the teardrops stop?
When will I love again?
Now I'm alone and deep in my sorrow.
How can I face each day without him.

When will the teardrops stop?
When will I live again?
He was my life, my love, my friend.
And now I cry, it seems without end.

Someday we will walk together
And the comfort that I need
Will come from Jesus Christ our Lord.
He will not leave me alone to grieve.

I know when my life is over
And I finally meet my friend
Christ will take me by the hand
And that's when my teardrops will end.

Margaret Rose Leisinger

Untitled

Is this how they treat you
When you fight to your end for them
Rest in peace, sweet dreams my friend
They were so unfair but they had you fight
Now they sit on their riches
Like gypsies and thieves
I know you'll return and make them die on their knees
She was every woman in the world to you but they took her away

You only wanted to share a dream with her
but for you there are no more days
She feels your magical eyes fill up with hate
She can hear your love call
She knows her own fate
With dagger, her hand flies to the air
Striking downward, freeing her heart from despair
They're no longer lost in love
Cause she heard his love call
Now they'll be together forever raise or fall!!

Michelle Magann

Untitled

It's not sad to see a heart hurt
When you know the path of the Road,
Its curvy sometimes with dips and Bumps.
Life's that way.
Through any age in one's life span,
We quite, and go on, only to find
another curve, or dip, or bump, and,
then in our old age with hair of grey,
We see the road our children take
We think when they're young, we've
taught them well, and we know the
Way of life's Road, then we can say, oh, well
So, its not sad to see a heart hurt.

Ruth R. Mata

Falling

To walk the line of fact and fiction
When you live in a fantasy
You start to lose your grip on life
And slip away from reality
You forget what's real and what is not
And start to bid the world goodbye
Losing the sanity you once had
When you decide to unfold your wings and fly
Away from decisions, wrong and right
Away from horrors and mysteries
Flying and soaring farther up till
You reach a world only you can see
Good-bye to the world, so long to life
Laughing from above while you wiggle and thrash
You start to fall slowly and then very soon
You come falling down faster and land with a crash

Mary Gentili

Peace Of Mind?

When I try to reach the sky I bring myself up;
When you try to reach your longing you see beyond yourself;
Were it not for you I would be alone, I have a hope;
Hope keeps me alive, love will always go on;
Days go on endlessly, my soul cries for peace;
The electricity is in my veins for what?
You are the universe, the substance, the only real truth;
My dreams must come true, but you will still be there;
My longing must become reality, but you will still survive;
Why is my pain great? Why are my eyes weak? Why is there such
love in my life?
I listen, I grieve, I know not what my life holds, but I have
power in my veins and soul, I will listen to the voice that speaks;
I will not be afraid, I will not doubt, I have the world, I will
look up and know.

Linda Rice

Entryways

The keeper of the key to the door to the place, where I once sat, thinking, words choked in my throat, linger among the falling leaves of the tree that shaded my thoughts.

The entrance to the hall in the house where I once lived, waiting, for the keeper of the key, to unlock the door, waiting to leave.

The gate to the garden with the cobblestone path, where I once walked, through the serene rose beds to my sanctuary, the willow tree, that protected me from the wrath.

If I went back, would those words reach my lips,
echo down the black slate foyer floor,
and disappear in the winds, withered leaves
floating peacefully to the ground?

Linda Mitchell

A Journey on a Gurney

There are many modes of travel
When you want to take a journey,
But none quite like the springless, antiseptic wagon
The doctors call a Gurney.

For this journey on a gurney
You'll be dressed quite in class,
In a swallow-tailed creation,
That won't quite cover up your - rump.

You will also have a Chauffeur, and if you have my sort of luck,
'Twill be a jolly little interne
Who drives it like a truck.

He will bang on doors and lintels
And cross thresholds with a bounce,
Which isn't really comfy on a wagon
With springing, not an ounce.

But you reach your out-bound destination
To be greeted very nice, by a nurse with a two-foot needle,
And hands she's packed in ice.

From here the path prows hazy, and the memories are dim,
But I thought I heard Doc say, "Lets go to work on Him."

Rev. Richard Lungren

Life

Life is like a giant clock
when you want you can make it stop
you sit and watch the hours go by
anxiously waiting for time to fly
watching the minutes tick by like the days
seeing yourself in so many ways
the clock may stop anytime, anywhere
when it does don't despair
the clock will start when a new life begins
and your hopes and dreams soon become his
but the time will come when the world
will stop, exactly like a giant clock.

Rachel Kostinko

Giggles of Happiness

There they are; I heard them again.
Where are they coming from, does anyone know.
They always just come and go.
Laughter of little children and happy people.
Now I can't hear the laughter, all
I hear now are tear drops falling,
falling down through the little cracks of life
The type of cracks left by hurt
and unfairness in someone's life.
Then suddenly through the hurt and unfairness
the sun glows like it's never glowed before.
And the giggles of happiness
return stronger then ever, never to be
broken by life's little mishaps again.

Kellie A. Richardson

Nature

The wind whispers whims into my ear,
While dancing in branches far and near.
The sun also shines high in the sky,
And dries my tears whenever I cry.
The clouds circle and come together,
And cause what we call cloudy weather.
The rain drops softly to the ground.
The clouds cry quietly and don't make a sound.
The sun and the wind whisk my tears away,
And clouds do my crying, so I'll be happy today.

Kathryn O'Kane

Missing You

Here I am...I have always been here,
Where are you? I don't feel your presence anymore.
It seems strange that you left an empty void in my heart.
Why must I feel this strongly about you,
When I know we are worlds apart.
You were just a passing fancy,
Yet you managed to come in and brought laughter into my life.

What have you done to me?
I find traces of you everywhere I go,
And wherever I looked, I see reminders of you.
Every time I gazed at the sky,
I would see the color of your eyes,
Whenever I see a tree, I think of your philosophy.

Why do I feel this way?
You don't know how much I yearned for your nearness,
Your caress, and the little things you used to do.
It seemed like only yesterday
When I delight in the comfort of your touch.
Where are you now...I'm missing you.

Marilene S. Kazior

Tribute To Jackie O.

Elegance is defined by experience
where grace has mingled with strength
where fear and pain can clench the heart
unmercifully while the body can stand strong
where the mind has swelled like a blistering
bruise exposed to the knowledge of
vulnerability and substitution of emotion
Where evolution becomes a trial of
beauty and the capability to "grin and bear it"
flow eloquently
From this we find admiration, intriguement
obsession and far more respect then any
king could imagine

Mercedes Griffin

"Life"

Is this the gift they call life?
Where homeless souls roam sadly in the night,
Where are the purple mountains
the vast fields of grain?
The songs of laughter, festive
dances in the warm summer rain.
I want to see love's association
with reality
The eye protrudes from the
portal of this mortal on its
maiden voyage.

Mike Keas

Mother's Love

Mother's are different in a special way.
They calm your fears and dry your tears.
And care for you everyday.

Mother's are always willing to help
With anything that's bothering you.
So hold on to that love,
'cause if you lose your mother like me,
you'll always wish you had.

Take your mother's love into your heart
and know matter what, don't ever let it part.

Shelley Gaugler

This Is The Street Where I Live

This is the street
where I live.
This is where
I sit on the street corner with a sign
and beg with my eyes for handouts
and get mean looks and laughs.

This is where
I dig through a can full of garbage
and collect the remains of anything
and willingly eat it for a supper.

This is where
I stay at night, in a dirty box
and force myself to try to get some sleep
and all night, I am frightened.
And you can hear the threats,
and see the tears,
and feel the hatred,
and not one soul cares.

Rachel L. Sumner

I Wish....

Starlight, starbright
Where is my love tonight?
I need someone to talk too,
Who will understand.
Will I ever meet my true love?
Sometimes an angel might come as a dove,
What shape is my love in?
I wish I knew what to do,
Who are you?
Is what I would ask,
All I want is someone to love me for who I am
I don't want to meet the wrong man,
And make the wrong choice.
I have a whole life ahead of me,
I just want to know I'll be cared for.
That's all I want to know
To give me something to look forward too.
I wish I may, I wish I might,
Meet my true love tonight.
I wish...

Melissa Hagerman

Three of a Kind

The child looked around, found silence.
Where is the lap to curl upon; the ears to share fears, hurts confusion and sometimes pleasure? A hug would make the world feel safe.
Oh, a hug would feel so good.

The adult looked about, so much needed to be done.
Anger surfaces everywhere; in the school, on the job, in the street and at home.
Where is the word of encouragement when spirits are low?
Where is the shoulder to lean on when times are tough? A hug would strengthen and support.
Oh, a hug would feel so good.

The elder exists, sometimes isolated, angry at the loss of youth and vigor, afraid of change, critical of the times, bitter because of lost opportunities, terrified when body functions diminish.
Where is the extended hand that offers a boost in courage, a sense of worth, a respect for shared experiences? A hug would be a comfort.
Oh, a hug would feel so good.

Lillian Garrity Edwards

Garden

Garden deserves our love and praise,
Where one may sit in peace and gaze
At trees and plants, or fragrant rose,
Some charm the eye, some please the nose.

Where folks in sorrow, pain or gloom
Are cheered by nature that's in bloom,
And veterans who lived through hell
Come to the garden to get well.

Garden where each can feel and see
How nature decorates a tree,
And every seed in fertile sod
Becomes a plant, the word of God.

Blessings and grace come from above
When garden work is done with love.
Garden is Adam's place of birth,
There is no better place on earth.

Nicholas P. Bird

Spring Dawn

In pelting rain's residual glow
Where sprightly April breezes blow
Spring trees strew storms of chartreuse snow
To open new portfolio.

Inviolate and fresh the morn
Aswirl with seedlings to adorn
The face of Earth yet winter-worn
And call, "Awaken! Be reborn!"

What splendid moment! Velvet green
Good Earth in new perspective seen
All tender, noble and serene
Saluting Spring, the pregnant queen.

Wilma Spellman

The Love Affair

Whatever this we are experiencing
Whether it be right or wrong
Whether it exists for a moment
Or lingers on for a while
It is there—It is real—It is Definite.

The glowing warmth
The inconcealable smile
The joy from within
Cannot be denied
For it truly is.

Who can establish what is our right
Or what is to be or not to be
Feelings, like the tide, change with passing time
Within the power of no soul
But they are there—they are real—they are definite.

Perhaps, like a rose
Its existence of short duration
Its beauty pouring forth
Only to fade into a memory
It was there—It was real—It was definite.

Jean J. Wiesmeth

Spring of Hope

There is a spring of hope
which waters me
during parched seasons
when all life seems to have
dried up,
and browned,
and crumbled,
and blown away
in the dust bowls of weary days
and lonely nights.
This spring trickles forth
in tiny tributaries
seeking out the roots of dissipated dreams,
and slowly seeps into the cytoplasmic mass,
revitalizing and nurturing the cells
until the branches and leaves
began
to grow
anew.

Sharon Cullars

Bloody Heart

Boom! Boom! Boom!
While drops of blood pierced
My aching heart
My heart was shouting out!
Mercy! Mercy!
The years of joy and pain raced through my mind
Like a speeding bullet
I thought I had died and went to heaven
As I reached and rubbed my hand across my head
I could feel an explosion taking place
Tears began to fall down my cheekbones
Lord! Lord! Ooohhh Lord! I screamed
Save me from my sins
Rescue me from my anger
Burn through me like lighting to a tree
I want to start over for I've endured enough pain
I laid down my old skin
I arise again

Patricia White

September Remembrance

He sleeps in body emptied like a cup
while mind-
emersed in duty still-
touches the willow,
and it does sing;
kisses the flower,
and it is spring,
lifts a child,
and it has pride, and peace abound
does thus abide,
and someone once failing is filled with joy
because he lived.

Parvella E. Gordon Coleman

If I Could Hitch A Ride Upon A Star

If I could hitch a ride upon a star,
would I stay near?
Or would I go far?
Would my dreams and wishes all come true?
Would you look out at night and see me?
Would I see you?
Would I spend eternity
hidden behind it's shadow?
Or would I become the star?

M. J. Lord

No Longer Alone People Like Arthur Kent Have To Fight

There truly is a man who gave his all
While on the job he did his best
And in the way he learned how
Using judgment was only part of the job
And he stuck to what he believed was right

He never lied as I recall
His way of words were different than the rest
He shouldn't of been fired I believe even now
And now I could see part of his life was rob
And for what is his he has a right to fight

He tried to tell many about it all
He felt he did his best
And he fought back the only way he knew how
And many don't know of the pain he endured on the job
and many don't understand this pain by right

This pain from day to day his mind may recall
And there will be many times his mind won't give him rest
And people like him need to know they're not alone now
They too feel life and happiness was rob
And no longer alone people like Arthur Kent have to fight.

Viviana Maria Teresa Diaz

As Clouds Go By

I looked at clouds and gazed at the sky,
While watching life pass me by.

No one to blame, I made my choices,
Most of the time ignoring my inner voices.

Tied to the material, after the buck,
Bemoaning my existence while trusting plane,
I wanted to do it, but couldn't bear the pain.

Life was so painful you'd think I'd welcome a change,
But in my fear I limited my range,

But things are better than they used to be,
In the last few years I've learned to like me.

I'm no longer a doormat, alone bearing guilt,
For the pains that have happened are part of life's crazy quilt.

I've made some peace with my inner self,
And put some of my fears on a temporary shelf.

Yet, I'm selfish, I've a long way to grow,
But for now, learning that it takes time is all I have to know.

Richard G. Wilde

Untitled

And when the hurt won't go away,
Whisper to me that it will.
and when my tired body aches all night,
Make my brain go still.

Let me cry until my face
Is slashed with teary streaks.
Hold my hand and tell me that
We are all God's freaks.

And when Death eats me inside out
And I have not even the strength to scream,
Look me in the eyes
And give me the strength to dream

Karen C. Borsotti

Winter

In these last summer days
Whistling wind a sparrow cries
Leaves die.
And fluid streams of rain pour upon us
as the wind drives the cold into our eyes.
And life goes on
the cruel demons few they are
follow the system of God
And change our lives uncontrollably.
Watchful creatures
always feeling out the negativity
Hatred runs thru their veins
They bring up points of nature
Only to constantly put it down.
They are true to their nature
the only thing I can credit them for.
But they live and die
no joy to feel,
and blast thru to the afterlife
condemning to life... Fear.

Kimberly M. Jenkins

White Bird

(Dedicated to Jesus)
White bird in her lonely cage, her golden age, her silent rage,
Freedom screams, His love redeems, breaks through these bars,
Removes the scars, her wings adjust, shakes off the dust,
Lifts up her head, discards the dread, the past is dead,
The future brings, salvation rings...

All is saved that's worthwhile memory,
The rest is thrown unto the throne,
Where He collects but not neglects...

To save to show His mercy though His heart wished not,
And quite distraught to save dismay for Judgement Day,
To show His love, into the Sea of Forgetfulness, Deliverance,
As one last pain engulfed in rain,
As mighty waves wash over me and then the calamity...

As Spirit stands, the naked fire within her prime reduced to claim,
Her love divine, the promised truth.
Her head bent low received the crown,
Then spread her wings as He gives word,
To mount to nearby Kingdom high,
To sing as other warriors sing,
Hosanna to the King of Kings.
Amen

Linda Lara

"Find Your Own Ways"

How can I find my way to
Who do I turn to
To get me there. Is it too much burden on you -
To take me there.
To take the time out for me.
Oh please tell me, who do I turn to
where am I going, How would I get back.
All I'm doing is turning in circles, going to and foe
and all they can say find your own way.
No, I'm sorry, that's all I need to know
did, anyone know I'll make it on my own
If its snowing raining or very hot water I know I can
make it, I'll get there by myself, no ways
no depending on same one.
When a guy cones by to give me a ride
I say no, don't accept rides from strangers
as I know I wont get there, that way
or anywhere. It just leads to trouble - shooting
I've been fooled again,
don't accept rides from strangers.

Theresa Ann Snider

Friend Or Enemy

What kind of friend lets you down?
Who does nothing but make you frown.
This person isn't a friend but an enemy,
Why you call him a friend is a mystery.
what gets me is why you take this from him,
Hey what happened did the light in your head go dim?
How could you be so blind?
And let this person take over your mind.
He's treating you like a wilting flower,
Which is draining your power.
How could this person be so mean?
You not leaving him isn't a good scene.
If you leave him you'd be doing a lot of good for yourself,
And when you looked in the mirror you'd be looking at a new self.
You'd be happier and more satisfied with what you see,
I know you'll make the right choice; but it's not up to me.

Mary Sanborn

Sadness

If we are spending millions on outer space,
Who is going to be benefited?
If we are making more powerful bombs,
Whom are we going to kill with all of these?
If we send more soldiers to foreign lands,
How are we going to bring them back?
And if we keep polluting this earth,
How are we going to explain it to our kids?

We explore outer space to see more stars?
To kill more people, we are making more bombs?
We send more soldiers, to come back in bags?
And we are polluting, I guess ... just for fun?

Questions with no answers, that is all we have
Abortions, and drugs, and drugs, and gangs
No kids in the schools, but who care for that
Parents, let me tell you ... those kids have rights
If you want some children, because you can provide.
Think before you bring them to uncertain life,
That even the children deserve to be loved
And need a good home not an empty house......

Marissa Munoz

Undying Friendship

This is a poem to my life long friend,
Whose love and friendship will never end,
Though I have moved and gone away,
In my heart you will always stay,
When I think of you and me,
I see two little girls playing dress up
and pretending to drink tea,
I see us dancing around in brightly
colored dresses,
And pretending our hair is long flowing
tresses.
I feel so happy when I am with you,
because our undying friendship is so
genuine and true,
To me you are a beautiful burning light,
that makes my life so wonderful and
bright,
In my heart you hold a very special spot,
That will always make me forget
you not.

Katie Felesina

Why?

Everyone is crying, they say there's a hole in their heart,
Why?
They say there has been a death, they say there has been a
death, They say that my Papa is gone,
Forever.....
Where is he? Why does he not come back?
I wish for him to be there, to sit me beside him, for me to hear
him say, just once, that all will be will again....
I wish for him to coax me, to plead with me not to cry, I wish to
see his wise old head turn to me and say...
Do not cry, all will be well again. They say to me, soon little
one, all will be forgotten. Why did my Papa leave us, what is this
death they speak of? They say that soon, they too, will leave,
why?
Hopefully, I ask them Why do you cry, did you fall, do you feel
pain? Tearfully, they tell me, no, little one, I did not fall,
but my heart is torn to pieces, and never will heal again, I ask
them, why?
They say there has been a death, they say that my Papa is gone,
Forever......

Jessica Leah Gilchrist Callinan

The World

The world seems always difficult, and hard to understand.
Why are we so far apart, when we could walk hand in hand.
Why is it that we're separated, in this world that we've created.
Can't I be your friend and not just learn to base,
The trust and the caring of your friends not only on their race.
Why are we different colors, why aren't we all as one?
We can live together, or do you think it can't be done.
If you can judge wisdom by the color of one's skin,
Then learn to be a loser, because you'll surely never win.
We've understood the glory, now we must understand the pain.
And if we're not persistent, then we'll never learn to gain.

Kelly Norton

Another Christmas Away from Home

Another Christmas away from home,
Why did I have to roam?
Now it's another Christmas alone.

I try to copy the way that it was,
But it can never be the same because,
I don't see Daddy teasin' Momma, no more,
Or Momma's turkey and dressing always better than the year
before,
Or all us kids playing those old games.
It'll never be the same.

Another Christmas away from home,
Why did I have to roam?
Now it's another Christmas alone.

But, I do have the family I've made,
The love I have for them will never fade.
So I'm really not alone,
There's just a part of me that's just not HOME.

Lucinda Hind

Christmas Lights

Lights beset this darkened night,
Twinkling, glowing, shimmering bright.
Inside, outside, whatever seems right.
Strung out and about the tree and house,
Dazzling one's eyes like the maze for a mouse.

A picturesque scene amongst all the green,
Giving the illusion of a long, lost dream.
Oh, the magic of these Christmas lights,
Beckoning one towards those inner sights!

Yame

Untitled

What is our purpose?
Why do we live?
It is not to take
It is only to give
When we pollute and damage our earth
The Planet that gave us our life, death and birth
If we were not here
There would be no fear
Why do we kill?
Just for the thrill
If we were gone, all would have fun
You see we ruin everything
Trees cannot grow birds cannot sing
It's just not fair for us to live
Humans must take
When all others give
The problem today is you and me
If we were gone all would be free

Kelly Haddow

Untitled

If all things decay
Why do we say
Our obsession
Is depression
Life is good but it seems
At times all we have is dreams
It doesn't matter what the dreams mean
As long as we wean ideas from their scenes
  If dreams are not real
  Then why do we feel?
  This is something you should know
Without dreams we'd feel as though
  That everything was quite low
  Mentally we'd be very slow
  For we'd have nothing to show
In our unworked imaginations here below.

Tim Wynne

I Do Not Understand

I do not understand
  Why people trudge on day after day
  Why fathers leave
  Why mothers cry.
But most of all
  I do not understand
  Why people do not understand each other
  When we can be so much alike
  And yet push others way.
What I understand is love
  Not man/woman love
  (That's too complicated for anyone)
  But love for your family
  The real, genuine love for your sibling
  And the people who created you.

D. J. Uithoven

Man in the Dark

What could you say to the Man in the dark?
What could you prove? Why does it matter to
the man in the dark? What could you say?
Be brave, be full? What could you do to the
man in the dark? You're hidden in his dark?
You're trapped and there's no way out?
  What can you say, what does it matter
what could you do to the man in the dark?
  You can run.

Sola Adesiji

My Long Lost Love

He came to tell me he'd soon be gone,
Why would he go after all we'd done?
But then I thought I'd get along,
Somehow, somewhere I'll sing my song!

Carry me back to Adams County,
Where I've run through grassy pastures plenty,
Barefoot and usually sorely hungry,
For the love of men and money.

Money proved to be elusive,
Men, however, weren't seclusive.
Perhaps I should have been more selective,
What the heck, he was defective...

...In love which is now departing,
Like the new day's sun, another starting.

Wilma Barney Burns Conley

Just a Thought for Tarz and Murph

What could we miss more than departed friends?
  Why would the merciless bell toll now their ends
And leave two weeping mothers for the boys,
  Who were their lives, their everything, their joys?

It seems to me that God, wherever hidden
  Could choose less nobler lives to stop, forbidden,
Or possibly could warn us years before,
  So while on earth we could appreciate them more.

But nay, He must for unknown reason
  Take them - a crime on earth that shadows treason,
And the worst is not for them who die in pain,
  But most for those whose aching hearts remain.

But we, who are so infinitely small
  Perhaps our thoughts far 'neath the truth do fall,
For though we suffer when our beloved departs
  The trust in God may reunite our hearts.

Scott Campbell

Embryo

Will the world sustain?
Will I loose my pain?
Will I see tomorrow?
And abandon yesterdays perils?
Will the Gods tell us why?
Will we swallow choke and die?
Will we get another hero to cling to?
Will we ever get back what was taken away?
and in the mean time be subjected to asbestos and decay?
Will this world survive the final blow.
Don't ask me, I don't know,
I'm just a young embryo.

Zeppelin Belladonna Zanzihari

Mother

Mother you are my library
You are the reference section that gives me advice
You are the children's center that raised me
The self help books that teach
The cookbooks that prepare meals
The mystery behind birthday surprises
The classics of your past childhood

Most of all mom, you gave me my library card
You brought me into the world
You are making me into a mom just like you
I wouldn't want it any other way

Nicole M. Tavares

Untitled

Will the pain ever stop, the sorrow ever cease?
Will my emotions and mind come to peace?
All I am is emptiness inside,
and bitterness that won't subside.
Is this the way I want to be?
Depressed instead of young and free.
I give no appreciation,
and in return I feel no joy or elation.
Does God want me to suffer and cry?
I question my faith because all I want to
do is die.
To me the world is one giant tear,
wet and cold and full of fear.
I gain confidence and understand,
that God and I go hand in hand.
I look around with a new sense of sight,
And suddenly the world turns bright.

Shanna McKiness

Vision of Prize

"All glory to Hump who shall
win the Prize,"
The old world has cried
for forty years,
But to Hump who trifled
away his life,
I give a great glory and
honor and tears.

Give fame and renown and pities of teaching,
To all who weaker or sicker,
Their spirit are many in the army of teaching,
They were born with vision of loveliness like a dream.

Oh, great is the teacher who wins the Prize,
But greater many and many of vision,
Some pale-faced teacher who dies in disgrace,
And lets Jesus finish the through supreme.

And great is Hump with a gun undrawn,
And good is Hump who refrains from prize fever,
But Hump who become weaker or sicker yet still fights on,
'Tis wealth, good Sir, makes honorable men.

Laurine Williams

In Search of Meaning

Through changing times and ages
Wisdom was not meant just for sages.
To realize one's own self principles
As a guide, this is invincible.

How does one grow up in a world of adults?
By example and models to produce some result.
Hopefully, the parent wants to see the child complete
And able to handle the road signs down life's street.

Ambitions of innocence push the child to explore
Blindly pursuing what life has in store.
Parent's words echo in the background - "right and wrong"
Facing life eye-to-eye is what makes one strong.

Guilt of what the parents want no longer drive the child,
For she's aware of who she is without being seen as wild.
"I've experienced a lot more life than you'll ever know.
If you don't think this way, take the time to ask "how so?"

You've given me strength from the head of which I'm grateful
But the feelings in my heart that I've learned are not debatable.
For I went out with my own map, compass and feet
In search of myself, I did not find down your street.

Tara Montoya

Christmas Wish!

Laying here looking at the Christmas tree,
wishing you could be here with me.
I know you want to be with me too,
but unfortunately dear our wish won't come true.
Don't be lonely or even sad, just remember the good times we had.
I know it hasn't been that long since you held me in your arm,
but the wonderful feelings you have left me with,
I'll always remember not to forget.
I wish you could be here with me night and
day it was only a wish but what can
I say, being apart at this time
hurts a little more because its Christmas.
For its almost Christmas twelve days away,
I'll be thinking of you on that special day and loving you in every way.
I wrote this poem just to say "Merry Christmas"
to you from my heart today.

Lydia L. Fontes

A Church Without Walls

A church is more than just a structure.
With a cross, an altar and some benches.
A church is more than a Pastor or two.
Whom one can confide their feelings too.

A church can be many things such as
choirs, youth groups, and bible study.
Prayer groups, caring for one another
and sharing in the Lord's supper.

It's a place where people gather to learn
about the Lord's work,
by singing his songs, reading his words,
and praying his prayers.

A church is a place to thank the Lord
for all that life has to offer.
And remember how he died for us.

Randy Triepke

Vampire In Love

His haunting glow took over my mind
with a pale light so cold that if froze within
moments of it touching
His corpse-like appearance was
terrifying, and then he laughed at me
It was cool and sleek and like a cut stone
and I cool feel his grin on the back of my neck
He had the look of a vampire in love
filled with lust and hungry for a kill he moved
forward with the grace of a black widow
and stretched out his hand towards me
I could see him like a dream
he caressed my cheek and stroke me neck
my hair was all in tangles and he brushed
it aside and kissed my shoulder tenderly
his kisses were icy and full of death
that he was
and he had the look of a vampire in love

Melissa Johnson

I Am Train

I'm the train roaring down the track
Whistle blaring "out of my way,
get back! Get Back!
My mournful moan in the still of the night
Dogs in chorus howling with all their might
Into the station with squealing brakes
majestic and shiny, what a sight I make

Eileen Reifsteck

He Was The One

(Dedicated to Shun Schneider of Slidell, LA.)

He was the one who made me feel that way
With all the warm loving words he would say

He was the one who gave me his class ring
All the sweet songs to me he would sing

He was the one that loved me.
Nobody understands
Maybe one day my life be in his hands.

He was the one who helped me in my time of need
Just to see him, with my dad I had to plead.

Now he is gone, I will never see him again.
He was the one.

Summer Robertson

Mime's Tears

She watches man's destruction through time,
With ancient knowledge in her eye's mirrors:
Emotions expressed by this mime,
With only silent tears.
And offers as comfort soft,
To man who initiates the pain,
Her wisdom in solitude not to be lost,
Her love always to remain.
And as man continue his perilous plight,
Sorrowfully desiring it's not too late;
Quiescent in stance, she displays her might,
Contemplating his inevitable fate.
But if in her insight man finds retreat,
Then in time, he will not defeat.

Mari Costell

Untitled

My life is like an ocean,
With drab and dreary days,
With waves as high as ten feet tall
And nothing gorgeous or gay.
My love is like an infant,
Easily destroyed,
Or like a little boat pushed and shoved
"till it gives away.
My family is like the sunshine,
That I welcome everyday,
And those who think I'm happy,
Must be looking the wrong way,
What I have just told you is my truth
and my fear
For this may be my future even though it
was my past
and I will have to live with it,
Until I'm gone at last.

Rachel McKinney

Art

Art isn't wrong or right.
You can do art any day or night.

Art isn't an exact science,
why it could be inspired by a
kitchen appliance.

Art comes in all shapes and sizes,
Art beautifies the things it capturizes.

Art can be anything for you and me,
Art can be a paper boat floating at sea.

Lakita Edwards

Your Pet

He sits patiently and waits till you come home
With empty rooms that surround him, still he sits there all alone

To him the day seems long but the knows you'll soon be there
To fill his world with happiness, he knows for him you care

Right now his dreams are quiet, the eyes are closed with sleep
His thoughts are calm and restful, as he guards the house to keep

His little tail lies still, no movement does it break
He's saving all his energy, for your entrance when you make

For you he gives wet kisses, a cold nose, he gives that too
His love, he doesn't hesitate, he gives unconditionally to you

He will not ask you questions, he cares not why you're late
He'll be happy just to see you, so for you he'll sit and wait

Those little legs start running, when he hears that open door
That little heart starts pounding, he wants his pets and more

Hello! Hello! Hello! His wagging tail does say
I'm hungry, feed and pet me and maybe later we can play

Remember the days you were sick and on nights, some cold and lonely
Who was always by your side, your faithful, one and only

So reward him with a smile, a pet and a praise or two
For no matter how you're feeling, he will always be there for you

Shirley Robideau

Mother Earth

You were green and beautiful
with flowers of every kind
There were trees that gave wonderful shade
Children played and enjoyed you
Then buildings went up
Black smog ruining the blue sky and clean air
Trees being taken down deteriorating rich brown soil
Hypodermic needles being dumped into lakes and
oceans where children and people once swam
Aids killing people left and right
What has the world come to!
Will there ever be no end?

Valerie Clifford

A House, My House, My Friend

A house, I grow up in,
With its creaking doors
And winding corridors,
I see this house as a friend, my friend,
Everlasting, and with no end.

A house, I wake up to,
with the smell of bacon and
the smell and aroma of fresh coffee,
I open my eyes with a smile.

Then, I leave my friend
an early bright morning,
And into my day when I'm feeling lonely,
I imagine a house, my house, my friend,
Everlasting and with no end.

Furthermore when I've grown up
and moved away,
I think of a house, my house, my friend,
Everlasting, and with no end.

Forever, a house I call to mind.

Matthew L. Carlton

Summer Storms

Summer rain falls gently to the ground
with it's pitter-patter, it rains all over town.
the plants look as if they're jumping as drops fall
the thunder, the rain, I love it all.
Summer storms, romance flows heavy, so heavy
It's possible summer storms, may be...
...the cause of summer love.
talking silently, making love or taking a walk
it doesn't matter, just don't speak don't talk.
body language it's the clue...so new
is love getting through to you?
on warm days tall grass blows side to side
on roller blades, holding hands, we guide.
I wish summer didn't have to end
it seems we've just started to begin.
the heat, the feeling of your hands touching my face
your touch takes me to another world, another place.
I feel so free, as free as I ever wanted to be.

Julie Anna Ming

Princess of the Nile

You made me feel like the princess of the Nile
with love so deep and pure as snow
I was the princess of the Nile
You gave me high hopes, joy and pleasure
you let me fall within
with all the faults I felt when it began
the hurt, the pain that's deep within
why did I let it begin
crying day and night
"Can't sleep" "Can't eat"
For the love I feel has gone astray
I feel alone this way
I know its one sided
but hope was there
For the love to begin on the other end
For I was the princess of the Nile
For a while

Laura L. Adams

I Love You So Much

All the pain and sorrow I've gone through, you've gone along right
with me
Not only pain but, also comfort and that's how it's supposed to be
I never thought that I could find myself in a love that's
'Oh so true!'
A love that's pure just like a virgin, a woman's dream that's
genuine and few
How could I gain a love so kind, so precious, constant and woo
A love many people cannot express, but I can because I found you
L - I love you because you loved me in a way no one else could
O - I love you in a special way, overpowering because I should
V - I love you because I have never experienced a love so valuable
and anew
E - I love you because you love me and exclusively me loving you
I love you with all my heart and soul I'm ready to say I do.
I treasure the moments that we've spent together, so lets settle down,
just me and you

Valerie Green

Mothers Life

Will this day roll unnoticed by?
With no events to steal your eye
No ships were launched - no mountain claimed
No bridges built - no lions tamed
I gaze back on these several years
Through bruises scrapes and salty tears
Thru tiny footsteps in the night
Chubby hands clasped round me tight
So many things for me to do
Read a story; tie a shoe
At times I sigh a weary sigh
How can days be so long; when time seems to fly?
Still I gaze at my darlings as I kneel by their beds
And ever so gently kiss three sleepy heads
And tho somewhat unnoticed my days seem to roll,
There's a peace still and deep inside of my soul,
I rest assured there is no better life
Than that of a mommy and a good mans wife
And when I'm aged I'll complete
With grand children still playing at my feet.

Tanya S. Alexander-Bourne

Just a Storm in the Night

Now he is gone to the store and he'll be back
with roses.
Yes, it has happened once more.
And Brooke, just a kid, knows; but she won't tell.
For she fears what comes from their room;
The screams of pain; the vicious yells.
"Help me" is the cry of the night covered by the
winds howling just right.
Now crouched in a corner filled with pain; tears
running down her face like the on-coming rain.
The lighting strikes hard; like his hand across
her face.
And like his deep, furious voice, the thunder roars.
Now crouched in a corner, she wonders —-
can I take this anymore?

Bissi

Love Is...

That special feeling you share
with someone for whom you really care

That special emotion that fills your soul
and makes you feel whole

That little tingling sensation you get in your heart
when you realize it's not just infatuation
It is the warmth of the sunshine on your face
it is that certain glow about you which shines all over the place

It is that feeling which makes you smile and glow inside
it is that special feeling that you just can't hide

It enriches the mind and the heart
it makes you feel wonderful right from the start

It is giving freely without expecting anything in return
it is something that cannot be bought but earned

It is that feeling which brightens your day
when you're feeling blue

It is that source of light for all hopes
and dreams come true

Love - My dear - Is Being With You!.

Michelle A. Lincoln

Darkness to Light

What do I think and what do I feel.
With the moonlight shimmering through the leaves,
Are things as dark as they seem?
When the sun arises and darkness falls,
will things seem different,
will they change as the days go on?
Will somber feelings fade away,
as darkness turns to bright lit days?
It is now time for new hope; for new fears.
I am growing stronger with each new day.
I find another piece of me,
that will get me through
the darkest of dark,
to bring me into the brightest of days.

Lori Ann Garrett-Bumba

So Many

Well you're on your own and you realize you're living
with the sad intention of blood, pain and fear.

A king's on his throne with his heart laced in stitches
for he feels for lives that have been overthrown.

If all your life is cutting to the quick
open your mind and gather your wits.

So with a truth for life may the children learn
feel the full moon's rays cause the tides to turn.

So many faces, so many thoughts, so many heart's beating feeling
the cost
So many within, so many without, so many like me without a doubt

If you hurt me again I just might wash up on shore
But I'm dying to see what life has in store

If this is a game I won't play by the rules
And we never keep score that's for loser and fools.
So many faces, so many thoughts, so many hearts beating feeling
the cost
So many within, so many without, so many like me without a doubt

Life is not a dream, it's a dream brought to life
So brush off all the dirt and put up a fight

Take my hand, we'll head towards the light
For lover and forever, we stand and unite.

Robert Bove

Untitled

When the day begins
With the tentative sunlight
Caressing the moist dew
On tiny misty green leaves,
And the birds sing songs
To it's red orb,
When the April air wafts
Through your open window,
Gentle as an angels' sigh
And the sounds of a small village
Carries through with it,
When the ice of winter
And the chill of spring rains are finally gone,
Oh, how fine is the earth then!
When the wind is as still as a sleeping babe—
Oh how fine is the earth!

Rose Rockwell

Beneath The Old Oak Tree

As I sit beneath old oak tree,
with the wind blowing against my warm face,

Listening to little children,
laughing and playing,
in their own special way.

Beneath the warm sun,
as I sit watching the seasons change,
spring, summer, fall,
then to winter.

As old mother nature,
changes her gown once more.

Thinking how very special it is,
for just a moment,

To be part of life's eternal time.

Katherine Lynne Van Cura

Blood from a Rose

Winter, my lover sings
with the wind over water, she breathes
like life, the stem carries a thorn
the blood is growing old
what happens to us
when our rose isn't red anymore

The birds are singing
with the air high and tight
bitter rose awakening
bleeds its last drop tonight

Bluer, my lover is
with ten for a dollar, she bids
lifeless train, running without a track
the wheel has come loose
what happens to us
when we can't make it back

I guess nothing really matters anymore
No, I can't hear the choir, the faulting wire
can't get blood from a rose

Keith J. Downey

Uncle S.E.M's Whaling City National Park

Today I salute my Eighty Years
With this whimsical ditty
About the place which I call Home,
Uncle S.E.M's New Bedford City.

You'll want to know "Who's Uncle S.E.M.?"
Is he in "Uncle Sam's Class?"
Uncle S.E.M.'s in "Uncle Sam's Family"!
Uncle S.E.M.'s "Uncle S.outh E.ast M.ass.

In the map of "Uncle S.outh E.ast M.ass.
Why does New Bedford make such a spark?
World History calls us "Whaling City."
Soon we'll be "Whaling National Park!"

A century ago, New Bedford's fleets,
As stated in world histories,
Hunted for Whales in all world oceans
Bringing home wealth from world's farthest seas!

Today we may visit, but not kill Whales!
Our courageous Whale Hunters forever are gone.
But the world still visits Uncle S.outh E.ast M.ass.
Brave Men's Memories in Uncle S.E.M. live on!

Manuel Almada

"Mom"

I'm sitting in your kitchen in your very home
With your phone on the table. I'm all alone.
You see, you're not here. You left us last week.
Sometimes all the pain makes me unable to speak.
I miss you already, mom, giver of life.
The pain that I feel cuts me just like a knife
You were hit very quickly, our lives fell apart
But you knew how I loved you right from the start.
I hated to see you in your current state
Oh, you triumphed and won just to succumb to this fate
The phone will ring, you're not on the line how I stop and I wish
that just maybe this time one more call from you, let me know you're
at peace for there's a safer place than this one you did lease.
It won't be the same you took a piece of my heart and I loved you,
dear mother, till death did we part. The calmness astounding -
I realized your pain to keep you alive - no one would have gained.
Thanks for my life and the things that you taught me.
Thanks for the patience and things that you bought me -
for the support and the love and the time that you gave;
I'll never forget and they'll go to my grave...

Linda Sigman

Reading

Through reading I can explore this great and
wonderful world of ours;
The meadows and hills in the country and the
bustling cities with their towers.

Books give pleasurable pastime, educate and
help to stretch my mind;
They lift me out of a monotonous life of
repetition, give height above the grind.

I am privileged to share the thinking of minds
of many that I could not know;
I am able to visit many foreign countries,
see places where I could not go.

Good books can be shared by people of all
races, religions and creeds;
There are special books to meet all occasions
and to fill each individual's needs.

Mava A. Spivey

"Believe (Side By Side)"

I don't know whether we are here to be spirits
wondering alone or if we were brought to this earth
to someday become one together.

I do know that there's too much hate in the world.

People turn to lives of crime and violence out of desperation;
the desperation to achieve power and status; to replace the
love never found at home; to escape their deepest fears; to
escape themselves.

The truth is that you can't escape yourself; you are who you
are, so why fight it?

I believe in the flight of the birds; the Eagle displaying pride and
majesty and the dove portraying peace, love, and hope.

I believe that someday we will all fly together-side by side; touching
the tops of snowcapped mountains and brushing our wings across the
flower painted meadows.

I know that somewhere someday shares my same feelings,
my same dreams.
I would like to tell her never to give up; to always believe in
something; and remember what I say....

My pen is my eagle, my words the dove; together we fly-side by side.

Jennifer E. Marvin

The Beauty Disappears

Leading into the sky, gazing at the deep blue.
Wondering if ever I could fly, or stay upon the earth glued.
The sunset was near, where shades of red would appear.
The light was becoming dim, and the beauty would look grim.
All of a sudden it was black, with only the moon to shed light.
I feared being attacked, the beauty of the day kept my hopes bright
The night went on, with increasing doubts.
Will I see the beauty again, or is it never to reappear.
I feared my own actions, because I didn't want to offend.
I needed to see the beauty, to make myself feel right again.
I wondered in my dreams for the rest of the night.
Praying to be blessed, once again with such vivid sights.
Inspired to yearn for more, my endurance lasted very long.
I held that beauty so dear, it allows my heart to feel clear.
I struggled with my own survival, hoping to be strong enough.
Letting loose other desires, made it hard to live with.
Keeping my main dream, was of utmost importance.
I realized all other desires, could not compare,
and waited until I had the chance, to find the beauty still there.

A. McNeff

Missing You

I worked many long hours into the night,
Wondering if I'd see you in the morning light.

Often I wasn't there to give a kiss
Or tell you how much you're missed.

I'd dream of your face glistened by the sun,
Catching a glimpse of your eyes and smile on the run

It's strange how our lives have changed,
Everything seems so rearranged.

Two lives very different yet living as one
together I know we'll make it a lot of fun.

Because you are who you are and I who I am,
together as one, we'll survive hand and hand

But if I should lye to rest
I'll wait for you, my blessed

For my heart is true,
Honey, I love you.

Patti Jany

You're The One

I use to sit here in front of the fire all alone
Wondering when I would find somebody to call my own
So when I finally found you, you were not like the
other boys I knew
Yes, you are the one that stole my heart
The times we spend together from my mind will never part
Deep inside my heart you've touched, you and only you
That's exactly why you could never be like the other boys I knew
You're the kind of guy that lots of women dream of
I can now proudly say that you're my one and only true love
The way you have touched my heart there will be no other
I long to be your friend and for you to be my lover

K. L. Hicks

"Kids"

I have a 3 yr. old, sometimes she doesn't do what she's told.
We begin to fuss, it really makes me want to cuss.
She means the world to me, she's all I've got you see.
I had two step-children too, but now I'm sad and blue.
Them I don't get to see my ex-husband turned them against me.
Between him and his first wife, and his new girl friend in his life.
I really want to shout, but I just shut my mouth.
My health is bad and I'm just sad.
I just feel down and out.

Sherry Lynn Barnett

Sitting on the Tracks

If my name was Fred
would I still eat celery
If I had a fork
would I still eat ice-cream with q-tips
If I had purple hair
would I still watch QVC
If I wore a condom on my head
would my toenails still grow
If I was computer generated
would I still wear underwear
If I was a moment in time
could I go to France
If I had a yellow ring
would I get twenty-two minutes
If I summoned Satan
could I get an artichoke
If I was a bean
could I smell your feet

A. P. Barilla

Last Words

If I told you I were to die tomorrow,
Would your last words to me be gentle and loving?
Or would they ring with disbelief and denial?
Would you try to soothe me, try to end my pain?
Or would your words sting with guilt making me need to live?
Would whatever you tell me be true and from the heart?
Or would it be words of pity-consolance to a dying ear?
Would your words fall softly on my ears like the caress of sunrise?
Or would your breath feel like ice and leave my heart frozen?
Hurry! Quickly tell me!!
A simple 'I loved you' will do.
Because no matter what you tell me,
"I love you, too!"

Stacey Strong

Confusion

There is a time were everything goes
wrong and you don't know how to deal
with it. It's called confusion.

It sticks in your mind until it all
explodes. Your in a dark room in peace
all alone, when everything starts to
explode and brings confusion.

Deep down inside, your heart feels empty
like an empty glass, that could be refilled
once again, and I want that empty heart
to be refilled once more.
There's a stingy burning deep down inside
that can't be put out by confusion.

All I need is to be heard out and understood.
To get rid of this confusion.

Stacey Corbeil

"A Request For Love"

Each day I find it harder to go on living,
Without a mother to talk to is killing.
It's been 5 yrs now and I have tried,
But all you do is run and hide.
You and I have had an unclear past,
A lot I wish to forget, some I wish could last.
I cry myself to sleep worrying about you,
And wondering if you love me too.
When will you realize what you're missing
And imagine us together again...

Robin Rebecca Longest

"I'm Wondering"

I'm wondering, what went
wrong between you and me?

Wondering, why our relationship could never be?

I wonder, why it felt like love at first sight?

Never realizing it was all ending by night.
I'm wondering, If I wouldn't of left, would it have end?
But that's now something I have to learn how to trend.
I'm wondering, what I did wrong for you to cheat on me?
I realize now, it was you and never me.

I wonder, where you are today?
waiting to tell you that I still
love you and your memories
still remain deep inside of me.

I hope, soon I'll get the
questions to my wonders from your own
sweet lips, and no lies, no lies.
But until that day, I'll still wonder....

Kathy E. Flores

Come In

Hey Stranger
Yes, you - deceit, anger, futility
You've cringed seeing us in our happiness
Ignorant of evil's charm
Stolen glances revealed
You on the edge
(Yes, we showed you the way)
Your whispers - all lies -
Still the distrust rose around us
Gasping for breath
Our vision became clouded
Your smile grew wider
Watching us call for help
Your hateful embrace
Enveloping us
Brought no shelter
From the cruelty you've bestowed upon our lives
So now I say to you the only thing I can:
Come in
For I have given up the fight.

Leslie Adams

Shiloh, April 7, 1862

Sister, you'll know if this letter reaches you.
Yesterday I carried our brother across the ridge
between heavy musket fire and cold rain
the trees bare—the very leaves shot off—
my back so slippery with his blood and weight
I couldn't keep my stride. Under a briar bush
I hollowed a space to rest, stripped my shirt
to press against the flow then tied it
with the scarf you knitted
before we left the farm. He moaned
and called for Ma and said some things
I'm afraid to tell about God and Mr. Lincoln.
These last two days
finished most of us, we fire at ghosts
our fingers frozen to the trigger,
our minds plead for quiet —
even dying.
I'll tuck this letter inside the pouch around my neck
and you'll see only me or read this.
Please tell Ma. Your loving brother Thomas.

Theresa Wilhoit

God's Calling One Of His Angels Home

She was as human as any
Yet her quiet wisdom and gentle touch
Shouted out loud she's not one of us

Her kindness, her warmth, her compassion for all
Proclaimed she was more than us all
For you see she was one of God's angels
And she's heeding his call

She'll be missed by many
Yet remember by all
For you see she was one of God's angels
And she's heeding his call

God has called one of his angels home
And now the time has come
For you see she's one of God's angels
And she's heeding his call

So now the time has come
To say good-bye to one of God's angels
For you see God's called for this angel to come home

Lorna Gladish

Untitled

You've hurt me more than I've ever been,
yet I still can't let go,
Maybe it's because I feel there's more
You must know.
Maybe its because of my feelings that
Block out all the lies,
Maybe its because of what rushes
Though me when I look into your eyes.
Maybe its because of what makes me
want to trust you,
Maybe it's because of what helps me see
The good in all you do.
Maybe it's because I want so much for
us to be together,
Maybe its because I'll always hope it
would of lasted forever.
Whatever the reason or explanation
may be,
I know I'll always love you and want
you here with me.

Krissy Palladino

Mom

Mom you never let me down,
you always help me when I frown,
If I ever start to cry,
I won't worry I'll just let you try,
Even though we have our doubts,
we always seem to work things out,
When I'm lonely you help me laugh,
you always lead to the right path,
Your not only my mother your my best friend,
I know you'll stick by me to the very end,
Mom your loving and ever so kind,
you know you'll always be first on my mind,
Your one of a kind no one else will do,
and I want you to know that I'll always love you!!!!!!!!

Katrina Howdyshell

Untitled

You got stabbed in the eye and shot in the side
You could have had me but you opted out
I could be sleeping I wanted to tell you
I wish I could have told you
I wish you were inside my head like I am
Too bored to be in love
I don't love anyone wish I could love you
Talk to me like you used to you have changed
Why didn't I
Sometimes I hate you
Wish I could love you

Jackie Havy

Untitled

When I was young and in my prime.
You could ride a train any time.
When Pearl Harbor was attacked
The railroad improved their act.
Trains moved swiftly to the Pacific and Atlantic
Helping our population control its panic.
When that unexpected war was ended
The population was no longer befriended.
The railroad industry's zealous greed
Has greatly exceeded the public need.
I sincerely hope the push for subsidation
Will never become one of realization.

William C. Gandert

To My Friends: My Advice

Life is like a dream I've found and once
you enter you can't turn back around.

You find yourself at the beginning
of your personal dream but before you know it,
it quickly ends and you lay still and quiet as
you get last good-byes from your friends.

While you're in this dream, live each
day as if it's your last and always look
back to good memories in the past.

Always keep compassion and understanding
in your heart and never think of hate.
Be kind and gentle and help all
you can before it's way too late.

Please, always say what's on your mind,
don't ever hold things in.
You will feel lots better and please remember
you may never get a chance again.

Katie Baker

Destiny

When I watch you sleep,
you lay there so still.
I can feel your breath against my face.
The pressure of your body to mine is getting deeper now,
And I wonder if you're going to stay.
Your lips look so tender and soft in the moonlight.
And your eyes look beautiful even closed.
As I turn away from you,
your image still lingers in my head.
When I wake will you be gone,
will I be left to face the world alone?
Before drifting to sleep I face you and
let destiny take it's toll.

Michelle Eckerman

Our Love

You loved me, you taught me, and swept me off my feet.
You let me love you, and for me that was a treat.

You saved my life when you asked to marry me.
Never did I dream of living so happy.

You are the most wonderful husband a woman could hope for.
I love you day by day, more and more.

You excite me, thrill me and you I adore.
I love you with a passion I have never felt before.

Love is hard, sometimes there are prices to pay.
Our love is a strong one, strong enough to stay.

You are my life, I will never let you go.
There is one thing you should always know,

I love you!!!

Sheila James

A Bit of Advice from a Most Treasured Friend

You entered my life at a time when I was down,
You lifted me up, and made me look around.
You said "life can be cruel, vicious and mean,
But you can control it if you dare to dream.

Focus yourself, set your own goals,
Then push onward, reach out and take hold.
Never look back, you can't change the past,
Always look forward, and hold your dreams fast.

Let go of the bad times, it's the good times you'll treasure,
Cherish good friendships, they'll be there forever.
Open your heart, trust the people who care,
They are the ones who will always be there.

There will be mistakes, but in them a lesson,
Learn from them, they can be a blessing.
Give of yourself freely, you have wisdom to share,
Let good advice show loved ones you care.

Then later in years, when old age has come,
Look back on life's battles, those lost and those won.
Pass on your wisdom to those in need,
Your words will be valued, you are an inspiration, indeed."

Lyn Martin

The Only Man For Me

My darling you are so adoring
You make life worth exploring
You are my one and only true love
Because you are my turtle dove
You make my life worth living
Because you are always so forgiving
You make each day a bright shiny day
That is why I love you in every way
You are the man that finished what you start
You make things look like a work of art
You are my man the joy of my life
That is why I am proud to be your wife
You make our children and me so proud
Because you have us living on a cloud
You fill our lives with joy and love every day
You make us happy in every possible way
You are so tender so kind so nice
I wouldn't want anyone better at any price
You are so loving and worth your weight in gold
That is why with you I will enjoy growing old.

Rebecca Renner

Life

Life is very confusing.
You never know which way to go.
Whether it be left or right, fast or slow.
You may take a lot of wrong turns.
You may end up with the right.
But all that it will determine,
Is if you used all your power and might.
Trying to get through the days,
Can be like a knife in the back.
But if you just hang in there long enough,
You will be repaid, it's a fact.
You will experience a lot of love.
Losses and pain will come too.
Just keep it together a little bit longer,
And that goodness will come back to you.
So try to keep this in mind,
When someone has wounded your soul.
It will come in handy someday,
When you are asked to pay the toll.

Stephanie Roulias

Untitled

I met you and you picked me up,
You scraped me off the floor.
I loved the way you listened to me.
You made everything seem so sure.
You made me feel special,
Secure,
And in place.
Nothing could touch me,
No one will ever erase,
The love I saw when I looked upon your face.
Obliterate became my feelings of confusion,
Frustration,
And hate.
You set my soul free.
I got to shine.
I felt as if nothing could withhold me from showing,
The deep affections hidden inside.
I never dreamed we would be this far apart.
I just want to you know that over all the miles,
You're still the one that holds my heart.

Linda Minarchin

God Gave Me A Gift

God gave me a gift,
You see He knew I needed a lift.
He gave me my first most beautiful thing,
It really did make me sing.
I sang a cradle song,
to a baby twenty one inches long.
The years, they sure did fly,
Believe me it did make me cry,
My baby is now twenty one (not inches)
A man fighting for his land,
Please Lord may I ask for one more lift?
Please protect my special gift.
Thank you Lord for my earthly gift,
Thank you Lord for my son's Heavenly lift.
Amen.

Mildred J. Simpson

A Poem For You

Mom you are the best
You take care of me and never rest
You are the sweetest and the nicest
And to me you are the finest
Your wisdom shines around the family
And you make sure everything is fine and dandy
You cook so good
You cook so well
It's like you have magic and did a spell
You need no reward like prizes or candy
BUT

This present to you
Is a little show of my gratitude
What I would like to do...
Is what I should do...
And that is say...
I LOVE YOU!!
HAPPY BIRTHDAY!!!
XOXOXOXO

James L. Ganz

From the Mist of Time

From the mist of time you weren't mine,
You took the breath from me
you set my soul free,
one day there will be just you and me,
As long as you are there
my heart will never need repairs,
You will always care,
The love you show is more than just fair,
Anyone can see that you
have changed me,
My love will never fail your
my inspiring male,
Come and spare your life so dear,
I know you will never bear
to let me shed any tears,
Make sure your always there
never leave me in despair.

Toi S. A. Wise

Jesus Heals

Ignoring your convictions, you gave in to carnal lust,
you turned your back in Jesus, where did you put your trust...

All sins carry a price tag, you thought for everyone but you,
But you're not ready to be a mother,
now you don't know what will you do...

Her husband was not faithful, but a child can't understand,
Why Daddy doesn't live here, and mom took off her wedding
band...

Some says everybody does it, but tell that to her heart,
She wakes up now alone again, dreading each new day that starts...

The woman that brought him into this world,
is the apple of her sons eye, she was there when no one else,
would hold him when he'd cry....

Now this mother is in the hospital, her prognosis is very poor,
With tear filled eyes he will watch her die,
Jesus stands at his hearts door...

Jesus heals, he knows and understands your fears,
those nail scarred hands of calvary,
want to wipe away your tears...

Jesus Heals, no matter great or small,
Jesus give it to the Lord above, his grace will conquer all...

Michael Farmer

Promises

From the beginning I knew exactly what you'd do
You walked away, when you say you'd stay

You promised me forever and I thought I was being clever
But you taught me something new
Something I really didn't expect from you

In my hour of need I was on my knees
Begging was only the beginning in trying to understand
The message you were sending

In the beginning it was so easy to justify my hoping
But after all the coping, I wonder how I managed
To let you do so much damage

Don't you come around here no more you're no longer adored
you don't know who I am or the circles I've been around
You don't know what I've been through to get to solid ground

I gave you my all and you gave me nothing at all

Thomas J. Barker

Last Night's Dream

Last night I had a terrible dream
You were here with me
But things were not the same

I saw the anger, the hatred, the fear
The emotions you hide so deeply
And never want to share

I will be here for you
I just want you to know
Please talk to me and tell me, I will listen

I think I heard your voice
A quiet cry for help
But the hint was not clear to understand

If I could tell you
Just how important you are
Just how much you mean

I think it might make things easier
Might pick up your life a bit, because...

I never want to have that dream again
Because... in last night's dream
You took your life

Kari Wellington

Never Ending Story

One night I had a never ending dream... I saw you.
You were very vague at first,
  but as time rolled on, it all became clear.

The characters were...you, me, and cupid.
You held your head so high, and me so dumb.

The setting was our hearts trying to find a way,
  but we needed a lot of memories for it to build as one.

I was lonely and you were determined to no more...to have none.
  When you looked into my eyes I felt my face grow burning.
When I looked into yours all I saw was the yearning.

Now I look back on those months, days, times,
  and all I find is a... Never ending story.

Janna Pomerantz

To You

Each day does not pass without a thought to you,
You, who are a part of my memory and life -
be it a moment or a collection of moments.

A token on the wall, friend or classmate,
faded picture or a blue ribbon;
A secret, a sentence, an emotion or a catastrophe.

Birth, death and rebirth of a person, attitude or
memory and how each one helps the next one grow,
Whether wrapped in wisdom or not.

So many things keep us from spilling our
thankful thoughts and blessings.
So if I fail to let you know just how grateful
I am to have met you, please let me tell you now.

For whatever fraction of time you have fit into my life,
It will multiply beyond myself and into the future
of dreams and reality.

May God Bless you,
And may you have a Wonderful Christmas.

Linda R. Bolene

To the Love of My Life

I see you in the morning, and in the night.
your face is what I see at first light.

Your everything I dream of, your everything
Above, your love fits me just like a glove.

Your there when I need you, and there when
I don't, you always show me love just when
I think you won't.

You may sometimes forget me or hurt me,
But you never desert me.

You have a hold on me I can't explain,
everyday your away, my love grows
more and more each day.

I miss you, I need you, I love you,
Is all I can say, so please say you'll
stay. Don't ever go away.

Marrianne L. Mitchell

Sue

As I close my eyes I begin to dream of you
Your hazel eyes sparkles in my
mind. Your short burgundy hair
brings forth light so that one
may admire your beauty. Your
gentle touch sends warmth through
my body and when you smile, you send
me into ecstasy—. The mere presence
of your company sends my heart running
with joy.

It is only a pity that I can only dream
of such things. For the love and desire
that I have for you I must conceal within
me, in fear of losing you, who is dear to
me as the air I breathe.

Roy Michael Guzman

Weeping Willow

Weeping willow why do you hang
your head and cry?
Here let me help you stand tall,
Yes he loved us so very dearly,
But now he can no longer be near thee,
He was our friend,
We confided in him, my dear friend,
He made me feel special inside,
So why, why do we still cry?
We must get on with our lives,
We can't just stand and hang our heads, and cry,
He would want us to stand nice and tall,
To remember him always with love,
Keeping him so near to our hearts,
Weeping willow come stand by me,
It's time we live our lives as they should be,
As long as we remember him always,
He's there to give us strength and courage,
So weeping willow, please dry your eyes
For there is no reason to cry.

Melissa Kough

If

If you ask them to crush the ice, to ease
Your swallowing, and it will spit back
At you with sharp edges and melting pieces.
If you ask them to clean up the white-colored trash,
They'll just dump rid on you instead.
If you ask them to untuck their starched shuts,
To loosen their ties - they'll end up compensating
With bigger boots and stiffer hats.
If you ask them to deepen their thoughts.
They'll drown.
What are they worth? Nothing, you say?
Well, challenge their mildewed minds —
Anyway.

Zoe Mader

Rain Today

Pursed through thickets of smog, I pass effortlessly around and down your thighs. Brand conscious and in need of your upstairs trembling stair. I love you, because the fugitive stands neatly and responds only to telepathic communication...probably speaking of a voyage. Your eyes, cool dreams peer into me and expose a history untold.

The maid, my God the maid. A little yawning and I deject my piercing scream. This is important and so is a clean bed...this is my something that wasn't here long.

Mark A. Schempp

Untitled

As you enter the room,
Your twinkling eyes pierce mine
with sunshine and happiness.
You reach forth your warm trembling hand,
And send tears of joy
running down my face.
Your smile, that of a child in a candy store,
brings forth laughter forgetting all problems.
As we embrace, leaving me with a feeling of security;
You then leave.
Blank, sad and full of sorrow.
Left only with the memories of your company
And a vague image of your face.

Merisa Taylor

A Final Prayer (To Absent Ears)

Shift your feet, adjust your weight,
You're getting nervous, it's getting late.
Down your drink, it's all you got
Get on your knees and find a spot.

There is no time for making love
Annihilation is looming above
Say a prayer to absent ears
Can't dust away my baby's fears.

Don't let the children worry now
Or see they're angels turning pale
I'll send my daughter up to bed
And hope to God He'll clear her head.

Oh my God! The hour has come!
Tears down your neighbors fence and run
To a spot where your remember bliss
Or received a distant lovers kiss.

There is no chance to save ourselves
Or turn our backs on private hells
We send ourselves on up to bed
And hope to God he'll clear our heads.

Mary Frances Manzo

Breaking Down the Walls

I've been in such a state of bliss since I've been with you,
you're honest, funny, and attractive;
You brought hope into a part of my life where I thought
all hope was lost,
If you weren't by my side, I don't know what I would do.
But, yes, love does have its faults,
You can be hurt pretty badly and I know that's happened to you;
But you must understand that I know exactly what that's like,
I've been through that, too.
But I've learned to go on with my life and leave all those
bad experiences crumbling in the dust,
And you can do the same, you can go on, my love, you can
rebuild your ability to trust.
I understand how hard it will be,
But, please, remove your blinders you really must see;
That if you break down these walls that you've been surrounding
yourself with since things with you and that one girl went wrong,
You will find that it's possible to love without pain and sorrow,
and you can tear down these walls that have been up for so long.

Sandra Hanan

The End

My wife and I, when we die, will march to a different band.
The Funeral Homes will not get to hold our cold and lifeless hand.
The Visitation, with it's long and endless line, who meet and greet
and some even tell jokes, of a different kind. And some will say,
"My don't they look nice, and well dressed, and they look so carefree
and well while they count the Flowers and remark of the Pleasant Smell

There will be no graveyard plot, or a gray and cold and printed stone,
while we lie under the ground - and so alone. No grave plot to tend,
and no flowers to bring, at each and every spring.

Bring us flowers, now while we are here, and we will hold each petal
near and dear. If we have to be seen in Death to be appreciated, then
our life has been overrated.

Yes, we will be cremated, a swift and antiseptic end, and we don't
want this to worry our Kin, or worry a valued friend. Our ashes will
be scattered, and will blow across this endless land, like blowing
sand, and if we're lucky might even visit some Foreign land.

We hope our life has touched you in some little way, while we lived
ours from Day to Day. If you can sometimes think of us with a smile
and a Happy tear, that would have been something we would have held
"Very Dear."

Raymond H. Stearley

Love Will Never Die

Love is like a perfume
that can be smelled and felt
when it arrives.
You might suffocate
when it's out of sight.
My dearest friend,
look up at the shinning stars
hanging in the moonlight.
They will tell you that
love will never die!

Love is like a wonderland.
In the right spot, it's not forgot!
With solid promises
love will never die!

Jimmy Z. Hu

"A Gift"

Buying a present
That doesn't cost much
Often means more
To the person you touch

It's not the present you buy
The thought is what counts
The cost isn't thought of
In whatever amounts

People who give
to people who care
Give from the heart
since they want to share

The person who gets
this gift from the heart
Receives a feeling of trust
That they'll never part

A husband and wife
share this love and the giving
Forever and always
and well after living

Alexander T. Findlay

Within

The sounds that echo in the night
That fill my mind with sweet delight
Neither shrill nor very sharp
No distant drums, no angel's harp
You cannot see the sounds I hear
No flashing lights or visions appear,
I meditate and then the sound
Within my head goes round and round.
It is a mantra all my own
That far surpasses any poem.
I hope the sound will never cease,
This wondrous sound of inner peace.

David Rothblat

I Am Searching

I am searching for a love,
that most people will never find.

A love to outlast all problems,
and grow strong with the ties that bind.

I pray that when I find this love,
I will never turn it away.

But maybe it will find me,
and never go astray.

Amanda Grainger

"Still Dreams"

It is of her face that still I dream, though more intently than it would seem
For the mask I wear is one of smiles, desperately pining all the while.
The dreams of her that come with sleep, are cherished pearls I long to keep
But I find at waking that they are gone, like fading darkness that flees the dawn.
I long to touch and hold her fast to a forgotten love recognized at last;
But the doubts I shoulder remain the same, of my worthiness to stake that claim.
The pierces through me with eyes that know the darkest secrets of my soul
And with that facade thrust aside, what have I left but foolish pride?
What may I give her? I cannot tell-perhaps a house built strong and well,
A tower composed of earth and stone and orchestrated by love alone.
And on that day of perfect grace, I'll lift from her a veil of lace;
To adore the face the veil would hide and to kiss the lips of my precious bride
In dew of the meadow we will know our love; while I gaze down as if above
And marvel as the years go by, how luck has touched one such I.
When in the autumn of my years, when frost has set upon my beard,
I will pull her close and whisper sweet; that she has made my life complete.
And as death engulfs in its fold' ne'er strong enough to breaks love's hold
I will lay me down as if to sleep, and implore my darling not to weep.
The grave's not as dark as it would seem; for it is of her face that I still dream.

Spencer Thomas Alexander

Time Has Come

Time has come for us to conclude our high school years
We've gone through many stages and many ages from learning how to walk
to learning how to drive

It took good and bad lessons for us to finally learn to strive
Our long path beginning with kindergarten is winding down
Years, Months, Days and Nights have past
Now we've traveled to our last
The day is upon us when we must stop acting like a clown,
Because something new has come to pick up where our parents left off;
That something new is time
Time has come to release that hand that has lead us for years,
Stop and listen, I'm sure you can hear time tick, tick, ticking,
within your ears.
Time is here to give us a push at saying good-bye to old and new found friends
And to release harsh feelings that's bottled within;
Time has come to make us shed uncontrollable tears,
This won't be an easy job but it must be done
We can't turn back the hands of time because it rings in our ears like
graceful wind-blowing chimes

Tonya Mills

Love And What It Sometimes Feels Like...

I sometimes feel feelings which are new to me. I don't know exactly where they come from, but I know that if I think and remember of other things I can somehow explain these new feelings inside. I feel the love coursing through my veins as like a flower growing...

The flower starts out upon its journey not knowing where it will go or what it will become. It lands upon the ground and sits upon the earth snugly until one day it starts to grow. It begins as a seed planted by no one, but there, and it starts to sprout, growing bigger every moment. It grows until a bud has formed and this is new to the flower, never before seen. The bud may stay dormant until finally one day it bursts open with expression of its color and life. The flower is complete and it continues to be forever, lest some day come where it withers away, but the flower resists this till the end...

And when I look upon my first love I see the flower in me. And my love for whom I have expressed to her, and she knows it, this is how I feel and will forever feel. Until my love will wither away, but I pray and hope that it will never wither. You will accept it my true love someday, and let my bud flower and burst with color.

Joseph Simard

Father Creator - I Love You

You are the only real true father
that I have ever known,
The only real true father
that I can call my own
The only one I can talk to
and tell my troubles to
The only one I can go to
and not feel all alone

I want to talk to someone,
I want to belong so bad,
I can feel it deep within my soul
the ache is so very bad
I want to turn to someone,
someone who understands
the beating of each heartstring
the good things and the bad

I've been searching and searching for
something
I found out what it is, and until
that day we meet face to face
I will feel that emptiness.

Doris Conway

My Blank Heart

I made my mark upon a tree
That now is many miles from me
With knife in hand I drew a heart
Inscribed my initials for a start
Love by plus I did indicate
Blank space to fill left into fate
I knew that I would one day find
One who I could in my heart enshrine
Many years have now passed by
I heard the tree still reaches high
The tree has always there remained
It there its larger size attained
My brands upon its bark still show
What others think I do not know
I believe I'll find
The one to fill this heart of mine

Donald W. Holton

Regret

Sometimes we forget to do things
that show loved ones how much we care
we start taking it for granted
that they will always be there

Then when they are taken from us
we beat our heads into the wall
in all the time they were with us
we never got to say it all

So listen up folks, listen good
take a bit of free advice
share little things with your loved ones
cause you don't get to do it twice

Debra Collman

Dream Maker

Follow your dreams in each every way: Take a journey with fate, but yet not denying misfortune. Reveal your character to those around you. Do not foretell all, for some secrets are best to be alone. May your mind be laced with enchanted thoughts while your heart is beating out the rhythm of the tango. It seems as though you found a true Paradise, but instead you found the path of dreams. You are so captivated on what you discovered you want to tell all. As you awake you are struck by reality just like the stroke midnight. Once again you left in the dark, or at least you think you are, but you can't be sure. Stumbling for the light switch to turn on, you hear a voice telling you that the dreamer's world does not only have to be an illusion, but it can also be an image. That voice you hear is running wildly, uncontrollable though your mind. Some say it's your conscience, but whatever it is it can not contained. Just as you are feeling tears of despair you reach high up into the sky, touching the soft, white painted, fluffy clouds of hope; hope for extended arms reaching toward you and the world. A bright lights shines though your mind just like the multi-color stained glass windows in the church. That light will never be explained. But yet it is so extraordinary you are able to find peace within yourself. Those wishes you wished so long ago have came true. You are no longer the visionary, but you are the dream maker!

Rene'e Freeman

A Song of Time

A timeless memory, the ancient barn abandoned stands,
The wood is faded, the paint no more, only a headless weather vane remains.
It is a testament to the years, of a day long gone.
Yet beneath that antiquated veneer, there is a song.

A faint but captivating tune, it portrays a vivid scene;
Rolling green fields, rippling like the ocean under an ethereal breeze,
Majestic oaks shading a meandering gravel lane, from the sun's dazzling rays,
Happily trilling meadowlarks, heralding another splendid summer day.

The music whispers of a day when the old barn resounded with life.
When a light gust of wind bore sounds of muffled snorts and carefree laughter;
When swishing tails flicked away irritating flies, if only for a while
And children chased farm dogs merrily down the aisle.

Now there is silence, a hush has fallen, the song has commenced.
The aged barn, tired and worn, stands deserted once more,
Waiting, pausing to rest, for soon time will play on.
Though its day has passed, there are more to come, and those memories still have a song.

Kimberly Dibble

Thee Game

It starts with a club, ball, thee and me
There's fairway, rough and even the duffer unlike eye
The object like us headed toward the hole
Say what you think to try and cajole

There is Arnie and Jack and way to many hack
And sooner or later it will affect your back
We try so hard to do our best and beat the rest
We do it with zest this little mental test

Anything but the bore, I've improved my score and depressed no more
Then got the old English lore, today's low score, to hell with work just play, don't say fore
Can't get enough you don't say, go watch the pros and lead with your hurray
Contrary to life a good lie is okay, don't like any delay, all I want to do is play play play

So you've listen to their tips, never paid nothing from their lips, done well with the chips
Sure do take your rips, know how to turn those hips, plays sin tennis and seldom slips
Well known that I've spoke, the future will hold a choke, yet to play with another bloke
Could put an egg and you'd see no yolk, I will keep at it 'till I lose the man made yoke

Maybe just a little cute, don't try and refute, unlike them it's score that I shoot
Maybe just a mind a little acute, out there never see a dispute, I play they toot
Another secret when they say your ill, you inherit this little skill, gets better still
So you overcome having nil, someone's bad will, oh what a game oh what a thrill

Mike Miner

"Love Speaks For Itself"

Love is not something
that simply grows on trees,
It is something that is earned,
yet we treat it like it's a disease.

Between a man and a woman,
it seems to come without warning,
And it's in this special way...
that makes it so lovely and warming.

Love is commitment,
without hesitating,
and if you really have true-love...
there's no such thing as waiting.

Love is full-time,
Love is being true,
Love is being able to wake up
and say "Baby I Love You!"

Love is a partnership,
more important than wealth,
Love is unconditional...
because "Love Speaks for itself!"

Andre Tucker

Bombay Bound

'Tis briefly concluded
that very well snooted
is the elephant of Bombay.
What his Indian friends
think he's got is the bends
and is in a terrible way.
But he don't give a hoot
what they might term his snoot
nor how funny he looks when in stride,
for still he has got
what might be termed, and why not,
a bit of pachyderm pride.
What he was given
he was bound to have gotten.
Surely he's not that funny to see.
Why with a little more time
and a bit more behind,
they too might be pompous as he.

Charles O. Rand

Who

Who are we to say
That we'll see another day,
God only know what awaits you tomorrow,
You may be happy or full of sorrow,
Pray each night when you retire,
Protect us from sickness and fire,
Thank God for a new day beginning,
Help those in need,
And then indeed,
You will be winning.

Harriet Alwin

Dubious

To watch the smoke rise
To see what's left
To not know when it will stop
You hope never
Because its the best
Maybe not then best you ever have had
But better then nothing
You feel it you know it there
It surrounds you.

Brian Fargnoli

A New Day Is Born

Have you ever stood in the middle of a great forest surrounded by all the sights and sounds of nature, looking up at the towering, majestic trees, the glittering light from the burning orange ball in the sky which filters softly through limbs of the great fir trees? If you close your eyes, you can hear the cold, clear running brook that splashes against the moss-covered stones that form a unique design that only nature itself could make. How about the delicate chirp of new-born birds as they snuggle against each other for protection and anxiously await the return of their mother since meal time grows near? Perhaps you catch a glimpse of a young fawn struggling to stand on its spindly legs. You might be fortunate enough to see a golden eagle soaring over a clear mountain lake outlined by white birch trees that reflect themselves in the clear blue water. What about the fresh fragrant scent of mountain laurels, their petals dripping from the fresh morning dew? To stand on a mountain top and to feel the churning wind as it works it's way up from the valley below, blowing gently against your face. If you were to hold your hand out, you could feel the warm hand of God touch you and after the Heavens had quenched the thirst of the great forest below, a golden rainbow would cast a glow of beautiful colors silhouetted against the dense foliage surrounding it. Yes, the love of nature and all living things - not to harm but to help, not to destroy but to build, and above all, to love and not to hate. To have a feeling like this is like being given a priceless gift.

Robert C. Welch

"That's My Mother"

A simple girl from a big city;
That's my mother.
A hard life but a wonderful wife;
That's my mother.

I have no doubt
she could make dreams come true.
Somebody like no other —
That's my mother.

Great big dreams
with no one to share.
Did she even know
if there was someone to care?

A lady that raised four children;
sometimes on her own.
Some say unsuccessfully,
but we know better at home.

Those four kids are almost grown;
some should even be gone.
But it is hard to leave a wonderful person.
That person — That's my mother!

Debra Sutphen

Untitled

When your time is up you'll be a bright shining star,
Your friends will love you no matter where you are.
You'll always be here within our heart,
Nothing, not even death, can make us apart.
You'll never be forgotten, but please try to see,
That death is not a bad thing, just a new place to be.
A safer, more happier place is where you're at,
Your friends and loved ones now realize that
When our time is up, we'll be able to say,
Everything we had forgotten, up to this very day.
We are not leaving you, so please don't cry,
Right now its just time to say goodbye.

Lesli Griekspoor

Taking the Moments Away

As with the moon to the earth and the sun to Jupiter, all relative to the size and order of things that characterize the universe, we huddle within the untamed masses, to be but a few from Earth's family of many livin' things; and yet in the inheritance of life abode, we have been given the unparalleled gift of knowledge, which reign us supreme over all others;

As in the blueprints of an inventor, to the dreams of a dreamer, as conceived by one or the other; to which the evolution of steam power to nuclear power, from the depths of the seas through the travels of space, quantitatively distinguish those of rags from those of riches, to become more of less relative to someone or another;
As with the raw indignities of earth-wide tyranny, that famine and disease forecast sudden death;
As in the entanglements of intolerance and consensus, and of conscience and persecution; as with the pressure to give birth to one, or deny the life of another;

Where with dwindlin' space from which uncertainty preoccupy our consciousness, and as Earth's population swell to explode in numbers, and the elderly becomes of age to gray longer, it seems that impulsive choices will prevail to a greater degree; of which the inequitable notion of not belongin' nor of bein' wanted, or the fragilities of free-wheeling hypocrisy, may draw us closer together, or separate us to drift faster away ...

Willie McDaniel

Third Stone From The Sun...

Voices raised in hate
the battle lines are drawn
the end of man would be at hand
even before the dawn
the men in charge made the choice
the people no longer have a voice
a deadly fight for power
ignorance breeds the hate
but what is the prize?
the certain demise of the human race
the survivors left to rule on high
even the vast armies of the dead
on our home, third stone from the sun
in a wasteland once so beautiful
we rot for eternity
the wise leaders of the world
gave us this fatal gift
one that can never be returned.

Heather D. Wood

Memories of Yesteryears

As we reminisce of days of old
The beautiful memories, we dearly hold
With our family album opened so wide
Remembering way back when
As we laughed and cried
Here we are now
Our hair turning grey
One thing for sure, we truly can say
Our lives have been gratefully fulfilled
Now we can relax
But not forgetting our daily pills
We have earned the enjoyment
Of our golden years
With the love and sorrows of memories
We hold so very dear.

Billie Metros

Death Of An Old Man

As I see him in a rocking chair,
The cool cool wind is,
Howling and blowing through his
Silver Hair!
The old man remembers his youth.
Everything he has ever done,
All of the lies, and even the truth.
He began to close his eyes,
His heart grew faint,
He put an end to all of his cries.
As he pulled me close and squeezed
My hand, I never forgot,
The death, of an Old Man!

Charles J. Hainline

Untitled

Call of the spirit
The eagle circles,
The wind blowers,
On that sad day when the horse
Want to fast,
Everybody mourned for her touch,
All is silent,
accept for the cry of the wolf

Elisa Kosbab

Without Warning

In the darkness of early morning
The earth shook and rolled.
Awakened from a deep and peaceful sleep,
Words cannot express the fear and panic.
The creaking and cracking
Seemed to ring in our ears for days.
Fear and depression would not let go.
Darkness brought a new wave of terror;
Daybreak seemed eons away.
Suddenly nature's fury relented.
Daylight appeared in the heavens,
Bringing the gift of a new day.

Jeannette Gobus Lamoutte

My Two Siamese Twins

Mao Mee
the evil one.
She will slash you
with her blood stained claws.
When he picks her up
he gets slashed.
When she picks her up
pain comes her way.
But when I pick her up,
I feel love.
Gismo,
the blood princess.
She will give pain
too and only too the evil.
When he picks her up
she hisses at him,
When she picks her up
she runs away,
When I pick her up,
I become loved

Aisha Rios

My Special Three

My children are my life,
The expressions of my love.
They mean so very much to me
They are my special three.

Only I will ever know
How very much my heart grows,
As all the years pass,
The memories will always last.

Each year they grow stronger,
Pretty soon needing me no longer.
So very proud I will always be,
As the future takes them away from me.

Please God, Let them see,
I am always there for them to need.
Give them strength to carry on,
And always know that they belong.

They are my life - all of me.
My days are filled with them.
They mean so very much to me,
They are my special three.

Carolyn R. Houlihan

Spring Happiness

Spring is here.
The flowers appear.
The birds begin their song.
Life is a joy to a girl and
a boy all day long.

Dripping ice cream cones
and pretty spring tones
all season long.
It gets so hot that we go for a swim
and stay there 'till the sun get's dim!

Jessica Grigalunas

Quiet Reflections

I love to lie and watch the sky;
The fluffy white clouds as they
Float by,
The sun through the trees
The birds on the breeze
Dipping and soaring high.

My thoughts seem to fly
Like the birds in the sky
Wandering ever so far;
To the places I've been,
To all of my friends,
And to times not yet arrived.

And when the hour comes
To get up and go home,
I linger just for a while
To reflect on the things
That this beautiful day brings,
Such as joy and peace to my mind.

Janet T. Boyer

Born Free

Listen man I didn't ask
to come here
Or pay the price of life
My battle's never won.
The fight I must survive
'Cause I'm supposed to be
born free.

Bernadine Fillmore

"The Great I Am"

The newness of each morning,
The fragrance after the shower,
Makes me know there is a loving God,
And marvel at His power.

The mountains that rise to meet the sky,
The rivers and streams that trickle by,
Were put in place by God's own hand,
And can never be done by any man.

God spoke this world into being,
He is still in full control,
He gave His life a ransom,
For every living soul.

He is the great "I AM,"
He is the one that holds the key,
To life and death and all eternity.

Cliffie R. Hubert

Leaves

When winter is near
The frost comes
like fingers
of icicles
Stealthily? I think not!
Only on time
Like windmills spin
and rhymes rhyme
and around we go
The sap in the tree
gets sleepy
And the world is red and gold
and brown
And then the snow
makes a blanket
for the leaves on the ground

Janet Faulkner

Ode to Memories

Spring, whence begins
the growing of seeds
As wonders of nature
begin to nurture and feed.

Their continuing growth,
the forming of trees,
As they tower thru summer
with their beautiful leaves.

Whence the coming of the Autumn,
the leaves begin to brown,
As they flutter thru the wind
till their ebbing reaches ground.

Swept into the corners of the world
under winter's flaking tomb,
Then drawn within the resting voids
of time's eternal womb.

Blain Allen Bohag

Behind The Face

The mask behind the face
Travels forward to a place
A place forgotten in the future
Hidden behind the face
The face forced to endure
A never winning race
A race only for the classical
Who marvel the masked face

Alex

Forever Long

If your stop to ponder inquires...
The how,
The what,
The why.

Then ask yourself to answer these...
Why must the children die?

Is it fate or destiny?
This for which I have no clue.

This can not be the End for them,
Is there nothing we can do?

How can we stop the endless cries...
of empty bellies and shattered lives?

What type of life is this we lead?
full of death and endless greed.

Why can't we stop this pain?
think of the lies for which we'll gain.

These Children have done nothing wrong,
yet — their sentence — is...
forever
long.

Audrey I. Berry

Depression

I would love to have a childhood,
The kind I'd never had,
With purity and innocence,
Where nothing's ever bad.

I would love to have a romance,
Where pain is not required,
And in the morning I would not wake
Always feeling very tired.

I would love to have one moment,
Without this binding shame,
So I could hold my head up high,
And be proud of who I am.

But all of this I've mentioned,
Is far beyond my reach,
For while among the living,
I'll know nothing but my grief.

Bonnie Andrews

Precious Child

If ever I forget to tell you of
the laughter that you've
brought within my soul;
Let me say now that you are
the star that brings me light;
you keep me going
whenever I've lost hope.
You are that special blessing
that He saw fit to let me keep.
If at times I seem unfair with
the restrictions I impose,
simply grow with me, since I've
never traveled this path before.
If at times you stumble off
that straight and narrow line
remember that I'll pick you up
oh precious child of mine.

Ann Vazquez

A Fall Day

The air turns crisp
The leaves change to
crimson and light shaded brown
They flutters gently to the ground
A different smell with in the air.
The birds in loud and plaintive cry.
In flocks begin to Southward fly.
The fields of green turn
and become Stark and Bare.
The flowers begin to fade and die.
As fall is soon to be replaced
by winters snowy face.

Brandy Andrews

Classical

Classical,
The lilting golden strands
Of a composition by Bach; Music.
Classical,
The soft glow of sun upon a leather cover,
Binding the words which survived ages.
Classical,
The rosy skin and velvet eyes,
Framed by copper beech curls; Beauty
Classical,
The mahogany desk, waiting, dustless,
With shiny fountain pen.
Classical,
The old man, with wispy white hair,
Rough, weathered skin,
And smiling grey eyes;
Which have seen the ages.
Classical
Those withstanding.

Ann Benton

No More Childhood Dream

The day has been black
The night can't even be seen
My fears are on their attack
I've lost my childhood dream
I've ran but never traveled far
With my shadow still behind
Who carries my ever growing scar
With my grieving emotions still inside.
The dream I'm dreaming now
Is to see the day shine blue
Discover the love I need some how
To feel my running is finally through
To let my eyes rest every night
To wake up to the morning light gleam
Which shines the whole day bright
Would be better than my childhood dream.

Christopher Cohen

Changing Of The Seasons

The winter air is setting in
The nights are getting colder
She's sitting by the fire
With her head upon his shoulder
The nights are now becoming long
As the leaves blow from the trees
And love will warm the shivering -
And knocking of the knees
People will come together
No one knows the reason
For love will only last as long
Till the changing of the seasons.

Cindy Musarra

I Will Always Be There

As heaven sits in
the palm of my hand
I would give all the
world to be with you.

On the edge of
a wakening dream
I will always shelter
you from the pain.

When you close your eyes
and are scared inside
I am on your side
and forever there.

When your trapped
and can't find your way out
I will guide the way
walking hand in hand.

Your the reason I
Breathe, I
Live and I
Die.

Heidi Wilson

Rage

How can one really express
The rage that you see,
Is all rage visible
Is there rage in me.

Is it like a turbulent force
Raging through endless time,
Searching through emptiness
Without silence of any kind.

Can a pounding heart beat
And a tingling in the soul,
Be rage living in me
Or am I hiding a story untold.

The mixture of my fiber
The explosion of energy within,
Can it be a rage gone mad
Or is it a yearning for one to win.

Is there rage in everyone
That is calmed by inevitable love,
When the storm of life is raging
Gentle peace rules rage to annul.

Ada C. Morris

The Tears On My Pillow

He doesn't see the tears on my pillow.
The secret that each one contains.
Every little drop has a story of its own.
All tell of something different - yet
the same.
Of something new - yet old.
Each one wants him to see the
story it tells.
So that he may know all the secrets
they hold.
Then he will see just how much I
love him.
And he will know how deep those
feelings go.
Maybe then he will wipe away
the tears on my pillow.

Jolie Lislegard

A Midsummer's Eve

Silver sparkles twilight sends
The sky a purple hue
The midnight hour never ends
When I'm alone with you

The gentle whisper of the breeze
Floats softly through the air
Sweet scent drifts from flowering trees
A summer's eve that's fair

Together we view the darkened sky
Our eyes are filled with awe
A flashing light goes streaking by
I'm shocked by what we saw

There's turbulence within my heart
There's pounding in my head
Mixed emotions spin in parts
That gather shades of red

Anthony J. Rego

My Special Place

Mesas tower on the horizon,
the song of a stream is heard,
And into the tree above me,
to his nest, flies a bird.

Indian paint brushes
in the sun, are all aglow.
Upon my face and through my hair
A gentle wind does blow.

Bluebonnets and honeysuckle
reach into deep blue skies.
And from somewhere beneath the sun,
fly a thousand butterflies.

For me this is a special place,
where only I can go.
Many are the happy memories here,
that only I can know.

Emma Garrison Smith

The Squirrel

There is a chill in the air.
The squirrels are gathering nuts.
Their tails wiggling madly,
As they dig and make ruts.
Some nuts go up the tree,
Others go in the ground.
They prepare for winter,
Hardly making a sound.
They are fun to watch,
As they scamper and run.
All their hard work,
Looks like a lot of fun.
How can people hunt squirrels,
And kill them to eat?
You can see at a glance,
They don't have much meat.
Sit and watch the squirrels.
Relax as they work and play.
Their antics will make you smile,
And brighten your entire day.

Daniel D. Howell

The Dreamer

The moon shown bright.
The stars gave light
When they came forth at night
In days of long ago.

Those nights were dear to me
As I sat beneath the tree
With life happy and carefree
When I was a boy.

On the crest of the distant hill
I could hear the whippoorwill.
The frogs down by the old mill
Filled the air with song.

Again, I sit upon the hill,
And with my heart to fill,
My thin body feels the chill
From many days of toil.

I dream of the coming day
When I am taken far away.
It is then I will hear Jesus say,
"Welcome home, my child, welcome
home."

Clinton E. Riddle

Life's Refrain

The breeze was blowing gently
The sun shone softly down
The Autumn leaves were turning
From gold to darker brown.

The lady in her bedroom
Was drawing her last breath
But a fleeting thought passed her mind
As she entered into death.

The plants, flowers and people
Are so very much the same
They grow they bloom then fade away
A verse from life's refrain.

Emily Addison Edgeworth

A Daughter:

Is the joy of life
the sweetness of the best tasting
wine; the very beauty of the
God given day; the very breath
of the Precious winds that blow.

A daughter is the sunlight
of a smile; the tear of a sad
song. A daughter is the daddy's
own dream and a Mom's
own virginity; a daughter is
a sacred stone never to
be left alone.

Thank - you Lord for a daughter
to call my own!

Debra Anne Knaak

Untitled

Some say that they were just
too perfect for this world
to die so young they did
So brave they must have
been. Never to see adulthood
for they died too soon.
Never to have children they fell too young,
too soon.

Andrea Sheppard-Brick

One Flag for All Nations

Each country has its colours
The symbol of its might.
Each country sings its anthem
And for its flag would fight.

One day a flag of colours
Will fly in every land -
The world will be its symbol
And for each country stand.

A dove of peace the centre -
A golden circle earth -
The cross for balanced payments
The signature of worth -

The triad of the earth plane
Of body, mind and soul -
The colours of the rainbow
Will merge behind the whole

May this dream not be a mirage -
May this prayer of hope come true
When the flag of every country
Is shared by me and you

Cecilia S. R. Rogers

The Misunderstanding

Why can't you hear
the things I hold dear?
Why won't you see
what life means to me?
Oh, how can I communicate
that it's not too late?
That it is meant to be....
a life together for you and me.

You have closed your mind
to enlightenment of any kind
on why and how we can mend
this relationship sure to end.
Please, my love, look around
and you'll find what I have found,
That it is meant to be....
our lives together, just you and me.

Carole L. Atkins

The Sunset of Life

The setting sun carries with it
The thought of the day which has past
The end of the day has beauty
And that is what once sees last

The greatest artist paints the sky
And sunset time is here
As this day draws to its close
We feel your presence near

You seem to be around us
The colorful closing draws nigh
In our solemnity, we will seek
To search for the reason why

God grant us faith to perceive
This sunset in a different way
Not as the end, but rather
The remembrance of a beautiful day

May the colorful sunset of your life
Always dawn upon my face
Reminding me that sun only sets
To rise in another place.

Heather D. Clough

When Gone

I sense the sadness in your dreams,
The tilt of your thought,
When you are away,
Missing the reality of touch,
Though near in heart.

When you return, I sense
Your voice, your smile,
Though tears of aloneness
Glisten on my cheek,
Like the bud of morning rose.

Tomorrow's dreams, I sense,
Will bring joy to you,
Even though apart,
And from your love,
Absence becomes the dream.

Herbert T. Smith

Another Year

You turn around and then it's gone
The time flies by so fast;
The youth you took for granted
Is now a memory of your past.
Another year - It just can't be
How quickly they appear;
Like the sun rising in the morning
Over a lake that once was clear.
Memories held deep within
Are kept in silk and lace;
And special thoughts of days gone by
Are to help me keep the pace.
Another year - It just can't be
How quickly they appear;
It seems like only yesterday
When my youth and I were near.

Gale M. Mazur

Porcelain Throne

The King stirs to contemplate,
The urge in him to hesitate.
But he must go where nature calls,
He wonders down the cold dark halls.

He quickly enters his private realm,
And sits upon his throne.
While reading dated manuscripts,
And issues mournful groans.

This throne is like all others,
In kingdom's far and wide.
It's where his majesty,
Often goes to hide.

The throne is like kingdom,
Over which royalty resides.
It's oh so pretty to look upon,
But full of shit inside.

Are toilets like the world we know?
Dressed to please the eye.
Yet, in the end, the purpose known,
We flush our lives Good-bye!

Jerald Schierling

Patchwork Land

The leaves rustle gently,
The wind feels cool against my face.
Trees sway with the breeze,
Wreath of soft, green lace.

Mountains go rolling on forever,
With veil of cold, gray sky.
Laurel blooms, trillium pink,
Golden eagles cry.

Soar on lofty wings of glass,
Against the patchwork land.
Tossed and turned the breezes blow,
Through immortal feeding ground.

Lift me up,
Over mountain, stony, soil
Where spirits unheeding, roam,
And farming ancestors toil.

Audrey Rinehart

Beyond the Desert

Beyond the desert lies the mountains,
Their purple majesty rising high;
Their ragged cliffs and jumbled rocks,
Hidden by our distant eye.

The morning sun, it's rays caresses
The mountain tops and sides so dear;
The noonday heat makes waves a-dancing,
And makes the hills so far so near.

But when the evening shadows come,
And close of day draws nigh the rest;
The Immortal Artist paints a picture,
That gladdens the eye as being the best.

Beyond the desert lies the mountains,
Beyond the drab a beauty there;
Beyond the heat a picture perfect,
Beyond Arizona my love so dear.

Janice L. Powell

Rose

In the veins of a rose
There are millions of tears
From the joy and pain of life

The joy: is for all the new life,
Love of happiness and memories
Of a past worth remembering

The pain: is for the sorrow of
loss and of the heart ache
That comes with it

Hopefully the tears of joy will
Overpower the pain
And the sorrow fade
But the memories of joy stay

Allison Diggett

The Baby

I saw this baby on the beach
with skin so very rough
Large protruding eyes that
Made her look quite gruff

A row of bony teeth and
A long gruesome smile
But that's not really bad...
For a baby crocodile

Harvey P. Smith

Morning Serenity

Beyond the darkness
There glows a light
The morning sun has come
To steal the night
Shades of purple
Replace the midnight blue
The sky is splashed with light
The grass is splashed with dew
Creatures begin to stir
And birds begin to sing
Nature feels a coming warmth
A new day is dawning.

Eric L. Snyder

Metal

Forty foot tall and full of hate
These machines will seal man's fate
With gatling gun and metal fists
Human flesh they tear and twist

Marching with their pounding feet
They grind the living into meat
Nothing can pierce their metal skin
Armageddon shall now begin

Black smoke and screams begin to rise
From the cities brutalized
Underneath the blackened sky
The tortured earth begins to die

Looking back at years gone past
The human race could never last
Building their machines of war
To kill each other by the score

And now the earth aglow with fire
Serves as mankind's funeral pyre
Although machines have scorched this land
Man has died by his own hand

George Dieterle

"Sounds of Summer"

I love the sounds of summer,
they are music to the ear,
Kinda makes me wish I was young again,
But there's no turning back the years!
I hear the children's laughter
As they play in the evening sun,
And the dogs frantic barking
As they join in the fun!
I hear the birds a singing
their sweet melodies,
Bringing back fond memories
that never more will be.
yet should these sounds begin to fade
with the March of Father time,
I still will always hear them
If only in my mind.

Cecil B. Pipkin

Untitled

I used to root for losers
Who only strove to lose.
Then I turned to winners
Because I needn't choose.
But, winners turned to losers.
They lost despite the cost.
Now, I root for no one.
I cannot bear the loss.

Jane Burch

Just Words

In the dark the shadows chime;
They speak from some forgotten time;
Like an old familiar rhyme;
but with the silence of a mime;

Some penciled words upon a page;
A single turn can bring them rage
Like a beast trapped in a cage
they devour up this simple stage

Through clever thought a message send
To move around and back and bend
Their possession alone we cannot lend
They move across the sea like wind

In birth and death and tragedy
Are we ever what we're born to be
As if we're blind and cannot see
They whisper now our dreams to be

Christian S. Vaughn

The Zebra

As I stare at his stripes,
they start to blend together
They mix and become,
a gray
The gray of a rainy day,
sad and meaningless
I wonder if this animal,
can see me
What is this creator thinking,
that my colors blend together—maybe
They must have feelings,
they must love and hate
They must need,
and want
Someday the zebra will gallop away
and leave me staring
into the distance

Denylle Lagasse

My Black Man

They say good black men do not exist
they're liars, cheats and thugs.
There's one black man upon my list
who should be spoken of.

A big, strong guy with chocolate skin,
full lips as sweet as wine.
It makes me very glad to know
that he is mine all mine.

He made a sacred vow to God
to love and honor me.
Devotion is his strong suit
I admire his loyalty.

I trust in him with everything
My child, my love, my life.
He has become a part of me
I am lucky to be his wife.

My heart discovered him by chance
He was closer than I thought.
A good black man, hard to find?
I really do think not.

Carolyn A. Dennis

What's Happening to the World Today

Times are changing,
Things go bad.
To look at the world,
It's pretty sad.

Kids on drugs,
Thinking they're cool,
Destroying their brains,
They're nothing but fools.

Jobs are scarce,
And poverty high.
People living on the streets,
I only ask why.

Countries are fighting,
Throughout the lands.
If only there was peace,
And people stood hand and hand.

Times are bad,
Goodness is rare.
If only we could all stand together,
And say the Lords Prayer.

April Haggard

Writing This

I just ramble all this off,
thinking of the moments lost.
I could have written a song,
or mowed my God-forsaken lawn.
I could have watched the tube,
or gone to the pool.
So much I could have done
this is just a break,
to have some real fun.
Enjoy this thoughtless work
it came straight from the heart.
As you read, you forget
all the time I wasted,
writing this
oh well, like always
opportunity passes me by.
By writing this
I'm taking one? (opportunity)
or letting one slip away,
either way, I guess, it's okay.

Justin Rogers-Cooper

Untitled

The monster emerges
This is his night.
He sees a small child
With his fading sight.

He lures the child to him,
Then takes him by the hand.
They disappear into the trees.
That night neither one is seen again.

In the woods the next day,
A small child is found,
A bullet through the head,
Yet no one heard a sound.

A witness to this execution
There surely must have been.
Letting this person kill again
Is nothing short of sin.

Brenda Bridgman

Lonely

I sleep alone tonight why is
this? Is it because you left on
such short notice? No it's because
you found someone new! The things
that I would have done for you!
If only you knew! These feelings
roam around in my head like circles,
The lightest touch of your hand
would set off a spark! But I sit here
and think about what could have
been. But you're just a memory now
and I know it will never happen,
The thoughts have not gone yet
But my love grows weaker and
weaker day by day! So now
I sit here lonely as ever thinking
of what could happen instead of what
would happen, I'm just a lonely
person now, I thank you!

Gina Campbell

LSD in a Lift

Nerves torment all through
this trip unkind.
Purple, orange, yellow, blue
hues dye my mind.

Amber button twenty is depressed,
cocoon-like I ascend.
Hum-thrum, vroom-zoom's the best
way for me to fend.

I birth breach my metal shell
To flit to the ledge,
Goggle down the maw of hell
Far below its edge.

Eight cylinder ants inch along,
naked neon notches night.
City sounds sing sinister song
to accompany my flight.

I know that man can fly,
for I live the dream!
A "Monarch" takes to sky
Just one long scream.

George B. Williams

Untitled

If you had ever looked at me with
those green eyes filled with love,
I would always see the stars and skies
All in the heavens above.

You would sleep with me at night
and still my quiet tears.
You always helped me through everything,
even calming my greatest fears.

Now I hope you went to heaven
and are not lying in hell.
For all the things you have done for me,
I will always wish you well.

Angela Olkey

"Let Me Go On...Dreaming"

Let me go on...dreaming,
Though never reach the goal...
Joy is in the waiting...
As you enrich your soul!...

Let me go on...dreaming,
As long as I can think,
Let me love forever:
The words that make me sing!...

Let me go on...dreaming,
Of friends I've yet to meet...
Walk, and talk with old ones,
On the phone, or in the street!...

Let me go on...dreaming,
Though my legs move slow,
My mind is an overtime...
As hopefully... I glow!.....

Angelina Pavese

Reaching Out

As you reached for my hand,
time stood still.
I felt so drawn to you
against my very will.
Years of friendship have
sealed our past.
Can we obtain another type of
relationship that will forever last?
Feelings for you have been locked
in my soul for years,
That now when I look at you
I can smile in spite of my tears.
One major obstacle stands
in our way,
So I am not able to tell you
about all my feelings this day.
My voice has been silenced
and we are apart,
But the words of this poem are
reaching out to your heart.

Cathy S. Gann

The Innocent

The innocent,
Tiny victims of the pain and punishment,
In so many prayers I've asked Him why.
Why do the children have to cry
For the thoughtless anger here?
Why are there those who justify,
Can you help them?

"What is was meant"
No, I don't understand at all.
Can't rules be bent?
So tender the life that has to fall.
Why do the children have to die
For the thoughtless violence here?
If there's a place where answers lie,
Let us find them.

'Cause when they laugh, we don't know them.
When they cry, we can't hear at all.
When there lost, we can't find them.
We just count them,
We just count them all.

Craig D. Lindhorst

Untitled

A map is the key
To a lock of confusion
Sit back with some tea
Save that mind that you're use'n
Just get out a map
And save you some time
Stop all that yap
It won't cost you a dime
So listen to me
And stop all your lose'n
'Cause a map is the key
To a lock of confusion

Angela Birchfield

You And I

It is always such a pleasure,
To be with you for a little while.
To share some conversation,
And to sometimes make you smile.
It seems to me a sorry thing,
That times together are few,
When it's so much pleasure being there,
Sharing some thoughts with you.
I think of you so often,
And I hope you do the same.
I picture your face and see your smile,
I feel pleasure just saying your name.
Our moments live in my memory,
And you know, time really does fly.
Soon, I hope, we can be together again,
To build more memories, You and I.

Dick King

Restoreth My Soul

Warm hope reaches out
To calm the delicate savagery
That rages within the tattered
Remains of my consciousness.

Hope, sent forth by caring souls
Weaving a tender web
Of protection, to repel thoughts
That could incite destruction.

Thoughts that flaunt through
The depths of debris,
Sanctimoniously seeking control
While projecting their devious battles.

But the featherduster of love
Held in the hand of a praying heart
Can overcome, sweep clean and restore
The vilest conflict, through faith.

Carrie Brady

Cry of the Bitter Wind

A bitter wind blows
To chill my aching heart.
I gave you my love,
My innocence,
In my young years.
I was too naive to know
That love and understanding
Could not be found with you.
And bitter tears fall
For all the unhappy years
I gave to you.
Now I have loneliness
But I am free
Of the cry of the bitter wind.

Eleanor B. Everett

Our Life

Three score and ten is what we have
to cultivate his plans
Of what we are and what we do
Are guided by his hands
There are so many things to do
from the cradle to the grave
From childhood on you'll find that you
Have wanting as well as craves
"I've done it all" I answer
As though it were a whim
But stop and ponder for a while
"Did I succeed because of Him?"

Donald Thurston

Time Marches On

It now takes twice as long
To do just half as much.
What is going wrong?
Are we out of touch?
Or could it possibly be
That years crept up on you and me?
The hearing is not so keen,
The eyes no longer gleam.
The hands tend to cramp,
When the weather is damp.
Often there's an ache in every bone,
And the halls have longer grown.
It now takes forever to get back home
Where we can sit and dream
About when we were a teen.

Gladys Stockl

You Think You Have Forever

You think you have forever
to do the things you want to do.
You want to say the things
you feel inside of you. You make
your plans for the future and each day
Before you know it everything,
fades away, and you don't have one
more day.
You feel so blue it just isn't
you. What else would you do? This
is the story of you sad and true.

Antoinette Nalezyty

Good-bye

To be held in his arms again
To feel his gentle lips
Against mine one last time
To hear his words of love
Or just a simple good-bye
Or to answer my question
Why? Why then? Why that way?
Could we have worked it out

I guess it's time
To expect the fact
That he ain't coming back.
I'll never be in his aims again
I'll never feel his gentle lips
Or hear his words of love
Never get my question answered

I guess that was his good-bye
I'll always wonder
If he's thinking of me
But for now here is my goodbye.

Jackie Sherry

"Sitting In My World"

Why was I put into this world?
To feel the pouring rain
To sit in my world, so all alone
So full of hate and pain.

No one cares,
I'll have to make it alone
Sitting in my hate-filled world
With a heart of cold cruel stone.

I can no longer feel the pain
I no longer really care
Sitting in my world of apathy.
Never going anywhere.

Now I'm as cold as steel
I can no longer feel hurt's cruel bite
Sitting in my isolated world
Staring into the cold dark night.

I never feel joy and happiness
I'd rather scream and cry
Sitting in my morbid world
Until the day I die.

Johnna Mathews

Christmas Savior

Christmas is a special time
to gather loved ones near,
to celebrate the birth of Christ,
with glad tidings of cheer.
We give each other gifts and sing,
glory hallelujah,
for on this day as God foretold,
was born the king of Jew(s).
He sent his son to live and die
that we through him might live,
so accept the gift of life,
which only God can give.
Christ is knocking on your heart
open up and let him in,
for Jesus Christ, the son of God,
will forgive us all our sin.
So as you celebrate Christmas
with all you holiday trim,
remember the reason for the season.
Have you opened your heart to him?

Jenine A. Low

Deceased

There is no memorial for me
To go to release my sorrow
I cannot return to a remembrance
Made of stone
To unleash my anger at the unfairness
Of this untimely death
I am not able to bring flowers
To the remains of that which is gone
Cannot reminisce
Over material objects
The good times or the happiness
Of what once flourished
In its short life span
No marble statue after this passing

It is only the death
Of your once sweet love

Jamie L. May

Falling

My journey started, I chose to escape
to look for you - to stop some hate
I don't know what happened
to living life and being glad
We were together it makes me sad
To see your face
It shows your thoughts
True to life, your guilts are caught
Did you want me? Yes you did
Did we come together?
No, I think we fell apart

Amanda L. Parish

The Innocent Stranger

A bundle of joy, that's who you are.
To many faces, you have brought smiles.
Though small, frail, and vulnerable.
Naked in our eyes.
Fully clothed in God's eyes.
Calmly wrapped and laid down.
Strangers we both are — in this world
Yet we see us in you, and you in us.
Your first cry, is our joy
As innocent as a drifting snow,
In the midst of sinners all.
All delighted you are here.
As one battle ends, so begins another,
Heading into a turbulence and cold world.
Yet determined to conquer.
A winner, you once are —
Well equipped for the battle ahead —
Only if enemies let be.
As we cherish this moment —
We can't help but ponder the future.

David Shominure

Lost Innocence

A sad time it is
to mourn a loss.
A death of twenty-two,
four and so innocent.

We were best friends until then
they called him Davey,
just like Davey Crocket,
which father called him.

Until my innocence was torn away,
like a twister ripping a tree,
root and all out of the Earth.
Twenty-two years a time gone by.

It's better they say,
what's better I ask?
No matter it's forgotten now.
Just never mind those days gone by.

So scared to know the truth
of all the greatest of lies
it's just a twisted dream of evil
only he lived thank God not I!

David Doctor

To My Love

Farewell! Farewell!
To my summer love.
It may be our last time
To say goodbye.
For what life thee has meant to me.

She is more golden, than the sunlight
on a beautiful summer's day.

And more beautiful than,
Springs May flowers.

For she is... my first love.

Greg "Bone" Bohnert

A Trip Down Memory Lane

I took a trip down Memory Lane,
To places I have been;
Met my good deeds and my sins.

Back through many years, came face
to face with my joys and my tears;
Saw much I regret.

I saw the pleasant things in my past.
Also the fear, anger and strife;
all a part of my life.

I do not grieve for what has been,
Today is mine in joy or sorrow,
In no past pain will I wallow,
No future pain will I borrow.

Past and future, joy or pain,
not in the flesh, but in the mind.
Memories past and hopes to be,
The choice is up to me.

Stepping stones of joy or pain,
Raise me to a higher plain.
I leave Memory Lane in the past;
To live this day is all I ask.

Diane Gallegos

"Feelings Of You"

I find myself looking forward
to seeing you each and everyday.
Each time I see you my heart
turns to dust.

In my dreams you are by my
side.
I am lonely in reality.
I am wishing you would save me
from my loneliness.
But only in my dreams you will
save me.
Never, in reality.

Dana Jay Smith

Passions

Passions need constant tending.
They are the threads of souls mending.
We push away,
Keep love at bay,
And all we have are endings.

I kept my passions by the door.
They gathered dust and were no more.
In reflection I see,
Passions like unwanted children,
Flee

George Ann Wishon

His Class Ring

Close by the door he stopped
to stand; as he took his
class ring off her hand.

all who were watching did
not dare to speak, as a
silent tear ran down his cheek

All through his mind memories
ran of the moments they
laughed and played in the sand

how her eyes looked cold,
he'll never again have her to hold.

they watched in silence as
he bent down near, to whisper
"I LOVE YOU" soft in her ear.

While touching her face he
started to cry, put the ring
on and wanted to die.

just as the wind started
to blow, they lowered her
casket deep in the snow.

Angela Korabek

"Sweet Surrender"

Sweet surrender
To that certain smile,
To eyes that illuminate the soul,
To a song of love, by chance.
To imagined ecstasy,
To unimagined fulfillment.

Sweet surrender
To a small hand extended.
To, "Mom, can I, please?"
To a chocolate cake for charity.
To volunteer at the nursing home,
To comforting someone slipping away,
To tears at their passing.

Sweet surrender
To a son going off to war,
To a daughter as she weds,
To a grand child's bright smile.
To all that life had to offer,
To all that you gained along the way,
To eternities bliss.

Deborah Faulks

Untitled

Rural welcome sign.
To the speckled grass
in which
your rusted legs
of iron
are pitched for the stranger.
To your white crumbling paint
facing the sun
several hours a day,
and a shade branch.
To your honest black print.

Craig Douglas

The Daisy

I prefer the daisy
To the tulip or the rose
Because it's independent
In the way it swiftly grows.

A daisy isn't confusing
And yet it isn't plain;
Representing simple beauty
Yet strong to withstand rain.

And when I think about it
Clearly I come to see;
A daisy is like many,
Individual as can be.

Brianna Marie Keilar

Life Is Just A Span

God gives to us a brief time
To walk this earth below.
To do our best to serve Him
Before it's time to go.

What we do with our life here
Is written down up there.
God keeps his books in order
So, friend, please have a care

Love your neighbor as yourself
Take time to lend a hand.
When he's fallen, lift him up
Until he learns to stand.

If he falters walk with him
Your strength will see him through.
Just as we in weaker times
Depend on God's strength too.

Our time here is just a span
Our life He'll one day sever.
Then we'll walk beyond the blue
To live with Him forever.

Amy Stoler

Endless Skies

Are we free
to wonder why
when we all see
is but endless sky
and distant stars
that tease our thought
then leave the scars
of lesson taught

How can we teach
or understand
when we can't reach
beyond our hand
to touch a soul
with-in its shell
or tears that roll
by a wishing well

Who are we, who laugh and cry
too blind to see, too young to die
withstand the pain and nix the sighs
to search the plains of the endless skies

Jesse Eaton

"Apology"

I'd like to take this chance,
to write a line or two.
to let you know how much;
I really do love you.
I know I haven't always been
the one you dreamt about.
I know that I have hurt you,
and filled you full of doubts.
So let me take this time
to show how sorry I am.
I'll try to be the person
that you deserve to have.
I love you so much more
than words could ever say,
that's why this apology,
comes to you today.

Gail Owen

Untitled

Today I walked another mile,
Today I smiled another smile.
Today I cried another tear.
Today I lived another year.

Without your face before my hand,
Without your hand to help me stand,
Without your love to be my guide
Without your right here by my side,

Today I failed in what I tried
Today I cried instead of smiled,
Today I wished with all my might,
That you'd be here again tonight.

Doris Grady

The Mother's Prayer

Oh Father, I'd like to ask you,
Tonight when I pray.
To answer this Mother's prayer,
In your tender loving way.

I pray tonight for my Children,
Heal their tender soul's
Keep them safe from harm Lord,
Restore health be it so.

The road of life is weary, Lord,
Help lighten my heavy load.
Oh father, when they were little,
That was so long ago.

Oh, Father, ease the heartbreak,
Give me strength from you.
Then I can be for my Children,
A pillar of your love too.

I'll close for now, sweet Jesus,
Oh, hear this Mothers prayer.
In the darkness of even hard times,
Oh God, I know your there.... AMEN

Donna Niedermeier

Words

Whisper high
Whisper low
Whisper in my ear just so.

Whisper words I want to hear
No matter what they be, for
they will linger in my ear
for all eternity.

Beth Napoleon

Untitled

As the moon is traveling swiftly
Toward an orange emblazoned sky
I lay and watch and wonder
A tear comes to my eye

The clouds are turning crimson
Floating slowly changing free
The Angels in the promised land
Are dancing over me

Guarding me from sorrow
Shielding me from pain
Waiting for me to let my heart
Just laugh and smile again

The silhouettes of sturdy trees
Standing century in the night
Are full of love strong promises
That all will be all right

The sun is all but gone now
This has been an awesome sight
The moon is shining brightly
To guide our spirits through the night

Brad J. Cloud

Comparison

Peace of mind is likened to
Tranquil waters; skies clear blue;
Peaceful 'til an ill wind blows,
Then, ah then, how fast it goes.

This endowment, seek and find,
Cherish and appreciate,
Joy in it while life is kind,
Ere fair tide too soon abate,
Leaving you perplexed, behind,
Restive for another fate.

This endowment, seek and find.
Beware lest you hesitate
Too long, before you enshrine
In your heart a gift so great,
And awake one day, to find
It gone, though you'd bid it wait.

Troubled minds are likened to
Wind-lashed waters; storms that brew;
Troubled 'til a fair wind reigns,
Yet the wreckage wrought remains.

Diana Behrens Swann

Grand Pa

Doughnut holes on doughnut days
Twins spirit all year round
Caring for your family
Or training another hound

My mom and all her siblings
Grandma your special wife
Everything is unique GrandPa
That you brought into my life

Concentrating on the good things
The memories you gave
Holding a place in time
For you it will be saved

When I look back upon the days
That you were still alive
I know that in my heart
You always will survive

I love you Grandpa.

Heidi Rademacher

Young Love

He strums his guitar -
under a shady tree.
She hums along -
Happy to be free.
He sings a song -
About the girl he loves.
She doesn't say "I love you"
But he knows that she does.
He looks into her eyes -
Now filled with joy.
She wonders why he plays with her heart
As if it were a toy.
He knows how she feels
But knows not what to do.
She wants to live her life with him.
But afraid of what he'll do.
He really does love her
Doesn't know why she feels that way.
He strums his guitar
But has nothing to say.

Catherine Amy Doldan

A Graveyard

Silhouetted spider legs
Upon a lichened grave,
Sitting there between a groove
Of dates that passed away.

Granite wears and still they lay
So silently beneath,
The lilies and the bleeding hearts
To comfort and to ease.

There are those that lie in leaves
Their graves have sunken in,
Where mother earth has grown so soft
And said, "please come on in."

The blanket from the evergreens
Pours gently down the sky,
And wraps round each and every grave
So they may sleep at night.

Erin Clements

Towards the Dawn

"In pensive mood I sat and gazed
Upon the clouds below.
Thoughtfully reviewing my lot,
Facing the eastern glow.

At 33,000 feet in space
Perceptions often seem to blur;
But thoughts of love and grace
Most frequently occur.

A blanket of clouds beneath
And rays of the rising sun
Combine to provide a treat
Both challenging and fun.

Travelling eastward
In the early light of day
One can truly feast
On nature's brightest ray.

So, shift your gaze from the depths of night
And fix your eyes on th'advancing morn
Prodding you gently towards the light —
And the brightness that follows the dawn."

Adrian T. Westney

White Swans Naked

You touched my breast and I fell soft
upon the shaded dandelion.
The old oak tree watched graciously,
as our legs became intertwined.
You kissed my lips like running streams
where lily pads lie soft and still,
and carved my name inside the tree
which guarded proud, the docile hill.
We gazed upon these bodies white
that ran and flew into the sun.
Making love upon each cloud
while we laid tranquil, so undone.
I held my breath, than grazed the grass,
and plucked a small rose looking on.
A breeze came in, her petals fell,
I turned and found that you were gone.
The bright sun parted suddenly,
my baron heart felt sudden chill,
I thought of how it used to be,
like white swans naked, running still.

Anna Maria Kline

Grafton, Ohio

Trains whistling
upon the tracks
As cars screech
and horns yell
Airplanes roar
when they go past
You could smell
the rain as it falls
Birds and chickens
Chirping as dogs bark
then hearing
ducks quacking
If you are really quiet
you can see
deer and rabbits
you could hear
the cars thumping
down the road
You could feel the
cool mist in the night.

Cathy Nieves

Untitled

You were once stately beings
Upright and strong
Who at times would shout...
Can now only hum a song
The elderly of today
Our parents of yesteryear
Whose advice on life
We seldom want to hear.
Now that you're growing old,
And cannot live alone...
Isn't it my turn, to give a home?
But now, in your "Golden Years"
When you should be treated like royalty
We often show the true extent.
Of our undying loyalty.
We no longer have the time
To give you "special care"
But when we needed it,
Weren't you always there?

Debera Ann Paschal

Old Warrior

In days gone by, you
Used to seize your fate...
Never a stranger to fame
You never had to wait.

Gone... Winning days, and prizes
Quick are the moments I dream...
The past revisited in happy recall
Enjoys much, upon waking, beams.

The lance and shield are put away
A rapid charge slowed down...
A serious walk replacing
A quickness to sit down.

My rusty box of memories
With pictures yellow from time...
Everything is wearing out
I age like a bottle of wine.

Bill Olesky

What's Up

Going home, I cant
wait, hope I'm not forgotten,
pray I'm not too late.
Watching the country
side slide by, thinking of you
makes me cry.
What has changed,
what part of my life has
been rearranged.
Does anyone think
of me? Not knowing what's
going on is driving me crazy.
I miss you, do you
miss me, when I get back I
guess I'll see.
I wish I was
there, does anyone care?
I hope the answer
is yes, I wish I weren't
so anxious!

Amber Evans

Our World God's World

Our world, God's world
Was it meant to be
Some bound by conflict
While others are free?

Our world, God's world
Was it meant to be
All bound by conflict
And nobody free?

God's world, our world
That means you and me.
Lord, grant us the grace
To help make it free.

Everyone free!

Geneva Kellon

The 90's

Bullet's flying everywhere,
watch your head and comb your hair,
kids catching everything,
parent's crying as they sing.
Guns on campus
what you say?
Knives cutting like filet.
90's kids who raise themselves,
Babies raising babies what the hell!
Crack, heroin, speedballs,
shooting needles in the arm.
Bodies laying on the ground,
Is there a pulse?
But no sound.
Parents watching as they play,
will they live another day,
trying make that paycheck stretch,
another bill they have to catch.
8 hour working days,
signs pointing "this way."

James Griffith

Our Lives Together

Fine day in July
Water warm - sunhigh
Handsome man - with grin
Meets girls in swim-
He say - "Me love" She coo like dove-
"Let's wed," he say she say "O.K"
Wedding bells - ring ring!
Honeymoon, everything
Settle down - married life-
Happy man - loving wife
Another day - mid July-
Hospital - baby cry-
Happy parents - little boy,
Fills our hearts with much joy
Five years later in July-
Again we hear, baby cry
Another son - joins our clan
Proud mother - happy man-
Sons Dale and Gary B
Have rounded out our family.

Ellie Brewen

Respect In Me

Respect.
We all say we need it.
We say we need it from others.
But what about ourselves?
Do I treat myself right?
Or is it someone else's voice
that seems to creep up,
Just to ridicule?
"Why wear that?
Doing that again?
Wait, does she approve?
Stop, does he like it?"
I think the only way
to even get respect from others
is to start by loving who we are.

Genevieve Ranieri

Ones Self Image

We are the product of our parents lives
We are created from our minds
Our chemistry we do create
Our souls do nothing to abate

The cross roads we travel
oh so alone
Our destiny calls us to come home
Imaginary creates of oneself
a picture capture in innocence
Put on a shelf
To just take one look
no one would know what is amiss
Politics of the heart
Shadows of bliss
Tangled webs to reminisce
We make us out to be what we are
The creators to do as we please
Being free to create a life of what we want
to be our self
Captured in the essence of our hearts

Christy L. Clark

"Lord, We Need Thee"

In these days of trouble and sorrow,
We call upon You, Lord.
Our souls are lost and hungry;
Feed us with Thy word.

Help us in our daily life
To do the best we can,
To show loving kindness
To all our fellow man.

Help us always wear a smile
And let a warm light glow,
So some lost soul might see it,
And come and want to know.

Just what it is that makes us shine
When they in darkness be.
We'll tell them they can see the light
By trusting, Lord, in Thee.

Brenda A. Trent

Remember the Holocaust

We all must remember
We can never forget
The pain, the suffering
the Death
All caused by
Hate, madness, and
Blame
Many died
Yet many lived
We must hear their stories
Feel their pain
We all must learn, be educated
About this torture
A fire must burn inside of us all
A fire of
Remembrance, knowledge, and
Prevention
So this will happen
Never again.

Jenni Grant

So Many, Many Times

We needed so much
we helped each other
so many, many times.

We comforted ourselves
little child; we tried
So many, many times.

We tried to be soft
we screamed in silence
So many, many times.

We still need
we try to comfort
So many, many times.

We scream not in silence
we scream from deep within
So many, many times.

This pain has buried itself
we need to see it
we need to comfort it..
So many, many times.

Christine Holley

See Me Grow

In September...
we meet
you are so
timid,
so shy
so excited.
As the year grows older
so do we...
we laugh,
we cry,
we learn together.
Each giving
Each taking...
And now it is June...
our time together grows
to an end...
our memories we carry in
our hearts
Forever...

Christine M. Young

"The Assistants"

Medicare - Medicaid
We need aide!
Aides, assistants, clerks,
Tutors, reading-math
Food service, health,
Detention, computers!
We worked for the board of Ed.
Now, we need to be fed!
Unemployment, S.S.I.
Social Security, Welfare who cares!
We put in our time
Now! We need the dimes! Who cares!
We, should march around the capital!
We, did our best for the child,
All the while! We, paid our dues!
So now, we are in the ranks;
Who gives us thanks!
Maybe one day you will meet
someone on the street!
They will say "Thank You!" I care!

Eleanor G. Paige

Life Cycles

Looking back upon our little lives,
We realize our petty strives.
Counting on one another-
But all alone, we soon discover.
Happy-Sad-Upset-Glad,
Angry-Hurt-Afraid -or Mad.
Life goes on- no time to spare,
So take a leap - if you dare.

We're all alone in this world,
'Round and 'round it will twirl.
Hold on tight-with all your might,
Another day-another fight.

Thoughts controlled by higher powers,
Possessions robbed by midnight prowlers.
It's a struggle to live in peace,
But don't give up-do not release.
Hope and joy-anxiety's toy,
Daily life-it's a ploy.
Life is here-it's here today,
So little time -just to play!!!

Dwight Gregory Jones

The Cosmic View

On a clear summer night
We scanned the star-studded heavens
With its complexity entwined.
In viewing the celestial dome
Our minds were filled with awe.
While we studied the starlit sky
and felt the thrill of wonderment,
As a streak of light flashed out—
And disappeared from sight;
It seemed as though the ARTIST,
Creator of all beauty,
Embroidered the heavens with diamonds
To reveal an immensity of love with
A message to this earthly realm.
Therefore, let this wondrous experience
Fill all hearts with jubilation
And capture these memories
As a treasured gift of life.

Helen Kroll, S.P.

Only Me

We hitched our wagon to a star,
We traveled near, we traveled far.

We had the moon, the sun, the stars,
We followed Jupiter and Mars.

We shared the days throughout the years,
The joys, the laughter, even tears.

We made a life
as a man and wife

We watched our progeny grow and grow,
Their love and caring gave us a glow.

We shared the sunshine and rainy weather,
We did all these things together.

We shared our lives from youth to old age,
The time now has come to turn the page.

Our star is in orbit and flying free
You unhitched our wagon and left without
me.

We are now no longer We,
My Love is gone,
there is only me.

June W. Morris

"He Was A Simple Man"

He was a simple man,
Well mannered and bred.
To all who dared to be his friend.
And loved ones, he shared his all to
them.

The race he just ran is not lost.
But was just won
His reward was sleep. A never ending
sleep.
Oh what a rejoicing there will be
if ever his awake.

Georgia Pern

A Dream

Am I a senior citizen?
Well, yes, I guess I am.
How I reached this venerable age
I'll never understand.

To me 'twas only just last year
I played with dolls and such;
So, how could I be eighty-three?
Am I confused that much?

And then about a month ago
I started going to school;
Enjoyed each day and learned so much,
You say I'm aging? Why, how cruel!

Just last week I married him,
A boy so good and kind;
I'm sure I'm in my twenties now,
Or have I lost my mind?

It's all a dream, I tell myself;
And time has fairly sped;
So guess I'll just forget my age,
And crawl back into bed.

Caryl Vyvyan

Good Grammar

What is a good grammar anyway
What does it mean?
Perhaps not using slang words
Or, do I have to orate clean?
If I say, Can I do it
When I know it should be "may"
What's the difference if I blew it
Tomorrow's another day.
Will they toss me in the clink
If I don't use real good grammar?
Or with they start to compare me
With Ice T or with Hammer.
Those rock group are making good money
Me? I'm only making scrap
So to hell with all that good grammar,
I'm gonna learn how to rap!

Elaine M. Sheahan

Leaving Home

Where are you going?
Why do you ask?

Are you ready for this?
Do you think it's too great a task?

Will you write?
Is there reason I shouldn't?

Why are you crying?
Did you think I wouldn't?

Anna Tait

Faith

I can't stand
What I can't have
Never knowing
the great feeling of love.

Faith can be there
someone who will care.
The constant staring
that will never go away.
But I will always want
him to stay in my heart
where he belongs.
My heart can only sing sad songs.

Give faith a thousand chances
and never up stand your stances.
For love will always be with you;
where your heart is.

Jeannie Murphy

What Life Would Be Like

I try to imagine
what life would be like
without the sound of your
voice, but all I do is cry.

I begin to think of the times
we shared, or the fights we had
and then how you were almost gone
forever without a warning.

I know sometimes I push and pry
it's just because I love you.
To imagine life without your smile,
Just breaks my heart in two.

Everything is different now,
I hardly think of when or how.
I try to imagine life without you,
But all I do is cry and cry.

Andrea Markham

My Unspoken Prayers

Oh, my precious Savior
What makes us so very blind?
What makes us do the things we do
Without you, Lord, in mind?
When things for us are going well
And all our cares are free
Why must we have the trials of life
Before we call on Thee?
When things are going our way
And we take credit for the good we do
Why can't we turn around and say.
The praise Lord, belongs to you
My trials my Lord seem many
Seem's there's nothing I can do
But than how little is my faith
I need but to call on you.

Beatrice A. Cheney

The Roses

White is the purity that was in you
Yellow is the friendship and the
friends you left behind.
Red is the love everyone showed
when you were around and now gone
No words can ever relieve the loss,
but the memories will always be there

Love Mom

Diana Roman

Priceless Gifts

What gifts can I give my mother?
What, to her, can I say?
She always has been there for me
In her own understanding way.
I'll give here a sincere hug
To show how much I care.
My mother offered much to life
By always being there.
I'll give some wildflowers like
I gave her as a child.
My mother has been so faithful;
She's loved me; shared her smile.
I'll confess to her that she
Was so often "right after all!"
I'll adore her as in childhood;
Always she was there when I called.
These inexpensive, priceless gifts
Are mine, and like none other;
It is I alone, who can give
These priceless gifts to my mother.

Elsie C. Hutto

If the Feather Could Speak

If the feather could speak
What would it say?
Courage - honor - conquer
The V. F. M. A. way
Lead by example
Reward, encourage, teach and counsel.
Always be worthy of emulation
Respect and guide with consideration
The feather would say this,
And the pips much more.
Do your best daily
Just as before.

Carroll Ann Funk

Christ Paid the Price

Christ paid the price
When He died on the cross
Can you imagine
How great the loss

To die as a sinner
When perfect as He
To take the sins
Of you and me

Of Him, you can stand in awe
For because of Him
We live under grace
Not the law

Can you imagine
How great the loss
When Christ paid the price
As He died on the cross

Jennifer Lynn Harlan (Jenn)

Untitled

'Tis the night to be happy
When at last I am with you
My thoughts are of you only
To be solely with you
To feel your arms around me
To touch your lips to mine
To have you come lovingly to me
To be lost in deep ecstasy
All alone with thee!

Helen M. Ashna

Bedtime Prayer

Often at night
When I go to bed,
I lie there thinking
Thoughts of you in my head.
If I ever do wrong,
or if I act bad,
If my heart is heavy,
or if I'm just sad,
A quick thought of you,
That's all it would take
To brighten my day
So my heart will not break.
If I close my eyes tight
To shut out this bad day,
If I just hold my hands
And my heart starts to pray,
If I think of your love
How you saved me from sorrow,
Lord, I'll just take your hand,
To give me strength for tomorrow.

Emily Kaufman

An Oak

At times
when I look back
There is this person
That's always there

I may have done
a lot of wrong
but that, first thought, of her
is one, that will, forever, be pure

And the wrong
that I, have done
is that I tried
to be a rose

When in fact
I am
an oak
At times when I look back

I found out
that I should of stood tall
but instead
I chose to fall

Joseph M. Parodi

Maybe If...

No one hears me
When I try and say
I'm crying.

No one hears me
When I say
I'm scared.

No one listens to me
when I say
I'm gonna die.

Maybe if someone would listen,
and not just to me
but to anyone in need
A soul wouldn't be left alone
to suffer and die.

People are too busy to care-
but they always stand and stare.

Dennis Keller

Always

Even when the pale moon fades away,
when the sun has gone to stay,
I will always love you.
We may fight and we may bicker,
we may say we hate each other,
but you and I both
know that through the barriers
of the world and the road
blocks up ahead we shall
always stay together,
because we love each other.
For you are my mother and I'm
your daughter and no matter
how much we grow apart
our hearts will keep us together.

Jeannette Hopster

Windy Day

Everyone's seen a windy day,
when the wind and trees
swing and sway,
looking like oceans play.

When the wind and trees make a
wispy sound,
as they cast their shadows
on the ground.

When the sun slowly sets,
but the trees are not wet,
for the wind has flown by
with the clouds in the sky,
leaving the trees cool but dry,
for the night has come.
and now my poem is done.

Alison C. Kennedy

A Fighting Chance

Why must we die,
when we can live?
Why must we fight,
when we can be happy?

Violence is bad,
not much is good.
But we can help,
help make peace,
in places like the "hood".

Violence is not rare
to people in this world;
to people like you and me,
including every boy and girl.

Peace can be shared,
throughout the world.
Peace can be shared,
by people who care.

Don't forget though,
we still have a fighting chance.

Anastasia Xinos

Our Cruel World

Clean earth, clean air,
When will people start to care?
What happened to the peace?
And when did love start to cease?
What is the point of all these wars?
Men and women getting sores
Love, hate, good, bad
Living life is really sad
Rape, murder, suicide
Her baby could of died
Little girls and little boys,
Playing with their little toys
Anger and fears
Teenagers crying tears
Sex and drugs in the schools,
All of this isn't cool
What is this world coming to?
What should we try to do?

Heather Hall

Life Is A Bitch!

Life is truly a bitch,
when you are not rich.
It causes you to itch
and twitch.

And when you are trying
to scratch your itch, in
just trying to make it,
or better yet, getting rich,
There is always someone
around to knock you
down with a switch

When you are twitching
with the itch, in
just trying to make it
and not even making it
rich, life will still be
a bitch, now isn't that
just rich?

Barbara Jean Wilder

Dreams

There are no dreams
when you're six-five
You're satisfied and happy
you're still alive
No planning, no scheming
no starting anew.
Because deep down in your heart,
you know you're all thru.
It hasn't been bad
living sixty-five years.
With it's ups and downs
in a valley of tears.
You can come out on top
in life's every battle.
'Til that cycle of time
knocks you out of the saddle.
So everything ends,
even this great poem.
As I open another beer,
before heading for home.

Art Williams

Lovescape

There is a place
where buttercups dance
and pixies prance
to a sprightly lovers' tune,
where the sun obeys
and bends its rays
to face the rising moon,
where shadows thrill
to the crickets' trill
and lonely lovers swoon,
where gremlins glide
and hitch a ride
upon a witch's broom.
To such a place
I bring our love
to dwell with angels 'till
the music box unwinds itself
and everything is still.

George Velkas

"Sleeping with the Stars"

Sleeping with the stars,
where I am going, it won't be that
far, in the sky's I'll be watching
you, down on the green grass
I'll be following you.
In the weather of rain I'll
be showering you
those are the tears I'll
be drowning in them
when the wind blows through
your hair, that's only me I hope
you take the time to care
what ever you do don't you fear
just make yourself be aware
I am an angel above
even though the trees are bare
and it doesn't seem as though
I'm here
for I still have so much more
that I can share.

Jessica Yevonne Quinn

This Place

This place
Where is this place?
Can you see it?
Can I?
Is it good? Is it Bad?
Is this what you call life?
Can you really call this life? Why?
Where is this place?
Why is there no colors?
Why is it so dark, so cold?
What is this pain?
Is it mine? Is it yours?
Why pain? Why me?
This place.
Where is this Place?

Jennifer Reddy

A World of Guns and Gunshots

A place of poverty
where money is a cause
and murder its effect
a world willing to change
a place where survival
is important
and protection is a
necessity
A world where
dreams hang on
A place where
nightmares are a reality
where darkness
ends a days fear...
Until ...Tomorrow.

Dina Caporale

A Faraway Place

I have a dream about a faraway place.
Where nothing matters; not even color,
nationality or race!
Where people are free to do as they
please.
Without the worry about being teased!
This place is a place where people can
go.
Without feeling afraid, sad or even low!
This is a place where all people are
happy and gay,
Because this is a place where people
having nothing negative to say!
Unfortunately this place is only in my
mind.
This wonderful place where everyone is
gentle, loving and kind!

Christen Orbanus

Life's Travels

Precious moments linger.
While the future, it begins.
Mother nature tests our patience,
While father time, he grins,
We struggle through existence,
As we grapple with our fears.
We travel down life's winding roads,
As we stack up all our years.
Sometimes the roads are rocky,
Sometimes the roads are fair.
Sometimes we turn down dead end streets,
Or the road need some repair.
Sometimes we find our crossroads meet,
With those who truly care.
We pander to our feelings,
And we make bonds, if we dare.
Don't worry 'bout past steps we've made,
Let's take it day by day.
Travel with an open heart,
Good things will come our way.

George A. Mihalke III

Family Album

the willow leaves
whisper
in the summer breeze

in the photo I am weightless

across the browning grass
they laugh
and grill burgers

they
never wanted
five children

and I was the last

Anne Armstrong

With; in the Living Trees

Something in the living trees
Whispers to me deeply
Standing there so all alone
locked within a space.

Something in the living trees
Pleads to me desperate
Swaying in the gentle breeze
dancing on a limb.

Something in the living trees
Questions to my soul
Why does man disrespect us
burn and trample me.

Oh something in the living trees
Somewhere deep inside
A living purpose a fragile thing
in the living trees.

Something in the living trees
Staring thru window
Seeing all my darkest fears
within the living trees.

Clarence E. Lippard

A New Beginning

The statue of Christ stood tall and lean.
White was what it wore.
It faced the ocean and looked as calm
As the water against the shore.

Looking into the marble eyes,
Stood a man in great despair.
Tears glistened in his hurting eyes.
He wondered if God was there.

Unknown to the man stood angels;
Numerous in amount and huge in size.
They fought against the demons
Who upheld the devil's lies.

The man looked up at the statue;
Blood stains on its hands and feet.
He wiped the dirt off the statue's hands.
The demons fled in defeat.

The statue brought his attention to Christ.
Jesus became his King.
Now he can say his life is new
With the joy that the Lord does bring.

Heather Hunt

Journalism

Who comes first?
Who comes last?
Who comes between
That goes so fast?

What is the moon?
What is the star?
What is the come?
That sails way afar?

Where comes the rain?
Where comes the snow?
Where comes the wind
That makes it blow?

When is the beginning?
When is the end?
When is the middle
That causes the blend?

Why comes the Spring?
Why comes the Fall?
Why comes the Winter
That ends it all?

Heidi M. Fisher

The Witch On Oak Road

There is a windowed witch
who lives on a oak road.
She once had a husband
but now he's a toad.

She comes out once in a while
usually around midnight.
You can see her on a broom
in the sky in the moonlight.

I'm going to go clown there
Somebody when I'm brave.
But before I go
I'm reserving a plot for my grave.

So that's the main story
of the witch on Oak Road.
If you want, go visit,
if you don't mind being turned
into a toad.

Emily Steffel

I Saw

I saw a youth with troubled eyes
Who smiled real big to hide his lies.

I saw a youth go from good to bad
From honor his parents, to hate his dad.

I saw a youth grow to a man
Who's troubles grew at a larger span.

I saw a man who's soul once hurt
Who finally found his peace in church.

I saw a man who reads and prays
His life has changed in every way.

I saw a man grow straight and strong
He praises God with his sweet song.

I saw this man almost every day
He's my son, I can proudly say.

Frankie Durrett

My Guardian Angel

I have a guardian angel
Who watches over me.
I know that it true because
often when I'm sleeping
And it's time for me to rise
I feel a hand upon my shoulder
Just as sure as I'm alive!

Many times when I've faced danger
That hand has pulled me back
And kept me from harm or injury
And left me still intact.

It's not imagination,
If it's not real as real can be
Why it keeps on happening
Is one more mystery!

Bertha Lee Jones

The Island of the Dead

Oh thou still Isle of mortal fears
whose icy halls are sweet.
Unsoiled by trivial human tears
Thy gift to mortal feet.
Receive this traveller come from earth
His feet have wandered far.
His spirit pleads now for rebirth
Where death's rare wonders are.
Let him enjoy the waters still —
The silvery stream of sleep,
Or wander on the shadowed hill
His life's rewards to reap.

Dorothea Frederich

That I May Know Him

That I may know Him
Whose life transforms us all
To give us peace and joy;
And lift us less we fall.

That I may know Him
Whose love indwells our hearts,
To forgive us our sins
And cleanse all our parts.

That I may know Him
And the power of His life,
That overcomes the world
And wipes away all strife.

That I may know Him
And the suffering He went through
To purchase redemption
For enemies like me and you.

That I may know Him
To put my life in His hand,
That when it seems impossible
With Jesus I know I can.

Charles R. Brown

A Friend

I imagine the future, what
Will happen to you? I
imagine our dreams, will
they ever come true?

I imagine the fun we've had
in the past. I imagine our
friendship will it always
last?

I imagine the times
you were always there. I
imagine the times I wasn't
always fair.

I imagine you
saying, "I'll help too,"
I imagine me saying, "I love
you."

Erin DeNardo

My Father

Does my father love me?
Will I ever know?
It's hard for me is see
What he really thinks of me?

Is he really caring?
For his one and only kid
Does he know my heart is tearing
Does he know, what he did?

Why does he hate me?
Was I a mistake?
Why don't he tell me?
His love for me is so fake.

I guess the one to ask,
is my father,
But don't you see
He doesn't want to bother,

Billie Winters

Upon Realizing That I'm An Idiot

When everything I own is destroyed,
Will I then be content?
The tally runs high
With the possessions that my,
Anger shown a thing or two.
The problem being
CD players and phones,
Can't be "shown a thing or two."
And that mass of wires,
And wooden splinters
With plastic connectors
On cracked, bent, decks of metal
Does me no good anymore,
I finally ask myself
"What am I trying to prove?"
And then...
It makes me angry

Josh Wolf

To Be With You

Here I am stuck again
Will my troubles ever end,
Lay down right here with me
So we can let our love run free,
Wanting so bad to be with you
Tell me please, what do I do?

Hold me in your arms tonight
To be with you it feels so right,
I can't explain just what I feel
Tell me is this feeling real,
Wanting so bad to be with you
Tell me please, what do I do?

My tired eyes don't want to see
The hurt and pain you're causing me,
My aching ears don't want to hear
My conscience filling up with fear,
Wanting so bad to be with you
Tell me please, what do I do?

Denise Calma

All Alone

Walking through the breeze
Wind through your hair
Looking up at the sky
With a thoughtful, gentle stare.
Trying to listen, but hear no sound
Watching the orange sunset,
Slowly go down.
Feeling at home in this quiet place
Like I just saw, a familiar face.
Here I feel so alive and true
I feel like I know everything
Like I have every clue.
Even if no ones with me
I've always known
That I'm never ever all alone.

Belinda Gutierrez

The sails are set

They seek nautical
winds,
As the waters speak
softly at the hull
Blindless compass, the
Captain caress
The rudder
Hushes sweet words to his lady,
"Easy now, just follow the horizon."
Then the majors voice
Bellows out, "Watch the boom!"
I wonder if he was just
Protecting his lady, or
his crew.

Christine Hovdal

Love - Discovered

I walked through a barren,
Windswept land,
Seemingly without hope
or promise.
I stopped, looked around
once, twice;
Then something beautiful happened;
- You came!

Al Stewart

Remembrance

Light a candle,
wipe the tears and look away.
Come back for memories,
to kiss, another day.
I'll remember your touch,
those smiling eyes that stray,
that dim my heart, my senses,
and tell, you will not stay.
My eyes close goodbye,
Lest the silent space betray,
the nothingness that fills me,
as you slip away.

June Heider-Bisson

Untitled

I don't know why God loves us
with all our many flaws.
We sit around and complain
when we don't have any cause.
We're never completely satisfied
with anything He does.
We ask Him for so much;
Then forget what it was.
I don't know why He listens
To anything we say;
we ask Him for forgiveness
each time we THINK to pray.
Then tomorrow comes around;
we do the same things again.
Just because He's understanding
And forgives us for our sins.
One day we'll be sorry
we didn't pay attention;
when we're standing in front of Him,
And our name He doesn't mention.

Janie Hornback

"SOUL MATE"

SOME BELIEVE IN ANGELS
WITH BROKEN WINGS
FALLING FROM BLUE SKIES
WITH IMMEASURABLE BEAUTY
AND UNMATCHED LOVE
THROUGH HYPNOTIZING EYES

SOME BELIEVE IN FATE
AND SOMETIMES EVEN DESTINY
COINCIDENCE OR CHANCE
YOU KNOW YOU STILL BELONG
WITH ME

SOME BELIEVE IN GOD
AND SOME BELIEVE IN HELL
I'D RATHER JUST BELIEVE IN YOU
THAT SUITS ME JUST AS WELL

YOU CAN CALL IT WHAT YOU WANT
YOU CAN CALL IT WHAT YOU WILL
I'D RATHER JUST BELIEVE IN YOU
EVEN BETTER STILL

Bradley E. Thomsen Jr.

Crystal Dawn

She's Crystal Dawn
With hair so bright,
a smile so sweet
a mother's delight.

Her eyes the color
of a pale blue sky,
she learns the wonders
of days gone by.

She sees the world
from a young girl's view,
she longs to find
a life so new.

She's Crystal Dawn,
a child fast growing;
she's learning of life
she's finding... she's knowing...

Hilda Weaver

O Lord

A world of pain
with nothing to gain
A bottle of torment with every drop
Power of alcohol so strong
Where did I go wrong
The pain of every drop
My soul cries to stop
O Lord O Lord
What do you have in store
My son My son
When you called out my name
You were not the same
You've been lying down
Long enough
Isn't it time you start
Relying on me and your
Soul will have victory

Charles Adams

Summer Days

The long summer days are filled
with picking wild flowers...
and endless talking hours,
They're reckless days of fishing..
and walking along a river wishing...
They're filled with making wooden boats..
and wondrous root beer floats.
They're the sounds of splashing water...
and watching a baby otter.
So when warm memories
start to fade away
and cool ones take their place,
and the snow falls and melts
on your face.
Remember there's a bright circle
beyond the clouds, waiting to shine through
and make all your warm memories come
true.

Jessica Weaver

Windward

Thank God for life's storms!
With the wind in my face
I have learned to travel
At a vigorous pace.

With the wind at my back
All might be ease.
I'd not need to struggle;
Adversities might cease.

Then how could I strengthen
My mind and my soul?
How could I know
That pain makes whole;

That courage comes
From grief and strife?
I need the storms
To know calm in my life.

Grethe G. Bichel

Wives of the Fifties

We strolled elm-shaded walks
with toddlers in our wake;
Spent lazy mornings drinking coffee,
engorging sticky sweets—
Comparing babies,
pregnant bellies,
husband's habits;
A coterie of provinciality,
circle closed and tightly guarded.

Our young engineers
were gods of plastic,
Vaguely, peripherally interesting.

Somewhere on the cliffs
across the river
Eagles built an aerie,
nurtured their young.

They, too, were an endangered species.

Joette McDonald

Untitled

Laying, thinking of things gone wrong.
Wondering, will they ever change?
Knowing, life will always be like this.
She stands up then walks to the
side of the ship. It moves swiftly
and silently through the night. Clouds
pass over the moon. For a split
second everything is dark. Then she
knows. The one way to make it
all stop, stop forever.

Alexandrea A. Bouska

Untitled

A Little white bushy cloud lies upon
woolen soft feathers and
lets out a soft whimper...
Lying by itself going to heaven
By finding a little feather, thinking
"Nobody understands me"
If only I could be noticed
My life would change,
Lonely and frightened
It drifts off...
to where it belongs

Courtney Smedley

Katie

Our Granddaughter Katie is seven
years old and what a joy to see
Big sparkling eyes, a beautiful smile
and as sweet as she can be
You never know how blessed you
are until a grandparent you become
When I look at her face, I'm
filled with love and all my worries
fade — for once again I can
feel hope for another day
God kept the best for last — a
grandparent to become
For in these blessings from above
a part of ourselves lives on

Helen Conwell

You And Me

I need your love; and you need mine.
You and me
That's the way its got to be.

Birds fly high in the sky,
When I think of you,
I'm just as high.

No words could explain
The way I feel; my pain
My sorrow; my guilt
for letting you go.

The bridge we built
between your heart and mine;
it broke so many months ago.

But together, we could shine
again; and build that bridge again
just so perfect, without a flaw,
That no other could tear us apart with their
claw.

You and Me
That's the way I want it to be!

Brandy Bullard

Purpose

We're all here for a purpose
You and you, and you and me
Don't let it run out
For that's all there will be.

It may be strength
For others to lean
Or just a smile
To begin the beguine.

Wisdom is important
Talent too
Notice niceness prevails
It gets through to you.

And along, the way
Sniff deep that sweet flower
Savor that tonic
You'll need it tomorrow.

Darlene Flood

Eternal Love

Dearly Beloved, I love but thee
You are my life, my self
My every waking thought is you
With thee I abound in wealth.

At night I dream of you
And all day long I sing
Your love is all I need
To make my life worth living.

And so - I'll still love you
Even after we are dead
And time and earth have covered us -
Eternally, Beloved!

Barbara Allenson

My Child

Yes, my child,
you asked me how you got here?
You were conceived from desire
and grew on longings.
When I thirsted to drink the passion
from your father's lips
your quivering inside
let me know he'd not gone.
When I searched the faces of passersby
with hope of seeing his,
it was your steady growth
that lent me comfort that he was there.
And when the day came
when I could not live without him
you were born unto me... I saw his eyes
kissed his lips... played with his nose.
My child, your are the gift of months of
longing
and the drink that quenches my thirst for
love.

Ercell H. Hoffman

Untamed Heart

Untamed heart you know not what you want
You base love on what is externally;
You know not the difference
of infatuation and reality.
There is a barrier between your mind
and your untamed heart,
Your course is never finished it only
begins to start .
Over and over you continue to search
for what really is not there,
only when you learn the difference
will you truly be aware.
The answer is quite simple, it isn't
hard to find
in real love there is a connection
of the heart and the mind.
Untamed heart it is impossible to give
what you, yourself do not possess,
only self - peace and understanding
will put your untamed heart to rest.

Cathy M. Brandt

"Night"

The night wind whispers
You can hear it sigh
Stars in the heaven
Are flyin' high

Shadows dance
Around the tree
The leaves are talking
About being free.

Pretty fire flies
Are lighting the way
The crickets are watching
As they sit down to play

They're all in harmony
So stay out of sight
Just watch and listen
It's all in the night.

Deby Grebe

"Alone"

Alone is good.
You can think of what
you want to do.
You can gather all of your
thoughts.
You can hide your secrets
from the world.
You can pick up pieces that
you have lost along the way.
Your also lonely when your alone.

Angel K. Fowler

Perfection on a Paper Plate

Steaming and bubbly
You emerge from the steel oven
Where you've been incubating.
You, a whole meal
Packed into a neat wedge.
I crave your oregano and garlic aroma
Which permeates the air
And plays with my nostrils.
I ache for your tangy red sauce
And greasy stringy cheese
To crawl slowly down my chin.
I long to scoop you up
And caress your gritty golden bottom
As I fold you and work you
Into my mouth
Which graciously accepts you,
Salivates for you,
Savors you
FINALLY releasing you
To my awaiting stomach.

Filomena Cocchiaro

Love Me Now

You take my hand or kiss my cheek
You hold me close when I am weak

You love me now when joy we take
You love me now when our hearts ache

You love me now while I'm still near
You love me now while life is dear

No need for tears on my day
You cried with me along the way

For death, we know, we cannot stave
No need for flowers on my grave.

John G. Jackson Jr.

Yes, Lotto

Oh lotto, oh lotto
you know you ought to
Come to my hand
that life may be grand
To pay off my car
now four years afar
Send some to my sons
may they have lots of fun
Mail a check to my Dad
all he gave when he had
Share much with the sick
let recovery be quick
Give alms to the poor
that they may have more
Yes, lotto
Oh, lotto
You know
You ought to!

Donna M. Heberling

Cheating

You told me that
You loved me
So I really don't understand
How you could go behind my back
And be someone else's man

You said you'd be
mine forever
But I have heard
that one before
you told me not
to be jealous
She was a friend
nothing more

You meant the
world to me
And I trusted you
with my heart
But now I have
opened my eyes and I see
It's time for us to part.

Christina Ortiz

Mother Dear

My memories of you are so sweet,
You mean so much to me,
I pray to be the kind of person
That you would have me be.

You've led me in the paths of right
You taught me how to pray,
I love you so much, Mother Dear,
Much more than words can say.

The time has come and gone so fast,
It seems just a year or two,
We'd go walking hand in hand
The way we would often do.

Now your hair is turning silver
Your eyes are fading too,
Please remember, Mother Dear,
I'll be patient, just like you.

Teardrops fall, my heart cries out
On earth there is no other
So sweet, so kind and loving
As you, my own Dear Mother.

Avola E. Parks

"Give Me Love"

You plucked me from the gutter
You picked me from my death
You helped me
You loved me
You gave me breath.

In the gutter I laid
No clothes on my back
Wondering if you'd come my way
Hoping that you'd come my way
Knowing that some day
You'd come my way
Give me love.

Days nights
Nights and days
Time flies by
Day by day
Help me guide me give me love
Keep me protect me
Give me love.

Adam Lemke

The Girl with the Curl

Hey girl!
You with the curl,
That titian silky swirl
In the middle, on your brow.
You with the lovely fluffy curl,
Walking so admirably straight and tall,
Never slouching never crouching,
Holding your head high unafraid,
Looking at the changing world
In a whirl.
Is the only thought in your mind
Of that furly furly curl?
Or is there the indomitable will to be,
And do good with sincerity?
If you have it, dear girl,
You are as a priceless pearl,
Along with your lovely, silky furly curl.

Fannie M. Coleman

"Wedding Poem"

Today is the day,
You'll say "I do."
Your life together;
will start a new,
Your hearts will forever sing,
As you put on your wedding ring,
God's face will shine,
with love from above,
a special day,
To pledge your love,

A happy life
You'll have together,
May your love last forever;

Ella M. Stephenson

"Young Mama"

Unaware of what's out there,
young mama must provide and care.
She questions her mistakes,
and then embraces joy as her child awakes.
Love managed to tease her,
and left her not as she were.
Memories without a baby are so far
and a blur.
"How many are like me by the same man!",
she cries.
Then she looks to her baby
and she dries both their eyes.
A baby with a father it may never know.
And a young mama who has no place to go.

Dale D. Hastie

Longing For...

I'm longing for you. I'm longing for
your body, longing for it to be
mine completely and longing for
your arms around me.

I'm longing for that touch, when
you touch my body gently.
I'm longing for that night when
you will enter me completely.

I'm longing for that kiss, your
lips pressing against mine.
I'm longing for the feeling of your
body next to mine.

I'm longing for that night when
you explain and ease my pain,
when you enter me deeply and
never, ever leave me.

Jessica Rybnick

A Poet's Cry

If poetry is the song of
your heart, then perhaps
I best go back to sleep.
My heart is full of wondrous
songs; some sad, some sweet,
some incomplete. But I
have never been able to
hear them clear; nor to
see their notes, to put them
to pose.

Perhaps my whole life will
be spent in slumber, never
opening the door to the
symphony inside of me.
What a tragedy that
would be. So, I must
try, at least this once.
Please hear me.

Debora Bischoff

Once in a Blue Moon

Once in a Blue Moon,
Your Parents say,
As you walk into your room.
The black sky covers the blue,
And a full moon shines above.
As I look into the sky,
I see one star that turns
into a thousand
And I wonder when the
world will come to an end,
And another will take its
place with a new life.

Casey Krug

"The Ageless Rose"

Little Rose Bud do not cry
Your petals reaching to the sky
You wish to grow up and tower
Just like all the other flowers
And most beautiful of all
Stands the rose so proud and tall
Through the soaked and pouring rain
She stands straight, though very vain
But you will grow, you will bloom
Till you lay inside your tomb
You will wilt, you will die
You will know the end is nigh
Then comes the pain, the sad, the fear
Grim Reaper comes, he's here
No one cares when you're gone
Others grow upon your lawn
They know not the beautiful rose
That once upon this lawn grows
So cherish time, it is your friend
Until you die, until the end.

Emily Sickelka

Death

Death,
You've stole my faith
With the lives you took.
You've destroyed my trust.

Death,
My flesh and heart fail
From the sadness I'm feeling.
But God's love rebuilt my heart.

Death,
Of you, I'm afraid no more,
I'll sleep peacefully and calmly
My heart and soul is safe with God.

Faye M. Noel

Regrets

Will I regret it,
Years from now,
When my youth takes a bow,
And old age lives with what is left.

After youth commits its theft
Will I be happy
Sitting here
Years from now when you're still near.
Or will I wish you'd run cover
While I sit and regret another.

Jacqueline M. Stevens

Oh Wolf

Oh Wolf, who walks on frozen snow, so proud and noble where you go.
Your eyes can see into the souls, of those you watch around you.

Oh Wolf, who sits upon the hill
In depths of winter's icy chill
You sing your songs much to the thrill,
Of all those who surround you.

Oh Wolf, the keeper of blue night
You sing to stars and full moon's light,
Songs from the heart with will and might,
The moon's energy astounds you.

Oh wolf, who guards with knowing eyes
You have the knowledge of the wise
Teaching lessons of how and why,
To all of those who've found you.

Oh Wolf, protector of the old, of family, young, and stories told,
With loyalty, so brave and bold, to everything, you're bound to.

Oh Great Spirit, I do pray,
That you and Wolf will guide the way,
And guard life's roads and always stay,
Watching every night and day.

Susie K. Nelson

Lillie B. — My Life

Like a refreshing summer breeze-she came into my life.
With her presence, my life encompassed new meaning.
My whole world became paradise-void of tension and strife.
She took over my heart-she became my reason for living.
By her loveliness I was enthralled-heard music when she spoke.
Right from the start I loved Lillie B.-she possessed my heart-my soul.
Now night and day-day and night- I pray with unceasing fervor, that
Lillie B., who is my life, will covenant to be my wife.
Be my soul companion through thick and thin-through storm and wind;
let me capture her heart, let me proclaim:
"She's my Lillie B.-- my life, my love, my everything."

Willie Ringold

Ghosts

Wisp of wind so feared so scorned
Your cries go unheard enveloped in your depthless sorrow
A cloud of dreams and memories
A cloth stitched of lives unsung and deaths unmourned
You bear the weight of ten thousand sins
Sightless eyes see futures yet to be decided
Your existence is as a stagnant pool of liquid silver
Constantly churned with blurred images of things not understand
but certain
And as the world and all it's trouble tell me that it's false
Somewhere in my mind I cannot help but believe in Ghosts.

Matt Cucullu

A Work of the Heart

Have you ever wanted someone so badly and knew you could never have
them?
To hold them in your arms and never let them go, to capture them with
your heart and dissolve them with your soul.
When you look into their eyes are you captivated by their inner being?
Always hoping, always praying to have what you're seeing.
Well never let go of your hopes and dreams, for with out them your
life is demeaning.
Though time will pass and lovers will leave, you heart always belongs
to them in that time of deceive!!!!

Melissa Delozier

Dreams And Hopes

Everybody has a dream
A dream deep within
A dream full of desires
A dream, only to be dreamed, by you
For when dreams are let known to others
They only become shattered, and forgotten

Everybody has a hope
A hope we will not share
A hope so high, we cannot reach
A hope for love, and dreams

But dreams are told, and shattered
And hopes, are sent too high
Too high, for either you or me, to reach
And they too, become only a dream
A dream, only to be dreamed, by you

If only people, like you and me, could not dream
And stop our thoughts, from becoming hopes
We'd have only today
Only today, to live for
And dreams would become, only a hope

Wanda W. Ainsworth

Love

There... in the park...
A lovely pair sit on the lawn green french
provincial bench under the shade of a great oak tree...

Up there... in the full branches... a movement...
a small winged fellow...
Spies the contented couple... whisks an arrow
out of his pack... draws his bow... fires.

He is caught in the watery depths of her eyes,
She steals glimpses of the strong masculine line of his jaw.

They draw closer; he guides her lips to his and
tenderly kisses her,
Taking her into his strong muscular arms,
Holding her gently as not to crush her love.

She pulls free, uncertain of her past,
Scared of the future.

He stares at her with hurt confusion in his eyes
As she rises and glides down the path.

Dayle Connor

Croc-A-Tate

On a croc's plate
A man named Tate
Was very nearly ate

In a bayou a-touristing
With camera click, click, clicking
Out flashed the croc's tail swing, swing, swinging

Tate's hair stood up
And he jumped up
And left the croc without his sup

Cherryl Hayes

Poetry:

A rainbow of words,
droplets of verse, a light flowing limerick
or humorous mirth!
An air of magnificence or
a shiver of rhyme,
whatever it is, poetry seems to
STOP time.

Monika Karpinska

Untitled

My longing for your touch smolders near the surface of my self.
Your kiss ignites a flame inside of me
My desire turns to a fire determined to engulf you.
My burning for you turns into molten lava craving to feel you...
Deep inside of me the lava flows freely.
Touch me now, with your cool stroking
fingers the burning will subside.
Love me as I love you.

Catherine Towner

My Special Best Friend

You're so smart, sweet, funny and caring
A shoulder always there to cry on when feeling blue,
You always seem to make me laugh,
When I've had a gloomy day.
You seem to put all my anger away.
Then make all my problems seem so clear.
You're always there for me,
Listen when I have something to say.
Through the good and bad,
Your sweet smile makes me happy again.
You gave me courage and lots of confidence.
Then give it all.
You will always be loved of who you; really are.
I am so glad that you're my best friend,
Someone who understands me.
We will always stick together,
That's why our friendship will never end,
Because you are my trusting friend.

Mary Sayegh

Spring

The smell of newness is on the breeze,
A tinge of green about the trees.
Baby calves frolic and songbirds sing,
While high above the wild geese wing.
Flocks of ducks join the stately swans
In a flight break as they rest on a nearby pond.
The gopher's whistle and the meadowlark's trill
Harmonizes with the call of a crow upon a hill.

Sights, sounds, and smells of spring abound
As once more our part of the world has found
That there is reason for our faith in God
For just as sure as crocuses nod.
The cycle is repeating, life is renewed,
And God smiles and says, "It is good!"

Karen Frayn

The Love of All Time...

The love that you seek is a heartbeat away
Across a wide ocean
From a land without name,

The love of all time has sought you afar
To join blood in blood
The ties strong they are,

You dance by the light of a pale blue moon
Hand in hand
Hunger in tune.
Body against each your tender silk lays
His charm will romance you
Your love is his prey,

Your eyes dance about like the fires of the sky
His touch will caress you
Your soul he will sooth
For he is the darkness that lives within you.

Ramona M. Ramkissoon

Coyote'

I watched him as he meandered his way
across the field getting closer where people dwelled;
His coat was in it's prime and shone like
polished silver;
I worried for him as man is often cruel to
that which is not understood;
I walked to possible to close to him but
within the safety of my yard;
I shouted "Go away from her so you may
stay free."
I watched him turn to run, stopping he
tipped his head and howled his defiance to the sun
I shivered as a thought ran through my head;
Is man the dying species?

Norma Jean Morin

Elegy To Luna

Come sing a melancholy air, you caller of the moon,
Alone this night in wild expanse
To stars and I, your tune.
Within your realm some human hand committed willful wrong,
Lament your grief and loneliness as tragedy in song.

To man you are a lonely shade but mourning in the night
Having paused along your away
To give your fancies flight.
Cry aloud for I can hear through chorus of your loss,
It resonates in saddest strains and disappears aloft.

Olympian twins of lyre and bow, protect your nightshade child;
A solitary crying voice
Still dwindling in the wild.
Bereft of mate for sadly now, companions all are done,
Victims to Prometheus' spawn by poison, trap and gun.

O tawny bard of heaven's round, your echo rings forlorn,
Carried 'loft into the void
A signal - all to mourn.
Thine eerie call and tale of woe this mortal's ear did lend
And now your loss is also his; thy charm has served to rend.

Brian Olajos

The Most Profound Moment

Was, what when, that I was born,
Amongst the nape of jewely corn;
That fertiled round my skin so clear,
Those seeds of fruit around so near.

That from that corn that I was raised,
Amongst pollute, jute and haze....
And voices dammed; 'twas burned the air:
My hairs all stood aloud to swear.

My mind — a beacon, ne'er stopped,
I erred and grew so tall.
Amongst the grasses milky glean;
Supported not to fall.

Burned and seared....where what was feared;
As I took hold of roots,
Coaxed them into deeper ground
With Corn, Jute and Fruits.

Yet...poured me on them water;
That I would burn no more.
'Twas the most profound moment;
Sweet water...healed the sore.

David J. Ridley

Lines Of Steel

When the ways of a man turn evil
And crime is the only life he knows
The man on the bench dictates his future
And a cage becomes his lonely home.

Freedom is now a fleeting memory
And your only friends are the thoughts inside your head
All tomorrows are the same as yesterdays
As you pray each night and wish that you were dead!

These lines of steel before my eyes
Seem to stretch for miles and miles
And the faces staring grimly from behind
Have forgotten what it is to smile.

Oh how I wish that things were different
And I could undo all that I have done
Now I vow that when I get my freedom
With God's help I'll become a better man.

D. Pearcey

Young Love Learns

Love lingers lost in a young man's fool heart
And here he devotes his whole entity,
Being everything for her from the start
Seeing her only in entirety.
Soaring free over the landscape of love,
Breathing air with exhilarated breath;
Touching white clouds with wings like a pure dove,
And vulnerable to the very death.
And yet, he lingers with his love and hope,
At the mercy of his lover's cold whim.
Struck down is he, bleeding and left to grope,
With a comforting thought left just for him:
It's not how long the spring, how wide the sky-
How sweet the time from 'hello' to 'good-bye.'

Chad A. Leaver

My Ode to Love

My love, a tender flower, buds
And opens wide to drink the floods
Of sunshine, poured within its folds,
Exposing deep and hallowed holds.

Oh, do you wish to span its breadth,
To scale its heights, or mine its depth,
To rest, enfolded in its wings
Or float upon its lilting springs?

Then come to me, my precious bride!
Be not remiss to step inside
This wondrous place, where we can ride,
The swelling and receding tide.

This glorious place: where eagles soar,
Where mountains peak, and thunders roar,
Holds banks that sleep, and brooks that purr,
And grassy beds, well-lined with fir.

Yes, come to me, my child-like bride,
Where none—my love—you'll be denied.
This ever-grateful heart fulfilled,
Forever more...to you be willed!

Denise Raleigh

In Rwanda... Cry the Forsaken Country

Tribal warfare between the Hutus
and the Tutsis verily savage and unkind
Leaving the village orphanage
children by the thousands behind.
Genocide, another act of appalling
cruelty, killing half a million Tutsis...
Exodus of refugees across the Zairean
border, dying of starvation, cholera, dysentery and meningitis.
To cede the land but take the
people with them was the Hutu leaders' strategy.
Western troops and U.N. aid workers
set up a humanitarian operation aftermath of the tragedy.
Trigger off a mass return? A must for
new leadership and rebuild trust for coming generation.
MAN must learn to deepen the sense of
brotherhood and of loyalty to a NATION.

Simon Leong

God Never Changes

Just as the sun moves across the sky,
And the waves and breakers move in the ocean,
Just as the sand changes,
As the wind blows,
As the trees sway,
So is my life.
At times all I feel is turmoil and depression,
I wish the Lord would just come, take me home.
People desert me. I feel lost, alone,
But, the Lord loves me.

God will always stay with me,
Stand by me.
He will never desert me.
If I run away from him, he will call me back.
He will hold out his arms, and I will run into them.
He will hold me as I let out my frustrations.
His love endures forever and ever.
His greatness reaches towards the sky.
His love is as great as the mountains.
Jesus is awesome.

Taraleigh Borne

The Last Time

Today we say goodbye for the last time
And we think of what we're leaving behind
We talk about the bad times
and we laugh about the good times
and as we hug for the last time
we cry for the first time.
We say good bye forever, as I walk out the door.
never to return, and a tear rolls down my cheek,
And my face starts to burn.

When I look back at you
I'm filled with so much sorrow,
I hope and pray that the pain is better by tomorrow
Although I know I'll never see you again,
deep in my heart, this isn't the end.

Audra-Marie Humphries

The Actors

It once was said; "The world's a stage,"
And this rings true through any age;

An endless play of pain and pleasure,
Where all receive their equal measure,
In vain pursuit of celestial crown,
Till the lights come up, and the curtain down.

S. F. McAllister

"You"

You bring out all the good in me,
And when we are together there's perfect tranquility
You are the warm sensation in my heart
Our love for one another will never part
I love you more than you will ever know
As time goes on our love will continue to grow
Life without you would be too much to handle
You are my light, yes my burning candle
And just like that flame
Our love will be the same
We are one, and one together
We have a love that will never ever severe
You keep me from falling apart at the seams
Reassuring me all will be fine if I just pursue my dreams
You show me my ideas are not insane
That I haven't got anything to lose, but only to gain
I think of you every moment of the day
I just stand there because you take my breath away
You are my everything
You are the only one I love, you.

Joe Levesque

Prayer For The Bride

She stands where once her mother stood
And where I stood before,
And my mother before me,
And all the women of our line.
Each has stood before an altar
With the man of her choice,
No tremble in her voice
Saying the age-old vows
Spoken time out of mind.
Each has smiled at the man by her side;
What an awesome thing it is to be a bride
As is my granddaughter now,
Confident in love,
Oh, God, let her know with him
The joy in life she hopes to find,
But most of all, please, Lord,
Through all their days together,
Grant that he be kind.

Anne Marron Rensel

Best Friend

Always there for me,
And willing to show me the way.
Now that you are gone, I cannot see.
Loosing you was more than words could say.

All the bike rides and games we played,
Were the best times in my life.
Now that we are apart, I am left in the shade.
As days go on deeper cuts the knife.

It feels like the end is near.
Without you life is not the same.
The day you passed on, I was left with a tear,
But now I know life is not a game.

There are a lot of friends, but only one best friend,
And that one is surely you.
You brought joy to me that I did not want to end,
But when you were here life was to good to be true.

Jimmy Arlia

Untitled

I love you more with each new day,
but it's sometimes hard to say.
So I'm writing in a poem the way I feel for you today.
Hold me tightly in your arm's,
don't every slip away.
For I shall need you more tomorrow then I ever did today.

Pauline Mammolite

Something

And sometimes it seems meaningless,
And you don't know why,
And you don't want to know why,
But give ignorance no satisfaction,
None of your time, none of yourself,
It will do what it can to bring you down,
But stop it, claw your way out of the misery,
Grab hold of every juice, every flavor of enjoyment,
Enjoy the ear tantalizing varieties of music,
Drink wine and be merry with friends,
Indulge your taste buds in orgasmic flavors from all
Corners of the earth. Laugh, joke, feel health
Beauty and strength. Treasure the good times
And stay strong through the bad. The bad
Are the least making you stronger. The good times
People and places are always just around the corner.
All questions have answers, the strong, the truly
Strong, give ignorance and understanding,
But no satisfaction.

Joe Daniels

"Each Day"

Each morning begins a new day.
Animals move, and children play.
Our souls awake and minds wonder
The sun shines, the dew and its saunter.

We walk miles to places we must go.
Take everything that happens and its toll.
We find someone to share these days.
Our hearts go numb, our minds a haze.

Love is life, and happiness is someone
To whom we devote and share each day.
Laugh and joke, we smile and play.
This is free to everyone.

Each night ends the day.
Children in bed, parent enjoy the day.
Our souls dim, and minds stop
The moon rises and a smile breaks.
To have and be with you, no mistake.

Raymond Peter Clinkard

Please Don't Hit Me!

Love loss, broken dreams, and shattered glass,
Are terrible memories that I hope will pass.

The sleepless nights, from anger to pain then sorrow,
Hoping everything will change tomorrow.

Why the mental and physical abuse, what did I do?
I tried my best, but it wasn't good enough for you!

You won't listen, and what it seems you do not care.
I'm a person too, this is so unfair.

Maybe it was all a dream, and I'd awake for real,
Maybe it's not, when will I heal?

There's no real escape, for the pain is everywhere.
This is truly a child's nightmare!

Jennifer Myers

The Crystal Lining Of A Heart

As fragile and shy is the heart,
As is a crystal in these parts.
So strong and yet so delicate,
Must be careful not to break it.

When a crystal is placed in your hands,
Do not wave it,
chip it,
or crush it,
But rather caress it,
pet it
and shine it.
Then a loving heart is in your hands.

A crystal beautifies your home;
A rainbow when the sun shines through.
A crystal, clear as a crystal
Will be everything shown to you.

But if your crystal were to fall,
Pick up the pieces, gather them all.
Place them back, close together,
Glue them back with feeling and laughter.

STAM

Who Says That Friendship Cannot Last?

In quiet solace, undisturbed,
As silently the years have passed,
Two nations, unified have dwelt,
And shown that friendship long can last.

Canada, and the U.S.A.,
Whose flags hang high on coupled mast,
A symbol of a mutual bond,
Who says that friendship cannot last?

A parallel, the forty-ninth,
Winds on through forest and field engrossed,
It's charted path is just a mark,
Of something greater, unsurpassed!

At times new leaders fill their posts,
Some unprepared, some true, some chaste,
In spite of this the bond has stood,
Who says that friendship cannot last?

Canada, and the U.S.A.,
The future, present or the past,
A monument of brotherhood,
Who says that friendship cannot last?

John W. Friesen

The Child

The old man passing along the dingy sidewalk pauses for just one moment.
He had seen a child, playing. No different from others, yet separated
by some strange force.
A beautiful child. Beautiful. Small. Fragile. Hair the color of the
sun on a warm spring day, floating down her back. Beautiful.
The child has a strange aura. A haunting beauty.
As if... As if...
He pauses in thought, and wipes a weary hand across strained eyes.
It can't be. It can't. She's gone. Never to return. Gone.
He slowly looks back to the spot last seen.
Empty!
The cold wind lifts the dust and crushed leaves across the pavement.
Rasping.
Rasping.
And yet. Could it be?
He hears a quiet and gentle humming. Then happy laughter.
As if all is right with the world once more.
The man quickly turns, and briskly walks away from the graveyard.

Debbie Flegg

"The Final Mile"

The old man, he gazed at the girl that the loved,
as the time for his ending drew near
and with tears in his eyes, to the girl that he loved,
he said, "Honey, he's dying I fear."

"But wasn't he special, so black and so fine,
and didn't he give us his all?
and wasn't he handsome, so sleek and so grand?
he made all other horses seem small!"

And he ran his last mile, with his heart and his soul,
Though his body kept crying to quit,
but he rode on to win for the old man who
gave to him, all of this spirit and love

"And sadly, I see, his time has now come
and with sorrow I say my goodbye,
but I know when the spring comes, I'll see him again

In the eyes of another black foal"

"Yeah, he ran his last mile, with his heart and his soul,
and a smile shall be my goodbye;
for I know when the spring comes, I'll see him again.
In the eyes of another black foal!"

John McNab

Harshness of Deaths

Wet are the tears, that fall from my eyes.
As your ears are deaf, so you can't hear my cries.
Thick is the blood, so dark and so red.
As you don't seem to care, if I'm alive or dead.
Bruised is my body, covered in blood.
Should I dare speak? Oh God, I never could.
Broken are my bones, my body falling apart.
But never as broken, as my dear broken heart.
I tremble with fear as you grab a clump of my hair.
Should I hit back? Oh God, I wouldn't dare.
My head is split open from the bang against the wall.
It will be over soon I prayed, so I'll have to take it all.
Weaker is my body,
Silence will soon come.
Twitching is my body,
But then my body all goes numb.

No longer wet are the tears, that will no longer fall from my eyes
No longer deaf are your ears,
that will no longer hear my cries.

Trish Zaremba

Ulcer

And I will never break.
Attempt to rape my mind
Molotov cocktail my dreams
Choke me with your pageantry sash
Maybe I'll regurgitate some phoney phrase.
Leave me out of the universal hug
In embracing yourself you won't be deceived.
You say you were in love once? (Patsy)
Merciless quisinant maceration of a meat cleaved heart.
And break me? I'll never break.
You can't hurt me, you can't grasp air.
Impenetrable celebration never really knew
Freedom is a state of mind
It touches stars and orchids and me.
Some blind, rigid strength found power in hiding
A simple mind found happiness in a box
Where the deaf hear the sweet, sweet melodies of silence
And the dead never had to die.
You try my patience
And you give me an ulcer.

W. R. Wacholtz

Called: Letting Go

Don't look back when you head for the door
Because if you do it will only hurt more
Don't stop to explain don't tell me why
If your going to leave just tell me good-bye

As I sit, I think of you believing the love we had will always be true
As I begin to think I start to cry for I don't know how to say
good-bye
It's hurting now a tear has fell
I don't know if I'll find another love I'll love as well

I love you I need you but I can make it alone
I want you I miss you but I'll find my one
Because I can't tie you down you got to be free
and I cannot make you love only me

I will always love you my whole life through
Finding in your tender love my dearest dreams come true
It tears me apart to let you go
I can't stop the hurt, I miss you so

Even though apart our love I'll remember by heart!

Valerie Stone

Illusions....

Behind every cloud there is sunshine
Beneath every frown you'll find a smile,
Sour grapes can make a sweet wine
Every step helps to make up a mile.

Each flower helps to make a bouquet
Every photo a joy from memories past,
Each minute is important in the day
Every actor just part of the cast.

Each puzzle is made up of pieces
And each person depends an another,
On our bodies we only hold leases
So be kinder next time to your brother.

Each union is made up of workers
But a family should be made up of friends,
Every failure is probably due to shirkers
How you see life through your eyes depends.

So if life gives you lemons, make lemonade
When adversity strikes, strike it back;
If you never give up, you've got it made
For God will always keep you on track.

Nora C. Slamp

Heart

Why are now some other sons
broke her heart?
Five sons
man of her own
they're all gone with madness of war.

On their graves
she was standing alone,
silent face of her own.
Only deaf man could hear
her invisible tears.

She gave them birth, she put them in grave.
Sky must be blind!
Wind must be deaf!
How many deaths will it take
till is enough?
Nor the sky is blind!
Nor the wind is deaf!
Answer lie
in mother heart.

Zvonimir Mrdalo

Buffalo

Buffalo, buffalo, you're so strong.
Buffalo, buffalo, where have you gone?

By the Indians you were understood
And provided them with daily goods.

You were a source of meat and hides
With which the Indians were satisfied.

They only took what they really needed,
Therefore your numbers were not depleted.

You roamed the plains for many a year
Until the white men began to appear.

They would shoot you for sport and fun,
Taking only your hide and tongue.

After several years of abuse and waste,
Your numbers have reduced with very great haste.

Even though only a few remain,
You're still regarded to as King of the Plains.

Buffalo, buffalo, you're so strong,
Buffalo, buffalo, where have you gone?

Nichole Langlois

Fire and Ice

Here, on the lake of love, two forbidden hearts lie
burning yet drowning by their temperatures, listen the quietness lurks
where hidden tears are withheld by her blue encirclement breathes
the air of freedom where these two stifled souls fly

Soaring like a lost leaf getting closer each time, yet painfully drawn
further apart
meeting by the moonlight yet melting in their touch - the forest knows
the animals share their sorrow, the wind, holds their heart

Their dire song played foolishly by raindrops, their secrets moments
invaded by the counting hand of time
The silence whispers for one shared deprived kiss, the appetite of
life a severe penalty for such an innocent crime

The passion princess caught in the flame of her own fire,
crying in matches laden tears, for that one guarded moment of truth
igniting in sacrificial love, for the ice prince of her fiery hearts
burning desire

Together, trapped in the cast against nature, the trees sigh, begging
for their will not to be done, but the bow of cupid is arched and sets
of into the sun, then there's a peaceful sizzle, as their chastity
ends forever - and fire and ice becomes one......

Michelle Nanan

Treasures

A dream shared by millions
but experienced by a chosen few.
A star so bright that it is seen by all,
yet, for a few, a star so far away it is impossible to define.
A world to be filled with happiness,
ends up filled with hurt and anger.
For those lucky enough the Treasure
should be appreciated not abused.
A Treasure that can never be replaced
but should forever be allowed to increase in value.
A Treasure which to some, is more
precious than even their own lives.
Look after our Treasures.
As they are the future.

Natalie Merritt Ramsay

Best At Rest

It was a cold, dark day
But I know in my heart
It was for the best

My grandpa was buried in the most beautiful and
peaceful place in the whole world.

He struggled,
And was a strong fighter
But his struggle grew weak
And he became sicker
One day he passed away

At his funeral, he looked so peaceful laying there
Almost alive
But I knew he would never be alive again

I swear he would have talked back to me
I just sat there, waiting... for him to respond
He never did

Angela Getson

The Henpecked Sportsman

Marriage sure is wonderful, and I guess it's all worth while.
But I must say as a sportsman, it can surely cramp your style. The
weekend comes, your thoughts are on that brook so nicely shaded, you
grab your gear, and she says "dear, our trees should all be spaded."

But this week will be different, we're going after bass, the boat's
all tuned, the reels restrung and the tanks are full of gas, and then
I think "To stay in good, I'd better kiss this lass". Then she looks
real sad, and she says "Dad, you just gotta cut this grass."

Then at last comes our vacation; a good trip we can take,
When we discussed location, I suggested Great Slave Lake.
I saw she wasn't buying, so I said "Perhaps Ear Falls?"
She said "Let's go to Toronto, they have such lovely shopping malls."

So I'm down here in the city, so sad I've nearly cried,
And I'm thinking "What a pity, all the fun I've been denied".
I guess I'll watch "Red Fisher" - then she dashes all my hopes,
She rushes in from shopping just in time to catch her soaps!

So young men take my warnings, though you think that girl's a saint,
When you rise up in the morning, you won't fish, you'll likely paint.
While hunting, fishing, boating and lovin' are all swell,
When you mix them all together, it's hard to do them well.

Lawrence Hutchinson

Goodbye

I've said goodbye a million times
But never quite like this
Goodbye's are shown through smiles & waves
Or maybe through a kiss.

But this time it is different
And hard to comprehend
That this goodbye's forever
And forever has no end.

I took you much for granted
I thought you'd always stay
But now you've left so suddenly
And a price I have to pay

I didn't get to see you
For that official "one last time".
You didn't think of that mountain of pain
You've left for me to climb

The hardest part in dealing with this
Is knowing now, about your grief
But the grief you never showed is gone
And as your life,it was too brief.

Tammy Berndt

Sex, Drugs And Rock And Roll

In all our minds they still live.
But no more great music will they give.
They were the greats, still many to come.
But will they catch this disease, I'm sure of some.
When will they realize that there is more to life,
Having a home, children and a wife.
So many hearts have been broken,
Just because you all have been smokin'.
It ain't cool in my mind to sniff lines
Can't they just leave it all behind?
I don't want to lose anymore.
You can't just buy this talent in a store,
It has to be given to you by powers above.
Why waste this talent? What ever happened to peace and love.
I guess drugs are a part of Rock.
That tradition I won't mock.
I just hope the rest stay around.
And not buried six feet underground.
This is in memory of all that have perished,
Their music many will still cherish.

Eric McGillis

Together

Hi! granny my feet are all sandy.
Can I wipe them off? She said. Sure I said.
I'm Linda Throne. That was my granddaughter.
She got divorced from her father.
They were not doing well. Her mother, my daughter died.
I still think about her we all do she's in our hearts.
Granny she said.
You promised me we would look at your picture album.
Okey. I said. Oh, I forgot to tell you
what my granddaughters name is it's Stephanie. GRANNY!!!!!
She's a little fussy sometimes.
Okey. look there's a picture of you and your mother.
There's me. Me and Stephanie had a great time.
We drank some tea I mean I did.
Stephanie drank orange juice.
It was great. I felt like me and my daughter were together.
Even if it was not we were together again.

Nisha Gupta

Worlds Apart

Snipers in the Market place again! We'll be hungry tonight.
But she won't! The heiress leaves for her charity ball.
Passionless in humiliation a beggar sweats beneath a Bangkok sun.
The remnants of fast food litter the empty football stands.
Worlds Apart!

Sun shimmering on a Mediterranean bay, all is peace!
Tranquil forests wasted in an orgy of fire.
Snow capped mountains rise triumphantly, calling us onward.
The earth is shaken, screams ring out, another widow is born.
Worlds apart!

We rest secure within our insulated boxes.
Sounds of laughter on the beach. Yet no! Not marching feet?
Once more the motherland takes our sons.
Once more the birds are silenced by their screams.
Worlds apart?

Wanting, we pass by the doors of want.
Our monuments to progress stare down upon our homeless.
Where now is your Enlightenment dream?
Yet one more silent scream!
Worlds apart? - No more.

Adam P. Kirby

Do You Really Know Me?

Do you really know me or only think you do
Can you creep into my mind
Or feel the pain within my heart
At the thought of losing you
Can you imagine for a moment how bleak the days have been
How empty and forbidding each night without you seems
Do you really know me, or was it just a dream I had
That we were kindred spirits our lives entwined forever more
Untouched by mortal woes and laws?
I could anticipate your wishes, read your every look
You said my face to you was like an open book
How many times you swore to me we'd never be apart
Until one day quite suddenly you left and broke my heart
And now you're gone while sadly I recall
In spite of all the love we shared
You really didn't know me at all.

Joan W. Gagnon

Untitled

Love is a whisper
Calling out through the stillness of the dark,
Calling out to you to embrace it with passion, lust.

Love is a song
Singing it reveals its secrets, it true meaning,
Singing it is heard by others, but is understood by only one.

He stands there hearing it, feeling it, understanding it,
But he does not answer its call.
His time is fading, fading.
Whispers in his ear, he hears, but does not listen,
The beauty, the music is overwhelming him now,
He cannot handle it...he turns it off.

Love is but an echo of what it once was
You still hear it, feel it, sense it,
But not as it should be, but how it will never be.

Serena Luchenski

A Gift

Here with me I hold a gift, something which is precious and cannot be given a price. I can only offer one, for there are no others. This gift is a one of a kind.

This gift is very fragile, yet can be so strong at the same time. It longs for attention, caring and devotion that can only be received from the same gift of another.

Everyone sets out each day in search of this gift, but it is all yours, I give it to you. Treat this gift as if it were gold and never let it go, for if it is lost there is no way in which you can retrieve it. I trust you with this gift.

My gift to you is a token and sign of my affection. It is to show you how much I care about you, to what extent I would go for you if you needed me, but most importantly of all... this gift is the ultimate indication as to how much I love you.

This gift my dear, you cannot see...
This gift you can only feel.

I give you my heart.

Jody Haidenger

Yellow Ribbons

Upon the fence and tied to trees
Car antennas, we all can see
Golden ribbons hanging bright
Remembering those through day and night

January fifteenth the war began
Caused and started by the dreadful Sadam
The world sent many to try and toy
To try and stop his deadly ploy

Home in the free and peaceful land
We pray for those in the desert sand
We hang our ribbons and do our part
The ribbons of love that come from the heart

The men and women who fight so brave
Peace on earth they try to save
The yellow ribbons for peace and friends
That someday soon the war will end.

Susan E. Smith

Unchained Heart

My heart beats to the rhythm of my soul, entwined in chains I can not let go.
As time goes on a man comes by, he is very nice though a little shy.
So my soul, my heart starts to cry, it feels without him it will surely die.
His kindness and warmth greatly overflow, oh in his arms my heart must go.
Times gone by to us were mean, which makes us afraid on him to lean.
For our future together comes with no guarantee, oh can this man truly love me.
I know future things cannot lie seen, I pray only to each other we are never mean.
At last to his arms I must quickly fly or I am sure I will truly die.
To his chest my heart must go, for it is only then we will ever know.
My unchained heart, now free to fly entwined with his will never die.

Lynn Kneller

Untitled

Two separate lives of Ice and Fire
come together with sweet desire.
The first so cold, with no compassion
is melted warm by Fires' passion.

Time would show they were not right,
the end was coming into sight.
Always together, the mix was wrong.
Fire took over before to long.
His heated rage tore Ice apart
and broke Ice of her solid heart.
Passion soon turned to obsession
and Ice soon realized a valued lesson.
Once a cold hard heart now tears would conquer
Fires' flame that always did haunt her.
They came together and left by a ploy,
showing loves' power can destroy.

Two separate lives of Ice and Fire
came together with sweet desire.
Bonded together; separate but one.
Bonded together until there was none.

Kelly Ambrose

Even Still

Ten years has not taken you from my heart,
Distance has not severed our souls,
It's still the same as it was from the start,
Without you near me how can I be whole.

Life's forces have tested us through and through,
And fate has surely been unkind,
But I've lived with the hope of it being me and you,
Even though it might only be in my mind.

Help me fill the emptiness and give me a sign,
Or my soul may just shrivel up and die,
For I've held on so long and put my heart on the line,
Cause I just can't tell you goodbye.

The ache that I have for you won't go away,
And the dreams come to haunt me at night,
Tell me I'm not fooling myself - show me the way,
I can hold on if you say our loves still right.

I'll go to my grave carrying your spirit in my heart,
I'll love you with every breath that I take,
And even if fate still insists we must be apart.
I won't give up the fight for love's sake.

Debra Lewis

Friendship

What is "friendship"?

Friendship is something rare, that you
don't find everywhere.

It is like constructing a building that
requires time and patience

Friendship is precious as our own life

It is shared between friends that
help each other out during times of suffering

It is an important aspects in our lives
today because without friendship,
you have nothing.

Annette Marina Gauthier

Mary Was

Mary was a sweet girl; quiet and shy.
"Don't speak till you're spoken to, mouthy Mary!"

Mary was a bright girl; studying and learning.
"Only a B! Such a stupid Mary!"

Mary was a pretty girl; slender and graceful.
"You're so fat, ugly Mary!"

Mary was just a child
scared and silent
"I'm not gonna hurt ya, little Mary!"

Mary was so gentle; no defense.
"Damn it! Don't scream, Mary!"

Mary was an innocent child; pure and untouched.
"Don't you like it, Mary?!"

Mary's silent; so still
Mary's so white
Cold
And dead

Mary always was a sweet girl
So quiet.

Sarah Styles

Repercussions

Want my freedom - choose to have sex.
Don't want to be pregnant - kill the child.
Birth rate too low.
Who'll pay the taxes - who'll pay for our pensions?
Bring in the immigrants - They're taking our jobs.
Send them back.
Who'll pay for our pensions?
Birth rate too low.

Want my freedom - choose to have sex.
Don't want to be pregnant - kill the child.
Birth rate too low.
Who'll pay the taxes - who'll pay for our pensions?
Bring in the immigrants - They're taking our jobs.
Send them back.
Who'll pay the taxes?
The children are dead.

Margaret C. Gostmann

The Poor Indian Laborers A Cheap Cigarette He Smokes

The laborers cigarette between his lips,
Exhale and eject blue pungent smoke,
Laced with marijuana's dope,
Perhaps bit by bit his bone breaking tiredness
Goes up with smoke,
He sleeps, the cancer in his throat creeps,
Then after a time, leaving family
Into the oblivion he leaps,
There he found the creator making universe,
with fiery bits,
And the indigents he hits,
And send them to the earth's snakepit
Against the creator we should file a suit.

D. D. Banerji

Jealousy

She spun me on the merry-go-round,
faster and faster,
and even though I was terrified
I didn't want her to stop.
With every turn, a strobe-like
fragmented flash revealed new emotions.
Her eyes turned dark, and her smile deepened.
I thought I actually saw in her smile
a glint of jealousy.
Jealousy towards who I've become
and how I've grown.
I held on hard and I cried
"won't you stop."
But her smile
sank further
into her face.
And she spun me
even harder
than she did before.

Kerry Trevelyan

The Little Bird

Little bird upon the tree;
Come sing a tune for me,
Don't ever fly away,
And if you do here I will stay.
I'll wait for you until it's spring;
So you can come and sing.
Little bird upon the tree;
Come say hello to me,
And you know I will always remember thee.
And when you finally leave we'll see,
if you too remember me.

Claudia Gonzalez

The Eternal Quest

What is love but a wondrous dream,
Flying through space on a heavenly beam?
At peace with oneself, and the world about.
Two people so happy they want to shout.

What is this trust that grows from this love,
Directed by powers we've seldom dreamed of?
We seek it, we find it, we tremble in awe
At the tumultuous feeling, the incredible draw.

Respect it, and share it, and treat it with care,
Bear this in mind, and love will stay there.
Bask in the sunshine,delight in its glow
For once you have found it, you won't let it to go!

Virginia M. Flaherty

Aliens On Earth

They've come from a place so far away.
For a certain while, they were meant to stay.
Watch them as they try to adapt.
Hear their whispers, so magical and apt.
These creatures who seem so different from you,
Have a heart, a body, and feelings, too,
Aims and wishes, smiles and tears,
Memories, insecurities, fears.
Aliens struggle to shout and call
All humanity to befriend their soul.
If you look around, you can surely see
Aliens who are living a life of misery.
Heavy threats are being raised more and more,
Warnings that have never been said before.
Hardly are they able to be provided with air,
Hardly would an alien complain of a life so unfair!
Earth was meant to be a plain dwelling place,
Made for every soul, made for every race.
Let all aliens on earth be
Loved and wanted, safe and free!

Hania Abed Rabbo

Alone

Our souls long for acceptance,
For a place to be loved
Where there is security,
A place where we belong
Safe within the fold
Like the time of a child with his mother
In a select group—tight and warm.
When we are alone,
The world is cold.
Who can we trust?
Where is there a place for us?

God's spirit comes and comforts,
He upholds with his hand.
Children, I love you.
Do not be afraid;
The time of rejoicing will come again;
Children will be happy as in days of old;
They will all know me.
I will be their God
And they shall be my people.

Jean Dorothy Cox

Star Bright

He is the power of the universe; She is the closest to Him,
for there she can feel his energy.

He is fire; She is fire; She is the leader; He is the organizer
She is the match that lights the fire, which is Him.

They have a choice, a choice of joining together and emerge,
which can cause disaster, or melt ice and be as one.

He is the King, therefore He walks with pride and grace.
Those who should follow Him when He roars He
means no harm, for they know it's only a calling of his kind.

She is the pretender, therefore when she walks she
gives anger but those who she should approach, she gives happiness.

She is an enemy but also a friend; She is a lover
but also a hater; She can lay with her enemy in
peace and harmony but yet sit with her friend in conflict and hate

He is the teaching; She is the learning; He is the water; She is the
sponge when they are together he is always pouring;
therefore she is always absorbing.

He is like an ocean, which is full of life, energy and wisdom
which will never run dry. She is like an infant, which is

hungry, young and innocent, which will always cry out.

Starr Babe

As One

As one we be as long our hearts are free,
free from the burdens of time and born
into eternity.

Emotions toss and turn like fall slipping into
winters frosty presence, despair not
for summer is in our own essence.

Fate has forced its mighty hands upon our souls
and helplessly we followed but one can't
toy with natures ways.
So be it our love through out our days.

Now joy and glee fill our hearts, for the air
we breathe and the things we see will always be.

So let the earth tremble, the waters dry, for to all is life
but the simple look from ones eyes.

Vincenzo Iapicco

Changing Seasons

Shades of autumn red orange and gold,
Glorious colours, a sight to behold.
Leaves are falling and branches are bare,
Birds are leaving one last moment to share,
Summer's past, a season's final glare.

Soon branches will be covered with a blanket of snow,
Glistening flecks and silhouettes all aglow.
Winter air is brisk fresh and clean,
Northern lights are now easily seen,
Nights are longer, but yet a bit more serene.

Birds are appearing and the snow will soon melt,
Animals are shedding that warm winter pelt.
Grass is growing and the colours of spring,
Are quite evident now as you hear the birds sing,
Bellowing to the sky, while brushing off his wing.

Leaves are appearing and it's getting warmer each day
Laughing sounds as children rush out to play.
We've come full circle, another year has past,
Moments to remember, they've gone so fast,
But like the seasons themselves, we know they can't last.

Dorothy MacKay

Untitled

I hold Her hand and in Her eyes I see Him.
Grandma was frail and old but her spirit is of a youthful vitality,
which gives me strength.
The flames around me dance: a flicker of golden hair,
the touch of His skin - warm and sensual
and eyes that manifest a desire so intense, so profound
for ours is an eternal love.

Her crystal ball illuminates brilliantly and Grandma's aroma envelops
my body.
My emotions are RACING, wildly, passionately, and tearful tremors
mask my eyes.
I look around me but no one is there - only Her;
She closes Her eyes.

I stare at Her intently; at the deepening furrows,
compelled by Her hypnotic overtones.
The archer lies entwined in the Tree of Life - a beautiful symbol of
wisdom and honor.
Above him the Dove of Peace takes flight
and the encircling cards uplift my soul in mystical splendor.
The Chalice is overflowing and She smiles.

I hand Her a dull and crumpled note: a reflection of my prior state
of mind,
and as I leave Her my fear is dispelled with a surreal purity
and I am at peace with myself.
I close my eyes and I can see the light.

Lakshmi Tummala

Take A Little Trip

Take a little trip beyond the stars
Guaranteed to soothe most any heart
Weave your web of tears an other day
Leave it all behind, come sail away.

Gentle is the morning slow to rise
Soft and silent burns the dew
A southern breeze caresses you
And in your heart I'll be there too

Wipe away the tears you cry tonight
Let your mind just wander through candlelight
The dawn will shine upon your brow
When that day comes walk on proud.

Like the phoenix rising from the flames
Brush away the scars and the shroud of shame
Calm the waters of your soul
Flood your heart and make it whole

Take a little trip beyond the stars
Leave it all behind, come sail away.

Heather Addie

Passage of Time

I never meant to imprison your self, your being, your soul
Had I known the many depths and levels my future held,
I would not have opened the door of my world for you,
I could not, with knowledge, hurt you this way,
Had I known...
You, my friend and lover, are falling victim to my world,
So much pleasure, so much pain
You never realized just how much was at stake.
The gifts I bring are intangible
The passage of time brings vision, comprehension, and heartache.
These are merely fuel to bring forth your flame, your light within,
As you adjust your sight and peer into the shadows
Cast forth by glorious dancing colors,
You will see me, my arms eternally open.

Lisa Coleman

He Will Never Leave Us Again

He showed his teaching to his follower
He descended upon us
He was resurrected
He obeyed his father without any doubt
In order for us his children to do the same
To be his sleep, so the shepherd will keep his
flocks by night
We will remember a man, a spirit so great
in thought.
Which will remain in our hearts
His courage, bravery & our spoken attitude
which we could hardly perform
In this our day and age our desire to
wait and see our majestic king
His demands for us is great we owe our lives to him
For I dedicate to you a poem at a love song
A poem that means so much to me
I'm here oh Lord, waiting for your presence.

Elizabeth Simpson

The Seventh Day

I am writing what the Lord told me tonight
He spoke to me with anger and fright
Say not to any woman or man you should know
But to me this world is one big show
This creation of mine will vanish some day
So take heed my son, for this I will say
I've given you life equal to any man
So you could live on this earth and understand.
But the people had a choice to linger and fight
And now this planet is one pitiful sight
So now the time's come to lay down my hand
To destroy the evil I've put on this land
I've been with you my son, you've tried your best
And I leave you now with no request
Six days have gone by and the seventh we all rest.

Cliff Caron

Jason

When my brother died
He was only four
I was very little
I don't remember my years with him.
I never really knew him.
My parents say that I would've loved him.
I do.
My father says that I knew when he died.
Dad was holding me in his arms when suddenly I cried.
When I look at the night sky
I talk to him
I know he can hear me
Because I see a shooting star.
I love him.
I cannot miss him.
But I try.
And I almost do.
Now I can.

Kathryn A. Hanen

Untitled

Edge of the dark side of star nine
The moon shone so dimly and pale.
The sun's radiance so did shine
Even shunned with harpoon lightning,
dolphin, shark and whale;
An ancient dendroid couldn't even define
The scientific basis of solstice equinox
saga and tale

Dorothy June Hamilton

No Food For Fatima

She was just a little ten-year-old,
Her whole life waiting to unfold;
But Hunger came with out-stretched paw
And took the life of Fatima.

Too late her families' desert walk,
Too weak to eat, too weak to talk;
Too weak a shallow breath to draw,
Too late! too late for Fatima.

With hopeful hearts and measures brave,
They tried in vain her life to save.
With loving hands her kinfolk saw
The struggle end for Fatima.

No tears were shed, though hearts did break.
No mourners gathered for her sake.
Just one more death in Africa -
No food! for little Fatima.

Ruth Taylor

War

The man laid still on the battle-scarred ground
His eyes were pale and stared up at the sky
There was no wind, not a noise, not a sound
His eyes seemed to hurt and want to ask why
Tears rolled down his face from the hurt he felt
This can't be it, he thought, his cannot be
Yet on his chest there was a growing welt
Which told a tale, a tale of destiny
Always as a child he loved his nation
He could not have known of what lay ahead
Forging ahead with grim contemplation
He vowed to follow where the others lead.
He was lead to his death, to slow decay;
He always knew there was another way.

Daniel Hirschkorn

Garden of My Life

Flower my garden!
Hold back the swirl of passing time.
Let me lie in your welcome shade
And contemplate my future life
Surrounded by your beauty and serenity.
Flower my garden,
Garden of my life.

And the garden of my life replied:
"Dear Nature's child, so sweet and mild,
I cannot make the time stand still,
That's not God's purpose or His will.
Dedicate your future years
To stamping out this earth's tears.
And when your life is through and done
You'll come and join me in the rays of the sun,
Shining and smiling as my wife
Onto the garden of your life.

Flower, flower, flower my garden,
Dearest, garden of my life.

Daphne Gulland

As the Tide

As the tide slowly rolls away
And the suns going down shows the end of day
I think of you and smile with grace
As a salty tear rolls down my face
I feel the pain you are going through
I wish you were here, if only you knew
I look up at the rising moon
Hoping you will get well soon

Mandy Heide

Lonely Love

Wanted to tell you so many times
How I feel when you're with me
Now that I found you, you are my destiny
I only wish I could read your mind
So I'd know just how you feel
I wish I could hold you in my arms
And tell you everything will be alright
But something is there
That has hurt you so which then hurts me
To see you go I'm not so sure just where I stand
I'm not looking for true love but now your looking at me
Your the only one I can think of your the only one I see
I don't mean to put you under pressure
But it's something that I can't control
And though I'd give you the world if I could
I'm afraid to let you know cause I don't want to lose you
The best of romances deserve second chances
I'll get to you somehow
Cause I will promise you now
You are all that I'll ever need.

Willi Jo Coblenz

Together

My life is so much different, since I fell in love with you.
I appreciate the finer things, I never used to do.
The stars are so much brighter, and the moon a greater glow
The birds they sing a sweeter song
because I love you so

When we walk together and I hold your hand in mine
I feel a gentle warmth flow slowly up my spine.
When I look into your eyes they sparkle like the stars
and when I kiss you darling, I'm floating like the clouds.

I think about you darling every moment of each day
you're always with me darling in a very special way.
I like it when your with me, my life feels so complete,
I'll always love you darling, you mean the world to me.

Lawrence C. Beaton

When I Dream

Whene'er I feel overwhelmed or forlorn
I dream of the Land of the Unicorn.
Feeling I'm one with both forest and stream,
I become immersed in my childhood's dream,
Drawn by a magical mystical breeze
Whisp'ring softly through forever green trees.

My one-horned friends oft frolic night and day
—I'm intrigued by the fairness of their play.
Their love and friendship permeate the air
And the hearts of all those who venture there.
Such peace and happiness rarely I feel,
'cept when amongst the Unicorn I kneel.

Some say 'tis not right to think such a thought
—They deem a Unicorn's existence naught.
All I know is that when I close my eyes
Much breathtaking beauty before me lies.
When days lack heart-felt, soul-felt ecstasy,
I choose a tireless, timeless fantasy...

Arwen Evenstar

Black Uncertainty

I look around and all I see is blackness,
I look inward and all I see is blackness,
Then I get so numb that I can't feel
And I can't tell what's fake from what's real.

Now I can no longer see a thing
Calmness this darkness does not bring,
But I'm not afraid, nor am I scared
When I get so low that I don't care

About life and death, or, joy and pain
But all emotions are not the same,
Pain and sorrow thrive at night
While love and joy both bring light.

But I don't see any light in here,
Nor any sounds do I hear,
Darkness darkens and agony pertains,
To a blackened heart and a soul that's maimed.

My eyes are open staring at the blackness,
My soul floats through nothing but blackness,
No longer numb, no emotions I feel,
But I still can't tell what's fake from what's real.

Hike McGowan

Because

Because you were my eyes
I never cried
Because you were my love
My heart was never broken
Because you were my life
I seemed interested in it
Because you were my soul
I was alive
You left...
You took all of this with you
Now that you have gone
How should I live without all of that
Sans eyes, Sans love, Sans life, Sans Soul...
Sans everything.

Lena Agha

A Disturbing Fact

Peeping around the corner
I saw my mother sitting
Her face was red
And tear swollen. A disturbing fact.

There had been an accident
A car accident;
Something had happened
Someone's dead. A disturbing fact.

Two cars racing
One ran a red light
The car was hit
And Auntie Cindy was dead. A disturbing fact.

They had been drinking
They were drunk
She was the victim
And now she was gone. A disturbing fact.

We have to face the truth
We have to realize the importance
Drinking and driving is a... Disturbing fact.

Lynnette Thompson

Untitled

When I wake up in the morning
I think of you,

When I go to bed at night,
I think of you,

When I look up in the sky at night,
I see the stars that shimmer,
I think of you,

Looking so anxiously in to the crystal ball,
looking to see as time goes by,

Looking, searching for a lifetime of happiness,
only to see what I dreamed would be.
I think of you.

All I can do is wait for your calls,
all I can is wait for your touch,
All I can do is hold onto your sweet,
gentle kiss,
all I can do is wait, and as time ticks by,
I think of you.

Angela Monte

Lonely Vigil in Desert Storm

I'm a lonely soldier, in a foreign land.
I wish I was holding my sweetheart's hand.
But I'm holding a gun, to kill or be killed,
As the enemy is dug in beyond the hill.

My thoughts of home whirl around in my head,
I'm on duty when I should be in bed.
The roar of the jets make the desert shake,
I need sleep, but I'm wide awake.

The safety of the regiment depends on me,
But the blowing sand makes it hard to see.
Being a prisoner of war is hell they say,
And a cease fire is expected any day.

When I get home to my family and friends.
I will never come back this way again.
The smoke is so thick, you never see the sun,
The environment will be polluted, for years to come.

Oil burning and flowing like a flood,
Forgotten is the price of human blood.
God works in His mysterious ways,
He has the power to amend mans ways.

Masie Edith Cavell Jackson

Saying Goodbye

Last night you passed beyond to joy supreme.
I won't despair today when sudden grief
Will come to frighten me beyond belief,
For I can call you to the land of dreams.

When comes the parting of the ways to bear,
Through night and day, I'll feel you ever near,
Your soothing voice shall I forever hear,
Beyond the grief and comfort friends can share.

For death gives way to great reality
And does not end our human destiny.

And life goes on in spite of grief and pain,
Within, my heart knows we shall meet again.

And though I should forget you for a while,
A vestige of your thoughts shall make me smile.

Christine Howald

If I Had One Wish

If I had one wish,
I'd wish to travel far.
In search of a distant planet,
To find the perfect star.

The wish I'd make upon this star,
Would be to always be with you.
But if this wish I could not have,
Then I guess wishes don't come true.

But people always told me,
To try tricks and magic things.
And never to give up,
'Cause wishes come on magic wings.

But I soon found out and realized,
That for my wish to come true,
It had to be wished straight from my heart,
So I came up with, "I love you."

Elizabeth Seguin

Addiction: Past And Present

I'm so happy here, I hope I can stay
I'm feeling clean and free
I'm trying to succeed at a special job
The job of just being me

I think of my friends that I left behind
They are talented, competent and kind
I wish they'd follow so they can be free
To use the best parts of their minds

Addiction has many faces
It's not just junk or blow
There's beer and pot or work and dreams
It's any place you go

To get away from that child within
And the memories of childhood too
It's the things you lean on or hide behind
To get away from just being you

I know there's still problems that lie ahead
So everyday I pray
And with luck and diligence and the grace of God
In this wonderful place I'll stay

Edi Brennan

Chief White Cloud

Chief of the sioux tribe speaks to me.
In dreams of tomorrow, so clear to see.
My mind opens wide for his voice to speak.
The answers to questions my soul does seek.
As a guide he came to me one night.
Majestically seated on his stallion of white.
He spoke not a word. But turned to me.
His eyes of brown, like the depth of the sea.
My soul was weightless and together we did soar.
Beyond all that is time and back once more.
He taught me the beauty of the pine trees so tall.
Of each living creature and insect so small.
The colours of the sunsets with their fiery hue,
have burned in my soul a spectacular view.
He taught that each creature has it's life to lead.
No matter how great, each must strive to succeed.
Chief white cloud my friend, my soul guide is he.
Teaching lessons of love beyond all eternity.

Bonnie Faber

"Pane Of Glass"

Naked against a pane of glass I look to you,
In my heart you've always lasted you remain true,
Naked in front of all nothing is to hide,
For nothing matters at all and I must survive.
So naked I remain in front of my pane of glass for all those to see,
But the heart ache that remains still continues to bleed.
Naked in front of the world where no one belongs,
I turn towards you and see that you have gone.
It is this cold world I reveal to,
Bleak as I may be
It is this world I live in that is naked to me.

K. Shmyr

My Grandmother

Nobody knows why she had to suffer so much
It just didn't seem at all right.
She was always so charitable, and friendly,
To everyone she saw.

She was born a Christian, and
Stayed strong until the end (and longer)
I know she appreciated all the prayers sent her way.
I'm even sure she sent prayers our way,
When she saw that we suffered her pain, too.

She loved us all very much,
Each with a whole different love.
I know she'll watch over us from Heaven,
And send us her love, and greetings,
Through our prayers, and in our dreams.

I wish they'd find a cure,
For that wretched disease,
Which has taken so many wonderful lives...

... Including the life of my dear Grandmother.

Gaylene Ann Giesbrecht

Nursing Home Dreams

Silently she waited for their footsteps at her door,
It seemed she did this so many times before.
She could see those tiny babies snuggled in her arms,
How they filled her heart with love,
And she fell captive to their charms.
She also sees those toddlers playing with their toys,
It seemed her home was always filled with little girls and boys.
Their teenage years were filled with many ups and downs,
They shared love and laughter,
Mixed with tears and frowns.
Then came the day when they left home,
Oh how it hurt her so,
But in her heart she knew she had to let them go.
Now she feels so lonely in her little room.
She hopes they will think of her and visit very soon.
She wakes up from her daydream to see them standing there,
She holds them closely to her heart,
An answer to her prayer.

Mary McDonald

Untitled

Little Robin fly, though come time and seasons,
Of goodwill; military flyers. Knock poor things from branch tip.

A countryside beautiful. Dwells its gorgeous scenery where live stock roam.

Farms and farmers in many "mediums." Maneuvers "auld times though new time," compete everyday.
Rigours: Runaway, landing zones.

John Manson

Mirror

Silence that echoes so deep inside,
It shows no faces, but has so much to hide.

The laughter and the thrill of breaking the rules,
But the mind concludes that this world is but cruel.

The happiness has faded so deep into one's soul,
A heart that once knew love, now feels so cold.

To the heavens and to the hells divides the beauty within,
The faces of hypocrisy as seen so paper thin.

To life the untold meaning so waiting to be desired,
To the outer physical being just beaten down and tired.

I am at war with my soul trying so hard to find,
The smiles and adoration that seem so far behind.

These walls inside me so easy to break down,
Just to find the joy to take this frown.

If there is a God let him be known,
Cause when I reach my heaven,
Please don't let me be alone.

Laura Laurent

Sadness And Strength

Sadness comes from deep within,
It takes all your strength to keep it in,
When letting go and feeling sadness,
Strength comes and keeps you from doing badness.
Sadness need not last forever,
Strength takes over and saves the day,
Sadness leads to deep depression,
Strength within is so impressive,
Sadness hurts deeply and makes you weep,
Strength is power so let it seep,
Don't give in to sadness,
For it will take you down,
Give all you got to strength,
It will carry you along,
Through all the sadness life will bring,
Strength will always conquer and win.

Mary Anne Creighton

Only Three

One day I walked through a little park,
It was early afternoon
The children were playing baseball
They had just go out of school
As I walked around the corner
Much to my surprise a little girl sat all alone
She was very beautiful, with pretty dark blue eyes.
I said "hello little girl," "Why are you all alone?"
With tear-filled eyes, she looked at me
And this is what she said,
"My mother went to heaven a short time ago,
My daddy has to go to work it's very hard you see.
Soon my Auntie Susan will come home
She will look after me.
I sit here till my Daddy comes,
He picks me up at noon".
As I stood back in the shade that day
I felt the teardrops start,
For that tiny little girl of 3
She really touched my heart.

Mae Cole

Untitled

I was trying to escape.
It was you I was leaving behind.
The thoughts were not in your mind,
But the feelings were taking over my soul.
My very existence was alive in you.
Escaping did not work.
I saw you everywhere.
You were in the stars.
You were my reality,
You are my reality.
I cannot escape you
Even though I put the distance between us.
It is a mystery the way thoughts and feelings,
Can control the way my body feels.
It aches...
It is numb.

Heather J. Milner

Love Forever Lost

Hold back the Spring—
Its tenderness might thaw my grieving heart
'Till now a part of winter's ice and snow,
Warmed only by the searing tears that ever ebb and flow.

Hold back the Spring—
The blossoming of bud and bough, unshared,
Yet cared for still, but bringing only pain,
Has all the sadness of a dying leaf caught in Autumn rain.

Hold back the Spring—
It's promise bright forever dimmed for me —
My soul's not free to hold such happiness and light —
It's lost in endless sorrow, and the deepest shadow of the night.

Diana D. Cliff

The Sea Is For Me

I must come around to the seas again,
it's waters deep and untold,
Secluded in it's slimy grasp,
Upon the ocean floor, treasures unfold,
The remains of relic, debris and bones
From people of long ago.

I must come around to the seas again,
It's sea green waves I adore,
As they wash upon the sand,
Like a mop across the floor.

I must come around to the seas again,
To feel the sea breeze blow ashore,
With salty taste, and smells of seaweed,
Nevermore will I forget the sea and Shore.

Leah Dore

Through All Time

We walk the path together, united our lost souls,
Joined our hearts together, who could ever know.

That I still shiver with desire, tremble in the night,
Anticipate our sweet touch, quiver in your sight.

Your touch alone can haunt me, with your breath you make me dance,
When you hold me in your arms, love, I haven't got a chance.

What power do you hold dear, over my aching soul?
To keep me by your side love, and with your love enfold?

If ever you should leave me, how could I go on?
You possess my only life breath, my love you are the one.

So please me with caresses, slowly, your body over mine,
Kiss me to our rapture, take me through all time.

Denise Limebeer

A Love Forgotten

I reach for you in the darkness
knowing that you are not there.
Perhaps wishing the dream I just awoke from had come true.

Everywhere I go I am forced to see you
never able to forget the past
never able to move on.

How is it that you have forgotten so easily the way things used to be?
while I remember every detail, and play the memories over and
over in my mind
wondering - What did I do? What could I have done?

Why don't you love me?
I still love you.

I feel I might burst from the loneliness around me,
so alone

Words cannot described the way I feel when I see you.
When I hear your voice.
When I remember the way things used to be.
With you.

Bridget Campbell

The Wag

All I can say to this wag of a lad (who I hear indiscreetly brags)
Let's be honest dear friend, do you really give a damn?. What 's
more, can you really trust a woman who is continually, ducking and
diving, cannoudling conniving normally appealing but to a certain few.

"Go forth and multiply" it has been boldly written but to my state
of mind do try and decline and don't let nature take its course.
Pandora's box hidden through the ages has been opened in the past by
a wag of a lad (who I hear indiscreetly brags) to find a less than
virtuous female trapped inside, what's more, could you escape from a
paradox that can only end up in someone's grief? "namely your own".

A woman's scorn is unmistakably relentless when life plays second
fiddle to her tune, now be advised and despite the sardonic lengths
that she will stage her play.
On your way-you wag of a lad the horizon calls you as one of its own
"Step lively now don't look back" Indeed to be quite honest and
sincere, "I never really thought you ever, ever bragged at all."

Andrew F. Dodds

Darkness

Once alone, forever scared.
Life's long road has left me dead.
Fire, water, air and land.
You rule the world with your magic hand.
The cards are dealt on the table they lay.
What's in store on deaths day?
Pain, Sorrow. Tears that fall.
The endless terror deaths call.
No more waiting, no more guilt.
Like a flower I begin to wilt.
Although I'm gone my spirit lives
  Once alone, forever scared.
Now I'm gone, forever dead.
No need for sadness, no need for tears
No hidden terror, no hidden fears.
Death has taken all that's in it's path.
My screams of terror, evil wrath.

Natasha Thyme Marois

Darkness enhanced the sea
Light was only that which shone
From the lighthouse afar

A soft rain fell moistening the sandy shoreline
All of existence seemed peaceful and content
Only anguish swelled in my heart
At the spectacle before me

Instantly the surf acting in rage
Pounded fiercely against shore and all that was near
Such beauty without meaning
Such vengeance and power
The Sea - Empress With Staff of Steel

Laura Farrugia

The Blue Wheel of Fate

The blue world of life has crashed to earth
like a giant hydronian of the septi

Which shows the seven deadly sins for all to worship

To cast off one of the seven is to leave six
which doesn't set with the tide of time

Which shifts and pulls, to and fro, the
perils of birth and the withering of the old

Bent and gnarled, who are laden with wisdom,
who are set aside for the fruitless plot

Which schemes for death and for the birth of life
with the wheel of fate

Which turns the mind of man

To fall in the mind of the blue which all men fear

The emptiness of one, to stand alone

in the blueness of this world

to fall again

In the tide of time to face again

the perils of birth

the withering of ages

And to spin the blue wheel of fate

Dan Cormier

In Love

During your life
Love may come and go.
And when you have it
You will know.

Love is strange
It fills the empty pit.
it is like a puzzle
It has a perfect fit.

Love involves pain
There may be ups and downs.
Arguments will happen
Some leave smiles while others leave frowns.

Then there is the happiness
Remembering moments together.
Discussing the future
And promising love forever.

Those without love
Just wait and see.
These things take time
And one day you'll be in love.

Debbie Henry

Bleeding Canvas

I cry where I once laughed,
miracle and music lost in the past,
pearls, stolen by the touch
of those betrayers of hope.

The sundrops are like a surgeon's deft hands
through which all the world has passed
and miracles are as common as death.

Before my death, I need to know
of broad rivers on the way
without you painting each day
When we started the sketch
we hurt and cried
and since then we feel no more
and since then we are slowly dying.

I slip once more from my place on the shelf,
Until the bruises hurt no more.

I need once more to laugh
in the face of the sun
simply to be every day
until no feeling need replace me.

Kendra Hanou

Hebrew Child

Dear Hebrew child, so fair so full of grace,
My conscience burns when now I look upon your face,
For sins committed, against your ancient, migrant race.

What madness, that smolders in the mind of few,
Entices men to do the things they do?
To murder the young, the old, the innocent Jew.

But justice is yours - for so long delayed,
Your race its price has paid,
Six million in their shallow graves were laid.

David's star so proudly still does shine,
Oppression's symbol is crushed, has failed the test of time,
"Live Israel" and all of David's line.

Kenneth J. Maclean

Another Love Poem

Love springs forth as does passages of the seasons.
My love for you is not in time with the falling of the leaves.
Nor the images of large white flakes,
As individual as a finger print that spiral downwards on a breezy winter day.

The scents and colours manifested in a garden of roses bloom, threatening to overtake one's senses, do not even begin to capture the essence of true love that I feel for you.

The sun.
Ever bright.
It's brilliant rays of light that spear through the clouds does not approach the adoration and passion that radiate from the depths of my soul and reaches of my mind.

My love for you exceeds and transcends the momentary lapses of time that continually relinquishes it's substance.
As the seasons come to pass and yield their unequivocal beauty,
My love for you shines within my heart,
For an eternity.

Bob Michon Jr.

I Call It....(Quilting Bee)

Women sitting round the table
Neatly sewing what there able
Each with there own unique style
All willing to go that extra mile
Some do this and some do that
Many like the latest fad
But all contribute what they can
Doing most of it by hand
Made into beautiful quilts of all kinds
When they are all finished, they usually are signed
Colors are picked out just so they match
Otherwise all of it would be a clash
Smiling and talking and happy to be
With all their good friends
At the quilting bee

Barbara Langley

Good Looking

Though I searched through the dead of the Winter,
Not a fragrant red rose could I find.
So I stopped at the old Corner Flower Shop,
And ordered a "store-bought-kind."

The Clerk said they too had a fragrance
And hoped they for me would suffice.
As she readied and tied them with ribbon,
I thought to myself; my how nice!

I asked then; to have them delivered.
The address, wrote down with a swirl.
'Said you won't need a name or a number,
Just look for a "Good Looking Girl."

Tim Turney

True Feelings

I dread to face the long black night
not knowing if I'll see the dawn's early light.
or hear "Good Morning" wishes from the Nurse's Aide.
I'm old, I'm alone, I'm so afraid.

So I find excuses to ring my bell.
Knowing I can do most things quite well on my own.

And that they're saying "It's him again I should have known"!
I've just been down to see that man!
Oh, but if only they could understand
that I'm really a very lonely old man,
Who'd like them to stay and chat a while
and maybe give me a friendly smile.
It would help me to face that long black night
not knowing if I'll see the dawn's early light...

Diane Cuillerier

Friends

Girls made mud pie and tea,
While boys played cops and cowboys.
All at the ripe, young age of three -
Their prize possession was their toys.

Age 13, the girls are done with dolls;
Boys are starting to look at girls
Wondering if they should call
And ask a girl to a dance, to twirl.

Now one is older and knows much better,
What a friend is supposed to mean.
They are happy to receive a letter
From a friend they have not seen.

A friend is someone close to the heart,
With whom no one wants to part.

Christi Jo Greiner

Tragedy Of Cherry

Sweet little cherry shaken from tree
Not quite ripe, nevertheless set free
Wandering throughout forests of adolescence
No Hansel or Gretel making woods less dense
Lacking patience for time's progression, why
You'd toss up an egg, expect it to fly
Waiting on fate at each clearing
Causes too much pain in the grass
Besides, one who breaks his compass
Dares not sit on the shards of glass

Enduring one full circle of pain, within half a season's time
Not finding some way home soon, might make cherry misplace her
mind
Then you and dates will never be in sync
Love surrounding, but poisonous to drink
Still, shed your last shred, dive right out of your skin
Forget testing water before you begin
Now only if pit was left with stem -
At the critical point of delivery
For although you've lost your faith in men
You'll never give up Christianity.

Carl Hines

Broken Hearts

No matter how much you are loved,
Nothing hurts more then your own beloved.
It's hard to love again,
knowing your heart still needs to mend.
When your heart is a shadow that never flows,
You still know love comes and goes.
You know deep inside your heart,
Nothing hurts more than a broken heart.
You've been hurt before,
Nothing so bad to stay so sore.
Although you know it takes time,
You don't want to wait a lifetime.
When your true love does arrive,
You know it was worth the heartache and cries.

Sandra O'Bumsawin

The Dreamers Dream

Yesterday the streets were wider
Now they're narrow I would go
To the place of mystery is gone
Truths revealed the wide-eyed wonder of a child
Is gone into the eyes of that distant dream
I had dreamt the visions of a peaceful life I live
The remnants of that child's dreams come true

Take my hand and take my feet
On the paths that no one has thread before
No one knows the pain that dreamers feel
I cross these rivers deep and wide
I search through valleys deep and wide
The other side starts where each new day begins

Now today I will walk the streets
Of yesterday has passed into a new beginning
Is in what I see from the bridges
On the rivers that flow from yesterday
It's clear that I am dreaming my reality
Dreams are real make them happen as a child
Plays the games that are reality at any age.

Dan Tucker

Out From The Dark

"Will you ever leave me?" said the small boy to his mom
"Oh no I'll always be here so don't you worry son."
The boy, contented, laughed, played and grew,
Two loving parents helping with the things he chose to do.
Then came the art of learning as he went off to school
There were holidays with trips, fun and hot dogs...
splashing in the pool.

The boy, now ten, felt a shadow start to fall
Sometimes his mom was lying down when he came in the hall
His dad was always looking sad then one day began to cry
"My son it's very hard to tell you this but mom is going to die".
"But dad she said she'd never leave me",
said the boy with plaintive voice
"Oh please don't ever blame her, she simply has no choice".
The days and nights were lonely, filled with bitterness and pain
Longing for a miracle to bring her back again

As time went by fond memories began to conquer grief.
The saying "time heals all things" became his firm belief.
And later on, a man now with family of his own
He knew the need and value of a safe and loving home
As he looked upon his children and traits began to show...
The legacy of a loved one gone so many years ago.

Rose Lindsay

Somalia

That million Dollar smile have I seen
on the face of a dying child in Somalia.
Every day is Christmas and each sunrise is New Year.

Nicholas begged his parents, "Mummy, Daddy,
tell them... I don't want to die."
"It is all right to die, my son.
In your next life, when peace will reign the world,
you will be a beautiful, healthy child."
Nicholas and Paul, twin brothers
got AIDS even before they were born.

Why Somalia? Why Sarajevo?
Why Nicholas and Paul?
Am I to change the channel
each time I see the dying faces?
They are dying by minutes and meters,
under the saffron, sorrel sun of Somalia and Sarajevo;
and I can't change those channels anymore.

Jay Banerjee

The House

Brown and green, ugly and old
Once put up for sale, but never sold.
Black cats wander 'round it at night —
And what's inside must be quite a fright.
The front door is always shut
The windows bares the face of a sorry mutt.
Then one day the door swings wide —
Revealing what's truly inside.
I blocked myself from the horrible sight
But then saw something different in that house in the light.
A woman sitting on the floor
No chairs or TV just a mat and no more
Two young children playing with the old mutt
Looking so happy in their little old hut.
Their clothes were all tattered, but the house very neat
No windows were shattered, and the dog ate meat
This house is no mansion that's filled with money
Just full of laughs when the weather is sunny.
This house is what no money can buy the rich or the poor —
For this house brings love beyond the tattered door.

Kyla Harwood

Light of God

As night falls upon the earth,
One by one people fall into a deep sleep;
Motionless,
As if death had come upon them.
Yet I do not,
For fear fills my heart,
Soul and state of mind,
For I may not wake.
It was my time,
Death himself has beckoned me,
Closer to him.
I can almost feel his cold fingers,
Slowly tighten around my fragile neck,
Yet I refuse to submit.
As his movements become slower and slower towards me,
I notice the sun slowly rising to the east.
I know I am safe;
For no one from the dark side can stand the light of God.

Christina Struthers

Xmas Tears

As we sat down at the table that snowy Xmas Day,
One chair was standing empty as we bowed our head to pray
'Twas a lost and lonely feeling not to see him sitting there,
But his spirit was there with us as we said our Xmas prayer.
And all through the Xmas season, though his face we could not see,
For it's a long long way to Heaven far past the tallest tree.
We knew that somewhere up there he was happy and content,
For to spend the Xmas season with God is Heaven sent.
I'm sure that he could see us as he looked down from above
And he knew our hearts were lonely as we longed for him with love
Yet if he could write a letter, I'm sure he'd tell us all,
that he's happy up in Heaven and our tears should cease to fall.

Ilsa Fleming

A Quiet Day in the World

It was a quiet day in the world today
Only a million guns fired
Only a million lives lost
Only a billion tears shed
And only a million infected
You take a breath of tainted air not knowing if it was your last
You see images on television that will never leave your heart
You can't sleep, haunted by their faces
The pain and sadness in their eyes
It hurts so much to see them so helpless
To know as much as you want to reach out to them, you can't
They're unreachable, untouched by the goodness of our world
A world we share in geography but not in peace and harmony
You've got to wonder how much it hurts to be alive
When all you see is darkness
When all you hear is torture
When all you smell is fear
And when you all taste is bitter
It was a quiet day in the world today.

Sharon Pereira

Tears Flow Freely And Often

The pain that grips my heart
  is like a cancer - all consuming.
It is eating away the very soul of who I am.
I am obsessed with it - I want to rip it out.
No amount of morphine can dull it.

  Meditation and prayer make it bearable
Will it go with me to my grave??
I look to God, Psychics, Astrologers
For answers, for PEACE

Debby Shaw

Peninsula

Semaphore scarlet of thoughts,
Opening you the way of its haven
Would like to be a wave, break in you,
Foam murmur full of promises
Sea, bathe you with a palpitating fluid,
Liquid case, split by a bubbling wake,as a torn fabric ...
Spray, whip you, O' gentle torture,
Sun,caress you, scorching tongue licking your offered flanks,
Tropic win your exiled heart,
Deserted island,shelter your wrecks,
Reef, that would smash your boredom,
Sand grain, adhere to your gilded skin pearled with salted moistness,
Glittering crystal on your amber body,
Breeze offer you ocean aromas,
Palm tree, A delectable heart,
Pearl, adorn you glistening,
Coral,blooming you with eternity,
Beach, at last, proud to raise your imprint,
But, anchored, earthman, I simply wait for tide.

Patrice Boqueho

Our Love

Some people say a rose is a symbol of
our love.

If it dies how can it be a symbol of
our love?

Does that mean that the same will happen
to our love?

I say the granite rock is a symbol of
our love.

Because it is strong, hard and unbreakable
like our love.

Ruthie Proudfoot

Mind Over Matter

What does it matter if the mind does wander
Over things gone by and time we did squander.
Our thoughts are with us both day and night
Some turn out badly and some turn out right.

For that is life to which we're born
To accept our future with little scorn.
To reject 'what-ifs' and lost chances
To accept 'what-is' with forward glances.

To keep our heads above our hearts
And in doing so, we make a start
To live, love and have peace of mind
For what really matters is the you, you'll find.

Joy Kenyon

The Great Escape

Pain, pain, it's in the corner of my brain.
Pain, pain, you think I'm insane?
Lock me up, take me away
I don't care if you throw away the key.
Pain, pain, it's in the corner of my brain
It's on the left, now on the right,
I whisper pain under my breath.
I start to swivel, then boom,
Now I'm being rolled on a bed into a room.
Tall man frowns, Mommy bends down, she kisses me.
I'm dead. Pain slips from under my head.
No more pain.
Pain, pain, you think I'm insane?
Pain, pain, it's in the corner of my brain.

Carrie Perreault

A Shakespearian Sonnet

Gentians I bring you from their Alpine cradle,
Praying they make love burgeon in your heart;
There 'tis my hope that they will light a candle,
Despite the alopecia of my art.
May this investment bring its dividend,
And I to my own devices be not left;
Helpless until my journey has its end,
Eternally of thy pure love bereft.
So allocate to me your true affection,
If my charisma moves you to be kind;
And by my Runcorn waters our election
To lasting bliss will leave dull self behind.
Then give your heed to this my cri de couer,
And I will love none but my only her.

E. W. Orr

Remember

Do not stand by my grave and weep,
remember that I'm only in a long, peaceful sleep.
I know that my death was a burden on you,
I could see you suffering as my illness grew.
The morning that I passed away,
I no longer wanted to stay.
Shining down on me were beams of light,
and I knew if I left it would be right.
You must always remember me in your heart,
for if you do we will never part.
Until the day you die I will watch over you,
and I think because of my death our friendship grew.
I will always remember the times we shared,
and how much for you I cared.
I hope that your feelings are the same,
and that our friendship to you wasn't just a game.
The times we shared were never a loss,
and one day our paths will cross.
But until then; do not stand by my grave and weep,
remember that I'm only in a long, peaceful sleep.

Erin Kinney

The Mind Journeys Into The Heavens

Man with piety and love of the Lord will wiser grow,
Restless will he be if love to his Lord he cannot show.

In journeys into the Lord's love, blessings will he meet,
And toiling to please the Almighty will to him be sweet.

Still waters shall a stale taste to their waters develop,
But to waters running, shepherds from far apart gallop.

Hungry Lions can only feed their cubs and find a prey,
When their own lands they desert and refuse to stay.
The sun will be abhorred if one day becomes motionless,
Like gold, unexploited, shall like earth be valueless.

Hilda Harbuk

Fudge

The mechanical smoothness of his movements,
Running like a new machine.
A distinguished, gentle animal;
With names in shows which gleam.
He shows appreciation
With the pleasure of his ride,
His complete and total disposition
Showing of his form of pride.
I can only sit and wonder
Of what life might be like,
A complete and total blunder,
Without my best friend,
Fudge.

Stacy Dyck

The Artist

There once was an artist, she called herself that;
She carried a bag and owned a stray cat.

She'd sit on a bench downtown on the street;
And say "come sit, take a load off your feet."

She'd talk and she'd listen to one and all;
No story too big, no story too small.

I said "an artist is a musician, painter or poet."
"Well I am a painter of people, I thought that you'd know it.."

"My art is quite different it's not on a sheet."
"I paint smiles on faces of people I meet."

"My work is rewarding, the pay really great;
I give out happiness and remove the hate."

Some call her the bag lady with the stray cat;
But she is an artist, no doubt about that!

Cindy Eakins

Hands Of Time?

Lone in love is hard for people to do.
She loves him and lets him know.
She tries to hold him tight,
But she knows she can't have him for life.
He is looking for more.
Some things she can offer and others out of reach
He wants to turn back the hands of time.
She knows if he could he wouldn't be with her.
Circumstances keeps him.
Although not by her intentions,
She tells him to go and then prays he won't,
for if she heard the door her heart would also go.
She's so afraid he will leave her someday
She tries to hurry him to go or stay.
But she knows someday she will face her biggest fear
And her eyes will be filled with tears.
She will set him free and try to let him be.
I know he can't be the one for me, he finds reasons not to be.

Lisa Card

Salmon Roses

Her favorite flower was a salmon colored rose;
she watered them, pruned them and helped them to grow.

She was kind and gentle in her own special way;
to some she wouldn't give them the time of day.

On the day of her death my world became dim:
I had lost my only grandmother, to Heaven, to Him.

I soon found out that she was happy and fine;
that she would always be with me, no matter the time.

I gave her a flower, a single salmon rose;
when placed in her hand, it began to blossom, to grow.

I know now you're with me, wherever I go;
in good times and bad, your spirit will show.

You're safe and you're happy and no longer in pain;
I'll love you and miss you...until we meet again.

All my love.

Diana L. Cross-Armstrong

Strangers When We Meet

Strangers when we meet
Shivering with thrills
Looking forward to a treat
Thinking what the other thinks

Sharing common feelings
Wondering what will be on the next reelings

We get coy and contemplate on our chances
When will be holding passionate dances

We have joy and fun
Which make our relationship to flourish on

Before we know, we are together
Loving and caring for each other

Now the stranger of yesterday
Are the happy lovers of today
That is the natural way
To strive for a life of happy way

Although the best thing in life is free
But that doesn't give happiness a guarantee

M. H. A. Farhad Amidi-Nouri

Still I Cannot Hate

I see bones and hair,
Shoes and glasses,
While in a Polish hell ruled by the devils brother,
But still I cannot hate.

I see women's brushes, men's talisim and babies tattered clothing,
But still I cannot hate.
I see splintered boards where people laid their weary bodies,
I see where people slaved and tried to exist,
And still I cannot hate.
I see the death and destruction,
But still I cannot hate.

I won't continue this tragedy,
I won't spread the disease.
I won't fan the flames,
That hate like this inspires.

Jennifer Staffenberg

Silence in Peace

The silence everything is silent.
Silence in the day
Silence in the night
Silence in my mind
The silence he hasn't always been here.
There use to be noises, music and violence,
screams of the dying and of the living.
There use to be voices of everything
until the silence came.
He took it all away.
Now there's silence in the noises
Silence in the music
Silence in the violence and
Silence in all the voices
Even my thoughts are silent as my voice begins to scream

The silence in the silence.
There is but one good thing in the silence.
In the silence there is peace.

K.C. Maranne Brown

Have You Ever Felt....

Have you ever felt... so sad it seems the world's come to an end?
so sad you feel you don't have a single friend?
or like your life has reached a dead end?
Have you ever felt... like the world's turned it's back on you?
like you have no one to turn to?
or that there was nothing anyone could do to help you?
even if they wanted to? (which they didn't.)
Have you ever felt... like nothing was going right?
or crying with all your might - throughout the entire night?
Have you ever felt... like you're facing the world alone?
or like no one cares and you're on your own? All alone?
Have you ever felt... so broken-hearted you'd rather die than take the pain?
only to love once more and have your heart broken again?
or like pretty soon love would drive you completely insane?
Have you ever felt... all whom you love turn their backs on you?
walk away and forget all about you?
like you'll never find someone to love you?
Have you ever felt... like you're sorrow would go on endlessly?
or have you ever felt, like me?

Alethea Pantoja

Someone To Care

Somewhere tonight hearts are breaking
somehow the pain just won't quit.
Someone has cried oceans of tears
and no one has noticed them yet.

Is there someone to care for the hurting
Is there someone to say, I do.
Is there someone to give a hug
and say dear one, I love you.

Then do it today while there's time
for tomorrow may be too late.
And the heart that was longing for love
decided no longer to wait.

Cora Herridge

What Is Love?

Love is something beautiful to define
sometimes impossible to describe
short as the word love is
deep as its meaning is

Love is born in heart and mind
sometimes difficult to find
the true meaning of love
here and around the world

For love and peace must be together
finding hearts to stay forever
planting seeds here and there
for a better future together

Like a mother feeding her beloved baby
the roots of love are born to grow
like an enormous ocean beyond the universe
flooding people without a heart

Please tell me, please tell me
What is love?
Here and around the world
Please no more blood stop the war

John Henao

One Summer Night

There I was on a calm summer night;
Standing in awe, of everything in sight...

The moon and it's glow,
The night and it's woe...

Vehicles of every kind passing by,
Planes in the sky...

Rapt from every past day,
An impression of regret gone astray.

There I was on a cool summer night;
Upright in wonder from everything in sight...

Stars radiant, bright and clear,
Stars distant, yet seeming so near.

People sauntering by,
Not a billow in the sky...

There I was on a calm summer night.
Standing in awe, of everything in sight.
The deep, mysterious eve. The fear of having to grieve.

Standing, alone; in a world so cold.
Lest, seemingly a being so bold.
There I was on a cool summer night...

Clinton W. J. Collins

The Loner

The girl walks along the sandy beach,
Staring longingly at the blue green ocean.
Her eyes bloodshot, the only proof that she shed a single tear.
Remembering how the evil loneliness crept upon her the night before;
Scarring her, leaving her with horrid nightmares,
In her already restless sleep.

There is no comfort, no more love inside.
Just the cold emptiness.

No sighs of life surround her.
The trees, the ocean and the sky are her only companions.
But they can't chase away the pain.

The girl is so fragile and weak,
For her soul left her years ago.
She yearns to find it but ends up in defeat.

Escaping the never ending misery is impossible.
But she knows that her search for sanity will soon come to an end.

Jessica Brantley

The Rose

So slowly has the summer gone by,
If I said this, it would be a lie,
Another year is soon to start,
And fall will come, as summer will part.
Leaves will fall from trees so green,
as old and new faces shall be seen.
New friendships are sure to take place,
With people from every possible race.
As year '95 grows to a close,
The new summer will unfold like a rose,
Then the next year shall be built,
And will grow old, just as a rose would wilt.

Sarah O'Sullivan

Water Is My Love

You are the water
That I drink, that I bathe in that I live

Your love flows within my veins
Without you I would go insane

You are the sweat
That lies above my pores
Your love is hidden
Behind closed doors

You are the rain
That washes away the flames
All evil, all sorrow
My heart untamed

You are like the river
That flows to the lake
There not much more
I can take

You have purified my soul
And set my love free
You have refused all I have offered
You have refused to love me...

Mirella Morrone

A Portrait Of Love

In faith's deep my eyes enfold the one true candle,
That lifts my weary soul to see rose breath dewing soft,
And nights keeping you from knowing that for you, I want to be...

What no one ever could before, but I as fools do,
Had dreams of being good enough to know your thoughts as mine,
What cry to heaven's ear,
Will tell me if I could

Now looking deeply into blue, blue eyes,
I think of your warmth, and cringe thinking of,
The chill in my heart at the price to be wise,
And the flow of my soul when I think of love.

Then I plead unto life, that He'll let me do
A portrait of truth, with portraits of you

Armand Urion

When I Sit Under The Moonlight

I wish upon a star
that you could be mine
to be around me every minute,
to be around me all the time.
I stare when you are near
yet, I dream when you are far.
I wish you were always close
when I wish upon a star

I look upon the sea
and all I picture is you,
your face shines in the water along with mine, too.
When the wind blows my way.
I feel your arms around me, so soft and so gentle
when I look upon the sea

I sit under the moonlight to rest on a hill.
When you lie down beside me,
the world seems so still.
I'd love if we were together going off in the night,
I wish it could be
when I sit under the moonlight.

Taryn Cramer

Untitled

Sitting in a shallow corner.
The darkness is my only friend.
For the dark does not judge me,
Even in my times of sadness.
The darkness holds me tightly
As I cry my tears for you.
It was there when you weren't.
The darkness fights the emptiness in my heart.
An emptiness that not even the love songs on
the radio can fill.
For those songs are a dull roar, drowned out by the crying.
Loud tears that only the dark can understand.
Soon enough the darkness dries my face.
Yet why am I being comforted by the darkness?
Why aren't you next to me?
Holding me, fending off the emptiness.
I reach out to touch you.
But the darkness is all that brushes my fingertips.
I must go now. The darkness is calling me.
Calling me when you should have.

Erin J. Brown

Somehow

Somehow I believe in dreams of the heart
The fairy tales of childhood
When a princess finds her prince
and lives happily ever after.

Somehow, I believe in movies of the long ago
When a cowboy finds his lass
and they ride off into the sunset.

Somehow each of us has a joy,
peace and love captured in our hearts
from our childhood past,
we hang onto this because in the
future when we are grown
We somehow find the dream of our dreams.

Kelly-Jo Cox

Summer Sonnet

The cookie jar's empty, there's crumbs on the floor,
The mirrors are murky, and gum's stuck to the door.
The coat hooks stand empty, like sentinels forlorn,
The deep freeze is ravaged, most everything's gone!
But the memories and shouts, the banging of doors,
The bouncing of balls, and babes on all fours——
Still lives in our hearts, memories time can't erase.
The grandkids are gone!!! There's a smile on our face!!

The smile lasts all day, while we pick up the toys.
We have time to think, there's not any noise!
The bedding's all washed, and hung out to dry,
The mud's swept away....but there's something awry!
The house seems so lonely, there's something alack,
It must be the grandkids....Please hurry back!!

Norma L. Smith

Medjugorje

The gentlest breath of wind blows through the young thorn trees.
Is Thy Holy Spirit coming to inspire and love us?

The sun blesses with its warmth
The breeze cools and refreshes
The countryside of Medjugorje
Takes our breath away.

Blow more, more, Holy Spirit
Replace the breath we have lost
And fill us with Thine Own.

Rosa Mills

The Pilot

The day was cold and dreary
The snow fell in a sheet,
As we laid our most beloved one
Down to his last long sleep.

A loving friend to man or beast
A smile that warmed the heart
A bitter foe to cruelty or sin
Ever a hand to help one win.

He flew the skies in time of strife
Many times risking limb or life
To keep his loved ones safe and sound
A better world for old or young.

How we miss his happy ways
The tricks and jokes he used to play
Bringing happiness from the day he was born
From our lives and hearts so ruthlessly torn.

J. Herbert

Father and Son

Since time began, the legacy of man
The torch it must be passed.
From flicker to flame, the family name,
It must be built to last.

The story goes that one reaps what one sows
And that mirrors never lie.
The apple, you see, falls not far from the tree;
A fallen apple am I.

Things become clearer as I turn to my mirror
With a concentrated stare.
If I look real close, I can see us both
And the endless traits we share.

Now I've been blessed with a newborn guest
He uses my mirror too.
The torch it is there for the family heir
With an image of me and you.

Dean Avery

The Upgrading School

Our country needs them, the ones without work.
The trucker, the helper, the maid, the young soda jerk.
To learn a new trade, there's no time to fool
So we turned up for class at the upgrading school
We take out our books and it all looks like Greek.
But we're adding and dividing by the end of the week.
Then comes the decimals and percentage too.
You'd think a few simple fractions would do! Now it's a circle,
and now it's a rule oh dear, we sure know it's an upgrading school.
There's Science and English, and they're both pretty deep.
If you don't understand them, try falling asleep.
When the ruler goes 'crack', you'll wish you were dead.
You'll get air pressure and clauses 'til they run out of your head.
You'll learn about nouns, and the odd molecule.
We'll, isn't it fun at the upgrading school.
Come down to the lunch room and hear all the chatter.
It's boy friends and hairdos, who cares about matter?
Or, atoms, or pistons, or air while we powder our nose, run a comb
thro' our hair. The buzzer will sound, we balk like a mule.
But it's room 14 at the upgrading school.

Ruby E. Schell

Winter

It's windy, it's dark, it's late...it's three A.M.
The wind is whipping around the house
as though it is trying to gift wrap us.
The snow is thick and very curly
It is as though we could finally touch the fog
only to have it melt in our fingers
and then...disappear.
The wind, the artist, creates an oil of ice,
As she whips designs gracefully in the snow,
She whistles around the corner of the house,
Trusting us to go and see her works,
Her majestic displays and her powers.
The snow becomes the foam on the ocean,
washing in and out with the strength of the wind.
Acting out the role of the earthly tide,
Always picking up and moving on.
How can it snow so much?
And leave such little evidence of it behind.
The wind, begs of her captured audience to
boldly glare at her majestic art.

Linda Knelsen

If Tears Could Only Talk

If tears could only talk,
they could tell you better than I
of the sadness that exhausts my soul.

They could tell you that I am my own
worst enemy, for I unconsciously fan
the fires beneath my fears.

They could tell you of the regret
that shudders through me and leaves me
raw with distress.

Their quantity will tell you of the hurt
that lies within my heart, aching
to be soothed and softened.

Their wetness will tell you of the waterfalls
of memories that bind me, yet yearning to
release and flow freely by.

If my tears could only talk,
they would tell me of their hidden powers,
that frees me to feel peace ...
If tears could only talk.

Sandra Howard

Whales

The ocean wide, the cries so sweet
They flip and turn in the water so deep

The fear grows more as another one dies
The sounds of cries as it closes its eyes

Another lost to the unforgiving, whose
Hearts and souls care not for the living

Extinction is a sickly word
That we have so often said and heard

We cringe at its sound and
Say when we hear it

What a terrible thing
But we soon forget it

The whales we hear will soon not be there
Unless we stand up and start to care.

Nadia Kolly

"I Have Feelings Too!"

In class I stumble over written words
They Trip me us and make me cross
The letters dance and jumble up
Pupils laugh and snigger at my mistakes
I blush then panic and this makes me worse!

My teacher then says "it doesn't matter".
But it matters a lot to me
I'd read that same page yesterday
And read all those words so perfectly
But not today.

Inside my head my thoughts are clear
And I know that I know those words to say
So reading aloud is torture for me
Spelling words in class is something I fear
And the pleasure of books is denied to me.

I dream of writing a school text book
That every school must use
Then I would get the last laugh you see
At all those pupils who laugh at me
Dyslexia rules - O.K.

Jonathan Charles Wood

In My Cage

I walk solemnly through the forest of dreams
Thinking of my life that's in the future and past
Watching the beautiful surroundings that lay
Not knowing if feelings are meant to last
I gaze upon the long road ahead
Wondering it someone will be in my heart
To hold me forever and never let go
To promise me nothing, will keep us apart
I stop to sit by a flowing stream
Looking at the fresh water that runs by
Alone with myself and the quiet wood
I hang my head and begin to cry
Experiencing pain in the depths of my soul
I reveal the tears that I held within me
I see the emptiness inside that will never grow old
I will remain in my cage, to never be free.

Leah Richter

The Rider

Through the depth of passion
Through the might of glory...he road
Through the abundant villages
To the roaming pebble-paved streets
In search of his treasure...he road
With a burgundy velvet cloak
And snake skin boots
With no map, just sense of direction...he road
Through the days in which bitter cold
Blew over the land
No nourishment was waiting in his path...he road
And yet he road to find his treasure
No clue of where, or why
But he kept his promise to his people
That ride he will, and never may he halt
Until he finds this treasure, this virtue
This exquisite, caressing and beguiling object
One that could bring much wealth to his people
One which would cause revelation to the world - the meaning of life -

Maya Honigman

Hopes of Peace Turn to War

(With special thanks to Kyle Smith)
Time is short, people grow weak,
The wars last long, leaders don't speak.
Night grow cold, while skies go dark,
The days are gray, and bombs make their mark.
People scream, while others die,
The terror is great, and the mourners cry.
Adults go hungry, and children starve,
Headstones are made, names are carved.
Fighting slows down, but the time isn't right,
The war was goes on, and becomes deadlier over night.
U.N. comes in, the tries to make peace,
The leaders listen, and fighting begins to cease.
But still people fall, as if they're lead,
The war is now over, millions are dead.
We realize how senseless this was,
Our dreams are ruined from what everyone does.
We hope for peace yet nothing comes through,
But if we try harder our dreams will come true.

Leanne Andre

Love Expressed

A young girl jumps into her mothers lap
To feel her warm embrace
The love, respect, the trust and joy
Is all there in her face.

A small boy reaches for his grampa's hand
They saunter across the field
With nature in it's finest realm
They see just what she yields.

The seasons pass,the kids grow older
The boy has noticed the girl
He gives her an engagement ring
The oyster's magnificent pearl.

Out on a Sunday drive one day
They pass bedside a temple
They stop the car and go inside
Surprised it was so simple.

They gave their hearts to God that day
Their love was everlasting
And when they die one thing their sure of
To heaven they will be passing.

Judy Butt

Opportunity

Opportunity beckons, you cannot resist.
Too much temptation for your feeble will.
You know the risks, you weigh up your chances,
You get the green light and use your skill.

Relax, you've done it, piece of cake really.
Why do it - excitement or greed?
You don't know, you just know that you must.
Are you fulfilling some primeval need?

From the touch on your shoulder, you know you've been caught.
Was it being careless that gave you away?
Or that age old maxim; there being right from wrong.
Did someone Up there have his say

J. L. Benson

Dreams of the Heart

Amidst our youthful dreams, reality is a fairy tale
We are all equal in our quest for the light,
Maturity evolves our limitations, like a ship in a gale,
Floundering with destiny in a windswept night.

Hearts are anchored to success and bliss,
We live not in fear, our ideals we will reach,
Till cruel reality marks us, like the black widow's kiss,
Eroding confidence, character, like colours in bleach.

Through life's wonder we hear power, wealth must be acquired
But love of family, friends and health are things
to GOD in our hearts far stronger to be admired,
Whilst eternity beckons with heavenly wings.

Remember our intellect allows us the choices,
to follow what's right within our inner most voices.

Peter Alexander Brandt

Being Human

We all exist somewhere in the past.
We merely linger through the present.
The fine line between our fantasies
And the harsh reality
Is but determined by our calculating conscience.
We only dream to achieve that
Which will be taken away from us,
Because our mere existence
Is determined by the ticking of the clock.
And so we strive to posses our future,
Which only soon becomes an element
Of an invisible past.

Diana Saakian

I'm Sorry

There are so many miles between us
What I'm trying to say is a must
I feel really sorry for hurting you
I never meant to put you through a lot of pain
I'm really sorry

It has been so long for you
to forgive me I was in the wrong to put your through
a lot of grief I'm really sorry

I wish, I could change the past but I can't
If I could, I would make it last
I'm really sorry

I have felt guilty over the years
for hurting you
All I wont is to hear
your voice again I'm really sorry

Nicole Buzikievich

Footprints In The Sand

The ocean roars in response to the cries of the gulls,
What is the meaning of their many calls?
Are they inviting their feathered friends to a feast?
Or are they protecting their territory like a savage beast?

Off on the horizon some crows are heard.
Dinner is wanted by each and every bird
Who will starve and who will eat?
Or will they learn to share in the summer heat?

It is now calm as the water laps against the shore.
Up in the sky the gulls all soar
The food is gone, silence surrounds the sands.
Many footprints are seen that were never planned.

Jennifer Prokop

"It's Christmas Time in the Bahamas"

'Twas the month of the long awaited day,
When family gatherings, parties with ham and turkey, and
Good cheer, would permeate the atmosphere.

Shops and businesses, employers all,
Glowed as they displayed their yuletide cloy.
Children's eyes all a-glow, as they envisioned
Santa's show, with his reindeers, sweets and many treats.

Music - sweet cry, flowed exorbitantly from every store,
House, car and individual lip, as they all proclaimed
With asserted pride the advent spirit.

The songs of cowbells ringing; costumes, the Valley, Saxons
And Music Makers - whistles, horns and drums and all,
Brought rushed memories of Junkanoo's enthrall.

The young and young at heart elegantly adorned
For the season's purport, proceed to worship
In our saviour's hour, to partake and pay homage to a
brother and stalwart.

Its joyous spirit and healthy cheer,
brings delicate memories of many years - all so special and very
divine, reminds us that it's Christmas Time.

Clover M. Bonamy

The Death Of A Mother

I was taking out the cattle,
When I heard the door rattle,
I looked around,
And saw a big coffin on the ground,
I became furious,
But inside I was curious,
I ran up to the door,
What I saw I couldn't take anymore,
My mother was dead;
I suddenly felt a pain in my head,
I knew she was no longer going to be there,
When she was alive, for her I didn't care,
Inside I felt the pain,
I knew she wouldn't live again,
As I cried and cried,
She died and died,
For now I know
The love I didn't show,
Has gone to waste,
In such great haste.

Rhea Woodroffe

Aging

Aging is but a state of mind
Life is like a highway yet
you fall behind
Coming upon death's road
Everyone knows your growing old
Your life long companion has gone away
You sit alone each passing day
Dependance has flown upon you fast
And you think how much longer will it last
As kids run to find a place to meet
You now need help to cross the street
As your time comes upon it's way
I hope to see you another day.

Melissa Bice

"It's Hard To Be A Hero"

It's hard to be a hero,
When life's going kind of rough.
It's hard to be a hero,
When you get the feeling of just giving up.

It's hard to be a hero,
When all you want to do is cry.
It's hard to be a hero,
When you're so sick you just want to die.

It's hard to be a hero,
When nothing stays the same.
It's hard to be a hero,
When you don't even known your Daddy's last name.

It's hard to be a hero,
When your inner strength gets weak.
It's hard to be a hero,
When darkness sets in deep.

I've had to be a hero,
Surely you can see, my downs almost destroyed me.
I've had to be a hero, to keep my spirit alive,
Because I've always been a hero, I've survived.

Angele Jacobson

In Sympathy

I've stood there too; on this lonely road
When someone dear has died
I've stood there too; with the ache in my heart;
With the pain, and I have cried.

I stand with you, in this time of grief.
It hurts me to see your sorrow.
I stand with you, in your time of need,
And pray for a bright tomorrow.

The void that the death of a loved one leaves,
Is a space that can never be named.
The pain in our chest at the time of the death,
Is the love that remains unclaimed.

Time is the healer; and God is the cure,
We know not what is in store,
But rest assured, those gone on before
Stand in peace at Eternity's door.

Rose Salsman

Dreaming

I have a dream
which stronger and stronger grows
That one day soon I'll celebrate
My Freedom Day — I've set the date
So I'll not have to meet another's demands
But set in place my own
My dreams - my wants - my have to's
I'd like to first just sit and gaze
Across the water shimmering, dancing
When touched by the sun's warm rays
To hear the slapping at the rocks
And watch the birds gather in flocks
To play their silly little games
In and out amongst the foam.
I'd like my home to be right here
With all this beauty very near
A never ending vista for the soul
To reverse the stressful ravages that take their toll.
A restoration for tired, tired eyes
An ever lasting solace for the heart.

Norma J. May

Deathblow (The Fatal Vision)

The blood-red sun blazes - struggling to pierce the darkness,
while giant man-made chimneys disgorge poison
into the murky sky above.
There is no sunrise or sunset - only never-ending obscurity
in a time and place where no one "Sees"...
or "Hears"...
or "Speaks"!
Rain forests lay barren
a "testimonial" to man's greed,
Fish float in grotesque artistry
a "tribute" to man's mindless ignorance,
Birds lay in oily cerecloths
a "reminder" of man's carelessness,
and carcasses of wild beasts lay scattered randomly
a "monument" to the mighty hand of "Humanity"!
The world is silent, save for the laborious grinding of machines
that generate synthetic, materialistic, "wealth"
for man, in his stupidity, to enjoy...
while the beauty of nature, goes "to sleep" forever!

Jennifer Marshall

Reflections of a Stranger

Why did you grow from that ideal age?
Why change so quick from a child?
The differences shock me. When looking at you
I expect innocence, meek and mild.

I see you're confused about who you should be.
The same old routine keeps you young.
Yet you've aged to adulthood, you're now breaking free,
But the ladder gets tougher each rung.

Show me yourself if you dare!
Can you do it? Do you know who you are?
You have matured and grown much too fast for my taste,
Yet on life's road you're still stuck in the tar.

Who are you today? Where will you be tomorrow?
Why are you avoiding my query?
You hide from my contact. You're open to none.
What is it that makes you so wary?

I look at you and what I see scares me.
You're a stranger staring right back.
Wait! Is that hope in those familiar eyes?
Or just the mirror reflecting a crack?

Jenn Thomas

Eagle in the Sky

Smooth and powerful,
wide and large,
splashing the water surface with the tip of his wings,
scooping, diving, leaving no trace.

As he stops,
he peers from a ledge, on high.

Scanning
for his next kill.

There it lays under a bush,
its brown jacket and floppy ears,
as he swoops down to pick up the rabbit
in his great talons,
it shoots out from under the bush,
and starts a chase.

The rabbit is no challenge for this
creature of the sky.

With one gigantic dive of speed,
the rabbit is violently jerked off his feet,
and taken to feed the mother's babies.

Christina Semak

Untitled

Sun twinkles - dances in the shade
Wind - light on the leaves
Fluttering green cool shade
Peace is just a touch away.

Laying, sitting talking
On the grass, together in the shade
Loneliness far, far away.

No past, no future
Just "now", together in the shade

Time races away but not together in the shade
Time is now young and old all together in the shade
If only for a twinkling - forever - together in the shade.

Barry Thacker

Guardian Angel

Together we reach the end of the earth
With each passing flower and tree we
grow closer together like the vines that connect them.
Our journey is constant like the rivers that flow
The wind and the rain urge us along
and it is the sun that guides us.
The skies are the heavens that give
us faith and the soil is what nurtures.
Dreams and visions lead us with insight
but it is the soul that takes us there.

Shana Wannamaker

Nature's Peace

Running wild through a field of daisies,
without a care in the world.

As free as a dove flying through the sky,
as free as a star amid the heavens.

The sun looking down upon the tenderness
of your being,

With rays of warmth whispering as you dance
with the flowers of spring.

What solitude and serenity in these meadows
so green and lush.

A feeling of belonging, as you speak with
nature so bountiful.

Trickling streams sing soft melodies,
as the mountains quietly sway.

The trees open their loving arms to cradle
the squirrels, and the eagle soars with manly stride.

Then, as the sun closes it's eyes to the world,
bright diamonds shine against a velvet sky.

The daisies hang their heads to rest, as you
dream of the peace you'll reclaim tomorrow.

Francine Kohut

My Night Angel

I'm awakened once again
by the gentle shudder
as you quickly fade into the night,
awakened by the whisper
of something taking flight...
and as I rise from out my sleep,
the memories through my mind do creep...
Did I encounter darkness
more powerful than even Death,
or is it but an illusion -
this taste of blood upon my breath?

Jared Bielby

Beauty Within

If someone came and turned off the light
Would there really be love at first sight
Perhaps with what they've let out from inside
But when your scared it can easily be denied
The best thing God created is definitely our mind
For intelligence, understanding but first to be kind
Some people you'll think it's only within
But we've learned it's o.k it's not a sin
If you do use someone's image in vain
You'll suffer the consequences which is usually pain
So do you really think there'd be love without light
I think beauties within and there actually might

Brooke Roy

Our Friendship

From climbing rocks, to first kisses;
You and I are just like sisses.
Sure we've argued, sure we've cried;
But we love each other deep inside.
Picnics and beaches and grand shopping spree's,
To enter our friendship we needed no keys.
If you left there'd be a hole,
Cut right from my life;
So I will be there 'til and after,
That your someone's wife.
I hope you'll be there when I walk down the isle;
Side by side, you and I,
Together we'll walk a mile.
Our friendship is like a barrier,
To protect me from all danger,
And to each other, you and I,
Shall never be called a stranger.

Amanda Dawn Apt

"To You My Friend"

Life is such a strange journey yet unknown,
You may withstand or you may fall,
but it all goes round like a ball.
Then one time I really felt lost
when a person came along.
That person was you, you lifted me up.
Then we've been friends ever since.
Sharing thoughts and feelings,
while our friendship grows stronger.
In joys and in pain, you were there beside me all the time.
Comforting me, while I comfort you.
And all the times we shared together
only memories can trace.
For five years now we've known each other.
Yes, its a long time but now you have to go.
With only memories to treasure and hopes to stand again.
But realizing, that we've gone a long way and longer we have to go
my friend... for friendship knows no distance.

Karen Bagadiong

Untitled

A gift's true value can only be totally realized once
you understand the dynamic potential it possesses.
A gift should never be taken for granted you may not get another.
Be one with your gift,
understand it like you would understand yourself.
Be careful, if the gift is powerful, treat it with respect.
Do not let it intimidate you.
Usually a gift is earned, do not give it away.
Use the gift with discipline, tact and skill.
Enjoy the gift,
This gift called..... Life!

Michael Schwenk

Untitled

To Whom It May Concern:
You'll never walk alone my dear
You'll always feel my presence near.
Even though we're far apart,
I love you so with all my heart.
Nights and days will pass to years
And this will soften all your fears
Sometimes you'll stroll down memory lane,
But let it go when causing pain
I want for you such happiness
You'll find your way through all this mist
So hug the children oh so tight
And kiss them gently both good night
And as the dawn comes breaking through
You'll find your way to start anew
Now let me go, don't hold me tight
For Jane, everything will be alright

Dolores Phelps

My Sweet Dream

It always seems you're in my thoughts, haunting all my dreams.
you're on my mind, in my heart, always there it seems.

Even though we're far apart, I'm in your thoughts I know.
you take me with you in your heart wherever you may go.

My heart is warm and loving when filled with thoughts of you.
you're in my hopes, you make me strong, you make me struggle
through.

Deep inside my sweetest dreams, I'm always loving you.
If I didn't have you, I'd know not what to do.

You've been there in my heart of hearts, waiting all along.
Waiting for the chance to meet to finally come along.

Often when I think of you a chill runs down my spine.
I sometimes stop to wonder if you're really mine.

If you're a dream, don't wake me up, I'd never want to know.
If you're a dream, and not for real, I'll sleep forever more.

Connie Chaput

A Precious Stone

Grandmother, a precious stone you are,
You shine like the sun on a summer day.
The greatest gem is you by far,
Your spirit and soul are like a Shakespearean play.
A diamond is adored on a lovely woman's finger,
A ruby is as red as love itself.
But your truth and honesty will always linger,
The emerald is a world of green all in itself.
The sapphire burns like fire in the night,
Gold and silver are queens and kings.
But in my eyes you are the most heavenly sight,
Always saying the most heavenly things.
Grandmother, we will never be alone,
Because grandmother, you are a precious stone.

Samuel Weissman

A Passive Passion

I can not say in words how much I want you
The sun couldn't shine long enough.
And the darkness would add a mood of solitude.
To you a flower should surrender, yet
The heavens troubled tears only broaden problems.
The burden of desire is like a fire on water,
You could comfort the strains of love
For I know I love, and need to show it.

Michael G. Van Walleghem

A Tear of Lamentation

It is
the same
rain that for
five days mourned
your death a year ago.
On this dreary night it
is impossible to prevent the
tears from welling in my eyes,
or the sadness from flooding my
thoughts. There is such a heaviness
in this mother's heart. The four seasons
have come and gone; all day there had
been no hint of rain. It is as if nature,
too, is lamenting (as did Demeter for her
daughter and I for my son) the loss of
your smile, your vibrancy, your love
of life. Or, does she come just to
comfort me in the fact that so
many of her sons have been
taken senselessly?

Joan A. Honeycutt

TIDES

Tides of joy and then of pain
Like sun that suddenly turns to rain
Tides of smiles and then of tears
Like memories turning fast to fears

Like screams of hate to songs of love
Tides of hell and heaven above
Like broken heart to helping hand
Tides, we need not understand

Marc D'Ambrose

Eternal Passion

Smiling eyes in a picture
A kiss free-floating in the wind
Your fragrance embedded in my sheets
Signify love without trite expressions.

Kissing in the darkness
A touch from your hand
Your unclothed body next to mine
Signify love without one-way pressures.

Copulating by the fire
A subtle moan from your lips
Your sex filled with my lust
Signify love without any inhibitions.

Whispering into your ear
A delicate flutter from my tongue
Your climax and mine simultaneous
Signify love with uninterrupted eternal passion.

Avery Kazuhiro Egerer

"For Robynne"

Under a chilled autumn sky,
As would a leaf, plucked
And carried by a breeze,
May your still heart one day turn,
And slowly drift to me.

Fergus Drake Smith

Circle

Chrysalis Embryo began dreaming. Her vision was of a sleeping girl who awakens to pen the following words:

I exist as an everlasting dream. I could be the World Soul itself, but I am not sure. This I do know: everything imaginable is alive in me.

Thus having written, the writer falls into another swoon. The mirage ended. Miss Embryo woke. She stepped to the desk and wrote her story. She returned to bed and slept.

Clay Norris

The Child Asleep

I tiptoe into the room wherein you sleep
Glide o'er the polished pine floors of the bedroom
Adroitly step between the toys aheap
And, swaying, skirt the frame of sturdy handloom
With reverence approach your hidden bower
Your antique cot, a golden-oak four-poster
And flanked each side by sprays of lilac flower
Abundant in their scent, as well their cluster
The damask canopy of midnight blue
Its drapery of muslin fine descending
Alike to starry heaven, of that same hue
Through archéd windows from the lintel pending
I view, as Peace within and Space without come blending.
The outspread starfish fingers on the quilt
From out a sleeper pink, its sleeves are peeping
The ash-brown hair, with auburn highlights gilt
From out the bonnet tulle a garland circling
Your face; as cherubim do fly unseen a watch for cherubs sleeping.

. . . . .

Softly I part the screen, a grace to seek
Bend low to steal a kiss from petal-soft cheek.

E. T. L. Evans

A Different Kind of Prayer

In June, in Africa, I planted a pepper tree.
Watering the sapling, I watched quick rivulets of water
stain the dry, brown African earth an even darker brown.

In July, a world away, I saw you leaning against the subway door.
Closer to death than to life - the husk only of a human being.

My God, I thought, which terrible illness has invaded you,
eating away at your body until nothing is left?

God, is it an insidious drug that has brought you
to this point of no return?

My God, is this what it has come to, is this the sum total
of your ancestors' suffering taking a physical shape?

Is this the memory of the dark hold of the ship,
the sound of the chain, the lash of the whip?

My God, I thought, but said: "Sit down".

My God, I thought, as from behind a closed eyelid
one single tear trickled down your brown, dry cheek
staining it a darker brown like the rivulets of water did
the soil beneath the newly planted pepper tree.

My God, I thought!!!

My God!!! Hast Thou now really forsaken us?!

Maria Kamins

Waiting

A candle in the window
Weird shadows on the wall
A spider in the corner
Toward the trapped fly began to crawl
A lonely vigil waiting
Footprints in the snow
Sinister nights of evil
Ill-fated winds do blow
The old man watches for death
He's dead but does not know
The candle in the window now is burning low
A lonely vigil waiting
Footprints in the snow

Tia Shawnté

"The Miracle of Life"

When a man, looks into a mirror of his life,
and he has no faith,
care or strength in himself,
he is considered a loser.
When a conqueror, looks into a mirror of his life,
and there is pain, anger, hate and sadness,
and still strive to look beyond that for joy,
peace, happiness and faith.
This man looks for the meaning of life, and in which,
some how he may endure an inner respect for whom he is.

Lorine Thompson

Dreamer

The moon floats, romantically down on
the calm, dark river.
Sitting on the old, wooden bridge a
cool gentle breeze brushes by.
I feel the warmth of his body,
the strength in his arms that hold me.
Hearing in the distance the relaxing,
comforting sounds of the night.
Everything is so peaceful and perfect.
Until, a tear falls from my face,
rippling the water, disturbing everything.
Jolting back to reality.

Carla Adloff

Goodbye

How hard it is to smile,
When inside you hurt so much.
How hard it is to stay calm,
Nearly melting at your touch.
You never call or send me cards,
Two of the reasons that makes it so hard.
Losing you is, losing a jewel,
That will always and forever shine bright.
I'll never quite get over you,
'Cause I had everything to lose.
I lost. You won.
Now the battle between us is won,
Sorrowfully,
Our journey together is done.

Danielle Duval

My America

The home of the brave and the land of the free.
As I walk each day, I see people of all races
ask for work and food each day. I see grown
people killing one another.

Oh, my America! What has become of thee?
As I walk, I see adults and children selling and
taking drugs. All races, you see, are trying
to make it through life even when it seems dark and painful.

As I walk, I see these children each day.
I see mothers and fathers crying and screaming.
I see old people walk alone and put in nursing homes,
and forgotten. Can you see? No job, no respect.

Oh, my America! What is happening to us?
As I walk, I see women's rights coming slowly. It doesn't
matter that she is a doctor or senator. She can be raped or
murdered and receive little justice.

I live in America and put up with the pain.
Why are we fighting race against race, hunger and poor?
Oh, my America! The land of the free. Home of the brave.
I hope some changes can someday be.

Dolly Davis

Once, Now, and Forever

Once I thought that I loved you
but now I know I was wrong.
What we share isn't love, it's much
too powerful; it's much too strong.
It is as long as the rivers and as deep
as the sea.
It is as everlasting as all of
eternity.
It is as abundant and plentiful
as the sand.
If only you (and I) could understand.
There isn't a word known to man that
describes what we share.
If you deny me that truth, it would
be too much to bear.
Together we can do anything; go to
the edge of the earth and beyond.
Just hold me and love me until we are
ashes and the earth is gone.

Hope Michaels

This Boy

There comes a time when, I must die.
But the time has not yet come
For I must live to carry on, the ghost that's found
deep down.

His name is found deep inside,
His name is in my heart,
His name is on my face and on the stone in front of me.

For when he died I cried and cried,
My eyes were swollen shut.
For the pain he left behind I cried, for the hurt deep
down inside.

Now he's gone and past remains have haunted me yet since.
I know he's out there somewhere,
He's my angel of dissent.

I loved this boy, I speak about,
He was my only one.
But now I cannot tell him
His grave stone is but bound.

Jolene Gettinger

Can You Hear Her Cry

Can you hear it
Can you hear her cry
She sings out in rolls of thunder
Hear them dance across the sky
There
There it is again
The bellow of her soul
Soon the heavens will respond to her
And let the raindrops go
Plummeting toward her sun parched lips
Freed from mystic clouds
They'll quench the thirst
Of Mother Earth
And cleanse her dusty brow

Chris Craig

A Galapagos Tortoise

A Galapagos Tortoise
Crawls alone
Through Equadorian-nights
Weighing a hundred pounds.

Seek it out—-
Through search light procession
There I am hiding in a tree-top
So to wonder why?

Prehistoric fauna
Live on
In the dream
Of a torrid zone —
Night!

Eugene Zaia

The Storm

I heard the pitter patter of rain
falling upon the ground.
I saw the rain dribbling down my window.
I saw a flash of eye blinding
Lightning with a touch of deafening
Loud thunder, swiftly following behind.
I turned out the light and fell a sleep.

Anica Heggelman

Untitled

Be not angrily silent with me
for I am tired of
being mute to that of which you know!

Frustration creeps throughout my veins
...thicker to mine blood.
Because of this, I have fallen short.

You have blocked my soul of love,
and chained my heart to this wall...
forcing me to hide from any other.

Yet it has been so long
that I have forgotten how to!
...Even with you!

Oh how longing tears at ones mind;
keeps one from knowing oneself,
And hides thee from a love so true.

'Tis scary to know!
...that of which is quite impossible,
has happened to mine own eyes!

Hillary Markgraf

Caress

For you, I will caress.
For you, I will undress.
For you, I will dive into
The sea of your soul and
Swim as if swimming were
All I had to live for .
I want you in my world of caress.
I want you in the moonlight.
I want you undressed.
Kiss me once, care me twice
Kiss me again, and caress me all night.
Caress

Marvin L. White

Soft Light Six

Her eyes glisten.
Her smile shines dimly.
Her hand twitches, barely perceptible.
My grip tightens.
The chair moves.
She undresses before me.
My forehead beads.
I move toward her,
and I
spill
my drink
and my popcorn.
The lights come on
And I drive home
Alone.

Kristopher Matthew Clifford

When I Was Born

When I was born,
I had lots of hair.
Then it all fell out,
Gee that wasn't fair!

When I was one,
At the beach I found a feather.
My Mom thought it was cute,
Because my name is Heather!

I had a Care Bear Cake,
When I turned three.
That was real neat,
Happy Birthday to me!

My Mom had Andrea,
When I was eleven.
The minute I saw her,
I knew she was from Heaven!

Heather Grudis

Mainland Ignorance

I saw a little boy
sitting in the café
of Mauna Loa
with brown hair,
brown skin,
and brown eyes,
like a Mexican boy
I once saw in Tijuana.
And I wondered
if he spoke English.

Wendy Watson

Untitled

Eyes of ice and hair the color of a late October thunderstorm
I start from that dream
tasted in steamy lectures and on dusty sidewalks and in the glide of a droning highway under whispering clouds burning in a diluted sky.
Feeling for more, I have dreamed and seen and heard and sensed and smelled and tasted the hunger for motion and I know its tendrils.
Yearning for more, I have dreamed. Recollected. Sighed.
Introspected.
Inertia is a thirst...
-distant mountains.
I stride forth crossing streams and forests towns sailing over these fields closing in on the alter where the moment of reckoning has come that should put the rusty demon-blade from its silken bed so that I may finally dive headlong into the warm blueness shimmering and crystalline. Full. Open. Boundless.
Beyond those lavender crags.

Somewhere.

History has a certain flavor.
The sieve ought to render sweetness because
Love is not a tragedy.

B. D. Robertson

The Travel Clock

Beginning as a compact black box, the partitive article discloses.
It is now a three-sided object, two of the sides ebony
in color, shiny, and smooth.
However it is the other side that is impressive.
It once told a story of time, a story of constant rush and stress.
Hidden behind its crystalline facade of glass, the
clock is no longer functional.
The small hands, once marching around in their unchanged pattern
Have ceased in their ritual motion.
Surrounded by a frame of gold, the clock was once a portrait of time.
However, the timekeepers seem to have forgotten about
their once-frequent voyage
Around the orbit of numbers that never budged;
Yet stood fast as the timekeepers trudged by,
Minute after minute, hour after hour, day after day, year after year.
Maybe someday they will be reminded of their long-forgotten journey
And begin counting again with their repetitive footsteps
through time.

Brooke Perrault

In a Flirtatious Mood

Hello Gorgeous, I, like what I, see and I, think that you are really fine,
A matter of fact, I, would like to make you mine.
All I, want to do is squeeze and hold you tight, shielding you from the wolves of the night.
I, want to kiss, caress, and tease you, while I'm doing my best to please you.
It is stated in God's, Holy word, that if I, delight my self in him.
He would give me the desires of my heart,
So I've delighted myself in him and he made you the desires of my heart, and forever more we will never part.
Raging storms, and the wicked sea could never separate my love from you,
Neither could wars, earthquakes, fires, can destroy my everlasting feeling that always seem to renew.
Times have changed and the generations have come and gone, but the love for you sweetheart still live on.
It's gotten stronger as time tick away, as we enter into the 20th century today.

Danny C. Coutee

Nature's Colors

All nature's colors are beautiful,
like a rainbow after a spring rain.
Yellow is the sun,
splashing it's warm rays onto the earth.
Red opens like a rose,
twinkling on a warm spring morning.
Blue splashes like the cool water,
from a glistening waterfall,
White floats within an enormous fluffy cloud,
sailing in the breezy sky.
Green glows from the sweet grass,
swaying in the air.
Pink blooms as an apple blossom,
Spreading out it's beautiful color.
Orange springs from the sun when it sets.
Making the last bright and soothing colors of day.
The colors of nature have the ability to spring
a beautiful day forth,
glowing bright colors all around and to end a day with
beautiful colors,
To say good night to the earth.

Amber Havermann

Hush Little Baby

Hush little baby, go to sleep.
Mamma doesn't want to here a peep!
Worked all day and worked all night
Don't mean to give you such a fright.

Hush little baby, Daddy's here
Sleep my little darling, don't you fear.
The angels are watching all night long
And getting ready to sing their song.

In the morning we'll play all day
You can have it all your way
But for now little baby, go to sleep
Mamma wants to see you fast asleep.

Carmella Donato

Belinda's Prayer

I will think not of the heartache that now fills my life
Nor of the emptiness in this time of great strife
I will think instead of the wonderful days gone by
Of my beautiful little boy with that twinkle in his eye
I will dwell on the good times we have had
I refuse to think only of the tragic and sad
My boy is now in heaven free of all his pain
Forever will he walk in sunshine never again in rain
Playing amongst the angels ever happy and free
With his sad passing he takes a big part of me
Always will he be in the depths of my soul
My precious little angel who was just six years old
Dear Lord I now place my boy in your loving care
Until the day you call me and allow me to come there
Trouble he will give you not, for he is gentle and kind
A sweet, loving child like him is very hard to find
I will raise my eyes to the Lord and hold my head up high
For I am only saying so long and not really good-by
Someday we will be together again through God's loving grace
To gaze once more upon his beautiful little face

Rita Corosanite

Hidden Love

I built a tall wall around my heart,
One that would never fall apart.

You tried to break down that wall,
But my wall stood tall.

You carved a message into my wall.
It said "I love you and I'll never let you fall."

Your message soon faded away,
But in my heart it would always stay.

Little by little my wall began to crumble.
and our love began to stumble.....

Upon a new imperfection,
which sent your love in another direction.

So my wall once again I'll build,
To shield,

The shattered pieces of love that hide.
Behind this wall my heart can never subside.

Aimee Edwards

Best Friends

I look beyond your physical appearance
Past the mirror imagine of who you really are...
But to the mental ryes you have proven to me.

I have taken to heart the person to be
Is not just a fake status of an image
In a sleeping fantasy.

As others gaze upon you with eyes of Sallowness
They neglect to differ you from your sense
of style and foresee to judge you on just that.

As of me I conceive your inner soul and find its beauty extreme
I see the courage held in your heart trickling with gleam.

I portray your minds quality with acceptance
And will forever carry you in my heart
As my best friend

Julie W. Tart

Untitled

Summertime blues,
Reverse the you,
Tattered ruins.

D. Allan J. Peterson

The Day Will Come!

"The day was so very long ago, it seems,
Since I heard pitter patters through the house by day,
And at night you were quiet as a mouse, I say.
I watched you smile, as you laid your head to rest.
I stayed awake at night and wept.
I miss you boys, so very much you see.
Your in my every move and thought to be.
I'd kiss your cheeks so very tenderly.
Your the best boys in the world to me.
To hold you close and hug your hurts away,
Was the best thing I've felt since you left that day.
I wonder if you remember our good times,
The way I do when times aren't so good sometimes.
It makes my hurts feel so much lighter
remembering when you'd hold my hand a little tighter.
I'll hold you close and watch you grow up strong,
We're a family that's where we belong.
To have my boys home again by my side.
The day will come you just wait and see,
You'll look around one day and it'll be me."

Liz Smith

Untitled

It lay on the road,
so cold,
so alone.
It never did any harm;
it was so innocent.
Man and his technology;
it's the creatures that suffer;
the innocent.
Don't chase the rocks on the street, kitten.
Don't chase the cars, puppies.
Deer, don't cross the roads at night.
Be careful little rabbit, raccoon, squirrel,
frog, gopher, bird...
These men just keep building;
they don't think;
they don't care.
Now that little kitten...
is dead.

Debbie Gilbertson

The Things We Did Not Say

Treasure every moment life has to give.
Take another look at the life that you live.
Today I found out that it can be taken away.
There were so many things that I didn't every say.

Always my friend no matter what I did.
So much love that you always have to give.
My sister, my buddy, my very best friend.
This bond of ours that will never ever end.

So soft and gentle and full of so much love.
Eyes that say I love you, yet quiet as a dove.
You have touched so many lives in your special way.
Always you knew just what you had to say.

Just call us selfish, but you weren't suppose to leave.
Life without you is so hard for us to believe.
You are never coming back and that is tearing us apart.
You will always hold a place deep within our hearts.

These words we didn't have time to say.
Before the angels came to take you away.
Never again will you feel any pain.
Never again will our lives be the same.

Deloris Hester

There in the Arms of Love

There in the heat of night I heard
The crying, of tears of love that was lying
There in the arms of love
There in the sun that is now burning,
There my heart is yearning
There in the arms of love
There on the ocean shore I see the
Making of the waves, of crashing waters
To the sweetness of what my soul craves.
There in the arms of love
There I speak for here I am if I should
Ever again fall, to grace the lining of
Love to where I call.
There in the arms of love
There in the distance of the moon lays
The stars they are so many they are a lot
There I was forgiven, there I felt the
Power of God
There in the arms of love

David Mossman

Cupid's Gift

At a christmas party: Ribbons and bows.
Under gold paper: A gift and a rose.
I looked at the present - what a surprise!
Music to my ears, a song for my eyes.
Love at first sight. Harmony for my heart.
Cupid shot his arrow just like a dart.
It crossed shining armor worn by my knight.
Landed on my soul - dancing through the night.
Notes... Tunes... Melodies... Cupids gift on wings.
Now, forever and always: Our love sings.

Maria Morales-Hendry

White Swans Naked

You touched my breast and I fell soft
upon the shaded dandelion.
The old oak tree watched graciously,
as our legs became intertwined.
You kissed my lips like running streams
where lily pads lie soft and still,
and carved my name inside the tree
which guarded proud, the docile hill.
We gazed upon these bodies white
that ran and flew into the sun.
Making love upon each cloud
while we laid tranquil, so undone.
I held my breath, than grazed the grass,
and plucked a small rose looking on.
A breeze came in, her petals fell,
I turned and found that you were gone.
The bright sun parted suddenly,
my baron heart felt sudden chill,
I thought of how it used to be,
like white swans naked, running still.

Anna Maria Kline

"A Lost Best Friend"

I should have known it was too good to be true
We were supposed to be best friends all the years through;
Now it seems that you're almost gone
We never even hardly talk on the telephone.
Do you realize? Do you understand?
It seems as though you do everything at your boyfriends command.
What is this? A lose - a - best - friend - game?
Soon you will probably forget my existence and my name.
I tried to save us;
But, I was afraid we would argue and fuss.
Maybe this poem is stupid, maybe it's sad;
It just goes to prove that losing a best friend is really bad.

Carla Jo Ball

Quiet Nights

(Dedicated to the memory of my Mother, Erma.)
In the still, dark hours before dawn,
When your feeling either total peace;
Or just how much you are really alone.

We see things in the still of the night, that can
sometimes be blurred by day;

When our minds and bodies are so busy with
What needs to be done, to make our way.

By day we're surrounded by people, places, and things;
But all too often the lonely nights show you the
truth, and you, just want to scream!

But if peace is what you find in the still, dark nights;
Then the day light hours shall always fill
you with new "Hope For Life."

Teresa Ann Young

Flying In Air

Some people cry. Some people shout. You just sit there and
watch it go by. Word after word, tear after tear. People
stare, people laugh... you just sit there with tears in your
eyes. All bundled inside, no where to go, no where to hide.
standing there, by yourself, watching the world pass right
in front of you. No one's shoulder to cry on, no one to share
the tears. Just all by yourself. Let it go, mind, soul, your
life. Tears rolling down my face, tears rolling down yours.
Let me come with you, for I feel the same. Now, our hands
embrace.....as we fly. Our one last glimpse of life.

Lisa Audenart

Getting in Touch

Let the child speak, if you dare. Let her come out, you know she's there.
What will she say after all the years and all the many unshed tears?
Are you afraid to face her now, frightened that you won't know how
To deal with the damned up emotion that may come rushing in like an ocean?
"Yes I am", I hear you say... "Leave me alone—please go away."
"No, I won't", the child replies. You look her squarely in the eyes,
Eyes that look back from the mirror, and suddenly it all looks clearer!
It's not your enemy you see, nor a child begging—"take care of me!"
It's a woman—grown—mature—okay. It's the person that you are today.
Yes, the child's still there, it's true. She'll always be a part of you.
Her need was but to be embraced, to have the silent years erased,
To know that she was kind and good; and that, from now on, you would
Nurture her and keep her safe, so the woman could emerge with grace.

Now here you stand, face to face with all those years — all that space.
You wonder why it took so long for the woman to let the child belong.
Perhaps the woman had much to learn......
So the child just had to wait her turn.

Nancy Donovan

A Parent's Tribute To Caregivers

We have seen the excitement in our child's face,
While he describes some exotic place.

Like the artist blending colors in his palette to create the perfect hues,
You carefully select words to help children see this world's wondrous views.

Enthusiastically he shares what "we talk about" in circle time,
Joyfully repeating each song, finger play, and nursery rhyme.

And those rare times our child has had a furrowed brow, he tells
of your comfort which eased the pain and vanished his small scowl.

Watching the art work of crayons, paper and paint,
Transform itself from shapes we're not quite sure of to "projects"
he decorates.

Observing you wipe little "critters" from a runny nose,
Curious how many children for you have repeated this same pose.

Allowing us to share in class meaningful items from home,
Gave our son a special sense of pride that came from you and you alone

Mere words cannot express our heartfelt gratitude,
Because you have helped to mold his loving attitude.

As a butterfly quickly emerges from his cocoon,
It seems like we just met and now we're moving on too soon.

For when good friends come together and then it's time to part,
Fondest memories of you we will carry in our hearts.

Julie Anne Banks

Long Distance

So close, but yet so far
I wish every night on the evening star
that you will be here by my side forever,
but that just can't come true.
I have dreams, these dreams are like songs,
that are all dedicated to you
and in these songs are the secrets I keep,
just so you know that my love is true-
So close, but yet so far,
It's like a lost love coming from afar.
Never to be seen, not to be heard-
Sometimes when you think about it,
it seems quiet absurd.
I know you love me, (deep inside)
in a special kind of way
and even though you don't know what I look
like I wait to see you day after day...
I've known you for about a year,
and when I think about you, a single tear
rolls down my cheek, in search for an answer.

Michelle Brotons

For Someone Special

I guess the best thing for me to do,
Is say how I truly feel about you,
I've tried to get it through your mind,
But I couldn't ever seem to find,
The words to say just how I feel,
'Cause my words to you are fake not real,
I need you deep inside my heart,
I wish we'd never have to part,
I'll miss you and your sweet affection,
I'm glad you dealt with my imperfection,
Now I must go on with life,
I feel held down, my heart cut with a knife,
I have many things to say and do
The easiest for me is I Love You!

Alishia M. Cox

Untitled

You're a wide eyed curious machine
Soaring, whirrrrling
on your one wheel luxury liner
thru time and space
fueled by a tireless spirit
and a dream
that will not die
growing weaker
and than stronger
after each galactic confrontation
stopping momentarily
to let your hot rubber
heated by the jet stream you create
caress
the sweet touch
of those shiny sometimes treacherous surfaces
a thousand and one disciplines and more to come
the essence of motion is your true joy
yesterday you were young today old and
tomorrow young again

Larry Steel

Friends

Tall friends, short friends
  Skinny and wide;
Red-haired, black-haired,
  All side by side.

Old friends, young friends,
  And in-betweens;
Moms and grandpas,
  Some tots and teens.

Doctors, lawyers,
  Soldiers, teachers;
Housewives, firemen,
  Students, preachers.

From Washington
  To Delaware,
Good friends are found
  Most anywhere.

Nancy Hammett

Vulnerability

Last night I took a dull knife,
slit open my essence,
carved out my heart and soul,
put them in a paper bag
along with anxiety, fear, love
and hope - Handed it to you and said,
"Please be careful."

Patricia C. Sturm

September Revelation

Maturity
Slowly creeping up,
Stalking me for years,
Suddenly striking
In one swift summer
Of new challenges,
Rich experiences,
And life-altering moves.

Maturity
Claiming me,
Capturing me,
Carrying me on
To a future
Unknown.

Lori L. Getz

Endless Pain

I feel like a candle
Slowly melting away,
The spark within me grows dimmer
With every passing day.
Depression has taken its toll on me,
Bright colours are losing their glow,
A constant fight within my soul
Help my emotions flow.

Perhaps as the candle can be spent
Before it melts away,
And then rekindled once again
On yet another day,
My body needs a change, a rest,
To help release the pain,
But will the strength and spark be back
Before it is too late?

Winnie Cardona

Metropolitan Rain

When it rains, the
smell of clean laundry comes
floating from my brain.
Lightning inside the rain drops:
blue bulbs clashing under
the wheels in their
rapid, vaporizing, momentum.
A searing and steam;
headlights illuminate the presence
of the ghost, disintegrate into odors,
mushrooms in pockets, viruses
taking knife and fork to the life of
the flesh dripping a
night pool, night sweats
in globes of sky, seeding
ripened bacteria on storming
leaves on a night of legs.

Thomas C. Trzaskos

Society

Bone cold January,
Snow boil freeze.

Trudge and gaze
At heavy feet.

Rap, rap, rap, rap, rap,
You green watch cap.

There close to me,
Thudding a young tree

Rich frizzy headpiece,
Deepened ruby.

On return, a study,
Two holes tanned free.

Lone winter bee,
Sweet philosophy.

Roger Sycamore

Ka' Boom!

Dark and cold with lights
  So bright from eons
  Past them came.

Man looks above and sees
  The lights the lights that
  Soon decay.

He ponders and wonders,
  Where have they gone?

He looks at your sun,
  No time to run!!

Our sun blew up that day.

Ronald Ted White

Inviolate Place to God and Me

I walked today among the lupines,
Where only God, the pronghorns,
and the longhorns have trod.
"Entrepreneur, with all my strength,
I beseech you,
Don't let the sprayers and
the pivots invade
this wild, sacred, purple glade."

Vilma L. Ball

Home

We had no home
  so he built one
Using hand
  and head and heart;
A vacant lot
  beside a lake
Seemed a likely
  place to start.

Plans grew flesh
  and now it stands
Strong and sturdy
  gentle wood
Blending man
  with mother earth,
Making life
  and living good!

Olive Sigler

Mattering

I did not matter—
So let me rush,
To find some good to do.
The years we lost
And spent in search
Of what - I never knew.
Blinded, hampered,
Apart from birth,
I felt betrayed.
The lack of mirth.
And so encased,
In deadly inspection,
Years passed by
Without affection.
And because of me
I did not matter.
So let me rush
To mend the tatter.
  Find another more in need.

J. Robinson

Without a Home

I've seen your face
So many times
On the Boardwalk,
At the drugstore
Waiting and watching
As people go by.

The sun beats down
Unwavering
As you reach out
To closed doors
In a sea of faces.

Set adrift
You're not alone
See the rainbow in the sky
Take my hand -
And let me show you
There is hope
and there is Life.

Susan Anne Mills

Yesterday And You

So many times I've missed you,
So many times I've cried,
If love could have saved you,
You never would have died.

The things we feel most deeply
are the hardest things to say.
My dearest one I've loved you,
In a very special way.

I often sit and think of you
And think of how you died,
to think we couldn't say good-bye
before you closed your eyes.

No one can know my loneliness,
No one can hear my weeping.
All the tears from my aching
heart while others are still sleeping.

If I had one lifetime wish,
a dream that could come true.
I'd pray to God with all my heart,
for Yesterday and You.

Sylvia Crompton

Think

How can something give us much
so much at a simple touch
a touch of gold
priceless to hold.

How can something hurt so deep
so deep without a peep
a peep of silence
rebellious violence

How can right be so wrong
so wrong and last so long
so long to future right
ironies are the dark of night.

How can closeness tear apart
tear apart the mighty heart
the mighty heart that is weakened
by jealousy and suspicion,

How can temptation outpower love
love that fits tight as a surgeons glove
a glove with a hole perhaps
leads to temptation's little mishaps.

Scott Hughes

New York

So much to do,
So much to see,
New York is the place for me.

Shows on Broadway
Night and day,
Seeing the skyline
From the bay.

Touring the sights,
Lady Liberty is one,
Seeing New York is never done!

Kristi L. Godin

Sister

For a sister on her birthday
So special and dear,
With my heart doing the talking
And you lending an ear.
Memories of yesterday
So... go through my mind,
How can I ever thank you
For that precious time.
In time of difference we had to bend,
Knowing what we had
We didn't want to end.
Together we share hugs
With smile for tomorrow,
And never forget the hugs
When tears were of sorrow.
Sister and Brother moments we shared,
With all my heart I really do care.
Signs of love poems, a heart, or a flower,
All there for a sister
Who in my eyes stands like a tower.

Larry J. Niese

Twilight Falls

Twilight falls. The darkness;
So tangible, I can feel as well
As see the black figure
Overshadowing the sun. With it,
The morning doves cooing
Sweet melodies are silenced.
Soon an owl's
Haunting call breaks the
empty silence of dusk and
reverberates in my eardrums.
Twilight falls.

Maura Buxton

Only Dreaming

Wanting to hold you
So tight in my arms,
I long to feel your moist
Kiss and your soft caress.
But, tonight, not wanting
To disturb the sleep you
Most desperately need,
I will only dream as you
Lie quietly in my arms.
Tomorrow, I will have another
Chance to share my love
With you; a chance to fulfill
The dreams I dream tonight.

Lori D. Johnson

Red Rose

A red rose you remind me of,
So tough, yet so gentle.
With thorns to hide your hurt
And to show your feelings, your petals.
The warmth and the love we share
Make me feel we're the perfect pair
Don't leave me now, I love you dear
Hold me in your arms all year
If roses can grow, so can we,
Together forever, you and me.

Melinda Marie Tomlinson

This Life

Little ring of flowers upon your head,
Soft clovers for your bed.
Honey suckle for you to drink,
Sweet berries for you to eat.
If only life was simple,
Problems that are rare.
Ring of thorns upon my head,
Nails for my bed.
Bitter water to drink,
Sour grapes to eat.
Life is not simple,
Problems more than some can bare.
If only this raging river,
Would turn into a stream.

Sarah Y. Goodman

Ours

Some say it with cards
Some say it with flowers
Some say it with gifts
I say, it's what's ours

Ours is a love that lasts
Ours is one that's true
Ours, a love forever
Ours is - me and you

Some say, we can do it
Yea, let's give it a try
But God, in us, will prove it
Ours - a love that won't die

Lawrence E. Parker

Untitled

The way I feel, I can't express -
Something rending me.
I'm in anguish for something
I have no control over.
Something I cannot change,
Cannot amend,
Is making me suffer.
I've come full circle,
I've gotten nowhere.
My mind knows
What my heart
Refuses to believe.
I now know which is the stronger.

Rebecca Knaur

Reflections

The pictures that I've painted,
soon, in springtime will appear.
As the landscapes
that I've planted for you, grow.
It's then, when I'm away;
that you will stop and think of me.
And I'll be there beside you,
in the afterglow.
And though you still may talk to me,
my voice you'll only hear;
In whispers;
as the wind blows through your hair.
And though you may not walk with me,
I always will be there.
Take a look around;
You'll find me, everywhere.

John J. Hurton Jr.

You Thought

You thought he was your love.

You thought he was your only
soul from up above.

You said to yourself he was mine.

You thought he would never
cross your bad line.

After you came closer
you thought you would always be together.

After he learned your secrets,
After he said he loved you,
After you told him he was your only,
He lied and left you lonely.

Safiyah Y. Jeanty

Life's Music

The freshness of a dawn
Sparkling of a dew drop
The early morn bird song
Coolness of a rain shower

The wind whispering in the leaves
The fragrance of the flowers
And the hum of honey bees.
The sunlight on the water

The fireflies in the twilight
Stars in a black velvet sky
The shimmering path of moonlight
A summer's eve so long

The changing of the season
A glorious sunset
Love without a reason
Life's music fills the air.

Mary Ann Meyers

Untitled

Think of all the life
split amongst the few
separated in a past
the days can not renew
Or is not life
what holds together
an everlasting
time to treasure
Or in return
the means to need
for is not LOVE
the "Growing Seed"

Richard Walsh II

Labels

Must we face
With bladed steel?
I fear to die
'n worse to kill.
Druther be scared together
than agin,
Facing those
who faced us so,
As labels and
not as men.

Bob Lennon

Nightwatchman

Nightwatchman,
Standing still among the shadows
spying on my dreams,
Invading my privacy
Please leave me be.

I can't sleep at night
Your always at my side
Haunting my mind.
Nightwatchman, Nightwatchman
My nightmares are your pleasure
You want me to endure your pain
Craving sleep, you make me weep
Then lick my tears away and laugh
Nightwatchman, Nightwatchman
Please leave me be.

Tonya Lee Zigon

Untitled

A young woman
stands at the mirror.
Filled with hope and promise,
she straightens her veil.
She dreams of the man
who waits at the foot of the stairs.
Her mother calls to her,
impatiently knocking at the door.
She folds the towel,
places it on the shelf,
and returns
a little girl.

Laura Sexton

Silence

Sometimes I sit in silence
staring out into the sky -
It fills with clouds
without a warning -
without explaining why.

As it cries on the Earth
Its long needed tears
I think to myself just how silent
I had been for years

And I admire the rain
With its constant refrain
For breaking the silence
that was there before
And for quenching the life
that lives below the clouds once more

Kimberly O'Toole

The Man On The Moon

Twilight Lingers
Stars endlessly stretch across the sky

A lonely Soul Reaches out
out into a nothingness

...Thousands of cries, cry out...

only One Tear is answered
only One Night is felt
only One Dream is dreamt
only One Wish is granted

Kristen Cless

Untitled

hauntingly near
still within
alive throughout
silently stirring
always lingering
reflectively present

a gift of YOU
i give myself
in loving remembrance...

Nancy Taylor

Scattered Feathers

Light a match watch the flame.
Strike another they're the same,
Till the flash that won't snuff out
Teaches you what love's about.

The curtains down, empty seats.
House lights out, deserted streets.
Tortured lover, flightless dove.
Scattered feathers, lost love.

Rainy days, clouded skies
Lonely nights, misty eyes.
Search the ashes find a spark
Fan it gently light the dark.

Roaring fire, raging flame
Love's desire, healing pain.
Grasp a torch hold it high,
Never, ever, let it die.

E. R. Beeman

Now

A vision of tomorrow
  suddenly it seems
maturing into yesterday
  abandoning all dreams

No procrastination
  precious time is under way
the journey vital to exist
  impatient is the day

Recognize the future, as yet to arrive
  the past reminisce
live today - be alive!

Miss Alisa S. Krug

Misunderstood Girls

  Girls are known to be
sugar and spice, and everything nice,
  Well, that's not the fact
Jack,
  Girls are mean and cruel,
and would sometimes like to be
in a duel,
  So don't treat us wrong,
or we'll sing a song,
  and go totally out of
control,
  Be sure to treat us
nice or we'll send out the mice,
  and you'll be anything
but gold!

Melissa Jane Runnels

The Best Things In Life Are Free

Each day's a new beginning
Sunshine, God's light by day.
Rainbow, his promise
Near us He will stay.
Raindrops so refreshing
Moonlight by night;
Smiles, gifts of kindness
Faith makes things all right.
Snowflakes soft and silent
Trust in a little child's eyes;
Prayer talking to Jesus
With hearts opened wide.

Mable Johnson

Summer Thought

The rain has cool the
summer - a breeze of
autumn near; quite contended
with it all -

The river flows -
we roam and play.
A morning day,
Flowers - Breeze
has been saith -
willow - vine

Michele M. Mena

The Walls Of Sanity

The walls of sanity,
surround our minds.
This new wave of life
is very profound.
People laugh and play,
but do they really know?
How everything began,
and how it will go.
So laugh on my brothers,
Laugh on my sisters.
But the days are numbered,
for you and me.
You can stick around and see.
I hope to go some place,
good where no one cries.
I hope to go somewhere,
good and not left here to die.
Only to find the dreams,
I wish so for
Only to find what I did not know

Rhonda Bell

Love

Love is a feeling
that burns deep inside.
A feeling you
just can't hide.
The feeling of everything
being so perfect and nothing
could harm the love I have inside.
A feeling of burning
that causes so much pain.
You can't run away from it
for it'll cause you more.
Love fulfills all your needs and wants.
And its a feeling like nothing
you've ever felt before.

Rachel Amos

"Neverending Ending"

Alabama ferns,
Swaying it green,
Where it looks,
Is all over,
A path of emeralds,
The green continues.
Neverending is defined,
Yet, it's near.
Surrounding nothing,
Nothing surrounds.
Breaking through neverending,
It's near.
Scars, and ugliness,
It can't be touched.
Flying far,
It can be touched.
You look at me.
Yet, the treasure has been found.

Nicholas Weston Hall

Firstborn

There were some dead flowers
Surrounding a tiny gray slab
of smooth stone
Embedded
In the moist, lush grass
Dirt was caked around
The raised letters
Of a name
I know well
Of someone I never knew
The name that brings grief
When spoken
The name that is never said
Out loud
The name of the one I replaced
The name I wish
Wasn't there

Paula Marie Wagner

Untitled

She left
Taking his heart out the door
Leaving him alone to cry
Leaving him alone to die
Making him face the imperfects
Fragile humanity
She gave him love
He showed her pain
She rescued him from a sea of despair
Now she returns him there
Gripping with a broken heart
He had from the start
Imperfect.

Reginald Zimmerman

Love

Love is red.
With the sound of a joyous song
The taste of sweet candies,
And the smell of fresh roses,
And the best part is the
feeling you get, like
You are walking on
air and nothing brings
you down.

Kimberly Weida

2001

Behold the Mighty Monolith
Tall against the sky
Standing there so solemn
One solitary column

Scanning all God's universe
From its stationary berth
Standing there steadfastly bound
By its moorings in the ground

In this vast menagerie
Masterpiece of the Deity
Pillar of wisdom for all to see
Sepulcher of eternity

Proud surveyor of the realm
Calculated to overwhelm
Its enigmatic dignity
Disguised in rare simplicity

This sedentary odyssey
Monument to destiny
Representing all there is
Or will ever be

L. L. Burke

Kirk

An aquamarine monument to
tempt the turquoise brush
of the master captain, and, upon
acceptance of the cannibal's gift
(wrapped for royalty)
saves the eggs, all of them,
Aeolian chimes ring ancient prayers
reflected from soft arizonan plateaus,
and built solely for the brothers
of the Gila monster's egg.
The pinning warble must be silenced
especially in Rotterdam, where
caution must be observed not to
disturb the hidden cult which
vaingloriously reveres pterodactyls.

Todd Garfinkel

Love

Love is like a flower
That blossoms all year long.
With loving care and tenderness,
It will only become more strong.
It's strong, it's sturdy, it's lasting
When nurtured every day.
But fragile when neglected
And left to wilt away.
So fill your cup with all those things
That drew you to each other.
And feed them daily to your love
And it'll blossom on forever.

Jean Sanders

Flowers In The Garden

Today is the day,
Two will join together as one.
With love and warmth,
Lit up from the ray's of the sun.
The flower's then danced all
around to the beautiful sound's,
While smiling faces of
family, and friend's watching,
from the garden surround's.

Linda B. Sjoquist

Tapestry

Woven cloth, oh! Renaissance
Textile history speak to me.
You Kings and Queens of ages past,
skilled fingers capture destiny.

So delicate your features form
of yarn through hue and tinge,
tender woven authority
bound within a fringe.

Astute, embroidered majesty,
incarcerated past,
great artisan of yesteryear
preserve, emblazon cast!

Louis S. LaCava

Land Of Dreams

As I drift into dreams, I'm
taken away to a far off
land on a bright sunny day.

A land filled with love,
that is never in vain.
Where there is no such thing
as hunger, homelessness, or pain.

A land free of violence, hate,
and fear; where honesty
and tolerance persevere.

A place where innocence is
allowed to be; and people
live in peace and harmony.

As I awake, and night
turns to day; I wonder....
Is this land really so far away?

Melissa Johnson

Love

Love is a flower
That blooms at night;
It has much power
To console or to fright.

Love is an emotion
As big as an ocean;
It makes one swing
And produces a ring.

Love is as deep
As it is steep;
It blows like the wind
And causes strength to be kind.

Love is immortal
And will bind
Our senses as portal
To happiness we find.

Marie Merenhole

The Smile in My Sky

When I'm with you,
The sky is always blue.

You make sunshine
out of raindrops;
and laughter
out of tear drops;

And for this,
I'll always love you.

Tracey Hawks

Love

It is like a butterfly,
That glides on through the air...
Without a worry in the world,
As if no one is there

A feeling that possesses you,
And think it cannot be...
But know that it is in your heart,
It's something you can't see.

A special something that is felt,
That can't be put aside...
That fills the heart with laughter,
And takes everything in stride.

You want to shout out all the joy,
As if to set it free...
Then realize that this special touch,
Is really inside me.

This feeling that you can't express,
But thank the Lord above...
Is happiness that you deserve,
The feeling that's called... LOVE.

Raymond Vieira

Living Seeds

Jesus I want to be your seed
that grows day by day;
One that is planted in good soil
to flourish along life's way.

Help me to keep on looking up
to see your light so bright;
Please keep those weeds away from me
every day and every night.

When I reach a full grown state
and seasons come and go;
The top of me may disappear
but the roots will grow and grow.

Michael K. Wybro

Easter Time

Easter is the time of year
That I always love
Every tang is shinning
Even heaven above

I love to see the children
With smiles on all their face
It's a time to thank Jesus
For his amazing grace

It is a time to thank Jesus
For he died on the cross
So this sinful world
Would not be lost

Now when this day is over
We can all bow our head
And give thanks to him
For he is not dead

We may not see another
But in our heart it will always be
Knowing our Heavenly father
Will keep us always close to thee.

Margaret Brown

Today

Today is the day
That I start my life
I could grow up
To be someone's wife

Today is the day
I came into the world
I'm momma's little baby
And daddy's little girl

Today is the day
I said my first word
Spoke very softly
For all to be heard

Today is the day
I took my first step
Done all alone
All by myself

Today is the day
I said goodbye
I laid in my crib
And gently closed my eyes

Kendra E. Sester

What Is Blue?

Blue is the ocean
That I swim in.
Blue is a whale
That has a fin.

When I think of blue
I think of boys.
I think boys
Make a lot of noise.

Blue is my sapphire ring
that I wear when I can.
My Uncle Jimmy
Has a striped blue van.

Blue is my necklace
That my dad gave me.
Blue are my blue jeans
With a label that says Lee.

The sound of the waves
That I hear at the beach.
They take my shovel away
That I try to reach.

Shannon M. Kelly

"Dad"

In my eyes, I see you there.
That look of yours,
That shows you care.
I'm your little girl,
And I always will be.
I love you so much.
That, you can see.

Not a day goes by,
When I don't think of you.
You're always on my mind.
And I hope I'm on yours, too.
Our love can only grow,
In every way.
I love you more and more
Each and every day.

I know I have the best dad ever.
And I will love you always,
Now and of course forever.

S. Willson

Christmas Day

Christmas day is the time of year
that makes people cheer.
It's when kids get out of school,
and the weather gets really cool.
It's when kids have snowball fights
All through vacation nights.
People's faces get rosy,
and they also get nosey,
to see what presents they got.
No classes are taught,
children are screaming,
and kitchens are steaming
to get ready for Christmas day.
And on Christmas day,
kids are up before I can say,
"It's Christmas morn!",
and nobody ever looks forlorn,
on Christmas Day.

Sara B. Smith

True Sense of Loss

In my soul there is a void
That nothing will ever fill
It is a part of me I have lost forever
Sometimes I wish for it to return
But it is impossible
I cannot reach out and grasp it
It won't come back in
I don't know where it went
I don't know if I ever will
It is out of my grasp
Never to be seen
Touched or felt
Always lost to me

Malissa Bradburn

The Light

Dying embers
That once blazed brilliantly
Having orange colored flame
That danced with joy
Among the logs
And crackled in a strange,
Lovely fashion.
Once eyes have glowed like the fire,
In frightful appearance
Or in love with its ability
To give light and warmth.
Now it flickers,
Every blowing wind
Threatens its existence,
Willing to smite that divine light
And warmth and blaze.
And no one can stop the wind.

Lisa Altschuler

My Country

My country tries to live in peace
We have independence.
Freedom, Justice, Liberty.
and this is what it means to me.

What my country means to me
This is fairly simple,
Justice and all liberty.
and free choice for all people.

Michelle Finn

Christmas Is A Gift

Christmas is a gift
That only you can bring
To the people who need it
And can't give anything.

Christmas is a gift
That is quite sensitive.
For the people who need it
We really need to give.

For the people with no shelter,
To the people with no home.
That there is the very reason
I am writing this here poem!

Kristin Sommers

The Hunt

Time be falls into a hall
That runs through a saw
Blood... dripping down
On the hollow ground

As morning calls
Nothing's dull
There I stand
With a torture knife in my hand

Bending low
Seeking slow

My victim
Looking for help
I say to him... to run
To save himself
From the monster
That I am.

Mai Pham

Wishing

Why does it seem,
that things run in slow motion.
When tragedies seem at their height,
and the worst they've been.
Everything seems to stop,
yet you go on living.
Waiting for reality,
to come and open my eyes.
To trust is to be deceived,
by a friend or companion.
To lose your faith and friendliness,
and want to hold it back.
Keeping it cold and worthless,
so no one wants your life.
Some things are better left alone,
than to be examined.
Why do I trust,
when I know I'll be used.
If I had one wish,
I'd wish for my happiness.

Jennifer McKnight

Leave A Memory

Better it is that you should go,
When you share your heart with another;
Better it is I should not know,
When you leave me for another;
Leave me a tear of the summer sea,
A song of spring and an autumn prayer;
Leave me with the morning breeze,
Memories will live on forever.

Julianne Belunas

It Must Have Been Love (But It's Over Now)

From the first day,
That we met again.
You rocked my world with your charm,
And captured my heart.

The way you teased,
Made me want you more.
But your denial,
Tore my heart apart.

For some never let their feelings show,
And pride gets in the way.
Friends or lovers?
I'm to choose one or the other!

What's one little kiss,
When I would miss,
Your friendship even more.

So your friend I will be,
If you'll let me.
But deep in my heart
Is where my love for you,
Will always be.

Rhonda Eidet

Push On

As avid walkers walk the way
The accomplished goal in site.
The rhythmic stride beats out the tune,
Push on with all might.

Life's journey with its obstacles
Will pass rapidly by.
The pain increase, the struggle long,
Persist becomes the cry.

Quick sweeping breath of our joys past
Are but a memory.
Forward we stamp the unknown ground,
Pace on in liberty.

Dig down for strength beyond belief
Amazingly there's more.
The distant stretch comes into view,
Pursue until you soar.

Complete the task, transcend the rest,
Clear vision help to win.
The load gets lighter near the end,
Push on from deep within.

Linda Schlavensky

Murder She Wrote

She was having a baby at
the age of sixteen and the
father of the baby was brutal
and mean. So she went to a
clinic to do what she thought
was best and at the clinic
they gave her pills to rest.

When her mother found out she
was quite mad but when the
baby's father found out he was
quite glad so she killed herself
caused she was confused as you
can see her life was abused.

Taheerah Abdul

Whispers at Twilight

Rest, weary traveler
The bed is soft, the fire is warm.
Rest, and dream of good things.
Do not worry for friends outside;
They did not find their way.
You left for them a special trust
And they will not forget
As the others once did,
Laughing amongst the apple trees
Not knowing, not caring.
Nearby a lion was hiding,
Catching those who would go astray
But never snaring you.
You thought you were just beginning;
Today it is all but finished
So rest, my friend, and gain in strength
Tomorrow you must move on.

Robert Andrew Divis

Summer Night

As I walked out into
the brisk summer evening,
The wet grass tickled
my feet.
All around crickets
chirped happily, and
lightning bugs made a
faint glow among the
horizon.
I looked up at
the twinkling stars
above me and smiled,
Knowing I'd always remember,
That Summer Night

Kim Galloway

Cat's Menu

She teased the warm and kindled light
The candled moth in her merry flight
Pitched and fluttered, tossed and dipped
No harmony in her beating wing
or direction for her fatal slip

The black mask cat with sapphire eyes
Unmerciful in the moth's demise
Waiting in the silent moon
Instinctively gives the "coup de grace"
In a playful paw of certain doom

In hunter's stance-like lions do
Cat-eye dominating each sinew
In a graceful air ballet
She surrenders to the dew kissed grass
and becomes a siamese cat's buffet.

Raven Feaster

I Love You

Words of power
Turns lovers to haters
Haters to lovers
Friends to soulmates
Soulmates to friends
End to wars
Wars started
I love you
Words of power

Larry Campbell

The Grand Canyon

The wonderful view in the sky,
The Colorado River shining in disguise.
In between there is nothing but,
Beauty and colors in a rut.

People coming in and out,
People hiking down and up.
Mule rides going on and off,
Helicopter flights climbing up.

White water rafting down below,
White puffy clouds up above.
Wildlife marching loud and near,
The river's current bright and clear.

Trees in the glare,
Clouds in the sky.
Dirt on the road,
Birds in the air.

There is one place on Earth,
Where everything can be.
There is one place on Earth,
Where you should see - the Grand Canyon.

Lisa Tseng

Not Another Tear

One day, across the nations,
The coming of the King,
To lift us out of this world
By the giving of a ring.

Remove the worry from our brows,
Take the fear from our eyes,
Give to us life again
And finally hear our cries.

Think not of our sins,
Or the mistakes from the past.
Know only of our love
That will forever last.

Rejoice now in laughter,
For happiness is here.
Join the celebration,
Shed not another tear.

Ronda Lauzon

Time I Sit and Watch

Time I sit and watch
the days go by.
Always thinking of you
I ask myself why.

Why do I always cry
Why do I always sigh
For the good times I had with you
And the joy you bring to me.

I need you beside me
to love me and guide me
and to always be my friend
my friend ...

Robert Arnold LaFrance Jr.

Bear

Beware of bear
the dog who doesn't care
If he eats everything there
Or runs and jumps like a mare.

He has no flair
For grooming his hair
But he sure can scare
When he gives you a stare.

And what makes him really queer
And quite unfair
Is that he will tear
What may be extremely rare.

He'll grab it, then glare
The swing it in the air
He'll rip it in two and make it a pair
I sure hope it wasn't something you wanted
to wear.

Though he's cute as a hare I warn you to
take care
And remember the dare
And the signs that declare
"Beware of bear."

Pamela Robins

The Earth

As round as a plum
The earth is with molten lava
Spewing out from the
Volcanoes with magma and rock
Like a lock the earth
Does not reveal her secrets
But all of her deep
Secrets are inlocked in a
Single rock. Minerals and
Oils the earth toils when
Sun is set and all is at
Rest, the birds will sing
The owls will dance, out will come
Ladybirds to prance
Amongst the tallest trees and
The brightest star a
Single scratch can leave a scar
Watch out! Watch out! Don't
Damage the earth because soon it will be
replaced
By a new birth. Save the Earth

Gina Jankelow

"Ocean Mystery"

The golden sun rises in
the east, flooding your crystal
waters with light, sandpipers
run startled by your frothy
waves, waves of mystery, revealing
secrets to the wind whispering
about the life beneath the
majestic blue waters, serene and
peaceful until the harshness of
fisherman nets wake the ocean floor

Kristen A. Foltz

Untitled

The passion of a once cherished promise
The forgiveness of a once done fault.
The love which once was true
Has now come to a halt.
The years spent together
The romance at on time forever.
Two people as one
Are now left sever.
A once cheerful smile
A once softened tear.
The sound of happiness and laughter
You can no longer hear.
A once gentle hand
With a once kind touch.
The words I love you
Will never mean so much.
The loveliness of a once had secret
The tenderness of a once sacred night.
The relationship two people once so
carefully shared
Is now out of their sight.

Kelly Johnson

I Met A Girl

I met a girl - one girl-
the girl whose the girl of my dreams.
A girl whom I would call baby-
as would any one else it seems.

Long golden brown hair
that the sun likes to play upon.
Nobody nor no place
ever set eyes on such a one.

Clear blue crystal eyes
that reflect the light.
My own eyes aren't so great-
but they see the glorious sight.

You know I'll always love her
I'll always see her in my mind.
And in my hectic-haunted life:
time for her I'll always find.

Michael J. Paddock

Spate

The sun is yellow.
The grass is green.
The sky is blue.
Earth unclean.

Cats say "meow."
Dogs say "woof."
Birds say "tweet."
Time not enough.

Black and white
Beautifully make gray.
Blending so right.
Earth decorated in a day.

Red, yellow, and brown.
Even colorless is fine.
We so fragile.
Earth and brine.

Peace not war.
Love not hate.
Sooner or later
No doom to wait.

Sheiron Sanchez

Surviving After the Holocaust

Little girl forget
The horrid torture
The constant beatings
The mental tyranny
The tear stained cheeks
The pained faces
It is over
No more screams
No more whipping
No more pain
Put your head up
You survived
But now the hard part, living
Living after so much death
After so much cruelty
Sleeping
Threw the night without fear
Conquering nightmares
Letting go of the terror
Being free

Traci Levesque

Fog

Locked in fog
  the houses are not there.
Although I try to see
  everywhere
    there is a blanket
      soft and cool
that wraps long arms around
  to fool me.

The houses, standing
  as they were before
    the tenuous arms engulfed them
remain secure.
  They endure.

Am I so blind
  to never know
I need not fear obscuring gray?
  The sun pouring round
    clears fog away.

Mary K. Allton

A Flower

The man with
  the inside scar

to whom the world
  owes something
extra

is now indifferent as
  he crushes
a flower

with a welfare boot
  grinding the petals
into the pavement where
  the scent is lost
forever.

Tina-Marie Miller

Circle of Love

One quarter of the circle
The life that I had led,
The person I'd become
Thinking love must lie ahead.
The second part and halfway
Was when I went to find,
A family brought together
A love I thought would bind.
The third part of the circle
When love would take a turn,
A love yet not fulfilling
Tough lessons to be learned.
The fourth and final chapter
Inside me all the time,
The love that I would realize
The love that I was looking for
Was not too far to find.

Toni Armson

Prose Of Repose

Basking in the sun
the lioness stretches
out and feels the warmth
of the sun radiating
against her long sleek body.

Content with the feeling
of freedom she rules
with the grace of her
predecessors and feels no fear.

She solemnly fades
into an oblivious state
of contentment and is
calmed into a deep and
well deserved rest.

Rebecca Rudolph

Feelings

Feelings float in the air,
the may take you anywhere.
Life is made for curves
and bends, sad times seem
like they never end.
Someday we will die and
go to heaven, where angles
lie and crying's forbidden.
Just remember God is
there when unwanted feelings
float in the air.

Mary Kulp

The Burning of Fire

The burning of fire,
The memory of pain,
A life so unused,
With so much to gain,
The melting of snow,
The lost of a life,
The pain that hurts you,
That cuts like a knife,
The fall of the rain,
The mourning of a death,
A life without a cause,
Gone in one breath,
The burning of fire,
The memory of pain,
A life so unused,
With nothing to gain.

Kerry Smith

Texas Falls

The emerald waters swirl and dance,
The mossy rocks speak
With echoes of the roar and hiss.

The day moves on, but not in here;
Time has no meaning.

The wet stones gleam
As the water runs
Over them, no rhyme or reason.

Crystal clear, the waters move,
The white power rushes
Without relenting.

It's only a matter of time.

The wood thrush sings,
But the song is mute
Under the sound of the waterfall.

Katie V. Lundquist

The Conquest (Night Flight)

Emperor of the blue,
the pilot surveys the skies.
His mission is sure and true —
he scans the runway with anxious eyes.

A chance that's well worth taking,
a deed that he must try —
it is a love he's making:
the child of land must start to fly.

The power has always been with him;
the course he now must set.
As this day's light begins to dim,
the challenge must be met.

He hesitates and listens
to the ones long gone before.
His eyes begin to glisten
as his heart begins to roar.

Enveloped in midnight,
the plane makes its ascent.
A noble scene is the night flight,
pounding the sky to make a dent.

Traci Johnson Mathena

Mother Earth

The towering mountains,
The raging waters,
The great trees,
Mother Earth is calling.

The lovely rose,
The peaceful doves,
The soft rain,
Mother Earth is calling.

The innocent children,
Their sorrowful cries,
They understand,
Mother Earth is calling.

With all the violence,
With all the crime,
With all the pain,
Mother Earth is calling.

We must listen,
We must understand,
We must know,
Mother Earth is calling.

Mariko Preston

Switchplate Love

When the light goes off:
The room is dark,
The darkness lonely,
And the eyes are blind.

When the light turns on:
The room is included,
The light shines bright,
And the eyes can see clearly.

But when the light is off:
The room is evil,
The darkness desperate,
And the eyes see only what they want.

And when the light is on:
The room is invaded,
The light shines too bright,
And the eyes can see too much.

Karin L. Presley

The Last Cry

The coldness of the air
The soaking sheets on the bed
The thoughts which remain
The deepest breath of a sad soul.

The loudest cry for a need
A need to be loved
The hand reaching for yours
Two lives which are one.

The horror of the thought
The cold heart pumping faster
The thought of being alone
The thought of being wrong.

The cup put to the nose and mouth
The voices of wrong which you hear
The cold sharp point to your body

The other heartbeat which just stopped.

Tina Klenzing

Forbidden

The look in your eyes,
the soft touch of your hands,
we're thinking the same thing.
We both want it so much
but to scared to admit.
What would they say,
What would they do?
Their talk would be harsh
the fight all up hill.
So we both turn away,
never to say
how much we care,
never to say
how much we feel.
For what would they say
what would they do
if they only knew how much
I Love You!

Melissa Gero

A Place Of

From a place of pain,
the soul cries out,
Stop your blizzard of rain,
forgive yourself now!
From a place of remorse,
the heart screams out,
Stop the hurt that is yours,
forgive someone now!
From a place that burns,
the mind calls out,
Stop these images of hurt,
see yourself now.
From a place of rage,
the abused person lashes out,
Stop living the same torn page,
see another now.
From a place of love,
holds captured belief,
Captured are all you're dreaming of,
all the hopes you dare to conceive.

Julia Ybarra

Always and Forever

Nothing can replace
The sparkle in your eyes
That look upon your face
The whisper of your sighs
The tenderness in your touch
The feel of you next to me
Are your feelings as such
Or just illusions to me?
Somehow you found your way
Into my heart and mind
As we danced the night away
Always side by side.
You'll be with me forever
No matter how far
And I do mean forever
Please, believe that you are.

Leigh Ann Kerwin

Black Velvet

Black velvet is the night
The stars are shining bright
Venus is the one I see,
It shines for you and me.
The Big Dipper is on show
If you know where to go.
I point at it and say
There it is a silver sight,
And it is up there for delight.
God is very bright as
you can see his paintings
In the night..
The fish for Pisces
The lion for Leo
And probably even an
unknown named Cleo.

Patti Glasgow

"Leaves"

God bless the leaves
that first spring forth
After weary winters night.
Produce a shade so ever green
A breeze with all their might.
Color laden do they fall
another winter's night.

Margaret Walker

Life Line

From the dark winds
the storm beckons
Calling on the powers of
all that bring fear
to the souls of child and man

Raging torrents of emotion
swallowing us whole
Brinking on the verge
of insanity lest we
falter in our despair

As the swells overcome
Those who lose their mooring
Still others grasp
to their precarious leads
Pulling against the wake

Lord, let me be one
who ties my lead to yours
Never going under
And never giving in.

Marcella Kate Gilbert

The Land Is Green

The sun shines, all is still
The sun makes one sparkle
in one drop of water before it falls
down into the mossy green
It lays there silent a long time
The land is green
Sparkle in the grass
Day then night, the sun then moon,
Year in year out.
Birds and butterflies fly over me—
I am the one who lives under the sky
riding on a horse.
How I enjoyed wild roses
And Honey suckle flowers
Climbing and growing in beauty.

Vivian Brown

Wash Day

This morning as I gather
the things that need
to be washed,
I remember the wash days
of my youth.

Carry water, fill the boiler,
Add soap, boil the clothes awhile.

Rub - rub on a wash board,
rinse and rinse again,
Hang them on the line to dry.
How white they are against the sky.

How sweet and clean they smell
as they are folded tenderly
and put away.

Velva Butterworth Davis

Untitled

As I step within your dream
the two of us become one
you take my hand, and we
begin threw an endless tunnel
of love. We finally found forever
that's what our love means
when ever I need you beside
me I'll step inside your dream.

Sherry Distefano

When the Moon Died

The stars no longer shined,
The trees no longer swayed,
The rivers no longer ran,

When the moon died.

The grass no longer grew,
The ocean no longer came to shore,
The raindrops fell no more,

When the moon died.

The world's soul wept,

When the moon died.

Stefanie Cleland

Untitled

The light shined
The water glistened
T'was all perfect
Until you came along
The light dimmed
The water went cloudy
Leave, leave this place;
This place were I rest
Let the light shine
Let the water glisten
The future rays in your hand.

Misty Dawn Perry

Daddy's Little Girl

I remember
The way things used to be
The way you always
Had time for me
The way I tagged
Behind your heels
Or told you how
A little girl feels
But now I'm growing up
And you seem miles away
And I wish I could change everything
Somehow, someway
So that you would be
The same dad you were then
And I would be
Your little girl again.

Stephanie McFarland

Soulwinds

The wind can see into your soul
The wind can read into your mind
Seeing emotions you hold
Thoughts that no one can find

Gently it waves green grasses
Then wildly tossing tree boughs
The storm of emotions passes
The wind of your soldiers down

Wind is filled with emotions
Blowing inside your soul
Disturbing the calm steady motions
Of holding yourself in control

You're free to be yourself now
Anything you dare to be
Trust your soul to show you how
For the wind has set you free

Ruth Shramek

The Fire

The clouds got darker and darker
the wind picked up, everything
was stirred up and every
animal around was running
for shelter, the fire came
closer and closer, hotter and
hotter it got then all of a
sudden it was out, everything
was still and everything was
dead, the fire
had killed again...

Trisha Smith

Beautiful Black and White

Oh, beautiful black and white,
The world is without true sight.
Ask it not to see your light,
For you shine too pure and bright.

You are not two, you are one.
From one, man was forgotten.
Each man is the Father's son,
And everyone is chosen.

Only mortal men divide
When in fear they reside.
Such men seek not God inside
And in truth cannot abide.

Know your wisdom made your choice
And in its lessons rejoice.
Listen to your inner voice;
There in mortal words unvoice.

Joan Carol

Snowbound

Winter trees stand stark and bare,
Their lacy arms uplifted
To greet the steeply falling snow
And the fitful winds
That blow across the hills,
The hedge rows and the wood.

Snug in the mothering earth
Dormant roots are resting,
Sheltered from the swirling snow
And the biting winds that blow
The color from the stars
Across the snowdrifts far below.

The wood lies silent, buried deep
Under an opalescent sky.
A solitary, ink-black crow
Skates undaunted on the snow,
His raucous cry the only sound
Echoing for miles around
Through the frosty air.

K. E. Barrington

The Last Dance

The music plays slowly,
The lights flicker softly,
My heart pounds steadily,
As your hand touches mine.
We dance gently swaying,
Our bodies taunt, aching,
Our lips touching, anticipating,
No more longing, waiting
At last, you are mine.

J. E. Coakley

?Just Things?

When I was a child all Things were toys,
then became tools and made much noise

—— which slowly turned a few
into dreams come true.

Then, along the way, came a day
when I no longer owned them
—— they owned me!

For finally they ceased to be
things at all,

Became treasured symbols of places
and faces,

Touchstones of times olden,
tangible transmuters
of memories golden.

Robert E. Fulton, Jr.

Flower

You start out as a seed
then spread your roots around
You begin to grow a stem
that comes up from the ground

I watch you grow each day
high in the air
Rain and sunshine is essential
for you must have love and care

Finally you become
what you're supposed to be
You open up your life
and show it all to me

I marvel at your beauty
The colors that you show
To everyone who looks
They can see a little soul.

Melody Wangemann

Winter Fun

We saw the snowflakes all around;
Then there was snow upon the ground.
My granddad took me out to play.
I wished that we could stay all day.
We rode the sled and threw snowballs
And ran and jumped with gentle falls.
We rolled three balls of snow real fat
Gave them some arms, a face, and hat.
My hands got very cold and iced,
But Granddad gladly sacrificed
And put his gloves upon my hands.
So now a snowman stoutly stands
In Grandma's yard for all to see
The remnants of his fun with me.

Phyllis Haynes

Night

The sun is now dead.
The moon has risen.

Night has now come.
The darkness reigns in the distance.
The stars fall from beyond the sky.
The air is damp
but yet I feel the day watching,
and waiting to come.

Stacee Stratton

The Secret Weapon

Through all the wars of mankind
There always seems to be
A secret weapon in the works
Assuring victory.
In Science and technology
Our blessings in disguise
The secret weapon lies within
If we can spot the prize
True wisdom in selection
Rule out Pandora's box
And seize the reins of paradise
To solve this paradox.
No jump starts, no quick fixes
There is no healing we can see
Without the understanding
Of a world wide harmony
Then all war fare in the future
Shall dissolve and bloodless be
And we in turn shall claim like gods
Our new found weaponry.

Jim Harding

My Special Friend

She was my first and most loving friend
There for me right from the start
And no one can ever take the place
That she holds within my heart.

At times when I was feeling down
My friend would always say
Don't give up, just look ahead
For tomorrow is a brand new day.

My friend was always there for me
No matter night or day.
To share with me good times and bad
In her special loving way.

So when it comes to friendship
There can never be another
That will ever be as special and true
As the one I shared with mother.

Sherry Lynn Adkins

Innocence

When life begins
There is innocence abound
There's a need to be nurtured
And a soul to be found

Then as we grow
And innocence departs
Our surroundings have taught us
To harden our hearts

Now we are old
Does this innocence exist
Can it really fulfill us
Or is it a hollow abyss

If we could regain
That innocence lost
When Judgment Day arrives
Our souls won't pay the cost

Wayne Turner

Untitled

Sweet spring breeze fills the air,
The bright pink flowers, falling
Off the branches like rain.
There I stole a little kiss,
A secret that hides,
In summers flame.

R. T. Lauer

In Your Eyes

I'm lost
there's no way out
A sea of blue
filled with emotion
I can't swim about

Drowning in the hue
that surrounds the black
where are you?
I'm held hostage, held back.

I ask 'Do you love me?'
your gaze reads neither yes
nor no

All is washed away
A wave of amusement crashes down
casting emotions astray
I don't understand
you smile, you laugh, than you frown

I'm lost,
I shout
Helpless, I realize
There's just no way out

Trish Nelson

Moving On

It has been nice
these past few years
and leaving this school
will bring many tears.

For we had our fun
our learning complete
our friends we have met
new challenges to meet

Our teachers, our friends
our fun time will end
and return or carry on
as times change or bend.

Linda Platt

Untold Dreams

My dreams are like the river,
They flow inside my heart.
I want so much to share them,
But my lips will never part.
The music I hold,
Is a symphony untamed.
I wish that I could share my song,
And I hold myself to blame.
My eyes will tell my story,
They burn with untold words.
But who would ever looked that deep,
For my dreams,
They come in herds.
Every tear that comes tumbling down,
Is one small wish my eyes let go.
The Goddess of love retrieves that wish.
Is she my friend or foe?

Marieke Tuthill

School Daze at the Center

In pairs, trios and bus loads
They gather at the Senior Center,
To attend the scheduled classes
Conducted by Sinclair mentors.

The Big Men on the campus
Are squat, portly and round,
while the snazzy-jazzy coeds
Are the cutest to be found.

At the Center there's enhancement
In esteem, ability and knowledge,
All students are most avid
At this All American college.

There are rules they must follow
No goofing - or sleeping in,
Even mini-skirts are banned
And no exposure of the skin.

So - join the Rah! - Rah! gang
Put your talents on display,
With all the "stuff" you get
You'll be a politician someday!

Larry Fogle

Untitled

They live in my town
They lived in my house
They're in my soul
Children
They're only children
I wanted to help them
But then they were gone
So I found an excuse
And politely moved on
Sometimes I feel compassion
Sometimes I feel indifference
O Lord
Please help me;
They're only children
How can I abandon them
They never asked
To be unwanted
They didn't deserve
To be unloved

Tracey Bohn

The Beginning, The End

At a milk shake with two straws,
they met.

At the Prom while dancing, they kissed.

At her house her parents
excepted him.

At the restaurant, he proposed.
At the chapel, they committed.
At parties, they met new couples.

At the doctor's, they're going,
to have a baby.

At the right time the baby
was ready to come.

Eighteen years later, they were
alone once again.

At the nursing home, she passed on.

At the house, he died.

Lindsey Ketchum

No Tomorrow

Coldness tonight,
They wrap up tight,
With faces of great sorrow,
They huddle long, singing a song
In hope for a tomorrow.

In clothes so old -
Out in the cold -
With faces that show great sorrow,
To sleep on ground, not make a sound
And die with no tomorrow.

They lose their strength
Their life short length,
The face of painful sorrow -
"Place for me, where can it be?"
They pray for a tomorrow.

Sleeping by fountains,
Death so soon,
They show faces of their sorrow,
Tried for a ride, no one replied,
One more night with no tomorrow.

Kristy A. Fradette

The Tide and the Fisherman

Sometimes, if you think of me,
think of flowers and sunshine.
Think of birds and trees.
Think of everything divine.

You were once mine
but she stole you away.
You made your decision
on that very eventful day.

So now I'm alone
and the loneliness overwhelms me.
I still think of you sometimes
and you remind me of the sea.

You are like the tide,
flowing in and out as you please.
I am like the fisherman,
waiting for the storm to ease.

Karla Flanery

You

I sit here empty;
thinking only of you.

You left with him, but you are here;
in my heart.

I miss you already;
words cannot describe how much.

You are so beautiful, so delicate;
like the petals of a rose.

Think of me tonight!

Allow me to occupy your heart
and soul.

Sleep my love, for tonight is
the night that our dreams
become our destination.

No boundaries; no limits!

Jeff Cochran

My Gift

Such a special gift we all possess,
This capacity to love.
It can lead you to the lowest place
Or to the skies above.

It can run you down a danger path,
With troubles high and low.
It can lead you into happiness
With all the beauty it can show.

Many times I've often wondered
Now I know that it can be,
Of all the gifts from God on high,
He gave this one to me.

It must have been to show His love,
That yes, He truly cares.
With all the problems of this world,
He is there to share.

Alone, you say, oh no I'm not,
For He can never leave
This human spirit, a piece of Him,
On this, I do believe.

Kimberly Claunch

Forever Young

Forever young
this child will be
Not like the others
who must soon be set free

Forever young
this child of mine
not in body
but in spirit and mind

Forever young
she will remain
but do not grieve
there is so much we gain

Forever young
she does not worry
Always laughing and loving
she is never in a hurry

Forever young
A child she'll be
But what love she gives
to her father and me

Suzanne Love

Intimate Secrets

Intimate secrets my dear friend
This is how our friendship ends.

In your eyes I can always see
I told too much about Lee and me.

You're over there
And I'm over here.

What are you telling them
About me and him?

Now I wish I'd never told you
Because everyday you make me feel so blue.

J. Scarlette Black

Part of Me

I see the future in your eyes
This kind of love you can't disguise
I see your soul
It pulls me in
I see your heart
I see your sins
I see the love all locked inside
I see the love you cannot hide
I see the fears
I see them grow
I see the tears you dare not show
I see the world as it should be
I see it all
It's part of me

Nikole Sturgis

Mother

She looked so small and fragile
This woman that I love
When I was just a child
She held the stars above

As I grew older
We had our share of fights
I remember how my knees would weaken
When I saw anger in her eyes

Soon she will be leaving
To be with God above
As I stand beside her
I pray she knows she's loved

We had our share of problems
And there were times I believed
I did not need a Mother
In the life I lead

Now that she has left me
And gone to heaven up above
What I would give for one more day
With the Mother that I love

Suzanne Marie Dozier

Music Enchanted

Music enchanted, cast your spell
This world will never know too well—
The magic of your charms.
In countless, and in varied moods
Disturbing strains—my soul intrudes
Responding, my heart warms.
Oh, Music Great, You give us life,
In Joy or Sorrow——
Wealth or Strife——
Eternal Music, haunting me,
With every single rhapsody
To Quell life's storms.

Thelma Hull

Shadows

I am shadowed by my own idols
those glistening goldfish
that slip from my hands
the moment I think I have them
and slither away
into the dark shadows
under the rocks
at the pond's edge
leaving only dark hints
and unanswered queries

Mary C. Bragg

Friends...

Friends for such a little while
thought you've gone away.
Keeping thoughts within your heart
remember who has stayed.

The love of friends is always dear
the closeness never fails.
I bring to you good luck in all
the green in hills and vales.

Though Teddy bears and sickening rides
will turn my mind to you.
Keep me in your memories
and I the same will do.

Susan A. Taylor

Ode to Love

Thanks for the leisure rambles
Through your rose garden.
The petals still covered with dew
Reflecting your youthful beauty.

A story that ends here
Is still unfolding.
Depending on what I
Alone can do.

Knight in shining armor
Set out to conquer.
Cast aside the signs of time
Which brands such an endeavor.

The years are gone
Left are dreams of love.
Warrior steadfast and true
Grant you the will to do.

Norah H. Webb

Time

There is so little time in life
To accomplish all one's dreams.
So much things one wants to do
So little time it seems.
The older one gets
The faster time flies
I wonder where all the years have gone
And keep on asking why.
It seems that it was only yesterday
That I was but a small child.
Running, playing, getting into trouble
Yes, I admit I was wild.
But now I am much older
Set firm in my own ways
Finding myself often dreaming
About those good old days.
And I pray to my God everyday
To show me some sort of sign
That when I look to the future
That He'll grant me some more time.

Theresa Monaghan-Muglia

Nature Is Lost

If a tree could bleed,
would we still cut it down?
When the sun explodes,
will we hear the sound?
In a thousands years,
will we still be around?
If nature is lost,
can it ever be found?

Sandra Pamplin

When

To conquer love is a journey,
to achieve love is a chore.
To experience love is a blessing,
the searcher of love explores.

To truly experience love,
is to love deep within.
To feel what you seek,
You must look from the outside in.

That's what we are taught,
when we read hearing the spirit.
The gift of love is from God,
you'll know it when you feel it.

To love another is to know,
that God is on your side.
with God, you share all your feelings,
because you'll have nothing to hide.

Patrick T. German

The Last Dance

Swaying, leaning
To and fro
Strains of music
High and low

Spinning 'round
Slowly and easily
Gentle like
But not feebly

Holding tight
To your love
Your easy swinging
Not known of

Silence again
And then you part
Your dance is done
Never ending in heart

Jillian Jaeger

Happiness Is

Happiness is
To be able to share
Show someone that you care
To be glad
When someone smiles
To give a hand
When somebody cries
To look for the best
In somebody's heart
To see the sun
Through the darkest cloud.
Without riches
To feel rich
To listen, to learn
And to teach.
To see beauty
In every little thing
To remember
That after winter
Always comes spring.

Ruth Goldberger

Love

Love is what everyone needs
to discover....
What most of the world
needs
Love is what the homeless people
need to receive, and not to be looked
at differently by the people
dressed nice
Love is what the whole country
needs to strive for so everyone
can live in
peace!

Katherine Vargas

Untitled

It's hard for me to write a song
To explain just how I feel
To separate my heart and mind
And find out what is real

A friend like you is hard to find
In a world where no one cares
Someone who I can talk to
And with my burdens share

Each night I go to sleep
With you on my mind
I search out every word you've said
For the wisdom I can find

I wake up in the morning
With a smile on my face
I've finally found someone who cares
And no one can take your place

Robert Grant

A Clean Sweep

The autumn winds just swept my porch
To make the world more tidy
And whispered softly - on its way
That he'd be back next Friday
At first I was aghast
To think it needed cleaning
On second thought - I knew it did
And set my soul to gleaning
For every year - as people do
We store things un-needed
And should - like autumn breezes do
Clean out the weeds we seeded
Keep only fertile thoughts and dreams
To plant in springtime's sod
And cast aside the lowly ones
'fore they've had time to pod!

Mary E. Austin

-Wildflower-

In a field alone,
Unlike the others.
Unique, natural, unartificial.
Delighting the senses,
Appealing to the mind
-Beautiful-
Sought after by many
For its exceptional beauty.
A beauty that far exceeds
that of the rose or daisy.
For myself I want-
This rare, This beautiful
-Wildflower-

Joseph Ferragamo Jr.

My Sister

She's always there
To pick you up,
A loving hand
No harsh words
Never criticizing or placing blame
But always loving you
Just the same

I've always loved her
And known she was special
But I didn't know how much
She meant to me
Till I heard her voice
On the phone, late one nite
She said she was calling
To make sure I was alright.

Linda Galbreath

Spirit Eagles

Spirit Eagles soar, not fly
To realms beyond the visions
of men.

To heights beyond the eye.
To distances far exceeding the
dreams of men.

Only to strike, when least expected
Found as one, not in a flock.

Spirit Eagles soar, not fly.

Paul S. Hickman

The Way I Feel

There are no words to speak of
to say just how I feel
I only know I feel this way
when ever I'm with you.

And I would gladly tell
anyone that asked,
in your heart there is a goodness
that erases all the past.

I am always thankful
in life you choose me first,
forsaking all the others
who would, have gladly took you first.

Sheri Maison

Love Is

Love is a starting
to say we're never parting,

Love is a feeling
sometime stops or never ending,

Love is an emotion
as big as the enormous ocean,

Love is sorrow
wishing there wasn't another tomorrow,

Love is a desire
that sets your heart a fire,

Love is hurtful
when it starts to get tearful,

Love is heart
heart is what makes love start,

Love is an ending
to stop the hate and start the mending.

Lisa Bartley

How Deep Is Our Love

Where to begin - oh how shall I start
to tell of the love for you
I hold deep in my heart

Of how wondrous it is to be swept away
by a knight on a charger
each and every day

Of how my heart fluttered
when asked how deep was my love
it began to grow wings
and to soar like a dove

A new life together
our wedding day will begin
and the love that we share
will be drawn from within
That day our hearts shall soar
on the wings of a dove
and the whole world shall I know
how deep is our love

M. K. Celentano

Where Is My Heart?

Blown away, with the north wind
torn into a thousand pieces
sent far and wide over land and sea
so many places, I can't find me.
Home is where my thoughts so wonder
family safe, and together
but dreams are crushed
reality, full of anguish
children, dear to my heart
are very, far....apart.
Places, I cannot go
my heart now blown in the four winds
will never mind
until, all my children are, home again

Nancy R. Binder

In Life

Go straight ahead
Try for what you want
Do what you want to do
Try something you've not.

Never pass a good opportunity
There might not be another chance
Go through with the experience
Always strive to enhance.

Use your strengths wisely
Don't give up your desired
You'll always be assured
You'll always be admired.

Live your short life
Always bearing good news
Bring out the best
You've got nothing to lose.

For you only live once
So be carefree and willing
And let it be known
That your life is fulfilling.

Wendy Kuhns

Try Smiling

When the weather suits you not
Try smiling
When your coffee is not hot
Try smiling
When your neighbors don't do right
And your relatives all fight
Sure it's hard, but then you might
Try smiling
Doesn't change the things, of course,
Just smiling
But it cannot make them worse,
Just smiling
And it seems to help your case,
Brightens up a gloomy place
Then it sort of rests your face
So try smiling.

Tina Brower

The Dance

As I'm here on the dance floor,
Trying to dance the pain away.
I look around the room,
Hoping to see you looking my way.

The nights you're not there,
Don't hurt quite as much.
But when I lay my eyes on you,
I need to feel your touch.

Please dance with me,
Let me love you once more.
Are you afraid you'll find,
It's still me you adore?

Don't tell me no this time,
Say yes, for sake of my heart.
Maybe then you'll find,
We really shouldn't be apart.

Just one last dance together,
That's all I'm asking of you.
One last time to hold the love,
That in my heart will always be true.

Shawn Marie Dillion

The Island

I long to sit beside the sea,
Upon the sand,
At bended knee.

I long to look out from the shore,
To watch the waves,
To hear their roar.

I long to feel the warm breeze blow,
Sand under-foot,
And rocks below.

I long to smell the salty air
Blown through the palms
And in my hair.

I long to touch the textured shells,
To feel its curves,
Hear what it tells.

I long to see this island rare,
To know this land,
And to be there.

Kathy Jean Elmgren

Roses

We start out in the ground,
Waiting for the right moment to spring.
As we start to grow,
Our journey through the earth begins.

Rumble! Rumble!
That is the sound we make.
Can you hear us?
If you listen hard, you might.

The time is ripe!
The hour has arrived!
It is the moment!
Here we come!

We leave the darkness behind.
We welcome the sunshine gleefully.
What is that we see?
Why, it's a single bud.

More anticipation, I presume.
But it's blooming.
There is a single rose,
And with more to come.

Shu Yu Chen

New Orleans Remembered

I thought I saw
Walt whitman
on the corner of Peter Street
in the city of
New Orleans.
Crawfish, beer and jazz
flowed through the
gutters of Bourbon Street
in the city of
New Orleans.
Purple, Gold and Green
doubloons, beads and banners
danced through the night
on Canal Street in the city of
New Orleans.
My body took a jet plane
back to California...
but my heart remained
in a Reveler's tear, in the city of
New Orleans.

JoAnne E. Yost

Kitten

Soft and fuzzy,
Warm and cuddly.
A good companion,
With friendship like a canyon,
Waiting to be filled,
With all the love you spill.
There to stay,
Always wanting to play,
A kitten's a pet,
That you won't soon forget,
So may we get one today?

Kristin A. Boles

Siren Silhouettes

The sunset from the train
  Was breathtaking
    As the dawn of night
      Consumed the incredible azure
        Clinging to days end

The flame out on the horizon
  Lent the day
    To the all encompassing darkness

Clearly an endless tribute
  To the sirens of the sun
    As silhouettes chased each other
      To a mindless rendezvous
        Somewhere behind me

I would journey forever
  Searching Gods' archives
    For an imprint of that moment

Awareness of mind a juncture in time
  When splendors of all that is
    Stands fixed then fade to dreams
      Thru portals made of sand

Rad Baxter

Left Behind

I stood at the gate,
Watched the truck drive away.
Taking my best friend,
That horrible day.

It seemed much too quiet,
No friends skipping rope,
Everything was gone,
Even my hope.

I walked to the stream,
Sat down on the bank,
Watched the current going steady,
As if turned by a crank.

I had been left behind,
By my very best friend,
My heart had been broken,
And would never mend.

Sara Crowell

Summer on the Beach

Long summers on the beach,
Waves crashing on the shore.
Sun umbrellas making shade.
Mothers chasing children,
And much more.

Sand beneath your feet,
Salt irritates your eyes,
Ocean taste in your mouth,
Sunburn from sunny skies.

Sun sets,
Can't keep eyes open.
Playing on the beach,
Hot summer sun,
Building castles,
No matter what age,
Is always fun!!

Stefanie Dungan

"As One"

In our sights
We are two doves
Happy and content
We share and we care
We enjoy and we love
The many things we have in common
Our every little surrounding
Such as the sky
So blue unlike our mood
The sun
So bright just like our smile
We are two doves
Who paired together
To fly our solo flight
And if a cloud shall darken our sky
In our hearts
We are one
Together or apart

Vanessa Trafton

Live Life to the Fullest

We go about our business,
We live from day to day
Unaware of the fleeting years
That pass us on the way.
Then one day, we get the message
And we comprehend
That we should get our act together
And on no one to depend
We must make the great decision
Before it is too late
To live our lives to the fullest,
Fabulous — first rate.
Since youth is a gift of nature
And age is a work of art
Live each moment to the utmost
And paint with all your heart

Lottie Lamm

Stars

As we grow up,
We may spend many nights,
Looking into the sky;
We notice the stars;
How some go away,
and new ones appear;
Then there are some,
that are always there;
We've come to depend on these,
Simply because we know,
They'll never go away;
Anytime we need them,
They will always be around;
We can count on them,
And never be alone.

Kevin A. Marez

"The Miracle Of Friendship"

There's a miracle of friendship
that remains within the heart,
you don't know how it happens
or where it gets its start
But the happiness it brings you always
gives a special lift,
and you realize that friendship
is God's most perfect.

Juanora C. Wheeler

Life Is A Wonder

Life is a wonder
We take for granted
Each and every day.
Always a new mystery
And ceaseless changes
Await us along the way.
Never knowing never seeing
The uncertainty that lies ahead.
Whether grandiose or melancholy
I choose Christ to be my stead.
My father our Lord,
Jesus always my surrogate
For with him and by him alone
Will I reach peace, peace in heaven
Beyond the pearl gate.

W. T. Osburn

Benediction

In the twilight,
Weary with disappointment,
August repacks his hamper,
Preparing to leave the picnic,
While Pan,
Just over the hill,
Pipes the ducks to sleep —
False security
Against the creeping
Night cats.

One backward look:
The lake is still;
An inquisitive breeze
Tests the thorn tree
And skitters away
With bleeding thumbs.
The old month stumbles
As Pan counts the stars,
Courts the moon,
And "tootles in" September.

Richard T. Hartshorn

To Mona

If we'd had a daughter
We'd have wanted one like you!
So bubbly and so caring,
Thoughtful, kind and true.
But since we weren't so lucky
The good Lord let us share
He put His arms around us all
And put you in our care.
The years passed, all too quickly,
And we were left alone.
We stopped to thank two little tykes
Who made our house a home.

F. J. Schlener

Untitled

The pen bends,
The mind expands,
Unleashing the voices
Within my head.
Where the hell ends,
The spirit begins,
And the ink flows to the page.
Then they begin to understand.

M. Scott Shumate

Weeping Willow

Weeping willow
Weeping willow
Why do you look so sad?
I wish I could see your branches
Sway in the breeze when you're glad.

Weeping willow
Weeping willow
Don't cry, it will be all right.
Let your branches wave in the
wind all night.

Weeping willow
Weeping willow
What a beautiful sight.
Even though you cry all night.

Weeping willow
Weeping willow
Do you ever think it will be all right?

Meredith L. Story

Guns Are Not Fun

So you think you're invisible
Well you are not
A gun can kill you
With just one shot

It can rip a hole
In your heart or kidney
It can paralyze you instantly

A gun doesn't care
If your young or old
It can go off by accident
Or the trigger can be pulled

So if your near someone
And they have a gun
Don't think its cool
And don't stick around

Because before you know it
You can be on the ground
Then the people who love you
Won't have you around

Natalie Bellerjeau

I Love Your Heart

I love your heart....
What a beautiful emotion.

To know someone's heart,
so many settle for less.

What a goal,
but what a price must be paid,
to devote one's life,
to every word said.

God,
I love your heart
do you love mine?

That's all that really matters
in everyone's time.

Lisa Socha

A Special Celebration

This is the year we celebrate
What can the difference be?
I feel the same, and look the same
Who can explain this mystery?
This is the year we celebrate
And family come from afar,
We rent a big house
With room for all
It's my 85th birthday
And I'm the star.
Everyone buzzes with happy planning
To make a special day
As we talk, and laugh,
And work together,
We know our love will stay.
I'm a woman blessed
These many years
I'm sure you all agree
The happiness in our lives
Comes from our family.

Mary Olivier

He That Is

What Wisdom can equal the Love;
What Faith can compare to the Belief;
What Passion can describe the Above,
And give the Mind and Soul that relief.

What Light will penetrate the Dark;
What form must the Spirit be;
What length of motion from the start,
And what purpose now until Eternity.

What Excellence and Beauty is seen;
Unmade and untouched by rational man;
Beyond mortality and senses keen,
Yet ever present in Nature's plan.

What Truth can show the way;
What doubt can smother the Fire;
What Glory and Honor any day,
For He that is that Will Inspire.

Peter G. Lotto

Faith

I can't stand
What I can't have
Never knowing
the great feeling of love.

Faith can be there
someone who will care.
The constant staring
that will never go away.
But I will always want
him to stay in my heart
where he belongs.
My heart can only sing sad songs.

Give faith a thousand chances
and never up stand your stances.
For love will always be with you;
where your heart is.

Jeannie Murphy

What Can This Be?

My heart pumps fast,
What's happening?
Can this last?

My friends say,
"Be reasonable - with time,
This will go away."

I've rationalized -
He's an ordinary type guy
But, I'm mesmerized.

Does he feel the same?
I can't really tell,
I hope it's not a game.

This feeling runs deep,
My heart is still thumping,
Won't let me sleep.

What's wrong with me?
Please give me a clue,
Love - can it be?

Ramona L. Beard

Wouldn't It Be Better?

Is there any justice?
What's it all about?
We're born onto this earth,
ignorant and kind
but as history has shown it,
that never lasts too long
unknowing the ways of life,
we seem to get along
or is this the way we don't belong?

God must be pretty selfish,
not to let us in on the plan
or have a sense of humor,
only He can understand

He made us to rule over all the others
big, mighty and strong
the honor we never see,
nor know how to command
with our perverted ego's,
we destroy God's great land
wouldn't it be better if we knew the plan?

Rosemary Eulo

Dear Santa ...

How calm it was in ages past ..
So easy to be merry ..
In laden sleigh — with magic team
Your burden light and airy -

It all seemed very simple then
To picture children's eyes
What joy it was for everyone
To share in your surprise.

How different is the world today ..
How fast the pace and scary ..
As silver space ships roam the skies ..
No wonder you are wary!

Yet there are things that never change
And one is, come December
Because of you, dear old friend
Our childhood, we remember —

And if today, you well may ask
Are mortals worth the fuss?
Dear Santa, we believe in you
So, please, believe in us.

Kathryn R. Blom

The Holy Bible

Dear God, this world is something
what's wrong with these people today
If only they had a, bible
and, would sit home, think, and pray

People, just don't know
that you are right above
and, looking down at all of us
with your faith, and love

That's why they need the, bible
to understand, and know
the true words that you tell us
you reap just what you sow

They're just killing one another
and, dying by the minute
It's not the world, God gave us
It's just the people in it

If people would only listen
and, try to understand
that, there's only, but one God
with the whole world in his hands
A-men

Marcia Barnett

I Need You!

Feelings in my mind
When I rewind (think back)
The way it all was
The way it all will stay
In a way it seems unreal
The way I'll always feel
As long as I have feeling
I'll have you in my heart
Don't you understand that I need more
I need your body
I need you
Why? ...
The reason is known
But only obvious to me
Sometimes I wonder if you too can see
The expression not only in my body
But in my eyes
As you pull me close to you
And fill me with the love we once shared

Michelle L. Negron

To My Papa

You came into my life
When I was very young, indeed
And at the time, on many things
We seemed to disagree

As time went by, I found
That I, had more than just a Dad
I have a friend who understands
And soothes me when I'm sad

You always seem to be right there
No matter what the cause
To pull me up and help me stand
And over-look my flaws

To me a Dad is more than a man
Who merely brought me in the world
A Dad is guidance, love and hope
And faith that will long endure

I hope that you know, for it's hard to express
The things you mean to me
But if I had it all to do over again
My papa, you definitely would be

Sue Erickson

My Love

It happened six years ago,
When my sister Leah died,
She was a sweet and lovable child.

We laughed, played, sung, and danced,
In the little time we had together,
Oh Leah, how I love you so!

If I could see you again,
I would squeeze you so tightly,
And tell you how much I love you,
Oh Leah how I love you so!

Now there is Samuel,
He is sweet and kind,
But no one could be like you,
Oh Leah how I love you so!
My sweet and loving sister.

Rachael Dean

My Husband

My Husband is a great friend.
When no one else is there.
My husband is a great companion
anytime of year.
My Husband is a great man,
just like his father was.
He sends me letters of love,
just because...

My Husband is a faithful
one, there's not to many out there
He devotes his love to only me,
which is good, because
I don't like to share.

The only thing that he forgets
Are some of the important dates.
But I will forgive him because we are soul
mates.
My Husband is the one I love.

Shaun Cornell

Call Of The Astronauts

On that great primordial morning,
When our parents first slithered free,
Broke the chains that held us prisoners,
To a life within the sea.

Saw the grass wave in the breezes,
Saw the towering mounts afar,
Jeweled upon the vault of heaven,
Saw and wondered, "what's a star?"

Heard we then a voice calling,
With a gentle urging plea,
"Turn your back upon the water,
Little man seed, come and see!"

Russell Faughn

The Lily Bowed

Along the pathway
to Calvary
Strewn with boughs
of branches, flowers
and weeds of essences
all hailing the power
of grace
The Lily bowed

Lena Robertson

Dreams

Where do dreams go
When they go away?
Will someone else
Dream them someday?
Dreams are wishes
Cast in your mind.
The answers to your dreams
In time you will find.
What happens to dreams
When they are through?
I hope you'll find out,
When your dreams come true.

Leslie Michele Miller

Tranquility

There is a secret garden
Where I sit in hushed repose,
And let the beauty of its stillness
Heal the turmoil in my soul.

Neath the cliff that overhangs me,
In the hollows of its face;
Living creatures show the meaning
Of a time, a gent'ler place.

Minute ferns and vines of ivy
Hang suspended from their urns,
Fans and tendrils intermingle
As they share a common berth.

Swallows flit around my garden,
Bleeding hearts profusely bloom;
Chickadees in earthen color
Warble forth a cheery tune.

Quiet times and secret places,
Tender memories of the soul;
Never fading live forever
In my garden of repose.

Lois Ball

My Son

Star light, star bright
Where is my son tonight?
Is he out, is he home?
Will he never cease to roam?

Sun-up, daybreak,
Where is he for goodness' sake?
Visions of horror fill my mind
I'm trying hard to unwind

Early evening, phone rings
I know bad news it brings
I close my ears, close my eyes
I cannot listen to these lies

Pick-up truck, smashed up
They say he was messed up
Hit a tree driving 73
My son and his wife-to-be

I can't believe he'd drink and drive
If not for that, he'd be alive
Was there something I should have said?
It's too late, my son is dead

Rhonda Frierson

Beach Of Omaha

Now only shadows remain,
where many of our men were slain.
Shots no longer sound,
on the beach of Omaha.

Tears may still be shed,
in memory of our men that are dead.
For no one will ever forget that day,
on the beach of Omaha.

Their bravery and courage stand out,
because they are heros without a doubt.
Who could ever forget that day,
on the beach of Omaha.

How could we repay,
the thing you did that day
on the beach of Omaha.

Wendy D. Fitts

White Or Black

White or Black is just another color
Whether your white or black doesn't
mean that one is better
White or black is just another name
White or black cannot be called a game

Any color, gender, shape or size
is just another excuse to despise
We may be different, but yet we
are the same
We have nothing or no one to ever
blame
We should be proud of who we are,
not who we could be
For you are you and I am me

White and black should not fight
White and black should not strike
White and black should stick together,
For white and black are Forever!!

Tish Dodds

"One Voice"

Spirits talk
While
Angels listen,

God sits back
Just comfortably
Whistling,

Mortals scream
While
Satan's laughing,

All one voice
Mildly stabbing.

Miranda A. Allen

Jill Is Gone

Lift your mind from the petal's edge
To let the flower bloom.
Steel your heart to the soul of life
To seal your loved one's tomb.
Feel the bramble's prickling spire
To braille the touch of moss.
Press your ear to a robin's breast
And you will know my loss.

Richard W. McVey

Dragons and Butterflies

Butterflies in my day
While dragons sweep the night
With the slit of dusk
At the end of day
And the green smell of lizard musk
In the wet straw fields they lay
Eyes of dull yellow gaze
There sounds from deep with in
To roam the skies for ever on
Our masters of the night
With the crack of day
So ends the night
From misty careless sleep
Awakes the tiny butterfly
With soft colored whispers
Of the day he brings
Then flutters on his way
And starts the sunny bright crescent day.

S. A. F. Testerman

The Shadow of Peace

Just before dawn,
While the people slept,
I saw a dark shadow,
Walking slowly, as it wept.

Its tears fell softly upon the dead.
Flowers came up where
the drops were shed.

It was merely a small vision of hope,
as it walked toward the war, and
its strangling rope.

I saw no person to the shadow.
It walked alone.
Against its foe.

Its journey was long.
Its life was hard,
but its purpose still walked,
It couldn't be scared.

Great walls of strength stood fast,
but the form would never cease.
And this bold shadow was the shadow, of
peace.

Tiffany Bauer

Obsessive Garden

Purple melancholy forgets me not,
white lilies intervene
before the red orange poppies
lusciously serene
mingle with yellow snapdragons
a kaleidoscopic scene
contrasting many colored iris
swaying bold in green.
Distorted trails of morning-glories
covered white trellises blue,
entertaining scarlet beauties
dressed in the evening's dew.
A blushing smile of apricot rose
and delphinium elatum grew
among the pink clematis
in the honeysuckle lieu.

Will Cline

My Dog "Bear"

You have always
been my steadfast,
malamute friend.

I owe you my grateful
thanks, now thirteen,
'til the very end.

Velma A. Thompson

So Many Questions

So many times I ask myself
Why am I here? And
So many times I can never
answer that question
So many times I ask
my self why people hate?
And so many times I can
never answer that question.
So many times in so many
years in so many days
in so many hours in so
many minutes in so many seconds
I ask my self so
many questions. Most of
my questions will remain
unanswered, for now. I guess
something just can't be
known. Maybe if every ones
questions were answered life
would be duel and lose it's mystery.

Miranda Esquivel

I'll Tell You

If you ask me,
"Why are you writing?"
I'll tell you,
"I read it in my horoscope"
if you ask me,
"Why are you thinking?"
I'll tell you,
"My fortune teller told me to."
if you ask me,
"Why are you smiling?"
I'll tell you,
"My lifeline said I should"
if you ask me,
"Why are you living?"
I'll tell you I want to.

Sarah Wittenbrink

"Love, Love, Love"

Love, love, love
Why do you hurt so?
Such a happy feeling
But then the hurt, Oh, no!

How painful it is
To love and then lose-
I don't understand life,
I guess, perhaps I'm confused.

Memories, will always be there
Oh, I am sure of that-
But, one day: hopefully
I will learn to adapt.

Michelle M. Tuzzolo

Man In The Moon

Man in the moon
Why do you look so blue?
Has your love left you too?
Man in the moon
Help me be strong
Help me forget everything
Help me please!!!
Man in the moon
Do you do wishes and dreams too?
Man in the moon
Is the end real soon
Will we have to build cocoons?
Man in the moon
Please give me love
Love I had before and evermore
Man in the moon
Shine bright and new.

Melissa M. Rollstin

Untitled

Everyone has their own beliefs
  Why does this cause so much grief?
We're not as different as we seem
  We have the same basic dreams
Whose wrong and whose right?
  We could argue that all night
Let's not fight nor yell
  Stop condemning everyone to hell
Let God figure it all out
  He knows what it's all about
Stop trying to guess
  You'll only cause a mess
Just let it all be
  And maybe you'll see
That all you need to do
  Is look inside of you.

Melinda Norris

Warrior And Friend

His pony's a paint,
Wide chested and tall.
He runs like the wind,
And never will fall.

The blanket he wears,
His master had sewn.
For the comfort of both,
the owner is known.

He'll take him to hunt,
Or lead him to war.
Whatever the work,
He will not ignore.

He's strong and he's spirited,
But knows his commands.
Till death do they part,
The Warrior and Friend.

Richard W. Brown

Ode to All

Wiggle In Need
Wobble In The Heat
Goggle Of Deed
Jobber Entered, Sat Up Seat
Togger Ran Under, Sacred Treed
Idler No Time Hath Entreat
Live On Royal Deed

Michael Timbrook

A New Day

Beyond me a field
  Wildflower tall
Grasses sweeping over
  In delight
A field filled with friends
Beckoning me forth
To come again
Run - and be free
Fly kites - and be free
And make the days yellow
To laugh - dance
Let my eyes - my being
Burst with life
And thrive on loving

Remember loving days in the sun
And the night time of their passing
And now run - kite in hand
A new day of loving
Of yellow
Is here

Pat Fischer

My First Love

Tonight I keep thinking of you
Will your memory remain in my
heart forever?
The moonlight is shining through
reminding me we will never
experience the thrilling ecstasy
of first love again
the love I have known and lost
moments of rapture I cannot attain
you have gone leaving only ghosts
of memories
Tonight my dreams disturbed
by emotion tender love
and devotion
Which out shines by far
the moon beams or even
the evening star.

Renois Gidcumb

When the Wind Blows

Lightning pierced darkened sky,
winter comes while summer dies.

  When the wind blows.

Leaves with color autumn spray,
breaking loose and drift away.

  When the wind blows.

Clouds of large shapely size,
drifting beauty to naked eye.

  When the wind blows.

Clothing whipped while hair is tossed,
something gained something lost.

  When the wind blows.

Misty Gail Akers

Pride

Does it go before the fall?
Is love the same as fall?
Why do we fall in love?

Suzanne Rentsch

La' Look

That little look.
That little glare.
I wonder if it means
How do you dare...

Diane Kuefler

God Brought You Together

God brought you together
With a love you could share
Give him praise daily
Show him you care
Be ever grateful
For what he has done
Love each other forever
As you're united as one
Be kind and loving
Give your all to the other
And guard and protect
What God brought together

Nancy Legg

Lonely Water

The sand through my toes
with brushing against my face
water up to my knees
and I give a shiver
a shiver of silence
a shiver of peace

The lawn chairs in a row
I look back as I go deeper
water up to my neck
and I give a shiver
a shiver of loneliness
a shiver of hope

The people with laughter in their eyes
me with no one
a tear drops from my eye
and I give a shiver
a shiver of heart ache
a shiver of emptiness

Sandy Da Silva

The World's Best Marksman

William Tell was a marksman
With careful aim he drew
And split an apple's center
His skill was matched by few

But there is one yet better
A youngster it is said
His bow has drawn on many
But not a one has bled

When cupid shoots his arrows
They always find their mark
Their tips contain no poison
Yet pierce the strongest heart

These arrows are invisible
For none has e'er been seen
Their power is immeasurable
Their accuracy - Supreme

You can salute this marksman
The greatest of all time
By wishing someone special
Happy St. Valentine's.

Tommy Edmondson

Untitled

Life has begun,
With child in womb.
Its meaning brings joy to all.

Taken for granted,
The mystery of its creation,
We forget the meaning.

Soon life has past,
But we only spent a second,
And now life must end.

But not all lost,
For the child left a legacy,
Its parents remembers forever.

And just a half a world away,
A new joy has been found
A cycle has formed, life has begun.

Terry Joseph Oliver

"First Day of School"

So many here
With frightened faces.
A held back tear
Will leave no traces.

With hands held tight,
A room we find.
Her eyes so bright
With tears that bind.

My heart has frayed,
But I must leave.
Who's really afraid
You or me?

J. E. Trevino

R. E. M.

I go to sleep
With my hopes and my fears
My loves and my dreams
My cries and my tears
In that state of sleep
I am perfectly at peace
No enemies are at war with me
No stresses, just release
I drift off to a world
Where fantasies come true
Everything is always happy
And I am never feeling blue
I dream of this world
Where my self-standards are matched
I have reached my perfection
The doors of bad times
Are locked and latched
Then I hear a bell...
It's time to wake up!

Nicole Palmer

Jennifer

Forlorn adoring through the
  transient separations
Banal pangs still wound
  the ever unstable heart.
Longing certitude; fond tranquility
Comfort with one, yielding security
Love with one, unyielding love.

Mark Smith

Grandpa

He sits all alone now
With no one to care
Just listening to the squeak
In that old rocking-chair
With tears in his eyes
And a trembling chin
He ponders in his mind
When his heart ache begin
Was it when the children left hone
Or when Mama passed on
He's nearing ninety now
And his legs are weak
So he just sit's and listens
To that old rocking-chair squeak

Vaughn W. Muncrief

Origin Belonging

I wait patiently
with relentless fervor

a pulsating glimmer of hope
on the edge of fruition

awaiting the gentle acceptance
of your essence

Then bond empathetically
the spirits - soul in grace

an overwhelming breathless union
suspended in unimaginable wholeness

enduring uncertain submission
to immortality's glow

Relinquish apprehension
commit to destined calm

an annunciation of common will
commanded by consenting instincts

believing
and belonging

Kevin Michael Kalinowski

A Marriage Toast

Blend heaping cups of kindness
With scoops of love and trust.
Add spontaneous bursts of laughter
To keep out any rust.

With every act of gentleness
Throw in deserving praise.
Be careful as you add advice.
Your voices, seldom raise.

A bucketful of cheerfulness
With help the marriage grow.
A pinch of sorrow now and then
Will even out the flow.

Nourish love with tenderness;
Pour into clean, pure hearts.
Bake until well matured,
While molding all the parts.

Share this recipe with others,
Pass on to all your kin.
May God bless and keep you.
Let your new life now begin.

Marilyn Schomburg

Here With Me

All alone just me and you
with the mood so right
And the thought of you holding me
close was undeniable

The look in your eyes,
The fire in your touch,
The love in your smile,
Told me that you loved me.

In time as the night went on,
The mood became more intense
And the thought of you holding me
close was no longer,
Now you were inside of me.

You were in my mind,
You were in my thoughts,
You were in my heart,
And most of all you were here
with me.

Now hours have gone by,
And so have the days
But now and forever you're still
here with me!

Patricia Long

Sea Gull

How free a sea gull feels inside
Without a suitcase by this side

To burden heavy with a load
Of things that make us fear for loss

The very thing we carry well
That never care who cares for them..

How strange we mortals be on earth
To love the things that give the least.

We should be more like gulls, you see
Who take the case of simple things,
Like sun and surf and winds blown free
Upon the sea gull that we see

No bills to pay
Or phones to ring that make a body
Wrench with pain.

A sea gulls life is simple sweet
Just flying, flapping, screeching glee.

Jackie Pastis Margoles

The Mirror That Lied

I see you there looking back at me
Wondering if you see what I see
Your disguise is so well hidden
Only you can set me free

I go along living my life
Being who you want me to be
But if I go on living this way
I'll never have a true identity

Your lines are so revealing
Your face is so well concealed
You make it so easy
My life is now revealed

If I could have one thing
Back to the way it was before
It would be my honesty
Because that's all I've been living for

Kevin Tiller

Mom

You are my mother,
Without any doubt,
you gave me a brother,
And he makes me shout.

You taught me plenty,
Throughout my life,
How to spend my twenties,
And how to deal with strife.

You've always been around
whenever I'm in need,
you taught me the sounds,
That I have to heed.

To me there is no one,
To ever take your place,
Everything I've done,
Is because of your grace.

You're the one I love,
and this day is for you
may God send down a dove,
To guide and direct you.

Lori Norton

Untitled

Sitting here looking out the window
wondering what life is all about.
Is there really a meaning for
this place we call earth? So many
questions but not enough answers.
What do you see when you walk
out your door? Do you see this
beautiful place we call earth?
Do you see all its beauty? Or do
you see how we are destroying
our land? Do you see violence?
Do you see war? So what is the
purpose of living? Do you not know?
Well neither do I. It's a long
journey a journey that takes a
lifetime to understand. But even
after that long journey do you know
the reason for living? Or was it
just a wasted trip you should never
have began?

Tiffany Hollingsworth

The Yearning

I always wanted a gal friend.
Wow - wouldn't that be a pal?
Well I just wasn't sure when
I'd find her around the bend.
It was always on my mind
when I'd find one that was kind.
I was anxious to meet her.
So I could treat her
It could be she's out of reach
or maybe she's at the beach.
I just need her to show her hide
so we could only go for a ride
I know she's hard to find
but you know I'm really in a bind.
I will always keep on hoping
and just stop all the moping
Stay away from the dope
so I would be able to cope
We will always stay in touch
because that would mean very, very much

Zachary Kramer

Obdurate

You are not made of Stone
yet words bounce off you
and do not Penetrate
the Shell around you
Put there
by yourself
to Protect yourself
from yourself
Not Me
Or the Others
who wish you were
Made of Stone

Karen A. Wynbeek

Untitled

I see faces in a sea of people,
Yet yours alone stands apart.
Slowly, it's becoming clearer,
Until I think I actually feel you.
Who are you?
Why me?
Isn't life beautiful?
Yes, two of us.
Free to love each other
And love ourselves.

Laurie Sidder

Utopian Lovers

We are Utopian Lovers.
You and I.
Born from Genesis and evicted from Eden.
To the eyes of some others
Our Love may be sin.
And when future days are so bleak,
I will protect you from times so dim.

Here in your arms in my Utopia.
A dwelling of Eden and Love.
Amorous means you my dear,
Utopia only happens when you are near.

Peter F. Daigle

Masters Are WE

Masters in the making,
You and me!
Life filters through
Windows new.
Freedom to Soar
Up and beyond;..

Masters in the Making,
You and Me!
Struggling and Striving
for promised - rewards!

New visions unfolding;
Awaken memories - past.

Progressing through-
Areas of growth.
Visions of grandeur,
Words...
Do not describe.

Masters In the Making
You And Me!!!

Rita Scherle

You Make It A Perfect Day!

You are the morning that I long for,
you are the one who lights my day.
You encourage me to laughter,
and make my heartaches go away.
You are the reason I'm living,
you make the storm clouds cease to be.
My heart swells within me,
as a glimpse of you I see.
You make my gray sky turn blue,
and your sweet smile is my cue.
It is so wonderfully precious,
in your presence just to be.
The day now is fleeting,
and very soon will end.
Now, I'm revealing my love for you —
no longer to pretend.
So hold me close my darling —
and never let me go.
I want no other —
for I love you so!

Paul E. Prock

Someday

The very day I met you
you become the owner of my heart.
My love grows even deeper
despite the fact that we're apart.
You touched my soul that very day
and made my life worth while.
The love I feel for you
grows stronger everyday.
Wandering what happened
to lead our love astray.
Everything was perfect
I thought our love was here to stay.
I've come to realize
our loves a thing of yesterday
still hoping that we'll meet again
someday...

Mary K. Pearson

Alone

You left me alone to die
You didn't care, you didn't cry
Why must you hurt me so
I cared for you
How can you be so low?

I am all alone to feel my pain
I'm all alone to face the rain
All alone am I
It's now time to say goodbye

Goodbye cruel world
Farewell
Wait for me Lord
Listen for my yell

See my pain
Feel my sorrow
I'm going insane
I won't be here tomorrow
Autumn

Maria Lisa Mule

Leave Me In A Memory

Just leave me in a memory if
you ever break my heart
The pain would be to intense
if we were to part.
I couldn't stand alone without
you by my side
From the pain of love,
there's nowhere to hide.

Just leave me in a memory,
no one will know.
Off to my place of rest, I
quietly go.
Come drink from my tears
as they fall like rain.
I am not dead just
running from pain.
No need for remorse or pity
for me,
You've just locked me inside
your memory.

Kimberly Bohannon

Untitled

Just once
you find a love that cares.

Just once
you see a rainbow
in her hair.

Just once
she drives the night
from the sky.

Just once
you tried to tell her
Goodbye.

Just once.

Tammy S. Smart

I Love You

For all those times
You gaze at me,
With steel-grey eyes
So lovingly..........
I love you.

When shadows fall,
You come to me
With care and warmth
So lovingly..........
I love you

The march of time
Won't alter me.
We'll keep our bond
So lovingly.........
I love you.

Marianne Hyatt

The Dance

The moon glows
wild, passionate
surpassing all auras of time.

And on earth
he dances
blind to the thoughts
of his goddess.

Joanne Gauthier

Love or Hate

When you don't know
You just want to go away
Where should you go?
Where should you hide?
When you're trapped
With one man or the other to
Choose from
Ones kind the other is away
Deeply in love
But trapped inside yourself
with love
One doesn't know
But you don't want more pain
inside your heart
You must not tell
You will get them in a war
For what?
Love a paresis love for both of them
Dearly you want them
But for what, love or hate?

Melanie N. Frady

One Precious Jewel Was Loaned To Me

"You must have lost your way!" I cried;
"You know that you're not welcome here.
Be gone at once!" Death merely sighed,
And as I caught my breath with fear,
My young son died —
His childhood gone so ruthlessly.
"What purpose this?" declaimed my grief.
"Nine futile years! 'Twere better he
Were never born than life so brief."

He was an earnest gifted child,
I reminisced, as solace came —
His humor keen, his manner mild.
And as I softly called his name,
I found I smiled
In gratitude that I could see
How much of joy and love were mine,
That all that he had meant to me
Could not be measured by mere time.

Pauline H. Kammet

"You Left Me That Night"

You left me that night
You left me in pain
You left me that night
in the cold dark rain

I lost your heart
I lost your love
I no longer hear
the sound from above

Why did you leave me
Why did you hurt me
Do I deserve this
Why did you desert me

You left me that night
You left me in fright
You left me that night
Why do we have to fight

Jami J. Mandill

J.I.S.

For so many things in life
You may not know what to do.
Maybe if your head stays clear
God will see you through.

There are two parts
For each choice every day.
Your happiness lies ahead,
So carefully choose your way.

Confusion is often a prelude
To success that lies ahead.
Just be sure that this success
Brings you happiness before your dead.

Sandra Kernstock

Ethics

To get to the top, on someone
you must climb
Then it must not be my time.
Competitive, no that's not me.
Instead helping others it must be.
Am I lost
Do I know who I am
Yes to both, I have found
Love my fellow man/woman to
A fault.
Teach what I have learned from
Dr King until someone else is taught.

Leonard Logan

When Friendship Lasts

When in life, friends are all you have
you need to treat them well.
If they're sweet, or if they smell
always treat them well.
If they're weird, or if they're gay,
always treat them well.
'cause remember...
"OPPOSITES ATTRACT,"
and believe me ya'll,
that's a fact!

Pamela Birchfield

Untitled

Me, wind
You, tree
Me blow life
Into your leaves

The tree thrust its branches
Down the wind's throat,
Grasped the hot air
From its lungs,
And whipped up a storm
That blew the wind away.

Steve Carlton

Mysterious

My beautiful Aunt Cerra
Youth she has no more
Soon to go to heaven
Talks to angels in her room
Enters the room her eyes sparkling
Reads from the big black book
Ignores the spider on the window sill
Opens a small box beside her chair
Upon her finger she slides a ring
Solid gold, his old wedding ring

Vince Branham

Dearest Amanda (Mandy)

We "touched" you and it was as if
you were here!! The circle of life
was eminent — the news of your
"pending birth" and in a blink of
an eye — "your untimely death"
— told us you were destined for
more heavenly things!!

We here on earth were very deeply
touched by your tiny being and the
promises to be fulfilled — alas
not to be fulfilled "here" but in
a more special place!!
Lullaby and Goodnight Little Mandy
Wherever you are!!

Grandma (Reva Marx)

My Country

My country means so much to me,
Young and old alike have fought
to keep it free
We have been involved in wars
throughout the years,
Our friends and loved ones have
shed many tears
If you have never been in a
country that isn't free
You may not know what it means to me
If you think I'm wrong, or
Just not right
Then go to hell, because
I'll fight!

Paul D. Layne

The Wind

Still but restless
young but old.
Whispering all the time
so all secrets are told.

Invisible to man
Invisible to all.
No one can see it
but you can hear it call.

It's untouchable
yes that's true.
But if you can't touch it
why can it touch you.

Light and gentle
forceful and strong.
Listen very carefully
and you'll hear what's wrong

So never be afraid
of the message it will send.
Who's sending all these messages?
Well we call it the wind.

Karen Woodberry

Untitled

We hear of the explosion,
of people, I mean.
But the people,
aren't people,
they're numbers
indeed.

Douglas R. Downie

How Wonderful

Your smiles are like rainbows,
Your eyes are like stars,
Your voice is like a dream
Calling to my heart.
Your hands are like old friends,
Comfortable to hold.
Your words are like gifts,
Precious to unfold.
Your laughter is joyous,
Musical and soft,
And all these things remain
Here, in my thoughts.
It's sad to be so far apart
When you belong here,
In my heart.
But I've suffered trials
And travelled far
Just to prove
How wonderful you are.

H. E. Wright

The Legacy

The wrinkles on your skin were deep,
Your face now poised as if asleep.
The life you led was one of love,
Flowing down from above.

Your hands were always touching others,
Sweetly each night you tucked my covers.
Your lips are now quiet and still
But with your words my heart is filled.

As I hear this last bell toll,
To be like you will be my goal.

Wendy Simms

Me

My body as one
My mind is me
With my sight, I can see you
With my hearing, I can listen to you
My touch, I can feel
Till death do we part
My body as one
My mind is me.

Teri-Dawn Wells

Passage of Time

New years and old years,
The passage of time,
Where are you going
With this youth of mine?
The old full of memories,
The new full of hope,
Tomorrows and yesterdays
With me have eloped.

Time keeps on passing,
I cannot deny,
I keep on changing
I think I know why.
I change 'cause the times do,
Sometimes without reason,
I change 'cause I want to
Keep up with the seasons.

Times given a treasure trove of things that I've seen.
It's given me the memories of places I've been.
It's broadened horizons through people I've known,
And left me to harvest the seeds that I've sown.

Patricia Hill

Missing a Friend

Sitting in my room,
your picture in my hand.
Smiling at the good ol' days.
Boy, were they grand!

But, as I sit there longer,
a tear rolls down my cheek.
How long has it been, best friend?
A month, a day, a week?

My, how time passes by,
without a friend to share it with.
Years just seem too go.
Seconds seem to quick.

But could it also be possible,
to feel the lapse will never end?
Anything is possible for one,
who misses her best friend.

Stacy L. Bell

Why Mommy?

Mommy, look at me,
You're gonna be so proud of me!

Thank you for bringing life to me!
Someday you'll see, I'm no mistake.
God has a plan for me.
By the time I die
I'll be known through the world.

Mommy, I can tell something is wrong.
What is it?
Daddy left didn't he?
I knew it, it's my fault.

Mommy please keep me anyway,
Don't kill me!

Please Mommy, don't hate me.
I know I was an accident to you,
But Mommy, to God, I'm no accident.

Mommy I just thought I'd let you know,
My life was going to be one of love and
encouragement,
But it's your loss now, because—
Mommy, today you aborted me.

Why Mommy?

Lynette Hawkins

Charlton Park

High heel shoes,
And swinging hips,
And beautiful blonde hair,
A tale of disappointment,
Is all that I found there,
For what was so attractive,
Retracts in the second sense,
A girl who had good looks to spare,
But no intelligence

S. Tarrant

Nowhere To Hide

In the corner of a dark room
Sits an innocent, little girl.
Her face streaked with teardrops.
His cold laughter in her mind.
Her mother knows all about it,
But she is too intoxicated to stop him,
When she tries to run and hide,
He always finds her.
There is no escape from it.
What did she do to deserve this?
These horrible nightly beatings.
"No", is not a word he likes
He just gets more abusive.
When will this pain end?

It has been a few years now.
She is older, practically a teen.
Still she receives his beatings.
No one listens to her frightened cries.
Will no one help her?
She has no where to hide.

Michelle Cook

Forever

40 years together
60 more to go
each and every year so far
has had a loving glow.

Because their love is natural
great and pure and true
they have made such a strong bond
will last forever too.

Love is indeed a force
the greatest one on earth
nothing can ever break this love
not even a strong curse.

There has been so many kinds
of friendship and young love
but nothing is as strong as this
cause this comes from above.

For all the years and years to come
no one knows what is in store
but what is known is that these two
will love forever more.

Janine Miller

Cease Complaining

Whene'er I begin to complain
About my troubles small,
It behooves me to pause,
And from grumbling refrain.
Lest into the trap I fall,
And Satan's glee cause.

For many others I know,
And millions unknown,
Have sorrows severe.
Thus strength should I show.
With God, I'm not alone.
Nothing should I fear.

Troubles can be overwhelming,
And solutions out of reach.
Yet many with less than I,
Are never found complaining.
They accomplish the impossible.
So silent should I be!

Mary Huggins Napier

Alex

My lovely little helper,
Alex is his name,
helps me in the garden
while waiting to play games.

We pick strawberries and tomatoes,
we water the flowers too;
now he is nearly five
there's so much he can do.

A treat is waiting for Alex,
his hard day's work is done.
Now it's time for strawberries
and a sticky bun.

Joyce Redman

Shelter from the Wind

Whene'er the winds of heartache blew
And aching filled my heart
I always could depend on you
My shelter from the wind.

Whene'er the winds of life blew cold
And sadness filled my soul
Your loving arms would me infold
My shelter from the wind.

Whate'er the winds would blow my way
Tears, joy and laughter, too
You'd wait to share my each new day
My shelter from the wind.

Where'er the winds of life send me
My age - it matters not
Dear mother you will always be
My shelter from the wind.

Mary Alice McHarg Royer

It

It caught me off my guard,
And crept up while I slept
When I awoke at dawn,
Through the window it slowly went.

It never said a word to me
Or whispered in my ear,
But it did do one thing,
To my eyes it brought a tear.

I knew one day it would arrive
But I didn't know how fast,
I was not prepared for it,
And I hoped it wouldn't last.

I wondered why it came at all,
What was its master plan?
To catch me off my guard
Not caring who I am.

The next night it arrived again,
But this time it didn't go,
It over took my body,
And to God it sent my soul.

Lynn Barany

The Trees,

Tall stately, yet bare,
Snow covering, their branches,
Like a mantle,
A peep of red,
A Robin, resting there

Nina Tyler

I Look At My Child

I look at your smiling face
And I see you are as refined as lace,
Unspoiled by modern truths,
The innocence of your youth.

I look at your crying eyes
And I realize,
That you are a child
And I should forgive and smile.

I look at your curious hands,
Wanting to learn and understand;
You see the world as something new,
Full of things to learn and do.

I look at your loving arms
And want to protect you from all harm;
Keep you safe within my heart
So we will never be apart.

I look at you smiling
And say "I would give anything
For you to have a happy life,
Free from everyday strife."

Barbara Comeau

If Only...

If I had seen your face
and kissed your eyes just once
they would be printed line for line
upon my memory.

If I had held your hands
cradled between my own
their touch would be impressed
upon my palms forever.

I know death is not final
but I miss you here
and my existence is unrounded
without you.

We would have grown together
laughed together, hand in hand,
instead, even your dying
was denied to me.

Yet you will live again
in everything I do
my grief transmuted
in creating love anew.

J. R. Biddulph

Crop Circles

The corn field glows
as it shows
circles spread upon its back.
What is that?
I wonder,
ponder.
Have aliens invaded?
Landed?
Or is it just a sign
saying this earth is mine
take care of it,
share it,
but don't abuse it
or misuse it.
Or is it just a stamp
saying
This earth is fresh.
Or is it a sell-by-date
mate?

Pamela Gorman-Sandry

The Two

As two they are lost,
As one they are found.

Once found, no THING can
break the one...

In the past,
The two are put
to test,

In the future,
The two are as one.

...From the two; one.
From the one; strength.

The bonds are
yet unbroken.

Lailanie Dolotallas

Abused...Wife? Alcohol? Hope?

He hit her in the mouth
As she wanted to scream
No sound came about
As though in a dream
She trembled in fear
As he came terribly near
The words that he spoke
Were of anger and pain
But when she awoke
Everything was the same
His constant drinking
Had not gotten better
Her husband is now
A fearful looking stranger
Everything stopped
Until all that was left
Was a wife and unborn
Beaten to death

Brigitte Loiselle

How's It Feel?

(Song to Dino)

How's it feel tonight
Being without me
Calling another yours

How's betrayal feel
Without my embraces
Giving another yours

How's no peace of mind feel —
Being without me
Calling another yours

Ljiljana Milice Zikic

Maude

A bright red boat at rest
Beside lobster traps
On a rocky beach
The tide is out

A young child throws stones
Splash
Blue cap blocks the sun
From her eyes

They wait for the tide

Lesha Heney

People Make Life Great

My life,
better than ever,
you're the one that makes it so great.

Every second, every minute,
I treasure time were together.

You, you make me a better person
because you always make me feel special

I always wanted to feel this,
Someone always by my side.

Your touch, your hug,
Makes my heart beat faster.

Everything about you makes me love you
day after day it gets stronger.

My life, would be nothing without you!

Stacey Merkley

Colors

Everyone is different
But we're also the same,
So why do some of us
Make others live in shame?

It's hard enough already
Being part of the human race,
So why do we judge others
By the color of their face?

Why do some of us believe
There's something we will gain
By trying our hardest day by day
To put others through the pain?

Will we ever get it through our heads
That this world is for us all?
Why do some of us find peace
In making others fall?

I hope our world will realize
We must live together as one;
And when we reach that day, we'll know
True life has just begun.

Shauna Borycki

History of the Wild Wild West

Boom boom, is Calgary our boom town.
Calgary, Calgary is our boom town:
Once upon a time sudbury was our,
boom town, sudbury and timmins:
Calgary, Calgary is our boom town.
Theirs Albertan, fields of wheat and
oil wells and gold in the hills:
Calgary, Calgary, is our boom town:
In town our gals are the greatest.
So guys and dolls, do not delay:
To Calgary, Calgary, our boom town.
Our Rodeo's will, thrill and chill you:
Our Rodeo's will, thrill and chill you:
Calgary, Calgary, is our boom town:
Calgary, Calgary, is our boom town:
Land of the Sundance kid:
Land of the Sundance kid: And that is the

History of the wild, wild, West:

Leo St. Gerard

Untitled

Unknown
Death stands above me, whispering low
I know not what into my ear.
Of this strange language all I know
Is, there is not a word of fear.

Francis MacDonald

Sometimes I See

"Chevrolet Celebrity"

Sometimes when I see
"Chevrolet Celebrity"
I think I will see
Your face.

Sometimes when I see
A white "Celebrity"
I hope we will meet
Again.

Nobody knows
Where you live
And I am looking
For your "Celebrity"
I hope I will find you
On the road.

I am the fastest on the road
I ride all around
I want to see you
For a moment
You are my fate
And my love.

Borislav Stanojevic

Eikon

I write with pain's darkened blood,
choosing words as weapons;
small daggers of amazement
that wound from beyond;
black screams
that cling to me
as rain to silence,
lurking in memory's twisted wreckage,
and clasping all my stories
within.

Neda Maria Brkic

Christmas Is.

The pretty gifts beneath the tree,
Could not mean half as much to me,
As the family who all gather near,
At this special time of year.

The friendly smiles of children grown
The happy memories we have known,
The caring words we seldom say,
Make this a very special day.

So let's enjoy this Christmas cheer,
And make a vow, throughout the year,
Remember how close we feel today,
And think about that everyday.
And so my wish to you today,
Is that forever come what may,
A family we will always be,
To gather round the Christmas tree.

William Waugh

Alone

They walk along
each in their own way.
Slow quiet steps
while their thoughts wonder.

Lonely, and by themselves
each, confused and angry.
Feeling churn, surfacing
then disappearing.
Cries of help float away
softly in the wind.
Their harsh whispers
are unheard.

Alone, and
by themselves
in a land surrounded
by loneliness.

Nicole Anderson

A Moment

Time begins here.
Everything is in its place.
The feeling lives
As a separate entity
Without fear, without hurt.
A connection so familiar
That you recognize yourself
Then reality is transformed
Into something whole
And stretches before you
And beyond
Lies the truth
It doesn't matter
Because I am left here
With your memory
Lingering in my mind
For what seems like eternity.

Kelly Binder

Rapture

She is beyond the gateway -
falling naked
in the stillness of
anticipation.
He enters the unknown,
her back arches
in the arms of ecstasy.
Inwardly, she moans.
Eyes flooded
with passion.
Tenderly she reaches for him,
eagerly she craves for him.
Unselfishly she gives herself,
and her world.
For he has taken her soul...
like no other -
Tread softly on her dreams.

Dina Simmons

True Friendship

Like a rainbow,
Friendship appears;
Through the glistening tears of a cloud.
Like a rose,
It blooms with promise.
Friendship comes true
from the heart and the spirit.
And, like a dream,
Can be easily shattered...

Rana Valenzuela

The Mountains

Majestically they rise,
far above the land.
Circling the valley,
like a solid granite band.

They rise into the clouds,
circling their tips.
The sky that is above,
seems to hold them in its grips.

Summer has arrived to them,
no longer is there snow.
Still their power and beauty,
creates security below.

Rebecca P. Strickland

Knock Softly

If you find yourself a runnin'
from the demons from behind
I'll bare you a brief message,
You must keep this thought in mind:

Knock softly on the door,
Do not go rushing in.
Reinstate your manners,
Intrusion is a sin.

You can't wait another moment!
Fiery shores breath down, your neck!
The demons are a comin'!
The demons come up quick!

Manners wait another time!
Throw caution to the wind!
You have to be one
Be one of those within!
Your mind can wait no longer!
It Snaps! Go charging in!

You've left the demons outside,
In exchange for those within.

Travis Zesmer

The Fair

What a wonderful thing is the fair,
Getting cotton candy in your hair,
Going on rides,
That churn the insides
What a wonderful thing is the fair.

What a wonderful thing is the fair,
Going on rides on a dare,
Playing the games,
All over again,
What a wonderful thing is the fair,

What a wonderful thing is the fair,
Winning prizes from the mayor,
Seeing the crafts,
And hearing the laughs,
What a wonderful thing is the fair!

Kathryn Baldwin

Imagine

I keep seeing things,
But then I cross them out.
Everything in the world I see,
But then cross out.
Until all I have left is YOU.

Kyle Chant

Mother Nature

Calm, quiet, pleasant,
hard to believe.
Breezy, cool, humid,
slowly changing.
Stronger, louder, cooler,
incoming storm.
Thunder, lightning, wind,
building up.
Rain, hail, gusts,
heading for cover.
Crops and trees trying,
to withstand unbearable odds.
Bending, fighting, dying,
succumbed to the storm.
Crushed, flattened, devastated,
nothing left.
Just shattered dreams,
broken plans, and a flattened crop.
To remind us just how strong
Mother Nature can be.

Vivian Nemish

You Could Never Deny

You could never deny
how far our wings were able to fly.

You could never deny
How deep our souls were unfree to cry.

You could never deny
how tender our lips whispered good-bye.

(You could never deny)
when we kissed-
the world turned up-side down
carrying our love to the blue-moon sky.

Bruria Schweitzer

Dreaming of You...Love

Oh how I have dreamed of loving you.
I always knew it would never be blue.
To hold you in my arms,
and dream of your charms.

The joy of having you near.
I will never forget you, dear.
To watch over you when you sleep.
My love for you runs so deep.

To know that you are there,
is something I will have to bare.
For I will smile and dream of us.
We both knew I would never make a fuss.

I will always remember your love.
You made me feel like those from above.
You know I was never sad,
even through the good and bad.

"I will always be thinking of your dear.
For in my heart you will always be near.
If by chance I do shed a tear,
its those beautiful thoughts of you...dear".

Diana L. Dew

Home Sweet Home

I could scale the highest mountain,
I could sail the deepest sea,
But town and hearth and family
Mean home sweet home to me.

I could indulge in high adventure,
And cross the desert sands,
But peace and great contentment
Are not found in foreign lands.

I could clothe myself in satins,
With gems my self adorn,
And think the greatest pleasure
Is dancing 'til the dawn.

But when all is said and done dears
And dreams have not come true,
The nearest place to heaven
Is home sweet home and you.

Ann Patricia Andrews

Untitled

Of it
I cried
Once again
To have
But oh, not to keep
You have come for me
Only to be shattered
In, of my fear
It would coil, the wrath
To feel it
Seething
So hot, passionate
Deadly
Do not touch, my dear
Fear of desolation
Destruction
It will come
Yes, it must

Laura Lowe

To The One

The days are long and lonely
I keep my problems inside
The things I feel so deep
Are the hardest things to say
I have lost my soul companion...
I loved you so much in so many ways
I needed you more and more each day
I wanted to spend my life with you
My love would never end...
These are a few of the things
I should have said
Before you gave up on me
I told you just as plain as it could be
How I needed to hear
Some words of love from you...
Oh why didn't I say things
I should have said
Now it's too late to confess
Now I'll never get a chance
But I will always love you.

Valerie Lynn Marie Zimmel

"A Poem for Love"

The first time I touched your lips
I kissed my heart goodbye
It's hard for me to give my love
But for you I'll surely try

You looked into my eyes
And I knew how much you cared
I knew that there would be special times
That you and I would share

Times with you are special
I'll keep them close to me
Memories remembered
Throughout eternity

And even though there's many miles
Between the two of us
The love we give each other
Will always be enough

And when we have to be apart
With help from above
Our love will build a bridge for us
It's called the bridge of love.

Laure Meyers

Secret Love

I do not what I love to do
I love to read and write
I wrote a book, a poem or two
But keep them out of sight

I worry what people think
About me all the time
I bring myself to the brink
Then keep silent, like a mime

Can words finally release me
From these silent prison walls
Put my thoughts for all to see
Shall I heed the inner calls

Will someone listen to my word
Find pleasure from my poem
Will I finally be truly heard
Will I find my literary home

Jean Chorney

Untitled

How many times will I have to say
I love you
Before you full comprehend
The meaning and the value
Of what my heart is truly trying to say
I will be a part of you
For always and forever
Just as you are all of me
Hidden from reality
What life is about
Is what we all need
To be held and cared for
With patience and understanding
No questions asked
Just to love and be loved
Forever

Kelly Morin

Goodbye

Memories crowd my mind,
I search for those easiest to find,
I think of you, Mike,
Remember what you were like,
But you moved on and left us behind.

Your death was so easy to deny,
To myself I tried to lie,
It's so hard to believe you are gone
Like the stars after dawn,
I never got to say goodbye.

Jennifer Schonhofer

Jokers Are Wild

Sometimes in the game of life
I'm dealt a rotten hand,
And when I least expect it
The "Joker" takes command.

Even though he laughs at me,
My heartache and my fears,
I know that I am strong enough
to wipe away my tears.

Even when the chips are down,
And the deck is stacked against me,
I look inside and try to find
A better way to see.

Melissa Grant

Innocence

I am born, Innocent.
In Innocence, I grow.
In Innocence,
  of those around
   I learn to Trust.
Of Those around,
  some Choose
   to take my innocence.
I'm Lost....?
  Dirty, Soiled, Discarded,
   ALONE!
I, can't get clean....?
  no longer Innocent.
I can,
  no longer Trust
   those around.
Must get away,
  ALL, the way
   back to my innocence.

Barry Goodwin

October Air

Autumn
In it's kaleidoscope
Of colour

Reminds me
Of being wrapped up
In a golden
Honey butter blanket

All warm and cozy
And happy to smell
The wood smoke
In the air

As crisp as
A Macintosh apple
In October.

Heather Barker

Baby's Grief

Life without a daddy,
Is the biggest of a tragedy.
No one special wants my love,
No one cares what I'm made of.

A little girls dreams go on endlessly,
But every one are about a daddy.
Her very first love so big and strong,
he made right everything that's wrong.

Somewhere along a lonely street,
My love's heart could no longer beat.
The tears that should have come,
Haven't yet for I'm just too young.

Now, in her life, mom has a new man,
And I guess he'll just never understand,
That having a daddy is as precious gold
And that, to give love, you're never too old....

Monica Hamilton

'Being'

Inside me lurks a being;
It is not my conscience,
It is not my fear,
  Yet
   it is not my friend.
It yells at me-
  Unlike my parents
It hits me, but only through words
It forces me to listen-
  It tells me there is no one
   who understands.
Inside me lurks a being;
in which I cannot describe...
It listens only through tears,
It sees through blind eyes,
It loves only itself.
Inside me lurks a being;
My hatred for it grows
And on that it thrives...
To dominate my soul

Cristina DeSilvio

Untitled

Have you ever felt
like you want to cry.
When you lose a friend
or your pet dies

Have you ever laughed
at a disabled man
the guy in a wheel chair
or the girl with no hand

Have you ever been angry
and want to strike out
I feel that way
but can't let it out

I'm a mother you see
and were different than you.
We have to be strong
and hide it from you.

But inside we feel it
like everyone else
Were only Human
Just like the rest

M. T. Norrie

The Crush

I stare at you from across the room,
looking into your eyes,
At night I dream of you,
a boy who knows no lies.

I catch you staring at me,
my heart skips a beat,
I wonder if you like me,
"did someone turn up the heat?"

People say you like me,
I wonder if it's true,
I wish I had the nerves to say,
"I like you, too."

As I stand there waiting,
for you to ask me out,
I'm too shy to ask you,
so I stand there and pout.

I want to break the silence,
I really like this guy,
What if he says no,
I don't want to cry.

April-Lee Dunk

Strong Love

Love can be strong
Love can be sweet
Love can knock you
Right off your feet

Love can be hard
Love can have pain
Love can do
Most anything

Love can hurt
Love can go
Love is trust
That you show

Love is special
Love is kind
Love is something
That takes time

John Smith

Love

Love is like a piece of art
love is drawn inside your heart
it is a peaceful picture of a dove
and colorful when you add the love
we use it everyday in every way
to make people happy
love is caring
love is kind
love is always in your mind

Love Born
The baby robin
free from it's pretty blue shell
hungry and crying
so fragile helpless and small
soon to be flying away

Jenny Pearson

Happy Birthday, Danny, Our Grandson!

Today is March 23, 1992.
Lovely weather and skies of blue.
Why is today a special day?
Because, Danny it's your birthday!

A grandson like you is hard to find,
This year your cake has candles nine.
To tell you something I feel free,
Remember what you said to me?

Grandma don't bake a cake for me,
But bake a pie will you agree?
This I promised I would do,
Thus I give this plate to you.

You are into sports and hockey,
We hope you will never be a jockey.
The hockey net is a gift to you,
So you can play hockey when you choose.

Danny, to you our wishes impart,
We love you with all our heart.
We wish for you good health and cheer,
With lots of fun, a happy year.

Clara Klassen

Untitled

Blue mixed with yellow
made green.
The tiny hand coloured
a sun speckled lake.
The sun was there,
you had to imagine.

Red mixed with blue
made mauve.
The crayons slowly coloured
everything on the page
into a crisscross of
iridescent rainbows.

When I mixed colours,
the world turned black.
The child said that
I coloured too fast.
That life was a masterpiece
of slow hours.

S. Guinn

You Touched Me

Like snowflakes caught in a whirlwind.
Mem'ries flutter 'round me,
Mem'ries of love that mesmerized.
O love, please set me free!
You made the moonlight magic
Caused me distant horizons to see,
While you deceived-while you possessed
You touched me love, you touched me!

Mem'ry would surely linger awhile...
It remained - not an unwelcome guest:
I could not embrace love anew
Whilst I harbored you deep in my breast.
What set you apart from others love
Keeps me chained forever to thee?
Saddens my eyes reflecting.
You touched me love, you touched me!

Brande Denis

Calm

Hazy mists.
Misty clouds.
Cloudy days.
Days are quickly over.
Over here.
Here it is!
Is that it?
It can't be!
Be calm.
Calm is impossible
Impossible is the truth.

Truth is never spoken.
Spoken words hurt.
Hurt does not leave.
Away with you! Go away!
You can't help me.

Jarra M. Church

Life

Life comes in many ways,
more than once in your time.
It comes and goes, asleep, awake
yet in rhythm of a rhyme.
The life that you hold is in your heart,
and passes in your mind.
Life in part or in a whole,
is only that you can find.
You are the one that run it,
taking so much everyday.
And are the one to end it,
to make it go away.
The world all around you,
is full of war and fear.
Yet life can be so wonderful,
more and more every year.
Life is what you make of it,
and the only thing to do.
It is the best you make of it,
it can only be up to you.

David Andrews

Into the Fire

Each word that I write,
Must be held to the light,
Each phrase I do speak,
Is void and bleak.

A poet I am not,
Because my morals are bought,
A fool I am,
Tempered by the lamb.

To each person of knowledge,
I resent the implication of college,
So I say to you tiresome liar,
Be gone into the fire.

Buster E. Martyn

The Dark

The dark is my friend,
It hugs me when I'm sad,
And keeps me warm when I'm cold.
It's there when I need it
And leaves me alone when I want.
It listens when I talk,
And holds the secrets forever,
But if you don't like it,
Turn on the light!

Angela Eisbrenner

The Glass Box

In a glass box,
my heart is encased.
A tiny gold lock,
on the outside is placed.
Awaiting the day,
for my knight to arrive.
His armor is shining,
a top a mustang to drive.
Around his neck,
placed close to his heart.
Is the gold key,
to break the lock apart.

Tanya Sawchuk

Your Hiding Love

The tear drops fall
my spirit gets weak,
as my heart and your heart
play hide n' go seek.

When I am close
you're far away,
as my heart and your
begin to stray.

When you're hiding
I begin to cry,
my heart can't find your heart
and I don't know why.

Then time after time
we find one another,
cause my heart and your heart
were made for each other.

Please tie our hearts together
before they get to weak,
so my heart and your heart
can't play hide n' seek.

Susanne Klassen

"Words"

My words are true my words are few
My words are simply I love you.
My words come... From the heart
Not any heart not any words
But my own. The strength I feel
I never felt before incredible things
I will do all for you.
Don't be untrue because, it is true
The love I feel for you.
My words are true
My words are few
My words are simply
I love you.

Wejdan Salem Almannai

Honesty Contains Charm

Honesty contains a charm
of a type all its own.

The honest word like a child
undeserving of harm.

Honesty borne out of trust
is the richest kind, indeed.

Honest men are rare to find
But once met always near.

The truth and lies both can hurt
But only honesty is mined.

Leonora J. Thompson

Stranger

People walk by
Never seeing him
Never caring about him
He hides his face from the cold
Hands cold and numb.
Raw to the touch
Clothes are tattered
face old and worn
By the cold night air
He prays for an angel
He begs to go home
But life keeps him there
Never seeing him
Never caring about him.

Rebecca Bernicky

Confidence

I do need no gun
no poison either
although love is gone
although I suffer

I do need no knife
I do need no rope
for when there is life
there is also hope.

Jocelyne Fortin

The Travelers of Life

Wherever you go
North, East, South or West
Water runs, trees will grow
You've tried, you've done your best.

Nowhere to run, nowhere to turn,
It's like an endless road
Full of twist and turns
Death, is sure to follow.

Until the light fades away
Until the last breath you take
Embrace the joys and the pains
For you have nothing else to gain
You deserve your rest.

Louisianne Gauthier

Alone

Alone
Nothing but alone
Hours go by
Four walls fall in on me
The phone doesn't ring
Silence....

I want to reach out
But no one is there
I telephone friends and family
And what can they do or say
They have their own lives
And mine is not included
Alone
Alone
I turn to Christ with my lament
He doesn't answer
And I sit
Alone
Alone

Anne Goodall

The Solitary Tree

It stands alone
one solitary tree
forced by fate and wind
to stand separate from the rest.
Shot at,
branches broken,
bark shorn off in sheets,
hacked by an ax,
yet still it stands.
A lone sentinel against the world
shivering with the wind.
Silently,
it lifts its stiff arms to heaven
and heaven reaches down to protect
what the world
would strive to steal.

Tammy Dasti

Like Children

I saw two children playing,
One was black, the other white;
They didn't notice color
Until they went home at night.

One family jeered and whispered
About the color of man's skin
And talked about how annoying
The "blacks" have always been.

The other family chose to pray
That equality soon would be
The "norm" that makes us brothers
In the human family.

How different things would be
If we watch the children play,
And take their attitude of love
To live by, day by day.

No one would need to mention
or care about his race,
For in this world, you'll notice,
Every person has a place!

Bessa McKaye

The Pain of Divorce

Open up your heart,
Open up your eyes.
It will all work out,
No need for good-byes.

The tears are building,
Emotions intense.
Love for this family,
Extremely immense.

Problems are growing,
We're all torn apart.
We're not all together,
But they're each in my heart.

Our last day together,
Involved way too much pain.
Saying "don't worry Daddy,"
"I'll see you soon again."

More hugs and more kisses,
Temporary good-bye.
No longer a family,
... I don't understand why.

Jennifer Woods

Unbroken Freedom

Dotted jewels falling from the sky
pelting the windowpane,
Scrutinizing the familiar face while
I stare into an endless haze,
Westwards I face, as a stampede of
memories return,
Of times never to be forgotten and our
sneaky sly fox pranks,
Mischief of the leprechaun with his
shamrocks and pots of gold,
Carefree and spirited like the
unbroken horses of the west,
Soon I found myself where I started,
slipping into the faceless crowd,
It seemed so long ago yet, it
could have been yesterday.

Kelly Thorarinson

AIDS

Death, pain, lost, hurt, love, hate
People die from AIDS
They feel lost
No hope
What do they do
Were do they go

Pain everyday
Knowing that soon
They have to go away

Loosing their loved ones
Hurting in side
Trying not to hate the world
On the outside

From dying to death
Tears falling from our eye
Why can't we find a cure
For love and for their lives.

Crystal Osmond

All the King's Men

All the King's men
really didn't know
why he was King
Was he stronger? Braver? Bigger?
Certainly, they
were as intelligent
so why did he
make all the decisions?
Ask the questions?
Sit on the throne?
The King's men
had shown courage, bravery, strength.
They fought together
looking out for each other
but still couldn't see
why he was King.
What they missed
in their speculation
was the second throne
belonging to the Queen.

Colleen Hanson

An Angel's Flight

Suns that rise to morning
Recall your shining way
Longed to turn the other cheek
To feel your warmth each day

Clouds that drift through heavens
Embrace the smiles you sold
Silver linings pave the hearts
Of souls you painted gold

Rainbows that have seen the calm
Sought shelter in your eyes
A welcome from an angel
Few colours could disguise

Moons that wake from slumber
Seek your ray of light
In corners of a heart you lit
Remain the dawns of night

Stars that fall one by one
Gather 'round your name
An angel's flight begins and ends
In lives you kept aflame.

Rosa Leo

Let Me Know How

Nectar from thy lips
Shall I sip
Thoughts of thee
I carry with me to sleep
Every night I dream of thee
Ye light the night for me
Let thy heart be not cold
To this love ye now behold
How shall I win thy love?
Speak my beloved
Whisper to me now
Let me know how
Speak my beloved
The sound of thy sweet voice
Makes my heart rejoice
Thy precious heart I seek to win
For in mine heart
Thou art the Queen
How may I be thy heart's King?
Whisper to me now let me know how.

Lourdes Jasmin P. Nisce

To Speak Thoughts

My voice -
sharp,
pointed -
glimmering icy on the reflective surface.
The thoughts
behind the words
winding and whirling
forever around and around
into a ball -
tight
confused
in a cramped space within myself -
then swept out
away
far over the ocean
lost
forgotten
merely a whisper
in time
in eternity.

Andrea Dymond

Rebecca

Rebecca was our Sunday guest
She had the virtues of a pest
Her selfishness would not play fair
With the swing we were to share

She took her turn and swung with glee
And wouldn't share it back with me
And on and on she swung to test
The patience of my childish best

Rebecca's laughter rung and rung
As higher up she swung and swung
She dragged her feet as back she gust
And showered me with dirt and dust

She called me sissy when I cried
And that's the word that turned the tide
I pounced upon the howling brat
As in my face she spat and spat

During the tussle my mother's call
Demand to know what caused her fall
I ran to hide beneath the table
Rebecca tattle tailed a fable.

Helen C. Gattinger

He'll Change

In the emergency room,
Sitting across the hall,
Leaning against the wall,
"He did this didn't he? He did!"
"No! Don't worry, he'll change,"
Broken ribs, cracked nose,
This is the life that you chose,
No way you can get out,
No way you can, without a doubt,
Don't get him mad, don't be bad,
I don't know how many drinks he's had,
Got stitches on your head,
Pretty soon you'll be dead,
He doesn't care, want a ride?
Get some bus fare, hitch a ride,
Written on your tombstone,
Big and bold, to love and to hold,
"DON'T WORRY, HE'LL CHANGE!"

Madona Jarbouh

Endless Pain

I feel like a candle
Slowly melting away,
The spark within me grows dimmer
With every passing day.
Depression has taken its toll on me,
Bright colours are losing their glow,
A constant fight within my soul
Helps my emotions flow.

Perhaps as the candle can be spent
Before it melts away,
And then rekindled once again
On yet another day,
My body needs a change, a rest,
To help release the pain,
But will the strength and spark be back
Before it is too late?

Winnie Cardona

God Is Everywhere

The skies are so blue
Songs of birds fill the air
Clouds float lazily by
I feel God everywhere.

In the touch of your hand
In your warm tender embrace
In the beat of my heart
In the smile on your face.

I pray that this happiness
Through our lives will endure,
That each moment together
Makes our love more secure.

I thank God for making
The skies so blue,
For the songs of the birds
For giving me you.

I know He is watching
Over all from above,
All I ask is His Blessing
On our home and our love.

Wilma B. Winter

Confession

On the crossroad of my life
Standing with arms turning
Helplessly to heaven looking
For something that has just gone
I feel nothing. But unlimited
Chaos of my own insanity.
Nothing but never ending passage
of complex sentences, which sense
Is lost in the speed of existence

In the middle of my life.
Considering direction to nowhere,
Glaring at the yellow pages of albums,
To save something that just disappeared
I Think nothing but escape,
From reality of nonsense
Being nothing but illusion
Of the promised land that turned
to be a living hell full of monsters

Lucyna Szabla

Untitled

I walked into a cemetery black,
Staring, glancing behind my back.
Terrible tremors going through my skin,
Wondering what's gonna do me in.

I walk slowly and unaware,
Feeling something touch my hair.
I don't dare look at this thing,
For what terror it will bring.

I pray to God, let me be ok,
And don't let me be touched on this day.
I feel sad, cold, and scared,
A thought as if no one cared.

I hear noises, and I can't see,
O God, please take care of me.
Thoughts of death in my head,
I've awaken in my bed.

Thoughts cluttered this has been,
Of times when I haven't grinned.
Memories I have never shared,
My mind holds yet unaware.

Ashley Davis

Lady Liberty

Silhouetted against crimson sky
Stately lady on pedestal high
She does not lament or sigh...
Her eye leaps to disclose a clue;
Ever scanning beyond the blue.
Firm hand clutching a light
Guiding through perilous night,
Robed in loose flowing gown
Donning a grand queenly crown.
In regal splendor at the shore
Freedom beckons at her door.
New opportunities and peace
War and hunger now can cease.
Those who enter have much to gain
'Liberty' is not a beacon in vain.
Ending many desperate plights
Beyond sapphire depths and heights.

Elizabeth Paetkau Krahn

Summer Thought

The rain has cool the
summer - a breeze of
autumn near; quite contended
with it all -

The river flows -
we roam and play.
A morning day,
Flowers - Breeze
has been saith -
willow - vine

Michele M. Mena

Time Rolls On

You gave me a rose
That made me smile
You gave me a kiss
That lasted a while
You gave me a moment
A moment in time

But the rose soon died
Along with my smile
And the kiss that lasted
Only a while
And for the moment of time
Time rolls on.

Tracy Shanahan

Oh! How I Wish!

Just write a poem
That's all you do
And you could win some money too!
Oh! How I wish that I could do
This wondrous thing you ask me to.
The words I know, are all about
If I could only think them out.
But twenty lines is not enough
For me to strut me out my stuff
In truth I haven't got a clue
How I can win a prize from you
But coming from the Emerald Isle.
I hope, at least I've made you smile

Mary V. McGivern

Language Of Silence

Nothing;
The dark vacant minds which once dreamt,
dream no longer
The vibrant earth which once turned,
now stands still.
The words which lovers once exchanged,
have ceased.
The guns which once boomed,
no longer speak.
The sun no longer shines down upon us,
the moon no longer dances
in the waves along the shore.
People no longer live,
people no longer die
for creation is no longer.
The day the world becomes silent,
will be the day the world
no longer exists;
BLACKNESS

Naomi Lilley

"Dunes"

In the scorching August heat,
the dunes were set ablaze.
They raced, the horizon to meet,
then vanished in the distant haze.

The sun glared over the land,
an angry, vengeful face.
Merciless, it tortured the sand,
this mighty teasing face.

A golden sea before me lay,
it burned to a fiery red.
It was true what they used to say.
This was a flaming death-bed!

Arabian desert in a fervent veil,
glowing on this torrid day,
set afire from thermal gale,
from many a scalding ray.

Arabian dunes all set alight but still the
fever grew.
The sun was high and proud and bright
above this sandy stew.

Storming scarlet, shiny gold and light of
every color
fought upon dunes ancient old-dunes that I
stand here and honor.

Rola Ali Hisham

Destiny

Rippling water flowing forcibly
Through a rocky canal, tumbling
And cascading over rocky ledges
On its long journey to the sea.
Wriggling and thrashing, flurries of
Movement. Light filters through
Crystalline water, turning vague
Images into definite likenesses.
With exhausted muscles yet with a
Courageous heart, the fish struggles on
Against the repelling current, to live
Or to die, its destination still far
Away but its determination unyielding.
To bring new existences to this world,
Its final purpose. Its aim:
To succeed.

Suma Reed

rem(ember)

you breathe
the grey dust
of memory
off my coral soul
dust off ash blushed ember
ignite the hot blue
flame

I remember

your breath
soft as a butterfly kiss
eyelashes brushing a peach fuzz check

I feel

the closeness hot in the
space between our skins
the airspace sandwiched, as
a desert
the oasis your lips,
    your mouth,
your tongue, the
ripe date, succulent and sweet
your teeth, the pit,
    hard, unyielding
your breath, the hot desert wind.

kathy fisher

A Gift of Love

I had no ribbons wrapped around it.
The loveliest thing I've ever seen
You gave to me the greatest treasure
"A gift" fit for a queen.

I wrapped my sorrow in your laughter
And slowly with each passing day.
Your understanding made it blossom.
Into the loveliest bouquet.

In all your giving and your sharing
You taught me all there is to caring.
The greatest gift that one could have.
That special gift, "The gift of love."

Judi Nigh

Mitzie

'Tis treachery I fear,
The one dumb thing I held so dear
Is squandered,
Her lovely fur her bug pecked ears
Her knowing........

To all intense and purposes
She did not matter
Who cared that she stood guard
Beside the door and waited,
Waited patiently for favors,

Never more dear friend of mine
Never more
If I could just once more
See you there beside the door
Guarding, waiting patiently for favors

And should there be a heaven
And a God who does exist
Would you please plant upon
My Mitzie's head a kiss
From me

Carole Zmenak

That Last Summer

Remember our Summer of Romance,
The songs we wrote together,
The long walks down by the beach
Strolling hand in hand,
And the countless talks we had until
late at night on the old porch swing.
I can't believe it is over.
You left, and I stayed behind.
What will happen next year?
Will you be back or will I be gone?
Our last summer of freedom,
Our last summer together,
Before we go our separate ways.

Katherinne Gruszecki

Insecure

If time is the wind,
Then I'm locked inside,
Waiting the years away.

I turn away from danger,
Back to somewhere safer.
Childhood, maybe, or earlier still.

Perhaps I should try to grow up,
But I'm scared, of life
Maybe if I pray, God will help.

He heeds to prayers, doesn't He?
He'll guide me, won't He?
Maybe I'm scared of the results.

Cindy Van Arnam

Destruction

Out of the tall quiet timber
There comes a whining sound,
Man is there with his chain saw
Giant trees fall to the ground,
Under his devastating dozer
The saplings trample down,
The animals, they are driven
But man not wears a frown,
He takes the best to offer
Without a second thought,
Leaving a barren hillside
The stumps to lie and rot.

Ross Urquhart

The Valley of Death

As you enter the valley of deadness
There is a silence in the air,
That forms a cloudy horizon
Which protrudes from everywhere.

In the night there is a shrillness
And everyone can hear,
The deathly scream of terror
That poisons them with fear.

As I walk through the valley of deadness
The following shadows in the sky,
Will fill my mind with insanity,
And soon, I too, shall die.

Sherry Villneff

Past

When the past leaves
There's no more feeling
The hurt, the pain
It all leaves
I lay here remembering
The time she left me
It hurts
But when I forget
It all leaves
Like nothing - blowing away in the air
The past can kill
And you wastingly await for the future
Like a song coming closer

William Clayton Stone

Friendship

Although I'm in love
  there's room for a friend
Someone to talk to
  when no one seems to care
My boyfriend comes first
  but there's always a second
Someone to fall back on
  when the going gets tough
You're a really nice guy
  but I'm already taken
Someone's filled my heart
  but there's no sense in breaking
A beautiful friendship
  that can last forever.

Jennifer Amy Curry

The Hands of Love

The hands of love are gentle and kind
They are also soft and sweet
Never they seek to overpower
Or to harm the weak
These hands were made to protect
To hold, to caress
To wipe tears off one's cheeks
They are made to express love
Or just to say I care

Sylvie Audet

Untitled

I built this wall around me
To keep me from the rain
I held this love inside of me
To protect me from the pain
the lightning and the thunder
Is like the love I feel
My heart is beating harder
wishing you were real
This love I've left inside of me
The sparks are in my soul
I used to wrap around me
To make my life feel whole
But now that you have left me
I have to face the pain
My wall has crumbled down on me
Now comes lightning, thunder and rain.

Aimee Young

Untitled

Tears come to my eyes
To look at you
All six feet.

Tears come to my heart
You're going away
I can't follow.

You head for a land.
Called Manhood
Leaving me behind.

I only had you
A few short years
Not really enough.

I long for the time
When I held you
On my lap.

Mothers are left
Sons go away,
Just like you.

Mary P. Maxie

Reward

Be not dismayed though storms arise,
To spoil a glorious enterprise;
But let your patience lead the way,
And drive away the grim dismay.

You say, "'tis hard to bear the load,
Upon a rough and rugged road."
'Tis true, but can it e'er surpass
The joy that you'll enjoy at last?

Can you enjoy the blessed light,
Unless you have a darkened night?
Or can you know the joy of spring.
Unless you know what winter bring?

Be not dismayed, the storm will cease,
And bring you everlasting peace;
Your patience then will lead the way,
And drive away the grim dismay!

Maurice A. Mallory

Best Friends

Loving
Understanding, caring
A special trust
A silent language
The unspoken word
And yet - you know.
Growing, sharing
Helping
A shoulder to lean on
To cry on - if need be.
A joy in despair
A hope in hopelessness
And strength in weakness.
Sunshine -
On the darkest day
Accepting without question.
Forgiving
Together as one
For now and forever
Us — Best Friends

Jackie Vanidour

Death

I am waiting
Waiting for what?

I am waiting for death
Will it ever come?

Does age matter?
Young or old?

Death, is it pretty
Ugly, torture, or madness?

Is it like a new
Life or a new beginning?

Or a total end,
Unendable darkness?

Life after death
Is it believable,
Will I die the come back
As someone else?

To me death is a huge question,
Does anyone really
Know what death is
Except the dead?

Penny-Lee Whitwell

Were My Mother Captured

It was early. I had been
walking with my father near
Widow's Creek.
He talked to me about the wars
and God,
when he lifted me off the earth
and taught me to fly.

Our home was a fusion of extremes
with people grieving, talking in whispers
laughter in other rooms.

Despite an attempted suicide
collapse and surrender...
  My father sick with
compassion and divorce
we survived.

But limp with the burden
of some untold debt, mother cried
murder

murder

Ron Moulden

Untitled

Our braids and bead are symbols
we wear them with great pride
to remind our young children
of how we once lived our lives.

We used to pass down stories
in the form of campfire chants
we sang tales of the hunt
as we celebrated with dance

But then there came the white man,
wit them we traded furs
who knew we would be trading
our lifestyle for their's

As time goes quickly past us
our way of life and customs gone
who will be left to remember
if the legends are not passed on.

Lori Summers

"Free Willy"

We were wary, at odds before we knew,
What good friends, as we grew,
We watched each other, every day,
Learned to trust, as we played.

We touched each other, we were drawn,
Close together, we grew fond.
I heard his cry, in the night,
I would try, to make things right.

We made a pact, him and I,
When we looked, into each others eyes,
When up from the depth, he came for me,
Saved from death, he knew I would see.

So together we had planned,
We would weather, and understand.
I watched for signs, so he could leave.
There'd come a time, to be set free.

We spoke the words, that set you on your path,
We knew you heard, it was time for the task,
He knew why, this would be when,
I'd say good-bye, to my best friend.

Christine Vonk

Wonder

Why do I wonder
when it only makes
me angry!? why do I
even bother! I guess
these are questions
that in time, will
find answers for.
Wonder... man what a
"thoughtful" world! What
does it mean! I think it has something
to do with thought .
People say,"that it's
the thought that counts."
But if wonder equals
thought, and thought
equals wonder. Then why
does it upset me so!
Maybe it's because I'm
confused easily...
or maybe ... maybe, it's just me!

Melissa P.

Roses

Roses swaying in the wind,
when will the first petal fall.
Even though I wonder,
When will the first petal fall.
The roses keep on swaying
and my suspense withdraws.
Now I am quiet, now I am calm
because the first petal
I think will not fall.
I went through the garden
a moment of fun. And when
I came back the roses only one.
I wanted to see the last petal fall.
And now the only rose had no
petals at all.

Shalyn A. Gurr

Elvis Wuss

Dear God let there be a cat heaven
Where cats are kittens forevermore
And never get caught in a closing door

May eat crabmeat and shrimp
To their hearts' content
Chase dogs around poles
And mice into vents

Chase birds through the air
On furry winged feet
Never catching their prey
Never feeling defeat

Let them play with the thread
Of a thousand spools
And think of us all
As silly human fools

Sandra Sutter

My Beloved One

I remember that day so clear
Where the one I loved stood so near;
The sun was shining, oh so bright
And every thing seemed so alright.

Until that very hour of night
When nothing we did was but fight;
The darkness of doom, it spelt for me
For my love, he has gone across the sea.

Letters we wrote of odds and ends
But never were we the same again;
My love will never return to me
And my heart will always yearn for thee.

Yes I remember that day so clear
Where the one I loved, He stood so near;
Those memories that make me sad and blue
But still my heart will always be true.

For He reminds me of a love so dear
That showered my heart, and shed my tears;
So remain with me, He always will
For I remember and love him still.

Mary Currie

The Meaning Of Love

A flame within your hearts
Will shine like the stars
You've found each other
Through love and all its power

You are now as one
Your new life has just begun
Take each others hand
And conquer together your new land

The beauty of love is an attitude
A feeling, of life and its meaning
An awareness, it's a sense of happiness
This is your chance to love each other
'Till the end of forever
Experience the magic
Within the spirit
Of Love

The life that you'll finally share is no fantasy
It's now becoming a reality
Open the door together
To start your new life of wonder...

Jennifer Cross

Pigeons

Coral-footed pigeons fly,
wings ephemeral thoughts;
feathers flashing in the sky
pale-blue forget-me-nots.

Far below, the children raise
their heads to watch the flight.
Numbered the innocent days
'till day gives way to night.

And I? I watch their faces
In desperate attempt
to capture back the graces
of innocence long spent.

Soon, I'll join the innocent
to watch the birds once more,
my ghostly presence spirit lent
to open heaven's door.

Anna Somerville

Untitled

As I walk along this lonely road,
With many burdens and a heavy load,
I think of times when I was small,
Without a care in the world at all.

To be the best was my only dream,
But failed repeatedly it seemed,
But as I grew and faced my fears,
A loving God dried up my tears.

I found some honest friends indeed,
That I could turn to when in need,
To share my sorrows and my pain,
To be without I saw no gain.

And as I walk this road content,
I know for sure my life was meant,
To be a beacon for my God,
To share his love here and abroad.

Carl Lirette

Heartbreak Street

I walk toward Heart Break Station
With my heart in pieces in my hands,
I lay it down on the tracks
And someone comes and takes it away.

I walk toward Heart Break Hotel,
With my tears cracking the sidewalk.
I walk in the door and break down
And someone takes me to my room.

At the Station I wait for the train
Which will help me through this mess.
It picks me up and takes me away.
It takes me far and wide.

And in the room, I cry for help
With people who are in pain.
The walls are gray to match my mood
Its the heartbreak kind of way.

These are where broken lovers go
Whose hearts are broken bad,
Heart Break Station, Heart Break Hotel
They're the places I go.

Melanie J. Reinhart

Life Is So Yellow

Have you ever felt so
yellow? You're overjoyed
and have a carefree spirit.
You're too happy to think,
or even speak. The yellow
shades you feel, fills your
life with hope and many
experiences. You think of
flags flowing in the air,
they are free. As the very
yellow color turns golden,
almost a different shade.
Life is vibrant, even worth
living for. You're inspired
with every feeling within
your very body, mind and
soul.

Stephanie Lynn Dugan

Treasure the Little Things

When love disappears
you lose all your hopes,
and remember your fears.
All those memories
that passed with the years.
Mixed with the heartaches
that caused all the tears.
Shining on the good times,
forgetting all our fears.
Treasure the little things
that were always so dear.
Like watching the stars
when the night was so clear.
After all this time
the end has come near.
But, through good times and bad,
I will always be here.

Antonia Chatzimihalis

When You Sleep

When you sleep
your face is prettier than everything
and I am able to love you
with all my heart

When you sleep
I am not afraid
and I give you all the tenderness
you ever dreamed of

When you sleep
warm and satisfied after we made love
are you and this moment
all my life

When you sleep
and I feel the warmth from your body
the scent of your skin
I want to kiss you all over and love you
once more

When you sleep
I fight my needs to touch and love you
I am afraid that you will wake up
and leave me

Tina Larsen

BIOGRAPHIES

ABDUL, TAHEERAH
[pen.] Khaliah; [b.] Anchorage, AK; [p.] Zaklyyah and John Miser; [ed.] Landis Intermediate, Vineland High; [memb.] African American Culture Club, Vineland High girls basketball team; [hon.] Dean's List, Honor Roll, Science Award, perfect attendance, graduation from 8th grade; [oth.writ.] Several poems that have to do with whatever is in my heart, mostly love poems;[pers.] If someone says to anyone that they aren't going to amount to anything that person should try their hardest to prove everyone wrong. [a.] Vineland, NJ.

ABOKO-COLE, CLAIRE
[pen.] "P" Girl; [b.] March 26, 1952, Freetown, Sierra Loone; [p.] William and Ophelia Aboko-Cole; [ed.] AWMS High School, Howard University, MD University; [occ.] Accountant; [memb.] Mt. Pleasant Baptist Church, Robert J. Nash, FAIF and Association PC., Red Cross, Girl Scouts; [hon.] Dean's List, Child of the Most Higher God; [oth.writ.] Several poems, some published in local newspapers, articles and short plays; [pers.] I strive to do the best I can when I can, and if I can't I strive to look for another way I can. [a.] Adelphi, MD.

ACUNA-NEELY, CARLA
[b.] June 24, 1976, Santiago, Chile; [p.] Carlos and Jenny Acuna; [ed.] Alamo Heights High School; [occ.] High school student, senior; [memb.] Trinity Baptist Youth Group, Dimension Club, C.A.U.S.E. Club, soccer organization; [hon.] Community service award, Spanish Honors, Honor Roll Student; [oth.writ.] Several poems and stories published in Dimension magazine in Alamo Heights High School; [pers.] Writing is the unique way to express myself and to build bridges for others to understand my complex being of thoughts and emotions; [a.] San Antonio, TX.

ADAMS, GORDON BRUCE
[pen.] "G.B." Adams, Wordman; [b.] October 16, 1946, New York City; [p.] Leonard and Nathalie Adams; [m.] Sharon Lynn Adams, February 17, 1980; [ed.] Life on the street; [occ.] The Adams Group Business Consultant; [memb.] Human Being, Earthling; [hon.] Still alive and striving for health, wealth and happiness; [oth.writ.] A life time full of personal writings; [pers.] (1) Share, (2) No hitting, (3) Learn something new everyday, (4) Lots and lots of laughing! [a.] Redondo Beach, CA.

ADESIJI, ADEBUSOLA
[pen.] Sola Adesiji; [b.] June 7, 1979, Minneapolis; [p.] Janice and Babatunde Adesiji; [ed.] Edison High School (10th grade), Minneapolis, MN; [oth.writ.] None, but I frequently write notes, stories and poems; [pers.] Remember, I don't view this as a poem. I view this a 1 possible way to write a written poem so it would sound like a poem to me, not to you. [a.] Minneapolis, MN.

ADOLFF, CARLA
[b.] December 15, 1976, Camrose; [p.] Erika and Helmut Adolff; [ed.] Finishing grade 12 in January at Camrose Composite High School; [occ.] A student and babysitting in the community; [hon.] Science 14, Enterprise and Innovations 20, work experience 25 and English 23; [oth.writ.] Trying to get several other poems published, had one poem published in a Vancouver magazine titled Chalk Talk; [pers.] My poems reflect my interests in human relations and I believe the world can be a better place. [a.] Ohaton, Alberta Canada.

ADONNINO, VICTORIA ANNE
[occ.] Teacher.

AGHA, LENA
[b.] January 15, 1978, Delhi; [p.] Monzen and Faten Agha; [occ.] Student at the American College in London; [memb.] Royal Festival Hall Poetry Library, England; [oth.writ.] Many other poems non really published, around 50 in total; [pers.] I believe that most of us have talent but to find it we have to look for it in ourselves and not wait for it to jump out into our heads. [a.] Delhi, U.A.E.

AGHA, VANESSA E.
[b.] January 12, 1978, Hornell, NY; [p.] Alice and Farooq Agha; [ed.] Deer Path Junior High, Lake Forest High School; [occ.] Student at Lake Forest High School; [hon.] Editor's Choice in 1994 poetry contest, National Library of Poetry, semi finalist in 1994 National Library of Poetry contest; [oth.writ.] An article in the Corba Chronicle, I write for the high school paper The Forest Scout; [pers.] If people put their thoughts in writing, the world would be a happier place. [a.] Lake Forest, IL.

AHEM-SAWYER, SARA HEATHER
[b.] May 11, 1980, Portland, OR; [p.] Pamela and Fredrick Sawyer; [ed.] Abigail Scott Dunway Elementary, Sellwood Middle, Grover Cleveland High; [occ.] High school student; [memb.] Girl Scout, Student Body Publicity Representative, Girl Scout Reporter; [hon.] Girl Scout Silver Leadership Award, selected for 10th Oregon Writing Festival; [oth.writ.] Article in Girl Scout current and school publications; [pers.] Writing is a remarkable way for people to understand and learn about themselves. I feel I have found myself within my own words. [a.] Portland, OR.

ALCORN, SAM J (AL)
[pen.] Al Howell; [b.] February 22, 1922, Saratoga, TX; [p.] Gladys Independence Spell Alcorn and Wendell Bertram Alcorn; [m.] Mary Lou Rohan Alcorn, September 8, 1972; [ch.] Kenneth J. Richards, Sam J. Alcorn Jr. and William "Billy" Alcorn; [ed.] Graduate Boiling High School 1940, Prep. Allen Military Academy, Bachelor of Science Degree Agriculture from Texas A & M College, January 1950; [occ.] Retired U.S. Coast Guard Reserve May 30, 1980, from Aluminum Company of America (Alcoa) November 1, 1984; [memb.] American Military Society, Fleet Reserve, Eagles, American Legion, American Poets Association, International Society of Poets, Top Records Songwriter's Association, Methodist Church; [hon.] WW II Victory Medal, Coast Guard Meritorious Service Medal, Honorable Discharges, Navy Air Branch Reserve 1946, Coast Guard Reserve 1980; [oth.writ.] "No Bed of Roses" and "Heck Whay The Heck" to be on Amerecord Album Star Route USA, "No Present, No Future, No Past" to be on Hilltop Records cassette album, "Great Navy Gray", "Corpus Christi Blues", "Out Of Navy Moth Balls", "What Is The Greatest Thing On Earth"; [pers.] Many poets go unpaid, but the honor belongs to the poets. Not all poets go unpaid. In 1374, Edward III decreed Geoggrey Chaucer be given a pitcher of wine every day/ Edgar Allen Poe used opium, alcohol and caffeine to influence his writing. Some say Chaucer's writing got better. [a.] Palacious, TX.

ALEXANDER, GEORGE
[pen.] George A. Green; [b.] October 23,1957, Jamaica; [p.] Ewin and Pearl Green; [ed.] Linstead All Age School, Lluidas Vale Industrial Vocational Training Center, American High; [occ.] Artist; [hon.] Bronze Medal, Honorable Mention, works published in National Fine Art Gazette; [oth.writ.] Songs; [pers.] True happiness comes from serving our Creator and being altruistic. Out-side of this is mere illusion. [a.] Miami, FL.

ALEXANDER, SPENCER THOMAS
[b.] November 23, 1970, Williamsport, PA; [p.] Ralph and Helen Alexander; [m.] Samantha, August 7, 1994; [ed.] Northpole High, UAF; [occ.] Owner, operator Apex Roofing Inc.; [pers.] God is in the details, so let him take care of them. [a.] Northpole, AK.

ALIFF, DAMITA LEA
[b.] May 31, 1967, Beckley, WV; [p.] Arthur and Juanita Herron; [m.] Lester Darrence Aliff, July 8, 1989; [ed.] Woodrow Wilson High, College of West Virginia, Tri-C College; [oth.writ.] Several poems published through American Collegiate Poems and through local college magazines; [pers.] In loving memory of my living mother and grandmother whom I will love forever and in loving memory of my late father whom I will miss forever. [a.] Cleveland, OH.

ALLEN, RICHARD NELSON
[pen.] Rick Allen, Col. Rick Allen; [b.] August 6, 1949, New Albany, IN; [m.] Fiance, Donna Jean MoLina; [ch.] Selena Rosemarie, step-son, John Paul II; [ed.] Manatee High, T.T.I. (Sigma Epsilon Theta), American Auctioneer College (Colonel diploma), C.G.M. (Doctor of Divinity), Tampa College (Associate in Business degree); [occ.] Poet, singer, songwriter, musician, music teacher, copyrights-author (30) music books, ASCAP publisher, performer, Elvis look-a-like; [hon.] Fla. Colonel, Auctioneer, Kentucky Col., TN. Col., credentials of Ministry Doctor of Divinity, hundreds of 1st place talent shows, radio and T.V., Stars of Tomorrow (spanning 30 years), sing out organizer performer, volunteer leadership, patriotic songwriter volunteer, fund raising organizations, groups and clubs; [oth.writ.] Several poems published in local newspapers, Elvis newsletter book, writer, author of hundreds of song-poems; [pers.] "Through my own play-write away music lessons books, my promise is to teach the world to play right away in minutes"! Thank you Edith and Fred McKenzie, for your faith and inspiration for several of my best poems. [a.] Madison, TN.

ALLGOOD, THERESA K.
[b.] February 22, 1970, Des Plaines, IL; [p.] Leo and Kathleen Golda; [m.] March Allgood, November 20, 1993; [ed.] Harvard High, Baylor University, Creighton University; [occ.] Pharmacist, Walgreen's, Omaha, Nebraska; [pers.] My poems are the result of expressing my creativity and feelings. I hope that other individuals will find them either entertaining or just plain interesting. [a.] Omaha, NE.

ALLIS, JAMES B.
[b.] October 14, 1911, Galveston, TX; [p.] Frank and Eula Mae Allis (deceased); [m.] Marie E. Allis, February 16, 1933; [ch.] James Barry and Lin Milan Allis; [ed.] Degree in Applied Science, State University of New York at Buffalo, 1963, additional courses completed in Business Administration, Electronic Theory, Structure Theory and Design, Industrial Engineering and Mechanical Engineering fields; [occ.] Retired; [memb.] Appointed member of Creative Leadership Council in 1964, selected from membership of the Society of American Value Engineers to serve on an "All Star Team" to assist the U.S. Department of Defense in appraising the Defense Automotive Supply Centers Value Engineering Program at Detroit, faculty member of Erie County Technical Institute, conducted Value Analysis course, faculty member of Cornell University, the New York State School of Labor and Industrial Relations; [hon.] Established and conducted Value Engineering courses at the State University of New York at Buffalo each semester, conducted seminar in Cre-

ative Problem Solving for the Western New York Section of American Institute of Chemical Engineers, conducted courses in Creative Problem Solving for Cornell University, the New York State School of Industrial and Labor Relations, courses given to management personnel at Trico, Carborundum, Sisters Hospital of Buffalo, Jamestown Management Club; [oth.writ.] Many poems in the past 2 years, prior to that when work, I wrote business papers, reports and articles for the Value Engineering Society and made presentations at our annual meetings; [pers.] Most of my poems and memories have been the result of visitations every day to see my wife who has alzheimer disease. It began about 10 years ago when the change occurred and gradually developed to a point of no return. She has been in the nursing home for nearly 2 years. [a.] Williamsville, NY.

ALSTON, TIFFANI
[pen.] T.J.; [b.] May 31, 1980, San Diego; [p.] Pamela and Ernest Alston; [ed.] Lincoln Middle School, Weequahic High School; [occ.] Student; [memb.] Angling Club, College Prep; [hon.] Citation from Yearbook Club, Certificate for Perfect Attendance, Certificate for Honor Roll; [oth.writ.] Short story on modern day "Little Red Riding Hood", several unique poems; [pers.] My writing is influenced by the things around me. In my writing I plan to tell the truth. [a.] Newark, NJ.

ALVEAR, JOE
[pen.] James Braxton; [b.] January 4, 1973, Quito, Ecuador; [p.] Douglas and Bonnie Alvear; [ed.] Fort Hamilton High School, Brooklyn College; [occ.] Full time student; [pers.] My writing emphasizes the need for all people to come together in a celebration of life. Likewise, we need to put aside our differences and replace them with love, understanding and laughter. [a.] Brooklyn, NY.

AMERSON, JOHNSIE P.
[pen.] J.P. Amerson; [b.] January 5, 1911, North Carolina; [p.] (Deceased) John M. Primm and Dora Dickens; [m.] Deceased, 1930; [ch.] W.P., T.L. and Saundra; [ed.] High school, 1 year Campbell College 1927-28, Buies Creek, NC; [occ.] Retired; [memb.] Methodist Church (active), Rebeccas (not active); [oth.writ.] Short stories and poems, had never submitted anything for publication before; [pers.] I give my parents credit for instilling in me the desire to write. My mother wrote beautiful poems and letters. My sister was a writer and maybe the fact that I am a great niece of Charles Dickens (the novelist) inspired me. [a.] Murfreesboro, TN.

AMOS, RACHELANN
[pen.] Rachel Amos; [b.] June 21, 1978, Barron; [p.] Susan and Harry Amos; [ed.] South Shore High School, right now I am a junior in high school; [occ.] Waitress; [memb.] South Shore SADD Club, 4-H (Gitchee Gumie); [hon.] Cheerleading, volleyball, softball, Elp, etc.; [oth.writ.] Written several poems, started them in a journal yet this is the first poem that actually is getting published and first I've sent somewhere; [pers.] I write poems to get things off my mind. If I'm depressed, I write about the thing I'm depressed about, they make me feel better by writing my feelings on paper. [a.] Iron River, WI.

AMSDER, JEFFERY GRANT
[b.] September 13, 1961, Elkhart County; [p.] Robert and Elizabeth (mother deceased); [ed.] Elkhart Area Career Center, (no college); [occ.] Chef-Peddlers Village, Chef-Elks Lodge; [memb.] International Society of Poets, Elks Lodge B.P.O.E. # 798, North American Yae Kwan Do Association, Fitness USA Health SPA's; [hon.] Outstanding Achievement Award (North American Tae Kwon Do Association), runner up 1992 Indiana State title P.K.C., (Professional Karate Commission), Certificate of Excellence, Sarasota Herald Tribune 1976, International Poet of Merit Award 1994, ISP; [oth.writ.] I am currently on schedule to write over 100 poems in 1994, that will make you wonder and believe "Forevermore". [a.] Goshen, IN.

ANDERSON, AARON
[b.] September 30, 1975, Dillon, MT; [p.] Scott and Mary Belle Anderson; [ed.] Gooding High School, Albertson College of Idaho; [occ.] Student (electric motor repair-summer); [memb.] Amnesty International, Sigma Chi Fraternity, International Association Sanzyuryu (martial arts); [hon.] Dean's List, Outstanding Mathematics Student 1993-1994. [a.] Gooding, ID.

ANDERSON, ADAM
[b.] April 29, 1977, Missoula, MT; [p.] Christi and Al Barnett; [ed.] Clinton Elementary (Montana), Lakewood Junior Senior High School (Washington); [occ.] Partner of Glass installation contractor; [oth.writ.] Just personal, unpublished short stories; [pers.] Be who you are deep down inside, the person who eats at your essence and let them thrive and rage with their voice, sooner or later people will listen. Everything happens for a reason. [a.] Arlington, WA.

ANDERSON, AVIS D.
[pen.] A. Denise; [b.] December 27, 1953, New Orleans, LA; [p.] Elder Richard E. Sr. and Elva A. Smith; [ch.] Albert L., Letitia O. and Juane' T. Blake; [ed.] Attending San Diego City College, attended Sawyers Business School, Pomona, CA., graduated Ganesha High School, Pomona, CA (1971); [occ.] Operations Control Co-ordinator at Teledyne Ryan Aeronautical, San Diego, CA; [memb.] National Authors Registry (Troy, Michigan), International Society of Authors and Artists (Painted Post, NY), Writers Digest Book Club; [hon.] Honorable mention (spring 1993) Iliad literary Award program and (1994) President's Award for literary excellence both for "You A Kid Too" (the National Authors Registry), Editor's Choice for (1993) "Heartaches Pain" (1994) "The Job", National Library of Poetry; [oth.writ.] Editors Preference Awards for Excellence (spring 1995) "Riders of The Paved Black Snow", Creative Arts and Science Enterprises; [pers.] Writing is fulfilling, no matter what mood I'm in I can get lost in a thought and create an experience on paper. [a.] San Diego, CA.

ANDERSON, BONNIE J.
[pen.] Bonnie J. Anderson; [b.] March 5, 1950, Arlington, VA; [p.] Frank H. and Florence V. Snyder; [m.] Ross M. Anderson, November 7, 1980; [ch.] Kristin Dawn and Michael Kevin; [occ.] Food Service Manager in elementary school; [memb.] American School Food Service Association; [oth.writ.] Several poems published in Food Service Journal; [pers.] Enjoy writing about lifestyles of today, mostly pertaining to children. [a.] Remington, VA.

ANDERSON, DAVID R.
[b.] May 15, 1954, Worcester, MA; [p.] Russell and Lorrainne Anderson; [m.] Single; [ed.] High school graduate; [occ.] Unemployed currently; [oth.writ.] Other one sent in and a few others since; [pers.] The one you've selected got its inspiration from two friends I know through a twelve step recovery program that I and they attend. It's anonymous (yes). [a.] Leominster, MA.

ANDERSON, ELLEN M.
[pen.] Cricket M. Anderson; [b.] October 30, 1964, Selma, CA; [p.] Bill and Lois Woodward; [m.] Mark A. Besgrove, December 19, 1985; [ch.] Anthony, Deseree' and Mark Besgrove; [ed.] Finished all the way to the middle of 12th grade.

ANDERSON, MEGAN ELIZABETH
[pen.] Megan Anderson; [b.] April 16, 1983, Elgion, IL; [p.] Adelbert and Margaret Anderson; [ed.] In 6th grade, gifted program; [occ.] Student at Huntley Elementary School; [memb.] Junior Girl Scouts; [pers.] I always see the beauty in things and then I want to share the beauty part not the bad part. [a.] Huntley, IL.

ANDERSON, ROBERT T.
[pen.] Bob Anderson; [b.] December 17,1923, Plainfield, NJ; [p.] Jennie S. Anderson (deceased); [m.] Phyllis Ploughman Anderson, August 2, 1946; [ch.] Marsha, Susan, Robin and Beth; [ed.] Plainfield High, Drew University, New Brunswick Theological Seminary, all New Jersey, M/Div., USA Cmd. and Staff College, Kansas; [occ.] US Army, retired Chaplain; [memb.] American Legion, VFW, UM church (ordained minister, M/Div.); [hon.] Colonel, US Army, highest military award, Legion of Merit with one leaf cluster, Valley Forge Freedom Foundation Award (Vietnam), Citizen of Year Ruritan Award, Friends and Neighbors Award, WHAP Radio Station, VA., NC Governor Award for voluntary work; [oth.writ.] " The Role of Special Forces' Chaplains in Counter-Insurgency" bound and placed in USA and SC Library, edited and compiled "TakeFive" for special forces soldiers, "Dear Mr. and Mrs. American", VFFF, other poems and writings; [pers.] To understand and love your neighbor makes you the most important person in the world! Your neighbor may be your husband or wife or children or even your relatives or people you dislike the most. To live is to love and love is to live. [a.] Sanford, NC.

ANDRE, LEANNE
[b.] September 6, 1977, Victoria General Hospital; [p.]Dorothy Severinski; [ed.] Grade 11 at Correlieu Senior Secondary; [occ.] Attending Correlieu; [pers.] I like to express in my poetry what's happening throughout the world and problems we're facing. I also enjoy expressing how I feel in my writing. [a.] Quesnel, BC.

ANDREWS, BRADNY CATHLEEN
[pen.] Brandy Andrews; [b.] April 3, 1979, Charrlot, MI; [p.] Rone and Joyce Andrews; [ed.] Olivet Elementary, Pennfield Junior High, Harrison High School; [oth.writ.] Published in Young Authors; [pers.] My writing reflect the way I feel and my surroundings. [a.] Harrison, MI.

ANDREWS, DAVID E.
[b.] March 16, 1970, Toronto, Ontario; [p.] Victoria Leetham (grandmother); [ed.] Twin Lakes S.S., Orillia, Ontario; [pers.] I just hope and dream the world and people in it will become united and help one another. [a.] Keswick, Ontario.

ANDREWS, JEFFREY
[b.] April 11, 1957, New Jersey; [p.] Gerald R. Andrews; [m.] Gillian D.C. Andrews; [ch.] Will and Victoria; [ed.] Master's-Cornell (Public Administration); [occ.] Army officer.

ANDREWS, SUSAN J.
[pen.] Susan; [b.] January 7, 1962, Fort Monmouth, NJ; [p.] Fred C. and Emiko Scxhoenagel Jr.; [ed.] B.S. Recreation and Parks, Penn State University (1984), A.S. Physical Therapist Assistant (1991) also Penn State University; [occ.] Physical Therapist's Assistant Rehabilitation of traumatic

brain injured clients, DuBois Regional Medical Center; [memb.] Water safety instructor, lifeguard training instructor of American Red Cross since 1985, Penn State Alumni Association, lifetime member (1984); [hon.] Voice of Democracy 2nd place (1979), Who's Who Among American High School Students (1980); [oth.writ.] Personal writings of my thoughts and dreams; [pers.] My feelings and thoughts form into rhymes and I write them down, some are better than others. [a.] DuBois, PA.

ANTHONY, R.W.
[pen.] R.W. Anthony; [b.] November 16, 1953, New Haven, CT; [p.] Robert W. Anthony Sr. and H. Barbara Edwards; [m.] Esther Figueroa, June 6, 1970; [ch.] Michelle Lyn, RObert W. III, Samara Rae and Steven Michael; [ed.] 1 year University of Maryland (European Division), 1 year Mount Wachusett Community College (MWCC), Gardner, MA, major, English; [occ.] Retired military; [oth.writ.] Several poems published in the local college poetry forum, several essays published in college magazines, a poem scheduled to be published in the Treasury of American Poetry Anthology; [pers.] Strongly influenced by the French symbolists i.e., Baudelaire, Verlaine, Rimbuad, Mallarme and comparisons of these with the French impressionist program. Symbolist poetry should evoke rather than describe the subjective objects of the subconscious. Should also develop free verse (verslibre) and liberate poetry from its traditional restrictions. [a.] Huntington, WV.

ANTHONY, WILLIAM N.
[b.] April 15, 1917, Chicago, IL; [p.] Nicolas and Lillian Anthony; [m.] Annbritt Anthony, October 21, 1947; [ch.] Linea Anthony Goodenough; [ed.] North Park College, DePaul University School of Law; [occ.] Lawyer; [memb.] Illinois State Bar Association; [hon.] 1992 from Illinois State Bar Association for 50 years of practice in the legal profession; [oth.writ.] Three other poems to complete the quatrenion of "Sounds of Evening", plus more in various subject matters, all reflecting my striving for precise meter and consonance; [pers.] I have a love of nature, its glories and the animal life that fills it. I am an environmentalist saddened by the unthinking and uncaring forces that will inevitably destroy the world as we know it now. [a.] Chicago, IL.

ANTONUCCI, JOHN M.
[b.] February 3, 1916, Chicago Heights, IL; [p.] Victor and Antonette; [m.] Deceased; [ch.] 4 children; [ed.] High school, business college, sales school; [occ.] Retired; [memb.] American Legion, St. Joseph The Worker Church, Loma Linda, CA; [hon.] Honor man award from Great Lakes Illinois Station; [oth.writ.] I have 3 songs recorded, I am in partnership with Lawrence Weld on 1 of the songs; [pers.] I have been writing poetry since high school. My love is music, I write the lyrics also, there aren't many writers who do. [a.] Redlands, CA.

APIKOS, DOM A.
[b.] March 12, 1932, New York City, NY; [p.] Anna and Stephen; [m.] Patricia, August 2, 1992; [ch.] Stephanie and Thomas; [ed.] B.S. Chemical Engineering, Drexel University, Philadelphia, PA; [occ.] Retired; [memb.] Nature Conservancy, National Committee to Preserve Social Security and Medicare (NCPSSM), National Taxpayers Union, Veteran of Foreign Wars, Greenpeace, the Concord Coalition; [hon.] Golden Poet Award 1989, 1990, 1991, Who's Who in Poetry-1992, World of Poetry, Editor's Choice Award-the Poetry Center; [oth.writ.] 10 U.S. patents; [pers.] I would like my poems to be read a long time from now and have people say, "I would like to have known this person". [a.] Villa Park, IL.

APPELL, SHARON
[pen.] Sharon McCarty; [b.] October 15, 1965, Ohio; [p.] Ruth Yocum and Robert McCarty; [m.] Tommy Appell, June 6, 1990; [ch.] Christopher, Patrick and Kimberly; [ed.] 10th grade but I'm taking classes to get my GED; [occ.] Homemaker; [memb.] I'm a member of the First Pentalcostal Church on Dakota Avenue, lead by Pastor Brother Joseph Stump; [oth.writ.] I wrote lots of poems in 7th and 8th grade at Holy Name, one was printed in a magazine called Jack and Jill and a couple in the church bulletin; [pers.] This poem was written for my friend Stella on her birthday. I know if God wasn't in my life I couldn't have come this far. I thank Him more and more each day for what He's given me. [a.] Columbus, OH.

APRILE, FRANK
[b.] August 13,1956, W. Germany; [m.] Ann Aprile, December 22, 1989; [occ.] Perfusionist (chief); [memb.] American Society for Extra Corporeal Technology; [oth.writ.] Articles for Society Journal, prose, etc.; [a.] Howell, MI.

ARMSTRONG, HARROLL
[b.] September 6, 1934, Norfolk, VA; [p.] Eunice and Anson Armstrong; [m.] Betty Armstrong, March 5, 1957; [ch.] Harry P., Helen, Doug, Glen and David; [ed.] High school, School of Life; [occ.] Retired; [memb.] Mason, Lodge 39, Norfolk, VA., 32 degree Scottish Rite Valley of Norfolk, VA.; [hon.] Editor's Choice Award, National Library of Poetry, U.S. Proficiency Flight team; [oth.writ.] Poems published in Navy News, Nadep paper, articles written in Navy newspaper; [pers.] I write what I feel and feel what I write. [a.] Virginia Beach, VA.

ARMSTRONG, YETTA N.
[b.] November 12, 1955, Rahway, NJ; [p.] Genorace and Alice Armstrong; [ed.] Linden High School, Rutgers University, B.A. in English; [occ.] Owner, Advanced Text Processing; [oth.writ.] Shayna , a short story and several poems published and non-published; [pers.] I strive to be completely honest with who I am, at all times willing to void out any contradictory associations that prohibit that honesty from flourishing.

ASHNA, HELEN M.
[pen.] Laura Elizabeth Ashley; [b.] December 26, 1944, West Virginia; [p.] Mary Elizabeth Neal and Harold C. Smith; [ch.] Jeanni, Thelesa, Kerry, Erin, Ashley and 6 grandchildren; [ed.] High school and 2 years college, graduate Huntington High School, West Virginia, Galveston Junior College, College on the Mainland; [occ.] Provide personal care services, specializing in the care of alzheimer patients, I love my work and am dedicated 260%; [oth.writ.] Personal poetry, eg., "Little Princes", "Laying On My Pillow", "Secrecy", this is my first attempt to send any of my writings in: [pers.] Love breaks down the walls that separate us. I believe that unconditional love and unselfishness are key ingredients that we are to demonstrate toward each other. Take time to listen and care for someone daily. [a.] Houston, TX.

ASHTON, NICOLE ALEXANDRIA;
[b.] January 4, 1975, Jamaica Plain, MA; [p.] Elizabeth Ann and Holbrook Theodore Ashton; [m.] Fiancee, Ryan O. Rice; [ed.] Brookline High School, Massachusetts Bay Community College, January 1995, I will be attending St. Elizabeth's Hospital School of Nursing; [occ.] Nutrition Assistant at Brigham and Women's Hospital, Boston, Massachusetts; [hon.] Honor Roll (senior year of high school), school spirit award, attendance award; [pers.] In my poetry I try to push the need for self-confidence. You can love no one until you love yourself. I find poetry as a form of self-expression. Most importantly I try to always send a message in my writing. I'd like to thank my parents as well as my boyfriend for their continuous support. [a.] Brookline, MA.

ASHTON, ROBERT DEREK
[pen.] Jimmy Berry; [b.] August 21,1977, San Diego; [p.] Sharon Harms and William Ashton III; [ed.] I am currently attending my senior year at West Hills High School; [occ.] Unemployed; [memb.] I belong to nothing; [hon.] I have received nothing; [oth.writ.] I am currently in the process of writing three other poems, other than that I have not done anything else; [pers.] Once a person believes that they can learn no more, that is the point in which they become stupid. I basically feel that everything is pretty. [a.] Santee, CA.

ASKEY, HENRY B.
[b.] July 9, 1925, Buffalo, NY; [p.] Winifred May, Benjamin Askey; [m.] Gladys Marie (Cramer) Askey, July 14, 1945; [ch.] Barbara Jean, Thelma Jane, Charles Benjamin, Gladys Marie; [ed.] Burgard VHS; Memphis State University; Jacksonville Florida Univ.; Univ. of Hawaii; Pensacola J.C.; [occ.] Retired Navy Commander; Retired Lockheed Engineer; [memb.] Masonic Blue Lodge #671; Shrine; Retired Officer Assoc.; YMCA; [oth. writ.] One play; 20 additional poems; [pers.] I try to understand and reflect on those things that are important in the great area we call the universe and how they affect life.; [a.] Burbank, CA.

ATKINS, CAROLE L.
[b.] March 5, Washington, DC; [p.] John and Jackie Law; [m.] Allen W. Atkins, May 27, 1978; [ch.] Brenda; [ed.] Prince George's Community College, Largo, Maryland; [occ.] Paralegal, Notary Public; [memb.] National Notary Association, Space Coast Art Festival Inc.-Publicity Director, Space Coast Network of Executive Women; [hon.] Listed in Who's Who Among Students in American Junior Colleges, several poems published in college literary magazine while serving as President of Student Government; [oth.writ.] Published poetry, several children's story books, yet unpublished, Condominium Association Newsletter Editor and Publisher since February 1994; [a.] Cape Canaveral, FL.

AVERITT, SHANNON MARIE
[b.] February 10, 1977, San Bernadino, CA; [p.] Malcom and Carolyn Averitt; [ed.] Dixie Elementary School (Texas), Stewart Middle School (Texas), John Tyler High from 9th -10th (Texas), Harizon High School; [occ.] Student; [memb.] Member of my high school Pep Squad (Blue Brigade); [hon.] Won 1st and 2nd place in a poetry contest in third grade; [oth.writ.] I have several poems that never been published before; [pers.] I feel that the best poems ever to be written are those written from the heart. I enjoy writing about my feelings and my thoughts but mostly from my heart. I thank God for this special talent that He's given me. I also thank my family and friends. [a.] Long Beach, CA.

AVERY, CHRISTINE CLARK
[pen.] Teenie, Mama Chris; [b.] November 17, 1934, Louisville, MS; [p.] Annie and Roy Edwards; [m.] Elton Clark and Glover Avery (both deceased) May 26, 1951 and April 1977; [ch.] Larry and Ken Clark; [ed.] 10-tenth grade, high school; [occ.] Retired, disabled hair stylist, barber; [memb.] Briarwood Baptist Church, American Legion Auxiliary for Ladies; [hon.] I am honored each day, I see a new sunrise, I reap many awards, much to my

surprise; [oth.writ.] I have written many poems, none published, some would make beautiful songs, also some philosophy painted deserts and mountain streams, etc.; [pers.] My heart is so big, there is room for much more. If only I would give it a chance. My life and others would be enhanced. [a.] Pearl, MS.

AYERS, SARAH J.
[b.] April 25, 1956, Winston-Salem, NC; [p.] Mel and Evelyn James (deceased); [m.] Divorced; [ch.] Will IV, age 19; [ed.] High school, Private Pilot Ground School, and some flight training; [occ.] Executive Assistant for a private household; [hon.] Purple Berries has been recognized before, I have had a lot of recognition at the workplace for my writing ability and hope to write a book someday soon, either poetry or short stories; [oth.writ.] "Thirty and Life Without Love" to be published in 1995, it has a "country" sound to it and I primarily want it recognized as song lyrics; [pers.] "I believe in the depths of our despair or at the heights of our joy, our "best" words are written". My current and future works are dedicated to my son, Will and my dear friend, Jimmie. [a.] Greensboro, NC.

BACHOFNER,, CAROL WILLETTE
[pen.] Carol Snow Moon; [b.] January 16, 1947, Portsmouth, NH; [p.] Charles and Dorothy Willette; [m.] Bill Bachofner, December 26, 1980; [ch.] Katherine, Kristin, Gina, Erin, Richard and Lauren; [ed.] York High School, Victor Valley College; [occ.] Retired R.N.; [memb.] Wordcraft Circle, California Writer's Club, Juan Diego Intertribal Circle; [oth.writ.] "Why Be Married" published in The Family magazine; [pers.] As a woman of Native American descent (Abenaki) my poetry reflects my Indian culture and the white culture in which I was raised. I ride the river of my own history. What a glorious ride! [a.] Victorville, CA.

BAKER, ARTHUR
[pen.] Sentell Cabrini; [b.] November 6, 1978, New Orleans, LA; [p.] Alvin and Anna Baker; [ed.] Finishing the degrading institution known as high school; [occ.] Musician, poet, and artist; [memb.] Amnesty International; [oth.writ.] Poem published in Reflections magazine; [pers.] I try to mutilate everyone's emotions in my writing. In short, I try to scare them in anyway possible. I'm too introspective and I think that I've decided to take everybody else down with me. [a.] Ocean Springs, MS.

BAKER, KATIE
[b.] August 18, 1979, Edina, MN; [p.] Melissa I. Vazzano and Danny L. Baker; [ed.] Currently a sophomore at Park Hill High School (15 years old); [occ.] Student; [memb.] Cheerleading, band, choir (Park Hill High School); [hon.] Who's Who Among American High School Students; [oth.writ.] 14 other unpublished poems; [pers.] Always work for what you want, always believe in yourself and everyone has a special talent, never hide it. [a.] Kansas City, MO.

BAKER, TINA M.
[b.] September 20, 1959, Redmond, OR; [p.] Rodney L. and D. Elouise Gregg; [m.] Divorced, March 4, 1977 to April 1992; [ch.] Odessa M., KayLynn M. and Charlene M.; [ed.] Madras Senior High, Madras, OR., Paraoptometric Assistance course, AOA CE program; [occ.] Registered Optometric Assistant, Madras Vision Clinic, Madras, OR.; [memb.] American Optometric Association; [oth.writ.] "Songs of Youth", American Poetry Press, July 1975; [pers.] I enjoy sharing my poetry and the many inspirations that life gives. [a.] Bend, OR.

BALDAZO, LIBRADA C.
[pen.] Lee; [b.] September 1, 1944, San Juan, TX; [p.] Ramiro and Zoila Cantu; [m.] Fidel Baldazo Jr., December 3, 1967; [ch.] Fidell III and Jorge Baldazo; [ed.] Graduated Pharr-San Jaun-Alamo High School and attended Pan American College; [occ.] Have worked for 22 years as an Office Clerk in the mail order department of Crest Fruit Company in Alamo, Texas; [memb.] Walkamerica (March of Dimes), have been member of various church choirs, attend Alpha and Omega Baptist Mission in San Juan, Texas; [oth.writ.] Numerous poems and several fairy tales, none have been published; [pers.] My writings reflect love toward God and mankind. My early writings date back to the 1960's and show carefree days of childhood. I have loved poetry since early childhood influenced by my mother who loved to recite poetry. [a.] Alamo, TX.

BALTEFF, GREGORY M.
[pen.] Gregory M. Balteff; [b.] September 23, 1962, Shelby Township, MI; [p.] Dale and Judy Balteff; [ed.] Oakland University, 2 years; [occ.] Mr. Positive on WHYT-FM Detroit Radio; [memb.] Powerhouse Gym of Garden City; [hon.] Bodybuilding and weight lifting titles, other sports related honors such tennis, chess, baseball etc.; [oth.writ.] Mostly Mr. Positive poetry, I deal with the dilemmas facing our youth of today, in hopes that they will in turn achieve the goals and hopes they set out to do; [pers.] You start with a dream and then you believe. Your thoughts become magic and then you achieve. [a.] Westland, MI.

BANAN, JULIETA
[b.] March 10, 1979, Rockville, MD; [p.] Jack and Regina Banan; [ed.] Rockville High School; [occ.] High school student; [memb.] School Drama Club; [hon.] 1988 Principal Award for outstanding writing, 1989 certificate of merit art show, letter of delight from First Lady Barbara Bush, 1990 Mathematical Olympiad Award, 1991 certificate of achievement for outstanding service, 1992 certificate of appreciation for services at Earle B. Middle School, 1994 certificate of appreciation for service on behalf of Girl Scouts of America, 1994 award on Science Fair Expo at Rockville High School; [oth.writ.] A poem published in Echoes magazine; [pers.] Write only what you want, not what others want. [a.] Rockville, MD.

BANASZAK, ANNA MONIKA
[b.] February 21, 1969, Szczecin, Poland; [ed.] Adam Mickiewicz University in Poznan, Poland; [occ.] Translator; [pers.] I never think of myself as a poet, I'm a traveler, whatever it may mean. [a.] New York, NY.

BANKS-BEY SR., SHONN L.
[b.] April 22, 1967, Cleveland, OH; [p.] Jerome E. Banks Sr. and Cheryl A. Baker; [ch.] Shonn L. Banks-Bey Jr; [ed.] West Tech High School, Wooster Business College; [occ.] Security specialist; [hon.] Dean's List, scholarship award (graduated Magna Cum Laude), class president, 4 Lamplighter Awards certificate of attendance; [oth.writ.] Songs and other poems which have not been published; [pers.] Knowledge is power, yet the road to achieving this power begins with knowledge of one's self. [a.] Cleveland, OH.

BANTEGUI, MIRLA C.
[pen.] Fatima B.; [b.] July 13,1937, Philippines; [p.] Anastacio Caedo and Florencia Beltran; [m.] Ralph J. Bantegui, June 18, 1969; [ch.] Abraham, Benjamin, Melissa and James; [ed.] B.s.H.E.; [occ.] Housekeeper; [memb.] Catholic Church, Fatima Crusader, I.T. member, N.P.C.A., W.W.F., N.S.A.L.; [oth.writ.] Quill Books published, poems "Red Shadow", "Are You In Love"; [pers.] What is true and good? What is holy and beautiful? My pen still upholds them all, with caressing lines I'll lay them down, should man's eyes fail to gaze upon them, joyfully to his ears, I will sing. David the shepherd inspires. [a.] Colonia, NJ.

BANTOM, SYDNEY
[b.] January 19, 1975, Philadelphia, PA; [p.] Dr. Walter and Gayl Bantom; [ed.] Philadelphia High School for Girls, Marymount Manhattan College, Temple University; [oth.writ.] Poems published in high school literary magazine and yearbook, Marymount Manhattan College literary magazine. [a.] Philadelphia, PA.

BARBOUR, BRIANNE LAUREN
[b.] November 21, 1982, Washington, DC; [p.] Neville and Carla Barbour; [ed.] 7th grade student, National Cathedral School, Washington, DC, also attended National Presbyterian School, Washington, DC.

BARITELL, SUSAN K.
[b.] July 1, 1947, Parkersburg, WV; [p.] Babe and Lois Baritell; [ch.] Robin Elizabeth and Joshua Miles; [ed.] Jamesville-DeWitt High School, Long Ridge Writers Group; [occ.] I show and breed Nubian Dairy goats under the herd name Moonshadow Farms and produce handmade Shaker style brooms, feather dusters and fans; [memb.] American Dairy Goat Association, New York State Dairy Goat Breeders Association, Central New York Dairy Goat Society, New York State Goat Youth Programs Committee at Cornell University, National Parks and Conservation Association, Planned Parenthood, Putting People First; [hon.] Several awards for service to the New York State Dairy Goat Industry; [oth.writ.] Articles for Dairy Goat Journal, United Caprine News, Great Lakes Goat Market, pamphlet-"Dairy Goats", History Milk, Cheese; [pers.] Home is a 170 year old cabin atop the hills of rural Central, New York where the only lights are the stars and imagination is set free to mingle with the wood elves and nature's magic. [a.] Fabius, NY.

BARKER, HARDEN
[b.] October 13, 1977, Fort Lauderdale, FL; [p.] Gale Barker and Harden Barker (deceased); [ed.] Will graduate from Northeastern High School in June 1995, plan to go to college and obtain a master's degree in English; [occ.] Student, I wish to become a high school English teacher; [memb.] Inducted into National Honor Society and Key Club, I'm also in Future Teachers of America, Science Club and Literary Club; [hon.] I won Honorable Mentions for short stories and poetry I've written for the local Junior Women's Club, recognized as Junior Marshal, I've won academic and athletic letters from high school; [oth.writ.] I write a monthly youth column for the local newspaper, I've had poetry printed in the school yearbook; [pers.] My goal as a writer is for people to read my works and thing, because thinking opens new possibilities in all of our minds. [a.] Elizabeth City, NC.

BARKER, LINDA
[pen.] Katie Barker; [b.] September 3, 1968, North Carolina; [p.] James and Betty Box; [m.] George Barker, March 27, 1987; [ch.] Brittany Sue and Malachi Alan; [ed.] Clinton High, Taylor county Vocational School; [occ.] Homemaker; [oth.writ.] I do personal poems for birthdays, weddings, funerals, anniversaries, etc. upon request; [pers.] Everything I write comes directly from the heart. I believe writing is the greatest way to express one's feelings and emotions. [a.] Perry, FL.

BARKER, THOMAS
[b.] August 13,1968, Danville, VA; [p.] Harriett Barker; [ed.] Thomas Jefferson High School; [oth.writ.] I have consistently written for just about all of my adult life, however, this poem will be the first ever published which is ironic because it's the only writing I've ever been proud of; [pers.] The poetry that I write must always be reality based and it must move me as well as the reader. My inspiration always has and always will be humanity. [a.] Richmond, VA.

BARLOW, L. FERN
[b.] September 17, 1941, Macksville, WV; [occ.] Bookkeeper; [oth.writ.] A book of poetry Appalachian Memories printed in 1994; [pers.] My book of poetry was done to share my feelings for the privilege of being raised by two very special people, my mom and dad, and a very special grandmother in a very small town U.S.A. [a.] Arlington, VA.

BARNES, BRITTNEY NICOLE
[pen.] Disney-Barnes; [b.] February 26, 1980, Olney, MD; [p.] Mr. and Mrs. Daniel L. Barnes Sr.; [ed.] 9th grade student, Quince Orchard High School; [occ.] Student; [memb.] St. James A.M.E. Church; [hon.] Honor Roll, Academic Awards; [oth.writ.] Composed modest variety of short poems including funny, sad, and sincere subject matter; [pers.] Mr grandmother, Mrs. Florence G. Disney, has utilized her knowledge, skills and abilities to enhanced my skills to be a professional writer with originality, motivation and creativity. [a.] Gaithersburg, MD.

BARNES, ELDER CHARLES
[pen.] The Greatest; [b.] January 20, 1952, Itta Benta, MS; [p.] Georgia Barnes; [m.] Naomi G. Barnes, April 2, 1993; [ch.] Malcom, Tabitha, Anna, Elvin and Nakesha; [ed.] Lincoln High, Leland, Mississippi, additional education California and the state Utah, attended business school at Riley College, Greenville, Mississippi; [occ.] Pastor of Prayer and Supplication World Ministries Inc.; [memb.] American Red Cross, Prayer and Supplication World Ministries Inc., High Dimension Church, United Christian Church, Ministerial Association, Universal Life Church Inc., National Audubon Society; [hon.] Several American Red Cross Awards and Honors, several Ministerial Awards and Honors, several awards and honors in high school and college for straight A's, Fire Department Award, Pleaston, California best performer and readiness; [oth.writ.] I write poems, essays, news columns, words of wisdom and lots of Biblical materials, few songs and hopefully some more poetry or songs; [pers.] I have written a lot of poems and songs alike but never had the courage to have any of this material published, but you all at National Library of Poetry have given me hope. [a.] Greenville, MS.

BARNES, KEVIN M.
[b.] June 22, 1983, Philadelphia, PA; [p.] Ed and Lynn Larkins; [ed.] Chestnut Ridge Middle School, 6th grade, Bells Elementary School, Sewell, New Jersey; [occ.] Student; [hon.] Presidential Physical Fitness Award; [pers.] Family, Keith, Debbie, Danny, Kasey, Sandy and Muffin. [a.] Sewell, NJ.

BARNETT, MARICA
[b.] March 9, 1946, Chester, PA; [p.] Dorothy and Alphonso Barnett; [m.] Single; [ch.] 1 son; [ed.] To 11th grade; [occ.] Homemaker; [memb.] Church of God; [pers.] One of thirteen children and mother of one son and two grandchildren. I have the Lord in my life and I am living for Him and I usually talk to other people about Him. [a.] Chester, PA.

BARNITT, RICHARD P.
[b.] December 7, 1945, Hackensack, NJ; [p.] Samuel C. and Elizabeth Ann Barnitt; [m.] Martha Oldham Barnitt, October 15, 1977; [ch.] Emily Jule Barnitt; [ed.] B.A., Syracuse University, New York, M.L.A., Middlebury College, Vermont; [occ.] Russian Linguist; [oth.writ.] "His Kiss" in The Desert Sun, 1994; [pers.] Enjoy writing poetry for family and friends. [a.] Hasbrouck Heights, NJ.

BARON, LYNNE
[b.] March 26, 1978; [ed.] High school junior, Redlands High School, Cope Junior High, McKinley Elementary; [occ.] Student trying to get out; [hon.] Nothing very special, mostly sports awards; [oth.writ.] I plan to write my own book of short stories and poems, I started my book around 12 years of age; [pers.] "Fear is the lack of knowledge..". Live life to the fullest, be happy now.. you may never have another chance. [a.] Redlands, CA.

BARR, JENNIFER L.
[b.] February 23, 1975, Exton, PA; [p.] John L. and Katherine Barr Jr.; [ed.] Bishop Shanahan High School, Westchester, PA., York College of Pennsylvania; [occ.] Student at York College of Pennsylvania; [memb.] Student Nurses' Association of Pennsylvania; [hon.] National Honors Society at Bishop Shanahan High School, Academic dean's Scholarship recipient to York College, PA., 1st place at state competition for piano, held at Elizabethtown College; [pers.] Poetry portrays my deepest emotions for peace and equality among mankind. "Beauty lies in the eyes of its beholder". My writing reflects the pressures within society. [a.] Exton, PA.

BARRAFORD-SOOBITSKY, MAUREEN
[b.] May 31, 1943, Gouverneur, NY; [p.] William and Jessie Barraford; [m.] Michael Soobitsky, September 23, 1989; [ch.] James; [ed.] Graduate high school 1960 Edwards High School, New York, Middlesex Community College; [occ.] Homemaker; [hon.] Middlesex Community College Dean's List; [oth.writ.] Several poems published by local papers; [pers.] I have learned through the illness of depression, that one must bring feelings out, however painful. Poetry has allowed me the communication vehicle I needed to express my feelings and become whole. [a.] Durham, CT.

BARRERA, MARGARET GUZMAN
[pen.] Margaret Guzman; [b.] October 28, 1956, East Chicago, IN; [p.] Maria A. and Anselmo Guzman; [ch.] Gabriel G., Christine B. and Michael B.; [ed.] Washington High, East Chicago, IN., Tech High Ham Ind.; [occ.] Uniform inspector, Arrow Uniforms, Ham, IN.; memb.] First Baptist Church of Hammond Indiana; [hon.] Victory Torch received (August 1994), Light House pin (running the race), (Phoster Club), First Baptist of Hammond, IN.; [pers.] (First) Let the Lord be magnify! It is God that giveth the talents; my poetry reflects all of our life's experiences to a point, so let me briefly say: "Experience is a hard teacher". "She gives the test first, the lesson afterwards", and then a talent is born. [a.] Hammond, IN.

BARRY, CAROL A.
[m.] George; [ch.] Five children, five step children and 14 grandchildren; [occ.] Licensed Practical Nurse, work with elderly and terminally ill; [oth.writ.] Poems about my children, life, my old folks in the nursing home, no attempts to publish these, they are in my book of "Hugs"; [pers.] I live a simple life, keep a journal and often a poem emerges as I write. My personal journey is to spread love and be of help wherever I am if only to give a hug. [a.] Canadaigua, NY.

BARTLEY, MEKESIA
[b.] June 9, 1981, Brooklyn, NY; [p.] Deserine and Hopeton Bartley; [ed.] Public School 78, Michealangels Intermediate School 144; [hon.] Honor Roll Student; [oth.writ.] Several poems; [pers.] I wish to be a role model to many of the young poets of the world today to follow their dreams. [a.] Bronx, NY.

BEAMESDERFER, DONNA
[b.] April 21, 1952, Lancaster, PA; [p.] Ben and Violet Keener; [m.] Harry Beamesderfer, June 7, 1975; [ed.] Annville-Cleona High School; [occ.] Housewife; [memb.] Myerstown Grace Brethren Church for over 20 years; [hon.] 3, 4-H 1st place awards; [oth.writ.] Wrote one other poem, and had is published in the poem book called At Days End; [pers.] Hope to write my own life story in the future and more books and poems. [a.] Newmanstown, PA.

BEAN, BOBBY J.
[pen.] Beaner; [b.] September 26, 1943, Laredo, TX; [p.] M.M. and B.B. Bean; [m.] Becky, March 20, 1965; [ch.] Kimberley and Amy; [ed.] Graduated Vidor High School, Vidor, Texas, graduated Lamar University, BBA, general business, Beaumont, Texas; [occ.] Contracts coordinator Tengizchevroil-Kazakhstan; [pers.] My family is my life and it has been blessed in so many ways, so I hope my writings will reflect my expression of love for my parents, wife and children. [a.] Katy, TX.

BEASON, TERANCE MIGUEL
[pen.] T.M. Beason; [b.] December 4, 1969, Oakland; [p.] Steve and Thelma Barrios Beason; [ed.] Attended St. Joseph Elementary, Saint Anthony High School and currently studying at California State University, Long Beach; [occ.] Student; [pers.] Thank you Alicia for your encouragement and belief, love M. My work comes from a place deep inside my heart, I make it that way so yours can hopefully be less burdened and more full of understanding.

BECK, EDITH
[pen.] Edith Beck; [b.] August 3, 1910, Moldavia; [p.] Reizel and Idel Eisman; [m.] Leon Beck, April 1, 1940; [ch.] Don; [ed.] P.S. 174 in Brooklyn, nite high, Washington Irving, Irving Place, NYC, sweatshops, life, picket lines, jails, Central Park, etc.; [occ.] Retired, but to circumvent Social Security checks, I work some on the L.A. Times, polls; [memb.] Jewish Cultural organizations, family, large, wonderful life, my occupation, living, observing, reflecting, put it down on paper; [hon.] I got printed in the labor press and journal--Yes, first story in a big book "Living Past", printed by L.A. Cita and American Profiles, its good-its fine, I'm in good company with American Doers, writers actors, Scientists, leaders; [oth.writ.] Poems, stories articles, leaflets and such, a book for my 65th birthday "Wrinkling Leaves", printed 3000 copies with the help of my union member, sold them out in a few months; [pers.] I nominated myself to tell young America of my generation and its contributions to life. America, the 40 hour week, unions, unemployment insurance, Social Security, the birth of the Civil Rights movement and more unique, we were and I was there. [a.] Los Angeles, CA.

BECKER, DAVINA F.
[b.] May 29, 1978, California; [p.] Anne and Michael Becker; [ed.] Junior in high school at South San Francisco High; [occ.] Salesperson and Assistant Teacher at Sunday School; [memb.] California Scholarship Federation; [oth.writ.] Poetry, "The Immortal", "Places We've Been", Togetherness"; [pers.] Treat life like a palm tree

to the wind, bend and twist but never break. [a.] South San Francisco, CA.

BECKER, JOHN L.
[pen.] John L. "Jack" Becker; [b.] May 13,1915, Pittsburgh, PA; [p.] Andrew A. and Theresa Becker; [m.] Jeanne L. Becker (deceased), December 31, 1938; [ch.] Theresa M. Kriek, John L. Becker Jr., Lynne L. Carlson and Brooke Vaughn; [ed.] Duquesne University and Polytechnic Institute of Brooklyn; [occ.] Retired, formerly Sales Manager for U.S. Steel; [memb.] Buffalo Athletic Club, Park Country Club (Buffalo, NY), Limestone Creek Hunt Club (Cazenovia, NY), Cavalry Club of Manlius (NY), Naples Bath and Tennis Club (FL); [hon.] Open Jumper Champion 1961, Erie County Fair; [oth.writ.] "Would You Listen", collection of poems; [pers.] After being very active in equestrian and tennis competition, I was incapacitated be a severe stroke at age 74. Clinging to the philosophy "When God closed the door, He always opens a window", I began writing poetry, which has given new meaning and hope to my life. [a.] Naples, FL.

BEECH, LINDA
[b.] October 29, 1958, Muskogee, OK; [p.] Mr. and Mrs. Jerry Hester and Mr. and Mrs. Clarence Gregory; [m.] Wallace Beck, October 29, 1993; [ch.] Jaime Henning, Thomas Westfall, Stephanie Henning and Billy Jack Westfall; [occ.] School bus driver; [oth.writ.] I have several but none that has ever been published; [pers.] I'm thrilled that my poem was picked. I started writing this kind of poems back in 1992 when I lost my husband.

BEEMAN, BOBBIE JO
[b.] February 11, 1972, Oakland, CA; [p.] Ray and Jencie; [ed.] Point Loma Nazarene College; [pers.] Always wear flowers in your hair and believe in love at first sight. [a.] Ocean Beach, CA.

BEEMAN, E.R.
[pen.] Al Beeman; [b.] September 10, 1922, Chicago, IL; [p.] Elmer and Irene Beeman; [m.] Wanda (deceased), December 30, 1952; [ch.] Jinx Lee and Jody Lee; [ed.] Retired from trucking industry, free-lance creative artist; [memb.] American Diabetes Association; [hon.] Numerous trucking industry safety awards; [oth.writ.] Humorous art sales, published cartoons, documented song lyric's; [pers.] Although memories can not be touched I strived to make them real. [a.] North Olmsted, OH.

BEHRENS, LIANA
[b.] June 12, 1977, Aurora, IL; [p.] Edwin A. Behrens Jr. and Sandra J. Klemencic; [ed.] West Aurora High; [oth.writ.] Several other poems (never published), which are made for people or kept with me; [pers.] My influence came from romance and love stories. These are my thoughts, some of my dreams and some of my difficulties. I would love to make a change in someone's life. I'm a romantic. I search for love, there's love in all. [a.] Aurora, IL.

BEHZADPOUR, ROSEMARIE SERRANO
[b.] August 30,1958, Mesa, AZ; [p.] Frank R. Serrano and Erlinda G. Valenzuela; [m.] Mahmound Behzadpour, July 3, 1981; [ch.] Talia; [ed.] McClintock High, Mesa Community College, Arizona Stat University; [occ.] Student, Arizona State University; [pers.] My love for God has brought me to a better understanding of this world we're living in and my fondness for reading and writing has educated my mind, opened my heart and strengthened my soul. [a.] Chandler, AZ.

BEISIGL, BRIAN
[b.] December 6, 1968, La Mesa, CA; [p.] Ray Starnes and April Beisigl; [ed.] Granite Hills Highs, Grossmont College; [occ.] Payroll clerk, Forte Hotels Inc., projectionist, Kirkorian el Cajon Cinema 8; [oth.writ.] Over 200 poems and 15 songs (none published) working on a book that I hope may be published someday; [pers.] Create in ones mind, but write to show dreams. [a.] El Cajon, CA.

BELL, ELIZABETH BRADNER
[b.] November 27, 1908, Philadelphia, PA; [p.] Blanche and W.H.G. Bradner; [m.] J. Elliott Bell (deceased), May 22, 1943; [ch.] Joan E. Bell (deceased); [ed.] Frankford High School, St. Mary's Hall, Burlington, New Jersey, Temple University, Philadelphia; [occ.] Retired 1968; [oth.writ.] Music, "Weep Not Dear Mary" (used Nativity Church, Media, PA.), children's poems, various topical poems; [pers.] Daughter of William H. G. Bradner, well known Philadelphia musician. I wrote for self amusement and to please my mother who hopes one of her three children would inherit dad's talent. Never tried to publish. [a.] Orlando, FL.

BELLERJEAU, NATALIE
[b.] August 18, 1965, Elkins Park, PA; [p.] Carol and Bill Bellerjeau; [ch.] Donald Flannigan; [ed.] George Washington High graduated 1983; [occ.] Homemaker; [pers.] My inspiration for this poem unfortunately came from a young boy I knew who died as a result of another youth's carelessness with a handgun. In memory of Billy Z. [a.] Philadelphia, PA.

BELTON, MARIE
[pen.] Mariah Lockett; [b.] June 29, 1980, Detroit, MI; [ed.] 9th grade student at Cass Technical High School; [memb.] Cass Tech Concert Band (percussion); [hon.] 3rd place area essay contest 1992, honored at Young Writer's program 1994, writer and artist in Bates Creates Middle School's publication or poems, essays and short stories 1993, 1994, 1991 essay contest Fox 50; [oth.writ.] Close to 100 poems, a few of which were published locally and dozens of essays and short stories, some which have won awards; [pers.] My vivid imagination takes me places I have never been, and lets me experience things I never have. This ability gives my writing such a realistic quality. "I love to write because it is an escape from the world around me. Through the power of words, I can be anywhere and do anything". [a.] Detroit, MI.

BENEDICT, REBECCA
[pen.] The Novelist; [b.] February 16, 1975, Euclid, OH; [p.] James and Joyce Benedict; [ed.] Aurora High School; [occ.] Student at University of Akron; [memb.] Tri-M Music Honorary Society, Baptist Student Union; [hon.] John Philip Sousa Award;[pers.] Proverbs 16:3, "Commit to the Lord whatever you do, and your plans will succeed". I know this is true for my plans have succeeded. [a.] Aurora, OH.

BENNETT, RICK
[b.] December 6, 1974, Louisville,KY; [p.] Dr. and Mrs. James Bennett; [ed.] Episcopal High School, University of Houston and Texas Christian University; [occ.] Student; [memb.] Sigma Mu; [oth.writ.] Personal poems which I have not submitted anywhere; [pers.] I strive to show the injustices of a society where love is taken for granted, ideals are changing and the soothing beauty of nature is being destroyed. [a.] Houston, TX.

BENNETT, SHERRILL
[b.] January 8, 1941, New Orleans, LA; [p.] Stanley and Louise Bennett; [m.] Suzanne, May 31, 1966; [ch.] Stan, Steve and Stuart; [ed.] B.S. Social Work from George Williams College, M.S. Counseling from Mississippi State University; [occ.] Minister, Elementary Counselor; [memb.] Mississippi School Counselor Association. [a.] Columbus, MS.

BENTLEY, RICKIE
[b.] February 13, 1959, Williamson, WV; [p.] Charles and Bonnie Bentley; [m.] Not married yet; [ed.] Mentor Public Schools, Auburn Career Center; [occ.] Woodworker, furniture restorations and repairs; [memb.] North American Fishing Club, Bass Anglers Sportsman Society, Trout Unlimited, Greenpeace, Mentor Methodist Church, National Rife Association; [hon.] "They're on the way"; [oth.writ.] In the creative stages; [pers.] Hope to dream, dare to do and pray your hopes and dreams come true. [a.] Novelty, OH.

BENTON, ANN
[pen.] Ann Benton; [b.] May 12, 1980, Stamford, CT; [p.] Marian and David Benton; [ed.] Gagi School 1985-1988, St. Augustines School 1988-89, St. Anne's School 1989-90, St. Joseph's school 1990-91, St. Francis of Assisi School 1991-93, Rye St. Anthony School, Oxford U.K. 1993; [occ.] Student, Rye St. Anthony School; [memb.] Diversability Theatre Group, Rye St. Anthony choir and Dramatics Society; [hon.] Guildhall level 4 acting. awarded with merit, certificate of Merit of Excellence at the 1993 Michigan Interscholastic Forensics Association in impromptu speaking; [oth.writ.] 1989 Friends of Poetry contest, an Honorable Mention Award, 1991 participation in Michigan Young Author's Conference, poem published in 1994 Rye St. Anthony School magazine; [pers.] Sometimes, my poetry is the only way to let out my feelings inside. Perhaps this is best summed up by a quote from Edgar Allen Poe "with me, poetry has not been a purpose, but a passion". [a.] Ypsilanti, MI.

BERGERON, OLIVIA ANN
[pen.] "Liver"; [b.] January 23, 1980, Louisiana; [p.] Angela and Kent Bergeron; [ed.] I'm in the 9th grade at Northeast Jones High School in Laurel, Mississippi; [memb.] Audubon Drive Bible Church, N.E. Student Council, freshman choir, French Club, Future Homemakers of America; [hon.] Honor Roll, reporter of the ninth grade class; [pers.] Anybody can do anything if you believe in yourself and God. [a.] Hiedelberg, MS.

BERMAN, SPRING MELODY
[b.] May 5, 1983, Morristown, NJ; [p.] Zoe and Jay Berman; [ed.] Heritage Middle School; [occ.] Student.

BERNDT, TAMMY
[b.] April 24, 1979, Kamloops, BC; [p.] Bernie and Yvonne Berndt; [pers.] My poem was written in loving memory of Michel (Mike) Robert Comte, October 6, 1979 -May 29, 1994. [a.] Kamloops, BC Canada.

BERNICKY, REBECCA LUISE
[pen.] Rebecca L. Bernicky; [b.] April; 29, 1975, Smith Falls, Ontario; [p.] Larry and Heidi Bernicky; [m.] Engaged to Jamie Hummel, summer of 1996; [ed.] High school; [occ.] Trying to be a writer; [oth.writ.] Several poems and short mystery stories, currently starting a novel, never been published; [pers.] I want my poems and stories to really touch people. One day I hope to be a real writer and have my work be known to the world. [a.] Brockville, Ontario.

BERNSTEIN, JENNIFER A.
[pen.] Jeanne Dossert; [b.] August 15, 1974, Syracuse; [p.] Dr. Arthur and Nancy; [ed.] Fayetteville, Manlius High School, SUNY Potsdam; [occ.] Student; [oth.writ.] None published so far; [pers.] Throughout my life I've found writing to be the truest and most effective way to express myself. A pen and paper are more powerful than anything, for with them you can create your own world. "I write, therefor I am". [a.] Manlius, NY.

BETLOW, ANN MARIE L.
[b.] October 2, Morristown, NJ; [p.] Leo and Olga Betlow; [occ.] Technology; [pers.] My writing has been greatly inspired by my mother. I am currently putting together my very own poetry book. Set forth with dignity and stay true to your dreams. [a.] Landing, NJ.

BIANCHI, MARIA A.
[pen.] (Nickname) Runt; [b.] August 16, 1980, Baltimore, MD; [p.] Johanna Bianchi; [ed.] Poly High School in 9th grade now, Canton Middle and Highlandtown Elementary # 215; [memb.] I am a member of Pompei Church and other community groups; [hon.] Have got writing awards through the years of school; [oth.writ.] I write poetry for fun, about what I see or to express my feelings; [pers.] This poem is dedicated to my loving father, Bruno Bianchi who passed away when I was only four. I also want to thank my loving family and friends. [a.] Baltimore, MD.

BIBLE, BETTY
[b.] February 16, 1954, Gettysburg, PA; [p.] Gayetta Bible and Worth H. Bible (deceased); [ed.] Graduate of New Oxford High; [occ.] Factory worker for Hanover Direct; [pers.] The poem "I Was Blue" is the truth, it says what I feel. [a.] New Oxford, PA.

BICE, MELISSA
[b.] July 24, 1978, Cherwynd, BC; [p.] Michele Ternent; [ed.] Chetwynd Secondary School, currently in grade 11; [occ.] I work at the Chetwynd Vet Clinic; [oth.writ.] I have written other poems but none have been read, they are poems that I write when I am in the mood to write; [pers.] I am 16 years old. I enjoy writing and horseback riding, I have won several trophies in riding. [a.] Chetwynd, BC Canada.

BICKTA, BRENDA L.
[b.] April 27, 1957, Reading, PA; [p.] Syd and Ardell Hirshland; [m.] Barry L. Bickta; [ch.] David Charles Bickta; [ed.] Wilson High School; [pers.] My poems have always been a result of personal experiences. I believe you should never give up on your dreams. Please teach your children well, they are our future. [a.] Leesport, PA.

BIEN-AIME, ALIX A.
[pen.] Antoine Day; [b.] January 14, Brooklyn, NY; [p.] Marlene Day; [ed.] South Shore High School, Auburn University; [occ.] Student, Computer Tech; [pers.] My writings are from the heart, trying to capture the elements and the passions of the soul. Inspired by the people in my life as well as the elements of my mothers, natural and earth.[a.] Brooklyn, NY.

BINKLEY, GINA MARIE
[b.] February 11, 1972, Inglewood, CA; [p.] George R. and Debbie M. Brinkley; [ed.] Newbury Park High School, currently enrolled at Cuesta College and will transfer to Cal Poly, San Luis Obispo; [occ.] Self-employed student; [hon.] Miscellaneous photography awards; [oth.writ.] Several poems and short writings published in a local literary magazine called Neopolition; [pers.] I dream that through my writing I can bring hope to people, for I feel that there is an overwhelming lack of hope in the world. [a.] Morro Bay, CA.

BIRCHFIELD, ANGELA
[pen.] Angela Birchfield; [b.] June 1, 1982, Christ Hospital; [p.] Ray and Elizabeth Birchfield; [ed.] Went to Winfield Elementary School for preschool through 1st grade, went to Roy DeShane for 2nd through 4th and now in Stratford Junior High 7th grade; [hon.] 1st place Reflections, 3rd place best dressed dog award for my dalmatian, accepted in Glen Ellen children's choir, an Honor Roll student, played in school "Wheel of Wisdom" game show; [pers.] Anything that can help you solve a problem is the map, the key to the lock of confusion.

BIRCHFIELD, PAMELA
[pen.] Pamela Birchfield; [b.] June 1, 1982, Oaklawn, IL; [p.] Ray and Elizabeth Birchfield; [ed.] Grades-pre-school 1st (Winfield Elementary) grades 2-4 (Roy DeShane), grades 5-6 (Jay Stream) grade 7, Stratford Junior High; [hon.] 1st place for Young Author's contest (grade 3), 1st place Reflections, on 7th grade volleyball team, accepted into Glen Ellen children's choir, an Honor Student; [oth.writ.] None are published, "Chucky To The Rescue", "The Dalmatian With No Spots", "The Hearts Who Were Never Loved"; [pers.] You must have friends who love you to stay alive. [a.] Winfield, IL.

BIRCZ, RORY (MRS.)
[b.] June 14, Freeport, NY; [ed.] B.S.C.I.S., DeVry Institute of Technology, Columbus, Ohio; [occ.] Writer; [memb.] The Dramatist Guild Inc., National Association for Female Executives (NAFE), Data Processing Management Association (DPMA); [hon.] DPMA Service Award, 7th place Writer's Digest annual stage play script contest-1994, Technical paper presented at the Project Management Institute's 1993 Seminar/Symposium; [oth.writ.] Articles, PMNET work magazine, Training and Development magazine, PMI Journal, poems; "The Best of Feelings 1993" and "The Best of Feelings 1994" poetry anthology books; [pers.] If you believe in your dreams and who you want to be eventually, fate will lead you down the path that you're destined to be on. [a.] West Chester, PA.

BISCHOFF, DEBORA
[b.] October 10, 1960; [oth.writ.] "Mother's Love" and "Forever Seeking" also published by National Library of Poetry, plus 3 songs.

BISHOP, JAMES E.
[b.] December 5, 1959, Barracksville, WV; [p.] Paul and Catherine Bishop; [ed.] N. Ridgeville High School; [occ.] CNC Mill operator, Ridge Tool Company, Elyria, Ohio; [oth.writ.] One as of yet unpublished book of poems; [pers.] My poetry is a reflection of my thoughts and feelings on life. [a.] Elyria, OH.

BITTERMAN, MARGARET CARROLL
[b.] November 23, 1941, Alma, MI; [p.] Floyd and Melissa Woodrow; [m.] John Bitterman, March 21, 1992; [ch.] Dwane, Victor, Janine and Marion; [ed.] Almay High, Alma Michigan; [occ.] Waitress, cook; [memb.] A.A.R.P. [a.] Bannister, MI.

BJORNN, SANDRA M.
[b.] October 5, 1968, Boise, ID; [p.] James and Teresa Peterson; [m.] Gordon, October 18, 1991; [ch.] Jerimiah and Denise; [ed.] Boise High School, Boise State University; [occ.] PFC US Army; [hon.] National Honor Society, Boise High School; [pers.] Everybody can create their own reality and this is mine. [a.] Ft. Ord, CA.

BLACK, DOROTHY G.
[pen.] Dorothy G. Black; [b.] August 27, 1904, Beaver Falls, PA; [p.] Frances and Thomas Carroll; [m.] Donald Black (deceased), first marriage to Frank Longsenkamp November 16, 1929, second marriage to Don Black September 23, 1972; [ch.] Frank Longsenkamp Jr.; [ed.] 4 years Butler University, majored in Journalism, taught at St Monica's School 1 year, sold real estate for 30 years in Indianapolis, retired 1982; [occ.] Retired; [memb.] Former member of Indianapolis Athletic Club moved to columbus four years ago, member of St. Andrews Catholic Church in Columbus member of Pi Beta Phi, Social Theta Sigma Phi-Journalist; [hon.] First girl editor of Butler newspaper, in several plays at Butler and at Civic Theater in Indianapolis; [oth.writ.] Mostly poems.

BLADES, CARA MONICA
[b.] February 23, 1970, Boston, MA; [p.] Dr. Brandon and Mrs. Elizabeth; [ed.] Yes; [occ.] Dental Assistant; [memb.] Women's Information Exchange; [oth.writ.] "The Landscape of Things", "The Battle of Newcastle", "Carpe Diem is Killing Her"; [pers.] I am human, hear me er. [a.] Teaneck, NJ.

BLAKE, JAMES R.
[b.] June 26, 1952, Spangler, PA; [p.] Quentin and Lydia (Santucci) Blake; [m.] Lisa Williams Blake, September 12,1987; [ch.] Anthony (6 years) and Matthew (14 months); [ed.] Elementary and secondary education was at Cambria Heights School District, my college education was 2 years at Penn State University and my final 2 years was at Saint Francis College, BA degree in English Education; [occ.] Substitute English teacher; [memb.] Veterans of Foreign Wars, American Legion, Patton volunteer Fire Company, Patton, PA; [oth.writ.] "Blue Skies of Autumn". [a.] Patton, PA.

BLESSINGER, GREGORY A.
[b.] October 29, 1950, Jasper Memorial Hospital; [p.] Roman and Sigrid Blessinger; [m.] Linda Blessinger, April 25, 1970; [ch.] Craig and Chad; [ed.] 12 years; [occ.] Disabled; [memb.] Jasper Jaycees, Arthritis Foundation, Knights of Columbus Council # 1584, Loyal Order of Moose, Jasper Outdoor Recreation, Sons of American Legion; [hon.] Jaycee of the Month, Jaycee of the Year, also awarded a Jaycee Scholarship; [oth.writ.] "Confusion" "Our Love For Each Other"; [pers.] The greatest joy in the world is to love and to be loved.

BLODGETT, REBECCA
[b.] March 31, 1963, Pert Amboy, NJ; [p.] Theodore K. Blodgett and Myrna Grohosky; [m.] Stephen Prokopiak, May 28, 1994; [ch.] Steven Dane Prokopiak; [ed.] Pert Amboy High School, Kean College, School of Data Programming; [occ.] Counselor, The ARC (Association for the Retarded Citizens); [hon.] The ARC, the first employee in the Ocean County Chapter to be named and honored for service to the ARC; [pers.] I write in honor of my 8 year old son, who has shown goodness, caring and love in his heart for all of his life. If we as parents bring up our children in this way, then yes one day the world will have peace. [a.] Bricktown, NJ.

BODE, BROOKE
[b.] March 20, 1980, Nebraska; [p.] Chuch and Kittie Lou Bode; [ed.] Freshman in the high school will continue on to be an Orthopedic Surgeon, high school Millard North High; [hon.] Scholar achievements and track sprinter; [oth.writ.] Written many poems and stories, none of these have been published; [pers.] Always be willing to try something new, you never know what it could lead to. Let your

heart and mind take you to your dreams and beyond. [a.] Omaha, NE.

BOE, LONNIE R.
[pen.] L.R. Boe; [b.] October 13,1970, Washington; [p.] Gary and Cheryl Boe; [ed.] Irving High; [occ.] Cook; [oth.writ.] Another poem "With My Eyes Behind Me" published in another anthology; [pers.] I write what I feel whether it be anger, sadness or love. I think it's important for putting true emotion in my work. [a.] Cashmere, WA.

BOGAN, DIANA
[b.] July 12, 1974, Bandung, Indonesia; [p.] David E. and Diane Bogan; [ed.] Drexel University; [occ.] Student; Sophomore at Drexel; [memb.] International Thespian Society, Gamma Sigma Sigma National Service Sorority, Drexel Concert Band; [hon.] Merit Award in Drexel's 1994 Freshman Writing Contest; [oth. writ.] Poems published in various school literary magazines; news articles for the Drexel paper the Triangle; [pers.] Strive for your dream and let the journey enrich you. I will always be grateful for my parent's endless encouragement in seeking my own dreams.; [a.] Philadelphia, PA

BOHNERT, GREG
[pen.] The Bone; [b.] December 20, 1969, Linton, IN; [m.] Single; [ed.] Indiana State University, Business Administration, Linton-Stockton High School; [occ.] Owner/salesman, Bone Sports; [hon.] Mouster's degree, Walt Disney World, college program Fall 1993; [oth.writ.] Songs based on my short poems and life experiences, daily life journal; [pers.] Greatest influences in my life are mom, dad and Anthony Robbins. My goal in life is being successfully happy. Favorite writer is S.E. Hinton. [a.] Linton, IN.

BOHRINGER, TAMANA L.
[pen.] Tam, Boo-Boo, Boh, Tiger; [b.] December 27, 1965, Illinois; [p.] Don and Kathy Bohringer; [m.] Divorced, August 26, 1986-September 1989; [ed.] High school, Downers Grove South, 1984 graduated, also attended classes at Triton College (computers); [occ.] Supervisor of laundry/assistant housekeeping at Colonial Manor Health Care Center; [memb.] Greenpeace, World Wildlife, Gun Club Target Shooting/Range; [hon.] Army Accommodation Medal, highest s. commr. physical fitness test U.S. Army, expert shooter; [oth.writ.] I have written other poems, this is the first to be published; [pers.] I write poems based on my own life experiences. [a.] Westmont, IL.

BOLENE, LINDA RAE
[b.] May 7, 1948, Danville, IL; [p.] J. Madelyn and John W. Yaeger; [m.] V. Martin Bolene, September 23, 1973; [ed.] Danville High School, University of Illinois; [occ.] Sales; [memb.] Phi Upsilon Omicron, Little Sister Alpha Rho Chi; [hon.] Honor Society, Dean's List; [oth.writ.] 2 poems; [pers.] I give my never ending love and thankfulness to my husband and family for their continued love, support and influence all of my life. [a.] Anaheim, CA.

BOLES, KRISTIN
[pen.] Kristin Boles; [b.] August 29, 1984, Riverside, CA; [p.] Bill and Genne Boles; [ed.] Telluride Elementary School; [occ.] Fifth grade student; [memb.] I am in WWF; [hon.] Kenpo Karate, orange belt; [oth.writ.] Story once published in newspaper; [pers.] I am only ten and am already inspiring myself to creative writing. [a.] Telluride, CO.

BOLKCOM, TELVA D.
[pen.] Telva D. Bolkcom; [m.] November 11, 1936, Missoula, MT; [p.] John and Laura Stone; [m.] Clarence L. Bolkcom, June 5, 1982; [ch.] Justin, Susan, Curtis and Linda Jackson, 4 stepchildren; [ed.] 2 years college at Spokane Community College, Spokane, Washington; [occ.] Housewife, poet and writer; [memb.] Southside Community Church and NRA; [hon.] 1989 Golden Poet, 1990 Silver Poet, 1990 Who's Who in Poetry, 1992 Golden Poet; [oth.writ.] 4 children books, 1 commercial assignment (Genealogy handbook); [pers.] I try to write about the Northwest and life as I see it. My greatest influence has been Ella Brooks Bolkcom, Paul Croy, Helen S. Rice and Edgar Guest. [a.] Athol, ID.

BOLOGNA, MARGRET POLACZYK
[b.] April 25, 1956, Nowy Targ, Poland; [m.] Vito Bologna, April 20, 1974; [ch.] Robert and Michael; [occ.] Writer and artist; [pers.] This poem was written in memory of my brother Edward Lawrence Polaczyk (1967-1988) on the sixt anniversary of his death. [a.] Casselberry, FL.

BOLON, LEIGH ANN
[b.] May 20, 1975, Salem, OH; [p.] Thomas and Linda Bolon; [ed.] Second year student The University of Akron, East Palestine City Schools K-12; [occ.] Student; [memb.] University of Akron marching and concert bands, Telcom Committee, Tuba-Euphonium Ensemble; [hon.] John Philip Sousa Honorary Bandsmen Award, five time solo and ensemble contest winner; [oth.writ.] "Senior Poem", "Jackass City", personal poems written to friends who meant a lot to me, my own personal thoughts and feelings, poem for friends' boyfriend, sold for $20.00; [pers.] My poetry comes from my heart. My inspirations come from the hard times and relationships I've had. My poems are one hundred percent from my experiences. [a.] East Palestine, OH.

BONDS, ADAM
[pen.] Even Greene; [b.] October 17, 1976, Clinton, KY; [p.] Rose and Fred Bonds (divorced); [ed.] High school dropout, G.E.D. received, studying to become an actor; [occ.] Stand up-comic; [memb.] Subscriber to different magazines, East Hickman Baptist Church; [hon.] Royal Patronage Award winner, poem published in this book; [oth.writ.] Movie scripts, books and several comic books and poems all unpublished, plus paintings; [pers.] My writing reflects who I am as a person, I just want to be a happy man, both in mind and spirit and to live in peace with everyone. [a.] Hickman, KY.

BONNETT, LOUISE
[b.] November 10, 1969, Manchester, England; [p.] Peter and Iris Bonnett; [m.] Richard Rampersaud as of May 1995; [ed.] State College Area High School, State College, PA., the University of Maryland, College Park, College of Journalism; [occ.] Account Executive; [memb.] Golden Key National Honor Society, Phi Kappa Phi Honor Society; [hon.] Kappa Tau Alpha Journalism Award; [oth.writ.] Short stories, nothing published. [a.] Silver Spring, MD.

BOODY, GEORGE FRANKLIN
[pen.] Ryan Allen Pierce; [b.] January 24, 1971, Jackson, MI; [p.] David Boody and Laura Riker; [ed.] Concord High School; [occ.] Resident in state correctional facility (H.M.T.U.); [oth.writ.] None, except personal poems not yet seen by society; [pers.] I want to thank my family and grandmother for the encouragement to keep on writing when the times had gotten hard in my life and the fact that the only criticism is good criticism. [a.] Ionia, MI.

BORDEN, CAROL
[b.] November 4, 1971; [p.] Calvin Borden and Sharon Rodriguez; m.] Single; [ch.] James Honaker Jr.; [ed.] South High School, MTI Business College; [occ.] Medical Assistant; [memb.] American Association of Medical Assistants; [pers.] My writings reflect the experiences encountered in life as well as the dreams that fill my heart and soul. [a.] Cleveland, OH.

BOROFF, BURTON H.
[b.] October 24, 1931, Minneapolis, MN; [p.] Beatrice J.K. and George A. Borofff; [ed.] B.S. Journalism and PR University of Maryland, MPA (Public Administration), American University, Washington, DC; [occ.] Teacher and Consultant in Human Resources; [memb.] mason and Ninai Brith; [hon.] Sigma Delta Chi, Journalism, Tau Kappa Alpa, Speech, Pi Sigma Alpha, Political Science; [oth.writ.] Poem "Baffling" National Poetry for Teachers and Libraries; [pers.] Mother's poetry was widely published in Mid-west anthologies and nationally. I have been influence by work of John Berryman and Robert Lowell and have been regarded as a moralist. [a.] Silver Spring, MD.

BOSWORTH, LISA
[b.] April 28, 1980, Baltimore, MD; [p.] Julia and David Bosworth; [ed.] Chesapeake Senior High School; [pers.] I'm usually depressed, so when I am , that's when I can write my feelings down. [a.] Pasadena, MD.

BOURGOIS, VAN T. (MRS.]
[pen.] Taylor Parker; [b.] April 17, 1958, Viet Nam; [p.] Robert and Cindy L. Fuller; [ch.] Dian Squire, Matthieu and Colin Bourgois; [ed.] Bloom Township High School, Western Illinois University; [occ.] Financial planner, the MONY Group, Orlando, FL; [memb.] American Cancer Society, outdoors and active, Track Shack Foundation, running 5k/10k races for various charity causes; [hon.] National Honor Society, Dean's List at Western Illinois University; [oth.writ.] Written 30 plus poems includes the one that's being published, editorial comments in Glamour; [pers.] I lived everyday to the fullest with my sons. I strive to reflect the love, the happiness, the pain I feel in my poems and my writings. [a.] Maitland, FL.

BOURNEA, ROBERT CHRISTOPHER
[pen.] R.C. Bournea; [b.] August 2, 1972, Columbus, OH; [p.] Rochelle Rensch and Fred Allen; [ed.] Currently pursuing a degree in communications from the Ohio State University; [occ.] Journalist at the Call and Post newspaper; [oth.writ.] Three previous published poems; [pers.] Writers write to discover the world and themselves. [a.] Columbus, OH.

BOUSEMA, CAROL
[pen.] S.B. Grace (Saved By Grace); [b.] September 16, 1938, Sheldon, IA; [p.] Gerritt and Anna Peters (deceased); [m.] Roy Bousema, February 27, 1959 (deceased); [ch.] Jerris, Dennis, David and Todd; [ed.] Western Christian High, Hull, IA; [occ.] Homemaker, part time sales clerk; [memb.] Christian Reformed Church, Iowa Right to Life Chapter, World Vision Sponsor; [oth.writ.] Poem published in church periodicals; [pers.] I strive to glorify God in my writing; [a.] Sheldon, IA.

BOWDITCH, BRADLEY
[b.] May 19, 1969, Defiance, OH; [p.] Darrell and Karen Bowditch;[m.] Beth Bowditch, October 30, 1993; [ed.] Woodlan High School, Indiana-Purdue University Fort Wayne; [occ.] College student; [pers.] I have been greatly influenced by H.P. Lovecraft. I feel that all people are born inherently good, but they all must deal with their "darkside".

Writing helps me to conquer and express my fears as well as the many joys that God has blessed me with. [a.] Fort Wayne, IN.

BOWEN, DIANA
[b.] March 18, 1979, Grantsville, WV; [p.] James Bennett and Tiny Bowen; [ed.] Romney Junior High and Hampshire (10th grade now, I want to go to Boston University); [occ.] Student at Hampshire High School; [oth.writ.] "Good Overcomes Bad", "Our Love" and "Endless Feelings" (not published); [pers.] I'd just like to thank my family and my best friend Dawn Crounse for being behind me in my work. I'd also like to thank Jonathan Knight and the rest of his group for my inspiration to write. Thanks for all your support. [a.] Slanesville, WV.

BOWERS, BECKY
[b.] December 16, 1975, Orange, CA; [p.] Michael and Elizabeth Bowers; [ed.] Sophomore at the University of Arizona, graduated from Marina High School in Huntington Beach, CA; [memb.] University of Arizona Gymnastics team, Gymnastics Hall of Fame for Arizona; [hon.] Graduated with honors from Marina High; [oth.writ.] Various other poems not published; [pers.] I believe one should remember and reflect on the past, reach for dreams in the future, but live each day by "carpe diem"! [a.] Tucson, AZ.

BOWERS, ORRIN
[pen.] Orrin Bowers; [b.] May 10, 1926, Kent, OH; [p.] Jess and Blanche Bowers; [m.] Divorced; [ch.] Scott, Robert and Michael; [ed.] Roosevelt High School, Kent State University, Northwestern University, MFA Program; [occ.] Retired; [memb.] American Academy of Poets, North Carolina Poetry Society; [hon.] Poems published in several newspapers, magazines and university publications; [oth.writ.] Chapbook, "Disappearances"; [pers.] In poems of this nature I strive to write of a precisely rendered moment; the thin membrane that separates the actual from the possible and to consider alternate destinies. [a.] Cary, NC.

BOWMAN, JOANNE M.
[pen.] Joanne M. Bowman; [b.] March 24, 1943, Monroe, MI; [p.] Eugene and Marie Bowman; [m.] Divorced from Keith J. Rother; [ch.] Karl A. Rother; [ed.] MBA-expected August 1995, University of North Florida, BA-June 1981, Metropolitan State University, Minneapolis-St. Paul, Minnesota; [occ.] Graduate student at UNF and graduate assistant for management department; [memb.] DAR-Daughters of American Revolution, Eastern Star, Jazz Board, Music Department at University of North Florida; [pers.] As a very sensitive person, I try to convey this in my writing in a positive and meaningful manner. [a.] Jacksonville, FL.

BOWSER JR., BARRINGTON H.
[b.] January 29, 1957, Richmond, VA; [p.] Dr. and Mrs. Barrington H. Bowser Sr.; [m.] Bonita L. Settle-Bowser MD. (deceased July 29, 1994), July 9, 1982; [ch.] William Settle Bowser, age 10; [ed.] MD Meharry Medical College 1982, BS Virginia Commonwealth University 1978; [occ.] Public Health Physician Richmond; [memb.] Medical Society of Virginia, Richmond Academy of Medicine, VA Public Health Association, Alpha Phi Alpha Fraternity, Inc.; oth.writ.] Co-author several medical journal articles and abstracts, I have resisted all prior attempts to have my poetry published since high school. [a.] Richmond, VA.

BOYES, AMANDA JO
[pen.] Joei; [b.] June 14, 1979, Ft. Wayne, IN; [p.] Michael and Dawn Boyes; [ed.] Sophomore at New Hanover High School, Wilmington, North Carolina; [occ.] Student; [hon.] Winner of 3 awards for my artwork; [oth.writ.] Two poems printed in school newspapers, 1 short story also published in school paper; [pers.] Be yourself, no matter what. Never let someone try to tell you how to be. You are you, that's how God intended it. [a.] Wilmington, NC.

BOYKIN, EDWINA DEBORAH
[b.] April 23, 1943, Hartselle, AL; [p.] James and Frances Sims; [m.] Glenys Boykin, February 15, 1963; [ch.] Eric, Lisa, Deborah, Cheryl and Kevin; [ed.] High school and various college computer courses; [occ.] System Administrator; [memb.] Federally Employed Women; [hon.] Certified Executive Secretary; [oth.writ.] A collection of poetry, slogans, organizational tributes; [pers.] I strive everyday of my life to get to know more about myself and how I can make a difference to mankind. [a.] Glen Burnie, MD.

BRADDOCK, PATRICIA
[pen.] Patricia Braddock; [b.] January 30, 1943, Pittsburg, KS; [p.] Ben and Rosetta Toenges; [m.] Ken Braddock, May 13, 1993; [occ.] Housewife; [hon.] Two healthy, happy grown children, five mischievously active grandchildren, a contented husband and a quiet peaceful home. [a.] Jackson, MS.

BRADFORD, DENA
[b.] July 1, 1965, Los Angeles, CA; [p.] Mildred Stringfellow and Ernest Cottrell; [m.] Divorced; [ch.] Crystal Marie, Christopher Wayne, Darrel Glen and Joshua Duke; [ed.] Mitchea Horean Elementary, Batavia High School, dropped out in 9th grade; [occ.] Owner, operator of Bradford's Animal Shelter, Reynolds, IN; [pers.] I grew up in a very abusive situation and writing became my escape. I love to write, it was my one true friend and got me through some very rough times. I always felt better after writing, when the world came down around me. I always had my pen and paper. My writing gave me courage and strength. It could also take me anyplace I wanted to be. I believe that without it I never would of survived. I've got well over 1000 poems I wrote since I was 11 years old. They are not all happy because life isn't always. When I write it comes from my heart. I'm honored to have my poem in your book, this poem was wrote due to a love gone bad. [a.] Monon, IN.

BRAGINSKY, CRAIG
[pen.] John "Jack" Redmond; [b.] May 14,1967, CT; [p.] Benjamin and Marilyn; [m.] Crisanta Q. Braginsky, May 5, 1993; [ed.] Self educated; [occ.] Owner-BMP Ltd., an entertainment corp/audio and film; [memb.] A.S.C.A.P., American Society of Composers and Publishers; [hon.] 1988 New York Festival of the Arts, "Best New Songwriter", billboard Certificate of Achievement Award for the song"Take Me Tonight"; [oth.writ.] "The Silver Lining" book with audio project, it features 23 of the world's most distinguished actor/stars reciting poetry to my musical score, Jeremy Irons, M. Caine etc., due to be released in 1995; [pers.] Has worked extensively in T.V. film for 12 years. All my friends are film stars, and wonderful people. There's no business like show business. [a.] New Haven, CT.

BRAITHWAITE, KENT
[b.] March 27, 1957, Fullerton, CA; [p.] Charles and Doeothy Braithwaite; [m.] Robin Jennifer, May 26, 1979; [ch.] Laura, Alexander and John; [ed.] B.A. Claremont McKenna College, M.A., Claremont Graduate School; [occ.] Lead teacher, Business Career Path Academy, Coachella Valley High School; [memb.] American Federation of Teachers, California Federation of Teachers, Coachella Valley Federation of Teachers, Living Desert Reserve, Claremont McKenna College Alumni Association and Third Millennium Literary Convocation; [hon.] "Teacher of the Year" 1989-selected by faculty, "Teacher of the Year" 1991-selected by graduating class, CUFT President 1989-1992; [oth.writ.] Over fifty publication credits including poetry and fiction which have appeared in Mabius, The Sonoma Mandala, The Poet's Voice, Red Herring Mystery magazine, Potpourri's Strictly Fiction, Sophomore Jinx, Renegade, Conflict of Interest, Oxalis among others; [pers.] Allow my life and my writings to speak for themselves. [a.] Palm Desert, CA.

BRANCH, JOYCE LYNN
[pen.] "Red"; [b.] September 16, 1955, New Orleans; [p.] Hazel and Joseph Branch Jr.; [m.] Single; [ch.] Three sons; [occ.] Disabled mother; [hon.] Award of Merit Certificate for poem "Smile"; [oth.writ.] Prestigious Golden Poet trophy for 1992 for poem "Smile" other poems are "New Orleans Own Frank Davis", "Money", "Smoking", "Terror on A Man-made Highrise"; [pers.] These poems were written because a wonderful lady that I'm very proud to call my mother she has inspired me in so many ways. "I Love You Mom"! [a.] New Orleans, LA.

BRANDT, PETER A.
[b.] April 27, 1957, Woodstock, Ontario; [p.] Gerd and May Brandt; [m.] Shelley Brandt, October 21, 1978; [ch.] Blake Alexander and Nathaniel Peter; [ed.] Norwell District High; [occ.] Aero Engine Technician with Canadian Armed Forces; [oth.writ.] This is my first poem since I was in school, I saw the ad for the contest and felt because of my interest in writing, I would give it a try; [pers.] With my military career near an end I began to reflect on my next career. Unfortunately I have been unable to fully understand what that is. I was beginning to become upset at my inability to find something I was interested in and this poem is of my inner feelings. [a.] Greenwood N.S., Canada.

BRANHAM, JENNIFER
[b.] July 1, 1981, Cleveland, OH; [p.] Ann Branham; [ed.] Franklin D. Roosevelt Junior High School, 8th grade; [occ.] Student at Franklin D. Roosevelt; [hon.] Honor Roll National Junior Honor Society; [oth.writ.] This is my first poem to be published in a book like this, I've had one other poem published but it was amateur publishing; [pers.] Writing poetry is a great talent to have. I am glad I've got that special talent. My sister Angelina is one of my influenced writers (she writes poems as well as I do). [a.] Cleveland, OH.

BRANHAM, VINCE A.
[pen.] Vince; [b.] January 3, 1985, Wichita Falls, TX; [p.] Doug and Phyllis Branham; [ed.] Currently in fourth grade; [occ.] Student; [memb.] First Baptist Church of Grandfield, OK, Royal Ambassadors, Grandfield Elementary's Gifted and Talented Program and 4-H; [hon.] National Honor Society, top 3% in Nation on Iowa Basic Skills test, Western Day King of 1993, class favorite and class president; [oth.writ.] One comic in my mom's newspaper that wasn't very funny because I accidentally wrote in the wrong words, but I've been planning to write a correction for it; [pers.] I would do anything to make good grades and to get a good job when I grow up. I would really like to be rich so I could give millions of dollars to the poor. If I were rich I would also strive to help all animals survive. [a.] Loveland, OK.

BRANN, MELODY
[b.] December 26, 1960, Augusta, ME; [p.] Donald and Frances Northup; [m.] Ronald Brann, September 22, 1979; [ch.] Nicole, Jesse and Ashley; [ed.] Lincoln Academy, Newcastle, ME; [occ.] Substitute teacher, Erskune Academy, Chuna, ME; [memb.] Bee Club, Chuna, ME.; [hon.] National Honor Society; [oth.writ.] Poems published in the Lincoln Academy newspaper; [pers.] I write mostly of personal experiences which have made a difference in my life. [a.] Windsor, ME.

BRANTLEY, JESSICA
[b.] August 15, 1981, Silver Springs, MD; [p.] David Brantley and Unchalee Krurgawath; [occ.] 8th grade student at the New International School of Thailand (NIST); [memb.] Student Council, yearbook committee, "Think Green" Environmental Club; [hon.] Best overall effort in year 8 (grade 7) 1993-94, best over all achievement award in year 8 (grade 7) in English 1993-94. [a.] Bangkok, Thailand.

BREWER, ARLETHA
[[pen.] Michaelah Whitmore; [b.] March 16, 1975, Lansing, MI; [p.] Virdia Brewer and George Wilson; [ed.] Eastern High School, Eastern Michigan University, Lansing Community College; [occ.] Library Aide, Lansing Community College, Lansing, MI; [hon.] Who's Who Among American High School Students (1991-92, 1992-93); [pers.] Writing poetry allows me to express what I feel when I'm momentarily afraid to approach a person or situation. It is therapy. I have been influenced by the life and work of Ms. Maya Angelou. [a.] Lansing, MI.

BRICKLE, GERRI
[pen.] Raygem; [b.] June 18, 1950; [m.] Raymond Brickle, May 1966; [ch.] 4 children and 5 grandchildren; [ed.] Pierce Junior College and Community College of Philadelphia; [occ.] Admissions clerk at Children's Hospital of Philadelphia; [memb.] Parent and Teacher Association, American Heart Association, Fox Chase Cancer Center, Veterans Association and Moonstone's Publishing Pen Inc.; [hon.] Employee of the Month at Children's Hospital, an accommodation citation for invaluable service during the blizzard of 1993 by Bryn Mawr Hospital; [oth.writ.] Poetry published by Vantage Press, 1985-New Voices volume 1, 1990-New Voices volume 2; [pers.] I dedicate this poem to the parents of # 4 young man who mysteriously drowned in the Schulkyll River. I hope their parents, family, friends and classmates find strength and comfort in these words. In addition, I would like to thank Gloria Delmar for her tireless support and encouragement. Both the workshops and conferences serve to enhance and develop my writing skills. Through her unwavering confidence she has taught me to continue striving and achieving.

BRINCK, INGER
[b.] November 20, 1975, Tucson, Az; [p.] Fritz and Norine Brinck; [pers.] What such pleasure speaks of pain thicker than the thickest fog? Not to see an inch ahead or feel an ounce of hope. Fear not, not alone we stand bare before our majesty of love once swallowed in the abyss of despair. Beneficiary of support, I return with thanks from the source of my words unspoken-to Janet Lever, Ph.D. and Antonia Ludwig, MFCC. [a.] King George, VA.

BRIXIE, ANGELA
[b.] August 11, 1977, Lorian, OH; p.] Steve and Tina Brixie; [ed.] Vermilion High School the tenth grade (still in school); [occ.] Full time student; [memb.] The International Thespian Society, speech and debate; [hon.] Thespian Award; [oth.writ.] 25 untitled poems; [pers.] My poems are written about my life around me, friends, family, etc. To me my life is a black hole and my poems help me get out. [a.] Vermilion, OH.

BRKIC, NEDA
[pen.] Agrippina; [b.] January 6, 1944, Italy; [p.] Ted Brkic and Ivana Moscovic; [m.] Leonardo Serrano (poet), January 15, 1994; [ch.] 4 (previous marriage); [ed.] Graduated from high school 1962, (P.K. Yonge Laboratory School), Gainesville, Florida, diploma in Communications Universidad Diego Portales, Santiago, Chile; [occ.] Secretary of General Manager, Castrol Chile S.A.; [memb.] Chilean Writers' Society (Sociedad de Escritoires de Chile), member of the Cultural Commission; [hon.] Jury (judge) at local poetry contest in honour of Nicanor Parra, a Chilean poet eligible for nobel prize; [oth.writ.] Poems published in local literary magazines and newspapers, a short story in an anthology of women writers, "Machismo se Escribe Con M de Mama"; [pers.] Uprooting, margination moves me, I strive to unveil meaning and purpose in its suffering and construct, create from there on. I have been influenced by Albert Camus, C. Dickens, Pablpo Neruda, I enjoy greatly Robert Frost, T.S. Eliot and the English romantics. [a.] Santiago, Chile.

BROADIE, OLA MAE (EVANS)
[pen.] Lil Princess; [b.] May 21, 1931, Raleigh, NC; [p.] Robert and Ronnie Mae Evans; [m.] Harvey W. Broadie Jr., March 25, 1952; [ch.] Bryan A. and Derrick (Ricky) Broadie; [ed.] Washington High, Raleigh, North Carolina, Shaws University, Bowie State, Morgan State University; [occ.] Retired supervisory Secretary, D.C.P.S.S., Business Woman Limousine Service, advisor JACS; [memb.] Chairman Global Mission Women Department Eastern Region Progressive National Baptist Conv., Deaconess Board First Baptist Church Highland Park, Maryland, Eastern Star, Queen Esther Chapter I, Washington, DC; [hon.] Service United Community Against Poverty, service-National Alumni Association, Washington High School, Cub Scout Troop # 1003, Carsondale, MD., letters appreciation, Mr. John White (farmer) chairman, Democratic National Committee, Mr. Bob Neuman Democratic National Committee, Congressman Steny H. Hoyer, Mayor Marion S. Berry, D.C. Outstanding Ser. Supt. D.C. schools; [oth.writ.] "The Bells of Bill Clinton" song original choral arrangement, sheet music and tape; [pers.] Uncover life meaning, see God's people in a beautiful world. See the good images of life thru love, joy, hope and happiness. The strength and courage of man works showing goodness of life. We gain thru serving, caring and sharing. Combating negative thoughts, images and deeds. Calmness, patience and determination brings trails of accomplishments. [a.] Lanham, MD.

BROCK, DENNIS
[b.] January 8, 1958, Harlan, KY; [p.] Bobby Ray and Eythelk Louise Brock; [m.] Teresa Lynn Brock, February 18, 1984; [ch.] Dennis, Jared, Franchesca, Daniell and Gregory Brock; [ed.] Wilbur Wright High; [occ.] Self employed, interior, exterior painting; [memb.] Boy's Club, as a child; [hon.] Camper of the Year, on the Ohio Buckeye trails, my mother, the day I met my wife, and my children; [oth.writ.] I have always been encouraged by a good friend to stay strong and to continue on, Mr. Edward J. Schaaf, a friend til the end; [pers.] The words I put on paper are gifts from heaven. These gifts I share with you! Only my wife, do I keep to myself. [a.] Burgin, KY.

BROKSTAD, STEPHANIE
[b.] August 29, 1977, Muskegon, MI; [p.] Cindy and Chuck Brokstad; [ed.] Mona Shores High School; [occ.] Student; [memb.] Mona Shores Acapella choir; [hon.] Honor Roll Student; [oth.writ.] Other poems not published; [pers.] Understanding one's art is understanding one's soul. [a.] Muskegon, MI.

BROPHY, TIMOTHY
[pen.] Garrett Jax; [b.] September 4, 1975, Baltimore, MD; [p.] Robert and Virginia Brophy; [ed.] Harford Christian High School, Harford Community College; [oth.writ.] Unpublished poems; [pers.] Love and trust have trite meanings today. I just look into my soul for their source and revel in them. [a.] Jarrettsville, MD.

BROWN-MAYO, ANEISE
[pen.] Anne Niesel B-Mayo; [b.] March 8, 1941, South Carolina; [p.] Ruley and Gertrude Brown; [m.] Milton A. Mayo Sr., November 19, 1961; [ch.] Timothy Alan, Donna Maria, Milton Jr. and Renee' Aneise; [ed.] Lincoln High, 6 months of business school, beauty school; [occ.] Housewife (retired); [memb.] American Museum of Natural History, Leonard Bernstein Society; [hon.] American Legion, Charmett, Profiles of Courage, Salutorian, Biology, Superior Accomplishment, letter of commendation from school, Honor Roll; [oth.writ.] Poems published in school newsletter, special poems by request, Mother's Day, Father's Day, obituaries, programs, etc.; [pers.] I try to reach the elderly, young children with simple poems while conveying a message of reality, understanding, hope and serenity to all who read my poems. [a.] Kew Gardens, NY.

BROWN-RICHARDSON, DEBORAH
[pen.] Niashia; [b.] October 20, 1962, Durham, NC; [p.] Frank and Elma Brown; [m.] Shawn A. Richardson, February 14, 1992; [ch.] Safhaan Brown and Ashanti Richardson; [ed.] Graduated from Brooklyn Technical High School, attended Megars Evers College for 1 year; [occ.] Security agent working for New York Transit Authority Police; [memb.] Oxford Club and High Landers Club; [hon.] Awards for playing the game of chess; [oth.writ.] Several poems unpublished; [pers.] I was once told "go with your passions the money will follow", so I love to write poetry because it gives me "passion". I'm inspired to write about love and other positive things because my husband and children believe in me. [a.] Brooklyn, NY.

BROWN, JOHN L.
[pen.] April 29, 1914, Ilion, NY; [p.] Leslie Beecher and Katherine L. Brown; [m.] Simonne L'Evesque Brown, August 25, 1941; [ch.] Michel S. and John H. Brown; [ed.] Hamilton College, A.B. Ecole des Chartes (Paris), University of Paris, (Docteur de l'universite) Catholic University of America (Ph.D.); [occ.] Consulting editor, lecturer, visiting professor, reviewer, writer and poet; [memb.] Phi Beta Kappa, Pen Club, Association International Critiques Litte-aires (former Vice President), Cosmos Club (Washington), Cercle Interallie (Paris), Chevaliers du Tastevin, Catholic Commission on Intellectual and Cultural Affairs; [hon.] Grand Prix de la Critique (Paris), Doctor honoris causa, Universidad de Queretaro (mexico), President Fulbright Commissions in Brussels and Paris, Corresponding member, Royal Belgian Academy; [oth.writ.] My Panorama de la litterature contemporaine aux Ee-UU (written directly in French), was awarded the Grand Prix de la Critique the first time that this prize was given to a non-Frenchman; [pers.] A romantic anarchist and marginal man. [a.] Washington, DC.

BROWN, MARGARET
[pen.] Little Head; [b.] November 27, 1944, Dillon, SC; [p.] John and Evelyn McClellan; [m.] Bernard Brown, September 20, 1962; [ch.] Lisa Tirena Brown; [ed.] James City E. School, J.T. Barbara Junior High; [occ.] Britthaven Nursing Home N.B., housekeeping; [memb.] St. Matthew's Church of Christ, Disciples of Christ Usher Board; [hon.] Britthaven Nursing Home N.B. 55 years service; [oth.writ.] Many poems written for church groups; [pers.] I enjoy reading and became inspired to write. It give me a feeling of confidence. [a.] New Bern, NC.

BROWN, TANYA
[b.] May 8, 1979, Springfield, MN; [p.] Steve and Julie Brown; [ed.] I attend Minnesota Valley Lutheran High School in New Ulm, MN., I plan to attend a college and major in Child Psychology; [oth.writ.] I pretty much write for fun, never had any of them published; [pers.] Smile, and always turn to God for help because He helps us through it all. [a.] Sleepy Eye, MN.

BROWNE, FRANCIS (WM)
[b.] December 26, 1935, Pittsburgh, PA; [p.] Deceased; [m.] Ellouise Foy Browne, October 31, 1986; [ch.] 7; [ed.] BA-1969, MA- all Long Island University, Brooklyn, NY, Ph.D.-graduate Ctr (CUNY) New York, New York 1979; [occ.] Associate Prof., English, Brooklyn College; [memb.] Association for the study of African American Life and History (ASAALH); [oth.writ.] House of Dips-Doodle, two kinds of course, Frederick Douglass and John Brown, a look at their relationship (critique) "When I Was A Boy" and other poem of memory , fun and respect (poems), articles in journals. Dictionary of American Bio, The Gissing newsletter, The American Book Review and fiction international; [pers.] Art is both hope and opportunity. [a.] Long Eddy, NY.

BRUCE, MARCIA T.
[b.] March 3, 1939, Lansing, MI; [p.] Maxine and Joseph Thomas; [ch.] Lisa Marie and Wendy; [ed.] BS, University of Maryland, College Park; [occ.] Real Estate Broker; [pers.] Bravo for word processors! Thoughts often swish through so rapidly I am unable to remember them in longhand. Most of what I write comes from personal experiences. This poem was written for my daughters when they were each at a crossroad in their lives. [a.] Irvine, CA.

BRUMMEL, JENNIEVE
[b.] December 13, 1979, Georgetown, Guyana; [p.]Lloyd and Lynette Brummel; [ed.] Beach Channel High School; [occ.] Student; [oth.writ.] I've written several other poems but they've never been published because I like to keep my writing to myself; [pers.] I attend Beach Channel High School. I am in the 10th grade, I plan on being a lawyer. I write poems when I feel depressed and I just write what I feel or what I want to feel. [a.] Far Rockaway, NY.

BUCHANAN, JUDITH ANN
[pen.] Jaz; [b.] May 7, 1945, Wilmington; [p.] Deceased; [m.] Divorced, remarried March 17, 1995; [ch.] Cheryl, Linda and Sharon, step-children, Joe, Josh and Jonathan; [ed.] Del-tech Community College, Ins. sales; [occ.] Hostess, cashier; [memb.] St. Anthony's choir; [hon.] Editor's Choice Award-1994, "Last Drink"; [oth.writ.] Written over 300 poems in 1 year, have had 3 published Delaware State Hospital Forum, Veterans of WWII Review, SADD and MADD American Cancer Society; [pers.] My poems are written on a day to day basis. As I perceive life, both in a good and positive fashion. [a.] Wilmington, DE.

BUFFORD, BEN F.
[b.] August 19, 1922, Jamestown, AR; [p.] Walter and Henrietta Manuel Bufford; [m.] Winnie Mildred Bell Bufford, December 28, 1947; [ch.] Christopher, Lex, and Blake, one grandchild, Emilie Rebecca; [ed.] BSE, Arkansas State University, MA (2) Memphis State University; [occ.] Retired high school teacher; [memb.] Sierra club, National Wildlife Federation, Masonic Lodge, SPCA, Fresno Alliance for the Mentally Ill (FAMI), California Retired Teachers Assocation, CRTA, AARP, CDCC; [oth.writ.] Poems, short stories, four novels; [pers.] "All things are relevant". After 35 years of public life, I treasure my privilege of being reclusive. English writers, especially the poets of the 19th Century influenced me greatly, but I love all writers with something important to say, particularly Whitman, Frost and Rod McKuen. [a.] Madera, CA.

BURGAN, JOANNA M.
[b.] December 31, 1954, Delano, CA; [p.] Jack T. and Martha R. Burgan; [ed.] AA Business, AA Avionics Technology, AA Instructor Technology; [occ.] Air Force Avionics Instructor, supervisor, 2nd job Emergency Medical Technician; [hon.] Numerous military commendations and service awards, honored for duty in Persian Gulf War; [pers.] I write for enjoyment and to reflect on family values and patriotic duty. [a.] Wichita Falls, TX.

BUKOVITZ, RICHELLE
[b.] July 6, 1978, Johnstown; [p.] Bryan and Cathi Pritt; [ed.] Windber Area High School, sophomore; [occ.] Student; [memb.] Art Club, Poetry Club, Scalp Level Church of the Brethren; [hon.] Editor's Choice Award; [oth.writ.] Poem entitled "Goodbye" published by National Library of Poetry, numerous unpublished short stories and poems; [pers.] I strive to make others lives happier by my poems and laughter. [a.] Windber, PA.

BULLARD, BRANDY
[pen.] Bee Bee; [b.] June 27, 1977, Marion, SC; [p.] Van and Terisa Tyndall and Robert and Vickie Bullard; [ed.] I am currently a senior in high school in Marion South Carolina; [occ.] Part time worker at Kids Konnection Day Care Center; [memb.] I am a member of the Zion Southern Methodist Children's League and have been for about eight years; [pers.] This poiem tells a story of my heart. It means a lot to me. [a.] Marion, SC.

BURBANO, MARK ANTHONIO
[pen.] Sir Valiant Mark Anthony Burbano; [b.] March 16, 1961, Ecaudor (S.A.); [p.] Alfredo and Sharon (Sanders) Burbano; [ed.] Florida High School, St. Petersburg Junior, U.S.F.; [occ.] Retired; [memb.] Life member D.A.V.; [hon.] Delta Theta Chi founder of United Federation of Earth - International Organization for college students, Hesperides - name of literary fraternity which I co-founded in Junior college; [oth. writ.] Several poems unpublished but treasured by family members; [pers.] I have been inspired by the early classical poets. I enjoy living life on the edge to the point of madness. [a.] Cupertino, CA.

BURKETT, BESSIE SHANNON
[pen.] Bessie Shannon; [b.] February 6. 1909, Mt. Erie, IL; [p.] Lewis and Mary Elizabeth Shannon; [m.] Walter Thomas Burkett, July 5, 1934; [ch.] Charles Robert Burkett; [ed.] Held lifetime certificate in K to high school II college at S.I.U, Carbondale, Il; [occ.] Taught 17 1/2 years, rural schools, subtaught afterwards until I was 70, retired school teacher, widow, housewife, live alone; [memb.] All Co. State organizations, national, of importance throughout teaching years; [hon.] None of importance except the joy I had in writing, that was my reason for writing; [oth.writ.] Have 5 books written comparable to Little House on Prairie, etc., but never had money to have edited, they are very interesting, publishers say; [pers.] I never wrote for money, I wrote for pleasure and have had it writing both prose and poetry. [a.] Fairfield, IL.

BURNS, JENNIFER M.
[pen.] Jennifer M. Burns; [b.] April 1, 1964, Lakewood, CA; [p.] Robert Lee Burns and Sylvia Burns; [ed.] High school, West Valley Occupational School of Cosmotolgy; [occ.] Hairdresser; [hon.] Cable documentary named "Lost and Found" on my life story, founder of Trajedies to Triumps a support group of all chronic illness; [oth.writ.] "Magic Carpet Ride" 1990 by American Poet Society; [pers.] I am a Cancer survivor, twenty (20) surgies, I just had another 2 days ago. I recovered from a stroke 4 years ago. I have learned to never give up, keet the faith, "If you think you can or if you think you can't you're right". [a.] Westwood, CA.

BURNS, JESSICA
[b.] November 9, 1979, Chicago, IL; [p.] Rosemarie and Andrew Burns; [ed.] Hinsdale Township High School, Central; [occ.] Student; [hon.] In the third grade, I won a gold medal for writing a true story about my dog; [pers.] I take pleasure in expressing my feelings through writing. [a.] Hinsdale, IL.

BURTON, LaSHONDA
[b.] December 23, 1973; [p.] Joyce Willis and Ernest Boose; [m.] Anthony Burton, July 6, 1992; [ed.] High school diploma; [pers.] I have a true love for poetry, it makes things seem so special and complete. [a.] W. Helena, AR.

BUSSE, RONALD A.
[b.] April 3, 1967; [p.] Ronald and Marylou Busse; [ed.] Massapequa High School, Associate degree in Business Adminsitration from Nassau Community College; [occ.] Assistant Underwriter for CNA Insurance Co.; [oth.writ.] Several poems and articles published in school newspapers and company newsletter, I have also written many songs, incorporating my poetry in the lyrics; [pers.] Just do it. What have you got to lose? [a.] Lindenhurst, NY.

BUSSE, LINDA L.
[b.] July 9, 1944, St. Lawrence Hosptial, Lansing, MI; [p.] Mr. and Mrs. Howard Joseph Martin; [m.] Richard James Busse, December 12, 1975; [ed.] High school graduate; [occ.] Housewife; [hon.] Certificates for Bible School, certificates for Wesley Crusader Choir, coloring contest 1953 to The Longlong Trailer, first place 1955 4-H, second and third place, youth talent exhibit; [oth.writ.] Wrote instructions to Tat A Peppermint Ring; [pers.] Strive to learn Cluny Tatting. [a.] Lansing, MI.

BUSSOLOTTA, EDLY
[b.] October 1, 1930, Norway; [p.] Emma and Sig Fredriksen; [m.] Anthony Gregor Bussolotta, January 14, 1961; [ch.] Ellen, Paul and David; [ed.] A.S. Business (1978), B.A. English Lit and Writing (1990), B.S. minor Psych, M.S. started 1993; [occ.] Secretary/Adm Assistant, Fairfield University; [memb.] Alpha Sigma Lambda, Delta Epsilon Sigma, Who's Who Among Students in American Unviersities and Colleges, Halsey Int. Scholarship Program; [hon.] From all of the 3 first above, Dean's List, Sacred Heart University Certificate of recognition for academic excellence, National Scholarship Honor Society, Sacred Heart University Certificate for academic recognition for completion of Adm. Assistant Program; [oth.writ.] Poetry and prose writings, with poetry

published for California Publisher, and some prose abroad, where I lived as a young girl and where I started writing in grammer school, non-fiction mostly; [pers.] I try to write from experiences in wartime Norway as well as writing for children and adolescents, based on the upbringing of my own children. I like my writings to be both educational and entertaining, sprinkled withh humor. [a.] Bridgeport, CT.

BUTLER, EMILIE JILL
[b.] February 14, 1975, Bremerton, WA; [p.] John and Moe Butler, Gary L. Butler; [ed.] Washington School for the Deaf, Gallaudet University, a sophomore; [occ.] Latin tutor at Gallaudet University; [memb.] Class of 1997, different committees; [hon.] America's Who's Who for the Dear 93, Dean's List; [pers.] There are times that I wished I had my mon, but wishing about it isn't going to do me any good. I would like to thank my familes, friends, my mom and God for their unconditional love and support. [a.] Kodiak, AK.

BYERLY, NORMAN J.
[pen.] N.J.B.; [b.] June 1, 1961, Brookville, PA; [p.] Thelma and John Byerly; [ch.] Michael John Byerly; [ed.] Dayton High School, Pittsburg Job Corps; [occ.] Part-time domestic; [hon.] Perfect attendance, unit of the month telecommunications for ability to wrik without supervision; [oth.writ.] I Reached Out To Touch You; [pers.] I have been greatly influenced by all the people in my life. [a.] Blairsville, PA.

CACCIATORE, JOHN
[b.] August 22, 1967, Malden, MA; [ed.] Lynnfield High, Merrimack College, North Andover, MA, Richmond College, London, UK.; [occ.] Senior Copywriter, Harv Johnson and Associates, Boston, MA., Freelance Writer, Advertising Consultant; [oth.writ.] Other poems include "X-Ray Eyes" (published), "Oak of Faith", "In The Cler", "Fly By Night Love", "The Blanket", "Dreamer's Ball", "Question in A Bottle (part I)", "Liquid Solution (part II)", "Lissome Is My Lily"; [pers.] "Morning Grace" is dedicated to those wonderful but elusive moments when all feels right in my life... when we feel as though we can overcome any obstacle with the utmost of ease and confidence. [a.] Lynnfield, MA.

CAGLE, ZELMA D.
[b.] September 30, 1963, Richmond Heights, OH;[p.] Walter A. and Myrtle V. Cagle; [ed.] High school graduate, trade school; [pers.] My poem is a true reflection of my life and reinforces within me that life holds no coincidences. [a.] Medina, OH.

CAHILL, JESSICA
[b.] November 13, 1981, Norristown, PA; [p.] Barbara Harvey and James Cahill; [ed.] Presently in eight grade, Pottsgrove Intermediate School, Pottstown, PA; [occ.] Student; [memb.] JV Field Hockey team; [hon.] Seventh grade perfect attendance award, seventh grade Honor Roll; [oth.writ.] I write on a regular basis; [pers.] People are more honest on paper. I express my feelings through my poetry. [a.] Pottstown, PA.

CAIN, JUANITA
[b.] January 29,1957, Ft. Thomas, KY; [p.] Donald and Loretta Fasse; [m.] Rick E. Cain, September 20, 1975; [ch.] Jason (age 15) and Ben (age 12); [ed.] Campbell County High; [occ.] Pre K Teacher, Kinder Academy, Alex., KY; [pers.] Most of my writings are of family and friends. I love children and also write many poems about them, and the things they do. [a.] California, KY.

CAINE, BRANDY
[b.] November 8, 1977, Barberton, OH; [p.] John and Janice Berenyi; [ed.] Junior at Northwest High School in Canal Fulton, Ohio; [occ.] Student; [oth.writ.] Northwest High newspaper, most personal and only shared with close friends; [pers.] All my writings come straight from my thoughts and feelings. I'd like to thank my Mom and Dad for being good parents and supporting me. I'd also like to thank my cousins Heather McRobie and James McFadden for the encouragement to send in a poem. And to the rest of my friends and family just for being them. Love you guys! [a.] Doylestown, OH.

CALANDRI; JANICE MAE WIENS
[b.] November 20,1926, Sterling, IL; [p.] Lepha Sherman and Clarence Humphrey; [m.] Ray Calandri, June 22, 1981; [ch.] Pamela Ann and Kevin Frances; [ed.] Sterling High and Blackhawk College, Sterling Beauty School and Anthony Real Estate School, Sterling Beauty School, Teachers Division; [occ.] Caretaker of my paraplegic husband, hit by a drunk driver; [memb.] St. John's Lutheran Church, United Methodist Church, Unity Church, graduated Magna Cum Laude from college, sing with Sweet Adelines International also church choir and choral group; [hon.] My honors and awards are just being able to put into words exactly what I want to say and hope the words help or make someone happy; [oth.writ.] I wrote and sent a poetry book to 130 school members of my class for our 50th class reunion 1994, I have since written poetry of my life, my newest poem addresses "ABUSE"; [pers.] I write about what I feel, includes all areas of life. I have a hilarious sense of humor, love to laugh. love my fellowman, to sing lustily, yes I love life. I have deep empathetic feelings about man's inhumanity to man. [a.] Byron, CA.

CALLIN, ELOISE N.
[b.] June 14,1920, Georgia (South); [p.] Thomas L. Edenfield and Olive E.; [m.] Glenn Thomas Callin, October 17, 1953; [ch.] James, Arthur, Thomas and David; [ed.] High school, St. Augustine, Florida, business school, Atlanta, Georgia, I've lived in Florida for 55 years; [occ.] Wife, homemaker and grandmother; [memb.] Greylady Red Cross, past president at elementary and middle school, Social Work, church, Downey Memorial Interdenominational, Association with C.M.A.; [oth.writ.] I've written many poems, I've never tried to get them published, although I've been encouraged by my family, I write when I'm inspired to do so, it does come from the heart; [pers.] I'm a grandmother with eight grandchildren. I would like to publish more poems if I have the opportunity. I have a least a dozen unpublished ones. [a.] Chuluota, FL.

CALON JR. RUPERTO V.
[pen.] Tambourine Man; [b.] February 4, 1969, Philippines; [p.] Ruperto and Ligaya Calon Sr.; [ed.] Associate of Arts in Computer Information Systems, Pasadena City College; [occ.] Computer operator, International Imaging, Azusa, CA; [pers.] I try to write the poetry I see in everyone to make us aware of the things going on within and around us. Because at times we are blind. We see not the beauty of life till we observe the ugliness of it. [a.] West Covina, CA.

CAMERON, KATHERINE ELIZABETH
[b.] November 3, 1973, Minnetonka, MN; [p.] Kathleen Flanagan and Douglas Cameron; [pers.] The publication of this poem is dedicated to my mother, an incredible artist and a very classy lady. I love and miss you "Mother Goose Harper". [a.] Ashford, CT.

CAMEROTA, SISTER ROSE MARIE
[b.] April 22, 1909, Province of Salerno, Italy; [p.] Biaggio and Theresa Camerota; [ed.] 8th grade, since my parents were poor immigrants, I was needed to help with the children at home, at 18 years I entered the Convent, continued my education on my own; [occ.] Retired, but continue to help and be of service in anyway I can; [memb.] None, however I have more or less been in leadership for many years in my religious order; [hon.] Have a diploma for interior decoration and design, the knowledge acquired in this field has been of much use in beautifying our Convent, and also in designing Vestment, banners, etc., for our chapel and churches, since we are a contemplate order we need to be self-supporting; [oth.writ.] None to speak of, a few times I wrote articles for our Province paper, "Women Still Make A Difference" published during Year of the Woman and a poem about the magic; [pers.] Hidden away for the most part in a cloister, I have none-the-less lived a fruitful and satisfying life. My love of people, especially close friends and family prompts me to pray for their spiritual welfare as well as for their temporal needs, now you too will be remembered. [a.] Springfield, MA.

CAMPBELL, BESSE M.
[pen.] Bessa McKaye; [b.] High Point, NC; [p.] Alonzo and Annabelle Mackey; [m.] Paul L. Campbell (deceased); [ch.] Paula Grett and Gloria Ward; [ed.] Associate in Science, B.S. in Mortuary Science and Business Economics; [occ.] Registered Cardiology Tech., and Licensed Mortician; [memb.] American Society of Cardiovascular Professionals, N.C. State Board of Morticians, International Society of Poets, American Association of Medical Assistants; [hon.] 5 Golden Poet Awards from World of Poetry, lifetime member of ISP, semifinalist x 2-ISP, recognition from Amir of Kuwait, and President Mubarak of Egypt; [oth. writ.] Books, Each Lasting Moment, Written in the Sand, contributor to "Sandscript" our hospital newspaper; [pers.] I call myself a poet of "feeling". I guess I deal with most types of emotions, love, world conditions, people problems and of course justice. It is my desire to "awake" people to what is happening. [a.] Fayetteville, NC.

CAMPBELL, BRIDGET
[b.] September 21, 1978, Oakville, Ontario; [p.] Michaelene and Al Campbell; [ed.] Grade eleven student at Georgetown District High School; [occ.] Full time student; [hon.] Honor student; [a.] Georgetown, Ontario Canada.

CAMPBELL, DANNY
[pen.] Maverick; [b.] March 30, 1975, Frankfurt, Germany; [p.] Roxanne and Danny Campbell; [ch.] Mathew Kenneth Lindsey; [ed.] Widefield High; [occ.] College part time, ironwork during day. [a.] Security, CO.

CAMPBELL, J.J.
[pen.] Wendy; [b.] January 21, 1976, Dayton, OH; [p.] Jim and Mary Ann Campbell; [ed.] Trohwood-Madison High School; [occ.] Dreamer, poet; [hon.] Graduated high school with honors; [oth.writ.] Poem published in Trohwood Madison High School fall program; [pers.] Influenced greatly by the Beatniks and anybody else who writes on pure emotion. I strive to write about being a teenager in today's world. [a.] Dayton, OH.

CAMPBELL, REGINA
[pen.] Skie-Gina; [b.] October 18, 1979, Weymouth; [p.] Julie and Frank Campbell; [ed.] Hull Junior Senior High School; [occ.] Student; [oth.writ.] More to come; [pers.] Life-"Life has a meaning" no one has found it yet. [a.] Hull, MA.

CAN, MARY
[b.] May 23, 1953, Massillon, OH; [p.] Edna and Ernest Hines; [ch.] Ebony (daughter), Vatese and Marcell Hines (nieces); [ed.] J.F. Kennedy High School, Sawyer's Business College; [occ.] Assembler at Ford Motor Company and launching toy company (Blackeye Peas and Cornbread -founder); [memb.] 9 to 5; [oth.writ.] Letter to the editor of local newspapers, other poems and short stories not yet published; [pers.] I bandaged life's hurts with my writing. I thank God for gifting me to do so. [a.] Cleveland, OH.

CANDELA, CAROL ANN
[b.] St. Louis, MO; [p.] Victor Pius and Thelma Coughlin; [m.] James Candela; [ch.] Michael Chandela; [ed.] Attended the University of Missouri at St. Louis, MO., musically educated by the Sisters of St. Joseph of Carondelet, MO.; [occ.] Private piano teacher; [oth.writ.] Various poems, family histories; [pers.] Thank you. [a.] Dale City, VA.

CANDLER, DWAYNE
[b.] March 21, 1968, Batesville, AR; [p.] Ernest and Edith Candler; [ed.] Midland High, two year course in freelance writing; [occ.] Baker; [oth.writ.] Over 200 poems and lyrics, several articles, most relating to music or Civil War History; [pers.] With no purpose in life, you struggle for achievements to fill the void. With a purpose, you struggle to simply be. Through constant being, you become. Having become is achievement. [a.] Judsonia, AR.

CANDLER, PAUL B.
[b.] June 25, 1961, Vineland, NJ; [p.] Bruce and Betty Candler; [m.] Charlene Candler, December 12,1981; [ch.] Emily Charlene and Matthew Champion; [ed.] Lander Valley High School, Cumberland County College; [occ.] Programmer/analyst; [oth.writ.] Several poems as yet unpublished; [pers.] I strive to honor God and bring glory to His name with my poetry. [a.] Newfield, NJ.

CARD, LISA
[pen.] Weize; [b.] December 15, 1973, Huntsville; [p.] Glen and Karen; [m.] Phil Quilter, common law; [ch.] Cole David Quilter; [ed.] Grade eleven; [occ.] Waitress. [a.] Huntsville, Ontario.

CARDINALE, VINCENT G.
[b.] February 21, 1921, Boston, MA; [p.] Ottone and Rosina Cardinale; [m.] Clarie Chaput, July 5, 1953; [ch.] Nicholas; [ed.] Suffolk University, Boston College; [occ.] Retired-former school teacher; [oth.writ.] Short stories, Mystery of the Black Stamp, a novel for young teens, Professional Reader Stint, April 1988, Military Intelligence magazine; [pers.] The aim of art is to represent not the outward appearance of things, but their inward significance... Aristotle. [a.] Belmont, MA.

CARDONA, WINNIE, (B.A., M.A.)
[b.] MAY 30, 1941, Malta; [p.] Samuel and Mary Grech-Marguerat; [m.] Carmel Cardona, September 19, 1965; [ch.] John, Jennifer and Christopher; [ed.] Two year course at Teachers' Training College in Malta, Ontario College of Arts, University of Toronto, B.A. Honors, M.A., Art Specialist certificate, Seneca college-photography; [occ.] Visual Arts/Photography, English high school teacher, taught kindergarten to grade 13, 5 years visual arts consultant; [memb.] Lifetime member, International Society of Poets, Canadian Wildlife Federation, McMichael Canadian Art Collection; [hon.] Distinction in Art, Editor's Choice Award-1993 National Library of Poetry, Poet of Merit award plaque 1994, International Society of Poets, poems included in The Sound of Poetry and Expression read by Ira Westrich; [oth.writ.] "Endless Pain" published in The Desert Sun 1993, 'Enchantment" in A Far Off Place 1994, poetry, short stories and children's books; [pers.] Nature is my main source of inspiration. To glance at the beauty of nature is a fleeting moment, but to observe more closely gives a lasting memory. [a.] Richmond Hill, Ontario Canada.

CARNEY, VICKI L.
[pen.] Vicki (Lewis) Carney; [b.] August 19, 1969; [p.] Ramey E. Lewis and Barbara L. Johnstone; [m.] Steven M. Carney, May 18, 1991, divorced October 6, 1994; [ch.] Keyra Lynn Carney; [ed.] Marion Center High School; [occ.] Deli production; [oth. writ.] Several other poems; [pers.] I write down my feelings and life experiences. [a.] Smicksburg, PA.

CARON, CLIFF
[a.] Blenheim, Ontario Canada.

CARPENTER, CORKY
[b.] October 15, 1965, Encino, CA; [p.] Patricia and Richard Lockman; [ed.] Corcona del Mar High, University of CA at Irvine and Western State Law School; [occ.] Book Sales and Volleyball Coach; [memb.] Phi Delta Theta, Fraternity and The Dead Poet's Society of Newport Beach; [hon.] Daughters of the American Revolution, Masonic Institution's Academic Achievements, Dean's List; [oth. writ.] Short stories, poems and novel; [pers.] Beauty plus love equals hope. [a.] Balboa Island, CA.

CARPINO, CRYSTAL
[b.] July 7, 1982, Oakland, CA; [p.] Bob and Brenda Carpino; [ed.] I attend a French American School in Berkeley, CA., and I am currently in the 8th grade; [memb.] I belong to the United States Figure Skating Association and the Ice Skating Institute of America; [hon.] I received a certificate for participating in the honor recital at Holy Names College in Oakland, California, a certificate from the French Consulate in San Francisco, California for participation in the Festival of Dramatic Arts and I have received numerous figure skating medals from competitions in Santa Rosa, California, Stockton, CA., and Berkeley, CA.; [oth.writ.] I have never had a poem or essay published before but I hope that my success in writing poetry will continue for years to come; [pers.] Although I am only 12 years old, I have ideas of what I would like to do in my life. I am planning on being a doctor and writing in what spare time I have. I plan on continuing to take French courses throughout my schooling and on traveling more to France and Italy. I have traveled to France six times and would like to go more often. [a.] Oakland, CA.

CARRASCO-GRANDE, MAFALDA
[b.] March 27, 1919, Farrell, PA; [p.] John and Catherine Grande (deceased); [m.] Miguel A. Carrasco, January 19, 1991; [ed.] Farrell High School, PA., Macom CC College and Wayne State University, Detroit, MI., certificate in foreginism, Guatemala, Methodology Certificate for EFL Teachers Santo Domingo, Dominican Republic; [occ.] Retired, USA Relief Officer, Michigan, Beat Reporter, Anchor Bay Beacon, Baltimore, MI., Peace Corps, Guatemala, English Teacher, El Dominco-Americano, Domician Republic (Santo Domingo); [memb.] Holy Name Cathedral, Chicago, IL; [hon.] Dean's List, outstanding performance USA, 1976-1977, 1978-1979, a letter of recognition, El Dominco Americano; [oth.writ.] Poems published in several Universities English Department, Illinois Review, The Poetry East Journal; [pers.] I try to reflect realism in my writing. I have been inspired with naturalism, the scientific objectivity in observing and depicting life. [a.] Chicago, IL.

CARROLL, ERIC W.
[b.] June 22, 1969, Dalton, GA; [p.] Larry and Geneva Carroll; [ed.] East Bay High School, ITT Technical Institute, University of South Florida; [occ.] Computer Systems Manager; [memb.] National Space Society; [oth.writ.] Political articles, poems and various essays mainly for personal amusement. [a.] Tampa, FL.

CARROLL, ERICA E.
[b.] December 13, 1975, Ellsworth, SD; [p.] Steven and Darlene Carroll; [ed.] Weimar High School; [occ.] Navy enlisted personnel; [memb.] National Honor Society, Golden Girls, Texas Educational Theatre Association; [hon.] Various dramatic awards; [oth.writ.] Several non-published works; [pers.] No matter how life treats you, if you smile, it will always seem a lot better than the way it really is. [a.] Weimar, TX.

CARSON, PHIL
[pen.] P.J. Carson; [b.] July 25, 1974, San Clemente, CA; [p.] Ann and Harold Carson; [ed.] Dava Hills High School, Saddle Back College; [occ.] Grocery; [memb.] Honor Thespian Society; [hon.] Honor Thespian, honor graduate of the Sea Cadet Corp; [oth.writ.] Several poems that I keep personal; [pers.] I give thanks to my parents for the gift of life, in which I believe is the greatest gift of all. [a.] San Juan Capistrans, CA.

CARTER, AMY
[b.] June 23, 1974, Dyersburg, TN; [p.] James and Glenda Brashier; [m.] Charles Carter, January 28, 1994; [ch.] Corey Robert and Casey Victoria; [ed.] Bolton High School, Union University; [occ.] Housewife and dance instructor; [pers.] I strongly believe that the things you do in the past will make you what you are tomorrow. [a.] Memphis, TN.

CARTER, RISA D.
[b.] April 15, 1963, Tiapai Tiawan; [p.] Gifford and Dorothy Carter; [ed.] Emergency Medical Tech (Aurora Presbyterian Hospital), EMT Refresher (St. Anthony's Hospital, Denver, CO.) travel trade school; [occ.] Travel agent and photographer; [hon.] "Colorado Summer Adventure Getaway" photo contest 1992 (3rd place); [pers.] Everyone has a little magic in their hearts. The magic gives you more strength and confidence than you can imagine. You just have to look deep down inside yourself and believe. [a.] Aurora, CO.

CARTER, THELMA J.
[b.] Virginia; [p.] Cornelius and Elsie Smith; [m.] Walter J. Carter Sr., July 29, 1972; [ch.] Walt, Cherita and Bernadette; [ed.] I C Norcom High School, Norfolk State University; [memb.] Public Relations Committee (church); [oth.writ.] Old Man Time, How Much Shall I Give, Fantastic Lady; [pers.] Thank God for giving me the gift, knowledge and ambition to share my thoughts with others as I write. [a.] Portsmouth, VA.

CASEY, MARISA
[b.] November 5, 1979, Bogota, Columbia; [ed.] Currently a sophomore in high school at Newton South High School. [a.] Newton, MA.

CASH, R. LAUREN
[pen.] Lauren Rodgers Cash; [b.] June 25, 1987, Upper Saddle River, NJ; [p.] Major and Louise Cash; [occ.] 1st Grade student in Reynolds Public School - Upper Saddle River, NJ; Robert Franchino - Principal/ Susan Tillman - 1st Grade Teacher; [memb.] Upper Ridgewood Tennis Club, Brownie Troop 421, Church of the Presentation; [hon.] Gold medals in: ice skating, skiing, swimming; blue

ribbons in horseback riding; played in 2 piano recitals, competed in 4 tennis tournaments, I bowl, play soccer and do Karate; [oth. writ.] Other poems submitted to The National Library of Poetry; [pers.] I love school, sports and most all other activities, and I love to have fun with my family and friends.; Upper Saddle River, NJ.

CASHEN, CORY
[b.] June 8, 1981, Springfield, IL; [p.] Beth and Tom Cashen; [ed.] I am currently in 8th grade; [occ.] Student in Pawnee Junior High; [memb.] I am a member in high school band, United Methodist Church; [hon.] Honor Roll, letter in basketball and track, Young Author Award in 5th grade; [oth.writ.] Down at the Pickle Juice Palace and Grill, written by Corey Cashen and Nathan Hall; [pers.] I write for the fun of it. I also write short stories.

CASSARINO, ANTHONY
[pen.] Saint Anthony; [b.] February 12,1939, New York; [p.] Antoinette Frank; [m.] Dorothy, November 22, 1956; [ch.] Ted, Elizabeth and Dorothy; [ed.] GED; [occ.] Photographer; [memb.] Madison Square Boys Club, E 29th Street, New York; [hon.] Poets workshop, FCI Butner, NC; [oth.writ.] Drive By, Rafters, Here and Now, Hip Hop, Psychotropic Connoisseur; [pers.] Poetry is the language of the soul.

CASTERTON, JENNIE
[b.] May 29, 1979, Sacramento, CA; [p.] Michael and Jan Casterton; [ed.] Sophomore at Bella Vista High; [occ.] High school sophomore; [memb.] Future Business Leaders of America, Global Impact, Peer Leaders United in Service; [hon.] Presidential Academic Fitness Award, Achievement in English, Honor Roll, Fleet Reserve Association; [pers.] A writer listens with their heart and writes with their soul. [a.] Fair Oaks, CA.

CAVARETTA III, LEONARD F.
[b.] December 9, 1971, Frankfort, NY; [p.] Leonard and Carol Cavaretta Jr.; [ed.] Mohawk Valley Community College, Herkimer County Community College, Sherman College of Straight Chiropractic, Frankfort Schuyler Central High; [occ.] Chiropractor student; [memb.] HCCC Alumni, National Youth Sports, Coaches Association, Federation of Straight Chiropractic Organizations; [oth.writ.] Several poems published in local magazines, short stories published in magazines; [pers.] That person proves his worth who can make us want to listen when he is with us, and think when he is gone. [a.] Spartanburg, SC.

CEESALY, JOHNNIE BEATRICE
[pen.] Bea; [b.] California; [p.] Catherine Williams; [occ.] I am a Clinical Associate at Mayview Medical Center; [oth.writ.] I wrote several poems, I was Golden Poet for 1990, it was presented in appreciation from the World of Poetry, name of poem "Captive To Your Love"; [pers.] I strive to reflect on the love this world needs, people loving and caring and the beauty of the planet we live on.

CEROSS, LUCIANA
[b.] December 30, 1959, Malta, Europe; [p.] Albert and Yvonne Zarb-Cousin; [m.] Zoltan Ceross, January 19, 1980; [ch.] Aaron, Daniel and Jourdan; [ed.] St. Joseph Convent School, Malta, courses in English Lit.; [occ.] CFO in CPC (a computer company my husband and I run); [oth.writ.] Poems, short stories; [pers.] The poem "Good Night Sweet Cousin" is written in memory of my cousin Darren Jones, who died tragically in 1992. He was one of my favorite people. [a.] Franklin Lakes, NJ.

CHALIF, JULIUS
[pen.] Jules Chalif; [b.] February 20, 1908, U.S.A. (Manhattan); [p.] Abraham and Helen Chalif; [m.] Deceased, 1934-5; [ch.] Ronald, Martin and Janet; [ed.] Graduate of Boro Hall Academy, Brooklyn 1930; [occ.] Active violinist council center orchestra (non profit) entertain hospital, nursing homes, schools and colleges; [memb.] Member of Flatbush Jewish Center, member of Torah Club, member of Albemarle Neighborhood Concerned Association; [hon.] Recipient of $ 1,000.00 (cash) award, as outstanding volunteer, as member of council center orchestra (violin) 1985, sponorsed by award committee of Chemical Bank; [oth.writ.] Ode To Brooklyn, Senior Citizens Resurrection, a poem "Contingent to Life Sneak Attack On Pearl Harbor, 1947-December 7, "Day of Infamy"; [pers.] I personally feel that when I write poetry and summarily picked for publication, no greater acclimation or praise becomes the writing as final publicity definitely shows to have found favor in humble appraise. [a.] Brooklyn, NY.

CHAN, GAY M.
[b.] September 11, 1952, Honolulu; [p.] Richard and Muriel Chan; [ed.] Elementary Sacred Hearts Convent, Stevenson (Robert Louis) Intermediate, Theodore Roosevelt High School; [occ.] Oahu Transit Service Authority; [oth.writ.] Submitted poem on a whim after reading ad in newspaper and am deeply honored to have poem published; [pers.] To love God, to experience life, to be one in mind, body and spirit. [a.] Kaneohe, HI.

CHAPIN, BESSIE RICHARDS
[b.] June 30, 1908, Anocortes, WA; [p.] Jesse M. Richards and Julia Dibble; [m.] Sherman L. Chapin, June 14, 1931; [ch.] Sharon Lee and Jennifer Kay; [ed.] Monmouth Oregon Teachers College, University of Oregon, Stanfield Oregon High School; [occ.] Retired; [hon.] High school Valedictorian, Delta Kappa Gamma, teacher's honorary; [oth.writ.] "Poems of The Heart", "My Trip Through The Century"; [pers.] My family and my teaching career have been very important to me and I have devoted time and energy to them-until these last years. [a.] Lake Elsinoe, CA.

CHEE-A-TOW, ENA R.
[pen.] Becky Chee; [b.] January 27, 1926, Guyana, S.A.; [p.] Samuel and Ellen Yhap; [m.] Claude E. Chee-A-Tow, October 9, 1949; [ch.] Cheryl Goldberg, Penelope Cruise, Keith Michael and Richard Gordon; [ed.] Modern High, Osborne's Secretarial College; [occ.] Retired Legal Secretary; [hon.] On June 9, 1961, I received an award for Meritorious Service by the United States Information Agency; [oth.writ.] Several unpublished poems and a few short stories; [pers.] I always endeavour to maintain a positive attitude and whenever I encounter any adversity I find comfort in Isaiah 40:31, "But they that wait...they shall walk and not faint". [a.] St. Cloud, FL.

CHENG, JENNIFER
[b.] February 28, 1982, Springfield, MA; [p.] Stephen and Samantha Cheng; [ed.] Redwood Middle School; [occ.] Student at Redwood Middle School; [hon.] Honor Roll, Young Authors Faire Award; [oth.writ.] Young Author's Fairs short stories. [a.] Saratoga, CA.

CHEVALIER, MARCELLOUS
[pen.] Zeppelin B. Zarzihaw; [b.] January 22, 1976, Washington, DC; [p.] Patricia M. Davis; [ed.] Graduate of Eleanor Roosevelt High School, will be attending college in California next year; [occ.] Waitress at a Pizza Hut Restaurant; [memb.] Member of the World Wildlife Fund an active sponsor of the Christian Children's Fund; [hon.] Awards for poetry contest in schools, awards for plays written in high school; [oth.writ.] Another poem published in The National Library of Poetry, 2 plays performed at my high school and an essay displayed; [pers.] My one life's goal is to become the world's everything. Everything I can accomplish before death. Writing is all I'm good at. [a.] Laurel, MD.

CHIEN, HELEN H.
[b.] February 7, 1927, Shanghai, China; [p.] S.T. Hsieh and C.F. Yang; [m.] Paul P. Chien, May 15, 1948; [ch.] Bernard, Annette, Bernadette, Colette, Clarence and Paul; [ed.] Aurora High, Shanghai University of Peking, Peking, China, University of Shanghai, Shanghai, China, Michigan State University, E. Lansing, MI; [occ.] Writer/translator; [memb.] Society of Professional Journalists, National Press Club, Asian American Journalists' Association, North Carolina Writers' Network; [oth.writ.] "The European Diary of Hsieh Fucheng", St. Martin's Press, New York, NY; [pers.] As a retired journalist, I devoted many hours in meditation. I find it is more exhilarating to express my spiritual experiences in poetry than in prose. I sincerely hope that I may convey such messages to the public. [a.] Chapel Hill, NC.

CHIPLEY, PATRICIA
[pen.] Buddy Kermit; [b.] March 2, 1980, Louisiana; [p.] Lori and David Miner, Patrick Chipley; [ed.] I am in the 9th grade, I plan to become a chef; [hon.] I've made Honor Roll a lot, I won an essay contest in the 4th grade; [oth.writ.] I've been all over Europe because my mom is in the Air Force, I used to be in a band in which I was a lead singer and studying bassist, it was called Scapegoats, I also wrote every song in it; [pers.] I really am not interested in philosophy. I just write when I'm in the mood which is not very often. When I am, I feel it's a work of art. [a.] Lewisville, NC.

CHRISTENSON, LAURIE
[ed.] Olympic Community College, AAS Evergreen State College, junior, leading to a Psychology degree; [occ.] Volunteer at Kitsap Mental Health Services and student; [oth.writ.] Writings published in college newspaper, poem written for a friend's wedding announcement, one poem in At Day's End, Editor's Choice Award, another poem in The Best Poems of 1995, currently writing a novel; [pers.] Set unrealistic expectations for yourself and others. Expect perfection today this way you can guarantee failure, this is one way to help you become depressed and miserable. Compare your worst traits with others best traits this will insure a marty complex. [a.] Port Orchard, WA.

CHRISTIAN, JACCIE DIANE
[pen.] Jaccie Thomas; [b.] July 31, 1975, Cedar City, UT; [p.] Henry and Tanya Thomas and James David Christian; [ed.] Panquitch High, Sevier Valley Applied Technology Center, Granite High; [occ.] Administrative Assistant at Rehar Services, Inc., Salt Lake City, Utah; [pers.] Thanks to my family for giving me my greatest inspiration, being my best friends and encouraging me all the while. I love you all very much. [a.] Salt Lake City, UT.

CHURCH, DONNA R.
[b.] June 18, 1978, Hanford, CA; [p.] Don and Brenda Church; [ed.] I am currently a junior at Hanford High School; [memb.] I belong to the Future Farmers of America and to the California Scholarship Federation; [pers.] The poems that I write tend to reflect the reality of today's world. [a.] Hanford, CA.

CLAIR, ALICIA ESTHER
[b.] December 28,1980, Freeport, IL; [p.] Gary and Veronica Clair; [ed.] Currently an 8th grade student at Lena -Winslow Junior High; [hon.] Art award,

cheerleading award; [pers.] In my free time I enjoy reading and watching television. I have 1 sister and a brother-in-law. My hobbies are collecting erasers. [a.] Lena, IL.

CLARK, ANDREA
[pen.] Andrea; [b.] October 10, 1980, Toronto, Canada; [ed.] 7th grade; [memb.] Member of Sugar Mill Gardens Club; [hon.] Sea Side Music Theatre, ($50.00 saving bond); [oth.writ.] Yes (drawings). [a.] Port Orange, FL.

CLARK, REGINA KAY
[b.] March 31, 1977, Chambersburg; [p.] Kay and James Clark Jr.; [ed.] Chambersburg Area Senior High School, Franklin County Area Vocational Technical School; [occ.] Ingersoll-Rand Company; [pers.] Special thanks to Brad, mom, Gennie and Jus. Don't let other people make your decisions for you and most importantly, don't ever let happiness pass you by. [a.] Chambersburg, PA.

CLARK, ROBBYN M.
[pen.] Robbyn M. Clark; [b.] February 17, 1974, Haverhill, MA; [p.] Glenn and Kathleen Clark; [ed.] Exeber High, Northern Essex Community College; [occ.] Cashier; [hon.] Dean's List; [oth.writ.] Published in Heart of Dreams anthology; [pers.] My inspiration comes from within and the wonderful world around me. Each poem is special and reflects my feelings. Every person is special and captured in words. [a.] East Kingston, NH.

CLARKE, SANDY
[b.] December 14, 1953, Philadelphia, PA; [p.] H.C. (Pete) and Mildred Calvert Wilson; [ed.] B.A.-English and Psychology, MA-English-Morehead State University -KY., Ed.D.-higher education (all but dissertation-University of Kentucky, Lexington; [occ.] Self employed; [memb.] Phi Delta Kappa, Choice in Dying, National Association of Female Executives; [hon.] William Danforth Leadership Award, Kiwanis Citizenship Award, outstanding graduate student in English, Outstanding Young Woman of America, President's Club-Xerox Corp; [oth.writ.] Poetry published in Appalachian Heritage magazine and Inscape literary magazine of Morehead State University, Kentucky, numerous newspaper and magazine articles; [pers.] The greatest thrill in writing poetry is to have someone read my work and for their reaction to be "I wish I had written that". "The respect of those we respect is worth more than the applause of the multitude" (unknown). [a.] Alexandria, VA.

CLAUNCH, KIMBERLY
[b.] April 14, 1960, Weatherford, TX; [p.] Rochelle and Perry Claunch, Glen Rose, Texas; [ed.] Presently involved in pursuing a career in medicine; [memb.] Phi Theta Kappa, Dean's List; [oth.writ.] Staff writer for college newspaper; [pers.] I believe that there are no meaningless details in this world. No matter your position, your actions and words do make a difference to others. I strive to make that experience a positive one. [a.] Cleveland, OH.

CLAYBORNE JR., WILLIAM P.
[pen.] Clyde;[b.] October 14, 1952, Pierce County, WA; [p.] William and Gwendolyn Clayborne Sr.; [m.] Carolyn B.Clayborne, October 17, 1992; [ch.] Dustin, Brandi and Whitley; [ed.] 1971 graduate of Gloucseter High School, served as a Military Policeman in German 1972-1974; [occ.] Crane operator at Newport News Shipbuilding Dry Dock Company; [hon.] Won Golden Poet Award in 1989 in a poetry contest sponsored by The World of Poetry, poem entitled "Uncertain Tomorrows"; [oth.writ.] "America, The Once Beautiful", "This Ole World" and "Uncertain Tomorrows"; [pers.] To me poetry was a God given gift which is very personal. I find it relaxing and soothing to the mind. Someday I want to win the "Nobel Prize" for literature. I hope the world can perceive my poetry from a positive view point and an awareness of the world as a society. [a.] Gloucester, VA.

CLELAND, STEFANIE
[b.] November 17, 1981, Poway, CA; [p.] Yolanda Osuna and Victor Cleland; [ed.[Currently in 8th grade at Warner Union School, Warner Springs, CA; [memb.] GATE (Gifted and Talented Education); [oth.writ.] Poetry published by National Library of Poetry; [pers.] We are all different, yet we are all the same, follow your heart and always be true. [a.] Santa Ysabel Indian Reservation, Santa Ysabel, CA.

CLEMENTS, ERIN LEIGH
[b.] February 19, 1977; [p.] Diane and William Clements; [ed.] Currently a student at Greenwich Central High School in upstate New York; [hon.] County winner in New York State First Annual essay contest, sponsored by the Democratic Committee, regional and state level winners to still be announced; [oth.writ.] None published; [pers.] My happiness is my own responsibility. [a.] Schaghticoke, NY.

CLEMENTS, THERESA L.
[b.] December 14, 1957, Hammond, IN; [p.] Robert B. and Carol Smith; [m.] Lawrence G. Clements, September 21, 1985; [ch.] Jacylny Nicole and Brittany Therese; [ed.] Graduate Crown Point High School, attended Purdue University; [occ.] Probate Paralegal; [memb.] Lake County Association for the Retarded, Church of the Four Seasons United Methodist; [oth.writ.] Numerous unpublished poems, songs and children's stories as this is my first writing ever submitted to a contest; [pers.] This poem was inspired by and is dedicated to my beloved grandmother, Loraine Colins, who departed this world on January 31, 1994. Her memory and spirit live on. [a.] Crown Point, IN.

CLENCH, ERIKA T.
[b.] February 29, 1972, Brooklyn, NY; [p.] Mr. and Mrs. Robert J. Clench; [ed.] Walt Whitman High, North Warren High; [occ.] Optical retailing; [memb.] American Legion Auxiliary; [oth.writ.] Several poems written and yet to be founded; [pers.] If I can touch just one person's heart with soft words, I will live forever with peace and love. [a.] Huntington Station, NY.

CLINE, WILLIAM M.
[pen.] Will Cline; [b.] August 31, 1952, Battle Creek, MI; [p.] Harlan and Vivian Cline; [ch.] Alicia Joy and Justin Lee; [ed.] Comstock Community Education (G.E.D.), Kalamazoo Valley Community College, Davenport College (Kalamazoo), mostly self educated; [occ.] Student at State Technical Institute (Michigan) Mechanical Drafting; [oth.writ.] Never been published; [pers.] My portrait bleeds from the heart of my soul, stroked and brushed with the Master's touch, expressions of the truth I've never told.

CLOUGH, HEATHER
[b.] March 5, 1963, Providence, RI; [p.] Rev. Maxwell and Rita Clough; [ed.] University of RI (BA), Rhode Island College (MSW); [occ.] Clinical Social Worker Adjunct Faculty-Rhode Island College; [memb.] Delta Delta Sorority, Camp Street Ministries-Board of Directors, Travelers Aid Society Youth Services Advisory Committee; [hon.] Completed honors program at University of Rhode Island; [pers.] I dedicate my life to serving others. I believe that love is the greatest gift one can give to another. [a.] Pawtucket, RI.

CLURMAN, JOANNE
[b.] November 7, 1949, Baltimore, MD; [m.] Michael Clurman Sr., May 9, 1977; [ch.] Anthony, Michael Jr. and Jason; [ed.] Parkville Senior High School; [oth.writ.] I am currently writing a book called "Crossroads" on my survival of breast cancer; [pers.] My poems and book are centered around "Breast Cancer" and dedicated to my husband who has given me the strength and love to pick up the pieces of my life again, without him... the road to survival would not have existed. [a.] Dunkirk, MD.

COBB, KENNETH
[pen.] K.C. Musical Composer; [b.] June 21, 1964, Georgetown, SC; [p.] Mr. and Mrs. Cobb; [ed.] Pleasant Hill High and self education; [occ.] Music composer, director, author, producer and writer; [memb.] Church of God and True Holiness, Sadie Agency and a membership to compose music; [hon.] I honor to be published in On The Threshold of A Dream Vol III, Journey of The Mind, Best Poems of 1995, all published by National Library of Poetry; [oth.writ.] Songs, poems, lyrics, scriptwriting, books, comedy writing, screenwriting, manuscript writing, all for K.C. Musical Composer and several poems published by the National Library of Poetry; [pers.] My name is Kenneth Cobb, I am highly intellectual writer with the ability to learn and understand words that can be composed to music. I am also the founder of K.C. Musical Composer, a business that help you to proceed in accomplishing your goal. [a.] Georgetown, SC.

COCHRAN, JEFF
[pen.] Angel Heart; [b.] August 15, 1969, Cincinnati, OH; [p.] Patricia and Charles Cochran; [ch.] Ryan Patrick; [ed.] Roger Bacon High, Moler Pickens Beauty College; [occ.] Nail artist and sculptor, bartender-Chi-Chics; [oth.writ.] Many other poems reflecting my feelings and emotions at a given point in time; [pers.] My poems are from the heart. They reflect my own idea of romance and love, two things that should be inseparable. [a.] Cincinnati, OH.

COCO, ODETTE
[b.] September 15, 1970, Wurzburg, Germany; [m.] Thomas Coco; [ed.] Washington State University; [occ.] Restaurant Manager. Larry's Markets, Seattle, WA; [pers.] Poetry, the one true expression that never inhibits the mind. If my words can open your mind, evoke your thoughts and create a new awareness, then my life is more complete. People everywhere have great things to say, their words must never go unsaid. [a.] Renton, WA.

COGGAN, LAWRENCE M.
[b.] August 3, 1938, Detroit; [p.] Samuel and Esther Wainger Coggan; [m.] Marci Ellyce Coggan, August 31, 1975; [ch.] Amanda and Adam Coggan; [ed.] University of Detroit, Doctor of Dental Surgery 1963; [occ.] DDS; [pers.] Our journey in life is determined by the love we feel, the luck we have and the intelligence we acquire. [a.] Redford, MI.

COLAIACOVO, CHRISTINE
[b.] April 12,1945, New Britain, CT; [p.] Deceased; [m.] Pat, December 1, 1973; [ch.] Alexander; [ed.] BS Central Conn State College, MA Trinity College Hartford, Admin. Central Conn State University; [occ.] Teacher of English, Sociology, English Department head; [memb.] POK, AAUW, Berlin Education Association, CEA, NEA, N.C.T.E., A.S.C.D.; [hon.] Celebration of Excellence in Conn, Teacher's Excellence Award,

CCSU Alumni Award, membership in Kappa Delta Pi, PDK, Trinity Fellow, ten scholarships as undergraduate at CCSU; [oth.writ.] Poetry published in Dover Beach Press 1994, Sparrowgrass, 1993, 1994, The World of Poetry, Golden Poet Award 1990, Honorable Mention 1991, National Poetry Press 1975, 1977; [pers.] Poetry is a natural part of my life. I can't exist without it, my mind fills with image and feelings that have to explore outward.

COLE, KAREN M.
[b.] August 1, 1946, Brooklyn, NY; [p.] Ralph and Evelyn Reda And Ray and Elvera Van Pelt; [m.] Single, mom for last 10 years; [ch.] Michael and Jason Cole, Nigel Cloke; [ed.] Canton High School and some college courses; [occ.] Entertainment agent "Cole Enterprises"; [memb.] National Arbor Day Foundation, Women of the Moose, Highlanders Club; [oth.writ.] Published in "Field of Dreams"; [pers.] I have been an avid reader since a very young age. Religious and inspirational poetry have always been my favorites. Most of my own poetry has resulted from inner feelings and personal experiences. [a.] Rapid City, SD.

COLE, SHIRLEY FORD
[b.] July 18, 1943, Murphy, NC; [p.] Jack R. and Geraldine M. Ford; [m.] Hugh W. Cole, September 11, 1966; [ch.] G. Scott Cole; [ed.] Honor graduate of Hayesville High, Young Harris Junior College, B.A. Mars Hills College; [occ.] Teacher of second grade at W.W. Estes Elementary School in Asheville, NC; [memb.] I am a member of the West Asheville Baptist Church, N.C. Association of Educators, a former member of Delta Kappa Gamma; [oth.writ.] None submitted for publication; [pers.] I search for the good in others and try to bring happiness and laughter to the lives I touch each day. [a.] Candler, NC.

COLE, SHYRLEE
[pen.] Shyrlee Rueter Cole; [b.] March 17, San Francisco; [p.] Aldp and Margaret Simonetti; [m.] Hal Cole, June 28, 1970; [ch.] Melodee and Paul; [ed.] Abraham Lincoln High School, Skyline and San Mateo College, Morris Pratt Institute; [occ.] Loan officer at West Coast Mortgage Co.; [memb.] American Business Women's Association, Business and Professional Women's Association, National Spiritualist Association of Churches; [hon.] California Scholarship Federation lifetime member, past Presidents of ABWA, BPW, SOuthern Hills Homeowners' Association, Woman of the Year; [oth.writ.] Several poems published in various magazines and children's adventures in clockland and lightland; [pers.] I am a spiritual loving child of the universe. Nothing is impossible and peace on earth begins with me. [a.] Cameron Park, CA.

COLEMAN, FANNIE
[b.] October 7, 1928, Covington, TN: [p.] Eugene and Minnie Epps; [m.] James Travis (deceased), September 1, 1963; [ch.] Amelia Anne; [ed.] Frazier High, Lane College; [memb.] The National Geographic Society, AARP. [a.] Covington, TN.

COLLINS, CLINTON WILLIAM JOHN
[pen.] CC Rock; [b.] June 14, 1970, Edmonton, Alberta; [p.] Bonita and William Collins; [ed.] Grade 12 diploma; [occ.] Carpet cleaning technician; [hon.] Troubador Award 1991 from Cornerstone Academy, Vancouver BC, Canada; [oth.writ.] Many poems such as "Love in Life", "Always A Friend", "Life" "True Friends", "Us, You and I", "Advice on Advice", "With You", "When The Morning Sunshines" and much more; [pers.] Life whether it be good or bad, happy or sad. Your destiny is for you to decide, so live your life and don't let it slide. [a.] Vancouver BC, Canada.

COLLINS, VICTORIA S. V.
[b.] June 21, 1975, Trenton, MI; [p.] Kathleen DeNardo and Steven Collins; [ed.] Riverview Community High School, Detroit College of Business, earning Bachelor's Degree in Office Administration; [occ.] Secretary; [hon.] Dean's List; [pers.] I usually write when I am depressed or stressed out. Writing helps me feel better. I try to figure out the meaning of life and each of my writings shows a little bit of what life is all about. [a.] Riverview, MI.

COLVIN, CYNTHIA L.
[b.] October 2, 1950, Ft. Meade, MD; [p.] Alexander and Bessie Colvin; [ed.] Patterson High School, Strayer Business College, New York Institute of Photography, Maryland Institute College of Art; [occ.] Photographer; [memb.] International Free Lance Photographers Organization, American Image Press Club. [a.] Baltimore, MD.

CONDON, RACHEL
[pen.] Sarai Nazorine; [b.] May 11, 1978, Concord, NH; [p.] William Condon and Denise Marchese; [ed.] Salem High; [occ.] Full time student; [oth.writ.] Numerous song, poems and stories unpublished as of yet; [pers.] "Many people complain about life's hardships but as I see it, if life was perfect then what would I have to write about"? [a.] Baldwinville, MA.

CONLEY, WILMA
[pen.] Wilma Barney Burns Conley; [b.] October 19, 1933, Adams Co., OH; [p.] Icey and Earl Barney (deceased); [m.] Lester Conley (deceased), August 17, 1962; [ch.] 9 step children; [ed.] Loucst Grove School, Peebles High School, Advancement Center; [occ.] Assembler of cabinets, volunteer receptionist for school for child advancement; [memb.] Pike County (OH) Senior Citizens volunteer, Special Olympics organization, Eagle Scouts Board of Directors for Post 301, Waverly, OH; [hon.] Employee of the Month, Advancement Center, Creative Writing Award, Pike County Board MR/DD; [oth.writ.] Children's stories for School for Child Advancement, read to children with developmental disabilities; [pers.] I am committed to use my gift of the written word to enhance the inclusion of persons with developmental disabilities into the mainstream of American life. [a.] Waverly, OH.

CONNER, CARRIE ANN
[pen.] Ann Sable; [b.] February 10, 1977, Anderson, IN; [p.] Roger and Robin Conner; [ed.] Alexandria Monroe High-11th; [memb.] Registered CPR; [hon.] Author's Aglow, German Teacher's Award, ADV. German Teacher's Award and class, German Award; [oth.writ.] Wrote a book in 3rd grade called "Halloween" and received Author's Aglow Award, also write poems to enter contests; [pers.] I write poems to explain myself without coming out and saying it. Also I write to show how life has effect on people and objects. [a.] Alexandria, IN.

CONNER, MERCEDES VIGIL
[b.] August 17, 1926, Ft. Garland, CO; [p.] Vicente and Lucia Vigil; [m.] Richard Conner, May 3, 1947; [ch.] Claudia, Jim, Patty, Dickie Jane;[ed.] College, high school, Greeley, Co., Ft. Garland High, (Adams State College Alamosa, CO. (B.A.) 1948); [occ.] Teacher, retired 33 years; [hon.] 4 year Scholastic Scholarship, Adam State College 1944-48; [oth.writ.] Translated from the Spanish Language to English the only instruction maintenance and pilot's manual for the Vintage Aircraft, HEIII Heinkel (German W.W.II) aircraft owned by the Confederate Air Force, this plane could not be flown without and English translation as required by the FAA for U.S.A. flights; [pers.] Children are the key to the world's future. We must teach them to be honorable and our worries will be over as they become tomorrow's citizens.[a.] Greenville, TX.

CONNOR, CHARLES R.
[pen.] Charles R. Connor; [b.] September 11, 1915, Savannah, GA; [p.] Charlie C. and Mollie Martin Connor; [m.] Frances Keller Connor, September 9, 1942; [ch.] Charles Robert Connor Jr.; [ed.] Savannah High School, Richards Business College, Officers Candidate School # 28, Fort Sill; [occ.] Retired; [memb.] Past President Savannah Vol. Guard, Board member Chatham Artillery, St. Peter the Apostle Church; [oth.writ.] "Father Neptune".

CONNOR, DAYLE
[b.] September 21, 1978, Thunder Bay , Ontario Canada; [p.] John and Sandra Connor; [ed.] Currently in grade 11; [occ.] Student; [memb.] Women's Hockey Association -Manitouwadge, United Church of Canada; [hon.] MHS Honor Rolls, most valuable player for both ringette and hockey; [pers.] I'd like to dedicate this poem to POPPA, we love you. [a.] Manitouwadge, Ontario Canada.

CONWAY, DORIS
[pen.] The Big D; [b.] B.] June 17, Bronx, NY; [p.] Mr. and Mrs. Joseph Mullin; [m.] John Conway, June 19, 1965; [ch.] Mary and Patrick; [ed.] St. Joseph's, Peekskill, New York; [occ.] Housewife, hobby writing to God; [memb.] Church Prayers Groups and varied charities; [hon.] My greatest honor in this life is to achieve blessings from the Lord by doing for others and reflecting God's love, compassion and mercy for mankind; [oth.writ.] I have hundreds of poems meditations and prayers to God that are unpublished at this time; [pers.] I love God so much that in my everyday meditations and prayers to the Lord, my inspirations turn into writings and become my love letters to God. [a.] Miller Place, NY.

COODY, LEE ANN
[pen.] Lee Ann Coody; [b.] May 9, 1979, Warner Robins; [p.] Barbara and Olin Coody; [ed.] Bleckley County High School; [oth.writ.] I love to write poetry; [pers.] If you let the little things in life get you down you'll never get anywhere. [a.] Cochran, GA.

COOK, JUILE ANNA MILLARD
[b.] February 1, 1965, Wheeling, WV; [p.] R.A. and C.E. cook; [ed.] Wheeling Jesuit College BS; [occ.] Pre-prof. program at UNCG; [pers.] To reflect the sights, smells, feelings and wonders of the struggle of nature to survive. The truth as my giving feels and hears. [a.] Whitsett, NC.

COONEY, WILLIAM A.
[b.] March 1, 1926, San Francisco, CA; [p.] William and Eileen Cooney; [m.] Velma M. Cooney, November 28, 1953; [ch.] Sandra Petersen, Nancy Baker and Denise Elfendahl; [ed.] Graduated University of California January 1950, graduate studies University of California and San Francisco State University Secondary Teaching credential;[occ.] Retired finance manager; [memb.] Past President Sunset Community Club San Francisco, Past President Horiega Merchants Association San Francisco, former member of the Sierra Club and The National Wildlife Association; [hon.] PSI Sigma Alpha, a World of Poetry Golden Poet of 1991; [oth.writ.] Sands of Salmon Creek and A Bottle Gone Dry. [a.] Santa Rosa, CA.

CORMAN, MICHAEL PAUL
[pen.] Michael Paul Corman; [b.] March 17, 1948, St. Louis, MO; [p.] Morris and Pearl Corman; [m.] Mary Louise Wilson, September 3, 1982; [ch.] Andrew Wilson Corman; [ed.] Bachelor of Science, Physical Education, Environmental degrees in Waste Management; [occ.] Environmental sales and consultation; [memb.] Association Professional Emergency Manager, San Diego Earth and Day Association; [oth.writ.] I have written over 1000 pages of edit, in the mist of the Desert Storm, what have we learned, NOTHING, the 91st year upon the 92nd, the 94th year onto 5755 within my reality; [pers.] I started writing because of my father. It began in mourning his death that allowed me to take up the noble art of poetry. I feel that he is still influencing me in my work from heaven above. My writing is in his honor as a man of strength of the past. [a.] San Diego, CA.

CORTES, RODRIGO
[pen.] Rod, Rodney; [b.] December 25, 1964, Costa Rica; [p.] Roberto and Maria Cortes; [ed.] Violette Elementary, Walton Junior High, Santiago High School, Pacific Coast Tech Institute; [occ.] Certified Auto Tech; [memb.] Children's Hospital of Orange Count, Red Cross volunteer; [hon.] Student mostly likely to succeed, high school; [oth.writ.] Had article in high school for quotes and sayings; [pers.] If the world would practice love, we would never lose the game of life. [a.] Anaheim, CA.

CORUM, JACQUELINE R.
[b.] November 21, 1965, Chester County, PA; [p.] I. Walter and Carol Ann Corum; [ed.] Unionville High, Widener University; [occ.] Draftsperson, Sevenson Environmental Services, Inc., Chadds Ford, PA; [oth.writ.] Personal memorandums published in local newspapers; [pers.] I reflect on personal experiences which have touched the lives of myself, my family and friends. [a.] Coatesville, PA.

COTT, EDNA
[b.] April 23,1924, London, England; [p.] Miriam and Joseph Goldberg (both deceased); [m.] Edgar Cott (1922-1990), October 29, 1944; [ch.] Bernice, Barry, Brad and Brian; [ed.] Primary and secondary schools in London, England, Business College in London, England; [occ.] Retired; [memb.] Pasadena Jewish Temple/Centre, St. Luke Hospital volunteer; [hon.] Honorable Mention and Certificate of Merit, World of Poetry, Sacramento, California, Golden Poet Award 1991, World of Poetry; [oth.writ.] Album of poetry, personal enjoyment; [pers.] Poetry becomes therapy and relief from stress. I adore romance novels and poetry by the Brownings and Emily Dickinson. Intrigued by recitations of Maya Angelou. [a.] Pasadena, CA.

COTTER, JOHN EDWARD
[b.] December 30, 1947, Cleveland, OH; [p.] Leona and James (deceased); [ed.] West Tech High, 4 years apprenticeship with NASA Lewis Research Center; [occ.] Aerospace laboratory mechanic for NASA; [memb.] Aircraft Owners and Pilots Association, Annunciation Parish Pastoral Council; [hon.] Numerous awards and accommodations for my work with NASA as well as from Aerospace industry award for longevity in teaching religion (PSR); [oth.writ.] Several poems but this is the first and only poem submitted for any consideration, attempting to complete a non-fiction book at this time; [pers.] "To Live In The Sunshine" was from the heart. I truly believe that if we trust God and strive to fulfill His will, we could solve many of our problems. [a.] Cleveland, OH.

COUTEE, DANNY CHARLES
[pen.] Gypsy Dan; [b.] May 29, 1945, Dallas, TX; [p.] Emmitt and Ermo Coutee; [m.] Renee Elaine Coutee, September 2, 1989; [ch.] Tracie, Lamor Coutee, Evelynia Richard; [ed.] Bachelor of Arts in Criminal Justice, Law Degree from U. of D., I hold 3 class broadcaster license, registered lobbyist, private investigator; [occ.] Legal Intelligence with the Defenders Justice Associates P.C.; [memb.] State Bar Association, Kappa Alpha PSI Fraternity, Trail Lawyers Association, Gable Block Club Association, The Mayor's Task Force on Juvenile Crime, D.P.O.A.; [hon.] Mayor's Neighborhood Watch, Police Marksman Association; [oth.writ.] Dreams, Beloved, Captured, I'm A Flitatous Mood, Wait On God, Here's To Good Friends, Out of Control, Don't Be Like Zack, Changes; [pers.] I don't know what the future hold, but I know that God holds the future to my life. [a.] Detroit, MI.

COVAN, TINA A.
[b.] November 3, 1978, Pensacola, FL; [p.] Theresa and James Enfinger; [ed.] Thomas Com. Central High School; [occ.] Student; [memb.] VOCA Club and FHA Club at school; [hon.] Presidential Academic Fitness Award, Drug Free Helper, Academic "Go For The Gold", fair, jump rope for heart, official "Dear Abby" and summer education; [pers.] I have tried all kinds of poems from the way I feel. Writing poems are one of my favorite things to do. I would like to thank the teacher's aid at TCCHS for telling me I should put my poem in a contest.[a.] Thomasville, GA.

COX, GENEVA M. WHITE
[pen.] Geneva M. White Cox; [b.]April 19, 1917, Ash Grove, MO; [p.] Rev. and Mrs. T.A. White; [m.] W.L. Cox, June 18, 1944; [ch.] Marilynn and W. Lane Cox; [ed.] High school Ash Grove High, Ash Grove, MO, Chaffee College in Ontario, California; [occ.] Writer, wife and mother; [hon.] Literary award presented for "I Want" from Beacon Publishing; [oth.writ.] "Time", "Rain", "Sun", "I Want", "Springtime in The Ozarks", "the Soul in Death", "The Soul", "Deaths Sleep of Nothingness", "Autumn", and "America"; [pers.] I am 77 years old and have enjoyed every year. Writing has been one thing I have to do. I get an idea in the night and Iget up and write just for my satisfaction. Even losing the sight in one eye and pooe vision in the other has not stopped that desire to put pen to paper. [a.] Shawnee Mission, KS.

COX, KATIE
[pen.] Byrd; [b.] April 26, 1980, Martinsville, VA; [p.] William L. and Sandra G; [ed.] Freshman at Martinsville High School; [occ.] Student; [memb.] Key Club, International Club; [hon.] President of freshman class, 1994 Virginia Senate Page, "Big M" academic award -4 years; [oth.writ.] Many, many poems (not published), one song published by a recording company, one poem published by a literary magazine; [pers.] I have two bibles, E.E.Cummings, Greatest Works and The Passion (by Jeannette Winterson). Expression through words is more real than fact. [a.] Ridgeway, VA.

COX, KELLY-JO
[b.] September 9, 1967,. Ottawa, Ontario; [p.] John and Colleen Cox; [ed.] Cairine Wilson S.S., Algonquin College; [occ.] Developmental Services worker. [a.] Ottawa Ontario, Canada.

COYLE, JOSEPH
[pen.] Joseph Coyle; [b.] June 25, 1939, Carroll Gardens, Brooklyn, NY; [p.] Anna Jacobson and Joseph Coyle; [ed.] Manual Training High School, Brooklyn, New York; [occ.] I am a disabled Civil Service worker; [memb.] P.A.L. and C.Y.O.; [oth.writ.] Dark Side of The Moon, and Best Poems of 1995 and Songs On The Wind; [pers.] Live and let live, because the man you harm, is a brother. [a.] Brooklyn, NY.

CRADDOCK, JAMES DAVID (DAVE)
[b.] May 8, 1949, Grand Saline, TX; [p.] James and LaVone Craddock; [m.] Divorced; [ch.] Aleshia Michelle; [ed.] High school, 3 years of college; [occ.] Mailroom clerk, Denton Record -Chronicle; [oth.writ.] Written some 80 poems, none submitted for publication except one "Rain"; [pers.] Wrote poems as a means of therapy while in prison and while recovering from a 24 year bout with alcohol. Have been sober since September 1992, and continue to write poetry on matters of life, old age and homeless people. [a.] Denton, TX.

CRAIG, DEBRA MAE
[pen.] Debi Craig; [b.] October 3, 1952, Evansville, IN; [p.] Robert and Dolores Gipson; [ch.] Scott, Rob, and Carrie Robertson, Chris Craig; [ed.] Brown Co. High School, Indiana University; [occ.] Dispatcher for Brown Co. Sheriff's Department; [memb.] New life Community Church, Fraternal Order of Police, Christian Singles; [hon.] Honorable mention certificate for poem submitted in a contest, semi-finalist in this poetry contest; [oth.writ.] Poems published in local newspaper and opportunity for publication in a book of "Great Western Poetry"; [pers.] I am a firm believer that "love makes the world go round". Without it one's life can be without meaning and one's heart as empty as an abandoned cave. I am a great fan of Helen Steiner Rice. Her poetry emanates beauty and love. [a.] Nineveh, IN.

CRAWFORD, WILLA G.
[pen.] Willa Crawford; [b.] February 15, 1915, Doxey, OK; [p.] R.H. and Della Green; [m.] Sherman Crawford, June 15, 1951; [ch.] Gay Crawford King; [ed.] BA and M.E.D. S.W. State University of Oklahoma; [occ.] Retired English Teacher, Eisenhower High School, Lawton, OK; [memb.] Westminster Presbyterian Church of Lawton , R.S.V.P., life member of Southwestern State Alumni Association; [hon.] Scholarship to Oklahoma City University 1933-34, Magna Cum Laude graduate from S.W. State University of OKlahoma, RSVP volunteer of the year 1993-Lawton; [oth.writ.]"Pretense", "Idea", "Dust Bowl", "Daze", "Mother", "Enigma", "You Are Very Special", "How Old Am I", "Helen", "Credits", "Debbie", "Engulfed", a few published in OKlahoma Poetry and National Poetry Anthology; [pers.] I believe in the Christian Fundamentals. Being alive and helping others is my joy. My husband and I served as Vista volunteers in Dale School, South Carolina 1973-74 and continue volunteer work today. [a.] Lawton, OK.

CREPEAU, PETER N.
[b.] April 19, 1949, Haverhill, MA; [p.] Norman and Doris Crepeau; [m.] Juanita (Kookie) Crepeau, July 29, 1978; [ch.] P.J. and Cynthia; [ed.] Sanborn Regional High, various Navy schools during 20 year career, Century Business College; [occ.] Assistant to the President of Vectec, Inc.; [memb.] Fleet Reserve Association, USGA; [hon.] Navy Achievement Medal, twice selected command "Sailor of the Year", school Valedictorian for Century Business College; [oth.writ.] Vast number of other poems, only publications have been in Military newspaper; [pers.] Writing poetry is such a personal thing that sharing it with others is tantamount to showing a very secret part of my being. Due to my gregarious nature and often times silly demeanor, it is sometimes difficult to convince people that "yes I wrote that". [a.] Orlando, FL.

CROMPTON, SYLVIA JOHN
[pen.] Sylven J.; [b.] June 24, 1981, Fallbrook, CA; [p.] John and Janice Crompton; [ed.] Attending 8th grade, Potter Junior High, Fallbrook, CA; [occ.] Student; [hon.] 6th grade Honor Roll-1993, Presidential Academic Fitness Award -1993, Exhibitor, KPBS Environmental Art contest 1990; [oth.writ.] Poems, short stories published in class collections (1990-93), short story entered in Mary Fay Pendleton School Library (1992). [a.] Fallbrook, CA.

CROSS, DIANA L.
[b.] May 30, 1963, Wakefield, Quebec Canada; [p.] Eric Cross and Vera Woodburn; [m.] Stephen H. Armstrong, September 28, 1991; [ch.] Natalie Cote'; [ed.] High school; [pers.] There is always a positive side to things, no matter how negative life gets. [a.] Alcove, Quebec, Canada.

CROSS, LISA
[b.] September 18, 1965, Middletown, NY; [p.] Joy and Janet Cross; [ch.] Brian Jay and Damian Joseph Torres; [ed.] Monticello High; [occ.] Presidential Counselor, Sullivan Diagnostic Treatment Center, Harris, NY; [oth.writ.] I have written several poems and at the present time, I am working on a book; [pers.] I wrote this particular poem in memory of my mother. She was always and still is a great inspiration in all of my writings. Every poem I wrote, she was the first to read them, not I read them to her. [a.] Harris, NY.

CROSS-ARMSTRONG, DIANA
[b.] May 30, 1963, Wakefield, Quebec; [p.] Vera Woodburn and Eric Cross; [m.] Stephen H. Armstrong, September 28, 1991; [ch.] Natalie Danielle; [ed.] High school diploma, ICS Journalism, short story, writing course; [occ.] Legal Secretary; [pers.] There is always a positive side to things in life, no matter how negative things can be. [a.] Alcove Quebec, Canada.

CROTTE. FERNANDO
[b.] May 16, 1955, Cheverly, MD; [m.] Karen, February 4, 1978; [ch.] Megan, Ginny, Kelly and Kevin; [ed.] B.S. Biology, University of Toledo (Ohio), 1977, Medical College at Ohio (Toledo) 1980, International Medicine, Mayo Clinic, 1983; [occ.] Physician; [memb.] American Medical Association, American College of Physicians, The Foundation for Life; [pers.] I enjoy creative writing, poetry and prose. By viture of education, I am task-oriented and can execute specific projects, including technical. I am easy to work with. [a.] Sylvania, OH.

CROWELL, SARA
[b.] March 12,1983, Bryn Mawr,PA; [p.] Linda and Robert Crowell; ed.] I'm in 6th grade at the Radnor Middle School; [occ.] Student; [memb.] Kehlers Gymnastics team, gifted program at school, orchestra; [pers.] Some of my other interests are piano, animals, art, violin and my friend. [a.] Bryn Mawr, PA.

CROWELL, TAMARA
[pen.] Buffy; [b.] April 19, 1972, Lakeland, FL; [p.] Geraldine Crowell; [m.] Garvin Banta, November 25, 1994; [ed.] Fort Lauderdale High School, Nova University, Gene A. Whiddon Adult Center, plan to go to college to become a Dental Hygienist; [occ.] Front desk clerk, night manager at a Time Share Resort; [memb.] Kids in Distress, Law Club, Accounting Club, chorus, Spanish Club, S.A.D.D., D.C.T.; [hon.] Outstanding Student and attendance; [pers.] This poem is dedicated to my fiance for the inspiration he gave me to write it. [a.] Fort Lauderdale, FL.

CRUM, BRENDA
[b.] August 20, 1957, Greeneville, TN; [p.] D.L. Smith and Rose Sellers; [m.] Gary C. Crum, May 3, 1986; [ch.] Robert L. Shelton; [ed.] Chuckey-Doak High School; [occ.] Housewife; [oth.writ.] Poem published by World Wide Christian Books Glory Bound; [pers.] I feel a poem is the hearts way of telling us how it feels. [a.] Bay Minette, AL.

CRUZ, FERNANDO M.
[b.] November 27, 1970, Coron, Palawan PI; [p.] Ricardo S. and Virginia L. M. Cruz; [ed.] St. Augustine's Academy High School, Philippine Normal College (now university), Palawan State College-Extramural Studies Center (taking up AB); [occ.] Municipal Gov't employee; [hon.] Consistent Outstanding Pupil from grades one to six, recipient of three Scholarship Awards (one from the gov't and two from private individuals); [oth.writ.] None, "The Wandering Heart" is my first published work; [pers.] Funny; considering today's all powerful computers' capacity and ability to perform. Still, they failed to decipher one of the age old human expressions... POETRY. [a.] Palawan, Philippines.

CUCULLU, MATTHEW A.
[b.] August 28, 1979, Anchorage, AK; [p.] Alan and Viola Cucullu; [ed.] High school freshman; [occ.] Student; [oth.writ.] "Dreams" (poem), "The Day of The Damned" (poem), "Night" (poem), "The First Hunt" (poem). [a.] Anchorage, AK.

CULVER JR., WILLIAM R.
[b.] September 10, 1956, San Diego, CA; [p.] Bill and Carmen Culver; [m.] Theresa L. Culver, April 29, 1978; [ch.] William Ross III, Seth Tyler and Sean Eldon; [ed.] Ramona High School, Riverside City College, San Bernardino Valley College;[occ.] Senior Engineering Technician, Parker Hannifin, CSD; [hon.] Dean's List, San Bernardino Valley College; [oth.writ.] Previously unpublished; [pers.] My writings reflect my own personal experiences and of those who are close to me. [a.] Lake Forest, CA.

CUMMINGS, ASHLEY
[b.] April 17, 1971, Evansville, IN; [p.] Charles and Barbara Cummings; [ed.] I'm in the 8th grade, currently attending South Junior High School in Henderson, KY; [occ.] I babysit 2 children and work for Neat-n-Tidy; [hon.] Honor Roll, Best Author, Best All Around, top 20 grades; [oth.writ.] I write short stories, a lot of short stories; [pers.] Someday I hope to begin my very own magazine. [a.] Henderson, KY.

CURRIE, MARY P.
[pen.] Marie Paul; [b.] May 23, 1957, Parrsboro, NS: [p.] Melborune and Pauline Currie; [ch.] Andrew, Crystal and Melissa Wood; [ed.] High school; [occ.] Single parent, homemaker; [oth.writ.] Poems, songs, children's stories just for family and friends; [pers.] I am an avid reader and love to sing for my community and church. I also like to create beautiful things like music, pictures of art and stories for the ones I love. [a.] Parrsboro N.S., Canada.

CURTIS, GREGORY SCOTT
[pen.] Scotty Curtis; [b.] January 19, 1969, Frankfurt, Germany; [ed.] Esperanza High School; [occ.] Bartender; [hon.] Life; [oth.writ.] Several poems, songs, and short stories that I would like to publish and record for the world; [pers.] This is the first poem I've ever sent anywhere and the first of many written about my love, Tamera Anne. I am inspired only by my passions. [a.] Norwalk, CA.

CUTRIGHT, ANGELA
[b.] November 27, 1977, Southfield, MI; [p.] Don and Marie Cutright; [ed.] Currently in 11th grade, attending Mio AuSable High School; [memb.] I play basketball along with volleyball for the Mio Lady Bolts; [oth.writ.] I have written for the school newspaper; [pers.] I tend to write about dreams and reality of life and love. [a.] Mio, MI.

CZEHUT, SUZANNE
[b.] March 8, 1971, Trenton, NJ; [p.] Alexander and Jacqueline Czehut; [ed.] Steinert High School, University of Scranton, B.A. English and Spanish; [occ.] Editorial Assistant, The Center for Applied Research, Inc., Philadelphia, PA; [hon.] Alpha Mu Gamma; [pers.] Truth lies within one's own heart. [a.] Hamilton Square, NJ.

DAHLKE, DERON JAY
[b.] December 13, 1966, San Diego, CA; [p.] Bryden Dahlke and Patti Dawson; [m.] Who knows her name, who knows when; [ch.] Eventually; [ed.] B.S. Psychology, University of Washington, B.S. Zoology, University of Washington, A.A.S. Premedical, Everett Community College; [occ.] English Teacher, South Korea; [memb.] Seattle Public Library, United States Tennis Association, Seattle Tennis Center, Ultra Slim-Fast Team Tennis; [hon.] 1994 Seattle Tennis center, Summer Singles Tournament Mens' "B" Champion, University of Washington-two time "high" scholarship status; [pers.] Usually, if one tries to become tolerant of others' differences, a relating experience takes hold, and soon establishes the common elements inherent in all human beings, which hopefully results in continued communication. [a.] Seattle, WA.

DAIGLE, PETER F.
[pen.] Pete Daigle; [b.] September 6, 1972, Berlin, NH; [p.] Ann-Marie and Raymond Daigle;[ed.] Berlin High School and NHTC-Laconia each with a major in Graphic Arts/Designs; [memb.] Waldenbooks, CD Club and the Berlin Bowling Center; [hon.] I am honored to be in this book and have been awarded my artistic abilities by God, as well as a supportive family; [oth.writ.] This is my first published writing; [pers.] I am influenced by the need for heroes in a hero based society and by ballads sung by Prince. This is my first published writing, I'm honored and hope to succeed more in the future with poems and stories alike. [a.] Berlin, NH.

DALE, HUGHIE
[b.[December 7, 1924, Stilwell, OH; [p.] Deceased; [m.] Helen Dale, May 5, 1956; [ch.] 2 sons; [ed.] BS degree from Oklahoma State University; [occ.] Retired. [a.] Houston, TX.

DALEY, APRIL
[b.] January 27, 1982, Hattiesburg, MS; [ed.] Currently in Junior High 7th grade South Forrest Elementary, honor student; [memb.] Beta Club, Horizons; [hon.] Superior Achievement and Excellence of Performance in Art 1993, Excellence in English 1993, Excellence in Science in 1993; [oth.writ.] I've had my art work published in local paper; [pers.] A poem is from the mind, the heart and the soul. I mainly get my poetry from the heart. [a.] Hattiesburg, MS.

DANIEL, JIMMIE G.
[pen.] Jimmie G. Daniel; [b.] April 9, 1939, McHenry, KY; [p.] Aruel Ray and Merle Daniel; [m.] Barbara Sue Daniel, July 5, 1961; [ch.] Jimmie G. Daniel Jr., Patricia D. Wiles, Stephen K. Daniel, David Glenn Daniel; [ed.] B.A. degree Kentucky Wesleyan College, grad. commano and general staff, grad work University Evansville, Evansville,

IN, master business adm.; [occ.] Self employed owner Multi-line Insurance Agency, V.P. Gas and Oil Drilling Co. Ret. Ltc. USAKTIY; [memb.] Hauson Methodist Church; [hon.] American National Red Cross Life Saving Award, Kentucky Colonel, selected Outstanding Young Man in American 1974; [oth.writ.] Published author, A Badge of Honor, 1980 police work; [pers.] I just sometime feel like expressing my feelings about life and the people and things I love. [a.] Hanson, KY.

DANIELS, JEFFREY
[pen.] Jeff Daniels; [b.] January 8, 1977, Wood County, Bowling Green, OH; [p.] Richard Daniels and Nancy Myers; [ed.] Senior, Elmwood High School, Bloomdale, Ohio; [occ.] Student; [memb.] F.T.A., Student Council, bowling league, freshman basketball, freshman golf; [hon.] Honor Student, a league high game bowling, 2nd place, Info Processing Assistant, region 6 Ohio Professional Business of America, 1994 Information Processing Assistant, state, fifth place, second division, certificate, business correspondence; [oth.writ.] This poem was written for 10th grade English; [pers.] An interest in basketball and other sports by participation and reading about the lives of the famous. Truly believing makes dreams come true. [a.] Cygnet, OH.

DANIELS, JOE
[b.] September 27, 1974, Victoria, BC; [p.] Susan Ferrie and Dean Daniels; [ed.] Currently attending Camosun College for a Psychology degree; [occ.] Waiter, White Spot Restaurant; [pers.] Work hard, play harder. I hope my poem makes someone's day. This is my first time published. [a.] Victoria, BC.

DARIMONT, LYNN
[b.] November 25, 1962; [p.] Gerald and Lillian Sronkoski; [m.] Steve Darimont, June 27, 1987; [ch.] Stephanie (13), Christopher (6) and Andrea (3); [ed.] Elk Grove High School-1980, Eastern Illinois University, B.S. in Education 1984, M.S. in Education 1985; [occ.] High school English teacher, Mattoon High School, Mattoon, IL; [memb.] Mattoon Education Association, Illinois Education Association, National Education Association, St. Charles Borromeo Catholic Church; [pers.] I dedicate this poem to my parents who, through their love for each other taught me what love is all about, and my husband, who "journeys" with me each and everyday. [a.] Charleston, IL.

DASTI, TAMMY ROSALIND
[b.] September 14, 1971, Hamilton, Ontario; [p.] Raised by grandparents, Charles and Rosalind Smith; [ch.] Only my dog, Kiska; [ed.] Parkside High, currently attending McMaster University where I will receive Hons. B.A. in 1995 and where I hope to do my graduate work; [occ.] Student; [memb.] Dundas Tennis Club, McMaster University Society of English (MUSE); [oth.writ.] Several poems published in high school literary books; [pers.] Literature is a way of either exploring or escaping our day-to-day life. It also permits us to touch however briefly, the souls of those we were not fortunate enough to meet during life. [a.] Dundas, Ontario Canada.

DAVIES, JOHN GERSON WILLIAM
[pen.] John Gerson; [b.] February 17, 1936, Caernarfon, Wales; [p.] Rev. William Clifford and Betty Davies; [m.] Norma Warren Davies, October 23, 1993, two previous marriages; [ed.] Sir Thomas Jones School, Amlwich, Anglesey, N. Wales, Institute of Bankers, London; [occ.] Realtor Associate, Lobland Realty, Palm desert, CA; [memb.] Free Mason (English Constitution), Welsh Baptist Church, Eastcastle Street, London, W1; [hon.] London Grand Bank, Deacon and Newsletter Editor; [oth.writ.] A novel not yet published, with a sequel in mind and a third started, my first anthology of poetry is about to be published by Janus Publishing Company, London under the title An Orchid Nosegay For My Love; [pers.] Peace, love and human understanding. My childhood love of poetry was lost by the need to work, first in banking, then military service and business, to be revived by my present wife who asked me to write her a poem. Few days pass without my writing one. [a.] La Qunita, CA.

DAVIES, WILLIAM
[pen.] Scouse; [b.] March 26, 1938, Liverpool; [ch.] Michael Alexander; [ed.] Our Lady's Eldon St. Liverpool England; [occ.] Tile Setter; [pers.] I laugh, I cry, I live, I die, Why? [a.] Midvale, UT.

DAVIS, ASHLEY
[b.] December 30, 1978, Halifax, Nova Scotia; [p.] Sharon and Robert Davis; [ed.] In grade 10 when poem was written, (Cole Harbour High School); [occ.] High school student; [memb.] Highland and tap dancer with Amethyst Highland dancer;[hon.] Honor Roll of junior high, all around student award; [pers.] Even though this poem was a catharsis following a past event, I've realized it alludes many of my experiences. [a.] Dartmouth, Nova Scotia.

DAVIS, CHERYL
[b.] November 13, 1950, Chanute, KS; [ch.] Jamie and Carrie Davis; [ed.] BA in Elementary Education from Southwest Baptist University, Bolivar, MO, Masters Degree in Elementary Education from Drury College, Springfield, MO; [occ.] Elementary teacher; [hon.] Who's Who in American Colleges and Universities; [pers.] Many of my writings are a result of my own search for peace during personal struggles and are a journey of my faith in God. It is my desire that through sharing my poems, others may learn that they, too can find peace and joy, even in their trials. [a.] Strafford, MO.

DAVIS, DAVID E.
[pen.] Dozer; [b.] November 14, 1962, C.B., IA; [p.] Mr. and Mrs. D.D. Davis; [ed.] Graduate of Glenwood High; [occ.] Manager Glenwood Bottle and Can Redemption Center; [memb.] ABATE of Iowa, District 2 (FOE) Eagles; [hon.] It was an honor to me, to have pictures of mine published by Easy Riders, just doing my thing with a Harley and a pen; [oth.writ.] Writing music, poetry all my life, actually since the age of 14, have written many, but never sent or enter any contest; [pers.] America should go back to being what we should be, Americans. The U.S. of A. not try to be a govern power over everyone outside the U.S.A., think about us first, your family, your friends, your life. [a.] Glenwood, IA.

DAVIS, JESSICA
[pen.] Jessica Davis; [b.] June 14, 1982, Houston, TX; [p.] Janet and Jeff Davis; [ed.] Elementary and junior high (7th grade); [occ.] Going to school; [pers.] Every today, 13 yesterdays'tomorrow. [a.] Northville, MI.

DAVIS, PHILIP B.
[b.] June 11, 1959, Cleveland, OH; [p.] Alberta and Sherman J. Davis; [ed.] B.A. Economics, Stanford University 1981, MBA, University of Virginia, Darden Graduate School of Business; [occ.] Entrepreneur, President and CEO of Bert Sherm Products Inc.; [memb.] Leadership Cleveland class of 1993, 1994, United Way Leadership Development 1990, Board of First Call For help; [hon.] Stanford University Lloyd W. Dinkelspiel Award for outstanding service to undergraduate education, Upward Bound, Distinguished Alumnus 1994, Baldun Wallace College; [oth.writ.] "Goodbye to Die", Essence magazine, April 1988; [pers.] Only if the world is different, slightly changed for the better because of what I have done while alive, can I die with no regrets. [a.] Cleveland, OH.

DAVIS, ROA
[b.] August 24, 1927, Lewistown, MT; [p.] Lee and Rhoda Davis; [m.] Edith Davis, March 29, 1952; [ch.] Carl Thomas and John Allen; [ed.] Denton High, Denton, MT., U.S. Trade School, Kansas City, MO.; [occ.] Retired farmer, ranch hand, fertilizer plant manager, janitor; [memb.] DAV, Lebannon, MO. chapter, local Southern Baptist Church; [hon.] Denton, MT. class of 1944 Valedictorian, Korean War, Purple Heart with 1st Oak Leaf Cluster, Bronze Star, Combat Inf Badge; [oth.writ.] Poem for high school annual, one published in Young America Sings 1944, one or two in local church bulletins, last year had one in Lebanon newspaper about the Korean War; [pers.] My first rule choosing a subject, write about something you know about. I wrote Sage Brush Memories in 1963 while working as a ranch hand on another ranch in the same area of Central Montana that my boyhood home was. It had been seventeen years then since we had sold and left that ranch. Being that close made the nostalgia almost overwhelming. [a.] Lebanon, MO.

DEAL, JANICE MARIE
[b.] March 27, 1964, Sacramento, CA; [p.] Ronald and Mazie Deal; [ch.] Carl, Lindsey, Megan and Tyler; [ed.] Weippe Elementary School, middle school, Nova and Pioneer High Schools; [occ.] Pallet tag clerk, Bell Carter Foods Inc; [pers.] I like to write about the precious and valuable things in life. It truly inspired me to write this poem. [a.] Corning, CA.

DECKER, DELORES
[b.] March 26, 1942, Bayonne, NJ; [p.] Helen Russell; [ch.] William, Michele and Delores; [occ.] Hospital of Bayonne; [pers.] Thanks to my summer up in Sun Air Camp Grounds.

DeFINA, JOHN R.
[b.] January 22, 1970, Weehawken, NJ; [p.] Bartholamea and Evelyn DeFina; [ed.] Union Hill High School; [occ.] Clerk, Liz Clairborne Inc.; [oth.writ.] "Cooperstown Bound", "Lost In Love", "Dear Michelle"; [pers.] I try to express the feeling of losing or the leaving of people who were dearly loved. [a.] Union City, NJ.

DeFORD, KRISTIE
[pen.] Kristie DeFord; [b.] October 8, 1973, Burlington, WI; [p.] Bonnie Hancock and Jerry Rodriquez; [ed.] 14 years at Tomah High; [occ.] Seamstress; [oth.writ.] Short (unfinished) stories. [a.] Tomah, WI.

DELAWARE, DOROTHY P.J.
[pen.] Marie Dela; [b.] April 13, 1945, Baltimore, MD; [p.] Mr. and Mrs. Herman Lee Jones, Sr.; [m.] Roland Leon Delaware, October 2, 1964; [ch.] (Parental guardian), Wanda, Pauline, Aaron, Tammy Angeline, Anglecia and Kara; [ed.] Paul Lawrence Dunbar Senior High School graduated June 8, 1964; [occ.] Poet, artist, philosopher and Entrepreneur; [oth.writ.] Children novel, "Sea Party" not published yet; [pers.] My personal philosophy is to respect, love and believe in God and yourself. Take care of you and yours. Take time out to stop, listen and look around you. Think about everything you have seen and heard. Learn from it. Don't stand and ponder the thought! Move on. Always desire more than you have and prepare

to work hard for it. [a.] Baltimore, MD.

DeMARCO, MAREA LYNNE
[b.] June 19,1980, Falls Church, VA; [p.] Ronald and Margaret DeMarco; [ed.] Currently in 9th grade at Lake Braddock Secondary School, Institute for the Arts 1994; [occ.] Student; [memb.] World Wildlife Fund, Earth Island Institute, International Order of Job's Daughters, National Junior Honor Society, Springfield Youth Club Soccer; [hon.] Honor Roll; [oth.writ.] Various poems for Reflections, a school poetry book; [pers.] "Touch the earth, love the earth, her plains, her valleys, her hills and her seas, rest your spirit in her solitary places". Henry Beston. [a.] Burke, VA.

DeMARTIN, MICHAEL
[pen.] Nebiros Andre Marcotte;[b.] March 10, 1953, Burbank, CA; [p.] Albert and Charlotte DeMartin; [m.] Dorothy DeMartin, October 14, 1989; [occ.] Meta Physician, Occult Philosopher, lecturer; [memb.] Ordain Minister of the faith "New World Temple For All Creation", October 12,1985, incorporated March 30,1978, California; [oth.writ.] Several privately published works, such as "The Magic of Numbers", "Life Scope Oracle" and "The Art of Divination"; [pers.] Each in their own time realizes the kinship of all things under heaven, and is thereby made whole. [a.] Hollywood, CA.

DEMING, TIMOTHY D.
[b.] December 3, 1968, Winfield, IL; [ed.] B.S. Columbia Bible College, Columbia, SC; [oth.writ.] Unpublished poems in personal file; [pers.] I received a "D" my first time through poetry class (Eng 102) at the University of Georgia. I believe that "every good and perfect gift is from above" and therefore that Christ Jesus deserves credit for our accomplishments, whether great or small. "Flights" is a reference to the U.S. Air crash in Pennsylvania in September of 1994. [a.] Wheaton, IL.

DeNARDO, ERIN
[b.] March 12, 1979, LaCrosse, WI; [p.] Judith and Charles DeNardo; [ed.] Presently a sophomore at Waukesha West High School, Waukesha, WI; [occ.] Student and cashier; [memb.] Drama Club; [pers.] I feel that my poems are to reflect the good times and the bad times in life. The poems I write contain many or the feelings I am going through as a teenager. I enjoy writing very much and hope others will enjoy my writing too. [a.] Waukesha, WI.

DENKER, ROBIN
[pen.] Rob; [b.] April 3, 1964, Sioux City, IA; [p.] Barb Parmeter; [m.] Rick Denker, November 23, 1985; [ch.] Tristan Wayne, Shaland Elyise and Mandi Leigh; [ed.] South Sioux Senior High; [occ.] Beautician-Cost-Cutters Hairdresser; [oth.writ.] 2 other poems and 1 letter which won my mother and stepfather a trip to Washington, DC in 1987 to the Welcome Home Concert for Viet Nam Vets; [a.] South Sioux, NE.

DENNIS, CAROLYN A.
[b.] February 7, Edenton, NC; [m.] Larry A. Dennis; [ch.] Tiffany Leanne; [ed.] Manor High, Tidewater Community College; [occ.] Career in Public Relations, city of Portsmouth, VA; [memb.] Vice President of the Hunt/Mapp Middle School PTSA-94/95 school year, Secretary of Hunt/Mapp Middle School PTSA 93/94 school year, Vice President of fundraising, Douglas Park Elementary School PTA 1990/91 school year; [oth.writ.] Numerous articles and feature stories published in local newspapers, have written and illustrated my first children's novel and am currently seeking a publisher; [pers.] Fictional writing is my escape. In my writings, I can go any place I choose and no matter what, things always turn out the way I want them to. [a.] Portsmouth, VA.

DENNIS, GLENDA (McINTOSH)
[pen.] Max Lee; [b.] November 26, 1945, Taylorsville, MS; [p.] Lee Roy and Hattie McIntosh; [m.] Gary Dennis, December 19, 1965; [ed.] Taylorsville High, Jones County Community College, East Central Community College; [occ.] Woodwork shop of yard decorations; [memb.] Zion Church of God; [hon.] Phi Beta Lambda, Philomathean Club Treasurer; [oth.writ.] Articles for local newspaper, chairperson and publisher of church cookbook, poems and writings for church paper, compiled family tree albums; [pers.] I believe a person's own experiences can also benefit other people's lives. The beauty of God's nature, and simply being alive inspires me. [a.] Philadelphia, MS.

DERENTHAL, JEFFREY BRYAN
[pen.] Jeff; [b.] October 19, 1978, Women's Hospital; [p.] Tom and Jean Derenthal; [ed.] Working on high school; [memb.] Social Studies Academic Society, Thespians; [pers.] No matter what the price always be yourself and always tell the truth. [a.] Seffner, FL.

DeSABATO, EDWARD
[b.] March 13,1931, Brooklyn, NY; [p.] Ernest and Mary; [ed.] George Westinghouse High School, P.S. 157 Elementary School; [occ.] Retired; [memb.] D.A.V., N.R.A., Florida Sheriffs Association, N.Y.C. Civil Service Retirees Association, St. Jude Children's Hospital Association; [hon.] D.A.V. Captain's club, St. Joseph's Indian School; [oth.writ.] "Christmas Comes But Once A Year", "You Took My Heart and Tore It Apart", "A Half Hour By Car", "As Time Passes"; [pers.] I try to bring to the attention of children that there is very little time to show love and respect for their mothers. [a.] Brooklyn, NY.

DeSILVIO, CRISTINA
[b.] July 11, 1977, Hamilton, Ontario; [p.] Sara and Vito; [sib.] Frank (12) and Leanne (14); [ed.] Student, St. Mary's Catholic High School in Hamilton; [oth.writ.] Other various poems and unpublished short stories; [pers.] Whoever has read the poem has had something to say about it. An English teacher asked me if I "needed to talk", that's when I knew I had achieved my purpose. This poem makes you think, maybe about something you've never considered before, that's what poetry is, a statement that makes you think. [a.] Ancaster, Ontario.

DESMARAIS, SHARON
[pen.] Stam; [b.] November 7, 1976; [p.] Rose Moreau and John Desmarais; [ed.] Cegep Education in commerce, assistant teacher for mentally and physically handicap children; [hon.] In high school I received 3 certificates of honor for volunteering to work with the handicap children of our school; [oth.writ.] Some poetry and articles published in school newspapers, other projects exposed in Science Fairs and bulletin board; [pers.] I'd like to thank my boyfriend and dearest friend Seb, who inspired me to write this poem, as well as my family for their support. [a.] Montreal, Quebec.

DESONIA, ALBERT
[b.] January 9, 1969, Subic Bay, Philippines; [p.] Perfecto and Victoria Desonia; [ed.] Goose Creek High School, United States Naval Academy, Clemson University; [memb.] American Mensa, Ltd., U.S. Naval Academy Alumni Association, U.S. Naval Institute; [hon.] Admiral John H. Sides Perpetual Award. [a.] Goose Creek, SC.

DEVLIN, NORA
[pen.] Nora Devlin; [pers.] Love Jesus, know God, show the world. [a.] Sunnyvale, CA.

DEYNES, MERIDA G.
[pen.] Memi; [b.] January 27,1975, Manhattan; [p.] Ismael Deynes and Rosalia Ramos; [hon.] 1st in city championship in handball and 2nd in the Bronx championships; [pers.] Without the love and support of the one person who influences me to write poetry from the heart. Jose Luis Valentine the love of my life, the one who brings out the best in me. [a.] Bronx, NY.

DeZELL, JACLYN
[pen.] Jaclyn DeZell; [b.] January 30, 1980, Livonia, MI; [p.] Elmer (Al) and Andrea DeZell; [ed.] Plymouth Salem High School; [occ.] Student; [hon.] Honor Roll, Artistic Achievement Award, Fashion Model, Certificate of Achievement; [pers.] I created "Eternal Love" in memory of my grandfather's death and the birth of my niece. I love my grandfather very much and missed him after his death. Two years later, my niece was born. My love for my grandfather was never forgotten and now I love my niece as much as my grandfather loved me. I'd like to dedicate this poem to my niece, Amanda Lombardo and my grandfather Joseph P. Billicic. [a.] Plymouth, MI.

DIAZ, VIVIANA MARIA TERESA
[pen.] Viviana Maria Teresa Diaz; [b.] September 26, 1953, Yakima, WA; [p.] Audelio P. and Carmen Diaz; [ed.] Kent Meridian High School; [occ.] Can't work because of my handicap and disability, can't drive; [memb.] In the past I was a member of the King County Epilepsy League, until KCEL merged with the Washington State Epilepsy Society and moved to Seattle; [oth.writ.] Many poems on Epilepsy for the King County Epilepsy League (First Aide For Seizures, You Need To Follow) 60 lines long, I wrote "A Brave and Strong Soldier" for David Anthony Cardenas, my cousin who was a Marine in the Persian Gulf War, 50 lines; [pers.] I like writing poems that can help others deal with personal problems. I believe if former NBC News Correspondent Arthur Kent were to read my poems about himself that he would feel better about himself inside and just ask Arthur Kent yourself if this is so. My cousin thanked me for all I did for him during the Persian Gulf War. My cousin gave me his medal that says on it, Yakima Valley says thanks, Operation Desert Shield/Storm 90-91. My cousin's first words to me when he got back from the war were, "YOU DID IT". [a.] Kent, WA.

DIBBLE, KIMBERLY
[b.] June 9, 1976, Kingston, NY; [p.] Michael and Raelyn Dibble; [ed.] Rhinebeck High, New York, Lindsay High, Oklahoma, Oklahoma State University; [occ.] Student at Oklahoma State University; [memb.] OSU Horsemen's Association, OSU Pre-vet Club; [hon.] Kelly Ann Eubank scholarship, Superintendent's Honor Roll, medals in Interscholastic meets, Who's Who Among High School Students in America; [oth.writ.] Poem published in town newspaper (Lindsay) for homecoming, all other writing is personal poems and original stories; [pers.] I base my writing greatly on emotions and feelings, and try to convey that feeling by creating a visual picture for the reader. [a.] Foster, OK.

DiCARLO JR., MICHAEL J.
[pen.] John Doe; [b.] April 12, 1973, Massachusetts; [p.] Michael J. DiCarlo; [ed.] Winthrop High School, University of Massachusetts at Amherst; [occ.] United States Marine; [memb.] United States

Marine Corps; [hon.] National Defense Award; [pers.] I see myself as a medium through which my emotions are channeled for I achieve sanctuary through my writings. [a.] Winthrop, MA.

DIGGETT, ALLISON RENEE
[b.] October 7, 1979, Pawtucker, RI; [p.] Michael E. and Alice R. Diggett; [ed.] Winter Haven High School, Winter Haven, FL. [occ.] Student; [hon.] P.C.C.T.E. Poetry Award 1992, Polk County Foreign Language competition, 1993 and 1994, National Library of Poetry, Editor's Choice, Tears of Fire, "What Is Sane" 1993; [oth.writ.] "Ice Garden" 1992, "What Is Sane" 1993, "And The Roses Clash" 1994; [pers.] "Rose" was composed with inspiration from and in memory of Rose Bergeron, February 14, 1949-March 8, 1993. [a.] Winter Haven, FL.

DiGREGORIO, JIM
[b.] May 14, 1924, Brooklyn, NY; [p.] Frank and Mary DiGregorio; [m.] Annette Faccenda, April 6, 1946; [ch.] Frank James DiGregorio and Mary Ann Zambito; [ed.] Long Island University, NY, Stony Brook State University, NY, NY American Institute of Banking, PA State University; [occ.] Retired New York City Firefighter, Congressional NY State Political Advisor; [memb.] Currently involved as Investment Executive, Banker Real Estate, Financial Marketing, member-actively formerly engaged on Long Island New York politically over 25 years during 1950's, 60's and 70's; [hon.] Never really tried, to complete for high honors or awards for financial gain, reason, some of my original ideas have been stolen from me since my birth and this has kept me from showing my complete writings or being involved as an adviser; [oth.writ.] Author of Vol 1 "Original (c) 1977 by Jim DiGregorio, (author writer), "To Balance The Natural Survival", A Hearthstone Book, Carlton Press Inc., New York, NY,. poem "The Balance of Nature" in above book pages 76, 77, also titled in 1976 National Society of Poets, poems, "The Eulogy of Mom", page 293, "The Shining Star" page 294, both in book "New Voices In American Poetry" 1976, Vantage Press, U.S.A. National Publisher; [pers.] The world of the young poor have many friends. As success come to some and they ascend out of poverty their comrade of misery are lost forever. The more successful we are the loner life could become. Success of one could mean failure to another. Who may wish for more, we need the wisdom to reach a day to day goal, gradually transforming "negatives" to "positive" needed. As I'm one who has not reached certain goals I am capable of, I personally feel I have the honor of being titled "the most successful failure you have ever met. [a.] Forest City, PA.

DILL, DIANNA
[pen.] Di; [b.] September 30, 1952, Johnstown; [p.] Owen and Delila Dill; [ed.] Jenner Boswell Junior Senior High School; [occ.] Horticulturist; [memb.] American Horticultural Society, Academy of Ornament Horticulture, National Association of Female Executives; [hon.] Silver Poet 1990 Award of Merit, Certificate 1988, Golden Poet Award 1989 Award of Merit Certificate 1992; [oth.writ.] Several poems not published, short stories not published; [pers.] I enjoy writing poems for friends. [a.] Jennerstown, PA.

DISBENNETT, TIMOTHY A.
[b.] January 17, 1952, Marion, OH; [p.] Walter H. and Ruth Disbennett; [m.] Brenda C. Disbennett, December 12, 1970; [ch.] Tracy and Robin; [ed.] Bucyrus High School, Ohio, Wayland Baptist University, University of Oklahoma; [pers.] "A Prayer for Granddaughter" was written for my granddaughter, Erin, shortly after her birth in April 1992. [a.] New Lebanon, OH.

DiSPIRITO, NADINE
[b.] March 14, 1977, Arlington Heights, IL; [p.] James J. and Nancy Dispirito Jr.; [ed.] Palatine High School; [oth.writ.] Several poems. [a.] Palatine, IL.

DiSTEFANO, SHERRY
[pen.] Sherry DiStefano; [b.] July 30, 1974, Providence; [p.] Joey and Debbie DiStefano; [occ.] I'm currently in sales and someday hope to be a poet; [pers.] The poems I write are to someone dear to my heart Vincent Voas, who has stood beside me when there was no-one else there. Our love is one of a kind and our friendship undesirable.[a.] Johnstown, RI.

DIVITO-NAHS, JONATHAN
[b.] February 14, 1978, Battle Creek; [occ.] High school student; [pers.] I believe poetry is a personal experience. Poetry should be used to express emotions and personal point of views. [a.] Elmhurst, IL.

DIXON, SHANNON
[b.] November 9, 1974, Canada; [p.] Pat and Alex Dixon; [ed.] Currently enrolled in University of South Florida; [occ.] Legal Assistant.

DODDS, ANDREW F.
[b.] July 19, 1949, Scotland; [p.] Andrew and Marion Dodds; [m.] Jayne, August 1990; [ch.] Steven Jamie and Marion; [ed.] Chryston Primary and Secondary Schools; [occ.] Merchant seaman; [oth.writ.] Various other poems and short stories with a variety of subjects; [pers.] I tend to write about my own experiences in life and find pleasure in other people enjoying my efforts.

DODDS, TISH
[pen.] Tish Dodds; [b.] February 26, 1979, Akron-St., Thomas Hospital; [p.] Larry Dodds and Sherry Carey; [ed.] Chippewa High School, sophomore; [hon.] A cheerleading achievement award, most improved cheerleading award; [oth.writ.] I write many poems now and then, but mostly they are for fun; [pers.] Who would ever think that a dream would come true right away. I never thought that a poem that I wrote could be liked by many. I didn't have much faith in myself, but now I do. Those of you who feel that you aren't good at anything, it's because you're holding yourself back. If you let yourself go, you could find so many hidden qualities, but they won't just appear you have to work for them, then grab it. You never know when it's too late, so you'd better start your life now. Go get it and live hard. [a.] Doylestown, OH.

DODSON, MARTHA L.
[b.] October 12, 1915, Tekoa, WA; [p.] Alphons and Ella Denoo; [m.] Charles Dodson, July 17, 1968; [ch.] Sally, Wallace, Susan, Gary and Stephen; [ed.] Tekoa High School graduate; [occ.] Retired; [oth.writ.] None that have been published; [pers.] My poem was inspired by Idaho's mighty Salmon River. Nature's beauty can warm the heart of all of us if we take the time to stop and look. [a.] Boise, ID.

DOLIN, EVA J.
[pen.] Eva Dolin, Eva Fisher; [pen.] April 29, Chicago, IL; [p.] Bertha and Ben Fisher; [m.] Deceased; [ch.] Dennis Alan and Dr. Edward Howard Dolin; [ed.] North Western University School of Journalism, Evanston, IL., Roosevelt High School, Chicago, IL., Off Campus Writer's Workshop, Winnetka, IL; [occ.] Columnist, freelance writer; [memb.] American Heart Association, Hadassah, Evelyn Steinberg Cancer Foundation, Publicity Club of Chicago, Off-Campus Writer's Workshop, Winnetka, IL, Public Relations Society, Phi Iota Zeta Sorority; [hon.] "Hall of Fame"-Publicity Club of Chicago, "Foremost Woman in Communications" (1970) Recording Industry Award, Best News Reporting and Public Relations; [oth.writ.] Newspaper, magazine columnist and feature writer, author of copywriter columns, "Garden of Eva", "The Amusement Wheel", "Teen Newsmakers", "Eva Dolin's Newsmakers", "The Shopping Wheel" appearing regularly in the Lerner newspaper chain, Bugle newspapers, Freeshopper News, Lakeview News and various teen and adult magazines, published feature articles in newspapers, magazines throughout the U.S.; [pers.] I hope my poem to my beloved son, Denny, (Dennis Alan Dolin) will reach deep into the hearts of mothers and fathers who have lost a child, so that they too can find peace and comfort as I have. There is no greater emotional outlet than the written words of a poem. [a.] Glenview, IL.

DOLOTALLAS, LAILANIE
[b.] November 14, 1978, Vancouver, BC; [p.] Luz Galdo Dolotallas and Matildo Dolotallas; [ed.] Lord Tweedsmuir Secondary School; [occ.] Grade 11 student at Lord Tweedsmuir Secondary School; [memb.] Lord Tweedsmuir Senior concert band, vocal jazz, rugby; [hon.] Musicianship awards, Honor Roll in grade 10; [oth.writ.] Many writings that are unknown; [pers.] For all of their support and encouragement, I dedicate this poem to my family and friends with love. [a.] Vancouver, BC Canada.

DONALDSON, DAWN M.
[b.] March 8, 1975, Lemore Naval Air Station, CA; [p.] Holly and Stephen Holland; [ed.] A.S. in Paralegal at College of the Sequoias, high school-Hanford High; [memb.] College of the Sequoias (C.O.S.) Paralegal Association; [hon.] Delta Kappa Gamma, Dean's List; [oth.writ.] Several poems written, never published; [pers.] I hope my writing touches others as deeply as it has myself. [a.] Visalia, CA.

DOUGLAS, SHARON KAY
[b.] May 20, 1952, Sarasota, FL; [p.] David and Joyce Minor; [occ.] Licensed Practical Nurse, specializing in medically complex pediatric patients; [oth.writ.] Although I have written to myself all of my life as my way of coping, this is my first public display of my most "inner thoughts"; [pers.] I deem my poems "Basics" because I write about life in it's simplistic form. Exactly the way I believe we as a society should view it. Inner knowledge is to me, the most valuable. [a.] Orlando, FL.

DOW, STEVEN
[b.] July 6, 1973, Philadelphia, PA; [p.] Robert F. Dow Jr. and Josephine Ann G. Dow (deceased); [ed.] Red Bank Catholic High School, Villanova University; [occ.] Engineering student; [hon.] Tay Beta Pi, Chi Epsilon; [oth.writ.] Several poems in campus publications and a few short stories I'm proud of; [pers.] I guess I try to get at the roots of things even when there may be no roots and even when it might not make a difference if there were. I like to flirt with both futurity and meaning and I suppose I'm very influenced artistically by people who attempt sincerity (i.e. Albert Camus, Kurt Cobain, Bruce Springsteen, etc.). [a.] Tinton Falls, NJ.

DOWDS, CAROLE A.
[b.] March 9, 1947, Barberton, OH; [p.] Susan and Frank Hahacky; [m.] Lawrence R. Dowds Jr., August 18, 1973; [ch.] Joyce Lynn, Daniel Scott and Kristen Sue; [ed.] St. John's College, Cleve-

land, Ursline College, Cleveland; [occ.] Licensed Social Worker; [memb.] Education Chairman of the Tri-County Association Nursing Home Social Workers, Board Member of Senior Rights and Advocacy and Chairman of Quality Assurance Committee for Senior Rights and Advocacy; [oth.writ.] Just recently started to write poetry at this time; [pers.] I strive to reflect the inner most thoughts of the mind and the soul and it response to life. [a.] Warren, OH.

DOWNEY, KEITH
[pen.] J.K. Downey; [b.] July 17, 1969, Jasper, IN; [ed.] Bedford North Lawrence High School; [occ.] Rock musician and member of rock group duo "Two of Us"; [pers.] Lennon and McCartney, Vie and Z'Nuff are responsible for inspiring me to become a writer. Lyrics are the language of infinity. If you have not reached that point yet you still have not tapped into your emotions. Take a ride with the Beatles and come into our world. [a.] St. Mary's, KS.

DOWNIE, DOUGLAS R.
[pen.] Douglas Alistair Biro, Einwood Salguod; [b.] January 2, 1953, Toronto, Ontario; [p.] Robert and Freda Downie (deceased); [m.] Divorced, April 2, 1977; [ch.] 1; [ed.] Successful completion of Anthropology course at McMaster University in Hamilton; [occ.] Unemployed writer of children's short stories, playwright; [memb.] T.H.I.A.C., Tenants and Homeless Information and Action Committee (steering committee member), Chairman of the board of the M.H.R.C., Mental Health Rights Coalition, Hamilton Poetry Club, Naturalists Club; [hon.] Graduation from the Connecticut Institute of Children's Literature; [oth.writ.] Children's short stories as yet unpublished and non-fiction articles as yet unpublished and science fiction stories as yet unpublished; [pers.] Healthy competition is good for the soul. [a.] Hamilton, Ontario.

DOWNIE, REBECCA GRACE
[b.] May 22, 1960, Roseville, CA; [p.] Carl and Margaret Winter; [m.] Tom Downie, April 25, 1981; [ch.] Amanda Jean and Caroline Annette; [ed.] Sacramento High School, Sacramento State University; [occ.] I'm the musician for the American Eurhythmy School in Weed, California, classical performing artist, professional pianist and violinist, teach music; [oth.writ.] Currently working on a children's book, and writing and illustrating my own poetry book; [pers.] I love to read and write. Children's literature is of great interest to me. I would like to present clean, non-violent, imaginative stories to children, so they can truly dream in this harsh world. [a.] Mount Shasta City, CA.

DOWNING JR., THOMAS
[pen.] Eric Nathaniel; [b.] December 13, 1958; [m.] Maria; [ch.] Ariel, Alisia, Bryanna; [oth.writ.] Currently seeking publication of a book of poetry and 2 children's books; [pers.] Aspire to the limitless! There are heights and depths within the mind begging to be discovered and each of us can provide a pathway through uncharted territory. Dare to quest! [a.] San Bernardino, CA.

DOYLE, RUTH M.
[pen.] Ruth McCumber; [b.] February 1, 1942, Tattnall County, GA; [p.] Troy and Cevera McCumber; [ch.] Doug, Dwain and Drew; [ed.] Graduated high school; [occ.] Secretary/bookkeeper; [oth.writ.] Many poems and short autobiographical "Moments to Remember" (none published); [pers.] My poems and writings are like children to me. I feel very protective of them and find it hard to share them with others. It's like giving away a part of myself. [a.] Metter, GA.

DOZIER, SUZANNE M.
[b.] February 26, 1960, Travis A.F.B., CA; [p.] Margaret B. and Robert E. Herrick; [oth.writ.] Several unpublished poems; [pers.] Transition begins with our first breathe and ends with our last. Some transitions pass through our lives with no more notice than the blink of an eye, other transitions touch us so deeply that we are left with hindsight and insight which changes our lives forever. Through these transitions I have been blessed with the ability to experience peace and solace through my writing. [a.] Vacaville, CA.

DRINKARD-HAWKSHAWE, DOROTHY
[b.] June 22, 1938, Greensboro, GA; [p.] Claudia Belle Ashe Drinkard and Junior Drinkard; [m.] Richard R. Hawkshawe (deceased), June 14, 1963; [ch.] Sharon B. Hawkshawe; [ed.] B.A. (Economics) at Howard University, M.A. (History), Ph.D. (history at the Catholic University of America); [occ.] University Professor and Administrator; [memb.] Phi Alpha Theta, International Honor Society in History, Association for the Study of Afro American Life and History, American Historical Society; [hon.] The poem in this collection was written at age 17 upon graduation from high school, it was selected as the class song in competition with others; [oth.writ.] Historical writings on the Civil War and construction and biographies of historical figures; [pers.] God given gifts should be developed and used to make the world a better place. [a.] Columbia, MD.

DRY JR., GEORGE
[pen.] George Dry; [b.] Lehighton, PA;[p.] George M. and Elsie M.; [ch.] Michael, Rodger and Gail; [ed.] 10 1/2 years; [occ.] Singer/songwriter currently not working; [memb.] A.F.M., A.A.R.P., American Heart Association, B.M.I.; [hon.] 1982 Wrangler contest 1st place, New Jersey state, American Heart fund awards, wrote special song for Desert Storm (Gulf War), special letter of praise from President Bush; [oth.writ.] Have written over 200 songs, some in poem form, recorded Christmas cassette of own songs, also country cassette of own songs, 2 albums, some singles all on own label; [pers.] Most if not all my songs and poems are true to life experiences. I give God all the credit for my writings. I am only the instrument that places the words on paper for without His help I could not write the things I do. [a.] Stroudsburg, PA.

DUCOTE, NICOLAS JOSEPH
[pen.] Nico Ducote; [b.] September 17, 1970, Buenos Aires, Argentina; [p.] Raymond Joseph Ducote and Patricia Ines Moche; [ed.] Escuela Escocesa San Andres, Universidad Catholica Argentina, Universidad De San Andres, Georgetown University; [occ.] Student of International Affairs; [oth.writ.] Unpublished poems in English, Spanish, Portuguese and others; [pers.] I have been greatly influenced by my father's hidden poetry and the soft romantic music of the world. [a.] Buenos Aires, Argentina and Arlington, VA.

DUNLAP, HELEN ELIZABETH
[pen.] Helen Brown Dunlap; [b.] August 23, 1937, Wellston, OH; [p.] Coleman Albert and Margie Brown; [m.] Jerry David Dunlap, June 16, 1985; [ch.] Timothy A. Voght, Margie Renee Voght and Kayse E. Hembree; [ed.] Jeffersonville High School, Jeffersonville, IN, IBM, Data Processing, Montgomery County Ohio Police Academy; [occ.] Domestic engineer; [memb.] Calvery Baptist Church, Richmond, IN; [hon.] Editor's Choice Award, The National Library of Poetry; [oth.writ.] A tribute to my dad Rev. C.A. Brown for his 60 years in the ministry, "Daddy", "Why Do We Wait", "Where Daddy Lives" has been published in the Calvary Baptist Church paper, "The Voice of Calvary", "Daddy" published in The Space Between, The National Library of Poetry, "Where Daddy Lives" published in Poetic Voices of America, Sparrowgrass Poetry Forum; [pers.] Once again I want to thank God for the talent He has given me. If I can brighten someone's day through the poetry that I write than I am happy. Everything that God originally put on this earth was beautiful, somehow things have went a little downhill. I would like to help bring some of that beauty back through poetry. [a.] Richmond, IN.

DUNLAP, JENNIFER
[b.] May 4, 1978, Ft. Worth, TX; [p.] Ronald and Paula Dunlap; [ed.] Presently a junior at Amarillo High School, Amarillo, Texas; [memb.] Office Aide at Amarillo High; [hon.] I received an award for Creative Writing as a sophomore at Judge Joe Edison High School; [oth.writ.] School projects and personnel poems; [pers.] I strongly feel that there is to much violence in the world and not enough love. I focus on writing poems about love and kindness. [a.] Ft. Worth, TX.

DUNLAP, PATRICIA ELMORE
[b.] October 10, 1927, Borger, TX; [p.] Frank B. and Theda Mize Elmore (both deceased); [m.] John M. Dunlap; [ch.] Mary Kathryn (Kate) Benson, Douglas Elmore Benson and Kelley Benson, stepchildren, Charles Shank Dunlap and Virginia Bell Dunlap Celentano, grandchildren, Rachell Eve and Garrett Cole Benson, Amanda Marie and Christopher Clarke Dunlap; [ed.] Borger High School, Borger, TX., West Texas State University, Canyon, YX., the University of Kansas, Lawrence, KS; [occ.] Retired landsman from CXY Energy Inc, Dallas, Texas; [hon.] Certified Professional Secretary 1965 and Certified Professional Landsman 1981; [oth.writ.] Numerous informational and technical reports and bulletins for the petroleum industry, poems in hometown newspaper; [pers.] In these days of war, famine and crime, I like to paint word pictures in either prose or poetry giving hope, humor and trust in the future of our nation and the world.

DUNN, JOE
[pen.] Joe Chuch; [b.] June 14, 1977, Lubbock, TX; [p.] Ray and Becky Dunn; [ed.] Coronado High School; [memb.] National Honor Society, Coronado marching and concert band, Indiana Avenue Baptist Church and youth choir; [hon.] Who's Who Among American High School Students. [a.] Lubbock, TX.

DUNNEBIER-FRAUENBERGER, MARTHA M.
[b.] Germany; [m.] Erich Frauenberger (painter-artist); [ch.] Five children; [ed.] M.A. English, CSU Sacramento, M.A. German, CSU Sacramento; [occ.] Retired German teacher; [memb.] Delta Phi Alpha; [oth.writ.] Several poems published on various poetry books, poem printed in a CSUS Literary magazine; [pers.] For me poetry is an emotional outlet to resolve conflicts within myself and my surroundings. Searching for a connection of the inner and outer world lets me maybe come closer to a truth. [a.] Fair Oaks, CA.

DUPLANTIS, KRISTY LYNN
[pen.] Kristy L. Duplantis; [p.] Erich and Faye Duplantis; [ed.] I am currently a sophomore in high school; [occ.] Student; [memb.] Key Club; [hon.] 1988 4th grade Citizenship Award, 1992 8th grade Spirit Award (drill squad); [oth.writ.] I have a notebook of poetry never published, I was waiting for an older age to show it out; [pers.] I started writing poems at the age of 8, but I wrote this poem after a tragic accident involving my brother. I write

poems to express the way I feel on things that happen or just ideas I get. [a.] Houma, LA.

DURBIN, HERBERT F.
[pen.] H. Fitzgerald; [b.] February 18, 1915, Todd, OK; [p.] W.R. Durbin and Bertha L. Romines; [m.] Nolda Juanita Walker, August 15, 1933; [ch.] Seven; [ed.] 8 years public school, 4 years Bible training; [occ.] Retired Christian Minister; [memb.] A.A.R.P., C.W.A., A.F.A., General Council of the Assemblies of God, Rutherford Institute, Christian Action Network; [hon.] Gold pin award for fifty years of ministry; [oth.writ.] The Man Last, My Life Story, poems published in local paper; [pers.] That my life and writings will portray the love and compassion of a creative God. [a.] Wyandotte, OK.

DURHAM, CLINT
[b.] November 9,1978, Hendersonville, TN; [p.] Alton and Kathy Durham; [ed.] Currently enrolled at Hendersonville High School; [pers.] I hope to make an impression on other people in poetry to help them overcome obstacles. [a.] Hendersonville, TN.

DURHAM, JAMIE
[b.] July 13,1984, Tacoma, WA; [p.] Jim and JoAnn Durham; [ed.] Endeavour Intermediate; [occ.] Student; [memb.] ASB Student Body, member of Dance Magic; [hon.] Treasurer of ASB and 2nd place in competitions; [oth.writ.] School newspapers and oral announcements; [pers.] I study a subject before writing about it. [a.] Auburn, WA.

DURNAN, AMANDA
[pen.] Mandy Durnan; [b.] August 11, 1980, Sacramento; [p.] Janice Johnson and Dan Durnan; [ed.] Woodcreek High School; [occ.] School/computers; [hon.] Various awards from school and certificates; [oth.writ.] Several poems that haven't been published; [pers.] I like to write about all the good things in life, beauty, nature, people, etc. I have been inspired by God. He gave me my talent and wanted me to make the best of it. I give thanks to my mom for never letting me give up. [a.] Roseville, CA.

DUSETTE, RUTHE M.
[pen.] Ruthe Dusette; [b.] January 30, 1947, Dobbs Ferry, NY; [p.] Charles M. and Fanchon W. Hollis; [m.] Christopher E. Dusette Sr., July 1, 1967; [ch.] Kit (Jr), Rudyard and Tobias S.; [ed.] Redford High, Detroit, Mi., University of Michigan School of Music; [oth.writ.] Children's stories; [pers.] There is something creative within us all we only need to tap into it. If one medium does not work try a different outlet, but never give up! [a.] Interlochen, MI.

DUVALL, SARAH WALL
[b.] August 30, 1946, Toccoa, GA; [p.] Frank and Mary Stone Wall; [m.] Julius Dean Duvall, December 25, 1966; [ch.] Jacquelyn Deanna and William Edward; [ed.] Bachelor of Music Ed-Columbus College, Columbus, GA., Masters of Curriculum and Instruction, University of Kansas, Western Maryland College, University of South Carolina; [occ.] Media Specialist-Oakland Elementary, Greenwood, SC; [memb.] NEA, National Associations of Story Tellers, SCEA, ALA, SCALA, ALA; [hon.] Distinguished Reading Oakland Elementary School, Distinguished Reading Teacher Piedmont Reading Council, Teacher of the Year 94-95, Greenwood District 50 Teacher of the Year 94-95; [oth.writ.] Several poems published in local paper; [pers.] Several of my poems were written after a gunman came into our school and killed two students and injured several others. My poems were written to hasten the healing process. [a.] Greenwood, SC.

DWELLO, CHELSIE
[b.] May 19, Great Falls, MT. [p.] Midge Cweleaux; [ed.] School of Aerospace Medicine, Brooks AFB, Texas; [occ.] Aero Medical Technician; [hon.] Editors Choice Award, National Library of Poetry; [oth.writ.] The Coming of Dawn, A Question of Balance, The Best Poems of 1995; [pers.] I would like to dedicate this poem and all future poems to a very close friend, Mark Christopher, Martin Hernandez (as you wish).

DYBER, W. JAMES
[b.] Hartford, CT; [p.] Walter J. and Beatrice M. Dyber (deceased); [m.] Elizabeth K. Dyber; [ch.] Kenneth and Nicholas; [ed.] Watkinson School, McMurray College; [occ.] Sales manager for Encyclopedia Britannica. [a.] West Hartford, CT.

DYCK, STACY
[b.] August 20, 1973, Morden, Manitoba; [p.] Ray and Eunice Dyck; [ed.] I am currently in grade 10 at Teulon Collegiate in Manitoba, Canada, I have passed all grades with honors; [occ.] I am a volunteer at a nursing home as well as a grade 10 student; [memb.] I am a member of the st. Andrews Horse Association and a member of 4-H; [hon.] I am an Honor Student as well as a high achiever in several classes, I have been awarded the O'Malley Award, most improved rider, sports leadership award as well as 4 speech contest awards and Equestrian awards; [oth.writ.] This is my first published poem, I'm very happy; [pers.] "Fudge" was my first horse, still is and always will be. This poem is to my best friend, "Fudge". [a.] Teulon, Maintoba Canada.

DYKES, JOSIE H.
[pen.] Josie H. Dykes; [b.] October 13, 1939, New Orleans; [p.] Mim-Charles W. Hanagriff; [m.] Hugh V. Dykes, September 27, 1967; [ch.] Elizabeth, Kimberly, Lynn Maureen; [ed.] Franklin University of South Louisiana; [occ.] Director of Activities, Franklin Nursing Home; [memb.] Grace Presbyterian Church; [hon.] BP&W, Woman of the Year 1967; [[pers.] Working with the elderly is a challenging and satisfying career. [a.] Franklin, LA.

EADIE, SHARON
[pen.] Siobhan Eadie; [b.] March 3, 1972, Glasgow, Scotland; [p.] Isabella F. and Jerry Eadie; [ed.] St. Saviours and St. Olaves Secondary School, London, Westchester High School, Los Angeles; [occ.] Writer (starving artist), unpublished; [memb.] People For The Ethical Treatment of Animals (PETA); [oth.writ.] El Camino College Warrior Life magazine, LD-50 magazine, Underground LA (both LD-50 and Underground LA published, in part by myself); [pers.] I like to write about the issues that are not being addressed (as unpleasant as they may be). I consider myself a realist. I try not to be too opinionated in my writing and let the reader make his\her own decisions. Influences Charles Bukowski and William S. Burroughs. [a.] Redondo Beach, CA.

EARLY, TERENCE J.
[pen.] Jay Earley; [b.] March 14, 1980, Burlington, NJ; [p.] Susan Helen and Terry James Earley; [ed.] 9th grade student, Shawnee High School, Burlington County, NJ; [oth.writ.] Numerous songs and poems written for either musical or personal reasons; [pers.] God didn't give us anything He didn't want us to have. So, when inspiration comes grab, hold on and never let go. It's not your life that depends on it... it's your soul. [a.] Medford, NJ.

EATON, JESSE
[b.] November 25, 1959, Los Angeles; [p.] Ed and Theresa Eaton; [m.] Cynthia Saxton, July 1991; [ch.] Candy, Jessica, Shane and Cody; [ed.] High school graduate, San Lorenzo High School (1978), San Lorenzo, California; [occ.] Retired Navy Chief; [memb.] Moose Lodge, Disabled Vets of America; [oth.writ.] Other unpublished poetry, "Limbo" book of poetry; [pers.] "The grass is always greener on the other side, until you have to mow it yourself". [a.] Lemon Grove, CA.

ECCLES, ANNETTE M.
[pen.] Nette; [b.] Washington, DC; [p.] Elsie M. Kenner; [ch.] Lamont, LaVonda, Tyrrell, LoToya and BJ; [oth.writ.] Several poems such as "The Image", "A Black American Women", "A Teenager In Love", "A Place Called Paradise", "My Blessed Child" and many more; [pers.] I look forward to having others read my work and to see if anyone could benefit in anyway from them. [a.] Clinton, MD.

EDGEWORTH, EMILY ADDISON
[pen.] Emily Addison; [b.] July 12, 1927, Brilliant, AL; [p.] Allen and Margie Mayes Addison (school teacher-poet); [m.] William (Bill) Edgeworth, September 24, 1972; [ed.]Brilliant High School, Alabama Business College, L.V.T.C. (Insurance) University of Alabama; [occ.] Retired-head of Emily Edgeworth Insurance Agency; [memb.] Unity Baptist Church, Southeast Writers Association; [oth.writ.] Poems of the 1930's by Aunt Emily (self published), Southeast Writers Association Chapbook Anthology; [pers.] It is my hope that in my writings, I can portray the relationship of God, nature and humanity. [a.] Tuscaloosa, AL.

EDWARDS, LAKITA NICOLE
[pen.] Katheryn Hastings; [b.] April 9, 1981, Monroe, LA; [p.] Arthur and Linda Edwards; [ed.] Little Flower Academy; [occ.] Student; [memb.] KSE (Kids for Saving Earth), F.A.C.E. (Kids For A Cleaner Environment), Girl Scouts Troop # 48, NSAL (North Shore Animal League); [hon.] First place in short story contest, second place in school poetry contest, first place in local spelling bee and fourth place in statewide spelling bee, three time recipient of school's Scholastic Achievement Award; [oth.writ.] Short stories published in school newspaper, story writing achievements published in local newspaper; [pers.] My philosophical statement is, today maybe filled with bloopers and blunders, but in tomorrow lies perfection. [a.] Monroe, LA.

EGERER, AVERY KAZUHIRO
[b.] July 8, 1967, Fresno, CA; [p.] Akihiro and Sawako Egerer; [ed.] Westlake High, UCLA, Loma Linda University; [occ.] Doctoral student; [pers.] I soulfully dedicate this poem to Yuki O.; her compassionate love and friendship could be the only inspiration an imprisoned heart needed to become rescued, allowing this poem to be created. If only her strength and will-power rivaled her uncompromising beauty, God only knows what kind of dimensions our lives would have infinitely propelled into. [a.] Westlake Village, CA.

EISENHAUER, PATRICIA
[pen.] Patricia Eisenhauer; [b.] January 15,1960, Philadelphia Naval Hospital; [p.] Hanalore and Wilfred "Ike" Eisenhauer; [ed.] Upper Dabry Senior High School; [occ.] Self employed "Eisehnauer's 5-star Sect. Srv." [oth.writ.] Several poems written, however this is my first publication, hopefully more to be seen published; [pers.] To me, poetry comes deep from within ones self. Words to most my poetry flow from my heart onto paper, releasing inner feelings and thoughts from me.

ELDRIDGE, ALETA J.
[pen.] A.J. Eldridge; [b.] May 24, 1955, Indianapo-

lis, IN; [p.] Harold and Dona Gibbs; [ed.] North Central High School, Ozark Christian College, Southwest Baptist University; [occ.] Teacher; [hon.] Dean's List; [pers.] I believe that human beings are able to understand God's nature through listening to and feeling compassion for their fellow travelers on earth. [a.] Sullivan, IN.

ELKIND, MORT
[pen.] Mort William Fenimore Cooper Elkind; b.] September 10, 1925, New York City; [ed.] Bronx High School of Science, B.S. Summa Cum Laude University of S.W. LA, M.A. Phi Kappa Phi LA State University, also attended C.C.N,Y., Cornell University, U.C.L.A., Georgetown University of Lang., Berkeley College; [occ.] Business and Creative Consultant, other occupations included newspaper reporter, feature writer, maitre d' at major mountain resort, intelligence officer for C.I.A., copywriter/copy supervisor for 3 small business-to-business and 3 major pharmaceutical ad agencies, Director of Professional Relations for the first automated, computerized clinical laboratory, editor of a major psychiatric calendar, Director of Marketing for a financial service company, Director of Advertising for an elite domestic slipper manufacturer, screen writer and movie script consultant, principal/co-founder of several small companies; [hon.] Prestigious Andy Award for advertising, Blue Key National Honor Fraternity, Phi Kappa Epsilon National Chemistry Honor Society, All-conference guard (3 years) in basketball at U.S.W. LA, All State AAU guard at Fort Belvoir, VA, elected to Athletic Hall of Fame at U.S.W. LA, listed in Who's Who Among Students in American Universities and Colleges, Who's Who in the East, Who's Who in Finance and Industry, Who's Who in the World (Marquis), also Sterling's International Who's Who; [oth.writ.] Writer and co-producer of "Billy Bang-Bang", a TV series for children, author of "Internecine", a novelette made into a major motion picture starring James Coburn and Lee Grant, creator of "Bringing Up Kids:, a TV series for syndication, currently writing the antithesis to "Schindler's List", tentatively titled "Elkind's List", based on personal activities following the liberation of the concentration camp at Buchenwald toward the end of World War II in Europe. [a.] Chestnut Ridge, NY.

ELMGREN, KATHY JEAN
[b.] December 2, 1975, Superior, WI; [p.] Davie and Virginia Elmgren; [ed.] Marantha Academy (private school open to K-12), graduated from, currently attending (UWS) University of Wisconsin Superior; [memb.] A member of Hermantown Community Church of Assembly of God in Minnesota; [hon.] Who's Who of American High School Students; [pers.] My love for God and appreciation for His creation is the inspiration for many of my poems. Also, my boyfriend Jonathan has been a constant source of strength and support in all I do. [a.] Superior, WI.

ELY, ELLA MARTIN
[pen.] Rhonda Ashworth; [b.] September 7, 1924, Columbia; [p.] Curvin and Florence Martin; [m.] Roland Price Ely, November 25, 1953; [ch.] Michael, Linda and Andrea; [ed.] High school, Brown University, Miami of Ohio University, etc.; [occ.] General Ely-Command In Chief of Battle of Armegeton; [memb.] Member of Round Table of Generals; [hon.] 15 Gold Medals; [oth.writ.] Article for Reader's Digest; [pers.] A true intellect is one who has the comfortable feeling of knowing. [a.] Washington, DC.

EMANUEL, DAWNTRELL M.
[b.] September 8, 1970, Minnesota; [ed.] High school graduation; [occ.] Journeywoman; [oth.writ.] Countless pieces written over the past nine years; [pers.] I am also a songwriter, it is through my writing that my deepest soul is set free. [a.] St. Paul, MN.

ENGBERG-MALUVAC, ROBIN L.
[pen.] R.L. Engberg; [b.] November 18, 1965, Indiana; [p.] Jean Engberg (father); [m.] Bryon M. Maluvac, September 25, 1993; [ed.] Administrative Assistant, National Steel Corporation; [memb.] Lifetime member of the International Society of Poets, member of the Center for Marien Conservation; [hon.] Published in The National Library of Poetry's Whispers in The Wind and At Day's End editions and received Editor's Choice Award; [pers.] During life's tragedies, we find strength through "Friendship". Thank you for letting me be your friend. [a.] Chesterton, IN.

ENGLISH, ROBERT G.
[b.] August 12, 1945, Portland, OR; [p.] Mr. and Mrs. Samuel English; [ed.] 12 years high school, 2 years college, 4 years Army; [occ.] Poetry writer; [memb.] National Library of Poetry , International Society of Poetry, Stormbelt-Paris, France; [oth.writ.] Books published, Only Yours, Susanna My Rose, Poetical Jest, My Gestful World, The Dream Catcher, all published by Carlton Press; [pers.] Catching the spirit, capture the dream. [a.] Albuquerque, NM.

ERNST, JULIE
[b.] August 11, 1979, Pensacola; [p.] John and Susan Ernest; [ed.] Brick Memorial High School; [occ.] Junior volunteer at Kimball Medical Center; [memb.] Explorers # 369, Key Club, Drama club, yearbook staff, Art and Poetry Society, J.C. field hockey; [hon.] High honor roll, Who's Who Among American High School Students, Honorable Mention in fall 1994 awards program for Iliad Press; [oth.writ.] Several poems published in school newspaper, poems published in Musings; [pers.] I personally believe, you can't change the past, but you can make a difference for your future. [a.] Brick, NJ.

EUBANKS, THELTON L.
[b.] May 20, 1919, Decatur, AL; [p.] Walter and Ella Mae Eubanks; [m.] Zola B. (R.) Eubanks, September 19, 1946; [ch.] Thelesa Susan (e.) Simmons; [ed.] Four years college; [occ.] Retired, Air Traffic Controller; [memb.] Member Alpha Kappa Psi Business Men's Fraternity; [oth.writ.] I've Ivy, My Friendly Frown, Haley's Comet, Ode to Geneva, Nippersaink, two short stories, "Friends" and "Home"; [pers.] Born Decatur, AL, May 20, 1919. Parents Walter L. and Ella Mae Eubanks, September 19, 1946. One child Thelesa Susan (E.) Simmons, spouse Zola R. Eubanks, education Okemah High School, Okemah, Oksamford University Birmingham, Alabama, occupation Air Traffic Controller Federal Aviation Administration. Although I know that there is much good in this world, I try to point up the inhumane treatment that some people have toward others. [a.] Birmingham, AL.

EULO, CHRISTINA
[b.] November 1, 1979, NAM; [p.] Marie Hickman and Mark Eulo; [ed.] Arcadia High School, grade 10; [memb.] Co-Ed Tri Hy Y, Flag Corps, Journalism staff, yearbook staff, sophomore class committee; [hon.] D.A.R. Essay Award; [pers.] To judge is to be blind, open your heart and you will find the greatest gift of an open mind. [a.] Hallwood, VA.

EVANS, AMBER
[pen.] Pepper; [b.] December 11, 1979, Olathe, KS; [p.] Tim and Lorena Evans; [sib.] Sarah and Erick Evans; [ed.] 9th grade; [occ.] I go to high school and write poems; [pers.] Poems or stories are thoughts in your mind that you let flow through your pen onto paper. [a.] Gardner, KS.

EVANS, ANN MARIE
[b.] June 30, 1945, Illinois; [p.] John A. and Margot Evans; [ed.] M.Ed., B.S., A.A.; [occ.] Retired Correctional Educ. Student, Wesley Theological Seminary; [memb.] AARP, AAA, WTS Covenant Disciples, First Baptist church Diaconate; [hon.] Who's Who in American Education, 1987-88, 1989-90; [oth.writ.] Poems published in campus newsletter, hymns sung in church; [pers.] Having been reunited with my father after 45 years. I know that if something is right, it will happen. All I need to do is do the footwork and be patient. [a.] Silver Springs, MD.

EVANS, CINDY
[b.] August 7, 1973, Willard, OH; [p.] Robert and Brenda Evans; [ed.] South Central High School; [occ.] Child care provider; [hon.] Who's Who Among American High School Students; [oth.writ.] Several stories and poems written for school; [pers.] My family influences my writing through their love and encouragement. [a.] Willard, OH.

EVERETT, ELEANOR B.
[pen.] E.B. Everett; [b.] April 24, 1922, Central Lake, MI; [p.] John Allen and Anna Murray Brown; [m.] July 3, 1944, divorced June 1970; [ch.] William, Bruce, Karl and James; [ed.] BFA-Michigan State University 1947, BS-Education, University of Minnesota 1970; [occ.] Retired, did clerical work for many years, also taught art in junior high school for a short time; [memb.] I was married for many years to a Geologist who was away from home, often months at a time, I did not join many organizations because much of the time I was both a mother and father to my sons; [oth.writ.] Articles, "Wild About Wildflowers" published in 1982 in Lake Superior Port Cities and CCC Boys Take A Nostalgia Trip published Lake superior Port Cities magazine 1983, poetry, Divers Beware, published in Nor' Easter 1983, also Downbound; [pers.] I have hoped through the years to repay my father for helping me get an education at MSU and by achieving what I could both as an artist and as a writer. [a.] Duluth, MN.

EVERETT, MARY B.
[b.] October 1, 1963, Hartford, CT; [p.] Jane and Fred Carnevale; [m.] Rory A. Everett, April 30, 1983; [ch.] Allen F. Everett; [ed.] Westbrook Junior Senior High School; [oth.writ.] Other unpublished poems and songs; [pers.] A lot of what I write reflects the love that lie deep within all our souls. [a.] Old Lyme, CT.

EVERSON, SARA MARIE
[b.] September 22, 1977, Oregon City; [p.] Bobbi Wilson and Doug Becker; [ed.] Clark College soon to graduate; [memb.] Oxford Athletic Club; [oth.writ.] "6 Feet Under" and "Jeremy Has Spoken"; [pers.] Writing our my problems and fears seems to help me face and conquer them. Without the expression of writing, I feel I would not be here today. [a.] Vancouver, WA.

FABRIZI, JANE S.
[pen.] Jane S. Fabrizi; [b.] April 6, 1921, Mass; [p.] Mr. and Mrs. Robert Shepardson; [m.] Deceased, November 4, 1940; [ch.] Peter, Jane and Kathy; [ed.] Art school, 8 years Teacher Leo Laskarism, New-Ark Del; [occ.] Housewife; [memb.] Wild Life Duck collection, worked on private school board-4 years, judged art painting in Army hospital; [hon.] Won art awards and prize for wild birds 1st place, art awards-2 wild horses 1 place running

across the dessert, from India religious festival of church people in their native dress -2nd place; [oth.writ.] I never sent any of my poems before, but like to write them. Thank you. [a.] Elkton, MD.

FADUL-CHEON, BARBARA
[pen.] Barbara Fine; [b.] June 17, 1953; [ch.] Joshua, Natasha and Frederick; [ed.] Clifton High School, Montclair State University; [occ.] Elementary school teacher; [memb.] P.E.A., NJEA, NEA; [hon.] Teacher of the Year 1994; [oth.writ.] A variety of songs for promoting self-esteem and global awareness, a variety of poems and jingles reflecting my attitudes of hope for our children - our future; [pers.] My writings express my focus on the wonder and beauty of our world. I am a very proactive and progressive thinker/doer. I am in awe of nature. [a.] Clifton, NJ.

FAGIOLINO, ROSA
[b.] June 5, 1965, Brooklyn, NY; [p.] Giuseppe and Loretta DiMeglio; [m.] Gianvito Fagiolino, June 10, 1984; [ch.] Damien Joseph; [ed.] John Jay High School; [occ.] Homemaker; [oth.writ.] This is my first poem and wish to write more; [pers.] My husband, my son, parents and whole entire family are my inspiration. [a.] Orlando, FL.

FARGNOLI, BRIAN C.
[b.] December 2, 1970, Plain View, NJ; [p.] Robert and Joanne Fargnoli; [ed.] High school and life; [occ.] The Pet and Exotic Animal Industry; [pers.] My love and desire to work with animals over whelms all other interest. My writings derive from everyday life and are meant to be taken as the reader sees it and not how I portrayed it. [a.] Levittown, NY.

FARRAH, CHRISTINE MARIE
[pen.] Christine, Chrissy; [b.] August 7, 1973, Framingham, MA; [p.] Ruth and Jack Walden; [ed.] Major-Business Law, minor-Foreign Language, no degree currently attained; [occ.] Legal Secretary; [oth.writ.] Several poems of several topics, I hope to have published someday; [pers.] If you do not feel, you cannot express. If you do not try, you'll never succeed. [a.] Naperville, IL.

FARRIS, DAVID L.
[pen.] David Standley-Farris; [b.] November 5, 1942, Sedalia, MO; [ed.] A-B, William Jewell College, Liberty, MO. (1965), M.Ed., University of Missouri, Columbia, MO. (1973);[occ.] A.G. Edwards and Sons Inc, Administrative Aide; [memb.] Leawood United Methodist Chancel Choir, Leawood, KS, Potpourri; [hon.] Bronze Star Medal, US Army 1968, Outstanding Young Men of America-1973; [pers.] I strive to communicate life, journey experiences psychologically, spiritually and mindfully. It's the most enjoyable facet of my life. I read poems of others from all periods and experiences. [a.] Overland Park, KS.

FAUGHN, RUSSELL PARKER
[pers.] Son of Rebuen and Bessie Alice Faughn, born Canalou, MO., January 2, 1924. Married to Helen Bernice, nee Kisner, July 18, 1945. Daughters, Brenda Sue Garman, electrical research engineer of Scottsdale, AZ. and Judy Diana Bundren, a teacher in Manchester, MO. Veteran, nightfighter air wing, 1st Div. U.S. Marines. Works have appeared in local paper, literary publications, and of course the Marines, "Leatherneck". I enjoy to write of things that is of interest to the people of rural Missouri and use the gentle vernacular they speak in, occasionally, to spice up a line, I quietly reach up and borrow a pretty word or two from our intelligentsia. It shows respect for them and their achievements. Longfellow and Sir Walter Scott is my favorites and I do mostly ballads, revisions of old songs, nature poems and some zany stuff too. [a.] Imperial, MO.

FAULK, RACHEL
[pen.] Tarie Newcomb; [b.] October 24, 1981, Dothan, AL; [p.] Judy Newcomb and Winn Faulk; [ed.] Spanish Fort Elementary, Spanish Fort Middle, Daphne Middle School (I am 13 years old); [occ.] Student; [memb.] Yearbook staff, Drama Club, Presbyterian choir; [hon.] Certificate of Scholastic Citizenship, graduated from Alabama School of Math and Science summer program, certificate of Academic Excellence; [oth.writ.] "In Search of A Dream" published in the Anthology of Poetry by Young Americans, I have also written poems such as "Lost Love" and "Alone"; [pers.] To write my poems, I try to reach deep in my soul and express my feelings with the magic of the pen. [a.] Spanish Fort, AL.

FAVUZZA, MARIA N.
[b.] December 8, 1967, Brooklyn; [p.] Giuseppe and Antonina; [ed.] Edward R. Murrow High School, Kingsborough Community College, Pace University (currently attending); [occ.] Legal Secretary, Haight, Gardner, Poor and Havens, New York; [hon.] Award, Random House Dictionary (only one is awarded), Dean's List, twice, Phi Beta Lamda Honor Society; [pers.] No matter how discouraging life becomes, never give up on your dreams. I have been greatly influenced by three wonderful and caring individuals, Salvatore and Madeline Vizzini, Carmella Puglisi.[a.] Brooklyn, NY.

FELESINA, KATIE
[b.] December 17, 1979, Reno, NV; [p.] Barbara Broyles and John Felesina; [ed.] Attending Carson High School; [pers.] To my undying friend Amber. [a.] Carson City, NV.

FERRARA, SABRINA
[b.] July 18, 1967, Bronx, NY; [p.] Carlo and Maria Calvanico; [m.] Walter Ferrara, June 2, 1990; [ch.] Robert Michael; [ed.] Msgr. Scanlon High School; [occ.] Homemaker; [pers.] Believer in yourself and the rest will follow. [a.] Palisades Park, NJ.

FERRIN, ROBIN J.
[b.] January 30, 1955, Kansas City, MO; [p.] Roy and Rhodora Simpson; [m.] Wayne R. Ferrin, February 21, 1987; [ch.] Bradley Scott and Quenten James; [ed.] Lyman Co. High, Preschool SD, Dakota Wesleyan University-Mitchell, SD.; [occ.] Dog breeder; [memb.] March of Dimes Foundation; [hon.] Dean's List, National Dean's List, Jerry M. Trimble Leadership Award; [oth.writ.] "Robin's Nest" (college newspaper column), "My House and Me" (college newspaper column); [pers.] Through examples in my own life, my writing attempts to encourage others to be the very best they can be and to remember that no matter what accomplishments you make in a lifetime, it is incomplete without Jesus. [a.] Mitchell, SD.

FESTER, BONNIE I.
[b.] Illinois; [m.] Earl Fester (deceased); [ch.] Dr. Steven Bomba, and Susan Bourne; [ed.] University of Illinois, University of Wisconsin, studied piano at Millikin Conservatory; [occ.] Retired Bane One employee, also piano teacher; [memb.] Advisory Program Committee for Public Television, Drury College President's club, volunteer for St. Johns Hospital, member of Springfield Symphony Guild, member of Art Museum Guild; [hon.] Won music scholarships to the University of Illinois; [oth.writ.] Many poems since 1973, never tried to publish any; [pers.] Most of my poems are filled with love of nature and love, written mostly to my husband. [a.] Springfield, MO.

FIEGER, JAMIE VIRGINIA
[b.] April 28, 1977, Virginia Beach; [p.] Robert and LuAnn Fieger; [ed.] Upper Perkiomen High School, graduation in June 1995; [occ.] Student; [memb.] Upper Perkiomen Field hockey and lacrosse teams; [hon.] Academic awards in English, academic honors throughout school; [oth.writ.] My first publication is this, also I have, "I Watch A Flower Pedal Drop To The", published in your book also; [pers.] There is only so much one can accomplish in time, but yet there is only so much time. Use the time aloud. "Truth is in the beholder". [a.] Red Hill, PA.

FILLMORE, BERNADINE
[pen.] Bonnie; [b.] May 25,1955, Newark, NJ; [p.] The late Flossie and Sam Fillmore; [ed.] High school graduate; [memb.] Trinity Reformed Church, Child-Free Networth; [pers.] I am one black voice in a million. [a.] Newark, NJ.

FINDLAY, ALEXANDER T.
[pen.] Tom Findlay; [b.] November 16, 1937, Detroit, MI; [p.] Archie and Frances Findlay;[m.] Chong Sun, August 3, 1973; [ch.] Kimberly Ann and Anthony Thomas; [ed.] Western High, Cameron University, Lawton, Oklahoma; [occ.] Maintenance Technician Goodyear Tire, Lawton, OK; [memb.] Veterans of Foreign Wars, Post 5263, Disabled American Veterans, Post 56, Lawton; [oth.writ.] Poems and articles for company newsletter.

FINKLE, DOLLY MARIE
[b.] March 20, 1955, Williamsport, PA; [p.] Betty and Robert Finkle; [m.] Michael S. Keas, May 8, 1993; [ed.] Some college, left due to illness at home; [occ.] Business owner and licensed certified Animal Health Tech.; [memb.] American Lung Association, Veterinary Technician Association of PA, Help The Homeless; [hon.] Dean's List, numerous first place awards in dog schools, confirmation and obedience; [oth.writ.] Several articles for local newspapers; [pers.] My inspiration comes from my mother, Betty Finkle, she passed away October 24, 1991. She was an inspiration to all. Kind, gentle, intelligent, never give up attitude who made you believe in yourself and who surrounded me with love. [a.] Williamsport, PA.

FIRESTONE, SARAH
[pen.] Sarah Firestone; [b.] March 10, 1978, Michigan; [p.] Mark and Barbara Firestone; [ed.] Working on GED, then I plan on going to junior college to earn an associate degree in Journalism; [occ.] Telemarketing; [oth.writ.] I have wrote a couple different editorials for various newspapers, magazines and radio stations; [pers.] The artistic talent comes from one's heart and soul. Those who limit art to just a painting or a sculpture are missing the meaning of unlimited expression. I use my gift of writing as a way to bring out my artistic side... to bring our my inner feelings... to bring our my true self. [a.] Overland Park, KS.

FISCHER JR., ASHTON JOHN
[b.] November 24, 1952, New Orleans, LA; [p.] Ashton and Elizabeth Fischer; [ed.] B.A., majored in English, M.A., majored in Theatre and drama, both degrees Tulane University; [occ.] Self-employed; [memb.] Lifetime member of International Society of Poets 1993; [hon.] Awarded Editor's Choice Award, Outstanding Achievement in Poetry by National Library of Poetry 1993, three Blue Ribbons Awards by the Southern Poetry Association. [a.] New Orleans, LA.

FISCHER, MARY E.
[b.] February 14, 1935, Buffalo, ND; [p.] Patrick and Elizabeth Killoraw; [m.] Clair A. Fischer, (deceased 1967), September 27, 1952; [ch.] 2 sons and 6 daughters; [ed.] BS Education majors in English and Biology Library, media and other classes before and since college graduation 1978; [occ.] Library Director/Librarian Valley City Barnes County Public Library; [memb.] The Human Race "God's Family", St. Catherine Church, Beginning Experience; [hon.] Summa cum Laude grad, President's Honor and Dean's List, 2 Honor Societies, Who's Who Among American College Students, recognition for success (financial aids recipient) Golden Poet Award 2 times; [oth.writ.] Lots of poetry, songs, Oh Tree; [pers.] I write what I feel, when inspired, when asked. I write for special occasions and for my patrons to inform, uplift and yes, enjoy. [a.] Valley City, ND.

FISHER, ANNE T.
[pen.] Anne Fisher; [b.] November 18, 1943, Charlottesville, VA; [p.] edward T. and Ruby D. Truslow; [m.] Wayne D. Fisher, May 14, 1963; [ch.] Dorcas Anne and Remonia Jean;[ed.] Graduate of Nelson County High School, Lovington, VA; [occ.] Assemble and Welder also part time pianist at Glen Kirk; [memb.] Presbyterian Church; [oth.writ.] "My Ole", "Piano", to be published in Poetic Voices of America, "The Rocking Chair" to be published in Treasured Poems of America" both to be published in 1995, many poems written for retirement of co-workers, 2 poems published in Relay newsletter, 1 published in church Worship of Advent; [pers.] Many of my emotions and much of my character are shown in my poetry. It gives me great pleasure to brighten other people's days and lives through my poetry, because I'm also a pianist and guitarist some poems become songs. [a.] Fishersville, VA.

FISHER, HEIDI M.
[b.] March 24, 1964, Concord, NH; [p.] Constance and Arthur Thurber; [m.] Jonathan Fisher, February 24, 1990; [ch.] Thomas, Mark, Jesse, Benjamin, Rebekah and Kurt; [ed.] Coe-Brown Northwood Academy, Coastal Carolina Community College; [occ.] Mother; [memb.] AWANA Leader, attend Epsom Baptist Church; [hon.] 1981 Miss New Hampshire's Miss United Teenager essay winner; [pers.] I enjoy writing poetry, especially those inspired by my Lord. I also have written several children's books that I hope to have published sometime in the future. Thanks be to God. [a.] Pittsfield, NH.

FITCH, AMANDA SUE
[pen.] Mandie Fitch; [b.] December 25, 1982, Muskegon, MI; [p.] Audrey and Steve Thies, Jim and Dee Dee Sorensen; [ed.] Whitehall Elementary 3-4, Montague Elementary 1-2, Montague Middle 5-6; [memb.] Montague Middle School Cadet band, St. James Lutheran Church; [hon.] Montague Middle School Whiz Kid Honor Roll all year, Presidential Academic Fitness Award, Knowledge Master competition award, Citizenship award, several attendance awards; [pers.] To read is to learn, and to write is to share your knowledge with others. I enjoy reading and I would like to share that joy with others. [a.] Montague, MI.

FLAHERTY, VIRGINIA
[b.] January 10, 1931, Toronto, Canada; [p.] George and Margaret Flaherty; [m.] Divorced; [ch.] Bob, Bruce, Brian and Ron Hamilton; [ed.] Grade XII, Western High School of Commerce, Toronto; [occ.] Bookkeeper; [hon.] Won 1st prize in poetry contest for local transit system last year, many honors and awards in high school for literary and poetic efforts; [oth.writ.] Other poems published in local newspapers, many poems and stories written for my own children while young; [pers.] I have always loved the rhythm and beauty of poetry and the challenge it represents to create it. Longfellow and Frost are particularly admired. [a.] Toronto, Ontario Canada.

FLANERY, KARLA
[b.] May 8, 1970, Fremont, MI; [p.] Kent Ward and Phyllis Garenflo; [m.] Rodney Flanery, July 14, 1989; [ch.] Alexander Gerald; [ed.] Walkerville High, New Yago County Area Vocational Center; [occ.] Owner of licensed home day care; [hon.] CDA (Child Development Associate) for preschool, certifies me to teach pre-school; [oth.writ.] First publication; [pers.] When I write I put a personal experience into it. I just write what I feel. [a.] Walkerville, MI.

FLANN, MARGIE
[b.] June 12, 1938, Pennock, MN; [p.] Henry and Florence Spletter; [m.] Marlin Flann, July 28, 1956; [ch.] Rhonda LeAnn, Rod Allen and Rachelle Jean; [ed.] Bird Island High School, Bird Island, Minnesota; [occ.] General clerk, First State Marketing-Lake Lillian, MI.; [hon.] My biggest honor is to be a wife and mother to a loving family; [pers.] This poem was written in loving memory of our son-in-law, Marty who was more like a son than a son-in-law. How blessed we were to have had him in our family for such a short time. [a.] Lake Lillian, MN.

FLEGG, DEBBIE
[b.] February 23, 1970, Edmonton, Alta; [p.] Sandra Flegg; [ch.] Alexandria Jennifer; [ed.] Grade XII, partial radio broadcasting; [occ.] Editor of local paper and reporter for another; [oth. writ.] This was the first time I have ever tried to have anything published. I have, although, been writing since I was 5 years old.; [a.] Kelvington, Sask., Canada.

FLEMING, ILSA A.M.
[pen.] Ilsa Fleming; [b.] April 27, 1926, Germany; [p.] Mr. and Mrs. H.Kraupner; [m.] Edward-GN Fleming, now divorced, 2nd marriage, January 25, 1986 (2nd); [ch.] Bill Fudger and Linda McLaren from 1st marriage to W.H. Fudger Sr.; [ed.] Grade eleven plus one year in convent for commercial; [occ.] Retired; [hon.] I was honored by Canadian Armed Services and called Sweetheart of the Services and presented with flowers by Commander Harreson RCNVR for entertaining troops all through the war Canadian and American, I was a dancer the Capital Theatre held 800 service men and my picture was published in a book in costume; [oth.writ.] Poems and songs, I have written songs, had a demo record sent to me but it arrived broken and my husband said don't bother anymore, it was called "Lonely Street" and was recorded by the Liberace Studio; [pers.] I write from the heart and to make people happy. It is just something I enjoy and a chance to express my feelings. [a.] Richmond BC, Canada.

FLOOD, DARLENE
[b.] Sign-Taurus, Chicago, IL; [m.] Yes, the greatest day of my adult life -2 times; [ed.] Began at a calligraphy lesson at the YMCA in Northbrook, IL., after having raised 3 boys. When the "Y" brochure detailed the art of artistic lettering and training your hand to perform the ABC's in a high state of the art presentation I was shocked. I always thought beautiful handwriting was inherited from a "book of Kells" monk, or a scribe from the castles of a King and Queen. My obsession with calligraphy took me around the U.S.A. to the greatest scribes and their classrooms. Yes, I studied, learned and practiced and combined my love of watercolor art and this sensuous combination created the first poem-prose. "Purpose". I have discovered an experience of tremendous emotion can bring our meaningful words... "Purpose" is my first written piece and was composed upon the death of my beloved father.

FLORES SR., ABEL JOSEPH
[b.] September 17, 1948; [occ.] Retired; [pers.] Hobbies, camping, furniture woodwork, reading, family wife (Molly) and four children. I am taking journalism classes at a local college, I would like to write a novel someday. My poem is entitled "E.T.P.".

FLORES, ALETA ELENA
[pen.] Ruffneck, Al; [b.] December 17, 1981, Charles Harword Hospital; [p.] Elviea V. and Isabelo Flores; [ed.] I am now attending the St. Patrick's School; [occ.] A student, model and a child; [memb.] I am a member of sports, cheerleading, modeling, poetry and many of animal wildlife; [hon.] I have many awards in sports and cheerleading, I have honors in the following subjects, Science, Math and English, etc.; [oth.writ.] When I finish school I would like to attend a college in Atlanta, Georgia, to become a doctor; [pers.] To all the young children or youths of the world keep your head up high, ignore the ignorant and get all the education possible. [a.] Fredericksted, St. Croix.

FLORES, KIMBERLEY LAINE
[b.] January 10, 1959, Hamilton; [p.] Ronald and Eva Statton; [ch.] Ronald Genaro and Christopher Dayne; [ed.] GED, University of Cincinnati, Associates Degree, major Paralegal; [occ.] Full time student at the University of Cincinnati; [hon.] Recipient of the 1994 Executive Women International Scholarship, Dean's List; [pers.] God sends the right people into your life at the right time. [a.] Cincinnati, OH.

FLORIO, FRANK JOSEPH
[b.] September 5, 1960, Oak Park, IL; [ch.] Alyissa Marie and Johanna Kay; [occ.] Poetic writer; [oth.writ.] "Life Is Like A Mountain Stream", "The Rose", "The Cheesmaster"; [pers.] For true love is filled with many sorrows but in the end all tears will be wiped away. [a.] Elmwood Park, IL.

FLOWERS, STACI DYAN
[b.] May 10, 1980, Fontana, CA; [p.] David A. and Shirlee J. Flowers; [ed.] 9th grade student at San Gorgonio High School, San Bernardino, CA; [occ.] Student; [memb.] NSF, National Scholastic Foundation, American Youth Soccer Organization, Junior Varsity San Gorgonio High School, Highland, CA.; [hon.] GPA 3.7; [oth.writ.] Many poems none published; [pers.] I strive to be an independent thinker, travel my own path of creativity. [a.] Highland, CA.

FLYNN, FRANK W.
[b.] November 29, 1965, Malone, NY; [p.] Frances Flynn and Walter Goodman; [m.] Girlfriend-Jill McCoy; [ch.] Jan T. Flynn; [occ.] Cat Scan Technologist; [oth.writ.] Many, none published; [pers.] I write to relax, while my regular job is very rewarding, it can also be incredibly stressful. This poem was written to my 5 year old son. [a.] Colchester, VT.

FLYNN, YVONNE AMELIA
[b.] May 31, 1955, Detroit; [p.] John and Patricia LaBrecque; [m.] Dennis Flynn, October 2, 1981; [ch.] Melanie Emily and Heather Elizabeth; [ed.] Fitzgerald High School, Wayne State University, University of New York Regent's College; [occ.]

Registered Nurse, Labor and Delivery, Grace Hospital-Detroit; [memb.] American Red Cross, Michigan Nurses Association; [oth.writ.] Editor of the school newsletter; [pers.] I try to give voice to what is in my heart. I never knew complete and unconditional love until I had my daughters. [a.] Royal Oak, MI.

FOGLE, LAWRENCE
[pen.] Larry; [b.] June 15, 1911 (twin), West Carrollton, OH; [p.] Marshall and Edith; [m.] Dorothy, October 25, 1943; [ch.] John and Millicent; [ed.] West Carrollton High, Ohio State University 1935; [occ.] Retired, publication printing ex.; [memb.] Miamisburg Historical Society, St. Jacob Lutheran Church, Miamisburg Senior Adult Center; [hon.] Miamisburg Poet Laureate, Miamisburg Man of the Year 1989, Citation for coordinating olympic writing project for third graders; [oth.writ.] Editor, employee publication, articles in Trade Journals, several booklets of poems, weekly letter writing to grandchildren while in college, on going narrative about the family, newspaper columnist; [pers.] A positive attitude with a sense of humor is the way to go. [a.] Miamisburg, OH.

FON, CARMEN
[pen.] Carmen Fon; [b.] September 8, 1980, St. Pete, FL; [p.] Dianne and Donald Fon; [ed.] Liberty Baptist, St. Pete Christian, Shore Acres Elementary, Northside Christian; [occ.] Student at Northside Christian; [memb.] Praise Cathedral Youth Group; [hon.] Honor Roll, Dean's List, Perfect Attendance, Most Creative Student, Graduating Writers Camp, Science Fair; [oth.writ.] Several poems and short stories along with other types of writings; [pers.] I have been influenced by my friends, parents and love songs I've heard on the radio. I would like to thank everyone that wouldn't let me quit when I wanted to. [a.] St. Pete, FL.

FONNER, PEGGY W.
[pen.] Peggy Steed; [b.] March 2, 1948, Durham, NC; [p.] Hazel and Luther Wilkins; [m.] Thomas R. Steed, February 11, 1973; [ch.] Sharyn Elizabeth and Thomas Wilkins; [ed.] Durham High, Watts Hospital School of Nursing; [occ.] LPN II, Durham Clinic, Durham, NC; [oth.writ.] Most writings are being kept private at this time; [pers.] My writings usually reflect my experiences in life. Most of the time when I can't vocalize how I feel, it is written easier in words. I have been influenced by the art of living. [a.] Durham, NC.

FORD, DANIELLE
[b.] March 14, 1983, Lebanon, KY; [p.] Gary L. and Kim Ford; [ed.] 6th grade student at Saint Augustine Grade School, Lebanon, KY; [memb.] St. Augustine Youth Choir; [hon.] Young Authors Award, 1993; [oth.writ.] 2 children's books, school project, "Grin and Bear It", "Bifocals for Patricia", two winning speeches-school projects, "Braceaphobia" and "Bifocalitis"; [pers.] I strive to show the beauty of the world around us and the humor found in everyday occurrences thru my writing. [a.] Lebanon, KY.

FORRESTER, MARY FRANCES ALL
[pen.] Mary All Forrester; [b.] October 17, 1938, Wilmington, NC; [p.] Mr. and Mrs. W.W. All; [m.] James Summers Forrester, M.D., March 12,1960; [ch.] 4 grown children and 4 grandchildren; [ed.] New Hanover High School, Butler University, Wake Forest University, Bowman Gray School of Medicine, School of Hytotechnology; [occ.] Homemaker, volunteer specialist Parliamentarian; [memb.] NSDAR, NC Medical Society Alliance, National Association of Parliamentarians; [hon.] Juliette Award for the arts, Silver Poet Award, World of Poetry (1986); [oth.writ.] Unpublished poems, articles in volunteer publications, usually pertaining to volunteer effort or motivational; [pers.] I write because I love the English language and I find words exciting. To find the right group of words that opens the window of my thinking and describes the contents that life has accumulated there, is very soothing. [a.] Stanley, NC.

FORTIN, JOCELYNE
[b.] June 5, 1948, Aylmer, Quebec; [p.] Leopold Fortin and Lucienne Charette; [ed.] BA (Linguistic), Ottawa University; [occ.] Teacher, Ecole St. Medard, Aylmer, Quebec; [memb.] Association des auteurs de l'Outaouais quebecois, Association des auteurs de l'Ontario; [oth.writ.] Three books of poems, Envers et en vrac in 1985, Tout feu tout femme, in 1990, En vers et contre toi, in 1993, two short stories and other poems published in anthologies, newspapers and magazines, in Canada and France; [pers.] My mother tongue being French, writing poetry in English has not been only a challenge, but also a real pleasure, an experience I will surely resume. [a.] Hull, Quebec.

FORTIN, PAUL
[b.] June 25, 1945, Lewiston, ME; [p.] Wilfred and Georgette Fortin; [ch.] Melissa Ivy; [ed.] Lewiston High, New York Institute of Photography, Rockport School of Photography, workshop; [occ.] Photographer artist, state of Maine; [memb.] Artists of the Androsgoggin, The L.A. Studio Emporium Group; [hon.] Numerous publications of photography, magazines, greeting cards, newspaper articles, television specials, numerous exhibitions, U.S. France; [oth.writ.] Photographs in conjunction with other poets, Maine publications, Great Raven Press, Association Press-New York; [pers.] Poetry inspires me to fashion my photographic images, a mixed media of words, paint photo onto paper from my journals, poems. I can reach into the heart and catch it on film both medias combined to tell a story. [a.] Lewiston, ME.

FORTUNATO, THOMAS J.
[b.] December 17, 1958, Brooklyn, NY; [p.] Nicholas T. and Grace Fortunato; [m.] Ann F. Fortunato, November 8, 1981; [ch.] Danielle Nicole; [ed.] Sewan Haka High School, Nassau Community College; [occ.] Correction Officer, Nassau County Sheriff's Department, East Meadow, NY; [memb.] Parents Teachers Association, Fraternal Order of Police; [hon.] (N.Y.S.) certified E.M.T., (N.Y.S.) certified Adult and Child C.P.R., commendation award U.S. Postal Service; [oth.writ.] None at Present; [pers.] Reflections of the heart profit love from those whom are loved. I have been moved spiritually by the loss of a loved one, thus inspiring forthcoming poetry. [a.] Elmont, NY.

FOSTER, CHRISTOPHER ALLAN
[pen.] Christopher Allan; [b.] April 1, 1969, Missouri; [p.] Amy Foster; [ch.] Hope Alexandria and Brittney Leigh-Ann Edwards; [ed.] Went to school at Lafayette High School in St. Joseph, quit at the 10th grade and passed G.E.D. in prison; [occ.] Plumber, painter, enrolled in college to study Psychology; [oth.writ.] I have written poetry for many years but I have never done anything with it, this is the first time that I got the nerve up to send one in; [pers.] If you sit around in life and "think" about doing something with your life, that's all you'll ever do is think, but, if you want to do something with your life then do it, life isn't going to hand you anything. If you want it you have to work for it. [a.] St. Joseph, MO.

FOSTER, ELIZABETH D.
[pen.] Beth Foster; [b.] September 5, 1975, Clarksdale, MS; [p.] Tommy and Sandra Foster; [ed.] Lee Academy, first year at Mississippi Delta Community College; [memb.] FCA-Fellow Christian Athletes at MDCC: [hon.] Most creative, softball scholarship, basketball scholarship to MDCC; [oth.writ.] Published in school paper, published in church articles; [pers.] The words of my poetry consist of my emotions on that particular subject. To share with others my feelings is to write them on paper. To share with others my poetry is to release my emotions. [a.] Clarksdale, MS.

FOSTER, ERNEST RICHARD
[pen.] Dick Foster, Richard Foster; [b.] May 27, 1956, Kansas City; [p.] Ralph and Ima Jean Foster; [ed.] Hall High, University of Maryland, Central Texas College, Writer's Digest School; [occ.] Independent contractor; [memb.] New Hope Nazarine Church; [hon.] Article about myself in Writer's Digest magazine; [oth.writ.] Articles published in a local paper, "Our Neighborhood", letters in the Arnies-AFEE's paper, local articles in the Arkansas democrat/Gazette paper; [pers.] I try to bring out the best of things in my writings. I encourage people to write. Anyone can be a writer. [a.] Little Rock, AR.

FOSTER, JEFFREY W.
[b.] December 25, 1958, Lebanon, TN; [p.] James A. Foster and June Marie; [m.] Patricia Foster, March 20, 1977; [ch.] Misty D. and Rock A.; [ed.] Henry Co. High School; [occ.] Manager fast food restaurant; [oth.writ.] Several poems and 1 song recorded by a recording studio and offered on cassette to the public for sale; [pers.] Discovered only in the past year that I had an ability to write, and I'm greatly inspired by my wife Pat of almost 20 years. [a.] Paris, TN.

FOWLER, ANGELICA KAY
[pen.] Angel Kay Fowler; [b.] August 12, Bakersfield, CA; [p.] Deborah Fowler and Charles; [ed.] Freshman in high school, working to be a Vet, 1st graduating class of Walter Stiern WPS; [occ.] Babysitter; [memb.] Spanish Club, Rainbow Girls; [hon.] Awards for G.P.A.; [pers.] I love animals and love to write poems and stories. [a.] Bakersfield, CA.

FOWLER, SUE C.
[b.] September 16, 1947, Gowensville, SC; [p.] Ruth and Jack Campbell; [m.] Kenneth Fowler, August 1, 1967; [ch.] Cassie Sue Fowler; [ed.] High school; [oth.writ.] "Barefoot Jack", unpublished; [pers.] Poem dedicated to my mother, which faith enriched her life to live to be 85 years old.

FOX, JAMES W.
[pen.] Bossie; [b.] July 10, 1930, Milo, OK; [p.] Samuel N. and Mary Francis Fox; [ch.] @ boys, 2 girls natural, 2 boys and 1 girl adopted; [ed.] 12th grade at Meadowbrook Oklahoma Love County; [occ.] Retired from Wilson Foods (meat packers) Oklahoma City; [memb.] A.A.R.P., Labor Unions, clubs, Arbor Day Foundation, National Parks Department and many others; [hon.] 12 diplomas from various schools, general education, labor, Presidential's, secretary and agriculture, many short courses; [oth.writ.] Many church writings such as Consecration, Limited Opportunity, and others for the Herald paper published worldwide, family poetry and etc., many others (none other published) also songs; [pers.] I strive to better my fellowman. I have many valuable inventions (all unpattened) some in model form to benefit others. [a.] Lebanon, OK.

FRADY, MELANIE
[b.] July 27, 1981, Shakopee, MN; [p.] Robert and Marie Frady; [ed.] Mound Westonka High School,

8th grade; [occ.] Babysitter; [memb.] Gymnastics Academy of Westona, 3 years, Minnesota Junior League bowling, 5 years, volleyball first year; [hon.] A and B Honor Rolls, gymnastics and bowling awards; [pers.] I thank my mother and dad, education, freedom and choice. I also thank my family and friends for always being there for me. [a.] Mound, MN.

FRANCIS, JANICE
[pen.] Jan Francis; [b.] September 21, 1948, Bangor, ME; [p.] Arthur and Muriel Hewes; [m.] Donald Francis; [ch.] Christopher, Joanne, Scot, Tanya and Micheal; [ed.] Brewer High School, Brewer, ME; [occ.] Customer Service Supervisor, JC Penney, Potomac Mills; [pers.] I write to express my innermost feelings which sometimes are too hard to express orally. [a.] Woodbridge, VA.

FRANK, DARA
[b.] November 4, 1980, New York City; [p.] Carol and Peter Frank; [sib.] David; [ed.] Saddle Rock Elementary, Great Neck South Middle and currently Great Neck South High School; [memb.] B'nai B'rith Youth Organization; [pers.] Love is more than one soul can bear or understand, yet the heart continues to explore. [a.] Great Neck, NY.

FRANTZ, KIMBERLY L.
[b.] December 17, 1964, Kailua, Oahu, HI; [p.] LeiLani Flick and Albert Mejia; [m.] Randy J. Frantz (1962-1988), July 29, 1982; [ch.] Heather Rae (14 years) and Robert Lewis (11 years); [ed.] Carson City High (Michigan); [occ.] Homemaker, full time mom, very involved in my neighborhood's safety, improvement and communication; [oth.writ.] Been writing a monthly neighborhood newsletter (The Venturian) for almost 3 years now, also several poems and short stories (Journals 1-2 pg) never published; [pers.] My inspiration for writing poems is complicated because it comes from deep within me. I cannot write them one after another, like clockwork. I only write a poem when the words come to me naturally. [a.] San Antonio, TX.

FREEMAN, APRIL
[pen.] Renee, Nee and Peaches; [b.] December 10, 1981, Detroit, MI; [p.] Ella Freeman and Matthew Robinson; [ed.] Barbour Magnet Middle School, 7th grade and Jhon Casablancas Model and Carrer Center; [hon.] Perfect Attendance and compact; [oth.writ.] Other names of poems that I wrote, "Finding Me", "Passion", "True" "Intispation" and "Forever" non-published; [pers.] I strive to reach my goals in life which are, being an actress, a model and a writer. In my writings I express the way I feel about someone, something and I write a lot of children's poems. [a.] Detroit, MI.

FRIEDEBERG-SEELEY, FRANK
[pen.] David Barraz; [b.] London, England; [p.] Emil Friedeberg and Lilly Seeler; [m.] Maria (Fragala), April 2, 1962; [ch.] Mark Alexander; [ed.] Privately and Oxford University, brassey scholar, first class honors, lit. hum., B.A., M.A., Oxon; [occ.] Retired (taught 25 years in English, 15 in U.S. Universities). [a.] Georgetown, TX.

FRIESEN, JOHN W.
[b.] March 23, 1935, Waldheim, Sask, Canada; [p.] Gerhard and Barbara Friesen; [m.] Virginia Agnes Lyons-Friesen, July 30, 1990; [ch.] Bruce, Karen, Gaylene, David and Beth Anne; [ed.] B.R.E., BA, M.S., Ph.D., D. Minn; [occ.] Professor the University of Calgary; [memb.] Multicultural Education Council, The Alberta Teacher's Association; [oth.writ.] Books, The Real (Riel) Story, Ottawa Bovealis 1994, When Cultures Clash, Calgary Temeron 1993, The Community Doukobors, Ottawa Bovealis 1989, Reforming The Schools-For Teachers, University Press of America 1987, Lanham, MD. [a.] Calgary, Alta.

FUERST, MARLENE
[b.] June 4, 1975, Hawthorne, CA; [p.] Martin Fuerst and Melinda Sehr; [ch.] Sharron Renee Fuerst; [ed.] Downey High School; [oth.writ.] None published; [pers.] To live is what we all do, but to love is something not many of us can feel. [a.] Downey, CA.

FUGATE, ELAINE Y.
[pen.] ELaine Y. Fugate; [b.] August 13, 1945, Fairview Hospital; [p.] Michael and Ann Siley; [m.] Ronald D. Fugate Sr., December 15, 1990; [ch.] Kimberly Ann and John Lawrence; [ed.] College, education; [occ.] Secretary at Cleve Employ Weekly; [oth.writ.] Cherokee Man, Proud Nation.

FULGHUM, LISA DOWNER
[b.] April 13, 1965, Chattanooga, TN; [p.] Jack Downer and Sharon Payne; [m.] Paul L,. Fulghum Jr., August 28, 1992; [ch.] Jonathon Raines and Misty Fulghum; [ed.] Northwest Georgia High School, Electronic Computer Programming Institute, Chattanooga State; [occ.] Delinquency Coordinator, Provident Life and Accident Insurance Co.; [pers.] I lost my baby daughter, Jackie to open spina bifida. She is my inspiration. I am completing a book in her memory. [a.] Chattanooga, TN.

FYFE, CAROL A.
[b.] September 29, 1943, Jersey City, NJ; [p.] Martha Lawrence and John Scherr; [m.] Frank E. Fyfe, November 19, 1955; [ch.] Debra, Janis, Susan and Melissa; [ed.] Union Hill High, Union City, NJ; [occ.] Retired in the Adirondack Mountains, seasonal work in a western theme park; [memb.] Vice President Schroon Lake Arts Council; [oth.writ.] Correspondence for people needing letter writing, this is my first competition for poetry; [pers.] The greater our gifts, the greater are our challengers. How we handle both is the summation of life. My poems seem to cry out this message. A true balance of joy and sorrow. Isn't this the story of all of our lives. [a.] Schroon Lake, NY.

GABRIELA, JAMES V.
[b.] November 14,1921, Nutley, NJ; [p.] Patrick and Rose Gabriela; [m.] Anna Garbiela, June 10, 1978; [ch.] Patricia Read; [ed.] Nutley High and Elementary School; [occ.] Retired employee of Public Service Electric and Gas Company. [a.] Nutley, NJ.

GALBREATH, LINDA HADDOCK
[b.] August 13, 1977, Marianna, FL; [p.] Pat and Vonothe Haddock; [ch.] Curtis, Clay, Jimmy Michael and Terry; [sib.] Alice, Tommy and Patty; [ed.] High school, photography; [occ.] Secretary; oth.writ.] Several poems, none published; [pers.] I would not be here today if not for my wonderful family. There is nothing greater in life than the people around you. [a.] Panama City, FL.

GALBREATH, TERRY WOOD
[b.] September 27, 1948, Meadville, PA; [p.] Leroy and Helen Wood; [ed.] Lakeland High, Southern College; [occ.] Student, major Dental Technology; [memb.] National Association of Dental Laboratories and National Guild of Hypnotists; [hon.] President's List, 1994 AWBA Scholarship; [oth.writ.] Credit for NGH thesis, Nature studies, poetry, fiction and non-fiction writing; [pers.] The question, "What oneness do I share with a tree, flower...?" Opens the mind to understanding all creation. [a.] Edgewater, FL.

GALLAVAN, ROB
[b.] March 20, 1975, Bremerton, WA; [p.] Robert and Ellen Gallavan; [ed.] Mount Saint Mary High School, Saint Gregory's College; [occ.] Student ad assistant to the Director of Public Relations at St. Gregs; [memb.] Editor of the college newspaper at St Gregory's College, member of the Residence Life staff, stage Greg, college Republicans; [hon.] Outstanding college freshman award, listed as Who's Who Among Students in American Junior Colleges; [oth.writ.] Sports and feature articles for the Shawnee News-Star; [pers.] Life...it's the greatest gift one will ever receive. It's never outdated, it's full of surprises and you can share it with everyone. [a.] Shawnee, OK.

GALLOWAY, KIM
[pen.] Kim Galloway; [b.] December 20, 1983, Houston, TX; [p.] Lu and Beverly Galloway; [occ.] Student, fifth grade, Radnor Middle School; [pers.] Writing for fun or competition, helps me touch the stars! It makes me feel good about myself. [a.] Bryn Mawr, PA.

GALVEZ, MANUEL A.
[pen.] Manny Andes; [b.] January 26, 1972, Santiago, Chile; [p.] Nora Granadino; [ed.] Brookline and Framingham High Schools, U.S. Army 92A; [occ.] U.S.A.R. and shift supervisor at store; [oth.writ.] Several unpublished love poems and life poems, working on a book of poetry "I Wish To Die In A Dream"; [pers.] Lost in hopes which childless denies to accept, facing reality and steps yet holding in the pain. Lost in the breeze a dream I became... in this timeless flow we breath awaiting an end. [a.] Allston, MA.

GANZ, JAMES L.
[b.] April 28, 1982, Hackettstown, NJ; [p.] Lynn and Richard Ganz; [ed.] I am currently a 7th grade student at Warren Hills Middle School, Washington, NJ.; [hon.] Academic Excellence Award, Ruddy Memorial Award for outstanding citizenship and achievement, Presidential Academic Fitness Award; [pers.] This poem is dedicated to my mom. I strive to excel in all my endeavors in my life. [a.] Hackettstown, NJ.

GARCIA, DAVID ANTHONY
[pen.] David Anthony; [b.] January 15, 1964, Spain (AF); [p.] Ernest and Clara Garcia; ed.] Judson High, San Antonio College, University of Texas at San Antonio, (B.F.A. candidate); [occ.] Artist, student, manager on duty-Timberhill Villa Retirement Co.; [memb.] San Antonio Art League; [hon.] Artwork selected for U.T.S.A. Juried Shows in 1993 and 1994, work selected, up coming show at the Artists Gallery at Aviart (December 8), poem and drawing recognized by Vatican (Given Apostolic Blessing); [oth.writ.] Several poems unpublished, this was my first attempt at publication; [pers.] Having studied the teachings of Joel Goldsmith, Carl Jung, Kahlil Gibran, Julia Cameron and many others, I realize that my works are manifestations of God and meant to be. The tremendous knowledge found in the written word has been stifled by the mesmerizing effect of electronic media on today's society. I strive to affect others in the interest of self awareness and higher consciousness regardless of race, creed or color. [a.] San Antonio, TX.

GARCIA-FINO, LUIS
[pen.] Luis Garcia-Fino; [b.] October 22, 1934, Ault, CO; [p.] Luis and Ritz Garcia; [m.] Single; [ed.] Colegio Palmore in Mexico, University of Michigan and Central Michigan University, masters degree in Administration; [occ.] Free lance writer/retired Administrator; [memb.] AmFar; [oth.writ.] Collection of short stories being con-

sidered for publication; [pers.] I am influenced by Gabriel Garcia Marquez, a man of incredible talent. [a.] El Paso, TX.

GARDINER, DOUG ANTHONY
[pen.] Doug Anthony; [b.] December 1, 1966, Nassau, Bahamas; [p.] Lester and Gladys Gardiner; [ch.] Doug Anthony Gardiner; [pers.] Achieve what you believe, believe in what you have achieved, then share it with others for God has given the gift to you. [a.] Miami, FL.

GARFIELD, SAMPSON MISSISSIPPI
[pen.] S.M. Garfield;[b.] November 3, 1977, Harlem, NY; [p.] Deceased; [ed.] Dropout, sophomore year high school; [occ.] Bicycle messenger for 2 companies in Manhattan; memb.] At times the human race, but never an equal member, but I'm not crying for nobody; [hon.] My only prize possession, winning the Julius Erving trophy at Mayor Dinkins Inner-city basketball challenge 1990; [oth.writ.] I write everyday, everywhere, on my shoe, on my hand, my walls, my sheets, my arms are tattoed with my sayings.

GARFINKEL, TODD
[pen.] Sven Fjelstad; [b.] May 14,1968, Providence, RI; [ed.] B.A. in Literature, Brown University; [occ.] Musician; [oth.writ.] "Brock's Joist"; [pers.] I leave my composition to my unconscious. [a.] Narragansett, RI.

GARNER, CARRIE
[b.] January 14, 1977, Charlotte, NC; [p.] Mike and Laura Garner; [ed.] High school senior, Lewisville High School, Lewisville, TX; [occ.] Student; [hon.] Who's Who Among American High School Students, 1992-1993, 1993-1994; [oth.writ.] High school literary magazine. [a.] Lewisville, TX.

GARRETT, MELISSA
[b.] July 9, 1980, Detroit, MI; [p.] Jim and Cathy Garrett; [ed.] Freshman at Brighton High School. [a.] Brighton, MI.

GARRETT, MELISSA
[b.] January 17, 1977, Cape Girardeau, MO; [p.] Ursula Reynolds and James Reynolds (stepdad), Raymond Garrett (father); [ed.] Senior at Anna-Jonesboro Community High School, studying nursing; [occ.] CNA at City Care in Anna, Illinois; [memb.] FHA Club; [hon.] Tech Prep Award for health occupations; [pers.] I base my writings on my personal feelings and thoughts about my life. This is to someone special who touched my heart in many ways. [a.] Cobden, IL.

GARRISON, CLAIRE B.
[pen.] Clarice; [b.] March 25, 1916, Perth Amboy, NJ; [p.] Esther and Edward J. Bachman; [m.] Irving C. Garrison, September 25, 1948; [ch.] Phyllis, Carl, Laura and John; [ed.] Perth Amboy High School, N.J. State Teacher's College, Rutgers University Extension School; [hon.] Silver Poetry Award 1990 from World of Poetry, American Guild of Organists; [oth.writ.] Many other poems on religious or philosophical subjects; [pers.] Prolific writing began after my first husband was killed in action in Germany in 1945-just 6 weeks before our baby was born on April 8, 1945. She was killed by a drunk driver at Penn State University on the very same date on which her father was killed.

GARRISON, FIONA JULIA
[b.] November 23,1978, Corvallis, OR; [p.] Hallie and Paul Sanders;[ed.] Orcas Island High School, currently a sophomore; [occ.] Horse trainer, 4-H member, student; [memb.] 4-H, Norgegian Fjord membership, Orcas Island basketball team, Orcas Island softball; [hon.] Awards in writing in my high school career; [pers.] "Behind every shadow is a dream". [a.] Eastsound, GA.

GARRITY, DOROTHY
[b.] December 21, 1908, Buffalo, NY; [p.] Peter and Anna Garrity; [ed.] Master's degree of Ed. Librarian-Special Ed.; [occ.] Retired; [memb.] I have written poetry for years and have over 200; [hon.] Several from public education; [oth.writ.] Hundreds of poems and journal of trips of Europe and US Jubilee Memorials, happy birthdays, etc.; [pers.] I love to write all kinds of materials. [a.] Hamburg, NY.

GARRITY, ELIZABETH ANN
[b.] January 11, 1976, Elemdorf AFB, AK; [p.] Robert and Denise Garrity; [ed.] Chugiak High School; [hon.] American Veterans ROTC Medal, Veterans and Foreign Wars ROTC Medal; [pers.] Poetry is the voice of the soul. Poetry is the anger, depression, joy, love and passion that is impossible to express in conversation. I believe poetry to be the essence of one's true self. The poetry of others that a person enjoys reading gives a hint of their character. The poetry a person writes is an intimate view of his most important thoughts, the essence of his being, the doorway to his soul. [a.] Provo, UT.

GARROD, JOHN Th.M.
[pen.] Arthur; [b.] May 5, 1929, Plymouth, England; [m.] Jeanne Garrod, December 24, 1993; [ed.] Th.M. (Magna Cum Laude); [occ.] Retired teacher, International Seminary Extension, part-time lecturer in Ocala, FL.; memb.] Ordained minister (Christ Gospel International); [oth.writ.] Write religious articles for newspapers, Christianity and Charisma, write letters on Bible topics, such as personal growth and biblical prophecy as it relates to TODAY; [pers.] I strive to exhibit high standards of the Torah, coupled with insight into giving the masses a spiritual education in a world of chaos and confusion! [a.] Ocala, FL.

GARTMAN, MYRTLE I.
[p.] Paul G. and Lillie M. Gartman; [ed.] Roanoke College, Salem, VA., George Washington University, Washington, DC., Berlitz School of Languages, Washington, DC.; [memb.] Life member, International Society of Poets; [hon.] 1994-Editor's Choice Award for poem published in The National Library of Poetry , At Day's End; [oth.writ.] Former community columnist for small town newspaper, poems published by The National Library of Poetry, 1994-At Day's End, 1995-Best Poems of 1995. [a.] Washington, DC.

GARZA, MERCEDES
[b.] December 12, 1977, Chicago, IL; [p.] Ruben and Angela Garza; [occ.] Junior at United South High School; [memb.] Communities in School (CIS); [hon.] Secondary Regional Science Fair-1994 UISD-1st place, United South High School Science Fair, Biological Level II, 3rd place 1993; [oth.writ.] Have written several other poems on feelings; [pers.] I write on what I feel and how I would have felt if it happened to me. [a.] Laredo, TX.

GASKINS, JENNIE SELLERS
[b.] September 28, 1944, Lumberton, NC; [m.] Thomas A. Gaskins, December 31,1983; [ch.] Sabrina Raye and Tracey John; [occ.] Housewife; [pers.] I wrote this poem after the death of my mother in 1985.

GASTON, SUSAN
[pen.] Susan Gaston; [b.] October 28, 1948, Big Spring, TX; [p.] Walter and Betty Heideman; [m.] Van Gaston, June 27, 1965; [ch.] Van Jr. and Vanessa Lynn Gaston; [ed.] Graduated Forsan High School, Christian Writer's Inst., Praise and Worship Leader's Inst.; [occ.] VP, Van's Well Service, Inc., Forsan, Texas; [memb.] Praise and Worship Team, Hillcrest Baptist , (AOSC) Association of Oilwell Servicing Contractors, Women's Aglow, (CWA) Concerned Women for America; [oth.writ.] Various church newsletters; [pers.] I wish to give God glory in all that I do. [a.] Forsan, TX.

GATES, SABRINA
[b.] February 13,1977, Bronx, NY; [p.] Gerald and Evelina Gates; [ed.] Convent of the Sacred Heart High School; [occ.] Student, current Senior Class President; [hon.] HOBY Leadership Foundation Ambassador, Wellesley College Book Award, Who's Who Among American High School Students; [pers.] I have drawn inspiration from three great women of this decade, Maya Angelou, Hillary Clinton, Mother Theresa, their ability to communicate and serve people has always served as a guide. [a.] Pelham, NY.

GAUTHIER, CARRIE L.
[b.] January 7, 1972, MA; [p.] Linda Rindal and Dennis Gauthier; [ed.] Cape Cod Community College, University of Mass, present pending decision transfer to Emerson College; [occ.] Entertainer; [hon.] Dean's List; [oth.writ.] Cape Cod Community College's "The Main Street" (co-editor and reporter/photographer); [pers.] Writing is an opportunity to capture one thought from the chaotic, cluttered whirlpool of my mind and come to an understanding with it. Considers the works of Salinger to be of God-like stature. [a.] Brighton, MA.

GAUTHIER, JOANNE
[b.] June 24, 1979, Virden Manitoba; [p.] Ray and Huguette Gauthier; [ch.] Yosep Woga (foster child); [ed.] Archbishop M.C. O'Neill High School; [hon.] Honor Roll, various academic, literary and music awards; [pers.] A child is the most precious sweetest form of human life. In the eyes of a true writer. I almost catch a glimpse of the innocence and magic of a child's soul. We have a lot to learn from children for they have within them the dance of life. [a.] Regina, Saskatchewan, Canada.

GAVIGAN, CAROLEE
[pen.] Carolee Gavigan; [b.] January 16, 1942, Brooklyn, NY; [p.] George and Loretta Reimann; [m.] John H. Gavigan, September 11, 1965; [ch.] Pierrette, John and Timothy; [ed.] St. Michael's High School, St. Joseph's College and State University of New York at Stony Brook; [occ.] Vice President Community Relations National Westminster Bank; [memb.] Public Relations Society of America, Long Island Transportation Management Board member, National Association for Female Executives. [a.] Port Jefferson, NY.

GEMMELL, TREY LABAN
[b.] March 30,1980, Tulsa, OK; [p.] Hugh and Jennifer Gemmell; [ed.] Booker T. Washington High School, Tulsa; [memb.] Tulsa Fencing Club, Scottish Club of Tulsa; [hon.] 1st place poetry in the Tulsa City-County Library's Young People's Creative Writing contest, 2nd place short story; [pers.] I've spent most of my life aborad, traveling throughout Australia, the Bahamas, England and Normandy, my travels invariably affecting and even inspiring my writing. There's poetry inside everyone, though we each express it differently, some have their music, others their painting, I rely on my verse. [a.] Tulsa, OK.

GENCO, NINA
[pen.] Lee Mack; [b.] March 9, 1942, Akron, OH; [p.] Virgie Sprinkle and George Mack; [ch.] Jacqueline and James Genco; [ed.] Patterson Park High School, Essex Community College; [occ.] Instructional Assistant, Maryland School for the Blind; [memb.] Eastern Yacht Club, Chi Sigma Sorority, Alpha Mu American Legion Auxiliary; [pers.] You're always with me dad, even though you're miles away, Nina.

GERMAN, PATRICK LA'RON
[b.] June 26, 1969, Oklahoma; [p.] Perry and Shirley German; [m.] Niecie LeAnne German, August 29, 1987; [ch.] Terrell, Jasmine and Brittany; [ed.] Associate of Arts, Bachelors in Psychology; [occ.] Asst. head Urology Department, Naval Hospital Rota Spain; [memb.] American Urologic Association; [hon.] Navy Achievement Medal for outstanding performance.

GERRY, RICHARD D.
[b.] September 9, 1972, Portsmouth, NH; [p.] Clifton and Eileen Gerry; [ed.] York High School, B.A. in Criminology at the University of Southern Maine; [occ.] Shipping clerk at Samuel Weiser's Warehouse, York, Maine; [memb.] Sigma Nu Fraternity, Alpha Kappa Delta (Sociology Honor Society); [hon.] Dean's List, highest G.P.A. in Sigma Nu for 2 years (93-94); [oth.writ.] A short story, Mealtime, in my high school yearly anthology, plus an undergraduate thesis, The S & L Crisis, A New Look At An Old Problem. [a.] York, ME.

GETSON, ANGELA
[pen.] Angela; [b.] November 13,1980, Summerside, P.E.I.; [p.] Elizabeth Alice and William Royce Getson; [ed.] Summerside, P.E.I.-grade 1 Cornwallis, Nova Scotia-grades 2-4, Fort Saskatchewan, Alberta 5-8, currently an honor student in grade 9; [hon.] Honor student in every grade; [oth.writ.] A poem published in Stepping Stones book at James Mowat School, Fort Saskatchewan; [pers.] The poetry I write reflects on, my innermost thoughts and feelings, beliefs, present world issues and personal experiences. [a.] Fort Saskatchewan, Alberta.

GETTINGER, JOLENE KAY
[pen.] Jolene Gettinger; [b.] January 3, 1979, Tomah, WI; [p.] Dennis and Marsha Gettinger; [ed.] Current Sophomore -- Royall High School, Elroy, WI; [memb.] Royall High School cheerleader, Royal High School track team; [hon.] Track; [a.] WI.

GEYER, BETTY
[pen.] Betty Geyer; [b.] May 21, Bridgeport, CT; [p.] Ethel Tubman and Nelson Geyer; [ed.] Masters in social work, University of California, Berkeley, Stamford High School, Stamford, CT.; [occ.] Studying fashion design; [memb.] Stamford YWCA, East Bay Science of Mind, Berkeley Zen Center, Sidlha Yoga; [hon.] American Institute of Architure Fellowship 1974, University of California Scholarship, 2nd prize in U.C. Berkeley art exhibit 1970; [oth.writ.] Book in progress-fiction, Confession of A Madwoman, articles for Fairfield Advocate, Hartford Inquirer, Sun Reporter, Chapbook, Faces of She, Moments in Jade; [pers.] To express inner ecstacy in joy of living that is all of ours to experience. [a.] Oakland, CA.

GIDEON, CAROL
[b.] November 14, 1934, Davies Co., IN; [p.] Ernest and Esther Myers; [m.] Bernard, April 23, 1954; [ch.] Stanley, Janet and David; [ed.] High school (Epsom); [occ.] Homemaker, I was church organist for many years; [memb.] Presbyterian Church of Montezuma, currently attending First Church of the Nazarene in Terre Haute, IN.; [oth.writ.] I had a front page by-line in the Terre Haute Tribune-Star Christmas Day 1988, it was an article in tribute to my father written for their column Christmases ago, I use many of my poems in making greeting cards for all occasions; [pers.] I feel God has given me a talent for expression with words. I write on many subjects but am more fulfilled with my inspirational writings. My parents instilled in me a love of expression through music and writing. [a.] Montezuma, IN.

GIEBRECHT, GAYLENE
[b.] May 31, 1978, Altona, MB; [p.] Ben and Lucille Giebrecht; [ed.] W.C. Miller Collegiate (grade 11); [occ.] Gas station attendant at Petro Canada (part-time); [hon.] Festivals of the Arts, organ trophies and speech arts trophies "Christmas" poem published in local newspaper (in contest); [oth.writ.] "Christmas" poem (1992); [pers.] I really wish the Cancer Research would find a cure for cancer and rid all cancer patients of this disease. This poem was written in memory of the only grandmother I ever knew. [a.] Altona, MB Canada.

GILBERT, VINCENT C.
[b.] October 3, 1957, Texas; [p.] Allan and Crass Gilbert; [m.] Kristy Gilbert; [ch.] Christopher, Casey, Richard, Brittan and Halye; [ed.] Tarleton State University; [occ.] English teacher, Van Uleck High School; [oth.writ.] Essays and poetry; [pers.] Creativity is the key to success and creative writing opens the mind so we may see opportunity when it appears. [a.] Pottsville, TX.

GILL, HEATHER P.
[pen.] Heather P. Gill; [b.] January 23, 1960, Barbados; [p.] Stanley Gill and Anita Stevenson; [ch.] Christopher Gill; [ed.] Modern High, Montgomery College, Dean's List; [occ.] Senior Library Assistant; [oth.writ.] Several poems; [pers.] Through my poetry, I hope to promote thoughtfulness in my readers. I would like my readers to benefit in some way from my insights. [a.] Silver Spring, MD.

GILLEY, SHIRLEY
[b.] May 18, 1958, Oklahoma; [p.] Edward and Betty Gilley; [ed.] Rogers State College, Hank Thompson School of Music, University of Kansas; [occ.] Surgical Tech for Surgical Services Tulsa, OK.; [hon.] 1991 Billboard song contest, Honorable Mention for song "A Circle Small" ; [oth.writ.] "For A Moment or So", short story in Uncommon Waters, an anthology of women's fishing stories; [pers.] I am a struggling singer/songwriter who strives to be understood through song, and hopefully people will see their lives too and not feel alone. [a.] Talala, OK.

GILLIS, COL. THOMAS D.
[pen.] Tom Gillis; [b.] October 29, 1912, Presidio of San Francisco, CA; [p.] Geo. S. and Lilian D. Gillis; [m.] Wilhelmine C. Carr, December 28, 1935; [ch.] Leah C. Campbell and George S. Gillis; [ed.] USMA, West Point, NY and Army War College; [occ.] Retired; [memb.] Sons of the American Revolution, Washington Family Association, Horse Cavalry Association, life member, Disabled American Veterans, American Legion, 4th Armored Division Association; [hon.] Silver Star with oak leaf cluster, Legion of Merit with oak leaf cluster, Bronze Star, Air Medal, Army Commendation Medal, Purple Heart, Combat Infantryman's Badge, National Defense Service Medal, United Nations Svc. Medal, Presidential Distinguished Unit Emblem, distinguished Marksman Badge, General staff identification badge, Republic of Korea Presidential Unit Citation, French Croix de Guerre with Palme, 5 service medals with 9 campaign stars; [oth.writ.] In process of writing autobiography, Sabers and Spurs; [pers.] I derive immense satisfaction from taking snapshots of friends on festive occasions and then sending them prints accompanied by a personal verse. Since retiring from the Army, I have devoted my life to serving and helping others. [a.] Greenbrae, CA.

GINDLESPERGER, ROSE
[b.] February 9, 1934, Meyersdale, PA; [p.] George and Catherine Brown; [m.] Willard Gindlesperger, February 9, 1952; [ch.] Ronald Eugene, James Lee, Katherine Ann (adopted) and Mildred Jean (adopted); [ed.] Meyersdale Public School; [occ.] Housewife; [oth.writ.] Limited to my children and grandchildren; [pers.] I strive to do as much as I can today, because tomorrow never comes. [a.] Streetsboro, OH.

GITTENS, CHERYL
[pen.] Cheryl Claire Gittens; [b.] January 21, 1963, Barbados, West Indies; [p.] Henderson and Elaine Gittens; [ed.] Early Education in Barbados, Art Students League of New York, California University, California Pennsylvania; [occ.] Student full time; [memb.] International Club California University, P.A., Art Student's League N.Y.C.; [oth.writ.] Short stories about my life in Barbados, poetry writings, diary compilations; [pers.] My life's goal is to be free from all repression and suppression, for freedom of spirit and to always stand up for what's just and right in this world. [a.] California, PA.

GLEASON, ANNE MARIE
[b.] May 16, 1948, Bay City, MI; [p.] Horace and Martha LaFramboise; [m.] Rolland V. Gleason, May 21, 1977; [ch.] Eliot, Michael, Joseph, Renee, Cynthia and Dorinda; [ed.] 12th grade; [occ.] Office worker at Cooley Law School; [memb.] Muscular Dystrophy Association, Mothers Against Drunk Drivers board of directors county chapter, and on the State Board; [hon.] Recognition of work as co-ordinator for the Muscular Dystrophy Telethon (4 years), Presidents Award for Leadership from the MADD chapter in Lansing; [oth.writ.] Brown Eyed Angel, Love Hurts and A Mom's Kiss, all dedicated to my two sons, one who died from MD and the other was killed by a drunk driver, My Brown Eyed Angel is to my grandson Niko, whose father was killed 4 months before his birth; [pers.] The poem chosen to be published is dedicated to Fr. Arthur Bosse, a wonderful friend who died. [a.] Lansing, MI.

GLICK, GRETCHEN B.
[b.] August 4, 1952, California; [p.] John and Hazel Glick; [ed.] BA Art History, MA Art History, C.S.D. Spiritual Direction; [occ.] Writer and water colorist; [oth.writ.] Currently writing non-fiction "Cloud of Glory" a 15 year account of spiritual experiences; [pers.] My writing is done to give glory to God.

GLODEK, PATRICIA A.
[pen.] Pat Zellem; [b.] July 27, Ralphton, PA; [p.] Stephen and Anna Zellem; [m.] John A. Glodke (deceased), April 8, 1939; [ch.] John A. Jr.; [ed.] Grace School, Somerset High School, Adele Allan Beauty School, editor of poetry in high school; [occ.] Retired writer and amateur poet; [memb.] AARP, Everett Senior Citizens, Bedford Bosum Buddies, Concerned Women of America, Christian Singles, Everett Assembly of God Church; [hon.] Was honored at Everett for being a charter member in helping start the Everett Assembly of God Church; [oth.writ.] My poems are published at least twice a month in the Bedford Sun Gazette; [pers.] I've studied the writing of many authors and especially poets Joyce Kilmer (my favorite), Henry W. Longfellow, I'm a bookworm. [a.] Everett, PA.

GLOTZER, MARGUERITE
[pen.] Maggie Horst, Mary Bell; [b.] December 23, 1917, Washington, DC; [p.] John and Daisy Steese Horst; [m.] Albert; [ed.] North High School, University of Akron, Ohio, B.A., Hunter College, New York, M.A., Columbia University, New York, poetry seminars, New School, NYU, Si Beagle Learning Center for Retired Teachers, United Federation of Teachers, New York City; [occ.] Editor, retiree, RTC-UFT, Board of Directors, Mortal Redevelopment Houses, Inc., a non -profit co-op; [memb.] OFT-RTC, Executive Board, Social Democrats, U.S.A., Educators Chapter, Jewish Labor Committee, Aubudon Society; [hon.] Art and literary editor, the Findleyite, elementary school mimeopaper, President Chi Delta Phi, literary honorary, University of Akron, columnist, the Buchtelite, University of A., newspaper, co-editor, Labor Action, executive director, Untied Cerebral Palsy of Queens, Inc., various awards as teacher unionist, sponsor of high school yearbook; [oth.writ.] Editorials, political commentary, poems in little magazines, administrative bulletins of many kinds in appropriate bureaucratese; [pers.] To push the boundaries of understanding of feelings and dreams of the rational genius of man, if the earth beneath our feet of laughs,of sighs of cries, all is grist. [a.] New York, NY.

GODERICH, ANGELA
[b.] July 8, 1978, Mobile, AL; [p.] Roberto Goderich (of Waukesha, WI) and Judy Wagner (of Deer Lodge, MT.); [ed.] 10th grade at Powell County High School, Deer Lodge, MT; [occ.] Student; [pers.] This poem means a lot to me for these reasons, one being I wrote this poem the night my grandma died and the last being it helped me cope with her death. We were really close, sometimes I wonder if it wasn't her trying to tell me everything is going to be all right. [a.] Deer Lodge, MT.

GOFF, ERINA
[pen.] Erina O. Goff; [b.] February 6, 36, Mulchatna River, Alaska; [p.] Yngvar and Minnie Engelstad; [ch.] David, Nina and Jenny; [ed.] Holy Cross, Alaska; [occ.] Contract Assistant U.S.D.A. Forest Service, Gresham, OR; [oth.writ.] Poems broadcast on the Armed Forces Service Network, through our local KGW Radio Station, for approximately 10 years, our radio program here in Portland, OR., was called "Open Door"; [pers.] I am Y'pik Eskimo, Norwegian and Russian. I feel a very close relationship with mountains, forests and wild creatures, nature affects me deeply, for she offers the soothing balm of profound peace and serenity that mankind can never duplicate. [a.] Portland, OR.

GOLDEN, KAREN A.
[b.] April 10, 1966, Kennett, MO; [p.] Jerry W. and Patsy J. cook; [m.] Bruce K. Golden, May 25, 1985; [ch.] John Kenneth and Amy Elizabeth; [ed.] Piggott High, Crowley's Ridge College; [occ.] Postmaster Relief; [pers.] I hope the life I live will inspire my children to reach for their dreams. [a.] Gregory, AR.

GOMEZ, LAURA
[b.] december 10, 1978, Oklahoma City, OK; [p.] Donna and George Gomez; [ed.] Casa Roble High School; [occ.] Babysitting; [oth.writ.] Several poems but none of them published; [pers.] Treat the earth well. It was not given to you by your parents, it was loaned to you by your children. [a.] Citrus Heights, CA.

GONZALES, CARMEN L.
[pen.] Mameng; [b.] July 16, 1928, Boac Marinduque, Philippines; [p.] Tomas Lara and Juan Labog; [m.] Emilio B. Gonzales, January 12,1954; [ch.] Arlene, Emilio Jr., Melisa, Freddie, Agnes and Odilon; [ed.] High school, etc., BSEED graduate; [occ.] Retired school teacher of the Philippines (40 years in service); [memb.] Teaching Forces, Teacher's Club, PPSTA, OMPSTA; [hon.] Graduated with honors in the high school (fourth honor), I finished college by means of Saturday classes and summers but often times I am exempted in some of my subjects; [oth.writ.] I often make poem in our district and my superior appreciated it, I create a poem for my pupils; [pers.] I love and appreciate poems. [a.] Jersey City, NJ.

GONZALEZ, LISA
[b.] August 11, 1980, Pawtucket; [p.] Gail and Angel Gonzalez; [ed.] Attending junior high school, Jenks Junior High; [oth.writ.] A Child's World, A Mother's Love and Loving Moments, all previously published in The Times on Monday, June 13, 1994; [pers.] Age is just a number and talent expands more with age. [a.] Pawtucket, RI.

GOODALL, ANNE
[pen.] Anne Goodall; [b.] May 10, 1949, Rosevalley, Sask; [p.] Jean and Glen Lucey; [ch.] Jean and Janell Hauzeneder; [ed.] University Agnew Shoe Store; [occ.] University student; [memb.] Art Work Galley, Nude Model University, University choir, Outdoor Club, Art Exhibit-The Grind Coffee House, producer Moxie Crew, playhouse-Neils Simons; [hon.] California Suite Public Relations for the "Dove"; [oth.writ.] Yes; [pers.] Love all people, creatures great small and all things and money too.

GOODMAN, SARAH Y.
[b.] June 11, 1964, Delhi; [p.] Paul Young and Ruth (Joann Fox and Sonny); [m.] David Goodman, July 19, 1987; [ch.] Jeremy, Heather, Doris and William; [ed.] Pioneer High School; [occ.] Wife and mother; [memb.] Ladies Auxiliary ; [pers.] Life and family are precious never take anything for granted. It can be gone in a blink of an eye. [a.] Pioneer, LA.

GORDEN, MITZI J.
[pen.] "MJG"; [b.] February 7, 1933, Carlsbad, NM; [p.] E.R.T. and Lela Hanez; [m.] Ralph Gorden Jr., February 2, 1953; [ch.] Shawn, Russell, Ralph and Tim, grandchildren, Lauren, Lia, James and Jenna; [ed.] Graduated Carlsbad High School, 3 years New Mexico State University; [occ.] Retired. [a.] Carlsbad, NM.

GOSTMANN, MARGARET C.
[b.] July 27, 1955, England; [p.] Marie and Peter Tierney; [m.] Hans H. Gostmann, July 31, 1976; [ch.] Brendan, Kieran and Kirsty; [ed.] Matriculated from Our Lady of Mercy Convent, Springs South Africa 1972, National diploma in Medical Laboratory Technology (Microbiology) 1976; [occ.] Writer, homemaker; [memb.] None at present (active) mail-list member of Burnaby Writers Society; [oth.writ.] None published, (some printed in school magazine) mostly short stories. [a.] Tsawwassen, BC.

GOUVEIA, LISA
[b.] April 16, 1981, Maui; [p.] Mae and Alfred F. Gouveia; [oth.writ.] Poems written for friends and family; [pers.] I write poems to express my feelings and they usually have happened to me. [a.] Wailuku, HI.

GRAFF, BRYAN T.
[b.] March 20, 1973, Buffalo, NY; [p.] Thomas and Rita Graff; [ed.] Currently a senior secondary English major at Cortland State New York; [pers.] This poem is dedicated to Allison, my love and inspiration.

GRAHAM, LYN M.
[b.] 1943, Riverside, CA; [ch.] Katherine Marie Reynolds Kelly of Byron, GA; [ed.] Riverside City College and Snead State University; [occ.] Master stylist; [hon.] Named one of the top 8 stylist in U.S. by Helen Curtis, 1992; [oth.writ.] "Hands of Time", is Ms. Graham's first published piece. Though she has been writing for her own pleasure for over 30 years and until very recently deemed her work to personal to share.

GRAHAM, RACHEL
[pen.] Rachel Graham; [b.] July 6, 1979, Louisville, KY; [p.] John and Debra Graham; [ed.] Center Grove High School, freshman year, Danville High School-sophomore year, Center Grove is in Greenwood, IN., Danville High is in Danville, KY.; [occ.] Student; [memb.] National Junior Beta Club, Church of Christ; [hon.] Author's contest awards, ages 8-11, school scholastic achievement; [oth.writ.] Poems published by school literary magazine, poems and short stories published by local newspaper at age 12, at age 11, won first place for poetry category in county young authors' contest; [pers.] I'd like to thank all those who first encouraged me to write, especially Mrs. Janice Suggs, Mr. Mark Culberth, Mrs. Linda Knight, Mrs. Dana Bowling and Mr. Steve Meadows. [a.] Danville, KY.

GRAHAM, TeQUAN SABRE
[b.] July 27, 1959, Newark, NJ; [p.] Shirley McCloud and Gertrude Banks; [m.] Carolyn Polite; [ch.] Latisha Sherri Graham; [ed.] Weequahic High School, Middlesex Community College, course Language Arts and basic computer; [occ.] Freelance writer; [memb.] President and founder of Pain Potions greeting cards, "subsidiary to the medical profession of love", Ex-internal Director for Wilderness Jaycees, G.E.D. tutor; [hon.] School essay champion, winner of English class writings of poetry and short stories, best seller of many poems to Dekalb C.J. Georgia; [oth.writ.] "Godly Grace", "Happy Daughter's Day", "Mirror Image", "In Heart of Mind", "What God Intend For Me", "Witness Of A Man's Tears"; [pers.] My dedication to Sherri, "Everybody need somebody's love". To the Grahams, Polites, Jones, Walkers, Banks and all who has faith in me. My deepest thanks to Jehovah. [a.] Tucker, GA.

GRAINGER, AMANDA
[b.] November 24, 1980, Fort Riley, KS; [p.] James Grainger and Frankie Stanley; [ed.] 8th grade at Johnsonville Middle School in Johnsonville, SC; [occ.] Student; [memb.] Junior Beta Club, Student Council, Academic Challenge Team, Pep Club, middle school chorus; [hon.] The National Honor Roll Society, United States Achievement Academy; [oth.writ.] Several short stories entered in writing contests, school newspaper articles; [pers.] "I can do all things through Christ which strengthens me"! Philippians 4:13. "Man that is born of a woman is of few days, and full of trouble". Job 14:1. [a.] Johnsonville, SC.

GRANT, JENNIFER A.
[b.] December 16, 1978, Lincoln, NE; [p.] Doug and Judy Grant; [ed.] Sophomore at Lincoln High; [memb.] Junior Achievement, Future Business Leaders of America, First Plymouth Church; [hon.] Nebraska Young Author's Award, most valuable swimmer 1991; [pers.] Believe in yourself and be who you want to be, not who others want you to be. [a.] Lincoln, NE.

GRANT, ROBERT D.
[b.] August 25, 1952, Kewanee, IL; [p.] Willis and Dorothy; [m.] Gale Lynn, October 31, 1994; [ch.] Stephen, Shane, Julie and Jessica; [ed.] High school;

[occ.] Cook; [oth.writ.] Several poems and songs never published; [pers.] All my poems and songs reflect the times I pounder in my past and hopes for the future. [a.] Newton, IA.

GREBE, DEBY
[b.] August 1, Lincoln, NE; [p.] C.L. Squires and Joyce Bermingham; [m.] Terry Grebe, June 30, 1984; [ed.] Rock Port R II High School; [occ.] Insurance agent; [oth.writ.] Although I have been writing for several years, this is the first one I have submitted; [pers.] Never lose faith in the power of dreams; [a.] Rock Port, MO.

GREEN, IRVIN J.
[pen.] "Grady"; [b.] August 29, 1969, Savannah, GA; [p.] Rev. William B. and Mazie Lee Green Sr. (both deceased); [ed.] Graduated, Savannah High, June 1987; [memb.] Coastal Jazz Association; [oth.writ.] Reflections, Songs For A Hoodoo Man (written in memory of deceased poet/author Larry Neal); [pers.] I always have been moved by the power of the written word to teach as well as entertain. Writers who have inspired and enlighten me are Ishmael Reed, Larry Neal, Amiri Baraka and Chester Himes. [a.] Savannah, GA.

GREEN, JACK D.
[b.] May 10, 1924, South Bend, IN; [p.] George and Lillian Green; [m.] Julie Ann Brackin, Luhrsen Green, April 28, 1975; [ch.] Philip George Green, Jacquelyn Green Lewkowich, Melissa Lynn Luhrsen Micari, Timothy Edward Luhrsen and 12 grandchildren; [ed.] Carl Schurz High School, Chicago, IL., 2 years U.S.A.F.I.; [occ.] Retired; [memb.] V.F.W., American Legion, Galena Neighborhood Watch, Stone County Historical Society; [oth.writ.] Poems published in local newspaper; [pers.] Veteran European Campaigns, World War II. [a.] Galena, MO.

GREEN, JAMES EDWIN
[b.] March 16, 1956, Ypsilanti, MI;[p.] Robert and Helen Green; [m.] Janet L. Green, May 4, 1984; [ch.] Colby Ryan Green and Duncan Ryan Green; [occ.] Ford's Saline Plant.

GREEN, SONIA
[b.] May 3, 1939, Detroit, MI; [m.] Richard; [ch.] 5 children, 11 grandchildren; [occ.] Retired Respiratory Therapist (Children Hospital, Michigan); [memb.] Foster Care Review Board # 8, (Vice Chair), Eastlake Baptist Church; [pers.] I'm striving for my writing to remind children to think and be aware of their surroundings at all times. Parents can not be with them always. [a.] Detroit, MI.

GREEN, VALERIE
[b.] November 3, 1975, New York City; [p.] Fannie Garnett and Willie Green; [ed.] Jane Addams Vocational High School, Mercy College; [occ.] Full time student; [memb.] Speech Club, I Had A Dream Scholarship Fund, Double Day Book Club; [hon.] Mervin H. Riseman, Hydroponics, Operation Success, Community Board of Harlem Hospital Merit Award; [oth.writ.] I've written several other poems, some of them are "Infatuation", "One Night Stand", "Where Did Love Go" and a few others; [pers.] Poetry is imaginative or creative writing that is designed to provoke one's interest, develop their thinking and help improve their writing skills. I hope, I am contributing to literature and to the minds of all intermediate poets. I wrote this poem when I experienced my 1st love, Kwabena Boama. [a.] New York, NY.

GREENE, VICTOR T.
[b.] March 6, 1960, Columbus A.F.B., MS; [p.] C.L. and Marion A. Greene Sr.; [ed.] Landrum High School graduate; [occ.] Disabled; [memb.] Gowansville Baptist Church, A.M.O.R.C., International Society of Poets, Poet's Guild, L.E.G.G.'s (Loyal Escorts of the Green Garter); [hon.] Golden Poet 1991 and 1992, several Honorable Mentions, twice chosen Editor's Choice; [oth.writ.] Several poems published, National Library of Poetry, Poet's Guild, International Library of Poets, Amhurst Society and Rainbow Records; [pers.] I hope to inspire. [a.] Landrum, SC.

GRIBOVICZ, DAN
[b.] January 30, 1961, Cleveland, OH; [ed.] Trinity High School, Ohio School of Broadcast Technique, National Radio Institute, Airco Technical Institute; [occ.] Owner/operator of Liger Studio and Music Affaire Disc Jockey Service; [pers.] Strive to be your best. [a.] Cleveland, OH.

GREINER, CHRISTI JO
[b.] March 29, 1975, Denver, CO; [p.] Donald P. and Tracey Greiner Jr.; [ed.] Northwood Public High, Northwood, ND., Altoona School of Commerce, Altoona, PA.; [occ.] Full time student at Altoona School of Commerce; [memb.] Member of St. Matthews Parish choir; [hon.] Who's Who Among America's High School Students; [oth.writ.] Several other poems, "Life", "The Tornado", "Changes In Season"; [pers.] My poetry shows many things of today's world. It wakes up a person and makes he or she aware of what they may feel. It maybe a topic on love, friendship or the beauty of the world around us. [a.] Tyrone, PA.

GREINER, SUSAN
[pen.] Samantha Martin; [b.] February 7, 1953, Woodstock, IL; [p.] Catherine and Bill Martin; [m.] Jack W. Greiner, October 21, 1972; [ch.] Jonathan and Katie; [ed.] Cary-Grove High School; [occ.] Photographer; [pers.] This poem was inspired by a need to be understood by two special friends. When I can't say the audible words, I let my heart dictate and my hand pens what I feel deep within. [a.] Rochester, MN.

GRIESEDIECK III, JOSEPH E.
[b.] September 28, 1970, St. Louis, MO; [p.] Joseph E. Griesedieck Jr. and Carolyn Rhett; [m.] Tara Boyd Griesedieck, August 20, 1994; [ed.] Kemper Military School, B.S. Bradley University; [occ.] Divinity student at Trinity Episcopal School for Ministry, Ambridge, PA.; [hon.] Cum Laude, 1992 Bradley University; [pers.] As a Christian, all of my writing is to the glory of God, the giver of all my gifts. I have been especially inspired by George Herbert and John Donne. [a.] Ambridge, PA.

GRIFFIN, GYNETH
[b.] July 8, 1921, Richland County, WI; [p.] Ernest and Ethel (Parfrey) Gray; [m.] Arno Griffin, June 10, 1989; [ch.] Gray Rubin, by former marriage; [ed.] Richland Center, Wisconsin High School, 2 years Wessington Springs Junior College, S.D., 1 year Teacher's College in Richland Center, Wisconsin; [occ.] Retired, dairy farmer, self employed, crocheting, knitting, baking and writing; [memb.] Member of Free Methodist Church; [hon.] Poem published by the National Library of Poetry; [oth.writ.] Just poems since the 1930's; [pers.] I try to find ways to help others. Am presently knitting mittens and caps for the Salvation Army and Olive Branch Mission in Chicago, also sponsor two children in Haiti. [a.] Richland Center, WI.

GRIFFITH, JAMES
[pen.] Scriptolight; [b.] June 16, 1956, Trenton, NJ; [p.] Mary and Eugene Gay; [ed.] Cedar Grove Academy, Philadelphia College of Bible, Manna Bible Institute; [occ.] Security guard at Stapeley in Germantown; [hon.] Timothy Christian Award at Cedar Grove Academy, year 1975; [oth.writ.] "To Lynn", "If My People"; [pers.] I endeavor to keep the bond of peace with all mankind through God. [a.] Philadelphia, PA.

GRIFFITH, LISA L.
[b.] February 6, 1965, Quantico, VA; [p.] Robert Griffith and Linda Fitch; [ed.] High school, some college, U.S. Army, (Loy Norrix High School, Madonna University); [occ.] Consumers Power Co., Street Utility worker, Livonia, Michigan; [oth.writ.] Some short stories, some lyrics, more poetry; [pers.] Writing is my personal therapy. Through writing I discover who I really am, what I truly feel and what I honestly can be. [a.] Livonia, MI.

GRIFFITHS, NELL J.
[b.] March 4, 1946, Thompson, MI; [p.] Bonnie and Arthur Choat; [m.] William J. Griffiths, October 26, 1974; [ch.] Brian J. Griffiths (30 years old, stepson); [ed.] Graduate-Champion High School, Champion, Michigan; [occ.] Executive Administrative Secretary; [oth.writ.] Authored poetry and art sections, high school newspaper (1962-64), authored "Poetry Corner", bi-weekly Muni newsletter, Anchorage, Alaska (1982-87); [pers.] My writings and poems reflect the human condition. I am a romantic, human nature, changing seasons and roses are the bases of my writings. New England poet, Robert Frost inspires me. [a.] Anchorage, AK.

GROOCH, JAMES V.
[b.] March 2,1973, Jefferson City, MO; [p.] James W. Grooch and Carla Roesger; [ed.] High school diploma from Jefferson City High School and currently attending University of Mo-Columbia with graduation date in December 1995; [occ.] Bookkeeping and data entry; [memb.] National Honor Society of Secondary Schools; [hon.] I have several medals for competition in football and track and field in high school; [oth.writ.] I have no other published writings, I just have some poems written to my girlfriend; [pers.] This world is cruel and anything can happen to you at anytime. I say hold your head up high and take it. You will get your reward in the end. [a.] Jefferson City, MO.

GROSS, JASMIN
[b.] December 29, 1980, Lewisburg, PA; [p.] Richard and Janice Gross; [ed.] Maclay Elementary, Sunbury Middle School; [occ.] Student; [memb.] National Junior Honor Society; [oth.writ.] Numerous unpublished poems and stories; [pers.] I write because i believe that nothing it louder, more honest or direct than a child's thought. A child's thought is the voice of tomorrow and I think people should pay a little more attention to a child's thoughts. [a.] Sunbury, PA.

GROTE, MICHELLE A.
[b.] March 6, 1977, Abington, PA; [p.] Mike and Marcy Grote; [sib.] Michael; [ed.] Bensalem High School, class of 96; [occ.] Breezy Point Day Camp (summer) counselor; [memb.] Bensalem High School, choir soloist, Captain Bensalem Color Guard, Students Against Driving Drunk; [oth.writ.] Poems published in school paper; [pers.] "No one is better than me, they just do a different job".

GRUDEN, JAYME R.
[b.] November 8, 1961, Oakland, CA; [p.] Nancy Hagen; [m.] henry Gruden Jr., April 26,1985; [ed.] Old Dominion University-B.S., University Southern Mississippi, M.Ed.;[occ.] Special Education Teacher. [a.] Biloxi, MS.

GRUDZINSLY, JIM
[b.] June 7, 1960, Philadelphia, PA; [p.] Walter and Bernadette; [ch.] Richard James and Cynthia Jean; [ed.] College Prep, Technical Schools, pursuing B.S. Computer Science (when time permits); [occ.] Programmer/analyst, consulting in Mid Range Systems; [memb.] Various computer user groups, museums, Zoological Society; [oth.writ.] Poetry, short stories, clever greetings, keeping my daytime job; [pers.] Writings inspired by a strong passion to overcome the struggles of life. Life is not eternal, but a lifetime last forever, make an impression. [a.] Philadelphia, PA.

GRUSZECKI, KATHY
[b.]July 27, 1973, Saskatoon, Sask (grew up in Archerwill, Sask); [p.] Mike and Beryl Gruszecki; [ed.] Rose Valley High School, Rose Valley, Saskatchewan, University of Regina, 3rd year, Psychology, Regina, Saskatchewan; [occ.] Student; [oth.writ.] Written a few other poems, none of which have been published; [pers.] Besides writing poetry I enjoy drawing, painting and listening to music. [a.] Regina, Saskatchewan.

GUCKENHEIMER, HELEN
[b.] March 9, 1945, Washington, DC; [p.] Dora and Louis Fox; [m.] Dan Guckenheimer, December 21, 1969; [ch.] Debra and Julie; [ed.] Shawnee Mission East High School, Massey Business College; [occ.] Self employed, Secretary-bookkeeper; [memb.] B'Nai B'rith Women, Women's American ORT, Hadassah, Board of Central Agency of Jewish Education, Chairman of Board of Education at Kehilath Israel Synagogue; [hon.] Award of Merit for Friends In Peace, December 12, 1990, World of Poetry, Sacramento, CA., Hadassah Service Award; [oth.writ.] Friends In Peace: [pers.] Believe in working together to make a difference. [a.] Overland Park, KS.

GUERNSEY, CHACE A.
[b.] January 17, 1977, Portland, OR; [p.] Betty Anne and John Cole Dempsey; [ed.] High school; [occ.] Landscaper; [oth.writ.] Several poems in my 7th grade class were put in a school magazine; [pers.] The rights are yours to make and you can make it all. The right is mine to make so I make it my all. [a.] Bear, DE.

GUTH, ALBERT
[b.] February 24, 1932, Newark, NJ; [p.] Herman and Eleanor Guth; [m.] Regina Guth, June 21, 1975; [ch.] Rob, Ken, Tim, Denise, Gina and Michael; [ed.] B.A> Social and Political Science; [occ.] President, RG Environmental Inc.; [hon.] American Legion Oratorical Awards, Citizenship Award; [oth.writ.] Several poems and writings; [pers.] As the highest priority, we must instill and strengthen the social attitudes of mankind. [a.] Cedar Grove, NJ.

HACKER, JEANETTE ELAINE LEGG
[b.] June 14, 1950; [p.] Jeanette L. Steadmen and Stanley A. Legg; [m.] Rick Alan Hacker, September 23, 1991; [ch.] Rachel Marie Schuster and Jacob John Schuster III, Rick Alan Hacker II; [ed.] Port Huron High and Sawyer School of Business; [pers.] Love, understanding and compassion make the world a better place to live in and without it we have nothing. [a.] Yale, MI.

HACKETT, PHILIP
[b.] Boston; [ch.] Dylan Thomas Hackett; [ed.] College educated, English Lit., (Art History) European, U.S. Colleges; [occ.] Poet; [memb.] California Poets In The Schools, World Affairs Council, Commonwealth Club, Press Club; [hon.] Varied honors and awards from U.S., Mid-East; [oth.writ.] Poetry published widely in U.S. and overseas newspapers, magazines and anthologies; [pers.] Founder, organizer and promoter of numerous poetry events in Boston, Laguna Beach, San Francisco. Developer of large audiences for such large events. [a.] San Francisco, CA.

HAESSIG, SUZANNE
[pen.] Suzanne Haessig; [b.] August 5, 1981, Parma, OH; [p.] Hans and Jalone Haessig; [ed.] Keystone Middle School; [occ.] Student; [memb.] Keystone Levy Committee which makes posters and buttons to support the school's levy; [hon.] Honor Roll since 4th grade, Citizenship and Scholastic Achievements; [pers.] Humor is important in life and I want to make people laugh through my poems. [a.] Grafton, OH.

HAGOOD JR., TALBOTT B.
[b.] July 15, 1946, Danville, VA; [occ.] Sculptor (of wildlife and people in outdoor related activities); [memb.] National Wildlife Federation, Nature Conservancy, Wilderness Society; [hon.] My sculptures have received numerous first place awards as well as several "Best and Second In Show" awards at wildlife art shows in the U.S. and my sculptures are found in private collections in the U.S and abroad; [oth.writ.] "Hatteras", (poem); [pers.] Through my sculptures and poems, I hope to create an awareness and appreciation of the beauty and importance of nature and our natural world. [a.] Clover, VA.

HAINLINE, CHARLES J.
[b.] December 20, 1970, Peoria, IL; [p.] Sharon A. Gomes; [ed.] I graduated the 8th grade from Whittier Grade School in Peoria, Il., I went to Elmwood High in Elmwood, IL., then I received my high school diploma at Spoor River College, in Canton, IL; [occ.]Self-employed general laborer; [memb.] I support the animals of the North Shore Animal League, I also sponsor a child in Columbia, through Children International, I have an annual Royal Patronage of the Order of Nobility of the Hutt River Province; [hon.] Top male speller in my 8th grade class, certificate for "Outstanding Effort and Academic Integrity", certificate of appreciation for the respect for the rights of others, certificate of accomplishment-"Project Business", judo achievement award, I'm an official white belt; [oth.writ.] Numerous poems which will be published in a book in the near future; [pers.] My thoughts of poetry is the description of life within itself. One man's thought could mean, many thoughts to others. [a.] Yates City, IL.

HALEY, CHRIS VOGEL
[b.] June 12, 1951, Terre Haute, IN; [p.] Abbie and Ken Vogel; [m.] Joseph A. Haley, July 1976; [ch.] Carey, Matt, Joe and Abbie; [ed.] BS Ohio State University, MS Indiana University; [occ.] Secondary English teacher, mom and "horsebuster"; [pers.] A typical Hoosier, I feel a closeness to the land that I count as a vital element in people's lives. [a.] Terre Haute, IN.

HALL, ERIC
[b.] December 28, 1974, Manhattan, KS; [p.] Donald and Brenda Hall; [ed.] Mattoon High School, sophomore at the University of Illinois; [occ.] College student and vocalist; [hon.] National Honors Society; [oth.writ.] Numerous poems and songs; [pers.] My poetry serves as a vessel in reaching the unobtrusive aspects of the human soul. Through my poetry and my music, I'll reach out to give hope to ones who feel lost in the modern world. [a.] Mattoon, IL.

HALL, KAREN L.
[b.] June 14, 1979, Maryland; [p.] William and Elizabeth; [ed.] Now in 10th grade, (prime), theatre, French, Geometry, World History, Carver Center for the Arts and Technology; [occ.] Babysitter; [memb.] Ft. Howard Haunted House Choir; [hon.] Talent shows, fashion shows, theatre plays, I won a contest from "Famous Poet's Society" and they want to publish one of my poems; [oth.writ.] Just a lot of other poetry; [pers.] Life is a game you need to learn how to play and win. Thanks to my mom, stepmom, Nikki and Brian, I love you all. [a.] Baltimore, MD.

HALL, LYNN CLARICE
[pen.] Little White Birch; [b.] May 9, 1950, Flint, MI; [p.] Mary Hills and Douglas Hall; [ed.] Charlevoix High, North Central Michigan College, Eastern Michigan University; [occ.] Homemaker, server for senior citizens; [hon.] Lou Grant Award from the Ypsilanti Arts Council; [pers.] I hope to show through my writing how humans can celebrate their inner strength and bring themselves closer to their own natural resources. [a.] East Jordan, MI.

HAMMOND, BRUCE
[b.] July 24, 1966, Miami, FL; [p.] Essie Hammond; [ed.] Masters of Science, Bachelor of Arts (Marshall University); [occ.] Occupational Safety and Health Director; [memb.] American Society of Safety Engineers, National Society of Black Engineers; [hon.] Football and track and field scholarship, Dean's List, 2 times student athlete (award). [a.] Huntington, WV.

HAN-JUERGEN, MICHAEL HARLE
[b.] March 6, 1971; [p.] Eleonore and Johann Harle; [occ.] Retired Naval Special Operations; [pers.] One must experience every situation attainable without going out too far past society's norms. It is not uncommon for one to have his social umbilicus severed due to insightful thinking. In closing, I would sell my soul to interview Arthur Rimbaud. [a.] Indianapolis, IN.

HANAN, SANDRA
[pen.] Sandra Stevens; [b.] November 9, 1976; [p.] Barbara and Steven Hanan; [m.] Single; [ed.] I'm currently attending Niles North High School in Skokie, I plan on going to college and majoring in acting and journalism; [oth.writ.] Right now, I'm in the process of trying to publish my first poetry book and my first novel; [pers.] When writing any piece of work, whether it's a poem or story, I like to write it in a way where others can relate to it and maybe even learn something about themselves and the way in which they view the world around them. [a.] Skokie, IL.

HANBERRY III, JAMES C.
[b.] February 5, 1974, Murfreesboro, TN; [p.] James and Lynne Hanberry Jr.; [ed.] Santa Maria High, Allan Hancock College, (Associates degree in Criminology); [occ.] Student; [pers.] My writings tend to consist of our future on this planet and what it beholds for us. I only hope that we can change our ways before its too late. [a.] Santa Maria, CA.

HANSCOM, MELODY L.
[b.] December 14, 1964, Waterloo, NY; [p.] Eva D. and Ronald L. Seeber; [m.] Dale E. Hanscom Jr., May 12, 1989; [ed.] High school graduate, some college; [occ.] Administrative Assistant; [memb.] The American Legion Auxiliary; [pers.] I wrote this poem, "A Wonderful Man Is Leaving Us" when a close family member of my husband's was dying of cancer. [a.] Woodbridge, VA.

HANSEN, BECKY
[b.] October 13, 1947, Wichita, KS; [p.] Ivan and Arlene Nelson; [m.] Cregg P. Hansen, January 11,

1965; [ch.] Mitch and Paul; [ed.] High school; [occ.] Housewife; [memb.] M.S. Society, VFW Auxiliary, American Legion Auxiliary; [oth.writ.] "A Letter From Home" sent to soldiers in Desert Storm, published in local paper, one verse of it is on Pow posters in rest areas across Kansas; [pers.] "Keri", the poem I entered was written for my niece who was killed in a car accident. I no longer can work due to multiple sclerosis, so I have been pursing my writing which has always been a joy in my life. [a.] Derby, KS.

HARBUK, HILDA
[b.] 1978, Jerusalem; [p.] Sam and Izador Harbuk; [ed.] High school; [occ.] 12th grade; [hon.] Awards of recognition of voluntary work to a number of societies and elderly homes and settlement programs; [pers.] My personal philosophy embodies a recognition of the existence and omnipotence of our Lord, the Creator, which forms a basis of our being a small universe in a larger one and from this springs our love to humanity and mankind. [a.] Halifax, Nova Scotia, Canada.

HARDEN, DIXIE
[b.] June 10,1957, Marengo, IA; [p.] Calvin and Beverly Davis; [m.] Jack Harden Jr., November 28, 1974; [ch.] Shawn Michael Harden; [pers.] Adopted children should never feel that they were unloved. A lost child is not a forgotten child, they remain a part of your life forever, whether or not you're ever to meet again. We did meet my husband's daughter, once she was grown and it meant more than words could ever express. [a.] Ladora, IA.

HARDING, JIM
[pen.] Jim Harding; [b.] May 29, 1928, Peterboro, Ontario Canada; [m.] Florence and Michael Harding; [m.] Allison Harding, October 15, 1977; [ch.] Amy and Jane;[ed.] K-W Collegiate Institute, Kitchener Ontario, Canada; [occ.] Salesman, retired cemetery industry, pre-need counselor 30 years; [oth.writ.] Too numerous to list, average two per week, perhaps over a thousand altogether, I do poems for fun and profit, for all occasions, births, marriages, eulogies, parties, etc.; [pers.] "Expect the unexpected". Favorite writer and philosopher, George Bernard Shaw. Statement, to the real meaning of life, to die young but postpone it as long as possible. [a.] Torrance, CA.

HARDY, DONALD EARL
[pen.] Donald Earl Hardy; [b.] July 15, 1961, Baltimore; [p.] Mr. and Mrs. William E. Hardy; [ed.] Northwestern Senior High, Morgan State University, Baltimore City Community College, Rets Electronic School, CAD Training, biology major; [occ.] Lab Tec., Johns Hopkins' Hospital 8 years; [memb.] Merrit Athletic CLub, Columbia House Video Club; [oth.writ.] "Longest Road", "My Treasured Pleasure", "The Seedless Fruit", these poems are my original work; [pers.] I try to express togetherness and self for fullment in my poems. Self influenced. [a.] Baltimore, MD.

HARGRETT, DONALD
[pen.] J.J. Alphine; [b.] February 12, 1965, Chicago, IL; [p.] Douglas and Willia Frank; [m.] Ramonia Lisa Hargrett, March 1, 1994; [ch.] Donald O'Neal and Jeasica Lhyn; [ed.] Chathsworth High, Chaffey College; [pers.] This world is for the children, we must make a change.. life inspires my writing.

HARPER, MISTY LEA
[b.] December 17, 1979, Fitzgerald, GA; [p.] Billy and Bonnie Brooks; [pers.] The heart of a fool is in his mouth, but the mouth of a wise man is in his heart. [a.] Fitzgerald, GA.

HARPT, SCOTT C.
[pen.] Katter; [b.] May 16, 1973, Michigan; [p.] Gerald and Karen Harpt; [occ.] Currently a student at Valley City State University in ND; [pers.] The only thing my writings have in common is that they are influenced by personal life experience. My favorite poet is John Lennon. [a.] Wallace, MI.

HARRIS, MARY
[b.] September 23, 1963, Shreveport, LA; [m.] Keith; [ch.] Ashley, Alexis and Robbie; [ed.] College-Louisiana State University, Shreveport.

HARRIS, SHIRLEY DENISE
[b.] December 25, 1968, St. Louis; [p.] Ora Mae Harris; [ch.] La Marr Harris; [ed.] Soldan High School, Dewey Middle School; [occ.] Aspiring poet; [memb.] YWCA; [oth.writ.] My Darling Jewel, The Golden Butterfly; [pers.] I just started writing poetry at the end of August. I write poems about love, loss, religion and what I desire in life. I have been reading and liking poetry every since grade school. I have been inspired to write poetry by the many beautiful poems I have read. I am currently taking up creative writing in poetry class at St. Louis Community College at Florissant Valley in St. Louis. I have gotten nice compliments on my poems from my teacher and classmates and other people I have showed them to. [a.] St. Louis, MO.

HARRIS, TIFFANY
[b.] February 24, 1981, Connecticut; [p.] Roland S. and Maria V. Harris III; [hon.] I am in Journey of the Mind and in Musings; [oth.writ.] Pearl's Jam's Last Jam, Kurt Cobain, A Fan's Tale, The Tale of Two Planets and Courtney, all above are poems; [pers.] My friends and family mean the world to me so I dedicate this to my dad, mom and my brother, and Courtney Jackson, Shannon Mayo, Kathleen Kave and Aleen Saunders. Thank you all. [a.] Rockville, MD.

HARTMANN, CARY WILLIAM
[b.] July 5, 1948, Ogden, UT; [p.] Bill and Donna Hartmann; [ch.] Jared Cary and Joshua Jack; [ed.] Weber State College, Utah State University, Southern Utah State University; [occ.] Journeyman, plumber; [memb.] American Heart Association, Corvette Club of America, Tennessee Squire, Vietnam Veteran, Ducks Unlimited; [hon.] I've been honored with the life of my oldest son Jared and the grace of my youngest son Joshua; [oth.writ.] Poems, short stories and verse with one publication; [pers.] I strive each and everyday to achieve something productive, with honor to God and my family. [a.] Ogden, UT.

HARTMANN-PHIPPS, HANNE
[pen.] Hanne Hartmann-Phipps; [b.] July 19, 1937, Copenhagen, Denmark; [p.] Helga and Geert Hartmann (father deceased in 1985); [m.] James A. Phipps, February 8, 1982; [ed.] Studied for Royal Danish Ballet in Denmark, private school in Denmark, high school and some college in USA, six scholarships to Art Institute of Chicago, IL; [occ.] Retired-formerly Adm. Assistant to President/ CEO of major insurance company; [memb.] National Honor Society, current interests, my husband, Jim and I are retired and live in the S/W Ozarks with 2 poodles (Max and Style) and a mutt (Bogart), we also have a killer cat named Tuxedo, Jim and I are happily retired, he does magnificent stained glass art for which he has won awards, I do writing and designing; [hon.] (Poetry) Award of Merit 1989, Golden Poet Award 1989, (poetry) Awards of Merit May and September 1990, Golden Poet Award 1990 and Who's Who in Poetry 1990, second prize for essay for city of Chicago sponsored by D.A.R., several Honorable Mention Awards in art as a student in Chicago, special commendation from the company where I worked for the Business English Grammar course I wrote and taught; [oth.writ.] Wrote and taught a Business English Grammar course for the company where I worked, I have had many editorial letters printed by newspapers and other publications, my article on crime was sent to the entire Lake county (IL) Judicial System by State Senator Carl Berning, have had poems published in the following, Great Poems of the Western World Vol II, World of Poetry Anthology, Poetic Voices of America, (Spring and Fall 1991), Am in Who's Who in Poetry Vol III (page 406); [pers.] I try to be the best person that I can be, and be helpful and kind to those I come in contact with. I truly believe that each of us CAN make a difference, and make our world a better place for all. [a.] Reeds Spring, MO.

HARVEY, DAVID
[pen.] D.A. Harvey, A.H. Davison; [b.] January 7, 1973, Largo, FL; [p.] Joan and Alfred Harvey; [m.] Maria Anne Harvey, December 27, 1993; [ch.] Celina Talon Harvey; [ed.] Private grammar and high schools, five semesters of junior college; [occ.] Security officer; [memb.] Chairman of recycling committee, in high school Via Earth Awareness Club; [hon.] Student of the Month (high school) for organizing a petition against the Sands Corporation and for founding the "Earth Awareness Club"; [oth.writ.] "Cycles", short story (horror) countless poems currently working on a Science fiction novel; [pers.] The muse seldom leaves me. [a.] Maple Heights, OH.

HASELY, ONETA
[b.]May 7, 1924, Luan, AR; [p.] Ora G. Lloyd; [p.] Johnnie Hasely (deceased), June 4, 1938; [ch.] 8; [ed.] 5th grade; [occ.] Housekeeper; [memb.] Church of Christ; [a.] Winnfield, LA.

HASTIE, DALE D.
[pen.] David L. Johnson; [b.] October 3, 1972, Detroit, MI; [p.] Donald and Evelyn Hastie; [m.] Synceria A. Hastie, October 2, 1993; [ed.] Life; [occ.] Freelance artist; [oth.writ.] Poetry books includes "Thoughts From The Inner City", "Colors of Madness", "Collage" selected poems;[pers.] "There's no such thing as luck only the Lord's will". [a.] Southfield, MI.

HAUPTMANN, BRANDY
[b.] April 10, Savannah, GA; [p.] Brenda Brewer and Michael Hauptmann; [ed.] 7th grader, North District Middle School, Varnville, SC; [memb.] Junior Beta Club, YAC Club, member of Acteens, Sunday School and Bible Drill class; [hon.] Honor Roll, Junior Beta Club, Duke Talent Identification program participant, Gifted and Talented class; [pers.] I am not one to tell people how I feel. When I write poems it gives me a chance to express my feelings as well as strengthen my vocabulary. [a.] Hampton, SC.

HAUSE, MELODY ROSE
[b.] November 20, 1953, Cleveland, OH; [p.] Frank and Ameila Hula; [m.] Jerry, June 2, 1972; [ch.] Stephanie Marie and Dale Allen; [ed.] Barkwill Elementary, Myron T. Herrick, South High; [pers.] To all of the young men who serve in my neighborhood of Hamm Avenue, Barkwill Avenue, Broadway, Dolloff, E 48 St., E 49 St., of Cleveland, Ohio and to all of the young men who serve in this war. [a.] Newburgh Heights, OH.

HAVERMANN, AMBER
[pen.] Amber Havermann; [b.] December 25, 1979, Sacred Heart Hospital, Yankton, SD; [p.] Karen and Leander Havermann; [ed.] Freshman at Yankton High School; [occ.] Freshman at Yankton

High School; [oth.writ.] I wrote a lot of poems but have never gotten any published before; [pers.] I think that poetry is a great way to express your thoughts and feelings. I often write to express myself and to help myself understand what's going on in my life. [a.] Mission Hill, SD.

HAVY, JACQUELINE
[pen.] Cats; [b.] July 29, 1979, Panama City, FL; [p.] Terry A. Aberle nd Yvan Havy (deceased); [ed.] Washington Community High School (sophomore); [occ.] Student; [memb.] St. Mark's Lutheran Church, Washington swim team. [a.] Washington, IL.

HAWKINS, LYNETTE R.
[b.] May 22, 1980, Pueblo, CO; [p.] Paul and Connie Hawkins; [ed.] Freshman in centennial High School; [occ.] Student. [a.] Pueblo, CO.

HAWKS, TRACEY L.
[b.] March 27, 1971, Kansas; [p.] Connie Ward; [m.] Divorced; [ch.] Jonathan, Jessica and Jennifer; [occ.] Medical Assistant, Lab Tech; [oth.writ.] Many in my own personal journal, none that are famous; [pers.] This poem was written for, inspired by and dedicated to my grandparents, John and Darlene Ward, two of the most wonderful people God ever created. [a.] Oakdale, NE.

HAYES, CHERRYL
[pers.] Cherryl Hayes, was born Marie Blanche Cherryl Martin on February 6, 1947 in Quebec, Quebec to Millicent Florence Webberley and Oram Alexander Martin. She married in 1969, the have one son.

HAYES, WALKER
[b.] February 28, 1971, Cleveland, OH; [p.] Raymond and Celestine Hayes; [ed.] Columbia Area Career Center (office technology); [hon.] American Legion Award in sixth grade, GED scholarship in 1991; [oth.writ.] Several poems, several position essays on educational and political topics, letters to magazines and TV shows; [pers.] I came up with the poem by playing with words in my mind. [a.] Columbia, MO.

HAZELWOOD, EDDIE
[b.] October 23, 1979, Richmond, VA; [p.] Ed Hazelwood; [ed.] Washington and Lee High School; [occ.] Student; [hon.] Published in Daily Press, Newport News, VA., published in Treasured Poems of America 1994, Swanson Middle School's career poem contest 2nd place; [oth.writ.] Miscellaneous; [pers.] I believe that we all need to make the best of what we've got and never give because I've learned that in this world there's a place for each and everyone of us. [a.] Arlington, VA.

HEGGELMAN, ANICA
[pen.] Anica C. Heggelman; [b.] May 17, 1981, Minnetonka; [p.] Renee' Heggelman; [ed.] Go to Minnetonka Middle School West, now in 8th grade; [memb.] Minneapolis Institute of Arts; [oth.writ.] I write all kinds of things, poetry, stories, etc.; [pers.] I believe that people should speak their mind, in other words say what they are thinking. [a.] Minnetonka, MN.

HEIDER-BISSON, JUNE
[b.] June 30, 1932, Utica, NY; [p.] Jacob Heider-deceased, and Marie Heider; [m.] George Bisson, July 1, 1989; [ed.] T.R. Proctor High School, Utica, NY., Syracuse University College of Nursing, B.S., M.S., Utica State Hospital School of Nursing, R.N.; [occ.] Clinical Specialist in Psychiatric Nursing and Mental Health, Consultant and Psychotherapist in Psychiatric Nursing/Psychiatric; [memb.] Associates of CNY, Liverpool, NY., New York State Nurses Association, American Nurses Association, Sigma Thea Tau Nursing Honorary, Nursing Honor Society, Health Science Cntr., Upstate Medical Center, Syracuse, NY.; [oth.writ.] Talk Music-, Heart, Talk Music-Bass, analysis of Dickens' "Christmas Carol" in process; [pers.] My poetry is the creative product of my work with patients, their struggles and their resolution of their problems in living. I am influenced by two romantic poets, John Keats and Percy Bysshe Shelley and novelist Charles Dickenson. I have long been an admirer of their writing talents. [a.] Liverpool, NY.

HEINZE, JO
[pen.] Jo Heinze; [b.] December 22, 1925, Chicago Heights, IL; [m.] John Heinze, July 26, 1947; [ch.] John, Mary Jo, Jane, Margaret, Marielle and Joan; [ed.] Attended Prairie State College, graduate Chicago Archdiocese Lay Ministry program, graduate American Floral Art School; [occ.] Semi-retired flower shop employee, high school clerical, kind active in church ministry-go to classes; [memb.] Ladies Society of VFW, many years ago, society at church, I have always worked part-time and raised 6 children, I'm not too much of a social butterfly or charity person; [hon.] I have recently been inducted into a Hall of Fame, thing for going out and helping people, I feel honored that you selected my poem; [oth.writ.] This is my first; [pers.] I understand the gift of giving in its truest sense, how we receive by giving, how we heal by sharing, and as we constantly grow and experience newness beyond the occurring joys and sadness, life and its surprises just get better and better. [a.] Chicago Heights, IL.

HENDERSON, HELEN MOORE
[pen.] Helen Henderson; [b.] January 28, 1923, Greenville, NC; [p.] Deceased; [m.] Deceased, October 9, 1948; [ch.] Hastings Henderson Jr. and Helen Henderson Barrett; [ed.] Peace Preparatory Department, St. Mary's Junior College; [occ.] Retired; [memb.] Emmanuel Episcopal Church; [hon.] Honor's List (Peace); [pers.] I glory in aging because I know in aging I am humbled. Oh, let me be less centered in self and immersed in the community of humankind. [a.] Southern Pines, NC.

HENSLEY, LARA SUE
[pen.] Lara Hensley; [b.] July 15, 1968, Colby, KS; [pets.] Dog-Teekona and mouse-Hanna; [m.] Terry lee Fuller, July 21, 1990; [ed.] BA in Sociology from Fort Hays State University, one year certificate degree in Rural Human Services at University of Alaska, Fairbanks (UAF); [occ.] Village based mental health counselor for Nondalton Alaska; [oth.writ.] This poem is the first poem or any writing I've ever submitted for publishing, however I have written many poems and articles reflecting my personal and spiritual experiences in my work and with nature; [pers.] I feel most complete when I'm in touch with the nature around me. I strive for peacefulness, serenity and simplicity in my life. I often find these through living off the land. [a.] Nondlaton, AK.

HENSON, RUBY
[b.] February 14, 1912, Gastonia, NC; [p.] Sarah Jane Boyles and Melvin A. Crigg; [m.] Deceased; [ch.] 3 (one is deceased); [occ.] Retired; [memb.] Silver Striders Walking Club, Raleigh, NC., Fitzgerald Church of God, Young at Heart Club; [oth.writ.] Poems in newspapers, church bulletins, senior citizens's papers, (poems published in Fitzgerald Herald Leader and Gaston Observer; [pers.] My desire is to share my talents with others hoping to help and inspire someone along the way. God has given me a talent and I feel that it's important to use it for His glory. [a.] Fitzgerald, GA.

HEPRIAN, VIRGINIA M.
[b.] JUNE 17, 21, Lakewood, OK; [p.] Deceased; [ed.] High school graduate, wrote for the school paper (West High School), two years of college with courses (Cleveland) in Journalism and Applied Psychology; [occ.] Retired; [memb.] American Red Cross, PBS-TV local channel, National Arbor Day Foundation, Disabled American Veterans, Friends of the Cleveland Libraries; [hon.] National Honor Society, high school, Thespian Dramatic Society, high school, penmanship certificate, grade school (Waverly Elementary), spelling bee contest, grade school, certificate of merit -college (2) years; [oth.writ.] Short stories (never published); [pers.] English was my favorite subject in school, and I had wonderful teachers who gave me the inspiration to read and to write.[a.] Cleveland, OH.

HERALD, DEANNA
[pen.] Dee; [b.] July 23,1981, Cookeville; [p.] Dayna and Dwight Herald; [ed.] Cookeville Junior High School; [occ.] Basketball player; [memb.] Basketball team for Cookeville Junior High School; [oth.writ.] Us, You, Best Friends Forever, Till The Water Runs Dry, It Will Only Be You And I, and The World Around Us; [pers.] I just want to thank my parents for raising me and my sister and brother. I also want to thank my real good friends, Emilie Owens, Stpehanie Bybee, Rhoda Goolsby, Dana Robertson and Tasha Woods. [a.] Cookeville, TN.

HERBERT, JESSIE
[b.] July 5, 1900, Vancouver, BC; [p.] John and Jessie Forrest; [m.] Gordon Brerton Herbert, June 3, 1919; [ch.] G.B. Herbert Jr.; [ed.] King Edward High School, Greg Shorthand-steno; [occ.] Retired; [memb.] Grimshaw W.I., Stony Plain OES (now disbanded); [hon.] Poem "Gentle Jesus" accepted by the World of Poetry and copyrighted by them.

HERBERT, MARGARET V.
[pen.] Margie Herbert; [b.] Seat Pleasant, MD; [occ.] Retired, R.N.

HERCULES, ANDREW T.
[pen.] Drew Sta.; [b.] March 30, 1965, Guyana; [p.] Nella Bristol and James Hercules; [ch.] Christopher, Mark Hercules; [ed.] Charles Evan High School, New York City Tech. College; [occ.] A mechanic; [pers.] It's not the size of your words that makes poetry. It's not the among to letters you use. It's not even the way you speak, poetry comes from the beauty within you. [a.] East Orange, NJ.

HERPIN, HOBERT F.
[pen.] H.F. Herpin "Hobie"; [b.] July 5, 1918, Glencoe, OH; [p.] Mamie and Fred Herpin; [m.] Eleanor S. Herpin, October 6, 1972; [ch.] None from current marriage; [ed.] Worthington, Ohio schools; [occ.] Retired from Supervision capacity of Physical Plant at Ohio State University 1970, and from Supervision of Housing at University of Southern California 1990; [memb.] American Legion and Veterans of Foreign Wars; [hon.] Received the lifetime award of the Paul Harris Fellow of the Rotary Foundation of Rotary International in 1988; [oth.writ.] I have written between 30 and 40 poems, none have been published until now; [pers.] In 1971, after my first wife of 30 years died, for the first time in my life, poetry began to flow from my pen during my lonesome and despondent days. During my second chance of happiness, my 22 years of marriage to Eleanor, has inspired me to continue writing a variety of poems, mostly about our grandchildren and life. [a.] Artesia, CA.

HERRIDGE, CORA
[b.] October 20, 1943, Little Hr. East, Newfoundland; [p.] Giles and Melinda Pardy; [m.] Russell Herridge; [occ.] Homemaker; [oth.writ.] Booklet, The Way He Led Me. [a.] Grand Band, Newfoundland.

HESTER, JOSEPH E.
[b.] April 17, 1951, New York, NY-Harlem; [p.] Audrey Glover and Joseph Hester (deceased); [ch.] Joseph Hester Jr. and Justin Hester; [ed.] City College of New York, York College; [oth.writ.] Have been personally read and performed in churches, and a variety of community and secular groups around New York, in addition, my poetry has been printed in various community newsletters; [pers.] My poetry seeks to capture the power of truth and love in everyday life situations. My poetry is based on love and teachings I received as a child and maintained through adulthood. My poetry is emotional expressions from the heart. I hope someday my children and others who read it learn "what it's all about". [a.] New York, NY.

HICKMAN, PAUL S.
[pen.] Mavros Paul; [b.] January 15, 1942, Muskogee, OK; [p.] Henry and Pauline Hickman; [m.] Maria-anna Macopoulos-Hickman, March 6, 1965; [ch.] Irene Melina and Alexander Obona; [ed.] Manual Training High, University of LaVerne, Golden Gate University, Claremont Graduate College, University of Vanderbilt; [occ.] Disabled Veteran Outplacement Counselor, College Park, Maryland; [oth.writ.] Several professional articles for local Air Force base newspapers, founder of "Educational Director", (unpublished); [pers.] My writings tend to provoke the mind to reflect and think. The strong influences in my writings are, John Milton and Langston Hughes. I am a poet philosopher. [a.] Largo, MD.

HILDENBRAND, MARK T.
[b.] April 18, 1960, Milwaukee, WI; [p.] Thomas and Sharon Hildenbrand; [ch.] Brianna M. Hildenbrand; [ed.] Working towards an A.A. in Logistics and a B.S. in Vocational Education Studies, graduate of James Madison Senior High School-1978; [occ.] United States Air Force Supply Training and Quality Management Supervisor; [memb.] Air Force Association, USTA, Who's Who Worldwide; [hon.] Distinguished graduate class 92-94, Non-Commissioned Officers Academy 650th Supply Squadron NCO of the Year 1992, 1994/95, Who's Who Worldwide Registry of Business Leaders; [oth.writ.] Several poems yet to be published; [pers.] Fine what you truly enjoy and pursue it extensively. Be a good role model for someone. My daughter Brianna is my inspiration. [a.] Rosamond, CA.

HILL, RANDOLF P.
[pen.] Randolf P. Hill; [b.] March 31, 1953, Sullivan, TN; [p.] Paul and Sylvia Hill; [m.] Sylvia L. Hill, August 15, 1970; [ch.] Randella, Randolf, Renee, Regina and Ryan; [ed.] High school, Sullivan Indiana; [occ.] Carpenter; [oth.writ.] Numerous unpublished poems and songs, and one published in newspaper in memory of my grandmother; [pers.] Everyone has a poem in their soul if they will open up their heart and put it on paper. [a.] Sullivan, IN.

HILLIARD, CHRISTOPHER M.
[b.] March 6, 1974, Honolulu, Oahu; [p.] Reta Spears (mom), David Spears (step-dad), Floyd Hilliard (dad) and Mildred Hilliard (stepmom); [ed.] Richmond Hill High School, Armstrong State College, Florida Baptist Theological College; [occ.] Student; [pers.] I write to express the struggles and joys of serving Jesus Christ and to persuade others to surrender to Him. [a.] Richmond Hill, GA.

HINKLE, GARRY
[b.] October 6, 1946, Watseka, IL; [p.] Floyd and Lee Hinkle; [m.] Maureen (Brasel) Hinkle, October 8, 1966; [ch.] Amy Lynn, Abby Jo and Angie Lee; [ed.] BS Pharmacy University of Illinois, College of Pharmacy, Chicago, IL; [occ.] Pharmacist, Gulick Pharmacy, Danville, IL; [memb.] St. James United Methodist Church, Illinois Pharmacists Association, American Pharmacist Association; [hon.] High school, National Honor Society, college, Dean's List; [pers.] Though our fast advancing technology has the capability of aiding in providing us with fuller lives, such lives remain empty until the heart's satisfied through the expression of art. [a.] Bismarck, IL.

HINTON, JACQUELINE
[b.] June 29, 1948, Kinston, NC; [p.] Thomas H. Harper (deceased) and L. Lucille Fraley Harper; [m.] Howard W. Hinton, June 6, 1970; [ch.] Jennifer L. Hinton Wiseman and Brooke L. Poe; [ed.] Eddystone High School, Eddystone, PA., 1966, Benedictine College, B.A., English 1987, Atchison, KS., Magna Cum Laude; [occ.] Atchison Area Chamber of Commerce-manager for the Atchison Trolley; [memb.] Presbyterian Church, Association of Kansas Theatre, American Association of Kansas Theatre, Theatre Atchison, Chapter J. P.E.O. Sorority, Atchison Art Association, Association of Community Arts Agencies; [hon.] Cray Family Award in recognition of contributions to the development of Theatre Atchison-1993, convention chairperson, Association of Kansas Theatre 1989, International Star Registry-Star Number Cassidreia RA3H7M25SD57 22' renamed Jackie Hinton, award from Theatre Atchison Board of Directors-1993, Delta Epsilon Sigma, Kappa Gamma Pi; [oth.writ.] Several poems and one short story published in Loomings, a magazine of the Arts-Benedictine College; [pers.] The gift of poetry writing is, for me a freedom flight. It helps me to define the essence of life experiences and in doing so makes me empathetic to others. [a.] Atchison, KS.

HINTON-SCOTT, JESSY
[b.] April 28, 1980, Oakland, CA; [p.] Leanne Hinton and Gary Scott; [ed.] Presently 9th grade; [occ.] Student; [hon.] Scholarship award, art award, Science award, scholarship trophy awards, 8th grade graduation awards; [pers.] I think that art and poetry are a way of getting inner anger and feelings out that you have on your mind. I write and draw as a kind of therapy or as a way to calm myself. [a.] Berkeley, CA.

HINTZ, RICHARD WILLIAM
[pen.] Bill Hintz; [b.] November 13, 1952, Detroit, MI; [p.] Joseph and Eleanor Hintz; [ed.] I graduated from UCLA with a B.A. in History in 1976; [occ.] Finance Agent; [hon.] I've bowled a 299 game and have a ring and watch as a reward, also I've bowled a 700 series and have a 700 patch as my trophy; [pers.] I would wish more people would take time to write something nice about someone who is special to them, than trying to vent their anger at other people. [a.] Trabuco Canyon, CA.

HIRSCHKORN, DANIEL J.
[b.] September 12, 1973, Saskatoon, Sask Canada; [p.] Norbert and Loretta Hirschkorn; [ed.] Stobart High School, University of Saskatchewan, pursuing B.A. in English; [occ.] Student, U of S; [memb.] Foster Parents Plan of Canada; [oth.writ.] Poems published in Provincial High School newspaper; [pers.] My goal is to make an impact on society by dealing with issues that mankind chooses to ignore. [a.] Duck Lake, Saskatchewan.

HITCHCOCKS, ELISABETH T.
[b.] September 21, 1923, Amherst, MA; [p.] Henry and Alfretta Thacher; [m.] Edward Hitchcocks, August 1952; [ch.] Tad and Daniel; [ed.] Eliot Pearson Early Childhood Education at Tufts University, many courses in literature and writing at University of Mass and Westbrook (Portland, ME.); [occ.] Writer and teacher, enrichment program for 3-5 years old, in my home; [memb.] Habit for Humanity, Arbor Day Foundation, Maine Writers and Publishers, W.C. Church, Nature COnservancy, A.A.R.P., Democratic Party; [oth.writ.] Essays, stories for young children, letters, letters, letters; [pers.] I am in love with words, the power of words, the beauty of words. [a.] Bethel, ME.

HOBBS, DIANA
[pen.] Diane Hobbs; [b.] September 11, 1962, Astoria Queens, NY; [p.] Edwin and Anna Oshman; [m.] David D. Hobbs, September 5, 1986; [ch.] Tara, Evan and Taylor; [ed.] Hillsborough High School; [occ.] Distribution clerk, Somerville Post Office, NJ; [oth.writ.] Other poems include, "Mother-In-Love", "It's Hard To Say Goodbye", "Remember The Good Times"; [pers.] Helen Steiner Rice is my favorite poet. I usually base my poetry on people or events that touch me deeply. Most of my best work has been written for friends and family. [a.] Somerville, NJ.

HOEFS, KATIE ANNIE
[pen.] Katie Hoefs; [b.] January 24, 1978, Palo Alto; [p.] Charles and Annie Hoefs; [sib.] Ginger Hoefs; [ed.] Attended St. Joseph's Schools in Menlo Park-Atherton for K-8 grade, now attending Palo Alto Senior High School as a junior, wish to go to college at UC Davis; [occ.] None, wish to become an equine (horse) vet; [memb.] California Dressage Society (CDS), United States Dressage Federation (USDF), United States Combined Training Association (USCTA), American Horse Show Association (AHSA), Combined Training Equestrian Team Alliance (CTETA), United States Badminton Association (USBA); [hon.] Many trophies and ribbons including 4th place for CDS and 3rd place for USDF at the 6th annual Junior Dressage championships, participated in CCS,/CIF state cross country meet, 3rd place in Mission Valley College short story contest with "Night Rider"; [oth.writ.] "Night Rider"; [pers.] My major goal is to become an olympic horseback rider and win a gold for the US. This is not just a dream, it ia almost reality. My motto is "I do it because I can". [a.] Palo Alto, CA.

HOFFMAN, ERCELL H. (M.A.,M.A., M.P.A.)
[b.] August 16, 1941, Cotton Valley; [p.] Adell and Rosie Harris; [ch.] Bonnie, Cynthia and Lisa; [ed.] MFCC Intern, Masters degree in Clinical Psychology, Masters degree in Education and a Master of Public Administration; [occ.] Outreach counselor/case manager; [memb.] CAMFT (California Association of Marriage and Family Therapists), PSI Chi (the National Honor Society in Psychology); [hon.] Honorable Mention Opinion essay, 6th annual Writers' Conference, September 17, 1994, Long Beach, California; [oth.writ.] Novel The Acknowledgement" published 1978, completed manuscript No Room Up", a completed manuscript of poems, entitled The Lament, selected poems and a complete non-fiction work Thoughts, Dreams and Impressions, with tips on how to stay fat; [pers.] All human beings strive for growth and self actualization, for it is the nature of life to thrust itself forward. Our goals in life then should be to remove those obstacles that impede that process. [a.] Compton, CA.

HOGAN, JENNIFER
[b.] March 28, 1973, Brooklyn, NY; [p.] John Hogan and Stella D'Aleo; [m.] John Quatrone, November 19, 1994; [ed.] Christ the King Regional High School, Queensborough Community College; [occ.] Billing clerk; [pers.] My poetry expresses my feelings in writing. My inspiration comes from nature. [a.] Staten Island, NY.

HOGAN, JOAN CAROL
[pen.] Joan Carol; [b.] August 25, 1947, Hershey, PA; [p.] Kathryn and Marlin Hetrick; [m.] Brooker T. Hogan Jr., August 8, 1978; [ch.] Bryon T. Hogan; [ed.] Shippensburg University, B.S., Southwestern University School of Law, J.D., A.A. White Dispute Resolution Institute Transpersonal Hypnotherapy Institute and Inner Guidance Center, C.H.T.; [occ.] Attorney Mediator and Faciliator; [memb.] State Bar of Texas, State Bar of California, American Council of Hypnotist Examiners, National Guild of Hypnotists; [hon.] Pi Nu Epsilon National Honor Society; [oth.writ.] Journey of Many Sojourns (a collection of poems-unpublished); [pers.] Our search for self knowledge is an expression of our inherent craving for unity with God. To truly know self is to remember our Oneness. [a.] Brenham, TX.

HOLLAHAN, ELEANOR J. LEAVER
[pen.] Nina; [b.] December 6, 1921, Pennsylvania; [m.] Deceased; [ch.] Pamela Elyssa Hollahan; [ed.] 4 years college, 6 years post graduate, M.A., B.A.; [occ.] Retired U.S. Federal Civil Service DOD; [memb.] Mensa, Circumnavigator's Association, Nature Conservancy, other environmental and animal protective organizations; [hon.] Numerous; [oth.writ.] Poetry, short stories, limericks, Haiku, Senryu, travel articles, published various newspapers, magazines and several anthologies; [pers.] I endeavor to stir the readers' emotions and strive to make the world a "kinder and gentler" place. [a.] Ocala, FL.

HOLLAND, JANE A.
[b.] October 30, 1951, Oakland, CA; [p.] Barbara Lucile and Jim Smith; [ch.] Heather; [ed.] The school of life; [occ.] Personnel Analyst, state of California; [pers.] I believe life is what we make of it, and each moment is a treasure that must be cherished and never taken for granted. [a.] Elk Grove, CA.

HOLLAWAY, SANDRA J.
[b.] March 3, 1952, Galesburg, IL; [p.] Floyd and Frances Jennings (both deceased); [m.] Thomas C. Hollaway, April 15, 1987; [ch.] James, Joshua, Jolene, Zachary and Marissa; [ed.] Graduated 1970 from Virden Community High School, Virden, IL; [occ.] Housewife, part-time student; [memb.] Mt. Olive Baptist Church, Crawford, MS; [pers.] I enjoy writing poetry and find it a way of expressing my deepest feelings. [a.] Crawford, MS.

HOLLOMAN, REBECCA
[b.] February 14, 1956, Lee County; [p.] The late Carrie Lee Holloman; [ed.] A graduate from Bishopville High School with a high school diploma and attended the Kershaw County Vocational Center; [occ.] Nurse Assistant; [memb.] A member of the Mount Herman Baptist Church and a born again believer; [hon.] Received a grant certificate for being one of the most talented drawers to go to art school; [pers.] I am grateful for the gifts and talent that I do have and I'm looking to find the very best one that will bring me up to a big money making level. [a.] Florence, SC.

HOLMAN, DEBORAH LOUISE
[b.] May 5, 1971, Russellvill, KY; [p.] Clarence and Annie Francis Holman; [ed.] Auburn Junior High School, Logan County High School, Professional Career Development Institute; [occ.] Machine operator at Red Kap Industry; [memb.] People for the Ethical Treatment of Animals, World Wildlife Fund; [pers.] I believe that if you work hard in everything you do, you can accomplish anything you try. I also wish for world peace. [a.] Russellville, KY.

HOLMES, CHARLI
[b.] March 27, 1957, Denver, CO; [ch.] Ajani and Kojo Holmes; [ed.] East High School, Syracuse University; [occ.] Inventory Management Specialist, Department of Defense, CECOM, Ft. Monmouth, NJ.; [memb.] Voice Center Baptist Church Board of Ushers and Sunday School Teacher, Ft. Monmouth Mentors Scholarship Committee, Booster Athletic Club; [hon.] Dale Carnegie, TOM Facilitator; [oth.writ.] Staff writer for the community newspaper; [pers.] I allow the spirit of God to guide my creativity. My sons provide encouragement and support for my writing. [a.] Eatontown, NJ.

HOLZBERG, CHERYL BRASSO
[b.] October 26, 1961, Woodbridge, NJ; [p.] Anthony and Dina Brasso; [m.] David Holzberg, March 7, 1982; [ch.] D.J. Taylor Holzberg; [ed.] Cooper City High School of Cooper City Florida, school of hard knocks; [occ.] Nursing Agency Receptionist; [memb.] Women Bowling Association, American Poolplayers Association; [hon.] Winner of "Best" wife and mother contest, awarded by both husband and son; [oth.writ.] "The Uncaught Butterfly" to be published in Seasons To Come by the National Library of Poetry, other artistry patiently awaiting publication; [pers.] "A negative experience can open up a whole new world of positive change. I should know..." [a.] Hollywood, FL.

HOOD, JENNA D.
[b.] October 31, 1979, Auburn, WA; [p.] Teresa L. and Edwin N. Hood; [ed.] I am currently a student in 9th grade at Rainier Junior High; [memb.] National Junior Honor Society; [hon.] Presidential Academic Award; [pers.] I believe poetry is a universal language. It is a way for me to voice the feelings I have on injustices. [a.] Auburn, WA.

HOPKINS, DESIREE
[b.] March 30, 1968; [p.] Mi; [m.] Kevin Hopkins, May 12, 1990; [ch.] Cassandra Marie; [ed.] Savannah High School; [occ.] Administration Office clerk, Ridgecrest Community Hospital; [pers.] It is my desire to touch the hearts of people. [a.] Ridgecrest, CA.

HOPKINS, DUD
[b.] April 11, 1941, Harvey, IL; [m.] Bobbi Hopkins, June 18, 1983; [ed.] Thornton High, junior college, Indiana University, USAF 3320th Tech School, ATC, Personnel Specialist course, seminars and workshops in rehab. counseling and guidance and job placement, in-service training,; [occ.] Unemployed, formerly employed as a junior and high school teacher, state and federal civil servant; [memb.] None currently, formerly National Rehab. and Counselor Associations, National Association of Rehab Secretaries, Voc. Rehab. Survivors Benefit Association, LA Mayors Committee on the Handicapped Member, Board of Directors, St. of LA., V.R., B.A., LA Equal Opportunity Association Inc., S.P.E.B.S.Q.S.A., Inc., the American Legion, Loyal Order of Moose, Bayou Legion of the Moose Lodge, the Federated Church of Harvey, IL., member of IL. Junior College Conference Championship tennis team (T.j.C.Harvey); [hon.] 2nd place award, IL. Junior Academy of Science, I.I.T., National High School Honor Society, lettered in tennis, Chicago Youth Orchestra member, selected for I.U. summer music clinic, French horn in orchestra, Air Force and Civil Service certificates of work appreciation and achievement over the years, 2nd place doubles competition, IL Junior College Conference tournament, TUSLOG singles and doubles tennis championship, Ankara, Turkey; [oth.writ.] Sociological paper studying the Palquan culture of the Southwestern Pacific Islands, paper on lecture demonstration techniques in organic chemistry lab for secondary school teachers, undergraduate research on paper on community health education, de-emphasis of saintly Science in school, a proposition legal defense paper on appealing a denial ruling of unemployment compensation; [pers.] Poetry is like a work of art of the soul and the mind. The music of expression translated into thought and put into words. [a.] S. Holland, IL.

HORNER, WANDA
[pen.] Wanie; [b.] January 23, 1948, Scioto County; [p.] Clyde and Alice Horner; [m.] Single; [ed.] Graduated from Green High School, Franklin FCE, Ohio; [occ.] Have been a cook for the past 16 years; [oth.writ.] I have written quite a few poems but have had nothing published as of yet; [pers.] I have been greatly influenced by Jesse Stuart who is my 3rd cousin. He was one of the great poets and authors who I would like to dedicate this poem.

HORTON, DOROTHY JEAN
[pen.] Jean Armstrong; [b.] June 26, 1904, Jackson, MI; [p.] DeWitt, Jennie M. [m.] Frederick F. Horton, June 20, 1930; [ch.] Ann Loraine, Ellie Jean and Ruth Altson; [ed.] Trumansburg High, New York, Baldwin-Wallace College, A.B., Western Reserve U.-B.S.; [occ.] Retired, formerly children's librarian; [memb.] Lakeside E.C. Church Missionary Correspondent, American Library Association, A.A.R.P., National Humane Society of U.S., American Red Cross; [hon.] National recognition certificate for A.A.R.P. World Book of Poetry, several poems, awards; [oth.writ.] Cat story-to "Cat Fancy", to local newspaper, church bulletin; [pers.] I write for the joy of writing and to bring a little cheer to the down-hearted. [a.] Greenville R.D., PA.

HOSACK, KATIE
[pen.] Katie Hosack; [b.] July 22, 1982, Harlan, IA; [p.] Carmen and Bill Hosack; [ed.] I am in 6th grade at Harlan Community Middle School; [oth.writ.] Poetry is my hobby, but this is the first time any of my poems have been published; [pers.] I love writing and I think it opens up a whole world of possibilities for the imagination and mind. [a.] Harlan, IA.

HOULIHAN, CAROLYN
[b.] November 1, 1943, Holyoke, MA; [p.] Doris L. and Stanley A. Brunell; [ch.] Kelli C., Stephen D. Jr. and Kimberly K.; [ed.] Holyoke High School, Springfield Technical Community College, Long Ridge Writers' Group, Holyoke Community College; [occ.] Nanny, EKG Technician; [memb.] MADD: [pers.] I write poetry for my own enjoyment. I dedicate this poem to my three children for they are my greatest joy, iI am very proud of them. [a.] Holyoke, MA.

HOUSE, NICOLE
[pen.] Nikki; [b.] July 13, 1979, Memphis, TN; [p.] LaVargia Smith; [ed.] St. Augustine Catholic School, Bellevue Junior High and Central High School; [memb.] Koinonia Baptist Church, usher board, choir member and Secretary Youth Council, Central High School, drill team, Spanish Club; [hon.] Perfect attendances, Honor Roll, Principal's Lists, certificate of appreciation for service-

Koinonia Baptist Church usher board, certificate of appreciation for participating in Tennessee Youth Summit Conference; [oth.writ.] Welcome for Youth and Young Adult Day at Koinonia Baptist Church, stories (spare time), rap lyrics (never published or song) and of course poems; [pers.] I strive to continuously imply, by words, that everyone has a hidden talent and if they put their entire being into it, they can write, sing, act and much much more, but we must keep searching believing in ourselves and mostly in God. [a.] Memphis, TN.

HOUSTON, CLIFF
[b.] July 6, 1953, Blakely, GA: [p.] Cary and Delma Houston; [m.] Karen Purvis Houston, January 1, 1979; [ch.] Amanda Nichole (19) and Emily Paige (12); [ed.] Early County High School, ABJ, University of Georgia, M.Div., Southeastern Baptist Theo. Seminary, currently enrolled in D-Min program at Canbler School of Theology at Emory University; [occ.] Pastor of Brinson Baptist Church; [memb.] Brinson Baptist Church, Georgia Baptist Convention's Advisory committee to Mercer University, Georgia Writers' Coalition for Literary in Georgia; [hon.] Voted most valuable teacher at Brianbridge Seminary in 1992; [oth.writ.] One poem published in American Legion magazine, weekly sermons, bible studies and responsive readings; [pers.] I believe writing should reveal who we are, how we feel and what we're about. That way it can lead us into dialogue with others. [a.] Brinson, GA.

HOWARD, IMILDA M.
[pen.] Amy Howard; [b.] March 24, 1926, Lanes Mills, PA; [p.] George and Laura Harding; [m.] Donald C. Howard, January 5, 1945; [ch.] Jerry, Penny and Mark; [ed.] Brockway High, currently enrolled in creative writing class here in Paul Spring Retirement Community; [oth.writ.] Recently had a story published in Mount Vernon Gazette, all my writing has been in creative writing here and this is the first poem I've attempted, my stories are memories of childhood, etc.; [pers.] I enjoy writing and only started to do so in the last year. I was always used to a very active life but am limited-in a wheelchair and use a walker since surgery two years ago. Writing keeps my mind active and busy. [a.] Alexandria, VA.

HOWARD, SANDRA
[b.] March 7, 1965, Prince George, BC; [p.] Robert and Barbara Purney; [ch.] Cass Wade and Meagan Amanda; [ed.] Hazelton Secondary, Malaspina College, Northwest Community College; [occ.] Bookkeeper; [memb.] Ksan House Society Association, Canadian Cancer Association/Society; [hon.] District Scholarship Award for Excellence, Rebakah Shield Award for service; [oth.writ.] Currently working on fiction novel; [pers.] My poems generally contain the elements of emotions we all feel at one point in time, creating a connection between strangers. [a.] Squamish, BC.

HOWELL, JOSEPH DAVID
[b.] September 27, 1967, Louisville, KY; [p.] Irvin and Shirley Howell; [ed.] Iroquois High, U.L. College, Institute Children's Lit. Conn., Cogitation Exp. USA Tank Colorado Div., self-educated (Fine Arts); [occ.] Auditor; [memb.] NRA, Knights R.T., Louisville, KY Humane Education Society, Big Brothers Elementary School Div.; [hon.] Rembrandt Honors, Honorable Mention Award, BBC-Creative Writing Award, the respect of family and friends; [oth.writ.] Short stories various magazines, art., sci.-fiction and horror novels, deserving love letters to my Gemini Cindy; [pers.] Give and take love and respect, friendship and caring, harmony and peace, live a life through creativity, find potentials, marry a soulmate, be real. [a.] Wilmington, OH.

HOWELL, STEVE
[pen.] Steve Howell; [b.] January 2, 1968, Walnut Creek, CA; [p.] Dorothy and William Howell; [ed.] Las Lomas High School CA., Diablo Valley College, CA., Saint Mary's CA-B.A. Communication; [memb.] American Diabetes Association, American Baseball Coaches Association; [oth.writ.] Several for my own personal saneness; [pers.] I write to express my feelings to help me deal with problems in life. It's my therapy. [a.] Walnut Creek, CA.

HU, JIMMY ZHIYU
[b.] December 23, 1960, Hubie, China; [p.] Shigian Hu and Guiying Wu; [m.] Christina Hu, September 9, 1994; [ed.] Wuhan University (China), Saarland University (Germany), Harvard University (law school), Vanderbilt University (law school); [occ.] Attorney at law (licensed in New York and New Jersey); [memb.] New York and New Jersey Bars and various Bar Associations, Phi Delta Phi, Roster of International Experts of United Nations Conference on Trade and Development (i.e. UNCTAD); [hon.] Awarded German Konrad Adenauer Scholarship by achieveing highest score for law school admission exam in China, first prize for International Year of Youth Essay contest, various sports prizes in college; [oth.writ.] Elvis and The Land, and other publications on Elvis Presley, several legal publications in English, German and Chinese; [pers.] I strive to absorb all goodness of mankind and develop my talents to benefit mankind. Various philosophers in 3 civilizations (Chinese, German and American) have influenced my thinking and devotion to writing. [a.] New York, NY.

HUBBARD, ERICA
[pen.] Erica Hubbard; [b.] May 4, 1979, St. Louis; [p.] Belinda Hubbard and Melvin Riley; [ed.] Sophomore in high school at Hazelwood East, Honor Roll student, current G.P.A. 4.143, honors math student (plan to attend a four year university or college); [memb.] Volleyball and basketball teams, Peer Leaders, Future Business Leaders of America, Mu Alpha Theta Math Club, Youth Excited About Salvation, G.A.N.G. (God's Anointed Generation), B.A.C.E. (back Ground of African Culture and Ethnics), Candystripper at local hospital over the summer; [hon.] Foreign language and P.E. Academic awards, first place intramural basketball, citizenship awards, lettermen awards; [oth.writ.] A collection of poems and writings in a personal portfolio; [pers.] I can do all things through Christ who strengthens me. Most of my poems and writings have been personal experiences or inspirations from God. [a.] St. Louis, MO.

HUESTIS, JOANNA
[b.] September 29, 1959, Pomona, CA; [p.] Bob and Scharlene Berry; [m.] Jim Huestis, September 27, 1986; [ch.] Christian and soon to come Zachary; [ed.] Graduate Hillcrest High School 1977, one semester Shelby State Community College; [occ.] Proud mother and wife; [oth.writ.] I have several poems I've written over the years but have never submitted any until now; [pers.] I believe your life can only be as good as the effort you put forth. If you sit back and wait for happiness, love, success it will not come-go get it yourself. [a.] Memphis, TN.

HUGG, JENNIFER ALLY
[b.] April 21, 1974, Chicago, IL; [p.] Roger and Sandie Hugg; [ed.] Graduate of Countryside High, class of 1992, St. Petersburg Junior College, aspiring to attend NYU or University of Southern California; [occ.] Surgery Tech, Morton Plant Eastlake; [hon.] Dean's List, Presidential Honor's List; [pers.] This poem I dedicate to Holly Johantgen. You are my inspiration. No matter how far apart we are, you are always in my heart. [a.] Dunedin, FL.

HUGHES, BARB
[b.] July 11, 1978, Newfane, NY; [p.] James and Tiia Hughes; [ed.] Newfane Middle School, Newfane High School, junior year; [oth.writ.] Many other poems and some short stories; [pers.] Although I am young, I am still able to compete with a nation and be chosen as a good poet. That, to me is amazing. [a.] Newfane, NY.

HUGHES, SCOTT
[b.] January 4, 1973, Dallas, TX; [p.] Howard and Judy Hughes; [ed.] University of Texas at Austin; [occ.] Student; [pers.] I write in order to better understand those things around me. [a.] Austin, TX.

HUGHES, SHERRI
[b.] May 20, 1981, California; [p.] Pamela Pacetti, (step-father John Pacetti) and (father) William Hughes; [ed.] Middle School Student at Williamsburg in Arlington Virginia; [memb.] Potomac Kiwanis soccer team; [hon.] Academic Achievement Awards; [oth.writ.] I have a personal journal of poetry I have been adding to since the fifth grade; [pers.] My interest in writing and desire to achieve has been influenced by my family, but most importantly, my mother. [a.] Arlington, VA.

HUMPHRIES, AUDRA-MARIE
[b.] May 16, 1979, St. Mary's Hospital, Montreal; [p.] Beverly and Christopher Humphries; [m.] Single; [ed.] Lake of Two Mountains High School; [occ.] Eight grade and babysitting; [pers.] Live life in a box and you shall die young, live life to the fullest and you will never grow old. [a.] Laval West, Quebec Canada.

HUNTER, KARTINA DENISE
[pen.] Trina; [b.] February 12, 1984, Memphis, TN; [p.] Jeraldine Baker-Hunter; [ed.] 1 5th grade student at South Park Elementary; [occ.] Student; [memb.] I was a member of the Girl Scouts of America; [hon.] I have been on the Honor Roll at school for four years, I have also been on the Principal's Honor Roll and received ribbons for perfect attendance; [pers.] I like to write poems. I get my inspiration from life or actual things that happens. I like to make people smile and the poems I write, seems to make them happy and I enjoy doing it. [a.] Memphis, TN.

HURDLE, LINDA
[b.] The early 1950's, Los Angeles, CA; [p.] Sam and Nelma Hurdle; [m.] Never married; [ch.] LaKeesha, Shawna and crystal Page; [ed.] Southwest Junior College, Pruitt Business College, Sacramento City College; [occ.] Daycare teacher; [hon.] Editor's Choice Award from The National Library of Poetry; [pers.] Somewhere there's a place for me in the sky. It hasn't come and I don't know why. I have the gift to pour out more but, if I don't get noticed soon to me life will forever be a total bore. [a.] Sacramento, CA.

HURLBURT, ANN BROWN
[b.] November 12, 1955, Spartanburg, SC; [p.] Howard W. Hurlburt; [ed.] Critical care RN Cardiac; [occ.] Nursing-RN; [memb.] Poets Society; [hon.] "Georgia Flood 1994" being published by the Famous Poets Society, Hollywood, California in "Today's Great Poems"; [oth.writ.] Publishing book that will be released in 1996; [pers.] Helen, Georgia with its beautiful mountains and rivers.

From my home I can see for miles, the beautiful scenery makes me feel very close to God. It inspires me to write. [a.] Helen, GA.

HUTCHESON, ROGER A.
[b.] June 10, 1955, Tulsa, OK; [p.] J.L. and Crystal Douglas Hutcheson; [m.] Sue Ann Beehler Hutcheson, December 28, 1974; [ch.] Robert Allan and Richard Allan Hutcheson; [ed.] High school, college; [occ.] Associate Pastor, Minister of Music; [memb.] National Piano Guild, Young Tulsans (International Young Musicians), (TAP) Tulsa Auxiliary Police, O.R.U. Male Ensemble; [hon.] Capitol State Page, Atlanta, Georgia, District and State Trumpet Soloist, Georgia, OK, President's Scholarship Liberty University , Trumpet with Bill Gaither trio; [oth.writ.] Two songs, one published in sheet music form, several arrangements for various choirs, etc.; [pers.] Written in dedication to my wonderful christian grandfather, Earl Douglas. His life was such an example and inspiration that when he died, we truly all knew he was "Homeward Bound". [a.] Chickamauga, GA.

HUTCHINSON, LAWRENCE
[b.] December 8, 1924, Euphrasia Twsp. Grey County, Ontario Canada; [p.] Eldridge and Fanny Hutchinson; [m.] Alma Hutchinson, May 1, 1965, Jean August 14, 1943-deceased; [ch.] Larry, Keith, Danny, Reid, Mark and Cindy; [ed.] Waterford High; [occ.] Retired heating and air conditioner contractor; [oth.writ.] Several poems mostly political, published in local papers, many, many roast poems for parties, weddings. etc., (not recorded for publication); [pers.] I love to find people's peculiarities and exaggerate them (as a cartoonist does) and create a roast or political poem. [a.] Waterford Ontario, Canada.

HUTCHISON, JAMES W.
[b.] October 22, 1918, Milwaukee, WI; [p.] Samuel and Laura Farr Hutchison; [m.] Single; [ed.] Riverside High (Milwaukee) Wisconsin, Conservatory Music, Northwestern University (B.M.and M.M.); [occ.] Prof. Emeritus, St. Lawrence University , Cantor, NY; [memb.] Phi Mu Alpha, American Musilogical Society; [hon.] Fulbright Scholar Austria, 62-63; [oth.writ.] Essays, short stories, piano music, songs; [pers.] The creative process of any level is a God given privilege (trust) and should never be debased.

HYDRICK, ASHLEY
[b.] May 12,1977, California; [p.] Carter and Kris; [ed.] I am currently finishing my senior year at Klein Oak High School in Spring, Texas; [occ.] Since I'm not yet graduated, I work at a movie theater; [hon.] I have help positions in church as a youth leader for my church, the Church of Jesus Christ of Latter Day Saints; [oth.writ.] I have never had anything published, although I would some day like to publish a children's story and possibly more poetry; [pers.] I firmly believe that by putting God first, all things will fall into their proper places. I also believe you can't improve, unless you can admit you need improvement. [a.] Spring, TX.

IAPICCO, VINCENZO
[pen.] "Picco"; [b.] August 28, 1967, Nocera Inferidre, Salerno, Italia; [p.] Lucia and the late Francesco Iapicco; [m.] Sandra Iapicco, September 18, 1993; [ch.] None yet, one due May 16, 1995; [ed.] O.S.S.G.D. (grade 12 diploma); [occ.] Custodian and professional painter (homes); [oth.writ.] "Carousel of Time", "River of Life", Life Can Be So Wonderful", "My Moon", etc.; [pers.] I am inspired by my natural surroundings and it was through the death of my father that I developed my early independence to deliver my thoughts on paper. I thank everyone I love. [a.] Niagara Falls, Ontario Canada.

IMERI, PAL
[pen.] P.I.; [b.] June 20, 1960, Albania; [p.] Mhill and Hana Imeri; [m.] Rusha Imeri, February 5, 1989; [ch.[Hana and Mhill Michael; [ed.] High school education; [occ.] Handyman; [oth.writ.] Albanian children poetry.

INFANTE, DAISY I.
[b.] August 3, 1946, Philippines; [p.] Jesus and Josefina Infante; [m.] Rosben R. Ogbac, June 7, 1987; [ch.] Desiree, Dante and Darrell; [ed.] M.A. in Human Communications, Fairfield University, Connecticut, B.S. Psychology, University of Santo Tomas, Magna Cum Laude, AB in English, University of Santo Matos, AA Notre Dame of Marbel College, highest honors; [occ.] Real Estate Broker, insurance sales, home based business networker; [memb.] National Association of Female Executives, American Society of Professional and Executive Women, Chicago Philippines Professional Club, Chicago Philippines Chamber of Commerce, Lions International, Christian Writers Guild, Bayanihan International Ladies Association; [hon.] BS Psychology, Magna Cum Laude, AA-Highest Honors, listed in Who's Who of American Women, Who's Who of Emerging Leaders in America, Who's Who in Professional and Executive Women, Two Thousand Notable American Women; [oth.writ.] Poems of my youth, my first twenty songs, feature writer and columnist for Pinoy News magazine, Philippine News and Via Times, published poems for American Poetry anthology and Best New Poets of 1989; [pers.] I believe in true love, in the fullness of life, in success and the fulfillment of one's dreams, but most of all I truly believe that unless and until we discover the source of such love, life, success and fulfillment and give God all the glory, then everything becomes meaningless. [a.] Orlando, FL.

INMON, JIMMIE NELL
[pen.] Lady "J"; [b.] April 7, 1948, Vardaman, MS; [p.] J.E. and Mary Scarbrough; [m.] Jimmy Ray Inmon, November 26, 1968; [ed.] B.A.E. University of MS, M.A.E. Mississippi State University, post graduate studies; [occ.] English department chair, Calhoun City High School, Rancher, coowner The Double J Ranch; [memb.] AQHA, Apha MAE, Midway Baptist Church, Eastern Star, past Worthy Matron, B and W Hunting Club-sec./treas., sponsor The Wildcat Prowler, NEA, active breeder of racing quarter horses since 1987; [hon.] Star Teacher, 1990 from the MS State Economic Council, Who's Who Among American Teachers-1993; [pers.] Trying to find some positive note in each of my students has always been the key to my teaching success. God is my constant companion. Robert Frost is my favorite poet. [a.] Vardaman, MS.

INSKEEP, ROBERT
[b.] October 27, 1921, Cleveland, OH; [p.] Arthur and Fern Inskeep; [m.] Martha Inskeep, February 1, 1947; [ch.] Kathy, Peggy and Fred; [ed.] Sidney Ohio High School, Ohio State University; [occ.] Retired; [memb.] Honorable Order of Kentucky Colonels, American Legion, Veterans of Foreign Wars, Buckeye Sheriffs Association; [oth.writ.] Autobiography "Ordinary Me" plus various poems not published; [pers.] My thoughts most often reflect my love of nature. [a.] Bellefontaine, OH.

IPPOLITO, MICHAEL JUSTIN
[b.] August 13,1942, Brooklyn, NY; [m.] Emelia Ippolito, May 30, 1987; [ch.] Michael Joseph and John Thomas; [ed.] B.S., M.A., John Jay College; [occ.] Fraud Investigator; [memb.] American Society for Industrial Security, Association of Certified Fraud Examiners, High Technology Crime Investigation Association; [pers.] Often, truth lies in feelings, not in beliefs. Thus, discover thyself. [a.] Ossining, NY.

IRICK JR., JAMES SHELLEY
[pen.] Jim Irick; [b.] July 20, 1936, Sumter, SC; [p.] Ola and Shelley Irick Sr.; [m.] Pearl Irick, April 9, 1960; [ch.] Ginger Irick Dewitt and Nora Irick Ogletree with two grands from each; [ed.] 7th grade, Sumter, South Carolina; [occ.] Retired from accident had on October 8, 1979, truck driver; [memb.] Ex-member of Sumter National Guards of 118 Infantry at rating of Buck Sergeant, 1951-1955, from Charleston, South Carolina; [oth.writ.] I thank my grandparents Mary and Ulysses Irick for my bringing up, to always respect other people's feelings, no matter who they were; [pers.] If one of my poems bring a smile to someone or even a tear then I know I have touched someone and that makes me happy. [a.] N. Charleston, SC.

ISSITT, CINDY
[pen.] Lou Miller; [b.] December 22, 1959, Loveland, CO; [p.] Frank and Thelma Mills; [m.] Stan Issitt, November 12,1982; [ch.] 1 girl, 4 boys (2 of which are twins); [ed.] Loveland High School, Loveland, CO., Abilene High School, Abilene, KS.; [occ.] Garfield Upper Elementary lunchroom supervisor, Abilene, Kansas; [memb.] 1st Methodist Church, Girl Scouts, United Way, American Heart Association; [hon.] (Hobbies) Outdoor activities, reading, writing, music, activities with my family, family is important; [oth.writ.] Many poems and songs (unpublished children's short story, series) unpublished-novelette-"Hidden Playgrounds; [pers.] My writing is a reflection of daily life and feelings. I try to capture deep feelings and express them so others can adapt and relate to my writings. [a.] Abilene, KS.

IVESTER, ELIZABETH JADE
[b.] November 20, 1984, San Francisco, CA; [p.] Jo and Jon Ivester; [ed.] 5th grade, Eanes Elementary; [occ.] Student; [pers.] I love writing and I'm good at it, so I write. [a.] Austin, TX.

IZAGUIRRE, CHARTA'E
[b.] August 20, 1973, Chicago, IL; [p.] Flora Brown and Charles Dixsion; m.] Joseph Izaguirre, October 15, 1994; [oth.writ.] "Who Are We", "Feelings"; [pers.] Dedicated, "Feelings' to my husband Joseph Izaguirre.

JACKSON, JIM
[b.] Wilmington, DE; [p.] Alice Hall; [ed.] University of MD-College Park; [occ.] U.S.C.G. Licensed Ships Master; [memb.] Balto Harbor Capt's Assoc.; [hon.] Several MD-DE-DC Press Association Awards; [oth. writ.] Several articles and poems published in the local press as well as a portfolio of songs; [pers.] My goal is simply to relate to the reader and try to get an emotional response. [a.] Baltimore, MD.

JACKSON, KATIE
[b.] November 8, 1960, Houston, TX; [p.] Don and Alice Jacobs; [m.] Mike Jackson; [ch.] Joshua, Kasey and Paige Gerjevic; [occ.] Housewife; [oth.writ.] Many, none submitted or published; [pers.] A special thank you to all who have influenced my writings. You're in my heart. [a.] Lincoln, NE.

JACKSON, MASIE EDITH CAVELL
[pen.] Masie Edith Cavell Jackson, Cavell Jackson; [b.] November 30, 1917, Glace Bay, N.S. Canada; [p.] Ben and Frances Barrett (deceased); [m.] Alexander R. Jackson (deceased), November 6,

1937; [ch.] Frances K. Parsons and son-in-law Gordon; [ed.] Grade 8, as I had three sisters, Shirley Christoff, Gussie Whiting, Edna Brown (deceased) and one brother, Max Barrett; [occ.] Retired, writings, paintings; [memb.] St. Mary's Anglican Church, Glace Bay, N.S. Canada, regular contributor to Amputees and War Amps of Canada; [ed.] Editors Choice Award from National Library of Poetry 1994, my favorite poet, Robert Louis Stevenson; [oth.writ.] I have written over forty poems for local newspapers, also memorials, all were published, I am still writing; [pers.] Poetry is one way I can express my inner feelings to bring joy to others who read it, as reading it is like an education in itself. [a.] Nova Scotia, Canada.

JACKSON, NANCY MARGARET CURL
[b.] January 24, 1948, Ft. Knox, KY; [p.] Richland H. and Marilyn Mylan Curl; [m.] Larry Ralph Jackson, January 15, 1977; [ch.] Marilyn, Richard, Shannon, Angela and Chris; [ed.] Norte Vista Riverside California Management and Direct Sales, Pasadena, CA., Health and Vitamin Therapy, Panama City, FL.; [occ.] Owner and manager day care center; [memb.] Disabled American Veterans, Commanders Club, Bronze Leader; [oth.writ.] Song-Traces of Tears, Nashville Co-Writers, Nashville Tennessee, lots of poems on Angels, not published; [pers.] Most of my poetry reflects life, people and the Lord. "I try to write on the feelings of the heart of others and myself". I was greatly influenced by my parents Richard and Marilyn Curl of Riverside, CA. [a.] Suisun City, CA.

JACKSON, SHERRY
[b.] May 18, 1964, Durham, NC; [p.] Curtis and Ella T. Jackson; [ed.] BA-University of Maryland, Paralegal certificate, University of Maryland University College; [memb.] national Capital Area Paralegal Association, Baltimore Association of Legal Assistants, National Federation of Paralegal Associations; [pers.] I only write what I feel. I wish to contribute in the tradition of my dear departed brother, Jeremiah Jackson who wrote poetry and encouraged me to write. [a.] Gaithersburg, MD.

JACKSON, WAYNE F.
[b.] May 3, 1973, New York, NY; [p.] Karen and Francis Jackson; [ed.] St. Rita Parochial School Long Island City, NY, Msgr. McClancy High School, Elmhurst, New York, presently attending St. John's University (St. Vincents College), Jamaica, NY; [hon.] St. Rita Midget Hockey 1981, Allstar Long Island City YMCA 1983, Lou Correas New York Shotokan karate International championship February 23, 1986, Msgr. McClany HS Tip-off tournament 2nd place 1990; [pers.] With thanks and appreciation for the teachings and guidance of my maternal grandmother Beulah R. Smith, who raised me. I strive to go forward in life taking "one step at a time", "one day at a time" and with "Blessed Assurance". [a.] Rego Park, NY.

JAKUBOWICZ, KATHLEEN
[pen.] Katy James; [a.] April 30, 1958, Ireland; [p.] Robert and Mary Duffy; [m.] Michael, November 15, 1980; [ch.] Lauren Mary, Devin Thomas; [ed.] Theatre Arts degree; [occ.] Mother and wife, starving singer and songwriter; [oth. writ.] Over 50 songs written in collaboration with my husband - recorded in our studio, some performed live by us in various clubs in New York City. Presently at work on first novel; [pers.] The words in my heart forever bursting into song, are birds of bliss meant to soar, not remain unheard. [a.] Cherry Hill, NJ.

JAMES, JENNIFER
[pen.] Jenny or Jen Marie; [b.] January 18, 1981, Oklahoma City, OK; [p.] Susan and (step-father) Ronnie Dinse (father) Kitok James, I live with Susan and Ronnie, my father lives in Del City, OK; [ed.] I'm going to Verden K-8th grade from there I'm going to Verden High School when I'm in the 9th grade; [occ.] I am an 8th grade student at Verden K-8th; [memb.] I'm a member and a fan of the Tear Street Book Club; [hon.] I've been awarded student of the month, I have been awarded with softball trophies, 3 first place, 1 second place and 1 participation, I've been honored with reading and language arts medals, also at an Engineer Fair for 7th grade, participating in "TIVY" a math game, I got 1st place there; [oth.writ.] The only other writings I've ever done have been in the classrooms (meaning 7th and 8th); [pers.] What comes from my writings is what comes from inside me. I've been influenced by many of my peers and their writings. Also, I've been influenced by many other writings from different authors. My poem "Love" is based on how I feel about someone I care about deeply. Always love with all your heart each day because you never know if you'll be able to the following day or the future. [a.] Verden, OK.

JANSSON, MARY L.
[b.] May 29, 1953, Nevada City, CA; [ed.] Rio Lindo Academy; [occ.] Nursing Assistant, Ketchikan General Hospital; [oth.writ.] Poem published in A Question of Balance; [pers.] Strive to be one with nature. [a.] Ketchikan, AK.

JANY, PATRICIA R.
[b.] October 16, 1966, Red Bud, IL; [p.] James and Kay Surman; [m.] Paul E. Jany, September 11, 1992; [ch.] Ashley Nicole and Dustin James; [ed.] Chester High School; [occ.] Molder (factory technician); [pers.] Just a poor farm girl writing about life as I see it. [a.] Chester, IL.

JARBOUH, MADONA
[pen.] Madona Jarbouh; [p.] George and Samia Jarbouh; [ed.] Immaculate High School, grade 8; [hon.] Champ swimmer, publication of story in the Ottawa Citizen paper, award for best French reader, writer and speaker; [pers.] My greatest influences are my parents, they helped me believe in all I do. A great thanks to my Aunt Terry, who I will always love and taught me how to write my feelings. [a.] Vanier, CA.

JAROS, COLLEEN ANN
[b.] June 3, 1975; [oth.writ.] Unpublished poems; [pers.] I dedicate this and all my other poems to my dearest friend David Sardina whom I love very much, without him I couldn't have written any of them. David, I love you always, your friend Colleen. I want to thank Stephanie Buchinski for encouraging me to send my poem which allowed me to get it published. Thank you. [a.] Holbrook, NY.

JEANTY, SAFIYAH YAMINAH
[pen.] Sofii; [b.] November 4, 1981, Brooklyn, NY; [p.] Yvrose Jeanty and Martin Raphael; [ed.] Yucca Elementary School and Juniper Intermediate School; [occ.] Doing homework and babysitting my little sister; [hon.] Kiwanis Club member for being student of the month in 1991 and 1992; [pers.] I like to write poetry because it helps me breakdown things that happen in many people's everyday life, and if I watch a movie or listen to a song, I'll make a poem about what the song/movie means to me. [a.] Palmdale, CA.

JEMMOTT, SEWELL T.
[pen.] Tommy Jemmott; [b.] December 1, 1921, Georgetown, Guyana; [p.] William A. and Lilian O (deceased); [m.] Nellie (deceased), May 24,1952; [ch.] Rowland Alfred, Jeffrey Scott and David Grant; [ed.] Progressive High School, Georgetown, Electronic Technology, Royal Technical College, Glasgow, Radar Mechanic, Royal Air Force; [occ.] Retired, New York City Housing Authority; [pers.] I have enjoyed reading and writing poetry from my youth and am blessed to be able to remember many that I committed to memory over the years. I still memorize any interesting ones that I encounter today. [a.] Lauderdale Lakes, FL.

JENKINS, KIMBERLY M.
[b.] November 10, 1973, Atlanta, GA; [p.] George and Brenda Jenkins; [pers.] What I wish to do with my writing is make others think about the world in which they live. [a.] Stockbridge, GA.

JOHNS, ALAN D.
[pen.] Jaques; [b.] March 24, 1932, Denver, CO; [p.] Alice Hazel Brown and Andrew Albert Johns; [m.] Beth Newcom Johns, February 14, 1982; [ch.] Eleven (6 his and 5 hers) 9 sons, 2 daughters; [ed.] Bachelor of Science U.S. NPGS, Monterey, California, Naval Officer (pilot) 20 years, Computer Programmer and Software Quality Analyst; [occ.] Retired, (volunteer on 11 boards) (elected Director and Presiding Board member on some); [memb.] Kiwanis, Weed Chamber of Commerce, County Delegate to Shasta Cascade Tourism Region; [hon.] Citizen of the year, Weed/Chamber of Commerce 1984, California; [oth.writ.] Successful Grant for Weed, Historic Lumber Town Museum, compulsive note taker, very useful habit in recalling details and documenting software flow charts; [pers.] The thyme and meter of inspired verse moves me to seek such a format for concise and lyric profundity when such needs regain my sense "There is something to say"! I am a faithful student of A Course in Miracles. [a.] Weed, CA.

JOHNSEN, CONSTANCE
[b.] October 5, 1963, Barrington, IL; [p.] Dale and Phyllis Miller; [m.] Michael Johnsen, May 12, 1984; [ch.] Branden Michael and Kyle Joseph; [occ.] Housewife, mom; [pers.] This poem is dedicated to my husband, Michael, who began his fight against cancer in November of 1992. At age 32, and whose fight began again in 1994. With love to you Michael, keep fighting. [a.] McHenry, IL.

JOHNSON, ADAM
[pen.] AJ; [b.] August 30, 1964, Fairfax, VA; [p.] Jim and Marie Reynolds; [ch.] Jason; [ed.] BS; [occ.] US Navy, Director Urology School; [oth.writ.] Poems "My Friends", "Brothers", "Never Give Up"; [pers.] The poem "If I Leave This Life" was during a trying time and listening to Jimmy Baffett songs brought me joy and inspiration. [a.] Porstmouth, VA.

JOHNSON, APRIL
[pen.] Hope Mornay; [b.] July 26, 1974, Amherst, OH; [p.] Larry and Oleta Johnson; [ed.] Marion L. Steele High, Lorain County Community College; [occ.] College student; [hon.] Dean's List, Amherst Democratic Women's Club Award; [pers.] Without dreams there isn't hope. Without hope there isn't life. Situations in life has greatly influenced my poetry. [a.] Amherst, OH.

JOHNSON, ARNOLD E.
[b.] May 29, 1973, Meadville, PA; [p.] Arnold E. and Linda L. Johnson III; [m.] Stacy N. Corbean Johnson, November 12, 1993; [ed.] Martial Arts instruction from age 3, Meadville Area Senior High, pursuing a career in respiratory therapy; [occ.] Short order cook, martial arts instructor, student; [memb.] American Shotokan Karate Club of Meadville, PA; [hon.] District, Regional and State Awards for PMEZ orchestral performance/ competition, various awards in martial arts competitions, awarded all state honors in Pennsylvania, forensics competition; [oth.writ.] A small

collection of poems, songs and other writings; [pers.] The heartfelt agony of love lost is sweeter than the silent pain of love never found. [a.] Meadville, PA.

JOHNSON, BONNIE JO
[b.] January 30, 1967, St. Paul, MN; [p.] Marvin and Claris Ohmann; [m.] Warren Johnson, October 21, 1989; [ch.] Trevor Scott Johnson. [a.] Burnsville, MN.

JOHNSON, JACOB G.
[b.] Westallis, WI; [p.] Val and Rosanne Johnson; [ed.] Grantsburg High School, Grantsburg; [occ.] U.S. Navy active duty; [pers.] To the sailor that never came home, and to the girl he left behind, love alone from death can save, love is death and is so brave, love can fill the deepest grave, love lives on beneath the wave. [a.] Lemoore (Naval Air Station), CA.

JOHNSON, JILL MARYE
[b.]June 2, 1978, Richmond, VA; [p.] Brenda and James Johnson Jr.; [ed.] Junior in high school, Henrico High School in Richmond, Virginia; [memb.] East Highland Park Baptist Church, National Honor Society, Spanish Club, Peer Helpers Group; [hon.] Ranked No. 1 in my class of 280, listed in Who's Who Among American High School Students; [pers.] I have been writing short stories and poems since I was a little girl. I enjoy writing and plan to continue. [a.] Richmond, VA.

JOHNSON, JOE C.
[b.] November 17, 1939, Glasgow, MT; [ed.] Helena Senior High; [occ.] Sculptor, furniture maker, inventor; [pers.] Life ought always be a continuing adventure, not cloaked in comfortable conformity's indenture. Hither to has the Lord brought me, hither to has the Lord preserved me. [a.] Mountain Park, NM.

JOHNSON, KRISTIN
[pen.] Justine Campion; [b.] April 29, 1971, Chicago; [p.] Dale and Laurel Johnson; [ed.] Currently attending Western Illinois University as a music therapy major and theatre minor; [occ.] Full time student; [oth.writ.] "Freedom", "Golden Day Dream"; [pers.] In everything I do, whether it is music, theatre or writing, my goal is to touch other people's lives in a positive way. Thank you, mom and dad for believing in me. [a.] McHenry, IL.

JONES, ANTONIO
[b.] March 1, 1978, Saluda; [p.] Juanita Jones; [occ.] High school student; [oth.writ.] Unpublished poems, "Didn't Even Speak", "Christmas Love", "Loving Memory", "Love", "The Love I Feel", "When Doves Cry", " Where Have You Been". [a.] Salunda, SC.

JONES, BETH
[pen.] Elisabeth Anne Jones; [b.] May 11, 1979, Phoenix, AZ; [p.] Bob and Suzie Jones; [ed.] Desert Valley Elementary, Ironwood High School; [occ.] Student; [memb.] National Junior Honor Society, Civil Air Patrol, National Association of Miniature Enthusiasts; [hon.] Principal's List, Honor Roll, Mitchell Award in Civil Air Patrol; [oth.writ.] Publication in this poetry book; [pers.] Thank you to mom for the encouragement and inspiration, DV Staff, IMS friends and staff for your support and friendship. [a.] Glendale, AZ.

JONES, CHRISTINA A.
[pen.] Christina A., C'de Baca Jones; [b.] July 20, 1959, Fort Sill, OK; [p.] Filadelfo and Ilse C'de Baca Jr.; [m.] Nelson I. Jones, April 22, 1994; [ch.] Michael David and Benjamin Ryan; [ed.] Lawton Senior High School; [occ.] Housewife and mother; [memb.] American Heart Association, PTA; [hon.] High school diploma, CPR training, Winnebago Automation for Library Facility; [oth.writ.] Several poems written solely for family members, friends on special occasions, not for publication; [pers.] My writings are created from the heart to express my feelings. I started writing poetry in greeting cards, which I created, since I was seven years old. [a.] Lawton, OK.

JONES, MELVIN L.
[b.] September 27, 1952, Milwaukee; [p.] Edward and Leola Jones; [ed.] Rufus King High, Milwaukee Area Technical College; [occ.] Professional driver; [oth.writ.] Several poems published in various books and magazines; [pers.] I will only write a poem when I can feel it deep inside of me. [a.] Milwaukee, WI.

JONES, MONICA
[b.] January 31, 1980, Nashville, TN; [.] Gordon and Faye Jones; [ed.] Student; [occ.] Student. [a.] Chapmansboro, TN.

JONES, VALERIE N.
[b.] March 12, 1981, Santa Fe, NM; [p.] Ella and Richard Jones; [ed.] Student at St. Michaels High School, 8th grade; [occ.] Student; [hon.] Won first place in the first grade for short story on animals, awarded $ 25.00. printed in local newspaper; [oth.writ.] This will be the first published poem, but I am constantly writing poems and songs; [pers.] I write about inside and mental feelings that are in kids my age. I also write about my feelings at the time of the writing. My generation is real messed up. [a.] Santa Fe, NM.

JULES, SHERRYANN LYDIA
[pen.] Sherryann Jules; [b.] February 9, 1982, Trinidad; [p.] George Jules and Monica Peters Jules; [ed.] P.S> 91, Bronx, NY, Northwood Elementary School, Baltimore, I am a 7th grade student at Chinquapin Middle School, Baltimore; [occ.] Middle school student, 7th grade; [memb.] I am a Fox 45 Clubhouse member, a member of the Towson Seventh Day Adventist Church; [hon.] I am a recipient of the 93/94 Baltimore City Schools' "Commonwealth Gold Card", an award of participation in 1994 National Youth Sports program at Morgan State University; [pers.] I hope that I'll be successful in helping others, and to teach good things to others and achieve myself, so they can recognize. [a.] Baltimore, MD.

JUMEL, D.
[pen.] Dickie; [b.] December 8, 1921, Kearney, NE; [p.] Altine and Albert Dixon; [m.] Bidwell Jumel (deceased 1973), February 24, 1946; [ch.] Mignon, Brent, Stephen and Jeffrey; [ed.] Salem High School, San Diego State College, Life Science Institute (minister); [occ.] Nutritionist, counselor; [memb.] Theological Science Society, Religious Science Church of San Juan, Capistrano, The Elisabeth Kubbe-Ross Center; [hon.] Formed NHF (National Health Federation), Sacramento, president 3 years, helped form preschool "Tiny Tots", Sacramento California, helped form Park District, Sacramento County; [oth.writ.] "The Child Mind" (under Reverend Jumel), Simon and Shuster; [pers.] I believe life is a great adventure and we as players come to give love, peace, joy and wisdom to our fellow players each day. Laughter and humor shared. [a.] San Juan Capistrano, CA.

JURAK, EILEEN L.
[pen.] Eileen L. Jurak; [b.] October 12, Grand Haven, MI; [p.] Joseph Martin and Mary Martha Jurak; [m.] Single; [ed.] 1974 B.S.Ed. and M.S. Ed. 1981, University of Southern California, Compton High School; [occ.] Administrative Assistant, University of Southern California; [memb.] Life membership USC, General Alumni Association; [oth.writ.] Local newspapers, holiday greetings and editorial; [pers.] I try to write from personal experience and include real life situations. I enjoy Elizabeth Barrett Browning, Robert Browing, Robert Frost and William Shakespeare. [a.] Garden Grove, CA.

KABORE, PATRICIA A.
[b.] February 11, 1940, Ann Arbor, MI; [p.] Helen Louise Cook and Gwnis Stafford; [ch.] Rema Felicia Kabore; [ed.] Art, education, none in writing; [occ.] Graphic artist, printmaker; [memb.] Founder, Kindred Souls, Ethnic Women Fine Artist Organization, Board of Directors, Arts Extended Gallery; [hon.] Honorable Mention the African American Crafts National, Kentucky Arts Center, Louisville, Kentucky; [oth.writ.] Published, (Theadum) presents poetry issue, Detroit, Michigan; [pers.] I have always written, even as a child I kept a journal. Writing for me is a part of my inner voice, as is my creation of visual arts. I want to share the experiences and feelings of women, especially black women. [a.] Detroit, MI.

KAKUK, MARY ELIZABETH
[pen.] Mary Beth; [b.] December 31, 1967, Indianapolis, IN; [p.] James and Violet Winkel; [m.] Sgt. Daniel Kakuk, July 19, 1986; [ch.] Joshua Daniel Kakuk; [ed.] 1 year of college, college of cosmetology; [occ.] Waitress; [memb.] P.T.A.; [hon.] Military Spouce Awards, award of appreciation for Spouce support during operation Desert Storm, an award for serving Generals, Captains, Lieutenants and other high ranking officers in the country Belgium; [oth.writ.] I have won items from local radio stations, by my writing of chorus lines, I have several other poems, I have written, but I have never published; [pers.] I feel that we should look at out mistakes as learning experiences and we will be stronger and wiser for them. I enjoy writings of any poet who speaks of real life experiences. [a.] White Pine, MI.

KALLY-WILLIAMS, JESSE
[b.] Accra, Ghana; [p.] Lawrence and Tawiah Kally; [m.] Single; [ed.] Presently pursuing my Ph.D. (doctoral) in Theology (Systematic Theology) in the University of Basel, Switzerland; [occ.] Student; [memb.] Ruschlikon Amnesty International, the Protestant Church and Gellerfskirche in Basel; [oth.writ.] Many unpublished writings including, poems, essays on democracy, justice, economics, world peace, religious symbols; [pers.] "The unexamined life is not worth living". This statement, attributed to Socrates, linked to the Delphic words "know thyself are reflected in my writings". I have been greatly influenced by the Hebrew Prophets, Luther-King and Lincoln. [a.] Basel, Switzerland.

KARNS, NANCY
[b.] May 6, 1935, Minneapolis, MN; [p.] Leilah and Harry Anderson; [m.] Patrick Karns, May 25, 1991 (second); [ch.] James Lee, Michael Bruce and Kenneth Charles; [ed.] Washburn High School, University of Minnesota, New Mexico State University, (graduate with B.S. in Social work) 1976; [occ.] Retired Legal Secretary (trying cottage industry); [memb.] Canada Creek Ranch Association, Atlanta MI., Int'l Children's Association, Audubon, Association for Research and Enlightenment (A.R.E.), Canada Creek Singers, ALM (Adoption Identify Movement), Cancer Society; [hon.] Dean's List, NMSU, piano award of Minnesota, Piano Teacher's Association when I was 12 years old (1947); [oth.writ.] Just a few letters to the editor, Christmas poems to friends and journal writing always; [pers.] What I want most in all this

world is PEACE ON EARTH FOR ALL OF MANKIND. What I want most for myself is a humorous attitude towards life. [a.] Atlanta, MI.

KARPINSKA, MONIKA
[b.] August 21, 1980, Warsaw, Poland; [p.] Andrzej and Grazyna Karpinski; [ed.] High school student in grade 9; [occ.] Student; [memb.] SPCA; [hon.] 1st place in grade 8 Science Fair; [oth.writ.] Several poems and short stories written mainly for family and school; [pers.] Live with nature, not against it. [a.] N. Vancouver, BC.

KARR, JENNIFER
[b.] December 18, 1978, Lincoln, NE; [p.] Vickie S. Klundt and Steven D. Karr; [ed.] Northeast High School, present grade 10th; [oth.writ.] I have written many poems and stories, but never had them published. [a.] Lincoln, NE.

KAUFFMAN, SHANNON
[pen.] Shannon; [b.] December 26, 1979, Stuart, FL; [p.] Doreen and Blake Kauffman; [ed.] I'm currently at East Hampton High School in the tenth grade; [oth.writ.] I write a whole bunch of poems, for instance one about love and feelings; [pers.] I really enjoy writing poems. I usually write when something happens in my life. I would like to dedicate it to my mom and my boyfriend Frank. [a.] East Hampton, CT.

KAUFMAN, SHERWIN
[pers.] My background is somewhat unique. I am a retired physician with a new career as a songwriter and loving it! In addition to composing music and lyrics, I also enjoy writing poetry and short stories. The poem in this volume, "My Child Drew A Picture" was inspired by my own children and more recently, grandchildren. [a.] New York, NY.

KEAS, MICHAEL S.
[b.] March 27, 1956, Williamsport, PA; [p.] Harry Miller and Loretta Shannon; [m.] Dolly Marie Finkle, May 8, 1993; [ed.] Grand Prairie High-Grand Prairie, TX; [occ.] Business owner/photographer; [memb.] National Rabbit Breeders Associations, National Association of Rocketry; [hon.] Numerous photographic awards; [oth.writ.] A few poems published in local newspapers; [pers.] Poetry is literature's main spring, an endless wealth of eternal beauty! [a.] Williamsport, PA.

KEATING, MARY T.
[b.] May 13, Oak Park, IL; [ed.] Siena High, Northeastern Illinois University, B.A., M.A.; [occ.] Asst. Principal Pulaski Community Academy, Chicago; [memb.] St. William Parish Concert Choir, Phi Delta Kappa, Alpha Delta Kappa, A.S.C.D., American Association University Women; [pers.] Poetry permits me to share my thoughts in a special way. It helps tear down the walls which divide us and helps us better understand one another. [a.] Chicago, IL.

KEDDIE, AMY SUE
[pen.] Susan Keddie; [b.] January 1, 1976, McKeesport; [p.] Larry and Pam Harden, Mark and Heidi Keddie; [ed.] Penn-Trafford High School graduate of 1994; [memb.] Champion Dance Studio, Girl Scouts, Acolyte Club at church, member of Circleville United Methodist Church, Young Sportsmen's Association; [hon.] Academic Fitness Award, Presidential Fitness Award, track relay medal and lettered in track and band in high school, I've also had poems published in my high school's literary magazine, Traces, sponsored by the English department at Penn-Trafford High School. [a.] Claridge, PA.

KEELS, KRISTEN ELIZABETH
[pen.] Cat, Kris; [b.] August 1, 1982, Gwinnet Community Hospital; [p.] Robert Edward Keels and Ann Elizabeth Russo; [ed.] Allgood Elementary; [occ.] 7th grade student; [memb.] Fox 36 Kids Club; [hon.] Chi Alpha, Honor Student, 1st place in 1 mile run (age group); [oth.writ.] Poems, Love, Fast, Slow, Him and Cats, short stories, Team and Me, books, Caller From Underneath, I'm working on "The Trocilbe"; [pers.] To get along in life be honest, learn to compromise, learn to be kind to mankind, and most of all get a good education. [a.] Stone Mountain, GA.

KEIM, LEE A.
[b.] September 29, 1969, Kansas City, MO; [p.] Judy Smith and Mike Schafer; [ch.] Nikki Lee Keim; [oth.writ.] Wind In The Night Sky, and Quest of A Dream; [pers.] I hope that my poems touch a lot of people. Please watch for future writings. I have many more waiting to be published. [a.] Wildwood, FL.

KELCH-GEAR, SUZANNE
[b.] February 3, 1964, Corpus Christi, TX; [p.] Penny LaForce and James L. Gear; [m.] Franklin L. Kelch, May 6, 1991; [ch.] Jacqueline Lee, Jessica Lynne and Jamie Lynlee; [oth.writ.] "Twenty One Gun Salute", Pacific Rims, Publication Inc., Seattle, Washington, 1992, Quest For A Dream.

KELLER, BILL
[pers.] Bill Keller, born in New York City in 1938 has spent most of his adult life in Northern Virginia where he worked in advertising. In 1992, after semi-retirement, he turned to his hobby of writing in a serious way. He recently had a screenplay considered by Warner Bros, and is currently editing his second novel for publication. He writes under the pen name of Scott Williams.

KELLY, JESS
[b.] October 2, 1942, Joshua, TX; [p.] Gladys Kelly; [ed.] I never finished high school; [pers.] I'm just a busted up ex-bull twisting drunk who likes words and phrases. [a.] Stamford, TX.

KENDRICK, CANDI
[b.] October 25, 1978, Meridian, MS; [p.] Bobby and Barbara Kendrick; [ed.] Newton County High School; [memb.] Chorus class and Beta Club at Newton County High School; [hon.] I am on the Honor Roll, I was a cheerleader, I'm a Beta member and a chorus singer; [oth.writ.] I have written close to 100 poems, my friends always like them but I never knew they ware good enough to be published, thank you; [pers.] I write poems when I have feelings inside that I sometimes can't talk about but I can write them down. [a.] Decatur, MS.

KENNEDY, ALISON
[b.] June 2, 1981, Buffalo; [p.] Bob and Nancy Kennedy; [ed.] Currently in junior high school, 8th; [occ.] Student; [hon.] Honor student for the past 3 years; [oth.writ.] First poem recognized to be good from another person, I have many more poems that I have written and that I am working on; [pers.] In my poems, I try to capture the feel for nature. [a.] Kingston, NY.

KENNEDY, LaNETTA
[b.] July 27, 1978, Chicago, IL; [p.] Mary and Henry Kennedy; [ed.] LaSalle High School; [occ.] Student; [hon.] Honor award, report card sophomore year; [oth.writ.] Wedding poems, short stories, freewrite; [pers.] The words I live by are "never say never, always say I can, I can". [a.] South Bend, IN.

KENYON, JOY
[b.] July 20, 1929, Victoria, BC; [p.] George and Jessie Cruickshank; [m.] Deceased, February 15, 1957; [ch.] 2 daughters; [ed.] Victoria High School, I.C.S. (accounting) and Camosun College; [occ.] Retired; [memb.] Past President of Victoria Credit Women-International, Kiwaniannes of Victoria; [hon.] Editor's Choice Award, National Library of Poetry; [oth.writ.] "Train of Thoughts" as published in Tears of Fire anthology, many poems, unpublished; [pers.] I use poetry to express the unspoken turmoil and self reflections of my generation. [a.] Victoria, BC.

KERRINGAN, JANEEN KAREN
[b.] January 14, 1976, Syossett, NY; [p.] Josephine and William Kerrigan; [ed.] Graduated Northport High School, June 1994, attending Plattsburg University; [hon.] Quill and Scroll Award for investigating reporting, News Day Award; [pers.] To Jackie with love, I dedicate my poem in loving memory of my sister Jacqueline Kristine, who died at age 16. She was my big sister and I wrote this poem when we lost her. I was 14 years old.

KESACK, DANIEL F.
[b.] July 24, 1949, Bethlehem; [p.] William and Margaret; [m.] Rochelle L. Kesack, March 7, 1981; [ch.] Daniel Jr., Matthew and Kristine; [ed.] Bethlehem Area, Liberty High School, School of Life; [occ.] Postmaster, Martins Creek, PA.; [memb.] MENSA (pending) National Association of Postmasters, 1st Baptist Church, Bethlehem, National ABC, Association of Quality Participation, Little League Manager; [hon.] Postmaster appointment Father of the Year; [oth.writ.] Articles for the Eagle Times, newsletter for the postal service on employee involvement; [pers.] Let your brain be the sponge of knowledge. Your eye the window to your soul. Your heart the pilot of your dreams, then life's mystery will unfold. [a.] Bethlehem, PA.

KETCHUM, LINDSEY
[pen.] D.D. Dudas; [b.] June 19, 1980, Lansing, MI; [p.] Jan Dudas and Mark Ketchum; [ed.] Kendon Elementary School, Eaton Rapids Middle School, Eaton Rapids High School; [memb.] Freshman Student Council President, 4-H Club (5 years), Eaton Rapids volleyball program; [hon.] Kendon Elementary School, Principal Award, all A's, Honor Roll, high point in dog obedience (4-H); [pers.] Love conquers all. [a.] Eaton Rapids, MI.

KETNER, SHIRLEY H.
[b.] April 29, 1937, Monroe, NC, Cabarrus, CO.; [p.] Franklin B. and Coral E. Henry; [m.] Garry L. Ketner, March 21, 1958; [ch.] Sherie Delanie and Richard Leon; [ed.] Graduated W.R. Odell High School; [occ.] Receptionist, Hospice of Cabarrus County; [oth.writ.] I have a poem entitled "Angelic Symphony" that will be published in the book Treasured Poems of America", published by Sparrowgrass Poetry Forum, in December 1994; [pers.] Poetry is the rhythm in each beat of my heart. It is music to my soul. My poems reflect the beauty of mankind and nature. Some poems are derived from life experiences, both funny and sad. My writing is truly a gift from God. [a.] Concord, NC.

KILLINGSWORTH, MINDY K.
[b.] October 28, 1970, Springfield, MO; [p.] Linda and Roscoe Killingsworth; [ed.] Parkview High School, Southwest Missouri State University; [occ.] Secretary, Killingsworth Feed Mill Inc.; [hon.] Melissa Daniels Award of leadership and service; [oth.writ.] Short essay published in Unicorns and Daisies; [pers.] I'm inspired by Robert Frost, an amateur writing friend, and by making something

good out of something bad. [a.] Springfield, MO.

KIMBRO, ADA BELLE
[pen.] Dr. A. Kem; [b.] April 18, Birmingham, AL; [p.] Earnest and Minnie Lamar Sr.; [m.] Widowed; [ch.] Lillian, Mary Theresa, Tommie Roosevelt, Earnestine, Anita Louise, Karen Lenore; [ed.] Elementary-Council School, Industrial High, Alabama, Wilkens School of Cosmetology and Clinic, Cleveland, Ohio; [occ.] Associate Doctorate of Cosmetology, graduate, B.A., M.A. Doc. I,II, III degree; [memb.] Triedstone Baptist Church, Cleveland, Ohio, Q.A.B. Inc. State-Chapter # 1, N.B.C.L. Inc., Alpha Theta Ohio Chapter, Theta Nu Sigma, National Sorority; [hon.] Service award, Artist Guild, adult tutor, volunteer at Karamu Theatre, Fin. Sec. Newlight Baptist Church, Nursing Guild management member of Shrine of, Madam C. J. Walker in Washington, D.C. cosme. etc.; [oth.writ.] December 19, 1988, something I jotted down when I was awakened on above date by the TV in the wee hours when I had left the TV on; [pers.] Personal reflection as my living caring and sharing not to be in vain while touching the lives of my fellowman, be it man, woman or child. Since childhood, spiritually influenced by many. [a.] Cleveland, OH.

KINDELL, MONTE L.
[pen.] Monte L. Kindell; [b.] May 24, 1970, Troy, OH;[p.] Merle R. and Mary Lou Kindell; [m.] Lisa R. Kindell, July 24, 1993; [ed.] Piqua High School, HFI (Hollywood Film Institute); [occ.] Welding Technician, F & P America, also a drum teacher; [memb.] Piqua Baptist Church, Piqua Dog Club; [hon.] Athletic Booster's Spirit Award in 1987, 1989; [oth.writ.] "One Hundred Stories" is my first poem to be published, currently writing a screenplay for motion picture and another script geared for national television (small screen); [pers.] My dream has always been to write to express how life is short and to reach for your dreams, which was inspired by the life of Michael Landon, hopefully my life will be an inspiration for others. [a.] Piqua, OH.

KING, JACQUELYN C.
[b.] February 26, 1957, Washington, DC; [p.] Esau and Sarah King; [ch.] Eric S. Roberts; [occ.] Information Systems Specialist, Government Systems Inc.; [oth.writ.] Numerous other poems and prose written for churches, organizations and individuals; [pers.] My writings are a gift from God, and if they touch anyone in a special way, then my reward is acknowledged and my blessing received. [a.] Suitland, MD.

KING, RICHARD
[pen.] Dick King; [b.] April 24, 1927, Reardon, WA; [m.] Virginia King, November 23, 1946; [ed.] 1 year high school, Odessa Washington, 1 year Yakima Valley Junior College, 3 years Tri State College; [occ.] Retired; [memb.] VFW-life, American Legion-life, National Rifle Association-life, Stueben Co. Humane Society-life; [oth.writ.] Book of poetry Oh Well published 1993, approximately 100 other poems, dissertations, etc.; [pers.] I write, primarily for my own entertainment. However, "While writing is satisfying and pleasure enough, to have others get a smile, a chuckle or a warm gentle thought would give me a sense of satisfaction that would indeed be a bonus to enjoying life, there are not many rewards greater than pleasing your fellowman" (from Oh Well). [a.] Howe, IN.

KIRBY, BECKY
[b.] September 6, 1975, Chillocothe, OH; [p.] Betty Clark; [m.] Stephen Kirby, February 28, 1993; [ed.] Vinton Co. High, Buckeye Hills Career Center, Columbus State Community College; [occ.] Student, retail associate; [memb.] Student organization of Legal Assistants, Business Professionals of America; [pers.] "Hourglass" is dedicated to my grandmother. She was my world, she taught me everything and though she is gone in my heart she will forever live on. [a.] Columbus, OH.

KITT JR., HARRY L.
[pen.] Kip; [p.] Jeannette and Harry Kitt; [ed.] Seward Park High School, BMCC Community College; [occ.] NY Team Federal Credit Union; [pers.] My writing helps to express my inner self to others. "If only you could read my mine". [a.] New York City, NY.

KLASSEN, CLARA
[pen.] Mary; [b.] February 3, 1918, Aberdeen, Sask; [p.] Henry and Abaneta (Schulz), Niessen; [m.] Cornelius H. Klassen, November 26, 1939, Aberdeen, Sask; [ch.] Trevor, Gerald, Diane and Ken; [ed.] School of Aberdeen, Sask, Nurses Aid, grade VIII, piano, seamstress, painter, 2 years Bethany Bible School choir pianist since age 13 to age 76 in Aberdeen, Hepburn Sask and B.C.; [occ.] Retired, pianist; [memb.] Nurses Union, Mennonite Brethren Church in Clearbrook, BC, Ladies Club; [hon.] In handwriting, at age 75 retired from playing for choirs, it was celebrated in my honor and gifts were presented, etc.; [oth.writ.] Books, size approximately 9x11, 500 "Niessen" Genealogy books, approximately 660, pictures 326 (soft cover) pages, 500 Schulz, Genealogy books approximately 1000 pictures, 525 pages (hard cover), 500 "Klassen Genealogy" books, 2000 pictures and 636 pages, hard cover.

KLASSEN, SUSANNE
[b.] April 28, 1978, Morden, MB; [p.] David J. and Mary Klassen; [ed.] Valley Mennonite Academy Private School, grade eleven; [pers.] My motive for writing poetry is to express the feelings in my heart, so they can also be placed in others. [a.] Winkler Manitoba, Canada.

KLEBS, DeANNA JO
[b.] February 11, 1979, Harvey, IL; [p.] JoAnn Klebs and late Richard Klebs; [ed.] Shackelford Junior High School; [oth.writ.] I have several poems, but I just keep them in my poetry book; [pers.] I enjoy writing poems they help me to get out my feelings. [a.] Arlington, TX.

KLINE, ANNA MARIA
[pen.] Annie; [b.] November 19, 1964, Red Bank, NY; [p.] Joseph Anthony and Pia Videtti; [m.] Jay William Kline, July 13, 1991; [ch.] Christian Joseph Kline; [ed.] Howell High School, Georgian Court College BA in Arts and Humanitian, Seton Hall University MAE in Psychology Education; [occ.] Psychiatric screener, artified in state of NJ, Kimball Medical Center, Lakewood, NJ; [memb.] Kappa Delta Pi, National Geographic Society; [hon.] Dean's Scholar-Georgian Court College; [oth.writ.] "Dear Mother" published in Our World's Most Beloved Poems, several honorable mentions and Silver and Golden Poet Awards from World of Poetry, outstanding effort award, Authors/Writers Network New Jersey, short short story contest; [pers.] It is through words, that we are able to share what is in our hearts. [a.] Jackson, NJ.

KMIEC, JAMIE
[b.] June 28, 1977, Houston; [p.] James and Jefferie Kmiec;[ed.] Inez Caroll Elementary, T.S. Grantham Middle School, currently a senior at Aldine Senior High School; [memb.] Ecology Club, Photography Club, varsity soccer, school literary magazine, National Honor Society, Social Studies, prep bowl, Help One Student to Succeed (HOSTS) program, 3rd grade mentor; [hon.] Photo Student of the Year, Texas Media Award, 3rd place, Soccer Booster Club appreciation award, Who's Who Among America's High School Student, 2 year honor; [oth.writ.] "The Betrayer", "Invisible Person"; [pers.] This poem is for the guys on the soccer team, for they have taught me the most important lessons, love and respect and to Christopher wherever you may be. [a.] Houston, TX.

KNUPP, DEAN
[b.] January 11, 1971, Chicago, IL; [p.] Fred and Sharon Knapp; [m.] Single; [ed.] Downers Grove South High School; [occ.] Journeyman meatcutter, assistant meat manager Omni Superstore; [memb.] United Food and Commercial Workers Union, United We Stand America, U.I.C.A., Vocational Industrial Career Advance; [hon.] Most improved bowler Argo Bowl Award, great inner strength and two wonderful parents; [oth.writ.] The Moon Is Over The Monarch and other miscellaneous sayings and short poems; [pers.] Nothing in life comes easy and expect no free rides. Life is what we make it no matter how grim things maybe. Look up believe that you can work to be free. Search for truth and believe in Jesus just like me. [a.] Hinsdale, IL.

KNELSEN (NEE GODARD), LINDA LOUISE
[b.] February 21, 1958; [p.] Felix and Mary Godard; [m.] Douglas Allan Knelsen, October 18, 1980; [ch.] Karen Yvonne and Daniel Amos; [ed.] Grade twelve, Queen Elizabeth Senor Second; [occ.] Wife, mother, homemaker; [oth.writ.] One poem published in a local newspaper; [pers.] Through the power of God and His creation, through the turning of the seasons, I try to see the beauty in all. [a.] Aldergrove, BC Canada.

KNIPP, DIANN M.
[[en.] Diann Wenger Knipp; [b.] October 31, 1948, South Bend, IN; [p.] Jodine and David E. Wenger; [m.] Frank L. Knipp; [ch.] Frank L. Knipp Jr; [ed.] Arizona State University at Tempe, Arizona, B.A. Elementary Education in 1971, M.A. Special Education 1971; [occ.] Special Education Teacher, grades 5 and 6; [memb.] Lattie Coor School, Avondale, Arizona. [a.] Glendale, AZ.

KNORR, DANA L.
[b.] December 12, 1970, Altoona, PA; [p.] Alfred D. and Patricia L. Knorr; [ed.] Altoona Area High School, Elizabethtown College; [occ.] Substitute elementary teacher, Altoona Area and Hollidaysburg Area School Districts; [memb.] Oterbein U.M. Church Youth Director, Children's Sunday School Teacher; [hon.] Honors graduate of Altoona Area High School, Elizabethtown College Dean's List 6 semesters, Cum Laude graduate of Elizabethtown College; [oth.writ.] Several poems published in high school and college literary magazines. [a.] Altoona, PA.

KNUTSON, NIKKI
[b.] September 2, 1980, Fresno, CA; [p.] John and Natalie Knutson; [ed.] Modesto Christian High School, freshman year; [memb.] American Holstein Association, neighborhood church youth group; [hon.] Superior award in Youth Authors of American two years ago; [oth.writ.] A small book of a total of eight poems (not published); [pers.] I like to write when I am depressed, therefore most of my writings are depressing with the exception of a very select few. [a.] Modesto, CA.

KOBBE, VIRGENE M.
[b.] June 13, 1947, Elmira, NY; [p.] Percy and Clara Brown; [m.] Donald E. Kobbe, March 7, 1970; [ed.] Elmira Free Academy graduated 1965; [occ.] Direct worker; [oth.writ.] Poetry for friends

and relatives for special occasions; [pers.] Anyone in emotional stress should express their opinions on paper in any form of writing. It is a necessary part of healing. [a.] Elmira, NY.

KOEHL, OPAL
[b.] January 15, 1909, Marthasville, MO; [p.] F. and Ida McVey Berg; [m.] Everett Koehl, April 27, 1937; [ch.] Timothy Koehl; [ed.] McAllen High, life; [occ.] Retired secretary; [memb.] American Association of Research and Enlightenment; [oth.writ.] 1 poem, published in high school annual; [pers.] When Bishop Warren Candler faced death, he was asked, "Do you dread to cross the river of death?" He replied, "My Fathers owns the land on both sides of the river! Why should I fear?" Emil A. Balliet, Pentecostal Evangelist. [a.] Houston, TX.

KOESTER, MARGARET E.
[pen.] Margaret E. Koester; [b.] December 21,1924, Ontario, OR; [p.] Clay and Grace Blakley; [m.] Widow, March 29, 1965; [ch.] John; [ed.] High school, extra courses in art and writing; [occ.] Retired, volunteer, craft teacher; [memb.] Gem State Writers Guild; [oth.writ.] Lots of articles on the news of the day and reflections on the state of everyday life; [pers.] I have written lots of letters "to the editor," our news letter also. [a.] Boise, ID.

KONITSNEY, LINDA A.
[b.] November 30, 1972, Warren, OH; [pers.] Poetry, for me is an expression of love, a release from stress and the most uplifting experience that comes from deep inside one's heart, mind, body and soul. [a.] Warren, OH.

KOSBAB, ELISA F.J.
[b.] October 12, 1980, Jansvill, WI; [p.] Elsa Labbs and Arnold Kosbab; [ed.] Wilson Elementary, Bowler; [hon.] Reading the most books in 2nd grade, good behavior, best singer; [oth.writ.] Short stories, "The Lavender horses" (not published); [pers.] "The world would be nothing without poetry or books. [a.] Bowler, WI.

KOSTRACH, MARIA
[b.] March 8, 1980, Pontiac General; [p.] Dane and Theresa, step-Sue and Wes; [ed.] Stevenson Junior High, 9th grade, Westland Public Schools; [occ.] Housecleaning and volunteer at Hope Nursing Center for the elderly; [hon.] Achievement awards, awards for 3.876 average and sport awards; [oth.writ.] Non-published poems and stories, also short novels; [pers.] I try to do helpful things for elderly people and my family. I use my family in some of my poems, especially my closest loved ones. [a.] Westland, MI.

KOUSEK, JENNIFER
[pen.] Raven; [p.] Dave and Kay Kousek; [ch.] Aaron Slayter; [pers.] Unknown to those who can not see beyond the reign of confusion. It is the mind that holds the purest phantoms of the soul. Dimension and control. [a.] Norcross, GA.

KOVAL, MARY L.
[b.] August 7, 1942, Kulpmont, PA; [p.] Ray and Mary Thomas; [ed.] Rollin College, Winter Park, FL.; [occ.] Banker, semi-retired; [pers.] I wish to dedicate this to my father who passed away in 1993. [a.] Leesburg, FL.

KRAHN, ELIZABETH PAETKAU
[pen.] Elizabeth paetkau Krahn; [b.] June 18, 1944, Winkler, MB; [p.] Both are deceased; [m.] Jim Krahn, July 14, 1973; [ch.] Lavonne Lynn and Julia Kaye; [ed.] Man. Teachers College, can. Menn Bible College, Bachelor of Chr. Education, Bethel College in Newton, Kansas, Bachelor of Science in Elementary Education; [occ.] At present I am a homemaker; [hon.] My poem published in The Space Between, I will have a poem in Best Poems of 1995, my poem is on the tape The Sound of Poetry, a collection of my work is on visions; [oth.writ.] I publish a poem in our church paper every month, I have published poetry in my alumni newsletter; [pers.] My desire is that people everywhere be free from tyranny and poetry. In my writing I attempt to portray the greatness and the love of God. [a.] Manitoba, Canada.

KRAUSER, TWILA
[b.] February 7, 1961, Denison, TX; [p.] Laurattea and Jerry Stowe; [ch.] Paul III, Nathan and Jim Lalley, Barbara and Emily Krauser; [ed.] Judson High School, Vouge Beauty College; [occ.] Dietary cook at Cantex Nursing Home; [oth.writ.] Have written a few poems but haven't had any of them published; [pers.] I have enjoyed poetry since the age of twelve. I was told to recite Eldarodo by Edgar Allen Poe and have enjoy his and many other poets works in my life. [a.] Denison, TX.

KRCULIC, SILVANA
[b.] October 20, 1949, Former, Yugoslavia; [p.] Ivan and Pierina Brkaric; [m.] Lino, July 29, 1968; [sib.] Mario; [ch.] Allen, Alexandra and Christopher; [ed.] Administrative Technician; [occ.] Clerical; [memb.] Belong to clubs of poetry (Europe and Australia); [hon.] Poetry published in Germany, Yugoslavia and Australia; [oth.writ.] I Came Here To Land of Plenty, Dreamers' Heart and other; [pers.] Poet, humanitarian, lover of mankind. [a.] Brooklyn, NY.

KROLL, HELEN M. S.P.
[pen.] Helen Kroll; [b.] February 12, 1909, Osceola Mill, PA; [p.] Anton and Helena Buchholz Kroll; [ed.] Jasonville Elementary Public School, St. Mary-of-the-Woods (IN) High School, St. Mary-of-the-Woods (IN) College, Indiana State University, Mark Tracey Overseas Scholarship, Credo Program Religious Studies at Gonzaga University, Spokane, Washington, German studies at Wanne, Germany; [oth.writ.] Several poems published in "Community" the newspaper of Sisters of Providence Religious Organization; [pers.] "Through the arts my life has been enriched, my self-awareness deepened, thereby adding richness to the lives of those I touch." [a.] St. Mary-of-the-Woods, IN.

KUHLMAN, BRIAN '
[b.] April 5, '942, Gothenburg, NE; [p.] Henry and Bessie Kuhlman; [ch.] Daniel; [ed.] Gothenburg High, Central Technical Institute, Kansas City; [occ.] Electronic Technician, Eglin Air Force Base, FL; [hon.] Your own 1994 Editors Choice Award; [oth.writ.] Poems published in books by the National Library of Poetry, Famous Poets Society and American Film Studios; [pers.] If people were like words the world could be a better place. One word by itself can be okay, but several of them working together tend to make things a lot better. [a.] Santa Rosa Beach, FL.

KYANTHONY, RAIGN
[b.] August 1, 1956, Corpus Christi, TX; [p.] Murphy and Esther Hamilton; [ch.] Nickema Nicole, James Henry and Erik Justin; [ed.] Roy Miller High, Prince George's Community College; [occ.] Customer Service Representative, Washington, DC.; [memb.] Cub Scout Leader (certified) prior Brownie Leader, NAFE member, Pastoral Anniversary Committee-New Macedonia Baptist Church; [oth.writ.] Several poems (unpublished); [pers.] Originating from a semi-tropical area, one has to but gaze upon nature's energy, beauty and intensity, hence flows unbountiful inspiration. [a.] Forestville, MD.

LACY, CLINT E.
[b.] May 25, 1972, Cape Girardeau, MO; [p.] Glen R. and Sharon L. Lacy; [m.] Michelle Lacy, March 19, 1994; [ed.] Currently attending Southeast Missouri State University; [occ.] Cashier; [oth.writ.] This is my first published writing, though I have co-written several songs with friends; [pers.] Songs often come to me by minor creates of actions, for example, a train whistle or leaves blowing across a road, or the weather can give me an idea for writing and set the mood of the writing. I try to paint a picture of an event or idea when I write. [a.] Jackson, MO.

LaFLEUR, ALICE R.
[b.] March 10, 1910, Massachusetts; [p.] George and Aurisie Berard; [m.] Edward E. LaFleur, April 15, 1929; [ch.] Edward Jr. and Paul B. LaFleur; [ed.] High school, several adult classes in Psychology, advanced English, etc.; [occ.] Retired Civil Service Records Clerk; [memb.] Business and Professional Women, Sweet Adeline, Toastmistress Int.; [hon.] Speech contest, Toastmistress full page recognition, Ridge Crest paper, superior performance award, Civil Service; [oth.writ.] School paper articles, personal auto-bios for friends, stories of people in my geology research book, have poems in "Visions", In The Desert Sun, etc.; [pers.] How great a world we live in if only people took time to realize its beauty and to see all the good things we can enjoy. [a.] Ridgecrest, CA.

LAKE, JOANNE MARIE
[b.] September 12,1945, Waukegan, IL; [p.] Frank and Audree Zalewski; [m.] Gerald Lake, September 2, 1967; [ed.] San Jose Community College, Teaching Certificate Religious Education, Reno/Las Vegas Diocese; [occ.] Teacher, first grade, Religious Education, Confraternity of Christian Doctrine; [memb.] Beta Sigma Phi and St. Anthony's Coffee hour server; [hon.] Won first prize in Beta Sigma Phi scrap book contest for the art work that I did; [oth.writ.] I have written poems and verses for the children I teach, also, I have written music to scripture verses for use by the children, I am currently in the process of writing a children's story; [pers.] For the mind to be open to goodness, it must be nourished with input that is good. [a.] Fall City, WA.

LAKE, JOHN
[b.] August 4, 1967, Denville, NJ; [m.] Chrissy Lake, May 18, 1991; [ed.] My teachers have been me, this life and the world around me; [occ.] Artist; [oth.writ.] Presently trying to get my first book published entitled "The Book of Life", which includes my poems and paintings; [pers.] The closed minded surround you. See the hate in their eyes, hear the anger in their words. They don't understand, if you understand... they will follow. [a.] Budd Lake, NJ.

LANADA, QUENNIE RAGADIO
[pen.] Quennie or Queen; [b.] June 13, 1977, Philippines; [p.] John Leo and Ofelia Desposito; [ed.] Holy Infant Jesus Study Center (high school, Philippines), PJC or Pensacola Junior College as a freshman student; [occ.] Freshman student; [pers.] Poetry cleanses the soul, it freshens the mind, it softens the heart. Reach for your dreams for everything lies in your hand, heart, soul and mind. Keep reaching for the stars. Success is the ladder that can't be climbed with hands in pocket. Do the best and show the world who's tough. The Lord is always with you/us. [a.] Pensacola. FL.

LANGE, JEREMY
[pen.] Jeremy Lange;[b.] August 18, 1979, Hayward; [p.] Brian and Keran Egan; [ed.] Sophomore high school student, Altimire Middle School graduate,

Camp Pendleton/US Marin Corps Leadership training and physical fitness; [memb.] Who's Who, Boy Scouts, Lutheran Church Youth Group; [hon.] Devil pups, Boy Scouts, Stare 6th grade student of the year award, Who's Who Among American High School Students, Honor Roll, Principal Honor Roll; [oth.writ.] Several poems and a couple short stories; [pers.] Time does not wait for anyone, so ride on it. Thanks Jackie for the inspiration, thanks grandma for helping. [a.] El Verano, CA.

LARA, LINDA
[pen.] Linda Lara; [b.] September 27, 1953, Clarendon, TX; [p.] Bert and Arva Smith; [m.] Joseph Lara; [ch.] Michael Noel Arnold, Alyisha Nicole Sutherland and Elias Miguel Verdalette; [occ.] Massage therapist and reflexologist; [memb.] World of Poetry, Sacramento, California; [hon.] Lady in Light written to my dear late grandmother Jodie, was a Golden Poet winner; [oth.writ.] Several poems published in World of Poetry, I have won 8 Golden Poets Awards and several honorable mentions; [pers.] Poetry has been my outlet and love since I was a small girl. It is and always has been an expression of the depths of my soul.

LARSEN, KRISTINA
[pen.] Kristina M. Larsen; [b.] July 23, 1972, Powell, WY; [p.] Lester and Pam Larsen; [ed.] American School, The Professional Paralegal program; [memb.] Jobs Daughters,Bethel # 23 from 1984 to 1991; [hon.] Honorary Honor Queen of Jobs Daughters in 1991; [oth.writ.] Various other unpublished poems and short stories; [pers.] Alex F. Osborn once said, "Creativity is so delicate a flower that praise tends to make it bloom, while discouragement often nips it in the bud. Any of us will put up more and better ideas if our efforts are appreciated." Many thanks to my family for their praise and support of my creativeness. THANK-YOU. [a.] Evanston, WY.

LaRUE, CORYELL
[b.] December 16, 1982, Waco, TX; [p.] Marjorie and Cleo LaRue; [hon.] Two academic excellence awards from West Windsor, Plainsboro African American parent support group; [pers.] I try to write about places I would like to go. My inspiration came from women like Zora Neal Hurston, Maya Angelou and Dori Sanders. I'm only 11 but maybe I make a difference later. [a.] Princeton, NJ.

LATHROP, MICHELLE
[pen.] Mesh, Mel; [b.] September 5, 1974, Clifton Springs, NY; [p.] Janet and Mahlon Lathrop; [ed.] Midlakes High School, Finger Lakes Community College (FLCC); [occ.] Wal-Mart Sales Associate, owner of beauty mart boutique; [memb.] Alateen, American Legion Unit 286, Midlakes Alateen, American Legion Junior's committee; [oth.writ.] Several poems including "Summer Breeze" and "Passion of Dreams", several short stories, am now writing "Secret of Eden", the autobiography of an adult child; [pers.] I have found writing to be my door to my spiritualness and serenity. We all have dreams but it takes a healthy person to accept the goals we have and pursue them. [a.] Newark, NJ.

LAWRENCE, ZELDA
[pen.] Zelda Lawrence; [b.] May 5, 1904, Foster, AL; [p.] Floyd and Clara Lindsey; [m.] C.L. Lawrence (deceased), February 2, 1929; [ch.] 6; [ed.] Completed high school and graduated in 1924; [hon.] My church in Mississippi honored me for 90th birthday, honored at my former church where my children were raised, I was the oldest living former member and was given a beautiful orchid corsage; [oth.writ.] A writing of some of my life work in a senior edition magazine published in our local newspaper; [pers.] My oldest brother was a gospel song writer and wrote words and music and was published in gospel song book.

LAWTON, GEORGE A.
[b.] August 13, 1922, Torrington, CT; [p.] Nellie O'Shaughnessy and George Lawton; [m.] Toshiko, March 30, 1956; [ch.] Maureen and Kimianne; [ed.] Nangatuck High School, University of Wisconsin Public Affairs Fellowship, Stanford University; [occ.] Management Analyst; [memb.] AARP; [hon.] Fellowship awards; [oth.writ.] Many poems, couple published in newspapers; [pers.] Life without love is barren, love without meaning is empty, love is the sole word of all religions, all else reflects man's greed, only true love survives. [a.] Lakewood, CO.

LAY, OCIE (MRS.)
[pen.] Ocie Tackett Lay; [b.] January 25, 1925, Caryville, TN; [m.] Dean Lay, August 30, 1946; [ch.] 2 sons and 1 daughter; [occ.] Retired; [memb.] Baptist Church; [oth.writ.] Poems published in anthologies, local newspapers and Ideals (which is presently being published in Nashville, Tennessee), have several of my poems in their files and have published 3 in separate books; [pers.] Inspiration for my writings are from everyday life, from my love of nature, from faith in a Supreme Being and from having a very strong imagination dating back to childhood. [a.] Knoxville, TN.

LEACH, ROSE MARIE
[b.] October 25, 1957, Philadelphia; [p.] Daniel and Theresa Corson; [m.] Kenneth A. Leach Jr., August 12, 1978; [ch.] Melissa, Sean and Scott; [ed.] North Penn High; [occ.] Title Clerk; [pers.] I believe we all are here to fill the destiny our Lord has prepared for us, each of us are here to change the world in our own special way. [a.] Florham Park, NJ.

LEBHERZ, RICHARD
[pen.] Richard Lebherz; [b.] November 3, 1921, Frederick, MD; [occ.] Novelist, short stories, art critiques, editor; [oth.writ.] 3 published novels, The Altars of the Heart, The Nazi Overcoat, The Man in The White Raincoat and Conversations with Practically Everybody; [pers.] I have been a columnist for the Frederick News and post, written article for the Washington Post and editor of diversions here in Frederick which is now known as Frederick magazine. I also write for the newspaper here in Frederick. [a.] Frederick, MD.

LEDGER, BONNIE
[b.] May 8, 1945, Lancaster, NH; [p.] Arnold and Evelyn Spencer; [m.] Charles Ledger-deceased; [ch.] Mark Arnold, Lori Lynn and Kim Marie-deceased; [ed.] Plymouth High School, Plymouth State College; [occ.] Housekeeping, Mill House Inn, Lincoln, NH.; [memb.] Rathkamp Matchcover Society, New England Matchcover Club; [oth.writ.] Poems; [pers.] When my oldest daughter was killed in 1974, I found it helpful to write down my feelings. Expressed emotions are easier to deal with.

LEE, MICHAEL E.
[b.] February 8, 1952, Little Rock, AR; [p.] Audrey and Glen Lee; [m.] Deborah S. Lee, December 13, 1985 (Friday the 13th); [ch.] Tammie, Cindy, step-children, Andy and Jessie Krongberg; [occ.] Finance Manager at GM Dealership; [oth.writ.] Unpublished poems and short stories. [a.] Little Rock, AR.

LEE, YOUA ALYSSA
[b.] April 6, 1973, Xiengkhougn, Laos; [p.] Phoua Kong Lee and Wangtoua Lee; [ed.] Garinger High School, University of North Carolina at Chapel Hill; [occ.] Student, University of North Carolina at Chapel Hill; [memb.] Emerging Leaders of America, Womentoring Program, Asian Students Association, Carolina Fever, International Society of Poetry-lifetime member, International society of Poetry Advisory Panel, Hmong Evangelical Church, Gigo Computer Club; [hon.] Editor's Choice Award 1993 and 1994 for poems entitled "Just Another Stranger" and "You Are So Far Away", lifetime member of ISP, first place Science Fair project, Art Award, Garinger National Honor Society, Vocational Honor Society, Junior Marshal, Art Honor Society; [oth.writ.] Poem entitled "Just Another Stranger" published in Where Dreams Begin, poem entitled "You Are So Far Away" published in The Space Between, poem entitled "The Miles Seem Too Far" published in Best Poems of 1995, several poems published in local newspapers during high school, several other non-published poems; [pers.] I want to thank God for making everything possible, for His love, for my family and my friends. I want to thank my parents, especially my dad who has been my greatest aspiration in my strive for excellence and self-improvement, and thanks to all who strengthens me with prayers, blesses me with love and encourage me with hope. [a.] Chapel Hill, NC.

LEGG, NANCY S.
[b.] November 8, 1942, Portsmouth, OH; [p.] Leonard and Pauline Evans; [m.] David Legg, February 14, 1993; [ch.] Karla, Shane (step-children, Tammy and Christy); [ed.] Glenwood High, Columbus Par-professional Institute; [occ.] Phlebotomist with the American Red Cross; [memb.] Whitehall Baptist Church; [hon.] Attendance award, Club 95 Award, Alpha Beta Kappa Honor Society; [oth.writ.] Several poems published in local newspaper, I give poems to my friends to share the gift God gave me; [pers.] This particular poem was written for my best friend who was getting married. I give God all the credit for my poems, before I knew Him as my Lord and Saviour I couldn't write poetry. [a.] Columbus, OH.

LeGORE, JEFFREY F.
[b.] September 9, 1956, Eau Claire, WI; [p.] Robert and Bertha LeGore; [ed.] Bachelor of Fine Arts, drawing and painting 1980, BS degree-Pharmacy 1990, UW-Eau Claire and UW Madison respectively; [occ.] Pharmacist; [hon.] None related to poetry or writing, various art and sports related awards and trophies; [oth.writ.] None-currently working with friends to put together a comic book anthology of stories and writings; [pers.] My poetry tends to wallow in the sadness of life. Largely this is because of a love of the image of morbidity as portrayed by Edgar A. Poe, the media portrayal of life, love of the autumn season, and watching and reading too darn many horror movies and comic books. [a.] Eau Claire, WI.

LEISINGER, MARGARET ROSE
[b.] January 23, 1934, Greensburg, PA: [p.] Michael and Ellen Casper; [m.] Widowed; [ch.] Brenda, Greg and Jeff; [ed.] College-Akron University and diploma Idabelle Firestone School of Nursing; [occ.] Registered Nurse in Dialysis Department at Arkon College Hospital; [memb.] ANNA, various committees in nursing; [pers.] I like to reflex the goodness of God and how I feel about love and trails of life. [a.] Akron, OH.

LEMKE, ADAM
[b.] January 19, 1978, Tiyuana, Mexico; [p.] Shelby Lemke; [ed.] I am a student at Campbellsport High School in Campbellsport, WI.; [oth.writ.] I have written numerous poems and songs about every aspect of my life; [pers.] One thing I have always believed in, is believing in yourself. You can

do anything you set your mind to, no matter what age, color or sex you are, you can accomplish anything. Anything is possible, never give up. [a.] Eden, WI.

LENGEL, BARBARA GABRIEL
[b.] March 3, 1941, Oceanside, NY; [p.] Frank and Gertrude Kaiser; [ch.] Stephen F. and Jon C. Gabriel; [ed.] South Side High School, NY, Baldwin-Wallace College, Ohio, Hofstra University, NY; [pers.] Poetry can be written anytime, anyplace. All you need is pen, paper and a little inspiration. [a.] Rockville Centre, NY.

LENNON, ROBERT H.
[b.] March 23,1931, Providence, RI; [m.] Single; [ed.] Master of Library Science, University of Denver 1953; [occ.] Retired; [memb.] American Library Association; [pers.] To fight racism, poverty and genocide is a "just" war. To turn the other cheek is also the ideal... It is the balancing of contradictions of ambiguities which make us responsible and human. [a.] Los Angeles, CA.

LEO, ROSA
[b.] July 7, 1970, Toronto; [p.] Antimo and Santina Leo; [ed.] Bishop Marrocco, Thomas Merton C.S.S. and St. Lucy Elementary School; [occ.] Reception, University of Toronto; [memb.] The International Society of Poets; [hon.] BMTM Honour Society and National Library of Poetry, Editor's Choice certificate; [oth.writ.] "Moonlit Waltz", Tears of Fire and "By Water's Edge', The Space Between; [pers.] "An Angel's Flight" is in loving memory of a dear friend and devoted husband, Joseph Robert Blakoe, whom at the age of 47 was suddenly taken from us on May 7, 1994, and to his loving wife Wendy Smith, it is through you, that his memory lives forever young. [a.] Toronto, Ontario.

LEONARDI, BETSY
[b.] Troy, NY; [ed.] B.A., The college of St. Rose, M.Ed., Marygrove College.

LePERA, JUDITH
[b.] August 9, 1981, Somers Point, NJ; [p.] Randi Brickman and Robert LePera; [ed.] Junior high, 8th grade; [occ.] School; [memb.] Statue of Liberty Collector's Club, SADD, drama club; [oth.writ.] Co-author of elementary school (6th grade) play; [pers.] I'm hoping to go to college and pursue a career in teaching. [a.] Shoemakersville, PA.

LESHAN, STEPHANIE
[pen.] Bob; [b.] May 24,1976; [p.] Lawrence and Bonnie Leshan; [ed.] Presently enrolled in the Columbus College of Art and Design, graduated from Plymouth Salem High School; [occ.] Student; [hon.] Art Honors Key (sculpture); [pers.] Your freedom, your identity, your space, your sanity. [a.] Plymouth, MI.

LESSARD, TRISHA J.
[pen.] Lanny Les'Sure; [b.] November 28, 1978, Fresno; [p.] Christopher and Jane Lessard; [ed.] California School for The Deaf, Fremont; [memb.] National Author's Registry; [oth.writ.] A poem published in "Musings" in upcoming release in 1995; [pers.] I am deaf, but I fight for my success and don't let my deafness pull me down. [a.] Fresno, CA.

LEV, MYER
[pen.] Michael Lev; [b.] August 10, 1913, London England; [p.] Leo and Jenny Lev; [m.] Betty, August 30, 1953; [ch.] Heather, Vivienne; [ed.] William Morris Sr. High School; [occ.] Retired; [hon.] Inducted as a freeman of the city of London; [oth. writ.] Monologues, songs, etc. unpublished.

LEVAULT, IRIS MARIE
[b.] September 22, 1939, Sesser, IL; [p.] Wanda and Orval Piper; [m.] Richard Gale Levault, June 9, 1957; [ch.] Todd Levault and Toni-Levault Morhet;[occ.] Housewife; [pers.] The love for a wonderful family and the love for nature have inspired me to write simply a few poems. I try to express in my writing only the feeling within my heart. [a.] Sesser, IL.

LEVESQUE, TRACI
[b.] November 5, 1974, Cedar Rapids, IA; [p.] Rogette Steele and Richard Levesque; [ed.] Washington High; [occ.] Manager in restaurant; [oth.writ.] Poems and photography in a high school publication; [pers.] My writing is inspired by my life and changes. It's my vision, but my ability is a gift from God. [a.] Cedar Rapids, IA.

LEWIS, DEBRA
[b.] September 26, 1962, Bermuda; [ch.] Tyrone Frederick Lewis; [ed.] Cavendish Hall, Saltus Junior, Whitney Institute; [occ.] Part-time Imagine Processor; [memb.] Song Authors Guild of America in 1978, (was then Debra Mello); [hon.] Had two songs recorded by the group "Ebb Tide" in 1979; [oth.writ.] At 10 years old had a poem in the school yearbook (the first poem I wrote the teacher didn't believe I did it by myself so she made me do another one in class while she was at her desk to watch me); [pers.] Poetry has always been the heart and soul of who I am. A God given talent that inspired me at age 10 to write my first poem and is still very much alive within. [a.] Paget East, Bermuda.

LEWIS, EDITH
[b.] June 20, Virginia; [p.] Lathan and Jessie Williams; [m.] Charles H. Lewis, April 26, 1929; [ch.] Mary Evelyn and Charles Jr.; [ed.] High school graduate; [occ.] Retired, designer, dressmaker; [memb.] St. Luke Baptist Church, where I am a deaconess, N.A.A.C.P., other charitable organizations; [pers.] My favorite poets are, Longfellow, Poe and Dunbar. I strive to see and feel beauty in all things. I receive blessings from God everyday, I am truly blessed. [a.] Washington, DC.

LEWIS, MARLINA L.
[b.] May 5, 1969, Washington, DC; [p.] Ira and Margaret Lewis; [ed.] Largo High School, Largo, Maryland, University of Maryland, College Park; [occ.] Television writer, producer, director; [memb.] National Association of Television Arts and Science; [oth.writ.] "Two World's Collide", a script, "Letters to My Therapist" (a collection of short stories), and "Remember, What's Past Is Prologue"; [pers.] Love God first because if you love God whom you've never seen then it's easier to love your brother who you see everyday. God first, you second and me third. [a.] Upper Marlboro, MD.

LEWIS, ROBERT D.
[pen.] Robert D. Lewis; [b.] August 7, 1961, Michigan City; [p.] Edward and Ernestine; [m.] Letha Lewis, January 6, 1994; [ch.] 10 loving kids; [ed.] Going to school now to get my G.E.D.; [occ.] Incarcerated at the Westville Corr.; [hon.] This is my first one; [oth.writ.] This is my only one and my very first.

LICHMAN, BRENDA
[b.] October 18, 1964, St. Joseph Mercy Hospital, Iowa; [p.] Don and Betty Lichman; [m.] Engaged-Mark Perkins, 1995; [ch.] Matthew Ryan and Brittany Ann; [ed.] North Central High School, Manly Iowa, Marshalltown Community College; [hon.] I entered one of my poems in the World of Poetry contest and was awarded a Silver Poet Certificate, Honor Roll student in high school; [oth.writ.] A couple of poems published in my high school newspaper; [pers.] Poetry is like a best friend to me. It's been there when others couldn't be. [a.] Aberdeen, MD.

LIE, KRISTIN
[pen.] Kristin Joy Lie; [b.] November 27, 1980, Renton, WA; [p.] Signar and Barbara Lie; [ed.] Leota Junior High; [occ.] Student; [hon.] Several district "Reflections" awards; [oth.writ.] A couple poems entered in "Reflections" contest; [pers.] I always try to bring out the innermost feelings and create a vivid image of people's emotions. [a.] Woodinville, WA.

LILLEY, NAOMI K.
[b.] August 7, 1974, North Vancouver, BC Canada; [p.] Keith and Bonnie Lilley; [pers.] I am influenced by my parents. They have always told me to be truthful with myself. Expressing my emotions through poetry comes naturally to me. [a.] North Vancouver, BC Canada.

LILLEY SR., THEODORE K. (DECEASED)
[pen.] Kermit Lilley; [b.] August 2, 1922, Reading, PA; [p.] Effie and William Lilley; [m.] Yolande A. Lilley, March 27, 1946; [ch.] Theodore Lilley Jr.; [ed.] Reading Senior High School graduate; [occ.] Deceased, August 4, 1984; [memb.] Deacon Holy Redeemer Lutheran Church; [hon.] The love and respect of his family, friends and community; [oth.writ.] Unpublished manuscript of poetry some of which were published in local newspapers; [pers.] Mr. Lilley was a man of immense love and deeply troubled by man's inhumanity to his fellowman. [a.] Reading, PA.

LIN, AUSTIN
[b.] February 11, 1977, Chattanooga, TN; [p.] Michell and Tzelan Lin; [ed.] The McCallie School; [occ.] Student; [pers.] For me, poetry is a live entity. It lives in the form of emotions, of Aurae, all of which surround the poet. Poetry is a craft, it is the ability to channel those emotions into this world and immortalize them for others to feel. [a.] Signal Mountain, TN.

LINDBERG, LAWRENCE D.
[b.] April 19, 1942, Iron Mountain, MI; [m.] Bernadette M. Lindberg; [ch.] Walter Dale, Loni Elizabeth and Candice Marie; [memb.] 1st Covenant Church, a member of the Family of God; [hon.] Everlasting life through Jesus Christ Deacon Committee of church; [oth.writ.] Six, seven page collection of poetry (none published); [pers.] I understand that God has a purpose for my life, God has a purpose for yours. When led by the Holy SPirit, your salvation is given to you by Jesus Christ. My ambition in life is to be found a man of God. [a.] Iron Mountain, MI.

LINCOLN, VALARIA JOAN McCAW
[pen.] Joan McCaw Lincoln; [b.] November 3, 1933, Omaha, NE; [p.] Arthur B. and Valaria Lee McCaw; [m.] James E. Lincoln (divorced) August 13, 1955; [ch.[Kim E'Lin Lincoln and Kent Arthur Lincoln; [ed.] Omaha Central High, Drake University, University of Nebraska; [occ.] Retired Specifications Engineer, U.S. Army Corps of Engineers (Civilian); [memb.] St. John's Episcopal Church, Los Angeles County Museum of Art, Honorary Citizen, Boys Town, NE, community volunteer, political volunteer; [hon.] Department of the Army Commendation, certificate of appreciation for Outstanding Community service, award from Personal Poetry; [oth.writ.] The Children's Column, The Omaha Guide Newspaper, "Fats" a novella, "Apollo 21" a play, a collection, poems, "An American Fly On Mexican Walls"", a nonfiction novel; [pers.] My writing began as a child, a

drive to be creative by a middle child who could not paint, perform ballet, nor successfully play a musical instrument. Positive creative inspiration and literary exposure when woven together, form the fabric of family values. [a.] Los Angeles, CA.

LINDGREN, GINA
[b.] November 15, 1971, Anchorage, AK; [p.] James Lindgren and Sue Godwin; [m.] Jesse Gallagher-engaged; [ch.] Darien Lindgren and Thor Gallagher; [ed.] 10th grade education never finished school, I'm getting my GED then I'm going to open my own day care; [occ.] Housemom; [memb.] Women of the Moose at Anchorage Moose Lodge; [hon.] My honor and award is both of my boys because without them I would of never written my poem, they are the best things to ever happen to me; [pers.] I think people should always follow their dreams and never give up even if you don't get it, right away. I have always believed in helping people without giving a second thought. [a.] Anchorage, AK.

LINDSAY, ROSE
[b.] Yorkshire England, UK; [p.] Henry and Beatrice M. Fortune; [m.] Arnold R. Lindsay, February 26, 1945; [ch.] Gary, June, Stanley and Melvin; [ed.] Limited, because of economical reasons, have not had any extended education or formal writing instruction; [occ.] Retired, widow; [memb.] United Church Women of Canada Army, Navy Air force Veteran in Canada, Assiniboia Unit 283; [oth.writ.] Poems published in "Poets Corner" of small town newspaper (several years ago), have written humorous poems for bridal showers, etc., was often asked to write speeches for different occasions, one time correspondent for "Neepawa Press", small town newspaper; [pers.] I came to Canada as a young war bride following WWII and lived in a small town 150 miles north of Winnipeg until recently. I wanted to put my thoughts on paper at an early age but didn't realize it as a talent but was often asked to read my essays to the class at school. Deep feelings for people in sadness and the underprivileged. [a.] Winnipeg, Manitoba.

LINDSEY, FRED ANTHONY
[pen.] Fred Anthony Lindsey; [b.] May 2, 1952, Detroit; [p.] Floyd Collins Lindsey and Mary Lois Lindsey; [m.] Valedia Lindsey, July 20, 1990; [ch.] O.J., Andrew, Lena and John; [ed.] King High, Wayne Community College, Christ Bible Institute; [occ.] Molding press operator; [memb.] Solomon's Temple Church, U.A.W. member; [hon.] Evangelical Training 1993 Association Award, Christian Workers Award, certificates; [oth.writ.] An essay called "The Rapture", not published; [pers.] I minister the gospel of Jesus to all people of the world and teach by the power of the spirit, to every heart that is in bondage by the darkness of men's sins. [a.] Detroit, MI.

LINSALATA, DAVID
[pen.] Dibbs; [b.] June 17, 1960, Philadelphia, PA; [p.] James Thomas and Jean Dorothy Linsalata Sr.; [sib.] James Thomas and Dean Joseph and the memory of our pet dog named Daisy; [ed.] Saint Thomas Aguinas, Oak Knoll, Williamstown High, Camden County College; [occ.] Student, Camden County College; [hon.] Achieved honor roll at Williamstown High for the first 2 years, Spanish Award for highest grade and Dean's List at Camden County College; [oth.writ.] I have written several other inspirational poems that I personally shared with others which they found very touching; [pers.] I believe I have a calling to the priesthood which I would like to pursue to increase my knowledge of God and to contribute to the betterment of mankind. I owe all my talent to the good Lord through the charismatic renewal in the Catholic Church and the born again experience. I feel the arts should not be underestimated. I think the arts excel all academic ability for it is the language of the soul. [a.] Williamstown, NJ.

LINVILLE, SHIRLEY
[b.] April 10, 1945, Logan CO; [p.] Tom and Laura May; [m.] Spurgeon Linville, June 7, 1921; [ch.] Nine; [ed.] Eight grade; [occ.] Mother and housewife; [memb.] Baptist; [hon.] Sending recipes to contest only, won several times; [oth.writ.] I am also a psychics; [pers.] I can tell you things comes to me. I was an orphan at age 12 and lived in a home for homeless children until I married. [a.] Danville, WV.

LIPSCOMB, DEBBIE ANN
[pen.] Debbie Ann Lipscomb; [b.] December 13,1976, Georgetown, SC; [p.] Donald J. Liscomb; [ed.] Currently a senior at Georgetown High School; [occ.] Sales Associate for Cato, a woman's clothing store; [memb.] DECA, FHA, NJROTC and Thespian Society; [hon.] Cadet Lieutenant Administration Officer, Fleet Reserve Medal, DECA Vice President and Color Guard Commander; [oth.writ.] No other publication, but several other writings; [pers.] There are no limits. [a.] Georgetown, SC.

LITTLE, MONICA
[b.] January 23, 1979, New Albany, IN; [p.] Monte and Nancy Little; [ed.] I am striving for an academic honors diploma to further my education after high school; [occ.] I am currently a sophomore at North Harrison High; [memb.] I am a member of Christian's Missionary Church and the varsity choir of my school; [hon.] I am an Honor Roll student and I was selected to have my picture and biography published in the Who's Who Among American Students' magazine; [oth.writ.] Several poems and this is my first attempt to publish one; [pers.] I like to write about the innermost secrets of every person's mind and soul. [a.] New Salisbury, IN.

LIVERMORE, ANGELA M.
[pen.] Angi Fedde; [b.] March 11, 1971, Ladysmith, WI; [p.] Barry and Barb Bartel; [m.] Jeremie Livermore, June 19, 1993; [ch.] Aerial Mae and Zavier Kane;[ed.] Graduated class of 1989 from Waupaca High School, Waupaca, Wisconsin; [occ.] Homemaker; [oth.writ.] Published in high school newspaper, The Paca Pacer and the high school's yearly creative magazine Comet Country; [pers.] Never be afraid to pursue your dreams. My dream was to be published in a major literary work and here I am. Thanks to all those who encouraged me to enter this contest. [a.] Waupaca, WI.

LIYANAGE, RAMILA ANNE
[pen.] Ramila Liyanage; [b.] March 31,1973, Sri Lanka; [p.] Maurice and Rukmal Liyanage; [m.] Single; [ed.] Bachelor of Arts, double degree in Communication (Advertising) and English; [occ.] Public Relations Co-ordinator; [memb.] Concordia College Alumni, International Student Scholarship Honors; [hon.] Dean's List student, Most Outstanding Student of the Year (90), Nedisa Finishing School for Ladies; [oth.writ.] Many published poems in local and college newspapers; [pers.] My inspiration and talent derives from my mother, my best friend, my writing is dedicated to God and my family. [a.] Fairfax, VA.

LOFTUS, BETH
[b.] September 5, 1978, Akron, OH; [p.] Barbara Loftus; [ed.] Our Lady of Mt. Carmel, Villa Joseph Marie High School; [occ.] Student; [memb.] Nativity of Our Lord Cyo, Vice President, PRo-life, CSC; [hon.] Honors, volleyball MVP; [oth.writ.] Several poems; [pers.] In my poetry I express exactly how I feel, it is an outlet for my feelings. [a.] Warminster, PA.

LOGAN, LEONARD
[pen.] Len Logan; [b.] August 15, 1957, Philadelphia; [p.] Welton and Delores Logan; [m.] Gwendolyn J. Logan, June 1, 1983; [ch.] Michael and Lynetta; [ed.] West Philadelphia High School, C.C.P.-Army, American Academy of Broadcasting, National School of Health Tech; [occ.] Mail clerk for P.R.W.T.; [oth.writ.] Short stories, screenplays, etc.; [pers.] Before I die if just one person can say they were glade they knew me, life will have been worth the trip. [a.] Philadelphia, PA.

LONG, KEITH KIMBALL
[pen.] K. Nicholas Long; [b.] July 6, 1967, Elizabeth; [p.] Gloria Long; [ed.] Linden High School, American Association for Laboratory Animal Science; [occ.] Chemical operator; [memb.] OCAW Local 8-575, Greenpeace; [oth.writ.] "Our Father", "Escape", "Without You", "Through A Child's Eyes", "Summer Lover", "My Boy"; [pers.] Once I was lost, but now I am found. I've learned that love is when you give someone something or yourself that no one else may possess, your heart and soul. [a.] Linden, NJ.

LONGEST, ROBIN REBECCA
[b.] December 4, Maryland; [p.] Mary E. Utley and George B. Fisher; [m.] Robert Courtney Longest Jr., August 27, 1994; [ch.] Steven Lawrence Longest; [ed.] 11th grade; [oth.writ.] I have written an editorial on child abuse, I sent it to the Columbia Flyer and it was published; [pers.] After all the things I've been thru, life has treated me well, but it would be better if my mother was in it. She is the reason for my writing the poem. [a.] Baltimore, MD.

LOPEZ, ADOLFO
[pen.] Al Lopez; [b.] December 26, 1953, Havana, Cuba; [p.] Jose and Aida Lopez; [m.] Anita Lopes, August 17, 1974; [ed.] Associate in Science degree with a major in Business Administration, Northern VA Community College; [occ.] Assembly manager; [memb.] Boy Scouts of America; [hon.] Outstanding Leader Award, 1990, 1991, 1992, George Washington District Boy Scouts of America; [oth.writ.] Several poems in English and in Spanish, none published; [pers.] I enjoy writing poetry both in English and Spanish. Most of my poems are about family, life and personal experiences and feelings. I like for my poems to describe something or tell a story and not necessarily to carry a message. [a.] Springfield, VA.

LOPP, BETTYE RUTH
[b.] February 19, 1931, Lexington, KY; [p.] Walter and Bettye Hiteshue; [m.] Eugene B. Lopp, December 19, 1948; [ch.] Ronald Eugene and Linda Marie; [ed.] Two and a half years, Albuquerque High School, Albuquerque, New Mexico, no college; [occ.] Retired homemaker; [memb.] Philanthropic Sorority organization, (Delta Omicrow) in Albuquerque, New Mexico, Stamp Club of Eureka, California; [hon.] The only honors and awards I have ever won were having two wonderful children, a great husband and knowing God is my help in every need; [oth.writ.] A short story written years ago, poems and writings of which none have been published; [pers.] I love good music, it inspires me greatly when I sit and write. I have a wish to bring to those who might read my poems an inner peace and a deep feeling of contentment. Authors I like, Anne Marrow Lindberg, Emily Dickinson and mystery writer Barbara Michaels. [a.] McKinleyville, CA.

LORENZO, AMY
[b.] December 9, 1974; [ed.] Graduated from Hereford High School in 1993 and is currently attending Duke University; [occ.] Student first, materials consultant for the Maryland State Department of Education; [hon.] Angier B. Duke Memorial Scholarship, American Academy of Achievement Golden Scroll, County Executives Award for service to youth; [oth.writ.] This is the first submission by Miss Lorenzo; [pers.] Always, I write for me. Occasionally I share with you. Rarely, I am understood, but that is the fate of everyone-eternally. [a.] Millers, MD.

LOVE, SUZANNE
[b.] February 22, 1946, Los Angeles; [m.] Marv Love; [ch.] Erin, Sean, Monica, Karl, Kelly and Matt; [ed.] Recently returned to college after 20 years, currently a senior at California State University, San Marcos, major Liberal Studies with a special field in Psychology; [occ.] Retired Deputy Sheriff; [memb.] Society of FBI Alumni; [oth.writ.] None published; [pers.] This poem was inspired by my daughter Erin, age 13. [a.] Murrieta, CA.

LOVELAND, GLADYS
[b.] October 23, 1910, Fayette, OH; [p.] Hudson and Hannah Paxson; [m.] Harley Loveland (deceased), December 27, 1927; [ch.] Robert, Joseph and James; [ed.] High school; [occ.] Retired; [memb.] First Baptist Church, American Heart Association; [hon.] First prize in essay on thrift; [oth.writ.] Several poems published in local newspaper; [pers.] I have always greatly enjoyed reading as well as writing poetry. [a.] Wauseon, OH.

LOW, JUSTIN
[b.] February 20, 1967, Edinburg, TX; [p.] Joan Eckert and Ronald Low; [m.] Carmen Low, July 13, 1991; [ed.] Candidate for J.D., St. Mary's University School of Law, San Antonio, TX., May 1995, B.A. Political Science, University of Texas of the Permian Basin; [memb.] Phi Delta Phi, American Bar Association, Student Division; [hon.] American Jurisprudence Award, Dean's List, top 20% class standing at St. Mary's School of Law; [oth.writ.] Poems and legal writings. [a.] San Antonio, TX.

LUCAS, SHARON J.
[pen.] Wife; [b.] December 12,1961, Ohio; [p.] Ted and Cathern Goins; [m.] Douglas W. Lucas, May 6, 1994; [ch.] Candid R. Austing; [oth.writ.] "Bottled Wives Tears" not yet released; [pers.] I want everyone to know that I am a very happy wife and mother. I just thought that there were a lot of women that have felt this way at some point or another in their lives.

LUCE, JENNIFER JEAN
[b.] November 4,1972, Aberdeen, SD; [p.] Robert and Wilma Luce; [ed.] Graduated from Redfield Public High School 1991; [occ.] Work at South Dakota Developmental Center with developmentally disabled people; [memb.] Our Saviors Lutheran Church, Amnesty International, Rock The Vote; [oth.writ.] I won 2 local poetry contests in grade school and had 2 poems published in Prairie Lalinds in junior high school; [pers.] Hates only construction is self destruction. [a.] Redfield, SD.

LUCKETT, RUTH
[pen.] Ruth Luckett; [b.] March 26, 1929, Canton, MS; [p.] Eleas Holbert Sutton and Gilse Sutton; [m.] Fred W. Luckett, February 17, 1951; [ch.] Fred W. Luckett Jr. and Pastor Kennedy C. Luckett; [ed.] B.S. degree and elementary education studies in Gerontology from Tougaloo College and Mississippi State University Ext., NINW (9) years experience as an elementary school teacher; [occ.] One year as counselor and initiator and director of the nutritious program for the elderly in Madison Co.; [memb.] Holy Child Jesus Catholic Church; [hon.] Twelve (12) awards from various state and county organizations; [oth.writ.] Several articles in the Clarion Ledger paper; [pers.] I am very much concerned about the plight of our youth throughout the nation. Love and want to help. [a.] Canton, MS.

LUDOLPH, LORRAINE J.
[pen.] "Raine; [b.] August 21, 1972; [p.] John and Kathleen Ludolph; [ed.] County College of Morris and William Paterson College as a Criminal Justice major; [occ.] Full-time student; [hon.] Dean's List at County College of Morris; [pers.] This poem is dedicated to Robert c. Acker, my inspiration. Robert, I love you. Love always, 'Raine. [a.] Pequannock, NJ.

LUKE, SHAUNA
[b.] November 11, 1980, Silver Spring, MD; [p.] Kathryn Luke; [ed.] Currently a freshman at Westlake High School; [occ.] Student. [a.] Waldorf, MD.

LUSK, KATHY
[b.] April 24,1953, Elkin, NC; [p.] Gwyn and Kathryn Lawrence; [m.] David Lusk, August 21,1993; [ch.] Travis Chipman (22 years), Justin Chipman (19 years); [ed.] Elkin High graduate 1971; [occ.] Officer Manager, Animal Hospital West Winston-Salem, NC; [pers.] On December 12, 1991, I at last found the love I needed or rather love found me. His name is David and I married him in the summer of 1993. [a.] East Bend, NC.

LYNCH, SHERYL SINGLETON
[b.] April 23, 1955, Bronx, NY; [p.] David Singleton and Janet Wooden; [m.] Humphrey Thomas Lynch, January 2, 1979; [ch.] Daniel Colin Lynch; [ed.] Samuel J. Tilden High School, City College of New York; [occ.] Activist for children with disabilities and their families; [memb.] International Women's Writing Guild, The Crystal Quil, Autism Society of America, NY Open Center; [hon.] Honorable Mention, Fresh Meadows Poets; [oth.writ.] Several poems, articles and essays have been published in literary journals and newsletters; [pers.] I strive to express the truth and reality of relationships in my work. [a.] Hollis, NY.

LYNNI, JESSA K.
[pen.] JKL; [b.] July 14,1981, Pueblo; [p.] Becky and step-dad Lee; [pets.] Three dogs Duke, Baby, Kristal, one cat Goto; [ed.] 8th grade, currently a student at Falcon Middle School, after graduation I will attend college to become a lawyer or veterinarian; [occ.] Student; [memb.] KCS Country Club and the L.B.F.R.; [hon.] At the El Paso County Fair I have won many awards for artwork, all fair awards total 4, 1st place, 1 3rd place, 1 reserve champion and the comsitioners trophy; [oth.writ.] I have many other unpublished poems and plan to write a book or two before I finish high school; [pers.] Believe in yourself, you may fail but never give up. If you never give up you can't fail. My poem was inspired by Ms. Meuller and class (thank you). [a.] Peyton, CO.

LYONS, ALLEN F.
[b.] November 8, 1936, E. Millinocket, ME; [p.] John Allen and Marie G. Lyons; [m.] Carol A. Belmore Lyons, February 16, 1968; [ch.] Mark (deceased), Matthew, Luke and Sean; [ed.] Attended Husson Business College (Bangor, ME.) and University of Hartford; [occ.] Senior Account Analyst or Liability Insurance for Fortune 1,000 Companies; [memb.] Currently Knights of Peter Claver (New Haven, CT.) Thresholds (CT), previous, Connecticut Jaycees (Crime Prevention Chairman), Madison (CT) Exchange Club, Madison Boy Scout (troop 491) Board of Directors; [hon.] Certified aids instructor (American Red Cross), certificate of appreciation (New Haven correctional center); [oth.writ.] None published; [pers.] Trust nature, when left alone it replenishes, even improves on itself. It defined what freedom truly is. [a.] New Haven, CT.

LYONS, CYNTHIA L.
[b.] September 16, 1964, Cincinnati, OH; [p.] Janet R. Helbig; [ed.] U.s. Air Force Technical School, Electro Environmental, current sophomore at University of Alaska Anchorage; [occ.] Full time student University of Alaska Anchorage; [hon.] USAF Airman of the quarter, January - March 1992, Honor graduate USAF basic training, National Honor Society graduate (high school), Dean's List University of Alaska Anchorage; [pers.] My poem "Golden One" published herein is a reflection of my philosophy of life. I try to be happy, think positive and feel my emotions, but not retain anger. I wish this for all people but especially for those I love. [a.] Anchorage, AK.

MACHOVER, MAURICE
[pen.] Mack The Knife; [b.] December 5, 1931, New York City; [p.] Ray Bernfeld and Fred Machover; [m.] Ruth Machover, 1964 (deceased); [ed.] Brooklyn College, Columbia University, New York University; [occ.] Professor at St. John's University; [memb.] Scientific Professional Societies, New Press Literary Society; [hon.] Sigma Xi, Pi Mu Epsilon, Magna Cum Laude; [oth. writ.] Scientific and Mathematics publications, including Mathematical poems and limericks in Math journals; [pers.] Favorite poets that inspired me are Edgar Allan Poe and Alexander Pope. [a.] Jamaica, NY.

MacKINNON, CATHY M.
[b.] September 17, 1979, South Africa; [p.] Denise and Anthony MacKinnon; [ed.] Dunvegan Primary School, St. Agnes School, Holy Rosary School, Qualters Middle School, Mansfield High School; [occ.] Student; [memb.] National French Honor Society, Who's Who of American Students; [hon.] Presidential Award, National French Honor Society, Top Scholastic Student; [pers.] Everything will be okay. [a.] Mansfield, MA.

MacLEAN, KENNETH J.
[b.] May 2, 1926, Scotland; [p.] John and Catherine MacLean; [m.] Eileen Vivian MacLean, April 22, 1949; [ch.] Dianne, Catherine, Frances, Vivian; [ed.] Waterloo Lutheran University, University of Toronto; [occ.] Retired high school teacher, counselor; [memb.] Ontario Secondary School Teachers Federation, Canadian Guidance and Counseling Association; [hon.] Royal Air Force, WW II; [oth. writ.] Twenty poems, six short stories, one novel, articles, essays; [pers.] Enjoy clean humour and literature. Like Robert Burns I try to "see ourselves as others see us" in my writing. [a.] Brantford, Ont, Canada.

MADDEN, SUE
[b.] September 16, 1944, Alton, MO; [p.] Everett and Ella Walters; [m.] Samuel, May 21, 1963; [ch.] Donna and Allen; [ed.] Couch High School, Franklin Tech College; [occ.] Social Worker - State of Kansas; [oth. writ.] Many poems, songs and short stories; [pers.] My writings are done by inspirations. I trust they will inspire those that read them also and be a blessing to them. [a.] Pittsburg, KS.

MADDOX, KAY
[b.] December 7, 1950, Rushville, IN; [p.] Raymond and Mildred Akers; [m.] Raymond, August 14, 1971; [ch.] Meredith, Matthew; [ed.] IU School of Nursing owner of "On-Site Training Service; [occ.] Public Health Educator, Adult Education; [memb.] Main Street Christian Church, American Heart Association, National Safety Council, Tri Kappa Sorority, Lladro Collection Society, Alliance of the Americans Dental Association, American Nurses Association; [hon.] "I Dare You Leadership" award, Pace Maker/Pacesetter awards, Tri Kappa of the Year, Richard G. Leegar Excellence in Public Service Series; [oth. writ.] Other poems have been published or given as personal gifts to friends and family; [pers.] This piece was written in honor of my daughter's sixteenth birthday to express her love for the piano and her car. "The Grand" it is lovingly dedicated to Meredith. [a.] Rushville, IN.

MAHON, MARINNA
[pen.] Marinna Mahon; [b.] December 27, 1950, Philadelphia, PA; [p.] Marie and Joseph (deceased); [ch.] Two daughters; [ed.] Rosemont College, John Carroll University, University Heights, American Bilingual Institute; [occ.] Teacher, writer (two national newsletters); [memb.] Philadelphia Writer's Organization, American Mensa LTD, American Association University Women, Friends of Rosemont Library; [hon.] BA-graduated department honors (Field of History), Teacher Development Scholarship, John Carroll University, University Heights, OH other awards-Humane Society in Mexico City, AAUW, Mensa positions; [oth. writ.] Two newsletters since 1991 within American Mensa Ltd, many poems published with Mensa, including Mensa Espana National magazine. Published own small book of poems in 1991 of published poems; [pers.] I believe in the basic goodness and loving nature of all people. As teacher, I try to make this part of my students shine to share. As a writer, my effort is to encourage growth in awareness. [a.] Philadelphia, PA.

MAHONEY, MICHAEL PATRICK
[b.] July 4, 1956, Amsterdam, NY; [p.] Patricia Mahoney; [m.] Denise Smith Mahoney, July 22, 1989; [ch.] Ryann Patricia, Kelly Lynn; [ed.] W.H. Lynch High School. Community College of Vermont; [oth. writ.] Several essays and short stories. [a.] Pittsford, VT.

MAHONY, CARMEN
[pen.] Elizabeth McKenna; [b.] March 10, 1984, Omaha, NE; [p.] Joe and Irma Mahoney; [ed.] Assumption Elementary School; [oth. Dreams. [a.] Omaha, NE.

MAHSHI, DINA
[b.] February 28, 1974, Ternuzen, Holland; [p.] Hana and George Mahshi; [pers.] This poem is dedicated to my brother, Omar Mahshi, who passed away in April '94 at 21 years old. I hope this poem helps, those who have lost a loved one, in making them realized that life can not stop. You have a job to be done on this earth. So when you feel like you can't go on --read this poem -- and do it for them. [a.] Woodland, CA.

MAJOR, GREG
[pen.] Gregory P. major; [b.] June 16, 1964, Lewiston, ME; [p.] Lawrence and Sally Ann Major; [ed.] High school, Heavy Equipment School in Navy; [occ.] Recovering from a Traumatic Brian Injury occurred in 1985; [memb.] Seabees of America, Paralyzed Veterans of America, New Hampshire Head Injury Association; [hon.] Chosen Achiever of the Year by Telephone Pioneers of America Region 12; [pers.] Even when life deals you a bad hand never give up. I was in a coma for eleven weeks after my accident in 1985. I was suppose to die or remain a vegetable. I still have a lot of obstacles to overcome, but I have also overcome starting over like an infant from the beginning. [a.] Peterboro, NH.

MALESON, LARRY
[b.] May 1, 1969, Baltimore, MD; [p.] Mark and Betty Maleson; [ed.] Steinert High, Mecer County College, Mecer County High School of the Performing Arts; [hon.] "McCarter Theatre Award" Top Actor in the Senior Class; [oth. writ.] I have many years worth of writing, none of which I have ever attempted to have published. My writing started out very personal and private, but that has started to change as I grow older; [pers.] To me, writing is a genuine release from regular life. I can kill, die, or exist at any level. I can move so slow it almost seems like returning. I am truly fascinated by the unknown. To me, nothing tests the brain like imagination. [a.] Trenton, NJ.

MALEWSKI, NICHOLAS
[b.] April 18, 1972, Columbia, MO; [p.] Ed and Connie Malewski; [ed.] Missouri Western State College; [pers.] I have been interested in writing since I was 15 years old. My other interests include songwriting, playing, guitar, painting, and reading philosophy. [a.] St. Joseph, MO.

MALLORY, MAURICE ALEXANDER
[b.] April 6, 1906, Santo Domingo; [p.] John and Clemencia Mallory; [m.] Murel Louise Mallory; [ch.] Marcella, Maxine, Ruth, Maurice, Leonard, Alfred, Yvonne, Helena; [ed.] Music teacher, High School Trinity College of Music, higher local University Extension Conservatory; [occ.] Piano tuning with diploma; [memb.] Church of God, member of Faculty of Church of God Bible School as Music Teacher, Teacher of Poem Writing, Song Writing, Vocal Music; [hon.] Church of God: 1967 Efficiency Award in Music, Outstanding Contribution the Field of Music 1990, Dedicated Service to the Church of God Convention Choir 1989, 20 Years of Dedicated Service as Music Instructor 1990, honors from Gospel Music Workshop of America; [oth. writ.] Layman of the Year 1991 award for Outstanding Service to Department of Lay Ministers. Many poems written for our theme songs of our conventions; [pers.] I strive to give a sermon in every poem I write. I have others that I will submit from time to time if you so advise. [a.] Nassau, Bahamas.

MALVEAUX, ROY L.
[pen.] Roy L. Malveaux; [b.] December 10, 1950, Beaumont, TX; [p.] Vivian and Mamie Malveaux; [m.] Kaffie Loraine Malveaux, November 10, 1984; [ch.] Roy Jr., Latedia, Michell, Tina, Felix and Leslie; [ed.] Hebert High School, Lamar University, Del Mar College, Guadalupe Theology Service School; [occ.] Machine Shop Inspector; [oth. writ.] Other writings in local newspapers, publish book "The Signs of the Times" Vantage Press; [pers.] I have only one life to live...and I will do my best to please God and serve mankind in hopes that my living may not be in vain...[a.] Corpus Christi, TX.

MANAL, CANDIDO M.
[pen.] Ed. M. Manal; [b.] October 3, 1930, Infanta, Pangasinan, Philippines; [p.] Juan M. Manal and Juana Minas; [m.] Sally M. Mozo, April 26, 1959; [ch.] Arlene, Teodoro, Angie Timerding, Ferdinand, BSEE, Janette and Monette; [ed.] Graduated from the Philippine School of Business Administration; [occ.] Materials/Warehouse Manager, Librarian, Russiaville Branch Library Volunteer; [memb.] Green Thumb Inc. and National Arbor Day Foundation; [hon.] Several community service awards, Dean's list, most outstanding member-Personnel Management Association; [oth. writ.] My Love is Like An Open Sea, Aurora (copyrighted songs)-both are unpublished and unrecorded; [pers.] Poetry is the real expression of the heart. It doesn't mature or die. In my writings, I intend to arouse feeling and emotion of love for the young and especially the older generation. [a.] Russiaville, IN.

MANDELBAUM, MICHELLE
[b.] December 9, 1975, Los Angeles, CA; [p.] Rick and Margo Mandelbaum; [ed.] Escondido High School, Palomar College; [occ.] Student; [memb.] California Scholarship Federation; [hon.] Who's Who Among American High School Students; [oth. writ.] First published poem; [pers.] In a world of change and isolation, we can't overlook our closest friend - the mind. Bryan - thank you for easing the burden of self-realization. You are an inspiration to me. [a.] Escondido, CA.

MANDILL, JAMI J.
[b.] August 15, 1981, Slidell, LO; [p.] James and Sandra Mandill; [ed.] St. Margarey Mary School; [pers.] No matter what age you are everyone can write poetry. [a.] Mandeville, LO.

MANN, MONISHA
[pen.] Monisha; [b.] August 2, 1979, London, England; [p.] Katie and Gurnam Mann; [ed.] Hoover High School; [occ.] Volunteer-Valley Children's Hospital; [memb.] Dance Works; [hon.] Honor Roll, Perfect Attendance. [a.] Fresno, CA.

MANNING, NORMA JEAN
[b.] November 22, 1931, Scranton, PA; [p.] Hilda and Floyd Depew; [m.] William J. (Deceased), December 20, 1952; [ed.] Clarks Summit/Clarks Green High School, Keystone Jr. College, Moses Taylor Hospital School of Medical Technology, University of California Long Beach; [occ.] Medical Technologist, FHP, California Regional Laboratory; [memb.] ASCP (American Society of Clinical Pathologists); [pers.] Appreciation of all that our creator has given us and dedication to preserving these gifts. [a.] Costa Mesa, CA.

MANSHACK, DUSTIN
[b.] July 27, 1979, Shreveport, LA; [p.] Thomas and Melanie Manshack; [ed.] Northwood High School; [memb.] National Junior Honor Society, Z Club, 4-H, National Wildlife Federation; [hon.] Principal's List, Presidential Academic Fitness Award; [oth. writ.] Terse Verse published in Ascending; [pers.] Its better to have tried and failed than to never have tried at all. [a.] Shreveport, LA

MANUEL-DONLEY, JOLEEN MARIE
[pen.] Jo-Jo; [b.] January 23, 1975, Salem, OR; [p. Robert L. Donley, Vickie L. Laderlich; [m.] John P., August 7, 1993; [ch.] Ashleigh Manuel (unborn child); [ed.] Douglas McKay High, Trend College [occ.] Legal Secretary and very busy mom; [memb. Christian Church Affiliations (non-denominational); [hon.] Awarded for basketball, volleyball 4-H and sewing. College awarded Spelling, English and most improved typing. Was honored on the Dean's list for a 4.0 and perfect attendance; [oth writ.] Only to my husband; [pers.] I will become successful and achieve the best to my ability. I wi never quit learning. [a.] Turner, OR.

MAPLESDEN, JANELLE
[pen.] Renee Johnson; [b.] February 8, 197 Houston, TX; [p.] Irene E. and Axel R. Maplesden [ed.] South Houston High School; [occ.] Sophomore student; [pers.] I wrote this poem because a or at least most of my friends like Science, but

didn't because my class was rude, loud and the teacher didn't control them. [a.] Houston, TX.

MAPUANA, KAHANU S.
[pen.] Mops/Tida; [b.] March 4, 1955, Cheyenne, Wyoming; [p.] Anthony Bee and Elvera K. Bee; [m.] Benjamin, March 30, 1974; [ch.] Benjamin Kanenui, Chad Keone, Starr Mapuana and Jarett Kawika; [ed.] Roosevelt High; [occ.] Secretary K.J.L. Associates Real Estate Business; [memb.] The Church of Jesus Christ of Latter-Day Saints; [oth. writ.] Several unpublished poems; [pers.] Attitude in life is important. Your Attitude will determine your Altitude. Get a head-start in life...SMILE!!! [a.] Honolulu, HI.

MARINO, ELIZABETH
[b.] March 13, 1959, Drexel Hill, PA; [p.] Samuel J., Elizabeth Mendicilo; [m.] Divorced; [ch.] Angela, Amamos; [ed.] 2 years college; [occ.] 2 part-time jobs; [memb.] 800 Market Research Interviewed; [oth. writ.] Several works of poetry, one soon to be published in newsletter for the disabled; [pers.] In my writing I seek to glorify Jesus Christ my savior and make the most of my gift. [a.] Drexel Hill, PA.

MARINO, LISA
[pen.] Lisa Marino; [b.] January 21, 1975, England; [p.] Cynthia Marino; [ed.] Little of this, little of that also a high school diploma; [occ.] Working with Westchester Association Retarded Citizens (W.A.R.C.) White Plains - Community Abulette Yonkers; [hon.] Too many to mention; [oth. writ.] None published but I write as it comes...; [pers.] I really don't call my thoughts poems, I think of them as "Lisa's mind explosions". They just pop into my mind, so I put them on paper. [a.] Yonkers, NY.

MARISSA, MUNOZ AGUILLON
[pen.] Marissa Munoz; [b.] November 1, 1944, Reynolds, Mex; [p.] Caretano Aguillon and Diana Morales; [m.] Pablo Munoz, Sept. 1991; [ch.] Sgt. Diana E. Tucker, Sanjuana M. Elvia I. Creamer, Dinora M., Manorao M., Maria M.; [ed.] GED/ Notary/Travel Advisor/Income Tax Prep/Public Relations Radio and Newspaper; [occ.] TRavel Advisor; [hon.] Red Cross - Internal Revenue Service; [oth. writ.] Songs, articles, poems (some have been published); [pers.] What are we doing to children? [a.] Houston, TX.

MARKHAM, ANDREA ELIZABETH
[b.] August 28, 1977, Osage, IA; [p.] Richard and Marge Markham; [ed.] Elementary and high school; [occ.] Student at Osage Community High School; [oth. writ.] Unknown stories and poems; [pers.] I dedicate this poem to my sister Angela with love. Angie was in a serious car accident which almost took her life at the young age of 18. Now 7 months later we are closer than ever. [a.] Osage, IA.

MARSAR, CHRISTOPHER J.
[b.] December 17, 1954, Sayville, NY; [m.] Jackie; [ch.] Zachary, Sammi and Raymond; [occ.] Caterer/chef; [pers.] My poem was inspired by my childhood experiences visiting my grandparents in Vermont. I was blessed to be part of a big family, with parents who in my eyes are the reason I can strive to keep going forward. To live life to the fullest. I dedicate this poem to my grandmother: Mary E. Phelon, and to Sammi, and Zachary. My heart will always be theirs.

MARSHALL, JENNIFER
[pen.] Jamie; [b.] February 18, 1946, Wetaskiwin, Alberta, CAN; [p.] Louis Gallie (deceased) and Alice Kerik; [m.] Marshall Stephen Brent, August 12, 1967-divorced 1978; [ch.] Wendy Lynn Marie, Sherri Lee Ann, Steven Michael Louis; [ed.] Bashaw Elementary -completed grade 8, Bashaw High School grade 10 1963, School for Nursing Aides, graduated as a Licensed Registered Nursing Aide April 1965, Licensed Practical Nurse in British Columbia 1971, Transition Training Program for Battered Women Calgary, Alberta, CAN 1985, BSN Training and Resources (Life Skills Program 1986), Kelsey Campus (ABE) completed grade 11 and 12 graduated 1991; [occ.] Registered Nursing Aide, Waitress, Bartender, Mother, Grandmother; [memb.] Saskatchewan Writer's Guild; [oth. writ.] Poetry assignment - published Kelsey Campus 1991, Christmas Reflections (Expository Essay) published Bashaw Star - Christmas 1992, descriptive Overview - published Bashaw Star 1993, Christmas Reflections - to be published in Western People (Western Producer) Christmas of 1993; [pers.] We have come to believe in man instead of God and in this belief have destroyed the beauty that is God-given: I see the changes - some good and some bad, and fear the bad, knowing that mankind is spinning out of control on his own ego and corruption. [a.] Calgary, Alberta, CAN.

MARSZALEK, VALERY
[pen.] Valery Marszalek; [b.] November 13, 1984, Resurrection Hospital Chicago; [p.] Stan and Donna; [ed.] Roy Elementary 4th grade; [occ.] Student; [memb.] American Girls Book Club; [oth. writ.] The Flying Car; [pers.] I love to read and write.

MARTIN, ANDY
[pen.] Andy Martin; [b.] August 19, 1952, Raton, N. Mex.; [p.] Mr. and Mrs. Billie Martin; [m.] Carmen Orlene Martin, August 20, 1983; [ed.] Portales High School; [occ.] New Mexico State Highway Department; [oth. writ.] I wrote about 30 of these and all are different; [pers.] I try to write things that will inspire other people and I hope they will like it. [a.] Portales, N.M.

MARTIN, CHRIS
[b.] August 13, 1979, Denver, CO; [p.] Howard Martin and Mary Schrodt; [ed.] Schooling in Brussels, Belgium; Arlington, VA; Zurich, Switzerland; Copenhagen, Denmark and now in high school at Potomac in VA; [occ.] Student; [oth. writ.] Several other short stories and poems written over the last 2 years; [pers.] A person should know that one is never completely tied down to one place or thing, and when you realize this, really see this, you'll find life easier and more enjoyable than you did before. [a.] Arlington, VA.

MARTIN, MARGARET C.
[b.] July 27, 1933, Hickory Grove, SC; [p.] James and Mary Wylie; [m.] Arthur, March 6, 1955; [ch.] Bonita Louann, Regina Sue, Matilda Kaye; [ed.] Blacksburg High School; [occ.] Housewife; [hon.] Received the Editors Choice award 1993 and in 1994 for poem "In My World" published by "The National Library of Poetry in "The Space Between". The poem "Little Ones" will be published in the special edition, "Best Poems of 1995". "Dear Bridget" will be published in "Journey of the Mind". [oth. writ.] A poem "I Love You My Dear" was published by The National Library of Poetry in "The Coming of Dawn". Have written three children's books, waiting to be published; [pers.] This poem was written in the memory of my dear little dog, Bridget. She was so protective of me and wanted to be with me every minute. She is missed and always will be in my heart and mind. I think of her often. Rest in peace my loving friend. [a.] Blackburg, SC.

MARTIN, MARTHA
[pen.] Martie Wiker; [b.] September 18, 1979, Chicago; [p.] Tracey Moats and Christ and Joann Wiker; [ed.] Washington Township High School; [pers.] My writings come from my heart. They are about my feelings and my outlook on life. Also, about my life experiences. [a.] Turnersville, NJ.

MARTINEZ, MARJORIE
[pen.] Giggles; [b.] March 8, 1975, Brooklyn; [p.] Carmen and Saturnino Martinez; [m.] Fiance' - Alexander W. Levy; [ed.] Satellite Academy High; [occ.] Student; [memb.] Intergenerational Services; [hon.] High school honor roll, educational award to further educational skills. Award for my time and dedication volunteering; [oth. writ.] Several poems published in I.G.S. yearbook, and some in my poetry class; [pers.] I strive to reflect the goodness of love and romance. I was influenced by Robert Frost. [a.] Brooklyn, NY.

MARTINEZ, MONICA
[pen.] Monica Martinez; [b.] January 14, 1978, Fresno, CA; [p.] David and Rosie Martinez; [ed.] Amistad High School; [occ.] Scholar; [pers.] I am a poet of myself and of family and friends. By receiving numerous amounts of encouragement I decided to enter your contest. [a.] Indie, CA.

MARTINI, PAUL
[b.] January 31, 1979, Los Angeles; [p.] Maria and Pete Martini; [ed.] Downey High; [memb.] Science Club, German Club; [hon.] Academic Fitness Award, Award for Honor 4.0 G.P.A.; [pers.] Strive for the best, success is waiting just around the corner. [a.] Downey, CA.

MARVIN, JENNIFER ELIZABETH
[b.] September 7, 1976, Jeannette, PA; [ed.] Hempfield Senior High School; [occ.] Attractions for Walt Disney World; [oth. writ.] I've had one other poem published. I write children's stories also; [pers.] Always keep love and hope in your heart. Believe in yourself and your dreams. Never give up and strive to do your best each day. [a.] Poinciana, FL.

MASON, DARRIN
[b.] July 22, 1969, San Francisco, CA; [p.] Claude and Norma Mason; [ed.] National College, Sioux Falls, SD; [occ.] Electronics Assembler at Raven Industries; [oth. writ.] Rose, published in The National Library of Poetry's book "The Space Between", other unpublished poems. [a.] Sioux Falls, SD.

MASON, NICOLE
[b.] December 8, 1979, Middlesex, NJ; [p.] Laurence and Nancy Mason; [ed.] Our Lady of Mt. Virgin, Von E. Manger Middle School, Middlesex High School; [occ.] Student. [a.] Middlesex, NJ.

MASON, THOMAS
[b.] October 30, 1971, Long Island, NY; [p.] William and Mary Jane Mason; [m.] Mary Lee; [ch.] Corinne Tiffany, Janine Elizabeth; [ed.] High school; [oth. writ.] I write poetry for my own personal satisfaction.. I hope to get my own book of poetry published; [pers.] I like to express good, evil and love of life in my writing. I'm influenced by Jim Morrison. [a.] Allentown, PA.

MATA, GENEVA
[b.] August 29, 1957, Houston, TX; [p.] Leroy and Edna Daley; [m.] Demos, October 30, 1985; [ch.] Cheryl and Paul Hernandez; [ed.] Milby High School, San Jacinto College; [occ.] Accounting Clerk; [memb.] Pasadena Civic Club, Greenpeace; [pers.] I also have 3 beautiful grandchildren Paula Marie and John Paul Hernandez and David Giovanni Soto. [a.] Pasadena, TX.

MATHENA, TRACI JOHNSON
[pen.] Traci Johnson Mathena; [b.] May 15, 1970, Baltimore, MD; [p.] Earl and Christine Johnson; [m.] Larry Richard Mathena, Jr., November 20, 1992; [ed.] University of Maryland College Park; [occ.] Freelance writer, teacher, master's degree candidate; [memb.] Society of Professional Journalists, Phi Beta Kappa; [hon.] SPJ Public Service Writing award; [oth. writ.] Various non-fiction articles for The Baltimore Sun (6 years employed with the paper), two cover stories for The Sun Magazine (freelance); [pers.] Writing is an extension of self. There can be no true "poems" or "stories" without the author's personality, reflections, or beliefs coming through in the writing. Through writing, we learn; through learning, we live. [a.] Owings Mills, MD.

MATKINS, BRADLEY
[m.] Vicky Matkins; [occ.] Owns landscaping business; [pers.] I believe in people. I look for their good qualities. I am partially disabled and I believe that causes me to have so much compassion for others. [a.] Omaha, NE.

MATTEI, LINETTE
[pen.] Giza; [b.] September 8, 1973, Ponce, PR; [p.] Ermitania Caraballo and Carlos J. Mattei; [ed.] Asuncion R. de Sala High School, University of Puerto Rico-Ponce; [occ.] Student-Psychology; [memb.] Fontecha Premier Modeling and Refining Academy; University of Puerto Rico in Ponce Choir; The National Arbor Day Foundation; [oth. writ.] Over 25 poems, unpublished; [pers.] What's written, is been written; And there's nothing more to say. [a.] Guayanilla, PR.

MATHEWS, JOHNNA
[pen.] Phoenix Ralston; [b.] April 25, 1980, Suffolk, VA; [p.] Nancy Larson and John Mathews III; [ed.] Nensemond River High School; [occ.] Volunteer at humane society; [memb.] Future Business Leaders of America, volunteer at Humane Society, United Colors Pen Pals, Adopt A Highway, Children International; [hon.] MVP 1993 Player for 'minor' Bay Harbor Dolphins football team; 1992 Queen Paper and Pollution; [pers.] I am quite unique although by some it is considered strangeness. I consider myself to be the one and only of me there is, was, or ever will be. So say I'm strange, I love bring different. [a.] Suffolk, VA.

MATTHEWS, BEVERLY
[pen.] Beverly Matthews; [b.] December 13, 1950; [p.] Jim Hall and Joyce Williams; [m.] Wayne Henry Matthews, September 18, 1987; [ch.] Stacey Sikes, Jason Sikes and Melinda Sikes and two stepchildren-Robert and Jessica Matthews; [ed.] Marion C. Early High School, Ozark Technical College; [occ.] Housewife and amateur writer; [memb.] Morrisville Assembly of God Church; [pers.] I am profoundly honored and proud to have my poetry chosen to be published by the National Library of Poetry. I have always admired the early poets, and find some of the poets of my generation fascinating. [a.] Springfield, MS.

MAURY, K.R. JR.
[pen.] K.R. Maury, Jr.; [b.] May 20, 1970, Lafayette, IN; [p.] Brenda Rollins and K.R. Maury, Sr.; [m.] Monica, June 27, 1992; [ch.] Alene Morgan Maury; [ed.] Woodlawn Senior, Catonsville Community College; [occ.] Certified Nursing Assistant; [memb.] Susquehanna Writer's Group, Writer's Reading; [oth. writ.] Susquehanna Writer's Group Journal, Western Digest; [pers.] Go, Go! Power Rangers! [a.] Lansdale, PA.

MAXBERRY, DENNIS LEE
[pen.] Flint T. Holliday; [b.] May 11, 1959, Lexington, KY; [p.] William Clay Maxberry and Evelyn Carter; [ed.] Southwestern College of Business, Southern Career Institute; [occ.] Freelance Writer; [memb.] National Writer's Association, Dean's List Southwestern College of Business, Newsletter Editor in 1987, Certificate of Achievement from Southern Career Institute, School of Paralegalism, Instructor is now Professor of Law at Harvard; [hon.] Presidential Citation 1977, The United States Third Armored Calvary Regimen; Dean's List Southwestern College of Business, Certificate of Merit Southern Career Institute, from Mr. Gorman of Harvard University; [oth. writ.] The Federal Financial Welfare Act-The Money (is) Gold Bill-The Amended Bill of Rights for Kentucky, Trademarks in 1985. Copyrighted Anti-Antons with its Trademarks; [pers.] A humanitarian don't have to be a philanthropic although, along with the need there will always be the want. To be influenced, brings along with it the demand, or the goal...[a.] West Allis, WI.

MAXSON, PAUL
[b.] March 21, 1955, Delano, Ca; [p.] Edwin and Mary Maxson; [ed.] Cal Poly San Luis Obispo, The Ohio State University; [occ.] Nutritionist/Sales Manager; [memb.] American Society of Animal Science, Dairy Science Association, California Scholarship Federation; [hon.] L.E. Kuncie Award, Outstanding Graduate Student, Ohio State University Animal Sciences.

MAXWELL, ELISHA
[pen.] Elly Maxwell; [b.] October 1, 1978, Salt Lake City, UT; [p.] Beth and Larry Maxwell; [ed.] Twin Falls High School; [occ.] Sophomore student; [hon.] Won first place in Idaho's Young Author;s in 1991; [oth. writ.] An article published in the Idaho Catholic Register in 1991; [pers.] My pen is the voice of my heart. [a.] Twin Falls, ID.

MAY, DEBORAH LAURSEN
[b.] February 4, 1954, Penn Yan, NY; [p.] Lynn and Vangie (Daggett) Laursen; [m.] Greg, August 13, 1978; [ch.] Don, Daryl and Jacquie; [ed.] U.S. Army, University of Maryland, Genesee Community College; [occ.] Inactive LPN, student, wife, mother and dreamer; [oth. writ.] Several notebooks of poems and essays, in the planning stage of writing a book about my experiences living with Manic Depression and living through and beyond It with the help of a therapist who refused to let me give up on myself; [pers.] In the immortal words of Steppenwolf: "It's Never Too Late to Start All Over Again". The group Chicago sung in "Skinny Box": "Love your brothers and sisters and love'll come back to you." I couldn't say it any better. [a.] Waterport, NY.

MAYHEW, KHRYSTINA KATHLEEN
[b.] November 27, 1972, Albuquerque, NM; [ed.] La Cueva High, New Mexico State University, New Mexico Art Center; [occ.] Student in commercial graphic and advertising art; [memb.] Communication Arts of New Mexico, President Student Chapter New Mexico Advertising Federation; [pers.] My grandmother read poetry to me every week, Robert Frost was my favorite, but she was who inspired me to create and write. Thank you always. [a.] Albuquerque, NM.

MAYLATH, MELISSA ANNE
[b.] December 11, 1973, North Bergen, NJ; [p.] Jayne F. Maylath; [ed.] Cliffside Peak High, Bergen Community College; [occ.] Student; [oth. writ.] High school literary magazine - Pegasus, high school newspaper-Cliffside Courier, high school yearbook staff; [pers.] I love to reach out through writing. [a.] Cliffside Park, NJ.

McCARTHY, MICHELLE JANINE
[b.] March 14, 1982, Fountain Valley; [p.] Justin and Kathleen; [ed.] Shorecliffs Middle School; [occ.] Student; [hon.] Citizenship awards, D.A.R.F. essay winner, Nuclear Challenge science project; [oth. writ.] Short stories and poems in a scrapbook; [pers.] I have been writing since I was four years old. Always thinking up new ideas for stories and poems. [a.] San Clemente, CA.

McCLURE, ALLISON
[b.] August 4, 1091, Corinth, MS; [p.] Kathleen McClure, Jerry McClure; [ed.] APAC Academic and Performing Arts School; [occ.] Student; [memb.] Children's choir of Mississippi, National Junior Honor Society, Duke University Talent Search program; [pers.] The art of writing is to make writing the art. [a.] Jackson, MS.

McCOLLUM, EUGENE H.
[pen.] Mac McCollum; [b.] December 26, 1923, Van Wert, OH; [p.] C.D. McCollum, Emma Johnson; [ed.] High School, art schools; [occ.] Retired ex-marine ; [memb.] All Veterans and Marine Corps League, Confederate Air Force, D.A.V.; [hon.] Six Gardener awards, the Renaissance Towers; [oth. writ.] "A Rose", published in this years Winter edition, "Amber Curtain" published 1976 in V.A. newspaper; [pers.] The works of God, in time, people, places and things, is my main inspiration, and helping to make others happy, and in turn helping myself and faith in the future. [a.] Hammond, IN.

McCOOL, YOLANDA
[p.] Migdonia and Aristides; [m.] William; [ch.] Barbara and Raquel; [ed.] 2 1/2 years of college; [hon.] Regents High School diploma, Citation of Honor, Certificate of Merit, Certificate of Excellence in Writing, Honors Certificate in Graphic Arts and Spanish; [oth. writ.] "The Sisters of Love" in Dusting Off Dreams, "Ursula, The Butterfly", in Dark Side of The Moon and "The Poet" in Best Poems of 1995"; [pers.] The inspiration to write this poem emerged from the special relationship I have with my dearest friends and my family members. [a.] Greenbelt, MD.

McDADE, DERRICK A.
[b.] January 21, 1976, St. Petersburg, Fl; [p.] Irene McDade; [ed.] Gibbs Senior High School; [occ.] U.S. Navy fire control man; [a.] St. Petersburg, FL.

McDANIEL, WILLIE
[b.] April 18, 1953, Houston, TX; [p.] Alex McDaniel and Norcie Schooler; [ch.] Ashley Monique Perkins; [ed.] Bishop College, El Campo High; [occ.] Spokesperson/Community Activist/ Freelance Writer; [oth. writ.] Several poems published in local newspapers, news columns in the El Campo Leader News, San Antonio Register and Houston Forward Times Newspapers; [pers.] I seek to express the sum total of those ideas and events by which life is bound. My writing pen have been and continues to be guided by incurred experiences and by the aspirations of others. [a.] Las Vegas, NV.

McDERMOTT, BETTY FOBAIR
[b.] April 16, 1930, Butte, NB; [p.] Dr. Roscoe Fobair, Annette Fobair; [m.] Dr. Donald Giffin (divorced, August 20, 1950; [ch.] Robert Bruce Giffen; [ed.] Univ of California Santa Barbara, California American University; [occ.] International management and human relations consultant, writer; [memb.] UCSB Alumni Association; [hon.] Who's Who of American Women, Who's Who of the West, Dictionary of International Biography, Two Thousand Women of Achievement; [oth. writ.] Co-author "California Cooks!", countless newspaper and magazine articles relating

to management and human behavior; [pers.] My life purpose is to assist in transforming negative energies into positive actions through improving communications by consulting, speaking, and writing. [a.] North Hollywood, CA.

McDONALD, BROOKE
[b.] July 31, 1979, Florence, AL;' [p.] Jerry and Emily McDonald; [occ.] Student; [pers.] I believe God made this possible for me and I wish to dedicate this to Him. [a.] Florence, AL.

McDONALD, S. RAMELLE
[b.] April 23, 1923, Albemarle, NC; [p.] Mr. and Mrs. L. C. Lowder; [m.] Rev. Howard F. McDonald, September 25, 1948; [ch.] Carla Elliott, Myra Gonino; [ed.] MSU, Scarrit College; [occ.] Retired elementary school teacher; [memb.] Delta Kappa Gamma, MEA, NEA, MARSP, editor, "Chatter That Matters"; [hon.] President, United Methodist Women, AARP Bouquet of Roses; [oth. writ.] Fast Spiritual Food; [pers.] My philosophy of life is to show your faith by your actions. They speak louder than words. [a.] Jackson, MI.

McDOW, ASHLEY MARIE
[b.] JUne 12, 1981, West Germany; [p.] Michael and Robin McDow; [ed.] Lynden Middle School; [occ.] Student; [hon.] 4.0 GPA, 1st place Isom Spelling Bee; [oth. writ.] "Devotion", "If I Were the Teacher"; [pers.] Life is too short, don't sweat the small stuff. And it's all small stuff. Enjoy life. [a.] Lynden, WA.

McDOWELL, WEBB RANDALL
[pen.] Randolph Webster McDowell; [b.] January 31, 1958, Minneapolis, MN; [p.] Leslie and Carol McDowell; [ed.] DeAnza College; [occ.] Self-employed electronic component broker; [memb.] NAFC, NRA, local library; [hon.] My first to be published; [pers.] Always be yourself. Never worry about what people think of you. Call your mother once a week. Be nice to all, and smile as often as yo can. [a.] Redondo Beach, CA.

McDUFFIE, CHARLES
[b.] November 14, 1922, Plant City, FL; [m.] Lathene McDuffie, November 9, 1975; [ch.] Charles McDuffie III, Florida AMU; [occ.] Retired;

McELROY, COURTNEY JANNINE
[b.] April 24, 1982, OH; [ed.] Kiddie College Headstart, Belle Haven Elementary, Shilohview Elementary, Trotwood Junior High; [occ.] Peer mediation; [memb.] Band, Honors Society; [hon.] Presidents Academic award, many other academic awards; [oth. writ.] Beautiful Flower, Sweet Revenge, One Race One Nation, and Peace For All, many other writings; [pers.] I continuously strive to do my best at everything I do to make my life a most successful one. [a.] Trotwood, OH.

McFARLAND, STEPHANIE
[b.] January 18, 1979, Bay City, MI; [p.] Catherine and George McFarland; [ed.] Western High School; [hon.] I graduated summa cum laude from my freshman class; [oth. writ.] Five poems published in Western Star literary magazine, 35 poems altogether; [pers.] My writing has never been an attempt to become a poet. It has always been an outlet for my feelings-like a diary. All of my poems are from my heart. [a.] Bay City, MI.

McGAHAN, PATRICIA
[pen.] P.J.; [b.] May 16, 1960, Pueblo, CO; [m.] Donovon Rieman, July 31, 1993; [ch.] Nathan, Isaiah, Ralph Michael; [ed.] GED; [occ.] Housewife; [hon.] Five honorable mentions, three Golden Poet awards, two Silver Poet awards; [oth. writ.] Riding on a Rainbow, Twinkle, Twinkle Little Star, Dreamland, Ashley's Prayer, Cotton Candy Land, Teardrops From Heaven, This Bitter Earth, Follow That Dream, God is Like; [pers.] Great Poets aren't made, they're born-Ralph Waldo Emerson. [a.] Skykomish, WA.

McGILLIS, ERIC
[b.] May 12, 1980, Toronto, Canada; [ed.] Turner-Fenton Campus, Brampton; [occ.] Student; [memb.] Brigades Baptist Church, Junior Trojans, Turner Fenton football team; [hon.] Regional Elementary School Wrestling competition, 2nd place, most improved Jr. wrestler, Olympia Sports Camp; [pers.] I only write my feelings and about what I have experienced. Also, I get by with a little help from my friends. [a.] Brampton, Ont, Canada.

McGOWAN, MIKE
[b.] January 7, 1976, Hamilton, Ont, Canada; [p.] Vincent McGowan, Lucia McGowan; [ed.] Barrie Central Collegate High School; [occ.] Student; [hon.] Honour Society, Economics award; [oth. writ.] Articles for school newspaper; [pers.] One can never be too strong, too wealthy, or too wise. Strive for excellence in every endeavor. [a.] Thornton, Ont, Canada.

McGOWEN, JAMIE
[b.] February 3, 1978, Poteau, OK; [p.] James and Paula McGowen; [ed.] High school; [occ.] Student; [memb.] Future Farmers of America, Future Homemakers of America; [oth. writ.] Other poetry; [pers.] Live your life to the fullest. Strive to do your best. Live and have fun throughout your life and leave your mark behind when you leave this world. [a.] Wister, OK.

McHENRY, DONNA
[ch.] David and Aaron; [ed.] John Carroll University, Cleveland State University; [pers.] Has been writing since the age of seven. [a.] Cleveland, OH.

McILHENNEY, CHRISTINA
[b.] March 13, 1981, Baltimore, MD; [p.] Helen McIlhenney, Robert McIlhenney; [ed.] Our Lady of Fatima School; [memb.] Safety Patrol; [oth. writ.] I haven't tried to published any before but I have written many. This is dedicated to my 8th grade teacher Sr. Anthony Leo; [pers.] I want to thank God for giving me this talent, my mom, dad, family, friends and of course my teachers and principal at Our Lady of Fatima School. [a.] Baltimore, MD.

McINTYRE, BOBBY
[b.] December 9, 1955, Shreveport, LA; [p.] Lottie Joyce; [ch.] 3; [ed.] High school, voc tech, college; [occ.] Social security disability; [hon.] Honor awards in high school, regular attendance, merit for outstanding in Army and school, scholarship in accounting; [oth. writ.] I have been writing poems over 20 years. I still write and love to write and read. I love to sign poem and write about people and God. Writing the truth; [pers.] Many people told me to write and many love my writing. Today I consider myself the lucky man in the world. I just need the world to see my work. This is something I never did. [a.] Pelican, LA.

McKINNEY, RACHEL N.
[b.] October 14, 1980, Battle Creek, MI; [p.] Rebecca and Ken McKinney; [ed.] Beadle Lake Elementary, Harper Creek Junior High; [pers.] I found out that my poem was being published on my 14th birthday. [a.] Ceresco, MI.

McLAUGHLIN, DELTA
[b.] May 12, 1939, Springtown, TX; [p.] Arthur Brown, Stella Brown; [m.] Widow; [ch.] Benita Julian, Jacquelyn Deaver; [ed.] Northside High School; [occ.] Dispatcher/clerical, Tri-County Electric Corp; [hon.] I've had poems in Christian papers and newsletters, poem in book "Heart of Dreams"; [pers.] I love poetry. I was near death in a car wreck. I had some miraculous divine healing from the Lord. I love to write poems about the Lord and how great he is. My poems come from the heart of how I feel. [a.] Azle, TX.

McMILLER, THERESA ROSE
[pen.] Therese Roset; [b.] July 16, 1971, IN; [p.] Norman and Gracie Mcmiller; [ed.] George Washington High School, Ivy Tech State College; [occ.] Salesclerk; [memb.] Ivy Tech College Secretarial Club; [hon.] Deans List; [oth. writ.] Three published letters in Ebony Magazine, one published letter in Star Magazine; [pers.] Poetry and creative writing is providing self-therapy for me. Writing reveals my deepest thoughts on paper. Poetry reveals the passionate, romantic side of me. [a.] Indianapolis, IN.

McMULLIN, MELISSA
[b.] January 14, 1980, Bryn Mawr, PA; [p.] James and Cynthia McMullin; [occ.] Student; [memb.] Bacton HIll Bible Church; [pers.] A time of pain is a time of growth. That will only result in making one stronger. [a.] Exton, PA.

McNEFF, A.A.
[b.] February 8, 1967, Woodstock, RI; [p.] Christopher A. McNeff, Huguetta M. Larrivee; [ed.] North Province High, Mar Vista High, Southwestern College; [occ.] Storeroom assistant/food service, University of California at San Diego; [memb.] Associated Student Organization, senator and lifetime member of Southwestern College, San Diego Maritime Museum, Society for Creative Anachronism; [hon.] Star of India sailing crew, Chi Epsilon; [oth. writ.] This is the poem I have put up for publication. I have however been to a few poetry readings with numerous amounts of poems and some short stories of adventure, science fiction and romance; [pers.] Poetry is the everlasting romantic search for the humanity buried deep within the heart. [a.] Imperial Beach, CA.

McNUTT, JEAN
[b.] May 20. 1925, Muskegon, MI; [p.] Beatrice Covell, Don J. Irwin; [ch.] Von, Roger, Barry, Douglas, Elaina; [ed.] Grand Ledge High School; [occ.] Retired; [memb.] American Legion Auxiliary, ISP lifetime member; [hon.] Award of merit from ISP; [oth. writ.] Poems to Ponder, unpublished, currently working on Poems to Ponder II; [pers.] Poetry is my way of expressing what I feel. Most of my poems are written from actual experiences. I am truly satisfied when a reader tells me they know how I feel. [a.] Saranac, MI.

McSWIGGAN, JENNIFER
[b.] June 21, 1982, Philadelphia, PA; [p.] Audrey and James McSwiggan; [ed.] Logan Elementary School; [occ.] Student; [pers.] I like to write poems and stories, and hope to have a career in this. [a.] Swedesboro, NJ.

McVICKER, ERMA
[b.] July 24, 1919, Hanna City, IL; [p.] George and Bertha (Johnson) Largent; [m.] W. Wesley McVicker, December 14, 1947; [ch.] Linda McVicker Feil, Paul McVicker; [ed.] Some college, Browns Business College; [occ.] Retired; [memb.] University United Methodist Church; [hon.] Honorable discharge from WW II; [oth. writ.] Just personal writings for anniversaries, farewells-a few have been in local papers, but not published.

MEADOWS, JAMIE
[b.] February 25, 1980, Anaheim, CA; [p.] Mike and Debbie Meadows; [ed.] Norco High; [occ.] Student; [oth. writ.] Friends; [pers.] Without my pen, my thoughts would still be thoughts. [a.] Corona, CA.

MECKLE, LAURA
[b.] August 3, 1981, Miles City, MT; [p.] Sally Meckle; [ed.] B.M. Hanson Elementary School; [occ.] 8th grade student; [memb.] First Lutheran Church, Luther League; [hon.] Honor roll student; [oth. writ.] Several poems which I hope to have published some day; [pers.] There are many young writers and I encourage them to continue writing and trying to get published. It does take hard work but someday you will get there, you just have to believe in yourself. [a.] Martin, ND.

MEECH-MAST, LAURIE
[pen.] Laurie Meech-Mast; [b.] November 13, 1960, Monterey, CA; [p.] L.R. and Billie Meech; [m.] Mark Mast, May 31, 1986; [ed.] Monterey High School, Monterey Peninsula College; [occ.] Homemaker; [memb.] Monterey United Methodist Church; [pers.] "Life is very short, and we have but far too little time"...My thoughts and writing are based on this belief, and, a constant yearning to remind others of how much they matter; and, that there is someone in this world, to love and appreciate them so..."We must make each day count". [a.] Marina, CA.

MEFRET, NICOLE
[pen.] Nadine Norman; [b.] March 10, 1960, Feurs (France); [p.] Georges and Adrienne Mefret; [ed.] St. Charles Lyon (France); [occ.] Assistant Editor-United Nations New York; [pers.] I'd like to be able to be accepted in this high world of poetry by my personal expression. [a.] New York, NY.

MELGUIST, CAROL O.
[pen.] Carol Joseph; [b.] April 15, 1946, Islesboro, ME; [p.] Doris and Wyman Hatch; [m.] Divorced; [ch.] Terry Lee, granddaughter-Patricia; [ed.] School Business, Manchester Comm. Teachers College; [occ.] Real Estate Entrepreneur and Lest We Forget Antique Curiosity Shop; [memb.] Wolf Pen Writer's Group, Manchester Chamber of Commerce; [oth. writ.] Published "Mirror'd Reflections" with companion piece "The Clown Crys" in progress. Published dialogue "Ballad's in Black, White Linen Pantomime"; [pers.] Thoughts and idea, when communicated in kindnesses that transcend the mind and body, can light one candle for good, which we each can carry and pass on light, in love, to all. [a.] Manchester, CT.

MESSER, SANDRA LEE
[pen.] SLM; [b.] February 22, 1962, Atlantic City, NJ; [p.] Tomiko and James Messer; [ed.] BA., English, Emphasis-Literary Analysis & Criticism; [occ.] Associate; Strategic Marketing Communications and Design Consulting; [oth. writ.] Other unpublished poems, quotes, musings; [pers.] I am very fortunate that on occasion I can, with the immense generosity of words, articulate something of the infinite intricacies of human thought and emotion, recognize it as my own, and have it be understood by someone else. This is the essence of satisfaction. [a.] San Francisco, CA.

METROS, BILLIE LOUISE
[b.] January 13, 1927, Glenrock WY; [p.] Robert and Maebelle Duncan; [m.] John, September 18, 1982 (2nd marriage); [ch.] Mickie Louise, Vickie Lee, Kathleen Marie, Carolyn Jean; [ed.] High school grad; [occ.] Retired (Retirement Home Housecleaning Supervisor) Housewife; [hon.] To have so many friends and relatives that love me; [oth. writ.] Writes poems for all grandchildren - daughter's and son in laws and friends for their birthdays, anniversary, etc. Several poems published at Retirement home I worked; [pers.] Everything that I write reflects the personal life of each person. [a.] Westminister, CA.

MEYER, RICHARD
[pers.] For Sigourney. [a.] Hawthorne, NJ.

MILAM, DELLE ELAINE
[b.] January 14, 1981, Monroe, LA; [p.] Tommy and Connie Milham; [ed.] Jesus Good Shepherd School; [occ.] Student 8th grade; [memb.] Monroe Youth Girls Softball, JGS Basketball and Volleyball, Girl Scouts Pathfinders (a special group in girl scouting); [hon.] Leadership pin and silver award (Girl Scouts), All Star Team for two years in softball. [a.] Monroe, LA.

MILLER, JANINE MARIE
[b.] June 14, 1981, Saskatoon, SASK; [p.] Delbert and Sheila Miller; [ed.] Speers Elementary School, Hafford High School; [occ.] Student; [memb.] Speers United Church; [hon.] 4-H award, Remembrance Day Literary award, Distinction award-Hafford School; [oth. writ.] Numerous poems and short stories. I have also written an anniversary poem and put it to music; [pers.] In my poetry I love to write serious poems about my family, life, and beliefs my poetry is always a way of reflecting the way I feel. [a.] Speers, SASK.

MILLER, JOSHUA RHETT
[b.] August 9, 1979, Philadelphia, PA; [p.] Richard and Dana Miller; [ed.] George Washington High School; [memb.] Mentally Gifted Program, various literature magazines and newspapers, swimming and diving team, Bustleton Bengal Youth Group, AZA Youth Group; [hon.] National Presidential Academic Award, Language Achievement Award; [oth. writ.] Several articles published in school newspapers, short stories, poetry, journalism; [pers.] All men are created equal, but its their heart and desire to win that sets them apart. [a.] Philadelphia, PA.

MILLER, KERRYANN
[pen.] Kerry Langston, Kerryann Langston; [b.] August 7, 1976, Long Island; [p.] Richard Miller and Eileen Fippinger; [m.] Robert Woodruff, June 3, 1994; [ed.] Hicksville Senior High School; [occ.] Writer; [hon.] Several music and writing awards provided by my high school; [oth. writ.] Several poems published in local or school newspaper; [pers.] The things I'd like to accomplish in my life are my goals to be a writer, and to bring all our veterans home from South East Asia, and stay well in the eyes of my goddess. I admire Edgar Allen Poe as a genius. [a.] Levittown, NY.

MILLER, MARJORIE P.
[b.] April 13, 1927, Berkeley Co., WV; [p.] Hunter and Alice Triggs; [m.] John A. Miller (deceased), October 31, 1942; [ch.] Seven; [ed.] 9th grade; [occ.] Homemaker; [pers.] This is the only poem I have written. The grief from the sudden death of my husband at the age of sixty-one inspired me to write this poem for our forty-third wedding anniversary. [a.] Martinsburg, WV.

MILLER, TINA MARIE
[b.] October 8, 1974, Tacoma, WA; [p.] Harold Gene Miller and Toni Lee (Wray) Miller; [ed.] Clonlara School, University of Maine at Farmington; [occ.] Writer; [hon.] Salutatorian Clonlara Graduating Class 1990; [pers.] I owe much thanks to the guidance and encouragement of my parents and my two favorite college instructors, Baron Wormser, poet, and Jay Hoar, author. Most of my poetry is based on personal observations to variety of environments. My father was the inspiration for "A Flower". I am currently on Sabbatical in the Middle East. After my visit in the Middle East, I intend to explore Central and South America before returning home to the United States. [a.] Arlington Heights, IL.

MILLS, TONYA
[pen.] Hrroganee LeShante; [b.] September 21, 1975, Eden, NC; [p.] Walter and Sylvia Mills; [ed.] Rockingham County Senior High, Rockingham County Community College, NRI Correspondence School; [occ.] Inserter, Eden Daily News and Student; [hon.] NRI Writer's Achievement Award; [oth. writ.] Several unpublished short stories and poems; [pers.] Follow your dreams. Never hesitate to see what may happen. Always allow your heart to lead you if your mind doesn't. Thanks for believing in me, Mom, Dad, Shortie and Ms. Murphy. [a.] Ruffin, NC.

MINER, MICHAEL A.
[b.] June 30, 1954, Detroit; [p.] David and Dorothy Miner; [ed.] 12th grade; [pers.] I dedicate this verse to psychiatrist and those who improve life. [a.] Mt. Clemens, MI.

MITCHELL, CLAYTON
[b.] June 14, 1933, Tonkawa, OK; [p.] Chelsie and Ada Mitchell-sister-Dolores Rieger; [ed.] The University of Central Oklahoma, The University of Oklahoma Law School; [occ.] Cild welfare, social worker for Oklahoma County Child Welfare; [memb.] Poetry Society of Oklahoma, Carey Heights Baptist Church; [hon.] Greatest honor is having won my sister's admiration as an author; [oth. writ.] Poems, fairy tales and short stories; [pers.] Poetry is The Heart Speaking For the Mind. I revere poet John Keats and I hold poet, Edgar Allan Poe in high esteem. They are my poetry mentors. [a.] Oklahoma City, OK.

MITCHELL, KRYSTAL ANN
[b.] January 18, 1977, Seldovia, AK; [p.] Dale Ann and Arthur Mitchell; [m.] Fiance'-Anthony Waterbury; [ed.] Susan B. English Elementary/high school, Highland View Middle School; [occ.] Senior student in high school; [hon.] 'A' and 'B' Honor Roll; [oth. writ.] One other poem published in the anthology "In A Different Light", also published in local newspaper; [pers.] My writing always reflects my personal life. I have been greatly inspired by my fiance, Anthony, who has always been there. [a.] Seldovia, AK.

MITCHELL, MARRIANNE LEANN
[pen.] Sunshine, Mary Mitchell; [b.] June 19, 1977, Austin, MN; [p.] LeAnn and Donovan Mitchell; [hon.] Won an award in 5th grade for writing an essay on What One Nation Under God Meant to Me; [oth. writ.] Many poems non-published, wrote for my friends, some short stories non-published; [pers.] I feel like if you feel upset or sad or peaceful it's a good time to write what you feel down, so that later if you get those feelings you can dream away. In short term smile a mile and laugh a while. [a.] Alberta, MN.

MITCHELL, MICHELLE LYNN
[b.] August 3, 1976, Montgomery, IL; [p.] Larry and Robin Mitchell; [ed.] Aurora University, West Aurora High School; [occ.] Full-time student; [hon.] Illinois State Scholar, Who's Who Among American High School Students, Presidential Academic Fitness Award; [oth. writ.] Personal collection of poems and short stories; [pers.] At first my work may seem simple, but it is simplicity that is most often complex. [a.] Montgomery, IL.

MIZRAHI, HAIM
[b.] July 13, 1959, Jerusalem; [p.] Mordechai and Latiffa Mizrahi; [ed.] Institute Goldman for physical rehabilitation, Hebrew University in Jerusalem, Slavic and Russian studies; [occ.] Painter, musician and writer; [hon.] Empire State nationals, 3rd, fighting division; [oth. writ.] Aphorisms titled: "Aphorisms of my uncle Abraham". Aphorisms post cards titled: "Think Cards"; [pers.] "Good digestion demands a certain amount of coarse food-refined and condensed aliment alone kills. Man should work and busy himself with the common place, rest himself for his flight, and when the moment of transfiguration comes, make the best of it." -Baruch Spinoza. Our oath to the reality of the almighty is our debt to it; to safe guard the portion of greatness that was given to us with a crisp sanity of intelligent and passionate human beings. [a.] East Hampton, NY.

MJELLELI, TERRY LEE
[pen.] Terry Lee; [b.] September 4, 1954, Auburn, WA; [p.] The late Frank Grispino and Eleanor Grispino; [m.] Martin S., May 29, 1976; [ch.] Marty Steven and Mario Franco; [ed.] Auburn High, Highline College and Bellevue College; [occ.] Homemaker formerly a kindergarten instructional assistant for Seattle school district; [hon.] Honor society (high school and college), finalist in the Miss Auburn Beauty Pageant, Phi Theta Kappa; [oth. writ.] Published books called "Dusting Off Dreams", a collection of verse by several contemporary authors including myself; [memb.] Most of my poems have a romantic theme. I give a light message of positive advice, even if the poem talks of great adversity. This reflects my outlook on life. My favorite poet is Carl Sandburg. [a.] Seattle, WA.

MOESER, ALICE E.
[b.] June 16, 1937, Huntington; [p.] Reinhold E. and Eleanor Beseler Moeser; [ed.] High school, University of Chicago, The Institute of Children's Literature, Century Business College, several night courses at Marshall University; [occ.] Controller at Ramada Inn; [memb.] St. Paul's Lutheran Church, past member of Beverly Hill's Juniors Womens Club, past Finance Committee at church, set up daily kindergarten school at church, taught kindergarten as supervisor and fifth graders for 12 years; [oth. writ.] Five Little Bears at Christmas 1984; [pers.] You're never too old to try something new. [a.] Huntington, W.VA.

MOLTHOP, SANDRA LYNN
[pen.] Sandra Molthrop; [b.] July 28, 1980; [p.] Robert L. and Deborah A.; [ed.] Mundelein High School; [memb.] Pom Pons School participant in school choir; [hon.] Two contest ribbons for spelling contest and running; [oth. writ.] This is my first entry although I have written quite a few; which I plan on submitting; [pers.] I enjoy writing and it comes pretty easy. I never really saw or thought I could do it. I have always and still have interest in like writing to make cards. The words can come as I write. Do I have a talent? [a.] Mundelein, IL.

MOMY, LEO ST. GERARD
[pen.] Leo St. Gerard; [b.] July 6, 1926, Mon Laurie, Moncerf, Quebec; [p.] Deceased; [ed.] High school Ottawa Technical High; [occ.] Self employed-sales of reports; [memb.] The Highlanders Club; [oth. writ.] I lived in Japan. I wrote "My Key to Geisha", "Life and Loves of The Professional Geisha" recorded in the Prof. BK (Great Poems of Today); [pers.] Rank professional poetry is liken to the light at the end of the tunnel. Only good can happen.

MONAGHAN-MUGLIA, THERESA
[pen.] Theresa Monaghan-Muglia; [b.] November 7, 1963, New Jersey; [p.] Bettie Jean and Joseph Daniel Monaghan; [m.] Alfred Muglia, March 5, 1994; [ch.] 3 step-children; [ed.] John F. Kennedy High School; [occ.] Secretary; [oth. writ.] Children's stories that I make up while telling them; [pers.] The most important people in my life are my mother and father who have helped me thru the toughest moments of my life. [a.] Edison, NJ.

MONETTI JR., STEVEN R.
[pen.] Steven R. Monetti, Jr.; [b.] November 29, 1972, Englewood; [p.] Steven and Carol Monetti, Sr.; [ed.] North Bergen High School; [occ.] Board of Education staff at North Bergen High School; [memb.] Madonna Catholic Church in Fort Lee, NJ., North Bergen Peer Group and N.J.E.A.; [hon.] North Bergen High School coaches award, two language appreciation awards, Peer Group award; [oth.writ.] Several poems published in high school newspaper and prelude yearbook at high school; [pers.] I strive to be the best at whatever I do. I take pride in my work and have a desire to fulfill my inner most thoughts that God has given me to enlight mankind. [a.] North Bergen, NJ.

MONROE, CHRISTIANE K.
[pen.] Christiane Gebauer Monroe; [b.] October 30, 1930, Wiesbaden, Germany; [p.] Alexander Gebauer; [m.] Henriette, October 2, 1965; [ch.] Joyce Christiane, Janice, Charles Alexander, Elizabeth Ann; [ed.] Madchen Realgymnasium (Germany), University of California, Holy Names College; [occ.] German/English Teacher; [memb.] University of California Alumni Association, California Library Trustees and Commissioners (CALTAC), Solano County Library Advisory Council (SCLAC); [hon.] Delta Phi Alpha/Theta Mu; Dean's Lists, graduation "With Honors"; [oth. writ.] Several letters to the editors published in local newspapers; [pers.] In my writing I attempt to reveal the monadic nuances of the human spirit, the poignancy and sanctity of each life, and the obligation each of us has to be worthy of the gift of life.. My literary models include Biblical authors, medieval masters, the periods of the enlightenment, romanticism, classicism, and T.S. Eliot of our century. [a.] Vacaville, CA.

MONTE, ANGELA
[b.] December 27, 1974, Toronto; [p.] Angela and Antonie Monte; [ed.] High school graduate; [occ.] Recruiting Officer for a telecommunications company; [pers.] Life is what you make it to be. Happiness and wealth is there if your determined enough and keep in mind that good things happen to those who wait. [a.] Richmond Hill, ONT.

MOONEY, ROBERT R.
[b.] June 21, 1933, Lake Charles, LA; [p.] Robert Brock and Rae Reisor Mooney; [m.] Paulene Roeder, February 16, 1963; [ch.] Kelly Mooney; [ed.] Beaumont High, Texas A&M University; [occ.] Retired Engineer; [pers.] Throughout my life, I have been striving as honesty and objectively as possible in search of answers to the great questions. Willy-nilly, the various religious, philosophies and sciences have influenced the cyclical path of my search. It is desired that my poems and writings can deatrophy and stimulate others to join me on this exploratory journey. [a.] College Station, TX.

MOORE, CJ
[b.] July 5, 1923, Blunt Co., TN; [p.] Glenn and Christine Moore; [m.] Thelma Evans Moore, October 31, 1942; [ch.] Carolyn, Rhea, Iris and Joyce; [ed.] High school GED 1948, two years college while in the United States Air Force, took courses at night and weekends; [occ.] Retired from USAF as a CMSgt in 1964 after 21 years and from Civil Service after 25 years; [hon.] None outside my military and civil service; [oth. writ.] I have written about 150 poems pertaining to religion, romance, nature and odds and ends. A few of my religious poems have been published in my church's paper. The poem that is being published was written in 1970; [pers.] Look forward to doing something each day that will awaken a weary or lonely heart)s) so that it(they) will, on some future day, remember pleasant memories of the past, and look forward to a brighter tomorrow. [a.] Van Ormy, TX.

MOORE, DANNY JR.
[pen.] Earl Pen; [b.] July 26, 1966, Akron, OH; [p.] Danny Moore and Sharon Kyle; [ed.] Central-Hower High; [occ.] Collection Examiner Rdwy; [oth. writ.] All others non-published; [pers.] Don't write just to write. Write to express, or encourage emotions. Solomon wrote his "Song of Songs" may every poet create such a work. [a.] Akron, OH.

MOORE, DELORES
[b.] July 8, 1957, Detroit, MI; [p.] Alfred and Gloria Moore; [ch.] Michael David; [ed.] Chadsey High, Detroit College of Business; [oth. writ.] Dean's List; [pers.] I would like to dedicate this poem to my mother, whose remarkable strength and love has truly inspired me. I will love you always. [a.] Detroit, MI.

MORAN, JARROD PAUL
[pen.] Paul; [b.] May 30, 1976, Wichita, KS; [p.] Dr. Paul and Barbara Moran;, [ed.] Senior High School; [occ.] Certified Nurse Aid; [hon.] Alumnus Cal. Farleys Boys Ranch Texas; [oth. writ.] Many; [pers.] My love of poetry is most supreme and my love of the gift it bring to others. [a.] Coleman, TX.

MORANTE, ROBIN ANN YALE
[pen.] R.A. Yale Morante; [b.] June 5, 1971, Syracuse, NY; [p.] John and Joyce Garris; [m.] Christopher Peter Morante, June 20, 1992; [ch.] Michael Hughes Morante; [ed.] State University of New York College at Potsdam, Suffern High School; [occ.] Fitness Instructor; [memb.] Omega Delta Phi; [oth. writ.] Collection of vignettes and poems. Two previously published in high school literary magazine; [pers.] The best way to enhance your life, is through enhancing the lives of others. [a.] Hillsborough, NJ.

MORGAN, CHRISTINA
[pen.] Pooky/Pebbles; [b.] July 7, 1978, Winston Salem, NC; [p.] Ray and Wanda Morgan; [ed.] Student 10th grade; [hon.] Miss Jr. America for 2 years in Martinsville, VA; [oth. writ.] Mommy Can You Hear Me Crys, Love And Faith, Can't Wait Until Spring, Love One Another No Matter, What, My Story of Love, Friends Forever, and I could Dream; [pers.] I try to reflect my feelings about life and how I see life in my eyes, then I try to put it on paper. [a.] Fayetteville, NC.

MORGAN, NICOLE DAWN
[pen.] Nikki Morgan; [b.] October 30, 1981, Tulsa; [p.] Kenny and Liz Morgan; [ed.] Oologahtalala Public Schools; [occ.] Dance and modeling teacher; [hon.] Masonic's "Student of the Year" award, "Student of the Month" three years in row; [pers.] I'm only twelve. [a.] Talala, OK.

MORGAN, SYLVIA
[b.] September 1, 1952, Floyd County, Rome, GA; [p.] Herman and Gamette Haynes; [m.] Harold Morgan, February 22, 1980; [ch.] Amber Renee; [ed.] East Rome High, Knoxville College, Georgia State University, Jacksonville State University;

[occ.] Case Educator Manager, Georgia School For The Deaf; [memb.] GAE, NEA, NAACP, GEHI, Greater Mt. Calvary Baptist Church, GA Health Decisions; [hon.] 1980-Who's Who, 1995-Who's Who In the South and Southwest; [pers.] I strive to express the pain and joy of being an African-American woman and mother of a disabled child. [a.] Rome, GA.

MORIN, NORMA JEAN
[b.] December 14, 1946, Foamlake, SASK CAN; [p.] Norman and Vera Bodie; [m.] Chris C., October 12, 1991; [ch.] Christian; [ed.] Seaton Secondary School - grade 10; [occ.] Salad Bar Chef; [oth. writ.] In memory verses for mother and brother in Quesnel paper; [pers.] My Love of Nature is a gift from my mother Vera who inspired me to see only the Beauty and find Goodness in all that was nature and life. [a.] Lumby, B.C., CAN.

MORRIS, ALI
[b.] July 8, 1979, Chicago; [p.] Dale and Irwin Morris; [ed.] Deerfield High School; [oth. writ.] I have about 400 pages of poetry, not yet published; [pers.] I love to write, especially romantic poems. I hope someday to be as good as the poets whom I admire. Advice to all- Live for today because there may not be a tomorrow. [a.] Deerfield, IL.

MORRIS, JERALD
[pen.] Jerry Morris; [b.] February 9, 1945, Woodbury, NJ; [p.] James and Estella Morris; [ch.] Galina, April 28, 1994; [ch.] Polina Nikulina; [ed.] Northeastern Bible College, International Seminary; [occ.] Computer Analyst; [memb.] American Society Writers, Northeastern Alumni Association, VFW Post 3620; [hon.] Certificate of honor International Seminary and Recognition of Appreciation Veterans of Foreign Wars 1990; [oth. writ.] Vantage Press 1989 "God's People-Reality & Myth" and articles for Northeastern's school newspaper; [pers.] I emphasize the spiritual nature of man to illustrate the mind's creativity. [a.] West Orange, NJ.

MORRISSEY, JEAN C.
[pen.] Trademark: Agapegrams; [b.] June 7, 1942, Berlin, PA; [p.] Paul and Ferne Christner; [m.] Patrick B., June 26, 1984; [ch.] Robin, David; [ed.] Dover High, University of Delaware; [occ.] Secretary, Excavation Management Co; [memb.] Phoenix First Assembly; [hon.] National Honor Society, Scholastic Yearbook, All-American Award; first place essay awards; first place slogan contest promoting the work ethic; [oth. writ.] Various magazine articles; Children's Bible Education quarterly materials; Songwriter; [pers.] To share the gift of inspiration through poetry is for me both a divine mandate and source of personal joy. [a.] Phoenix, AZ.

MOSENTHINE, BERT
[pen.] Bert Von Suppe; [b.] November 14, 1962, Fords, NJ; [p.] Bert and Dorothy Mosenthine; [ed.] Woodbridge High School, St. John's University; [oth. writ.] A collection of my own writings which include songs and poems for instance: Melody Winds, Blossom, Essence, Nowhere, etc. [a.] Edison, NJ.

MOSS, KELLY S.
[b.] February 6, 1968, New Castle, IN; [p.] Earl and Carolyn Thrasber; [m.] Jeffrey, June 23, 1988; [ch.] Amanda; [ed.] New Castle High School; [occ.] Housewife; [hon.] Dean's List, Spanish National Honor Society; [pers.] I have a musical background and eventually would like to write songs. [a.] Elkart, IN.

MOULDEN, RON
[b.] November 19, 1949, London, ONT; [p.] John and Joyce Moulden; [m.] Vicki Masse, May 24, 1979; [ch.] Jennifer Rae Moulden; [ed.] Northern Collegiate, Lambton College; [occ.] Life Underwriter Mutual Life of Canada; [memb.] Arthur Rimbaud Poetic Society; [oth. writ.] Several poems published throughout United States and Canada, collected poems, Little Beggar Boy, The Angels Are White. [a.] Tecumseh, ONT.

MOULDOVAN, DINA E.
[b.] June 15, 1979; [p.] Judith and Noel Mouldovan; [ed.] SSDS High School. [a.] Teaneck, NJ.

MOYE, EVONNE
[pen.] MOYE; [b.] July 22, 1962, Bronx, NY; [p.] Beatrice and Henry Moye; [ed.] Mabel Dean Bacon Vocational School, Bernard M.Baruch College; [occ.] Representative-Hilton Hotels; [memb.] Zion Hill Church, St. Jude Hospital; [hon.] Teachers medal in Business education; [pers.] Faith is the key to life's promises and the path to excel in all that may challenge you. God Bless You. [a.] Carrollton, TX.

MUCHISON, CHARON
[b.] October 26, 1980, Naples, Italy; [p.] John and Janet Muchison; [hon.] 1st place county and district awards in band (1st chair flutist) school honors in academics, phys. ed., L. Arts, and Social Studies. Honorable mentions in acrylic paintings, displays at fairs and community library; [oth. writ.] Several miscellaneous poems and stories, some published in school newsletters or books; [pers.] I believe writing is a talent not all of us have, so we who have the gift should use it. [a.] FPO, AE.

MUELLER, WILLIAM J., JR.
[b.] March 25, 1955, Chicago, IL; [p.] William and Ruth Mueller; [m.] Polly, April 11, 1992; [ch.] William J. Mueller III; [ed.] Lemoore High, College of the Sequsias, Cal Poly San Luis Obispo, Southwest Missouri State University; [occ.] Student, soon to be Secondary Education Science Teacher; [hon.] Kappa Delta Pi, Dean's List; [pers.] Living proof that you can accomplish whatever you set your mind to do. [a.] Heritage, MO.

MUENZLER, MICHELLE LYNN
[b.] December 9, 1976, Freeport, TX; [pers.] Life is the pile of wood stacked in the bottom of the fireplace; inspiration is the spark which sets is aflame. [a.] Conroe, TX.

MULLIGAN, LISA L.
[b.] April 25, 1976, Corry, PA; [p.] Paul and Darleen Mulligan; [m.] Fiance-Joseph Cerce, Jr.; [ed.] High school; [occ.] Unable to work because I suffer, like many others, from cystic fibrosis; [oth. writ.] Numerous poems that have not been seen by any publishers; [pers.] Everyday I am challenged by the life threatening disease, cystic fibrosis, which I have. This disease makes me look at life differently and this is where my poems come from. [a.] Corry, PA.

MULLINS, ANN SAYLOR
[b.] December 9, 1919, Corbin, KY; [m.] Jack P., July 24, 1940; [ch.] Constance M. Evans; [ed.] Berea College; [occ.] Retired teacher 30 years; [memb.] Berea United Methodist Church, Kappa Delta, Phi Kappa Phi, American Association University Women; [oth. writ.] I've written many poems for relatives and friends birthdays or anniversaries. Have never before submitted one for publication; [pers.] In my opinion, love is the most important force in one's life. [a.] Berea, KY.

MUNCRIEF, VAUGHN W.
[pen.] Von W. Muncrief; [b.] March 23, 1922, Madill, OK; [p.] Walter and Lillie Muncrief; [m.] Lowana, May 17, 1944; [ch.] Dennis, Lavona, Linda; [ed.] 7th grade only; [occ.] Retired from Lone Star Gas Co. TX; [memb.] Prostestant; [hon.], Expert Rifleman Badge, Expert Inf. Man Badge; [oth. writ.] Veteran of WWII served in France, Belgium, Luxumburg, Holland. Served in 104 Inf. Division The Timber-wolf Division.

MUNN, COURTNEY TAYLOR
[b.] June 13, 1983, Mt. Clemens, MI; [p.] Rae and Larry Paperd; [ed.] John F. Kennedy Middle School; [occ.] Student; [hon.] Michigan Physical Fitness award, D.A.R.E. award, Student of the Week awards, Champion Softball "94" award, All-Star Game Award, Bowling awards; [oth. writ.] Several other poems. [a.] St. Clair Shores, MI.

MUNOZ, GERARDO
[b.] February 9, 1977, Denver, CO; [p.] Dora M. Garcia; [ed.] Dona Ama Community College; [occ.] Writer/musician; [oth. writ.] Two independently published poem books: "Saints, Sinners, and the Sunshine People" and "All I See Is Black"; [pers.] My influences include: Jim Morrison, Edgar Allan Poe, Walt Whitman, and William Blake. "In a fevered dream, thing are never what they seem." [a.] Las Cruces, NM.

MURPHEY, RODGER D., SR.
[b.] October 28, 1947, Atlanta, GA; [p.] Mrs. Polly Maxwell-Murphey; [ch.] Rodger D. Murphy, Jr.; [ed.] Public Affairs Office, U.S. Dept. of Education, Georgia State University; [occ.] Public Affairs Officer; [hon.] 4th Estate award, U.S. Dept of Army; [oth. writ.] Listed are poems not published. The Trickster, Rain on the Street, Dribble and Goo, Talks, A Bee in the Bonnet, Do Say, Voice, In Harmony, Run into the Light, An Un-Adorned Animal; [pers.] The written word is a gift only man or woman can leave as testament of their existence. [a.] Silver Spring, MD.

MURPHY, DONNA LEE
[b.] September 9, 1941, Mt. Zion, IA; [p.] Darrell Loeffler and Laura Reddick Loeffler; [m.] J. Barney Murphy, March 22, 1959; [ch.] Daryl Udell and Michael John; [ed.] Keosauqua High School, trained dance instructor and choreographer - various schools; [occ.] Area freelance newspaper feature writer, dance author of articles for Dance School Trends, Denton, TX, Marketing Dance Manuals to Instructors over USA and independent professional musicians; [memb.] Presb. Church, Arts Council Coop (ACCOP), Chamber of Commerce, Keosauqua; [hon.] Biography in 1st and 2nd editions of Marquis Who's Who in Entertainment; [oth. writ.] Author of Following Dance Books: Tip Top Dancing, Dance Varieties, Jazz/Break Dance, Tap-Ballet-Jazz, and the Ins and Outs. Freelance Dance Articles for Dance School Trends, freelance feature articles for area newspapers; [pers.] You are able to accomplish any goal you set in life-- The only obstacle in reaching your goals is yourself. [a.] Keosaugua, IA.

MURPHY, MARGARETHA
[pen.] Margaretha Murphy; [b.] April 23, 1931 Linz, Austria; [p.] Rosina and Rudolf Sauer (step father); [m.] Patrick; [ch.] Chris, Lori, Edie, Jack Pat, Mick and Hugh; [ed.] 8th grade; [occ.] House wife, mother and writer; [oth. writ.] Poems published in World of Poetry; [pers.] I write poems lyrics, and fictions and I love it. 1975 I had cancer and was operated. I talk with Esophageal Speech I speak well. [a.] El Paso, TX.

MURPHY, MICHAEL G.
[b.] October 30, 1961, Denville, NJ; [p.] Barbara Ann and Richard Paul; [m.] Yvonne Le Compte Murphy, August 31, 1989; [ch.] Nichole B. Guidry, Sally A.; Britta N.; Simone A.; [ed.] East St. John High; [occ.] A/C & Heating Mechanic; [hon.] Who's Who Among American High School Students, Society of Distinguished American High School Students; [oth. writ.] Currently unpublished, however, working on a Sci-Fi book entitled "The Dream" due to be completed by early 1995; [pers.] "LIfe is a gift. Enjoying it is a bonus." [a.] Gretna, LA.

MURRAY, NELLIE HAZEL
[pen.] Nell; [b.] September 6, 1933, Memphis, TN; [p.] Luther and Mary White; [m.] Joe W., October 27, 1956; [ch.] Marilyn Allen; [ed.] B.T. Washington High, Olive Harvey College, Chicago State; [occ.] Retired.

MURRELL, SARAH I.
[b.] November 12, 1970, Ontario; [p.] Norm and Barb Murrell; [ed.] Niagara College, Welland Ontario CAN in the Print Journalism Program; [hon.] English Proficiency award; [oth. writ.] Currently writing first novel; [pers.] As a future journalist I hope to use my pen or computer to change the world for the better, even if in a small way. [a.] Ontario, CAN.

MUSANA, CYNTHIA M.
[b.] April 14, 1964, Cleveland, OH; [p.] Sam and Frances Musana; [m.] James D. Adam, June 2, 1984; [ch.] Amber and Kara Adam; [ed.] Strongville Senior High School; [occ.] VP of S.F.&C Electric, Inc.; [memb.] National Multiple Sclerosis Society; [oth. writ.] I've written many poems as a teenager but never pursued publication; [pers.] Live in "Today" not yesterday or tomorrow. [a.] Medina, OH.

MYERS, LURA J.
[pen.] Lura Maness Myers; [b.] March 21, 1924, Bailey, TN; [p.] W.J. (Bee) and Dolly Maness; [m.] Divorced, August 3, 1946; [ch.] Terry Myers; [ed.] High school equivalent, and other training; [occ.] Security; [memb.] Rector Heights Baptist Church, Second Baptist Church, Various String Instruments Groups; [hon.] Job related; [oth. writ.] Several poems published in newspapers, church affiliated papers - poetry and short stories in Dark Starr magazine. I write country and western songs (one recorded) and various type songs; [pers.] I believe life is a master teacher some things are meant to be, while others cannot. Being willing to accept the cannots, are the test of human metal. [a.] Hot Springs, AR.

NAGLE, CRISTY COPELAND
[b.] November 12, 1957, Coldwater, MI; [p.] Arthur L. & D. Gene (Wood) Copeland; [m.] Earl Charles, June 21, 1980; [ed.] Kellogg Community College, Spring Arbor College; [occ.] Program Assistant for the Gifted/Talented; [memb.] International Waterlily Society, Jackson & Perkin's Rose Test Panel member, Christian church; [hon.] National Honor Society; [pers.] I am interested in English Puritan theology; the writings of the Puritans; and church history. I enjoy painting and gardening. [a.] Tekonsha, MI.

NAKAMURA, TRA
[b.] April 18, 1961, Honolulu, HI; [p.] Raymond and Edna Nakamura; [ed.] Aircraft Mechanic and Electronic technician. Bible College courses via correspondence; [occ.] US Post Office mail handler; [memb.] Band Servant of Christ Jesus, attends Calvary Chapel West Oahu; [hon.] By God's grace I've been awarded the free gift of eternal life through his son Christ Jesus; [oth. writ.] I wrote this poem in about 2-3 minutes while reading the newspaper and inspired by the holy spirit; [pers.] I pray that people will come to know Jesus Christ as their personal Lord and Savior. [a.] Ena Beach, HI.

NAPOLI, LEO III
[b.] January 11, 1949, Cleveland, OH; [p.] Leo and Betty Napoli, Jr.; [m.] Marilyn, August 27, 1982; [ch.] Lauren, Rachel, Marisa, Samuel; [ed.] Reading the Psalms and Proverbs; [occ.] Disciple of Jesus Christ; [memb.] I belong to the body of Christ; [hon.] Child of God, Servant of God, eternal life awarded through the blood of Jesus Christ the King; [pers.] I can do all things through Christ who strengthens me. Phil. 4:13. [a.] Cleveland, OH.

NASSER, JEFF
[b.] December 6, 1955, Louisville, KY; [p.] Mitchell and Lucy Nasser; [ed.] Ballard High School, Purdue University, University of Louisville, University of Louisville Law School; [occ.] Attorney; [memb.] Kentucky and American Bar Association; [oth. writ.] Poems and time jokes; [pers.] I started writing poetry in March 1971, about when Muhammad Ali had his first fight with Joe Frazier. It was Ali who made it respectable enough to write poetry. I started writing to amuse people, or writing about shooting pool. I write about people now on request. [a.] Louisville, KY.

NAVAGE, ERICA ASHLEY
[b.] May 28, 1986, Dammam, Saudi Arabia; [p.] Americans living abroad Sharon J. and S. Phil Navage; [ed.] International School of Kuala Lumpur, in Malaysia, Burnett Elementary; [occ.] Student 3rd grade; [memb.] Odessa Soccer Association, Permian Playhouse Theater Elementary Group, Dulcimar Club of Texas, Girl Scout in Malaysia 3 years; [hon.] 2 periods on the Honor Roll at Burnet, numerous soccer trophies, t-ball trophies and several blue ribbons for pottery and art projects; [pers.] I write because I enjoy it.

NAVARRA, THOMAS
[pen.] Thomas Fulton Navarra; [b.] March 29, 1956, New Castle, PA; [p.] Constantino and Mary Navarra; [m.] March 1977, Divorced 2/87; [ch.] Tracy Marie, Christina Michelle and Maria Deanne; [ed.] Warren Harding High, City College of Chicago, Youngstown State University, US Navy 13 years; [occ.] Steelworker, Thomas Steel Strip; [memb.] United Steelworkers of America; [hon.] 2 Navy Achievement Medals, several letters of commendation; [oth. writ.] Unpublished; [pers.] As a single working father, raising three daughters, I have become keenly aware of my purpose in life; "Learning to love unconditionally"; no matter what my children or others say or do to cause me pain, I try to forgive and love as I want to be forgiven and loved. [a.] Warren, OH.

NAYLOR, JESSICA
[pen.] Bissi; [b.] June 6, 1980, McAllen, TX; [p.] Keith and Bobette Naylor; [ed.] Riviera Kaufer High School; [occ.] Student; [memb.] Child Abuse Prevention Council of South Texas, Riviera Two 4-H Club, Riviera Seahawk Band; [hon.] Honor student; [oth. writ.] Poems and short stories dealing sexual child abuse and battering; [pers.] Because I was sexually abused by my natural father and suffered sever depression, I turned to writing in hopes of not only helping myself, but also the many children affected by abuse. I now have a wonderful stepfather Keith Naylor and I have nothing to do with my natural father.

NEAL, HEATHER M.
[b.] October 17, 1980, Wiesbaden W. Germany; [p.] Diane and David Neal; [ed.] Kingston High School; [occ.] Student; [memb.] Kingston High Field Hockey Team; [hon.] NYSSMA for flute award of excellence and outstanding. NYSSMA for voice award of excellence. [a.] Ulster Park, NY.

NEAL, JOHNNY
[b.] August 28, 1978, Gary, IN; [p.] Annie Neal and Johnny Bynum; [ed.] Pike High School; [occ.] 10th grade honor student, employed at Fazoils Fast Food Restaurant; [memb.] Red Ribbon Ambassador; [hon.] Honor Roll, MVP Basketball 3 years straight; [pers.] In my poetry I like to write positive this nothing negative. [a.] Waldron, IN.

NEDD, BEULAH
[pen.] Beulah Nedd; [b.] September 26, 1936, Trinidad, W.I.; [p.] Mr. and Mrs. Evy Reece; [m.] December 21, 1959 - Divorced; [ch.] Patsy, Sherma and Denise; [ed.] St. Francis RC, Modern Academy High, Mercy College; [occ.] License Practical Nurse Teacher (Kindergarten); [memb.] Mental Health Association, National Council of Negro Women, Mt. Carmel Spiritual Baptist Church; [hon.] Scholarship to Modern Academy High, ASA degree in Arts, Assoc. degree in Theology; [pers.] I enjoyed reading Stevenson as a child. By him I'm inspired to write for the joy and knowledge of the seen and unseen things.

NEEDLES, DORIS POSTELL
[pen.] Doris Needles; [b.] April 15, 1924, OH; [p.] Andrew and Lillian Postell; [m.] Widowed; [ch.] George T. Needles; [ed.] Retired-Engineering Fielder; [occ.] Volunteer for mentally disabled - care and transportation; [memb.] Independent Telephone Pioneer Association (ITPA); [hon.] United Way, Cerebral Palsy, General Telephone, Communications Workers of America (CWA); [pers.] One of sixteen children was a great inspiration to excel. Our father was a poet and didn't know it. [a.] Perris, CA.

NEGRON, MARIANA
[b.] April 23, 1980, Madison, WS; [p.] Doris Quinones and Jorge Negron; [ed.] Parkville School, Academia Maria Reina; [occ.] Student 9th grade; [pers.] I write things as I see them. In my own different ways. [a.] San Juan, PR.

NELSON, CLARA I.
[b.] November 30, 1926, Madison, SD; [p.] Arthur and Esther Kirstein (both parents deceased); [m.] Leo T., November 12, 1948; [ch.] Sidney Nelson and Sharon Nelson; [ed.] High school, Northwestern Bible College, and Southwestern Technical College; [occ.] Former church secretary, now nursing assistant and hospice; [hon.] Church bulletin, local newspaper, National Library of Poetry the last three years; [oth. writ.] I didn't begin to write poems and songs until 1972. Now I share these with friends all for God's glory; [pers.] I want to give God all the praise for these songs and poems. My prayer is that they will all reflect my love for God and his precious word. Jesus is my saviour, he wants to be yours too. The poem "God's Trees" tell us God's purpose for creating trees. [a.] Windom, NM.

NELSON, GREGORY ALLEN
[pen.] G. Allen Nelson; [b.] November 6, 1965, Los Angeles, CA; [p.] Eloise and Bennie Nelson; [m.] Charleen R., July 20, 1991; [ch.] Christina Jene' and Christopher Joel Allen; [ed.] Crenshaw High School, Sierra College of America; [occ.] Sales Associate-WalMart, Chattanooga, TN; [memb.] Secretary-New Generation Young Peoples Group, Union Hill Baptist Church, Past President-Progressive Baptist State Convention Young Peoples

Department of CA and NV; [oth. writ.] Currently writing a collection of poetry based on my life experiences over the course of one year; [pers.] I thank God for the talent given me, the gift of freeing my mind through poetry. [a.] Chattanooga, TN.

NELSON, JANN
[ch.] Rick, Felicia and Shallon; [ed.] Leslie High, Sue Bennett College; [occ.] Field Assistant for U.S. Senator; [hon.] Golden Poet Award, World of Poetry 1989, Silver Poet Award World of Poetry 1988; [oth. writ.] One poem published "No Choice" by World of Poetry. [a.] London, KY.

NELSON, SUSIE K.
[pen.] Little Fawn; [b.] February 3, 1959, Waterloo, IA; [p.] Barbara Hanslik and Joe Hanslik - (niece and nephew Briana May and Joshua Lee Hanslik); [oth. writ.] Several poems published in high school yearbook and I have a collection of poems that I hope to have published as a book. I also have made a poster of one of my poems; [pers.] I strive to help enlighten people with my writing. I like to present new ways of thinking and I especially like to encourage people to grow spiritually. My poems about animals strive to teach people about their medicine (power, totem) animals, and how important they are. [a.] Plymouth, MN.

NELSON, TRISH
[b.] December 19, 1978, Denison, TX; [p.] Bill and Debbie Nelson; [ed.] Denison High School; [occ.] Student; [memb.] Spanish Club, Future Homemakers of America, Yearbook Staff; [hon.] Story published in the high school writer. Entered University Interscholastic League literature competition the past 2 years; [oth. writ.] Story published in the High School Writer and local newspaper. Current author of articles in the high school newspaper "Jacket Racket" and high school year book.

NERYS, MADELINE
[pen.] Madeline Nerys; [b.] May 22, 1976, Newark, NJ; [p.] Lizette and Carlos Nerys; [ed.] Bay Path College, Easthampton High School; [occ.] Cashier at Jim Dandy's Restaurant; [hon.] Honor roll senior year in high school community foundation of Western Mass Scholarship, citizens of Easthampton Scholarship. Easthampton Education Association Scholarship; [pers.] My poetry, my talent comes from within (my happiness and my sadness). I owe it all to God for bringing me to the world and letting me be someone. The world has many of us. [a.] Easthampton, MA.

NEWTON, MICHELLE
[pen.] Diamon; [b.] October 7, 1968, Chicago; [p.] Willie and Mary Newton; [ch.] Carlan and Christopher Newton; [ed.] Richard's Vocational High School, Metropolitan Junior College; Data processing computer certificate; [occ.] Vocalist, model, actress, designer and author; [memb.] The First Baptist Church, A.C.O.R.N. since 1989, F.B.L.A. since 1982; [oth. writ.] "You Will Survive: Speaking From Experience" (unpublished). I also write all of my songs and currently finished a screenplay entitled, "Diamon Life: The Movie"; [pers.] My writings are the conscious reflections of my life's experience through mental and physical abuse and rape. I feet through all negativity, we all must realize, we can and will survive! [a.] Chicago, IL.

NGUYEN, QUANG X.
[b.] July 20, 1968, Saigon, Vietnam; [p.] Nhi X. (father) and Hoi T. (mother) Nguyen; [ed.] High school valedictorian, BS in Aerospace Engineering at UMCP, MS in Information Systems (part of MBA/MS program) at UMCP; [occ.] Department of Energy; [memb.] Sigma Gamma Tau, an Aerospace Honors Society; [hon.] Bausch & Lomb Science Award, Dean's List, scholarships, high school Phi Beta Kappa; [pers.] From my favorite poet, Alexander Pope: Thus let me live, unseen, unknown, Thus unlamented let me die, Steal from the world, and not a stone Tell where I lie. [a.] Silver Spring, MD.

NIESS, TINA
[b.] May 5, 1981, Mitchell County, Memorial Hospital; [p.] Vernon and Cindy Niess; [ed.] Sacred Heart Elementary, Osage Middle School; [occ.] 8th grade student; [hon.] Honor Roll. [a.] Osage, IA.

NISCE, LOURDES JASMIN P.
[pen.] Henri Dubec; [b.] September 23, 1964, Manila; [p.] Camilo Z. Nisce and Zenaida Panlilio; [ed.] University of Philippines; [occ.] Freelance writer; [memb,] UGAT AGHAM PANTAO, anthropological association of the Philippines; [hon.] Dean's list, PI Gamma MU, International Honor Society for the Social Sciences; [oth. writ.] Several poems published in American Anthology of Poetry, a poem published in the Literary Apprentice; articles published in SAY Magazine and Asenso newsletter; [pers.] I seek to portray in my writings the values in life that we cherish most. [a.] Quezon City, Philippines.

NISHIMARA, ALEXANDER MATTHEW, JR.
[b.] December 21, 1974, Bronx, NY; [p.] Antoinette and Alexander; [ed.] "More to come..."; [pers.] We, in this human universe, are nothing but the bacterial existence of and on a greater life-essence. [a.] Sousville, WY.

NOEL, FAYE MICHELLE
[b.] July 1, 1969, Carriacou, Grenada West Indies; [p.] Elevthan and Grace Noel; [ed.] Zephyrhills High School, Pasco Hernando Community College, Taylor Business Institute; [occ.] Poet, Receptionist; [oth. writ.] The Children, Essence of Love, Rainbow's End, Unseen Blessings. Recently finished writing my first book of poetry (52 poems) still looking for a publisher; [pers.] It is through poetry that the world can get acquainted with my deepest thoughts and feelings. Poetry is the mind. Talent is the soul. Now the world can see the inner me! [a.] Brooklyn, NY.

NOLAN, AMY
[b.] August 14, 1980, Fredricksburg, VA; [p.] Bill and Paige Nolan-siblings Ricky and Lisa Nolan; [ed.] High school; [occ.] 9th grade; [memb.] Student Government 2 years, '92-'93 Associated Student Body Class President, and Secretary; [hon.] 1993-94 City Queen, 1991-92 Presidential Academic Fitness Award, 1992 San Bernardino CO. Academic Pentathlon, 1992 Nestle Beich Sales Achievement Award; [pers.] The poems I wrote which goes untitled, was written in loving memory of a friend and teacher who had recently died. All of the poems I write come from my heart and reflect my thoughts and emotions. [a.] Fontana, CA.

NOONE, DEMIAN
[b.] January 27, 1947, New Jersey; [p.] Ruth and Joe (deceased); [ed.] High school, art school, Wayne State University; [occ.] Printing Co.; [memb.] American Society of Portrait Artists; [oth. writ.] Currently working on a book of my poems what work, by me; [pers.] A desire for people to feel, experience and understand the power, beauty and color of language as expressed in the written word. Poetry is one these expressions. [a.] Chicago, IL.

NORBERG, MARYAN G.
[b.] August 18, 1902, Rockford, IL; [p.] Nima and George Sundberg; [m.] Everett C. Norberg (deceased), October 3, 1929; [ch.] Charles E. Worber; [ed.] High school, 2 years college, musical education, singer, wedding consultant; [memb.] Presbyterian Church, U.S.A. Historian United Church Women; [hon.] Lifetime membership in Presbyterian Church, given black and gold pin, silver bowl; [oth. writ.] Compose all my own greeting cards - also for others writing for high school - stories, poems composed songs, wrote short dramas - comedies; [pers.] To follow my Lord God - to find good in everyone - to be friendly and helpful to all to respect everyone's religious beliefs. To "wear a smile" and not be envious of others. [a.] Reston, VA.

NORMAN, VAN HORNE
[b.] October 10, 1919, Hampton, NH; [p.] Foster child at age 4; [ed.] Grammar 4 years high 2 years accounting college; [occ.] Disabled Household mover and packer - teamster Union Local 191; [memb.] VFW Post #145 Bridgeport, CT; [hon.] Golden Poet award 1989 in Washington DC, Post Poet VFW Post #145 Bridgeport, CT (appointed) Outstanding mover and packer from Mayflower Moving and storage Co.; [pers.] I was inspired by my neighbor, Henry Wardsworth Longfellow of Congress St. Portland, ME. [a.] Bridgeport, CT.

NORRIS, ANGELA D.
[pen.] Angie Norris; [b.] November 28, 1980, Dayton; [p.] Naomi and Richard Norris; [ed.] Kettering Junior High School; [memb.] Christian Life Center Church, Power of the Pen; [hon.] KJH Writing Award for Writing Best Children's Story Power of the Pen; [oth. writ.] Over 100 poems, 50 songs, many stories; [pers.] I write about good things like love. I write what I really feel inside and writing allows me to express myself to the fulles extent. [a.] Kettering, OH.

NORRIS, HENRY CLAY II
[b.] July 3, 1959, Monroe, LA; [p.] Mr. and Mrs Henry C. Norris; [ed.] Neville High School, Northeast Louisiana University; [occ.] Various temp agencies; [hon.] In 1981 my short story "Adam & Eve All Over Again" won honorable mention in th Louisiana College Writer's Contest; [oth. writ.] am the author of three self-published books: Philosophical Fictions, Movies For Your Mind and Se Inscriptions.

NORRIS, MARIA GABRIELLA
[b.] August 10, 1964, Camden, NJ; [p.] Edward an Nancy Randow; [m.] Joseph D., September 1 1988; [ch.] Thomas Edward, Michael Decla Sarah Danielle. [a.] Woodbury, NJ.

MOUR, BRENDA
[pen.] Beta Jean; [b.] February 13, 1957, Bel flower, CA; [p.] Fred Rock and Janet Podell; [m Gamal Nour; [ch.] Joyce Yeh and Jason Trun [ed.] GED and some dental assistance educatio [occ.] Housewife; [memb.] American Heart Ass ciation, American Cancer Society; [hon.] Go Student Award from Brea Library and El Po Loco chicken, Certificate of Merit for particip tion in Parent Education classes, award from Unit States Purchasing Exchange; [oth. writ.] I wri songs and sing them in my home; [pers.] I ha been involved in my own child custody case and see other children being used, as pawns, toys and I feel for them all. [a.] Brea, CA.

NOURI, MOHAMMAD HOSSEIN AMIDI
[pen.] Farhad; [b.] November 15, 1942, Tehra [p.] Abolhassan and Anisdoleh; [m.] Mitra, 197 [ed.] Business Administration degree and Mark

ing diploma both from England; [occ.] Business-man/poet; [memb.] Lifetime member International Society of Poets (ISP), Institute of Marketing of England; [hon.] Finalist in 1992 and 1994 North American Open Poetry Contest, with my poems "Who Rules Our World" and "Strangers When We Meet", the former was published in the anthology book of "Where Dreams Begin", in 1993. My poem "Peace Please" was published in the Tehran Times, January 1994; [oth. writ.] My various original poems notably "The Way We Are", "Strangers When We Meet", and "Reflection", have been entered into poetry contests of ISP awaiting results, my poem "Life" is to be published in the anthology book named THE BEST POETS, in spring 1995; [pers.] I strive to wipe out the barriers to communications and count on your supports. [a.] Tehran, Iran.

NOWICKI, GERALDINE FRISCIO
[pen.] Geri; [b.] May 9, 1945, Brooklyn, NY; [p.] Mary and Salvatore Friscio; [m.] Joe, May 28, 1966; [ch.] Joseph and Scott; [ed.] Maxwell Vocational High School; [occ.] Sales Representative for National Fed. of Ind. Business in Boca Raton, FL; [memb.] Abundant Life Christian Center, Calvert Chapel in Pompano, Ministry For the Homeless; [hon.] The Finest Award I could ever be blessed with is having God in my life, the best husband (Joe), 2 fine sons Joey and Scott. All whom I could not be more proud of - 2 loving parents and 3 sisters Annette, Carol and Judy; [oth. writ.] I have written several poems. This is my first to be published. God has inspired me to write from the deepest part of my heart for the problems we face today - My poems I truly hope will open everyone's eyes; [pers.] I feel it's my responsibility to relay a strong and powerful message I receive from God which my poems reflect about today's problems in our society regarding: The Homeless - Our abused children and the elderly. [a.] Tamarac, FL.

NOWICKI, KAREN
[b.] July 30, 1981, Willingboro; [p.] Barbara and John Nowicki; [ed.] Westfield Friends School; [hon.] Summa cum laude for Latin contest, 7th grade; [oth. writ.] None other than school; [pers.] I really don't care what people think about me. I'm not afraid to be myself. [a.] Palmyra, NJ.

NTAL-I'MBIRWA, ALIMASI
[b.] September 27, 1962, Bukavu (Zaire); [p.] Alimasi Byasi and M'Lushere; [ed.] MS Community Development with International Specialization (New Hampshire College), M.Ed. with specialization in African Literature (Institut Superieur Pedagogique, Bukavu), BA Applied Education w/ majors in African Culture and English; [occ.] Research Associate, Inst. for International Research, consultant (Int'l Community Econ. Development); [oth. writ.] Deep Waters of Life (poems), Deaf Talk (poems), Feuilles d'Amour ou la Souffrance d'aimer (poems), Christianity and Monotheism in the Bushi. A study of the Shi Divinity (thesis); Characterization in Bonnie Lubega's The Outcasts and Mbella Sonne Dipoko's Because of Women (thesis); [pers.] One who stands at the edge of a cliff is wise to define progress as one step backward. [a.] Arlington, VA.

O'BRIEN, CHARLOTTE ANDERSON
[b.] October 13, 1950, Los Angeles, CA; [p.] Chester and Grace Anderson; [m.] Jonathan Dorr O'Brien, July 18, 1981; [ch.] Lauren Elizabeth; [ed.] Santa Monica High School, Santa Monica College, University of California Los Angeles; [occ.] Advertising Assistant; [memb.] UCLA Alumni Association; [hon.] Clifton Webb Grant, President's Undergraduate Fellowship, Teaching Assistant Fellowship, Master Teaching Assistant Fellowship, Sam Briskin award, Bilbao International Film Festival participant; [oth. writ.] Several unproduced screenplays; [pers.] I'm a firm believer in the power and magic of love. This poem is dedicated to my parents who are now deceased. [a.] Ventura, CA.

O'BRIEN, MERRY E.
[pen.] Merry E. O'Brien; [b.] October 28, 1979, Palo Alto, CA; [p.] Donald E. and Rebecca L. O'Brien; [ed.] Notre Dame High School; [occ.] Student; [hon.] Optimist Oratorical Awards, Principal's award, Athletics award; [oth. writ.] A poem published in the "Anthology of Poetry by Young Americans", called "RED" 1993 edition. A poem for the Literary magazine of Notre Dame High School called "A Drop So Deep"; [pers.] The feelings of my mind, body, soul reflect onto the writings of my poetry. What I feel from my heart does not come out in works, but on paper. To explain the experiences of my life. I give you a unique way to understand. [a.] Gilroy, CA.

O'CLISHAM, TULLY MACLIAM
[b.] January 8, 1985, Falls Church, VA; [p.] Liam Conor and Cealaig Byrne O'Clisham (sisters-Maire'ad, Maura McCealaig, Maeve, Maigida-Cait; [ed.] 5th grade home schooled; [occ.] Vocation-priest; [memb.] St. Joseph Roman Catholic Church Children's Choir, Blue Claw Marine Science Club, Sea Isle City Little League, Sea Isle City Soccer; [hon.] First honors 3rd and 4th grade; [oth. writ.] Am currently working on poetry and a story about the future; [pers.] Before I write, I like to wonder about the people, places and ideas in my stories. I especially like to wonder about the future. [a.] Sea Isle City, NJ.

O'CONNOR, TERRY
[b.] August 15, Springfield, MO; [p.] Terry and Margueret O'Connor; [m.] Shirley (Lake) O'Connor, June 1974; [ch.] Daughter 16 and son 14; [ed.] Elementary, high school, Marine Corps, Audiology; [occ.] Recently sold files in 15 years of practice fitting hearing instruments work patient mentally retarded; started herb farm; [memb.] Medicinal Herbs Building Greenhouse, Lions Club, USCG Flotila Boy Scouts, Sailing Club; [oth. writ.] Used to write in '60's underground, political, alternative estacology study of last days; [pers.] Business taught me what people do to other people for money, studying medicinal herbs and plants that doctor's and pharmaceuticals do not want to be known. [a.] Springfield, MO.

OHANNESIAN, TIFFANY
[b.] July 26, 1981, Los Angeles; [p.] Dorn and Rose Ohannesian; [ed.] Currently 8th grade student; [occ.] Student/8th grade; [hon.] Armenian Mesrobian School Honor Roll, sports awards - Volleyball and Basketball; [oth. writ.] Poems, short stories; [pers.] My goal in life is to treat everyone with love and respect and achieve peace. In doing so, all other good things will follow. I do believe in this philosophy which has been taught to me at an early age by my mother. [a.] Whittier, CA.

O'HAWK, KRISTINA
[pen.] Krissy, Kristoff; [b.] April 2, 1980, Allentown, PA; [p.] Bernard and Diane; [ed.] Lincoln Middle School Catasauqua; [occ.] Student; [memb.] Church choir; [hon.] Presidential awards, track awards, student of the month; [pers.] Someday I hope to become a teacher and author. [a.] Catasauqua, PA.

O'HAYER, MARYKATHLEEN
[b.] September 7, 1973; [ed.] University of Indianapolis, Warren Central High School; [oth. writ.] Published previously in Poetic Voices of America Spring 1994, Contemporary Poets of America and Britain Winter 1994, Sequaya 1990 and 1991; [pers.] C.S. Lewis once wrote "God whispers to us in our pleasures, speaks in our conscience, but shouts in our pain". I've learned to recognize God's voice in my pain and how He uses that pain. God tells me to put my pain into prose and hear what He has to say. He's speaking to us all of the time if only we would stop and listen. [a.] Indianapolis, IN.

O'NEIL, MARIE HOLMAN
[b.] August 1933, Pittsburgh, PA; [p.] Deceased Mr. and Mrs. R. Earl Holman; [m.] John W., August 1953; [ed.] 40 years experience as Secretary/ Manager in industry, social agencies, churches and school; [occ.] Writing a series of novels. The Chapel Road Series, seven novels; [hon.] Numerous certificates of appreciation for volunteer entertainment at nursing homes and retirement centers. Play the keyboard and sing with husband; [oth. writ.] Novel: The Whispering Winds of Chapel Road 40,000 words; [pers.] We may not realize how much of our life is spent marching to the beat of someone else's drum. When, in fact, we are free to develop our own traditions, beauty, and fun. [a.] Ocala, FL.

O'SHEA, CAROL J.
[pen.] Carol Berry O'Shea; [b.] March 23, 1926, Kansas City, KS; [p.] Madge and Andrew Berry; [m.] Maurice V., November 24, 1945; [ch.] Maurine, Michael, Kathleen, Kelly, Erin; [ed.] High school and continuous reading, including many of the "Great Books", encyclopedia and an average of five books per week on varied subjects; [occ.] Homemaker, worked for two years as paraprofessional in the Lawrence, KS school system; [hon.] Not many awards, but many gifts. The greatest gift of course was life. Those that follow in importance are love and the ability to feel deeply what that life has presented to me, and wonderful family and friends; [oth. writ.] I had two poems published in a small poetry quarterly called, "Reflections" that was published in Conway, AR in 1993; [pers.] I was given much encouragement by teachers from elementary school on, to continue writing and was told I had a gift for writing. Though I married young and did not pursue a career, I never lost my love for writing about the beauty and the sadness in life. Writing is recording what the eye can behold, what the mind can imagine and what the heart and soul can feel. Written words may capture what is startlingly real or something so fleeting as a dream. [a.] Springfield, MO.

OAKLEY, JUANITA COLOMB
[b.] October 13, 1946, New Orleans; [p.] Edgar George and Joyce Coleman Colomb; [m.] Francis C. Oakley, Jr., November 25, 1967; [ch.] Scott and Rebecca; [ed.] High School; [occ.] Legal Secretary; [pers.] This is my personal goodbye to a man I love deeply in my heart. It's my way of letting go of my life with him. [a.] New Orleans, LA.

OBAWOLE, DEBO
[pen.] Debo Obawole, Debor Richards; [b.] October 13, 1957, Lagos-Nigeria; [p.] S.A. Richards and A.N. Richards; [m.] A.B. Obawole, April 2, 1983; [ch.] Jimi and Emmanuel Obawole; [ed.] BA & MA Philosophy; [occ.] Studying to become a nurse; [oth. writ.] Many unpublished poems and short stories; [pers.] I wish this earth would go back to its original state of purity in nature and man to live purity of mind. [a.] Austin, TX.

OBERHOLTZER, TERESA
[b.] September 3, 1958, Ephrata, PA; [p.] George and Faye Walter; [m.] William J. Jr., June 26, 1983; [ch.] Alicia Marie Oberholtzer; [ed.] Ephrata High

School; [occ.] Sunline Coach Co-Cabinet Maker; [oth. writ.] I have written other poems for gifts and special occasions; [pers.] I wrote this poem for my father's 60th birthday. I think all parents deserve this kind of tribute. [a.] Denver, PA.

OLIVIER, MARY ELIZABETH
[b.] may 29, 1908, Terre Haute, IN; [p.] Elizabeth Patterson and George Wilber; [m.] Oliver Michael, July 16, 1937; [ch.] Lee, George, Lynne Olivier; [ed.] High school McKees Rocks, PA, Duquesne University; [occ.] Retired as reading specialist in 1973. Began first remedial reading program in the Stowe Twp School Dist. Last three years of teaching I ran a reading clinic; [memb.] AARP, PSEA, Andrus Foundation; [oth. writ.] Short stories and poems of incidents in my life; [pers.] I have lived my life as an honorable, trustworthy person in all situations and given help to others including family when possible. My children have followed my example. [a.] Daly City, CA.

OLSEN, ANGELA MARIE
[b.] December 6, 1968, Iron Mountain, MI; [p.] Jerry and Patricia Olsen; [ed.] Hamilton College, Georgetown University, Catholic University of America; [pers.] I thank my parents for their encouragement and my professors at Hamilton College for their inspiration and support.

OLSON, BETSY
[b.] May 12, 1983, Waterstown S.D.; [p.] John and Helen Olson; [ed.] Clark Elementary School; [memb.] Piano, gymnastics band, odyssey of the mind, and just say no; [hon.] I was on the B honor roll 3 quarters and A honor roll one quarter in the 5th grade. And so far in the 6th grade I've been on the B honor roll once; [oth. writ.] I am 11 years old and ever since I was born I have had asthma. Some people treat me different but I still have the ability of doing everything any normal person can do; [pers.] I inherit my writing skills from my mother and both of my parents are always cheering me on. And one thing I believe in is that if you put your heart into it, no matter who you are you can do it. [a.] Clark, SD.

ONDIGI, SAMSON
[pen.] Sam'; [b.] March 21, 1959, Kisii-Kenya; [p.] George and Jemimah Abere; [m.] Alice N., July 21, 1992; [ch.] Olivia K. Ondigi; [ed.] University of Minnesota; [occ.] Writers; [memb.] Treasurer of NASA Cooperation, Seventh Day Adventist Church, Youth Organizing Secretary; [hon.] Community Volunteer award, Dean's List; [oth. writ.] A research on the effect of 8-4-4 education system on Harambee Secondary schools in Kenya; several inspiring poems published in high school newsletters; [pers.] Olivia will poeticize my writing. Since my high school, I have been greatly interested in romantic and misery poems. [a.] Columbia Heights, MN.

ORPHANOUDAKIS, JOYCE G.
[pen.] Joyce G. Orphanoudakis; [b.] March 9, 1941, Salem, NJ; [p.] David and Violet Husted; [m.] George A., march 1, 1964; [ch.] Andrew and Alan; [ed.] High school, Brookdale College; [occ.] Hairstylist and artist - watercolorist; [hon.] Wife, mother, career woman, business owner. Just write what I feel about people I love and life. Brookdale College high honors in art, watercolors; [oth. writ.] Just started to write in 1993, after I lost my husband George. I write to express my feelings to get thru the grief. It helped greatly. Thank you.; [pers.] I write from the heart, my family was very easy to love; but each one of them had strong minds and good hearts. I always was helpful to my fellowman and walked with God always.

ORTIZ, CHRISTINA
[pen.] Cuddles; [b.] June 10, 1980, Newark; [p.] Migdalia and Ruben Ortiz; [ed.] Grammar School and grade student Wilson Ave School; [pers.] Beyond the lightness laids the darkness, beyond the darkness laids my thought. [a.] Newark, NJ.

OSBORNE, MOZELLE
[pen.] Mo Oaborne; [b.] April 13, 1939, Kemp, OK; [p.] Mamie and John May; [m.] Mike, October 29, 1966; [ch.] Ray, Wayne, Natalie, John; [ed.] Kemp High School; [occ.] Manicurest; [memb.] Church of Christ, Heart Association, Quilting Club; [hon.] 2 song awards 1972 (copyrighted); [oth. writ.] Several poems though unpublished. Two songs copyrighted entitled "My Love", and "Fraction of A Heartache"; [pers.] I'm just thankful to God. I have been blessed by him to write. I'll do my best in this life. [a.] Big Spring, TX.

OSEGUERA, CEJA ELVIRA
[b.] March 19, 1969, Mexico; [p.] Enrique and Juana Ceja; [ed.] CSLA BA in Child Development; [occ.] Teacher in elementary; [oth. writ.] Publications in Alchemy, Statement, RiverSedge and Untitled. [a.] Huntington Park, CA.

OSTER, ANGELA M.
[pen.] Angie Oster; [b.] August 12, 1975, West VA; [p.] Darren and Louise Shambough; [ed.] Paw Paw High School; [pers.] I owe my achievements to God, and my mother who gave me her honest opinion, whether I liked it or not. I love to read and write and will, until I die.

OSTRANDER, AMANDA
[b.] June 2, 1976, Lansing, MI; [p.] Paul and Linda Ostrander; [ed.] Leslie High School; [occ.] Student; [memb.] Big Brothers/Big Sisters of Jackson, MI; 4-H Council, Student Class treasurer, Forensics (drama) treasurer, Varsity Girls Tennis team, 1994 4-H Ambassador, NHS National Honor Society; [hon.] "Excellence in Art" at 1994 Ingham County Fair, "Coach's Award" for '93 team, many other Forensics and tennis awards; [oth. writ.] Several personal poems that are unpublished; [pers.] This poem is about a resident at Jackson County Medical Care Facility in Jackson, MI, that passed away. I volunteer there in there ceramics activities and loved her with all my soul. [a.] Leslie, MI.

OUTLAW, WANDA C.
[b.] October 17, 1954, Washington, DC; [p.] Mary L. and Augustus King Brown (deceased); [ch.] Stephen T. Outlaw, Jr.; [ed.] ST. Patricks Academy (high school), Trinity College; [ed.] HRD Specialist; [memb.] AACC (African American Catholic Congregation-Imani Temple); Imani Temple Poet Laureate, Temple Coordinator Lector Ministry, National Association for Female Executives; [hon.] 1987 Outstanding Young Woman of America; Toastmasters Bulletin Editor of the Year 1986, Outstanding Volunteer Employee-Veterans Administration 1985; Partnership Award from OPM 1985; [oth. writ.] "a loss" American Poetry Anthology 1985; "A Visitor" "in passing" in the University of Kansas Cottonwood publication 1986; "I Mean No Disenchantment, But..." self-published '91-'93.

PACK, SHERRY
[b.] October 4, 1975, Portsmouth, OH; [p.] John and Shirley Howard; [m.] Kevin, April 5, 1993; [ch.] Kayla Nichole Pack; [ed.] Minford High, Shawnee State University; [occ.] Cashier, Rally's Hamburgers; [hon.] National Honor Society; [pers.] I believe that the best poetry comes from within your heart, and is most greatly influenced by those you love. [a.] Portsmouth, OH.

PAIGE, ELEANOR G.
[b.] June 3, 1928, Cleveland, OH; [p.] Rose L. and Archie Johnson; [m.] Charles Paige Jr. (deceased), September 29, 1956; [ch.] Roger Paige; [ed.] High School, computer classes, line dancing - senior group cleve, housing mgmt class; [occ.] Educational Aide (laid off); [memb.] AARP, Cleveland Northeast Ohio Credit Union, Cleveland Teachers Union, Home Base Senior Group, Friends of Shaken Space; [hon.] Project Learn - Reading Certificate, Educational Aide Certificate, Housing Management Certificate; [oth. writ.] Letters to the Cleveland Board of Education concerning my employment for 23 years; [pers.] You're never too old to learn or teach! This poem is for all the paraprofessionals, clerks, lunch aides who worked for the Cleveland Board of Education. Looking forward to the day one student will thank them for their help. [a.] Cleveland, OH.

PALACIOS, PAMELA
[b.] October 5, 1979, Chattanooga, TN; [p.] Joyce and Ed Palacios; [ed.] Red Bank High School 10th grade; [hon.] Honor student.

PALAZZOLO, TONI
[b.] October 23, 1990, Elk Grove, IL; [p.] Frank Palazzolo and Vita Owen; [pers.] I usually write my poems when I'm depressed and there is no one to listen to me. [a.] Streamwood, IL.

PALLADINO, LENORE MIRIAM
[b.] August 24, 1980, Worcestor, WA; [p.] Stephanie and Arthur Palladino; [ed.] Amherst Regional High School; [occ.] Student; [memb.] B'nai B'rith Youth Organization, Amherst Writers Association, MSPCA and Humane Society of the United States; [hon.] Jones Library of Amherst Writing Contest, Honor Roll of Amherst High School; [oth. writ.] Poem, Anthology of Young Americans. [a.] Amherst, MA.

PALMA, PAUL ALVAREZ
[b.] January 2, 1920, Philippines; [p.] Cecilio L. Palma and Severa Alvarez; [m.] Evangeline M., July 4, 1956; [ch.] Gloria, Rainier, Charles, George, Romeo, Henry, Winston, Shirley, Lenn; [ed.] Ilocos Sur High, School of Arts and Trade; [occ.] Retired Const. Supvr.; [memb.] Ilocano Association of Guam; [pers.] Coming to this country, American culture has greatly influenced me. This transition stage have given me inspiration in creating this poem, an awareness what is actually happening in our lives today. [a.] Suisun, GA.

PALMER, CINDY L.
[b.] March 18, 1957, Manchester, NH; [p.] Beverly and Harry Brown; [m.] William E. Burfeind; [ch.] Jeremy R.; [ed.] Drug High Whitman's Academy of Hair Design, Southwest Vermont College; [occ.] Assistant Treasurer for the Town of Bennington and Bennington School District, Mount Anthony Union High School District, and Southwest Vermont Supervising Union; [pers.] I strive to love my neighbor, and hope to find that in return. [a.] Bennington, VT.

PALMER, LISA GOODIN
[b.] May 30, 1961, Louisville, MS; [p.] Jack and Ree Goodin, grandmother-Alice P. Whitehead; [m.] Joe W. Palmer, Jr., February 26, 1990; [ch.] Jason Warner, Lindsay Rigdon (step-Jason Palmer and Arin Palmer; [ed.] 9th grade, GED diploma, Mississippi State University; [occ.] Sales Manager for Lumber Company; [memb.] Harmont Baptist Church; [pers.] My grandmother is 83 years young and I feel her love and teachings has put me well beyond my years in strength and support of dealing with situations of Day to Day living. [a.] Louisville, MS.

PALMER, RON
[b.] January 30, 1940, OH; [p.] Walter and Gladys Palmer; [m.] Sandra Palmer, April 25, 1966; [ch.] Rhonda Jean, Maria Lynn and Nicole; [ed.] Keifer Jr. High School; [occ.] Meat packing farmland - Foods Crete Nebraska; [oth. writ.] 200 unpublished poems some placed in newspapers - some placed in hospitals across country; [pers.] I'd like to believe my poetry is inspired by my experience in life of Good and bad times as well as Happy and sad times. And by the Greatness of those who tried to change things for the betterment of mankind. [a.] Wilber, Nebraska.

PALMIERI, DEBORAH LUCILLE
[b.] may 1, 1966, Brooklyn, NY; [p.] Vince and Carolyn Lois Palmieri; [ed.] Desert Institute of the Healing Arts; [occ.] Massage Therapist; [pers.] The more I understand myself the more compassion I have for others. I pray we all touch the depths of our soul and remember that we all make a difference and that our love make flowers grow. [a.] Tucson, AZ.

PALUMBO, LARAINE F.
[occ.] Astrologer Researcher; [memb.] American Federation of Astrologers, Inc., Ocala Civic Theater/Marion Players; [oth. writ.] My astrology poetry has been published in "Today's Astrologer". A variety of other poetry has appeared in local newspapers. Writing short story books for children is also a favorite hobby; [pers.] My type of astrology requires research and composing extensive indepth manuscripts, yet I find that poetry represents a flowing creativity easily expressed from the depths of the soul. [a.] Ocala, FL.

PAMIN, DIANA
[pen.] Diana DolhancyK; [b.] December 13, Cleveland, OH; [p.] Peter and Diana Dribus Dolhancyk; [m.] Leonard Pamin; [ch.] Diana Anne, Louis Peter; [ed.] West Tech High, Titus College of Cosmetology; [occ.] Hobbies-Interior Decorating Art; [memb.] A girl in India for 14 years; roots begin in Europe (Russia); [pers.] Always give someone a smile, you'll never know who's heart you might lighten. I can't say I was influenced by any poet in particular. I wrote my first poem at age 12. It came naturally. [a.] North Royalton, OH.

PANZA, KATHY
[b.] June 27, 1974, Arcadia, CA; [p.] Jacque and Frank Panza; [ed.] Mead High School, Spokane Falls Community College, Simpson College; [oth. writ.] "California Summer" in Of Diamonds and Rust" school newspaper; [pers.] Writing poetry helps me to clear my head. When I need to vent or express my feelings, I grab a pen and paper. [a.] Spokane, WA.

PARDOE, ROBERT C.
[b.] September 4, 1934, Franklin, PA; [p.] Mr. and Mrs. B.H. Pardoe; [ed.] Academy of Psychiatry, Medical and Surgical Academy, Air Force Base; [occ.] Retired; [memb.] The American Legion, The Veterans of Foreign Wars, The Loyal Order of Moose, Associate member Faternal/Order of Police; [hon.] Two academy awards World of Poetry, Korean Service medal, national Defense Service Medal, United Nations Service medal; [oth. writ.] Fifty seven poems; [pers.] A life, is but a moment in time. May a poem, make someone happy in that moment. [a.] Grove City, PA.

PARISH, AMANDA LYNN
[b.] November 3, 1975, Decatur, IL; [p.] Scott and Rosemarie Parish; [ed.] St. Teresa High School, Parkland College; [memb.] World Wildlife Federation, The Nature Conservancy; [pers.] I try to let people know me through my poetry. [a.] Weldon, IL.

PARKER, DANI ELAINE
[b.] February 7, 1981, Madison, WS; [p.] Fran Norman Parker; [ed.] Black Hawk Middle School in Madison; [occ.] Student; [memb.] Blackhawk Student; [oth. writ.] Column for Wisconsin State Journal about my school (a daily Madison newspaper); [pers.] My Mom is a writer I must take after her. I have 3 sisters and one brother so I learned how to communicate effectively at an early age. [a.] Madison, WS.

PARKER, DOROTHY CERVANTES
[pen.] D.C. Parker; [b.] September 15, 1949, Troy, NY; [p.] John L. Cervantes and Dorothy C. Potter; [m.] John Avery Parker, Jr.; [ch.] Williamjohn A. Polidoro, Karin Elizabeth Sekela, Nicole Carmela Polidoro - (grandchildren-Michael, Cody, Ashley, Katelyn and two more yet to be born); [oth. writ.] The Golden Chain, We Need The Rain, I Remember You, Jennie Elizabeth's House; [pers.] I write about what I know best my family. I write so that my grandchildren will know about me and so that our family history will go on for another generation. And if I am lucky, one of my grandkids will write about me. [a.] Brevard, NC.

PARKER, LAWRENCE E.
[pen.] Larry Parker; [b.] December 22, 1938, Washington, DC; [p.] Fred and Evelyn Parker; [m.] Alice, September 11, 1961; [ch.] Wesley Charles, Pamela Jewel, Patricia Michele, Jay Lawrence; [ed.] USAF Tech schools, Barstow Jr. College, NASA Equipment; [occ.] Gospel Singer/retired aerospace; [memb.] First Assembly of God Church; [hon.] Cum Laude, National Dean's List, Christian Ministries award, STS-2 Shuttle Flag award; [oth. writ.] The Chronological Revelation - not yet published; [pers.] The most important thing in life is a personal relationship with our Creator God through his son Jesus Christ. [a.] Barstow, CA.

PARRIS, CHRIS
[b.] August 23, 1966, Harrisonville, MO; [p.] Ray and Millie Parris; Don and Jackie Waterman; [m.] Colleen, November 6, 1994; [ch.] Erica Christen; [ed.] Pleasant Hill High School, Sam Houston State University; [occ.] Air Traffic Controller; [pers.] My subject material generally is centered on family and memories of yesteryear. I have been greatly influenced by my grandmother Della, my late grandpa Leroy and mom. [a.] Spring, TX.

PARSONS, MARY LOU
[pen.] Lou; [b.] February 15, 1946, Aurora; [p.] Edward J. and Mary Ellinghusen Sr. (dad passed away 6/10/79); [m.] Divorced both husbands deceased; [ch.] Richard Allen and Brian Edward Anderson; [ed.] West Aurora Schools; [occ.] Laundry at The Super 8 Motel; [pers.] I've never won anything in my whole life, and this is just wonderful that I've finally won something or even came in running for something. "Praise the Lord". [a.] Aurora, IL.

PASCHALL, DAVID
[pen.] David Thomas; [b.] October 23, 1977, Brooklyn, NY; [p.] Debbie Paschall-Thomas and Robert Thomas (step father) - David Paschall (father); [ed.] Redon High School; [memb.] Redon Junior ROTC; [oth. writ.] Story- The Mysterious Macrocosm Smiling Faces, When The Inability is Yours, America The Beautiful, Childs Dream...; poems-Reversed, Indifferent, Mind Power, Faight and Chance, Star Gazer, Dedicated to Dad, Mother and many more; [pers.] Words on paper that are not from the heart are dead words without soul or meaning. Words on paper that are true in definition carry a man like wings of feather laced lightly with gold. [a.] Stone Mountain, GA.

PATTERSON, CELESTINE J.
[pen.] Tina Jay; [b.] April 29, 1939, Chicago, IL; [p.] Opral and Wardell Sutton; [ch.] Michael, Michelle, Crystal, Jacquelynne and Steven; [ed.] High school - Clep Credit currently enrolled Daley College; [occ.] Office Manager - Nursing Administration; [memb.] Professional Secretaries International; [oth. writ.] Many - done on request for persons I know and special events; [pers.] My gift of writing is God given. I want to always reflect pride, love and gratitude in all my writing. It's like "putting a hug on paper". [a.] Chicago, IL.

PATTERSON, DIANE S.
[b.] July 9, 1951, Monongahela, PA; [p.] Margaret and Stefan Seydor; [ed.] Monessen High School, Robert Morris College, State University of New York; [occ.] Teacher for the Department of Defense Dependent Schools; [memb.] Alpha Iota Sorority, OEA, NEA; [hon.] Received acknowledgement for photographs submitted to local photo contest. Teacher of the Year for DC Department of Corrections at Central facility; [pers.] Don't give in to the madness around you. Be true to yourself, follow your heart, and listen to the quiet spirit within you. [a.] Keflavik, Iceland.

PATTERSON, JR., HAROLD LINTON
[pen.] Nickname "Howie"; AKA Lot; [b.] August 13, 1959, Wauchula, FL; [p.] Betty Reid and Harold Patterson, Sr.; [ed.] Electronics Technician, WSMC; [occ.] Retired; [oth. writ.] Author of poem "Engima" my vert favorite and best; [pers.] My works tend to serve as reminders of the pureness and permanency of the virtues, honor and truth. My readers will often remember, occasionally foresee and always review for focus. Main influencer, the Holy Bible. [a.] Lakeland, FL.

PATTERSON, MINNIE B.
[pen.] Ms. Pat Patterson; [b.] September 25, 1909, Huntington, OR; [p.] Frank and Ida Bryant; [m.] Widow, October 18, 1939; [ed.] The Youngest of Family of 13; [occ.] Retired from Production Engineer at Lockheed; [memb.] American Legion, The Womens Memorial of Service - Wash., DC; [hon.] Picture with Womens Ball team - with President Hoover at The White House 1931; [oth. writ.] Only in school and for pleasure one published in Lockheed Paper 1941; [pers.] In air corp army war #2 coached women's softball team also airplane electrician. [a.] Montclair, CA.

PATTON, GRACE N.T.
[b.] October 6, 1974, Philippines; [p.] Paul Z. and Angeles C. Patton; [ed.] South High School, Columbus State Community College; [a.] Columbus, OH.

PAUL, JEAN C.
[b.] May 9, 1922, Mineola, NY; [p.] Theodore and Charlotta Schmidt (deceased); [m.] Frank C., July 15, 1943 (deceased); [ch.] Harvey M. and Steven F. Paul - 4 grandchildren; [ed.] Adelphi University; [occ.] Retired Hospital Ward Clerk; [memb.] St. Alfred's Episcopal Church and church choir, Volunteer Mease Hospital, Aux. of the Reserve Officers Association of USA, "Cursillo" an Episcopal Renewal of Faith Group; [hon.] Honor given for one thousand hours as a volunteer at Mease Hosp., Soprano soloist with many choirs and choral groups while living in NY; [oth. writ.] "The Touch Divine" pub. in "Outstanding Poets of 1994"; [pers.] If I can lead someone to believe in God, through my poems. I will feel truly blessed. [a.] Palm Harbor, FL.

PAYNE, RICHARD JAMES JR.
[pen.] Rick Payne; [b.] September 24, 1952, Gloversville, NY; [p.] Diana H. Melita and Richard J. Payne Sr.; [m.] Kathleen A., September 24, 1984; [ch.] James and Jennifer; [ed.] Gloversville High, Fulton Montgomery Community College, Alfred State Ag. and Tech., Zenger-Miller Management Consulting School; [occ.] Production Coordinator for a leather manufacturer; [memb.] Board member of Literacy Volunteers of America of Fulton County New York; [hon.] Dean's List, School Literary Magazines, nominated for American Spirit award at U.S. Navy Training Center Great Lakes, Chicago IL; [oth. writ.] Short stories for Scholastic Literary Magazines and Christian songs; [pers.] The Memories and lives of Senior Citizens have so much to offer a younger generation if they will take the time to listen to the richness and full experience of wisdom that older persons want and need to share. [a.] Johnstown, NY.

PAYNE, SHIRLEY M.
[b.] September 4, 1952, Savannah, GA; [p.] John and Ora Faust; [m.] James E. (Gene), April 9, 1971; [ch.] James and Jenny Payne; [ed.] Groves High School, St. Leo College; [occ.] Housewife, past volunteer for American Red Cross, Army Community Service, PTA and various community counsel activities, and spouse of a retired service member; [hon.] All volunteer related; [oth. writ.] Poems written for school newspapers, an article for local paper; [pers.] The inspiration for all of my poems has come from real life experiences. Reading them, one would think that I am leading a very sad and depressing life, but not so, on the contrary, I think I am wiser and more compassionate having lived each event. [a.] Faulkville, GA.

PEAKE, RUSSELL C.
[pen.] RC Peake; [b.] May 20, 1949, Detroit, MI; [p.] Geraldine Biel and Russell Peake; [m.] Christine Peake, June 18, 1988; [ch.] Jessica Julia and Cynthia Eileen; [ed.] Lincoln Park High School; [occ.] Clerk - Ford Motor Company; [memb.] Vietnam Veteran Marines; [pers.] My influence stems from Sara Teasdale's writings. [a.] Taylor, MI.

PEARCE, MELVIN MICHAEL
[pen.] Mike Pearce; [b.] July 13, 1943, LaMesa, TX; [p.] Melvin and Jane Pearce; [m.] Ann Roether Pearce, October 3, 1964; [ch.] John, Todd, Doug; [ed.] Hobbs High School, Eastern NM University, University of IA, University of Nor. CO; [occ.] Public School Band Teacher, Community College Anthropology Teacher; [memb.] Colorado Music Educators Association, Music Educators National Association, National School Orchestra Association, Colorado Bandmasters Association, American String Teachers Association, National Association of Jazz Educators, National Education Association, Colorado Historical Society, Denver Museum of Natural History, Smithsonian; [hon.] Lakewood HS Teacher of the Year, Jefferson County Teacher of the Year, MAC Award - Distinguished Band Directors, Business Week Award for Creative Teaching; [oth. writ.] Many unpublished poems, unpublished music arrangements and anthropology monographs. [a.] Littleton, CO.

PEARSON, EVELYN JEAN
[pen.] Granny (sometimes); [b.] April 29, 1928, Mystic, IA; [p.] Mr. and Mrs. Emery Dickey; [m.] Karl W., August 29, 1945; [ch.] Thomas, Kathleen, Sandra (deceased), Danny (deceased); [ed.] High school; [occ.] Greeter at K-Mart was Cardio Pulmonary 17 years and worked for the State of Florida approx. 9 years; [memb.] Inactive member of Baptist church; [oth. writ.] Many approx. 100; [pers.] See a person beyond materialistic appearances...acceptance of others as they are...influenced by my teacher of yesteryear Bessie Stout. Most writings based on experienced of living. [a.] Native, IL.

PENNY, RADWA
[b.] October 1, 1983, Cairo, Egypt; [p.] James and Maha Penny; [ed.] Public School 188, New York City 1989-94; Butterfield Trail Elementary School; [occ.] 6th grade student; [hon.] Woman's History Month Poem award - Principal's honors list (5th grade) - various scholastic awards; [oth. writ.] Several poems and short stories; [pers.] My poem portrays the never ending struggle between man vs nature. Though my poem is rather solemn, most of my other writings include tidbits of humor here and there about life. [a.] Fayettesville, AR.

PEREZ, BELKIS
[pen.] Belkis Perez; [b.] January 7, 1979; [p.] Pedro E. Perez and Barbara Planehart; [ed.] St. Brendan High; [occ.] Full-time high school student; [pers.] I view writing as a way of expressing myself. My family and close friends have been a great support and influence, I would like to thank them all. [a.] Miami, FL.

PERKING, MARIA G.
[b.] August 20, 1934, Mexico; [p.] Mr. and Mrs. Jose Villescas; [m.] Sgt. First class David G. Perkins (retired army), August 3,1 963; [ch.] Lisa Ann, Joseph, Michael, David II; [ed.] McAllen High School, Pan American College, Our Lady of The Lake; [occ.] Records Specialist; [memb.] Tax Assessor Collector of Rio Grande Valley Secretary, Catholic Altar Society, Confratority of Christian Doctrine, AARP; [hon.] Poet of the Year (World Book of Poetry), Poet of Merit from International Poet Society, First place Creative Writing International Adult Talent Awards; [oth. writ.] In the Company of God, I'll Cry Tomorrow, My Daughter Lisa, Love Dreams In the Rain, If I Had A Magic Wand, and many other unpublished poems and short stories "Only God" poem published by Fine Arts Press; [pers.] Day dreams are our best friends; they take us wherever we want to be, (be what we want to be), love wherever we want to love - any day, any hour, any minute of the day - we can soar like a bird, bloom like a flower, swim the deepest ocean, dreams have no boundaries - it sets no limits. [a.] Edinburg, TX.

PERL, TOBI
[b.] October 14, 1970, Cali, Columbia; [p.] Charles and Janice Perl; [ed.] University of South Florida, Nova High School, Nova Southeastern University School of Law; [occ.] Law student; [memb.] Phi Kappa Phi, Jewish Law Students Association, Golden Key National Honor Society; [hon.] Graduated from high school and college with honors, Dean's list USF, BCC, University of South Florida honors; [oth. writ.] High school newspaper - entertainment section editor; [pers.] Every event in life becomes a memory. I write what I have lived because it comes from my memories, and my imagination. [a.] Plantation, FL.

PERRY, MATTHEW EYAN
[pen.] Matt Perry; [b.] January 6, 1982, Charleston, WV; [p.] Douglas D. and Kimberley A. Perry; [ed.] 7th grade student at Ocoee Middle School; [occ.] Student; [memb.] School band (trombone); [hon.] "Principal's award (4.0 G.P.A.); [oth. writ.] Various poems and short stories, also participated in writing anthologies at school; [pers.] I feel that there would be "peace on earth" if everyone treated each other as an equal. [a.] Orlando, FL.

PERRY, MISTY
[b.] January 29, 1980, Sturgis, MI; [p.] David and Gayla Perry; [ed.] Sturgis Middle School, Sturgis High School; [occ.] Student; [memb.] Student Council; [hon.] Awarded for writing poetry; [oth. writ.] Several poems published in school newspaper; [pers.] I feel sad yet there is a smile on my face. I feel tired yet I am still running. Never underestimate my power. [a.] Sturgis, MI.

PESONEN, JENNIFER
[b.] October 23,1 981, Kingston, NY; [p.] James and Patricia Pesonen; [ed.] Navesink Elementary School, Bayshore Middle School; [occ.] Student; [memb.] Middletown Traveling Soccer Club, Challenger Program Buddy - a group of young adults teaching mentally and physically handicapped children how to play soccer, Student Council; [hon.] Presidential Academic Award, Honor Roll. [a.] Navesink, NJ.

PETERS-GOLDEN, REBECCA
[b.] March 1, 1982, Baltimore, MD; [p.] Marc and Holly Peters-Golden; [ed.] Clague Middle School; [occ.] 7th grader; [memb.] Hobb-Young People's Theater Acting Troupe and have been in various plays, including Casey at the Bat, Orpheus and Candice, and You're A Good Man Charlie Brown; [hon.] I am very interested in art, and have won some awards for a joint project. I love music and poetry and have won an award at my school for one of my poems; [oth. writ.] Some assorted short stories, poetry and currently working on another; [pers.] Always assume the worsts and when something good comes along, you'll appreciate it even more. [a.] Ann Arbor, MI.

PETERSON, JOYCE
[b.] August 13, 1956, Elkhorn, WI; [p.] James R. and Esther M. Peterson; [ed.] East Troy High School; [occ.] Poetry Writer; [hon.] Editor's Award for the poem "My Soul at Peace"; [oth. writ.] My Soul at Peace, Being Lost & Mother's Love; [pers.] My hope is to help the world find peace through my poems. [a.] Dousman, WI.

PETERSON, KAREN A.
[b.] July 18, 1946, Minneapolis, MN; [p.] John and Doris Branger; [m.] Dennis, September 10, 1966; [ed.] College of St. Scholastica; [occ.] Program Manager for Lutheran Social Service; [memb.] AARM, AAMR, Prader Wille Association, MN Foster Providers Association; [hon.] Benediction Scholarship graduated cum laude from St. Scholastica, 1990 MSSA Foster Provider of the Year; [oth. writ.] Numerous poems and short essays, two books in progress. [a.] Motley, MN.

PHELPS, DOLORES
[b.] July 7, 1935, Chemainus, BC; [p.] Victor and Fanny Ordano; [m.] Allan, December 20, 1969; [ch.] Ricky, Sharon, Susan, Rudy, Holly and Judy; [ed.] Elementary 8th grade; [occ.] Housewife; [pers.] For my children whom I love. [a.] Chemainus, CAN.

PHILBRICK, LISA
[pen.] Lisa Philbrick; [b.] June 28, 1982, Cleveland, OH; [p.] Anthony and Vicky Philbrick; [ed.] Riverside Elementary, Gracemount Elementary, Wilbur Wright Middle School; [memb.] National Junior Honor Society; [hon.] National Junior Honor Society, Honor Roll for two years in a row; [oth. writ.] Other poems are titled: How Short A Life Could Be and other poems; [pers.] Youngest of five children, four older brothers. Our society which troubles me - inspired me to write this poem, along with my grandfather (Richard Singer) who always said he'd buy my first book. [a.] Cleveland, OH.

PHILLIPS, CLIFFORD W. JR.
[b.] October 31, 1956, Moses Lake, WA; [p.] Clifford and Shirley Phillips; [m.] Divorced; [ch.] Ashley and Amanda Phillips; [ed.] Auburn High; [occ.] Ambulance Driver for 20 years; [pers.] To the millions of loving, caring, dads who have to miss out on alot through no fault of their own. God bless each and everyone of you; and to Ashley and Amanda. Daddy loves you. [a.] Auburn, WA.

PHILLIPS, COLLEEN
[b.] January 22, 1928, Delta, UT; [m.] Widow; [ch.] Ken, Deborah Phillips; [ed.] Jefferson High School; [occ.] Retired; [memb.] Choir member of Hope Lutheran Church, American Cancer Society, Foreign Affairs Council; [oth. writ.] Poem published in 1994 San Mateo Co. Contest for "Poetry on Aging" short stories for several publications. Short story in Skyline College Creative Writers Contest; [pers.] My inspiration for writing comes from my family and grandchildren and the ever present hand of God. [a.] Colma, CA.

PHILLIPS, JOHN E.
[pen.] Too Tall; [b.] November 12, 1955, Dallas, TX; [p.] Avery and Pat Jones, J.E. Phillips; [m.] Geri, December 31, 1994; [ch.] Melissa Lacy; [ed.] Sharpstown High, Thompson Tech; [occ.] AC and Heating, Painting; [memb.] Lakewood Church, NA, CA, AA; [oth. writ.] Several; [pers.] I write about personal experiences, beliefs and my feelings recovering from a life of addiction, I try to help others. [a.] Humble, TX.

PHILLIPS, KENNETH O.
[pen.] Kenn Phillips; [b.] October 31, 1972, Cherry Pt., NC; [p.] Robert and Donna Phillips; [ed.] Garinger High School; [occ.] 3rd shift receiving Wal-Mart; [memb.] Hickory Grove Baptist Church; [hon.] Golden Poet (World of Poetry) 1990; [oth. writ.] Various unpublished poetry and songs; [pers.] I live to please no one but myself, if I happen to please a few people just by doing that - good for them. [a.] Charlotte, NC.

PHILLIPS, SUSAN STOWE
[b.] September 22,1964, Burlington, VT; [p.] Richard K. and Nancy M. Stowe; [m.] Greg O., October 28, 1986; [ch.] Travis, Jasmine, Chelsea, Brooke; [ed.] Champlain Valley Union High, Brigham Young University, American Institute of Medical/Dental Technology; [occ.] Marina/Resort Operator, Strawberry Reservoir, UT; [oth. writ.] Several Children's Stories written as a hobby; [pers.] I believe that a writer is like a photographer, capturing impressions reflecting from the mind and soul. [a.] Orem, UT.

PHILPOT, LONA M.
[pen.] Lona M. Lawson; [b.] May 19, 1945, Bentonville, AR; [p.] Millard F. and Marjorie Lawson; [ed.] Siloam Springs High School; [occ.] Administrative Assistant to Dick W. Dick of ECA Companies, a financial services corporation; [memb.] Treasurer and member of Westside Christian Church of El Paso; [hon.] Citation from the Oklahoma Senate for service above and beyond the call of duty at the bank where I was employed; [oth. writ.] My first was written about 13 years ago, but I have only written for family and friends. I have written quite a number, but not has any published; [pers.] My grandmother Arvilla Pratt wrote poetry and I feel my inspiration is a "gift" from her and a blessing from the Lord. [a.] El Paso, TX.

PHIPPS, DEBRA LYNN
[pen.] Storm; [b.] March 27, 1966, Zimbabwe; [p.] Ann and Mike Phipps; [ed.] Hallingbury Junior School, Mabelreign Girls High School; [occ.] Security Supervisor - Sight and Sound Security Services; [oth. writ.] None published - one poem written for a friend that died and it was read out at his funeral; [pers.] I have never read or studied poetry. I write feelings and try to touch people's emotions. I try not to categorize my poems but leave them 'open' to the readers interpretations. My writing is influenced by my previous (R)SPCA work. [a.] Southampton, UK.

PICKENS, GLENDA JOYCE COOK
[b.] October 31, 1941, Knoxville, TN; [p.] Mr. and Mrs. Lowell E. Cook, Sr.; [m.] Fred Mayford Jr., March 24, 1961; [ch.] Gregory Keith, Randall Curtis; [ed.] Young High, Knoxville Business College, University of Tennessee credits; [occ.] Administrative Assistant, U.S. Department of Energy; [memb.] Toastmasters International (Area 8 Governor '94-'95), Stock Creek Baptist Church (altar counselor); [hon.] I will receive Toastmasters International's highest award - Distinguished Toastmaster (DTM)--spring 1995; National Honor Society, Young High, First Place Area 8 Speech Contest 1990; several awards for outstanding service to USDOE; [oth. writ.] Several inspirational poems and speeches. I have been greatly influenced by the writing of Helen Steiner Rice; Norman Vincent Peale; and Robert Schuller; [pers.] "Life's greatest treasures are: faith, hope, and love. Life's greatest treasures can never be bought; they can never be sold; they can never be lost or stolen; they can only be given away. Life's greatest treasures are treasures of the heart!". [a.] Knoxville, TN.

PIFER, ANGELA ANDREWS
[b.] October 12, 1964, Abilene, TX; [p.] Shirley K. Brown and The Late Doyle Wayne Andrews; [m.] Richard D. Pifer, Jr., December 11, 1982; [ch.] Justin Donald, LaTrisha Renee; [ed.] Charlotte High School, Manatee Community College; [occ.] Co-Owner, Tie-Beams Unlimited; [memb.] Charlotte Builders & Contractors Association; [oth. writ.] Essays/short stories in YOU Magazine, several poems and prose published in other anthologies dating back to 1984. Currently working on a children's novel; [pers.] In reference to what I write..."It comes from within; some deep feeling place. My hand is only the messenger, for what the paper hears." The written word does not get lost in the noise. [a.] Port Charlotte, FL.

PINGLEY, JENNIFER
[b.] January 9, 1981, Newport News, VA; [p.] Don and Betty Pingley; [ed.] 8th grade Heritage Middle; [hon.] None for my writing but I have been awarded many ribbons and medals for track and field events and I am also part of many school sports teams; [oth. writ.] I have written several other poems and short story's and have been for many years. But none have been published or noted for anything; [pers.] Just write what you feel and it will be great. I think that the thing that influenced me to write is certain things that happen in my life, such as happiness or sorrow. [a.] Westerville, OH.

PINSON, BETTY D.
[b.] May 28, 1925, Alabama; [p.] C.L. and Lela Duke; [pers.] I try to write what I feel. Sometimes with laughter - sometime with tears - sometimes with a feeling of serene peace. [a.] Decatur, AL.

PIONTEK, DAWN M.
[b.] September 2, 1975, Milwaukee, WI; [p.] Thomas and Catherine, brothers-Mark and Kyle; sisters-Cartney and Stacie; [ed.] University of WI-Milwaukee, Thomas More High School, Institute of Children's Literature; [hon.] Dean's List; [pers.] I'm inspired by the writings of Anne Dillard and Ayn Rand's philosophy of Objectivism. [a.] Milwaukee, WI.

PITTINGER, LINDA K. (BOONE)
[b.] November 29, 1944, PA; [p.] Ora and Hazel Boone; [ch.] Arthur Pittinger, Jr., Anthony Pittinger, Adam Pittinger; [ed.] Bermudian Springs High School, Thompson School of Business and Technology; [occ.] Buyer at SKF USA, Inc.; [memb.] Calvary Bible Church, The American Business Women's Association, Adams/Hanover Parents Without Partners; [hon.] National Honor Society in H.S., Dean's List in Business College, 1994 Chapter member of the Year in the American-Business Women's Association; [oth. writ.] On the staff of company newsletter doing "Getting to Know You" interviews - also creating puzzles and looking for an outlet, as a source for additional income. [a.] Hanover, PA.

PITTOCK, TINA
[b.] January 8, 1980, Cleveland, OH; [p.] Tama Braswell and Tom Pittock; [ed.] Morristown Hamblen High School West; [occ.] High school student; [memb.] Red Cross Club; [hon.] 4-H awards; [pers.] You get out of life what you put into it. [a.] Morristown, TN.

PIZZOLANTE, ADRIENNE
[b.] February 3, 1934, Brooklyn, NY; [p.] Sol Larry and Mae Blaustein; [m.,] Francesco, December 30, 1966; [ed.] Brooklyn College of C.U.N.Y.; [occ.] Retired elementary school teacher - 26 years; [memb.] Actors and others for Animals, Friends of Neil Diamond; [oth. writ.] Only personal poems, for friends and relatives on their special occasions; [pers.] Even at this age I still trust in the innate goodness of the human race. And I just love animals! We are "parents" to 4 cats. I also love music - soft rock. [a.] Rye, NY.

PLATT, LINDA
[pen.] Linda Platt; [b.] July 7, 1979, New York City; [p.] Sharon and Christopher; [ed.] Humanities High School in 10th grade; [occ.] Student; [memb.] Greenpeace, Sierra Club, Nature Society, New York Zoological Society, Wildlife Conservation Society, school newspaper; [hon.] Won the Science Fair award for 1st place 2 years in row; [oth. writ.] Have written other poems and short stories but never before have they been published but published in school newspaper; [pers.] A positive outcome of a situation can only be true if positive energy is released and negative energy is contained. [a.] New York City, NY.

PLOURDE, WILLIAM J.
[b.] June 5, 1972, Concord, MA; [m.] Jennifer R. Fuller, August 28, 1994; [occ.] Novelist. [a.] Ayer, MA.

PLUMLEE, CRAIG DOUGLAS
[pen.] Craig Douglas; [b.] April 4, 1975, Tulsa, OK; [hon.] Various writing awards from high school; [oth. writ.] Plays: McKinnley and the Locksmith, Bagboy, collection of personal poems. [a.] Broken Arrow, OK.

PLUMLEY, KAREN
[b.] New York, NY; [pers.] I am a true optimist, and took forward to every new day. I greatly admire writers of fiction; such as Fitzgerald and O. Henry. I am influenced heavily by Joyce Carol Oates, Stephen King, and Raymond Carver. [a.] Washington, DC.

PLUNKETT, JOHN WILLIAM
[pen.] JWP; [b.] October 16, 1947, Philadelphia, PA; [p.] William and Catherine Plunkett; [m,.] Linda, November 12; [ch.] Dawn and Michele; [ed.] Thomas Edison High; [occ.] Office Manager; [memb.] Messiah Church-Deacon; [oth. writ.] The Tree and Me to be printed n Echoes of Yesterday;

[pers.] Let your life be open to Jesus. [a.] Philadelphia, PA.

POCHRON, CAROL
[b.] November 6, 1956, Bethlehem, PA; [p.] James and Anna Marie Hallman; [m.] Michael, August 27, 1977; [ch.] Joe, Jeff, Lauren; [ed.] Salisbury High School, St. Lukes School of Nursing; [occ.] Registered Nurse; [memb.] Harry S. Truman PTA, Salisbury Alumni Association, Salisbury Parent Organization, St. Andrews Church Council; [oth.writ.] Over 30 poems which I have not submitted for publication; [pers.] My poems reflect the way events and people have touched me in my life. My hope is that by writing - I can touch others. [a.] Allentown, PA.

POE, JASON MIKHALL
[b.] March 13, 1978, Parkersburg, WV; [p.] Larry Poe and Cheryl Mace; [ed.] Parkersburg Catholic High School; [occ.] Student; [memb.] National Honor Society, Youth Ministry Team, Student Council, President, Parkersburg Catholic High School Choir; [hon.] Daughters of the American, Revolution Citizenship Award, Who's Who Among America's High School Students, Rotary Youth Leadership Awareness Camp representative; [oth. writ.] Short stories and poems published in county competitions; [pers.] I don't see myself as a very good writer. It just happens to be that life has given me a plethora of great experiences to write about. [a.] Parkersburg, WV.

POLING, CHRISTINA
[pen.] Christina Crandall; [b.] September 30, 1966, Akron, OH; [p.] Adelaide Arp and Tom Crandall; [m.] Divorced; [ch.] Casandra, Joshua, Lauren; [ed.] Ellet Sr. High School; [occ.] Clerk, Advanced Auto Parts Store; [oth. writ.] I've written several poems, never published. One was published in a memorial in the newspaper for a friends late mother; [pers.] I have always loved writing poems. It is easier to express myself on paper than with speech. [a.] Rock Hill, SC.

POLLY, JESSICA
[b.] May 16, 1981, Kendallville, IN; [p.] Larry and Tina Polly; [ed.] Rome City Middle School; [occ.] 7th grade student; [memb.] Cheerleading squad, volleyball team and basketball team; [hon.] Academic Awards and honor student; [oth. writ.] Short stories and poems; [pers.] My ultimate goal is to make the world a better place for my generation and each an everyone thereafter. I have been greatly influenced by my mom's humor and my dad's discipline. [a.] Rome City, IN.

POMERLEAU, NORA
[pen.] Nora Pomerleau; [b.] October 31, 1980, Arcadia; [p.] Carol and Roger; [ed.] DeSoto Middle School; [occ.] Student. [a.] ARcadia, FL.

POPAL, HEELA
[b.] July 14, 1979, New York; [p.] Rona M. and Abdullah Popal; [ed.] 10th grade high school; [occ.] Student; [memb.] Afghan Womens Association - International; [hon.] Honor student; [pers.] I am an Afghan born in U.S.A., but throughout the years I have heard about the wars and killings of the innocent children, and it made me sad to see those children suffer. I dedicate this poem to the children of Afghanistan. [a.] Dublin, CA.

PORTER, DEVAN
[b.] September 12, 1980, Exeter, NH; [p.] Jim and Diane Melville (guardians); [ed.] Grades 1-7 public school, currently being homeschooled for the 8th grade; [occ.] Student at home; [pers.] My writing is greatly influenced by my life experiences and encouraged by my home school teachers. [a.] Rochester, NH.

POTTS, JOE
[b.] November 11, 1956, Philadelphia, PA; [p.] Catherine and Edward Potts, Sr.; [m.] Nora, July 11, 1981; [ch.] Joseph Michael, Bridget Marie; [ed.] St. Henry's Elementary, Cardinal Dougherty High, Olney High; [occ.] Letter carrier USPS Branch 157; [pers.] My writing to date has been influenced by the relationship I have with my wife, Nora. [a.] Phila., PA.

PRATER, VIOLET
[pen.] Vi; [b.] April 2, 1930, Palmer, MO; [p.] Ozzie Callahan and Laymond and Allie Hollinsworth; [m.] Lewis Prater II, December 23, 1946; [ch.] Gilbert, Bobby, Beverly, Barbara, Jessie, Donna, Gary, Rose, Lewis III; [ed.] Grassy Hollow School graduated 8th grade; [occ.] Deceased; [memb.] Grassy Hollow Baptist Church; [oth. writ.] 23 poems, before her death at the age of 35. Most poems were wrote for her children and family; [pers.] Remember always that everyday is a new day. Never give up your faith. God can hear prayers! Live everyday and hour to the fullest. Even minutes are precious, be glad you have them. [a.] Potosi, MO.

PRATT, AMANDA
[b.] March 3, 1983, Fontana, CA; [p.] Daniel and Andria Pratt; [ed.] Ranch Hills Elementary; [occ.] 6th grade student; [memb.] Girl Scouts, Awanas (church Bible group); [hon.] Guard of the Year (awanas), 3rd place Awana Olympics; [oth. writ.] "The Rose I Lay On Nicks Grave", "My Love for my Family"; [pers.] The poem "There Sits A 5 Year Old Girl" was written during my 5th grade year, about my dad's death. He was a Los Angeles Police Officer killed in the line of duty Sept. 1988 when I was 5 years old. [a.] Pomona, CA.

PRATT, JENNIFER
[pen.] Fantaisla Watters; [b.] June 30, 1981, Los Angeles; [p.] Rod and Myra Pratt; [ed.] St. Anselm School; [occ.] Student 8th grade; [memb.] Volleyball, cheerleading, and school newspaper; [hon.] Music, sports, academics and poetry; [oth. writ.] One poem in the school newspaper; [pers.] Accept nothing but your absolute best.

PRESTON, MARIKO
[pen.] Lazzette Preston; [b.] 1981, Okinowa, Japan; [p.] Rosalyn and Ray Preston; [ed.] St. Francis of Assisi School; [occ.] 8th grade student; [hon.] Semi-finalist in another school wide poem contest; [pers.] The things I reflect on or use as inspiration are all of the fine works of Jesus and his father. I also like to use, sometimes, the works of Shakespeare and Edgar Allen Poe to reflect on. [a.] Midway Park, NC.

PRICE, GRACE
[b.] march 25, 1911, E.TN; [p.] W.F. and Alice Williams; [m.] October 4, 1929; [ch.] Two sons and two daughters; [ed.] Knoxville High (GED), LPN Nursing; [occ.] Retired; [oth. writ.] Songs for my own pleasure; [pers.] It's hard to choose a favorite poet. I have enjoyed the old and the new and writing my own gives me pleasure too. I touch on whatever comes to mind. [a.] Knoxville, TN.

PRICE, JENNIFER
[pen.] Jen, Jennie; [b.] April 19, 1980, Fortsmith, AR; [p.] Donna and Dale Bloxham; [ed.] Oroville High School; [occ.] 9th grade student; [hon.] Top Noch; [pers.] It's my original poem I wrote it. [a.] Oroville, CA.

PRILL-GREBNER, BERNICE
[pen.] Bernice Prill-Grebner; [b.] May 23, Peoria, IL; [p.] Emma Duhs Prill and Jo Elmer Prill; [m.] Divorced; [ch.] Marjorie Welsch, David Grebner; [occ.] Accredited Astrologer, author of Eight Astrology books; [memb.] American Federation of Astrologers, 3rd Generation Astrology, Composer of Music; [hon.] Poet Performer of my own compositions; [oth. writ.] Books - Lunar Nodes, Decanotes, Everything Has a Phase, Mercury, The Open Door Part I, Mercury, The Open Door Part II, Day of Your Birth, Bee's Flight, ABC's of Astrology and Astronomy; [pers.] Be all you can be in this life - keep body, mind and spirit in balance and you will leave this life whole.

PROUDFOOT, RUTH
[b.] May 24, 1980, Midland, ONT; [p.] Diane Manning and Ross Proudfoot; [ed.] Midland Secondary School; [occ.] Video Store (Video Plus); [hon.] Valedictorian for grade school, Environmental awards, awards from fall fairs for various things; [oth. writ.] I've had poems published in yearbooks; [pers.] I'd like to thank my friends and family for encouraging me to enter. A special thanks to my teacher Mrs. Fraser who encourage me to write poems to express our feelings. [a.] Victoria Harbour, ONT.

PROVOST, TERRY L.
[pen.] T.; [b.] December 17, 1959, Rapid City, SD; [p.] Donald and Janet Provost; [ch.] Shawnda Marie; [ed.] St. Regis Falls Ctrl. North Franklin Education Center, North Country Community College; [occ.] Mental Health Field; [hon.] Dean's list, Professional Excellence Award in Health Occupations, NCS Home Bureau Scholarship in Mental Health; [oth. writ.] 1st place in Essay Contest in Health Occupations; [pers.] My poem published within "Mama's Pearl" is truly a gift from God, and is dedicated to my precious daughter Shawnda, who's love and beauty never ceased to amaze me. [a.] Satsuma, FL.

PRUE, PATRICK EUGENE
[pen.] Patrick Prue; [b.] October 27, 1963, Wichita, KS; [p.] Mr. and Mrs. Edmund Patricia Prue; [ed.] Completed 10th grade; [occ.] Part-time window cleaner; [memb.] Republican Presidential Task Force; [hon.] Medal from Task Force that haven't proclaimed into my personal possession; [oth. writ.] Main writing lyrics; [pers.] God Bless You and America. [a.] Greensburg, KS.

PRUSKI, DANIEL
[pen.] Daniel Pruski; [b.] January 18, 1969, Ft. Meade, MD; [p.] Casimer and Marcia Pruski; [ed.] Notre Dame High, Albany College of Pharmacy; [occ.] Pharmacist, Researcher and Healthcare Consultant; [memb.] National Eagle Scout Association, National Order of the Arrow, American Pharmaceutical Society, American Society of Hospital Pharmacists, Phi Delta Chi Leaders in Pharmacy; [hon.] Eagle Scout, Vigil member of the Order the Arrow; [oth. writ.] Articles written for Oncology and Healthcare research; [pers.] Life is what You make of it. [a.] Albion, NY.

PRZELENSKI, JOYCE ANN
[b.] September 17, 1940, Wheeling, WVA; [p.] Andrew and Mary Przelenski; [ed.] St. Joseph's Academy; [occ.] Shareholder Services Representative - COMSAT Corporation; [oth. writ.] A few other poems specifically for family and friends to celebrate a special birthday, graduation, family Christman, retirement; [pers.] I enjoy writing, creating something that might bring some pleasure to others. [a.] Arlington, VA.

QUELL, DOROTHY M.
[b.] March 30, 1915, Pennside, PA; [p.] Deceased; [m.] Leroy C., June 17, 1939; [ch.] Three; [ed.] 9th grade but worked for the visiting nurse and got many awards for good work in skilled nursing; [occ.] Housewife; [memb.] Calvary Luther Church, 25 Bridge Club, Sunday School teacher for 26 years; Visiting Nurse Association; [hon.] Wrote at least 10-15 Sunday school songs, wrote a poem Little Girls 2/25/81, A Parent Prayer, DAddy's Boy, Proud of Our State; [oth. writ.] I wrote at least 25 poems but never afford to send the money to try to get an award. Autumn, Beatitudes for the Aged, 10 Reasons to Take Time; [pers.] I am getting pretty old now and have lots of time to write poems if only I could get someone interested to buy them. [a.] Reading, PA.

QUICK, JILL K.
[b.] Waco, TX; [p.] Gordon Bruce and Audie Puckett Bruce; [m.] Frederick S., July 30, 1982; [ch.] David John Moore, Glen Gordon Moore, Vince Edward Moore; [ed.] The University of Texas at Arlington; [occ.] Business Consultant; [memb.] Fort Worth Chamber of Commerce (Board of Directors), ACE member of S.C.O.R.E.; [hon.] Texas Volunteer Award (Texas Department of Human Services), Omicron Delta Kappa (UTA); [oth. writ.] FEature writer in Southwest Life Magazine and The Shorthorn, publicity and newsletters for organizations, business plans, marketing plans and other technical writing for businesses; [pers.] With loving appreciation to my husband, Fred Quick; my sister, Cherry Kay Beckworth, and my brother-in-law, Edward Beckworth. [a.] Arlington, TX.

RACE, LOIS JANE "PUDDIN"
[pen.] pr; [b.] October 27, 1945, Birmingham, AL; [p.] Red and Lila Houston; [ch.] Roger Houston Race, Ben Charles Race; [ed.] 12 years of school in Orlando, FL, Indian River Community College; [occ.] Public Education Specialist-St. Lucie County -Ft. Pierce Fire District; [memb.] St. Andrews Episcopal Church; [pers.] The world is happier when people laugh together...gentler when they share their understanding.

RADATZ, TERESE' V.
[b.] October 14, 1948, Blomberg, Germany; [p.] Anele DeMist, Divorced; [ch.] Rebecca H. Radatz, Brian N. Radatz; [ed.] Holy Cross High School, St. Clair County Community College; [occ.] Licensed Practical Nurse, Cashier; [memb.] Disabled American Veterans; [hon.] Golden Poet 1991; [oth. writ.] Several poems published by two other publishers; [pers.] My inspiration has been my children and grandchildren: James (Jewel) and Amanda (Pretty Girl). [a.] Port Huron, MI.

RADIN, CONSTANCE E.
[b.] November 26, 1962, Festus, MO; [p.] Duane P. and Billie J. Huck; [m.] Anthony E., April 25, 1987; [ch.] Pet-Hank, a 100 lb pit bull terrier; [ed.] Festus Senior High School, Arkansas State University; [occ.] ABB Combustion Engineering (Nuclear Fuel Manufacturing); [memb.] Jefferson County Writers Guild of Missouri; [hon.] Knights of Columbus Scholarship to Jefferson College (declined), School Compositions Recognition for Merit; [oth. writ.] Honorable Mention in By-Line Magazine for poem "Adam". I have a portfolio of poetry that I have kept for my own enjoyment or sometimes close friends; [pers.] Much of my writing is inspired by natures aura, a personal aura, an animal's aura. Love, Passion, and mirrors to the soul. I'll try anything once. Mothers best advice, "Just do it". [a.] Festus, MO.

RAEL, VALERIE
[b.] February 7, 1976, Albuquerque, NM; [p.] Freddy and Pauline Rael; [ed.] Valley High School, T.V.I. Community College; [occ.] Administrative Assistant Rael's Masonry; [memb.] United Faith Youth Group, VICA Club; [hon.] Participation and Attendance for Youth Group various awards from school; [oth. writ.] Poems in school literary magazine. Short story in Who's Who of American Book in 7th grade; [hon.] I have learned alot at an early age. But the two most important are: to have faith in God and believe in yourself. [a.] Albuquerque, NM.

RAGSDALE, JON (JONATHAN)
[pen.] Jonathan Jones; [b.] June 20, 1955, Kerrville; [ed.] Schreiner College; [occ.] Disabled; [oth. writ.] No previous publications. [a.] Ingram, TX.

RAGSDALE, MARIA VICTORIA
[pen.] Victoria Ragsdale; [b.] October 23, 1968, Argentina; [m.] William F., March 9, 1988; [ch.] Patrick N., Samuel E., Duncan W.; [ed.] St. Nicholas English School (Argentina), National Extension College and Merces College; [occ.] Teacher as English as a Foreign Language to Adults; [pers.] As long as there are people who bring light to those who live in the darkness of ignorance, there will be hope for the future. [a.] Kissimmee, FL.

RAM, BISSOONDAT
[pen.] Japs; [b.] February 15, 1951, Guyana, SA; [p.] Lakhan and Budhni Ram; [m.] Lilaoti Ram; [ch.] Ganesh, Naresh, Vishnu, Malinie; [ed.] Cornelia Govt. School, Handicraft Center, National Assessment Institute; [occ.] Construction Manager of Ram's Construction; [memb.] MN Hindu Dharmic Sabha, "Swarsattie Cultural Group", American Songwriter Organization; [hon.] Lyric Writing Excellence Platinum Records, Certificate of Merit - Talent and Associated Companied, Editor's Choice award National Library of Poetry; [oth. writ.] I have an album to release on November 18, 1994 - "Tell Me De Numba Ayu Fone" my lyrics - singer and producer; [pers.] My thoughts and vision comes from beyond the stars. The Almighty Father has chosen me to spread his word of love and peace and I will do so as long as I lived. [a.] Minneapolis, MN.

RAMIREZ, REBECCA
[pen.] Becca; [b.] August 1, 1980, Santa Paula, CA; [p.] Guillermo and Beverly Ramirez; [ed.] Attending school and modeling classes; [hon.] 3 plaques for best written essay, first place in self defense, first place sparring in Karate; [oth. writ.] What I see in life and how I feel is written into poetry; [pers.] The meanings of my poetry is my feelings, either it has to do with anger, sadness, loneliness, confusion, etc. It makes me feel a lot better just to write my feelings and make it out into a poem. [a.] Piru, CT.

RAMSEY, WILLIAM C.
[b.] December 8, 1933, Fruckey, CA; [p.] Kathern E. and Richard Dee; [ch.] Richard, Debbie, (Curt); [ed.] Anary Union High School, Aquanaut Training Sea Lab, Cinima Oxnard College; [occ.] Retired, gopher, fish, sucker; [memb.] S.P.I.C.E., NASA, Science and education; [hon.] Presidential Unit Citation, SecnaV-Combination for 1200 ft. Free dive, Atomic Energy Communication; [pers.] For my mother who is like the handy old oak tree, or the giant redwood, standing strong, weathering the winds of changing times. Also for my friend Jamie, the best calligrapher that makes it all happen. [a.] Oxnard, CA.

RANDALL, BRIAN GERARD
[b.] February 1, 1973, New York, NY; [p.] Prince and Deborah Randall; [ed.] Rice High School, Borough of Manhattan Community College; [occ.] Student; [memb.] The Greater Faith Baptist Church, Usher Board Treasurer; [oth. writ.] I have written several poems and a screenplay they have not yet been published; [pers.] Give me a pen and pad and I will work wonders. [a.] Bronx, NY.

RAYBURN, JANICE
[pen.] MJ; [b.] July 26, 1932, Columbia, MS; [p.] Ruth and John Rayburn; [m.] Harry Barrios (deceased), August 23, 1949; [ch.] Danny, Mark, Don, Melanie, Perry; [ed.] Lumberton High School, Nichols State College; [occ.] Artist; [memb.] South MS Art Association, VP in Charge of shows and exhibits Southern Poetry Society, Tinicial Worker Association; [hon.] Poem placed in Southern Poetry Society and published. One woman exhibitions (art), group exhibitions in LA, NM, MS, AZ and CA; [oth. writ.] Twelve poems published; [pers.] Beauty is what we have, what we share, what gives human beings dignity." Be always searching, always looking for the unexpected in nature. [a.] Hattiesburg, MS.

RECTOR, GAIL ELAINE ROSE
[b.] October 11, 1951, Springfield, IL; [p.] Mr. and Mrs. William Rose; [m.] James Dean, November 25, 1979; [ch.] Mary Elizabeth, Nick; [ed.] Lanphier High, Parkland College, University of Illinois; [occ.] Rural Mail carrier; [memb.] Countryside Methodist Church, Girl Scout Leader; [hon.] Best Artist in 5 Media, Student Citywide 1965, Betty Crocker Homemaker of the Year 1969; [oth. writ.] Journals.

REED, SUMA
[b.] December 23, 1978, London, England; [p.] Richard and Sheila Reed; [ed.] Howe Sound Secondary School; [occ.] Grade 11 student; [pers.] My poems reflect my love of wildlife and the respect I have for it. I hope that they will have a positive influence on the way people feel towards the natural world. [a.] Squamish, CAN. BC.

REESE, CHAR M.
[pen.] Char Hare; [b.] July 15, 1948, Shelbyville, IN; [p.] Dorothy and James Hare; [m.] February 20, 1967; [ch.] Candance Kohler, Gregory Hare; [ed.] Howe High School; [occ.] Agoraphobic-don't go outside my home; [memb.] Indiana Genealogy Society,, Jennings Co. Genealogy Club, Eagles Club (Robert Schuellen) Crystal Ministry; [hon.] To be a parent to two children - whom I adore and grandmother to Christopher, Christian and Austin. (soon to have a fourth grandchild); [oth. writ.] I have written over 150 poems about loved ones, my happiness, "feelings" mostly. I have had one article published on Genealogy (newspaper). My life story Snyder Cemetery and Snyder Cemetery Inc.; [pers.] Since I was orphaned by 10 years of age two dreams: children to love and grandchildren to hold. Also to be a journalist or a published poet. My feelings are "my inspiration" for poems. [a.] Greenwood, IN.

REESE, LORETTA JEAN
[pen.] Hardy Reese; [hon.] In nomination for membership in the International Society of Authors and Artists; [oth. writ.] "Postmortem Blues", Memories/Summer '93 and Honorable Mention certificates, "Close To The One You Love", Poetic Voices of America/Spring '94, "Released", The Poet's Pen/FAll '93, "No Fault Love Insurance", '94 President's Award for Literary Excellence Certificate, "Untitled", Perceptions/'94 Parting Shots, "Happy Birthday Sweetheart", Poetic Voices of America/Fall '94, "Always You

and Me, Babe" Remembrances/Fall '94 and Honorable Mention Browning Competition/Semi-Annual; "Happy Anniversary", Cader Publishing/'94 Longfellow Award of Merit, "Open Your Mind", National Library of Poetry's Dark Side of the Moon/Fall'94.; [pers.] At the memorial service for my husband in November '92, a poem was read that I had written to him several years before. Everyone commented on how beautiful it was and if I had ever thought of publishing my works. That was the beginning.

REESE, ROBERT JR.
[pen.] Robert Reese, Jr.; [b.] August 9, 1946, Cincinnati, OH; [p.] Robert and Wenell Reese, Sr.; [ch.] Charles Michael Reese; [ed.] El Camino College; [occ.] Owner Security Business; [hon.] Who's Who 198-87 In California; [oth. writ.] A few things in school, that instructor kept Mrs. Anderson, paper on prejudice; [pers.] Tried to make this world a better place. [a.] Los Angeles, CA.

REEVES, KEITH
[b.] May 28, 1961, NJ; [p.] Joseph and Nancy Reeves; [ed.] SUNY Fredonia; [occ.] Manager-Residential Money Centers; [pers.] I drink to make people more interesting. [a.] Pearl River, NY.

REGO, ANTHONY J.
[b.] May 20, 1967, Newark, NJ; [p.] John and Ann Rego; [ch.] Alexandra Noel Rego; [ed.] Kearny High School, Montclair State College; [occ.] Office Manager, Freelance Photo Journalist; [memb.] American Philatelic Society, Germany Philatelic Society, North American Fishing Club; [hon.] World of Poetry - Golden Poet 1988, Ebon Research Systems - Merit Award 1990, Ebon Research Systems - Presidential Award 1991, DynCorp - Appreciation Award 1994; [oth. writ.] "The Mountain Peak", "Alone With You 1987, American Poetry Anthology, articles and photos for lost treasure magazine; [pers.] Never take for granted the many gifts life brings, make time to enjoy them before they ship away. [a.] Kearny, NJ.

REID, LORIEN
[b.] January 11, 1979, Walnut Creek, CA; [p.] Thomas and Judith Reid; [ed.] California High School; [memb.] California Scholarship Federation, School magazine-Protagonist, French Club, Rotary Club-Interact; [hon.] Numerous English, French, Math, History awards, dance scholarship, Junior High Valedictorian; [oth. writ.] Various poems, short stories; [pers.] Our world holds many wonders, and all we have to do is appreciate them and cherish them with all our hearts. [a.] San Ramon, CA.

REINDL, HOLLY RENEA
[b.] October 30, 1970, Weatherford, OK; [p.] Jerry and Sheron Douglas; sibling-Jerry Dale Douglas; [m.] Creighton Scott Reindl, September 3, 1993; [ch.] Brennen; [occ.] Housewife; [oth. writ.] Several poems; [pers.] Thank you to my husband, Creighton, for being the love of my life and giving me the strength to write again. [a.] Yukon, OK.

REMBOLD, DEBORAH KAUFMAN
[pen.] Dusty; [b.] November 13, 1949, Los Angeles, CA; [p.] Richard and Margaret Kaufman; [m.] Fred W., July 1, 1973; [ch.] 13 animals; [ed.] Hollywood High School, Licensed Insurance Underwriter; [occ.] Artist; [memb.] National Lupus Foundation, American Lupus Society; [hon.] Hollywood Presbyterian Church Choir 10 year award; [oth. writ.] Poem published in local paper as part of feature article, including photograph, Volumes of personal poetry as Daily Journals; [pers.] I live a lot in my mind because I'm confined due to illness but poetry allows me to consider myself an active person, my journals are 100% poetry which flows to me. I don't rework any poem it would spoil the effect. I strive to reflect the spirit of hope and determinations. I love and life with my devoted husband of 21 years and 13 pets. [a.] Genoa, NV.

RENFRO, TERRIS
[b.] May 24, 1979, Oklahoma, OK; [p.] Tommy and Linda Renfro, Sr.; [ed.] Tulsa Central High; [memb.] Prayer meetings, church, orchestra; [hon.] Honor Roll, Tulsa Metro-Honor Orchestra; [oth. writ.] I have been writing poems almost all of my life; [pers.] I have been influenced by poets such as Edgar Allen Poe, and Robert Frost and also my friends and family. "It is time for a new beginning". [a.] Tulsa, OK.

RENFROW, JAN
[pen.] The Folktress; [ed.] High school graduate, two years of community college, some trade and correspondence schooling, private workshops, music lessons, etc; [occ.] Professional massage practitioner, desktop publisher, songwriter, musician, poetess, art model, artist; [memb.] BMI, Carlsbad/Oceanside Art League, National Writers Club, Libertarian Party of California; [hon.] "Silver Poet Award", honorable mention in the "Third Annual Stump House Poetry Competition", several honorable mentions in Byline Magazine contests, first place ribbon in the March, 1994 exhibition in the Carlsbad/Oceanside Art League gallery; [oth. writ.] Poetry volumes: Stranger In The Wind, Songs of Love, For The Feeling Heart, What Compassionate Men Need To Know About Women, Within & Beyond, Cryptoverse! Audio Tapes: Jan Renfrow Singer Her Own, You's In Song, Stranger in the Wind, audio version; [pers.] I strongly feel that full creative control over one's own original work is a God-given right and NOT some special privilege granted by those publishers who just happen to feel like giving it to us. For that reason, I self-publish. [a.] Oceanside, CA.

RENNER, REBECCA MARY
[b.] October 18, 1943, Mt. Carmel, PA; [p.] Robert and Catharine Hornung; [m.] Robert Allen, June 21, 1970; [ch.] Three; [ed.] Junior Senior High School; [occ.] Housewife; [memb.] Primitive Methodist Church, B.P.O.E. Elks Club; [hon.] Win a lot of cooking contests; [oth. writ.] First poem I ever wrote. I wrote lots of recipes and I even got some published; [pers.] I would like to write more poems about love, because I have the best family in the world, and they could inspire anyone to write. [a.] Girardville, PA.

RENSEL, ELLA ANNE MARRON
[pen.] Anne Marron Rensel; [b.] July 3, 1918, Washington, DC; [p.] Owen and Ella Marron; [m.] Vincent Jerome Rensel, May 1, 1943; [ch.] Three sons and two daughters; [ed.] St. Petersburg Senior High School, Tomlinson Business School, U.S. Navy, Yeoman School; [occ.] Freelance Writer; [memb.] International Society of Poets, National Association of Retired Federal Employees; [hon.] One first, two second, and one third prizes, Northwest Pacific Writers Contest, runner-up prize, International Society of Poets Symposium, 1992; [oth. writ.] Three published novels, one novel - Ette, three short stories, poetry in magazines, collection of poetry, "Lifelines" 1993 by Ink Drop Press (Road Publishers), numerous magazine and newspaper articles; [pers.] I have been "in love with" poetry all my life, since age three and composed my first poem at age five. [a.] Madrid, Spain.

RETELL, DEBRA
[pen.] Debra Collman; [b.] October 30, 1967, Spokane, WA; [p.] Ronald Collman/Phyllis Winfield; [m.] Jason Retell, June 13, 1987; [ed.] Newburgh Free Academy; [occ.] Laborer on Construction Crew; [oth. writ.] I've got 4 books of poems that are unpublished. Another poem was published in my high school yearbook; [pers.] I write poetry based on my personal feelings and experiences. It's my way of expressing myself. Every word is a part of me. [a.] Warren, MI.

RETTER, SHANE
[b.] March 21, 1972, Winchester; [p.] Mary Margaret Hawley Retter and Ward Retter; [ed.] Winchester Community High, Ball State University; [memb.] Math Club (Ball State Chapter), Sigma Zeta, Methodist Youth Counselor, Methodist Administrative Council; [hon.] Dean's List; [oth. writ.] Philosophical writings and other poetic literature published by local newspaper, some theological poems in Methodist Lenten Book; [pers.] A poem is a subject of reflective thoughts about descriptive concepts that are understood and admired only by those who exist in the poet's world. Let the world be my resource. Deny me nothing! [a.] Winchester, IN.

REUSSER, THELMA L.
[pen.] Thelma La Vern Reusser; [b.] February 24, 1913, Laurel, OR; [p.] Myrtle and Ben Collins (deceased); [m.] Alexander C.; [ch.] Myrtle, Mead-Sheriff Fred Reusser, William Reusser; [ed.] Grade, high school and private schooling; [occ.] Retired printer and fine jeweler, Dept. head; [hon.] Presented before Board Directors for poetry high honors and 8 awards, honors in art, watercolor paintings - State of Medal of Oregon, also Grant County Sweepstakes, 12 Ribbons; [oth. writ.] Have written book "Thelma's Love" also did illustrating of some - have not sent in for public viewing; [pers.] Ill health has hampered me some since I have Multiple Sclerosis. On the other had it has been wonderful therapy. [a.] Fossil, OR.

REVILLE, ANNETTE MARIE
[b.] October 9, 1960, San Francisco, CA; [p.] William Dean and Janet E. Reville; [ed.] Brooke Haven, Yalloupe Ave, Longwood Elementary, Winton Grove, Rancho Arroyo Jr. High, Sunset High, Chabot Jr. College; [hon.] Girls Athletic Association, Merit for the Arts and Honorable mention, third place in music at Jazz Festival in Reno; [oth. writ.] Poetry magazine in high school; [pers.] Love is the only thing that out last all of the battered from others. [a.] Tracy, CA.

REYNOLDS, ELIZABETH
[b.] September 14, 1948, Cincinnati, OH; [m.] William, April 12, 1969; [ch.] George, Robert, Roy. [a.] Folkston, GA.

REYNOLDS, GLADYS R.
[b.] September 4, 1951, Essex County, Va; [p.] John and Elsie Richardson; [m.] Melvin D., February 12, 1971; [ch.] Lavar Kinta, Melvin Gerard; [ed.] Essex Cop. High School, Tidewater Memorial Hospital - Nurses Aide Training; [occ.] Paraprofessional Tappahannock Elementary School; [memb.] Past pres. Essex High Band Boosters, Pres Essex High Football Boosters, various school committees; [oth. writ.] I so far have only written for my own enjoyment. I have also written poems for different occasions such as funerals, memorials, church programs. [a.] Tappahannock, VA.

RHODES, NATALIE
[b.] February 7, 1981, Hammond, IN; [p.] Karen and Nathaniel Rhodes; [ed.] Harrison Elementary, Franklin Elementary, Washington Elementary,

Black Jr. High; [occ.] Student; [hon.] Other poetry writing contests, Science Olympiad medal, Spelling Bee trophy; [oth. writ.] "So Sad Am I" and "Between You & Me" both unpublished; [pers.] "People often say, "Wow, how'd you come up with that?" I just smile and say, "It just came to me all of the sudden. As a matter of fact, it came to me, when I wasn't trying to think of a poem." [a.] East Chicago, IN.

RICHARD, DEBORAH E.
[b.] December 14, 1957, Parkersburg, WV; [ed.] Walton High, WV Career College, Horry Georgetown Technical College; [occ.] Office Assistant with Kelly Temporary Services; [hon.] National Honor Society, Dean's List; [oth. writ.] I strive to project a positive nature in my writing. I especially enjoy capturing childhood memories and the valuable relationships in my day-to-day living. [a.] Longs, SC.

RICHARDS, DONNA
[pen.] D'a; [b.] August 12, 1952, Wilmington, OH; [p.] Donald and Lucille Snider; [m.] Doug Richards, January 30 1992; [ch.] Ronnie, Zachary and Mary; [ed.] Fayetteville High School, Delta College, Mich for English, Psychology, Raymond Walters College, English, Math, NKU-Speech, Chatfield College-Sciences; [occ.] Medical Secretary; [pers.] I find a great inspiration in writing. I strive to express a message of deep love and caring for others. A peace fullness and a thought to carry forward. [a.] Blanchester, OH.

RIDDLEBAUGH, MARGARET
[pen.] Margaret Campbell Riddlebaugh; [b.] August 5, 1940, Newark, OH; [p.] Ann and Lloyd Campbell; [ch.] Rose, Cheri, Jackie, Jennifer and Kate (grandchildren-Randy, Robin, Shawn, Chet, Lisa and Colten; [ed.] Utica High School, North Central Tech.; [occ.] Personal Caregiver; [memb.] Tabernacle of Praise, The Advisory Board for Building Committee; [oth. writ.] I've only recently started to write so I haven't had any other of my poems published, except in the church's weekly newsletter. In May of 1994 I wrote my first poem and since then I have written over 100 in all; [pers.] The inspiration for my poetry has come from my desire to let others know of the love of God; And my love for God, family, and friends. I have been greatly encouraged and supported by Linda VanBuren, Jackie Bryant, Clata Lockhart, and Brenda VanBuren in my quest to reach this goal. [a.] Mansfield, OH.

RIDLEY, DAVID J.
[b.] April 16, 1956, Northumberland, England; [p.] Norman and Anne Ridley; [m.] Louise, December 17, 1993; [ch.] Colin Kenneth Megan; [ed.] Love vrs Life, Life vrs Love; [occ.] Man of God/poet writer; [memb.] Life (The Real Reality); [oth. writ.] An extension of the worlds printing press; to numerous to mention; [pers.] For Love: Who Could See The Sun? If Not From The Shadow's. For Life: Knowledge Is Of Mankind, Wisdom Comes From God (Who Would Stand In The Fire of Truth?). [a.] Terrace Bay, ONT., CAN.

RIES, BARBARA
[pen.] barni; [b.] September 18, 1974, Chicago, IL; [p.] Ted Ries and Barbara McDonagh; [occ.] Ameri-Tech Operator.

RIGGINS, SALINA
[b.] August 22, 1979; [p.] Donna and Sylvia Plath; [ed.] Carver Center for Arts and Technology; [pers.] Favorite poet - Sylvia Plath. In memory of my favorite act and hero, River Phoenix, who died from a drug overdose last year. Quote: "I feel that my writing inspires death which plays a lead instrument in everyone's band." Thank you for this honor to have my poem published.

RIGGLE, GLORI ANN
[pen.] Ann; [b.] February 21, 1946, Borger, TX; [p.] Mary Watson and Monroe Moore; [m.] Frank, December 22, 1967; [ch.] Shane Riggle, BJ Riggle; [ed.] 12th grade plus college courses; [occ.] Secretary-bookkeeper for Riggle Seal Soup; [hon.] Only from my family; [oth. writ.] No writings ever published; [pers.] I write about the ordinary people, so the largest majority can identify with what I'm putting on paper. [a.] Borger, TX.

RIGGLEMAN, MARY ANN
[b.] August 2, 1945, Cumberland, MD; [p.] T.P. Liller and Helen (Gardner) Liller; [m.] Norris L., February 12, 1977; [ch.] 4 sons and 3 grandsons; [ed.] Keyser High, Catherman's Business School; [occ.] Service Master as cashier at Potomac State College; [memb.] Charter member of Victory Baptist Church where I teach Sunday school and hold office of treasurer of Ladies Christian Fellowship; [hon.] Recognition by Service Master as Employee of the Month for Sept. 1993. Certificate of appreciation from Victory Baptist Church having served as church secretary from 1990-93; [oth. writ.] All other writings have been for personal enjoyment by friends and family; [pers.] Inspiration for this writing came after losing my best friend to cancer in February of 1992. [a.] Keyser, WVA.

RILEY, LAURA
[b.] December 22, 1956, Berwyn, IL; [p.] John and Adeline Pasateri; [m.] Michael D., July 22, 1979; [ch.] Michael and Brian; [occ.] Trucking; [oth. writ.] A bunch of unpublished poems; [pers.] Go with the moment, you never know when it will end.

RINEHART, AUDREY HOPE
[b.] October 2, 1982, Marion, NC; [p.] Doug and Sandra Rinehart; [ed.] West McDowell Junior High; [occ.] Full-time 7th grade student; [oth. writ.] My first poem to be published; [pers.] Through my poetry I attempt to paint a picture of the beauty of the Appalachian Mountains, her heritage, and her people. The great love I have for them. [a.] Marion, NC.

RINEY, HEATHER
[b.] Heather Riney; [b.] June 18, 1975, Hannibal, MO; [p.] Mike and Debbie Riney; [m.] Darren Thomure, June 1995; [ed.] Hannibal Senior High; [occ.] Cashier at Gas Station Pick 'a' Dilly; [oth. writ.] Only poetry been writing since 4th grade. [a.] Hannibal, MO.

RINGWOOD, KATHLEEN LEORA MARIE
[pen.] Kat Wood; [b.] June 27, 1946, Morristown, NJ; [p.] Arthur and Blanche Ringwood; [ch.] "Rocky" (Peter Shawn); [ed.] Hatboro-Horsham High School, West Chester University, University of Houston, University of Houston of Doctoral Candidate; [occ.] TV Host/Producer; Commentator, teacher, instructor: San Jacinto College, South and U. of Houston, lecturer, writer, trainer, actress, DJ; [memb.] Pasadena Little Theatre, Texas Junior College Teachers Association, San Jacinto College Speakers Bureau, Gulf Coast Intercollegiate Consortium Literary Arts Committee, Library Resources Committee, SJS South; [hon.] Who's Who of American Women, Who's Who in America; Two Thousand Most Notable American Women, Who's Who in Entertainment, Spirit of San Jacinto Award, Who's Who of Emerging Leaders in America, Who's Who in Society; [oth. writ.] Newsletters: "Vocare", "Access", "Cub Reporter", TV Programs: "ACCESS", "Dear Subscriber", "Reaching Reality"; Songs: Ballad for Billy", "Renegade", "Avenger", "Champion"; Poetry-stories, working on a children's book series; [pers.] I believe that everyone should have an opportunity to learn how to and be able to express themselves creatively. Fine arts (like poetry) are vital links to the past, present, and future...they are crucial expressions of our talents and abilities. [a.] Houston, TX.

RISLEY, KARIN LEE
[pen.] Karin Lee; [b.] June 22, 1967, Barre, VT; [p.] Donna Edson and Harry Gallagher; [m.] Divorced; [ch.] Cameron J. Risley; [ed.] Spaulding High, Wabash Valley College; [occ.] Log Technician - Military Helicopter Sales/Foreign Sales; [memb.] Florida Army National Guard; [hon.] Dean's List, Good Conduct Award, 2 Safety Awards, 2 Battle E. Awards, Meritorious Unit Commendation award, National Defense Medal (all military); [oth. writ.] Have 30 original poems unpublished as of yet - wrote 1 song; [pers.] My innermost thoughts are best shared with others through my poems. I strive to comfort or inspire through my writing and hope to become an established writer one day. Writing is my escape. [a.] Pensacola, FL.

RITCHEY, PATSY FIELDS
[pen.] Paka; [b.] September 10, 1952, Arkansas; [p.] Louis C. and Carrie M. Fields; [m.] Mark R. Ritchey; [ed.] Kilgore College, WTCC, Richmar High; [occ.] Security Officer; [oth. writ.] Poems and songs; [pers.] My interest in poetry was greatly influenced by Grace Monie. Teacher Richmar High. Thank you Ms. Grace for a wonderful gift. [a.] Chandler, TX.

RIVERS, DEE
[pen.] Aszie Dean Rivers, (Wilbern, Burton-maiden name); [b.] November 20, 1950, Leslie, GA; [p.] Bertha Wilbern; [m.] Ulton, April 24, 1976 and Jerome Rivers (divorced), April 24, 1986 divorced 1989; [ch.] Shawn Jerome Rivers, Keyana Bettina; [ed.] High School, Business Education Writing Skills, secretarial training and KAD classes; [occ.] Document Coordinator, Kodak (Eastman) Co.; [hon.] A Demo for a record, I have many more poems; [oth. writ.] Marriage Road, Self, Will, Tomorrow, Pretended Love, Regain the Dream, Troubles of World and etc.; [pers.] I strive to write about true life. The meaning of the poem are reflected to help the reader. I admire Miss Maya Angelou the poet. [a.] Rochester, NY.

RIVET, NIMAI
[b.] September 28, 1977, Honolulu, HI; [p.] Roberta and Jaques Rivet; [ed.] High school junior; [occ.] Student; [memb.] Drama Club, Poetry Club, Hilo Swim Team; [oth. writ.] Other poems, 3 notebooks full; [pers.] The smile holds the key to everyone's heart. The smile holds the key to opening your heart. The laughter reminds us why we smile, and the decision us up to us! (to smile or not). [a.] Foster City, CA.

ROARK, DIANNE KAYE
[b.] April 18, 1944, San Antonio, TX; [p.] Clyde and Emma Kepple; [m.] Daniel E., November 13, 1965; [ch.] Darla (and John) Unterzuber, and Danny (and Sherry) Roark-grandchildren-J.J and Kevin Unterzuber; [occ.] Instructional Assistant - El Dorado Elementary School; [oth. writ.] Poems and stories for children, and inspirational poems about daily life; [pers.] Much of my writing has been influenced and inspired by my family. The Lord has blessed me greatly and has surrounded me with the love and encouragement of family and friends. [a.] Lancaster, CA.

ROBBINS, ANITA KAY
[pen.] Kay Robbins; [b.] December 28, 1944, Scranton, PA; [p.] Raymond and Kathryn Robbins; [m.] Deceased; [ch.] Thomas, April, August, Stephen; [ed.] High school, School of Beauty Culture, Colorist Education, Clairol, Logics International; [occ.] Hairstylist part-time, full-time Supervisor Rescue Mission; [memb.] American Cosmetology Association; [hon.] Customer service awards, JC Penney Sales Competition awards, Speaking at Rotary Clubs, The Optimist Clubs - tv related to operation of Women and Children's Shelter; [oth. writ.] Poetry, songs, editorials, devotionals, short articles speech and seminar on Domestic Violence Christian Tracts; [pers.] To be a blessing to those who enjoy reading. Sharing the inspiration of my Creator's gifts to me.

ROBBINS, MARY A.
[b.] February 21, 1914, Jamestown, PA; [p.] Joseph and Mary Gordian; [m.] Deceased.

ROBERTS, BOBBY J.
[b.] March 27, 1940, Coleman, TX; [p.] Archie and Eleanor Roberts; [m.] Dessie Ree Roberts; [ch.] Bobby Lamoure Roberts Sr., Shawn Jacqueline Roberts; [ed.] Coleman Colored High School; [occ.] Disabled since Nov. 1991; [oth. writ.] "Little Fishes In the Brook", sometimes, "Me Am I Am". [a.] Phoenix, AZ.

ROBERTS, MARIE
[pen.] Lily Marie; [b.] November 19, 1960; [p.] Frances Julia Roberts, George Walter Roberts; [m.] Brent Daniel; [ch.] Danny and Brianna; [ed.] Rockdale County High, Bryman School of Nursing; [occ.] Quality Control Manager; [memb.] The Band Talk Show; [hon.] First honors for every module in medical school; [oth. writ.] Book titled - Absolution, poems-Centuries in Love, The Well Wishers Hiding. Co-writer for of songs for other musicians; [pers.] Look beyond the mirror for beauty and you will always find it staring back at you. Inspired by 2 singer songwriters Brent Daniel, Neil Finn of Crowded House. [a.] Conyers, GA.

ROBERTS, STEVEN A.
[b.] November 25, 1955, Alton, IL; [p.] Jack and Rosemary Roberts; [ch.] Anthony, Jason and Amy; [ed.] Alton High School, Webster University; [occ.] Mental Health Tech II (Alton Mental Health Developmental Center); [pers.] Dedicated to the two people who inspired me to write my poem, Amy and Raquel. [a.] Cottage Hills, IL.

ROBIDEAU, SHIRLEY
[b.] May 31, 1951, Little Rock, AR; [m.] Richard, September 25, 1993; [ch.] James Robert; [ed.] McClellan High, Communications Specialist Sheppard AFB, TX; [occ.] Corrections Officer; [hon.] Criminal Justice Training Academy, Highest Overall and Highest Mock Scenes; [oth. writ.] I have a three volume set I would like to publish, "Emotions of the Heart"; [pers.] My inspiration for poetry started when I tried to deal with my own 'Emotions of the Heart' and it came out in writing form. [a.] Lake Stevens, WA.

ROBINSON, FRED E. JR.
[pen.] FE2, "BubbaLawn" "Baby Slim"; [b.] October 7, 1950, Sarasota, FL; [p.] Fred and Gladys Robinson; [m.] Renita D., September 1975; [ch.] Fred III, Desire, Richard, April and Dallas, Christina; [ed.] High school; [occ.] Disabled; [memb.] ASCAP, Worldwide Church of God, Right to Life, NAACP; [oth. writ.] Article title, "Dirt in America" rap songs - "It's Cracking Up America" and "Immipre', I Got a Ticket For You" and poems "Time Will Stop" Where Is My Road" and "MY Family"; [pers.] Easier said "and" done?? Why do we say, It's easier said "than" done, when when you say what is to be done, you are doing just by saying what's to be done, and when you done finished doing something what's to be done, It is easier said and done, because...You Done Said It! [a.] Cape Coral, FL.

ROBINSON, JEAN ANN
[b.] October 19, Morris, IL; [ed.] University of Wisconsin-Madison, University of Illinois; [occ.] Solid Waste Coordinator of Grundy; [memb.] Board of Directors, Canal Corridor Association, Morris Business and Professional Womens Club, Sierra Club, Nature Conservancy, National Wildlife Federation; [hon.] Delegate to First State Conservation Congress, 1994, Outstanding BPW member; [oth. writ.] Two regular newspaper columns, Waste Matters and Earthsense appearing in area papers.

ROBINSON, JERRY B.
[b.] April 4, 1930, Lawrenceville, IL; [p.] Mable and Stanley Robinson; [m.] Divorced; [ed.] Eastern Illinois State, Trinity University-San Antonio, University of Illinois, University of Southern California; [occ.] Financial Counselor-Univ. of CA; [memb.] Sigma Pi Fraternity, Church of Religious Science and Honorary Journalist; [hon.] Graduated cum laude from University of Illinois School of Journalism, Korean War Medals; [oth. writ.] One biography piece to St. Louis Post Dispatch - I have otherwise never submitted anything of my cartoon, short stories or poems written for my own amusement; [pers.] It seems to me that people general are courageous people and strong in their dealing with the pains they face in life, and I am encouraged when I see this strength of character that obsesses the writer's thoughts. [a.] Los Angeles, CA.

ROBINSON, LORISA
[b.] June 29, 1976, Fredericksburg, VA; [p.] Virginia and Howard Robinson; [ed.] James Monroe High School; [pers.] The youth of the world has a voice that desperately wants to be heard. Listen and help them learn to speak louder. [a.] Fredericksburg, VA.

ROBY, KEVIN PATRICK
[b.] June 12, 1971, Washington, DC; [p.] James Michael and Marion Clare Roby; [m.] Mitzi Dawn Roby, June 20, 1992; [ed.] Maryland High school graduate, Computer Learning Center; [occ.] Inside Sales Representative; [memb.] 82nd Airborne Aviation Unit and 1st COSCOM Unit in the US Army Ft. Bragg, NC; [pers.] Poetry has been a hobby of mine for quite awhile now. I felt that through my poetry my wife could see what I felt for her much easier. Although I have written quite a few poems, I felt this was my most meaningful since I wrote it while sitting in the desert waiting to hear when I would get to see Mitzi (my girlfriend at the time) again. [a.] Dunkirk, MD.

ROBY, VALERIE
[b.] October 22, 1971, Forrest City, AK; [p.] Jimmie Childress; [m.] Dorothy Childress, June 1, 1992; [ch.] Kannie and Ledra Roby; [ed.] Batesville High; [occ.] CB Mold Operator in Gen Corp Automotives; [oth. writ.] I've written poem for church I attend and for a poem contest in Batesville High; [pers.] I put forth time, tears, and prayers for my poem. I've got religious, love, and exotic poems for adults and a few of children poems. Also, I have a quite of few poetic short stories. (true short stories). [a.] Batesville, AR.

ROCCIO, ANTOINETTE I.
[pen.] Toni; [b.] September 22, 1925, Highland, NY; [p.] Maria Cremi and Lodonico Indelicotto (deceased); [m.] Armond C. (deceased), November 10, 1946; [ed.] Highland Grade School; [occ.] Seamstress now retired; [memb.] St. John Church, Senior Center; [oth. writ.] I have published two small books privately, not for book stores. 1) My Walk Along With Life, 2) Against The Wind; [pers.] I express my feelings in poetry and hopefully I will have the opportunity to share them with others. [a.] Beacon, NY.

RODNEY, DARRELL
[pen.] Darrell D.; [b.] May 11, 1972, Chicago, IL; [p.] Charles and Nellie Rodney; [ed.] Proviso West High, American Airlines Maintenance Academy; [occ.] United Parcel Driver; [hon.] Dean's List, Bronze Scholarship Award; [oth. writ.] Ace of Spade song on Music of America album produced by Hollywood Record Company, Tape Country Boy MC by Disc Makers; [pers.] I write about the things that I have been affected by in my life. I have been greatly influenced by late great blues players. [a.] Bellwood, IL.

RODRIGUEZ, ALAN
[b.] February 28, 1963, NYC; [p.] Kathleen and Israel Rodriguez; [m.] Kathleen T., May 29, 1987; [ch.] Daniel Albert; [ed.] Uniondale High School, Suburban Technical School; [occ.] Pest Control Operator, own business; [oth. writ.] Numerous songs and poems unpublished; [pers.] I always write from my heart and soul to reach the heart and soul of others. I have always learned from the journey of life to keep things simple. [a.] Sayville, NY.

RODRIGUEZ, LIZ
[pen.] Amber Marie Rodriguez; [b.] September 26, 1979, San Antonio, TX; [p.] Bernardo and Junie Martinez; [ch.] Jesus Barbosa IV; [ed.] Las Palanas Elementary, Gus Garcia Jr. High, Central Independent High School; [memb.] BMG Mucic Service; [hon.] For poetry Contest and Art, for drawing in the Drug Resistance Program; [oth. writ.] Several poems and compositions published in high school, newspaper. Awarded $100.00 for writing a composition in the Hacemos program; [pers.] Dedicated to the Rodriguez Family and in loving memory of Guadalupe Don Rodriguez. [a.] San Jose, CA.

RODRIGUEZ, RAFAEL JR.
[pen.] Chino; [b.] July 20, 1972, Chicago, Il; [p.] Rafael and Carmen Rodriguez; [ed.] High school, Roberto Clemente Community Academy; [occ.] Disabled bed bound with M.S.; [memb.] American Heart and Lung Association, Kedzie United Methodist Church; [hon.] Award on July 22, 1992, when graduated school, got the Spirit of Clemente award for attending classes even though I was very ill. I couldn't even walk right, but I struggled through it and graduated.; [oth. writ.] When my grandmother passed away - I wrote this letter for her. In loving memory. Remembering the times, you held my hands. No pain, no worries, not even tears could break the closeness I felt inside. Remembering the times we share together, seeing your smiling face has always filled my heart with joy. Remembering the holiday season and other holidays we have spent together. And all your home made cures, that worked! But most of all, remembering that you will always be a big part of my life. As the nights get colder and my tears begin to fall, I wonder how my life would be without you. As I see you in my mind, one day is sure to come when the Lord's angels will come for me and only that day would be the day that I would feel you holding my hands again. Mami abuela (grandmother) I will always love you and I will never forget you; [pers.] What I write comes from deep down memories that I have kept in my heart. I'm so happy that I will get to share my feelings. Getting my poem published is a dream come true. [a.] Chicago, IL.

ROGERS, CECILIA STELLA RIDLEY
[b.] January 6, 1908, Cheshire, England; [p.] General and Mrs. H.S. Rogers; [ed.] The Knoll, Camberly, Surrey Eng.; [occ.] Sculptor; [hon.] Sculpture Awards to mention a few - 1960 3rd prize "Wings of Thought" Outdoor Fair, 1968 1st prize "Pearl Fisher" Washington Miniature Show, 1970 1st prize "Aware" Washington Miniature Show, 1975 3rd place "A Dream Come True" Washington Miniature Show, 1980 honorable mention "The Messenger" New Jersey Miniature Show, 1986 1st place "Sea Voices" Montana Miniature Show, 1989 awarded membership to Miniature Artists of America Society, 1994 honorable mention "I Pray For You" Washington Miniature Art Show; [pers.] Whatever I create - sculpture or writing - I hope that it will bring light to the world. [a.] Washington, DC.

ROGERS, JOHNNY JR.
[b.] May 19, 1946, Florence, SC; [p.] Johnny Rogers Sr. and Katie Elizabeth Price Rogers; [m.] Divorced; [ed.] Brevard Community College, Francis Marion College; [occ.] Registered Respiratory Therapist - Duke University Medical Center; [memb.] The American Association for Respiratory Care and The National Board for Respiratory Care, charter lifetime member and Sapphire Poet, The International Society of Poets; [hon.] World of Poetry: Golden Poet 1990, 1991, 1992; five honorable mentions 1990, 1991; The International Society of Poets: Poets of Merit 1992, 1993, 1994 and four Editor's Choice Awards, 1993 and 1994; [oth. writ.] World of Poetry Press: 13 poems, World of Poetry Anthology 1991, 13 poems selected world of our World's Best Poets 1992, 1 poem Poems That Will Live Forever 1992; [pers.] I strive to reflect humanity, nature, and I write lyrics for song poems - on a wide variety of subjects. [a.] Durham, NC.

ROGERS, MANDY
[pen.] Mandy Rogers; [b.] January 18, 1980, Jacksonville, Passavant Hospital; [p.] Nancy Credit and Steve Rogers; [ed.] Jacksonville High School. [a.] Jacksonville, IL.

ROGERS, MELISSA
[pen.] Melissa B. Rogers; [b.] November 13, 1976, Brooklyn, NY; [p.] Ellen and Abraham Prig; [pers.] I've been writing poetry since I was thirteen years old. Writing helps me stay in tuned with myself and maintain stability within. For when the self is lost all is lost. [a.] New York, NY.

ROGERS, SHANNON ELIZABETH
[b.] November 13, 1977, Arlington Heights, IL; [p.] Larry and Marian Rogers; [ed.] Clover Hill High School, Amila County High School; [pers.] Most of my poems are an influence and a remembrance of a dear, close friend lost to suicide. Poetry has become my best way to relieve all my thoughts, feelings, heartaches, and memories. [a.] Amelia, VA.

ROIZEN, JENNY (JENNIFER LYN ROIZEN)
[b.] August 3, 1981, San Francisco, CA; [p.] Drs. Nancy J. and Michael F. Roizen; [ed.] 8th grade student The University of Chicago Laboratory Schools; [occ.] 8th grade student; [pers.] My writings are all, or almost all based on my life, and all the good things and happy moments in my adolescence. [a.] Chicago, IL.

ROJAS, MELVIN
[b.] March 24, 1948, Arecibo, PR; [p.] Julio Rojas and Andrea Caban; [m.] Virginia, April 11, 1970; [ch.] Melvin Raul, Sindy E., and Melsavir; [ed.] Arecibo High School (Dra Maria Cadilla), University of Catholic of Ponce; [occ.] City of Hartford-Tax Investigator; [memb.] Female Softball Team Melvin Magic Girls Founder and Coach, PR Owner and Coach of two softball teams, male and female. Movement for a better world, home Manresa, PR, Sacred Heart Church, family sheep founder and member; [hon.] Bronze star recipient, US Army Overseas Medal, US Army Vietnam Service Medal, National Defense Medal, Merit Certification of US Army and plaque and trophy awards; [oth. writ.] I have over three dozen of poems not published, like Mothers Day, Father's Day, Teacher, Cupid, Puerto Rico my Island, God, Woman, Anniversary, Virgin Mary, Best Friend, etc.; [pers.] Once you reach deep down and find the sweetness, tender, peace and love within you, the daily struggle to be successful powerful, rich and important. It mean nothing compared with the kindness of your heart. [a.] Hartford, CT.

ROLLSTIN, MELISSA M.
[pen.] Missy; [b.] March 6, 1971, Knoxville, IA; [p.] Don and Janet Rollstin; [ed.] High Desert High School, Victor Valley College; [hon.] Scholarship for the Best grades from High Desert High School; [pers.] I enjoy writing, this is a way I like to show my feelings. [a.] Victorville, CA.

ROMAN, DIANA
[b.] June 9, 1954, Limestone, ME; [ch.] David Roman, Jr.; [pers.] Dedicated to my daughter, Daviann. She died in a motorcycle accident at the age of 21 and will always be remembered. [a.] Newton, UF, MA.

ROONEY, JOEL P.
[b.] October 10, 1969, Chippewa Falls, WS; [p.] Dale P. Rooney and Barbara Shafer; [ed.] Chippewa Falls High School, Towson State University, Wesley College; [occ.] Student; [hon.] President's List, Dean's List, United Methodist Scholarship; [pers.] There is something positive to be drawn out of all of life's experiences. The poem was written in the memory of Melissa Norquist. [a.] Dover, DE.

ROOSA, BERTHA
[pen.] Bertha "Bert" Roosa; [b.] April 3, 1928, Middletown, OH; [p.] Anna and Felix Evans; [m.] Fred, May 4, 1946; [ch.] 3 sons; [ed.] High school; [occ.] Self employed Hobert Bear maker, painter, musical performer, wood carver, quilter, rug maker; [memb.] Allison Ave. Baptist Church; [oth. writ.] Book "The Hobert Bears Big Surprise", songs - "Willie", "My Sweet Ohio Dream", "O-hi-O-oo", many poems, stories, etc.; [pers.] To find the truth and proclaim it! Whether in music performances, gardening, crafts, art, writing...to see how things really are and to promote truth and honesty. Entrepreneurial independence! [a.] Middletown, OH.

ROOT, LAURA
[b.] June 20, 1979, Lewiston, IN; [p.] Lee Root and Judith Aplin; [ed.] Lewiston Hgh School [occ.] Student, child care; [hon.] Student of the Month; [oth. writ.] Fall's Rose, Lead Me To You, Where Are You Now? and others; [pers.] My friends and family have influenced my writing more than anything. I'd be lost without them. [a.] Lewiston, ID.

ROSE, SHERRY
[b.] August 1, 1979, Sacramento, CA; [p.] Gregory and Carla Rose; [ed.] Elk Grove High School; [occ.] Babysitting; [memb.] California Scholarship Federation (CSF); [hon.] Received award for getting 4.0 GPA during K-8; [oth. writ.] Poems published in local church newsletters, autobiographic published in school collages. [a.] Elk Grove, CA.

ROSEMANN, JEFFERY A.
[b.] November 5, 1960, Ft. Stewart, GA; [p.] Floyd and Virginia Rosemann; [ed.] Bradwell Institute High School, [oth. writ.] A few poems but only one other published in a local paper; [pers.] I'm just the fifth of six very talented brothers and sisters. [a.] Hinesville, GA.

ROSS, ANDRIA
[b.] May 11, 1980, Salina, KS; [p.] Bill and Felicia Ross; [ed.] Concordia, KS; [occ.] Freshman student; [hon.] Having my poem published is the only honor I ever had; [oth. writ.] Many other poems such as the others that were sent into difference poetry contests; [pers.] I love to write down my feelings and turn them into poetry. [a.] Concordia, KS.

ROSS, MELISSA
[b.] October 23, 1980, San Pedro; [p.] Ronald and Julia Ross; [ed.] Lorenze Hillside; Taper Elementary and Dodson Junior High; [hon.] Honor Roll 8th grade, Allstars Softball. [a.] San Pedro, CA.

ROTHMAN, HARRY E.
[b.] September 28, 1910, New York City, NY; [p.] Max and Dora Schanman Rothman; [m.] Hortense Hart Rothman, June 3, 1944; [ch.] David and Dorothy; [ed.] New York University; [occ.] Artist-current Contemporary Painting, Photographer Black and White, Color Photographic Work; [memb.] National Artists Equity Association, Eastman Kodak Pro Passport; [pers.] My art work is in collection of Presidents Jimmy Carter, Gerald R. Ford, John F. Kennedy, Ronald Reagan, and approximately 20 public collections. [a.] Alexandria, VA.

ROWLAND, SHAWNA LYNN
[pen.] Shawna Lynn Rowland; [b.] January 5, 1981, Huntington B.; [p.] Jack and Joni Rowland; [m.] Victor Hernandez; [ed.] Middle School student; [occ.] Babysitting; [memb.] Tarra Cotta Middle School 7th grade helper; [hon.] 1st place Beauty Contest, Honor Roll; [oth. writ.] I love writing anything; [pers.] I made this poem for people who have no love. And to let them know there is people who do love them. [a.] Canyon Lake, CA.

RUDOLPH, RITA
[b.] March 29, Chicago; [p.] Rita and Bruno Bellucci; [m.] Charles, October 6, 1956; [ch.] Marita, Mary, Chuck, Stephen, Breanne, Anthony, Chandler, Ashley; [ed.] Providence High School, DePaul University; [occ.] Homemaker; [oth. writ.] Poem published in local newspapers; [pers.] I want the words of my poem to touch the hearts of all who read it. [a.] Bedford, TX.

RUEDA, LINA
[pen.] Sylin Taylor; [b.] August 5, 1965, West Covina, CA; [p.] Isabel and Hector Rueda, Sr.; [ed.] Bishop Amar High School, Nogales High School and Life; [occ.] Working as singer/songwriter (lyricist); [memb.] APLA (AIDS Project LA); [oth. writ.] "Debut Collection of Hall & Taylor" (10 song catalog) with Library of Congress March 1994; [pers.] Live, Love, Laugh, Learn and never lose faith in yourself. Everything I write is a reflection of everyone who has touched my life. [a.] West Covina, CA.

RUFF, CYNTHIA J.
[b.] September 24, 1955, Northampton, PA; [p.] Alma and Wilson Smith; [m.] Divorced; [ch.] Daniel and Sarah; [ed.] Northampton High School, Northampton County Community College; [occ.] Dietary Aide at Nursing Home; [hon.] Golden Poet Award for 1990 - awarded by World of Poetry,

award of Merit Certificate for "The One That Got Away", Golden Poet Award for 1991 from World of Poetry; [oth. writ.] Manuscript of 116 spiritual poetry. Book is copywrited and entitled "Bound In His Glory" not yet published; [pers.] God has been the lighthouse in my life. His love has directed me when life's seas remain calm and protected me when the storms became threatening. [a.] Whitehall, PA.

RUHL, DARIN C.
[b.] March 31, 1973, Oregon City, OR; [p.] George and Judie Ruhl; [ed.] Rex Putnam High; [occ.] US Army, 11Bravo Infantry; [hon.] Military; Army Achievement Medal, Southwest Asia Service Medal; [oth. writ.] Personal writings; [pers.] Through my experiences in the military, I've come to the realization of how lucky every living being is to live on this earth today. I try to display that concept through my writings and often question it through the observation of different lifestyles. Nature from a mystical view and mankind relations with nature are other subjects I enjoy exploring. [a.] Clackamas, OR.

RUPLEY, JILL RENEE
[b.] June 26, 1978, Huntington, IN; [p.] Kevin and Dian Rupley; [ed.] Huntington North; [occ.] Student; [memb.] Co-people editor of our yearbook DEKA; [hon.] Who's Who Among High School Students 1995; [oth. writ.] "You Did It" a murder mystery comedy. Other short stories and poems (high school). I've also written a few stories and have done designs of pages for the D-issue of the campus; [pers.] Poetry is not only an expression of words, but of the heart and soul. I've always been partial to the writing of Emerson and Therowe. [a.] Huntington, IN.

RUSH, DON
[b.] March 10, 1938, Atlanta, GA; [p.] Charles and Bessie Rush; [b.] Charlotte, November 14, 1959; [ch.] Donna, Carolyn, Tammy; [ed.] Fort Lauderdale High School, Stetson University, Union University; [occ.] Employment and Training Specialist-North Central FL Planning Council; [memb.] First Baptist Church of Lake City, Southern Employment and Training Association; [hon.] Community Education Coordinator of 1982-83 Florida Association of Community Education Professional of the Year 1993 - Florida Association for Retarded Citizens; [oth. writ.] God's Reason, published 1976 in newspaper, I Was There; [pers.] But now abide faith, hope love, these three, but the greatest of these is love. 1 Cor. 13:13. [a.] Lake City, FL.

RUSH, STEPHEN L.
[pen.] Steve LeRoy Rush; [b.] November 15, 1965, Riverside, CA; [p.] Vernon and Betty Bergfalk; [m.] Raquel S. (Abreu) Rush, May 23, 1992; [oth. writ.] "God Laughs", "Love in the Ballads" (series), "Critters", "Cotton Seed" - books currently writing "Character Witnessing: The Moral History Dilemma"; [pers.] Mr. Rush used to suffer form a "hint handicap". This learning disability retards inter-personal skills and is partially caused by a negative parental instruction and omitting the suggestion, "That's a hint." Subtle communication skills become impaired further when answering matter-of-fact, rather than presuming what was meant. Society has chosen to rebel against hyprocrisy the poem speaks of. When the next generation rebels against the corruption and deceit of this generation, you will have anarchy - unless, someone shows you a way out. My example is clear: the man who abstains until marriage proves he loves his wife and her body, but just "hot". Compatibility therefore, is not "Mr./Mrs. Right", but "Do Right". [a.] Yucaipa, CA.

RUSSELL, MILDRED E.
[b.] January 23, 1915, Elmira, NY; [p.] Mr. and Mrs. Frank L. Clearwater (deceased); [m.] 1945; [ch.] One; [occ.] Housewife; [memb.] VFW and DAVA; [oth. writ.] "Scars Are Lonely, Without Touch". [a.] Lake Havasu City, AZ.

RUSSO, JAMIE
[b.] September 28, 1980, Bethel, CT; [p.] Bill and Cathy Palinchak; [hon.] National English Merit award, 4 English reading certificates, A-B Honor Roll; [pers.] Dreams are kept in a hidden door once you find the key cherish it all your life. [a.] Easley, SC.

RUTHERFORD, MARTHA HAYDEN
[b.] January 29, 1933, Smyth County; [p.] Roby and Virgie H. Hayden; [m.] Curtis H., January 27, 1994; [ch.] 8 by former marriage; [ed.] 7th grade; [occ.] Housewife; [hon.] My mother Virgie H. Hayden never won any awards or honors but she should have. The best mother a child could have. She raised 14 of us. 10 girls and 4 boys. There was no time for her to do much else. But we never heard her or daddy ever complain or say an unkind word to each other; [oth. writ.] An unpublished book of poems; [pers.] This poem was written by my mother in 1920. The only one, she ever wrote. She gave ut to me with the request that I do nothing with it, until after her death. [a.] Troutdale, VA.

RUZICKA, PATRICIA
[b.] November 25, 1963; [ch.] 3; [ed.] Washburn University; [occ.] US Army Reserves; [hon.] Few medals for my participation in the Persian Gulf War and for my time in the army.

RZESZUT, REBECCA
[b.] November 30, 1973, Cleveland, OH; [p.] Anthony and Jimmy Rzeszut; [ed.] Portage Area High School; [occ.] At 13 became handicapped. Every day is a fight to want to live. More than anything else I love to write; [oth. writ.] I've written other poems, short stories and one novel. Only now am I sending my material to publishers; [pers.] Although I dwell in this Cimmerion darkness, I will draw strength from the hope within. [a.] Portage, PA.

SAAKIAN, DIANA
[b.] November 11, 1968, Russia; [p.] Anna Saakian; [ed.] Saint Mary's School, New York Trafalgar High for Girls, Montreal Bois de Boulogne College; [occ.] Telecommunications and Translation; [hon.] Spring 1982, Awarded first place medal by the United Nations at the National Junior High Poetry and essay competition for Nuclear Disarmament; [oth. writ.] Several poems that I am hoping to publish in the near future; [pers.] If even a single word that I have uttered in my lifetime has struck a similar cord in another's soul, I have attained my immortality. [a.] Montreal, CAN. Quebec.

SAENZ, ABIANNE PATRICIA
[b.] March 25, 1982, Metairie, LA; [p.] Rose M. Alvarado and Felix Saenz, Jr.; [ed.] St. Gregory, 7th grade; [memb.] Church choir, Youth Group, Math Counts; [pers.] I feel one of the ways I can express my feelings is by poetry. Therefore I try my best to feel what I don't but will in the future through my writing. [a.] VA Beach, VA.

SALAMEY, MICHAEL
[pen.] Miko Starr; [pers.] I find that all in life is poetry in motion. Any experience can be adventured on paper in the hands of an inspired poet. [a.] Dearborn, MI.

SALZER, GREGORY SCOTT
[b.] February 25, 1969, Miami, FL; [p.] Grover Salzer and Cecilia Baggett; [ed.] Hialeah-Miami Lakes Senior High School, Broward Community College, Florida International University; [occ.] Student; [memb.] Sigma Tau Delta English Honor Society; [hon.] Honorable mention service award for Sigma Tau Delta; [oth. writ.] Several notebooks of unpublished writing; [pers.] "I write because my inner voice rises above my spoken words." Influences included The Romantics and The Beat Generation Writers. [a.] Miami Lakes, FL.

SALTZMAN, STEFANI
[b.] September 28, 1976, Dayton, OH; [p.] Nick and Robyn Saltzman; [ed.] Vandalia-Butler High School; [occ.] Wash clothes, Cintas; [hon.] My diploma; [oth. writ.] I was in writing class my senior year. I write my own personal poetry in a book of my own; [pers.] Have confidence and put effort into everything you do and you will accomplish more today than was possible yesterday. [a.] Vandalia, OH.

SANGRAM, AMARDEEP
[pen.] Mar-D; [b.] May 18, 1980, Chicago, IL; [p.] Aruna Sangram; [ed.] Currently in 8th grade graduating on June 8, 1994; [hon.] Young Authors Award, Historical Museum Award; [oth.writ.] Poem in Apna Ghar newsletter; [pers.] Writing is nothing more than emotions expressed without hurting someone elses. My writing has been influenced through my parent's divorce. I try to express my emotions without hurting someone. [a.] Skokie, IL.

SANTIAGO, JOHN
[pen.] Glenn Paul, Paul Santiago, John Glenn; [b.] May 20, 1979, Belleville, NJ; [p.] Mr. and Mrs. Ramon Santiago, Sr.; [ed.] St. Benedicts Prep High School, Immaculate Heart of Mary Elementary School; [occ.] Student; [hon.] Voted to Math team in 8th grade and District Free Throw Champion in 8th grade, voted as photographer for yearbook; [pers.] I'm in the Drama Guild, last year played JV Baseball, now I am playing tennis. Loves sports and wants to major in communications. [a.] Newark, NJ.

SANTOS, PETER
[b.] August 3, 1978, Cape Cod, MA; [p.] JoAnn and Ferdinand F. Santos; [ed.] Dennis - Yarmouth Regional High School; [occ.] Student-Junior; [memb.] Dennis-Yarmouth High School Marching Band; [hon.] Who's Who Among American High School Students; [pers.] I had a dream where I won a million dollars on a scratch ticket. The next day when I bought one I won nothing...[a.] Yarmouthport, MA.

SAPIEN, MARDESIA
[pen.] Mardesia Sapian; [b.] February 28, 1976, San Jose; [ed.] North Ranchito Element, North Park Middle, El Rancho High, Whittier College; [memb.] Wild Life National Geographics, School Poetry Publications; [hon.] Youth Feast award winner - writing awards; [oth. writ.] Several poems published in local newspapers, articles in school paper, published poems in magazines; [pers.] I only wish to reflect the evil reality of mankind as well as the minds wondrous imagination through poetry as Edgar Allan Poe accomplished. [a.] Hacienda Heights, CA.

SARDINA, ANNA MARIA
[pen.] Casandra; [b.] June 9, 1963, Monterey, CA; [p.] FRank and Agnes Sardina; [ed.] St. John's High School, City College, Sonoma State; [occ.] Graphic Art, Printing Industry; [memb.] Friend of Bill

Wilson and Dr. Bob; [pers.] I want people to know there's hope, no matter what the problems are. And that life is full of wonder and possibilities if you only believe. [a.] Rohnert Park, CA.

SAUBLE, KARA L.
[b.] October 13, 1982, Marshall, MO; [p.] Vicki and Michael Sauble; [ed.] Bueker Middle School; [occ.] Student; [memb.] Religion class and softball team; [hon.] A honor roll, P.E. award, several reading circle certificates, and an art award, award for poem in 3rd grade; [oth. writ.] I have written other stories and poems but none of these stories and poems have ever been published; [pers.] I write because I love to entertain people and I like to touch them or make them have some kind of emotion. [a.] Marshall, MO.

SAUERS, NORMA JEAN
[b.] May 4, 1944, Lewisburg, PA; [p.] Charles C. Boop and Ruby J. Gutelius; [m.] Lee R., May 22, 1965; [ch.] Anthony Sauers, Chad Sauers; [ed.] Milton High, Imperial Private School, Ambassador College, Empire Beauty School; [occ.] Housewife, volunteer at American Rescue Workers; [memb.] Mifflinburg Church of the Nazarene, Nazarene World Missionary Society Council, Outreach Sunday School class, L.I.F.T. (Ladies in Fellowship Together); [hon.] High school honor student, 1st place Hairdresser Trophy; [oth. writ.] Several poems published in local newspapers and church publications; [pers.] Poetry is an excellent avenue of expressing my deep inner feelings of today's controversial issues. Before writing, I pray for God's guidance so that each poem may cause the reader to be inspired to live a life of morality and compassion. [a.] Mifflinburg, PA.

SAUPAN, JAMES FRANCIS
[b.] October 10, 1959, Honolulu, HI; [p.] Roberto and Dolores Saupan, Sr.; [ch.] Briana Marie Loleina Saupan; [ed.] Radford High; [occ.] Flight Attendant; [oth. writ.] "Words From the Heart" a collection of poems, unpublished. "Plane and Simple" Airline Travel Planning Tips, unpublished; [pers.] My family is my inspiration and I cherish each one of them unconditionally for they are my greatest source of love and support. [a.] San Juan, PR.

SAYEED, RIAZ
[pen.] Riaz Fatima; [b.] January 11, 1957, Hyderabad, India; [p.] Hasan and Bilquis Reza; [m.] Vilayat, April 16, 1984; [ch.] Nageen, Nazneen, Najeeb; [ed.] Granada Hills High, California State University/Northridge; [occ.] Operations Officer; [memb.] Jafria Society, National Geographic Society, PTA, Girl Scouts; [hon.] Dean's List; [oth. writ.] Editor-in-Chief of religious magazines "The Message" and "Guide". [a.] Monrovia, MD.

SAYEGH, MARY
[b.] April 5, 1975, Windsor; [p.] Nimer and Faridah Sayegh; [ed.] Catholic Central High School, St. Clair College; [occ.] Student; [hon.] Perfect Attendance award, Evening of Excellence award - for getting highest mark in classes in; English, Math, Religion, Science, and Family Studies; [oth. writ.] Young Author's Contest for writing a story; write a poem and publish it in the newspaper, poetry contest; [pers.] I have been influenced by looking back on my childhood memories and on my self-image. My parents encouraged me to work hard and to exceed my goal. [a.] Windsor, ONT., CAN.

SCANLON, JOSHUA J.
[b.] November 21, 1972, Milwaukee, WI; [p.] Patrick and Janice Scanlon; [ed.] Ridge Road Elementary School and Horseheads High School, St. Bonaventure University; [occ.] Full-time student; [hon.] Kappa Delta Pi; [oth. writ.] Several poems published in St. Bonaventure's Literary, semester publication The Laurel; [pers.] I owe much to my life's experiences with people in influencing my poetry. My greatest influence has been Bob Dylan, and as long as he keeps writing, his affect will continue to be felt in my works as well. If this is to be my 15 minutes, then...Hi, Mom. [a.] St. Bonaventure, NY.

SCARRY, JENNIFER L.
[b.] September 29, 1974; [p.] Donald and Janet Maley Scarry-siblings-Kathy Scarry Smith, Don Scarry Jr., Brian Scarry and Shawn Lee Laughlin; [ed.] SLHS Intensive Business; [occ.] Operator-Worthington Custom Plastics; [pers.] I am greatly inspired by people in my past that I have loved and lost. [a.] Salineville, OH.

SCHELL, RUBY
[b.] May 25, 1920, Manitoba; [ed.] Swan River Valley, University of Manitoba; [occ.] Retired; [memb.] Retired Teacher's of Manitoba, Little Woody Baptist Church; [pers.] Whether its an about turn, or foraging ahead. After 30 years the young ones are still studying to improve their mind and lot. [a.] Swan River, MB, CAN.

SCHICK, DELORES E.
[pen.] Dee Whitmore Schick; [b.] October 3, 1931, Kenosha, WI; [p.] Allen and Della Whitmore; [m.] Jack Maurice, February 5, 1955; [ch.] John Eric, Robert Charles; [ed.] Stephens College, Northwestern University, Governors State University; [occ.] Secretary for Husband, a civil engineer and land surveyor; [memb.] MUSE-Local Writer's Group, Friends with Acorn Public Library Dist., Stephens College Alumnae Club; [hon.] Bi-Centennial Anthem Award 1975, winning anthem published on front page of "Oak Forest Times Herald", co-author of The Muse Newsletter; [oth. writ.] "Tone Poem in Prose" Stephens College Literary Magazine 1952, "I Wrote A Poem" high school paper interviewed and wrote biographies for Oak Forest Historical Commission 1969 -1972 for Oak Forest History; [pers.] I try to be brief and humorous. Also, I try to be positive. Influence classical Japanese poets. Inspiration - people, nature, classical music. [a.] Oak Forest, IL.

SCHILPP, AMY KATHLEEN
[b.] June 29, 1982, Baltimore; [p.] Paul and Kathleen Schilpp; [ed.] St. Clare's Catholic School; [occ.] Student; [memb.] Girls Scouts Troup 1983, Student Council; [hon.] Library Aide Effort awards in all school subjects. Many, many girl scout badges. Creative writing badge and reading badge; [oth. writ.] Life, Dreams; [pers.] I write about the worlds needs in a spiritual sense. [a.] Baltimore, MD.

SCHMIDT, CHRIS
[b.] June 17, 1982, Pittsburgh, PA; [p.] Tim and Martha; [ed.] Bessie Ellison Elementary School, Bode Middle School; [occ.] Student; [oth. writ.] The Revenge of Jack-the-Ripper, Home Alone 3; [pers.] I've been writing since 4th grade. I hope someday, I write entertaining books for adults. This has been a great honor to have my poem published in a poetry book. [a.] St. Joseph, MO.

SCHNEIDER, STEVEN
[b.] October 20, 1945, Bronx, NY; [p.] Lillian and Abe Schneider; [ed.] Jamaica High School, Queensborough Community College; [occ.] Office Services; [hon.] Honorable Discharge, United States Army 1968; [pers.] I write from the heart so that I don't sugar coat my words. [a.] Jamaica, NY.

SCHONHOFER, JENNIFER
[b.] December 6, 1976, Maidstone, SASK, CAN.; [p.] Jack and Beverly; [ed.] Maidstone High School, University of Saskatchewan; [occ.] Student; [memb.] Waseca United Church; [hon.] Eidness Scholarship, Nesbit Scholarship, Honor Roll; [oth. writ.] Poem published in local newspapers Maidstone Mirror; [pers.] My feelings have always been expressed through my poetry, such as Goodbye. This was written on the one year anniversary of my brother's death. [a.] Maidstone, SASK.

SCHRIEDER, JACKIE
[pen.] Jackie Schroeder; [b.] July 25, 1979, Cleveland, OH; [p.] Mark and Roberta Schroeder; [ed.] Chamberlin High; [memb.] Cheerleading, Key Club, Student Government; [hon.] Published in "Who's Who Among American High School Students" finalist in "Power of the Pen" state competition, 4 year principal's and honor roll; [oth. writ.] Several short stories and poems on various subjects one of which is copyrighted and will possibly be used for Hallmark Greeting cards; [pers.] Think no evil, see no evil, hear no evil - and you will never write a best-selling novel. [a.] Aurora, OH.

SCHROEDER, JAMIE
[b.] June 14, 1963, San Gabriel, CA; [p.] Paul and Judith Garcia; [m.] Michael, September 19, 1987; [ch.] Tamara, Brandi, and Michael; [ed.] Bonita High School; [occ.] Beauty and Health Consultant; [oth. writ.] National Library of Poetry, My Dear Sweet Mother, published in "Seasons to Come"; [pers.] This poem was written for my mother who recently passed away. It was very important for me to tell her exactly how I felt about her because I had a feeling this would be the last Mother's Day together and my last chance to tell her I thank the Lord for that chance. [a.] Azusa, CA.

SCHUBERT, JEAN
[b.] April 8, 1933, Peoria, IL; [p.] Deceased/Mr. and Mrs. John G. Kook; [m.] Divorced; [ch.] X5 "The Best"; [ed.] Manual Training High, St. Francis School of Nursing, Glendale College, Phoenix College; [occ.] Retired RN; [oth. writ.] Articles and poetry for gifts and personal pleasure - usually in Calligraphy. None have been published yet but many have been sold, also; [pers.] My feelings are expressed thru writings and oil paintings, so the variety is tremendous. [a.] Phoenix, AZ.

SCHULTZ, CATHY GENE
[pen.] Cathy Gene Schultz; [b.] April 12, 1945, Weston, W.VA.; [p.] William K. and Arretta M. Wright; [m.] James E., November 23, 1985; [ch.] Jill, Lorri, Jennifer and Julie Jurkoshek and Theresa, Ann, Janet and Marsha Schultz (stepchildren); [ed.] Stow High; [occ.] Medical Receptionist; [memb.] Former-P.T.A., C.A.R.E., M.A.D.D.; [pers.] I have been greatly influenced by my children, my family and the writings of Helen Steiner Rice. [a.] Bowling Green, OH.

SCHUYLER, GRETHCHEN
[b.] December 28, 1951, Rochester, NY; [ed.] New York State RN,; [occ.] Freelance Writer; [memb.] Bay Hundred Ducks Unlimited, Miles River Yacht Club, American Red Cross Nurse; [pers.] I want my writings to be a hand to hold on the journey we all travel. Traditional American music and my life's adventures have been my greatest influences. [a.] Bozman, MD.

SCHWAB, MARILYN
[pen.] Marilyn Schwab; [b.] Minneapolis, MN; [p.] Rose and Gunnar Thorkelson; [m.] Ted; [ch.] Laura, Christine and Vikki Anne; [occ.] Legal Office Administrator; [oth. writ.] None published but I write children's books and poems also; [pers.] I love life and nature and write best when all alone and in some beautiful park or serene setting. [a.]

Diamond Bar, CA.

SCHWETER, CAROLINE K.
[pen.] Caroline Anne Kelly; [b.] July 26, 1962, Cleveland, OH; [p.] Mary Louise and James Kelly; [m.] Marco Polo, August 20, 1994; [ch.] Grace Maegan; [ed.] Holy Name High; [occ.] Paralegal (Irwin M. Frank & Thomas G. Longo; [memb.] National Shrine of St. Jude, Church of St. Michael; [oth. writ.] Published poetry in Cleveland State University (book 1979), Contemporary Poets of America and Great Britian - 1993 Anthology; [pers.] My poems reflect past experiences and have had a tremendous effect on the person I have become. The sadness and tragedy of my past writings dating to 1974. Have become poems of celebration because of the love of my husband. [a.] Euclid, OH.

SCHWINGEL, ANGELA
[pen.] Angie Mae; [b.] June 12, 1978, Rochester, NY; [p.] Sara and Donald Schwingel; [ed.] Livonia High School (Junior); [occ.] West Shurfine - Cashier; [memb.] Bulldog Bullentin (newspaper), The Wild Dolphin Project, President of my Junior class, Run Track.

SCOTT, AUTRILLA WATKINS
[pen.] Autrilla Watkins Scott; [b.] May 24, 1930, Hope, AK; [p.] Mary Ella and Louis Watkins; [m.] Olen M. Scott, Sr., September 30, 1950; [ch.] Sharon S. Gillis and Olen M. Scott Jr.; [ed.] Yerger High School, Yerger Typing School, Long Beach City Nursing Class; [occ.] Retired LVN; [memb.] St. Vestal C.M.E. Church, Victoria Temple #609, Long Beach Central Area Association-Community Improvement Chairperson, Democratic National Committee; [hon.] St. Vestal C.M.E. Church So. CA Conf. 9th Dist. (1994) Outstanding and Dedicated Christian Service, Dept. of Vet. Affairs (Excellence in Nursing; 9th National Veterans Wheelchair Games, 1993 AT&T Silver Spirit Award, L.B. City 1990 Comm. Development Achievements; [oth. writ.] Poems published in local newspaper - Long Beach Times and Los Angeles Sentinel; [pers.] "Respect", we will be able to get along better with others, if we would respect each other. [a.] Long Beach, CA.

SCOTT, SAUNDRA RENEE
[b.] November 9, 1962, Washington, DC; [p.] Miles and Betty Scott; [ch.] Christopher James Scott; High school and a semester of Junior College; [occ.] Homemaker-getting job training; [memb.] Sooka Gaika International (Buddhist Organization); [oth. writ.] Keep a notebook of blank paper, and proceed to write whenever the words flow from my heart and mind, down to the page; [pers.] I try self motivation and harmony that can be flowing through the universe like water flowing over a cluster of rocks I achieve this through chanting. [a.] District Heights, MD.

SCOVILLE, TAMAH
[pen.] Tamah Frances Scoville; [b.] September 24, 1963, Waterbury, CT; [p.] Anita Frances and Sherwood Robert Scoville; [ed.] Union Thirty Two High School, ADP Vermont College, Burlington Academy of Music; [occ.] Singer, Songwriter, Musician, Waitron; [oth. writ.] One poem published in 1973 in "I Found A Cat in A Box of Pillows" - Vermont Public Schools Poetry and Prose; recorded 12 song tape, "Virgin Soul" at Star Studios in 1989 of Original Works; [pers.] Listen. Om Namah Shivaua! [a.] Burlington, VT.

SEARS, CARROLL L.
[pen.] Hank Sears; [b.] March 7, 1930, Paris, IL; [p.] Minnie and Henry Sears; [m.] Betty Jean, September 6, 1959; [ch.] Seven; [ed.] 10 years; [occ.] Retired; [memb.] The American Legion Post No. 0233; [oth. writ.] 3 years U.S. A. Air Force; [pers.] I love horseback riding hunting and fishing and write poetry.

SECRIST, CAROL M.
[b.] June 15, 1958, Marietta, GA; [p.] Dr. Noah and Jeanne Meadows; [m.] Don, May 16, 1987; [ch.] Mark Samuel; [ed.] Auburn University, Marietta High School; [occ.] Dealer Review Analyst, GE Capital Auto Lease; [hon.] Alpha Psi Omega - Theatre Honor Society, Dean's List; [pers.] I enjoy writing creative poems from the heart and soul. I find my inspiration from special people and situations. [a.] Matthews, NC.

SEIFULLAH, AJEENAH
[pen.] Nina; [b.] March 2, 1979, Cincinnati; [p.] Lateefah and Roland Littlejohn; [ed.] The Rayen High School; [memb.] School Science Club, H.U.G.S., Youngstown Striders Track Club; [oth. writ.] "Respect"; [pers.] Through my Lord and Savior Jesus Christ all things are possible if you just believe. [a.] Youngstown, OH.

SEIGLE, DAVID JOEL
[b.] May 8, 1930, Detroit, MI; [p.] Albert and Virginia Seigle; [m.] Divorced; [ch.] Sara, Ruth, Laura Seigle; [ed.] Michigan State University, Northern University; [occ.] Retired; [memb.] Phi Alpha Theta, Omicron Mu Chapter; [hon.] History Honorary 1975; [oth. writ.] Masters papers - "The Good Society" and "Civil Liberties" 1975; [pers.] We are a part of nature and have more in common with each other than otherwise. [a.] Port Huron, MI.

SERNA, DAWN
[b.] February 16, 1970, Beale Air Force Base, CA; [p.] Pedro and Virginia Serna, Jr.; [ed.] William B. Travis High School, St. Edward's University; [memb.] Delta Sigma Pi, Alpha Chi, Delta Mu Delta, Kappa Gamma Pi; [hon.] Several academic scholarships, University Honors Program, Dean's List, graduated Magna Cum Laude, Who's Who Among Students in American Universities and Colleges, Aesthetic Voice Vol. #1 - published drawing; [pers.] That which has previously profoundly touched my life is the fuel behind my writings. Hobbies: I sew, bake, cook, draw, decorate, garden, flower, walk, play piano and design my thoughts and dreams. [a.] Austin, TX.

SESTER, KENDRA ELAINE
[b.] February 9, 1976, Somerset, KY; [p.] Kenneth and Paulene Sester; [ed.] Clay County High School, Eastern Kentucky University; [occ.] Deputy Clerk-Clay County Circuit and District Clerks Office; [hon.] National Merit Scholar, published in Who;s Who in America's High School Students; [oth. writ.] Poems published in school newspaper; [pers.] If you're going to walk on thin ice, you might as well dance. [a.] Manchester, KY.

SHAFFER, HEATHER
[pen.] Heather Shaffer; [b.] January 30, 1981, Lincoln City, OR; [p.] Doug and Tami Shaffer; [ed.] Mt. View Intermediate School; [occ.] 8th grade student; [hon.] Won a Blazer Writing Contest for my school in 7th grade; [oth. writ.] Poem published in Anthology of Poetry of Young Americans; [pers.] My writings take thought and when I write them I add metaphors as sort of a test for the reader. If they figure out, they truly understand my writing. [a.] Aloha, OR.

SHAFFER, JAMES WILLIAM JR.
[b.] September 4, 1914, Savannah, GA; [p.] William and Ida Shagger; [m.] Blanca R. Freeman, June 29, 1948; [ch.] 3; [ed.] American Society of Industrial Security; [occ.] Security Officer, Great Western Bank; [memb.] Baptist Church; [oth. writ.] Several poems published in local papers and church papers; [pers.] Retired officer, U.S. Marine Corps 32 years service. Retired Executive of Security Guard Agency - 24 years. [a.] Pacifica, CA.

SHAMALEY, ROCHELLE LEE
[b.] January 19, 1976, El Paso, TX; [p.] Lee J. Shamaley and Angelina Uranga; [ed.] The University of Texas at El Paso; [pers.] Life is full of chances and if you do not take them, then you will never see how things could have been. [a.] El Paso, TX.

SHANKLES, LAURA
[b.] June 4, 1981, Kennansville, NC; [p.] Debbie Smith; [ed.] Sylvania High School; [memb.] Jr. Beta Club, FHA; [hon.] Woodmen of the World History award and Co-Salutatorian in Jr. High graduation.

SHAPIRO, LAURA
[b.] July 30, 1982, CT; [p.] Barbara and Gary Shapiro; [ed.] Lake Ridge Academy; [occ.] Student, 7th grade; [memb.] Charter member of Oberlin Choristers a community children's chorus, Lake Ridge Academy Middle School Girls Field Hockey TEam; [oth. writ.] Several poems published in school publication. [a.] Oberlin, OH.

SHARP, CAROL J.
[b.] June 9, 1943, Springfield, MO; [p.] Letha Colley and William Oliver Mays; [m.] Jerry A., July 19, 1963; [ch.] Jeffrey Allen and Michael Scott (deceased) Sharp; [occ.] Secretary; [oth. writ.] Poetry written and published in "Bereavement: a magazine of hope and healing and in the local chapter newsletter of The Compassionate Friends; [pers.] My writing of poetry came about from the death of my 22 year old son. He was killed in an automobile accident 9/7/91. I was inspired to do poetry, because of this loss and of my love for my son. All words come from my heart and soul. [a.] Springfield, MO.

SHARP. GWENDOLYN J.
[pen.] Gwen Sharp; [b.] August 7, 1980, Guam; [p.] Brenda and Thomas Sharp; [ed.] James Logan High School; [occ.] 9th grade student; [hon.] Young Author's AWard, School Achievement Awards, poetry award, Free Speech Television Announcement; [oth. writ.] Three small stories, other poems; [pers.] I always try to put a little bit of myself in each of my writings or poems. Also, I've always had a love for reading, and I feel it has greatly helped all of my writing. [a.] Union City, CA.

SHAWELL, TODD EDWARD MICHAEL
[pen.] Mason Shawell; [b.] April 15, 1974, Pottstown, PA; [p.] Edward C. and Kim E. Shawell; [m.] Theresa Lynn, June 18, 1993; [ch.] Tabitha Anne; [ed.] Westmont Christian Academy, Valley Forge Christian College; [occ.] Blue Collar Worker; [memb.] PA Army National Guard, Boy Scouts of America, United States Army Chemical Corps Regiment; [hon.] Various training awards acquired through the US Army Chemical Corps Regiment; [oth. writ.] Editorials published in local newspapers concerning the Vietnam War and to also include the various Vietnam Memorials; [pers.] In Buddhism, there is no place for using effort. Just be ordinary and nothing special. Eat your food, move your bowels, pass water and when you're tired go and lie down. The ignorant will laugh at me, but the wise will understand. Bruce Lee. [a.] Pottstown, PA.

SHAWNTE, TIA
[b.] August 14, 1949, Elmore City, OK; [p.] Henry and Catherine Roller; [ed.] East Central University, University of Tennessee; [occ.] Co-owner of Zarcon RoCo Publishing Company; [memb.] Broadcast Music Inc., Chickasaw Nation; [hon.] Recognized for Environmental and American Indian issues by Ned McWherter, Phil Bredesen, Bruce Todd, Dallas Morning News, Austin American Statesman, San Bernardino Sun, Kellogg Fellow; [oth. writ.] Four original musical compositions have aired nationally; [pers.] We must all return to the ways of the Ancient Ones and live in peace and harmony with Mother Earth. [a.] Seminole, FL.

SHEEHAN, MARK
[b.] June 28, 1927, Wallingford, CT; [p.] Dr. and Mrs. Mark T. Sheehan; [m.] Widowed; [ed.] Brown University, Princeton University, George Washington University - National Law Center; [occ.] Vice President National Newspaper Association; [memb.] National Press Club; [pers.] Living well is the best resource. [a.] Rockville, MD.

SHELANSKEY, SUZETTE
[b.] March 16, 1951, Elmira, NY; [p.] Henry and Ruth Shelanskey; [ch.] Sherry and Chad Fulmer; [ed.] Thomas A. Edison High School, Elmira Business Institute; [occ.] Resident Counselor - Association for Retarded Citizens of Chemung County; [pers.] My writings are greatly influenced by a special guy, my grandchildren, Amanda and Ashley; along with the natural beauty of the area in which I live. [a.] Wellsburg, NY.

SHEPPARD-BRICK, ANDREA
[b.] February 27, 1982, Northampton, MA; [p.] Bob Brick and Janet Sheppard; [ed.] John F. Kennedy Middle School; [occ.] Student; [memb.] Congregation B'nai Isreal Conservative Synagogue; [hon.] D.A.R. Citizens award, George Rutherford award; [pers.] The loss of a friend greatly influenced me to write this poem and since you never know what can happen live life to its fullest. [a.] Northampton, MA.

SHERMAN, WILLIAM K.
[b.] August 5, 1933; [m.] Carol M.; [ch.] Four; [hon.] The greatest of all, to carry God's message of love, help and mercy to others through the special gift of writing poems He has given me; [oth. writ.] Most important - spiritual poems shared with people through out the country (not published) but on a personal level; [pers.] With all the great problem in the world we tend to overlook the heartache and suffering of the one's around us. (Did you hear it). Did you hear a cry for help, did you answer the call? [a.] Westmont, IL.

SHERWIN, HELEN
[pen.] Illeanna Dazar; [b.] March 10, 1924, Aurora, IL; [p.] George and Illeanna Lazar; [m.] Deceased; [ch.] David, Bonnie Jean, Dennis; [ed.] Self-educated; [occ.] Retired.

SHIPLEY, RYAN LEE
[b.] December 19, 1968, Martinville, IN; [p.] Riley O. and Ruby L. Shipley II; [ed.] E. Manuel High; [occ.] Construction Worker; [oth. writ.] 130 plus additional poems waiting to be noticed; [pers.] With palpitations of the heart, deep chasms of the mind are discovered. Expressing the invisible, I write with emotions as a Lover. [a.] Nashville, IN.

SHOMINURE, OLUWOLE DAVID
[pen.] Daivd Shominure; [b.] September 24, 1954, Abeotuka, Nigeria; [p.] Alfred and Ruth Shominure; [m.] Abimbola Mary, August 27, 1983; [ch.] Anthony, Michael, Lola Shominure; [ed.] Egba High School, Northeastern Illinois University, Governor's State University; [occ.] President, Optimo International Investment, LTD Lagos Nigeria; [memb.] Egba Youth Association, International Marketing Association, Nigerian Youth Association; [hon.] Dean's List; [oth. writ.] None - Dedicated to: Tony, Michael and Lola; [pers.] I'm deeply concerned about the plight of children born to poor families. I'm troubled by the plight of homeless among us. [a.] Silver Spring, MD.

SHONES, JAMES
[b.] March 29, 1973, Pittsburgh, PA; [oth. writ.] Several other unpublished works reflecting our intricate minds; [pers.] In my work I try to probe these questions: Where were we before?, Where are we now? and Where will we be tomorrow? [a.] Carnegie, PA.

SHOPE, JILL
[b.] October 30, 1970, Coshocton, OH; [p.] Kenneth and Peggy Shope; [ed.] Centre County Christian Academy, The Pennsylvania State University; [occ.] Substitute teacher; [memb.] National Education Association; [hon.] Dean's List; [oth. writ.] Currently writing a novel; [pers.] The writings of Madeline L'Engle have influenced me to use my God-given talent by translating emotion into words. [a.] Snow Show, PA.

SHOWS, BARBARA
[b.] March 17, 1951, Hattiesburg, MS; [p.] Robert and Bernice Morgan; [m.] Richard Shows, January 5, 1979; [ch.] Jenny, Brian, Dana, Amanda; [ed.] Seminary High, Jones Co. Junior College; [occ.] Police Dispatcher; [memb.] Bethel Baptist Church, MS Law Enforcement Association; [oth. writ.] Several poems, none published as yet; [pers.] The inspiration I have comes from family and friends. I write what is in my heart. Writing about something or someone you care about makes the words come easily. [a.] Seminary, MS.

SHRAMEK, RUTH MARIE
[b.] May 22, 1977, Glennallen, AK; [p.] Gerry and Jan Shramek; [ed.] Calvert Correspondence School, Kenny Lake High School; [occ.] Student, struggling author; [hon.] Who's Who Among American High School Students, 2 years Academic Decathlon, honors group 1 year high honor roll 4-years, writing award for publication of a short story; [pers.] Poem published in a school correspondence magazine; short story published in <u>The Senior High Writer</u>; articles in school newspaper and community newspaper, many, many unpublished works; [pers.] Have fun. Get the most out of life. Be happy and always look up. Under every black thunder cloud is a brilliant silver lining. [a.] Copper Center, Alaska.

SHREVE, CATHERINE AMANDA
[pen.] Kimerly Halle, Kelli Readman; [b.] May 6, 1983, Suffolk, England; [p.] Rick and Susan Shreve; [ed.] Clarkson Elementary, W.R. Neill; [occ.] Student; [memb.] Junior Optimist Club, Beta Club, Adventure Club; [oth. writ.] I usually write stories or scripts for series shows; Snowy River, The McGregor Saga (family), Ocean Girl (Disney); [pers.] I love writing. It's my life. If you see me at recess, you'll see me writing away in my notebooks. But I don't know where I'd be today without writing. [a.] Bowling Green, KY.

SHY, SHARON M.
[b.] April 6, 1981, Orlando, FL; [p.] Kiyomi Shy; [ed.] Still in school; [occ.] Student; [hon.] Participant in 1994, National Spelling Bee, Johns Hopkins University Talent Search Participant; [oth. writ.] "How to Make the World a Better Place" essay won third place in Piedmont Young Author's Contest 1994; [pers.] I like to find a certain kind of peace in my writing. To write about places you can't just go physically, but mentally and emotionally. [a.] Lynchburg, VA.

SICKELKA, EMILY
[b.] August 14, 1981, Cherokee, IA; [p.] Mark and Patricia Sickelka; [ed.] Sioux Central Jr. High; [occ.] 7th grade student; [memb.] 4-H. [a.] Peterson, IA.

SIERRA, CHARLES F.
[b.] December 29, 1954, Chicago Heights, IL; [occ.] Proofreader, C.P.A. firm; [oth. writ.] Many not yet published; [pers.] My writings are merely perceptions on life, not meaning that they are necessarily correct or incorrect, nor do I want to influence others. Look at them as my reflections on the way of things. [a.] Crown Point, IN.

SIMMONS, PAUL JEROME
[pen.] Jerome Paul; [b.] February 17, 1953, Cleveland, OH; [p.] Irma L. Hamm; [ch.] Paul Rashad and Somer Rae Simmons; [oth. writ.] Unpublished book of poetry and 2 children's book; [pers.] You must reach for what's inside to touch the stars above. There's always tomorrow. [a.] Beachwood, OH.

SIMMONS, TAKISHA K.
[b.] September 22, 1973, New York City; [p.] Dianne Simmons; [ed.] Port Royal Primary, Warwick Secondary, Morris Brown College; [occ.] After school teacher's aide at Port Royal Primary School; [pers.] Take every experience in life, not as a stepping stone, but more as a guide to maturity and understanding to the real world. [a.] Somerset, Bermuda.

SIMONS, WILLIAM (BILL) M.
[b.] August 22, 1942, Carlisle, PA; [p.] Malcolm Simons and Louise Yenser; [m.] Thelma, May 13, 1989; [ch.] Juna, Eric, Heather, Amara, David, Mike, Christopher, Luens; [ed.] University of Kansas; [occ.] Disabled; [pers.] I suffer from a long-term mental illness (Obsessive-Compulsive Disorder with Agoraphobia) and I write as an outlet for the struggle and despair I sometimes feel. [a.] Lawrence, KS.

SIMPSON, AUSTIN J.
[b.] June 11, 1931, Houston, TX; [p.] Walter M. and Irma L. Simpson; [m.] Mary Lena (Lewis) Simpson, August 6, 1955; [ch.] Linda Peterson and Saxa Worsham; [ed.] Bosse High, Elmhurst College, Belmont Abbey College, Queens College, Duke University; [occ.] Retired; [memb.] Veterans of Foreign Wars, American Legion, NC State Employees Association; [hon.] Distinguished Service Award; [oth. writ.] Poem, National Poetry Anthology, 1960; [pers.] A man stands tallest when he bends down to help another. [a.] Cary, NC.

SINAGRA-SMITH, LINDA M.
[b.] January 13, 1957, Groton, CT; [p.] Bob and Rose Sinagra; [m.] C. Frank B., November 18, 1978; [ch.] Mark, Adrianne and Robert; [ed.] Daniel Hand High School, attending college majoring in Elementary Education; [occ.] Full-time mom, part-time student; [hon.] National Honor Society, Who's Who in American High Schools, Brown University Associated Alumni Award, Dean's List; [oth. writ.] Many poems, stories, a play; nothing published until in my heart; [pers.] My best writings are inspired by those closest to me. I hope my poems and stories touch their lives the way they have touched mine. [a.] Huntingtown, MD.

SINGLETON, MURIEL GRIGSBY
[pen.] Muriel Grigsby Singleton; [p.] Rosaria and Ruby L. Grigsby; [m.] Edward Lawrence Singleton, June 19, 1960; [ch.] Kenneth Lawrence, Tara Desiree; [ed.] West Phila High School, LaSalle College, Community College of Philadelphia; [occ.] City of Philadelphia retired from Free Library of Philadelphia; [hon.] President's award Free Library of Philadelphia, Employees Typifying the Spirit and performance of highest quality, Concerned Citizens of Wynefield Award 1977; [oth. writ.] Poem published in Dawn Magazine December 1983, two poems published in Limited Editions 1986-87, magazine Community College of Philadelphia; [pers.] My poetry depicts issues of life, evoking the emotions affected; the good, bad, poignancy and ecstacy also the drama of nature, deliciously spectacular with its power to sustain and potential for wreaking havoc. Intricately intertwined in these writings is my mind's stand. [a.] Philadelphia, PA.

SJOGREN, DOROTHY IRENE HJELLE
[b.] December 5, 1926, Brooklyn, NY; [p.] Anna and Oscar Hjelle; [m.] Karl Aron Sjogren, July 1, 1952; [ch.] Karl Martin, Annalisa, Margit; [ed.] Lutheran Medical Center, Wayne State University, University of Michigan; [occ.] Retired from Nursing, co-owner of small business; [memb.] Lutheran Med. Center alumni, Wayne State University Alumni, Ward Evangelical Presbyterian Church, Sons of Norway, U.S. English; [oth. writ.] Most of my poems have been for the pleasure of friends and family. I am presently writing a child's story book, whether it will be published is another matter; [pers.] I have been very blessed to have learned from others whether by personal interaction or through books. Whether one's life is long or short - it is not the length of the symphony that counts, but rather the quality. [a.] Livonia, MI.

SJOQUIST, LINDA
[pen.] Linda Bartoli; [b.] April 13, 1960, Eureka, CA; [p.] Charley and Edythe Bartoli; [m.] Andrew, July 1, 1979; [ch.] Nathan, Nicholas, Brigitte; [ed.] Eureka High School; [occ.] Cook, Homemaker, mother; [hon.] Rhody queen contestant, employee of the month, first place ribbon in woodwork; [oth. writ.] I have five other poems that I have written, not yet submitted for acknowledgment; [pers.] I have found in living threw life and experience I offer in my poems a part of myself, family, relatives, friends. Love family, friends and values. My inspiration, my poems. [a.] Eureka, CA.

SKELTON, DONNA MARIE
[pen.] Donna Skelton; [b.] October 19, 1961, Statesboro, GA; [p.] Melrose Lucille Hurst and J.D. Clifton; [m.] Gregory Lane Skelton, September 18, 1982; [ch.] Alisha Dawn Skelton; [ed.] North Augusta Sr. High, Lee College, Holmes Community College; [occ.] Registered Nurse; [hon.] Dean's List 1988, 1980-Who's Who of American High School Students; [pers.] God gave me the finest things on earth - my husband Greg, my daughter Dawn, and my mother - who sacrificed the good things in life for me and my siblings. [a.] Grenada, MS.

SLAMP, NORA COLLEEN
[pen.] Nora C.; [b.] May 16, 1949, Fairview, Alta CAN; [p.] Albert and Sybil Sundby-sister Lynn Stenhouse; [m.] Richard, July 30, 1983; [ed.] Fairview High, N.A.I.T./Royal Alexandra Hospital; [occ.] Retired X-ray Technician; [memb.] Scleroderma International, Plura Hills United Church, Beacon, Connector - Scleroderma Organizations; [oth. writ.] "Dreams" published in Scleroderma Magazine...(International) - other poems printed in local "Sclerodata" magazine...one poem in hometown newspaper; [pers.] I am striving to get my book of poetry published about "dealing with a chronic illness", to inspire and help others through the poems I have written (for my friends and family for their love and support.) [a.] Kamloops, BC., CAN.

SLAPPY, PAMELA SUE COX
[b.] June 7, 1958, Sewickley, PA; [p.] Harold J. Cox and Alvera M. Cox; [m.] John L., December 31, 1986; [ch.] Kevin and Ashley Slappy; [ed.] Crestview High School; [occ.] Homemaker; [memb.] Mount Calvary Chapel Church, NAACP; [oth. writ.] A variety of poems; [pers.] I thank the Lord from whom all things are made possible. I cherish my gift of poetry and the Lord is my inspiration. I'm thankful to be an encouragement through my poems to others through all sorts of emotions and trials. [a.] Midland, PA.

SLUDER, CANDACE MICHELLE
[b.] February 20, 1973; [p.] Donna Dodds and Kim Sluder; [m.] Engaged to Bobby Schofield; [ed.] Bedford North Lawrence High School; [pers.] I use writing and Black and White photography as a means of self-expression. [a.] Heltonville, IN.

SMILEY, MARJORIE W.
[b.] November 7, 1923, Charleroi, PA; [p.] Peter and Clara Wallace, decd.; [m.] Thomas M. (deceased), April 6, 1942; [ch.] Thomas W., Gregory M. and Deborah Kay Consavage; [ed.] Charleroi High School; [memb.] PTA President 1953, Past church choir member, presently Presbyterian Church; [oth. writ.] "With Blessings to Spare" story of tornado that struck our farm on 6/24/76. About 70 other personal message poetry, poetry printed in local newspaper; [pers.] I have been a multiple sclerosis victim for 31 years and currently reside at the Washington County Health Center. I keep my mind occupied by compiling poetry and storing my thoughts until someone can write it down as I dictate it to them. [a.] Washington, PA.

SMITH, ANGELA G.
[b.] January 2, 1966, Pensacola, FL; [p.] Ted McLain and Juanita Moore; [m.] Troy Smith, Sr., January 4, 1986; [ch.] Troy Smith Jr. and Alissa Smith; [ed.] Catherine Everett and Turlock High SChool; [occ.] Day Care Assistant; [oth. writ.] Poetry written for our neighborhood newsletter; [pers.] My poetry is for those who like inspiration and positive words to read. [a.] Ceres, CA.

SMITH, CATRA LYNETTE
[b.] July 6, 1974, Springfield, IL; [p.] Paul and Trudy Ayappa; [m.] David Russell Smith, April 4, 1994; [ed.] Calvary Academy High School, Southern Illinois University at Carbondale; [occ.] STudent; [hon.] Wo's Who Among America's High School Students (Spring 1991), USAF-ROTC Math and Science award, Golden Laurel, National Honor Society, Dean's List; [pers.] Bliss was it in the dawn to be alive...[a.] Carterville, IL.

SMITH, FERGUS DRAKE
[b.] November 15, 1972, Brattleboro, VT; [p.] Fergus S. Smith and Catherine S. Toomey; [ed.] Deerfield Academy, Middlebury College; [occ.] Student; [hon.] Chosen by writer John McPhee as the most promising writer in Deerfield Academy. This personal accolade was one of the turning points in my life; [pers.] Anyone can learn how to write well. The only thing that prevents people from doing so is a lack of resources, conviction and desire. [a.] Brattleboro, VT.

SMITH, JAMES JR.
[b.] July 24, 1912, Rahway, NJ; [p.] James and Jean Smith; [m.] Bessie Spear Smith, July 22, 1939; [ch.] James Spear and David Cameron; [ed.] Phillips Academy, Andover Agricultural College at Rutgers, New Jersey Agricultural School; [occ.] Retired; [memb.] Plainfield C.C., Life membership Board of Rahway Hospital Board; [oth. writ.] Many years of writing advisory literature for my Fertil-Soil Company. I had a book (handwritten) of many poems written through the years. Unfortunately, when we moved from Plainfield many of my personal records and my book of poems were lost; [pers.] At 82 years of age I am thankful that my wife (81) and I am reasonably healthy and happy and thankful that we are. [a.] Jamesburg, NJ.

SMITH, JODELL R.
[pen.] JoDell, Jodi and Renee Hill; [b.] April 3, 1970, Medina, OH; [p.] Linda Anderson and Steve Hill; [m.] Divorced; [ed.] Highland High School, Cuyahoga Community College; [occ.] Lab. Technician at Environmental Control Lab; [memb.] National Arbor Day Foundation, Rainy Forest Rescue; [pers.] Through my writings I try to share my love for natures wonders and my appreciation for the simple things in life. So many people rush through the days never pausing to ponder the glory of life. My goal through poetry is to help people realize that all things are truly precious. [a.] Brunswick, OH.

SMITH, LATASHA H.
[b.] April 18, 1980, Emanuel County; [p.] Leretha P. Smith; [ed.] 9th grade; [memb.] Basketball team, Flag Core and Track Team (formal cheerleader); [hon.] Basketball awards, flag core awards, and track awards (cheerleading award); [oth. writ.] Songs, cheers; [pers.] Thanks for selecting my poem. [a.] Wrightsville, GA.

SMITH, NICOLE
[b.] October 13, 1980, Sacramento, CA; [p.] Loretta Smith and Noel Perez; [ed.] Starr King Middle School, El Camino High School; [occ.] 9th grade student; [pers.] The key to living life is balance. Be true to yourself and follow your heart and all your dreams can come true. [a.] Carmichael, CA.

SMITH, PATRICK T.
[b.] April 21, 1964, Brooklyn, NY; [p.] Thomas and Dorothy Smith; [ed.] Northeast Bradford High, Lock Haven and Mansfield Universities; [occ.] First grade teacher, Athens Area School District; [memb.] American Cancer Society; [hon.] Kappa Delta Pi, National Honor Society, President's List, Dean's List; [oth. writ.] Currently have two children's books in the works; [pers.] My writings come from the heart and reflect my personal feelings. Life experiences have been my greatest influence. [a.] Ulster, PA.

SMITH, POLLY
[pen.] Polly Bell Boy; [b.] December 9, 1923, Kingsport; [p.] Leota and Charles Lane; [m.] Deadrick Boy; [ch.] CD and Brenda (boy and girl); [ed.] High school, Nurse Aide School, Beautician License; [occ.] Housewife; [oth. writ.] Wrote a book Life Beyond Tragedy, Polly Bell Boy, also a poem book, Poems of Thanks and Praise. They are also in the office copyright 1987; [pers.] Book and poems written by help of God. I love writing empties the soul. [a.] Kingsport, TN.

SMOCK, STEVEN L.
[b.] July 7, 1964, Indianapolis; [p.] William L. Smock and Elizabeth A, Smock; [m.] Sue A. Yocum, September 12, 1992; [ch.] Watson and Snickers; [ed.] Delran High, University of Pittsburgh, Southern Illinois University, University of Massachusetts Medical Center; [occ.] Molecular Biologist, Pfizer Central Research; [memb.] Sigma Xi Scientific Research Society, American Association For

the Advancement of Science; [pers.] I miss you Dad. [a.] Baltic, CT.

SMOKER, SHERRY ANN
[b.] November 28, 1961, Cherokee, NC; [p.] Owen and Ida I. Smoker, Sr.; [m.] Divorced; [ch.] DJ and Dakota; [ed.] Robbinsville High School, Tri-County Community College; [occ.] Cosmetologist; [oth. writ.] Personal library, but none published; [pers.] My words are from my deepest heartfelt feelings. My words come naturally through life's experiences, striving for happiness for the ones I love is my life's foal. I'm very deeply connected with my heritage as a Cherokee Indian and saddened by the Native American Extinction. [a.] Robbinsville, NC.

SNAPKA, DAVID L.
[pen.] Coach, Dave, Snappy; [p.] July 14, 1942, Corpus Christi, TX; [p.] Louis and Edith Snapka (deceased); [m.] Mary Ann, September 8, 1991; [ch.] John, Melanie, Sharon, Joe, April; [ed.] Texas A&I University; [occ.] Coach/teacher high school; [memb.] Texas High School Coaches, Texas Association Basketball Coaches, AFTE Texas Association Science Teachers; [hon.] Outstanding Teacher of the Quarter, American Legion Award; [oth. writ.] None published but many hopefuls; [pers.] I try to spread good cheer everywhere I go. Humor is good for the soul! [a.] Corpus Christi, TX.

SNELL, JENNY
[b.] December 4, 1978, Alexandria, VA; [p.] Robin and David Snell; [ed.] Chantilly High School; [oth,. writ.] Short stories. [a.] Chantilly, VA.

SNELLGROSE, RENI
[b.] September 18, 1962, Kalamazoo, MI; [p.] Raymond Snellgrose and Anna Logan - Russell Logan (step Dad); [ed.] Gladstone High School; [occ.] Nanny; [memb.] New Apostolic Church, Youth and Choir, Redwings Horse Sanctuary; [pers.] I hope that one day soon, all people will see each other for who they are, instead of what they are; And that they will let 'God' back into their lives. [a.] LaVerne, CO.

SNIDER, THERESA ANN
[pen.] Terri; [b.] February 14, 1953, Zanesville, OH; [p.] Bernard and Pauline Himmelspach; [m.] Douglas Richard Snider (divorced), May 18, 1974; [ch.] James Richard Snider, Marcus Snider; [ed.] St. Nicholas Grade School, Maysville High School, taking GED classes now; [occ.] Homemaker; [memb.] Eagles 302, The National Library of Poetry and Songwriters; [hon.] Won Editor's Choice award for poem published in Days End called "To The Day's Ahead"; [oth. writ.] "To The Day's Ahead", "When You're All Alone" published in Liltingly...when you're all...); [pers.] Take life as it is, some hard some easy. Get as much as you can in life. Work at it. [a.] Zanesville, OH.

SNOW, DIANE
[b.] July 26, 1974, Chillicothe, OH; [p.] Bob and Belva Snow; [ed.] Chillicothe High School, Ohio University, Ohio State University; [occ.] Journalism major at Ohio State. [a.] Chillicothe, OH.

SOMDAH, MARIE ANGE
[b.] October 19, 1959, Burkina Faso, West Africa; [p.] Adrien and M. Claire Somdah; [m.] M. Yanick, August 1992; [ed.] University of Franche-Comte'; [occ.] Literary Critic - translator - writer - professor; [memb.] Couleur Locale (France), Graf (Boston University), PEN International (England); [oth. writ.] "Demainserabeau" (Tomorrow) a collection of poetry - "Adjoa, l'Aorore" , a novel - "Campus Blues", a novel - "Le Nowbril de la Terre" - (published L'Harattau). All books published in Lan's (France); [pers.] Fly in quest, a deep quest of human being. So I'm writing in order to find a space of peace inside. [a.] Boston, MA.

SOMMERS, KRISTIN
[pen.] K.M. Sommers; [b.] August 17, 1982, Syracuse, NY; [p.] John and Sharon Sommers; [ed.] Roxboro Road Middle School; [occ.] Student; [memb.] Lifesavers Club (we help stop drugs and stop suicidal attempts); [hon.] I've gotten 2 gold passes (for being good in school). I've been in the Spelling Bee and on the Honor Roll and now this!; [oth. writ.] Nine poems and 2 stories. 1 story has 6 chapters, 1 has 4 - none to be published; [pers.] A smile is a curve that can set a lot of things straight. [a.] North Syracuse, NY.

SORGE, MAXINE K.
[pen.] Max Sorge; [b.] Altoona, PA; [p.] Allen and Elsie M. Kennedy; [m.] Roland H. Sorge (deceased), April 6, 1947; [ch.] Lynn Wayne, Gary Lee, Alan Pauln (all Deceased) - Tammy Dawn; [ed.] High school; [memb.] Former-ASA 80's Photography Club, Alto Artist Guild member; [hon.] Numerous awards in art and photography including 1985 Photographer of the Year, first place in state for Colored Pencil Drawing 1993, same drawing published in North Light Magazine Spring of 1994; [oth. writ.] Countless poems, three short stories, one song, poem, Ode to a Library published in National Library of Poetry 1994 two more accepted for Journey of the Mind and Best Poems of 1995; [pers.] Dare to be Different! That bit of advice was given to me by a friend and it works. I am constantly discovering new and exciting things about myself! Never say Never! [a.] Altoona, PA.

SOSTARICH, JODI
[b.] February 29, 1980, Livonia, MI; [p.] James and Nancy Sostarich; [ed.] Cimarron Memorial High School; [occ.] Student; [memb.] Cimarron Memorial Cheerleader, 1993-94 Becker Middle School Yearbook Staff, State Championship Soccer Team; [pers.] Never underestimate the capabilities of the youth. [a.] Las Vegas, NV.

SOUCY, MARY ELLEN
[b.] May 29, 1969, New Haven, CT; [p.] Loyd H. Cole and Jean H. Cole, Sr.; [m.] Francis R., May 5, 1990; [ed.] Casey Cole, Francis Soucy II, Tabitha Soucy; [ed.] Madison Memorial Area High School, Skawhegan Vocational School-CNA; [occ.] Homemaker; [hon.] National Honor Society, Vocational Tech, Certified Nurses Aide; [oth. writ.] Other poems I've written has been sent to other poetry companies; [pers.] As a single parent of three children, I write poems that show the true feelings from our hearts, the loneliness we've experienced. I want other people to feel, through the poems, that "yes" someone else is like you. [a.] Anson, ME.

SOUDER, BRENDA
[pen.] Brenda Lee; [b.] February 23, 1946, Washington, DC; [p.] Walter and Callie Clark; [m.] Divorced; [ch.] Sheila Lurean Souder; [ed.] Erwin High School, Howard County Community College; [occ.] RN on Mental Health Unit at Peninsula Regional Hospital; [oth. writ.] I sold another poem to a musician and it was used for a song; [pers.] I am also true to myself. I don't put expectations on other people to make me happy. People aren't perfect. I must stand alone before other people can stand beside me. [a.] Ocean City, MD.

SOUKUP, BETTIE
[pen.] Bettie Soukup; [b.] June 19, 1930, Dallas, TX; [p.] John and Libbie Palich; [m.] Jimmie, June 11, 1949; [ch.] Vicki Marlene, Claron Elizabeth, James Brian; [ed.] Waco High School, Houston Community College; [occ.] Retired Manger, Personnel & Administration; [memb.] Briarmeadow Garden Club, Sugar Land Garden Club, St. Laurence Catholic Church; [pers.] I am inspired by the beauty of nature and mysteries of life. Living by the "Golden Rule" has made my life rewarding. [a.] Sugar Land, TX.

SPEER, ELEANOR
[b.] September 12, 1929, Plymouth, NC; [p.] Louis and Nettie Exum; [occ.] Retired NY State Supreme Court Reporter; [memb.] Rochdale Players, Carr-Hill Singers, Clark Family Singers - numerous church choirs; [oth. writ.] Personal experiences during foreign travels, which are sent to many seniors and shut-ins; [pers.] People seem to love my travel stories. And that makes me happy because I think I make them happy. [a.] Jamaica, NY.

SPENCER, JENNETTE
[b.] January 7, 1954, Sunflower, MS; [p.] Mrs. Willa Beatrice Spencer; [ed.] Kenwood High, Dawson Skill Center, Kennedy King College; [occ.] Signal Person: Local 130 at Chicago North Western Railroad; [memb.] Big Sister Volunteer for teenage girl and women on drugs. At The Women Resident and City Girl, Women Treatment Center; [pers.] My life has always been filled with challenges. Today I believe God is in control and has given me the ideas to write through my dreams. I now share my writing with society.

SPENCER, LISA
[b.] October 11, 1980, Bangor, ME; [p.] Garry and Deborah Spencer; [ed.] Old Town High School; [pers.] I like to write in my free time, but have never been published anything. I am working on a book and I don't know how that will turn out.

SPERRY, SANDRA
[b.] November 13, 1970, Glendale, AZ; [p.] Pamela and John R. Potts; [m.] Daron Dean Sperry, April 26, 1993; [ch.] 2 girls; [ed.] Twin Lakes High School; [occ.] Homemaker - volunteer at Will Beckley Elementary school; [memb.] St. Anne's Catholic Church; [oth. writ.] Several unpublished poems and short stories; [pers.] I believe that the children of our country are our future and that they deserve only the best. Once we die, they take our places in the chain of life. [a.] Las Vegas, NV.

SPIVACK, JERRY
[b.] November 30, 1961, Chicago, Il; [p.] Irving and Adeline Spivack; [ed.] Glenbard East High SChool, College of DuPage, Illinois State University; [hon.] State Champion (Illinois) Poetry Reading, Bronze medal (National) Championships - Oral Interpretation; Mortar Board, National Honor Society (college), Dean's List, President's List; [oth. writ.] Lyrical journals: A collection of thoughts and musings. Novel: Another Green World, Screenplays - Another Green World, The Saviour Treatment: My Sister and Me (My Everything); play-The Cheaters. [a.] Tolucalk, CA.

SPIVEY, EUNICE TONEY
[pen.] Toni; [b.] NC; [ch.] Vickie, Randy, Paul; [ed.] Thomasville High School; [occ.] Mail Processing Clerk, Forsyth Hosp.; [oth. writ.] Article published in True Story Magazine. Write poems for special people and special occasions; [pers.] God gives me the poems I write. I want to honor him. I dedicate this poem to the memory of Jack Renegan of Forsyth Hospital, friend and coworker. [a.] Winston-Salem, NC.

SPRAGUE, ANGELA T.S.
[b.] August 25, 1979, Manchester, NH; [p.] Brenda and Frederick Sprague; [ed.] Memorial High School; [memb.] Merrimack Community Concert Band, Memorial High Chorus, Vernacular Foreign Language Magazine; [hon.] Who's Who Among American High School Students, High honors twelve consecutive quarters; [oth. writ.] Many more poems kept in a personal collection, and several short stories; [pers.] If you wish to have a long life, learn now so that you may have knowledge as your companion when you grow old. [a.] Manchester, NH.

SPRING, KRISTEN MARIE
[pen.] K.M. Spring; [b.] February 13, 1972, Wadsworth, OH; [p.] Robert and Linda Spring; [ed.] Medina First Baptist High School, Lee College; [memb.] Harvest Time Assembly of God, Fellowship of Lee College Historians; [pers.] God is alive and powerful. The realization of this has changed my life, and can change the life of any that would seek this truth. Hate pnly eats at the soul, we must therefore love our fellow man. [a.] Wadsworth, OH.

SPRINKEL, WES
[b.] December 9, 1962, Baltimore, MD; [p.] James and Trixiew Sprinkel; [m.] Deborah, October 10, 1992; [ch.] Angela Fout; [ed.] University of Baltimore, Essex Community College; [hon.] Wilson Highability Meritorious Award, Dean's Highest Honors; [pers.] This poem is dedicated to my loving wife Debbie, who's courageous, determined and valiant fight against cancer inspired me. [a.] Whitemarsh, MD.

STACY, HELEN
[pen.] Helen Stevenson Stacy; [b.] July 3, 1923, Fredericktown, MO; [p.] Lawrence and Margaret Stevenson; [m.] Finley P. (deceased), September 8, 1950; [ch.] Glenn Russell, Steve Roger; [ed.] High school, nurse aide training for new born babies; [occ.] Retired to my sister's farm; [hon.] Knowledge that some of my poems were framed and hung on walls, also a number were read at gatherings; [oth. writ.] All poems written since I was 8 years old are printed in a book (not published). I also have written six children stories. I wrote a story of my "Growing Up" days on the farm; [pers.] If I have any talent at all, it because God gave it to me. I think of my poems as tiny mustard seeds, one of them may comfort or help someone. Then again, maybe not, but who knows, it might.

STANOJEVIC, BORISLAV
[b.] Yugoslavia; [p.] Jelena and Nikola Stanojevic; [ed.] University of Belgrade, Europe; [occ.] Musician; [memb.] Society of Composers-Europe (Yugoslavia and Croatia), Songwriters Club of America (Sarasota, FL); [hon.] Silver Oyster award, 3rd prize at The University of Belgrade 1970 and 1971; [oth. writ.] "To Somebody" 1980 Europe, "Memories" 1984, "The Old Musicians", "Ana", "Anne"; [pers.] I write about musicians, criminals and music. I was a judge, lawyer, and rock and roll player. I write about love, life, and death. My heart writes with tears. I live with music and for music. My best friend is my guitar. [a.] Hamilton, ONT., CAN.

STARKWEATHER, DIANNA L.
[b.] August 14, 1970, Springville, NY; [p.] Carol and Richard Starkweather; [ed.] Western New England College; [occ.] Associate, AT&T; [memb.] Women of AT&T, National Association of Female Executives (NAFE), Women on the Move, The New Jersey Ballet Co., Trilogy; [hon.] Dean's list, Golden Goose Award; [pers.] I keep my thoughts loud, colorful, and lively, I live through imagination and not my memory. [a.] Bridgewater, NJ.

STARRETT, ELAINE
[b.] October 22, 1946, Palo Alto, CA; [m.] November 25, 1967; [ch.] Michael Jason Layes; [occ.] Artist, Art Consultant; [oth. writ.] Book (unpublished): No One Taught Me How To Be A Mom; [pers.] To bring humor and a compassionate understanding toward those who find themselves a single parent in a modern day world. And mostly, to encourage devotion and reverence toward our precious children. [a.] Kihei, Maui, HI.

STEARLEY, RAYMOND H.
[b.] August 17, 1927, Brazil, IN; [p.] Harold and Sylvia Stearley; [m.] Ellen, February 10, 1950; [ch.] Nancy Jane, Eric Vaughn; [ed.] Brazil High; [occ.] Retired; [oth. writ.] Several poems never sent any before working on short novel; [pers.] A monetary inheritance might last several years - the printed word can last forever. [a.] Brazil, IN.

STEELE, RICHARD H.
[b.] August 1, 1919, Buffalo, NY; [p.] Henry G. and Nancy Emil Steele; [m.] Iona, June 13, 1952; [ch.] Richard Henry, Scott Douglas; [ed.] Woodlawn High School, University of Alabama, Tulane University; [occ.] Retired; [memb.] American Chemical Society, American Soc. Biochemistry and Molecular Biology, Sigma Xi, American Association for Advancement of Science, Soc. Photo Chemistry - Club Biology; [oth. writ.] Scientific Publications; [pers.] The Watch is the Watchmaker. [a.] Metiarie, LA.

STEFFEL, EMILY
[b.] September 28, 1980, Shakopee; [p.] Joe and Margo Steffel; [ed.] St. John's Chaska; [occ.] Student; [memb.] 4-H; [hon.] Outstanding Youth of Chaska nomination; [oth. writ.] Anthology of Poetry by Young Americans; [pers.] This poem is dedicated to my school, St. John's. To my teacher Mr. Al Dutcher and my fellow 8th grade class. [a.] Chaska, MN.

STEPHENS, JAMES A.
[pen.] James A. Stephens; [b.] August 18, 1926, Bulland, TX; [p.] James Polk and Maudie Kilgore Stephens; [m.] Mickie M., January 29, 1944; [ch.] Dianna, Nancy, Pamela; [ed.] High school and self learning books; [occ.] Retired; [memb.] Telephone Pioneer America (life), Moose Lodge, (National Geographic member), School band, Christian church; [oth. writ.] Published (The Awakening Dawn), in the Desert Sun, many other in local papers and in telephone papers; [pers.] I believe the every person is born equal - its what you do in between that makes us all different. [a.] Clarkston, WA.

STEPHENS, MARIE TINA
[b.] November 6, 1949, Bronx, NY; [p.] Remo and Mildred Florio; [m.] Paul Ashley Stephens, August 26, 1978; [ed.] Southern Connecticut State University; [occ.] Technical Documentation Specialist (self-employed); [memb.] Society for Technical Communication; [oth. writ.] Over 20 years of experience in writing computer hardware and software documentation, marketing material, and proposals. Several unpublished children's stories and poems; [pers.] I believe in Easter, in the power of Love and in doing my best - always. [a.] Colleyville, TX.

STERNAL, JENNIFER M.
[pen.] Jennifer Sternal; [b.] March 7, 1981, Melrose Park, IL; [p.] Anthony and Maria Sternal. [a.] Chicago, IL.

STEVENS, RUSSELL
[b.] February 9, 1918, Georgia, USA; [p.] John Y. Stevens and Pattie Josie Ogburn; [m.] Divorced, 1950; [ch.] one son previous marriage; [ed.] 2 years college (business); [occ.] Retired; [oth. writ.] Miscellaneous poetry published in hometown newspaper. No copies available. Poem "Graveyard Reflection" to be published by The National Library of Poetry's Echoes of Yesterday in 1994-95; [pers.] I believe in the ultimate triumph of good over evil and the perpetuity of life. [a.] Thomaston, GA.

STEWARD, MICHAEL P.
[pen.] Byron Ruff; [b.] November 19, 1969, Lafayette, IN; [p.] Paul and Mary Ann Steward; [ed.] Louisiana Tech University, Tulane University; [occ.] Graduate student; [oth. writ.] Personal journals, essays, and a growing collection of poems; [pers.] Poetry to me is viewed in the most traditional sense, that is I use it simply to woo women. [a.] River Ridge, LA.

STWEART, AL
[b.] February 10, 1942, West Monroe, LA; [p.] Troy and Myrtle Stewart; [m.] Sandra, May 27, 1972; [ch.] Allen, Larisa; [ed.] West Monroe High, Southwestern College; [occ.] Service Manager; [memb.] N.R.A., A.A.R.P., M.D.A.; [hon.] National Sales Achievement award, Cum Laude College graduate, Who's Who in American Colleges; [oth. writ.] 3 Gospel songs; [pers.] I try to be there for others, especially my family, strive to do the right thing in all situations of life, to treat others like I want to be treated. I was influenced most by my mother, who taught me to be myself. [a.] Pine Bluff, AR.

STEWART, ELIZABETH
[b.] April 4, 1927, Rushville, IN; [p.] Forrest E. and Rosa L. Glover; [m.] Paul G. (deceased), March 3, 1950; [ed.] High school, some college experience and hard knocks; [occ.] Tax accountant and financial advisor; [memb.] Hint Hunters Homemakers Club, NFIB; [hon.] Honorable mention for story concerning the environmental impact of the future; [pers.] This poem came to me the day my favorite sister-in-law was known to be dying. This was her eulogy. I believe that if life hands you a lemon, make lemonade. [a.] Rushville, IN.

STICKMAN, EILEEN M.
[pen.] Ei; [b.] January 7, 1960, Tanana, AK; [p.] Leonard R. Stickman and Paulina A. Ambrose; [m.] Companion-Bennett D. Madros; [ch.] Jessica, Traci and Michelle Lohmer and Shannon and Bennett D. MaDros II; [ed.] 3 years college; [occ.] Laborer/supervisor - Nuclear Water/Sewer Project; [memb.] Mayor/City of Nulato; [hon.] National Dean's List 1978-79; [oth. writ.] Poems and short stories for the Sheldon Jackson College Newsletter 1977-78, Northland News - front page news; [pers.] I strive to capture in my poems, the beauty in life and this wondrous Alaska all around me. [a.] Nulato, Alaska.

STINE, TOMMY L.
[pen.] Tommy L.; [b.] November 29, 1948, Kokomo, IN; [p.] Fred L. and Frieda J. Stine; [ch.] Misty Renee and Christina J.; [ed.] IU and Ivy Tech, apprenticed pipefitter; [occ.] Pipefitter - Delco Electronic - General Motors; [memb.] All Secret; [oth. writ.] Write about 250-300 poems per year; [pers.] To be able to write and reach all walks of life; rich and poor alike. [a.] Kokomo, IN.

STOCKETT, DARREN
[b.] November 21, 1974, Fairmont, W.VA.; [p.] James L. Stockett and Helen L. Stockett-Carr; [ed.] Anna Jarvis Elementary, Grafton Middle, Frankfort High, Potomac State College; [memb.]

Holy Cross U.M. Church Youth Group, Church Administrative Council; [hon.] Sigma Phi Omega (Pres.) and Dean's List; [oth. writ.] Many other unpublished poems; [pers.] If I can touch one persons heart with my poems, then I have succeeded. [a.] Ridgeley, W.VA.

STOLER, AMY
[b.] September 3, 1922, Akron, OH; [p.] Jacob and Elizabeth Schad; [m.] Deceased-Milton, July 29, 1943; [ch.] Gary (deceased), Steve, Vicki; [ed.] High school; [memb.] Ashland Christian Center Church, Ashland Art Club, Mansfield China Painters; [oth. writ.] Process of writing a novel; [pers.] I strive to do my best with my God-given talent in writing, china painting and oil painting. [a.] Ashland, OH.

STONE, BARBARA L.
[pen.] Barbie; [b.] November 24, 1994, Portland, ME; [p.] Evelyn Griffin; [m.] Carl, July 13, 1992; [ch.] Patty William, Laura, Jimbo, Billy, Patty H.; [ed.] High school; [occ.] Disabled; [hon.] New writer; [oth. writ.] Yes, but not in publisher's hands at this time. I love to write poems it comes from the heart; [pers.] I think when I write my poems it is real person speaking from my heart and soul. [a.] Sandford, ME.

STONE, JAMES
[b.] January 30, 1978, Sturgis, MI; [p.] Cheryl and John Stone; [ed.] Lafayette High; [occ.] Student; [memb.] Parliamentarian for The Technology Student Association; [pers.] I strive to write poetry that shows the struggles and tribulations of the human heart. [a.] Toano, VA.

STONE, VALERIE
[b.] February 21, 1978, Manitoba; [p.] Selby and Doreen Stone; [ed.] Menihek International High School; [oth. writ.] Poems published at school, in newspaper; [pers.] What I write comes from my heart. It's about what I see in life, happiness, pain and sorrow and love. I write poems to express the way I see things. It makes me understand the way things are.

STONE, WILLIAM CLAYTON
[b.] June 13, 1979, Etobicoke, ONT; [p.] Wayne and Elizabeth Stone; [ed.] Grade 9; [occ.] Student; [oth. writ.] Several other poems; [pers.] I do not know when my inspiration came from. I guess you could say it was a gift from God. I wrote my first poem when I was 11, and will continue to write. It helps me express my feelings about the world. [a.] London, ONT.

STOOKEY, ROSANNA
[pen.] Savanaha Nichols; [b.] May 1, 1951, Downey, CA; [p.] Betty Hodge; [ch.] Ona, Aleta, April and Brian; [ed.] Western High, Pasco/Hernado Community College for CNA training; [occ.] Assistant Baker at TomThumb in Dallas; [oth. writ.] Currently working on 2 fiction novels; [pers.] Never give up on your dreams, always strive for your best. [a.] Dallas, TX.

STOTT, IVY K.
[b.] February 8, 1921, South Wales, Great Britian; [p.] Hugh and Eva Stott (both parents deceased); [ed.] High school graduate, 2 years college; [occ.] Retired legal secretary - studying medical transcription; [memb.] St. Christopher's Church (Episcopal) Choir member, Chicago Park District Outing Club, The Prairie Club, YMCA Women's Health Center, YMCA Prime Time Class (Aerobics); [hon.] Dean's List, Oak Park Twp. Lunch Program volunteer, Senior Companion Program, two one year awards; [oth. writ.] Poems previously published in church newspaper in Elmhurst, IL. (First Baptist) article published in Chicago Daily News at age 9; [pers.] Very much like poems of John Keats, etc. and Elizabeth Barrett Browning also enjoyed books by Elizabeth Goudge. Enjoy hiking in words and hiking for hunger (crop) 6.2 miles. [a.] Oak Park, IL.

STOWE, ROBERT L.
[pen.] Robert L. Stowe; [b.] January 5, 1921, Social Circle, GA; [p.] Joe and Frankie Stowe; [m.] Madge, February 16, 1990; [ch.] Jane, Joyce and Robert; [ed.] High school, some college; [occ.] Retired; [hon.] Inventor, National Honor Roll of Inventors, Society of American Inventors; [oth. writ.] Other poems published by National Library.

STRICKLAND, MELLISA C.
[b.] December 14, 1979, Tampa, FL; [p.] Shirley James and James Strickland; [ed.] Stanton College Preparatory School; [occ.] 9th grade student; [memb.] Mt. Calvary MB Church, School Chorus, School Basketball Team; [hon.] For Mathematics, Science, Language Arts; [oth. writ.] The Killing, published by National Library of Poetry, book A View From the Edge; [pers.] He who fails to prepare, prepares to fail. [a.] Miami, FL.

STRICKLAND, REBECCA PAIGE
[b.] March 16, 1971, Powell River; [p.] Ernest and Sandra Strickland - siblings - Richard and David Strickland; [ed.] Max Cameron High School, University of Victoria; [occ.] Student; [oth. writ.] Nothing, but enjoy writing for myself and my friends; [pers.] I feel poetry is an emotional outlet in which a poet can express their feelings about the world around them. [a.] Victoria, BC, CAN.

STRIMPLE, DENNIS
[b.] May 23, 1951, Buffalo, NY; [p.] Dale and Clare Strimple; [m.] Elizabeth, June 30, 1973; [ch.] Rebecca, Jaclyn, Russell; [ed.] Alden Central School, SUNY at Fredonia, NY, Health Services University; [occ.] Account Manager; [hon.] Dean's list; [oth. writ.] Many poems and songs. I greatly enjoy singing as well; [pers.] "I don't wanna go to sleep tonight" is really a song I wrote more than 20 years ago about the end of the world. It was edited considerably for this book. [a.] Orlando, FL.

STROME, DES'RAE L.
[b.] September 2, 1967, Denver, CO; [p.] Cheryl Dennis; [m.] Timothy D., August 30, 1993; [ch.] Joshua S. Burke; [ed.] Diploma in Dental Assistance; [occ.] Orthodontist Assistant; [memb.] Sheppard Sensations, First Church of Christ; [hon.] Martin Luther King award; [oth,. writ.] I have written a book for children entitled The Land of Numbers (unpublished numerous poetry) articles; [pers.] My writings tends to reflect on issues going on in today's world. Hopefully I will be able to make a difference in society through my writing. [a.] Sheppard, TX.

STROMP, LUCILLE LALANDA
[b.] February 14, 1923, OH; [m.] Michael; [ch.] Lalanda and Donald; [ed.] High school and a diploma to teach cosmetology; [occ.] Dealing in antiques and collectibles; [oth. writ.] Several poems published in local newspaper Geauga Times Leader; [pers.] Just finished writing a book of humorous poems. The laughable aspects of life, called "The Patchwork Quilt". Hope to find a publisher. [a.] Mentou, OH.

STROUP, ROBERTA
[b.] March 27, 1980, Berwyn; [p.] Penny and Robert Schwass; [ed.] Westmont Junior High; [oth. writ.] This is my second publishing. I have written 27 poems in all but only one has been published in a small camp newspaper.

STRUTHERS, CHRISTINA
[b.] April 27, 1978, Picton, ONT, CAN; [p.] Mervin and Carol Struthers; [ed.] Napanee District Secondary School; [occ.] Student; [oth. writ.] Several other poems that are unpublished and currently in my possession; [pers.] My writings are an escape from reality but not life. [a.] Napanee, ONT., CAN.

STUMPF, GEORGE R.
[pen.] Jolly G., George R. Stumpf; [b.] December 27, 1942, Long Island City, NY; [p.] George and Pat Stumpf; [m.] Nora P., September 23, 1969; [ch.] Gary P. Stumpf; [ed.] Long Island City High School, St. John's University College; [occ.] University North Carolina Asheville Management; [oth. writ.] Author of 1993 - Penalla The Magic Pencil - book for all to enjoy - 1993 Professor Wee Willie Appleworm (book) 1994 book and soon to be in a movie - The Mermaid and The Dolphins; [pers.] I have always tried to help kids, parents and anyone who's in need, and now bringing them together in life with the help of my cartoon characters to try to make a better world. [a.] Flat Rock, NC.

SUBER, ARIKA
[b.] April 14, 1980, San Diego, CA; [p.] Joyce and Willie Suber; [ed.] Chula Vista High School; [occ.] 9th grade.

SUBLETT, EVELYN JEAN KEMP
[pen.] Jean Sublett; [b.] December 23, 1919, Uniontown, PA; [p.] Walter Lewis and Grace Collier Kemp; [m.] Arthur Paul, July 7, 1946; [ch.] Michael, Sam and Paula; [ed.] Pittsburgh Academy, Hunter College, Oklahoma A&M, Miami-Dade Junior University Nevada; [occ.] Hostess - Arizona Family Restaurant - previously legal secretary, notary public in CO, CA and NV; [memb.] Episcopal Church; [hon.] Scouting, Swimming, CID for typing War Crimes, and Top Secret work in Bureau of Ships. Hiking the Narrows (Virgin River) on the North Rim of the Grand Canyon; [oth.writ.] Published 30 poems "Power of Love" 1975; [pers.] After my husband's death I had several unusual experiences that inspired me to write poetry that had to come from him. The awareness of the power of eternal love is forever a challenge to the mind. [a.] Green Valley, AZ.

SUDORE, THOMAS BRUCE
[pen.] Thomas Bruce; [b.] May 11, 1970, Rochester, NY; [p.] Joseph and Florence Sudore; [ed.] Monroe Community College, Brockport State College; [occ.] Perpetual Student of Life, Assistant Editor-Backflash Magazine, Free-lance Writer and poet; [oth. writ.] Many poems reflecting thoughts and feelings on love, politics and everything in between. Also works in progress including several screenplays. Plus articles and essays published in various newspapers and magazines; [pers.] My curiosity lies in finding ways to destabilize what's ordinarily stable. In creating change with words, or whatever, by reflecting on my past, and the past, while remaining aware of the future. And just to live passionately awake, instead of living restless and silent. I want to be inspired by it all, and be part of the inspiration. [a.] Rochester, NY.

SUITER, SUMMER MAGEE
[pen.] Summer/Magee/Suiter; [b.] August 24, 1979, Lake Havasu City, AZ; [p.] Gary and Bonnie Suiter; [ed.] Parker Dam Elementary School, Lake Havasu High School - Training - Commercials: Power Development Center; [occ.] Student; [memb.] Kay Club, "S" Club, Art Club; [hon.] Valedictorian of 8th grade class, winner of a $50.00 savings bonds in the Havasu Chapter NSDAR Essay Contest; [oth. writ.] Friends that are friends forever, Miss-

ing You, I Love You.

SULLIVAN, GENTRY C.
[pen.] Isham Caheen; [b.] February 5, 1947, Detroit, MI; [p.] Isham C. and Lillie M. Sullivan; [ch.] Monseille, Shavonne, Genique, Maleece, Ashley; [ed.] Central High, Ferris State University, Shaw College; [occ.] Internal Auditor, AAA Michigan-Retired; [memb.] Word of Faith International Christian Center, WOFICC Outreach Ministry, Christian Leadership Ministries, North Shore Animal League; [oth. writ.] The very first of the very beginning; [pers.] As a Christian, I strive to acquaint people with the Lord, Jesus Christ, for He is definitely the Way, the Truth and the Life. And the Truth will set you free. [a.] Detroit, MI.

SUMWATT, HILDA
[b.] January 26, 1925, Richland County; [p.] Chester and Lillie (Keller) Elliott; [m.] Delma D., October 5, 1942; [ch.] Lusna, Lanette, Lily, Luellem, Lila, Lavonne/Chester, Dennis and James; [ed.] High school; [occ.] Housewife (retired resident manager and social services; [memb.] American Legion Auxiliary Homemakers; [hon.] Have poem published in "The Space Between" and one entered and to be published in "Best Poems of the 90's"; [oth. writ.] Have had written a lengthy poem "Christmas in Heaven". Have had four poems published in local paper; [pers.] I have always been inspired by Carl Sandburg's poem "Fog" while in high school. I feel this is a God-given talent to me. [a.] Richland Center, WS.

SURATT, MARILYN SEMIDEY
[pen.] Meechie; [b.] October 13, 1966, Brooklyn; [p.] Maria and Antonio Semidey; [m.] Andrew A., September 4, 1990; [ch.] Alicia, Shamel, Taquan and Matika; [ed.] Roosevelt Junior, Sr. High School; [occ.] Housewife; [oth. writ.] I have several poems I've written, but none submitted to any contest until now; [pers.] I enjoy writing poems it's one of my ways of releasing stress. I've been influenced by personal experiences and my surroundings. [a.] Oakland, CA.

SWANN, DIANA ELIZABETH BEHRENS
[pen.] Diana Swann; [b.] September 22, 1923, Norfolk, VA; [p.] Admr. C.R. Behrens and Emma Spencer Behrens; [m.] Melvin J., March 17, 1969; [ch.] Marianne Diana Bennett, Lorraine Marie Finch, Ellen Alicia Rice, Steve Stuart and Janet and Jeffrey Swann (spouses' kids); [ed.] Woodrow Wilson High School, Corcoran School of Fine Art, Strayers Business School; [occ.] Helping Disabled Adults - champion swimmer and ice skater; [memb.] Grace Episcopal Church Choir; [hon.] "Golden Trophy" award for "Legacy"; [oth. writ.] Award winning "Legacy" in Haiti. I wrote my first poem at age 5 "I like to think that when it rain with all the fury born of wrath, that God in anger tries to cleanse this world of sins, with a bath." [a.] Milford, DC.

SWANSON, AVA
[b.] January 16, 1956, Terre Haute, IN; [p.] Sidney and Audrey Blankenbaker; [m.] Jay, July 21, 1985; [ch.] Angela, Mitchell and Marlies; [occ.] Employee at Pizza Pirate; [memb.] Trinity Baptist Church, Body Works Fitness Club, Volunteer Teacher of Art Awareness, Recording Secretary for Parent Group at School; [pers.] I wrote from that place inside myself that seems to need a voice, and if I do not let this voice be heard then something shrivels up within me. [a.] Benieia, CO.

SWIFT, LIZ
[b.] July 4, 1947, AR; [p.] Clyde and Viola Howard; [m.] Bert, May 19, 1989; [ch.] Gilbert, Libby, Andy, Dennis and Danny; [ed.] 11th; [occ.] Resident Manager for National Church Residences; [memb.] HEB, Chamber of Commerce; [hon.] One of my poems was selected for The Best of '95, the poem title is "A Field of Dreams". I have the Editor's Choice Award six times; [oth. writ.] My Love, Dad With Love and Gratitude, Mount Carmel, The Little Bag Lady, A Daughter's Love, A Prayer Just For My Son; [pers.] Our dear Montaysia was written for my little niece Montaysia September 6, 1993 - September 2, 1994. She now one of God little angels. We love you Montaysia. [a.] Bedford, TX.

SYMLAR, J. LEE
[pen.] Jaye Symlar; [ed.] Baldrige and Weiss Fellowship in Urban & Regional Planning, Kramer Fellowship for Fine Arts and Literature; [occ.] Program Systems Analyst - Mgt. Analysis for Software Development/Engineering; [memb.] National Writers Association, Poets Guild, National Conference of Artists, Amherst Society, National Forum for Public Administrator, International Financial Management Consortium, Brother-to-Brother Mentoring Group, Voices, The Spoken World; [hon.] Feldman Award, Smithsonian Fellow (Art & Poetry), Carnegie Award -1991, Kramer Award for Holographic Art 1985, Hirschorn Prize Award - Poetry/Art 1992, Carey Quality Award 1994; [oth. writ.] Change to Survive, A Call to Service, Into Focus, To Look Within, Dignity; [pers.] Somewhere between here and there lies the Rapture, which is the silent voice of wisdom, that is often closed except to the open mind and eager ears of understanding. [a.] Upper Marlboro, MD.

TAITT, VALERIE Y.
[b.] October 18, 1959, Trinidad, W.I.; [p.] Irma Ruth Keane-Taitt; [ch.] Renee', Anthony, Alexander; [pers.] I wish to thank John Marshall, my sweetheart, for his inspiration and encouragement in my writing.

TAFFI, MADELAINE
[b.] March 7, 1930, Sacramento, CA; [p.] Walter Blaine Felger and Elfrieda Thomas Felger; [m.] Donald James Taffi, January 20, 1951; [ch.] Scott Crawford, Gina Marie and David James; [ed.] Immaculate Heart High School, University of So. California, University of So. CA Medical Center, CA Family Study Center and Azusa Pacific College, UCLA; [occ.] Marriage, Family and Child Therapist; [memb.] California Association of Marriage, Family and Child Therapies; [oth. writ.] Wrote extensively as a child and adolescent. Have returned to writing in the 7th decade of my life. I was greatly influenced by my mother who was an artist and poet and died when I was 13 years old. Also, I have been influenced and deeply moved by the Psalms and Proverbs of the Old Testament; [pers.] Interested in Gerontology as the 65 and over age group will double in 40 years. A special interest in Altzheimer's, which will double by 2020 and triple by 2050. I am in the process of dedicating a poem to President Reagan who's poignant letter to his Fellow Americans appeared 11/6/94 in the LA Times. In my writing, I wish that my life experiences and those of others whose lives have touched mine would reflect the <u>BEING</u> rather that the <u>DOING</u> part of each of us and that the <u>CHILD</u> that is within us would emerge, causing us to move from one decade to the next with wonder and anticipation. [a.] Santa Monica, CA.

TALLMAN, EVELYN T.
[b.] November 13, 1922, So. Westerlo, NY; [p.] Hazel F. Mabie; [m.] Deceased, January 23, 1940; [ch.] Ralph R. Tallman; [ed.] Greenville Central High School, National Baking School; [occ.] Retired Cook and Baker; [memb.] Social Security Pension; [hon.] Golden Poetrygram; [oth. writ.] World of Poetry.

TANNER, CRYSTAL
[b.] May 27, 1977, Auburn, NY; [p.] Geri and Pete Tanner; [ed.] Port Byron High School; [occ.] Student; [memb.] 4-H Horse Club, Barrell Racing Association, Teen Council 4-H, North Eastern Appaloosa Association; [hon.] 4-H Sportsmanship, Hipoints for English Western and Game Shows school motto and first place in crafts; [pers.] I am striving to be one of the equestrian riders and trainers around and I also enjoy writing poems. [a.] Port Byron, NY.

TARDIF, STEVE
[b.] November 20, 1970, New Britian, CT; [p.] Huguette Veilleux and Fernand Tardif; [ed.] Berlin High School; [pers.] If anyone would have asked me if I would write poetry when I grew up. I would have said no. Thanks to all who have supported and encouraged me to keep trying. [a.] Plainville, CT.

TARRANT, S.
[b.] July 19, 1926, London; [p.] George William and Mary; [m.] Elsie Irene, 1953; [ch.] Ann, Kirk, Donna; [ed.] A London School; [occ.] Gardening Supervisor (Mental Health Services Company); [memb.] Sports Clubs; [hon.] Poems published in health magazines and programmes. Small book of poems published 1952 (self-financed); [oth. writ.] All types of articles, on future, short stories, children stories, philosophy. Influenced by Omar Kyyam, W.B. Yeats and William Blake; [pers.] One of ten children my father won small prizes in newspapers, for his humorous verse.

TAYLOR, CHARLES JR.
[pen.] James Ridgeway; [b.] December 14, 1972, Bainbridge, GA; [p.] Charles and Linda Taylor-sister - Carla Taylor; [ed.] Bainbridge High School, Bainbridge College, Thomas Technical Institute; [occ.] Respiratory Therapist; [memb.] American Association of Respiratory Care, Georgia Society of Respiratory Care; [hon.] V.F.W., Voice of Democracy Script Writing Award 1989 and 1990; [oth. writ.] Several country songs presently out as demo's; [pers.] I love to write about southern life and the never dying "old-fashioned" southern tradition. I have been influenced most by my family and my Christian upbringing. [a.] Stockbridge, GA.

TAYLOR, ERIKA STARR KRELING
[pen.] Starr Kreling-Taylor; [b.] August 21, 1981, Palo Alto, CA; [p.] A.S. Taylor and P.E. Kreling-Taylor; [occ.] Student; [memb.] Advance Band, Martial Arts; [oth. writ.] Two poems published in Iliad Press "Musings", 15th limited edition anthology; [pers.] I believe everyone has their own dreams and beliefs and they should follow them, despite what other people think. [a.] Oak Harbor, WA.

TAYLOR, JEANIECE
[b.] July 28, 1963, Philip, SD; [p.] Ed and Bonnie Morgan; [m.] Lance Taylor, October 1, 1983; [ch.] Lester Anna, Kelly Lynn, Hillary Kay, Kyle Richard; [ed.] Billings West High School; [occ.] Housewife, mother; [oth. writ.] Keeps a notebook of other writing I've done since high school and beyond, none published; [pers.] I find the written word is truly the most marvelous way of expressing myself. Quite often my tongue will fail me, but my pen provides me with the medium to thoroughly relate what is in my mind and heart. [a.] Valley City, ND.

TAYLOR, MATTHEW S.
[b.] February 3, 1974, Cleveland, OH; [p.] L. Kenneth and Elaine Taylor; [ed.] Ohio State University; [occ.] Student; [memb.] Delta Chi Fraternity, D.A.R.E., charter member of Adopt-a-School; [hon.] Choral Boosters Music Performance Scholarship; [oth. writ.] Working on a novel as well as a collection of my poetry works; [pers.] Thank you to my family for your love and support, especially during my hard times. Also to the gentlemen of Delta Chi for all they've taught me about life. There are too many other things in life to worry about besides ignorant hatred of others. Learn to live life through love and learn to love life! [a.] Strongville, OH.

TAYLOR, PENNY
[b.] February 7, 1933, Elyria, OH; [p.] Ed and Bea Sturtevant; [m.] Divorced; [ch.] Eric Taylor, Margi Osborne; [ed.] Elyria High School, Lorain County Community College; [occ.] Courier; [memb.] Unity Church; [hon.] Dean's list; [oth. writ.] Many poems pertaining to family and/or friends also short stories. Nothing before this submitted for publication; [pers.] My poetry is all based on heartfelt feeling. I would like to dedicate this piece to the friend for whom it was written, Barbara Ihrig, a great lady. [a.] Elyria, OH.

TAYLOR, RUBY
[pen.] Nell, Nellie, Ruby Taylor; [b.] April 18, 1946, Lundale, Logam W.VA; [p.] Blanche Lee Wright Taylor and John Otis Taylor; [m.] Divorced; [ch.] Ivan Lee Hurt Jr. and Bradley Allen Hurt; [ed.] Rio Grande College, Southeastern Business College, Hocking Technical College; [occ.] Assist principal (Building Administrator) at James Ford Rhodes High School; [memb.] Founder and President of Mental Education and Nutrition Corporation, author of "Mental Education and Nutrition"; [hon.] 1988 Golden Poetry award for "Tis Dawn) World of Poetry, Royal Proclamation August 14, 1994 from Hutt River Principality, The Prince Regent, Prince Kevin (for my lineage and deeds worthy of noble mention); [oth. writ.] Several poems, published for Ohio Child Conservation League, local newspaper, World of Poetry, The Mental Education and Nutrition Organization; [pers.] I want everyone to see as much of the world as one can see in a lifetime. I strive to see it, learn from it, enjoy it, profit from it, share it, write of it, and be most grateful to who gave it to us. My influences King Solomon, Queen Elizabeth, Queen Esther and Presidents Zachary Taylor and Bill Clinton and my mother and father. [a.] Cleveland, OH.

TELIS, GISELA ANGELA
[b.] March 9, 1983, Elizabeth, NJ; [p.] Reina and Daoiz Telis; [ed.] Victor Mravlag School #21, William F. Halloran School for the Gifted and Talented #22; [occ.] Student; [hon.] 1992-first place winner for AAA National School Traffic Safety Poster Contest, 1993-awarded medal for Artwork featured in book "Art for Every Kid", 1994 awarded medal for Highest fifth grade score on C.T.Y. exam in city of Elizabeth; [pers.] As an amateur poet, and considering my age, I feel that poetry is a way to reach people and life their spirits and to help them see the idyllic beauty which is sometimes hard to find in our everyday lives. [a.] Elizabeth, NJ.

TENA, ROBIN A.
[pen.] Jane Anne Niles; [b.] February 25, 1959, Des Moines, IA; [m.] Married; [occ.] Free lance writer; [hon.] First work published in grade school - like to concentrate on matters that affect women and children; [oth. writ.] Fitness, Health Care and Aging Process; [pers.] To continuously search for the best that I can be and inform and educate through words and actions. [a.] Fullerton, CA.

TERREBONNE, TODD
[pen.] Todd Hippie Terebone; [b.] July 1, 1976, Houma, LA; [p.] Perry and Grace Terrebonne; [ed.] Central LaFourche High School; [occ.] Starving artist/Supermarket Night Stocker; [memb.] Dead Poets Society - just a group of friends who read poetry; [hon.] I've never won any awards or been honored for my work, but it has made people smile. It has made people think and that matters more than any awards; [oth. writ.] Unpublished poems and songs for my band Baditude; [pers.] My art (music, poetry, and paintings) is my release. All my joys, pains and emotions go into my writings. My biggest influence is senior English teacher, Mr. Dally Breaux. He taught the difference between classical and romantic. Finally: just love everybody and it'll all be alright. [a.] Houma, LA.

TERRELL, WILLIAM H.
[pen.] Will E. Tea; [b.] William O, and Ruby; [ch.] Patrick and Angela; [ed.] Casa Grande High, Central Arizona College, University of Phoenix; [occ.] Maintenance Specialist at Ross Laboratories; [memb.] IBEW, O'Odham Tash Council, Sawtooth Mountain Men; [hon.] Citation of merit from The Governor of Arizona for Heroism, first vice president of O'Odham Tash Council; [oth. writ.] Several poetry published in local printings; [pers.] Never give up. Persistence and determination will carry you through. A retreat is not a defeat if you return to finish the job. [a.] Casa Grande, AZ.

TESTERMAN, SONJA A.F.
[b.] March 16, 1966, Germany; [p.] Arno Fels and Barbara Washborn; [m.] Randall, July 22, 1989; [ch.] Kasi Skie, Wendy Ariel; [ed.] Wurzburg American High School (Germany), Harford Community College; [occ.] Family business Soft Ice Cream Truck; [pers.] To me, writing is an emotion left on paper to last through out eternity. [a.] Aberdeen, MD.

TEXEIRA, GLENN R.
[b.] March 15, 1970, New Bedford, MA; [p.] Sylvester (deceased) and Mary Texeira; [ed.] New Bedford High School, Army; [occ.] Correctional Officer; [memb.] Deputy Sheriff's Association; [oth. writ.] "For the Ones Who Are There", "Only You", "Forgiven", "In the Name Of", "The Light".

THACKER, BARRY
[b.] July 30, 1951, Medicine Hat, AB; [p.] Joe and Lorraine; [m.] Slyvia, April 4, 1970; [ch.] Kari Lynn, Tammy Joanne, Darcy Jay; [ed.] Senior Matriculation (grade 12 advanced diploma), Power Engineering Technology (Medicine Hat College); [occ.] Power Engineer 2nd class at Chevron Fox Creek; [oth. writ.] Photos published in 75th anniversary book of Alberta; [pers.] Life is a road you must walk along to move ahead. [a.] Fox Creek, AB, CAN.

THOMAS, BRENDA JO
[pen.] Brenda Brammer; [b.] August 18, 1956, Balto City; [p.] Francis and Dorothea Crouse; [m.] Fiance-Joseph D. Twigg; [ch.] William A. Crouse; [ed.] Patterson High School, BCC and DCC; [occ.] Letter carrier; [memb.] NALC; [oth. writ.] Articles published in the East Baltimore Guide and the Enterprise, local newspapers; [pers.] For me, poetry is the way I can express my innermost thoughts into a verbal picture. [a.] Baltimore, MD.

THOMAS, ELIZABETH
[pen.] Liz; [b.] December 17, 1959, McKenzie, TN; [p.] Mrs. Mary Williamson and Herman Hines; [ch.] Brittany Thomas, Charles Johnson Jr.; [ed.] McKenzie High, West TN Business College; [occ.] Machine Operator - Atwood, TN; [memb.] Jehovah's Witness; [oth. writ.] Several poems written from personal experiences, none entered in contests; [pers.] This poem is dedicated to my son, Charles Johnson Jr. 19 years old who died on June 18, 1994. I write from experience when emotionally moved. [a.] Milan, TN.

THOMAS, JOHN
[pen.] John Thomas; [b.] November 29, 1981, Elmira, NY; [p.] John H. and Kelly Thomas; [ed.] Campbell-Savona Central School; [occ.] Student; [hon.] 1986 won third place in Science Fair, 1990 won 3rd place in Science and 1994 4th place in Science; [oth. writ.] Wrote one book in first grade, other small poems for fun and family; [pers.] I wrote this poem for my cousin Josh Lanning who died in the spring of 1994. He died with cancer he was only 12 years old - one month before his 13th birthday. [a.] Savona, NY.

THOMAS, JOSEPH SCOTT
[pen.] Joseph Scott Thomas; [b.] September 25, 1972, Odessa, TX; [ed.] Permian High, Baylor University; [occ.] United States Marine Corps: Computer Clerk; [pers.] Inspiration: James Douglas Morrison (1949-1971), my poetry reflects the sadness, chaos and disorder in the world I live in. Pain is full of emotion so I turn it around in poetry and make it something beautiful. [a.] Kaneohe, HI.

THOMAS, LLOYD H. SR.
[b.] January 7, 1938, New York City; [p.] P.B. and A.M. Thomas; [m.] Delores Thomas; [ch.] Lloyd Jr. and Leslie B. Favor; [ed.] Haaren High; [occ.] Minister, Retired Train Operator; [memb.] Abbeville Literacy Association; [oth. writ.] Poems for the Healing Journey, The Treasury of Christian Verse, Star Light 20, Our Divine Arranger, Mature Living Magazine, several poems published in church paper; [pers.] God is good. [a.] Abbeville, SC.

THOMAS, LYELL E.
[pen.] Let; [b.] February 20, 1926, Sears; [p.] Ray and Opal; [m.] Geneva Louise, May 7, 1950; [ch.] Leslie, Connie and Michael; [ed.] High school, Naval Service School at University of Illinois, Michigan State; [occ.] Retired from The Diary Business and Township Supervisor and Assessor; [memb.] V.F.W.; [hon.] Served my country in WWII; [oth. writ.] Some poems entered for award and publication consideration. My first year so a new comer. An article about serving in the Naval Special Forces and the occupation of Japan. Accepted for publication in a Naval History book; [pers.] You never get a second chance to make a first impression. [a.] Sears, MI.

THOMPSON, CRYSTAL
[b.] June 15, 1981, Havre, MT; [p.] Laura and Ken Thompson; [ed.] KG High School; [occ.] Student 8th grade; [hon.] $10 award for one poem in Rural Montana; [oth. writ.] 7 poems published in "Rural Montana", a monthly magazine. One poem in the American Academy of Poetry's "Anthology of poetry by Young Americans", 1993 edition. One poem previously published in the National Library of Poetry's "In the Desert Sun"; [pers.] First of all, thanks to my family and friends and the class of '99 for inspiring me. Always remember to go into your heart and find your talents - don't hold back the natural gifts that God has given you. [a.] Gildford, MT.

THOMPSON, EUGENE E.
[b.] April 8, 1930; [p.] Nora and Emery Thompson; [m.] Patsy, April 7, 1992; [ed.] High school; [occ.] Retired; [memb.] Legion Icks Walton League;

[oth. writ.] Song - "Because I Had Your Babe." [a.] Sigourney, IA.

THOMPSON, LEONORA J.
[pen.] Li Kum Tu; [b.] December 1, 1969, Three Hills, AB, CAN; [p.] Kenneth and Barbara Thompson; [ed.] Three Hills High School, Red Deer College; [occ.] Cook; [oth. writ.] Several poems and articles in the college newspaper and local newspaper; [pers.] Poetry is an art. It is easier to understand if it's simple and reflects common truths. [a.] Red Deer, AB, CAN.

THOMPSON, LYNNETTE MARIE
[pen.] Nickname - Sgt. Roo; [b.] July 19, 1978, Calgary, AB; [p.] Barb Blakley; [ed.] High school; [occ.] Babysitting, busing tables; [memb.,] Royal Canadian Air Cadets, Drama Club, Badminton; [hon.] Honors in Drama; [oth. writ.] I write poems to communicate my thoughts and feelings; [pers.] My Auntie Cindy's death greatly influences my writing. I try to live each day to the fullest knowing that at any point in time life can end; and when it's the worst it can go, it's got to get better. [a.] Olds, Alberta, CAN.

THOMPSON, STACIE
[b.] September 21, 1976, Ft. Gordon, GA; [p.] Richard Thompson and Victoria Zietlow; [ed.] Dora High School; [occ.] Waitress at Billy's Cafe; [oth. writ.] I have been writing since I was 12. I have been published in school newspapers and have contracts pending with Tin Pan Alley; [pers.] I write to express myself, to let my emotions run free on paper, while my mind explores it's darkest dreams. [a.] Mt. Dora, FL.

TICE, CHRISTOPHER G.
[b.] December 26, 1973, Pottsville, PA; [p.] George Tice and Margaret Minchoff; [ed.] Pottsville Area High School; [occ.] P.C. Technician, Schoeneman Corp; [hon.] United States Achievement Academy National Art Award 1987; [pers.] I've found that if you strive to do the things in life that you really feel, then success, no matter how small, is inevitable. [a.] Pottsville, PA.

TILMAN, JUDITH
[pen.] Judith T. Shelton Tilman; [b.] January 16, 1947, Wheeling, W.VA; [p.] Margaret M. Shelton; [ch.] Michelle Lynn Griffin; [occ.] Nurse; [pers.] A poem a day keeps the blues away. [a.] Peninsula, OH.

TOBIA, JOSEPH A.
[b.] January 24, 1942, New York City; [p.] Anthony and Madeline; [ed.] Catholic School, Richard Stockton College; [occ.] Owner/operator/chef "Ragin Cajun Restaurant"; [memb.] St. Augustine Parish, National Geographic Society, Greenpeace; [hon.] Who's Who in American Universities and Colleges 1993; [pers.] As we walk along the road of life, let's take time to help each other to see our divine expression. [a.] St. Augustine, FL.

TOLAN, MARY JO CARDER
[pen.] Mary Jo Carder Tolan; [b.] April 30, 1942, Artesia, NM; [p.] Ted Carder and Evelyn Dixon Carder; [m.] James Charles (deceased), September 18, 1962; [ch.] Rene Cathaline, James Marvin, Ronald Thomas; [ed.] Artesia High School; [occ.] Self-employed; [memb.] American Legion and Auxiliary Post 95, Veterans Foreign Wars, Auxiliary Post 5871, Navy Wives Club of America; [hon.] American Legion, Sgt. of Arms, V.F.W. Aux. 2nd Vice, Conductress, Guard and the several other offices and committees, Navy Wives Club of America, Chaplain, Secretary, President 2 terms; [oth. writ.] "The Wedding Vow" 1991 - another poetry contest; [pers.] I was born on my parents 9th wedding anniversary and country singer Willie Hugh Nelson's 9th birthday. [a.] Magnatia, TX.

TOLEDO, MICHELLE
[b.] August 1, 1977, San Juan, PR; [p.] Cesar Toledo and Raquel Cainas; [ed.] Southwest Miami Sr. High; [occ.] Student and part-time worker at Miami Seaquirium; [memb.] Greenpeace and Wildlife Rescue; [hon.] Award for leadership for the class of '95; [pers.] I like to say that by never giving up, and always working hard, you can accomplish your dreams. [a.] Miami, FL.

TONDERA, ERIC K.
[b.] December 27, 1966, Houston, TX; [p.] Harold and Patricia Tondera; [m.] Keesha Ramey, August 17, 1991; [ed.] Texas Tech University, Texas Chiropractic College, Rotations at Hermann Hospital in the Medical Center Houston; [occ.] Chiropractic Physician; [memb.] American Chiropractic Association, Texas Chiropractic Association, Texas Chiropractic College Alumni Association, Board of Director, National Eagle Scout Association; [hon.] 1992 Outstanding Clinical Internship Award; [pers.] Education is the key. [a.] Missouri City, TX.

TORIELLI, ANN MARIE
[pen.] Ann Marie; [b.] August 2, 1915, West, VA; [p.] Louis and Anna Parrinelli; [m.] John Blaise, April 21, 1940; [ch.] Joan and Robert; [ed.] Drakes Business School; [occ.] Mother, grandmother and great grandmother; [occ.] Club of all races and religions; [hon.] The love and respect of all my children, friends and a warm handshake from people I meet; [oth. writ.] Many stories and children's poems which are read on local radio station and the school my daughter teaches in. I teach understanding and tolerance; [pers.] I have two children, 7 grandchildren and 6 great grandchildren. They are all highly educated. I'm a widow. My husband and I were married for 50 years love and compassion is what we taught. [a.] New Windsor, NY.

TORME', KATHRYN B.
[pen.] Kathy Torme'; [b.] April 18, 1941, Bristol, VA; [p.] Hildred Knight and James B. Brown; [m.] Marvin R., March 10, 1963 (divorced); [ch.] Gregory Michael Torme'; [ed.] Jefferson State Junior College, University of Alabama; [occ.] Telemarketing/American Heart Association, Government Legal/Medical Word Processing; [memb.] The Club; [hon.] Eight cash awards/US Government Oil paintings shown at Birmingham Botanical Gardens, Alabama Real Estate Broker 1982; [oth. writ.] Unpublished songs "Another Man", "We're Three of the Biggest Fools on Earth", "Choo Choo Train Vacation" At Days End 1993; [pers.] Freedom of thought and freedom of publication should be available to everyone. Children should not have unlimited access to everything. [a.] Birmingham, AL.

TOWNER, CATHERINE ANNE
[pen.] Kitten Angel; [b.] June 1, 1969, Port Arthur; [p.] Ken Towner and Linda Lyytinen; [m.] Two full-time beaus Michel Bois and Walter McCallum; [ch.] Jennifer, Amanda, Rayann, Crystal, Michelle Bois; [ed.] Queen Elizabeth/Hillcrest; [occ.] Mother, aspiring writer and soon to be horse trainer (Kitty Wagon Ranch); [oth. writ.] My Bubble Bath: poem type article - currently unpublished, It Could Be You - currently unpublished - short story; [pers.] I enjoy writing it releases my creative mind. I just hope to bring happiness to other readers as other writers have done for me. [a.] Dyment, ONT, CAN.

TRANCUCCI, CRISTY
[b.] November 13, 1981, Staten Island, NY; [p.] Diane and Frank Harun; [ed.] Newtown Jr. High School; [occ.] Student; [memb.] S.A.D.D. (Students Against Doing Drugs), Jr. High Field Hockey, Link and Wing St. Andrews Parrish of Newtown, Pa; [pers.] I'm 13 years old and I love to write, especially poems. [a.] Newtown, PA.

TRAPP, DOLORES M.
[b.] May 31, 1926, Newman, KS; [p.] Harry D. and Melva (Fletcher) Workman; [m.] Leonard F., December 31, 1946; [ch.] Phillip Wayne, Karen Louise, Craig Lynn; [ed.] Perry High, Perry K.S. with honors at age 16; [occ.] Retired with 34 years Civil Service as typist and computer word processor; [memb.] Christian Church, Ladies of the Moose, NARFE, Husband and I belong to Coast to Coast Camper Club, and travel several months a year in our Four Winds motorhome. We love it.; [hon.] I received several awards for job performance, I crocheted "The Last Supper" wall hanging which is 11 ft. high and 14 ft. wide in 1985 and donated it to our church in Topeka, KS. It is hanging now in Highland Heights Christian Church; [oth. writ.] Over 100 friends and relatives on my correspondence list. I have a home computer. Also wrote a poem about our trip to Alaska in 1991 while driving our motorhome there; [pers.] I try to live by the Golden Rule. I enjoy baking, knitting, crocheting, gardening and reading the Urantia Book and true Angel experiences. I have 3 sisters, 1 brother and enjoy family gatherings. My mother is 89 I have 3 grandchildren. [a.] Camdenton, MO.

TRAUTH, JEANETTE
[pen.] Angelica White Mother; [b.] December 22, 1957, Norton, VA; [p.] Kyle and Helen Jones; [m.] Dennis, February 14, 1987; [ch.] Walt Massengill and Adam Massengill; [ed.] Appalachia High School, Chaffey Adult School; [occ.] Bookkeeper/office manager/electricians helper; [memb.] North Shores Animal Shelter; [hon.] Honor Roll High school and grade school; [oth. writ.] there are no other writings at this time, This poem was guided by my unconditional love for my son, who needed me at that time in his life; [pers.] If I can be a positive influence in at least 1 person's life everyday, I am serving a useful purpose in life. [a.] Torrance, CA.

TRIANA, KRIS
[pen.] Kris Triana; [b.] July 16, 1977, Long Island, NY; [p.] Richard and Kathleen; [hon.] Superior awards from county acting festival for monologues and duo interpretations. Most of which I wrote myself; [oth. writ.] Novels, Nolvilla's and poems, Some of my novels include "Scarecrow", "Purgatory", "Death of the Iron", and about 27 more. I also write screenplays and plays as well as songs; [pers.] The world of reality if not always satisfactory to the untameable mind. That's why writing is so important to me, with it I can take anyone, anywhere and make them do anything. [a.] Palm Bay, FL.

TRIPLETT, CAROL S.
[b.] March 12, 1959, Chillicothe, OH; [p.] Robert and Mary (Harley) Triplett; [ed.] Bellefontaine High School, Ohio Northern University; [occ.] WBNS-TV. [a.] Columbus, OH.

TRIPP, MICHAEL M.
[pen.] Tripp, Mike; [b.] May 17, 1955, Washington, DC; [p.] Barbara and Mayhew Tripp; [ch.] Robin Rene Tripp; [ed.] Morgan State University, Bowie State, Trinity College; [occ.] MD State Parole Officer Senior; [memb.,] Kappa Alpha Psi Fraternity, Alex-Fairfax Alumni Chapter; [hon.] Writing contest winner in high school; [oth. writ.] Several poems to be released soon/upon request;

[pers.] Poems are life's experiences and so is storywriting. [a.] District Heights, MD.

TROWERS, MIRIAM A.
[b.] October 31, 1951, Jamaica, W.I.; [p.] Peter and Mabel Trowers; [ch.] Megan D. Hamilton; [ed.] St. Catherine High, Community College, Institute of Children's Literature; [occ.] Salesperson; [oth. writ.] Several poems, unpublished; [pers.] I must strive to attract others to experience the beauty associated with life and love, and by reading from my work. They will be able to re-live the reality of it all. [a.] Washington, DC.

TRZASKOS, THOMAS C.
[b.] December 1961, Hartford; [p.] Theresa Trzaskos; [ed.] University of Connecticut; [occ.] Existence Philosopher; [hon.] Scholarship to Sarah Lawrence Col. Via Poetic Thomas Lux; [oth. writ.] Poems appeared in Larrals, Gulf Coast, Phobe, One Mead Way, articles in The Hartford Currant and North East Magazine; [pers.] My reason for writing is a reason for living and I breath the air of the French Poets of the 19th century, but mostly with the lungs of Jules Laforgue and Americans: Wallace Stevens and T.S. Eliot. [a.] Wethersfield, CT.

TSANG, YANKEE P.
[pen.] Bai fuh; [b.] December 25, 1927, Shanghai, China; [p.] Yangtse Tsang and Yuepao Liu (deceased); [m.] Divorced, 1962; [ed.] University of Shanghai and University of Southern California; [occ.] Land development and business consultant (part-time); [memb.] Honolulu Elks Lodge #616; [hon.] AKD, National Honorary Sociological Fraternity, life member; [oth. writ.] Bai fuh's published works: Two booklets of poetry; two fictions, two movie scripts and one song (all in Mandarin). Pending publications (potpourri biographies): "Bai-kwang and I" (in Mandarin); "A Yankee from Shanghai" (in English); [pers.] I strive to reflect beauty and truth in all objects, animate or inanimate, or imaginary. [a.] Honolulu, HI.

TSCHUMPERLIN, AMY
[b.] September 2, 1974; [p.] Bill and Rita Tschumperlin; [ed.] Eden Valley-Watkins High School, St. Cloud Technical College for Advertising; [memb.] In high school I was in FLA, SADD, Peer Helper, Peer Tutor, Volleyball and Softball. In college in DECA; [hon.] Placed in the top 12 finalists for DECA at Nationals for Advertising Campaign; [pers.] When things go wrong, during a day, I think to myself that tomorrow is a new day. [a.] Eden Valley, MN.

TUBBS, BOBBYE J.
[b.] January 12, 1930, Bay Springs, MS; [p.] Earl and Fleeta Vanderslice; [m.] Pascal B., August 11, 1984 (third marriage); [ch.] Johnny Read, Sherry Williams, and Marsha Bankston (8 grandchildren and 2 great grandchildren); [ed.] Bay Springs High School; [occ.] Housewife; [memb.] Care Wear Volunteers and Sylverena Baptist Church; [oth. writ.] Several poems published in local and out of state newspapers; [pers.] I always remember the things dear to my heart are mine to hold only by the Grace of God. [a.] Bay Springs, MS.

TUBELLO-CASSINARI, LORI
[b.] February 15, 1967, Brooklyn, NY; [p.] John and Maureen Tubello; [m.] Peter Joseph Cassinari, November 26, 1994; [ed.] New Utrecht High School; [occ.] Electrical Technician; [pers.] For me poetry is an exceptional form of expression. One in which nothing in this world could possibly inspire me more than the love I share with my husband. [a.] Vero Beach, FL.

TUCKER, DAN
[b.] August 17, 1960, Oshawa, ONT; [p.] Irwin and Ruth Tucker; [m.] Laura, June 21, 1978; [ch.] Sarah Lynn, David Daniel; [ed.] Riverside High; [occ.] Drug and Alcohol Counselor, Writer/singer/songwriter; [memb.] Canadian Liver Foundation, Associate member Ontario Metis and Aboriginal Association; [oth. writ.] Poems and articles published in small magazines and local newspapers; [pers.] I strive to relate in my writing the evolution of the human race in light of the evolution of moral and ethical principles which I believe are still evolving today, and how this affects our present and future. [a.] Strathroy, ONT., CAN.

TUCKER, LOU LEANN
[pen.] L. "Leann" T.; [b.] September 7, 1938, Ridgely, TN; [p.] Ora and Curry Hilliard; [m.] Carl, February 18, 1957; [ch.] Rhonda Akins, Danny Tucker and Greg Tucker; [occ.] K-Mart Employee; [memb.] Church of God of Prophecy; [hon.] 1969 won youth director for West TN in local church and worked closely with youth and enjoyed the work greatly; [oth. writ.] Written poems, songs my best friend and her family sings. (Unrecorded) and I write a byline for our church in our local newspaper The Dickson Herald; [pers.] I love writing, and I love working with young people they are my heart. I always say "God" is the writer, I'm only the "pen".

TUCKER, SHIRLEY M.
[b.] August 18, 1934, Essex, CT; [p.] Val Miller and Helen Miller Lee; [m.] James H., /april 20, 1979; [ch.] Kurt Grandsire, Peter Grandsire, Karen Hill; [ed.] Valley Regional High School; [occ.] Self-employed Gifts from the Sea; [memb.] First Congregational Church, Essex, CT Women's Club; [hon.] Various awards for Shell Flower Arrangements; [oth. writ.] Personal poems written for family and friends; [pers.] I was inspired while walking along the seashore in search of shells for my Shell Flower Arrangements, plus reading Poems by Robert and Louis Stevenson and Helen Steiner Rice to my granddaughter, Krista. [a.] Jersen Beach, FL.

TURNER, TRAYCE D.
[b.] June 6, 1962, Washington, DC; [p.] Anne Harris-Turner and Robert L. Turner, Sr.; [ch.] Travis Michael, Tyler Anthony; [ed.] Dunbar Senior High School; [occ.] Office Manager/Receptionist Bread for the World, Inc.; [oth. writ.] Currently working on my first book; [pers.] In my writing I always try to touch the soul by revealing the truth. I have been greatly influenced by my Heros: my mother and grandmother, the late Dorothy Belton-Harris. [a.] Washington, DC.

TUTHILL, MARIEKE
[pen.] Renee Tuthill; [b.] September 13, 1981, Wilmington, DE; [p.] Walter and Jantina Tuthill; [ed.] Tatnall Middle School; [occ.] Student and poet; [hon.] Won a place in a regional private school poetry collection with the same poem that is being published here, was chosen for "Young Authors Workshop" 2 years in a row, received awards for a short story and a poem by "Child's Play Touring Theater" in 4th grade; [oth. writ.] Articles written for school newspaper, and poems written for various contests and pieces sent to magazines; [pers.] In my writing, I express my inner emotions the only way I am able to, with pen and paper. I have trouble talking about my feelings, but when I write, everything comes out naturally. [a.] Kennett Square, PA.

TUZZOLO, MICHELLE MARIE
[b.] June 10, 1974, Lakenheath, England; [p.] Charles J. Tuzzolo and Linda G. Okruhlica; [ed.] San Joaquin High School, Solano Community College; [occ.] Shoe Pavillion in Vocaville, CA; [hon.] National Defense Medal U.S, Navy, 1st place Washington State Convention (radio program), most improved student - Bible Baptist School 1990, Scripture Memory 2 Tim., Pastors award 1989m, Bible memory Matt. 5-6, 1990, "A" honor roll 1993; [oth. writ.] I have written many poems at school and in my spare time. I have never had these poems published; [pers.] The poems I usually write reflect the way I feel at that particular time. My poems are real and original. [a.] Vocaville, CA.

TYKESON, DEISEL A.
[b.] June 6, 1926, Kennedy, MN; [p.] John and Nettie Tykeson; [m.] Jean, December 28, 1956; [ch.] Christine, Cindy, Valerie; [ed.] Bachelor of Philosophy majoring in teaching; [occ.] Retired; [memb.] Moose and American Legion and National Horseshoe Pitching Association; [oth. writ.] Several poems and plays to be put on tape by students in Social Studies and History. A tape recorded play called "A Lantern Held at Midday" Univ. of N.D. Radio Station; [pers.] Live each day to its fullest no matter how rotten it gets. And - A man may die a thousand deaths but a cell bug never gets cancer. [a.] Lompoc, CA.

TYLER, NINA
[pen.] Nina Tyler; [b.] January 28, 1927, Newcastle Upon Tyne, England.

TYNAN, DON
[b.] May 10, 1932, Dobbsferry-on-Hudson, NY; [p.] John and Edris Tynan; [ch.] Mike, Pat, Erk, Shelly, Ed, Dan; [ed.] Hackley, Georgetown Alliance Francaise, NYU, OSU, Grossmont, UNH, Harvard; [occ.] Retired, USAF pilot - captain, American Airlines; [memb.] National Museum of the American Indian (Smithsonian); [hon.] Dean's List, Grossmont College; [oth. writ.] "Paean to Patience" re: NY Public Library Lions; [pers.] I've long sought to fine tune my mind - by interacting with others' on our journey. [a.] Boscawen, NH.

UITHOVEN, DALE J. III
[pen.] D.J. Uithoven; [b.] January 5, 1979, Big Rapids, MI; [p.] Dale and Deborah Uithoven; [ed.] Whitehall High School; [occ.] Student; [memb.] Spanish Club, High School Soccer Team, Church Youth Group, Band; [hon.] Academic Awards, Honor carrier - local newspaper, Participation in Odyssey of the Mind; [oth. writ.] Short stories and poems written for high school honors writing class. [a.] Whitehall, MI.

URSILLO, STAR
[b.] January 7, 1978, Indianapolis, IN; [p.] Linda, Robert Ursillo; [ed.] Troy High; [memb.] Flutes in the Troy High Symphony Band and in the Oakland Community College Youth Band, on the Troy High Colorguard, Saint Thomas More Youth Group, Business Professionals of America; [hon.] Classic Colt Award, Who's Who Among American High School Student Award, Magna Cum Laude honors award and Cum Laude honors award; [pers.] I feel poetry is one of the most beautiful forms of art imaginable. [a.] Troy, MI.

UTSO, SARAH
[pen.] Sarah Lynn; [b.] February 16, 1981, Fullerton, CA; [p.] Dave and Pat Utso; [ed.] High School; [occ.] Student; [hon.] Presidential Award and in honors classes; [pers.] I have always loved poetry and writing short stories. I would like to touch and make a change in people with my writing. [a.] Sylmar, CA.

VAIL, KEVIN MICHAEL
[b.] July 21, 1955, Syracuse, NY; [p.] Malcolm Dack and Ruth Haskell; [m.] J. David Starn; [ed.] C.W. Baker High School; [occ.] Computer Systems Consultant; [pers.] The unseen world that lives around us all: to show it is the poet's only call. [a.] Bethesda, MD.

VALDES, CARMEN
[pen.] Bobim; [b.] April 1, 1982, Bayamon, P.R.; [p.] Ruben and Marta Valdes; ed.] Coral Park Elementary, Emerson Elementary and King's Christian; [occ.] Student; [memb.] Precious Moments; [oth. writ.] I have written other poems. I write mostly when I have problems or feel bad or happy. [a.] Miami, FL.

VALOVE, CHARLOTTE
[b.] June 30, 1980, California; [p.] Ellen and Joe Valove; [ed.] High school; [occ.] Writer/Student; [oth. writ.] Several poems and short stories published in books in Santee California; [pers.] I owe my writing to my biggest inspiration my mother and father. Life is too short to spend it without love. [a.] Jacksonville, NC.

VAN WALLEGHEM, MICHAEL
[b.] August 17, 1959, Winnipeg, CAN; [p.] George and Frances; [ch.] Bradley Charles and Kristen Michelle; [ed.] University of Montana; [occ.] Entrepreneur; [memb.] Winnipeg Chamber of Commerce, Canadian Environment Industry Association, Canadian Council for Human Resources in the Environmental Industry, Manitoba Environmental Industries Association, Inc.; [hon.] Recipient of a certificate of recognition for valuable contributions towards Sustainable Development 1994; [pers.] Reflected in his obvious commitment to creating an environment in which his children, their friends, and their families can live successfully and happily in the future.

VAN WINKLE, EARL
[b.] December 9, 1930, Hamilton, OH; [p.] Ellis and Dixie Van Winkle; [m.] Jerilyn; [ch.] Truman and Molli; [ed.] Wilmington Indiana Elementary, Moores Hill Indiana High School, various mechanical and operator schools; [occ.] Retired Construction Millwright; [memb.] American Legion Post #292, Loomoose Lodge #1464; [hon.] Honorably discharges US Army 10 years, Korean War Vet, Berlin Air lift; [oth. writ.] Editors Choice Award "At Days End" page 461; [pers.] Write for my own enjoyment life to write about everyday events. [a.] Vejay, IN.

VAN WINKLE, TAMMY
[pen.] Tabi or TVW; [b.] October 3, 1963, Kennett, MO; [ed.] Vatterott and Sullivan-Commercial Sign Painting-diploma, Rocky Mountain College of Art and Design-Graphic/Commercial Art ASOC., Platt College-Computer Graphic Designer-diploma; [occ.] Van Winkle Productions owner/designer of a freelance graphic design company; [pers.] "There are many different forms of art. As I see it, to succeed, art must come from deep down in your heart of hearts". [a.] Broomfield, CO.

VANDERMEER, DAWN-MICHELLE
[b.] June 27, 1968, Anaheim, Ca; [p.] Richard and Anne-Marie Simon; [m.] James, June 22, 1991; [ch.] Nicole Catherine; [ed.] Palos Verdes High School, University of San Diego; [occ.] Housewife/mother; [hon.] Cum Laude, Dean's list, Departmental honors - School of Education. [a.] Silverdale, WA.

VANA, THOMAS J.
[pen.] Thomas J. Vana; [b.] March 16, 1949, Chicago, IL; [p.] Marion and Richard; [m.] Mary Karen, October 8, 1988; [ch.] Thomas R. and Michael J.; [ed.] One year college and Harper and Oakton Community Colleges, Notre Dame High School for Boys; [occ.] Maint. Cast - U.S. Postal Service; [memb.] A.P.W.U. Vice Pres. Local 1788; [hon.] 5 times given special awards for service and valor US Army and U.S.P.S.; [oth. writ.] Poems and stories for children poem published in seasons to come 1995. Writings published in local papers; [pers.] I'd like my writings to represent hope and love for restored personal relationships between women and men. [a.] Des Plains, IL.

VANCE, JODI LEE
[pen.] Jade; [b.] November 28, 1976, Cincinnati; [p.] Marcia and Wendell Vance; [ed.] Got to 9th grade and family was having problems, my mother got very sick, I took care of her in her last days; [oth. writ.] I've written numerous poems over my years. I started writing when I was around 11 or 12. My mother had a very good influence on me. She wrote too!; [pers.] I've been very nature all my life. My mother was through a lot of operations. She was sick since I was born. Starting with a kidney transplant up to a brain tumor. She died on March 19, 1994. [a.] Fairfield, OH.

VARGAS, CARLOS
[b.] May 4, 1971, Lynwood, CA; [p.] Migual and Ana Maria Vargas; [ed.] St. Raphael's School, Bishop Mora Salesian High School, Cal-State Pominguez Hills; [occ.] Hup-person at United Parcel Service; [pers.] Life is too short, don't let it slip away because when you finally find what you want in life its too late. [a.] Los Angeles, CA.

VASQUEZ, EUGENE A.
[pen.] Thunder Bear Talking; [b.] July 29, 1968, Pontiac, MI; [p.] Louis and Juanita Vasquez; [m.] Fiance - Amy Sanderson; [ed.] Brandon High School; [occ.] Designer for Odysey, Inc.; [oth. writ.] Many poems waiting for the right publisher; [pers.] My writing is high influenced by the great spirit and the past, present and future of the Native American people. I hope to enlighten people of a tragedy forgotten. [a.] Waterford, MI.

VASQUEZ, MARY LOU
[pen.] Mary Lou Bakersville; [b.] April 10, 1945, Cedar Rapids, IA; [p.] Trevor Bakersville and Lois Hill; [ch.] Damian, Marcos, Danny; [ed.] Spirit Lake High, West Texas State University, Texas Tech University; [occ.] Educator, Counselor; [hon.] Elected member of Alpha Chi Honorary Sorority; [pers.] I attempt to reflect the human condition in its glory and sorrow, joy and pain. I am greatly influenced by the memory of my beloved father and his love of poetry. [a.] Lubbock, TX.

VASQUEZ, NAOMI R.
[b.] April 8, 1968, Alameda; [p.] Daniel and Ruth Vasquez; [ed.] San Lorenzo High, Chabot College; [occ.] Restaurant Supervisor; [memb.] Fairmont Hospital Service League; [pers.] When the turkey's get you down, fly solo! [a.] San Lorenzo, CA.

VEGA, DEBRA L.
[b.] November 23. 1964, Chicago; [p.] Donald G. and Margaret Koehler; [m.] Francis J., February 14, 1992; [ch.] Joseph Luis; [ed.] Kelly High School, Daley College; [occ.] Customer Service Rep.; [oth. writ.] Several poems inspired by the late Donald G. Koehler, through him I found another side of myself, which I never knew existed; [pers.] One must search deep inside oneself to ignite their unique talent, everyone has one. [a.] Chicago, IL.

VENABLE, ANNETTE
[pen.] Annette Venable; [b.] March 23, 1947, Indianapolis; [p.] William J. and Rosalie Glennon; [ch.] Mary Jane and Jerri Lynn; [ed.] Saint Agnes Academy; [occ.] Security Guard for 18 years at Allison Gas Turbine; [memb.] Indiana Interpreters for the Deaf, "Right to Life" Society, Saint Anthony's Catholic Church; [hon.] National Honor Society, National Interpreters for the Deaf; [oth. writ.] "Coleen's Miracle" a short story printed in an Irish magazine. "A Book of Poems" written by myself. A short story printed in the Indianapolis "Star"; [pers.] I have always loved poetry, and I've always dreamed of becoming a well known poet. Maybe someday, my dream will come true. [a.] Indianapolis, IN.

VENEMA, RHONDA
[b.] June 20, 1965, Upland; [p.] Charles and Penny Venema; [ch.] Raydrian, Justine, Michael and Kris; [pers.] I lived in an era of cons, individual competition; self-independence, free sex, drugs, strong moral breakdown in family structure. I believe in hardwork, honesty, responsibility, a helping hand and love. [a.] Moreno Valley, CA.

VERDALETTE, LINDA
[pers.] "White Bird," is dedicated to Jesus. Thank you for not giving up on me. For all the times you saved my very life. For giving me Grace which I clearly did not deserve. But you saw worth in this piece of earth... My soul lay down, my spirit free, with you in Eternity... I love you, Lord.

VERNOOY, SANDRA WHITEMAN
[b.] December 10, 1959, Middletown, NY; [p.] Clement and Dorothy Whiteman; [m.] John M., November 10, 1985; [ch.] Sarah Elizabeth, Michael John; [ed.] Orange County Community College; [occ.] Personal Care Aide; [oth. writ.] Unpublished sentimental poems and stories; [pers.] Really, where would we be, if God had no time for us? [a.] Middletown, NY.

VILLNEFF, SHERRY M.
[b.] November 16, 1962, North Bay, ONT; [p.] Joan and Harvey Villneff; [m.] Darrell Deering; [ch.] Sonya Deering; [ed.] Temiskaming District Secondary School, Northern College; [occ.] Single mom, taking correspondence courses; [hon.] Math 4 point average, Dean's list, Accounting 4 point average, Dean's list; [oth. writ.] Several different types of my work has been published in local newspaper, Temiskaming Speaker and The Northern Daily News; [pers.] I put everything I can in my work. My feeling are greatly enhanced. I thank my mother for all of her support and encouragement to continue my writing. [a.] New Liskeard, ONT.

VILLWOCK, SPENCER C.
[pen.] Spenser; [b.] September 4, 1974, Milwaukee, WI; [p.] Van and Teresa Villwock; [ed.] Ames High, Des Moines Area Community College; [occ.] Carpenter/student; [memb.] American Video; [hon.] 1992 State of Iowa Sales and Marketing Achievement Award, Dean's List, President's List; [oth. writ.] A fine essay influencing continued support of a child-published in a Parents Without Partners newsletter. Most of my poetry is written for myself, influenced by my feelings for significant others (everyone and everything is significant); [pers.] Make yourself the best individual that you can be, love that individual, and pass your wisdom onto others...hugs can hold two people together. [a.] Ames, IL.

VINCENT, JIMMY W.
[pen.] Brother Jimmy; [b.] April 10, 1952; [p.] John and Essie; [m.] Special friend - Kathleen T.; [ch.] 1 daughter and 2 sons; [ed.] Public schools, college and The Life of Survival; [memb.] Pentecostal Church of God; [oth. writ.] On Track Bible Information Service, ministry; [pers.] Jimmy is a

Pentecostal Midwestern brother. My poems and writings are based on life's experiences, "The Pentecostal Experiences". The ups and downs overcame by the ever present faith and hope in Jesus Christ. [a.] Kalamazoo, MI.

VINCENT, KAREN M.
[b.] July 26,1 945, Los Angeles, CA; [ed.] University of Akron; [occ.] Advertising Sales Rep, The Akron Beacon Journal; [oth. writ.] Have enjoyed writing poems for a long time, but this is the first one submitted for publication; [pers.] I have chosen the Zen philosophy of awareness and living in the moment to guide my thoughts and experience and those principles are often reflected in my poetry. [a.] Barberton, OH.

VINE, WILLIAM GEORGE
[b.] July 16, 1952, Placerville, CA; [occ.] Student, SMCC; [pers.] If you don't dance your dance. It doesn't get done, since I was 10 years old in 1962, I've wanted to write. The National Library of Poetry opened the door for me, my job is to step through. You'll be reading a lot of my future work.

VIRAY, ANNA
[b.] 1968; [p.] Commander Wilfredo D. and Angela Mansour Viray; [occ.] Correspondent, Philippine News, the largest Filipino American newspaper in North America and Canada; foreign correspondent for newspapers in the Philippines.

VITALE-COX, D.
[b.] November 5, 1965, Pomona,CA; [p.] Edward T. Pettit II and Janet F. Smith; [m.] Keifer D. Fox, August 6, 1993; [ch.] Peter Keigwin Vitale; [ed.] Fairvalley High School, Saddleback College, Irvine Valley College, Art Institute; [occ.] Independent consultant working in the fields of Communication Arts, Information Sciences, Business Management and Systems and Procedures; [memb.] Specialties-Executive Production, Video Production and Graphic Layout and Design, Production Research and On-Line Services, Start-Up; [oth. writ.] Corporate Video Scripts, Television Program Research, unpublished fiction, screenplays and lyrics; [pers.] There is nor reality without communication. The artist most worthy of reverence is he who is adept enough to create (and enjoy) his own unique existence. [a.] Seattle, WA.

VIVISSIMO, NATALIE
[b.] September 3, 1976, San Diego, CA; [p.] Anthony and Yvette Vivissimo; [ed.] University of San Diego High School, Johnson and Wales University; [occ.] Full-time student; [hon.] Scholarship to Johnson and Wales, U.P.S.E.S. YOuth Group Award for Dedication; [oth. writ.] This is my first poem I ever wrote. I did this for an English assignment in high school; [pers.] Just do it, because you don't know what is going to come out of it unless you try it. You'll be surprised. [a.] San Diego, CA.

VOIGHT, JUNE E.L.
[pen.] June E.L. Voight; [b.] January 22, 1925, Baltimore, MD; [p.] George and Marie Lueckert; [m.] Thomas O. (deceased), January 31, 1948; [ch.] Gale Charlotte Carter, Paula Jean, Dawn Lynn Kerner (deceased), Sandra Leeann Trimble (all married); [ed.] Southern High School; [occ.] Widowed, housewife; [hon.] Best All Around Girl Class of Feb. 1945; [oth. writ.] At the age of 15 "Sunshine" was published Balto Ohio Railroad Magazine, other poems I have written have been for the pleasure of my family over the years; [pers.] I have written poems since my early teens and over the years I have found that this is my way of expressing my inner feelings, of life and those who have blessed my life. [a.] Baltimore, MD.

VOLK, VIVIAN
[pen.] "Bianca"; [b.] October 17, 1915, La Salle, IL; [p.] Vincent Kurkowski and Mary Zimney; [m.] Frank, April 6, 1940; [ch.] Vivian Volk; [b.] La Salle Pery Twp High School, formal education was restricted to the public library where I read wall to wall books constantly; [occ.] Retired in 1993 after owning a bar and grill since 1946; [hon.] The only honor I wish bestowed upon me is to have my poetry live on even when I do not; [oth. writ.] First two poems in 1932 ISP yearbook. Over 300 poems in 3 Chicago Tribune columns (1952-1968). Editors: Chas. Collins, John McCutheon Jr., Arch Ward, and Delos Avery. In "Ideals" many times, religious magazines and 100s of poems in local News Tribune; [pers.] If songs of my heart make one life more glad - what greater reward is there to be had? [a.] La Salle, IL.

VOLKMAN, IRENE
[pen.] Irene Volkman; [b.] Milwaukee, WS; [p.] Alice and John Mitchell; [m.] Kenneth; [ed.] High school plus continuous education in psychology, philosophy, religion, theater, writing, music, etc.; [occ.] Real Estate Broker and hopeful composer of music/lyrics; [hon.] High school honors, recognition for theater performance and newspaper correspondence, real estate achiever awards, recognized as outstanding Marketing Director of 2 subdivisions; [oth. writ.] I have written hundreds of newspaper articles, humanitarian pieces. I just finished composing songs with lyrics and orchestral arrangements on master tapes - relating to man's emotions. Now ready to publish; [pers.] I cannot rest! I devote my entire being to reach deep into my heart and soul for guidance - as many do - to pacify my unquenchable quest for knowledge, wisdom, and fulfillment of this mysterious life. [a.] Inverness, FL.

VOLLMER, RICHARD G.
[pen.] Richard Gee; [b.] July 8, 1938, Denver Twp, MI; [p.] Alice Aaron Benner and Nina Vollmer; [m.] Sara Blakley Vollmer, September 26, 1981; [ch.] Richard E., Fawn Marie, Beverly R.; [ed.] Southern Missionary College; [occ.] Truck Driver 22 years with Consolidated Freight; [memb.] Teamsters Union, Greater Dickson Co. Writers Society; [hon.] Scholarship for Public Speaking; [oth. writ.] Luck, Cowboy Hat, One Night Stand, 3rd Floor Barbourville, One Thing I'll Never Do, Where Bot Road Go Daddy?, Monkey and the Bull Dog, I Thank You, A Flower for Mother and hundreds more; [pers.] Make sure you find the right mate the first time! [a.] Charlotte, TN.

VONK, CHRISTINE CAROL ANNE
[b.] December 25, 1955, Ottawa, CAN; [p.] Leonard and Clarisse Paul; [m.] John G., October 5, 1985; [occ.] Computer telephone operator; [oth. writ.] Personnel writings that have been written for family, none have ever been published; [pers.] My father, Leonard Paul, in passing, I have been given strength and courage to carry on, my mother, Clarisse Paul for her support and love throughout and my husband John Vonk for never giving up on me. [a.] Orleans, ONT., CAN.

WADDELL, HELEN
[b.] January 2, 1973, Haddington, East Lothian, Scotland; [p.] Helen and Dr. James Lindsay Waddell; [ed.] Knox Academy, Glasgow University, degree not completed; [occ.] Freelance writer; [hon.] Editor's Choice Award presented by The National Library of Poetry; [oth.writ.] Reviews, interviews and features in several publications. [a.] Glasgow, Scotland.

WAGNER, TENA M.
[b.] April 19, 1961, Bremerton, WA; [p.] Barbara J. McGinnis; [m.] Charles Wagner, February 9, 1992; [ch.] Jeremy, Levi and Fawn; [ed.] Olympic College (retraining); [occ.] Disabled carpenter; [memb.] Forever Processing on the Path of Recovery; [hon.] Being a mother is the most important thing I will ever do; [oth.writ.] "Gratitudes and Attitude", "Hope To Cope", "A Friend In Deed"; [pers.] Life has been my greatest teacher. Success is not what I gain but rather what I overcome. Favorite poet, Robert Service. [a.] Kingston, WA.

WALKER, JAMES E.
[b.] July 6, 1970, Denver, CO; [p.] Mallory Walker and Irene Nicolai; [occ.] I do photography at weddings, on occasions I do models and artists who want work photoed; [oth.writ.] Journey of The Mind is my 1st published work, but many of my friends and loved ones enjoy me work both in writings and photography; [pers.] I try to share my experience, strength and hope with my fellow man, I write on other subjects but am greatly influenced to write about my spiritual experiences in life and how I hit a bottom in life but have found an answer and a higher power. [a.] Clifton, NJ.

WALKER, JANET
[b.] March 20, 1974, Shreveport, LA; [p.] K.E and the late Lavern Walker; [m.] Single; [ed.] Joaquin High, Panola College, Associate of Arts; [occ.] Student and office manager, manager for Century 21, Center, Texas; [memb.] Phi Rho Pi, Delta Psi Omega, Mims Springs Baptist Church; [hon.] Who's Who Among Students in American Junior College, Dean's List, College Public Address Captain; [oth.writ.] Articles published in local newspapers; [pers.] This poem was written for my mother who passed away November 20, 1990 for her love and support. [a.] Joaquin, TX.

WALKER, KELLEY
[b.] November 17, 1984, Kansas City, KS; [p.] Jay V. and Sandra G. Walker; [ed.] Presently in 4th grade; [occ.] Student at Piper Elementary East, Kansas City, Kansas; [memb.] Wy Co 4-H (Chapparel Club), American Junior Quarter Horse Association; [hon.] Young Author's Conference at Pittsburgh, Kansas 1993, Most Improved 4-H Girl, Wy Co 1994, General Motors Achievement Award 1994; [oth.writ.] Annette and Dundee's Big Race, The Journey To Unicorn Land, The Frisky Cat, Adorable Puppies. [a.] Kansas City, KS.

WALKER, KIMBERLY NAKISHA
[b.] June 12, 1974, Washington, DC; [p.] Tyrone and Mary Walker; [ed.] Calvin Coolidge Senior High School, The American University; [occ.] Junior at the American University pursuing B.A. in Psychology (major) Education (minor); [memb.] American University Gospel Choir; [pers.] God is my true inspiration and guides me in all that I do. He lives in me and uses me for His service. I hope that whatever I write will have some impact on it's reader, even if it just makes someone think about themselves, someone else or nothing at all. [a.] Washington, DC.

WALKER, MARGARET
[b.] July 25, 1929, St. Paul, MN; [p.] Joseph A. Perron and Margaret O'Connor; [ch.] James M. Sproles and Martin V. Rhoades; [ed.] High school, St. Joseph's Academy, St. Paul, MN., college, Monterey Pennisula College, Montere, California; [occ.] Dental Therapy Assistant, Ft. L. Wood, MO.; [memb.] Catholic church, St. Theresas Dixon, and Visitation, Vienna, MO, certified Dental Assistant, American Dental Assistants Association, ADAA; [hon.] Many exceptional performance awards, several official commendations and letters

of appreciation from the Dental Organization at Ft. L. Wood, MO; [oth.writ.] Several poems and songs; [pers.] Trust in God. Look for good in other people. Influenced by my loving family who praise and pray. [a.] Vienna, MO.

WALKER, STEPHEN L.
[b.] July 10, 1963, Jonesboro, LA; [m.] Cynthia Walker, November 21, 1987; [ed.] Ball State University, B.S. degree in Psychology; [occ.] Policeman, Indianapolis Police Department; [memb.] Omega Psi Phi Fraternity, Eastern Star Baptist Church; [oth.writ.] Book, Inner Most Thoughts of A Black Man; [pers.] Psalm 23. [a.] Indianapolis, IN.

WALLACE, EVELYN S.
[pen.] Evelyn; [b.] May 19, 1951, Lee Co; [p.] Andrew and Pinkie Strickland; [m.] Divorced; [ch.] horace Jr., Melvin J. and Kelvin T.; [ed.] J.W. Darden High School; [occ.] Home Care Aide for Department of Human Resources; [oth.writ.] A Modern Free Prayer, A Better Tomorrow, Not For Sale; [pers.] A lovely smile is a quiet expression of (thoughts). [a.] Opelika, AL.

WALLACE, MAVIS
[ch.] Audrey (17) and Andrew (13); [occ.] Nurse; [hon.] Several Editor's Choice Awards, published in brochure, pamphlets; [oth.writ.] Short stories and career choice; [pers.] To become the best me each day. Striving to create "Art" in the great form of poetry and writing. [a.] Post Falls, ID.

WALLER, COLLEEN
[b.] August 25, 1979, Alexandria, LA; [p.] Jan and Stan Waller; [ed.] Sophomore at T.C. Roberson High School; [occ.] Corn Dog 7; [pers.] Writing poetry gives me great pleasure. I hope that you enjoy it as much as I do. [a.] Asheville, NC.

WALLER, DIANE POPE
[pen.] Pope, Diane; [b.] June 15, 1955, Bessmer, AL; [p.] Nathaniel and Lillie Mae Bell Pope Sr.; [m.] Kevin Scott Waller, December 26, 1991; [ch.] Alicia Veleda Pope Waller; [ed.] Jess Lanier High, Alverson Draughon Business College, Prince Georges Community College and the Community College of the Air Force; [occ.] Engineer-Utility Systems Repairer\operator, Master Sergeant U.S. Air Force Reserves; [memb.] Maple Springs Baptist Church, Board of Directors, Great Ideas, Inc.; [oth.writ.] Several poems copywritten, "Reflections". [a.] Forestville, MD.

WALLS, CHARLIE MICHELE
[b.] December 20, 1984, Antlers, OK; [p.] Tony Walls and Michele Chastain; [ed.] I am a 4th grade student at the Brantly Elementary School in Antlers, OK; [memb.] 4H Club, Youth Barrel Racing, gymnastic team, Gifted and Talented class; [hon.] My mom started entering me in pageants when I was 2 months old, so I have lots of trophies for that and gymnastics and soccer; [oth.writ.] I had a poem published in an anthology of children's poetry when I was in 2nd grade; [pers.] I like to write stories and poems but I love to do so many things I don't know what I want to do when I grow up. I love animals so I might be a veterinarian. [a.] Antlers, OK.

WALSH SR., JERRY ALAN
[b.] April 21, 1939, Bradford, PA; [p.] Vincent and Leah Walsh; [m.] Marlene Dingwell Walsh, June 10, 1972; [ch.] Jerry, Mark, Alan, David, Patricia, Deborah Brett; [ed.] Salamanca C. H.S., Salamanca, New York, Alfred State College, Alfred, NY; [occ.] Retired U.S. Navy, U.s. Postal Service, Hornell, New York; [memb.] V.F.W. Post 2250; [hon.] 67-68 Viet Nam Campaign Medal, Navy Expeditionary Medal-79, good conduct U.S. Navy (3), good conduct USAF (1), U.Su meritorious unit commendation (2), Coast Guard Meritorious Unit Commendation, Navy E (3), expert rifle medal; [oth.writ.] None published; [pers.] Those who serve and sacrifice in the military should not be forgotten. Honor and respect should be shown to them especially by the people whom they serve. [a.] Hornell, NY.

WALSH, TANYA KAY
[b.] May 14, 1974, Del Rio, TX; [p.] Skip and Debbie Sturges; [m.] Patrick H. Walsh, December 18, 1993; [ed.] Thomas Dale High, Richard Bland College, Fayetteville Tech Community College; [occ.] Secretary, Mid-South Insurance Company; [oth.writ.] Numerous poems and short stories; [pers.] Anyone can be a writer. It's a great way to express yourself and your feelings. [a.] Fayetteville, NC.

WALTERS, JEFF
[b.] December 16,1969, Oklahoma City, OK; [oth.writ.] Damonisch Welt (not published); [pers.] I write whatever comes to mind out of the blue, I don't force or plan it. A phrase will come along and imprison my thoughts until it's written down. When I start writing a phrase down more follows never pay much attention to it till I'm done. [a.] Moore, OH.

WALTON, BEN
[b.] February 28, 1972, Lubbock; [p.] Belinda Walton Gillispie and Jack C. Walton Jr.; [m.] Deborah Walton, May 7, 1993; [ed.] Pursuing a degree in Criminology and English; [occ.] College student; [pers.] Dreams are our only source of true freedom. [a.] Lubbock, TX.

WAMPLER, STEFANIE NICHOLE
[pen.] Stef and Nikki Wampler; [b.] July 12, 1983, Morehead, KY; [p.] Paul and Barbara Wampler; [ed.] 6th grade student at Bloom Middle School, South Webster, Ohio, 4th year in academically gifted classes; [occ.] Elementary student; [memb.] Girl Scouts, 4-H; [hon.] Fraternal Order of Police, Meritorious Service Award, Buckeye State Sheriff's Association civilian Citation, Civil Achievement Award, Top Performance Award for Art, several Academic Excellence Awards; [pers.] I was greatly influenced my third grade teacher, Mrs. Patsy Graff, which at this time I would like to thank. [a.] Wheelersburg, OH.

WAMSTEKER, SACHA MARIANNE C.
[b.] July 13, 1970, Haarlem, Netherlands; [p.] Kees Wamsteker and Yvonne Wamsteker-Bijlsma; [ed.] Stedelijk Gymnasium, Haarlem the Netherlands, National Bartending School, Los Angeles; [occ.] Actress, anything that pays the rent; [oth.writ.] Nothing published yet, this is my debut; [pers.] I search to find a way out of the beautifully intricate maze of life without having to give in to death. [a.] West Hollywood, CA.

WARD, KEVIN J.
[b.] September 3, 1955, Anoka, MN; [p.] Bernard and Darlene Ward; [m.] Julie Ward, February 6, 1981; [ch.] Erin Anne, Ryan Kevin and Megan Mary; [ed.] Anoka High, BS Engineering from University of Minnesota; [occ.] Project manager, Select Comfort Inc.; [oth.writ.] Several poems and one novel "The Seduction of Paradise" currently awaiting publication; [pers.] i try to depict the inner struggle of people dealing with their own human weaknesses, particularly in the family environment. [a.] Anoka, MN.

WARD, SARAH
[b.] June 4, 1983, Manitowoc; [p.] Scott and Kathy Ward; [ed.] Jefferson Elementary School currently a 6th grade student; [occ.] Student; [hon.] Honor Roll Student, Good Citizenship Award. [a.] Manitowoc, WI.

WARE, MARIANNE
[b.] October 28, 1973, Quantico, VA; [p.] Mary and Samuel Ware; [ed.] California State University, San Marcos, Capistrano Valley High School; [occ.] Student; [memb.] MCAS Historical Foundation, International Society of Poets; [hon.] International Poet of Merit Award; [oth.writ.] Several poems in anthologies. [a.] Mission Viejo, CA.

WARNER, RUTH
[b.] October 6, 1923, Toledo, OH; [p.] David B. and Pearl (Beyer) Edwards; [m.] Neal E. Warner, October 27, 1945; [ch.] Craig A. Warner; [ed.] Woodward High School and Stautzenberger Secretarial School; [occ.] Housewife, former secretary; [memb.] International Society of Poets, International Society of Authors and Artists and the National Authors Registry; [hon.] 1993 International Poet of Merit Award from Iliad Press, 1993 Literary Award, an Honorable Mention Award of Excellence and an accomplishment of merit certificate from Creative Arts and Science Ent., 1994 Editor's Choice Award from The National Library of Poetry; [oth.writ.] "The Long Road Back" published in "Odysses" Fall 1993 by Cader Publishing Ltd., "Zest For Living" published in "Treasured Poems of America", Fall 1994 by Sparrowgrass Poetry Forum, "the Separation" published in "Pen Etched Memories" by Creative Arts and Sciences Ent. 1994, "Fragile Flower" published in The Space Between by The National Library of Poetry (1994); [pers.] Writing poetry can be great therapy. A sense of well-being accompanies the finished product. [a.] Northwood, OH.

WASZ, AMY
[b.] April 1, 1976, Porter Memorial; [p.] Mr. and Mrs. R.G. Wasz;[ed.] Chesterton High School 1990-1994; [occ.] Unemployed; [pers.] I just love to write, it comes easy for me. [a.] Portage, IN.

WATKINS, SUSAN PAULA POWELL
[pen.] Susan Paula Powell; [b.] July 20, 1929, Towns Co., GA; [p.] T.O. and Daisy Ramey Powell; [m.] Divorced, October 12, 1964; [ch.] F. Stephen; [ed.] Towns County High, Knoxville Business College, Southside Community College; [occ.] Business Management; [memb.] Catholic Church, past Chairperson Justice and Peace Committee, Prison Ministry, Crisis Pregnancy Counsel; [hon.] Governor volunteer award; [oth.writ.] Several newspaper articles; [pers.] I strive to treat others as I wish to be treated. [a.] Blackstone, VA.

WATSON, ANN L.
[b.] January 14, 1953, Hanover, PA; [p.] Bernadine and Roy Masenheimer; [m.] James W. Watson, January 4, 1975; [ch.] Peyton Mackenzie Watson; [ed.] B.A. York College of PA, MLA Western MD College; [occ.] English teacher, New Oxford Senior High School; [hon.] Finalist for PA Teacher of the Year in 1989, Outstanding Ed. guest lecturer at Shippensburg University-1989; [pers.] My writing began with graduate courses taken during my Sabbatical leave after the adoption of my son. My parents raised me with a love of reading and my husband and I wish the same for our son. [a.] Hanover, PA.

WAYLAND, VIRGINIA
[pen.] Former professional-Virginia Phillis; [b.] Pasadena, CA; [p.] Howard Dunlap Phillis and Edna Bradford Phillis; [m.] (1) William F. Heinzelman (deceased 1964), (2) Russell G. Wayland, 1965;

[ch.] Step-children, Nancy and Paul Wayland; [ed.] Polytechnic School, Pasadena High, Pomona College B.A., Phi Beta Kappa; [occ.] Retired, former writer/editor and executive in the fields of advertising, publicity, highway safety and public service; [hon.] I am gratified to say i have won a great many scholastic and professional honors and awards, I even, to my vast astonishment won first prize in a local contest for an official city march, conducted by our neighbor community Fairfax City; [oth.writ.] At the age of two, I began writing poems, stories, skits, plays and songs, but only for my own gratification or the entertainment of friends --including fellow students and club members. After college and until recent retirement I earned my living writing advertising copy and publicity, plus innumerable newspaper and magazine articles on behalf of community and national causes. In the course of this career I have turned out countless millions of words, most of them anonymous or often, attributed to the titular spokesperson for some worthy movement of event.

WEAVER, JESSICA
[pen.] Rachel Weaver; [b.] October 2, 1980, Connecticut; [p.] Cindy and Tracy Weaver; [ed.] Hoggard High School; [oth.writ.] Blue Eyes, Never Again, Connecticut Memories; [pers.] I write about past and present experiences, about what I see around me and what I would like to see around me. [a.] Wilmington, NC.

WEBB, BESSIE
[b.] October 13, 1977, Carbondale, IL; [p.] Glen J. (deceased) and Martha Webb; [ed.] I am a senior at Anna Jonesboro Community High School; [occ.] CNA at the Anna City Care Nursing Home; [memb.] Anna First Baptist Youth, Future Business Leaders of America, Future Homemaker of America; [hon.] I have received many awards for my poetry and short stories, such as a story written about my mother on Mother's Day; [oth.writ.] "Missing You" At day's End, The National Library of Poetry, written in memory of my father; [pers.] I write poetry to express my emotions about my life. My poem "Who Would Have Thought..These Two" was written about my dear friend Abe Cain. [a.] Anna, IL.

WEBB, NORAH H.
[pen.] Norah Hall Webb; [b.] August 17, Kentucky; [p.] John A. and Sally Ann Hall; [m.] Ballard W. Webb, September 12, 1936; [ch.] John A. Webb; [ed.] B.S. and M.A. degrees from the University of Louisville State of Kentucky, Louisville, Kentucky; [occ.] Retired; [memb.] American Association of University Women, Local Writer's Group, Retired Educators of Florida; [oth.writ.] Short stories, travelogues, book review, fiction; [pers.] My writing is lacking in imagination. [a.] Gainesville, FL.

WEIDA, KIMBERLY
[pen.] Kimberly Weida; [b.] July 31, 1979, Kokomo, IN; [p.] Donald and Mary Ann Weida; [ed.] Washington Elementary, Maple Crest Middle School, Kokomo High School; [memb.] STAND (Students Taking A New Direction), Kokomo High School marching band, Spanish Club; [oth.writ.] "Confused", "My Feelings", "Love", "Let Me Be", "Hurt", "My Love For You", "Miss You Much", "Our Times", "Love"; [pers.] I write about love. Adults think love only happens when you're older. My poems are about the best boyfriend Josh, whom I love and admire and trust. [a.] Kokomo, IN.

WEIDNER, JOE C.
[pen.] Joe C. Weidner; [b.] November 23, 1948, Mineral Wells, TX; [p.] Alvin and Frances Weidner; [ed.] BFA in painting and design, trade degree in Silversmithing, trade degree in Jewelry Design, and trade degree Vehicular Customizing; [occ.] Jewelry designer/silversmith, musician, songwriter; [memb.] Tularosa Chamber of Commerce, Alamogordo Chamber of Commerce, "Singles Together" ABC Bowlers Association, Bros Club, Tularosa Chapter of ABATE, Retread's International; [hon.] Acceptance in National Library of Poetry anthology Journey of The Mind, assorted ABC Bowler's Association Awards; [oth.writ.] 15 published songs (lyrics and music), 3 released on musical albums, articles for local newspapers, an article for magazine "Mi Amigo", in Dallas, Texas, plus other numerous unpublished songs, music/lyrics and screenplays; [pers.] I write songs about real emotions and feelings, my poems reflect the struggle for Self-Awareness/Healing, Love and Relationships and the Human Condition. My screenplays are "semi-autobiographical" with overtones of love, fantasy and undertones of danger and despair for "commercialism" (as mankind reaches for the stars, some fall short or settle for less, while others preservers till their final breath). [a.] Tularosa, NM.

WELCH, WARD BRADFORD
[b.] January 24, 1961, Philadelphia, PA; [p.] William and Barbara Welch; [m.] Benita J. Welch, March 6, 1987; [ch.] Brianna Kaitlin Welch (September 11, 1992); [ed.] Academy of The New Church College, Jacksonville State University; [occ.] Toronado Grant Coordinator Calhoun County, Alabama; [memb.] General Church of The New Jerusalem; [hon.] Alabama Associated Press Broadcasters Association Awards, Best Radio News Anchor-1989, Best Radio News Feature-1990, Best Creative Use of Medium-1990; [oth.writ.] This is my first, many more to follow; [pers.] Influenced greatly by the many wonderful writings of Emanuel Swedenborg. [a.] Jacksonville, AL.

WELLMAN, REYNARD JAY
[pen.] Reynard Jay Wellman; [b.] March 15, 1942, Dallas, TX; [p.] James Walter and Edna Earl Wellman Jr.; [m.] Elizabeth Ann Wellman, August 17, 1982; [ch.] Jennifer and Erica; [ed.] Alameda High, Denver, Western State College, Taos Institute of Creative Orientation, College of Marin, San Anselmo, California; [occ.] Interface designer Motorola, Austin; [hon.] Excellence in Engineering Award 1991, Motorola; [oth.writ.] Many letters to the Editor, published in Austin American Statesman; [pers.] In art I seek to establish links between human consciousness and the consciousness in the natural world and through the vehicle of art to revitalize the spiritual and emotional message of our shared existence. [a.] Austin, TX.

WELLS, JESSICA LYNN
[b.] July 14, 1981, New Hanover Memorial; [p.] Michael and Gena Wells; [ed.] I'm an eight grade student at Penderlea School; [memb.] I'm an academically gifted student and have been for seven years; [hon.] Honor Roll Awards, band award, cheerleading award; [oth.writ.] Many poems written but not published; [pers.] In this writing, I try to make people see that spending a life spent hating others is a life not worth living. Love is everything. [a.] Watha, NC.

WELLS, TERI-DAWN
[b.] November 19, 1978, Nanimo, BC; [p.] Randy and Tom Wells; [ed.] Grade 10; [occ.] School; [memb.] Quarterway Gym. [a.] Nanimo, BC Canada.

WENIG, HAROLD
[b.] December 10, 1921, Brooklyn, NY; [p.] Jacob and Henrietta Wenig; [m.] Dorothy Wenig, June 19, 1980; [ch.] Richard Jay and Ronald Brett; [ed.] Thomas Jefferson High School, Lafayette University, N.Y.C. Police Academy, Treasury Agents Academy; [occ.] Retired N.Y.C. Police Lt., retired U.S. Treasury Agent; [memb.] Joseph Warren Gothic Masonic Lodge, Broward County 10-13 Club, Shields of Nassau County, Retired Lieutenant's Association N.Y.C. P.D.; [hon.] Albert Gallatin Awards, U.S. Treasury, meritorious duty N.Y.C.P.D.; [oth.writ.] Several short stories published in the Anthology of American Authors; [pers.] I try to instill realism in my writings. My 40 years in law enforcement has provided me with an unlimited source of material. [a.] Sunrise, FL.

WERNER, EVAN
[pen.] Evan Werner; [b.] June 5, 1977, Salem, OR; [p.] Elaine and William Werner; [oth.writ.] Circle of Stones, Outside The Bramble Patch, The Writer Within; [pers.] I enjoy reading and composing fiction because it is an antidote to my immediate surroundings. [a.] Portland, OR.

WESTFALL, JOHN BENTON
[b.] September 7, 1927, Kansas City, MO; [p.] Marguerite and B.F. Westfall; [m.] Barbara Jean Westfall, June 26, 1949; [ch.] Mark Benton and Barbara Ellen; [ed.] Independence, Kansas High School, Pittsburg State University of Pittsburg, Kansas; [occ.] Retired from Phillips Petroleum Company; [memb.] St. Luke's Episcopal Church, Bartlesville Lions Club, Bartlesville Civic Ballet Board of Directors, Youth and Family Services Board of Directors, Sigma Tau Gamma, Alpha Phi Omega, Boy Scouts of America; [hon.] Lions Club Melvin Jones Fellowship, Bartlesville Outstanding Citizen Award; [oth.writ.] The Philmont Hymn (words and music). [a.] Bartlesville, OK.

WHITE, BRENDA
[b.] December 20, 1954, New York; [p.] Willie and Leona White; [m.] William Richardson, May 4, 1990; [ch.] Wakenda, Shaquon, Shakima and William; [ed.] George Washington High School, Monroe College; [occ.] Housewife; [oth.writ.] One of my poems was printed in the Leake and Watts newsletter, the title was called "Undecided" which I wrote for my daughter; [pers.] My poetry deals with the struggles of life, love and relationships. I deal with the inner feelings which one might feel, such as myself, after a painful or joyful experience. I want my poetry to reach all people. Men, women and children to let them know that there is someone else out there who cares. [a.] Bronx, NY.

WHITE, GAIL
[b.]december 4, 1940, Blue Island, IL; [p.] Bernard and Elizabeth Perryman (both deceased); [m.] Ronald White (deceased), May 16, 1959; [ch.] Thomas Robert, Sherry Lynn and Natalie Ann; [ed.] High school; [occ.] Secretary to Guidance Coordinator at Homewood-Flossmoor High School; [pers.] I strive to bring out other people's emotions and to put into words what they themselves cannot say. "If you listen with your heart, you can always hear the better side of life". [a.] Blue Island, IL.

WHITE, KAREN B.
[b.] February 27, 1966, San Antonio, TX; [p.]Jay and Susan Weiner; [m.] George William White Jr., October 20, 1989; [ch.] Danielle Jean (4 years old); [ed.] Merritt Island High School, Brevard Community College, University of Central Florida; [occ.] Inmate Information Specialist, Brevard County Sheriff's office. [a.] Cocoa, FL.

WHITE, PATRICIA R.
[pen.] Searcher of Love; [b.] April 16, 1963; [p.] Macie and Wesley Franklin Jr.; [ch.] Steven D White Jr.; [ed.] Custer High School, MATC College (word processing specialist-clerk typist); [occ.] Switchboard operator/receptionist; [hon.] A modeling award and Honor Roll student; [pers.] Through my poems is a hidden deed that I feel may be to reach other people's hearts, expressions of life's trials and tribulations and long searches of life beckoning for happiness. [a.] Milwaukee, WI.

WHITE, PATTY
[pen.] P.J. White; [b.] May 10, 1948, Silsbee, TX; [p.] Tom and Marie Tennison; [m.] Bob White, August 6, 1979; [ch.] Darin Ashley Griggs; [ed.] Silsbee High in Silsbee, Texas, Lamar University in Beaumont, Texas; [occ.] Songwriter, poet; [memb.] Lifetime member of International Society of Poets, Chancel Choir at First United Methodist Church in Jasper, TX; [hon.] National Library of Poetry Editor's Choice Award for one poem chosen for "The Sound of Poetry" cassette for two poems, chosen for National Library of Poetry's The Best Poems of 1995 anthology; [oth.writ.] Poems for National Library of Poetry and for International Society of Poets and for greeting cards for family and friends; [pers.] I enjoy writing family and faith-oriented poems, and also silly poems about life situations that we all seem to experience. Family, faith and friendships are a very important part of my life. [a.] Sam Rayburn, TX.

WHITING JR., WILLIE LEE
[pen.] Jesse Williams; [b.] May 19, 1958, Pensacola, FL; [p.] Willie L. and Martha Whiting Sr.; [ed.] Washington High, Pensacola Junior College, California State University Los Angeles, American Technical Institute; [occ.] President, Global Alliance Productions; [memb.] International Traders Association, Mid-San Fernando Valley Chamber of Commerce, American Entrepreneurs Association, 82nd Airborne Division Association; [hon.] Pensacola Junior College Academic Honors, American Technical Institute Academic Achievement Award; [pers.] The truth is found in the hearts of all.. you have to strive for it through the inspiration of your realization for life's quest. [a.] Rialto, CA.

WHITLOCK, ANNAROSE
[b.] February 28, 1947, Manheim, Germany; [p.] Loyd and Marie Breazeale; [m.] Terry Samuel Whitlock, June 18, 1966; [ch.] Eva Marie, Angela Rene and Terri Leann; [ed.] Pickens High School, Draughon's Business College; [occ.] Administrative Assistant, Department of Disabilities and Special Needs; [pers.] I strive to help others through my writing. My writing reflects what I feel and how I see things in general. [a.] Pickens, SC.

WHITTED, MATTHEW ALEXANDER
[pen.] Alex; [b.] November 24, 1974, Fayetteville, NC; [p.] Mr. and Mrs. Duncan J. Whitted III; [ed.] 1993 graduate of E.E. Smith High School, Fayetteville, NC., currently enrolled at Fayetteville Technical Community College; [memb.] John Wesley United Methodist Church; [hon.] Recipient of the Presidential Academic Fitness Award in the 9th grade; [oth.writ.] Had poems published in the "Mimi Page" of local newspaper; [pers.] If at first you don't succeed, try and try again. [a.] Fayetteville, NC.

WHITTLE, PATRICK L.
[pen.] R.L. Idaho; [b.] March 17, 1918, Salt Lake City, UT; [p.] Newell P. and Elizabeth Whittle; [m.] Gloria Whittle, January 1, 1986; [ch.] Mary Beth Essex and Louise Isham; [ed.] Madison High 1936, Ricks College Assoc.-ED 1938, Blair Junior College, attended 1946-1947 didn't graduate, Washington University, Saint Louis, MO, B.S. 1953, Washington University, Saint Louis, MO, MBA 1955; [occ.] Writer (retired accountant); [memb.] National Library of Poetry, 8th A F Historical Society, Utah Sons of Pioneer, etc.; [hon.] Distinguished Flying Cross Air Medal and 3 clusters from W.W.II (others in business, military and writing); [oth.writ.] Monthly poem in real estate paper, poem in The Friend magazine, children two nostalgic pieces in Colorado Springs Gazette Telegraph; [pers.] I try to catch the goodness of people and the beauty of my surroundings in my writing.

WICKS, MARIE A.
[b.] August 4,1952, Baltimore, MD; [p.] Joseph E. and Marie E. Wicks; [ed.] Western High, Community College of Baltimore; [occ.] Administrative Assistant, professional organizer, freelance desktop publisher, vocalist; [memb.] National Association of Professional Organizers, (NAPO), National Association of Female Executives (NAFE). [a.] Baltimore, MD.

WIDMAR, EDWARD
[pen.] Fast Eddie; [b.] April 11, 1939, Kenosha, WI; [p.] Yes; [m.] Divorced; [ch.] 3; [ed.] High school; [occ.] Retired; [memb.] NRA; [oth.writ.] Publisher of "Journal Of Serious Drinker: [pers.] God knew what He was doing when He made woman. [a.] Kenosha, WI.

WIGGINS, TAMALA T.
[b.] July 11,1982, Miami, FL; [p.] Joseph and Barbara Wiggins Jr.; [ed.] Carol City Elementary, Miami Carol City Middle (present); [occ.] Student; [hon.] High Academic Achievement 1992-93, Academic Excellence classes, honor classes, perfect attendance from grade 1 up to this point, Citizenship Awards grade 1-6, cheerleading competition award 105 lbs., 1st place 93-94; [oth.writ.] Poem sent to Washington, DC Peace Hero essay contest, trophy (Bethune contest poetry winner 2nd place N.C., N.W. Gr. Miami section 1991); [pers.] What I feel in my heart I express it in poetry or other writings. I believe if you put your mind, heart, soul and dedication in any talent you have you can achieve what you are looking for. [a.] Pembroke Pines, FL.

WIIG, JEANETTE E.
[pen.] Inspirations by Jnet; [b.] Joplin, MO; [p.] Henry and Edna Kennedy Clevenger; [m.] Harold; [ch.] Ronald, Donna and Rex; [ed.] Licensed Vocational Nurse; [occ.] Disabled, debilitating bone disease; [memb.] My own personal memberships with my children and 8 grandchildren, membership between myself and God gives me great strength, dearly admire Maya Angelo; [hon.] Being a Navy wife for 20 years of 39 years of marriage, being a loving sister to 6 sisters and 3 brothers, having them to share my life with is a great honor; [oth.writ.] Several poems, Honorable Mention into World of Poetry in 1991, enjoy writing song lyrics, none published; [pers.] I am very family oriented, love to write, my writings have helped me deal with hurdles in life. "Shiny Brass Ring" was written in memory of daughter Brenda who died of brain cancer at 19 years of age.[a.] Ontario, CA.

WILBURN, JIM
[b.] July 30, 1975, Manhattan, KS; [p.] Bill and Joyce Wilburn; [m.] Single; [ed.] Living Word Christian School, Manhattan Christian College (freshman); [occ.] Student; [memb.] Trinity Baptist Church (Wamego, Kansas), The Family of God; [hon.] The Strong Heart Award (runner-up), Honor Roll; [oth.writ.] The majority of my poems are lyrics of songs that will be completely written sometime in the future; [pers.] As a born again Christian I write my poems for the glory of my Saviour Jesus Christ. I strive to praise God in my writings, evangelize and (or) a positive or a Christian aspect of life. I have been greatly influenced by my uncle who is also a poet. [a.] Manhattan, KS.

WILDT, DOROTHY
[pen.] Dorothy Koeller Wildt; [ch.] Nick Edward Nico; [ed.] Eastern High School, Lansing, MI; [occ.] Private duty nurse; [memb.] Former Mission Director and Preacher; [hon.] Echo Your Love-Kennedy Museum, The Eye (50-plus magazine), You Will Never Then Be old (magazine), Riding On The Joy of God (magazine), American Ring Those Bells (50-plus magazine); [oth.writ.] America Ring Those Bells, You Will Never Then Be Old, Abiding Love, The Eye, Our God Will Save The Day, God's Own True Plan; [pers.] I wanted the world to see what I believe in. How I feel about our America and life, as one of God's gospel poets. Riding On The Joy of God, was written after having a vision of Jesus. [a.] Vero Beach, FL.

WILHELM, VALERIE
[pen.] Vie; [b.] 1959, Detroit; [oth.writ.] I have written many pieces in seeking healing and enlightenment, some have been published by those reflecting the same; [pers.] This poem was inspired by my teenage daughter. [a.] Boulder Creek, CA.

WILHOIT, THERESA
b.] November 9, 1933, Phoenix, AZ; [p.] Evelyn and Vernon Moynahan; [m.] Bill Wilhoit, June 6, 1953; [ch.] Katherine and William; [ed.] Glendale Community College, Arizona State University, summer school Oxford University; [occ.] Writer, homemaker; [hon.] Annual Literature Award, Glendale Community College, Dean's List-Arizona State University, Phi Alpha Theta, Sigma Tau Delta, Magna Cum Laude-Arizona State University 1993; [oth.writ.] Unpublished as yet, but I write poetry and short fiction; [pers.] I have never thought age should be a barrier to success or realization of dreams and it hasn't been. [a.] Phoenix, AZ.

WILKS, MARY COOKSEY
[b.] June 26, 1948, Rockville Center, NY; [p.] Carlos and Marian Meehan Cooksey; [ed.] Graduate of Verona High School; [occ.] Owner of Tailwaggers Pet Sitting Service, part time School Crossing Guard, part time Dental Receptionist; [memb.] Chairman of Verona Recreation Department Advisory Committee, Sub-committee Chairman of Verona Community Center, member-Handgun Control, member-National Wildlife Federation; [oth.writ.] I have never had any of my work published but have, for many years written poems or satiric compositions for friends on birthdays, anniversaries and other occasions; [pers.] I hope someday to be able to spend more time writing and perhaps have other works published, but in the meantime I thoroughly enjoy working with children, caring for animals and serving on local committees. [a.] Verona, NJ.

WILLIAMS, BETTY
[pen.] Betty James Sexton Williams; [ed.] BS in Medical Technology from Arizona State University; [occ.] Writer; [oth.writ.] "Rosy Thoughts for Cross Cultural Living" ISBN 0-9626728-0-7, "The Lovers" published in Short Story International; [pers.] I have experienced that it is in commonplaceness where one finds poetry and beauty. Poor is the soul that requires unusual situations for inspiration. [a.] Fresno, CA.

WILLIAMS, CANDICE
[b.] September 6, 1982, Denton, TX; [p.] Beverly and Carl Williams; [ed.] Sam Houston; [occ.] Full time student; [memb.] N.A.A.C.P.; [oth.writ.] Other poems and stories; [pers.] I love to read and write. Try hard and will achieve success. [a.] Denton, TX.

WILLIAMS, ELLA
[b.] July 20, 1953, Osceola, AR; [p.] Ella Bell Anderson; [m.] Richard Williams Sr., August 18, 1979; [ch.] Richard Jr. and Renee; [ed.] Osceola High, Arkansas State University; [occ.] Assistant Principal, Franklin Elementary School, Port Arthur, Texas; [memb.] Texas Elementary Principals and Supervisors Association, American Association of School Administrators, Phi Delta Kappa, Golden Triangle Writer's Guild, Toastmasters International; [hon.] Lawrence A. Davis Scholarship, PAISD "Plus Award", District Table Topics winner; [oth.writ.] Educational article published in the TEPSA Journal; [pers.] I want to be all that God intended me to be and want to encourage others to do the same. [a.] Port Arthur, TX.

WILLIAMS, EVERETT L.
[b.] November 23, 1912, Monroe, LA; [p.] Oscar and Ada Williams; [m.] Francis, August 17,1940; [ch.] Mrs. Robert McCulley and Everett II; [ed.] B.A., M.A., plus; [occ.] Retired college Dean; [memb.] MENSA, Phi Delta Kappa, N.R.T.A., T.S.T.A.; [hon.] High school Valedictorian, 25 years Kiwanis plaque, 3 year Bible Teacher plaque, 75 year old Texas Doubles Tennis Champion, Asst. St. Supervisor Adult Ed., Army General's recommendation; [oth.writ.] Numerous newspaper letters, occasional columns, literacy writings, vocational courses of study; [pers.] To be truly great, one must lead the way into the unknown for the good of all mankind. [a.] Ingram, TX.

WILLIAMS, JANICE NELDA
[b.] June 20, 1945, Orange, TX; [p.] Nathan and Cora Ferguson; [m.] Clarence R. Williams, November 7, 1970; [ch.] Tammy Nadine Powell; [ed.] Kirbyville High School, Chenier Business College; [occ.] Housewife, mother; [memb.] Daughters of the Republic of Texas (D.R.T.), and also Daughters of the American Revolution (D.A.R.), Roganville Baptist Church; [hon.] I graduated Salutatorian of my class at Kirbyville High School; [oth.writ.] Personal poems only; [pers.] Never let go of your dreams in life. At the age of 40 I was diagnosed with muscular dystrophy. I thought my world had ended, but God opened up a new window of light, new dreams, new horizons. [a.] Kirbyville, TX.

WILLIAMS, KEITH E.
[pen.] Saleem the Poet; [b.] May 22, 1962, Newark, NJ; [m.] Gladys A. Williams, January 12, 1988; [ch.] Isaam Taalib and Jawhara Najlaa; [ed.] Irvington High School, Essex County College; [occ.] Senior Trust Clerk, First Fidelity Bank, Newark, NJ; [memb.] Camp Counselor 1980, Key Club 1980, International Bowling Association; [hon.] World of Poetry's Golden Poet Award 1990 and Certificate of Merit 1990; [oth.writ.] Numerous unpublished poems of various subjects; [pers.] I am trying to open America's eyes and ears to the plights of the America within. I would like to thank my wife and children for their love and support. I sent special thanks to Istawa Angervien (New Orleans, LA) for his friendship and encouragement. [a.] Newark, NJ.

WILLIAMS JR., LOUIS ALLEN
[b.] January 2, 1970, Vineland, NJ; [p.] Mildred and Louis Williams Sr.; [ed.] Millville Senior High School class of 1988; [occ.] Certified home health aide VNASNJ; [pers.] Love like luscious fruit dangling from the tree of hope, painfully out of my grasp. It seems that I am cursed to forever feel it, see it grow all around me, but never to have it as my own. Writing eases the pain. Special thanks to Steven Pitts and of course "Big" Allen Williams, my brother. [a.] Millville, NJ.

WILLIAMS, PATRICK
[b.] August 5, 1977, Algona, IA; [p.] Ann and Jack Williams; [ed.] Currently attending Algona High School; [occ.] Pizza Baker, part time student; [memb.] First United Methodist Church; [oth.writ.] None published; [pers.] I believe in the reality of man. There are too many people faking their way through it. [a.] Algona, IA.

WILLIAMS, ROBERT H.
[b.] September 24, 1959, Agana, Guam; [p.] Robert and Elizabeth Williams; [ed.] Orange Park High School; [occ.] Serving overseas in the U.S. Air Force; [memb.] Presbyterian Church of America, Save the Manatee Club, Gator Boosters; [hon.] Semi-finalist, 1994 North American Open Poetry contest. [a.] Middleburg, FL.

WILLIAMS, WILLIE C.
[b.] January 30, 1938, Coolidge, TX; [p.] Edward and Dollie Williams; [ed.] Waco High, TSTI (now TSTC), graduate Waco High, TSTC; [occ.] Retired U.S. Navy, presently attempting to establish a small business plus creditably as a poet, other interests include sketching and photography; [hon.] Award in East Junior High School for an essay on soil conservation; [oth.writ.] Other writing have been written but I have never entered any contest except for the essay in East Junior High School; [pers.] Hopefully in each poem someone will gain by their experience from reading one of my poems. [a.] Waco, TX.

WILLS, NATHAN ALAN
[pen.] Nathan Alan Wills; [b.] February 17, 1978, Carbondale, IL; [p.] Terrie Schaefer and Kerry Wills; [ed.] Currently a junior at Shawnee High School, Wolf Lake, Il; [oth.writ.] Have written many poems since "The Old Tree" some of my works include "Dreams", "Release", "The Last One", "Awaiting", "In The Mirror", "Drowned", "Cheshire Frost", "Black Winged Dove"; [pers.] I've always believed life is a gamble and you'll never know what you'll become if you don't roll the dice. [a.] Grand Tower, IL.

WILTSHIRE III, OXFORD S.
[b.] January 24, 1977; [ed.] Omaha North High School; [oth.writ.] 1 poem previously published, many short stores and screenplays, nonpublished. [a.] Omaha, NE.

WINHAM, MARY
[b.] January 11, 1943; [p.] Cecil and Ruth Grady; [m.] Harry Winham (July 7, 1940), September 30, 1966; [ch.] Anthony and Michael Winham; [ed.] Anthony Winham-Gainesville High, (U.S. Army), Michael Winham (assembly worker); [oth.writ.] I'm still writing other poems. Maybe someday they can all be published. I will keep them for my kids and grandkids.

WINTERS, CARRIE LELA
[b.] July 9, 1963, Lansing, MI; [p.] Donald and Delores Grimes; [m.] Kevin L. Winters, April 13, 1985; [ch.] Lela Vaness Ann Winters; [ed.] Eaton Rapids High School, Lansing Community College; [occ.] Associate at J.C. Penney's; [memb.] Moose Lodge # 288, MI; [oth.writ.] A couple of poems published in a church newsletter, Arise newsletter, July 1994; [pers.] To my grandmother, Gretchen A. Sumerix, she has books published in the Library of Congress. She is my inspiration to write the best I can. [a.] Eaton Rapids, MI.

WITT, VALERIA MICHELLE
[pen.] Mimi Michael Vincent; [b.] January 16, 1965, Washington, DC; [p.] Dorothy and Mircea Georgescu; [m.] Paul Nolan Witt, January 19, 1992; [ch.] Vincent Michael Joseph Cerda; [ed.] Crestwood High School, Mountain Top, Pennsylvania, Liberty College, Lynchburg, Virginia; [occ.] Administrative Supervisor, Combined Properties, Washington, DC,. and Fitness Instructor at IMF (International Monetary Fund, Washington, DC); [memb.] American Indian Relief Council, American Society of Notaries; [oth.writ.] Short stories, magazine articles, preparing my first novel; [pers.] Learn to have a traveling spirit, when you feel beaten run with the wind not against it. It's amazing how simple life can be if you think and feel positive things come easy. [a.] Washington, DC.

WITTE, JILL R.
[b.] July 29, 1976, Willingboro, NJ; [p.] Paul and Barbara Witte; [ed.] Shawnee High School, Cedarville College; [occ.] Student, Nursing major, Cedarville College, OH; [memb.] First Baptist Church of Medford, NJ; [pers.] "Delight thyself also in the Lord, and He shall give thee the desires of thine heart". Psalm 37:4. I desire to create beauty in a world where simple pleasures are seen as a waste of time-to dream! [a.] Medford Lakes, NJ.

WOESSNER, KIMBERLY A.
[b.] April 23,1975, Pottstown, PA; [p.] Walter and Candace Woessner; [ed.] Owen T. Roberts High School, Eastern College; [occ.] Student; [oth.writ.] This was first time published; [pers.] It's hard to be honest with others if you cannot be honest with yourself. My poetry reflects me. [a.] Pottstown, PA.

WOLFORD, ALEXA ELIZABETH
[b.] July 2, 1983, Atlanta, GA; [p.] Arol and Jane Wolford; [ed.] Holy Innocents Episcopal School, Atlanta, Georgia; [occ.] Student; [memb.] Atlanta Lawn Tennis Association, Holy Innocents Girls basketball team, Dan't Co., Jazz dancing.

WOLTER, NADINE MORRIS
[pen.] Zelta Morris; [b.] December 4, 1912, Freeport, KS; [p.] Harvey and Nellie Morris; [m.] Floyd Wolter, February 10, 1932; [ch.] Glenn, Gary, LaVon and LaRene; [ed.] Graduate senior high school, Lindsay, California; [occ.] Retired; [memb.] Dob O'Link Club, a publication of poetry; [hon.] Having one of my poems "The Guns of Heaven" published in Dob O'Link; [oth.writ.] Many, many poems some published over the years, some not; [pers.] I have a great love of writing and reading poetry. [a.] Ocheyedan, IA.

WONG, STACY
[pen.] Helen Joan; [b.] September 30, 1979, San Francisco, CA; [p.] Arthur and Helen Wong; [ed.] Lowell High (current student, class of 1997...I hope); [occ.] Literary genius; [hon.] 1994 N. California Junior Classical League "Ludi Octobres" Convention, 1st-level II grammar, 2nd-level II mythology, 1st-level II certamen, 1980 SF's Mom of the Year-essay contest-Honorable Mention, 1991-SF Shakespeare Festival/SF Chronicle Shakespeare contest runner-up, 1993-Daughters of the American Revolution American History month essay contest, 1st in CA Chapter, 1st in District III, 2nd in the state of California; [pers.] "God is love, love is blind. I am blind, therefore I am God". The Robin and the Kestrel by Mercedes Lackey. Moral of the story, I wouldn't rely on logic that much. It doesn't make any sense. [a.] San Francisco, CA.

WONGNGAMNIT, NARIN
[b.] May 20, 1979, Bangkok, Thailand; [p.] Suchai and Cynthia Wongngamnit; [ed.] Presently a sophomore in high school at Evansville Day School; [occ.] Student; [memb.] World Tae Lwon Do Federation, Korean Tae Kwon Do Association; [hon.] Black belt in Tae Kwon Do, High Honor Roll, in 1988 I placed 3rd in the Nation of Thailand in the 14 year old and under Tae Kwon Do tournament, Presidential Academic Fitness Award; [a.] Evansville, IN.

WOOD, JONATHAN CHARLES
[b.] December 13, 1978, Newcastle/England; [p.] Michael and Pamela Hales Wood; [ed.] Newlands Preparatory School, Gosforth High School; [memb.] Dyslexia Institute, Newcastle, England; [oth.writ.] Poems for children's magazines and competitions; [pers.] Dyslexia can slow my learning but not stop it. I can always make improvements in my performance with effort, help, love and understanding. [a.] Newcastle, England.

WOODBERRY, KAREN RENA
[pen.] Mikey; [b.] November 30, 1976, Marion, SC; [p.] Frankie and Julia Woodberry; [ed.] Britton's Neck High class of 1995; [occ.] Senior high school student; [memb.] Editor: BNHS Annual Staff, Science Club, Future Teachers of America, National Beta Club, Student Government Organization, Future Business Leaders of America; [hon.] Who's Who Among American High School Students, National Honor Roll, National Beta Club; [oth.writ.] I write and have written many other poems as my hobby, some of the names are as follows: "Colors", "Senior", "What About Us", "Little Jasmine", "Sealed With A Kiss", "To Ease", "Overcome", "Stand By Me'; [pers.] Poetry is written in many styles. The best style you can write in is the one you know how. The success to write is inside of you so believe in it and yourself. [a.] Greshan, SC.

WOODHURST, ELLEN JUDITH
[pen.] Judy, judy, judy, judy...(Cary Grant); [b.] September 13, 1957, Montreal; [p.] Jean Melanson, Richard Woodhurst (deceased), step-father, Geoff Sutton; [ch.] Jason Lee and Regan Daniel; [ed.] Dunton High, Lambton College, Rosemount Nursing School, Microbiology Lab training, Academy of Art, commercial-corporate design, darkroom B&W, color; [occ.] Acting director for Lee-Daniels' Public's (the Freelance Factory); [memb.] National Press Card Association (#17993 N.P.C.A.), International Freelance Photographer Organization (IFPO-ID # 50461), St. John Ambulance (93-52362) (emergency first aide-CPR); [hon.] Most Valuable Player, team competitions baseball, "literary achievement"; [oth.writ.] With photo work local newspapers, wrote for small local paper-Ontario English Lit. papers were kept by professor for examination from future students also some art; [pers.] The book of life is brief and once a page is read, all but love is dead. That is my belief. It was only after my father's death that I came to know he had special ability in journalism and photography which he gave up for family reasons. I have always had keen interest in literature art and especially photography but pursued a career in the medical field. I am now doing what I love most photography, illustrations, design and journalism. [a.] Sutton, Quebec.

WOODROFFE, RHEA
[b.] December 28, 1979; [ed.] Luther Thorne Memorial Primary School, The Lodge School Secondary; [oth.writ.] Several other poems that have not yet been published; [pers.] I love writing poetry and one day I hope to have my own poetry book. Writing poetry is my life and I hope my dream of my own poetry book comes true. [a.] St. Michael, Barbados.

WORMACK, MARIA
[b.] April 16, 1979, New Brunswick, NJ; [p.] Elsa Nunez and Les Wormack; [ed.] Woodbridge High School, sophomore; [occ.] High school sophomore; [memb.] Track Varsity, X-Country Varsity, School of Creative Arts; [hon.] Honor Roll; [pers.] I love to write but, I never really wrote. So I leave you with this poem and hope that you acknowledge its true meanings. [a.] Sewaren, NJ.

WORRELL, WENDY
[b.] October 7, 1972, Austin, TX; [p.] Russell and Bette Bowie; [m.] William Worrell, December 31, 1991; [ch.] Brittany Nichole; [ed.] Delvalle High School, Jacki Nell Secretary School, International Correspondence School-Photography; [occ.] Van driver, Williamson-Burnet County Opport. (WBCO); [hon.] My greatest honor and award is having a wonderful husband and a beautiful daughter; [pers.] I love expressing my thoughts in poems. I want everyone to feel compelled by my expressions and feelings through my use of poetry. [a.] Burnet, TX.

WRIGHT, DALE K.
[b.] June 10, 1962, Wilmington, DE; [p.] Wilbur D. and Patricia E. Wright; [ed.] College of The Albemarle; [occ.] Laborer; [pers.] A south wind-o production.

WRIGHT, JOHN
[b.] September 20, 1931, Village Mills, TX; [p.] George and Mary Wright; [m.] Long divorced; [ch.] Carolyn, Larry, Robert, Roger, James, Karron and Therisa; [occ.] Retired roustabout foreman; [hon.] 1994 Editor's Choice, National Library of Poetry, also selected to write a poem for The Best Poems of 1995, National Library of Poetry; [oth.writ.] "The Rose I Planted", "Remembering Daddy", "Send Me Flowers Now", "That Ol Rose Tree", "Clean Your Own House", "I Thank You Lord", "The World", "My Wife;s Cooking", "Traveling " and many more, published by The National Library of Poetry and in local and semi local newspapers; [pers.] Through a few of my poems are humorous, I mostly write poems to touch the heart and soul of the reader. As I feel the poet's pen is his mouthpiece, therefore, I try to write most of my poems with a message or advice, etc. [a.] Liberty, TX.

WRIGHT, WARNER ERIC
[b.] December 24, 1975, Seaford, DE; [p.] Warner L. and Carol M. Wright; [ed.] I completed high school at Delmar Junior Senior High, now I am currently enrolled as a AG major in University of Delaware; [occ.] Full time student; [pers.] I have taken what life has given me. I reflect my inner most feelings, my actions and the actions of others around in my writing. I use it as a release and a wy to share with others what I feel and see. [a.] Delmar, DE.

WYBRO, MICHAEL K.
[pen.] Michael; [b.] June 4, 1982, Houston, TX; [p.] Pieter and Suzanne Wybro; [ed.] Faith Lutheran School, grades 1-3, Southwest Christian Academy -grade 4, Manford Williams grade-5 and Bellville Junior currently grade 6; [occ.] Student; [memb.] Leader of the Science Club, 6th grade; [hon.] Straight A student, blue ribbons in art at ACSI programs orange belt in Karate; [pers.] God knows the plans He has for me. (Jre. 29:11). Greatly influenced by all my wonderful teachers especially Mrs. Thames (3rd grade) and Mrs. Post (5th grade) who I so dearly admire and love. [a.] Bellville, TX.

WYCHE, THOMAS C.
[pen.] Tom Wyche; [b.] December 24, 1949, Washington, DC; [p.] Chanel W. and Dimple D. Wyche; [m.] Margaret S. Wyche, June 30, 1973; [ch.] James Edward and Nicole Michelle; [ed.] McKinley High, B.S, Columbia Union College, MBA Averett College; [occ.] Manager, Bell Atlantic Corporation; [memb.] Consortium of Information and Telecommunications Executives, African American Writer's Guild, Association of Telecommunications Managers and Associates-Metro Washington; [hon.] National Dean's List, Spirit of Service; [oth.writ.] "Musings of an Average African-American Man", "Ruminations in Black", INCITE column appears in ATMA-Metro Intelligence Report; [pers.] With my writing I seek to provide a view of the world from the eyes of a black "every man" to show his thoughts on himself, his world, his people and America. [a.] Washington, DC.

WYMAN, MELISSA
[b.] May 21, 1981, Rochester, NH; [p.] Ann and Jay Wyman; [occ.] Student at Kingswood Regional Middle School; [hon.] 1992 Carroll County Robert Frost Youth Poet, recipient of the Presidential Academic Fitness Award and Honor Roll 2 years in a row; [oth.writ.] Several unpublished personal narratives; [pers.] The only way to achieve in life is to stop dreaming and going for what you want. [a.] Wolfeboro, NH.

YACOUB, CHRISSY
[b.] March 17, 1978, Beverly Hills, CA; [p.] Nabil and Cicil Yacoub; [ed.] Montebello High School; [memb.] Key Club, Junior States of America, California Scholarship Federation; [hon.] Student of the Month; [oth. writ.] Various short stories, and poems; [pers.] Writing is the form of inner expression that only words can describe. Through my writing I try to express different human emotions. [a.] Montebello, CA.

YAME'
[b.] April 16, 1955, VA; [p.] William H. and Mildred N. Barba; [ch.] All the spiritual beings in small bodies on this planet; [ed.] Masters in Social Work, teacher/student of the universe; [occ.] Purpose-Nurturer of life; [memb.] Divine Oneness, Human Race; [oth. writ.] Several poems published in Women's Newsletters; letters to the editor in local newspapers, article for hospital publication; [pers.] "To Thine Own Self Be True" and from there the journey of the heart begins. It is from this space that my poetry flows. [a.] Asheville, NC.

YARBROUGH, ADONIA M.
[pen.] Adonia M. Yarbrough; [b.] October 12, 1972, Kerville, TX; [p.] Terrie J. Moheny and Roy F. Wyatt; [ch.] Paul A. Saldana; [ed.] 9th grade at Oxford High; [oth. writ.] Have a notebook of poems I have written over the years. Some are happy, sad and some passionate; [pers.] I basically write about what I am going through and how I feel. I write for those who have the misfortune of being singled out and can relate to. [a.] McAllen, TX.

YATES, SCOTT A.
[pen.] S.A. Yates; [b.] October 20, 1963, Titusville, FL; [p.] Charles and Sandra Yates; [occ.] Offset Pressman, Sir Speedy Printing; [memb.] Melbourne Seventh-Day Adventist, Discaliber Disc Golf Club; [pers.] I believe I have a God given gift with words. I have a desire to share my gift and my philosophy with the world. My poetic style I derived from Roger Waters and Pink Floyd. [a.] Melbourne, FL.

YATSKO, GLORIA SUSAN
[b.] February 10, 1956, Morristown, NJ; [p.] Donato P. and Rosanna M. Battista; [m.] Andrew C., Sr.,

February 13, 1988; [ch.] Angela Lisa, Anthony Joseph, Andrew C. Jr., Alyxandra Suzanne; [ed.] Mt. Olive High, Morris County Vocational Technical School; [occ.] Homemaker; [pers.] A smile breaks through the dark clouds obscuring my emotions and like the brilliant sunbeams inviting flowers to blossom and birds to sing; it beckons me to reach beyond my incomplete and imperfect world to share it with others. [a.] Bangor, PA.

YOHANNES, BEMNET
[b.] February 8, 1977, Addiabeba, Ethiopia; [p.] Yohannes Hailemariam, Genet Beyene; [ed.] Piney Woods Mississippi; [occ.] High school student; [memb.] International Food Club, Drama Club, French Club, Student Ambassador, Student Government; [hon.] National Honors Society, Outstanding Student of Business, Honor Student, President's List; [oth. writ.] Essays based on the Cultural Diversity of my Country, Ethiopia, published in the school's newspaper; [pers.] I write when I want to admire what's around me. I express my thoughts and feelings better in writing than in any other way. I always admire nature's beauty and its infinite surprises. [a.] Piney Woods, MS.

YOHE, MARILYN J.
[b.] March 4, 1962; [p.] Wayne and Doristella Kennedy; [m.] Stanley J., December 31, 1981; [ch.] Laura M. Yohe, Ashley R. Yohe; [ed.] Evans High School, Aiken Technical College; [occ.] Housewife; [oth. writ.] Several other writings, never submitted for publication this is first one I have submitted; [pers.] Strong interest in Biblical poetry. [a.] Augusta, GA.

YOST, JOANNE E.
[pen.] JEY; [b.] October 3, 1954, Gardena, CA; [p.] Ray and Caroline Lnk; [m.] Daniel, May 11, 1979; [ed.] Torrance and Los Amigo High Schools, Orange Coast College; [occ.] Dietetic Technician by trade; [memb.] American Dietetic Association, Inland Valley Dietetic Association; [hon.] Dean's list Orange Coast College, Certificates of Appreciation from University of CA Cooperative Extension and California 4-H Program, certificate of Commendation state of California Department of Developmental Services; [oth. writ.] Several poems not yet published, I have been writing singe age 11; [pers.] I write about personal life experiences and feelings, hoping others may relate and benefit from them in some small way. I have been greatly influenced by current and early writers. [a.] Perris, CA.

YOUNG, AIMEE
[b.] March 1, 1979, Campbelford, ONT., CAN; [p.] Danny and Melanie Young-sister-Renee and brother - Kurtis; [ed.] Campbelford District High School; [occ.] Student; [hon.] Standard School Awards, Friendship, Sports, Computer; [oth. writ.] Had a couple in the local newspaper about Remembrance Day, also school newspapers; [pers.] Work had to achieve but have fun doing it. [a.] Workworth, ONT., CAN.

YOUNG, DEBORAH L.
[b.] June 9, 1959, Crossnore, NC; [p.] Peggy J. Vance and Robert F. Young (stepfather), Kenneth L. Beard (biological father); [ch.] Jennifer Angel Young; [ed.] Avery County High School, Maryland Tech. College; [occ.] Clerk/receptionist at Linville River Nursery; [hon.] National Honor Society in 1977; [oth. writ.] Several songs and poems, but none have been submitted for publication; [pers.] I am only a reflection of the people in my life. I thank God for all these special people, from my 4th grade teacher to my grandmother. May they always live in my memory, in my heart and in my work. [a.] Crossnore, NC.

YOUNG, EUSTATIA
[b.] November 23, 1931, Foreman, AR; [ch.] Quon Young; [ed.] Douglass High, Oklahoma City University; [hon.] Outstanding senior in the field of sociology in 1981; [oth. writ.] This is the first of my writings submitted for publication; [pers.] I have watched with great joy the slow climb of this mighty nation. I write, in horror, of its ever rapid fall. [a.] Oklahoma, OK.

YOUNG, JANET LYNN
[b.] May 16, 1971, Camden, NJ; [p.] Robert C. and Mary E. Young; [ed.] Haddon Twp High, The Restaurant School (Pastry Arts); [occ.] Baker; [hon.] Johnson and Wales Scholarship; [oth. writ.] I write only for the sole purpose of sorting out my feelings and bettering myself to grow (me and my child within); [pers.] Dreams of the heart will never die - unless you aren't a believer of those dreams: till the end of time life will always just be what you (we) make it. [a.] Westmont, NJ.

YOUNG, TERESA A.
[b.] August 27, 1964, Ephrata, PA; [p.] Harold and Erma Oberholtzer; [m.] Richard R. Young, August 16, 1991; [ch.] Harley David Young, Amanda Christine Young; [ed.] Boyertown Area Sr. High School; [occ.] General laborer/ Mother; [hon.] Varsity Cheerleader, Boyertown High Varsity Lacrosse; [oth. writ.] "Dear Friend"; "Gone Bad"; "The Rocks"; "Life's Road"; "Little One's"; "Inner Thoughts"; [a.] Boyertown, PA.

ZAIA, EUGENE
[b.] March 12, 1931, Corona, NY; [p.] John and Mary Zaia; [ed.] William Cullen Bryant High School, Rockland Community College, City College; [occ.] Unemployed; [pers.] I strive to reflect the goodness of Fauna preservation, I have been influenced by modern poetry and poets.

ZAJICEK, JESSICA LYNN
[b.] February 16, 1981, Lafayette, LA; [p.] Paulette L. Zajicek; [ed.] Marshall Middle School; [occ.] 8th grade student; [hon.] Honor Roll at Rabat American School; [oth. writ.] School work published in school magazine - Rabat American School. [a.] Warrenton, VA.

ZAMMIKIEL, SUSAN M.
[b.] 1970; [oth. writ.] Types of poetry - Christian - Christ centered, Love, Friendship, Inspirational, Wedding, Bereavement/Funeral etc. Styles of Poetry - Several. Constantly filling requests for family and friends. Published in newspaper (memorial). Poems have been read at weddings and funerals; [pers.] Psalm 18:2 "The Lord is my rock, and my fortress, and my deliverer; my God, my strength, in whom I will trust; my buckler, and the horn of my salvation, and my high tower. [a.] White Plains, NY.

ZEABART, DONNA JEAN
[b.] July 9, 1924, Vincennes, IN; [p.] Henry and Margaret Zeabart; [ed.] St. Rose Academy High School, Institute of Children's Literature; [occ.] Retired Telephone Operator from IND. Bell Tel. Co.; [memb.] St. John Baptist Catholic Church, Telephone Pioneers of America; [oth. writ.] Poetry and short stories for children. Nothing has been published; [pers.] I am the eighth child in a family of twelve children. I have lived my entire life in the house where I was born. [a.] Vincennes, IN.

ZENOBY, DEBBIE
[b.] January 9, 1960, Lancaster, OH; [p.] Norma Jean and Late Robert M. Johnson; [m.] John L., May 26, 1989; [ed.] Lancaster High School, Circleville Bible College; [occ.] Administrative Assistant, Westminster Thurber Retirement Community; [pers.] Whether reading poetry or writing poetry, it has always provided a place to which I can escape to examine my deepest feelings. Poetry should not just be read, it should be felt. [a.] Lancaster, OH.

ZIARNOWSKI, MICHELE
[b.] November 27, 1979, Somerville, NJ; [p.] Maureen Bradley and Richard Ziarnowski; [ed.] Hunterdon Central Regional High School; [occ.] Student; [hon.] High honor roll; [oth. writ.] Several other poems; [pers.] You can go beyond any limitations you desire if you believe you can do it. [a.] Flemington, NJ.

ZIKIC, LJILJANA (ZHIKICH(
[b.] September 3, 1957, Kragujevac; [p.] Milica Zikic; [ch.] Deni, Marko Vuletic, Dino, Mauro, Alberto and Dina Galorini; [ed.] College graduate; [occ.] Does design work for fashion magazines and TV commercials; [memb.] Writer's Association in Belgrade[hon.] Held many titles in 12 years, was chosen as Miss Yugoslavia, represented her country in London at Miss World Pageant; [oth. writ.] Writes comedies, novels, poetry, songs and is writing a book about her life.

ZILLERUELO, MARIO
[b.] February 15, 1953, Colombia, SA; [p.] Mario and Arleene Zilleruelo; [ch.] John Delmoyne, Anthony, Christopher; [ed.] High school, college; [occ.] Business Adm., Fairfax, VA; [oth. writ.] Several poems (unpublished) articles for "The Nation" a Washingtonian newspaper (Spanish); [pers.] Life as the universe has limits that are beyond human comprehension. Therefore we must strive to acquire the key to unlock reality and evolve illusion. [a.] Fairfax, VA.

ZIMMEL, VALERIE
[pen.] Valerie Lynn Marie Zimmel; [b.] August 3, 1970, Daysland, AB; [p.] Jerome and Cheryl Zimmel; [ed.] Strome School, Daysland High School, Augustana University College; [occ.] Farm Hand, Assistant Butcher, Chamber maid and working with horses; [hon.] Numerous horse show ribbons and silver medal in 1987 Alberta Summer Games in field hockey; [oth. writ.] First time published waiting four years; [pers.] I believe in writing what comes from the heart. I like writing about feelings, love, romance, and things that affect me. [a.] Stome, AB., CAN.

ZIMMERMAN, JULIE K.
[b.] April 10, 1970, Kendallville, IN; [p.] Dan and Jacqueline Zimmerman; [ed.] DeKalb High School; [occ.] Marketing, Kruse International Auction Company; [memb.] Helmer United Methodist Church; [oth. writ.] Several poems written for friends and family; [pers.] This poem in particular was inspired by my best friend, Deborah Smith, for without her there would be no "magic". Thank you, Deborah. [a.] Corunna, IN.

ZIMMERMAN, REGINALD
[pen.] Kirk James; [b.] February 12, 1976, Boston; [p.] Mary Zimmerman and Reggie Williams;[ed.] John D. O'Bryant High School; [occ.] Student; [memb.] Young Critics Institute, Eye of the Tiger; [oth. writ.] Screenplay for cablevision, articles for the Eye of the Tiger, including poetry, Review for Young Critics Institute; [pers.] Carpe Diem. [a.] Boston, MA.

ZIOLKOWSKI, HEATHER MICHELE
[b.] May 18, 1980, Princeton, NJ; [p.] Sally and Andy Martin (step-father) John Ziolkowski (father); [ed.] Toll Gate Grammar School, Timberlane, Hopewell Valley Central High School; [occ.] Stu-

dent; [hon.] I wrote a theme for the Pennington Memorial Day Parade when I was in sixth grade (it was a contest and my theme won); [oth. writ.] Other unpublished poems; [pers.] My poetry is everything to me. It is my art form. I draw with words, not pictures. My art brings pictures to the thoughts of the readers. These images are a gift of who I am inside. [a.] Pennington, NJ.

INDEX